P9-ART-695

JOHN MUIR

THE EIGHT WILDERNESS–DISCOVERY BOOKS

JOHN MUIR

THE EIGHT WILDERNESS
DISCOVERY BOOKS

Introduction by Terry Gifford

The Story of My Boyhood and Youth
A Thousand Mile Walk to the Gulf
My First Summer in the Sierra
The Mountains of California
Our National Parks   The Yosemite
Travels in Alaska   Steep Trails

DIADEM BOOKS · LONDON
THE MOUNTAINEERS · SEATTLE

also in this series

JOHN MUIR
HIS LIFE AND LETTERS AND OTHER WRITINGS

This 912-page companion title contains William Frederic Badè's acclaimed 1923 biography *The Life and Letters of John Muir* and Muir's magnificent essay series *Studies in the Sierra* that successfully challenged the geological orthodoxy of the day about the formation of the High Sierra and Yosemite region.
The compendium also contains *Cruise of the Corwen, Stikeen* and other Muir books and essays. Apart from being very entertaining reading they provide an effective commentary on Muir's growing influence on Conservation / National Parks matters.
(See fuller description on page 1027)

H.W. TILMAN
THE SEVEN MOUNTAIN-TRAVEL BOOKS

ERIC SHIPTON
THE SIX MOUNTAIN-TRAVEL BOOKS

H.W. TILMAN
THE EIGHT SAILING / MOUNTAIN-EXPLORATION BOOKS

FRANK SMYTHE
THE SIX ALPINE AND HIMALAYAN BOOKS

Published simultaneously in Great Britain and the United States by Diadem Books (Bâton Wicks Publications) London and The Mountaineers, Seattle.

Introduction and Appendix II –
Copyright © 1992 by Diadem Books

First published 1992. Reprinted 1993, 1995, 2000, 2004 2008, 2010

Steep Trails – Copyright © 1918 by the Muir-Hanna Trust. Reprinted with permission.

Photographic copyrights and permissions as credited.

All trade enquiries in Great Britain, Europe and Commonwealth (except Canada) to:-
Bâton Wicks, c/o Cordee, 11 Jacknell Road, Hinkley Leicester LE10 3BS.

All trade enquiries in the U.S.A. and Canada to The Mountaineers, 1001 SW Klickitat Way, Seattle, WA 98134, U.S.A.

British Library Cataloguing in Publication Data:
Muir, John
    John Muir: The eight wilderness–discovery books.
    I. Title
    333.7
978-0-906371-34-3

United States Library of Congress Catalog Card No:
    92-053740

ISBN 0-89886-335-2 (North America)

Printed in Singapore, under the supervision of MRM Graphics Ltd, Winslow, Bucks.

Contents

Illustrations in the Text

Illustrations at the beginning of each book

Illustrations between pages 582 and 583

Group photographs featuring Muir and others;
Relevant landscape photographs

Jacket photos

Front cover: Bridalveil Falls, Yosemite. *Photo: Doug Scott*

Back cover: President Theodore Roosevelt and John Muir in Yosemite in
1903. *Photographer unknown* (Sierra Club Library collection)

ACKNOWLEDGEMENTS Terry Gifford suggested this omnibus volume, wrote the introduction, compiled
the appendices, guided the ordering of the books and advised on other editorial matters. Photo research in the
United States was carried out by Mary Atterberry of The Mountaineers and the following photographers and
libraries and archivists are thanked for their help, advice and contributions: Doug Scott, John Cleare, John Dill,
Ian Fullerton, Shirley Sargent, H. Bradford Washburn and Leo Dickinson; The Huntington Library (San
Marino, California); John Muir Papers, the Holt-Atherton Special Collections (University of the Pacific
Libraries); The Yosemite National Park Reference Library; The University of California Library. Other
editorial assistance was provided by Janis Tetlow and Gloria Wilson.

INTRODUCTION

by Terry Gifford

On a May morning in 1903 two men pose for a photograph at Glacier Point, above the Yosemite Valley in the heart of the Sierra Nevada of California. They have slept the night in the open and have woken under a blanket of four inches of snow. Down in the valley a banquet is being prepared for them, together with fireworks and a lightshow to be projected onto the two thousand foot high granite walls. Up here, in the clear morning air, they are escaping all that. They pose for a camera, nevertheless, perhaps with a sense that this could be an important moment for the future of the landscape behind them. It is certainly a turning point in the history of American conservation.

The stocky man on the left, hand on hip and dressed as a frontier hunter, is the President of the United States, Theodore Roosevelt. The lean, long-bearded man on the right is John Muir, wilderness sage and founding father of the American conservation movement. What this photograph symbolises is the end of the frontier and its rediscovery as an essentially inner experience in National Parks. Roosevelt, the previous hunter of game, had asked to talk for four days 'out in the open' with John Muir, the founder of the Yosemite National Park and the man whose writings would make him a guru of conservation. Late in the afternoon they descended to the Valley, politely avoided the artificial entertainments arranged by the local politicians who administered the Valley, and camped out under the natural wonder of the orange evening walls of El Capitan. They were backpackers playing truant. What they were doing was following a pattern of short-term renewal, by seeking to reconnect their inner nature with external nature, that was to become a model for human survival in urbanised societies.

Muir had written: "Going to the mountains is going home". Starting on that day in 1903, policy makers and conservationists throughout the century have battled over the implications of Muir's ideas. His vivid writing has had a profound influence because it represents a challenging example: a visionary botanist, geologist, mountaineer, lobbyist and instinctive ecologist had integrated his caring curiosity into a lifestyle that was at home in the wilderness. For us, over a hundred years later, John Muir still represents the possibility of accommodated man, at home in the universe and actively participating in its continued well-being – the continuing challenge of the new frontier.

Who was John Muir?

Muir was born in 1838 in the Scottish coastal town of Dunbar, forty kilometres east of Edinburgh. In those early years of play, between the seashore and the inland meadows, he developed his sense of adventure and wonder in the natural world. He learned to climb on the walls of the fifteenth century castle that sits above the sea. Looking back in 1903 he might have recognised in his shared adventure with the President, evading the hotel-bound

13

politicians, an echo of his childhood "scootchers", the risky games Muir played with his brother that required the outwitting of parental discovery.

At the age of eleven he emigrated with his family to a farm in Wisconsin, where, although forced to work from dawn to dusk by a tyrannical Calvinist father, John Muir found opportunities to explore the open, unfenced landscape. To circumvent his father's suspicion of books, he arose at 1 am to develop his intellectual self-education. In the early hours of winter mornings he turned his hand to making inventions, which eventually gained him entry to the University of Wisconsin for two and a half years of studies, including some botany and geology. But his studies were interrupted by his draft-dodging from the Civil War. Muir decided to 'skedaddle' to Canada where he first learned to survive alone whilst botanising through forests and swamps.

When the war was over Muir returned home and immediately began plans to get to South America. First he would walk to the Gulf of Mexico by the 'wildest, leafiest, and least trodden way'. His writing during this journey of self-discovery established an interplay between observation and reflection that re-examined common assumptions. This was to become an exciting feature of Muir's later writing. Equally important was the discovery of a style that could celebrate an integrated vision of the natural world and the place of the human species in it. The journal of this early quest was posthumously published as the book *A Thousand Mile Walk to the Gulf*.

John Muir might well have gone on to write books about South America, or Canada had he not been first fortuitously engaged by one of the most dramatic natural sites of the planet, the Yosemite Valley. California had been, in his own mind, just a detour on his journey to South America. But he took a walk into the Yosemite Valley at the age of thirty and stayed six years. His journal of *My First Summer in the Sierra*, still his most widely read book, conveys and inspires humility in the process of learning to read the ecology of a landscape. In it he identifies the human destruction of that ecology and accepts the pressing need to fight for responsible management policies.

As well as the plants and trees, Muir observed the wild goats and the water ouzels, the storms and the earthquakes. But it was his reflections on his detailed observations of rocks and ice that brought him his first publication and with it his first taste of fierce public controversy. The commonly held view at the time was that the Yosemite Valley had been formed by a single cataclysmic fall of the valley floor. Josiah Whitney, for example, Head of the California Geological Survey, was committed to this view. No less a newspaper than the *New York Tribune* published John Muir's first article, "Yosemite Glaciers", in 1871, in which he declared that his painstaking records showed that the Valley had been formed by a slow process of glaciation. Whilst Whitney dismissed the evidence of 'that shepherd', his young assistant geologist, Clarence King, replied to 'that ambitious amateur' by accusing him of 'hopeless floundering'. Perhaps King, author of the then recently published *Mountaineering in the Sierra Nevada*, had been stung by Muir's casual references in his article to climbs King had retreated from! In the end it was the professionals who had to eat their words.

Across the nation the word grew about the eccentric mountain philosopher and naturalist living all year round in Yosemite Valley. Muir received visits from the famous and the curious. Ralph Waldo Emerson had made a graveside speech at the funeral of Henry David Thoreau, hinting at his disappointment that Thoreau's nature philosophy did not extend to conservation politics. Muir was now visited by Thoreau's mentor, Emerson, who disappointed him by not sleeping out under the stars as the later President did. A leading geologist, Joseph Le Conte, brought a party of his students to learn directly from Muir. The novelist Thérèse Yelverton walked and talked with Muir before writing her novel *Zanita: Tale of the Yo-semite* (see Appendix I).

Muir was persuaded to become the country diarist of Yosemite Valley. A series of "Studies in the Sierra" for the *Overland Monthly* immediately gained the sympathy of readers by the writer's self-effacing attitude towards the land-scape. By 1876 he was able to take his readers with him down the difficult trail of calling for conservation legislation. Freedom to destroy irreplaceable forests had to be curtailed. Popular opinion, as well as commercial interests, had to be persuaded that the frontier was at an end. From this point on, Muir became the centre around which the conservation movement began to grow.

At the age of forty-one Muir became engaged to Louie Strentzel and promptly left on his first Alaskan trip. The following year he married her and went on his second journey of Alaskan exploration. But for the next ten years, during which his two daughters Wanda and Helen were born, Muir disappeared from public view. He put all his energy into building up his father-in-law's fruit farm north of Oakland. When, under his wife's urging, he returned to public life, it was to campaign for a Yosemite National Park.

Conservation Activist

The New York editor of *The Century*, Robert Underwood Johnson, travelled to California to recruit Muir as a writer and inevitably found himself sleeping out in Yosemite discussing the future conservation of the Sierra Nevada. Beside a campfire the two men made a strategic plan to use Muir's writing to influence public opinion and, at tactical moments, the politicians in particular. Muir's essays and Johnson's lobbying in Washington resulted in the establish-ment of Yosemite National Park in 1890, the State of California retaining jurisdiction over Yosemite Valley itself.

Muir was not the first to use the term 'national park'. In 1832 George Catlin had proposed that American Indian way of life be preserved in 'a nation's park'. Yellowstone National Park had been formed in 1872 for commercial reasons. But Yosemite was effectively the first National Park established mainly for conservation reasons, the Valley itself having been made a state park in 1864, 'for public use, resort and recreation'. It was Muir who developed a National Park philosophy and is regarded as founder of the National Park movement.

It was obvious that some form of organisation would be necessary to defend the Park from the threats that Muir feared would soon come. There was also a need to educate regular Park visitors in Muir's principles of conservation. So in 1892 the Sierra Club was founded with John Muir as its first President.

Within two years Muir could offer club members his first book, *The Mountains of California*. Here he collected his early articles, infused with the spirit of his first years of self-discovery in that landscape, and produced a book that became a Bible for the growing conservation movement. Muir's reputation was by now nationally recognised. After receiving an honorary degree from Harvard, he joined the Forestry Commission which toured the forests of the West before making recommendations to Congress.

The debate about forests was ostensibly about exploitation or conservation. Muir realised that the debate was really about what would now be called the ecology of a landscape. He also quickly learned that "conservation" could include, for some of his fellow-travellers, controlled commercial exploitation. He therefore changed the terms of the debate through a series of articles into a choice between exploitation and recreation – between vested interests and leisure interests – thus forcing the politicians to listen to the people. In 1901 those essays were published in the influential book, *Our National Parks*.

The Commission's recommendations resulted in the creation of thirteen new forest reserves totalling 21 million acres. This set in motion a long-running debate about their management which was, as Muir recognised, essentially the same debate as that concerning the management philosophy for national parks.

Muir wanted improved access because he wanted the public to be moved by the mountains to support their preservation. Muir believed that such landscapes should be preserved for recreation. By the time he took Roosevelt camping in Yosemite Valley in 1903 he had come to despair of the way the State managed the Valley as a spectacle. Fireworks and searchlights playing on the majestic walls were typical. Of two political items on his agenda for discussion with the President, one must have been the need for the management of the Valley to be taken out of the hands of the local politicians. Two years later Yosemite Valley was returned by the State of California to the United States.

The second item that must have been on Muir's agenda was the city of San Francisco's proposal to extend its water supply by flooding Hetch Hetchy, a valley similar to Yosemite within the National Park. This was to be a long battle that threatened the integrity of the Park. It was also to split the Sierra Club and produce the bitter attacks on Muir. William Kent for example, who had made a public gift of a grove of redwoods and named it "Muir Woods", came to describe Muir as 'a man entirely without social sense'.

When Muir toured South America and Africa in 1911, reporters followed him as an international wilderness sage. Indeed he had gained an international perspective on mountains, from the Scottish Highlands, which he visited in 1893, to the Himalaya, which he saw in 1903. At home he became as much a part of American culture as Buffalo Bill. But in California he became increasingly isolated, particularly after the death of his wife in 1905. The former Mayor of San Francisco, James Phelan, said at a House hearing on Hetch Hetchy that Muir would 'sacrifice his own family for the preservation of beauty', an ironically hurtful jibe to one who had been persuaded out of family life to fight battles such as this.

When, in 1913, Hetch Hetchy was formally granted to San Francisco, Muir was worn out by the fight. He rallied himself and returned to his writing, but the loss of the integrity of Yosemite National Park seems to have had a demoralising effect that effectively shortened his life. A year later he took a short trip to see his daughter, Helen, and his new grandson at their family ranch on the edge of the Mojave Desert. He walked in the desert with Helen, but in the evening he was taken ill and died of pneumonia on Christmas Eve 1914. In a 1913 journal Muir had written presciently 'I only went out for a walk, and finally concluded to stay out till sundown, for going out, I found, was really going in.'

Muir's books

Muir's immediate fame and influence stemmed from his engaging and immensely popular writing. In America his books are regarded as classics and have rarely been out of print. But although Muir was a natural diarist and essayist he was a reluctant writer of books (see Appendix III). He wrote reflectively all his adult life, in a total of sixty journals, and he wrote enthusiastically in letters. He had to be persuaded to write articles at first, and only wrote his first book at the age of fifty-five. What makes many of his books so readable is the fact that they are often collections of either fresh and vivid journal writing, or articles that were written to both entertain and make a point.

After writing *The Mountains of California*, with its characteristic combination of information and anecdote, and *Our National Parks* as a celebration of what the conservation movement could achieve, Muir finally turned, in later life, to reconcile public demands for autobiography and political demands for the defence of wilderness. First he published the journals of his early lessons from the landscape that had become Yosemite National Park as *My First Summer in the Sierra*. This was quickly followed by a guidebook, *The Yosemite*, which concluded with a fighting chapter on Hetch Hetchy. His only autobiographical writing was forced out of him by way of dictation resulting in *The Story of my Boyhood and Youth*. On his deathbed he was correcting the almost completed *Travels in Alaska*, based upon the journals of three Alaskan trips. After Muir's death his literary executor, Frederick Badè, published Muir's first journal as *A Thousand Mile Walk to the Gulf* then brought together a collection of his essays as *Steep Trails*.

These books are published here for the first time in one volume and are ordered so that the first three books tell Muir's own story of his journey towards the discovery of his commitment to wilderness. The following books, from *The Mountains of California* onwards, are in their published order.

Americans will be amazed to find that most of Muir's books are virtually unknown in the country of his birth. In Scotland Muir's name is largely known through the work of the John Muir Trust (see Appendix V). Muir always thought of himself as a Scot, speaking with a Scottish accent all his life, and regarded by Dunbar folk as another Scotsman making a contribution to the world. In the rest of Britain, and indeed the rest of the world, the work of this internationally important writer about ecology, conservation, mountaineering is a literature largely awaiting discovery. Muir's thinking can bring fresh light on the major issue of our time: how to manage the ills of the present for ourselves and our planet in such a way as to reduce the ills of the future. In many ways the eccentric tramp portrayed as "Kenmuir" was developing in these books a vision of responsibility for an integrated world that was scientifically ahead of his time.

Ecological Writer

Muir's writings invited individuals to rediscover the natural in themselves by reconnecting with the ecological web of which they had forgotten they were a part. Before the photographs of first Ansel Adams (the visual equivalent of Muir) and later Bradford Washburn and Elliot Porter could show people the heart of the wilderness, Muir's writing not only walked readers sensuously and slowly into the wild, but gave them a warm sense of their rightful place there. The wilderness, their wilderness, was not threatening, it did not deserve the ignominy of conquest or exploitation, it was a resource for their self-discovery. Nature, in Muir's writing, assumed the possibility of actually including urbanised 'denatured' readers who lived in cities. Indeed, he himself continually experienced the tensions of moving between the city and the wilderness. His books continue to mediate that tension over a hundred years later. They also pass on to us the moral imperative to take responsibility for the management of our planetary ecosystem.

'Our planetary ecosystem' is not, of course, a phrase that Muir could have used. But the importance of Muir's writing for contemporary environmental debates is underpinned by his actually deploying ecological concepts before our current vocabulary for them was developed. In 1889, writing to Robert Underwood Johnson, Muir classified himself as a 'self-styled poetico-trampo-geologist-bot. and ornith-natural etc.!' Ultimately Muir cannot be satisfactorially described as only a naturalist, or writer, or conservationist, and certainly not as an intellectual. He persisted in calling himself a 'mountaineer'. In fact Muir has to be seen as what would now be called an ecologist, not only in his vision, in his method of enquiry, in his way of writing, but in his complete way of living. Although Ernst von Haechel (1834–1919) introduced the word "Oekology" in 1866 as a descriptive term, John Muir was independently developing a practical example of what that meant as a way of living. He was a naturalist who, according to one writer, had developed an ecological model of the Sierra 'at least fifteen years before such models were introduced to scientific theory in the 1890s' (Michael Cohen, p. 191. See Appendix IV).

In his books Muir was not an explicit theorist. He was a populariser of an ecological way of seeing. His vision is woven into the language of his description of external and internal experience. The features of his working notion of ecology can perhaps best be illustrated in two brief passages, firstly from his earliest published journal, *A Thousand Mile Walk to the Gulf*, and secondly from the last book he wrote, *Travels in Alaska*. The basis of Muir's view of nature was discovered in the swamps of Florida where he reflected upon the human association of alligators and snakes with evil:

The antipathies existing in the Lord's great animal family must be wisely planned, like balanced repulsion and attraction in the mineral kingdom. How narrow we selfish, conceited creatures are in our sympathies! how blind to the rights of the rest of all creation! . . . although alligators, snakes, etc., naturally repel us, they are not mysterious evils. They dwell happily in these flowery wilds, are part of God's family, unfallen, undepraved, and cared for . . .

Fundamental to Muir's philosophy is an attitude of humility. This he regarded as a pre-requisite to learning from natural things. At the other end of his life he was able to say of his dog Stickeen, his companion in *Travels in Alaska*, 'He enlarged my life, extended its boundaries. I saw through him down into the depths of our common nature.' Muir goes further in this passage from *A Thousand Mile Walk to the Gulf* by making the radical declaration that alligators and snakes had rights. In *The Rights of Nature* (p. 39), Roderick Nash says that Muir's comment was 'the first association of rights with what a later generation would call *environment*'. The notion that reptiles had rights must have appeared as absurd in 1867 as the idea that flowers or rocks had rights. Muir's later work would be to protect the rights of 'all the rest of creation', but always within a notion of contextual balance.

'Balance' and 'harmony' are key words in the intuitive ecology of Muir's writing. That the alligator played its carnivorous role in the balance of nature was not to assume that it was intrinsically evil, any more than mountains could ever be viewed as 'foul'. (Muir objected to John Ruskin's argument that mountains were 'foul . . . dead unorganised matter'.) Muir's remarkably advanced expression of balance in the animal kingdom assumes a *dynamic* process of continually interactive balancing. In this case he takes his analogy from the mineral kingdom.

For Muir mountains were not dead. For one thing, minerals interacted with each other in 'repulsion and attraction'. It is typical of his ecological vision that he explains a process at work in animals by reference to a dynamic at work in minerals. Nothing is static in Muir's description of it. Everything is literally alive in his view of the world, continuously interacting with every-thing else: 'When we try to pick out anything by itself, we find it hitched to everything else in the universe.'

Towards the end of *Travels in Alaska* Muir reflected on the paradox of the huge destructive power of the glaciers creating superbly beautiful landscapes: 'Out of all the cold darkness and glacial crushing and grinding comes this warm abounding beauty and life to teach us that what we in our faithless ignorance and fear call destruction is creation finer and finer.' In this image of creative-destructiveness is held the core of Muir's ecological vision. His favourite word for this transformation process is 'flowing'. In *My First Summer in the Sierra* he wrote: 'Contemplating the lace-like fabric of streams outspread over the mountains, we are reminded that everything is flowing – going somewhere, animals and so-called lifeless rocks as well as water.'

Muir writes with a disarming simplicity of vision. He makes his sense of the living unity of nature seem obvious. In fact, his vision of a dynamic ecology is essentially contained in his style. What better image of interconnected growth patterns, for example, could be devised by scientific discourse than that in *The Mountains of California* of the Merced River as an elm tree?

Throughout his work what appear to be descriptive metaphors – rather flowery language some might say – are really products of a larger vision. In the early writing they seem to be spontaneous flourishes: a storm is charac-terised as 'a flowering of clouds'; winter storms bring a 'springtime of snow-flowers'. In the later writing a simple image, such as a dewdrop, can be used to represent a unified vision of the universe, as in *Travels in Alaska*:

When we contemplate the whole globe as one great dewdrop, striped and dotted with continents and islands, flying through space with other stars all singing and shining together as one, the whole universe appears as an infinite storm of beauty.

The sense of cosmic unity which Muir conveys here within the dynamics of 'an infinite storm of beauty' is one which includes himself. It is not just that he knows himself to be part of ecology, he has actually experienced those natural forces at work. What doubles the power of the vision contained in these books is the writer's eagerness to physically enter the elements at their most dynamic, to learn about those processes from the heart of the storm, the earthquake, the waterfall, the avalanche, the iceflow, the mountain range.

After climbing a tree to share its experience in a storm Muir wrote: 'We all travel the milky way together, trees and men; but it never occurred to me until this storm-day, while swinging in the wind, that trees are travellers, in the ordinary sense.' The expression of this almost naive discovery puts no pressure on the reader. Muir is content to open the reader's mind to new ways of seeing with a deft and deliberate tact, offering a distance from the writer by his playing the naive eccentric.

Thinking like a Mountain

Muir can be playful, enthusiastic, apparently simplistic, but he is no fool. He is never complacent about either himself in the environment, or about its future. Aldo Leopold (1887–1948), Muir's successor in the American conservation movement, may have coined the phrase 'thinking like a mountain', but a generation earlier John Muir's books vividly reflect the ideas of a person who learned to 'think like a mountain'. Unlike Clarence King, Muir does not emphasise the dangers in his mountaineering. On the only occasion that Muir fell in the mountains he was knocked unconscious and awoke on a steep slope above Tenaya Canyon. He had just returned from the city and his comment to himself, recorded in *Steep Trails*, was: 'That is what you get by intercourse with stupid town stairs, and dead pavements.' Through a discipline of tuning-in to wildness, Muir could take risks and trust his judgement of the conditions. The essays within his books chart the exercise of that discipline and act as allegories of attuned ecological living.

That Muir could turn a life-style into a powerful and enduring social movement is largely due to the influence of his eight wilderness–discovery books. His writing, with its rich diversity, has something to say to many of our contemporary environmental issues. In a global sense the frontier still has not ended. We are told that we are all conservationists now. Fashions in environmental ideas may grow and change. This year's Gaia Theory may become next year's Psychic Ecology. But John Muir's books will be reinterpreted by successive generations because they contain the possibility of accommodated man, at home in the universe, facing the difficult decisions, and knowing why.

Part of the reason why is contained in Muir's opening words of *Our National Parks*, written over one hundred and ten years ago:

Thousands of tired, nerve-shaken, over civilised people are beginning to find out that going to the mountains is going home; that wildness is a necessity; and that mountain parks and reservations are useful not only as fountains of timber and irrigating rivers, but as fountains of life.

THE STORY OF MY BOYHOOD AND YOUTH

The Story of My
Boyhood and Youth

First published by Houghton Mifflin Co., Boston, 1913

Contents

CHAPTER ONE

A Boyhood in Scotland

WHEN I was a boy in Scotland I was fond of everything that was wild, and all my life I've been growing fonder and fonder of wild places and wild creatures. Fortunately around my native town of Dunbar, by the stormy North Sea, there was no lack of wildness, though most of the land lay in smooth cultivation. With red-blooded playmates, wild as myself, I loved to wander in the fields to hear the birds sing, and along the seashore to gaze and wonder at the shells and seaweeds, eels and crabs in the pools among the rocks when the tide was low; and best of all to watch the waves in awful storms thundering on the black headlands and craggy ruins of the old Dunbar Castle when the sea and the sky, the waves and the clouds, were mingled together as one. We never thought of playing truant, but after I was five or six years old I ran away to the seashore or the fields almost every Saturday, and every day in the school vacations except Sundays, though solemnly warned that I must play at home in the garden and back yard, lest I should learn to think bad thoughts and say bad words. All in vain. In spite of the sure sore punishments that followed like shadows, the natural inherited wildness in our blood ran true on its glorious course as invincible and unstoppable as stars.

My earliest recollections of the country were gained on short walks with my grandfather when I was perhaps not over three years old. On one of these walks grandfather took me to Lord Lauderdale's gardens, where I saw figs growing against a sunny wall and tasted some of them, and got as many apples to eat as I wished. On another memorable walk in a hayfield, when we sat down to rest on one of the haycocks I heard a sharp, prickly, stinging cry, and, jumping up eagerly, called grandfather's attention to it. He said he heard only the wind, but I insisted on digging into the hay and turning it over until we discovered the source of the strange exciting sound – a mother field mouse with half a dozen naked young hanging to her teats. This to me was a wonderful discovery. No hunter could have been more excited on discovering a bear and her cubs in a wilderness den.

I was sent to school before I had completed my third year. The first schoolday was doubtless full of wonders, but I am not able to recall any of them. I remember the servant washing my face and getting soap in my eyes, and mother hanging a little green bag with my first book in it around my neck so I would not lose it, and its blowing back in the sea wind like a flag. But before I was sent to school my grandfather, as I was told, had taught me my letters from shop signs across the street. I can remember distinctly how proud I was when I had spelled my way through the little first book into the second, which seemed large and important, and so on to the third. Going from one book to another formed a grand triumphal advancement, the memories of which still stand out in clear relief.

The third book contained interesting stories as well as plain reading- and spelling-lessons. To me the best story of all was 'Llewelyn's Dog', the first animal that comes to mind after the needle-voiced field mouse. It so deeply interested and touched me and some of my classmates that we read it over and over with aching hearts, both in and out of school and shed bitter tears over the brave faithful dog, Gellert, slain by his own master, who imagined that he had devoured his son because he came to him all bloody when the boy was lost, though he had saved the child's life by killing a big wolf. We have to look far back to learn how great may be the capacity of a child's heart for sorrow and sympathy with animals as well as with human friends and neighbours. This auld-lang-syne story stands out in the throng of old schoolday memories as clearly as if I had myself been one of that Welsh hunting party – heard the bugles blowing, seen Gellert slain, joined in the search for the lost child, discovered it at last happy and smiling among the grass and bushes beside the dead, mangled wolf, and wept with Llewelyn over the sad fate of his noble, faithful dog friend.

Another favourite in this book was Southey's poem 'The Inchcape Bell', a story of a priest and a pirate. A good priest in order to warn seamen in dark stormy weather hung a big bell on the dangerous Inchcape Rock. The greater the storm and higher the waves, the louder rang the warning bell, until it was cut off and sunk by wicked Ralph the Rover. One fine day, as the story goes, when the bell was ringing gently, the pirate put out to the rock, saying, 'I'll sink that bell and plague the Abbot of Aberbrothok.' So he cut the rope, and down went the bell 'with a gurgling sound; the bubbles rose and burst around', etc. Then 'Ralph the Rover sailed away; he scoured the seas for many a day; and now, grown rich with plundered store, he steers his course for Scotland's shore.' Then came a terrible storm with cloud darkness and night darkness and high roaring waves. 'Now where we are,' cried the pirate, 'I cannot tell, but I wish I could hear the Inchcape bell.' And the story goes on to tell how the wretched rover 'tore his hair', and 'curst himself in his despair', when 'with a shivering shock', the stout ship struck on the Inchcape Rock, and went down with Ralph and his plunder beside the good priest's bell. The story appealed to our love of kind deeds and of wildness and fair play.

A lot of terrifying experiences connected with these first schooldays grew out of crimes committed by the keeper of a low lodging-house in Edinburgh, who allowed poor homeless wretches to sleep on benches or the floor for a penny or so a night, and, when kind Death came to their relief, sold the bodies for dissection to Dr Hare of the medical school. None of us children ever heard anything like the original story. The servant girls told us that 'Dandy Doctors', clad in long black cloaks and supplied with a store of sticking-plaster of wondrous adhesiveness, prowled at night about the country lanes and even the town streets, watching for children to choke and sell. The Dandy Doctor's business method, as the servants explained it, was with lightning quickness to clap a sticking-plaster on the face of a scholar, covering mouth and nose, preventing breathing or crying for help, then pop us under his long black cloak and carry us to Edinburgh to be sold and sliced into small pieces for folk to learn how we were made. We always mentioned the name 'Dandy Doctor' in a fearful whisper, and never dared venture out of doors after dark. In the short winter days it got dark before school closed, and in cloudy weather we sometimes had difficulty in finding our way home unless a servant with a lantern was sent for us; but during the Dandy Doctor period the school was closed earlier, for if detained until the usual hour the teacher could not get us to leave the schoolroom. We would rather stay all night supperless than dare the mysterious doctors supposed to be lying in wait for us. We had to go up a hill called the Davel Brae that lay between the schoolhouse and the main street. One evening just before dark, as we were running up the hill, one of the boys shouted, 'A Dandy Doctor! A Dandy Doctor!' and we all fled pellmell back into the schoolhouse to the astonishment of Mungo Siddons, the teacher. I can remember to this day the amused look on the good dominie's face as he stared and tried to guess what had got into us, until one of the older boys breathlessly explained that there was an awful big Dandy Doctor on the Brae and we couldna gang hame. Others corroborated the dreadful news. 'Yes! We saw him, plain as onything, with his lang black cloak to hide us in; and some of us thought we saw a stickenplaister ready in his hand.' We were in such a state of fear and trembling that the teacher saw he wasn't going to get rid of us without going himself as leader. He went only a short distance, however, and turned us over to the care of the two biggest scholars, who led us to the top of the Brae and then left us to scurry home and dash into the door like pursued squirrels diving into their holes.

Just before school skaled (closed), we all arose and sang the fine hymn 'Lord, dismiss us with Thy blessing'. In the spring when the swallows were coming back from their winter homes we sang –

> Welcome, welcome, little stranger,
> Welcome from a foreign shore;
> Safe escaped from many a danger ...

and while singing we all swayed in rhythm with the music. 'The Cuckoo', that always told his name in the spring of the year, was another favourite song, and when there was nothing in particular to call to mind any special bird or animal, the songs we sang were widely varied, such as

> The whale, the whale is the beast for me,
> Plunging along through the deep, deep sea.

But the best of all was 'Lord, dismiss us with Thy blessing', though at that time the most significant part I fear was the first three words.

With my school lessons father made me learn hymns and Bible verses. For learning 'Rock of Ages' he gave me a penny, and I thus became suddenly rich. Scotch boys are seldom spoiled with money. We thought more of a penny those economical days than the poorest American schoolboy thinks of a dollar. To decide what to do with that first penny was an extravagantly serious affair. I ran in great excitement up and down the street, examining the tempting goodies in the shop windows before venturing on so important an investment. My playmates also became excited when the wonderful news got abroad that Johnnie Muir had a penny, hoping to obtain a taste of the orange, apple, or candy it was likely to bring forth.

At this time infants were baptized and vaccinated a few days after birth. I remember very well a fight with the doctor when my brother David was vaccinated. This happened, I think, before I was sent to school. I couldn't imagine what the doctor, a tall, severe looking man in black, was doing to my brother, but as mother, who was holding him in her arms, offered no objection, I looked on quietly while he scratched the arm until I saw blood. Then, unable to trust even my mother, I managed to spring up high enough to grab and bite the doctor's arm, yelling that I wasna gan to let him hurt my bonnie brither, while to my utter astonishment mother and the doctor only laughed at me. So far from complete at times is sympathy between parents and children, and so much like wild beasts are baby boys, little fighting, biting, climbing pagans.

Father was proud of his garden and seemed always to be trying to make it as much like Eden as possible, and in a corner of it he gave each of us a little bit of ground for our very own in which we planted what we best liked, wondering how the hard dry seeds could change into soft leaves and flowers and find their way out to the light; and, to see how they were coming on, we used to dig up the larger ones, such as peas and beans, every day. My aunt had a corner assigned to her in our garden which she filled with lilies, and we all looked with the utmost respect and admiration at that precious lily-bed and wondered whether when we grew up we should ever be rich enough to own one anything like so grand. We imagined that each lily was worth an enormous sum of money and never dared to touch a single leaf or petal of them. We really stood in awe of them. Far, far was I then from the wild lily gardens of California that I was destined to see in their glory.

When I was a little boy at Mungo Siddons's school a flower-show was held in Dunbar, and I saw a number of the exhibitors carrying large handfuls of dahlias, the first I had ever seen. I thought them marvellous in size and beauty and, as in the case of my aunt's lilies, wondered if I should ever be rich enough to own some of them.

Although I never dared to touch my aunt's sacred lilies, I have good cause to remember stealing some common flowers from an apothecary, Peter Lawson, who also answered the purpose of a regular physician to most of the poor people of the town and adjacent country. He had a pony which was considered very wild and dangerous, and when he was called out of town he mounted this wonderful beast, which, after standing long in the stable, was frisky and boisterous, and often to our delight reared and jumped and danced about from side to side of the street before he could be persuaded to go ahead. We boys gazed in awful admiration and wondered how the druggist could be so brave and able as to get on and stay on that wild beast's back. This famous Peter loved flowers and had a fine garden surrounded by an iron fence, through the bars of which, when I thought no one saw me, I oftentimes snatched a flower and took to my heels. One day Peter discovered me in this

mischief, dashed out into the street and caught me. I screamed that I w
steal any more if he would let me go. He didn't say anything but just dragged
me along to the stable where he kept the wild pony, pushed me in right back
of its heels, and shut the door. I was screaming, of course, but as soon as I was
imprisoned the fear of being kicked quenched all noise. I hardly dared
breathe. My only hope was in motionless silence. Imagine the agony I endured! I
did not steal any more of his flowers. He was a good hard judge of boy nature.

I was in Peter's hands some time before this, when I was about two and a
half years old. The servant girl bathed us small folk before putting us to bed.
The smarting soapy scrubbings of the Saturday nights in preparation for the
Sabbath were particularly severe, and we all dreaded them. My sister Sarah,
the next older than me, wanted the longlegged stool I was sitting on awaiting
my turn, so she just tipped me off. My chin struck on the edge of the bath-tub,
and, as I was talking at the time, my tongue happened to be in the way of my
teeth when they were closed by the blow, and a deep gash was cut on the side
of it, which bled profusely. Mother came running at the noise I made,
wrapped me up, put me in the servant girl's arms and told her to run with me
through the garden and out by a back way to Peter Lawson to have something
done to stop the bleeding. He simply pushed a wad of cotton into my mouth
after soaking it in some brown astringent stuff, and told me to be sure to keep
my mouth shut and all would soon be well. Mother put me to bed, calmed my
fears, and told me to lie still and sleep like a gude bairn. But just as I was
dropping off to sleep I swallowed the bulky wad of medicated cotton and with
it, as I imagined, my tongue also. My screams over so great a loss brought
mother, and when she anxiously took me in her arms and inquired what was
the matter, I told her that I had swallowed my tongue. She only laughed at
me, much to my astonishment, when I expected that she would bewail the
awful loss her boy had sustained. My sisters, who were older than I, oftentimes said when I happened to be talking too much, 'It's a pity you hadn't
swallowed at least half of that long tongue of yours when you were little.'

It appears natural for children to be fond of water, although the Scotch
method of making every duty dismal contrived to make necessary bathing for
health terrible to us. I well remember among the awful experiences of childhood being taken by the servant to the seashore when I was between two and
three years old, stripped at the side of a deep pool in the rocks, plunged into it
among crawling crawfish and slippery wriggling snake-like eels, and drawn up
gasping and shrieking only to be plunged down again and again. As the time
approached for this terrible bathing, I used to hide in the darkest corners of
the house, and oftentimes a long search was required to find me. But after we
were a few years older, we enjoyed bathing with other boys as we wandered
along the shore, careful, however, not to get into a pool that had an invisible
boy-devouring monster at the bottom of it. Such pools, miniature maelstroms,
were called 'sookin-in-goats' and were well known to most of us. Nevertheless we never ventured into any pool on strange parts of the coast before we
had thrust a stick into it. If the stick were not pulled out of our hands, we
boldly entered and enjoyed plashing and ducking long ere we had learned to
swim.

One of our best playgrounds was the famous old Dunbar Castle, to which King Edward fled after his defeat at Bannockburn. It was built more than a thousand years ago, and though we knew little of its history, we had heard many mysterious stories of the battles fought about its walls, and firmly believed that every bone we found in the ruins belonged to an ancient warrior. We tried to see who could climb highest on the crumbling peaks and crags, and took chances that no cautious mountaineer would try. That I did not fall and finish my rock-scrambling in those adventurous boyhood days seems now a reasonable wonder.

Among our best games were running, jumping, wrestling, and scrambling. I was so proud of my skill as a climber that when I first heard of hell from a servant girl who loved to tell its horrors and warn us that if we did anything wrong we would be cast into it, I always insisted that I could climb out of it. I imagined it was only a sooty pit with stone walls like those of the castle, and I felt sure there must be chinks and cracks in the masonry for fingers and toes. Anyhow the terrors of the horrible place seldom lasted long beyond the telling; for natural faith casts out fear.

Most of the Scotch children believe in ghosts, and some under peculiar conditions continue to believe in them all through life. Grave ghosts are deemed particularly dangerous, and many of the most credulous will go far out of their way to avoid passing through or near a graveyard in the dark. After being instructed by the servants in the nature, looks, and habits of the various black and white ghosts, boowuzzies, and witches we often speculated as to whether they could run fast, and tried to believe that we had a good chance to get away from most of them. To improve our speed and wind, we often took long runs into the country. Tam o'Shanter's mare outran a lot of witches – at least until she reached a place of safety beyond the keystone of the bridge – and we thought perhaps we also might be able to outrun them.

Our house formerly belonged to a physician, and a servant girl told us that the ghost of the dead doctor haunted one of the unoccupied rooms in the second story that was kept dark on account of a heavy window-tax. Our bedroom was adjacent to the ghost room, which had in it a lot of chemical apparatus – glass tubing, glass and brass retorts, test-tubes, flasks, etc – and we thought that those strange articles were still used by the old dead doctor in compounding physic. In the long summer days David and I were put to bed several hours before sunset. Mother tucked us in carefully, drew the curtains of the big old-fashioned bed, and told us to lie still and sleep like gude bairns; but we were usually out of bed, playing games of daring called 'scootchers', about as soon as our loving mother reached the foot of the stairs, for we couldn't lie still, however hard we might try. Going into the ghost room was regarded as a very great scootcher. After venturing in a few steps and rushing back in terror, I used to dare David to go as far without getting caught.

The roof of our house, as well as the crags and walls of the old castle, offered fine mountaineering exercise. Our bedroom was lighted by a dormer window. One night I opened it in search of good scootchers and hung myself out over the slates, holding on to the sill, while the wind was making a balloon of my nightgown. I then dared David to try the adventure, and he did. Then I went out again and hung by one hand, and David did the same. Then I hung by one finger, being careful not to slip, and he did that too. Then I stood on the sill and examined the edge of the left wall of the window, crept up the slates along its side by slight fingerholds, got astride of the roof, sat there a few minutes looking at the scenery over the garden wall while the wind was howling and threatening to blow me off, then managed to slip down, catch hold of the sill, and get safely back into the room. But before attempting this scootcher, recognizing its dangerous character, with commendable caution I warned David that in case I should happen to slip I would grip the rain-trough when I was going over the eaves and hang on, and that he must then run fast downstairs and tell father to get a ladder for me, and tell him to be quick because I would soon be tired hanging dangling in the wind by my hands. After my return from this capital scootcher, David, not to be outdone, crawled up to the top of the window-roof, and got bravely astride of it; but in trying to return he lost courage and began to greet (to cry), 'I canna get doon. Oh, I canna get doon.' I leaned out of the window and shouted encouragingly, 'Dinna greet, Davie, dinna greet, I'll help ye doon. If you greet, fayther will hear, and gie us baith an awfu' skelping.' Then, standing on the sill and holding on by one hand to the window-casing, I directed him to slip his feet down within reach, and, after securing a good hold, I jumped inside and dragged him in by his heels. This finished scootcher-scrambling for the night and frightened us into bed.

In the short winter days, when it was dark even at our early bedtime, we usually spent the hours before going to sleep playing voyages around the world under the bedclothing. After mother had carefully covered us, bade us goodnight and gone downstairs, we set out on our travels. Burrowing like moles, we visited France, India, America, Australia, New Zealand, and all the places we had ever heard of; our travels never ending until we fell asleep. When mother came to take a last look at us, before she went to bed, to see that we were covered, we were oftentimes covered so well that she had difficulty in finding us, for we were hidden in all sorts of positions where sleep happened to overtake us, but in the morning we always found ourselves in good order, lying straight like gude bairns, as she said.

Some fifty years later, when I visited Scotland, I got one of my Dunbar schoolmates to introduce me to the owners of our old home, from whom I obtained permission to go upstairs to examine our bedroom window and judge what sort of adventure getting on its roof must have been, and with all my after experience in mountaineering, I found that what I had done in daring boyhood was now beyond my skill.

Boys are often at once cruel and merciful, thoughtlessly hard-hearted and tender-hearted, sympathetic, pitiful, and kind in ever changing contrasts. Love of neighbours, human or animal, grows up amid savage traits, coarse and fine. When father made out to get us securely locked up in the back yard to prevent our shore and field wanderings, we had to play away the compara- tively dull time as best we could. One of our amusements was hunting cats without seriously hurting them. These sagacious animals knew, however, that, though not very dangerous, boys were not to be trusted. One time in

particular I remember, when we began throwing stones at an experienced old
Tom, not wishing to hurt him much, though he was a tempting mark. He soon
saw what we were up to, fled to the stable, and climbed to the top of the hay
manger. He was still within range, however, and we kept the stones flying
faster and faster, but he just blinked and played possum without wincing
either at our best shots or at the noise we made. I happened to strike him
pretty hard with a good-sized pebble, but he still blinked and sat still as if
without feeling. 'He must be mortally wounded,' I said, 'and now we must kill
him to put him out of pain,' the savage in us rapidly growing with indulgence.
All took heartily to this sort of cat mercy and began throwing the heaviest
stones we could manage, but that old fellow knew what characters we were,
and just as we imagined him mercifully dead he evidently thought the play
was becoming too serious and that it was time to retreat; for suddenly with a
wild whirr and gurr of energy he launched himself over our heads, rushed
across the yard in a blur of speed, climbed to the roof of another building and
over the garden wall, out of pain and bad company, with all his lives wide-
awake and in good working order.

After we had thus learned that Tom had at least nine lives, we tried to
verify the common saying that no matter how far cats fell they always landed
on their feet unhurt. We caught one in our back yard, not Tom but a smaller
one of manageable size, and somehow got him smuggled up to the top story of
the house. I don't know how in the world we managed to let go of him, for as
soon as we opened the window and held him over the sill he knew his danger
and made violent efforts to scratch and bite his way back into the room; but
we determined to carry the thing through, and at last managed to drop him. I
can remember to this day how the poor creature in danger of his life strained
and balanced as he was falling and managed to alight on his feet. This was a
cruel thing for even wild boys to do, and we never tried the experiment again,
for we sincerely pitied the poor fellow when we saw him creeping slowly
away, stunned and frightened, with a swollen black and blue chin.

Again – showing the natural savagery of boys – we delighted in dog-fights,
and even in the horrid red work of slaughter-houses, often running long
distances and climbing over walls and roofs to see a pig killed, as soon as we
heard the desperately earnest squealing. And if the butcher was good-natured,
we begged him to let us get a near view of the mysterious insides and to give
us a bladder to blow up for a foot-ball.

But here is an illustration of the better side of boy nature. In our back yard
there were three elm trees and in the one nearest the house a pair of robin-
redbreasts had their nest. When the young were almost able to fly, a troop of
the celebrated 'Scottish Grays' visited Dunbar, and three of four of the fine
horses were lodged in our stable. When the soldiers were polishing their
swords and helmets, they happened to notice the nest, and just as they were
leaving, one of them climbed the tree and robbed it. With sore sympathy we
watched the young birds as the hard-hearted robber pushed them one by one
beneath his jacket – all but two that jumped out of the nest and tried to fly,
but they were easily caught as they fluttered on the ground, and were hidden
away with the rest. The distress of the bereaved parents, as they hovered and

screamed over the frightened crying children they so long had loved and sheltered and fed, was pitiful to see; but the shining soldier rode grandly away on his big gray horse, caring only for the few pennies the young songbirds would bring and the beer they would buy, while we all, sisters and brothers, were crying and sobbing. I remember, as if it happened this day, how my heart fairly ached and choked me. Mother put us to bed and tried to comfort us, telling us that the little birds would be well fed and grow big, and soon learn to sing in pretty cages; but again and again we rehearsed the sad story of the poor bereaved birds and their frightened children, and could not be comforted. Father came into the room when we were half asleep and still sobbing, and I heard mother telling him that 'a' the bairns' hearts were broken over the robbing of the nest in the elm'.

After attaining the manly, belligerent age of five or six years, very few of my schooldays passed without a fist fight, and half a dozen was no uncommon number. When any classmate of our own age questioned our rank and standing as fighters, we always made haste to settle the matter at a quiet place on the Davel Brae. To be a 'gude fechter' was our highest ambition, our dearest aim in life in or out of school. To be a good scholar was a secondary consideration, though we tried hard to hold high places in our classes and gloried in being Dux. We fairly revelled in the battle stories of glorious William Wallace and Robert the Bruce, with which every breath of Scotch air is saturated, and of course we were all going to be soldiers. On the Davel Brae battleground we often managed to bring on something like real war, greatly more exciting than personal combat. Choosing leaders, we divided into two armies. In winter damp snow furnished plenty of ammunition to make the thing serious, and in summer sand and grass sods. Cheering and shouting some battle-cry such as 'Bannockburn! Bannockburn! Scotland forever! The Last War in India!' we were led bravely on. For heavy battery work we stuffed our Scotch blue bonnets with snow and sand, sometimes mixed with gravel, and fired them at each other as canon-balls.

Of course we always looked eagerly forward to vacation days and thought them slow in coming. Old Mungo Siddons gave us a lot of gooseberries or currants and wished us a happy time. Some sort of special closing-exercises – singing, recitations, etc – celebrated the great day, but I remember only the berries, freedom from school work, and opportunities for runaway rambles in the fields and along the wave-beaten seashore.

An exciting time came when at the age of seven or eight years I left the auld Davel Brae school for the grammar school. Of course I had a terrible lot of fighting to do, because a new scholar had to meet every one of his age who dared to challenge him, this being the common introduction to a new school. It was very strenuous for the first month or so, establishing my fighting rank, taking up new studies, especially Latin and French, getting acquainted with new classmates and the master and his rules. In the first few Latin and French lessons the new teacher, Mr Lyon, blandly smiled at our comical blunders, but pedagogical weather of the severest kind quickly set in, when for every mistake, everything short of perfection, the taws was promptly applied. We had to get three lessons every day in Latin, three in French, and as many in

English, besides spelling, history, arithmetic, and geography. Word lessons in particular, the wouldst-couldst-shouldst-have-loved kind, were kept up, with much warlike thrashing, until I had committed the whole of the French, Latin and English grammars to memory, and in connection with reading-lessons we were called on to recite parts of them with the rules over and over again, as if all the regular and irregular incomprehensible verb stuff was poetry. In addition to all this, father made me learn so many Bible verses every day that by the time I was eleven years of age I had about three fourths of the Old Testament and all of the New by heart and by sore flesh. I could recite the New Testament from the beginning of Matthew to the end of Revelation without a single stop. The dangers of cramming and of making scholars study at home instead of letting their little brains rest were never heard of in those days. We carried our school-books home in a strap every night and committed to memory our next day's lessons before we went to bed, and to do that we had to bend our attention as closely on our tasks as lawyers on great million-dollar cases. I can't conceive of anything that would now enable me to concentrate my attention more fully than when I was a mere stripling boy, and it was all done by whipping – thrashing in general. Old-fashioned Scotch teachers spent no time in seeking short roads to knowledge, or in trying any of the new-fangled psychological methods so much in vogue nowadays. There was nothing said about making the seats easy or the lessons easy. We were simply driven pointblank against our books like soldiers against the enemy, and sternly ordered, 'Up and at'em. Commit your lessons to memory!' If we failed in any part, however slight, we were whipped; for the grand, simple, all-sufficing Scotch discovery had been made that there was a close connection between the skin and the memory, and that irritating the skin excited the memory to any required degree.

Fighting was carried on still more vigorously in the high school than in the common school. Whenever any one was challenged, either the challenge was allowed or it was decided by a battle on the seashore, where with stubborn enthusiasm we battered each other as if we had not been sufficiently battered by the teacher. When we were so fortunate as to finish a fight without a black eye, we usually escaped a thrashing at home and another next morning at school, for other traces of the fray could be easily washed off at a well on the church brae, or concealed, or passed as results of playground accidents; but a black eye could never be explained away from downright fighting. A good double thrashing was the inevitable penalty, but all without avail; fighting went on without the slightest abatement, like natural storms; for no punishment less than death could quench the ancient inherited belligerence burning in our pagan blood. Nor could we be made to believe it was fair that father and teacher should thrash us so industriously for our good, while begrudging us the pleasure of thrashing each other for our good. All these various thrashings, however, were admirably influential in developing not only memory but fortitude as well. For if we did not endure our school punishments and fighting pains without flinching and making faces, we were mocked on the playground, and public opinion on a Scotch playground was a powerful agent in controlling behaviour; therefore we at length managed to keep our features in smooth repose while enduring pain that would try anybody but an

American Indian. Far from feeling that we were called on to endure too much pain, one of our playground games was thrashing each other with whips about two feet long made from the tough, wiry stems of a species of polygonum fastened together in a stiff, firm braid. One of us handing two of these whips to a companion to take his choice, we stood up close together and thrashed each other on the legs until one succumbed to the intolerable pain and thus lost the game. Nearly all of our playground games were strenuous – shin-battering shinny, wrestling, prisoners' base, and dogs and hares – all augmenting in no slight degree our lessons in fortitude. Moreover, we regarded our punishments and pains of every sort as training for war, since we were all going to be soldiers. Besides single combats we sometimes assembled on Saturdays to meet the scholars of another school, and very little was required for the growth of strained relations, and war. The immediate cause might be nothing more than a saucy stare. Perhaps the scholar stared at would insolently inquire, 'What are ye glowerin' at, Bob?' Bob would reply, 'I'll look where I hae a mind and hinder me if ye daur.' 'Weel, Bob,' the outraged stared-at scholar would reply, 'I'll soon let ye see whether I daur or no!' and give Bob a blow on the face. This opened the battle, and every good scholar belonging to either school was drawn into it. After both sides were sore and weary, a strong-lunged warrior would be heard above the din of battle shouting, 'I'll tell ye what we'll dae wi' ye. If ye'll let us alane we'll let ye alane!' and the school war ended as most wars between nations do; and some of them begin in much the same way.

Notwithstanding the great number of harshly enforced rules, not very good order was kept in school in my time. There were two schools within a few rods of each other, one for mathematics, navigation, etc, the other, called the grammar school, that I attended. The masters lived in a big freestone house within eight or ten yards of the schools, so that they could easily step out for anything they wanted or send one of the scholars. The moment our master disappeared, perhaps for a book or a drink, every scholar left his seat and his lessons, jumped on top of the benches and desks or crawled beneath them, tugging, rolling, wrestling, accomplishing in a minute a depth of disorder and din unbelievable save by a Scottish scholar. We even carried on war, class against class, in those wild, precious minutes. A watcher gave the alarm when the master opened his house-door to return, and it was a great feat to get into our places before he entered, adorned in awful majestic authority, shouting 'Silence!' and striking resounding blows with his cane on a desk or on some unfortunate scholar's back.

Forty-seven years after leaving this fighting school, I returned on a visit to Scotland, and a cousin in Dunbar introduced me to a minister who was acquainted with the history of the school, and obtained for me an invitation to dine with the new master. Of course I gladly accepted, for I wanted to see the old place of fun and pain, and the battleground on the sands. Mr Lyon, our able teacher and thrasher, I learned, had held his place as master of the school for twenty or thirty years after I left it, and had recently died in London, after preparing many young men for the English Universities. At the dinner-table, while I was recalling the amusements and fights of my old schooldays, the minister remarked to the new master, 'Now, don't you wish that you had been teacher in those days, and gained the honour of walloping John Muir?' This pleasure so merrily suggested showed that the minister also had been a fighter in his youth. The old freestone school building was still perfectly sound, but the carved, ink-stained desks were almost whittled away.

The highest part of our playground back of the school commanded a view of the sea, and we loved to watch the passing ships and, judging by their rigging, make guesses as to the ports they had sailed from, those to which they were bound, what they were loaded with, their tonnage, etc. In stormy weather they were all smothered in clouds and spray, and showers of salt scud torn from the tops of the waves came flying over the playground wall. In those tremendous storms many a brave ship foundered or was tossed and smashed on the rocky shore. When a wreck occurred within a mile or two of the town, we often managed by running fast to reach it and pick up some of the spoils. In particular I remember visiting the battered fragments of an unfortunate brig or schooner that had been loaded with apples, and finding fine unpitiful sport in rushing into the spent waves and picking up the red-checked fruit from the frothy, seething foam.

All our school-books were extravagantly illustrated with drawings of every kind of sailing-vessel, and every boy owned some sort of craft whittled from a block of wood and trimmed with infinite pains – sloops, schooners, brigs, and full-rigged ships, with their sails and string ropes properly adjusted and named for us by some old sailor. These precious toy craft with lead keels we learned to sail on a pond near the town. With the sails set at the proper angle to the wind, they made fast straight voyages across the pond to boys on the other side, who readjusted the sails and started them back on the return voyages. Oftentimes fleets of half a dozen or more were started together in exciting races.

Our most exciting sport, however, was playing with gunpowder. We made guns out of gas-pipe, mounted them on sticks of any shape, clubbed our pennies together for powder, gleaned pieces of lead here and there and cut them into slugs, and, while one aimed, another applied a match to the touch-hole. With these awful weapons we wandered along the beach and fired at the gulls and solan-geese as they passed us. Fortunately we never hurt any of them that we knew of. We also dug holes in the ground, put in a handful or two of powder, tamped it well around a fuse made of a wheat-stalk, and, reaching cautiously forward, touched a match to the straw. This we called making earthquakes. Oftentimes we went home with singed hair and faces well peppered with powder-grains that could not be washed out. Then, of course, came a correspondingly severe punishment from both father and teacher.

Another favourite sport was climbing trees and scaling garden-walls. Boys eight or ten years of age could get over almost any wall by standing on each others' shoulders, thus making living ladders. To make walls secure against marauders, many of them were finished on top with broken bottles imbedded in lime, leaving the cutting edges sticking up; but with bunches of grass and weeds we could sit or stand in comfort on top of the jaggedest of them.

Like squirrels that begin to eat nuts before they are ripe, we began to eat apples about as soon as they were formed, causing, of course, desperate gastric disturbances to be cured by castor oil. Serious were the risks we ran in climbing and squeezing through hedges, and, of course, among the country folk we were far from welcome. Farmers passing us on the roads often shouted by way of greeting, 'Oh, you vagabonds! Back to the toon wi' ye. Gang back where ye belang. You're up to mischief, Ise warrant. I can see it. The gamekeeper'll catch ye, and maist like ye'll a' be hanged some day.'

Breakfast in those auld-lang-syne days was simple oatmeal porridge, usually with a little milk or treacle, served in wooden dishes called 'luggies', formed of staves hooped together like miniature tubs about four or five inches in diameter. One of the staves, the lug or ear, a few inches longer than the others, served as a handle, while the number of luggies ranged in a row on a dresser indicated the size of the family. We never dreamed of anything to come after the porridge, or of asking for more. Our portions were consumed in about a couple of minutes; then off to school. At noon we came racing home ravenously hungry. The midday meal, called dinner, was usually vegetable broth, a small piece of boiled mutton, and barley-meal scone. None of us liked the barley scone bread, therefore we got all we wanted of it, and in desperation had to eat it, for we were always hungry, about as hungry after as before meals. The evening meal was called 'tea' and was served on our return from school. It consisted, as far as we children were concerned, of half a slice of white bread without butter, barley scone, and warm water with a little milk and sugar in it, a beverage called 'content', which warmed but neither cheered nor inebriated. Immediately after tea we ran across the street with our books to Grandfather Gilrye, who took pleasure in seeing us and hearing us recite our next day's lessons. Then back home to supper, usually a boiled potato and piece of barley scone. Then family worship, and to bed.

Our amusements on Saturday afternoons and vacations depended mostly on getting away from home into the country, especially in the spring when the birds were calling loudest. Father sternly forbade David and me from playing truant in the fields with plundering wanderers like ourselves, fearing we might go on from bad to worse, get hurt in climbing over walls, caught by gamekeepers, or lost by falling over a cliff into the sea. 'Play as much as you like in the back yard and garden,' he said, 'and mind what you'll get when you forget and disobey.' Thus he warned us with an awfully stern countenance, looking very hard-hearted, while naturally his heart was far from hard, though he devoutly believed in eternal punishment for bad boys both here and hereafter. Nevertheless, like devout martyrs of wildness, we stole away to the seashore or the green, sunny fields with almost religious regularity, taking advantage of opportunities, when father was very busy, to join our companions, oftenest to hear the birds sing and hunt their nests, glorying in the number we had discovered and called our own. A sample of our nest chatter was something like this: Willie Chisholm would proudly exclaim, 'I ken (know) seventeen nests, and you, Johnnie, ken only fifteen.'

'But I wouldna gie my fifteen for your seventeen, for five of mine are larks and mavises. You ken only three o' the best singers.'

'Yes, Johnnie, but I ken six goldies and you ken only one. Maist of yours are only sparrows and linties and robin-redbreasts.'

Then perhaps Bob Richardson would loudly declare that he 'kenned mair nests than onybody, for he kenned twenty-three, with about fifty eggs in them and mair than fifty young birds – maybe a hundred. Some of them naething but raw gorblings but lots of them as big as their mithers and ready to flee. And aboot fifty craw's nests and three fox dens.'

'Oh, yes, Bob, but that's no fair, for naebody counts craw's nests and fox holes, and then you live in the country at Belle-haven where ye have the best chance.'

'Yes, but I ken a lot of bumbee's nests, baith the red-legged and the yellow-legged kind.'

'Oh, wha cares for bumbee's nests!'

'Weel, but here's something! Ma father let me gang to a fox hunt, and man, it was grand to see the hounds and the lang-legged horses lowpin the dykes and burns and hedges!'

The nests, I fear, with the beautiful eggs and young birds, were prized quite as highly as the songs of the glad parents, but no Scotch boy that I know of ever failed to listen with enthusiasm to the songs of the skylarks. Oftentimes on a broad meadow near Dunbar we stood for hours enjoying their marvellous singing and soaring. From the grass where the nest was hidden the male would suddenly rise, as straight as if shot up, to a height of perhaps thirty or forty feet, and, sustaining himself with rapid wing-beats, pour down the most delicious melody, sweet and clear and strong, over-flowing all bounds, then suddenly he would soar higher again and again, ever higher and higher, soaring and singing until lost to sight even on perfectly clear days, and oftentimes in cloudy weather 'far in the downy cloud', as the poet says.

To test our eyes we often watched a lark until he seemed a faint speck in the sky and finally passed beyond the keenest-sighted of us all. 'I see him yet!' we would cry, 'I see him yet!' 'I see him yet!' 'I see him yet!' as he soared. And finally only one of us would be left to claim that he still saw him. At last he, too, would have to admit that the singer had soared beyond his sight, and still the music came pouring down to us in glorious profusion, from a height far above our vision, requiring marvellous power of wing and marvellous power of voice, for that rich, delicious, soft, and yet clear music was distinctly heard long after the bird was out of sight. Then, suddenly ceasing, the glorious singer would appear, falling like a bolt straight down to his nest, where his mate was sitting on the eggs.

It was far too common a practice among us to carry off a young lark just before it could fly, place it in a cage, and fondly, laboriously feed it. Some-times we succeeded in keeping one alive for a year or two, and when awakened by the spring weather it was pitiful to see the quivering imprisoned soarer of the heavens rapidly beating its wings and singing as though it were flying and hovering in the air like its parents. To keep it in health we were taught that we must supply it with a sod of grass the size of the bottom of the cage, to make the poor bird feel as though it were at home on its native meadow – a meadow perhaps a foot or at most two feet square. Again and again it would try to hover over that miniature meadow from its miniature sky just underneath the top of the cage. At last, conscience-stricken, we carried the beloved prisoner to the meadow west of Dunbar where it was born, and, blessing its sweet heart, bravely set it free, and our exceeding great reward was to see it fly and sing in the sky.

In the winter, when there was but little doing in the fields, we organized running-matches. A dozen or so of us would start out on races that were simply tests of endurance, running on and on along a public road over the breezy hills like hounds, without stopping or getting tired. The only serious trouble we ever felt in these long races was an occasional stitch in our sides. One of the boys started the story that sucking raw eggs was a sure cure for the stitches. We had hens in our back yard, and on the next Saturday we managed to swallow a couple of eggs apiece, a disgusting job, but we would do almost anything to mend our speed, and as soon as we could get away after taking the cure we set out on a ten or twenty mile run to prove its worth. We thought nothing of running right ahead ten or a dozen miles before turning back; for we knew nothing about taking time by the sun, and none of us had a watch in those days. Indeed, we never cared about time until it began to get dark. Then we thought of home and the thrashing that awaited us. Late or early, the thrashing was sure, unless father happened to be away. If he was expected to return soon, mother made haste to get us to bed before his arrival. We escaped the thrashing next morning, for father never felt like thrashing us in cold blood on the calm holy Sabbath. But no punishment, however sure and severe, was of any avail against the attraction of the fields and woods. It had other uses, developing memory, etc, but in keeping us at home it was of no use at all. Wildness was ever sounding in our ears, and Nature saw to it that besides school lessons and church lessons some of her own lessons should be learned, perhaps with a view to the time when we should be called to wander in wildness to our heart's content. Oh, the blessed enchantment of those Saturday runaways in the prime of the spring! How our young wondering eyes revelled in the sunny, breezy glory of the hills and the sky, every particle of us thrilling and tingling with the bees and glad birds and glad streams! Kings may be blessed; we were glorious, we were free – school cares and scoldings, heart thrashings and flesh thrashings alike, were forgotten in the fullness of Nature's glad wildness. These were my first excursions – the beginnings of lifelong wanderings.

CHAPTER TWO

A New World

OUR GRAMMAR-SCHOOL reader, called, I think, 'Maccoulough's Course of Reading', contained a few natural-history sketches that excited me very much and left a deep impression, especially a fine description of the fish hawk and the bald eagle by the Scotch ornithologist Wilson, who had the good fortune to wander for years in the American woods while the country was yet mostly wild. I read his description over and over again, till I got the vivid picture he drew by heart – the long-winged hawk circling over the heaving waves, every motion watched by the eagle perched on the top of a crag or dead tree; the fish hawk poising for a moment to take aim at a fish and plunging under the water; the eagle with kindling eye spreading his wings ready for instant flight in case the attack should prove successful; the hawk emerging with a struggling fish in his talons, and proud flight; the eagle launching himself in pursuit; the wonderful wing-work in the sky, the fish hawk, though encumbered with his prey, circling higher, higher, striving hard to keep above the robber eagle; the eagle at length soaring above him, compelling him with a cry of despair to drop his hard-won prey; then the eagle steadying himself for a moment to take aim, descending swift as a lightning-bolt, and seizing the falling fish before it reached the sea.

Not less exciting and memorable was Audubon's wonderful story of the passenger pigeon, a beautiful bird flying in vast flocks that darkened the sky like clouds, countless millions assembling to rest and sleep and rear their young in certain forests, miles in length and breadth, fifty or a hundred nests on a single tree; the overloaded branches bending low and often breaking; the farmers gathering from far and near, beating down countless thousands of the young and old birds from their nests and roosts with long poles at night, and in the morning driving their bands of hogs, some of them brought from farms a hundred miles distant, to fatten on the dead and wounded covering the ground.

In another of our reading-lessons some of the American forests were described. The most interesting of the trees to us boys was the sugar maple, and soon after we had learned this sweet story we heard everybody talking about the discovery of gold in the same wonder-filled country.

One night, when David and I were at grandfather's fireside solemnly learning our lessons as usual, my father came in with news, the most wonderful, most glorious, that wild boys ever heard. 'Bairns,' he said, 'you needna learn your lessons the nicht, for we're gan to America the morn!' No more grammar, but boundless woods full of mysterious good things; trees full of sugar, growing in ground full of gold; hawks, eagles, pigeons, filling the sky; millions of birds' nests, and no gamekeepers to stop us in all the wild, happy land. We were utterly, blindly glorious. After father left the room, grandfather gave David and me a gold coin apiece for a keepsake, and looked very serious for he was about to be deserted in his lonely old age. And when we in fullness of young joy spoke of what we were going to do, of the wonderful birds and their nests that we should find, the sugar and gold, etc., and promised to send him a big box full of that tree sugar packed in gold from the glorious paradise over the sea, poor lonely grandfather, about to be forsaken, looked with downcast eyes on the floor and said in a low, trembling, troubled voice, 'Ah, poor laddies, poor laddies, you'll find something else ower the sea forbye gold and sugar, birds' nests and freedom fra lessons and schools. You'll find plenty hard, hard work.' And so we did. But nothing he could say could cloud our joy or abate the fire of youthful, hopeful, fearless adventure.

Nor could we in the midst of such measureless excitement see or feel the shadows and sorrows of his darkening old age. To my schoolmates, met that night on the street, I shouted the glorious news, 'I'm gan to Amaraka the morn!' None could believe it. I said, 'Weel, just you see if I am at the skule the morn!'

Next morning we went by rail to Glasgow and thence joyfully sailed away from beloved Scotland, flying to our fortunes on the wings of the winds, carefree as thistle seeds. We could not then know what we were leaving, what we were to encounter in the New World, nor what our gains were likely to be. We were too young and full of hope for fear or regret, but not too young to look forward with eager enthusiasm to the wonderful schoolless bookless American wilderness. Even the natural heart-pain of parting from grandfather and grandmother Gilrye, who loved us so well, and from mother and sisters and brother was quickly quenched in young joy. Father took with him only my sister Sarah (thirteen years of age), myself (eleven), and brother David (nine), leaving my eldest sister, Margaret, and the three youngest of the family, Daniel, Mary and Anna, with mother, to join us after a farm had been found in the wilderness and a comfortable house made to receive them.

In crossing the Atlantic before the days of steamships, or even the American clippers, the voyages made in old-fashioned sailing-vessels were very long. Ours was six weeks and three days. But because we had no lessons to get, that long voyage had not a dull moment for us boys. Father and sister Sarah, with most of the old folk, stayed below in rough weather, groaning in the miseries of seasickness, many of the passengers wishing they had never ventured in 'the auld rockin' creel', as they called our bluff-bowed, wave-beating ship, and, when the weather was moderately calm, singing songs in the evenings – 'The Youthful Sailor Frank and Bold', 'Oh, why left I my hame, why did I cross the deep', etc. But no matter how much the old tub tossed about and battered the waves, we were on deck every day, not in the least seasick, watching the sailors at their rope-hauling and climbing work; joining in their songs, learning the names of the ropes and sails and helping them as far as they would let us; playing games with other boys in calm weather when the deck was dry, and in stormy weather rejoicing in sympathy with the big curly-topped waves.

The captain occasionally called David and me into his cabin and asked us about our schools, handed us books to read, and seemed surprised to find that Scotch boys could read and pronounce English with perfect accent and knew so much Latin and French. In Scotch schools only pure English was taught, although not a word of English was spoken out of school. All through life, however well educated, the Scotch spoke Scotch among their own folk, except at times when unduly excited on the only two subjects which Scotchmen get much excited, namely religion and politics. So long as the controversy went on with fairly level temper, only gude braid Scots was used, but if one became angry, as was likely to happen, then he immediately began speaking severely correct English, while his antagonist, drawing himself up, would say 'Weel, there's na use pursuing this subject ony further, for I see ye hae gotten to your English.'

As we neared the shore of the great new land, with what eager wonder we watched the whales and dolphins and porpoises and seabirds, and made the good-natured sailors teach us their names and tell us stories about them!

There were quite a large number of emigrants aboard, many of them newly married couples, and the advantages of the different parts of the New World they expected to settle in were often discussed. My father started with the intention of going to the backwoods of Upper Canada. Before the end of the voyage, however, he was persuaded that the States offered superior advantages, especially Wisconsin and Michigan, where the land was said to be as good as in Canada and far more easily brought under cultivation; for in Canada the woods were so close and heavy that a man might wear out his life in getting a few acres cleared of trees and stumps. So he changed his mind and concluded to go to one of the Western States.

On our wavering westward way a grain-dealer in Buffalo told father that most of the wheat he handled came from Wisconsin; and this influential information finally determined my father's choice. At Milwaukee a farmer who had come in from the country near Fort Winnebago with a load of wheat agreed to haul us and our formidable load of stuff to a little town called Kingston for thirty dollars. On that hundred-mile journey, just after the spring thaw, the roads over the prairies were heavy and miry, causing no end of lamentation, for we often got stuck in the mud, and the poor farmer sadly declared that never, never again would he be tempted to try to haul such a cruel, heart-breaking, wagon-breaking, horse-killing load, no, not for a hundred dollars. In leaving Scotland, father, like many other home-seekers, burdened himself with far too much luggage, as if all America were still a wilderness in which little or nothing could be bought. One of his big iron-bound boxes must have weighed about four hundred pounds, for it contained an old-fashioned beam-scales with a complete set of cast-iron counterweights, two of them fifty-six pounds each, a twenty-eight, and so on down to a single pound. Also a lot of iron wedges, carpenter's tools, and so forth, and at Buffalo, as if on the very edge of the wilderness, he gladly added to his burden a big cast-iron stove with pots and pans, provisions enough for a long siege, and a scythe and cumbersome cradle for cutting wheat, all of which he succeeded in landing in the primeval Wisconsin woods.

A land-agent at Kingston gave father a note to a farmer by the name of Alexander Gray, who lived on the border of the settled part of the country, knew the section-lines, and would probably help him to find a good place for a farm. So father went away to spy out the land, and in the meantime left us children in Kingston in a rented room. It took us less than an hour to get acquainted with some of the boys in the village; we challenged them to wrestle, run races, climb trees, etc., and in a day or two we felt at home, carefree and happy, notwithstanding our family was so widely divided. When father returned he told us that he had found fine land for a farm in sunny open woods on the side of a lake, and that a team of three yoke of oxen with a big wagon was coming to haul us to Mr Gray's place.

We enjoyed the strange ten-mile ride through the woods very much, wondering how the great oxen could be so strong and wise and tame as to pull so heavy a load with no other harness than a chain and a crooked piece of wood on their necks, and how they could sway so obediently to right and left past roadside trees and stumps when the driver said *haw* and *gee*. At Mr Gray's house, father again left us for a few days to build a shanty on the quarter-section he had selected four or five miles to the westward. In the meanwhile we enjoyed our freedom as usual, wandering in the fields and meadows, looking at the trees and flowers, snakes and birds and squirrels. With the help of the nearest neighbours the little shanty was built in less than a day after the rough bur-oak logs for the walls and the white-oak boards for the floor and roof were got together.

To this charming hut, in the sunny woods, overlooking a flowery glacier meadow and a lake rimmed with white waterlilies, we were hauled by an ox-team across trackless carex swamps and low rolling hills sparsely dotted with round-headed oaks. Just as we arrived at the shanty, before we had time to look at it or the scenery about it, David and I jumped down in a hurry off the load of household goods, for we had discovered a blue jay's nest, and in a minute or so we were up the tree beside it, feasting our eyes on the beautiful green eggs and beautiful birds – our first memorable discovery. The handsome birds had not seen Scotch boys before and made a desperate screaming as if we were robbers like themselves; though we left the eggs untouched, feeling that we were already beginning to get rich, and wondering how many more nests we should find in the grand sunny woods. Then we ran along the brow of the hill that the shanty stood on, and down to the meadow, searching the trees and grass tufts and bushes, and soon discovered a bluebird's and a woodpecker's nest, and began an acquaintance with the frogs and snakes and turtles in the creeks and springs.

This sudden plash into pure wildness – baptism in Nature's warm heart – how utterly happy it made us! Nature streaming into us, wooingly teaching her wonderful glowing lessons, so unlike the dismal grammar ashes and cinders so long thrashed into us. Here without knowing it we still were at school; every wild lesson a love lesson, not whipped but charmed into us. Oh, that glorious Wisconsin wilderness! Everything new and pure in the very prime of the spring when Nature's pulses were beating highest and mysteriously keeping time with our own! Young hearts, young leaves, flowers, animals, the winds and the streams and the sparkling lake, all widely, gladly rejoicing together!

Next morning, when we climbed to the precious jay nest to take another admiring look at the eggs, we found it empty. Not a shell-fragment was left, and we wondered how in the world the birds were able to carry off their thin-shelled eggs either in their bills or in their feet without breaking them, and how they could be kept warm while a new nest was being built. Well, I am still asking these questions. When I was on the Harriman Expedition I asked Robert Ridgway, the eminent ornithologist, how these sudden flittings were accomplished, and he frankly confessed that he didn't know, but guessed that jays and many other birds carried their eggs in their mouths; and when I objected that a jay's mouth seemed too small to hold its eggs, he replied that birds' mouths were larger than the narrowness of their bills indicated. Then I asked him what he thought they did with the eggs while a new nest was being prepared. He didn't know; neither do I to this day. A specimen of the many puzzling problems presented to the naturalist.

We soon found many more nests belonging to birds that were not half so suspicious. The handsome and notorious blue jay plunders the nests of other birds and of course he could not trust us. Almost all the others – brown thrushes, bluebirds, song sparrows, kingbirds, hen-hawks, night-hawks, whip-poor-wills, woodpeckers, etc. – simply tried to avoid being seen, to draw or drive us away, or paid no attention to us.

We used to wonder how the woodpeckers could bore holes so perfectly round, true mathematical circles. We ourselves could not have done it even with gouges and chisels. We loved to watch them feeding their young, and wondered how they could glean food enough for so many clamorous, hungry, unsatisfiable babies, and how they managed to give each one its share; for after the young grew strong, one would get his head out of the door-hole and try to hold possession of it to meet the food-laden parents. How hard they worked to support their families, especially the red-headed and speckledy woodpeckers and flickers; digging, hammering on scaly bark and decaying trunks and branches from dawn to dark, coming and going at intervals of a few minutes all the livelong day!

We discovered a hen-hawk's nest on the top of a tall oak thirty or forty rods from the shanty and approached it cautiously. One of the pair always kept watch, soaring in wide circles high above the tree, and when we attempted to climb it, the big dangerous-looking bird came swooping down at us and drove us away.

We greatly admired the plucky kingbird. In Scotland our great ambition was to be good fighters, and we admired this quality in the handsome little chattering flycatcher that whips all the other birds. He was particularly angry when plundering jays and hawks came near his home, and took pains to thrash them not only away from the nest-tree but out of the neighbourhood. The nest was usually built on a bur oak near a meadow where insects were abundant, and where no undesirable visitor could approach without being discovered. When a hen-hawk hove in sight, the male immediately set off after him, and it was ridiculous to see that great, strong bird hurrying away as fast as his clumsy wings would carry him, as soon as he saw the little, waspish kingbird coming. But the kingbird easily overtook him, flew just a few feet above him, and with a lot of chattering, scolding notes kept diving and striking him on the back of the head until tired; then he alighted to rest on the hawk's broad shoulders, still scolding and chattering as he rode along, like an angry boy pouring out vials of wrath. Then, up and at him again with his sharp bill; and after he had thus driven and ridden his big enemy a mile or so from the nest, he went home to his mate, chuckling and bragging as if trying to tell her what a wonderful fellow he was.

This first spring, while some of the birds were still building their nests and very few young ones had yet tried to fly, father hired a Yankee to assist in clearing eight or ten acres of the best ground for a field. We found new wonders every day and often had to call on this Yankee to solve puzzling questions. We asked him one day if there was any bird in America that the kingbird couldn't whip. What about the sandhill crane? Could he whip that long-legged, long-billed fellow?

'A crane never goes near kingbirds' nests or notices so small a bird,' he said 'and therefore there could be no fighting between them.' So we hastily concluded that our hero could whip every bird in the country except perhaps the sandhill crane.

We never tired listening to the wonderful whip-poor-will. One came every night about dusk and sat on a log about twenty or thirty feet from our cabin door and began shouting 'Whip poor Will! Whip poor Will!' with loud emphatic earnestness. 'What's that? What's that?' we cried when this startling visitor first announced himself. 'What do you call it?'

'Why, it's telling you its name,' said the Yankee. 'Don't you hear it and what he wants you to do? He says his name is "Poor Will" and he wants you to whip him, and you may if you are able to catch him.' Poor Will seemed the most wonderful of all the strange creatures we had seen. What a wild, strong, bold voice he had, unlike any other we had ever heard on sea or land!

A near relative, the bull-bat, or night-hawk, seemed hardly less wonderful. Towards evening scattered flocks kept the sky lively as they circled around on their long wings a hundred feet or more above the ground, hunting moths and beetles, interrupting their rather slow but strong, regular wing-beats at short intervals with quick quivering strokes while uttering keen, squeaky cries something like *pfee, pfee*, and every now and then diving nearly to the ground with a loud ripping, bellowing sound, like bull-roaring, suggesting its name; then turning and gliding swiftly up again. These fine wild grey birds, about the size of a pigeon, lay their two eggs on bare ground without anything like a nest or even a concealing bush or grass-tuft. Nevertheless they are not easily seen, for they are coloured like the ground. While sitting on their eggs, they depend so much upon not being noticed that if you are walking rapidly ahead they allow you to step within an inch or two of them without flinching. But if they see by your looks that you have discovered them, they leave their eggs or young, and, like a good many other birds, pretend that they are sorely wounded, fluttering and rolling over on the ground and gasping as if dying, to draw you away. When pursued we are surprised to find that just when we were on the point of overtaking them they were always able to flutter a few yards further, until they had led us about a quarter of a mile from the nest; then, suddenly getting well, they quietly flew home by a roundabout way to their precious babies or eggs, o'er a' the ills of life victorious, bad boys among the worst. The Yankee took particular pleasure in encouraging us to pursue them.

Everything about us was so novel and wonderful that we could hardly believe our senses except when hungry or while father was thrashing us. When we first saw Fountain Lake Meadow, on a sultry evening, sprinkled with millions of lightning-bugs throbbing with light, the effect was so strange and beautiful that it seemed far too marvellous to be real. Looking from our shanty on the hill, I thought that the whole wonderful fairy show must be in my eyes; for only in fighting, when my eyes were struck, had I ever seen anything in the least like it. But when I asked my brother if he saw anything strange in the meadow he said, 'Yes, it's all covered with shaky fire-sparks.' Then I guessed that it might be something outside of us, and applied to our all-knowing Yankee to explain it. 'Oh, it's nothing but lightnin'-bugs,' he said, and kindly led us down the hill to the edge of the fiery meadow, caught a few of the wonderful bugs, dropped them into a cup, and carried them to the shanty, where we watched them throbbing and flashing out their mysterious light at regular intervals, as if each little passionate glow were caused by the beating of a heart. Once I saw a splendid display of glow-worm light in the foothills of the Himalayas, north of Calcutta, but glorious as it appeared in pure starry radiance, it was far less impressive than the extravagant abounding, quivering, dancing fire on our Wisconsin meadow.

Partridge drumming was another great marvel. When I first heard the low, soft, solemn sound I thought it must be made by some strange disturbance in my head or stomach, but as all seemed serene within, I asked David whether he heard anything queer. 'Yes,' he said, 'I hear something saying *boomp*, *boomp*, *boomp*, and I'm wondering at it.' Then I was half satisfied that the source of the mysterious sound must be in something outside of us, coming perhaps from the ground or from some ghost or bogie or woodland fairy. Only after long watching and listening did we at last discover it in the wings of the plump brown bird.

The love-song of the common jack snipe seemed not a whit less mysterious than partridge drumming. It was usually heard on cloudy evenings, a strange, unearthly, winnowing, spiritlike sound, yet easily heard at a distance of a third of a mile. Our sharp eyes soon detected the bird while making it, as it circled high in the air over the meadow with wonderfully strong and rapid wing-beats, suddenly descending and rising, again and again, in deep, wide loops; the tones being very low and smooth at the beginning of the descent, rapidly increasing to a curious little whirling storm-roar at the bottom, and gradually fading lower and lower until the top was reached. It was long, however, before we identified this mysterious wing-singer as the little brown jack snipe that we knew so well and had so often watched as he silently probed the mud around the edges of our meadow stream and spring-holes, and made short zigzag flights over the grass uttering only little short, crisp quacks and chucks.

The love-songs of the frogs seemed hardly less wonderful than those of the birds, their musical notes varying from the sweet, tranquil, soothing peeping and purring of the hylas to the awfully deep low-bass blunt bellowing of the bullfrogs. Some of the smaller species have wonderfully clear, sharp voices and told us their good Bible names in musical tones about as plainly as the whip-poor-will. *Isaac, Isaac*; *Yacob, Yacob*; *Israel, Israel*; shouted in sharp, ringing, far-reaching tones, as if they had all been to school and severely drilled in elocution. In the still, warm evenings, big bunchy bullfrogs bellowed, *Drunk! Drunk! Drunk! Jug o'rum! Jug o'rum!* and early in the spring, countless thousands of the commonest species, up to the throat in cold water, sang in concert, making a mass of music, such as it was, loud enough to be heard at a distance of more than half a mile.

Far, far apart from this loud marsh music is that of the many species of hyla, a sort of soothing immortal melody filling the air like light.

We revelled in the glory of the sky scenery as well as that of the woods and meadows and rushy, lily-bordered lakes. The great thunderstorms in particular interested us, so unlike any seen in Scotland, exciting awful, wondering admiration. Gazing awe-stricken, we watched the upbuilding of the sublime cloud-mountains – glowing, sun-beaten pearl and alabaster cumuli, glorious in beauty and majesty and looking so firm and lasting that birds, we thought, might build their nests amid their downy bosses; the black-browed storm-clouds marching in awful grandeur across the landscape, trailing broad grey sheets of hail and rain like vast cataracts, and ever and anon flashing down vivid zigzag lightning followed by terrible crashing thunder. We saw several trees shattered, and one of them, a punky old oak, was set on fire, while we wondered why all the trees and everybody and everything did not share the same fate, for oftentimes the whole sky blazed. After sultry storm days, many of the nights were darkened by smooth black apparently structureless cloud-mantles which at short intervals were illumined with startling suddenness to a fiery glow by quick, quivering lightning-flashes, revealing the landscape in almost noonday brightness, to be instantly quenched in solid blackness.

But those first days and weeks of unmixed enjoyment and freedom, revelling in the wonderful wildness about us, were soon to be mingled with the hard work of making a farm. I was first put to burning brush in clearing land for the plough. Those magnificent brush fires with great white hearts and red flames, the first big, wild outdoor fires I had ever seen, were wonderful sights for young eyes. Again and again, when they were burning fiercest so that we could hardly approach near enough to throw on another branch, father put them to awfully practical use as warning lessons, comparing their heat with that of hell, and the branches with bad boys. 'Now, John,' he would say – 'now, John, just think what an awful thing it would be to be thrown into that fire – and then think of hellfire, that is so many times hotter. Into that fire all bad boys, with sinners of every sort who disobey God, will be cast as we are casting branches into this brush fire, and although suffering so much, their sufferings will never, never end, because neither the fire nor the sinners can die.' But those terrible fire lessons quickly faded away in the blithe wilderness air; for no fire can be hotter than the heavenly fire of faith and hope that burns in every healthy boy's heart.

Soon after our arrival in the woods someone added a cat and puppy to the animals father had bought. The cat soon had kittens, and it was interesting to watch her feeding, protecting and training them. After they were able to leave their nest and play, she went out hunting and brought in many kinds of birds and squirrels for them, mostly ground squirrels (spermophiles), called 'gophers' in Wisconsin. When she got within a dozen yards or so of the shanty, she announced her approach by a peculiar call, and the sleeping kittens immediately bounced up and ran to met her, all racing for the first bite of they knew not what, and we too ran to see what she brought. She then lay down a few minutes to rest and enjoy the enjoyment of her feasting family, and again vanished in the grass and flowers, coming and going every half-hour or so. Sometimes she brought in birds that we had never seen before, and occasionally a flying squirrel, chipmunk, or big fox squirrel. We were just old enough, David and I, to regard all these creatures as wonders, the strange inhabitants of our new world.

The pup was a common cur, though very uncommon to us, a black and white short-haired mongrel that we named 'Watch'. We always gave him a pan of milk in the evening just before we knelt in family worship, while daylight still lingered in the shanty. And, instead of attending to the prayers, I too often studied the small wild creatures playing around us. Field mice scampered about the cabin as though it had been built for them alone, and their performances were very amusing. About dusk, on one of the calm, sultry nights so grateful to moths and beetles, when the puppy was lapping his milk, and we were on our knees, in through the door came a heavy broad-shouldered beetle about as big as a mouse, and after it had droned and boomed round the cabin two or three times, the pan of milk, showing white in the gloaming, caught its eyes, and, taking good aim, it alighted with a slanting, glinting plash in the middle of the pan like a duck alighting in a lake. Baby Watch, having never before seen anything like that beetle, started back, gazing in dumb astonishment and fear at the black sprawling monster trying to swim. Recovering somewhat from his fright, he began to bark at the creature, and ran round and round his milk-pan, wouf-woufing, gurring, growling, like an old dog barking at a wild-cat or a bear. The natural astonishment and curiosity of that boy dog getting his first entomological lesson in this wonderful world was so immoderately funny that I had great difficulty in keeping from laughing out loud.

Snapping turtles were common throughout the woods, and we were delighted to find that they would snap at a stick and hang on like bull-dogs; and we amused ourselves by introducing Watch to them, enjoying his curious behaviour and theirs in getting acquainted with each other. One day we assisted one of the smallest of the turtles to get a good grip of poor Watch's ear. Then away he rushed, holding his head sidewise, yelping and terror-stricken, with the strange buglike reptile biting hard and clinging fast – a shameful amusement even for wild boys.

As a playmate Watch was too serious, though he learned more than any stranger would judge him capable of, was a bold, faithful watch-dog and in his prime a grand fighter, able to whip all the other dogs in the neighbourhood. Comparing him with ourselves, we soon learned that although he could not read books he could read faces, was a good judge of character, always knew what was going on and what we were about to do and liked to help us. We could run nearly as fast as he could, see about as far and perhaps hear as well, but in sense of smell his nose was incomparably better than ours. One sharp winter morning when the ground was covered with snow, I noticed that when he was yawning and stretching himself after leaving his bed he suddenly caught the scent of something that excited him, went round the corner of the house and looked intently to the westward across a tongue of land that we called West Bank, eagerly questioning the air with quivering nostrils, and bristling up as though he felt sure that there was something dangerous in that direction and had actually caught sight of it. Then he ran toward the Bank, and I followed him, curious to see what his nose had discovered. The top of the Bank commanded a view of the north end of our lake and meadow, and when we got there we saw an Indian hunter with a long spear, going from one muskrat cabin to another, approaching cautiously, careful to make no noise, and then suddenly thrusting his spear down through the house. If well aimed, the spear went through the poor beaver rat as it lay cuddled up in the snug nest it had made for itself in the autumn with so much far-seeing care, and when the hunter felt the spear quivering, he dug down the mossy hut with his tomahawk and secured his prey – the flesh for food, and the skin to sell for a dime or so. This was a clear object lesson on dogs' keenness of scent. That Indian was more than half a mile away across a wooded ridge. Had the hunter been a white man, I suppose Watch would not have noticed him.

When he was about six or seven years old, he not only became cross, so that he would do only what he liked, but he fell on evil ways, and was accused by the neighbours who had settled around us of catching and devouring whole broods of chickens, some of them only a day or two out of the shell. We never imagined he would do anything so grossly undoglike. He never did at home. But several of the neighbours declared over and over again that they had caught him in the act, and insisted that he must be shot. At last, in spite of tearful protests, he was condemned and executed. Father examined the poor fellow's stomach in search of sure evidence, and discovered the heads of eight chickens that he had devoured at his last meal. So poor Watch was killed simply because his taste for chickens was too much like our own. Think of the millions of squabs that preaching, praying men and women kill and eat, with all sorts of other animals great and small, young and old, while eloquently discoursing on the coming of the blessed peaceful, bloodless millennium! Think of the passenger pigeons that fifty or sixty years ago filled the woods and sky over half the continent, now exterminated by beating down the young from the nests together with the brooding parents, before they could try their wonderful wings; by trapping them in nets, feeding them to hogs, etc. None of our fellow mortals is safe who eats what we eat, who in any way interferes with our pleasures, or who may be used for work or food, clothing or ornament, or mere cruel, sportish amusement. Fortunately many are too small to be seen, and therefore enjoy life beyond our reach. And in looking through God's great stone books made up of records reaching back millions and millions of years, it is a great comfort to learn that vast multitudes of creatures, great and small and infinite in number, lived and had a good time in God's love before man was created.

The old Scotch fashion of whipping for every act of disobedience or of simple, playful forgetfulness was still kept up in the wilderness, and of course many of those whippings fell upon me. Most of them were outrageously severe, and utterly barren of fun. But here is one that was nearly all fun.

Father was busy hauling lumber for the frame house that was to be got ready for the arrival of my mother, sisters, and brother, left behind in

Scotland. One morning, when he was ready to start for another load, his ox-whip was not to be found. He asked me if I knew anything about it. I told him I didn't know where it was, but Scotch conscience compelled me to confess that when I was playing with it I had tied it to Watch's tail, and that he ran away, dragging it through the grass, and came back without it. 'It must have slipped off his tail,' I said, and so I didn't know where it was. This honest, straightforward little story made father so angry that he exclaimed with heavy, foreboding emphasis, 'The very deevil's in that boy!' David, who had been playing with me and was perhaps about as responsible for the loss of the whip as I was, said never a word, for he was always prudent enough to hold his tongue when the parental weather was stormy, and so escaped nearly all punishment. And, strange to say, this time I also escaped, all except a terrible scolding, though the thrashing weather seemed darker than ever. As if unwilling to let the sun see the shameful job, father took me into the cabin where the storm was to fall, and sent David to the woods for a switch. While he was out selecting the switch, father put in the spare time sketching my play-wickedness in awful colours, and of course referred again and again to the place prepared for bad boys. In the midst of this terrible word-storm, dreading most the impending thrashing, I whimpered that I was only playing because I couldn't help it; didn't know I was doing wrong; wouldn't do it again, and so forth. After this miserable dialogue was about exhausted, father became impatient at my brother for taking so long to find the switch; and so was I, for I wanted to have the thing over and done with. At last, in came David, a picture of open-hearted innocence, solemnly dragging a young bur-oak sapling, and handed the end of it to father, saying it was the best switch he could find. It was an awfully heavy one, about two and a half inches thick at the butt and ten feet long, almost big enough for a fence-pole. There wasn't room enough in the cabin to swing it, and the moment I saw it I burst out laughing in the midst of my fears. But father failed to see the fun and was very angry at David, heaved the bur-oak outside and passionately demanded his reason for fetching 'sic a muckle rail like that instead o' a switch? Do ye ca' that a switch? I have a gude mind to thrash you instead o'John.' David, with demure, downcast eyes, looked preternaturally righteous, but as usual prudently answered never a word.

It was a hard job in those days to bring up Scotch boys in the way they should go; and poor overworked father was determined to do it if enough of the right kind of switches could be found. But this time, as the sun was getting high, he hitched up old Tom and Jerry and made haste to the Kingston lumber-yard, leaving me unscathed and as innocently wicked as ever; for hardly had father got fairly out of sight among the oaks and hickories, ere all our troubles, hell-threatenings and exhortations were forgotten in the fun we had lassoing a stubborn old sow and laboriously trying to teach her to go reasonably steady in rope harness. She was the first hog that father bought to stock the farm, and we boys regarded her as a very wonderful beast. In a few weeks she had a lot of pigs, and of all the queer, funny, animal children we had yet seen, none amused us more. They were so comic in size and shape, in their gait and gestures, their merry sham fights and the false alarms they got up for the fun of scampering back to their mother and begging her in most persuasive little squeals to lie down and give them a drink.

After her darling short-snouted babies were about a month old, she took them out to the woods and gradually roamed farther and farther from the shanty in search of acorns and roots. One afternoon we heard a rifle-shot, a very noticeable thing, as we had no near neighbours, as yet. We thought it must have been fired by an Indian on the trail that followed the right bank of the Fox River between Portage and Packwaukee Lake and passed our shanty at a distance of about three quarters of a mile. Just a few minutes after that shot was heard, along came the poor mother rushing up to the shanty for protection, with her pigs, all out of breath and terror-stricken. One of them was missing, and we supposed of course that an Indian had shot it for food. Next day, I discovered a blood-puddle where the Indian trail crossed the outlet of our lake. One of father's hired men told us that the Indians thought nothing of levying this sort of blackmail whenever they were hungry. The solemn awe and fear in the eyes of that old mother and those little pigs I never can forget; it was as unmistakable and deadly a fear as I ever saw expressed by any human eye, and corroborates in no uncertain way the oneness of all of us.

CHAPTER THREE

Life on a Wisconsin Farm

COMING DIRECT from school in Scotland while we were still hopefully ignorant and far from tame – notwithstanding the unnatural profusion of teaching and thrashing lavished upon us – getting acquainted with the animals about us was a never-failing source of wonder and delight. At first my father, like nearly all the backwoods settlers, bought a yoke of oxen to do the farm work, and as field after field was cleared, the number was gradually increased until we had five yoke. These wise, patient, plodding animals did all the ploughing, logging, hauling and hard work of every sort for the first four or five years, and, never having seen oxen before, we looked at them with the same eager freshness of conception as we did at the wild animals. We worked with them, sympathized with them in their rest and toil and play, and thus learned to know them far better than we should had we been only trained scientific naturalists. We soon learned that each ox and cow and calf had individual character. Old white-faced Buck, one of the second yoke of oxen we owned, was a notably sagacious fellow. He seemed to reason sometimes almost like ourselves. In the autumn we fed the cattle lots of pumpkins and had to split them open so that mouthfuls could be readily broken off. But Buck never waited for us to come to his help. The others, when they were hungry and impatient, tried to break through the hard rind with their teeth, but seldom with success if the pumpkin was full grown. Buck never wasted time in this mumbling, slavering way, but crushed them with his head. He went to the pile, picked out a good one, like a boy choosing an orange or apple, rolled it down on to the open ground, deliberately kneeled in front of it, placed his broad, flat brow on top of it, brought his weight hard down and crushed it, then quietly arose and went on with his meal in comfort. Some would call this 'instinct', as if so-called 'blind instinct' must necessarily make an ox stand on its head to break pumpkins when its teeth got sore, or when nobody came with an axe to split them. Another fine ox showed his skill when hungry by opening all the fences that stood in his way to the corn-fields.

The humanity we found in them came partly through the expression of their eyes when tired, their tones of voice when hungry and calling for food, their patient plodding and pulling in hot weather, their long-drawn-out sighing breath when exhausted and suffering like ourselves, and their enjoyment of rest with the same grateful looks as ours. We recognized their kinship also by their yawning like ourselves when sleepy and evidently enjoying the same peculiar pleasure at the roots of their jaws; by the way they stretched themselves in the morning after a good rest; by learning languages – Scotch, English, Irish, French, Dutch – a smattering of each as required in the faithful service they so willingly, wisely rendered; by their intelligent, alert curiosity, manifested in listening to strange sounds; their love of play; the attachments they made; and their mourning, long continued, when a companion was killed.

When we went to Portage, our nearest town, about ten or twelve miles from the farm, it would oftentimes be late before we got back, and in the summer-time, in sultry, rainy weather, the clouds were full of sheet lightning which every minute or two would suddenly illumine the landscape, revealing all its features, the hills and valleys, meadows and trees, about as fully and clearly as the noonday sunshine; then as suddenly the glorious light would be quenched, making the darkness seem denser than before. On such nights the cattle had to find the way home without any help from us, but they never got off the track, for they followed it by scent like dogs. Once, father, returning late from Portage or Kingston, compelled Tom and Jerry, our first oxen, to leave the dim track, imagining they must be going wrong. At last they stopped and refused to go farther. Then father unhitched them from the wagon, took hold of Tom's tail, and was thus led straight to the shanty. Next morning he set out to seek his wagon and found it on the brow of a steep hill above an impassable swamp. We learned less from the cows, because we did not enter so far into their lives, working with them, suffering heat and cold, hunger and thirst and almost deadly weariness with them; but none with natural charity could fail to sympathize with them in their love for their calves, and to feel that it in no way differed from the divine mother-love of a woman in thoughtful, self-sacrificing care; for they would brave every danger, giving their lives for their offspring. Nor could we fail to sympathize with their awkward, blunt-nosed baby calves, with such beautiful, wondering eyes looking out on the world and slowly getting acquainted with things, all so strange to them, and awkwardly learning to use their legs, and play and fight.

Before leaving Scotland, father promised us a pony to ride when we got to

America, and we saw to it that this promise was not forgotten. Only a week or two after our arrival in the woods he bought us a little Indian pony for thirteen dollars from a store-keeper in Kingston who had obtained him from a Winnebago or Menominee Indian in trade for goods. He was a stout handsome bay with long black mane and tail, and, though he was only two years old, the Indians had already taught him to carry all sorts of burdens, to stand without being tied, to go anywhere over all sorts of ground fast or slow, and to jump and swim and fear nothing – a truly wonderful creature, strangely different from shy, skittish, nervous, superstitious civilized beasts. We turned him loose, and, strange to say, he never ran away from us or refused to be caught, but behaved as if he had known Scotch boys all his life; probably because we were about as wild as young Indians.

One day when father happened to have a little leisure, he said, 'Noo, bairns, rin doon the meadow and get your powny and learn to ride him.' So we led him out to a smooth place near an Indian mound back of the shanty, where father directed us to begin. I mounted for the first memorable lesson, crossed the mound, and set out at a slow walk along the wagon-track made in hauling lumber; then father shouted, 'Whup him up, John, whup him up! Make him gallop; gallopin' is easier and better than walkin' or trottin'.' Jack was willing, and away he sped at a good fast gallop. I managed to keep my balance fairly well by holding fast to the mane, but could not keep from bumping up and down, for I was plump and elastic and so was Jack; therefore about half of the time I was in the air.

After a quarter of a mile or so of this curious transportation, I cried, 'Whoa, Jack!' The wonderful creature seemed to understand Scotch, for he stopped so suddenly I flew over his head, but he stood perfectly still as if that flying method of dismounting were the regular way. Jumping on again, I bumped and bobbed back along the grassy, flowery track, over the Indian mound, cried 'Whoa, Jack!', flew over his head, and alighted in father's arms as gracefully as if it were all intended for circus work.

After going over the course five or six times in the same free, picturesque style, I gave place to brother David, whose performances were much like my own. In a few weeks, however, or a month, we were taking adventurous rides more than a mile long out to a big meadow frequented by sandhill cranes, and returning safely with wonderful stories of the great long-legged birds we had seen, and how on the whole journey away and back we had fallen off only five or six times. Gradually we learned to gallop through the woods without roads of any sort, bareback and without rope or bridle, guiding only by leaning from side to side or by slight knee pressure. In this free way we used to amuse ourselves, riding at full speed across a big 'kettle' that was on our farm, without holding on by either mane or tail.

These so-called 'kettles' were formed by the melting of large detached blocks of ice that had been buried in moraine material thousands of years ago when the ice-sheet that covered all this region was receding. As the buried ice melted, of course the moraine material above and about it fell in, forming hopper-shaped hollows, while the grass growing on their sides and around them prevented the rain and wind from filling them up. The one we performed in was perhaps seventy or eighty feet wide and twenty or thirty feet deep; and without a saddle or hold of any kind it was not easy to keep from slipping over Jack's head in diving into it, or over his tail climbing out. This was fine sport on the long summer Sundays when we were able to steal away before meeting-time without being seen. We got very warm and red at it, and oftentimes poor Jack, dripping with sweat like his riders, seemed to have been boiled in that kettle.

In Scotland we had often been admonished to be bold, and this advice we passed on to Jack, who had already got many a wild lesson from Indian boys. Once, when teaching him to jump muddy streams, I made him try the creek in our meadow at a place where it is about twelve feet wide. He jumped bravely enough, but came down with a grand splash hardly more than halfway over. The water was only about a foot in depth, but the black vegetable mud half afloat was unfathomable. I managed to wallow ashore, but poor Jack sank deeper and deeper until only his head was visible in the black abyss, and his Indian fortitude was desperately tried. His foundering so suddenly in the treacherous gulf recalled the story of the Abbot of Aberbrothok's bell, which went down with a gurgling sound while bubbles rose and burst around. I had to go to father for help. He tied a long hemp rope brought from Scotland around Jack's neck, and Tom and Jerry seemed to have all they could do to pull him out. After which I got a solemn scolding for asking the 'puir beast to jump intil sic a saft bottomless place'.

We moved into our frame house in the autumn, when mother with the rest of the family arrived from Scotland, and, when the winter snow began to fly, our bur-oak shanty was made into a stable for Jack. Father told us that good meadow hay was all he required, but we fed him corn, lots of it, and he grew very frisky and fat. About the middle of winter his long hair was full of dust and, as we thought, required washing. So, without taking the frosty weather into account, we gave him a thorough soap and water scouring, and as we failed to get him rubbed dry, a row of icicles formed under his belly. Father happened to see him in this condition and angrily asked what we had been about. We said Jack was dirty and we had washed him to make him healthy. He told us we ought to be ashamed of ourselves, 'soaking the puir beast in cauld water at this time o' year'; that when we wanted to clean him we should have sense enough to use the brush and curry-comb.

In summer Dave or I had to ride after the cows every evening about sundown, and Jack got so accustomed to bringing in the drove that when we happened to be a few minutes late he used to go off alone at the regular time and bring them home at a gallop. It used to make father very angry to see Jack chasing the cows like a shepherd dog, running from one to the other and giving each a bite on the rump to keep them on the run, flying before him as if pursued by wolves. Father would declare at times that the wicked beast had the deevil in him and would be the death of the cattle. The corral and barn were just at the foot of a hill, and he made a great display of the drove on the home stretch as they walloped down that hill with their tails on end.

One evening when the pell-mell Wild West show was at its wildest, it made father so extravagantly mad that he ordered me to 'Shoot Jack!' I went to the house and brought the gun, suffering most horrible mental anguish, such as I suppose unhappy Abraham felt when commanded to slay Isaac. Jack's life was spared, however, though I can't tell what finally became of him. I wish I could. After father bought a span of work horses he was sold to a man who said he was going to ride him across the plains to California. We had him, I think, some five or six years. He was the stoutest, gentlest, bravest little horse I ever saw. He never seemed tired, could canter all day with a man about as heavy as himself on his back, and feared nothing. Once fifty or sixty pounds of beef that was tied on his back slid over his shoulders along his neck and weighed down his head to the ground, fairly anchoring him; but he stood patient and still for half an hour or so without making the slightest struggle to free himself, while I was away getting help to untie the pack-rope and set the load back in its place.

As I was the eldest boy I had the care of our first span of work horses. Their names were Nob and Nell. Nob was very intelligent, and even affectionate, and could learn almost anything. Nell was entirely different; balky and stubborn, though we managed to teach her a good many circus tricks; but she never seemed to like to play with us in anything like an affectionate way as Nob did. We turned them out one day into the pasture, and an Indian, hiding in the brush that had sprung up after the grass fires had been kept out, managed to catch Nob, tied a rope to her jaw for a bridle, rode her to Green Lake, about thirty or forty miles away, and tried to sell her for fifteen dollars. All our hearts were sore, as if one of the family had been lost. We hunted everywhere and could not at first imagine what had become of her. We discovered her track where the fence was broken down, and, following it for a few miles, made sure the track was Nob's; and a neighbour told us he had seen an Indian riding fast through the woods on a horse that looked like Nob. But we could find no further trace of her until a month or two after she was lost, and we had given up hope of ever seeing her again. Then we learned that she had been taken from an Indian by a farmer at Green Lake because he saw that she had been shod and had worked in harness. So when the Indian tried to sell her the farmer said, 'You are a thief. That is a white man's horse. You stole her.'

'No,' said the Indian, 'I bought her from Prairie du Chien and she has always been mine.'

The man, pointing to her feet and the marks of the harness, said, 'You are lying. I will take that horse away from you and put her in my pasture, and if you come near it I will set the dogs on you.' Then he advertised her. One of our neighbours happened to see the advertisement and brought us the glad news, and great was our rejoicing when father brought her home. That Indian must have treated her with terrible cruelty, for when I was riding her through the pasture several years afterward, looking for another horse that we wanted to catch, as we approached the place where she had been captured she stood stock still gazing through the bushes, fearing the Indian might still be hiding there ready to spring; and she was so excited that she trembled, and her heartbeats were so loud that I could hear them distinctly as I sat on her back, *boomp, boomp, boomp*, like the drumming of a partridge. So vividly had she remembered her terrible experiences.

She was a great pet and favourite with the whole family, quickly learning playful tricks, came running when we called, seemed to know everything we said to her, and had the utmost confidence in our friendly kindness.

We used to cut and shock and husk the Indian corn in the autumn, until a keen Yankee stopped overnight at our house and among other labour-saving notions convinced father that it was better to let it stand, and husk it at his leisure during the winter, then turn in the cattle to eat the leaves and trample down the stalks, so that they could be ploughed under in the spring. In this winter method each of us took two rows and husked into baskets, and emptied the corn on the ground in piles of fifteen to twenty basketfuls, then loaded it into the wagon to be hauled to the crib. This was cold, painful work, the temperature being oftentimes far below zero and the ground covered with dry, frosty snow, giving rise to miserable crops of chilblains and frosted fingers – a sad change from the merry Indian-summer husking, when the big yellow pumpkins covered the cleared fields: golden corn, golden pumpkins, gathered in the hazy golden weather. Sad change, indeed, but we occasionally got some fun out of the nipping, shivery work from hungry prairie chickens, and squirrels and mice that came about us.

The piles of corn were often left in the field several days, and while loading them into the wagon we usually found field mice in them – big, blunt-nosed, strong-scented fellows that we were taught to kill just because they nibbled a few grains of corn. I used to hold one while it was still warm, up to Nob's nose for the fun of seeing her make faces and snort at the smell of it; and I would say 'Here, Nob,' as if offering her a lump of sugar. One day I offered her an extra fine, fat, plump specimen, something like a little woodchuck, or muskrat, and to my astonishment, after smelling it curiously and doubtfully, as if wondering what the gift might be, and rubbing it back and forth in the palm of my hand with her upper lip, she deliberately took it into her mouth, crunched and munched and chewed it fine and swallowed it, bones, teeth, head, tail, everything. Not a single hair of that mouse was wasted. When she was chewing it she nodded and grunted, as though critically tasting and relishing it.

My father was a steadfast enthusiast on religious matters, and, of course, attended almost every sort of church-meeting, especially revival meetings. They were occasionally held in summer, but mostly in winter when the sleighing was good and plenty of time available. One hot summer day father drove Nob to Portage and back, twenty-four miles over a sandy road. It was a hot, hard, sultry day's work, and she had evidently been over-driven in order to get home in time for one of these meetings. I shall never forget how tired and wilted she looked that evening when I unhitched her; how she drooped in her stall, too tired to eat or even to lie down. Next morning it was plain that her lungs were inflamed; all the dreadful symptoms were just the same as my own when I had pneumonia. Father sent for a Methodist minister, a very energetic, resourceful man, who was a blacksmith, farmer, butcher and horse-doctor as well as minister; but all his gifts and skill were of no avail. Nob was doomed. We bathed her head and tried to get her to eat something, but she couldn't eat, and in about a couple of weeks we turned her loose to let her come around the house and see us in the weary suffering and loneliness of the shadow of death. She tried to follow us children, so long her friends and workmates and playmates. It was awfully touching. She had several haemorrhages, and in the forenoon of her last day, after she had had one of her dreadful spells of bleeding and gasping for breath, she came to me trembling, with beseeching, heartbreaking looks, and after I had bathed her head and tried to soothe and pet her, she lay down and gasped and died. All the family gathered about her, weeping, with aching hearts. Then dust to dust.

She was the most faithful, intelligent, playful, affectionate, human-like horse I ever knew, and she won all our hearts. Of the many advantages of farm life for boys one of the greatest is the gaining a real knowledge of animals as fellow-mortals, learning to respect them and love them, and even to win some of their love. Thus godlike sympathy grows and thrives and spreads far beyond the teachings of churches and schools, where too often the mean, blinding, loveless doctrine is taught that animals have neither mind nor soul, have no rights that we are bound to respect, and were made only for man, to be petted, spoiled, slaughtered, or enslaved.

At first we were afraid of snakes, but soon learned that most of them were harmless. The only venomous species seen on our farm were the rattlesnake and the copperhead, one of each. David saw the rattler, and we both saw the copperhead. One day, when my brother came in from his work, he reported that he had seen a snake that made a queer buzzy noise with its tail. This was the only rattlesnake seen on our farm, though we heard of them being common on limestone hills eight or ten miles distant. We discovered the copperhead when we were ploughing, and we saw and felt at the first long, fixed, half-charmed, admiring stare at him that he was an awfully dangerous fellow. Every fibre of his strong, lithe, quivering body, his burnished copper-coloured head, and above all his fierce, able eyes, seemed to be overflowing full of deadly power, and bade us beware. And yet it is only fair to say that this terrible, beautiful reptile showed no disposition to hurt us until we threw clods at him and tried to head him off from a log fence into which he was trying to escape. We were barefooted and of course afraid to let him get very near, while we vainly battered him with the loose sandy clods of the freshly ploughed field to hold him back until we could get a stick. Looking us in the eyes after a moment's pause, he probably saw we were afraid, and he came right straight at us, snapping and looking terrible, drove us out of his way, and won his fight.

Out on the open sandy hills there were a good many thick burly blow snakes, the kind that puff themselves up and hiss. Our Yankee declared that their breath was very poisonous and that we must not go near them. A handsome ringed species common in damp, shady places was, he told us, the most wonderful of all the snakes, for if chopped into pieces, however small, the fragments would wriggle themselves together again, and the restored snake would go on about its business as if nothing had happened. The commonest kinds were the striped slender species of the meadows and streams, good swimmers, that lived mostly on frogs.

Once I observed one of the larger ones, about two feet long, pursuing a frog in our meadow, and it was wonderful to see how fast the legless, footless, wingless, finless hunter could run. The frog, of course, knew its enemy and was making desperate efforts to escape to the water and hide in the marsh mud. He was a fine, sleek yellow muscular fellow and was springing over the tall grass in wide-arching jumps. The green-striped snake, gliding swiftly and steadily, was keeping the frog in sight and, had I not interfered, would probably have tired out the poor jumper. Then, perhaps, while digesting and enjoying his meal, the happy snake would himself be swallowed frog and all by a hawk. Again, to our astonishment, the small specimens were attacked by our hens. They pursued and pecked away at them until they killed and devoured them, oftentimes quarrelling over the division of the spoil, though it was not easily divided.

We watched the habits of the swift-darting dragonflies, wild bees, butterflies, wasps, beetles, etc., and soon learned to discriminate between those that might be safely handled and the pinching or stinging species. But of all our wild neighbours the mosquitoes were the first with which we became very intimately acquainted.

The beautiful meadow lying warm in the spring sunshine, outspread between our lily-rimmed lake and the hill-slope that our shanty stood on, sent forth thirsty swarms of the little grey, speckledy, singing, stinging pests; and how tellingly they introduced themselves! Of little avail were the smudges that we made on muggy evenings to drive them away; and amid the many lessons which they insisted upon teaching us we wondered more and more at the extent of their knowledge, especially that in their tiny, flimsy bodies room could be found for such cunning palates. They would drink their fill from brown, smoky Indians, or from old white folk flavoured with tobacco and whisky, when no better could be had. But the surpassing fineness of their taste was best manifested by their enthusiastic appreciation of boys full of lively red blood, and of girls in full bloom fresh from cool Scotland or England. On these it was pleasant to witness their enjoyment as they feasted. Indians, we were told, believed that if they were brave fighters they would go after death to a happy country abounding in game, where there were no mosquitoes and no cowards. For cowards were driven away by themselves to a miserable country where there was no game fit to eat, and where the sky was always dark with huge gnats and mosquitoes as big as pigeons.

We were great admirers of the little black water-bugs. Their whole lives seemed to be play, skimming, swimming, swirling, and waltzing together in little groups on the edge of the lake and in the meadow springs, dancing to music we never could hear. The long-legged skaters, too, seemed wonderful fellows, shuffling about on top of the water, with air-bubbles like little bladders tangled under their hairy feet; and we often wished that we also might be shod in the same way to enable us to skate on the lake in summer as well as in icy winter. Not less wonderful were the boatmen, swimming on their backs, pulling themselves along with a pair of oar-like legs.

Great was the delight of brothers David and Daniel and myself when father gave us a few pine boards for a boat, and it was a memorable day when we got that boat built and launched into the lake. Never shall I forget our first sail over the gradually deepening water, the sunbeams pouring through it revealing the strange plants covering the bottom, and the fishes coming about us, staring and wondering as if the boat were a monstrous strange fish.

The water was so clear that it was almost invisible, and when we floated slowly out over the plants and fishes, we seemed to be miraculously sustained in the air while silently exploring a veritable fairyland.

We always had to work hard, but if we worked still harder we were occasionally allowed a little spell in the long summer evenings about sundown to fish, and on Sundays an hour or two to sail quietly without fishing-rod or gun when the lake was calm. Therefore we gradually learned something about its inhabitants – pickerel, sunfish, black bass, perch, shiners, pumpkin-seeds, ducks, loons, turtles, muskrats, etc. We saw the sunfishes making their nests in little openings in the rushes where the water was only a few feet deep, ploughing up and shoving away the soft grey mud with their noses, like pigs, forming round bowls five or six inches in depth and about two feet in diameter, in which their eggs were deposited. And with what beautiful, unweariable devotion they watched and hovered over them and chased away prowling spawn-eating enemies that ventured within a rod or two of the precious nest!

The pickerel is a savage fish endowed with marvellous strength and speed. It lies in wait for its prey on the bottom, perfectly motionless like a waterlogged stick, watching everything that moves, with fierce, hungry eyes. Oftentimes when we were fishing for some other kinds over the edge of the boat, a pickerel that we had not noticed would come like a bolt of lightning and seize the fish we had caught before we could get it into the boat. The very first pickerel that I ever caught jumped into the air to seize a small fish dangling on my line, and, missing its aim, fell plump into the boat as if it had dropped from the sky.

Some of our neighbours fished for pickerel through the ice in midwinter. They usually drove a wagon out on the lake, set a large number of lines baited with live minnows, hung a loop of the lines over a small bush planted at the side of each hole, and watched to see the loops pulled off when a fish had taken the bait. Large quantities of pickerel were often caught in this cruel way.

Our beautiful lake, named Fountain Lake by father, but Muir's Lake by the neighbours, is one of the many small glacier lakes that adorn the Wisconsin landscapes. It is fed by twenty or thirty meadow springs, is about half a mile long, half as wide and surrounded by low finely-modelled hills dotted with oak and hickory, and meadows full of grasses and sedges and many beautiful orchids and ferns. First there is a zone of green, shining rushes, and just beyond the rushes a zone of white and orange water-lilies fifty or sixty feet wide forming a magnificent border. On bright days, when the lake was rippled by a breeze, the lilies and sun-spangles danced together in radiant beauty, and it became difficult to discriminate between them.

On Sundays, after or before chores and sermons and Bible-lessons, we drifted about on the lake for hours, especially in lily time, getting finest lessons and sermons from the water and flowers, ducks, fishes and muskrats. In particular we took Christ's advice and devoutly 'considered the lilies' – how they grow up in beauty out of grey lime mud, and ride gloriously among the breezy sun-spangles. On our way home we gathered grand bouquets of them to be kept fresh all the week. No flower was hailed with greater wonder and admiration by the European settlers in general – Scotch, English and Irish – than this white water-lily (*Nymphaea odorata*). It is a magnificent plant, queen of the inland waters, pure white, three or four inches in diameter, the most beautiful, sumptuous and deliciously fragrant of all our Wisconsin flowers. No lily garden in civilization we had ever seen could compare with our lake garden.

The next most admirable flower in the estimation of settlers in this part of the new world was the pasque-flower or wind-flower (*Anemone patens* var. *Nuttalliana*). It is the very first to appear in the spring, covering the cold grey-black ground with cherry blossoms. Before the axe or plough had touched the 'oak openings' of Wisconsin, they were swept by running fires almost every autumn after the grass became dry. If from any cause, such as early snow-storms or late rains, they happened to escape the autumn fire besom, they were likely to be burned in the spring after the snow melted. But whether burned in the spring or autumn, ashes and bits of charred twigs and grass stems made the whole country look dismal. Then, before a single grass-blade had sprouted, a hopeful multitude of large hairy, silky buds about as thick as one's thumb came to light, pushing up through the black and grey ashes and cinders, and before these buds were fairly free from the ground they opened wide and displayed purple blossoms about two inches in diameter, giving beauty for ashes in glorious abundance. Instead of remaining in the ground waiting for warm weather and companions, this admirable plant seemed to be in haste to rise and cheer the desolate landscape. Then at its leisure, after other plants had come to its help, it spread its leaves and grew up to a height of about two or three feet. The spreading leaves formed a whorl on the ground, and another about the middle of the stem as an involucre, and on the top of the stem the silky, hairy long-tailed seeds formed a head like a second flower. A little church was established among the earlier settlers and the meetings at first were held in our house. After working hard all the week it was difficult for boys to sit still through long sermons without falling asleep, especially in warm weather. In this drowsy trouble the charming anemone came to our help. A pocketful of the pungent seeds industriously nibbled while the discourses were at the dullest kept us awake and filled our minds with flowers.

The next great flower wonders on which we lavished admiration, not only for beauty of colour and size, but for their curious shapes, were the cypripe-diums, called 'lady's-slippers' or 'Indian moccasins'. They were so different from the familiar flowers of old Scotland. Several species grew in our meadow and on shady hillsides – yellow, rose-coloured and some nearly white, an inch or more in diameter, and shaped exactly like Indian moccasins. They caught the eye of all the European settlers and made them gaze and wonder like children. And so did calopogon, pogonia, spiranthes and many other fine plant people that lived in our meadow. The beautiful Turk's-turban (*Lilium superbum*) growing on stream-banks was rare in our neighbourhood, but the orange lily grew in abundance on dry ground beneath the bur-oaks and often brought Aunt Ray's lily-bed in Scotland to mind. The butterfly-weed, with its brilliant scarlet flowers, attracted flocks of butterflies and made fine masses of colour. With autumn came a glorious abundance and variety of asters, those beautiful plant stars, together with goldenrods, sunflowers, daisies and liatris of different species, while around the shady margin of the meadow many ferns in beds and vaselike groups spread their beautiful fronds, especially the osmundas (*O. claytoniana, regalis*, and *cinnamomea*) and the sensitive ostrich ferns.

Early in summer we feasted on strawberries, that grew in rich beds beneath the meadow grasses and sedges as well as in the dry sunny woods. And in different bogs and marshes, and around their borders on our own farm and along the Fox River, we found dewberries and cranberries, and a glorious profusion of huckleberries, the fountain-heads of pies of wondrous taste and size, coloured in the heart like sunsets. Nor were we slow to discover the value of the hickory trees yielding both sugar and nuts. We carefully counted the different kinds on our farm, and every morning when we could steal a few minutes before breakfast after doing the chores, we visited the trees that had been wounded by the axe, to scrape off and enjoy the thick white delicious syrup that exuded from them, and gathered the nuts as they fell in the mellow Indian summer, making haste to get a fair share with the sapsuckers and squirrels. The hickory makes fine masses of colour in the autumn, every leaf a flower, but it was the sweet sap and sweet nuts that first interested us. No harvest in the Wisconsin woods was ever gathered with more pleasure and care. Also, to our delight, we found plenty of hazelnuts, and in a few places abundance of wild apples. They were desperately sour, and we used to fill our pockets with them and dare each other to eat one without making a face – no easy feat.

One hot summer day father told us that we ought to learn to swim. This was one of the most interesting suggestions he had ever offered, but precious little time was allowed for trips to the lake, and he seldom tried to show us how. 'Go to the frogs,' he said, 'and they will give you all the lessons you need. Watch their arms and legs and see how smoothly they kick themselves along and dive and come up. When you want to dive, keep your arms by your side or over your head, and kick, and when you want to come up, let your legs drag and paddle with your hands.'

We found a little basin among the rushes at the south end of the lake, about waist-deep and a rod or two wide, shaped like a sunfish's nest. Here we kicked and plashed for many a lesson, faithfully trying to imitate frogs; but the smooth, comfortable sliding gait of our amphibious teachers seemed hopelessly hard to learn. When we tried to kick frog-fashion, down went our heads as if weighted with lead the moment our feet left the ground. One day it occurred to me to hold my breath as long as I could and let my head sink as far as it liked without paying any attention to it, and try to swim under the water instead of on the surface. This method was a great success, for at the very first trial I managed to cross the basin without touching bottom, and soon learned the use of my limbs. Then, of course, swimming with my head above water soon became so easy that it seemed perfectly natural. David tried the plan with the same success. Then we began to count the number of times that we could swim around the basin without stopping to rest, and after twenty or thirty rounds failed to tire us, we proudly thought that a little more practice would make us about as amphibious as frogs.

On the fourth of July of the swimming year one of the Lawson boys came to visit us, and we went down to the lake to spend the great warm day with the fishes and ducks and turtles. After gliding about on the smooth mirror water, telling stories and enjoying the company of the happy creatures about us, we rowed to our bathing-pool, and David and I went in for a swim, while our companion fished from the boat a little way out beyond the rushes. After a few turns in the pool, it occurred to me that it was now about time to try deep water. Swimming through the thick growth of rushes and lilies was somewhat dangerous, especially for a beginner, because one's arms and legs might be entangled among the long, limber stems; nevertheless I ventured and struck out boldly enough for the boat, where the water was twenty or thirty feet deep. When I reached the end of the little skiff I raised my right hand to take hold of it to surprise Lawson, whose back was toward me and who was not aware of my approach; but I failed to reach high enough, and, of course, the weight of my arm and the stroke against the overleaning stern of the boat shoved me down and I sank, struggling, frightened and confused. As soon as my feet touched the bottom, I slowly rose to the surface, but before I could get breath enough to call for help, sank back again and lost all control of myself. After sinking and rising I don't know how many times, some water got into my lungs and I began to drown. Then suddenly my mind seemed to clear. I remembered that I could swim under water, and, making a desperate struggle toward the shore, I reached a point where with my toes on the bottom I got my mouth above the surface, gasped for help, and was pulled into the boat.

This humiliating accident spoiled the day, and we all agreed to keep it a profound secret. My sister Sarah had heard my cry for help, and on our arrival at the house inquired what had happened. 'Were you drowning, John? I heard you cry you couldna get oot.' Lawson made haste to reply, 'Oh, no! He was juist haverin (making fun).'

I was very much ashamed of myself, and at night, after calmly reviewing the affair, concluded that there had been no reasonable cause for the accident, and that I ought to punish myself for so nearly losing my life from unmanly fear. Accordingly at the very first opportunity, I stole away to the lake by myself, got into my boat, and instead of going back to the old swimming-bowl for further practice, or to try to do sanely and well what I had so ignominiously failed to do in my first adventure, that is, to swim out through the rushes and lilies, I rowed directly out to the middle of the lake, stripped, stood up on the seat in the stern, and with grim deliberation took a header and dove straight down thirty or forty feet, turned easily, and, letting my feet drag, paddled straight to the surface with my hands as father had at first directed me to do. I then swam round the boat, glorying in my suddenly acquired confidence and victory over myself, climbed into it, and dived again, with the same triumphant success. I think I went down four or five times, and each time as I made the dive-spring shouted aloud, 'Take that!' feeling that I was getting most gloriously even with myself.

Never again from that day to this have I lost control of myself in water. If suddenly thrown overboard at sea in the dark, or even while asleep, I think I would immediately right myself in a way some would call 'instinct', rise among the waves, catch my breath, and try to plan what would better be done. Never was victory over self more complete. At a slow gait I think I could swim all day in smooth water moderate in temperature. When I was a student at Madison, I used to go on long swimming-journeys, called exploring expeditions, along the south shore of Lake Mendota, on Saturdays, sometimes alone, sometimes with another amphibious explorer by the name of Fuller.

My adventures in Fountain Lake call to mind the story of a boy who in climbing a tree to rob a crow's nest fell and broke his leg, but as soon as it healed compelled himself to climb to the top of the tree he had fallen from.

Like Scotch children in general we were taught grim self-denial, in season and out of season, to mortify the flesh, keep our bodies in subjection to Bible laws, and mercilessly punish ourselves for every fault imagined or committed. A little boy, while helping his sister to drive home the cows, happened to use a forbidden word. 'I'll have to tell fayther on ye,' said the horrified sister. 'I'll tell him that ye said a bad word.' 'Weel,' said the boy, by way of excuse, 'I couldna help the word comin' into me, and it's na waur to speak it oot than to let it rin through ye.'

A Scotch fiddler playing at a wedding drank so much whisky that on the way home he fell by the roadside. In the morning he was ashamed and angry and determined to punish himself. Making haste to the house of a friend, a gamekeeper, he called him out, and requested the loan of a gun. The alarmed gamekeeper, not liking the fiddler's looks and voice, anxiously inquired what he was going to do with it. 'Surely,' said he, 'you're no gan to shoot yoursel.' 'No-o,' with characteristic candour replied the penitent fiddler, 'I dinna think that I'll just exactly kill mysel, but I'm gaun to tak a dander doon the burn (brook) wi' the gun and gie mysel a deevil o' a fleg (fright).'

One calm summer evening a red-headed woodpecker was drowned in our lake. The accident happened at the south end, opposite our memorable swimming-hole, a few rods from the place where I came so near being drowned years before. I had returned to the old home during a summer vacation of the State University, and, having made a beginning in botany, I was, of course, full of enthusiasm and ran eagerly to my beloved pogonia, calopogon, and cypripedium gardens, osmunda ferneries, and the lake lilies and pitcher-plants. A little before sundown the day-breeze died away, and the lake, reflecting the wooded hills like a mirror, was dimpled and dotted and streaked here and there where fishes and turtles were poking out their heads and muskrats were sculling themselves along with their flat tails making glittering tracks. After lingering a while, dreamily recalling the old, hard, half-happy days, and watching my favourite red-headed woodpeckers pursuing moths like regular flycatchers, I swam out through the rushes and up the middle of the lake to the north end and back, gliding slowly, looking about me, enjoying the scenery as I would in a saunter along the shore, and studying the habits of the animals as they were explained and recorded on the smooth glassy water.

On the way back, when I was within a hundred rods or so of the end of my voyage, I noticed a peculiar plashing disturbance that could not, I thought, be made by a jumping fish or any other inhabitant of the lake; for instead of low regular out-circling ripples such as are made by the popping up of a head, or like those raised by the quick splash of a leaping fish, or diving loon or muskrat, a continuous struggle was kept up for several minutes ere the outspreading, interfering ring-waves began to die away. Swimming hastily to the spot to try to discover what had happened, I found one of my woodpeckers floating motionless with outspread wings. All was over. Had I been a minute or two earlier, I might have saved him. He had glanced on the water I suppose in pursuit of a moth, was unable to rise from it, and died struggling, as I nearly did at this same spot. Like me he seemed to have lost his mind in blind confusion and fear. The water was warm, and had he kept still with his head a little above the surface, he would sooner or later have been wafted ashore. The best aimed flights of birds and man 'gang aft agley', but this was the first case I had witnessed of a bird losing its life by drowning.

Doubtless accidents to animals are far more common than is generally known. I have seen quails killed by flying against our house when suddenly startled. Some birds get entangled in hairs of their own nests and die. Once I found a poor snipe in our meadow that was unable to fly on account of difficult egg-birth. Pitying the poor mother, I picked her up out of the grass and helped her as gently as I could, and as soon as the egg was born she flew gladly away. Oftentimes I have thought it strange that one could walk through the woods and mountains and plains for years without seeing a single blood-spot. Most wild animals get into the world and out of it without being noticed. Nevertheless we at last sadly learn that they are all subject to the vicissitudes of fortune like ourselves. Many birds lose their lives in storms. I remember a particularly severe Wisconsin winter, when the temperature was many degrees below zero and the snow was deep, preventing the quail, which feed on the ground, from getting anything like enough of food, as was pitifully shown by a flock I found on our farm frozen solid in a thicket of oak sprouts. They were in a circle about a foot wide, with their heads outward, packed close together for warmth. Yet all had died without a struggle, perhaps more from starvation than frost. Many small birds lose their lives in the storms of early spring, or even summer. One mild spring morning I picked up more than a score out of the grass and flowers, most of them darling singers that had perished in a sudden storm of sleety rain and hail.

In a hollow at the foot of an oak tree that I had chopped down one cold winter day, I found a poor ground squirrel frozen solid in its snug grassy nest, in the middle of a store of nearly a peck of wheat it had carefully gathered. I carried it home and gradually thawed and warmed it in the kitchen, hoping it would come to life like a pickerel I caught in our lake through a hole in the ice, which, after being frozen as hard as a bone and thawed at the fireside, squirmed itself out of the grasp of the cook when she began to scrape it, bounced off the table, and danced about on the floor, making wonderful springy jumps as if trying to find its way back home to the lake. But for the poor spermophile nothing I could do in the way of revival was of any avail. Its life had passed away without the slightest struggle, as it lay asleep curled up like a ball, with its tail wrapped about it.

CHAPTER FOUR

A Paradise of Birds

THE WISCONSIN oak openings were a summer paradise for song birds, and a fine place to get acquainted with them: for the trees stood wide apart, allowing one to see the happy homeseekers as they arrived in the spring, their mating, nest-building, the brooding and feeding of the young, and, after they were full-fledged and strong, to see all the families of the neighbourhood gathering and getting ready to leave in the autumn. Excepting the geese and ducks and pigeons, nearly all our summer birds arrived singly or in small draggled flocks, but when frost and falling leaves brought their winter homes to mind they assembled in large flocks on dead or leafless trees by the side of a meadow or field, perhaps to get acquainted and talk the thing over. Some species held regular daily meetings for several weeks before finally setting forth on their long southern journeys. Strange to say, we never saw them start. Some morning we would find them gone. Doubtless they migrated in the night time. Comparatively few species remained all winter: the nuthatch, chickadee, owl, prairie chicken, quail and a few stragglers from the main flocks of ducks, jays, hawks and bluebirds. Only after the country was settled did either jays or bluebirds winter with us.

The brave, frost-defying chickadees and nuthatches stayed all the year wholly independent of farms and man's food and affairs.

With the first hints of spring came the brave little bluebirds, darling singers as blue as the best sky, and of course we all loved them. Their rich, crispy warbling is perfectly delightful, soothing and cheering, sweet and whisperingly low, Nature's fine love touches, every note going straight home into one's heart. And withal they are hardy and brave, fearless fighters in defence of home. When we boys approached their knot-hole nests, the bold little fellows kept scolding and diving at us and tried to strike us in the face, and oftentimes we were afraid they would prick our eyes. But the boldness of the little housekeepers only made us love them the more.

None of the bird people of Wisconsin welcomed us more heartily than the common robin. Far from showing alarm at the coming of settlers into their native woods, they reared their young around our gardens as if they liked us, and how heartily we admired the beauty and fine manners of these graceful birds and their loud cheery song of *Fear not, fear not, cheer up, cheer up*. It was easy to love them for they reminded us of the robin redbreast of Scotland. Like the bluebirds they dared every danger in defence of home, and we often wondered that birds so gentle could be so bold and that sweet-voiced singers could so fiercely fight and scold.

Of all the great singers that sweeten Wisconsin one of the best known and best loved is the brown thrush or thrasher, strong and able without being familiar, and easily seen and heard. Rosy purple evenings after thunder-showers are the favourite song-times, when the winds have died away and the steaming ground and the leaves and flowers fill the air with fragrance. Then the male makes haste to the topmost spray of an oak tree and sings loud and clear with delightful enthusiasm until sundown, mostly I suppose for his mate sitting on the precious eggs in a brush heap. And how faithful and watchful and daring he is! Woe to the snake or squirrel that ventured to go nigh the nest! We often saw him diving on them, pecking them about the head and driving them away as bravely as the kingbird drives away hawks. Their rich and varied strains make the air fairly quiver. We boys often tried to interpret the wild ringing melody and put it into words.

After the arrival of the thrushes came the bobolinks, gushing, gurgling, inexhaustible fountains of song, pouring forth floods of sweet notes over the broad Fox River meadows in wonderful variety and volume, crowded and mixed beyond description, as they hovered on quivering wings above their hidden nests in the grass. It seemed marvellous to us that birds so moderate in size could hold so much of this wonderful song stuff. Each one of them poured forth music enough for a whole flock, singing as if its whole body, feathers and all, were made up of music, flowing, glowing, bubbling melody interpenetrated here and there with small scintillating prickles and spicules. We never became so intimately acquainted with the bobolinks as with the thrushes, for they lived far out on the broad Fox River meadows, while the thrushes sang on the tree-tops around every home. The bobolinks were among the first of our great singers to leave us in the fall, going apparently direct to the rice-fields of the Southern States, where they grew fat and were slaughtered in countless numbers for food. Sad fate for singers so purely divine.

One of the gayest of the singers is the redwing blackbird. In the spring, when his scarlet epaulets shine brightest, and his little modest grey wife is sitting on the nest, built on rushes in a swamp, he sits on a nearby oak and devotedly sings almost all day. His rich simple strain is *baumpalee, baumpalee*, or *bobalee* as interpreted by some. In summer, after nesting cares are over, they assemble in flocks of hundreds and thousands to feast on Indian corn when it is in the milk. Scattering over a field, each selects an ear, strips the husk down far enough to lay bare an inch or two of the end of it, enjoys an exhilarating feast, and after all are full they rise simultaneously with a quick birr of wings like an old-fashioned church congregation fluttering to their feet when the minister after giving out the humn says, 'Let the congregation arise and sing.' Alighting on nearby trees, they sing with a hearty vengeance, bursting out without any puttering prelude in gloriously glad concert, hundreds or thousands of exulting voices with sweet gurgling *baumpalees* mingled with chippy vibrant and exploding globules of musical notes, making a most enthusiastic, indescribable joy-song, a combination unlike anything to be heard elsewhere in the bird kingdom: something like bagpipes, flutes, violins, pianos, and human-like voices all bursting and bubbling at once. Then suddenly someone of the joyful congregation shouts *Chirr! Chirr!* and all stop as if shot.

The sweet-voiced meadowlark with its placid, simple song of *peery-eery-ódical* was another favourite, and we soon learned to admire the Baltimore oriole and its wonderful hanging nests, and the scarlet tanager glowing like fire amid the green leaves.

But no singer of them all got further into our hearts than the little speckle-breasted song sparrow, one of the first to arrive and begin nest-building and singing. The richness, sweetness and pathos of this small darling's song as he sat on a low bush often brought tears to our eyes.

The little cheery, modest chickadee midget, loved by every innocent boy and girl, man and woman, and by many not altogether innocent, was one of the first of the birds to attract our attention, drawing nearer and nearer to us as the winter advanced, bravely singing his faint silvery, lisping, tinkling notes ending with a bright *dee, dee, dee!* however frosty the weather.

The nuthatches, who also stayed all winter with us, were favourites with us boys. We loved to watch them as they traced the bark-furrows of the oaks and hickories head downward, deftly flicking off loose scales and splinters in search of insects and braving the coldest weather as if their little sparks of life were as safely warm in winter as in summer, unquenchable by the severest frost. With the help of the chickadees they made a beautiful stir in the solemn winter days, and when we were out chopping we never ceased to wonder how their slender naked toes could be kept warm when our own were so painfully frosted though clad in thick socks and boots. And we wondered and admired the more when we thought of the little midgets sleeping in knot-holes when the temperature was far below zero, sometimes thirty-five degrees below, and in the morning, after a minute breakfast of a few frozen insects and hoarfrost crystals, playing and chatting in cheery tones as if food, weather and everything was according to their own warm hearts. Our Yankee told us that the name of this darling was Devil-downhead.

Their big neighbours the owls also made good winter music, singing out loud in wild, gallant strains bespeaking brave comfort, let the frost bite as it might. The solemn hooting of the species with the widest throat seemed to us the very wildest of all the winter sounds.

Prairie chickens came strolling in family flocks about the shanty, picking seeds and grasshoppers like domestic fowls, and they became still more abundant as wheat- and corn-fields were multiplied, but also wilder, of course, when every shotgun in the country was aimed at them. The booming of the males during the mating-season was one of the loudest and strangest of the early spring sounds, being easily heard on calm mornings at a distance of a half or three fourths of a mile. As soon as the snow was off the ground, they assembled in flocks of a dozen or two on an open spot, usually on the side of a ploughed field, ruffled up their feathers, inflated the curious coloured sacks on the sides of their necks and strutted about with queer gestures something like turkey gobblers, uttering strange loud, rounded, drumming calls – *boom! boom! boom!* interrupted by choking sounds. My brother Daniel caught one while she was sitting on her nest in our corn-field. The young are just like domestic chicks, run with the mother as soon as hatched, and stay with her until autumn, feeding on the ground, never taking wing unless disturbed. In winter, when full-grown, they assemble in large flocks, fly about sundown to selected roosting-places on tall trees, and to feeding-places in the morning – unhusked corn-fields, if any are to be found in the neighbourhood, or thickets of dwarf birch and willows, the buds of which furnish a considerable part of their food when snow covers the ground.

The wild rice-marshes along the Fox River and around Pucaway Lake were the summer homes of millions of ducks, and in the Indian summer, when the rice was ripe, they grew very fat. The magnificent mallards in particular afforded our Yankee neighbours royal feasts almost without price, for often as many as a half-dozen were killed at a shot, but we seldom were allowed a single hour for hunting and so got very few. The autumn duck season was a glad time for the Indians also, for they feasted and grew fat not only on the ducks but on the wild rice, large quantities of which they gathered as they glided through the midst of the generous crop in canoes, bending down handfuls over the sides, and beating out the grain with small paddles.

The warmth of the deep spring fountains of the creek in our meadow kept it open all the year, and a few pairs of wood ducks, the most beautiful, we thought, of all the ducks, wintered in it. I well remember the first specimen I ever saw. Father shot it in the creek during a snowstorm, brought it into the house, and called us around him, saying, 'Come, bairns, and admire the work of God displayed in this bonnie bird. Naebody but God could paint feathers like these. Juist look at the colours, hoo they shine, and hoo fine they overlap and blend thegether like the colours o' the rainbow.' And we all agreed that never, never before had we seen so awfu' bonnie a bird. A pair nested every year in the hollow top of an oak stump about fifteen feet high that stood on the side of the meadow, and we used to wonder how they got the fluffy young ones down from the nest and across the meadow to the lake when they were only helpless, featherless midgets: whether the mother carried them to the water on her back or in her mouth. I never saw the thing done or found anybody who had until this summer, when Mr Holabird, a keen observer, told me that he once saw the mother carry them from the nest in her mouth, quickly coming and going to a nearby stream, and in a few minutes get them all together and proudly sail away.

Sometimes a flock of swans were seen passing over at a great height on their long journeys, and we admired their clear bugle notes, but they seldom visited any of the lakes in our neighbourhood, so seldom that when they did it was talked of for years. One was shot by a blacksmith on a millpond with a long-range Sharp's rifle, and many of the neighbours went far to see it.

The common grey goose, Canada honker, flying in regular harrow-shaped flocks, was one of the wildest and wariest of all the large birds that enlivened the spring and autumn. They seldom ventured to alight in our small lake, fearing, I suppose, that hunters might be concealed in the rushes, but on account of their fondness for the young leaves of winter wheat when they were a few inches high, they often alighted on our fields when passing on their way south, and occasionally even in our corn-fields when a snowstorm was blowing and they were hungry and wing-weary, with nearly an inch of snow on their backs. In such times of distress we used to pity them, even while trying to get a shot at them. They were exceedingly cautious and circumspect; usually flew several times round the adjacent thickets and fences to make sure that no enemy was near before settling down, and one always stood on guard, relieved from time to time, while the flock was feeding. Therefore there was no chance to creep up on them unobserved; you had to be well hidden before the flock arrived. It was the ambition of boys to be able to shoot these wary birds. I never got but two, both of them at one so-called lucky shot. When I ran to pick them up, one of them flew away, but as the poor fellow was sorely wounded he didn't fly far. When I caught him after a short chase, he uttered a piercing cry of terror and despair, which the leader of the flock heard at a distance of about a hundred rods. They had flown off in frightened disorder, of course, but had got into the regular harrow-shape order when the leader heard the cry, and I shall never forget how bravely he left his place at the head of the flock and hurried back screaming and struck at me in trying to save his companion. I dodged down and held my hands over my head, and thus escaped a blow of his elbows. Fortunately I had left my gun at the fence, and the life of this noble bird was spared after he had risked it in trying to save his wounded friend or neighbour or family relation. For so shy a bird boldly to attack a hunter showed wonderful sympathy and courage. This is one of my strangest hunting experiences. Never before had I regarded wild geese as dangerous, or capable of such noble self-sacrificing devotion.

The loud clear call of the handsome bob-whites was one of the pleasantest and most characteristic of our spring sounds, and we soon learned to imitate it so well that a bold cock often accepted our challenge and came flying to fight. The young run as soon as they are hatched and follow their parents until spring, roosting on the ground in a close bunch, heads out ready to scatter and fly. These fine birds were seldom seen when we first arrived in the wilderness, but when wheat-fields supplied abundance of food they multiplied very fast, although oftentimes sore pressed during hard winters when the snow reached a depth of two or three feet, covering their food, while the mercury fell to twenty or thirty degrees below zero. Occasionally, although shy on account of being persistently hunted, under pressure of extreme hunger in the very coldest weather when the snow was deepest they ventured into barnyards and even approached the doorsteps of houses, searching for any sort of scraps and crumbs, as if piteously begging for food. One of our neighbours saw a flock come creeping up through the snow, unable to fly, hardly able to walk, and while approaching the door several of them actually fell down and died; showing that birds, usually so vigorous and apparently independent of fortune, suffer and lose their lives in extreme weather like the rest of us, frozen to death like settlers caught in blizzards. None of our neighbours perished in storms, though many had feet, ears and fingers frost-nipped or solidly frozen.

As soon as the lake ice melted, we heard the lonely cry of the loon, one of the wildest and most striking of all the wilderness sounds, a strange, sad, mournful, unearthly cry, half laughing, half wailing. Nevertheless the great northern diver, as our species is called, is a brave, hardy, beautiful bird, able to fly under water about as well as above it, and to spear and capture the swiftest fishes for food. Those that haunted our lake were so wary none was shot for years, though every boy hunter in the neighbourhood was ambitious to get one to prove his skill. On one of our bitter cold New Year holidays I was surprised to see a loon in the small open part of the lake at the mouth of the inlet that was kept from freezing by the warm spring water. I knew that it could not fly out of so small a place, for these heavy birds have to beat the water for half a mile or so before they can get fairly on the wing. Their narrow, finlike wings are very small as compared with the weight of the body and are evidently made for flying through water as well as through the air, and it is by means of their swift flight through the water and the swiftness of the blow they strike with their long, spear-like bills that they are able to capture the fishes on which they feed. I ran down the meadow with the gun, got into my boat, and pursued that poor winter-bound straggler. Of course he dived again and again, but had to come up to breathe, and I at length got a quick shot at his head and slightly wounded or stunned him, caught him and ran proudly back to the house with my prize. I carried him in my arms; he didn't struggle to get away or offer to strike me, and when I put him on the floor in front of the kitchen stove, he just rested quietly on his belly as noiseless and motionless as if he were a stuffed specimen on a shelf, held his neck erect, gave no sign of suffering from any wound, and though he was motionless, his small black eyes seemed to be ever keenly watchful. His formidable bill, very sharp, three or three and a half inches long, and shaped like a pickaxe, was held perfectly level. But the wonder was that he did not struggle or make the slightest movement. We had a tortoise-shell cat, an old Tom of great experience, who was so fond of lying under the stove in frosty weather that it was difficult even to poke him out with a broom; but when he saw and smelled that strange big fishy, black and white, speckledy bird, the like of which he had never before seen, he rushed wildly to the farther corner of the kitchen, looked back cautiously and suspiciously, and began to make a careful study of the handsome but dangerous-looking stranger. Becoming more and more curious and interested, he at length advanced a step or two for a nearer view and nearer smell; and as the wonderful bird kept absolutely motionless, he was encouraged to venture gradually nearer and nearer until within perhaps five or six feet of its breast. Then the wary loon, not liking Tom's looks in so near a view, which perhaps recalled to his mind the plundering minks and muskrats he had to fight when they approached his nest, prepared to defend himself by slowly, almost imperceptibly drawing back his long pickaxe bill, and without the slightest fuss or stir held it level and ready just over his tail. With that dangerous bill drawn so far back out of the way, Tom's confidence in the stranger's peaceful intentions seemed almost complete, and, thus encouraged, he at last ventured forward with wondering, questioning eyes and quivering nostrils until he was only eighteen or twenty inches from the loon's smooth white breast. When the beautiful bird, apparently as peaceful and inoffensive as a flower, saw that his hairy yellow enemy had arrived at the right distance, the loon, who evidently was a fine judge of the reach of his spear, shot it forward quick as a lightning-flash, in marvellous contrast to the wonderful slowness of the preparatory poising, backward motion. The aim was true to a hair-breadth. Tom was struck right in the centre of his forehead, between the eyes. I thought his skull was cracked. Perhaps it was. The sudden astonishment of that outraged cat, the virtuous indignation and wrath, terror and pain, are far beyond description. His eyes and screams and desperate retreat told all that. When the blow was received, he made a noise that I never heard a cat make before or since; an awfully deep, condensed, screechy, explosive *Wuck!* as he bounced straight up in the air like a bucking bronco; and when he alighted after his spring, he rushed madly across the room and made frantic efforts to climb up the hard-finished plaster wall. Not satisfied to get the width of the kitchen away from his mysterious enemy, for the first time that cold winter he tried to get out of the house, anyhow, anywhere out of that loon-infested room. When he finally ventured to look back and saw that the barbarous bird was still there, tranquil and motionless in front of the stove, he regained command of some of his shattered senses and carefully commenced to examine his wound. Backed against the wall in the farthest corner, and keeping his eye on the outrageous bird, he tenderly touched and washed the sore spot, wetting his paw with his tongue, pausing now and then as his courage increased to glare and stare and growl at his enemy with looks and tones wonderfully human, as if saying, 'You confounded fishy, unfair rascal! What did you do that for? What had I done to you? Faithless, legless, long-nosed wretch!' Intense experiences like the above bring out the humanity that is in all animals. One touch of nature, even a cat-and-loon touch, makes all the world kin.

It was a great memorable day when the first flock of passenger pigeons came to our farm, calling to mind the story we had read about them when we were at school in Scotland. Of all God's feathered people that sailed the Wisconsin sky, no other bird seemed to us so wonderful. The beautiful wanderers flew like the winds in flocks of millions from climate to climate in accord with the weather, finding their food – acorns, beechnuts, pine-nuts, cranberries, strawberries, huckleberries, juniper berries, hackberries, buckwheat, rice, wheat, oats, corn – in fields and forests thousands of miles apart. I have seen flocks streaming south in the autumn so large that they were flowing over from horizon to horizon in an almost continuous stream all day long, at the rate of forty or fifty miles an hour, like a mighty river in the sky, widening, contracting, descending like falls and cataracts, and rising suddenly here and there in huge ragged masses like high-plashing spray. How wonderful the distances they flew in a day – in a year – in a lifetime! They arrived in Wisconsin in the spring just after the sun had cleared away the snow, and alighted in the woods to feed on the fallen acorns that they had missed the previous autumn. A comparatively small flock swept thousands of acres perfectly clean of acorns in a few minutes, by moving straight ahead with a broad front. All got their share, for the rear constantly became the van by flying over the flock and alighting in front, the entire flock constantly changing from rear to front, revolving something like a wheel with a low buzzing wing roar that could be heard a long way off. In summer they feasted on wheat and oats and were easily approached as they rested on the trees along the sides of the field after a good full meal, displaying beautiful iridescent colours as they moved their necks backward and forward when we went very near them. Every shotgun was aimed at them and everybody feasted on pigeon pies, and not a few of the settlers feasted also on the beauty of the wonderful birds. The breast of the male is a fine rosy red, the lower part of the neck behind and along the sides changing from the red of the breast to gold, emerald green and rich crimson. The general colour of the upper parts is greyish blue, the under parts white. The extreme length of the bird is about seventeen inches; the finely modelled slender tail about eight inches, and extent of wings twenty-four inches. The females are scarcely less beautiful. 'Oh, what bonnie, bonnie birds!' we exclaimed over the first that fell into our hands. 'Oh, what colours! Look at their breasts, bonnie as roses, and at their necks aglow wi' every colour juist like the wonderfu' wood ducks. Oh, the bonnie, bonnie creatures, they beat a'! Where did they a' come fra, and where are they a' gan? It's awfu' like a sin to kill them!' To this some smug, practical old sinner would remark, 'Aye, it's a peety, as ye say, to kill the bonnie things, but they were made to be killed, and sent for us to eat as the quails were sent to God's chosen people, the Israelites, when they were starving in the desert ayont the Red Sea. And I must confess that meat was never put up in neater, handsomer-painted packages.'

In the New England and Canada woods beechnuts were their best and most abundant food, farther north, cranberries and huckleberries. After everything was cleaned up in the north and winter was coming on, they went south for rice, corns, acorns, haws, wild grapes, crab-apples, sparkle-berries, etc. They seemed to require more than half of the continent for feeding-grounds, moving from one table to another, field to field, forest to forest, finding something ripe and wholesome all the year round. In going south in the fine Indian-summer weather they flew high and followed one another, though the head of the flock might be hundreds of miles in advance. But against head winds they took advantage of the inequalities of the ground, flying comparatively low. All followed the leader's ups and downs over hill and dale though far out of sight, never hesitating at any turn of the way, vertical or horizontal, that the leaders had taken, though the largest flocks stretched across several States, and belts of different kinds of weather.

There were no roosting- or breeding-places near our farm, and I never saw any of them until long after the great flocks were exterminated. I therefore quote, from Audubon's and Pokagon's vivid descriptions.

'Toward evening,' Audubon says, 'they depart for the roosting-place, which may be hundreds of miles distant. One on the banks of Green River, Kentucky, was over three miles wide and forty long.

'My first view of it,' says the great naturalist, 'was about a fortnight after it had been chosen by the birds, and I arrived there nearly two hours before sunset. Few pigeons were then to be seen, but a great many persons with horses and wagons and armed with guns, long poles, sulphur pots, pine pitch torches, etc., had already established encampments on the borders. Two farmers had driven upwards of three hundred hogs a distance of more than a hundred miles to be fattened on slaughtered pigeons. Here and there the people employed in plucking and salting what had already been secured were sitting in the midst of piles of birds. Dung several inches thick covered the ground. Many trees two feet in diameter were broken off at no great distance from the ground, and the branches of many of the tallest and largest had given way, as if the forest had been swept by a tornado.

'Not a pigeon had arrived at sundown. Suddenly a general cry arose – "Here they come!" The noise they made, though still distant, reminded me of a hard gale at sea passing through the rigging of a close-reefed ship. Thousands were soon knocked down by the pole-men. The birds continued to pour in. The fires were lighted and a magnificent as well as terrifying sight presented itself. The pigeons pouring in alighted everywhere, one above another, until solid masses were formed on the branches all around. Here and there the perches gave way with a crash, and falling destroyed hundreds beneath, forcing down the dense groups with which every stick was loaded; a scene of uproar and conflict. I found it useless to speak or even to shout to those persons nearest me. Even the reports of the guns were seldom heard, and I was made aware of the firing only by seeing the shooters reloading. None dared venture within the line of devastation. The hogs had been penned up in due time, the picking up of the dead and wounded being left for the next morning's employment. The pigeons were constantly coming in and it was after midnight before I perceived a decrease in the number of those that arrived. The uproar continued all night, and anxious to know how far the sound reached I sent off a man who, returning two hours after, informed me that he had heard it distinctly three miles distant.

'Toward daylight the noise in some measure subsided; long before objects were distinguishable the pigeons began to move off in a direction quite different from that in which they had arrived the evening before, and at sunrise all that were able to fly had disappeared. The howling of the wolves now reached our ears, and the foxes, lynxes, cougars, bears, coons, opossums and polecats were seen sneaking off, while eagles and hawks of different species, accompanied by a crowd of vultures, came to supplant them and enjoy a share of the spoil.

'Then the authors of all this devastation began their entry amongst the dead, the dying and mangled. The pigeons were picked up and piled in heaps until each had as many as they could possibly dispose of, when the hogs were let loose to feed on the remainder.

'The breeding-places are selected with reference to abundance of food, and countless myriads resort to them. At this period the note of the pigeon is coo coo coo, like that of the domestic species but much shorter. They caress by billing, and during incubation the male supplies the female with food. As the young grow, the tyrant of creation appears to disturb the peaceful scene, armed with axes to chop down the squab-laden trees, and the abomination of desolation and destruction produced far surpasses even that of the roosting places.'

Pokagon, an educated Indian writer, says: 'I saw one nesting-place in Wisconsin one hundred miles long and from three to ten miles wide. Every tree, some of them quite low and scrubby, had from one to fifty nests on each. Some of the nests overflow from the oaks to the hemlock and pine woods. When the pigeon hunters attack the breeding-places they sometimes cut the timber from thousands of acres. Millions are caught in nets with salt or grain for bait, and schooners, sometimes loaded down with the birds, are taken to New York where they are sold for a cent apiece.'

CHAPTER FIVE

Young Hunters

IN THE older eastern States it used to be considered great sport for an army of boys to assemble to hunt birds, squirrels, and every other unclaimed, unprotected live thing of shootable size. They dived into two squads, and, choosing leaders, scattered through the woods in different directions, and the party that killed the greatest number enjoyed a supper at the expense of the other. The whole neighbourhood seemed to enjoy the shameful sport especially the farmers afraid of their crops. With a great air of importance, laws were enacted to govern the gory business. For example, a grey squirrel must count four heads, a woodchuck six heads, common red squirrel two heads, black squirrel ten heads, a partridge five heads, the larger birds, such as whip-poor-wills and nighthawks two heads each, the wary crows three, and bob-whites three. But all the blessed company of mere songbirds, warblers, robins, thrushes, orioles, with nuthatches, chickadees, blue jays, woodpeckers, etc., counted only one head each. The heads of the birds were hastily wrung off and thrust into the game-bags to be counted, saving the bodies only of what were called game, the larger squirrels, bob-whites, partridges, etc. The blood-stained bags of the best slayers were soon bulging full. Then at a given hour all had to stop and repair to the town, empty their dripping sacks, count the heads, and go rejoicing to their dinner. Although, like other wild boys, I was fond of shooting, I never had anything to do with these abominable head-hunts. And now, the farmers having learned that birds are their friends, wholesale slaughter has been abolished.

We seldom saw deer, though their tracks were common. The Yankee explained that they travelled and fed mostly at night, and hid in tamarack swamps and brushy places in the daytime, and how the Indians knew all about them and could find them whenever they were hungry.

Indians belonging to the Menominee and Winnebago tribes occasionally visited us at our cabin to get a piece of bread or some matches, or to sharpen their knives on our grindstone, and we boys watched them closely to see that they didn't steal Jack. We wondered at their knowledge of animals when we saw them go direct to trees on our farm, chop holes in them with their tomahawks and take out coons, of the existence of which we had never noticed the slightest trace. In winter, after the first snow, we frequently saw three or four Indians hunting deer in company, running like hounds on the fresh, exciting tracks. The escape of the deer from these noiseless, tireless hunters was said to be well-nigh impossible; they were followed to the death.

Most of our neighbours brought some sort of gun from the old country, but seldom took time to hunt, even after the first hard work of fencing and clearing was over, except to shoot a duck or prairie chicken now and then that happened to come in their way. It was only the less industrious American settlers who left their work to go far a-hunting. Two or three of our most enterprising American neighbours went off every autumn with their teams to the pine regions and cranberry marshes in the northern part of the State to hunt and gather berries. I well remember seeing their wagons loaded with game when they returned from a successful hunt. Their loads consisted usually of half a dozen deer or more, one or two black bears and fifteen or twenty bushels of cranberries; all solidly frozen. Part of both the berries and meat was usually sold in Portage; the balance furnished their families with abundance of venison, bear grease and pies.

Winter wheat is sown in the autumn, and when it is a month or so old the deer, like the wild geese, are very fond of it, especially since other kinds of food are then becoming scarce. One of our neighbours across the Fox River killed a large number, some thirty or forty, on a small patch of wheat, simply by lying in wait for them every night. Our wheat-field was the first that was sown in the neighbourhood. The deer soon found it and came in every night to feast, but it was eight or nine years before we ever disturbed them. David then killed one deer, the only one killed by any of our family. He went out shortly after sundown at the time of full moon to one of our wheat-fields, carrying a double-barrelled shotgun loaded with buck-shot. After lying in wait an hour or so, he saw a doe and her fawn jump the fence and come cautiously into the wheat. After they were within sixty or seventy yards of him, he was surprised when he tried to take aim that about half of the moon's disc was mysteriously darkened as if covered by the edge of a dense cloud. This proved to be an eclipse. Nevertheless, he fired at the mother, and she immediately ran off, jumped the fence, and took to the woods by the way she came. The fawn danced about bewildered, wondering what had become of its mother, but finally fled to the woods. David fired at the poor deserted thing as it ran past him but happily missed it. Hearing the shots, I joined David to learn his luck. He said he thought he must have wounded the mother, and when we were strolling about in the woods in search of her we saw three or four deer on their way to the wheat-field, led by a fine buck. They were walking rapidly, but cautiously halted at intervals of a few rods to listen and look ahead and scent the air. They failed to notice us, though by this time the moon was out of the eclipse shadow and we were standing only about fifty yards from them. I was carrying the gun. David had fired both barrels but when he was reloading one of them he happened to put the wad intended to cover the shot into the empty barrel, and so when we were climbing over the fence the buckshot had rolled out, and when I fired at the big buck I knew by the report that there was nothing but powder in the charge. The startled deer danced about in confusion for a few seconds, uncertain which way to run until they caught sight of us, when they bounded off through the woods. Next morning we found the poor mother lying about three hundred yards from the place where she was shot. She had run this distance and jumped a high fence after one of the buckshot had passed through her heart.

Excepting Sundays we boys had only two days of the year to ourselves, the 4th of July and the 1st of January. Sundays were less than half our own, on account of Bible lessons, Sunday-school lessons and church services; all the others were labour days, rain or shine, cold or warm. No wonder, then, that our two holidays were precious and that it was not easy to decide what to do with them. They were usually spent on the highest rocky hill in the neighbourhood, called the Observatory; in visiting our boy friends on adjacent farms to hunt, fish, wrestle and play games; in reading some new favourite book we had managed to borrow or buy; or in making models of machines I had invented.

One of our July days was spent with two Scotch boys of our own age hunting redwing blackbirds then busy in the corn-fields. Our party had only one single-barreled shotgun, which, as the oldest and perhaps because I was thought to be the best shot, I had the honour of carrying. We marched through the corn without getting sight of a single redwing, but just as we reached the far side of the field, a redheaded woodpecker flew up, and the Lawson boys cried, 'Shoot him! Shoot him! he is just as bad as a blackbird. He eats corn!' This memorable woodpecker alighted in the top of a white oak tree about fifty feet high. I fired from a position almost immediately beneath him, and he fell straight down at my feet. When I picked him up and was admiring his plumage, he moved his legs slightly, and I said, 'Poor bird, he's no deed yet and we'll hae to kill him to put him oot o' pain,' – sincerely pitying him, after we had taken pleasure in shooting him. I had seen servant girls wringing chicken necks, so with desperate humanity I took the limp unfortunate by the head, swung him around three or four times thinking I was wringing his neck, and then threw him hard on the ground to quench the last possible spark of life and make quick death doubly sure. But to our astonishment the moment he struck the ground he gave a cry of alarm and flew right straight up like a rejoicing lark into the top of the same tree, and perhaps to the same branch he had fallen from, and began to adjust his ruffled feathers, nodding and chirping and looking down at us as if wondering what in the bird world we had been doing to him. This of course banished all thought of killing, as far as that revived woodpecker was concerned, no matter how many ears of corn he might spoil, and we all heartily congratulated him on his wonderful, triumphant resurrection from three kinds of death – shooting, neck-wringing and destructive concussion. I suppose only one pellet had touched him, glancing on his head.

Another extraordinary shooting-affair happened one summer morning shortly after day-break. When I went to the stable to feed the horses I noticed a big white-breasted hawk on a tall oak in front of the chicken-house, evidently waiting for a chicken breakfast. I ran to the house for the gun, and when I fired he fell about halfway down the tree, caught a branch with his claws, hung back downward and fluttered a few seconds, then managed to stand erect. I fired again to put him out of pain, and to my surprise the second shot seemed to restore his strength instead of killing him, for he flew out of the tree and over the meadow with strong and regular wing-beats for thirty or forty rods apparently as well as ever, but died suddenly in the air and dropped like a stone.

We hunted muskrats whenever we had time to run down to the lake. They are brown bunchy animals about twenty-three inches long, the tail being about nine inches in length, black in colour and flattened vertically for sculling, and the hind feet are half-webbed. They look like little beavers, usually have from ten to a dozen young, are easily tamed and make interesting pets. We liked to watch them at their work and at their meals. In the spring when the snow vanishes and the lake ice begins to melt, the first open spot is always used as a feeding-place, where they dive from the edge of the ice and in a minute or less reappear with a mussel or a mouthful of pontederia or water-lily leaves, climb back on to the ice and sit up to nibble their food, handling it very much like squirrels or marmots. It is then that they are most easily shot, a solitary hunter oftentimes shooting thirty or forty in a single day. Their nests on the rushy margins of lakes and streams, far from being hidden like those of most birds, are conspicuously large, and conical in shape like Indian wigwams. They are built of plants – rushes, sedges, mosses, etc. – and ornamented around the base with mussel-shells. It was always pleasant and interesting to see them in the autumn as soon as the nights began to be frosty, hard at work cutting sedges on the edge of the meadow or swimming out through the rushes, making long glittering ripples as they sculled themselves along, diving where the water is perhaps six or eight feet deep and reappearing in a minute or so with large mouthfuls of the weedy tangled plants gathered from the bottom, returning to their big wigwams, climbing up and depositing their loads where most needed to make them yet larger and firmer and warmer, foreseeing the freezing weather just like ourselves when we banked up our house to keep out the frost.

They lie snug and invisible all winter but do not hibernate. Through a channel carefully kept open they swim out under the ice for mussels, and the roots and stems of water-lilies, etc., on which they feed just as they do in summer. Sometimes the oldest and most enterprizing of them venture to orchards near the water in search of fallen apples; very seldom, however, do they interfere with anything belonging to their mortal enemy, man. Notwithstanding they are so well hidden and protected during the winter, many of them are killed by Indian hunters, who creep up softly and spear them through the thick walls of their cabins. Indians are fond of their flesh, and so are some of the wildest of the white trappers. They are easily caught in steel traps, and after vainly trying to drag their feet from the cruel crushing jaws, they sometimes in their agony gnaw them off. Even after having gnawed off a leg they are so guileless that they never seem to learn to know and fear traps, for some are occasionally found that have been caught twice and have gnawed off a second foot. Many other animals suffering excruciating pain in these cruel traps gnaw off their legs. Crabs and lobsters are so fortunate as to be able to shed their limbs when caught or merely frightened, apparently without suffering any pain, simply by giving themselves a little shivery shake.

The muskrat is one of the most notable and widely distributed of American animals, and millions of the gentle, industrious, beaver-like creatures are shot and trapped and speared every season for their skins, worth a dime or so – like shooting boys and girls for their garments.

Surely a better time must be drawing nigh when godlike human beings will become truly humane, and learn to put their animal fellow mortals in their hearts instead of on their backs or in their dinners. In the mean time we may just as well as not learn to live clean, innocent lives instead of slimy, bloody ones. All hale, red-blooded boys are savage, the best and boldest the savagest, fond of hunting and fishing. But when thoughtless childhood is past, the best rise the highest above all this bloody flesh and sport business, the wild foundational animal dying out day by day, as divine uplifting, transfiguring charity grows in.

Hares and rabbits were seldom seen when we first settled in the Wisconsin woods, but they multiplied rapidly after the animals that preyed upon them had been thinned out or exterminated, and food and shelter supplied in grain-fields and log fences and the thickets of young oaks that grew up in pastures after the annual grass fires were kept out. Catching hares in the winter-time, when they were hidden in hollow fence-logs, was a favourite pastime with many of the boys whose fathers allowed them time to enjoy the sport. Occasionally a stout, lithe hare was carried out into an open snow-covered field, set free, and given a chance for its life in a race with a dog. When the snow was not too soft and deep, it usually made good its escape, for our dogs were only fat, short-legged mongrels. We sometimes discovered hares in standing hollow trees, crouching on decayed punky wood at the bottom, as far back as possible from the opening, but when alarmed they managed to climb to a considerable height if the hollow was not too wide, by bracing themselves against the sides.

Foxes, though not uncommon, we boys held steadily to work seldom saw, and as they found plenty of prairie chickens for themselves and families, they did not often come near the farmer's hen-roosts. Nevertheless the discovery of their dens was considered important. No matter how deep the den might be, it was thoroughly explored with pick and shovel by sport-loving settlers at a time when they judged the fox was likely to be at home, but I cannot remember any case in our neighbourhood where the fox was actually captured. In one of the dens a mile or two from our farm a lot of prairie chickens were found and some smaller birds.

Badger dens were far more common than fox dens. One of our fields was named Badger Hill from the number of badger holes in a hill at the end of it, but I cannot remember seeing a single one of the inhabitants.

On a stormy day in the middle of an unusually severe winter, a black bear, hungry, no doubt, and seeking something to eat, came strolling down through our neighbourhood from the northern pine woods. None had been seen here before, and it caused no little excitement and alarm, for the European settlers imagined that these poor, timid, bashful bears were as dangerous as man-eating lions and tigers, and that they would pursue any human being that came in their way. This species is common in the north part of the State, and few of our enterprising Yankee hunters who went to the pineries in the autumn failed to shoot at least one of them.

We saw very little of the owlish, serious-looking coons, and no wonder, since they lie hidden nearly all day in hollow trees and we never had time to hunt them. We often heard their curious, quavering, whinnying cries on still evenings, but only once succeeded in tracing an unfortunate family through our corn-field to their den in a big oak and catching them all. One of our neighbours, Mr McRath, a Highland Scotchman, caught one and made a pet of it. It became very tame and had perfect confidence in the good intentions of its kind friend and master. He always addressed it in speaking to it as a 'little man'. When it came running to him and jumped on his lap or climbed up his trousers, he would say, while patting his head as if it were a dog or a child, 'Coonie, ma mannie, Coonie, ma manie, hoo are ye the day? I think you're hungry,' – as the comical pet began to examine his pockets for nuts and bits of bread – 'Na, na, there's nathing in my pooch for ye the day, my wee mannie, but I'll get ye something.' He would then fetch something it liked – bread, nuts, a carrot, or perhaps a piece of fresh meat. Anything scattered for it on the floor it felt with its paw instead of looking at it, judging of its worth more by touch than sight.

The outlet of our Fountain Lake flowed past Mr McRath's door, and the coon was very fond of swimming in it and searching for frogs and mussels. It seemed perfectly satisfied to stay about the house without being confined, occupied a comfortable bed in a section of a hollow tree, and never wandered far. How long it lived after the death of its kind master I don't know.

I suppose that almost any wild animal may be a pet, simply by sympathising with it and entering as much as possible into its life. In Alaska I saw one of the common grey mountain marmots kept as a pet in an Indian family. When its master entered the house it always seemed glad, almost like a dog, and when cold or tired it snuggled up in a fold of his blanket with the utmost confidence.

We have all heard of ferocious animals, lions and tigers, etc., that were fed and spoken to only by their masters, becoming perfectly tame; and, as is well known, the faithful dog that follows man and serves him, and looks up to him and loves him as if he were a god, is a descendant of the blood-thirsty wolf or jackal. Even frogs and toads and fishes may be tamed, provided they have the uniform sympathy of one person, with whom they become intimately acquainted without the distracting and varying attentions of strangers. And surely all God's people, however serious and savage, great or small, like to play. Whales and elephants, dancing, humming gnats, and invisibly small mischievous microbes – all are warm with divine radium and must have lots of fun in them.

As far as I know, all wild creatures keep themselves clean. Birds, it seems to me, take more pains to bathe and dress themselves than any other animals. Even ducks, though living so much in water, dip and scatter cleansing showers over their backs, and shake and preen their feathers as carefully as land-birds. Watching small singers taking their morning baths is very interesting, particularly when the weather is cold. Alighting in a shallow pool, they oftentimes show a sort of dread of dipping into it, like children hesitating about taking a plunge, as if they felt the same kind of shock, and this makes it easy for us to sympathise with the little feathered people.

Occasionally I have seen from my study-window red-headed linnets bathing in dew when water elsewhere was scarce. A large Monterey cypress with broad branches and innumerable leaves on which the dew lodges in still nights made favourite bathing-places. Alighting gently, as if afraid to waste the dew, they would pause and fidget as they do before beginning to plash in pools, then dip and scatter the drops in showers and get as thorough a bath as they would in a pool. I have also seen the same kind of baths taken by birds on the boughs of silver firs on the edge of a glacier meadow, but nowhere have I seen the dew-drops so abundant as on the Monterey cypress; and the picture made by the quivering wings and irised dew was memorably beautiful. Children, too, make fine pictures plashing and crowing in their little tubs. How widely different from wallowing pigs, bathing with great show of comfort and rubbing themselves dry against rough-barked trees!

Some of our own species seem fairly to dread the touch of water. When the necessity of absolute cleanliness by means of frequent baths was being preached by a friend who had been reading Combe's Physiology, in which he had learned something of the wonders of the skin with its millions of pores that had to be kept open for health, one of our neighbours remarked, 'Oh! that's unnatural. It's well enough to wash in a tub maybe once or twice a year, but not to be paddling in the water all the time like a frog in a spring-hole.' Another neighbour, who prided himself on his knowledge of big words, said with great solemnity, 'I never can believe that man is amphibious!'

Natives of tropic islands pass a large part of their lives in water, and seem as much at home in the sea as on the land: swim and dive, pursue fishes, play in the waves like surf-ducks and seals, and explore the coral gardens and groves and seaweed meadows as if truly amphibious. Even the natives of the far north bathe at times. I once saw a lot of Eskimo boys ducking and plashing right merrily in the Arctic Ocean.

It seemed very wonderful to us that the wild animals could keep themselves warm and strong in winter when the temperature was far below zero. Feeble-looking rabbits scud away over the snow, lithe and elastic, as if glorying in the frosty, sparkling weather and sure of their dinners. I have seen grey squirrels dragging ears of corn about as heavy as themselves out of our field through loose snow and up a tree, balancing them on limbs and eating in comfort with their dry, electric tails spread airily over their backs. Once I saw a fine hardy fellow go into a knot-hole. Thrusting in my hand I caught him and pulled him out. As soon as he guessed what I was up to, he took the end of my thumb in his mouth and sunk his teeth right through it, but I gripped him hard by the neck, carried him home, and shut him up in a box that contained about half a bushel of hazel- and hickory-nuts, hoping that he would not be too frightened and discouraged to eat while thus imprisoned after the rough handling he had suffered. I soon learned, however, that sympathy in this direction was wasted, for no sooner did I pop him in than he fell to with right hearty appetite, gnawing and munching the nuts as if he had gathered them himself and was very hungry that day. Therefore, after allowing time enough for a good square meal, I made haste to get him out of the nut-box and shut him up in a spare bedroom, in which father had hung a lot of selected ears of Indian corn for seed. They were hung up by the husks on cords stretched across from side to side of the room. The squirrel managed to jump from the top of one of the bed-posts to the corn, cut off an ear, and let it drop to the floor. He then jumped down, got a good grip of the heavy ear, carried it to the top of one of the slippery, polished bed-posts, seated himself comfortably, and, holding it well balanced, deliberately pried out one kernel at a time with his long chisel teeth, ate the soft, sweet germ, and dropped the hard part of the kernel. In this masterly way, working at high speed, he demolished several ears a day, and with a good warm bed in a box made himself at home and grew fat. Then naturally, I suppose, free romping in the snow and tree-tops with companions came to mind. Anyhow he began to look for a way of escape. Of course he first tried the window, but found that his teeth made no impression on the glass. Next he tried the sash and gnawed the wood off level with the glass; then father happened to come upstairs and discovered the mischief that was being done to his seed corn and window and immediately ordered him out of the house.

The flying squirrel was one of the most interesting of the little animals we found in the woods, a beautiful brown creature, with fine eyes and smooth, soft fur like that of a mole or field mouse. He is about half as long as the grey squirrel, but his wide-spread tail and the folds of skin along his sides that form the wings made him look broad and flat, something like a kite. In the evenings our cat often brought them to her kittens at the shanty, and later we saw them fly during the day from the trees we were chopping. They jumped and glided off smoothly and apparently without effort, like birds, as soon as they heard and felt the breaking shock of the strained fibres at the stump, when the trees they were in began to totter and groan. They can fly, or rather glide, twenty or thirty yards from the top of a tree twenty or thirty feet high to the foot of another, gliding upward as they reach the trunk, or if the distance is too great they alight comfortably on the ground and make haste to the nearest tree, and climb just like the wingless squirrels.

Every boy and girl loves the little fairy, airy striped chipmunk, half squirrel, half spermophile. He is about the size of a field mouse, and often made us think of linnets and song sparrows as he frisked about gathering nuts and berries. He likes almost all kinds of grain, berries and nuts – hazel-nuts, hickory-nuts, strawberries, huckleberries, wheat, oats, corn – he is fond of them all and thrives on them. Most of the hazel bushes on our farm grew along the fences as if they had been planted for the chipmunks alone, for the rail fences were their favourite highways. We never wearied watching them, especially when the hazel-nuts were ripe and the little fellows were sitting on the rails nibbling and handling them like tree-squirrels. We used to notice too that, although they are very neat animals, their lips and fingers were dyed red like our own when the strawberries and huckleberries were ripe. We could always tell when the wheat and oats were in the milk by seeing the chipmunks feeding on the ears. They kept nibbling at the wheat until it was harvested and then gleaned in the stubble, keeping up a careful watch for their enemies – dogs, hawks and shrikes. They are as widely distributed over the continent as the squirrels, various species inhabiting different regions on the mountains and lowlands, but all the different kinds have the same general characteristics of light, airy cheerfulness and good nature.

Before the arrival of farmers in the Wisconsin woods the small ground squirrels, called 'gophers', lived chiefly on the seeds of wild grasses and weeds, but after the country was cleared and ploughed no feasting animal fell to more heartily on the farmer's wheat and corn. Increasing rapidly in numbers and knowledge, they became very destructive, especially in the spring when the corn was planted, for they learned to trace the rows and dig up and eat the three or four seeds in each hill about as fast as the poor farmers could cover them. And unless great pains were taken to diminish the numbers of the cunning little robbers, the fields had to be planted two or three times over, and even then large gaps in the rows would be found. The loss of the grain they consumed after it was ripe, together with the winter stores laid up in their burrows, amounted to little as compared with the loss of the seed on which the whole crop depended.

One evening about sundown, when my father sent me out with the shotgun to hunt them in a stubble field, I learned something curious and interesting in connection with these mischievous gophers, though just then they were doing no harm. As I strolled through the stubble watching for a chance for a shot, a shrike flew past me and alighted on an open spot at the mouth of a burrow about thirty yards ahead of me. Curious to see what he was up to, I stood still to watch him. He looked down the gopher hole in a listening attitude, then looked back at me to see if I was coming, looked down again and listened, and looked back at me. I stood perfectly still, and he kept twitching his tail, seeming uneasy and doubtful about venturing to do the savage job that I soon learned he had in his mind. Finally, encouraged by my keeping so still, to my astonishment he suddenly vanished in the gopher hole.

A bird going down a deep narrow hole in the ground like a ferret or a weasel seemed very strange, and I thought it would be a fine thing to run forward, clap my hand over the hole, and have the fun of imprisoning him and seeing what he would do when he tried to get out. So I ran forward but stopped when I got within a dozen or fifteen yards of the hole, thinking it might perhaps be more interesting to wait and see what would naturally happen without my interference. While I stood there looking and listening, I heard a great disturbance going on in the burrow, a mixed lot of keen squeaking, shrieking, distressful cries, telling that down in the dark something terrible was being done. Then suddenly out popped a half-grown gopher, four and a half or five inches long, and, without stopping a single moment to choose a way of escape, ran screaming through the stubble straight away from its home, quickly followed by another and another, until some half-dozen were driven out, all of them crying and running in different directions as if at this dreadful time home, sweet home, was the most dangerous and least desirable of any place in the wide world. Then out came the shrike, flew above the runaway gopher children, and, diving on them, killed them one after another with blows at the back of the skull. He then seized one of them, dragged it to the top of a small clod so as to be able to get a start, and laboriously made out to fly with it about ten or fifteen yards, when he alighted to rest. Then he dragged it to the top of another clod and flew with it about the same distance, repeating this hard work over and over again until he managed to get one of the gophers on to the top of a log fence. How much he ate of his hard-won prey, or what he did with the others, I can't tell, for by this time the sun was down and I had to hurry home to my chores.

CHAPTER SIX

The Ploughboy

AT FIRST, wheat, corn and potatoes were the principal crops we raised; wheat especially. But in four or five years the soil was so exhausted that only five or six bushels an acre, even in the better fields, was obtained, although when first ploughed twenty and twenty-five bushels was about the ordinary yield. More attention was then paid to corn, but without fertilizers the corn-crop also became very meagre. At last it was discovered that English clover would grow on even the exhausted fields, and that when ploughed under and planted with corn, or even wheat, wonderful crops were raised. This caused a complete change in farming methods; the farmers raised fertilizing clover, planted corn, and fed the crop to cattle and hogs.

But no crop raised in our wilderness was so surprisingly rich and sweet and purely generous to us boys and, indeed, to everybody as the watermelons and muskmelons. We planted a large patch on a sunny hill-slope the very first spring, and it seemed miraculous that a few handfuls of little flat seeds should in a few months send up a hundred wagon-loads of crisp, sumptuous, red-hearted and yellow-hearted fruits covering all the hill. We soon learned to know when they were in their prime, and when over-ripe and mealy. Also that if a second crop was taken from the same ground without fertilizing it, the melons would be small and what we called soapy; that is, soft and smooth, utterly uncrisp, and without a trace of the lively freshness and sweetness of those raised on virgin soil. Coming in from the farm work at noon, the half-dozen or so of melons we had placed in our cold spring were a glorious luxury that only weary barefooted farm boys can ever know.

Spring was not very trying as to temperature, and refreshing rains fell at short intervals. The work of ploughing commenced as soon as the frost was out of the ground. Corn- and potato-planting and the sowing of spring wheat was comparatively light work, while the nesting birds sang cheerily, grass and flowers covered the marshes and meadows and all the wild, uncleared parts of the farm, and the trees put forth their new leaves, those of the oaks forming beautiful purple masses as if every leaf were a petal; and with all this we enjoyed the mild soothing winds, the humming of innumerable small insects and hylas, and the freshness and fragrance of everything. Then, too, came the wonderful passenger pigeons streaming from the south, and flocks of geese and cranes, filling all the sky with whistling wings.

The summer work, on the contrary, was deadly heavy, especially harvesting and corn-hoeing. All the ground had to be hoed over for the first few years, before father bought cultivators or small weed-covering ploughs, and we were not allowed a moment's rest. The hoes had to be kept working up and down as steadily as if they were moved by machinery. Ploughing for winter wheat was comparatively easy, when we walked barefooted in the furrows, while the fine autumn tints kindled in the woods, and the hillsides were covered with golden pumpkins.

In summer the chores were grinding scythes, feeding the animals, chopping stove-wood, and carrying water up the hill from the spring on the edge of the meadow, etc. Then breakfast, and to the harvest or hay-field. I was foolishly ambitious to be first in mowing and cradling, and by the time I was sixteen led all the hired men. An hour was allowed at noon for dinner and more chores. We stayed in the field until dark, then supper, and still more chores, family worship, and to bed; making altogether a hard, sweaty day of about sixteen or seventeen hours. Think of that, ye blessed eight-hour-day labourers!

In winter father came to the foot of the stairs and called us at six o'clock to feed the horses and cattle, grind axes, bring in wood, and do any other chores required, then breakfast, and out to work in the mealy, frosty snow by daybreak, chopping, fencing, etc. So in general our winter work was about as restless and trying as that of the long-day summer. No matter what the weather, there was always something to do. During heavy rains or snow-storms we worked in the barn, shelling corn, fanning wheat, thrashing with the flail, making axe-handles or ox-yokes, mending things, or sprouting and sorting potatoes in the cellar.

No pains were taken to diminish or in any way soften the natural hardships of this pioneer farm life; nor did any of the Europeans seem to know how to find reasonable ease and comfort if they would. The very best oak and hickory fuel was embarrassingly abundant and cost nothing but cutting and common sense; but instead of hauling great heart-cheering loads of it for wide, open, all-welcoming, climate-changing, beauty-making, Godlike ingle-fires, it was hauled with weary heart-breaking industry into fences and waste places to get it out of the way of the plough, and out of the way of doing good. The only fire for the whole house was the kitchen stove, with a fire-box about eighteen inches long and eight inches wide and deep – scant space for three or four small sticks, around which in hard zero weather all the family of ten persons shivered, and beneath which in the morning we found our socks and coarse, soggy boots frozen solid. We were not allowed to start even this despicable little fire in its black box to thaw them. No, we had to squeeze our throbbing, aching, chilblained feet into them, causing greater pain than toothache, and hurry out to chores. Fortunately the miserable chilblain pain began to abate as soon as the temperature of our feet approached the freezing-point, enabling us in spite of hard work and hard frost to enjoy the winter beauty – the wonderful radiance of the snow when it was starry with crystals, and the dawns and the sunsets and white noons, and the cheery, enlivening company of the brave chickadees and nuthatches.

The winter stars far surpassed those of our stormy Scotland in brightness, and we gazed and gazed as though we had never seen stars before. Oftentimes the heavens were made still more glorious by auroras, the long lance rays, called 'Merry Dancers' in Scotland, streaming with startling tremulous motion to the zenith. Usually the electric auroral light is white or pale yellow, but in the third or fourth of our Wisconsin winters there was a magnificently coloured aurora that was seen and admired over nearly all the continent. The whole sky was draped in graceful purple and crimson folds glorious beyond description. Father called us out into the yard in front of the house where we had a wide view, crying, 'Come! Come, mother! Come, bairns! and see the glory of God. All the sky is clad in a robe of red light. Look straight up to the crown where the folds are gathered. Hush and wonder and adore, for surely this is the clothing of the Lord Himself, and perhaps He will even now appear looking down from his high heaven.' This celestial show was far more glorious than anything we had ever yet beheld, and throughout that wonderful winter hardly anything else was spoken of.

We even enjoyed the snowstorms; the thronging crystals, like daisies, coming down separate and distinct, were very different from the tufted flakes we enjoyed so much in Scotland, when we ran into the midst of the slow-falling feathery throng shouting with enthusiasm, 'Jennie's plucking her doos! Jennie's plucking her doos (doves)!'

Nature has many ways of thinning and pruning and trimming her forests – lightning-strikes, heavy snow and stormwinds to shatter and blow down whole trees here and there or break off branches as required. The results of these methods I have observed in different forests, but only once have I seen pruning by rain. The rain froze on the trees as it fell and grew so thick and heavy that many of them lost a third or more of their branches. The view of the woods after the storm had passed and the sun shone forth was something never to be forgotten. Every twig and branch and rugged trunk was encased in pure crystal ice, and each oak and hickory and willow became a fairy crystal palace. Such dazzling brilliance, such effects of white light and irised light glowing and flashing I had never seen before, nor have I since. This sudden change of the leafless woods to glowing silver was, like the great aurora, spoken of for years, and is one of the most beautiful of the many pictures that enriches my life. And besides the great shows there were thousands of others even in the coldest weather manifesting the utmost fineness and tenderness of beauty and affording noble compensation for hardship and pain.

One of the most striking of the winter sounds was the loud roaring and rumbling of the ice on our lake, from its shrinking and expanding with the changes of the weather. The fishermen who were catching pickerel said that they had no luck when this roaring was going on above the fish. I remember how frightened we boys were when on one of our New Year holidays we were taking a walk on the ice and heard for the first time the sudden rumbling roar beneath our feet and running on ahead of us, creaking and whooping as if all the ice eighteen or twenty inches thick was breaking.

In the neighbourhood of our Wisconsin farm there were extensive swamps consisting in great part of a thick sod of very tough carex roots covering thin, watery lakes of mud. They originated in glacier lakes that were gradually overgrown. This sod was so tough that oxen with loaded wagons could be driven over it without cutting down through it, although it was afloat. The carpenters who came to build our frame house, noticing how the sedges sunk beneath their feet, said that if they should break through, they would probably be well on their way to California before touching bottom. On the contrary, all these lake-basins are shallow as compared with their width. When we went into the Wisconsin woods there was not a single wheel-track or cattle-track. The only man-made road was an Indian trail along the Fox River between Portage and Packwauckee Lake. Of course the deer, foxes, badgers, coons, skunks, and even the squirrels had well-beaten tracks from their dens and hiding-places in thickets, hollow trees and the ground, but they did not reach far, and but little noise was made by the soft-footed travellers in passing over them, only a slight rustling and swishing among fallen leaves and grass.

Corduroying the swamps formed the principal part of road-making among the early settlers for many a day. At these annual road-making gatherings opportunity was offered for discussion of the news, politics, religion, war, the state of the crops, comparative advantages of the new country over the old and so forth, but the principal opportunities, recurring every week, were the hours after Sunday church services. I remember hearing long talks on the wonderful beauty of the Indian corn; the wonderful melons, so wondrous fine for 'sloken a body on hot days'; their contempt for tomatoes, so fine to look at with their sunny colours and so disappointing in taste; the miserable cucumbers the 'Yankee bodies' ate, though tasteless as rushes; the character of the Yankee, etc. Then there were long discussions about the Russian war, news of which was eagerly gleaned from Greeley's *New York Tribune*; the great battles of the Alma, the charges at Balaklava and Inkerman; the siege of Sebastopol; the military genius of Todleben; the character of Nicholas; the character of the Russian soldier, his stubborn bravery, who for the first time in history withstood the British bayonet charges; the probable outcome of the terrible war; the fate of Turkey and so forth.

Very few of our old-country neighbours gave much heed to what are called spirit-rappings. On the contrary, they were regarded as a sort of sleight-of-hand humbug. Some of these spirits seem to be stout able-bodied fellows, judging by the weights they lift and the heavy furniture they bang about. But they do no good work that I know of; never saw wood, grind corn, cook, feed the hungry, or go to the help of poor anxious mothers at the bedsides of their sick children. I noticed when I was a boy that it was not the strongest characters who followed so-called mediums. When a rapping-storm was at its height in Wisconsin, one of our neighbours, an old Scotchman, remarked, 'They puir silly medium-bodies may gang to the deil wi' their rappin' speerits, for they dae nae gude, and I think the deil's their fayther.'

Although in the spring of 1849 there was no other settler within a radius of four miles of our Fountain Lake farm, in three or four years almost every quarter-section of government land was taken up, mostly by enthusiastic homeseekers from Great Britain, with only here and there Yankee families from adjacent states, who had come drifting indefinitely westward in covered wagons, seeking their fortunes like winged seeds; all alike striking root and gripping the glacial drift soil as naturally as oak and hickory trees; happy and hopeful, establishing homes and making wider and wider fields in the hospitable wilderness. The axe and plough were kept very busy; cattle, horses, sheep and pigs multiplied; barns and corn-cribs were filled up, and man and beast were well fed; a schoolhouse was built, which was used also for a church; and in a very short time the new country began to look like an old one.

Comparatively few of the first settlers suffered from serious accidents. One of our neighbours had a finger shot off, and on a bitter, frosty night had to be taken to a surgeon in Portage, in a sled drawn by slow, plodding oxen, to have the shattered stump dressed. Another fell from his wagon and was killed by the wheel passing over his body. An acre of ground was reserved and fenced for graves, and soon consumption came to fill it. One of the saddest instances was that of a Scotch family from Edinburgh, consisting of a father, son and daughter, who settled on eighty acres of land within half a mile of our place. The daughter died of consumption the third year after their arrival, the son one or two years later, and at last the father followed his two children. Thus sadly ended bright hopes and dreams of a happy home in rich and free America.

Another neighbour, I remember, after a lingering illness died of the same disease in mid-winter, and his funeral was attended by the neighbours in sleighs during a driving snowstorm when the thermometer was fifteen or twenty degrees below zero. The great white plague carried off another of our near neighbours, a fine Scotchman, the father of eight promising boys, when he was only about forty-five years of age. Most of those who suffered from this disease seemed hopeful and cheerful up to a very short time before their death, but Mr Reid, I remember, on one of his last visits to our house, said with brave resignation, 'I know that never more in this world can I be well, but I must just submit. I must just submit.'

One of the saddest deaths from other causes than consumption was that of a poor feeble-minded man whose brother, a sturdy, devout, severe puritan, was a very hard taskmaster. Poor half-witted Charlie was kept steadily at work – although he was not able to do much, for his body was about as feeble as his mind. He never could be taught the right use of an axe, and when he was set to chopping down trees for firewood he feebly hacked and chipped round and round them, sometimes spending several days in nibbling down a tree that a beaver might have gnawed down in half the time. Occasionally when he had an extra large tree to chop, he would go home and report that the tree was too tough and strong for him and that he could never make it fall. Then his brother, calling him a useless creature, would fell it with a few well-directed strokes, and leave Charlie to nibble away at it for weeks trying to make it into stove-wood.

His guardian brother, delighting in hard work and able for anything, was as remarkable for strength of body and mind as poor Charlie for childishness. All the neighbours pitied Charlie, especially the women, who never missed an opportunity to give him kind words, cookies and pie; above all, they bestowed natural sympathy on the poor imbecile as if he were an unfortunate mother-less child. In particular, his nearest neighbours, Scotch Highlanders, warmly welcomed him to their home and never wearied in doing everything that tender sympathy could suggest. To those friends he ran gladly at every opportunity. But after years of suffering from overwork and illness his feeble health failed, and he told his Scotch friends one day that he was not able to work any more or do anything that his brother wanted him to do, that he was tired of life, and that he had come to thank them for their kindness and to bid them good-bye, for he was going to drown himself in Muir's lake. 'Oh, Charlie! Charlie!' they cried, 'you mustn't talk that way. Cheer up! You will soon be stronger. We all love you. Cheer up! Cheer up! And always come here whenever you need anything.'

'Oh, no! my friends,' he pathetically replied, 'I know you love me, but I can't cheer up any more. My heart's gone, and I want to die.'

Next day, when Mr Anderson, a carpenter whose house was on the west shore of our lake, was going to a spring he saw a man wade out through the rushes and lily-pads and throw himself forward into deep water. This was poor Charlie. Fortunately, Mr Anderson had a skiff close by, and as the distance was not great he reached the broken-hearted imbecile in time to save his life, and after trying to cheer him took him home to his brother. But even this terrible proof of despair failed to soften his brother. He seemed to regard the attempt at suicide simply as a crime calculated to bring harm to religion. Though snatched from the lake to his bed, poor Charlie lived only a few days longer. A physician who was called when his health first became seriously impaired reported that he was suffering from Bright's disease. After all was over, the stoical brother walked over to the neighbour who had saved Charlie from drowning, and, after talking on ordinary affairs, crops, the weather, etc., said in a careless tone, 'I have a little job of carpenter work for you, Mr Anderson.' 'What is it, Mr – ?' 'I want you to make a coffin.' 'A coffin!' said the startled carpenter. 'Who is dead?' 'Charlie,' he coolly replied. All the neighbours were in tears over the poor child man's fate. But, strange to say, the brother who had faithfully cared for him controlled and concealed all his natural affection as incompatible with sound faith.

The mixed lot of settlers around us offered a favourable field for observation of the different kinds of people of our own race. We were swift to note the way they behaved, the differences in their religion and morals, and in their ways of drawing a living from the same kind of soil under the same general conditions; how they protected themselves from the weather; how they were influenced by new doctrines and old ones seen in new lights in preaching, lecturing, debating, bringing up their children, etc., and how they regarded the Indians, those first settlers and owners of the ground that was being made into farms.

I well remember my father's discussing with a Scotch neighbour, a Mr George Mair, the Indian question as to the rightful ownership of the soil. Mr Mair remarked one day that it was pitiful to see how the unfortunate Indians, children of Nature, living on the natural products of the soil, hunting, fishing and even cultivating small corn-fields on the most fertile spots, were now being robbed of their lands and pushed ruthlessly back into narrower and narrower limits by alien races who were cutting off their means of livelihood. Father replied that surely it could never have been the intention of God to allow Indians to rove and hunt over so fertile a country and hold it forever in unproductive wildness, while Scotch and Irish and English farmers could put it to so much better use. Where an Indian required thousands of acres for his family, these acres in the hands of industrious, God-fearing farmers would support ten or a hundred times more people in a far worthier manner, while at the same time helping to spread the gospel.

Mr Mair urged that such farming as our first immigrants were practising was in many ways rude and full of the mistakes of ignorance, yet, rude as it was, and ill-tilled as were most of our Wisconsin farms by unskillful, inexperienced settlers who had been merchants and mechanics and servants in the old countries, how should we like to have specially trained and educated farmers drive us out of our homes and farms, such as they were, making use of the same argument, that God could never have intended such ignorant, unprofitable, devastating farmers as we were to occupy land upon which scientific farmers could raise five or ten times as much on each acre as we did? And I well remember thinking that Mr Mair had the better side of the argument. It then seemed to me that, whatever the final outcome might be, it was at this stage of the fight only an example of the rule of might with but little or no thought for the right or welfare of the other fellow if he were the weaker; that 'they should take who had the power, and they should keep who can', as Wordsworth makes the marauding Scottish Highlanders say.

Many of our old neighbours toiled and sweated and grubbed themselves into their graves years before their natural dying days, in getting a living on a quarter-section of land and vaguely trying to get rich, while bread and raiment might have been serenely won on less than a fourth of this land, and time gained to get better acquainted with God.

I was put to the plough at the age of twelve, when my head reached but little above the handles, and for many years I had to do the greater part of the ploughing. It was hard work for so small a boy; nevertheless, as good ploughing was exacted from me as if I were a man, and very soon I had to become a good ploughman, or rather ploughboy. None could draw a straighter furrow. For the first few years the work was particularly hard on account of the tree-stumps that had to be dodged. Later the stumps were all dug and chopped out to make way for the McCormick reaper, and because I proved to be the best chopper and stump-digger I had nearly all of it to myself. It was dull, hard work leaning over on my knees all day, chopping out those tough oak and hickory stumps, deep down below the crowns of the big roots. Some, though fortunately not many, were two feet or more in diameter.

And as I was the eldest boy, the greater part of all the other hard work of the farm quite naturally fell on me. I had to split rails for long lines of zigzag fences. The trees that were tall enough and straight enough to afford one or two logs ten feet long were used for rails, the others, too knotty or cross-grained, were disposed of in log and cordwood fences. Making rails was hard work and required no little skill. I used to cut and split a hundred a day from our short, knotty oak timber, swinging the axe and heavy mallet, often with sore hands, from early morning to night. Father was not successful as a rail-splitter. After trying the work with me a day or two, he in despair left it all to me. I rather liked it, for I was proud of my skill, and tried to believe that I was as tough as the timber I mauled, though this and other heavy jobs stopped my growth and earned for me the title 'Runt of the family'.

In those early days, long before the great labour-saving machines came to our help, almost everything connected with wheat-raising abounded in trying work – cradling in the long, sweaty dog-days, raking and binding, stacking, thrashing – and it often seemed to me that our fierce, over-industrious way of getting the grain from the ground was too closely connected with grave-digging. The staff of life, naturally beautiful, oftentimes suggested the grave-digger's spade. Men and boys, and in those days even women and girls, were cut down while cutting the wheat. The fat folk grew lean and the lean leaner, while the rosy cheeks brought from Scotland and other cool countries across the sea faded to yellow like the wheat. We were all made slaves through the vice of over-industry. The same was in great part true in making hay to keep the cattle and horses through the long winters. We were called in the morning at four o'clock and seldom got to bed before nine, making a broiling, seething day seventeen hours long loaded with heavy work, while I was only a small stunted boy; and a few years later my brothers David and Daniel and my older sisters had to endure about as much as I did. In the harvest dog-days and dog-nights and dog-mornings, when we arose from our clammy beds, our cotton shirts clung to our backs as wet with sweat as the bathing-suits of swimmers, and remained so all the long, sweltering days. In mowing and cradling, the most exhausting of all the farm work, I made matters worse by foolish ambition in keeping ahead of the hired men. Never a warning word was spoken of the dangers of over-work. On the contrary, even when sick we were held to our tasks as long as we could stand. Once in harvest-time I had the mumps and was unable to swallow any food except milk, but this was not allowed to make any difference, while I staggered with weakness and some-times fell headlong among the sheaves. Only once was I allowed to leave the harvest-field – when I was stricken down with pneumonia. I lay gasping for weeks, but the Scotch are hard to kill and I pulled through. No physician was called, for father was an enthusiast, and always said and believed that God and hard work were by far the best doctors.

None of our neighbours were so excessively industrious as father; though nearly all of the Scotch, English and Irish worked too hard, trying to make good homes and to lay up money enough for comfortable independence. Excepting small garden-patches, few of them had owned land in the old country. Here their craving land-hunger was satisfied, and they were naturally proud of their farms and tried to keep them as neat and clean and well-tilled as gardens. To accomplish this without the means for hiring help was impossible. Flowers were planted about the neatly kept log or frame houses; barnyards, granaries, etc., were kept in about as neat order as the homes, and the fences and corn-rows were rigidly straight. But every uncut weed distressed them; so also did every ungathered ear of grain, and all that was lost by birds and gophers; and this overcarefulness bred endless work and worry.

As for money, for many a year there was precious little of it in the country for anybody. Eggs sold at six cents a dozen in trade, and five-cent calico was exchanged at twenty-five cents a yard. Wheat brought fifty cents a bushel in trade. To get cash for it before the Portage Railway was built, it had to be hauled to Milwaukee, a hundred miles away. On the other hand, food was abundant – eggs, chickens, pigs, cattle, wheat, corn, potatoes, garden vegetables of the best, and wonderful melons as luxuries. No other wild country I have ever known extended a kinder welcome to poor immigrants. On the arrival in the spring, a log house could be built, a few acres ploughed, the virgin sod planted with corn, potatoes, etc., and enough raised to keep a family comfortably the very first year; and wild hay for cows and oxen grew in abundance on the numerous meadows. The American settlers were wisely content with smaller fields and less of everything, kept indoors during excessively hot or cold weather, rested when tired, went off fishing and hunting at the most favourable times and seasons of the day and year, gathered nuts and berries, and in general tranquilly accepted all the good things the fertile wilderness offered.

After eight years of this dreary work of clearing the Fountain Lake farm, fencing it and getting it in perfect order, building a frame house and the necessary outbuildings for the cattle and horses – after all this had been victoriously accomplished, and we had made out to escape with life – father bought a half-section of wild land about four or five miles to the eastward and began all over again to clear and fence and break up other fields for a new farm, doubling all the stunting, heartbreaking chopping, grubbing, stump-digging, rail-splitting, fence-building, barn-building, house-building and so forth.

By this time I had learned to run the breaking plough. Most of these ploughs were very large, turning furrows from eighteen inches to two feet wide, and were drawn by four or five yoke of oxen. They were used only for the first ploughing, in breaking up the wild sod woven into a tough mass, chiefly by the cordlike roots of perennial grasses, reinforced by the tap-roots of oak and hickory bushes, called 'grubs', some of which were more than a century old and four or five inches in diameter. In the hardest ploughing on the most difficult ground, the grubs were said to be as thick as the hair on a dog's back. If in good trim, the plough cut through and turned over these grubs as if the century-old wood were soft like the flesh of carrots and turnips; but if not in good trim the grubs promptly tossed the plough out of the ground. A stout Highland Scot, our neighbour, whose plough was in bad order and who did not know how to trim it, was vainly trying to keep it in the ground by main strength, while his son, who was driving and merrily whipping up the cattle, would cry encouragingly, 'Haud her in, fayther! Haud her in!'

'But hoo i' the deil can I haud her in when she'll no *stop* in?' his perspiring father would reply, gasping for breath between each word. On the contrary, with the share and coulter sharp and nicely adjusted, the plough, instead of shying at every grub and jumping out, ran straight ahead without need of steering or holding, and gripped the ground so firmly that it could hardly be thrown out at the end of the furrow.

Our breaker turned a furrow two feet wide, and on our best land, where the sod was toughest, held so firm a grip that at the end of the field my brother, who was driving the oxen, had to come to my assistance in throwing it over on its side to be drawn around the end of the landing; and it was all I could do to set it up again. But I learned to keep that plough in such trim that after I got started on a new furrow I used to ride on the crossbar between the handles with my feet resting comfortably on the beam, without having to steady or steer it in any way on the whole length of the field, unless we had to go round a stump, for it sawed through the biggest grubs without flinching.

The growth of these grubs was interesting to me. When an acorn of hickory-nut had sent up its first season's sprout, a few inches long, it was burned off in the autumn grass fires; but the root continued to hold on to life, formed a callus over the wound and sent up one or more shoots the next spring. Next autumn these new shoots were burned off, but the root and calloused head, about level with the surface of the ground, continued to grow and send up more new shoots; and so on, almost every year until very old, probably far more than a century, while the tops, which would naturally have become tall broad-headed trees, were only mere sprouts seldom more than two years old. Thus the ground was kept open like a prairie, with only five or six trees to the acre, which had escaped the fire by having the good fortune to grow on a bare spot at the door of a fox or badger den, or between straggling grass-tufts wide apart on the poorest sandy soil.

The uniformly rich soil of the Illinois and Wisconsin prairies produced so close and tall a growth of grasses for fires that no tree could live on it. Had there been no fires, these fine prairies, so marked a feature of the country, would have been covered by the heaviest forests. As soon as the oak openings in our neighbourhood were settled, and the farmers had prevented running grass-fires, the grubs grew up into trees and formed tall thickets so dense that it was difficult to walk through them and every trace of the sunny 'openings' vanished.

We called our second farm Hickory Hill, from its many fine hickory trees and the long gentle slope leading up to it. Compared with Fountain Lake farm it lay high and dry. The land was better, but it had no living water, no spring or stream or meadow or lake. A well ninety feet deep had to be dug, all except the first ten feet or so in fine-grained sandstone. When the sandstone was struck, my father, on the advice of a man who had worked in mines, tried to blast the rock; but from lack of skill the blasting went on very slowly, and father decided to have me do all the work with mason's chisels, a long, hard job, with a good deal of danger in it. I had to sit cramped in a space about three feet in diameter, and wearily chip, chip, with heavy hammer and chisels from early morning until dark, day after day, for weeks and months. In the morning, father and David lowered me in a wooden bucket by a windlass, hauled up what chips were left from the night before, then went away to the farm work and left me until noon, when they hoisted me out for dinner. After dinner I was promptly lowered again, the forenoon's accumulation of chips hoisted out of the way, and I was left until night.

One morning, after the dreary bore was about eighty feet deep, my life was all but lost in deadly choke-damp – carbonic acid gas that had settled at the bottom during the night. Instead of clearing away the chips as usual when I was lowered to the bottom, I swayed back and forth and began to sink under the poison. Father, alarmed that I did not make any noise, shouted, 'What's keeping you so still?' to which he got no reply. Just as I was settling down against the side of the wall, I happened to catch a glimpse of a branch of a bur-oak tree which leaned out over the mouth of the shaft. This suddenly awakened me, and to father's excited shouting I feebly murmured, 'Take me out.' But when he began to hoist he found I was not in the bucket and in wild alarm shouted, 'Get in! Get in the bucket and hold on! Hold on!' Somehow I managed to get into the bucket, and that is all I remembered until I was dragged out, violently gasping for breath.

One of our near neighbours, a stone mason and miner by the name of William Duncan, came to see me, and after hearing the particulars of the accident he solemnly said, 'Weel, Johnnie, it's God's mercy that you're alive. Many a companion of mine have I seen dead with choke-damp, but none that I ever saw or heard of was so near to death in it as you were and escaped without help.' Mr Duncan taught father to throw water down the shaft to absorb the gas, and also to drop a bundle of brush or hay attached to a light rope, dropping it again and again to carry down pure air and stir up the poison. When, after a day or two, I had recovered from the shock, father lowered me again to my work, after taking the precaution to test the air with a candle and stir it up well with a brush-and-hay bundle. The weary hammer-and-chisel-chipping went on as before, only more slowly, until ninety feet down, when at last I struck a fine, hearty gush of water. Constant dropping wears away stone. So does constant chipping, while at the same time wearing away the chipper. Father never spent an hour in that well. He trusted me to sink it straight and plumb, and I did, and built a fine covered top over it, and swung two iron-bound buckets in it from which we all drank for many a day.

The honey-bee arrived in America long before we boys did, but several years passed ere we noticed any on our farm. The introduction of the honey-bee into flowery America formed a grand epoch in bee history. This sweet humming creature, companion and friend of the flowers, is now distributed over the greater part of the continent, filling countless hollows in rocks and trees with honey as well as the millions of hives prepared for them by honey-farmers, who keep and tend their flocks of sweet winged cattle, as shepherds keep sheep – a charming employment, 'like directing sunbeams', as Thoreau says. The Indians call the honey-bee the white man's fly; and though they had long been acquainted with several species of bumblebees that yielded more or less honey, how gladly surprised they must have been when they discovered that, in the hollow trees where before they had found only coons or squirrels, they found swarms of brown flies with fifty or even a hundred pounds of honey sealed up in beautiful cells. With their keen hunting senses they of course were not slow to learn the habits of the little brown immigrants and the best methods of tracing them to their sweet homes, however well hidden. During the first few years none were seen on our farm, though we sometimes heard father's hired men talking about 'lining bees'. None of us boys ever found a bee tree, or tried to find any until about ten years after our arrival in the woods. On the Hickory Hill farm there is a ridge of moraine material, rather dry, but flowery with goldenrods and asters of many species, upon which we saw bees feeding in the late autumn just when their hives were fullest of honey, and it occurred to me one day after I was of age and my own master that I must try to find a bee tree. I made a little box about six inches long and four inches deep and wide; bought half a pound of honey, went to the goldenrod hill, swept a bee into the box and closed it. The lid had a pane of glass in it so I could see when the bee had sucked its fill and was ready to go home. At first it groped around trying to get out, but, smelling the honey, it seemed to forget everything else, and while it was feasting I carried the box and a small sharp-pointed stake to an open spot, where I could see about me, fixed the stake in the ground, and placed the box on the flat top of it. When I thought that the little feaster must be about full, I opened the box, but it was in no hurry to fly. It slowly crawled up to the edge of the box, lingered a minute or two cleaning its legs that had become sticky with honey, and when it took wing, instead of making what is called a bee-line for home, it buzzed around the box and minutely examined it as if trying to fix a clear picture of it in its mind so as to be able to recognize it when it returned for another load, then circled around at a little distance as if looking for something to locate it by. I was the nearest object, and the thoughtful worker buzzed in front of my face and took a good stare at me, and then flew up on to the top of an oak on the side of the open spot in the centre of which the honey-box was. Keeping a keen watch, after a minute or two of rest or wing-cleaning, I saw it fly in wide circles round the tops of the trees nearest the honey-box, and, after apparently satisfying itself, make a bee-line for the hive. Looking endwise on the line of flight, I saw that what is called a bee-line is not an absolutely straight line, but a line in general straight made of many slight, wavering, lateral curves. After taking as true a bearing as I could, I waited and watched. In a few minutes, probably ten, I was surprised to see that bee arrive at the end of the outleaning limb of the oak mentioned above, as though that was the first point it had fixed in its memory to be depended on in retracing the way back to the honey-box. From the tree-top it came straight to my head, thence straight to the box, entered without the least hesitation, filled up and started off after the same preparatory dressing and taking of bearings as before. Then I took particular pains to lay down the exact course so I would be able to trace it to the hive. Before doing so, however, I made an experiment to test the worth of the impression I had that the little insect found the way back to the box by fixing telling points in its mind. While it was away, I picked up the honey-box and set it on the stake a few rods from the position it had thus far occupied, and stood there watching. In a few minutes I saw the bee arrive at its guide-mark, the overleaning branch on the tree-top, and thence came bouncing down right to the spaces in the air which had been occupied by my head and the honey-box, and when the cunning little honey-gleaner found nothing there but empty air it whirled round and round as if confused and lost; and although I was standing with the open honey-box within fifty or sixty feet of the former feasting-spot, it could not, or at least did not, find it.

Now that I had learned the general direction of the hive, I pushed on in search of it. I had gone perhaps a quarter of a mile when I caught another bee, which, after getting loaded, went through the same performance of circling round and round the honey-box, buzzing in front of me and staring me in the face to be able to recognize me; but as if the adjacent trees and bushes were sufficiently well known, it simply looked around at them and bolted off without much dressing, indicating, I thought, that the distance to the hive was not great. I followed on and very soon discovered it in the bottom log of a corn-field fence, but some lucky fellow had discovered it before me and robbed it. The robbers had chopped a large hole in the log, taken out most of the honey, and left the poor bees late in the autumn, when winter was approaching, to make haste to gather all the honey they could from the latest flowers to avoid starvation in the winter.

CHAPTER SEVEN

Knowledge and Inventions

I LEARNED arithmetic in Scotland without understanding any of it, though I had the rules by heart. But when I was about fifteen or sixteen years of age, I began to grow hungry for real knowledge, and persuaded father, who was willing enough to have me study provided my farm work was kept up, to buy me a higher arithmetic. Beginning at the beginning, in one summer I easily finished it without assistance, in the short intervals between the end of dinner and the afternoon start for the harvest- and hay-fields, accomplishing more without a teacher in a few scraps of time than in years in school before my mind was ready for such work. Then in succession I took up algebra, geometry and trigonometry and made some little progress in each, and reviewed grammar. I was fond of reading, but father had brought only a few religious books from Scotland. Fortunately, several of our neighbours had brought a dozen or two of all sorts of books, which I borrowed and read, keeping all of them except the religious ones carefully hidden from father's eye. Among these were Scott's novels, which, like all other novels, were strictly forbidden, but devoured with glorious pleasure in secret. Father was easily persuaded to buy Josephus's *War of the Jews*, and D'Aubigné's *History of the Reformation*, and I tried hard to get him to buy Plutarch's *Lives*, which, as I told him, everybody, even religious people, praised as a grand good book; but he would have nothing to do with the old pagan until the graham bread and anti-flesh doctrines came suddenly into our backwoods neighbourhood, making a stir something like phrenology and spirit-rappings, which were as mysterious in their attacks as influenza. He then thought it possible that Plutarch might be turned to account on the food question by revealing what those old Greeks and Romans ate to make them strong; and so at last we gained our glorious Plutarch. Dick's *Christian Philosopher*, which I borrowed from a neighbour, I thought I might venture to read in the open, trusting that the word 'Christian' would be proof against its cautious condemnation. But father balked at the word 'Philosopher', and quoted from the Bible a verse which spoke of 'philosophy falsely so-called'. I then ventured to speak in defence of the book, arguing that we could not do without at least a little of the most useful kinds of philosophy.

'Yes, we can,' he said with enthusiasm, 'The Bible is the only book human beings can possibly require throughout all the journey from earth to heaven.'

'But how,' I contended, 'can we find the way to heaven without the Bible, and how after we grow old can we read the Bible without a little helpful science? Just think, father, you cannot read your Bible without spectacles, and millions of others are in the same fix; and spectacles cannot be made without some knowledge of the science of optics.'

'Oh!' he replied, perceiving the drift of the argument, 'there will always be plenty of wordly people to make spectacles.'

To this I stubbornly replied with a quotation from the Bible with reference to the time coming when 'all shall know the Lord from the least even to the greatest', and then who will make the spectacles? But he still objected to my reading that book, called me a contumacious quibbler too fond of disputation, and ordered me to return it to the accommodating owner. I managed, however, to read it later.

On the food question father insisted that those who argued for a vegetable diet were in the right, because our teeth showed plainly that they were made with reference to fruit and grain and not for flesh like those of dogs and wolves and tigers. He therefore promptly adopted a vegetable diet and requested mother to make the bread from graham flour instead of bolted flour. Mother put both kinds on the table, and meat also, to let all the family take their choice, and while father was insisting on the foolishness of eating flesh, I came to her help by calling father's attention to the passage in the Bible which told the story of Elijah the prophet who, when he was pursued by enemies who wanted to take his life, was hidden by the Lord by the brook Cherith, and fed by ravens; and surely the Lord knew what was good to eat, whether bread or meat. And on what, I asked, did the Lord feed Elijah? On vegetables or graham bread? No, he directed the ravens to feed his prophet on flesh. The Bible being the sole rule, father at once acknowledged that he was mistaken. The Lord would never have sent flesh to Elijah by the ravens if graham bread were better.

I remember as a great and sudden discovery that the poetry of the Bible, Shakespeare and Milton was a source of inspiring, exhilarating, uplifting pleasure; and I became anxious to know all the poets, and saved up small sums to buy as many of their books as possible. Within three or four years I was the proud possessor of parts of Shakespeare's, Milton's, Cowper's, Henry Kirke White's, Campbell's and Akenside's works, and quite a number of others seldom read nowadays. I think it was in my fifteenth year that I began to relish good literature with enthusiasm, and smack my lips over favourite lines, but there was desperately little time for reading, even in the winter evenings – only a few stolen minutes now and then. Father's strict rule was, straight to bed immediately after family worship, which in winter was usually over by eight o'clock. I was in the habit of lingering in the kitchen with a book and candle after the rest of the family had retired, and considered myself fortunate if I got five minutes' reading before father noticed the light and ordered me to bed; an order that of course I immediately obeyed. But night after night I tried to steal minutes in the same lingering way, and how keenly precious those minutes were, few nowadays can know. Father failed perhaps two or three times in a whole winter to notice my light for nearly ten minutes, magnificent golden blocks of time, long to be remembered like holidays or geological periods. One evening when I was reading Church history father was particularly irritable, and called out with hope-killing emphasis, '*John, go to bed!* Must I give you a separate order every night to get you to go to bed? Now, I will have no irregularity in the family; you *must* go when the rest go, and without my having to tell you.' Then, as an afterthought, as if judging that his words and tone of voice were too severe for so pardonable an offence as reading a religious book he unwarily added, 'If you *will* read, get up in the morning and read. You may get up in the morning as early as you like.'

That night I went to bed wishing with all my heart and soul that somebody or something might call me out of sleep to avail myself of this wonderful indulgence; and next morning to my joyful surprise I awoke before father called me. A boy sleeps soundly after working all day in the snowy woods, but that frosty morning I sprang out of bed as if called by a trumpet blast, rushed downstairs, scarce feeling my chilblains, enormously eager to see how much time I had won; and when I held up my candle to a little clock that stood on a bracket in the kitchen I found that it was only one o'clock. I had gained five hours, almost half a day! 'Five hours to myself!' I said, 'five huge, solid hours!' I can hardly think of any other event in my life, any discovery I ever made that gave birth to joy so transportingly glorious as the possession of these five frosty hours.

In the glad, tumultuous excitement of so much suddenly acquired time-wealth, I hardly knew what to do with it. I first thought of going on with my reading, but the zero weather would make a fire necessary, and it occurred to me that father might object to the cost of fire-wood that took time to chop. Therefore, I prudently decided to go down to the cellar, and begin work on a model of a self-setting sawmill I had invented. Next morning I managed to get up at the same gloriously early hour, and though the temperature of the cellar was a little below the freezing point, and my light was only a tallow candle the mill work went joyfully on. There were a few tools in a corner of the cellar – a vice, files, a hammer, chisels, etc., that father had brought from Scotland, but no saw excepting a coarse crooked one that was unfit for sawing dry hickory or oak. So I made a fine-tooth saw suitable for my work out of a strip of steel that had formed part of an old-fashioned corset, that cut the hardest wood smoothly. I also made my own bradawls, punches and a pair of compasses, out of wire and old files.

My workshop was immediately under father's bed, and the filing and tapping in making cogwheels, journals, cams, etc., must, no doubt, have annoyed him, but with the permission he had granted in his mind, and doubtless hoping that I would soon tire of getting up at one o'clock, he impatiently waited about two weeks before saying a word. I did not vary more than five minutes from one o'clock all winter, nor did I feel any bad effects whatever, nor did I think at all about the subject as to whether so little sleep might be in any way injurious; it was a grand triumph of will-power over cold and common comfort and work-weariness in abruptly cutting down my ten hours' allowance of sleep to five. I simply felt that I was rich beyond anything I could have dreamed of or hoped for. I was far more than happy. Like Tam o'Shanter I was glorious, 'O'er a' the ills o' life victorious'.

Father, as was customary in Scotland, gave thanks and asked a blessing before meals, not merely as a matter of form and decent Christian manners, for he regarded food as a gift derived directly from the hands of the Father in heaven. Therefore every meal to him was a sacrament requiring conduct and attitude of mind not unlike that befitting the Lord's Supper. No idle word was allowed to be spoken at our table, much less any laughing or fun or story-telling. When we were at the breakfast-table, about two weeks after the great golden time-discovery, father cleared his throat preliminary, as we all knew, to saying something considered important. I feared that it was to be on the subject of my early rising, and dreaded the withdrawal of the permission he had granted on account of the noise I made, but still hoping that, as he had given his word that I might get up as early as I wished, he would as a Scotchman stand to it, even though it was given in an unguarded moment and taken in a sense unreasonably far-reaching. The solemn sacramental silence was broken by the dreaded question:

'John, what time is it when you get up in the morning?'

'About one o'clock,' I replied in a low, meek, guilty tone of voice.

'And what kind of a time is that, getting up in the middle of the night and disturbing the whole family?'

I simply reminded him of the permission he had freely granted me to get up as early as I wished.

'I *know* it,' he said, in an almost agonized tone of voice, 'I *know* I gave you that miserable permission, but I never imagined that you would get up in the middle of the night.'

To this I cautiously made no reply, but continued to listen for the heavenly one-o'clock call, and it never failed.

After completing my self-setting sawmill I dammed one of the streams in the meadow and put the mill in operation. This invention was speedily followed by a lot of others – water-wheels, curious doorlocks and latches, thermometers, hygrometers, pyrometers, clocks, a barometer, an automatic contrivance for feeding the horses at any required hour, a lamp-lighter and fire-lighter, an early-or-late-rising machine and so forth.

After the sawmill was proved and discharged from my mind, I happened to think it would be a fine thing to make a timekeeper which would tell the day of the week and the day of the month, as well as strike like a common clock and point out the hours; also to have an attachment whereby it could be connected with a bedstead to set me on my feet at any hour in the morning; also to start fires, light lamps, etc. I had learned the time laws of the pendulum from a book, but with this exception I knew nothing of timekeepers, for I had never seen the inside of any sort of clock or watch. After long brooding, the novel clock was at length completed in my mind, and was tried and found to be durable and to work well and look well before I had begun to build it in wood. I carried small parts of it in my pocket to whittle at when I was out at work on the farm, using every spare or stolen moment within reach without father's knowing anything about it. In the middle of summer, when harvesting was in progress, the novel time-machine was nearly completed. It was hidden upstairs in a spare bedroom where some tools were kept. I did the making and mending on the farm, but one day at noon, when I happened to be away, father went upstairs for a hammer or something and discovered the mysterious machine back of the bedstead. My sister Margaret saw him on his knees examining it, and at the first opportunity whispered in my ear, 'John, fayther saw that thing you're making upstairs.' None of the family knew what I was doing but they knew very well that all such work was frowned on by father, and kindly warned me of any danger that threatened my plans. The fine invention seemed doomed to destruction before its time-ticking commenced, though I thought it handsome, had so long carried it in my mind, and like the nest of Burns's wee mousie it had cost me mony a weary whittling nibble. When we were at dinner several days after the sad discovery, father began to clear his throat to speak, and I feared the doom of martyrdom was about to be pronounced on my grand clock.

'John,' he inquired, 'what is that thing you are making upstairs?'

I replied in desperation that I didn't know what to call it.

'What! You mean to say you don't know what you are trying to do?'

'Oh, yes,' I said, 'I know very well what I am doing.'

'What, then, is the thing for?'

'It's for a lot of things,' I replied, 'but getting people up early in the morning is one of the main things it is intended for; therefore it might perhaps be called an early-rising machine.'

After getting up so extravagantly early all the last memorable winter, to make a machine for getting up perhaps still earlier seemed so ridiculous that he very nearly laughed. But after controlling himself and getting command of a sufficiently solemn face and voice he said severely, 'Do you not think it is very wrong to waste your time on such nonsense?'

'No,' I said meekly, 'I don't think I'm doing any wrong.'

'Well,' he replied, 'I assure you I do; and if you were only half as zealous in the study of religion as you are in contriving and whittling these useless, nonsensical things, it would be infinitely better for you. I want you to be like Paul, who said that he desired to know nothing among men but Christ and Him crucified.'

To this I made no reply, gloomily believing my fine machine was to be burned, but still taking what comfort I could in realizing that anyhow I had enjoyed inventing and making it.

After a few days, finding that nothing more was to be said, and that father after all had not had the heart to destroy it, all necessity for secrecy being ended, I finished it in the half-hours that we had at noon and set it in the parlour between two chairs, hung moraine boulders that had come from the direction of Lake Superior on it for weights, and set it running. We were then hauling grain into the barn. Father at this period devoted himself entirely to the Bible and did no farm work whatever. The clock had a good loud tick, and when he heard it strike, one of my sisters told me that he left his study, went to the parlour, got down on his knees and carefully examined the machinery, which was all in plain sight, not being enclosed in a case. This he did repeatedly, and evidently seemed a little proud of my ability to invent and whittle such a thing, though careful to give no encouragement for anything more of the kind in future.

But somehow it seemed impossible to stop. Inventing and whittling faster than ever, I made another hickory clock, shaped like a scythe to symbolize the scythe of Father Time. The pendulum is a bunch of arrows symbolizing the flight of time. It hangs on a leafless mossy oak snag showing the effect of time, and on the snath is written, 'All flesh is grass.' This, especially the inscription, rather pleased father, and, of course mother and all my sisters and brothers admired it. Like the first it indicates the days of the week and month, starts fires and beds at any given hour and minute, and, though made more than fifty years ago, is still a good timekeeper.

My mind still running on clocks, I invented a big one like a town clock with four dials, with the time-figures so large they could be read by all our immediate neighbours as well as ourselves when at work in the fields, and on the side next the house the days of the week and month were indicated. It was to be placed on the peak of the barn roof. But just as it was all but finished, father stopped me, saying that it would bring too many people around the barn. I then asked permission to put it on the top of a black-oak tree near the house. Studying the larger main branches, I thought I could secure a sufficiently rigid foundation for it, while the trimmed sprays and leaves would conceal the angles of the cabin required to shelter the works from the weather, and the two-second pendulum, fourteen feet long, could be snugly encased on the side of the trunk. Nothing about the grand, useful timekeeper, I argued, would disfigure the tree, for it would look something like a big hawk's nest. 'But that,' he objected, 'would draw still bigger bothersome trampling crowds about the place, for who ever heard of anything so queer as a big clock on the top of a tree?' So I had to lay aside its big wheels and cams and rest content with the pleasure of inventing it, and looking at it in my mind and listening to the deep solemn throbbing of its long two-second pendulum with its two old axes back to back for the bob.

One of my inventions was a large thermometer made of an iron rod, about three feet long and five eighths of an inch in diameter, that had formed part of a wagon-box. The expansion and contraction of this rod was multiplied by a series of levers made of strips of hoop iron. The pressure of the rod against the levers was kept constant by a small counterweight, so that the slightest change in the length of the rod was instantly shown on a dial about three feet wide multiplied about thirty-two thousand times. The zero-point was gained by packing the rod in wet snow. The scale was so large that the big black hand on the white-painted dial could be seen distinctly and the temperature read while we were ploughing in the field below the house. The extremes of heat and cold caused the hand to make several revolutions. The number of these revolutions was indicated on a small dial marked on the larger one. This thermometer was fastened on the side of the house, and was so sensitive that when anyone approached it within four or five feet the heat radiated from the observer's body caused the hand of the dial to move so fast that the motion was plainly visible, and when he stepped back, the hand moved slowly back to its normal position. It was regarded as a great wonder by the neighbours and even by my own all-Bible father.

Boys are fond of the books of travellers, and I remember that one day, after I had been reading Mungo Park's travels in Africa, mother said, 'Weel, John, maybe you will travel like Park and Humboldt some day.' Father overheard her and cried out in solemn deprecation, 'Oh, Anne! dinna put sic notions in the laddie's heed.' But at this time there was precious little need of such prayers. My brothers left the farm when they came of age, but I stayed a year longer, loath to leave home. Mother hoped I might be a minister some day; my sisters that I would be a great inventor. I often thought I should like to be a physician, but I saw no way of making money and getting the necessary education, excepting as an inventor. So, as a beginning, I decided to try to get into a big shop or factory and live a while among machines. But I was naturally extremely shy and had been taught to have a poor opinion of myself, as of no account, though all our neighbours encouragingly called me a genius, sure to rise in the world. When I was talking over plans one day with a friendly neighbour, he said, 'Now, John, if you wish to get into a machine-shop, just take some of your inventions to the State Fair, and you may be sure that as soon as they are seen they will open the door of any shop in the country for you. You will be welcomed everywhere.' And when I doubtingly asked if people would care to look at things made of wood, he said, 'Made of wood! Made of wood! What does it matter what they're made of when they are so out-and-out original. There's nothing else like them in the world. That is what will attract attention, and besides they're mighty handsome things anyway to come from the backwoods.' So I was encouraged to leave home and go at his direction to the State Fair when it was being held in Madison.

CHAPTER EIGHT

The World and the University

WHEN I told father that I was about to leave home, and inquired whether, if I should happen to be in need of money, he would send me a little, he said, 'No; depend entirely on yourself.' Good advice, I suppose, but surely needlessly severe for a bashful, home-loving boy who had worked so hard. I had the gold sovereign that my grandfather had given me when I left Scotland, and a few dollars, perhaps ten, that I had made by raising a few bushels of grain on a little patch of sandy abandoned ground. So when I left home to try the world I had only about fifteen dollars in my pocket.

Strange to say, father carefully taught us to consider ourselves very poor worms of the dust, conceived in sin, etc., and devoutly believed that quenching every spark of pride and self-confidence was a sacred duty, without realizing that in so doing he might at the same time be quenching everything else. Praise he considered most venomous, and tried to assure me that when I was fairly out in the wicked world making my own way I would soon learn that although I might have thought him a hard taskmaster at times, strangers were far harder. On the contrary, I found no lack of kindness and sympathy. All the baggage I carried was a package made up of the two clocks and a small thermometer made of a piece of old washboard, all three tied together, with no covering or case of any sort, the whole looking like one very complicated machine.

The aching parting from mother and my sisters was, of course, hard to bear. Father let David drive me down to Pardeeville, a place I had never before seen, though it was only nine miles south of the Hickory Hill home. When we arrived at the village tavern, it seemed deserted. Not a single person was in sight. I set my clock baggage on the rickety platform. David said good-bye and started for home, leaving me alone in the world. The grinding noise made by the wagon in turning short brought out the landlord, and the first thing that caught his eye was my strange bundle. Then he looked at me and said, 'Hello, young man, what's this?'

'Machines,' I said, 'for keeping time and getting up in the morning, and so forth.'

'Well! Well! That's a mighty queer get-up. You must be a Down-East Yankee. Where did you get the pattern for such a thing?'

'In my head,' I said.

Someone down the street happened to notice the landlord looking intently at something and came to see what it was. Three or four people in that little village formed an attractive crowd, and in fifteen or twenty minutes the greater part of the population of Pardeeville stood gazing in a circle around my strange hickory belongings. I kept outside of the circle to avoid being seen, and had the advantage of hearing the remarks without being embarrassed. Almost every one as he came up would say, 'What's that? What's it for? Who made it?' The landlord would answer them all alike, 'Why, a young man that lives out in the country somewhere made it, and he says it's a thing for keeping time, getting up in the morning, and something that I didn't understand. I don't know what he meant.' 'Oh, no!' one of the crowd would say, 'that can't be. It's for something else – something mysterious. Mark my words, you'll see all about it in the newspapers some of these days.' A curious little fellow came running up the street, joined the crowd, stood on tiptoe to get sight of the wonder, quickly made up his mind, and shouted in crisp, confident, cock-crowing style, 'I know what that contraption's for. It's a machine for taking the bones out of fish.'

This was in the time of the great popular phrenology craze, when the fences and barns along the roads throughout the country were plastered with big skull-bump posters, headed, 'Know Thyself', and advising everybody to attend schoolhouse lectures to have their heads explained and be told what they were good for and whom they ought to marry. My mechanical bundle seemed to bring a good deal of this phrenology to mind, for many of the onlookers would say, 'I wish I could see that boy's head – he must have a tremendous bump in invention.' Others complimented me by saying, 'I wish I had that fellow's head. I'd rather have it than the best farm in the State.'

I stayed overnight at this little tavern, waiting for a train. In the morning I went to the station, and set my bundle on the platform. Along came the thundering train, a glorious sight, the first train I had ever waited for. When the conductor saw my queer baggage, he cried, 'Hello! What have we here?'

'Inventions for keeping time, early rising and so forth. May I take them into the car with me?'

'You can take them where you like,' he replied, 'but you had better give them to the baggage-master. If you take them into the car they will draw a crowd and might get broken.'

So I gave them to the baggage-master and made haste to ask the conductor whether I might ride on the engine. He good-naturedly said, 'Yes, it's the right place for you. Run ahead, and tell the engineer what I say.' But the engineer bluntly refused to let me on, saying, 'It don't matter what the conductor told you. *I* say you can't ride on my engine.'

By this time the conductor, standing ready to start his train, was watching to see what luck I had, and when he saw me returning came ahead to meet me.

'The engineer won't let me on,' I reported.

'Won't he?' said the kind conductor. 'Oh! I guess he will. You come down with me.' And so he actually took the time and patience to walk the length of that long train to get me on to the engine.

'Charlie,' said he, addressing the engineer, 'don't you ever take a passenger?'

'Very seldom,' he replied.

'Anyhow, I wish you would take this young man on. He has the strangest machines in the baggage-car I ever saw in my life. I believe he could make a locomotive. He wants to see the engine running. Let him on.' Then in a low whisper he told me to jump on, which I did gladly, the engineer offering neither encouragement nor objection.

As soon as the train was started, the engineer asked what the 'strange thing' the conductor spoke of really was.

'Only inventions for keeping time, getting folk up in the morning, and so forth,' I hastily replied, and before he could ask any more questions I asked permission to go outside of the cab to see the machinery. This he kindly granted, adding, 'Be careful not to fall off, and when you hear me whistling for a station you come back, because if it is reported against me to the superintendent that I allow boys to run all over my engine I might lose my job.'

Assuring him that I would come back promptly, I went out and walked along the foot-board on the side of the boiler, watching the magnificent machine rushing through the landscapes as if glorying in its strength like a living creature. While seated on the cow-catcher platform, I seemed to be fairly flying, and the wonderful display of power and motion was enchanting. This was the first time I had ever been on a train, much less a locomotive, since I had left Scotland. When I got to Madison, I thanked the kind conductor and engineer for my glorious ride, inquired the way to the Fair, shouldered my inventions, and walked to the Fair Ground.

When I applied for an admission ticket at a window by the gate I told the agent that I had something to exhibit.

'What is it?' he inquired.

'Well, here it is. Look at it.'

When he craned his neck through the window and got a glimpse of my bundle, he cried excitedly, 'Oh! *you* don't need a ticket – come right in.'

When I inquired of the agent where such things as mine should be exhibited, he said, 'You see that building up on the hill with a big flag on it? That's the Fine Arts Hall, and it's just the place for your wonderful invention.'

So I went up to the Fine Arts Hall and looked in, wondering if they would allow wooden things in so fine a place.

I was met at the door by a dignified gentleman, who greeted me kindly and said, 'Young man, what have we got here?'

'Two clocks and a thermometer,' I replied.

'Did you make these? They look wonderfully beautiful and novel and must, I think, prove the most interesting feature of the fair.'

'Where shall I place them?' I inquired.

'Just look around, young man, and choose the place you like best, whether it is occupied or not. You can have your pick of all the building, and a carpenter to make the necessary shelving and assist you every way possible!'

So I quickly had a shelf made large enough for all of them, went out on the hill and picked up some glacial boulders of the right size for weights, and in fifteen or twenty minutes the clocks were running. They seemed to attract more attention than anything else in the hall. I got lots of praise from the crowd and the newspaper-reporters. The local press reports were copied into the Eastern papers. It was considered wonderful that a boy on a farm had been able to invent and make such things, and almost every spectator foretold good fortune. But I had been so lectured by my father above all things to avoid praise that I was afraid to read those kind newspaper notices, and never clipped out or preserved any of them, just glanced at them and turned away my eyes from beholding vanity. They gave me a prize of ten or fifteen dollars and a diploma for wonderful things not down in the list of exhibits.

Many years later, after I had written articles and books, I received a letter from the gentleman who had charge of the Fine Arts Hall. He proved to be the Professor of English Literature in the University of Wisconsin at this Fair time, and long afterward he sent me clippings of reports of his lectures. He had a lecture on me, discussing style, etc., and telling how well he remembered my arrival at the Hall in my shirt-sleeves with those mechanical wonders on my shoulder, and so forth, and so forth. These inventions, though of little importance, opened all doors for me and made marks that have lasted many years, simply, I suppose, because they were original and promising.

I was looking around in the meantime to find out where I should go to seek my fortune. An inventor at the Fair, by the name of Wiard, was exhibiting an iceboat he had invented to run on the upper Mississippi from Prairie du Chien to St Paul during the winter months, explaining how useful it would be thus to make a highway of the river while it was closed to ordinary navigation by ice. After he saw my inventions he offered me a place in his foundry and machine-shop in Prairie du Chien and promised to assist me all he could. So I made up my mind to accept his offer and rode with him to Prairie du Chien in his iceboat, which was mounted on a flat car. I soon found, however, that he was seldom at home and that I was not likely to learn much at his small shop. I found a place where I could work for my board and devote my spare hours to mechanical drawing, geometry and physics, making but little headway, however, although the Pelton family, for whom I worked, were very kind. I made up my mind after a few months' stay in Prairie du Chien to return to Madison, hoping that in some way I might be able to gain an education.

At Madison I raised a few dollars by making and selling a few of those bedsteads that set the sleepers on their feet in the morning – inserting in the footboard the works of an ordinary clock that could be bought for a dollar. I also made a few dollars addressing circulars in an insurance office, while at the same time I was paying my board by taking care of a pair of horses and going errands. This is of no great interest except that I was thus winning my bread while hoping that something would turn up that might enable me to make money enough to enter the State University. This was my ambition, and it never wavered no matter what I was doing. No University, it seemed to me, could be more admirably situated, and as I sauntered about it, charmed with its fine lawns and trees and beautiful lakes, and saw the students going and coming with their books, and occasionally practising with a theodolite in measuring distances, I thought that if I could only join them it would be the greatest joy of life. I was desperately hungry and thirsty for knowledge and willing to endure anything to get it.

One day I chanced to meet a student who had noticed my inventions at the Fair and now recognized me. And when I said, 'You are fortunate fellows to be allowed to study in this beautiful place. I wish I could join you.' 'Well, why don't you?' he asked. 'I haven't money enough,' I said. 'Oh, as to money,' he reassuringly explained, 'very little is required. I presume you're able to enter the Freshman class, and you can board yourself as quite a number of us do at a cost of about a dollar a week. The baker and milkman come every day. You can live on bread and milk.' Well, I thought, maybe I have money enough for at least one beginning term. Anyhow I couldn't help trying.

With fear and trembling, overladen with ignorance, I called on Professor Stirling, the Dean of the Faculty, who was then Acting President, presented my case, and told him how far I had got on with my studies at home, and that I hadn't been to school since leaving Scotland at the age of eleven years, excepting one short term of a couple of months at a district school, because I could not be spared from the farm work. After hearing my story, the kind professor welcomed me to the glorious University – next, it seemed to me, to the Kingdom of Heaven. After a few weeks in the preparatory department I entered the Freshman class. In Latin I found that one of the books in use I had already studied in Scotland. So, after an interruption of a dozen years, I began my Latin over again where I had left off; and, strange to say, most of it came back to me, especially the grammar which I had committed to memory at the Dunbar Grammar School.

During the four years that I was in the University, I earned enough in the harvest-fields during the long summer vacations to carry me through the balance of each year, working very hard, cutting with a cradle four acres of wheat a day, and helping to put it in the shock. But, having to buy books and paying, I think, thirty-two dollars a year for instruction, and occasionally buying acids and retorts, glass tubing, bell-glasses, flasks, etc., I had to cut down expenses for board now and then to half a dollar a week.

One winter I taught school ten miles south of Madison, earning much-needed money at the rate of twenty dollars a month, 'boarding round', and keeping up my University work by studying at night. As I was not then well enough off to own a watch, I used one of my hickory clocks, not only for keeping time, but for starting the school fire in the cold mornings, and regulating class-times. I carried it out on my shoulder to the old log school-house, and set it to work on a little shelf nailed to one of the knotty, bulging logs. The winter was very cold, and I had to go to the schoolhouse and start the fire about eight o'clock to warm it before the arrival of the scholars. This was a rather trying job, and one that my clock might easily be made to do. Therefore, after supper one evening I told the head of the family with whom I was boarding that if he would give me a candle I would go back to the schoolhouse and make arrangements for lighting the fire at eight o'clock, without my having to be present until time to open the school at nine. He said, 'Oh! young man, you have some curious things in the school-room, but I don't think you can do that.' I said, 'Oh, yes! it's easy,' and in hardly more than an hour the simple job was completed. I had only to place a teaspoonful of powdered chlorate of potash and sugar on the stove-hearth near a few shavings and kindling, and at the required time make the clock, through a simple arrangement, touch the inflammable mixture with a drop of sulphuric acid. Every evening after school was dismissed, I shovelled out what was left of the fire into the snow, put in a little kindling, filled up the big box stove with heavy oak wood, placed the lighting arrangement on the hearth, and set the clock to drop the acid at the hour of eight; all this requiring only a few minutes.

The first morning after I had made this simple arrangement I invited the doubting farmer to watch the old squat schoolhouse from a window that overlooked it, to see if a good smoke did not rise from the stovepipe. Sure enough, on the minute, he saw a tall column curling gracefully up through the frosty air, but instead of congratulating me on my success he solemnly shook his head and said in a hollow, lugubrious voice, 'Young man, you will be setting fire to the schoolhouse.' All winter long that faithful clock fire never failed, and by the time I got to the schoolhouse the stove was usually red-hot.

At the beginning of the long summer vacations I returned to the Hickory Hill farm to earn the means in the harvest-fields to continue my University course, walking all the way to save railroad fares. And although I cradled four acres of wheat a day, I made the long, hard, sweaty day's work still longer and harder by keeping up my study of plants. At the noon hour I collected a large handful, put them in water to keep them fresh, and after supper got to work on them and sat up till after midnight, analysing and classifying, thus leaving only four hours for sleep; and by the end of the first year, after taking up botany, I knew the principal flowering plants of the region.

I received my first lesson in botany from a student by the name of Griswold, who is now County Judge of the County of Waukesha, Wisconsin. In the University he was often laughed at on account of his anxiety to instruct others, and his frequently saying with fine emphasis, 'Imparting instruction is my greatest enjoyment.' One memorable day in June, when I was standing on the stone steps of the north dormitory, Mr Griswold joined me and at once began to teach. He reached up, plucked a flower from an overspreading branch of a locust tree, and, handing it to me, said, 'Muir, do you know what family this tree belongs to?'

'No,' I said, 'I don't know anything about botany.'

'Well, no matter,' said he, 'what is it like?'

'It's like a pea flower,' I replied.

'That's right. You're right,' he said, 'it belongs to the Pea Family.'

'But how can that be,' I objected, 'when the pea is a weak, clinging, straggling herb, and the locust a big, thorny hardwood tree?'

'Yes, that is true,' he replied, 'as to the difference in size, but it is also true that in all their essential characters they are alike, and therefore they must belong to one and the same family. Just look at the peculiar form of the locust flower; you see that the upper petal, called the banner, is broad and erect, and so is the upper petal of the pea flower; the two lower petals called the wings, are outspread and wing-shaped; so are those of the pea; and the two petals below the wings are united on their edges, curve upward, and form what is called the keel, and so you see are the corresponding petals of the pea flower. And now look at the stamens and pistils. You see that nine of the ten stamens have their filaments united into a sheath around the pistil, but the tenth stamen has its filament free. These are very marked characters, are they not? And, strange to say, you will find them the same in the tree and in the vine. Now look at the ovules or seeds of the locust, and you will see that they are arranged in a pod or legume like those of the pea. And look at the leaves. You see the leaf of the locust is made up of several leaflets, and so also is the leaf of the pea. Now taste the locust leaf.'

I did so and found that it tasted like the leaf of the pea. Nature has used the same seasoning for both, though one is a straggling vine, the other a big tree.

'Now, surely you cannot imagine that all these similar characters are mere coincidences. Do they not rather go to show that the Creator in making the pea vine and locust tree had the same idea in mind, and that plants are not classified arbitrarily? Man has nothing to do with their classification. Nature has attended to all that, giving essential unity with boundless variety, so that the botanist has only to examine plants to learn the harmony of their relations.'

This fine lesson charmed me and sent me flying to the woods and meadows in wild enthusiasm. Like everybody else I was always fond of flowers, attracted by their external beauty and purity. Now my eyes were opened to their inner beauty, all alike revealing glorious traces of the thoughts of God, and leading on and on into the infinite cosmos. I wandered away at every opportunity, making long excursions round the lakes, gathering specimens and keeping them fresh in a bucket in my room to study at night after my regular class tasks were learned; for my eyes never closed on the plant glory I had seen.

Nevertheless, I still indulged my love of mechanical inventions. I invented a desk in which the books I had to study were arranged in order at the beginning of each term. I also made a bed which set me on my feet every morning at the hour determined on, and in dark winter mornings just as the bed set me on the floor it lighted a lamp. Then, after the minutes allowed for dressing had elapsed, a click was heard and the first book to be studied was pushed up from a rack below the top of the desk, thrown open, and allowed to remain there the number of minutes required. Then the machinery closed the book and allowed it to drop back into its stall, then moved the rack forward and threw up the next in order, and so on, all the day being divided according to the times of recitation, and time required and allotted to each study. Besides this, I thought it would be a fine thing in the summer-time when the sun rose early, to dispense with the clock-controlled bed machinery, and make use of sunbeams instead. This I did simply by taking a lens out of my small spy-glass, fixing it on a frame on the sill of my bedroom window, and pointing it to the sunrise; the sunbeams focused on a thread, burned it through, allowing the bed machinery to put me on my feet. When I wished to arise at any given time after sunrise, I had only to turn the pivoted frame that held the lens the requisite number of degrees or minutes. Thus I took Emerson's advice and hitched my dumping-wagon bed to a star.

I also invented a machine to make visible the growth of plants and the action of the sunlight, a very delicate contrivance, enclosed in glass. Besides this I invented a barometer and a lot of novel scientific apparatus. My room was regarded as a sort of show place by the professors, who oftentimes brought visitors to it on Saturdays and holidays. And when, some eighteen years after I had left the University, I was sauntering over the campus in time of vacation, and spoke to a man who seemed to be taking some charge of the grounds, he informed me that he was the janitor; and when I inquired what had become of Pat, the janitor in my time, and a favourite with the students, he replied that Pat was still alive and well, but now too old to do much work. And when I pointed to the dormitory room that I long ago occupied, he said, 'Oh! then I know who you are,' and mentioned my name. 'How comes it that you know my name?' I inquired. He explained that 'Pat always pointed out that room to newcomers and told long stories about the wonders that used to be in it.' So long had the memory of my little inventions survived.

Although I was four years at the University, I did not take the regular course of studies, but instead picked out what I thought would be most useful to me, particularly chemistry, which opened a new world, and mathematics and physics, a little Greek and Latin, botany and geology. I was far from satisfied with what I had learned, and should have stayed longer. Anyhow I wandered away on a glorious botanical and geological excursion, which has lasted nearly fifty years and is not yet completed, always happy and free, poor and rich, without thought of a diploma or of making a name, urged on and on through endless, inspiring, Godful beauty.

From the top of a hill on the north side of Lake Mendota I gained a last wistful, lingering view of the beautiful University grounds and buildings where I had spent so many hungry and happy and hopeful days. There with streaming eyes I bade my blessed Alma Mater farewell. But I was only leaving one University for another, the Winsconsin University for the University of the Wilderness.

A THOUSAND-MILE WALK TO THE GULF

A Thousand Mile Walk to the Gulf

First published by Houghton Mifflin Co., Boston, 1916

Contents

CHAPTER ONE

Kentucky Forests and Caves

I HAD long been looking from the wild woods and gardens of the Northern States to those of the warm South, and at last, all drawbacks overcome, I set forth (from Indianapolis) on the first day of September, 1867, joyful and free, on a thousand-mile walk to the Gulf of Mexico. (The trip to Jeffersonville, on the banks of the Ohio, was made by rail.) Crossing the Ohio at Louisville (2 September), I steered through the big city by compass without speaking a word to any one. Beyond the city I found a road running southward, and after passing a scatterment of suburban cabins and cottages I reached the green woods and spread out my pocket map to rough-hew a plan for my journey.

My plan was simply to push on in a general southward direction by the wildest, leafiest, and least trodden way I could find, promising the greatest extent of virgin forest. Folding my map, I shouldered my little bag and plant press and strode away among the old Kentucky oaks, rejoicing in splendid visions of pines and palms and tropic flowers in glorious array, not, however, without a few cold shadows of loneliness, although the great oaks seemed to spread their arms in welcome.

I have seen oaks of many species in many kinds of exposure and soil, but those of Kentucky excel in grandeur all I had ever before beheld. They are broad and dense and bright green. In the leafy bowers and caves of their long branches dwell magnificent avenues of shade, and every tree seems to be blessed with a double portion of strong exulting life. Walked twenty miles, mostly on river bottom, and found shelter in a rickety tavern.

3 September. Escaped from the dust and squalor of my garret bedroom to the glorious forest. All the streams that I tasted hereabouts are salty and so are the wells. Salt River was nearly dry. Much of my way this forenoon was over naked limestone. After passing the level ground that extended twenty-five or thirty miles from the river I came to a region of rolling hills called Kentucky Knobs – hills of denudation, covered with trees to the top. Some of them have a few pines. For a few hours I followed the farmers' paths, but soon wandered away from roads and encountered many a tribe of twisted vines difficult to pass.

Emerging about noon from a grove of giant sunflowers, I found myself on the brink of a tumbling rocky stream (Rolling Fork). I did not expect to find bridges on my wild ways, and at once started to ford, when a negro woman on the opposite bank earnestly called on me to wait until she could tell the 'men folks' to bring me a horse – that the river was too deep and rapid to wade and that I would 'sartain be drowned' if I attempted to cross. I replied that my bag and plants would ballast me; that the water did not appear to be deep, and that if I were carried away, I was a good swimmer and would soon dry in the sunshine. But the cautious old soul replied that no one ever waded that river and set off for a horse, saying that it was no trouble at all.

In a few minutes the ferry horse came gingerly down the bank through vines and weeds. His long stilt legs proved him a natural wader. He was white and the little sable negro boy that rode him looked like a bug on his back. After many a tottering halt the outward voyage was safely made, and I mounted behind little Nig. He was a queer specimen, puffy and jet as an India rubber doll and his hair was matted in sections like the wool of a merino sheep. The old horse, overladen with his black and white burden, rocked and stumbled on his stilt legs with fair promises of a fall. But all ducking signs failed and we arrived in safety among the weeds and vines of the rugged bank. A salt bath would have done us no harm. I could swim and little Afric looked as if he might float like a bladder.

I called at the homestead where my ferryman informed me I would find 'tollable' water. But, like all the water of this section that I have tasted, it was intolerable with salt. Everything about this old Kentucky home bespoke plenty, unpolished and unmeasured. The house was built in true Southern style, airy, large, and with a transverse central hall that looks like a railway tunnel, and heavy rough outside chimneys. The negro quarters and other buildings are enough in number for a village, altogether an interesting representative of a genuine old Kentucky home, embosomed in orchards, corn fields and green wooded hills.

Passed gangs of woodmen engaged in felling and hewing the grand oaks for market. Fruit very abundant. Magnificent flowing hill scenery all afternoon. Walked southeast from Elizabethtown till wearied and lay down in the bushes by guess.

4 September. The sun was gilding the hilltops when I was awakened by the alarm notes of birds whose dwelling in a hazel thicket I had disturbed. They flitted excitedly close to my head, as if scolding or asking angry questions, while several beautiful plants, strangers to me, were looking me full in the face. The first botanical discovery in bed! This was one of the most delightful camp grounds, though groped for in the dark, and I lingered about it enjoying its trees and soft lights and music.

Walked ten miles of forest. Met a strange oak with willow-looking leaves. Entered a sandy stretch of black oak called 'Barrens,' many of which were sixty or seventy feet in height, and are said to have grown since the fires were kept off, forty years ago. The farmers hereabouts are tall, stout, happy fellows, fond of guns and horses. Enjoyed friendly chats with them. Arrived at dark in a village that seemed to be drawing its last breath. Was guided to the 'tavern' by a negro who was extremely accommodating. 'No trouble at all,' he said.

5 September. No bird or flower or friendly tree above me this morning; only squalid garret rubbish and dust. Escaped to the woods. Came to the region of caves. At the mouth of the first I discovered, I was surprised to find ferns which belonged to the coolest nooks of Wisconsin and northward, but soon observed that each cave rim has a zone of climate peculiar to itself, and it is always cool. This cave had an opening about ten feet in diameter, and twenty-five feet perpendicular depth. A strong cold wind issued from it and I could hear the sounds of running water. A long pole was set against its walls as if intended for a ladder, but in some places it was slippery and smooth as a mast and would test the climbing powers of a monkey. The walls and rim of this natural reservoir were finely carved and flowered. Bushes leaned over it with shading leaves, and beautiful ferns and mosses were in rows and sheets on its slopes and shelves. Lingered here a long happy while, pressing specimens and printing this beauty into memory.

Arrived about noon at Munfordville; was soon discovered and examined by Mr Munford himself, a pioneer and father of the village. He is a surveyor – has held all country offices, and every seeker of roads and lands applies to him for information. He regards all the villagers as his children, and all strangers who enter Munfordville as his own visitors. Of course he inquired my business, destination, et cetera, and invited me to his house.

After refreshing me with 'parrs' he complacently covered the table with bits of rocks, plants, et cetera, things new and old which he had gathered in his surveying walks and supposed to be full of scientific interest. He informed me that all scientific men applied to him for information, and as I was a botanist, he either possessed, or ought to possess, the knowledge I was seeking, and so I received long lessons concerning roots and herbs for every mortal ill. Thanking my benefactor for his kindness, I escaped to the fields and followed a railroad along the base of a grand hill ridge. As evening came on all the dwellings I found seemed to repel me, and I could not muster courage enough to ask entertainment at any of them. Took refuge in a log schoolhouse that stood on a hillside beneath stately oaks and slept on the softest looking of the benches.

6 September. Started at the earliest bird song in hopes of seeing the great Mammoth Cave before evening. Overtook an old negro driving an ox team. Rode with him a few miles and had some interesting chat concerning war, wild fruits of the woods, et cetera. 'Right heah,' said he, 'is where the Rebs was a-tearin' up the track, and they all a sudden thought they seed the Yankees a-comin', obah dem big hills dar, and Lo'd, how dey run.' I asked him if he would like a renewal of these sad war times, when his flexible face suddenly calmed, and he said with intense earnestness, 'Oh, Lo'd, want no mo wa, Lo'd no.' Many of these Kentucky negroes are shrewd and intelligent, and when warmed upon a subject that interests them, are eloquent in no mean degree.

Arrived at Horse Cave, about ten miles from the great cave. The entrance is by a long easy slope of several hundred yards. It seems like a noble gateway to the birthplace of springs and fountains and the dark treasuries of the mineral kingdom. This cave is in a village (of the same name) which it supplies with an abundance of cold water, and cold air that issues from its fern clad lips. In hot weather crowds of people sit about it in the shade of the trees that guard it. This magnificent fan is capable of cooling everybody in the town at once.

Those who live near lofty mountains may climb to cool weather in a day or two, but the overheated Kentuckians can find a patch of cool climate in almost every glen in the State. The villager who accompanied me said that Horse Cave had never been fully explored, but that it was several miles in length at least. He told me that he had never been at Mammoth Cave – that it was not worth going ten miles to see, as it was nothing but a hole in the ground, and I found that his was no rare case. He was one of the useful, practical men – too wise to waste precious time with weeds, caves, fossils, or anything else that he could not eat.

Arrived at the great Mammoth Cave. I was surprised to find it in so complete naturalness. A large hotel with fine walks and gardens is near it. But fortunately the cave has been unimproved, and were it not for the narrow trail that leads down the glen to its door, one would not know that it had been visited. There are house-rooms and halls whose entrances give but slight hint of their grandeur. And so also this magnificent hall in the mineral kingdom of Kentucky has a door comparatively small and unpromising. One might pass within a few yards of it without noticing it. A strong cool breeze issues constantly from it, creating a northern climate for the ferns that adorn its rocky front.

I never before saw Nature's grandeur in so abrupt contrast with paltry artificial gardens. The fashionable hotel grounds are in exact parlour taste, with many a beautiful plant cultivated to deformity, and arranged in strict geometrical beds, the whole pretty affair a laborious failure side by side with Divine beauty. The trees around the mouth of the cave are smooth and tall and bent forward at the bottom, then straight upwards. Only a butternut seems, by its angular knotty branches, to sympathize with and belong to the cave, with a fine growth of *Cystopteris* and *Hypnum*.

Started for Glasgow Junction. Got belated in the hill woods. Inquired my way at a farmhouse and was invited to stay overnight in a rare, hearty, hospitable manner. Engaged in familiar running talk on politics, war times, and theology. The old Kentuckian seemed to take a liking to me and advised me to stay in these hills until next spring, assuring me that I would find much to interest me in and about the Great Cave; also, that he was one of the school officials and was sure that I could obtain their school for the winter term. I sincerely thanked him for his kind plans, but pursued my own.

7 September. Left the hospitable Kentuckians with their sincere good wishes and bore away southwards again through the deep green woods. In noble forests all day. Saw mistletoe for the first time. Part of the day I travelled with a Kentuckian from near Burkesville. He spoke to all the negroes he met with familiar kindly greetings, addressing them always as 'Uncles' and 'Aunts'. All travellers one meets on these roads, white and black, male and female, travel on horseback. Glasgow is one of the few Southern towns that shows ordinary American life. At night with a well-to-do farmer.

8 September. Deep, green, bossy sea of waving, flowing hilltops. Corn and cotton and tobacco fields scattered here and there. I had imagined that a cotton field in flower was something magnificent. But cotton is a coarse, rough, straggling, unhappy looking plant, not half as good-looking as a field of Irish potatoes.

Met a great many negroes going to meeting, dressed in their Sunday best. Fat, happy looking, and contented. The scenery on approaching the Cumberland River becomes still grander. Burkesville, in beautiful location, is embosomed in a glorious array of verdant flowing hills. The Cumberland must be a happy stream. I think I could enjoy travelling with it in the midst of such beauty all my life. This evening I could find none willing to take me in, and so lay down on a hillside and fell asleep muttering praises to the happy abounding beauty of Kentucky.

9 September. Another day in the most favoured province of bird and flower. Many rapid streams, flowing in beautiful flower-bordered canyons embosomed in dense woods. Am seated on a grand hill-slope that leans back against the sky like a picture. Amid the wide waves of green wood there are spots of autumnal yellow and the atmosphere, too, has the dawnings of autumn in colours and sounds. The soft light of morning falls upon ripening forests of oak and elm, walnut and hickory, and all Nature is thoughtful and calm. Kentucky is the greenest, leafiest State I have yet seen. The sea of soft temperate plant-green is deepest here.

Comparing volumes of vegetable verdure in different countries to a wedge, the thick end would be in the forests of Kentucky, the other in the lichens and mosses of the North. This verdure wedge would not be perfect in its lines. From Kentucky it would maintain its thickness long and well in passing the level forests of Indiana and Canada. From the maples and pines of Canada it would slope rapidly to the bleak Arctic hills with dwarf birches and alders; thence it would thin out in a long edge among hardy lichens and liverworts and mosses to the dwelling-places of everlasting frost. Far the grandest of all Kentucky plants are her noble oaks. They are the master existences of her exuberant forests. Here is the Eden, the paradise of oaks. Passed the Kentucky line towards evening and obtained food and shelter from a thrifty Tennessee farmer, after he had made use of all the ordinary anti-hospitable arguments of cautious comfortable families.

10 September. Escaped from a heap of uncordial kindness to the generous bosom of the woods. After a few miles of level ground in luxuriant tangles of brooding vines, I began the ascent of the Cumberland Mountains, the first real mountains that my foot ever touched or eyes beheld. The ascent was by a nearly regular zigzag slope, mostly covered up like a tunnel by overarching oaks. But there were a few openings where the glorious forest road of Kentucky was grandly seen, stretching over hill and valley, adjusted to every slope and curve by the hands of Nature – the most sublime and comprehensive picture that ever entered my eyes. Reached the summit in six or seven hours – a strangely long period of up-grade work to one accustomed only to the hillocky levels of Wisconsin and adjacent States.

CHAPTER TWO

Crossing the Cumberland Mountains

I HAD climbed but a short distance when I was overtaken by a young man on horseback, who soon showed that he intended to rob me if he should find the job worth while. After he had inquired where I came from, and where I was going, he offered to carry my bag. I told him that it was so light that I did not feel it at all a burden; but he insisted and coaxed until I allowed him to carry it. As soon as he had gained possession I noticed that he gradually increased his speed, evidently trying to get far enough ahead of me to examine the contents without being observed. But I was too good a walker and runner for him to get far. At a turn of the road, after trotting his horse for about half an hour, and when he thought he was out of sight, I caught him rummaging my poor bag. Finding there only a comb, brush, towel, soap, a change of under-clothing, a copy of Burns's poems, Milton's Paradise Lost, and a small New Testament, he waited for me, handed back my bag, and returned down the hill, saying that he had forgotten something.

I found splendid growths of shining-leaved *Ericaceæ* (heathworts) for which the Alleghany Mountains are noted. Also ferns of which *Osmunda cinnamomea* (Cinnamon Fern) is the largest and perhaps the most abundant. *Osmunda regalis* (Flowering Fern) is also common here, but not large. In Wood's[1] and Gray's Botany *Osmunda cinnamomea* is said to be a much larger fern than *Osmunda Claytoniana*. This I found to be true in Tennessee and southward, but in Indiana, part of Illinois, and Wisconsin the opposite is true. Found here the beautiful, sensitive *Schrankia,* or sensitive brier. It is a long, prickly, leguminous vine, with dense heads of small, yellow fragrant flowers.

Vines growing on roadsides receive many a tormenting blow, simply because they give evidence of feeling. Sensitive people are served in the same way. But the roadside vine soon becomes less sensitive, like people getting used to teasing – Nature, in this instance, making for the comfort of flower creatures the same benevolent arrangement as for man. Thus I found that the *Schrankia* vines growing along footpaths leading to a backwoods schoolhouse were much less sensitive than those in the adjacent unfrequented woods, having learned to pay but slight attention to the tingling strokes they get from teasing scholars.

It is startling to see the pairs of pinnate leaves rising quickly out of the grass and folding themselves close in regular succession from the root to the end of the prostrate stems, ten to twenty feet in length. How little we know as yet of the life of plants – their hopes and fears, pains and enjoyments!

---

[1] Alphonso Wood, *Class-book of Botany, with a Flora of the United States and Canada.* The copy of this work, carried by Mr Muir on his wanderings, is still extant. The edition is that of 1862.

Travelled a few miles with an old Tennessee farmer who was much excited on account of the news he had just heard. 'Three kingdoms, England, Ireland, and Russia, have declared war agin the United States. Oh, it's terrible, terrible,' said he. 'This big war comin' so quick after our own big fight. Well, it can't be helped, and all I have to say is, Amerricay forever, but I'd a heap rather they didn't fight.'

'But are you sure the news is true?' I inquired. 'Oh, yes, quite sure,' he replied, 'for me and some of my neighbours were down at the store last night, and Jim Smith can read, and he found out all about it in a newspaper.'

Passed the poor, rickety, thrice-dead village of Jamestown, an incredibly dreary place. Toward the top of the Cumberland grade, about two hours before sundown I came to a log house, and as I had been warned that all the broad plateau of the range for forty or fifty miles was desolate, I began thus early to seek a lodging for the night. Knocking at the door, a motherly old lady replied to my request for supper and bed and breakfast, that I was welcome to the best she had, provided that I had the necessary change to pay my bill. When I told her that unfortunately I had nothing smaller than a five-dollar greenback, she said, 'Well, I'm sorry, but cannot afford to keep you. Not long ago ten soldiers came across from North Carolina, and in the morning they offered a greenback that I couldn't change, and so I got nothing for keeping them, which I was ill able to afford.'

'Very well,' I said, 'I'm glad you spoke of this beforehand, for I would rather go hungry than impose on your hospitality.'

As I turned to leave, after bidding her goodbye, she, evidently pitying me for my tired looks, called me back and asked me if I would like a drink of milk. This I gladly accepted, thinking that perhaps I might not be successful in getting any other nourishment for a day or two. Then I inquired whether there were any more houses on the road, nearer than North Carolina, forty or fifty miles away. 'Yes,' she said, 'it's only two miles to the next house, but beyond that there are no houses that I know of except empty ones whose owners have been killed or driven away during the war.'

Arriving at the last house, my knock at the door was answered by a bright, good-natured, good-looking little woman, who in reply to my request for a night's lodging and food, said, 'Oh, I guess so. I think you can stay. Come in and I'll call my husband.' 'But I must first warn you,' I said, 'that I have nothing smaller to offer you than a five-dollar bill for my entertainment. I don't want you to think that I am trying to impose on your hospitality.'

She then called her husband, a blacksmith, who was at work at his forge. He came out, hammer in hand, bare-breasted, sweaty, begrimed, and covered with shaggy black hair. In reply to his wife's statement, that this young man wished to stop over night, he quickly replied, 'That's all right; tell him to go into the house.' He was turning to go back to his shop, when his wife added, 'But he says he hasn't any change to pay. He has nothing smaller than a five-dollar bill.' Hesitating only a moment, he turned on his heel and said, 'Tell him to go into the house. A man that comes right out like that beforehand is welcome to eat my bread.'

When he came in after his hard day's work and sat down to dinner, he solemnly asked a blessing on the frugal meal, consisting solely of corn bread and bacon. Then, looking across the table at me, he said, 'Young man, what are you doing down here?' I replied that I was looking at plants. 'Plants? What kind of plants?' I said, 'Oh, all kinds; grass, weeds, flowers, trees, mosses, ferns – almost everything that grows is interesting to me.'

'Well, young man,' he queried, 'you mean to say that you are not employed by the Government on some private business?' 'No,' I said, 'I am not employed by any one except just myself. I love all kinds of plants, and I came down here to these Southern States to get acquainted with as many of them as possible.'

'You look like a strong-minded man,' he replied, 'and surely you are able to do something better than wander over the country and look at weeds and blossoms. These are hard times, and real work is required of every man that is able. Picking up blossoms doesn't seem to be a man's work at all in any kind of times.'

To this I replied, 'You are a believer in the Bible, are you not?' 'Oh, yes.' 'Well, you know Solomon was a strong-minded man, and he is generally believed to have been the very wisest man the world ever saw, and yet he considered it was worth while to study plants; not only to go and pick them up as I am doing, but to study them; and you know we are told that he wrote a book about plants, not only of the great cedars of Lebanon, but of little bits of things growing in the cracks of the walls.[1]

'Therefore, you see that Solomon differed very much more from you than from me in this matter. I'll warrant you he had many a long ramble in the mountains of Judea, and had he been a Yankee he would likely have visited every weed in the land. And again, do you not remember that Christ told his disciples to "consider the lilies how they grow," and compared their beauty with Solomon in all his glory? Now, whose advice am I to take, yours or Christ's? Christ says, "Consider the lilies." You say, "Don't consider them. It isn't worthwhile for any strong-minded man."'

This evidently satisfied·him, and he acknowledged that he had never thought of blossoms in that way before. He repeated again and again that I must be a very strong-minded man, and admitted that no doubt I was fully justified in picking up blossoms. He then told me that although the war was over, walking across the Cumberland Mountains still was far from safe on account of small bands of guerrillas who were in hiding along the roads, and earnestly entreated me to turn back and not to think of walking so far as the Gulf of Mexico until the country became quiet and orderly once more.

I replied that I had no fear, that I had but very little to lose, and that nobody was likely to think it worth while to rob me; that, anyhow, I always had good luck. In the morning he repeated the warning and entreated me to turn back, which never for a moment interfered with my resolution to pursue my glorious walk.

11 September. Long stretch of level sandstone plateau, lightly furrowed and dimpled with shallow groove-like valleys and hills. The trees are mostly oaks, planted wide apart like those in the Wisconsin woods. A good many pine

---

[1] The previously mentioned copy of Wood's Botany, used by John Muir, quotes on the title page I Kings iv, 33: 'He spake of trees, from the cedar of Lebanon even unto the hyssop that springeth out of the wall.'

trees here and there, forty to eighty feet high, and most of the ground is covered with showy flowers. Polygalas (milkworts), solidagoes (goldenrods), and asters were especially abundant. I came to a cool clear brook every half mile or so, the banks planted with *Osmunda regalis, Osmunda cinnamomea,* and handsome sedges. The few larger streams were fringed with laurels and azaleas. Large areas beneath the trees are covered with formidable green briers and brambles, armed with hooked claws, and almost impenetrable. Houses are far apart and uninhabited, orchards and fences in ruins – sad marks of war.

About noon my road became dim and at last vanished among desolate fields. Lost and hungry, I knew my direction but could not keep it on account of the briers. My path was indeed strewn with flowers, but as thorny, also, as mortal as ever trod. In trying to force a way through these cat-plants one is not simply clawed and pricked through all one's clothing, but caught and held fast. The toothed arching branches come down over you and above you like cruel living arms, and the more you struggle the more desperately you are entangled, and your wounds deepened and multiplied. The South has plant fly-catchers. It also has plant man-catchers.

After a great deal of defensive fighting and struggling I escaped to a road and a house, but failed to find food or shelter. Towards sundown, as I was walking rapidly along a straight stretch in the road, I suddenly came in sight of ten mounted men riding abreast. They undoubtedly had seen me before I discovered them, for they had stopped their horses and were evidently watching me. I saw at once that it was useless to attempt to avoid them, for the ground thereabout was quite open. I knew that there was nothing for it but to face them fearlessly, without showing the slightest suspicion of foul play. Therefore, without halting even for a moment, I advanced rapidly with long strides as though I intended to walk through the midst of them. When I got within a rod or so I looked up in their faces and smilingly bade them 'Howdy.' Stopping never an instant, I turned to one side and walked around them to get on the road again, and kept on without venturing to look back or to betray the slightest fear of being robbed.

After I had gone about one hundred or one hundred and fifty yards, I ventured a quick glance back, without stopping, and saw in this flash of an eye that all the ten had turned their horses towards me and were evidently talking about me; supposedly, with reference to what my object was, where I was going, and whether it would be worth while to rob me. They all were mounted on rather scrawny horses, and all wore long hair hanging down on their shoulders. Evidently they belonged to the most irreclaimable of the guerrilla bands who, long accustomed to plunder, deplored the coming of peace. I was not followed, however, probably because the plants projecting from my plant press made them believe that I was a poor herb doctor, a common occupation in these mountain regions.

About dark I discovered, a little off the road, another house, inhabited by negroes, where I succeeded in obtaining a much needed meal of string beans, buttermilk, and corn bread. At the table I was seated in a bottomless chair, and as I became sore and heavy, I sank deeper and deeper, pressing my knees against my breast, and my mouth settled to the level of my plate. But wild hunger cares for none of these things, and my curiously compressed position prevented the too free indulgence of boisterous appetite. Of course, I was compelled to sleep with the trees in the one great bedroom of the open night.

12 September. Awoke drenched with mountain mist, which made a grand show, as it moved away before the hot sun. Passed Montgomery, a shabby village at the head of the east slope of the Cumberland Mountains. Obtained breakfast in a clean house and began the descent of the mountains. Obtained fine views of a wide, open country, and distant flanking ridges and spurs. Crossed a wide cool stream (Emory River), a branch of the Clinch River. There is nothing more eloquent in Nature than a mountain stream, and this is the first I ever saw. Its banks are luxuriantly peopled with rare and lovely flowers and overarching trees, making one of Nature's coolest and most hospitable places. Every tree, every flower, every ripple and eddy of this lovely stream seemed solemnly to feel the presence of the great Creator. Lingered in this sanctuary a long time thanking the Lord with all my heart for his goodness in allowing me to enter and enjoy it.

Discovered two ferns, *Dicksonia* and a small matted polypod on trees, common farther South. Also a species of magnolia with very large leaves and scarlet conical fruit. Near this stream I spent some joyous time in a grand rock-dwelling full of mosses, birds, and flowers. Most heavenly place I ever entered. The long narrow valleys of the mountainside, all well watered and nobly adorned with oaks, magnolias, laurels, azaleas, asters, ferns, Hypnum mosses, Madotheca (Scale-mosses), etc. Also towering clumps of beautiful hemlocks. The hemlock, judging from the common species of Canada, I regarded as the least noble of the conifers. But those of the eastern valleys of the Cumberland Mountains are as perfect in form and regal in port as the pines themselves. The latter abundant. Obtained fine glimpses from open places as I descended to the great valley between these mountains and the Unaka Mountains on the state line. Forded the Clinch, a beautiful clear stream, that knows many of the dearest mountain retreats that ever heard the music of running water. Reached Kingston before dark. Sent back my plant collections by express to my brother in Wisconsin.

13 September. Walked all day across small parallel valleys that flute the surface of the one wide valley. These flutings appear to have been formed by lateral pressure, are fertile, and contain some fine forms, though the seal of war is on all things. The roads never seem to proceed with any fixed purpose, but wander as if lost. In seeking the way to Philadelphia (in Loudon County, Tennessee), I was told by a buxom Tennessee 'gal' that over the hills was much the nearer way, that she always went that way, and that surely I could travel it.

I started over the flint-ridges, but soon reached a set of enchanted little valleys among which, no matter how or in what direction I travelled, I could not get a foot nearer to Philadelphia. At last, consulting my map and compass, I neglected all directions and finally reached the house of a negro driver, with whom I put up for the night. Received a good deal of knowledge which may be of use should I ever be a negro teamster.

14 September. Philadelphia is a very filthy village in a beautiful situation. More or less of pine. Black oak most abundant. *Polypodium hexagonopterum* and *Aspidium acrostichoides* (Christmas Fern) most abundant of ferns and most generally distributed. *Osmunda claytoniana* rare, not in fruit, small. *Dicksonia* abundant, after leaving the Cumberland Mountains. *Asplenium ebeneum* (Ebony Spleenwort) quite common in Tennessee and many parts of Kentucky. *Cystopteris* (Bladder Fern), and *Asplenium filix-fœmina* not common through the same range. *Pteris aquilina* (Common Brake) abundant, but small.

Walked through many a leafy valley, shady grove, and cool brooklet. Reached Madisonville, a brisk village. Came in full view of the Unaka Mountains, a magnificent sight. Stayed over night with a pleasant young farmer.

15 September. Most glorious billowy mountain scenery. Made many a halt at open places to take breath and to admire. The road, in many places cut into the rock, goes winding about the knobs and gorges. Dense growth of asters, liatris,[1] and grapevines.

Reached a house before night, and asked leave to stop. 'Well, you're welcome to stop,' said the mountaineer, 'if you think you can live till morning on what I have to live on all the time.' Found the old gentleman very communicative. Was favoured with long 'bar' stories, deer hunts, etc., and in the morning was pressed to stay a day or two.

16 September. 'I will take you,' said he, 'to the highest ridge in the country, where you can see both ways. You will have a view of all the world on one side of the mountains and all creation on the other. Besides, you, who are travelling for curiosity and wonder, ought to see our gold mines. I agreed to stay and went to the mines. Gold is found in small quantities throughout the Alleghanies, and many farmers work at mining a few weeks or months every year when their time is not more valuable for other pursuits. In this neighbourhood miners are earning from half a dollar to two dollars a day. There are several large quartz mills not far from here. Common labour is worth ten dollars a month.

17 September. Spent the day in botanizing, blacksmithing, and examining a grist mill. Grist mills, in the less settled parts of Tennessee and North Carolina, are remarkably simple affairs. A small stone, that a man might carry under his arm, is fastened to the vertical shaft of a little home-made, boyish-looking, back-action water-wheel, which, with a hopper and a box to receive the meal, is the whole affair. The walls of the mill are of undressed poles cut from seedling trees and there is no floor, as lumber is dear. No dam is built. The water is conveyed along some hillside until sufficient fall is obtained, a thing easily done in the mountains.

On Sundays you may see wild, unshorn, uncombed men coming out of the woods, each with a bag of corn on his back. From a peck to a bushel is a

[1] Wood's Botany, edition of 1862, furnishes the following interesting comment on *Liatris odoratissima* (Willd.), popularly known as Vanilla Plant or Deer's Tongue: 'The fleshy leaves exhale a rich fragrance even for years after they are dry, and are therefore by the southern planters largely mixed with their cured tobacco, to impart its fragrance to that nauseous weed.'

common grist. They go to the mill along verdant footpaths, winding up and down over hill and valley, and crossing many a rhododendron glen. The flowers and shining leaves brush against their shoulders and knees, occasionally knocking off their coon-skin caps. The first arrived throws his corn into the hopper, turns on the water, and goes to the house. After chatting and smoking he returns to see if his grist is done. Should the stones run empty for an hour or two, it does no harm.

This is a fair average in equipment and capacity of a score of mills that I saw in Tennessee. This one was built by John Vohn, who claimed that he could make it grind twenty bushels a day. But since it fell into other hands it can be made to grind only ten per day. All the machines of Kentucky and Tennessee are far behind the age. There is scarce a trace of that restless spirit of speculation and invention so characteristic of the North. But one way of doing things obtains here, as if laws had been passed making attempts at improvement a crime. Spinning and weaving are done in every one of these mountain cabins wherever the least pretensions are made to thrift and economy. The practice of these ancient arts they deem marks of advancement rather than of backwardness. 'There's a place back heah,' said my worthy entertainer, 'whar there's a mill-house, an' a store-house, an' a still-house, an' a spring-house, an' a blacksmith shop – all in the same yard! Cows too, an' heaps of big gals a-milkin' them.'

This is the most primitive country I have seen, primitive in everything. The remotest hidden parts of Wisconsin are far in advance of the mountain regions of Tennessee and North Carolina. But my host speaks of the 'old-fashioned unenlightened times,' like a philosopher in the best light of civilization. 'I believe in Providence,' said he. 'Our fathers came into these valleys, got the richest of them, and skimmed off the cream of the soil. The worn-out ground won't yield no roastin' ears now. But the Lord foresaw this state of affairs, and prepared something else for us. And what is it? Why, He meant us to bust open these copper mines and gold mines, so that we may have money to buy the corn that we cannot raise.' A most profound observation.

18 September. Up the mountain on the state line. The scenery is far grander than any I ever before beheld. The view extends from the Cumberland Mountains on the north far into Georgia and North Carolina to the south, an area of about five thousand square miles. Such an ocean of wooded, waving, swelling mountain beauty and grandeur is not to be described. Countless forest-clad hills, side by side in rows and groups, seemed to be enjoying the rich sunshine and remaining motionless only because they were so eagerly absorbing it. All were united by curves and slopes of inimitable softness and beauty. Oh, these forest gardens of our Father! What perfection, what divinity, in their architecture! What simplicity and mysterious complexity of detail! Who shall read the teaching of these sylvan pages, the glad brotherhood of rills that sing in the valleys, and all the happy creatures that dwell in them under the tender keeping of a Father's care?

19 September. Received another solemn warning of dangers on my way through the mountains. Was told by my worthy entertainer of a wondrous gap in the mountains which he advised me to see. 'It is called Track Gap,' said he, 'from the great number of tracks in the rocks – bird tracks, bar tracks, hoss tracks, men tracks, all in the solid rock as if it had been mud.' Bidding farewell to my worthy mountaineer and all his comfortable wonders, I pursued my way to the South.

As I was leaving, he repeated the warnings of danger ahead, saying that there were a good many people living like wild beasts on whatever they could steal, and that murders were sometimes committed for four or five dollars, and even less. While stopping with him I noticed that a man came regularly after dark to the house for his supper. He was armed with a gun, a pistol, and a long knife. My host told me that this man was at feud with one of his neighbours, and that they were prepared to shoot one another at sight. That neither of them could do any regular work or sleep in the same place two nights in succession. That they visited houses only for food, and as soon as the one that I saw had got his supper he went out and slept in the woods, without of course making a fire. His enemy did the same.

My entertainer told me that he was trying to make peace between these two men, because they both were good men, and if they would agree to stop their quarrel, they could then both go to work. Most of the food in this house was coffee without sugar, corn bread, and sometimes bacon. But the coffee was the greatest luxury which these people knew. The only way of obtaining it was by selling skins, or, in particular, 'sang,' that is ginseng,[1] which found a market in far-off China.

My path all today led me along the leafy banks of the Hiwassee,[2] a most impressive mountain river. Its channel is very rough, as it crosses the edges of upturned rock strata, some of them standing at right angles, or glancing off obliquely to right and left. Thus a multitude of short, resounding cataracts are produced, and the river is restrained from the headlong speed due to its volume and the inclination of its bed.

All the larger streams of uncultivated countries are mysteriously charming and beautiful, whether flowing in mountains or through swamps and plains. Their channels are interestingly sculptured, far more so than the grandest architectural works of man. The finest of the forests are usually found along their banks, and in the multitude of falls and rapids the wilderness finds a voice. Such a river is the Hiwassee, with its surface broken to a thousand sparkling gems, and its forest walls vine-draped and flowery as Eden. And how fine the song it sings!

In Murphy (North Carolina) I was hailed by the sheriff who could not determine by my colours and rigging to what country or craft I belonged. Since the war, every other stranger in these lonely parts is supposed to be a criminal, and all are objects of curiosity or apprehensive concern. After a few minutes' conversation with this chief man of Murphy I was pronounced harmless, and invited to his house, where for the first time since leaving home I found a house decked with flowers and vines, clean within and without, and

[1] Muir's journal contains the following additional note: 'M. County produces $5000 worth a year of ginseng root, valued at seventy cents a pound. Under the law it is not allowed to be gathered until the first of September.'
[2] In his journal Muir spells the name 'Hiawassee,' a form which occurs on many of the older maps. The name probably is derived from the Cherokee Indian 'Ayuhwasi,' a name applied to several of their former settlements.

stamped with the comforts of culture and refinement in all its arrangements. Striking contrast to the uncouth transitionist establishments from the wigwams of savages to the clumsy but clean log castle of the thrifty pioneer.

20 September. All day among the groves and gorges of Murphy with Mr Beale. Was shown the site of Camp Butler where General Scott had his headquarters when he removed the Cherokee Indians to a new home in the West. Found a number of rare and strange plants on the rocky banks of the River Hiwassee. In the afternoon, from the summit of a commanding ridge, I obtained a magnificent view of blue, softly curved mountain scenery. Among the trees I saw *Ilex* (Holly) for the first time. Mr Beale informed me that the paleness of most of the women in his neighbourhood, and the mountains in general hereabouts, was caused chiefly by smoking and by what is called 'dipping'. I had never even heard of dipping. The term simply describes the application of snuff to the gum by means of a small swab.

21 September. Most luxuriant forest. Many brooks running across the road. Blairsville (Georgia), which I passed in the forenoon, seems a shapeless and insignificant village, but grandly encircled with banded hills. At night I was cordially received by a farmer whose wife, though smart and neat in her appearance, was an inveterate smoker.

22 September. Hills becoming small, sparsely covered with soil. They are called 'knob land' and are cultivated, or scratched, with a kind of one-tooth cultivator. Every rain robs them of their fertility, while the bottoms are of course correspondingly enriched. About noon I reached the last mountain summit on my way to the sea. It is called the Blue Ridge and before it lies a prospect very different from any I had passed, namely, a vast uniform expanse of dark pine woods, extending to the sea; an impressive view at any time and under any circumstances, but particularly so to one emerging from the mountains.

Travelled in the wake of three poor but merry mountaineers – an old woman, a young woman, and a young man – who sat, leaned, and lay in the box of a shackly wagon that seemed to be held together by spiritualism, and was kept in agitation by a very large and a very small mule. In going down hill the looseness of the harness and the joints of the wagon allowed the mules to back nearly out of sight beneath the box, and the three who occupied it were slid against the front boards in a heap over the mules' ears. Before they could unravel their limbs from this unmannerly and impolite disorder, a new ridge in the road frequently tilted them with a swish and a bump against the back boards in a mixing that was still more grotesque.

I expected to see man, women, and mules mingled in piebald ruin at the bottom of some rocky hollow, but they seemed to have full confidence in the back board and front board of the wagon-box. So they continued to slide comfortably up and down, from end to end, in slippery obedience to the law of gravitation, as the grades demanded. Where the jolting was moderate, they engaged in conversation on love, marriage, and camp-meeting, according to the custom of the country. The old lady, through all the vicissitudes of the transportation, held a bouquet of French marigolds.

The hillsides hereabouts were bearing a fine harvest of asters. Reached

Mount Yonah in the evening. Had a long conversation with an old Methodist slaveholder and mine owner. Was hospitably refreshed with a drink of fine cider.

CHAPTER THREE

Through the River Country of Georgia

23 SEPTEMBER. Am now fairly out of the mountains. Thus far the climate has not changed in any marked degree, the decrease in latitude being balanced by the increase in altitude. These mountains are highways on which northern plants may extend their colonies southward. The plants of the North and of the South have many minor places of meeting along the way I have travelled; but it is here on the southern slope of the Alleghanies that the greatest number of hardy, enterprising representatives of the two climates are assembled.

Passed the comfortable, finely shaded little town of Gainesville. The Chattahoochee River is richly embanked with massive, bossy, dark green water oaks, and wreathed with a dense growth of muscadine grapevines, whose ornate foliage, so well adapted to bank embroidery, was enriched with other interweaving species of vines and brightly coloured flowers. This is the first truly southern stream I have met.

At night I reached the home of a young man with whom I had worked in Indiana, Mr Prater. He was down here on a visit to his father and mother. This was a plain back-woods family, living out of sight among knobby timbered hillocks not far from the river. The evening was passed in mixed conversation on southern and northern generalities.

24 September. Spent this day with Mr Prater sailing on the Chattahoochee, feasting on grapes that had dropped from the overhanging vines. This remarkable species of wild grape has a stout stem, sometimes five or six inches in diameter, smooth bark and hard wood, quite unlike any other wild or cultivated grapevine that I have seen. The grapes are very large, some of them nearly an inch in diameter, globular and fine flavoured. Usually there are but three or four berries in a cluster, and when mature they drop off instead of decaying on the vine. Those which fall into the river are often found in large quantities in the eddies along the bank, where they are collected by men in boats and sometimes made into wine. I think another name for this grape is the Scuppernong,[1] though called 'muscadine' here.

Besides sailing on the river, we had a long walk among the plant bowers and tangles of the Chattahoochee bottom lands.

---

[1] The old Indian name for the southern species of fox-grape, *Vitis rotundifolia*, which Muir describes here. Wood's Botany listed it as *Vitis vulpina* L. and remarks, 'The variety called "Scuppernong" is quite common in southern gardens.'

25 September. Bade good-bye to this friendly family. Mr Prater accompanied me a short distance from the house and warned me over and over again to be on the outlook for rattlesnakes. They are now leaving the damp lowlands, he told me, so that the danger is much greater because they are on their travels. Thus warned, I set out for Savannah, but got lost in the vine-fenced hills and hollows of the river bottom. Was unable to find the ford to which I had been directed by Mr Prater.

I then determined to push on southward regardless of roads and fords. After repeated failures I succeeded in finding a place on the river bank where I could force my way into the stream through the vine tangles. I succeeded in crossing the river by wading and swimming, careless of wetting, knowing that I would soon dry in the hot sunshine.

Out near the middle of the river I found great difficulty in resisting the rapid current. Though I braced myself with a stout stick, I was at length carried away in spite of all my efforts. But I succeeded in swimming to the shallows on the farther side, luckily caught hold of a rock, and after a rest swam and waded ashore. Dragging myself up the steep bank by the overhanging vines, I spread out myself, my paper money, and my plants to dry.

Debated with myself whether to proceed down the river valley until I could buy a boat, or lumber to make one, for a sail instead of a march through Georgia. I was intoxicated with the beauty of these glorious river banks, which I fancied might increase in grandeur as I approached the sea. But I finally concluded that such a pleasure sail would be less profitable than a walk, and so sauntered on southward as soon as I was dry. Rattlesnakes abundant. Lodged at a farmhouse. Found a few tropical plants in the garden.

Cotton is the principal crop hereabouts, and picking is now going on merrily. Only the lower bolls are now ripe. Those higher on the plants are green and unopened. Higher still, there are buds and flowers, some of which, if the plants be thrifty and the season favourable, will continue to produce ripe bolls until January.

The negroes are easy-going and merry, making a great deal of noise and doing little work. One energetic white man, working with a will, would easily pick as much cotton as half a dozen Sambos and Sallies. The forest here is almost entirely made up of dim-green, knotty, sparsely planted pines. The soil is mostly white, fine-grained sand.

26 September. Reached Athens in the afternoon, a remarkably beautiful and aristocratic town, containing many classic and magnificent mansions of wealthy planters, who formerly owned large negro-stocked plantations in the best cotton and sugar regions farther south. Unmistakable marks of culture and refinement, as well as wealth, were everywhere apparent. This is the most beautiful town I have seen on the journey, so far, and the only one in the South that I would like to revisit.

The negroes here have been well trained and are extremely polite. When they come in sight of a white man on the road, off go their hats, even at a distance of forty or fifty yards, and they walk bare-headed until he is out of sight.

27 September. Long zigzag walk amid the old plantations, a few of which are still cultivated in the old way by the same negroes that worked them before the war, and who still occupy their former 'quarters'. They are now paid seven to ten dollars a month.

The weather is very hot on these sandy, lightly shaded, lowland levels. When very thirsty I discovered a beautiful spring in a sandstone basin overhung with shady bushes and vines, where I enjoyed to the utmost the blessing of pure cold water. Discovered here a fine southern fern, some new grasses, etc. Fancied that I might have been directed here by Providence, while fainting with thirst. It is not often hereabouts that the joys of cool water, cool shade, and rare plants are so delightfully combined.

Witnessed the most gorgeous sunset I ever enjoyed in this bright world of light. The sunny South is indeed sunny. Was directed by a very civil negro to lodgings for the night. Daily bread hereabouts means sweet potatoes and rusty bacon.

28 September. The water oak is abundant on stream banks and in damp hollows. Grasses are becoming tall and cane-like and do not cover the ground with their leaves as at the North. Strange plants are crowding about me now. Scarce a familiar face appears among all the flowers of the day's walk.

29 September. Today I met a magnificent grass, ten or twelve feet in stature, with a superb panicle of glossy purple flowers. Its leaves, too, are of princely mould and dimensions. Its home is in sunny meadows and along the wet borders of slow streams and swamps. It seems to be fully aware of its high rank, and waves with the grace and solemn majesty of a mountain pine. I wish I could place one of these regal plants among the grass settlements of our Western prairies. Surely every panicle would wave and bow in joyous allegiance and acknowledge their king.

30 September. Between Thomson and Augusta I found many new and beautiful grasses, tall gerardias, liatris, club mosses, etc. Here, too, is the northern limit of the remarkable long-leafed pine, a tree from sixty to seventy feet in height, from twenty to thirty inches in diameter, with leaves ten to fifteen inches long, in dense radiant masses at the ends of the naked branches. The wood is strong, hard, and very resinous. It makes excellent ship spars, bridge timbers and flooring. Much of it is shipped to the West India Islands, New York, and Galveston.

The seedlings, five or six years old, are very striking objects to one from the North, consisting as they do, of the straight, leafless stem, surmounted by a crown of deep green leaves, arching and spreading like a palm. Children fancy that they resemble brooms, and use them as such in their picnic playhouses. *Pinus palustris* is most abundant in Georgia and Florida.

The sandy soil here is sparingly seamed with rolled quartz pebbles and clay. Denudation, going on slowly, allows the thorough removal of these clay seams, leaving only the sand. Notwithstanding the sandiness of the soil, much of the surface of the country is covered with standing water, which is easily accounted for by the presence of the above-mentioned impermeable seams.

Travelled today more than forty miles without dinner or supper. No family would receive me, so I had to push on to Augusta. Went hungry to bed and awoke with a sore stomach – sore, I suppose, from its walls rubbing on each other without anything to grind. A negro kindly directed me to the best hotel, called, I think, the Planter's. Got a good bed for a dollar.

1 October. Found a cheap breakfast in a market-place; then set off along the Savannah River to Savannah. Splendid grasses and rich, dense, vine-clad forests. Muscadine grapes in cart-loads. Asters and solidagoes becoming scarce. Carices (sedges) quite rare. Leguminous plants abundant. A species of passion flower is common, reaching back into Tennessee. It is here called 'apricot vine,' has a superb flower, and the most delicious fruit I have ever eaten.

The pomegranate is cultivated here. The fruit is about the size of an orange, has a thick, tough skin, and when opened resembles a many-chambered box full of translucent purple candies.

Toward evening I came to the country of one of the most striking of southern plants, the so-called 'Long Moss' or Spanish Moss (Tillandsia), though it is a flowering plant and belongs to the same family as the pineapple (Bromelworts). The trees hereabouts have all their branches draped with it, producing a remarkable effect.

Here, too, I found an impenetrable cypress swamp. This remarkable tree, called cypress, is a taxodium, grows large and high, and is remarkable for its flat crown. The whole forest seems almost level on the top, as if each tree had grown up against a ceiling, or had been rolled while growing. This taxodium is the only level-topped tree that I have seen. The branches, though spreading, are careful not to pass each other, and stop suddenly on reaching the general level, as if they had grown up against a ceiling.

The groves and thickets of smaller trees are full of blooming evergreen vines. These vines are not arranged in separate groups, or in delicate wreaths, but in bossy walls and heavy, mound-like heaps and banks. Am made to feel that I am now in a strange land. I know hardly any of the plants, but few of the birds, and I am unable to see the country for the solemn, dark, mysterious cypress woods which cover everything.

The winds are full of strange sounds, making one feel far from the people and plants and fruitful fields of home. Night is coming on and I am filled with indescribable loneliness. Felt feverish; bathed in a black, silent stream; nervously watchful for alligators. Obtained lodging in a planter's house among cotton fields. Although the family seemed to be pretty well-off, the only light in the house was bits of pitch-pine wood burned in the fireplace.

2 October. In the low bottom forest of the Savannah River. Very busy with new specimens. Most exquisitely planned wrecks of *Agrostis scabra* (Rough Hair Grass). Pines in glorious array with open, welcoming, approachable plants.

Met a young African with whom I had a long talk. Was amused with his eloquent narrative of coon hunting, alligators, and many superstitions. He showed me a place where a railroad train had run off the track, and assured me that the ghosts of the killed may be seen every dark night.

Had a long walk after sundown. At last was received at the house of Dr Perkins. Saw Cape Jasmine (*Gardenia florida*) in the garden. Heard long recitals of war happenings, discussion of the slave question, and Northern politics; a thoroughly characteristic Southern family, refined in manners and kind, but immovably prejudiced on everything connected with slavery.

The family table was unlike any I ever saw before. It was circular, and the central part of it revolved. When any one wished to be helped, he placed his plate on the revolving part, which was whirled around to the host, and then whirled back with its new load. Thus every plate was revolved into place, without the assistance of any of the family.

3 October. In 'pine barrens' most of the day. Low, level, sandy tracts; the pines wide apart; the sunny spaces between full of beautiful abounding grasses, liatris, long, wand-like solidago, saw palmettos, etc., covering the ground in garden style. Here I sauntered in delightful freedom, meeting none of the cat-clawed vines, or shrubs, of the alluvial bottoms. Dwarf live-oaks common.

Toward evening I arrived at the home of Mr Cameron, a wealthy planter, who had large bands of slaves at work in his cotton fields. They still call him 'Massa.' He tells me that labour costs him less now than it did before the emancipation of the negroes. When I arrived I found him busily engaged in scouring the rust off some cotton-gin saws which had been lying for months at the bottom of his mill-pond to prevent Sherman's 'bummers' from destroying them. The most valuable parts of the grist-mill and cotton-press were hidden in the same way. 'If Bill Sherman,' he said, 'should come down now without his army, he would never go back.'

When I asked him if he could give me food and lodging for the night he said, 'No, no, we have no accommodation for travellers.' I said, 'But I am travelling as a botanist and either have to find lodgings when night overtakes me or lie outdoors, which I often have had to do in my long walk from Indiana. But you see that the country here is very swampy; if you will at least sell me a piece of bread, and give me a drink at your well, I shall have to look around for a dry spot to lie down on.'

Then, asking me a few questions, and narrowly examining me, he said, 'Well, it is barely possible that we may find a place for you, and if you will come to the house I will ask my wife.' Evidently he was cautious to get his wife's opinion of the kind of creature I was before committing himself to hospitality. He halted me at the door and called out his wife, a fine-looking woman, who also questioned me narrowly as to my object in coming so far down through the South, so soon after the war. She said to her husband that she thought they could, perhaps, give me a place to sleep.

After supper, as we sat by the fire talking on my favourite subject of botany, I described the country I had passed through, its botanical character, etc. Then, evidently, all doubt as to my being a decent man vanished, and they both said that they wouldn't for anything have turned me away; but I must excuse their caution, for perhaps fewer than one in a hundred, who passed through this unfrequented part of the country, were to be relied upon. 'Only a short time ago we entertained a man who was well spoken and well dressed, and he vanished some time during the night with some valuable silverware.'

Mr Cameron told me that when I arrived he tried me for a Mason, and finding that I was not a Mason he wondered still more that I would venture into the country without being able to gain the assistance of brother Masons in these troublous times.

'Young man,' he said, after hearing my talks on botany, 'I see that your hobby is botany. My hobby is e-lec-tricity. I believe that the time is coming, though we may not live to see it, when that mysterious power or force, used now only for telegraphy, will eventually supply the power for running railroad trains and steamships, for lighting, and, in a word, electricity will do all the work of the world.'

Many times since then I have thought of the wonderfully correct vision of this Georgia planter, so far in advance of almost everybody else in the world. Already nearly all that he foresaw has been accomplished, and the use of electricity is being extended more and more every year.

4 October. New plants constantly appearing. All day in dense, wet, dark mysterious forest of flat-topped taxodiums.

5 October. Saw the stately banana for the first time, growing luxuriantly in the wayside gardens. At night with a very pleasant, intelligent Savannah family, but as usual was admitted only after I had undergone a severe course of questioning.

6 October. Immense swamps, still more completely fenced and darkened, that are never ruffled with winds or scorched with drought. Many of them seem to be thoroughly aquatic.

7 October. Impenetrable taxodium swamp, seemingly boundless. The silvery skeins of tillandsia becoming longer and more abundant. Passed the night with a very pleasant family of Georgians, after the usual questions and cross questions.

8 October. Found the first woody *compositæ,* a most notable discovery. Took them to be such at a considerable distance. Almost all trees and shrubs are evergreens here with thick polished leaves. *Magnolia grandiflora* becoming common. A magnificent tree in fruit and foliage as well as in flower. Near Savannah I found waste places covered with a dense growth of woody leguminous plants, eight or ten feet high, with pinnate leaves and suspended rattling pods.

Reached Savannah, but find no word from home, and the money that I had ordered to be sent by express from Portage (Wisconsin) by my brother had not yet arrived. Feel dreadfully lonesome and poor. Went to the meanest looking lodging-house that I could find, on account of its cheapness.

CHAPTER FOUR

Camping Among the Tombs

9 OCTOBER. After going again to the express office and post office, and wandering about the streets, I found a road which led me to the Bonaventure graveyard. If that burying-ground across the Sea of Galilee, mentioned in Scripture, was half as beautiful as Bonaventure, I do not wonder that a man

should dwell among the tombs. It is only three or four miles from Savannah, and is reached by a smooth white shell road.

There is but little to be seen on the way in land, water, or sky, that would lead one to hope for the glories of Bonaventure. The ragged desolate fields, on both sides of the road, are overrun with coarse rank weeds, and show scarce a trace of cultivation. But soon all is changed. Rickety log huts, broken fences, and the last patch of weedy rice-stubble are left behind. You come to beds of purple liatris and living wild-wood trees. You hear the song of birds, cross a small stream, and are with Nature in the grand old forest graveyard, so beautiful that almost any sensible person would choose to dwell here with the dead rather than with the lazy, disorderly living.

Part of the grounds was cultivated and planted with live-oak, about a hundred years ago, by a wealthy gentleman who had his country residence here. But much the greater part is undisturbed. Even those spots which are disordered by art, Nature is ever at work to reclaim, and to make them look as if the foot of man had never known them. Only a small plot of ground is occupied with graves and the old mansion is in ruins.

The most conspicuous glory of Bonaventure is its noble avenue of live-oaks. They are the most magnificent planted trees I have ever seen, about fifty feet high and perhaps three or four feet in diameter, with broad spreading leafy heads. The main branches reach out horizontally until they come together over the driveway, embowering it throughout its entire length, while each branch is adorned like a garden with ferns, flowers, grasses, and dwarf palmettos.

But of all the plants of these curious tree-gardens the most striking and characteristic is the so-called Long Moss (*Tillandsia usneoides*). It drapes all the branches from top to bottom, hanging in long silvery-grey skeins, reaching a length of not less than eight or ten feet, and when slowly waving in the wind they produce a solemn funereal effect singularly impressive.

There are also thousands of smaller trees and clustered bushes, covered almost from sight in the glorious brightness of their own light. The place is half surrounded by the salt marshes and islands of the river, their reeds and sedges making a delightful fringe. Many bald eagles roost among the trees along the side of the marsh. Their screams are heard every morning, joined with the noise of crows and the songs of countless warblers, hidden deep in their dwellings of leafy bowers. Large flocks of butterflies, all kinds of happy insects, seem to be in a perfect fever of joy and sportive gladness. The whole place seems like a centre of life. The dead do not reign there alone.

Bonaventure to me is one of the most impressive assemblages of animal and plant creatures I ever met. I was fresh from the Western prairies, the garden-like openings of Wisconsin, the beech and maple and oak woods of Indiana and Kentucky, the dark mysterious Savannah cypress forests; but never since I was allowed to walk the woods have I found so impressive a company of trees as the tillandsia-draped oaks of Bonaventure.

I gazed awe-stricken as one new-arrived from another world. Bonaventure is called a graveyard, a town of the dead, but the few graves are powerless in such a depth of life. The rippling of living waters, the song of birds, the joyous confidence of flowers, the calm, undisturbable grandeur of the oaks, mark this place of graves as one of the Lord's most favoured abodes of life and light.

On no subject are our ideas more warped and pitiable than on death. Instead of the sympathy, the friendly union, of life and death so apparent in Nature, we are taught that death is an accident, a deplorable punishment for the oldest sin, the arch-enemy of life, etc. Town children, especially, are steeped in this death orthodoxy, for the natural beauties of death are seldom seen or taught in towns.

Of death among our own species, to say nothing of the thousand styles and modes of murder, our best memories, even among happy deaths, yield groans and tears, mingled with morbid exultation; burial companies, black in cloth and countenance; and, last of all, a black box burial in an ill-omened place, haunted by imaginary glooms and ghosts of every degree. Thus death becomes fearful, and the most notable and incredible thing heard around a death-bed is, 'I fear not to die.'

But let children walk with Nature, let them see the beautiful blendings and communions of death and life, their joyous inseparable unity, as taught in woods and meadows, plains and mountains and streams of our blessed star, and they will learn that death is stingless indeed, and as beautiful as life, and that the grave has no victory, for it never fights. All is divine harmony.

Most of the few graves of Bonaventure are planted with flowers. There is generally a magnolia at the head, near the strictly erect marble, a rose-bush or two at the foot, and some violets and showy exotics along the sides or on the tops. All is enclosed by a black iron railing, composed of rigid bars that might have been spears or bludgeons from a battlefield in Pandemonium.

It is interesting to observe how assiduously Nature seeks to remedy these laboured art blunders. She corrodes the iron and marble, and gradually levels the hill which is always heaped up, as if a sufficiently heavy quantity of clods could not be laid on the dead. Arching grasses come one by one; seeds come flying on downy wings, silent as fate, to give life's dearest beauty for the ashes of art; and strong evergreen arms laden with ferns and tillandsia drapery are spread over all – Life at work everywhere, obliterating all memory of the confusion of man.

In Georgia many graves are covered with a common shingle roof, supported on four posts as the cover of a well, as if rain and sunshine were not regarded as blessings. Perhaps, in this hot and insalubrious climate, moisture and sunheat are considered necessary evils to which they do not wish to expose their dead.

The money package that I was expecting did not arrive until the following week. After stopping the first night at the cheap, disreputable-looking hotel, I had only about a dollar and a half left in my purse, and so was compelled to camp out to make it last in buying only bread. I went out of the noisy town to seek a sleeping-place that was not marshy. After gaining the outskirts of the town toward the sea, I found some low sand dunes, yellow with flowering solidagoes.

I wandered wearily from dune to dune sinking ankle-deep in the sand, searching for a place to sleep beneath the tall flowers, free from insects and snakes, and above all from my fellow man. But idle negroes were prowling about everywhere, and I was afraid. The wind had strange sounds, waving the heavy panicles over my head, and I feared sickness from malaria so prevalent here, when I suddenly thought of the graveyard.

'There,' thought I, 'is an ideal place for a penniless wanderer. There no superstitious prowling mischief maker dares venture for fear of haunting ghosts, while for me there will be God's rest and peace. And then, if I am to be exposed to unhealthy vapours, I shall have capital compensation in seeing those grand oaks in the moonlight, with all the impressive and nameless influences of this lonely beautiful place.'

By this time it was near sunset, and I hastened across the common to the road and set off for Bonaventure, delighted with my choice, and almost glad to find that necessity had furnished me with so good an excuse for doing what I knew my mother would censure; for she made me promise I would not lie out of doors if I could possibly avoid it. The sun was set ere I was past the negroes' huts and rice fields, and I arrived near the graves in the silent hour of the gloaming.

I was very thirsty after walking so long in the muggy heat, a distance of three or four miles from the city, to get to this graveyard. A dull, sluggish, coffee-coloured stream flows under the road just outside the graveyard garden park, from which I managed to get a drink after breaking a way down to the water through a dense fringe of bushes, daring the snakes and alligators in the dark. Thus refreshed I entered the weird and beautiful abode of the dead.

All the avenue where I walked was in shadow, but an exposed tombstone frequently shone out in startling whiteness on either hand, and thickets of sparkleberry bushes gleamed like heaps of crystal. Not a breath of air moved the grey moss, and the great black arms of the trees met overhead and covered the avenue. But the canopy was fissured by many a netted seam and leafy-edged opening, through which the moonlight sifted in auroral rays, broidering the blackness in silvery light. Though tired, I sauntered a while enchanted, then lay down under one of the great oaks. I found a little mound that served for a pillow, placed my plant press and bag beside me and rested fairly well, though somewhat disturbed by large prickly-footed beetles creeping across my hands and face, and by a lot of hungry stinging mosquitoes.

When I awoke, the sun was up and all Nature was rejoicing. Some birds had discovered me as an intruder, and were making a great ado in interesting language and gestures. I heard the screaming of the bald eagles, and of some strange waders in the rushes. I heard the hum of Savannah with the long jarring hallos of negroes far away. On rising I found that my head had been resting on a grave, and though my sleep had not been quite so sound as that of the person below, I arose refreshed, and looking about me, the morning sunbeams pouring through the oaks and gardens dripping with dew, the beauty displayed was so glorious and exhilarating that hunger and care seemed only a dream.

Eating a breakfast cracker or two and watching for a few hours the beautiful

light, birds, squirrels, and insects, I returned to Savannah, to find that my
money package had not yet arrived. I then decided to go early to the graveyard and make a nest with a roof to keep off the dew, as there was no way of
finding out how long I might have to stay. I chose a hidden spot in a dense
thicket of sparkleberry bushes, near the right bank of the Savannah River,
where the bald eagles and a multitude of singing birds roosted. It was so well
hidden that I had to carefully fix its compass bearing in my mind from a mark
I made on the side of the main avenue, that I might be able to find it at
bedtime.

I used four of the bushes as corner posts for my little hut, which was about
four or five feet long by about three or four in width, tied little branches
across from forks in the bushes to support a roof of rushes, and spread a thick
mattress of Long Moss over the floor for a bed. My whole establishment was
on so small a scale that I could have taken up, not only my bed, but my whole
house, and walked. There I lay that night, eating a few crackers.

Next day I returned to the town and was disappointed as usual in obtaining
money. So after spending the day looking at the plants in the gardens of the
fine residences and town squares, I returned to my graveyard home. That I
might not be observed and suspected of hiding, as if I had committed a crime,
I always went home after dark, and one night, as I lay down in my moss nest, I
felt some cold-blooded creature in it; whether a snake or simply a frog or toad
I do not know, but instinctively, instead of drawing back my hand, I grasped
the poor creature and threw it over the tops of the bushes. That was the only
significant disturbance or fright that I got.

In the morning everything seemed divine. Only squirrels, sunbeams, and
birds came about me. I was awakened every morning by these little singers
after they discovered my nest. Instead of serenely singing their morning songs
they at first came within two or three feet of the hut, and, looking in at me
through the leaves, chattered and scolded in half-angry, half-wondering tones.
The crowd constantly increased, attracted by the disturbance. Thus I began to
get acquainted with my bird neighbours in this blessed wilderness, and after
they learned that I meant them no ill they scolded less and sang more.

After five days of this graveyard life I saw that even with living on three or
four cents a day my last twenty-five cents would soon be spent, and after
trying again and again unsuccessfully to find some employment began to think
that I must strike farther out into the country, but still within reach of town,
until I came to some grain or rice field that had not yet been harvested,
trusting that I could live indefinitely on toasted or raw corn, or rice.

By this time I was becoming faint, and in making the journey to the town
was alarmed to find myself growing staggery and giddy. The ground ahead
seemed to be rising up in front of me, and the little streams in the ditches on
the sides of the road seemed to be flowing up hill. Then I realized that I was
becoming dangerously hungry and became more than ever anxious to receive
that money package.

To my delight this fifth or sixth morning, when I inquired if the money
package had come, the clerk replied that it had, but that he could not deliver
it without my being identified. I said, 'Well, here! read my brother's letter,'

handing it to him. 'It states the amount in the package, where it came from, the day it was put into the office at Portage City, and I should think that would be enough.' He said, 'No, that is not enough. How do I know that this letter is yours? You may have stolen it. How do I know that you are John Muir?'

I said, 'Well, don't you see that this letter indicates that I am a botanist? For in it my brother says, "I hope you are having a good time and finding many new plants." Now, you say that I might have stolen this letter from John Muir, and in that way have become aware of there being a money package to arrive from Portage for him. But the letter proves that John Muir must be a botanist, and though, as you say, his letter might have been stolen, it would hardly be likely that the robber would be able to steal John Muir's knowledge of botany. Now I suppose, of course, that you have been to school and know something of botany. Examine me and see if I know anything about it.'

At this they laughed good-naturedly, evidently feeling the force of my argument, and, perhaps, pitying me on account of looking pale and hungry, he turned and rapped at the door of a private office – probably the Manager's – called him out and said, 'Mr So and So, here is a man who has inquired every day for the last week or so for a money package from Portage, Wisconsin. He is a stranger in the city with no one to identify him. He states correctly the amount and the name of the sender. He has shown me a letter which indicates that Mr Muir is a botanist, and that although a travelling companion may have stolen Mr Muir's letter, he could not have stolen his botany, and requests us to examine him.'

The head official smiled, took a good stare into my face, waved his hand, and said, 'Let him have it.' Gladly I pocketed my money, and had not gone along the street more than a few rods before I met a very large negro woman with a tray of gingerbread, in which I immediately invested some of my new wealth, and walked rejoicingly, munching along the street, making no attempt to conceal the pleasure I had in eating. Then, still hunting for more food, I found a sort of eating-place in a market and had a large regular meal on top of the gingerbread! Thus my 'marching through Georgia' terminated handsomely in a jubilee of bread.

CHAPTER FIVE

Through Florida Swamps and Forests

OF THE people of the States that I have now passed, I best liked the Georgians. They have charming manners, and their dwellings are mostly larger and better than those of adjacent States. However costly or ornamental their homes or their manners, they do not, like those of the New Englander, appear as the fruits of intense and painful sacrifice and training, but are entirely divested of artificial weights and measures, and seem to pervade and twine about their characters as spontaneous growths with the durability and charm of living nature.

In particular, Georgians, even the commonest, have a most charmingly cordial way of saying to strangers, as they proceed on their journey, 'I wish you well, sir.' The negroes of Georgia, too, are extremely mannerly and polite, and appear always to be delighted to find opportunity for obliging anybody.

Athens contains many beautiful residences. I never before saw so much about a home that was so evidently done for beauty only, although this is by no means a universal characteristic of Georgian homes. Nearly all well-to-do farmers' families in Georgia and Tennessee spin and weave their own cloth. This work is almost all done by the mothers and daughters and consumes much of their time.

The traces of war are not only apparent on the broken fields, burnt fences, mills and woods ruthlessly slaughtered, but also on the countenances of the people. A few years after a forest has been burned another generation of bright and happy trees arises, in purest, freshest vigour; only the old trees, wholly or half dead, bear marks of the calamity. So with the people of this war-field. Happy, unscarred, and unclouded youth is growing up around the aged, half-consumed, and fallen parents, who bear in sad measure the ineffaceable marks of the farthest-reaching and most infernal of all civilized calamities.

Since the commencement of my floral pilgrimage I have seen much that is not only new, but altogether unallied, unacquainted with the plants of my former life. I have seen magnolias, tupelo, live-oak, Kentucky oak, tillandsia, long-leafed pine, palmetto, schrankia, and whole forests of strange trees and vine-tied thickets of blooming shrubs; whole meadowfuls of magnificent bamboo and lakefuls of lilies, all new to me; yet I still press eagerly on to Florida as the special home of the tropical plants I am looking for, and I feel sure I shall not be disappointed.

The same day on which the money arrived I took passage on the steamship Sylvan Shore for Fernandina, Florida. The daylight part of this sail along the coast of Florida was full of novelty, and by association awakened memories of my Scottish days at Dunbar on the Firth of Forth.

On board I had civilized conversation with a Southern planter on topics that are found floating in the mind of every white man down here who has a single thought. I also met a brother Scotchman, who was especially interesting and had some ideas outside of Southern politics. Altogether my half-day and night on board the steamer were pleasant, and carried me past a very sickly, entangled, overflowed, and unwalkable piece of forest.

It is pretty well known that a short geological time ago the ocean covered the sandy level margin, extending from the foot of the Alleghanies to the present coast-line, and in receding left many basins for lakes and swamps. The land is still encroaching on the sea, and it does so not evenly, in a regular line, but in fringing lagoons and inlets and dotlike coral islands.

It is on the coast strip of isles and peninsulas that sea-island cotton is grown.

Some of these small islands are afloat, anchored only by the roots of mangroves and rushes. For a few hours our steamer sailed in the open sea, exposed to its waves, but most of the time she threaded her way among the lagoons, the home of alligators and countless ducks and waders.

15 October. Today, at last, I reached Florida, the so-called 'Land of Flowers,' that I had so long waited for, wondering if after all my longings and prayers would be in vain, and I should die without a glimpse of the flowery Canaan. But here it is, at the distance of a few yards! – a flat, watery, reedy coast, with clumps of mangrove and forests of moss-dressed, strange trees appearing low in the distance. The steamer finds her way among the reedy islands like a duck, and I step on a rickety wharf. A few steps more take me to a rickety town, Fernandina. I discover a baker, buy some bread, and without asking a single question, make for the shady, gloomy groves.

In visiting Florida in dreams, of either day or night, I always came suddenly on a close forest of trees, every one in flower, and bent down and entangled to network by luxuriant, bright-blooming vines, and over all a flood of bright sunlight. But such was not the gate by which I entered the promised land. Salt marshes, belonging more to the sea than to the land; with groves here and there, green and unflowered, sunk to the shoulders in sedges and rushes; with trees farther back, ill defined in their boundary, and instead of rising in hilly waves and swellings, stretching inland in low water-like levels.

We were all discharged by the captain of the steamer without breakfast, and, after meeting and examining the new plants that crowded about me, I threw down my press and little bag beneath a thicket, where there was a dry spot on some broken heaps of grass and roots, something like a deserted muskrat house, and applied myself to my bread breakfast. Everything in earth and sky had an impression of strangeness; not a mark of friendly recognition, not a breath, not a spirit whisper of sympathy came from anything about me, and of course I was lonely. I lay on my elbow eating my bread, gazing, and listening to the profound strangeness.

While thus engaged I was startled from these gatherings of melancholy by a rustling sound in the rushes behind me. Had my mind been in health, and my body not starved, I should only have turned calmly to the noise. But in this half-starved, unfriended condition I could have no healthy thought, and I at once believed that the sound came from an alligator. I fancied I could feel the stroke of his long notched tail, and could see his big jaws and rows of teeth, closing with a springy snap on me, as I had seen in pictures.

Well, I don't know the exact measure of my fright either in time or pain, but when I did come to a knowledge of the truth, my man-eating alligator became a tall white crane, handsome as a minister from spirit land – 'only that.' I was ashamed and tried to excuse myself on account of Bonaventure anxiety and hunger.

Florida is so watery and vine-tied that pathless wanderings are not easily possible in any direction. I started to cross the State by a gap hewn for the locomotive, walking sometimes between the rails, stepping from tie to tie, or walking on the strip of sand at the sides, gazing into the mysterious forest,

Nature's own. It is impossible to write the dimmest picture of plant grandeur so redundant, unfathomable.

Short was the measure of my walk to-day. A new, canelike grass, or big lily, or gorgeous flower belonging to tree or vine, would catch my attention, and I would throw down my bag and press and splash through the coffee-brown water for specimens. Frequently I sank deeper and deeper until compelled to turn back and make the attempt in another and still another place. Oftentimes I was tangled in a labyrinth of armed vines like a fly in a spider-web. At all times, whether wading or climbing a tree for specimens of fruit, I was overwhelmed with the vastness and unapproachableness of the great guarded sea of sunny plants.

Magnolia grandiflora I had seen in Georgia; but its home, its better land, is here. Its large dark-green leaves, glossy bright above and rusty brown beneath, gleam and mirror the sunbeams most gloriously among countless flower-heaps of the climbing, smothering vines. It is bright also in fruit and more tropical in form and expression than the orange. It speaks itself a prince among its fellows.

Occasionally, I came to a little strip of open sand, planted with pine (*Pinus palustris* or *Cubensis*). Even these spots were mostly wet, though lighted with free sunshine, and adorned with purple liatris, and orange-coloured *Osmunda cinnamomea*. But the grandest discovery of this great wild day was the palmetto.

I was meeting so many strange plants that I was much excited, making many stops to get specimens. But I could not force my way far through the swampy forest, although so tempting and full of promise. Regardless of water snakes or insects, I endeavoured repeatedly to force a way through the tough vine-tangles, but seldom succeeded in getting farther than a few hundred yards.

It was while feeling sad to think that I was only walking on the edge of the vast wood, that I caught sight of the first palmetto in a grassy place, standing almost alone. A few magnolias were near it, and bald cypresses, but it was not shaded by them. They tell us that plants are perishable, soulless creatures, that only man is immortal, etc.; but this, I think, is something that we know very nearly nothing about. Anyhow, this palm was indescribably impressive and told me grander things than I ever got from human priest.

This vegetable has a plain grey shaft, round as a broom-handle, and a crown of varnished channelled leaves. It is a plainer plant than the humblest of Wisconsin oaks; but, whether rocking and rustling in the wind or poised thoughtful and calm in the sunshine, it has a power of expression not excelled by any plant high or low that I have met in my whole walk thus far.

This, my first specimen, was not very tall, only about twenty-five feet high, with fifteen or twenty leaves, arching equally and evenly all around. Each leaf was about ten feet in length, the blade four feet, the stalk six. The leaves are channelled like half-open clams and are highly polished, so that they reflect the sunlight like glass. The undeveloped leaves on the top stand erect, closely folded, all together forming an oval crown over which the tropic light is poured and reflected from its slanting mirrors in sparks and splinters and long-rayed stars.

I am now in the hot gardens of the sun, where the palm meets the pine, longed and prayed for and often visited in dreams, and, though lonely to-night amid this multitude of strangers, strange plants, strange winds blowing gently, whispering, cooing, in a language I never learned, and strange birds also, everything solid or spiritual full of influences that I never before felt, yet I thank the Lord with all my heart for his goodness in granting me admission to this magnificent realm.

16 October. Last evening when I was in the trackless woods, the great mysterious night becoming more mysterious in the thickening darkness, I gave up hope of finding food or a house bed, and searched only for a dry spot on which to sleep safely hidden from wild, runaway negroes. I walked rapidly for hours in the wet, level woods, but not a foot of dry ground could I find. Hollow-voiced owls were calling without intermission. All manner of night sounds came from strange insects and beasts, one by one, or crowded together. All had a home but I. Jacob on the dry plains of Padanaram, with a stone pillow, must have been comparatively happy.

When I came to an open place where pines grew, it was about ten o'clock, and I thought that now at last I would find dry ground. But even the sandy barren was wet, and I had to grope in the dark a long time, feeling the ground with my hands when my feet ceased to plash, before I at last discovered a little hillock dry enough to lie down on. I ate a piece of bread that I fortunately had in my bag, drank some of the brown water about my precious hillock, and lay down. The noisiest of the unseen witnesses around me were the owls, who pronounced their gloomy speeches with profound emphasis, but did not prevent the coming of sleep to heal weariness.

In the morning I was cold and wet with dew, and I set out breakfastless. Flowers and beauty I had in abundance, but no bread. A serious matter is this bread which perishes, and, could it be dispensed with, I doubt if civilization would ever see me again. I walked briskly, watching for a house, as well as the grand assemblies of novel plants.

Near the middle of the forenoon I came to a shanty where a party of loggers were getting out long pines for ship spars. They were the wildest of all the white savages I have met. The long-haired ex-guerrillas of the mountains of Tennessee and North Carolina are uncivilized fellows; but for downright barbarism these Florida loggers excel. Nevertheless, they gave me a portion of their yellow pork and hominy without either apparent hospitality or a grudge, and I was glad to escape to the forest again.

A few hours later I dined with three men and three dogs. I was viciously attacked by the latter, who undertook to undress me with their teeth. I was nearly dragged down backward, but escaped unbitten. Liver pie, mixed with sweet potatoes and fat duff, was set before me, and after I had finished a moderate portion, one of the men, turning to his companion, remarked: 'Wall, I guess that man quit eatin' 'cause he had nothin' more to eat. I'll get him more potato.'

Arrived at a place on the margin of a stagnant pool where an alligator had been rolling and sunning himself. 'See,' said a man who lived here, 'see, what a track that is! He must have been a mighty big fellow. Alligators wallow like hogs and like to lie in the sun. I'd like a shot at that fellow.' Here followed a long recital of bloody combats with the scaly enemy, in many of which he had, of course, taken an important part. Alligators are said to be extremely fond of negroes and dogs, and naturally the dogs and negroes are afraid of them.

Another man that I met today pointed to a shallow, grassy pond before his door. 'There,' said he, 'I once had a tough fight with an alligator. He caught my dog. I heard him howling, and as he was one of my best hunters I tried hard to save him. The water was only about knee-deep and I ran up to the alligator. It was only a small one about four feet long, and was having trouble in its efforts to drown the dog in the shallow water. I scared him and made him let go his hold, but before the poor crippled dog could reach the shore, he was caught again, and when I went at the alligator with a knife, it seized my arm. If it had been a little stronger it might have eaten me instead of my dog.'

I never in all my travels saw more than one, though they are said to be abundant in most of the swamps, and frequently attain a length of nine or ten feet. It is reported, also, that they are very savage, oftentimes attacking men in boats. These independent inhabitants of the sluggish waters of this low coast cannot be called the friends of man, though I heard of one big fellow that was caught young and was partially civilized and made to work in harness.

Many good people believe that alligators were created by the Devil, thus accounting for their all-consuming appetite and ugliness. But doubtless these creatures are happy and fill the place assigned them by the great Creator of us all. Fierce and cruel they appear to us, but beautiful in the eyes of God. They, also, are his children, for He hears their cries, cares for them tenderly, and provides their daily bread.

The antipathies existing in the Lord's great animal family must be wisely planned, like balanced repulsion and attraction in the mineral kingdom. How narrow we selfish, conceited creatures are in our sympathies! how blind to the rights of all the rest of creation! With what dismal irreverence we speak of our fellow mortals! Though alligators, snakes, etc., naturally repel us, they are not mysterious evils. They dwell happily in these flowery wilds, are part of God's family, unfallen, undepraved, and cared for with the same species of tenderness and love as is bestowed on angels in heaven or saints on earth.

I think that most of the antipathies which haunt and terrify us are morbid productions of ignorance and weakness. I have better thoughts of those alligators now that I have seen them at home. Honourable representatives of the great saurians of an older creation, may you long enjoy your lilies and rushes, and be blessed now and then with a mouthful of terror-stricken man by way of dainty!

Found a beautiful lycopodium today, and many grasses in the dry sunlit places called 'barrens,' 'hummocks,' 'savannas,' etc. Ferns also are abundant. What a flood of heat and light is daily poured out on these beautiful openings and intertangled woods! 'The land of the sunny South,' we say, but no part of our diversified country is more shaded and covered from sunshine. Many a sunny sheet of plain and prairie break the continuity of the forests of the North and West, and the forests themselves are mostly lighted also, pierced with direct ray lances, or (the sunlight) passing to the earth and the lowly plants in filtered softness through translucent leaves. But in the dense Florida forests sunlight cannot enter. It falls on the evergreen roof and rebounds in long silvery lances and flashy spray. In many places there is not light sufficient to feed a single green leaf on these dark forest floors. All that the eye can reach is just a maze of tree stems and crooked leafless vine strings. All the flowers, all the verdure, all the glory is up in the light.

The streams of Florida are still young, and in many places are untraceable. I expected to find these streams a little discoloured from the vegetable matter that I knew they must contain, and I was sure that in so flat a country I should not find any considerable falls or long rapids. The streams of upper Georgia are almost unapproachable in some places on account of luxuriant bordering vines, but the banks are nevertheless high and well defined. Florida streams are not yet possessed of banks and braes and definite channels. Their waters in deep places are black as ink, perfectly opaque, and glossy on the surface as if varnished. It often is difficult to ascertain which way they are flowing or creeping, so slowly and so widely do they circulate through the tree-tangles and swamps of the woods. The flowers here are strangers to me, but not more so than the rivers and lakes. Most streams appear to travel through a country with thoughts and plans for something beyond. But those of Florida are at home, do not appear to be travelling at all, and seem to know nothing of the sea.

17 October. Found a small, silvery-leafed magnolia, a bush ten feet high. Passed through a good many miles of open level pine barrens, as bounteously lighted as the 'openings' of Wisconsin. The pines are rather small, are planted sparsely and pretty evenly on these sandy flats not long risen from the sea. Scarcely a specimen of any other tree is to be found associated with the pine. But there are some thickets of the little saw palmettos and a magnificent assemblage of tall grasses, their splendid panicles waving grandly in the warm wind, and making low tuneful changes in the glistening light that is flashed from their bent stems.

Not a pine, not a palm, in all this garden excels these stately grass plants in beauty of wind-waving gestures. Here are panicles that are one mass of refined purple; others that have flowers as yellow as ripe oranges, and stems polished and shining like steel wire. Some of the species are grouped in groves and thickets like trees, while others may be seen waving without any companions in sight. Some of them have wide-branching panicles like Kentucky oaks, others with a few tassels of spikelets drooping from a tall, leafless stem. But all of them are beautiful beyond the reach of language. I rejoice that God has 'so clothed the grass of the field.' How strangely we are blinded to beauty and colour, form and motion, by comparative size! For example, we measure grasses by our own stature and by the height and bulkiness of trees. But what is the size of the greatest man, or the tallest tree that ever overtopped a grass! Compared with other things in God's creation the difference is nothing. We all are only microscopic animalcula.

18 October. Am walking on land that is almost dry. The dead levels are interrupted here and there by sandy waves a few feet in height. It is said that not a point in all Florida is more than three hundred feet above sea-level – a country where but little grading is required for roads, but much bridging, and boring of many tunnels through forests.

Before reaching this open ground, in a lonely, swampy place in the woods, I met a large, muscular, brawny young negro, who eyed me with glaring, wistful curiosity. I was very thirsty at the time, and inquired of the man if there were any houses or springs near by where I could get a drink. 'Oh yes,' he replied, still eagerly searching me with his wild eyes. Then he inquired where I came from, where I was going, and what brought me to such a wild country, where I was liable to be robbed, and perhaps killed.

'Oh, I am not afraid of any one robbing me,' I said, 'for I don't carry anything worth stealing.' 'Yes,' said he, 'but you can't travel without money.' I started to walk on, but he blocked my way. Then I noticed that he was trembling, and it flashed upon me all at once that he was thinking of knocking me down in order to rob me. After glaring at my pockets as if searching for weapons, he stammered in a quavering voice, 'Do you carry shooting-irons?' His motives, which I ought to have noted sooner, now were apparent to me. Though I had no pistol, I instinctively threw my hand back to my pistol pocket and, with my eyes fixed on his, I marched up close to him and said, 'I allow people to find out if I am armed or not.' Then he quailed, stepped aside, and allowed me to pass, for fear of being shot. This was evidently a narrow escape.

A few miles farther on I came to a cottonfield, to patches of sugar cane carefully fenced, and some respectable-looking houses with gardens. These little fenced fields look as if they were intended to be for plants what cages are for birds. Discovered a large, treelike cactus in a dooryard; a small species was abundant on the sand-hillocks. Reached Gainesville late in the night.

When within three or four miles of the town I noticed a light off in the pine woods. As I was very thirsty, I thought I would venture toward it with the hope of obtaining water. In creeping cautiously and noiselessly through the grass to discover whether or no it was a camp of robber negroes, I came suddenly in full view of the best-lighted and most primitive of all the domestic establishments I have yet seen in town or grove. There was, first of all, a big, glowing log fire, illuminating the overleaning bushes and trees, bringing out leaf and spray with more than noonday distinctness, and making still darker the surrounding wood. In the centre of this globe of light sat two negroes. I could see their ivory gleaming from the great lips, and their smooth cheeks flashing off light as if made of glass. Seen anywhere but in the South, the glossy pair would have been taken for twin devils, but here it was only a negro and his wife at their supper.

I ventured forward to the radiant presence of the black pair, and, after being stared at with that desperate fixedness which is said to subdue the lion, I was handed water in a gourd from somewhere out of the darkness. I was standing for a moment beside the big fire, looking at the unsurpassable simplicity of the establishment, and asking questions about the road to

Gainesville, when my attention was called to a black lump of something lying in the ashes of the fire. It seemed to be made of rubber; but ere I had time for much speculation, the woman bent wooingly over the black object and said with motherly kindness, 'Come, honey, eat yo' hominy.'

At the sound of 'hominy' the rubber gave strong manifestations of vitality and proved to be a burly little negro boy, rising from the earth naked as to the earth he came. Had he emerged from the black muck of a marsh, we might easily have believed that the Lord had manufactured him like Adam direct from the earth.

Surely, thought I, as I started for Gainesville, surely I am now coming to the tropics, where the inhabitants wear nothing but their own skins. This fashion is sufficiently simple, – 'no troublesome disguises,' as Milton calls clothing – but it certainly is not quite in harmony with Nature. Birds make nests and nearly all beasts make some kind of bed for their young; but these negroes allow their younglings to lie nestless and naked in the dirt.

Gainesville is rather attractive – an oasis in the desert, compared with other villages. It gets its life from the few plantations located about it on dry ground that rises islandlike a few feet above the swamps. Obtained food and lodging at a sort of tavern.

19 October. Dry land nearly all day. Encountered limestone, flint, coral, shells, etc. Passed several thrifty cotton plantations with comfortable residences, contrasting sharply with the squalid hovels of my first days in Florida. Found a single specimen of a handsome little plant, which at once, in some mysterious way, brought to mind a young friend in Indiana. How wonderfully our thoughts and impressions are stored! There is that in the glance of a flower which may at times control the greatest of creation's braggart lords.

The magnolia is much more abundant here. It forms groves and almost exclusively forests the edge of ponds and the banks of streams. The easy, dignified simplicity of this noble tree, its plain leaf endowed with superb richness of colour and form, its open branches festooned with graceful vines and tillandsia, its showy crimson fruit, and its magnificent fragrant white flowers make *Magnolia grandiflora* the most lovable of Florida trees.

Discovered a great many beautiful polygonums, petalostemons, and yellow leguminous vines. Passed over fine sunny areas of the long-leafed and Cuban pines, which were everywhere accompanied by fine grasses and solidagoes. Wild orange groves are said to be rather common here, but I have seen only limes growing wild in the woods.

Came to a hut about noon, and, being weary and hungry, asked if I could have dinner. After serious consultation I was told to wait, that dinner would soon be ready. I saw only the man and his wife. If they had children, they may have been hidden in the weeds on account of nakedness. Both were suffering from malarial fever, and were very dirty. But they did not appear to have any realizing sense of discomfort from either the one or the other of these misfortunes. The dirt which encircled the countenances of these people did not, like the common dirt of the North, stick on the skin in bold union like plaster or paint, but appeared to stand out a little on contact like a hazy, misty, half-aerial mud envelope, the most diseased and incurable dirt that I ever saw, evidently desperately chronic and hereditary.

It seems impossible that children from such parents could ever be clean. Dirt and disease are dreadful enough when separate, but combined are inconceivably horrible. The neat cottage with a fragrant circumference of thyme and honeysuckle is almost unknown here. I have seen dirt on garments regularly stratified, the various strata no doubt indicating different periods of life. Some of them, perhaps, were annual layers, furnishing, like those of trees, a means of determining the age. Man and other civilized animals are the only creatures that ever become dirty.

Slept in the barrens at the side of a log. Suffered from cold and was drenched with dew. What a comfort a companion would be in the dark loneliness of such nights! Did not dare to make a fire for fear of discovery by robber negroes, who, I was warned, would kill a man for a dollar or two. Had a long walk after nightfall, hoping to discover a house. Became very thirsty and often was compelled to drink from slimy pools groped for in the grass, with the fear of alligators before my eyes.

20 October. Swamp very dense during this day's journey. Almost one continuous sheet of water covered with aquatic trees and vines. No stream that I crossed today appeared to have the least idea where it was going. Saw an alligator plash into the sedgy brown water by the roadside from an old log.

Arrived at night at the house of Captain Simmons, one of the very few scholarly, intelligent men that I have met in Florida. He had been an officer in the Confederate army in the war and was, of course, prejudiced against the North, but polite and kind to me, nevertheless. Our conversation, as we sat by the light of the fire, was on the one great question, slavery and its concomitants. I managed, however, to switch off to something more congenial occasionally – the birds of the neighbourhood, the animals, the climate, and what spring, summer, and winter are like in these parts.

About the climate, I could not get much information, as he had always lived in the South and, of course, saw nothing extraordinary in weather to which he had always been accustomed. But in speaking of animals, he at once became enthusiastic and told many stories of hairbreadth escapes, in the woods about his house, from bears, hungry alligators, wounded deer, etc. 'and now,' said he, forgetting in his kindness that I was from the hated North, 'you must stay with me a few days. Deer are abundant. I will lend you a rifle and we'll go hunting. I hunt whenever I wish venison, and I can get it about as easily from the woods nearby as a shepherd can get mutton out of his flock. And perhaps we will see a bear, for they are far from scarce here, and there are some big grey wolves, too.'

I expressed a wish to see some large alligators. 'Oh, well,' said he, 'I can take you where you will see plenty of those fellows, but they are not much to look at. I once got a good look at an alligator that was lying at the bottom of still, transparent water, and I think that his eyes were the most impressively cold and cruel of any animal I have seen. Many alligators go out to sea among the keys. These sea alligators are the largest and most ferocious, and sometimes attack people by trying to strike them with their tails when they are out fishing in boats.

'Another thing I wish you to see,' he continued, 'is a palmetto grove on a rich hummock a few miles from here. The grove is about seven miles in length by three in breadth. The ground is covered with long grass, uninterrupted with bushes or other trees. It is the finest grove of palmettos I have ever seen and I have oftentimes thought that it would make a fine subject for an artist.'

I concluded to stop – more to see this wonderful palmetto hummock than to hunt. Besides, I was weary and the prospect of getting a little rest was a tempting consideration after so many restless nights and long, hard walks by day.

21 October. Having outlived the sanguinary hunters' tales of my loquacious host, and breakfasted sumptuously on fresh venison and 'caller' fish from the sea, I set out for the grand palm grove. I had seen these dazzling sun-children in every day of my walk through Florida, but they were usually standing solitary, or in groups of three or four; but today I was to see them by the mile. The captain led me a short distance through his corn field and showed me a trail which would conduct me to the palmy hummock. He pointed out the general direction, which I noted upon my compass.

'Now,' said he, 'at the other side of my farthest field you will come to a jungle of cat-briers, but will be able to pass them if you manage to keep the trail. You will find that the way is not by any means well marked, for in passing through a broad swamp, the trail makes a good many abrupt turns to avoid deep water, fallen trees, or impenetrable thickets. You will have to wade a good deal, and in passing the water-covered places you will have to watch for the point where the trail comes out on the opposite side.'

I made my way through the briers, which in strength and ferocity equalled those of Tennessee, followed the path through all of its dim waverings, waded the many opposing pools, and, emerging suddenly from the leafy darkness of the swamp forest, at last stood free and unshaded on the border of the sun-drenched palm garden. It was a level area of grasses and sedges, smooth as a prairie, well starred with flowers, and bounded like a clearing by a wall of vine-laden trees.

The palms had full possession and appeared to enjoy their sunny home. There was no jostling, no apparent effort to outgrow each other. Abundance of sunlight was there for every crown, and plenty to fall between. I walked enchanted in their midst. What a landscape! Only palms as far as the eye could reach! Smooth pillars rising from the grass, each capped with a sphere of leaves, shining in the sun as bright as a star. The silence and calm were as deep as ever I found in the dark, solemn pine woods of Canada, and that contentment which is an attribute of the best of God's plant people was as impressively felt in this alligator wilderness as in the homes of the happy, healthy people of the North.

The admirable Linnæus calls palms 'the princes of the vegetable world.' I know that there is grandeur and nobility in their character, and that there are palms nobler far than these. But in rank they appear to me to stand below both the oak and the pine. The motions of the palms, their gestures, are not very graceful. They appear to best advantage when perfectly motionless in the noontide calm and intensity of light. But they rustle and rock in the evening wind. I have seen grasses waving with far more dignity. And when our northern pines are waving and bowing in signs of worship with the winter storm-winds, where is the prince of palms that could have the conscience to demand their homage!

Members of this palm congregation were of all sizes with respect to their stems; but their glorious crowns were all alike. In development there is only the terminal bud to consider. The young palm of this species emerges from the ground in full strength, one cluster of leaves arched every way, making a sphere about ten or twelve feet in diameter. The outside lower leaves gradually become yellow, wither, and break off, the petiole snapping squarely across, a few inches from the stem. New leaves develop with wonderful rapidity. They stand erect at first, but gradually arch outward as they expand their blades and lengthen their petioles.

New leaves arise constantly from the centre of the grand bud, while old ones break away from the outside. The splendid crowns are thus kept about the same size, perhaps a little larger than in youth while they are yet on the ground. As the development of the central axis goes on, the crown is gradually raised on a stem of about six to twelve inches in diameter. This stem is of equal thickness at the top and at the bottom and when young is roughened with the broken petioles. But these petiole-stumps fall off and disappear as they become old, and the trunk becomes smooth as if turned in a lathe.

After some hours in this charming forest I started on the return journey before night, on account of the difficulties of the swamp and the brier patch. On leaving the palmettos and entering the vine-tangled, half-submerged forest I sought long and carefully, but in vain, for the trail, for I had drifted about too incautiously in search of plants. But, recollecting the direction that I had followed in the morning, I took a compass bearing and started to penetrate the swamp in a direct line.

Of course I had a sore weary time, pushing through the tanglement of falling, standing, and half-fallen trees and bushes, to say nothing of knotted vines as remarkable for their efficient army of interlocking and lancing prickers as for their length and the number of their blossoms. But these were not my greatest obstacles, nor yet the pools and lagoons full of dead leaves and alligators. It was the army of cat-briers that I most dreaded. I knew that I would have to find the narrow slit of a lane before dark or spend the night with mosquitoes and alligators, without food or fire. The entire distance was not great, but a traveller in open woods can form no idea of the crooked and strange difficulties of pathless locomotion in these thorny, watery Southern tangles, especially in pitch darkness. I struggled hard and kept my course, leaving the general direction only when drawn aside by a plant of extraordinary promise, that I wanted for a specimen, or when I had to make the half-circuit of a pile of trees, or of a deep lagoon or pond.

In wading I never attempted to keep my clothes dry, because the water was too deep, and the necessary care would consume too much time. Had the water that I was forced to wade been transparent it would have lost much of its difficulty. But as it was, I constantly expected to plant my feet on an alligator, and therefore proceeded with strained caution. The opacity of the water caused uneasiness also on account of my inability to determine its depth. In many places I was compelled to turn back, after wading forty or fifty yards, and to try again a score of times before I succeeded in getting across a single lagoon.

At length, after miles of wading and wallowing, I arrived at the grand cat-brier encampment which guarded the whole forest in solid phalanx, un-measured miles up and down across my way. Alas! the trail by which I had crossed in the morning was not to be found, and night was near. In vain I scrambled back and forth in search of an opening. There was not even a strip of dry ground on which to rest. Everywhere the long briers arched over to the vines and bushes of the watery swamp, leaving no standing-ground between them. I began to think of building some sort of a scaffold in a tree to rest on through the night, but concluded to make one more desperate effort to find the narrow track.

After calm, concentrated recollection of my course, I made a long explora-tion toward the left down the brier line, and after scrambling a mile or so, perspiring and bleeding, I discovered the blessed trail and escaped to dry land and the light. Reached the captain at sundown. Dined on milk and johnny-cake and fresh venison. Was congratulated on my singular good fortune and woodcraft, and soon after supper was sleeping the deep sleep of the weary and the safe.

22 October. This morning I was easily prevailed upon by the captain and an ex-judge, who was rusticating here, to join in a deer hunt. Had a delightful ramble in the long grass and flowery barrens. Started one deer but did not draw a single shot. The captain, the judge, and myself stood at different stations where the deer was expected to pass, while a brother of the captain entered the woods to arouse the game from cover. The one deer that he started took a different direction from any which this particular old buck had ever been known to take in times past, and in so doing was cordially cursed as being the 'd——dest deer that ever ran unshot.' To me it appeared as 'd——dest' work to slaughter God's cattle for sport. 'They were made for us,' say these self-approving preachers; 'for our food, our recreation, or other uses not yet discovered.' As truthfully we might say on behalf of a bear, when he deals successfully with an unfortunate hunter, 'Men and other bipeds were made for bears, and thanks be to God for claws and teeth so long.'

Let a Christian hunter go to the Lord's woods and kill his well-kept beasts, or wild Indians, and it is well, but let an enterprising specimen of these proper, predestined victims go to houses and fields and kill the most worthless person of the vertical godlike killers – oh! that is horribly unorthodox, and on the part of the Indians atrocious murder! Well, I have precious little sympathy for the selfish propriety of civilized man, and if a war of races should occur between the wild beasts and Lord Man, I would be tempted to sympathize with the bears.

CHAPTER SIX

Cedar Keys

23 OCTOBER. Today I reached the sea. While I was yet many miles back in the palmy woods, I caught the scent of the salt sea breeze which, although I had so many years lived far from sea breezes, suddenly conjured up Dunbar, its rocky coast, winds and waves; and my whole childhood, that seemed to have utterly vanished in the New World, was now restored amid the Florida woods by that one breath from the sea. Forgotten were the palms and magnolias and the thousand flowers that enclosed me. I could see only dulse and tangle, long-winged gulls, the Bass Rock in the Firth of Forth, and the old castle, schools, churches, and long country rambles in search of birds' nests. I do not wonder that the weary camels coming from the scorching African deserts should be able to scent the Nile.

How imperishable are all the impressions that ever vibrate one's life! We cannot forget anything. Memories may escape the action of will, may sleep a long time, but when stirred by the right influence, though that influence be light as a shadow, they flash into full stature and life with everything in place. For nineteen years my vision was bounded by forests, but today emerging from a multitude of tropical plants, I beheld the Gulf of Mexico stretching away unbounded, except by the sky. What dreams and speculative matter for thought arose as I stood on the strand, gazing out on the burnished, treeless plain!

But now at the seaside I was in difficulty. I had reached a point that I could not ford, and Cedar Keys had an empty harbour. Would I proceed down the peninsula to Tampa and Key West, where I would be sure to find a vessel for Cuba, or would I wait here, like Crusoe, and pray for a ship. Full of these thoughts, I stepped into a little store which had a considerable trade in quinine and alligator and rattlesnake skins, and inquired about shipping, means of travel, etc.

The proprietor informed me that one of several sawmills near the village was running, and that a schooner chartered to carry a load of lumber to Galveston, Texas, was expected at the mills for a load. This mill was situated on a tongue of land a few miles along the coast from Cedar Keys, and I determined to see Mr Hodgson, the owner, to find out particulars about the expected schooner, the time she would take to load, whether I would be likely to obtain passage on her, etc.

Found Mr Hodgson at his mill. Stated my case, and was kindly furnished the desired information. I determined to wait the two weeks likely to elapse before she sailed, and go on her to the flowery plains of Texas, from any of whose ports, I fancied, I could easily find passage to the West Indies. I agreed to work for Mr Hodgson in the mill until I sailed, as I had but little money. He invited me to his spacious house, which occupied a shell hillock and commanded a fine view of the Gulf and many gems of palmy islets, called 'keys,' that fringe the shore like huge bouquets – not too big, however, for the spacious waters. Mr Hodgson's family welcomed me with that open, unconstrained cordiality which is characteristic of the better class of Southern people.

At the sawmill a new cover had been put on the main driving pulley, which, made of rough plank, had to be turned off and smoothed. He asked me if I was able to do this job and I told him that I could. Fixing a rest and making a tool out of an old file, I directed the engineer to start the engine and run slow. After turning down the pulley and getting it true, I put a keen edge on a common carpenter's plane, quickly finished the job, and was assigned a bunk in one of the employee's lodging-houses.

The next day I felt a strange dullness and headache while I was botanizing along the coast. Thinking that a bath in the salt water might refresh me, I plunged in and swam a little distance, but this seemed only to make me feel worse. I felt anxious for something sour, and walked back to the village to buy lemons.

Thus and here my long walk was interrupted. I thought that a few days' sail would land me among the famous flower-beds of Texas. But the expected ship came and went while I was helpless with fever. The very day after reaching the sea I began to be weighed down by inexorable leaden numbness, which I resisted and tried to shake off for three days, by bathing in the Gulf, by dragging myself about among the palms, plants, and strange shells of the shore, and by doing a little mill work. I did not fear any serious illness, for I never was sick before, and was unwilling to pay attention to my feelings.

But yet heavier and more remorselessly pressed the growing fever, rapidly gaining on my strength. On the third day after my arrival I could not take any nourishment, but craved acid. Cedar Keys was only a mile or two distant, and I managed to walk there to buy lemons. On returning, about the middle of the afternoon, the fever broke on me like a storm, and before I had staggered half-way to the mill I fell down unconscious on the narrow trail among dwarf palmettos.

When I awoke from the hot fever sleep, the stars were shining, and I was at a loss to know which end of the trail to take, but fortunately, as it afterwards proved, I guessed right. Subsequently, as I fell again and again after walking only a hundred yards or so, I was careful to lie with my head in the direction in which I thought the mill was. I rose, staggered, and fell, I know not how many times, in delirious bewilderment, gasping and throbbing with only moments of consciousness. Thus passed the hours till after midnight, when I reached the mill lodging-house.

The watchman on his rounds found me lying on a heap of sawdust at the foot of the stairs. I asked him to assist me up the steps to bed, but he thought my difficulty was only intoxication and refused to help me. The mill hands, especially on Saturday nights, often returned from the village drunk. This was the cause of the watchman's refusal. Feeling that I must get to bed, I made out to reach it on hands and knees, tumbled in after a desperate struggle, and immediately became oblivious to everything.

I awoke at a strange hour on a strange day to hear Mr Hodgson ask a

watcher beside me whether I had yet spoken, and when he replied that I had
not, he said: 'Well, you must keep on pouring in quinine. That's all we can
do.' How long I lay unconscious I never found out, but it must have been
many days. Some time or other I was moved on a horse from the mill quarters
to Mr Hodgson's house, where I was nursed about three months with unfailing
kindness, and to the skill and care of Mr and Mrs Hodgson I doubtless owe
my life. Through quinine and calomel – in sorry abundance – with other
milder medicines, my malarial fever became typhoid. I had night sweats, and
my legs became like posts of the temper and consistency of clay on account of
dropsy. So on until January, a weary time.

As soon as I was able to get out of bed, I crept away to the edge of the
wood, and sat day after day beneath a moss-draped live-oak, watching birds
feeding on the shore when the tide was out. Later, as I gathered some
strength, I sailed in a little skiff from one key to another. Nearly all the shrubs
and trees here are evergreen, and a few of the smaller plants are in flower all
winter. The principal trees on this Cedar Key are the juniper, long-leafed
pine, and live-oak. All of the latter, living and dead, are heavily draped with
tillandsia, like those of Bonaventure. The leaf is oval, about two inches long,
three fourths of an inch wide, glossy and dark green above, pale beneath. The
trunk is usually much divided, and is extremely unwedgeable. The specimen
on the opposite page[1] is growing in the dooryard of Mr Hodgson's house. It is
a grand old king, whose crown gleamed in the bright sky long ere the Spanish
shipbuilders felled a single tree of this noble species.

The live-oaks of these keys divide empire with the long-leafed pine and
palmetto, but in many places on the mainland there are large tracts exclusively
occupied by them. Like the Bonaventure oaks they have the upper side of
their main spreading branches thickly planted with ferns, grasses, small saw
palmettos, etc. There is also a dwarf oak here, which forms dense thickets.
The oaks of this key are not, like those of the Wisconsin openings, growing on
grassy slopes, but stand, sunk to the shoulders, in flowering magnolias,
heathworts, etc.

During my long sojourn here as a convalescent I used to lie on my back for
whole days beneath the ample arms of these great trees, listening to the winds
and the birds. There is an extensive shallow on the coast, close by, which the
receding tide exposes daily. This is the feeding-ground of thousands of waders
of all sizes, plumage, and language, and they make a lively picture and noise
when they gather at the great family board to eat their daily bread, so
bountifully provided for them.

Their leisure in time of high tide they spend in various ways and places.
Some go in large flocks to reedy margins about the islands and wade and stand
about quarrelling or making sport, occasionally finding a stray mouthful to
eat. Some stand on the mangroves of the solitary shore, now and then
plunging into the water after a fish. Some go long journeys inland, up creeks
and inlets. A few lonely old herons of solemn look and wing retire to
favourite oaks. It was my delight to watch those old white sages of immaculate

[1] Of the original journal.

feather as they stood erect drowsing away the dull hours between tides, curtained by long skeins of tillandsia. White-bearded hermits gazing dreamily from dark caves could not appear more solemn or more becomingly shrouded from the rest of their fellow beings.

One of the characteristic plants of these keys is the Spanish bayonet, a species of yucca, about eight or ten feet in height, and with a trunk three or four inches in diameter when full grown. It belongs to the lily family and develops palmlike from terminal buds. The stout leaves are very rigid, sharp-pointed and bayonet-like. By one of these leaves a man might be as seriously stabbed as by an army bayonet, and woe to the luckless wanderer who dares to urge his way through these armed gardens after dark. Vegetable cats of many species will rob him of his clothes and claw his flesh, while dwarf palmettos will saw his bones, and the bayonets will glide to his joints and marrow without the smallest consideration for Lord Man.

The climate of these precious islets is simply warm summer and warmer summer, corresponding in time with winter and summer in the North. The weather goes smoothly over the points of union betwixt the twin summers. Few of the storms are very loud or variable. The average temperature during the day, in December, was about sixty-five degrees in the shade, but on one day a little damp snow fell.

Cedar Key is two and one half or three miles in diameter and its highest point is forty-four feet above mean tide-water. It is surrounded by scores of other keys, many of them looking like a clump of palms, arranged like a tasteful bouquet, and placed in the sea to be kept fresh. Others have quite a sprinkling of oaks and junipers, beautifully united with vines. Still others consist of shells, with a few grasses and mangroves, circled with a rim of rushes. Those which have sedgy margins furnish a favourite retreat for count-less waders and divers, especially for pelicans that frequently whiten the shore like a ring of foam.

It is delightful to observe the assembling of these feathered people from the woods and reedy isles; herons white as wave-tops, or blue as the sky, winnow-ing the warm air on wide quiet wing; pelicans coming with baskets to fill, and the multitude of smaller sailors of the air, swift as swallows, gracefully taking their places at Nature's family table for their daily bread. Happy birds!

The mockingbird is graceful in form and a fine singer, plainly dressed, rather familiar in habits, frequently coming like robins to doorsills for crumbs – a noble fellow, beloved by everybody. Wild geese are abundant in winter, associated with brant, some species of which I have never seen in the North. Also great flocks of robins, mourning doves, bluebirds, and the delightful brown thrashers. A large number of the smaller birds are fine singers. Crows, too, are here, some of them cawing with a foreign accent. The common bob-white quail I observed as far south as middle Georgia.

Lime Key is a fair specimen of the Florida Keys on this part of the coast. The cactus, *Opuntia*, sketched on another page,[1] is from the above-named key, and is abundant there. The fruit, an inch in length, is gathered, and made

[1] Of the original journal.

into a sauce, of which some people are fond. This species forms thorny, impenetrable thickets. One joint that I measured was fifteen inches long.

The mainland of Florida is less salubrious than the islands, but no portion of this coast, nor of the flat border which sweeps from Maryland to Texas, is quite free from malaria. All the inhabitants of this region, whether black or white, are liable to be prostrated by the ever-present fever and ague, to say nothing of the plagues of cholera and yellow fever that come and go suddenly like storms, prostrating the population and cutting gaps in it like hurricanes in woods.

The world, we are told, was made especially for man – a presumption not supported by all the facts. A numerous class of men are painfully astonished whenever they find anything, living or dead, in all God's universe, which they cannot eat or render in some way what they call useful to themselves. They have precise dogmatic insight of the intentions of the Creator, and it is hardly possible to be guilty of irreverence in speaking of *their* God any more than of heathen idols. He is regarded as a civilized, law-abiding gentleman in favour either of a republican form of government or of a limited monarchy; believes in the literature and language of England; is a warm supporter of the English constitution and Sunday schools and missionary societies; and is as purely a manufactured article as any puppet of a halfpenny theatre.

With such views of the Creator it is, of course, not surprising that erroneous views should be entertained of the creation. To such properly trimmed people, the sheep, for example, is an easy problem – food and clothing 'for us,' eating grass and daisies white by divine appointment for this predestined purpose, on perceiving the demand for wool that would be occasioned by the eating of the apple in the Garden of Eden.

In the same pleasant plan, whales are storehouses of oil for us, to help out the stars in lighting our dark ways until the discovery of the Pennsylvania oil wells. Among plants, hemp, to say nothing of the cereals, is a case of evident destination for ships' rigging, wrapping packages, and hanging the wicked. Cotton is another plain case of clothing. Iron was made for hammers and ploughs, and lead for bullets; all intended for us. And so of other small handfuls of insignificant things.

But if we should ask these profound expositors of God's intentions, How about those man-eating animals – lions, tigers, alligators – which smack their lips over raw man? Or about those myriads of noxious insects that destroy labour and drink his blood? Doubtless man was intended for food and drink for all these? Oh, no! Not at all! These are unresolvable difficulties connected with Eden's apple and the Devil. Why does water drown its lord? Why do so many minerals poison him? Why are so many plants and fishes deadly enemies? Why is the lord of creation subjected to the same laws of life as his subjects? Oh, all these things are satanic, or in some way connected with the first garden.

Now, it never seems to occur to these far-seeing teachers that Nature's object in making animals and plants might possibly be first of all the happiness of each one of them, not the creation of all for the happiness of one. Why should man value himself as more than a small part of the one great unit of creation? And what creature of all that the Lord has taken the pains to make is not essential to the completeness of that unit – the cosmos? The universe would be incomplete without man; but it would also be incomplete without the smallest transmicroscopic creature that dwells beyond our conceitful eyes and knowledge.

From the dust of the earth, from the common elementary fund, the Creator has made *Homo sapiens*. From the same material he has made every other creature, however noxious and insignificant to us. They are earth-born companions and our fellow mortals. The fearfully good, the orthodox, of this laborious patchwork of modern civilization cry 'Heresy' on every one whose sympathies reach a single hair's breadth beyond the boundary epidermis of our own species. Not content with taking all of earth, they also claim the celestial country as the only ones who possess the kind of souls for which that imponderable empire was planned.

This star, our own good earth, made many a successful journey around the heavens ere man was made, and whole kingdoms of creatures enjoyed existence and returned to dust ere man appeared to claim them. After human beings have also played their part in Creation's plan, they too may disappear without any general burning or extraordinary commotion whatever.

Plants are credited with but dim and uncertain sensation, and minerals with positively none at all. But why may not even a mineral arrangement of matter be endowed with sensation of a kind that we in our blind exclusive perfection can have no manner of communication with?

But I have wandered from my object. I stated above that man claimed the earth was made for him, and I was going to say that venomous beasts, thorny plants, and deadly diseases of certain parts of the earth prove that the whole world was not made for him. When an animal from a tropical climate is taken to high latitudes, it may perish of cold, and we say that such an animal was never intended for so severe a climate. But when man betakes himself to sickly parts of the tropics and perishes, he cannot see that he was never intended for such deadly climates. No, he will rather accuse the first mother of the cause of the difficulty, though she may never have seen a fever district; or will consider it a providential chastisement for some self-invented form of sin.

Furthermore, all uneatable and uncivilizable animals, and all plants which carry prickles, are deplorable evils which, according to closet researches of clergy, require the cleansing chemistry of universal planetary combustion. But more than aught else mankind requires burning, as being in great part wicked, and if that transmundane furnace can be so applied and regulated as to smelt and purify us into conformity with the rest of the terrestrial creation, then the tophetisation of the erratic genus Homo were a consummation devoutly to be prayed for. But, glad to leave these ecclesiastical fires and blunders, I joyfully return to the immortal truth and immortal beauty of Nature.

CHAPTER SEVEN

A Sojourn in Cuba

ONE DAY in January I climbed to the housetop to get a view of another of the fine sunsets of this land of flowers. The landscape was a strip of clear Gulf water, a strip of sylvan coast, a tranquil company of shell and coral keys, and a gloriously coloured sky without a threatening cloud. All the winds were hushed and the calm of the heavens was as profound as that of the palmy islands and their encircling waters. As I gazed from one to another of the palm-crowned keys, enclosed by the sunset-coloured dome, my eyes chanced to rest upon the fluttering sails of a Yankee schooner that was threading the tortuous channel in the coral reef leading to the harbour of Cedar Keys. 'There,' thought I, 'perhaps I may sail in that pretty white moth.' She proved to be the schooner Island Belle.

One day soon after her arrival I went over the key to the harbour, for I was now strong enough to walk. Some of her crew were ashore after water. I waited until their casks were filled, and went with them to the vessel in their boat. Ascertained that she was ready to sail with her cargo of lumber for Cuba. I engaged passage on her for twenty-five dollars, and asked her sharp-visaged captain when he would sail. 'Just as soon,' said he, 'as we get a north wind. We have had northers enough when we did not want them, and now we have this dying breath from the south.'

Hurrying back to the house, I gathered my plants, took leave of my kind friends, and went aboard, and soon, as if to calm the captain's complaints, Boreas came foaming loud and strong. The little craft was quickly trimmed and snugged, her inviting sails spread open, and away she dashed to her ocean home like an exulting war-horse to the battle. Islet after islet speedily grew dim and sank beneath the horizon. Deeper became the blue of the water, and in a few hours all of Florida vanished.

This excursion on the sea, the first one after twenty years in the woods, was of course exceedingly interesting, and I was full of hope, glad to be once more on my journey to the South. Boreas increased in power and the Island Belle appeared to glory in her speed and managed her full-spread wings as gracefully as a sea-bird. In less than a day our norther increased in strength to the storm point. Deeper and wider became the valleys, and yet higher the hills of the round plain of water. The flying jib and gaff topsails were lowered and mainsails close-reefed, and our deck was white with broken wave-tops.

'You had better go below,' said the captain. 'The Gulf Stream, opposed by this wind, is raising a heavy sea and you will be sick. No landsman can stand this long.' I replied that I hoped the storm would be as violent as his ship could bear, that I enjoyed the scenery of such a sea so much that it was impossible to be sick, that I had long waited in the woods for just such a storm, and that, now that the precious thing had come, I would remain on deck and enjoy it. 'Well,' said he, 'if you can stand this, you are the first landsman I ever saw that could.'

I remained on deck, holding on by a rope to keep from being washed overboard, and watched the behaviour of the Belle as she dared nobly on; but my attention was mostly directed among the glorious fields of foam-topped waves. The wind had a mysterious voice and carried nothing now of the songs of birds or of the rustling of palms and fragrant vines. Its burden was gathered from a stormy expanse of crested waves and briny tangles. I could see no striving in those magnificent wave-motions, no raging; all the storm was apparently inspired with nature's beauty and harmony. Every wave was obedient and harmonious as the smoothest ripple of a forest lake, and after dark all the water was phosphorescent like silver fire, a glorious sight.

Our luminous storm was all too short for me. Cuba's rock-waves loomed above the white waters early in the morning. The sailors, accustomed to detect the faintest land line, pointed out well-known guiding harbour-marks back of the Morro Castle long before I could see them through the flying spray. We sailed landward for several hours, the misty shore becoming gradually more earthlike. A flock of white-plumaged ships was departing from the Havana harbour, or, like us, seeking to enter it. No sooner had our little schooner flapped her sails in the lee of the Castle than she was boarded by a swarm of daintily dressed officials who were good-naturedly and good-gesturedly making all sorts of inquiries, while our busy captain, paying little attention to them, was giving orders to his crew.

The neck of the harbour is narrow and it is seldom posible to sail in to appointed anchorage without the aid of a steam tug. Our captain wished to save his money, but after much profitless tacking was compelled to take the proffered aid of steam, when we soon reached our quiet mid-harbour quarters and dropped anchor among ships of every size from every sea.

I was still four or five hundred yards from land and could determine no plant in sight excepting the long arched leaf banners of the banana and the palm, which made a brave show on the Morro Hill. When we were approaching the land, I observed that in some places it was distinctly yellow, and I wondered while we were yet some miles distant whether the colour belonged to the ground or to sheets of flowers. From our harbour home I could now see that the colour was plant-gold. On one side of the habour was a city of these yellow plants; on the other, a city of yellow stucco houses, narrowly and confusedly congregated.

'Do you want to go ashore?' said the captain to me. 'Yes,' I replied, 'but I wish to go to the plant side of the harbour.' 'Oh well,' he said, 'come with me now. There are some fine squares and gardens in the city, full of all sorts of trees and flowers. Enjoy these today, and some other day we will all go over the Morro Hill with you and gather shells. All kinds of shells are over there; but these yellow slopes that you see are covered only with weeds.'

We jumped into the boat and a couple of sailors pulled us to the thronged, noisy wharf. It was Sunday afternoon,[1] the noisiest day of a Havana week.

---

[1] Doubtless 12 January 1868.

Cathedral bells and prayers in the forenoon, theatres and bull-fight bells and bellowings in the afternoon! Lowly whispered prayers to the saints and the Virgin, followed by shouts of praise or reproach to bulls and matadors! I made free with fine oranges and bananas and many other fruits. Pineapple I had never seen before. Wandered about the narrow streets, stunned with the babel of strange sounds and sights; went gazing, also, among the gorgeously flowered garden squares, and then waited among some boxed merchandise until our captain, detained by business, arrived. Was glad to escape to our little schooner Belle again, weary and heavy laden with excitement and tempting fruits.

As night came on, a thousand lights starred the great town. I was now in one of my happy dreamlands, the fairest of West India islands. But how, I wondered, shall I be able to escape from this great city of confusion? How shall I reach nature in this delectable land? Consulting my map, I longed to climb the central mountain range of the island and trace it through all its forests and valleys and over its summit peaks, a distance of seven or eight hundred miles. But alas! though out of Florida swamps, fever was yet weighing me down, and a mile of city walking was quite exhausting. The weather too was oppressively warm and sultry.

16 January. During the few days since our arrival the sun usually has risen unclouded, pouring down pure gold, rich and dense, for one or two hours. Then islandlike masses of white-edged cumuli suddenly appeared, grew to storm size, and in a few minutes discharged rain in tepid plashing bucketfuls, accompanied with high wind. This was followed by a short space of calm, half-cloudy sky, delightfully fragrant with flowers, and again the air would become hot, thick, and sultry.

This weather, as may readily be perceived, was severe to one so weak and feverish, and after a dozen trials of strength over the Morro Hill and along the coast northward for shells and flowers, I was sadly compelled to see that no enthusiasm could enable me to walk to the interior. So I was obliged to limit my researches to within ten or twelve miles of Havana. Captain Parsons offered his ship as my headquarters, and my weakness prevented me from spending a single night ashore.

The daily programme for nearly all the month that I spent here was about as follows: After breakfast a sailor rowed me ashore on the north side of the harbour. A few minutes' walk took me past the Morro Castle and out of sight of the town on a broad cactus common, about as solitary and untrodden as the tangles of Florida. Here I zigzagged and gathered prizes among unnumbered plants and shells along the shore, stopping to press the plant specimens and to rest in the shade of vine-heaps and bushes until sundown. The happy hours stole away until I had to return to the schooner. Either I was seen by the sailors who usually came for me, or I hired a boat to take me back. Arrived, I reached up my press and a big handful of flowers, and with a little help climbed up the side of my floating home.

Refreshed with supper and rest, I recounted my adventures in the vine tangles, cactus thickets, sunflower swamps, and along the shore among the breakers. My flower specimens, also, and pocketfuls of shells and corals had to be reviewed. Next followed a cool, dreamy hour on deck amid the lights of the town and the various vessels coming and departing.

Many strange sounds were heard: the vociferous, unsmotherable bells, the heavy thundering of cannon from the Castle, and the shouts of the sentinels in measured time. Combined they made the most incessant sharp-angled mass of noise that I ever was doomed to hear. Nine or ten o'clock found me in a small bunk with the harbour wavelets tinkling outside close to my ear. The hours of sleep were filled with dreams of heavy heat, or fruitless efforts for the disentanglement of vines, or of running from curling breakers back to the Morro, etc. Thus my days and nights went on.

Occasionally I was persuaded by the captain to go ashore in the evening on his side of the harbour, accompanied perhaps by two or three other captains. After landing and telling the sailors when to call for us, we hired a carriage and drove to the upper end of the city, to a fine public square adorned with shady walks and magnificent plants. A brass band in imposing uniform played the characteristic lance-noted martial airs of the Spanish. Evening is the fashionable hour for aristocratic drives about the streets and squares, the only time that is delightfully cool. I never saw elsewhere people so neatly and becomingly dressed. The proud best-family Cubans may fairly be called beautiful, are under- rather than over-sized, with features exquisitely moulded, and set off with silks and broadcloth in excellent taste. Strange that their amusements should be so coarse. Bull-fighting, brain-splitting bell-ringing, and the most piercing artificial music appeal to their taste.

The rank and wealth of Havana nobility, when out driving, seems to be indicated by the distance of their horses from the body of the carriage. The higher the rank, the longer the shafts of the carriage, and the clumsier and more ponderous are the wheels, which are not unlike those of a cannon-cart. A few of these carriages have shafts twenty-five feet in length, and the brilliant-liveried negro driver on the lead horse, twenty or thirty feet in advance of the horse in the shafts, is beyond calling distance of his master.

Havana abounds in public squares, which in all my random strolls throughout the big town I found to be well watered, well cared for, well planted, and full of exceedingly showy and interesting plants, rare even amid the exhaustless luxuriance of Cuba. These squares also contained fine marble statuary and were furnished with seats in the shadiest places. Many of the walks were paved instead of gravelled.

The streets of Havana are crooked, labyrinthic, and exceedingly narrow. The sidewalks are only about a foot wide. A traveller experiences delightful relief when, heated and wearied by raids through the breadth of the dingy yellow town, dodging a way through crowds of men and mules lumbering carts and carriages, he at length finds shelter in the spacious, dustless, cool, flowery squares; still more when, emerging from all the din and darkness of these lanelike streets, he suddenly finds himself out in the middle of the harbour, inhaling full-drawn breaths of the sea breezes.

The interior of the better houses which came under my observation struck me with the profusion of dumpy, ill-proportioned pillars at the entrances and in the halls, and with the spacious open-fielded appearance of their enclosed square house–gardens or courts. Cubans in general appear to me superfinely polished, polite, and agreeable in society, but in their treatment of animals they are cruel. I saw more downright brutal cruelty to mules and horses during the few weeks I stayed there than in my whole life elsewhere. Live chickens and hogs are tied in bunches by the legs and carried to market thus, slung on a mule. In their general treatment of all sorts of animals they seem to have no thought for them beyond cold-blooded, selfish interest.

In tropical regions it is easy to build towns, but it is difficult to subdue their armed and united plant inhabitants, and to clear fields and make them blossom with breadstuff. The plant people of temperate regions, feeble, unarmed, unallied, disappear under the trampling feet of flocks, herds, and man, leaving their homes to enslavable plants which follow the will of man and furnish him with food. But the armed and united plants of the tropics hold their rightful kingdom plantfully, nor, since the first appearance of Lord Man, have they ever suffered defeat.

A large number of Cuba's wild plants circle closely about Havana. In five minutes' walk from the wharf I could reach the undisturbed settlements of Nature. The field of the greater portion of my rambling researches was a strip of rocky common, silent and unfrequented by anybody save an occasional beggar at Nature's door asking for a few roots and seeds. This natural strip extended ten miles along the coast northward, with but few large-sized trees and bushes, but rich in magnificent vines, cacti-composites, leguminous plants, grasses, etc. The wild flowers of this seaside field are a happy band, closely joined in splendid array. The trees shine with blossoms and with light reflected from the leaves. The individuality of the vines is lost in trackless, interlacing, twisting, overheaping union.

Our American 'South' is rich in flowery vines. In some districts almost every tree is crowned with them, aiding each other in grace and beauty. Indiana, Kentucky, and Tennessee have the grapevine in predominant numbers and development. Farther south dwell the greenbriers and countless leguminous vines. A vine common among the Florida islets, perhaps belonging to the dogbane family, overruns live-oaks and palmettos, with frequently more than a hundred stems twisted into one cable. Yet in no section of the South are there such complicated and such gorgeously flowered vine-tangles as flourish in armed safety in the hot and humid wild gardens of Cuba.

The longest and the shortest vine that I found in Cuba were both leguminous. I have said that the harbour side of the Morro Hill is clothed with tall yellow-flowered composites through which it is difficult to pass. But there are smooth, velvety, lawnlike patches in these *Compositæ* forests. Coming suddenly upon one of these open places, I stopped to admire its greenness and smoothness, when I observed a sprinkling of large papilionaceous blossoms among the short green grass. The long composites that bordered this little lawn were entwined and almost smothered with vines which bore similar corollas in tropic abundance.

I at once decided that these sprinkled flowers had been blown off the encompassing tangles and had been kept fresh by dew and by spray from the sea. But, on stooping to pick one of them up, I was surprised to find that it was attached to Mother Earth by a short, prostrate, slender hair of a vine stem, bearing, besides the one large blossom, a pair or two of linear leaves. The flower weighed more than stem, root, and leaves combined. Thus, in a land of creeping and twining giants, we find also this charming, diminutive simplicity – the vine reduced to its lowest terms.

The longest vine, prostrate and untwined like its little neighbour, covers patches of several hundred square yards with its countless branches and close growth of upright, trifoliate, smooth green leaves. The flowers are as plain and un-showy in size and colour as those of the sweet peas of gardens. The seeds are large and satiny. The whole plant is noble in its motions and features, covering the ground with a depth of unconfused leafage which I have never seen equalled by any other plant. The extent of leaf-surface is greater, I think, than that of a large Kentucky oak. It grows, as far as my observation has reached, only upon shores, in a soil composed of broken shells and corals, and extends exactly to the water-line of the highest-reaching waves. The same plant is abundant in Florida.

The cacti form an important part of the plant population of my ramble ground. They are various as the vines, consisting now of a diminutive joint or two hid in the weeds, now rising into bushy trees, wide-topped, with trunks a foot in diameter, and with glossy, dark-green joints that reflect light like the silex-varnished palms. They are planted for fences, together with the Spanish bayonet and agave.

In one of my first walks I was laboriously scrambling among some low rocks gathering ferns and vines, when I was startled by finding my face close to a great snake, whose body was disposed carelessly like a castaway rope among the weeds and stones. After escaping and coming to my senses, I discovered that the snake was a member of the vegetable kingdom, capable of no dangerous amount of locomotion, but possessed of many a fang, and prostrate as though under the curse of Eden, 'Upon thy belly shalt thou go and dust shalt thou eat.'

One day, after luxuriating in the riches of my Morro pasture, and pressing many new specimens, I went down to the bank of brilliant wave-washed shells to rest awhile in their beauty, and to watch the breakers that a powerful norther was heaving in splendid rank along the coral boundary. I gathered pocketfuls of shells, mostly small but fine in colour and form, and bits of rosy coral. Then I amused myself by noting the varying colours of the waves and the different forms of their curved and blossoming crests. While thus alone and free it was interesting to learn the richly varied songs, or what we mortals call the roar, of expiring breakers. I compared their variation with the different distances to which the broken wave–water reached landward in its farthest-flung foam-wreaths, and endeavoured to form some idea of the one great song sounding forever all around the white-blooming shores of the world.

Rising from my shell seat, I watched a wave leaping from the deep and coming far up the bevelled strand to bloom and die in a mass of white. Then I followed the spent waters in their return to the blue deep, wading in their spangled, decaying fragments until chased back up the bank by the coming of another wave. While thus playing half studiously, I discovered in the rough,

beaten deathbed of the wave a little plant with closed flowers. It was crouching in a hollow of the brown wave-washed rock, and one by one the chanting,
dying waves rolled over it. The tips of its delicate pink petals peered above
the clasping green calyx. 'Surely,' said I, as I stooped over it for a moment,
before the oncoming of another wave, 'surely you cannot be living here! You
must have been blown from some warm bank, and rolled into this little hollow
crack like a dead shell.' But, running back after every retiring wave, I found
that its roots were wedged into a shallow wrinkle of the coral rock, and that
this wave-beaten chink was indeed its dwelling-place.

I had oftentimes admired the adaptation displayed in the structure of the
stately dulse and other seaweeds, but never thought to find a highbred
flowering plant dwelling amid waves in the stormy, roaring domain of the
sea. This little plant has smooth globular leaves, fleshy and translucent like
beads, but green like those of other land plants. The flower is about five
eighths of an inch in diameter, rose-purple, opening in calm weather, when
deserted by the waves. In general appearance it is like a small portulaca. The
strand, as far as I walked it, was luxuriantly fringed with woody *Compositæ*,
two or three feet in height, their tops purple and golden with a profusion of
flowers. Among these I discovered a small bush whose yellow flowers were
ideal; all the parts were present regularly alternate and in fives, and all
separate, a plain harmony.

When a page is written over but once it may be easily read; but if it be
written over and over with characters of every size and style, it soon becomes
unreadable, although not a single confused meaningless mark or thought may
concur among all the written characters to mar its perfection. Our limited
powers are similarly perplexed and overtaxed in reading the inexhaustible
pages of nature, for they are written over and over uncountable times, written
in characters of every size and colour, sentences composed of sentences,
every part of a character a sentence. There is not a fragment in nature, for
every relative fragment of one thing is a full harmonious unit in itself. All
together form the one grand palimpsest of the world.

One of the most common plants of my pasture was the agave. It is sometimes used for fencing. One day, in looking back from the top of the Morro
Hill, as I was returning to the Island Belle, I chanced to observe two poplar-
like trees about twenty-five feet in height. They were growing in a dense patch
of cactus and vine-knotted sunflowers. I was anxious to see anything so
homelike as a poplar, and so made haste towards the two strange trees,
making a way through the cactus and sunflower jungle that protected them. I
was surprised to find that what I took to be poplars were agaves in flower, the
first I had seen. They were almost out of flower, and fast becoming wilted at
the approach of death. Bulbs were scattered about, and a good many still
remained on the branches, which gave it a fruited appearance.

The stem of the agave seems enormous in size when one considers that it is
the growth of a few weeks. This plant is said to make a mighty effort to flower
and mature its seeds and then to die of exhaustion. Now there is not, so far as
I have seen, a mighty effort or the need of one, in wild Nature. She accomplishes her ends without unquiet effort, and perhaps there is nothing more

mighty in the development of the flower-stem of the agave than in the development of a grass panicle.

Havana has a fine botanical garden. I spent pleasant hours in its magnificent flowery arbours and around its shady fountains. There is a palm avenue which is considered wonderfully stately and beautiful, fifty palms in two straight lines, each rigidly perpendicular. The smooth round shafts, slightly thicker in the middle, appear to be productions of the lathe, rather than vegetable stems. The fifty arched crowns, inimitably balanced, blaze in the sunshine like heaps of stars that have fallen from the skies. The stems were about sixty or seventy feet in height, the crowns about fifteen feet in diameter.

Along a stream-bank were tall, waving bamboos, leafy as willows, and infinitely graceful in wind gestures. There was one species of palm, with immense bipinnate leaves and leaflets fringed, jagged, and one-sided, like those of *Adiantum*. Hundreds of the most gorgeous-flowered plants, some of them large trees, belonging to the *Leguminosæ*. Compared with what I have before seen in artificial flower-gardens, this is past comparison the grandest. It is a perfect metropolis of the brightest and most exuberant of garden plants, watered by handsome fountains, while gravelled and finely bordered walks slant and curve in all directions, and in all kinds of fanciful playground styles, more like the fairy gardens of the Arabian Nights than any ordinary man-made pleasure-ground.

In Havana I saw the strongest and ugliest negroes that I have met in my whole walk. The stevedores of the Havana wharf are muscled in true giant style, enabling them to tumble and toss ponderous casks and boxes of sugar weighing hundreds of pounds as if they were empty. I heard our own brawny sailors, after watching them at work a few minutes, express unbounded admiration of their strength, and wish that their hard outbulging muscles were for sale. The countenances of some of the negro orange-selling dames express a devout good-natured ugliness that I never could have conceived any arrangement of flesh and blood to be capable of. Besides oranges they sold pineapples, bananas, and lottery tickets.

CHAPTER EIGHT

By a Crooked Route to California

AFTER PASSING a month in this magnificent island, and finding that my health was not improving, I made up my mind to push on to South America while my stock of strength, such as it was, lasted. But fortunately I could not find passage for any South American port. I had long wished to visit the Orinoco basin and in particular the basin of the Amazon. My plan was to get ashore anywhere on the north end of the continent, push on southward through the wilderness around the headwaters of the Orinoco, until I reached a tributary of the Amazon, and float down on a raft or skiff the whole length of the great river to its mouth. It seems strange that such a trip should ever have entered the dreams of any person, however enthusiastic and full of youthful daring, particularly under the disadvantages of poor health, of funds less than a hundred dollars, and of the insalubrity of the Amazon Valley.

Fortunately, as I said, after visiting all the shipping agencies, I could not find a vessel of any sort bound for South America, and so made up a plan to go north, to the longed-for cold weather of New York, and thence to the forests and mountains of California. There, I thought, I shall find health and new plants and mountains, and after a year spent in that interesting country I can carry out my Amazon plans.

It seemed hard to leave Cuba thus unseen and unwalked, but illness forbade my stay and I had to comfort myself with the hope of returning to its waiting treasures in full health. In the mean time I prepared for immediate departure. When I was resting in one of the Havana gardens, I noticed in a New York paper an advertisement for cheap fares to California. I consulted Captain Parsons concerning a passage to New York, where I could find a ship for California. At this time none of the California ships touched at Cuba.

'Well,' said he, pointing toward the middle of the harbour, 'there is a trim little schooner loaded with oranges for New York, and these little fruiters are fast sailers. You had better see her captain about a passage, for she must be about ready to sail.' So I jumped into the dinghy and a sailor rowed me over to the fruiter. Going aboard, I inquired for the captain, who soon appeared on deck and readily agreed to carry me to New York for twenty-five dollars. Inquiring when he would sail, 'Tomorrow morning at daylight,' he replied, 'if this norther slacks a little; but my papers are made out, and you will have to see the American consul to get permission to leave on my ship.'

I immediately went to the city, but was unable to find the consul, where-upon I determined to sail for New York without any formal leave. Early next morning, after leaving the Island Belle and bidding Captain Parsons good-bye, I was rowed to the fruiter and got aboard. Notwithstanding the north wind was still as boisterous as ever, our Dutch captain was resolved to face it, confident in the strength of his all-oak little schooner.

Vessels leaving the harbour are stopped at the Morro Castle to have their clearance papers examined; in particular, to see that no runaway slaves were being carried away. The officials came alongside our little ship, but did not come aboard. They were satisfied by a glance at the consul's clearance paper, and with the declaration of the captain, when asked whether he had any negroes, that he had 'not a d——d one.' 'All right, then,' shouted the officials, 'farewell! A pleasant voyage to you!' As my name was not on the ship's papers, I stayed below, out of sight, until I felt the heaving of the waves and knew that we were fairly out on the open sea. The Castle towers, the hills, the palms, and the wave-white strand, all faded in the distance, and our mimic sea-bird was at home in the open stormy gulf, curtsying to every wave and facing bravely to the wind.

Two thousand years ago our Saviour told Nicodemus that he did not know where the winds came from, nor where they were going. And now in this

Golden Age, though we Gentiles know the birthplace of many a wind and also 'whither it is going,' yet we know about as little of winds in general as those Palestinian Jews, and our ignorance, despite the powers of science, can never be much less profound than it is at present.

The substance of the winds is too thin for human eyes, their written language is too difficult for human minds, and their spoken language mostly too faint for the ears. A mechanism is said to have been invented whereby the human organs of speech are made to write their own utterances. But without any extra mechanical contrivance, every speaker also writes as he speaks. All things in the creation of God register their own acts. The poet was mistaken when he said, 'From the wing no scar the sky sustains.' His eyes were simply too dim to see the scar. In sailing past Cuba I could see a fringe of foam along the coast, but could hear no sound of waves, simply because my ears could not hear wave-dashing at that distance. Yet every bit of spray was sounding in my ears.

The subject brings to mind a few recollections of the winds I heard in my late journey. In my walk from Indiana to the Gulf, earth and sky, plants and people, and all things changeable were constantly changing. Even in Kentucky nature and art have many a characteristic shibboleth. The people differ in language and in customs. Their architecture is generically different from that of their immediate neighbours in the north, not only in planters' mansions, but in barns and granaries and the cabins of the poor. But thousands of familiar flower faces looked from every hill and valley. I noted no difference in the sky, and the winds spoke the same things. I did not feel myself in a strange land.

In Tennessee my eyes rested upon the first mountain scenery I ever beheld. I was rising higher than ever before; strange trees were beginning to appear; alpine flowers and shrubs were meeting me at every step. But these Cumberland Mountains were timbered with oak, and were not unlike Wisconsin hills piled upon each other, and the strange plants were like those that were not strange. The sky was changed only a little, and the winds not by a single detectible note. Therefore, neither was Tennessee a strange land.

But soon came changes thick and fast. After passing the mountainous corner of North Carolina and a little way into Georgia, I beheld from one of the last ridge-summits of the Alleghanies that vast, smooth, sandy slope that reaches from the mountains to the sea. It is wooded with dark, branchy pines which were all strangers to me. Here the grasses, which are an earth-covering at the north, grow wide apart in tall clumps and tufts like saplings. My known flower companions were leaving me now, not one by one as in Kentucky and Tennessee, but in whole tribes and genera, and companies of shining strangers came trooping upon me in countless ranks. The sky, too, was changed, and I could detect strange sounds in the winds. Now I began to feel myself 'a stranger in a strange land.'

But in Florida came the greatest change of all, for here grows the palmetto, and here blow the winds so strangely toned by them. These palms and these winds severed the last strands of the cord that united me with home. Now I was a stranger, indeed. I was delighted, astonished, confounded, and gazed in wonderment blank and overwhelming as if I had fallen upon another star. But in all of this long, complex series of changes, one of the greatest, and the last of all, was the change I found in the tone and language of the winds. They no longer came with the old home music gathered from open prairies and waving fields of oak, but they passed over many a strange string. The leaves of magnolia, smooth like polished steel, the immense inverted forests of tillandsia banks, and the princely crowns of palms – upon these the winds made strange music, and at the coming-on of night had overwhelming power to present the distance from friends and home, and the completeness of my isolation from all things familiar.

Elsewhere I have already noted that when I was a day's journey from the Gulf, a wind blew upon me from the sea – the first sea breeze that had touched me in twenty years. I was plodding along with my satchel and plants, leaning wearily forward, a little sore from approaching fever, when suddenly I felt the salt air, and before I had time to think, a whole flood of long-dormant associations rolled in upon me. The Firth of Forth, the Bass Rock, Dunbar Castle, and the winds and rocks and hills came upon the wings of that wind, and stood in as clear and sudden light as a landscape flashed upon the view by a blaze of lightning in a dark night.

I like to cling to a small chip of a ship like ours when the sea is rough, and long, comet-tailed streamers are blowing from the curled top of every wave. A big vessel responds awkwardly with mixed gestures to several waves at once, lumbering along like a loose floating island. But our little schooner, buoyant as a gull, glides up one side and down the other of each wave hill in delightful rhythm. As we advanced the scenery increased in grandeur and beauty. The waves heaved higher and grew wider, with corresponding motion. It was delightful to ride over this unsullied country of ever-changing water, and when looking upward from the shallow vales, or abroad over the round expanse from the tops of the wave hills, I almost forgot at times that the glassy, treeless country was forbidden to walkers. How delightful it would be to ramble over it on foot, enjoying the transparent crystal ground, and the music of its rising and falling hillocks, unmarred by the ropes and spars of a ship; to study the plants of these waving plains and their stream-currents; to sleep in wild weather in a bed of phosphorescent wave-foam, or briny scented seaweeds; to see the fishes by night in pathways of phosphorescent light; to walk the glassy plain in calm, with birds and flocks of glittering flying fishes here and there, or by night with every star pictured in its bosom!

But even of the land only a small portion is free to man, and if he, among other journeys on forbidden paths, ventures among the ice lands and hot lands, or up in the air in balloon bubbles, or on the ocean in ships, or down into it a little way in smothering diving-bells – in all such small adventures man is admonished and often punished in ways which clearly show him that he is in places for which, to use an approved phrase, he was never designed. However, in view of the rapid advancement of our time, no one can tell how far our star may finally be subdued to man's will. At all events I enjoyed this drifting locomotion to some extent.

The tar-scented community of a ship is a study in itself – a despotism on the small territory of a few drifting planks pinned together. But as our crew consisted only of four sailors, a mate, and the captain, there were no signs of despotism. We all dined at one table, enjoying our fine store of salt mackerel and plum duff, with endless abundance of oranges. Not only was the hold of our little ship filled with loose, unboxed oranges, but the deck also was filled up level with the rails, and we had to walk over the top of the golden fruit on boards.

Flocks of flying fishes often flew acros the ship, one or two occasionally falling among the oranges. These the sailors were glad to capture to sell in New York as curiosities, or to give away to friends. But the captain had a large Newfoundland dog who got the largest share of these unfortunate fishes. He used to jump from a dozing sleep as soon as he heard the fluttering of their wings, then pounce and feast leisurely on them before the sailors could reach the spot where they fell.

In passing through the Straits of Florida the winds died away and the sea was smoothed to unruffled calm. The water here is very transparent and of delightfully pure pale-blue colour, as different from ordinary dull-coloured water as town smoke from mountain air. I could see the bottom as distinctly as one sees the ground when riding over it. It seemed strange that our ship should be upborne in such an ethereal liquid as this, and that we did not run aground where the bottom seemed so near.

One morning, while among the Bahama dots of islands, we had calm sky and calm sea. The sun had risen in cloudless glory, when I observed a large flock of flying fish, a short distance from us, closely pursued by a dolphin. These fish-swallows rose in pretty good order, skimmed swiftly ahead for fifty or a hundred yards in a low arc, then dipped below the surface. Dripping and sparkling, they rose again in a few seconds and glanced back into the lucid brine with wonderful speed, but without apparent terror.

At length the dolphin, gaining on the flock, dashed into the midst of them, and now all order was at an end. They rose in scattering disorder, in all directions, like a flock of birds charged by a hawk. The pursuing dolphin also leaped into the air, showing his splendid colours and wonderful speed. After the first scattering flight all steady pursuit was useless, and the dolphin had but to pounce about in the broken mob of its weary prey until satisfied with his meal.

We are apt to look out on the great ocean and regard it as but a half-blank part of our globe – a sort of desert, 'a waste of water.' But, land animals though we be, land is about as unknown to us as the sea, for the turbid glances we gain of the ocean in general through commercial eyes are comparatively worthless. Now that science is making comprehensive surveys of the life of the sea, and the forms of its basins, and similar surveys are being made into the land deserts, hot and cold, we may at length discover that the sea is as full of life as the land. None can tell how far man's knowledge may yet reach.

After passing the Straits and sailing up the coast, when about opposite the south end of the Carolina coast, we had stiff head winds all the way to New York and our able little vessel was drenched all day long. Of course our load of oranges suffered, and since they were boarded over level with the rail, we had difficulty in walking and had many chances of being washed overboard. The flying fishes of Cape Hatteras appeared to take pleasure in shooting across from wave-top to wave-top. They avoided the ship during the day, but frequently fell among the oranges at night. The sailors caught many, but our big Newfoundland dog jumped for them faster than the sailors, and so almost monopolised the game.

When dark night fell on the stormy sea, the breaking waves of phosphorescent light were a glorious sight. On such nights I stood on the bowsprit holding on by a rope for hours in order to enjoy this phenomenon. How wonderful this light is! Developed in the sea by myriads of organised beings, it gloriously illuminates the pathways of the fishes, and every breaking wave, and in some places glows over large areas like sheet lightning. We sailed through large fields of seaweed, of which I procured specimens. I thoroughly enjoyed life in this novel little tar-and-oakum home, and, as the end of our voyage drew nigh, I was sorry at the thought of leaving it.

We were now, on the twelfth day, approaching New York, the big ship metropolis. We were in sight of the coast all day. The leafless trees and the snow appeared wonderfully strange. It was now about the end of February and snow covered the ground nearly to the water's edge. Arriving, as we did, in this rough winter weather from the intense heat and general tropical luxuriance of Cuba, the leafless, snow-white woods of New York struck us with all the novelty and impressiveness of a new world. A frosty blast was sweeping seaward from Sandy Hook. The sailors explored their wardrobes for their long-cast-off woollens, and pulled the ropes and managed the sails while muffled in clothing to the rotundity of Eskimos. For myself, long burdened with fever, the frosty wind, as it sifted through my loosened bones, was more delicious and grateful than ever was a spring-scented breeze.

We now had plenty of company; fleets of vessels were on the wing from all countries. Our taut little racer outwinded without exception all who, like her, were going to the port. Toward evening we were grinding and wedging our way through the ice-field of the river delta, which we passed with difficulty. Arrived in port at nine o'clock. The ship was deposited, like a cart at market, in a proper slip, and next morning we and our load of oranges, one third rotten, were landed. Thus all the purposes of our voyage were accomplished.

On our arrival the captain, knowing something of the lightness of my purse, told me that I could continue to occupy my bed on the ship until I sailed for California, getting my meals at a near-by restaurant. 'This is the way we are all doing,' he said. Consulting the newspapers, I found that the first ship, the Nebraska, sailed for Aspinwall in about ten days, and that the steerage passage to San Francisco by way of the Isthmus was only forty dollars.

In the meantime I wandered about the city without knowing a single person in it. My walks extended but little beyond the sight of my little schooner home. I saw the name Central Park on some of the street-cars and thought I would like to visit it, but, fearing that I might not be able to find my way back, I dared not make the adventure. I felt completely lost in the vast throngs of people, the noise of the streets, and the immense size of the buildings. Often I thought I would like to explore the city if, like a lot of wild hills and valleys, it was clear of inhabitants.

The day before the sailing of the Panama ship I bought a pocket map of California and allowed myself to be persuaded to buy a dozen large maps, mounted on rollers, with a map of the world on one side and the United States on the other. In vain I said I had no use for them. 'But surely you want to make money in California, don't you? Everything out there is very dear. We'll sell you a dozen of these fine maps for two dollars each and you can easily sell them in California for ten dollars apiece.' I foolishly allowed myself to be persuaded. The maps made a very large, awkward bundle, but fortunately it was the only baggage I had except my little plant press and a small bag. I laid them in my berth in the steerage, for they were too large to be stolen and concealed.

There was a savage contrast between life in the steerage and my fine home on the little ship fruiter. Never before had I seen such a barbarous mob, especially at meals. Arrived at Aspinwall–Colon, we had half a day to ramble about before starting across the Isthmus. Never shall I forget the glorious flora, especially for the first fifteen or twenty miles along the Chagres River. The riotous exuberance of great forest trees, glowing in purple, red, and yellow flowers, far surpassed anything I had ever seen, especially of flowering trees, either in Florida or Cuba. I gazed from the car-platform enchanted. I fairly cried for joy and hoped that sometime I should be able to return and enjoy and study this most glorious of forests to my heart's content. We reached San Fransisco about the first of April, and I remained there only one day, before starting for Yosemite Valley.[1]

I followed the Diablo foothills along the San José Valley to Gilroy, thence over the Diablo Mountains to the valley of the San Joaquin by the Pacheco Pass, thence down the valley opposite the mouth of the Merced River, thence across the San Joaquin, and up into the Sierra Nevada to the mammoth trees of Mariposa, and the glorious Yosemite, and thence down the Merced to this place.[2] The goodness of the weather as I journeyed toward Pacheco was beyond all praise and description – fragrant, mellow, and bright. The sky was perfectly delicious, sweet enough for the breath of angels; every draught of it gave a separate and distinct piece of pleasure. I do not believe that Adam and Eve ever tasted better in their balmiest nook.

The last of the Coast Range foothills were in near view all the way to Gilroy. Their union with the valley is by curves and slopes of inimitable beauty. They were robed with the greenest grass and richest light I ever beheld, and were coloured and shaded with myriads of flowers of every hue, chiefly of purple and golden yellow. Hundreds of crystal rills joined song with the larks, filling all the valley with music like a sea, making it Eden from end to end.

The scenery, too, and all of nature in the Pass is fairly enchanting. Strange

[1] At this point the journal ends. The remainder of this chapter is taken from a letter written to Mrs Ezra S. Carr from the neighbourhood of Twenty Hill Hollow in July, 1868.
[2] Near Snelling, Merced County, California.

and beautiful mountain ferns are there, low in the dark canyons and high upon the rocky sunlit peaks; banks of blooming shrubs, and sprinklings and gatherings of garment flowers, precious and pure as ever enjoyed the sweets of a mountain home. And oh! what streams are there! beaming, glancing, each with music of its own, singing as they go, in shadow and light, onward upon their lovely, changing pathways to the sea. And hills rise over hills, and mountains over mountains, heaving, waving, swelling, in most glorious, over-powering, unreadable majesty.

When at last, stricken and faint like a crushed insect, you hope to escape from all the terrible grandeur of these mountain powers, other fountains, other oceans break forth before you; for there, in clear view, over heaps and rows of foothills, is laid a grand, smooth, outspread plain, watered by a river, and another range of peaky, snow-capped mountains a hundred miles in the distance. That plain is the valley of the San Joaquin, and those mountains are the great Sierra Nevada. The valley of the San Joaquin is the floweriest piece of world I ever walked, one vast, level, even flower-bed, a sheet of flowers, a smooth sea, ruffled a little in the middle by the tree fringing of the river and of smaller cross-streams here and there, from the mountains.

Florida is indeed a 'land of flowers,' but for every flower creature that dwells in its most delightsome places more than a hundred are living here. Here, here is Florida! Here they are not sprinkled apart with grass between as on our prairies, but grasses are sprinkled among the flowers; not as in Cuba, flowers piled upon flowers, heaped and gathered into deep, glowing masses, but side by side, flower to flower, petal to petal, touching but not entwined, branches weaving past and past each other, yet free and separate – one smooth garment, mosses next the ground, grasses above, petalled flowers between.

Before studying the flowers of this valley and their sky, and all of the furniture and sounds and adornments of their home, one can scarce believe that their vast assemblies are permanent; but rather that, actuated by some plant purpose, they had convened from every plain and mountain and meadow of their kingdom, and that the different colouring of patches, acres, and miles marks the bounds of the various tribes and family encampments.

CHAPTER NINE

Twenty Hill Hollow[1]

WERE WE to cross-cut the Sierra Nevada into blocks a dozen miles or so in thickness, each section would contain a Yosemite Valley and a river, together with a bright array of lakes and meadows, rocks and forests. The grandeur and inexhaustible beauty of each block would be so vast and over-satisfying

---

[1] This is the hub of the region where Mr Muir spent the greater part of the summer of 1868 and the spring of 1869.

that to choose among them would be like selecting slices of bread cut from the same loaf. One bread-slice might have burnt spots, answering to craters; another would be more browned; another, more crusted or raggedly cut; but all essentially the same. In no greater degree would the Sierra slices differ in general character. Nevertheless, we all would choose the Merced slice, because, being easier of access, it has been nibbled and tasted, and pronounced very good; and because of the concentrated form of its Yosemite, caused by certain conditions of baking, yeasting, and glacier-frosting of this portion of the great Sierra loaf. In like manner, we readily perceive that the great central plain is one batch of bread – one golden cake – and we are loath to leave these magnificent loaves for crumbs, however good.

After our smoky sky has been washed in the rains of winter, the whole complex row of Sierras appears from the plain as a simple wall, slightly bevelled, and coloured in horizontal bands laid one above another, as if entirely composed of partially straightened rainbows. So, also, the plain seen from the mountains has the same simplicity of smooth surface, coloured purple, and yellow, like a patchwork of irised clouds. But when we descend to this smooth-furred sheet, we discover complexity in its physical conditions equal to that of the mountains, though less strongly marked. In particular, that portion of the plain lying between the Merced and the Tuolumne, within ten miles of the slaty foothills, is most elaborately carved into valleys, hollows, and smooth undulations, and among them is laid the Merced Yosemite of the plain – Twenty Hill Hollow.

This delightful Hollow is less than a mile in length, and of just sufficient width to form a well-proportioned oval. It is situated about midway between the two rivers, and five miles from the Sierra foothills. Its banks are formed of twenty hemispherical hills; hence its name. They surround and enclose it on all sides, leaving only one narrow opening toward the southwest for the escape of its waters. The bottom of the Hollow is about two hundred feet below the level of the surrounding plain, and the tops of its hills are slightly below the general level. Here is no towering dome, no Tissiack, to mark its place; and one may ramble close upon its rim before he is made aware of its existence. Its twenty hills are as wonderfully regular in size and position as in form. They are like big marbles half buried in the ground, each poised and settled daintily into its place at a regular distance from its fellows, making a charming fairy-land of hills, with small, grassy valleys between, each valley having a tiny stream of its own, which leaps and sparkles out into the open hollow, uniting to form Hollow Creek.

Like all others in the immediate neighbourhood, these twenty hills are composed of stratified lavas mixed with mountain drift in varying proportions. Some strata are almost wholly made up of volcanic matter – lava and cinders – thoroughly ground and mixed by the waters that deposited them; others are largely composed of slate and quartz boulders of all degrees of coarseness, forming conglomerates. A few clear, open sections occur, exposing an elaborate history of seas, and glaciers, and volcanic floods – chapters of cinders and ashes that picture dark days when these bright snowy mountains were clouded in smoke and rivered and laked with living fire. A fearful age, say mortals, when these Sierras flowed lava to the sea. What horizons of flame! What atmospheres of ashes and smoke!

The conglomerates and lavas of this region are readily denuded by water. In the time when their parent sea was removed to form this golden plain, their regular surface, in great part covered with shallow lakes, showed little variation from motionless level until torrents of rain and floods from the mountains gradually sculptured the simple page to the present diversity of bank and brae, creating, in the section between the Merced and the Tuolumne, Twenty Hill Hollow, Lily Hollow, and the lovely valleys of Cascade and Castle Creeks, with many others nameless and unknown, seen only by hunters and shepherds, sunk in the wide bosom of the plain, like undiscovered gold. Twenty Hill Hollow is a fine illustration of a valley created by erosion of water. Here are no Washington columns, no angular El Capitans. The hollow canyons, cut in soft lavas, are not so deep as to require a single earthquake at the hands of science, much less a baker's dozen of those convenient tools demanded for the making of mountain Yosemites, and our moderate arithmetical standards are not outraged by a single magnitude of this simple, comprehensible hollow.

The present rate of denudation of this portion of the plain seems to be about one tenth of an inch per year. This approximation is based upon observations made upon stream-banks and perennial plants. Rains and winds remove mountains without disturbing their plant or animal inhabitants. Hovering petrels, the fishes and floating plants of ocean, sink and rise in beautiful rhythm with its waves; and, in like manner, the birds and plants of the plain sink and rise with these waves of land, the only difference being that the fluctuations are more rapid in the one case than in the other.

In March and April the bottom of the Hollow and every one of its hills are smoothly covered and plushed with yellow and purple flowers, the yellow predominating. They are mostly social *Compositæ*, with a few claytonias, gilias, eschscholtzias, white and yellow violets, blue and yellow lilies, dodecatheons, and eriogonums set in a half-floating maze of purple grasses. There is but one vine in the Hollow – the *Megarrhiza (Echinocystis* T. & D.) or 'Big Root.' The only bush within a mile of it, about four feet in height, forms so remarkable an object upon the universal smoothness that my dog barks furiously around it, at a cautious distance, as if it were a bear. Some of the hills have rock ribs that are brightly coloured with red and yellow lichens, and in moist nooks there are luxuriant mosses – *Bartramia, Dicranum, Funaria,* and several *Hypnums.* In cool, sunless coves the mosses are companioned with ferns – a *Cystopteris* and the little gold-dusted rock fern, *Gymnogramma triangularis.*

The Hollow is not rich in birds. The meadowlark homes there, and the little burrowing owl, the killdeer, and a species of sparrow. Occasionally a few ducks pay a visit to its waters, a few tall herons – the blue and the white – may at times be seen stalking along the creek; and the sparrow hawk and grey eagle[1] come to hunt. The lark, who does nearly all the singing for the Hollow,

---

[1] Mr Muir doubtless meant the golden eagle (*Aquila chrysaëtos*).

is not identical in species with the meadowlark of the East, though closely resembling it; richer flowers and skies have inspired him with a better song than was ever known to the Atlantic lark.

I have noted three distinct lark-songs here. The words of the first, which I committed to memory at one of their special meetings, spelled as sung are, 'Wee-ro spee-ro wee-o weer-ly wee-it.' On the 20th of January, 1869, they sang 'Queed-lix boodle,' repeating it with great regularity, for hours together, to music sweet as the sky that gave it. On the 22nd of the same month, they sang 'Chee chool chee-dildy choodildy.' An inspiration is this song of the blessed lark, and universally absorbable by human souls. It seems to be the only bird-song of these hills that has been created with any direct reference to us. Music is one of the attributes of matter, into whatever forms it may be organized. Drops and sprays of air are specialized, and made to plash and churn in the bosom of a lark, as infinitesimal portions of air plash and sing about the angles and hollows of sand-grains, as perfectly composed and predestined as the rejoicing anthems of worlds; but our senses are not fine enough to catch the tones. Fancy the waving, pulsing melody of the vast flower-congregations of the Hollow flowing from myriad voices of tuned petal and pistil, and heaps of sculptured pollen. Scarce one note is for us; nevertheless, God be thanked for this blessed instrument hid beneath the feathers of a lark.

The eagle does not dwell in the Hollow; he only floats there to hunt the long-eared hare. One day I saw a fine specimen alight upon a hillside. I was at first puzzled to know what power could fetch the sky-king down into the grass with the larks. Watching him attentively, I soon discovered the cause of his earthiness. He was hungry and stood watching a long-eared hare, which stood erect at the door of his burrow, staring his winged fellow mortal full in the face. They were about ten feet apart. Should the eagle attempt to snatch the hare, he would instantly disappear in the ground. Should long-ears, tired of inaction, venture to skim the hill to some neighbouring burrow, the eagle would swoop above him and strike him dead with a blow of his pinions, bear him to some favourite rock table, satisfy his hunger, wipe off all marks of grossness, and go again to the sky.

Since antelopes have been driven away, the hare is the swiftest animal of the Hollow. When chased by a dog he will not seek a burrow, as when the eagle wings in sight, but skims wavily from hill to hill across connecting curves, swift and effortless as a bird-shadow. One that I measured was twelve inches in height at the shoulders. His body was eighteen inches, from nose-tip to tail. His great ears measured six and a half inches in length and two in width. His ears – which, notwithstanding their great size, he wears gracefully and becomingly, have procured for him the homely nickname, by which he is commonly known, of 'Jackass rabbit.' Hares are very abundant over all the plain and up in the sunny, lightly wooded foothills, but their range does not extend into the close pine forests.

Coyotes, or California wolves, are occasionally seen gliding about the Hollow, but they are not numerous, vast numbers having been slain by the traps and poisons of sheep-raisers. The coyote is about the size of a small shepherd-dog, beautiful and graceful in motion, with erect ears, and a bushy tail, like a fox. Inasmuch as he is fond of mutton, he is cordially detested by 'sheep-men' and nearly all cultured people.

The ground-squirrel is the most common animal of the Hollow. In several hills there is a soft stratum in which they have tunnelled their homes. It is interesting to observe these rodent towns in time of alarm. Their one circular street resounds with sharp, lancing outcries of 'Seekit, seek, seek, seekit!' Near neighbours, peeping cautiously half out of doors, engage in low, purring chat. Others, bolt upright on the doorsill or on the rock above, shout excitedly as if calling attention to the motions and aspects of the enemy. Like the wolf, this little animal is accursed, because of his relish for grain. What a pity that Nature should have made so many small mouths palated like our own!

All the seasons of the Hollow are warm and bright, and flowers bloom through the whole year. But the grand commencement of the annual genesis of plant and insect life is governed by the setting-in of the rains, in December or January. The air, hot and opaque, is then washed and cooled. Plant seeds, which for six months have lain on the ground dry as if garnered in a farmer's bin, at once unfold their treasured life. Flies hum their delicate tunes. Butter-flies come from their coffins, like cotyledons from their husks. The network of dry water-courses, spread over valleys and hollows, suddenly gushes with bright waters, sparkling and pouring from pool to pool, like dusty mummies risen from the dead and set living and laughing with colour and blood. The weather grows in beauty, like a flower. Its roots in the ground develop day-clusters a week or two in size, divided by and shaded in foliage of clouds; or round hours of ripe sunshine wave and spray in sky-shadows, like racemes of berries half hidden in leaves.

These months of so-called rainy season are not filled with rain. Nowhere else in North America, perhaps in the world, are Januarys so balmed and glowed with vital sunlight. Referring to my notes of 1868 and 1869, I find that the first heavy general rain of the season fell on the 18th of December. January yielded to the Hollow, during the day, only twenty hours of rain, which was divided among six rainy days. February had only three days on which rain fell, amounting to eighteen and one-half hours in all. March had five rainy days. April had three, yielding seven hours of rain. May also had three wet days, yielding nine hours of rain, and completed the so-called 'rainy season' for that year, which is probably about an average one. It must be remembered that this rain record has nothing to do with what fell in the night.

The ordinary rainstorm of this region has little of that outward pomp and sublimity of structure so characteristic of the storms of the Mississippi Valley. Nevertheless, we have experienced rainstorms out on these treeless plains, in nights of solid darkness, as impressively sublime as the noblest storms of the mountains. The wind, which in settled weather blows from the northwest, veers to the southeast; the sky curdles gradually and evenly to a grainless, seamless, homogeneous cloud; and then comes the rain, pouring steadily and often driven aslant by strong winds. In 1869, more than three fourths of the winter rains came from the southeast. One magnificent storm from the northwest occurred on the 21st of March; an immense, round-browed cloud came sailing over the flowery hills in most imposing majesty, bestowing water as from a sea. The passionate rain-gush lasted only about one minute, but was nevertheless the most magnificent cataract of the sky mountains that I ever beheld. A portion of calm sky toward the Sierras was brushed with thin, white cloud-tissue, upon which the rain-torrent showed to a great height – a cloud waterfall, which, like those of Yosemite, was neither spray, rain, nor solid water. In the same year the cloudiness of January, omitting rainy days, averaged 0.32; February, 0.13; March, 0.20; April, 0.10; May, 0.08. The greater portion of this cloudiness was gathered into a few days, leaving the others blocks of solid, universal sunshine in every chink and pore.

At the end of January, four plants were in flower: a small white cress, growing in large patches, a low-set, umbelled plant, with yellow flowers; an eriogonum, with flowers in leafless spangles; and a small boragewort. Five or six mosses had adjusted their hoods, and were in the prime of life. In February, squirrels, hares, and flowers were in springtime joy. Bright plant-constellations shone everywhere about the Hollow. Ants were getting ready for work, rubbing and sunning their limbs upon the husk-piles around their doors; fat, pollen-dusted, 'burly, dozing humble-bees' were rumbling among the flowers; and spiders were busy mending up old webs, or weaving new ones. Flowers were born every day, and came gushing from the ground like gaily dressed children from a church. The bright air became daily more songful with fly-wings, and sweeter with breath of plants.

In March, plant-life is more than doubled. The little pioneer cress, by this time, goes to seed, wearing daintily embroidered silicles. Several claytonias appear; also, a large white leptosiphon(?), and two nemophilas. A small plantago becomes tall enough to wave and show silky ripples of shade. Towards the end of this month or the beginning of April, plant-life is at its greatest height. Few have any just conception of its amazing richness. Count the flowers of any portion of these twenty hills, or of the bottom of the Hollow, among the streams: you will find that there are from one to ten thousand upon every square yard, counting the heads of *Compositæ* as single flowers. Yellow *Compositæ* form by far the greater portion of this goldy-way. Well may the sun feed them with his richest light, for these shining sunlets are his very children – rays of his ray, beams of his beam! One would fancy that these California days receive more gold from the ground than they give to it. The earth has indeed become a sky; and the two cloudless skies, raying toward each other flower-beams and sunbeams, are fused and congolded into one glowing heaven. By the end of April most of the Hollow plants have ripened their seeds and died; but, undecayed, still assist the landscape with colour from persistent involucres and corolla-like heads of chaffy scales.

In May, only a few deep-set lilies and eriogonums are left alive. June, July, August, and September are the season of plant rest, followed, in October, by a most extraordinary outgush of plant-life, at the very driest time of the whole year. A small, unobtrusive plant, *Hemizonia virgata,* from six inches to three feet in height, with pale, glandular leaves, suddenly bursts into bloom, in patches miles in extent, like a resurrection of the gold of April. I have counted upward of three thousand heads upon one plant. Both leaves and pedicles are so small as to be nearly invisible among so vast a number of daisy golden-heads that seem to keep their places unsupported, like stars in the sky. The heads are about five eighths of an inch in diameter; rays and disk-flowers, yellow; stamens, purple. The rays have a rich, furred appearance, like the petals of garden pansies. The prevailing summer wind makes all the heads turn to the southeast. The waxy secretion of its leaves and involucres has suggested its grim name of 'tarweed', by which it is generally known. In our estimation, it is the most delightful member of the whole Composite Family of the plain. It remains in flower until November, uniting with an eriogonum that continues the floral chain across December to the spring plants of January. Thus, although nearly all of the year's plant-life is crowded into February, March, and April, the flower circle around the Twenty Hill Hollow is never broken.

The Hollow may easily be visited by tourists *en route* for Yosemite, as it is distant only about six miles from Snelling's. It is at all seasons interesting to the naturalist; but it has little that would interest the majority of tourists earlier than January or later than April. If you wish to see how much of light, life, and joy can be got into a January, go to this blessed Hollow. If you wish to see a plant-resurrection – myriads of bright flowers crowding from the ground, like souls to a judgment – go to Twenty Hills in February. If you are travelling for health, play truant to doctors and friends, fill your pocket with biscuits, and hide in the hills of the Hollow, lave in its waters, tan in its golds, bask in its flower-shine, and your baptisms will make you a new creature indeed. Or, choked in the sediments of society, so tired of the world, here will your hard doubts disappear, your carnal incrustations melt off, and your soul breathe deep and free in God's shoreless atmosphere of beauty and love.

Never shall I forget my baptism in this font. It happened in January, a resurrection day for many a plant and for me. I suddenly found myself on one of its hills; the Hollow overflowed with light, as a fountain, and only small, sunless nooks were kept for mosseries and ferneries. Hollow Creek spangled and mazed like a river. The ground steamed with fragrance. Light, of unspeakable richness, was brooding the flowers. Truly, said I, is California the Golden State – in metallic gold, in sun gold, and in plant gold. The sunshine for a whole summer seemed condensed into the chambers of that one glowing day. Every trace of dimness had been washed from the sky; the mountains were dusted and wiped clean with clouds – Pacheco Peak and Mount Diablo, and the waved blue wall between; the grand Sierra stood along the plain, coloured in four horizontal bands: – the lowest, rose purple; the next higher, dark purple; the next, blue; and, above all, the white rows of summits pointing to the heavens.

It may be asked, What have mountains fifty or a hundred miles away to do with Twenty Hill Hollow? To lovers of the wild, these mountains are not a hundred miles away. Their spiritual power and the goodness of the sky make them near, as a circle of friends. They rise as a portion of the hilled walls of the Hollow. You cannot feel yourself out of doors; plain, sky, and mountains ray beauty which you feel. You bathe in these spirit-beams, turning round and round, as if warming at a camp-fire. Presently you lose consciousness of your own separate existence: you blend with the landscape, and become part and parcel of nature.

MY FIRST SUMMER IN THE SIERRA

My First Summer in the Sierra

First published by Houghton Mifflin Co., Boston and Constable, London, 1911

Contents

YOUNG SUGAR PINE BEGINNING TO BEAR CONES.

CHAPTER ONE

Through the Foothills with a Flock of Sheep

IN THE great Central Valley of California there are only two seasons – spring and summer. The spring begins with the first rain-storm, which usually falls in November. In a few months the wonderful flowery vegetation is in full bloom and by the end of May it is dead and dry and crisp, as if every plant had been roasted in an oven.

Then the lolling, panting flocks and herds are driven to the high, cool, green pastures of the Sierra. I was longing for the mountains about this time, but money was scarce and I couldn't see how a bread supply was to be kept up. While I was anxiously brooding on the bread problem, so troublesome to wanderers, and trying to believe I might learn to live like the wild animals, gleaning nourishment here and there from seeds and berries, sauntering and climbing in joyful independence of money or baggage, Mr Delaney, a sheep-owner, for whom I had worked a few weeks, called on me and offered to engage me to go with his shepherd and flock to the headwaters of the Merced and Tuolumne Rivers – the very region I had most in mind. I was in the mood to accept work of any kind that would take me into the mountains whose treasures I had tasted last summer in the Yosemite region. The flock, he explained, would be moved gradually higher through the successive forest belts as the snow melted, stopping for a few weeks at the best places we came to. These I thought would be good centres of observation from which I might be able to make many telling excursions within a radius of eight or ten miles of the camps to learn something of the plants, animals and rocks; for he assured me that I should be left perfectly free to follow my studies. I judged, however, that I was in no way the right man for the place, and freely explained my shortcomings, confessing that I was wholly unacquainted with the topography of the upper mountains, the streams that would have to be crossed, and the wild sheep-eating animals; in short that, what with bears, coyotes, rivers, canyons and thorny, bewildering chaparral, I feared that half or more of his flock would be lost. Fortunately these shortcomings seemed insignificant to Mr Delaney. The main thing he said, was to have a man about the camp whom he could trust to see that the shepherd did his duty, and he assured me that the difficulties that seemed so formidable at a distance would vanish as we went on; encouraging me further by saying that the shepherd would do all the herding, that I could study plants and rocks and scenery as much as I liked, and that he would himself accompany us to the first main camp and make occasional visits to our higher ones to replenish our store of provisions and see how we prospered. Therefore I concluded to go, though still fearing, when I saw the silly sheep bouncing one by one through the narrow gate of the home corral to be counted, that of the two thousand and fifty many would never return.

I was fortunate in getting a fine St Bernard dog for a companion. His master, a hunter with whom I was slightly acquainted, came to me as soon as he heard that I was going to spend the summer in the Sierra and begged me to take his favourite dog, Carlo, with me, for he feared that if he were compelled to stay all summer on the plains the fierce heat might be the death of him. 'I think I can trust you to be kind to him,' he said, 'and I am sure he will be good to you. He knows all about the mountain animals, will guard the camp, assist in managing the sheep and in every way be found able and faithful.' Carlo knew we were talking about him, watched our faces and listened so attentively that I fancied he understood us. Calling him by name, I asked him if he was willing to go with me. He looked me in the face with eyes expressing wonderful intelligence, then turned to his master, and after permission was given by a wave of the hand toward me and a farewell patting caress, he quietly followed me as if he perfectly understood all that had been said and had known me always.

3 June 1869. This morning provisions, camp-kettles, blankets, plant press etc., were packed on two horses, the flock headed for the tawny foothills, and away we sauntered in a cloud of dust: Mr Delaney, bony and tall, with sharply hacked profile like Don Quixote, leading the packhorses, Billy the proud shepherd, a Chinaman and a Digger Indian to assist in driving for the first few days in the brushy foothills, and myself with notebook tied to my belt.

The home ranch from which we set out is on the south side of the Tuolumne River near French Bar, where the foothills of metamorphic gold-bearing slates dip below the stratified deposits of the Central Valley. We had not gone more than a mile before some of the old leaders of the flock showed by the eager, inquiring way they ran and looked ahead that they were thinking of the high pastures they had enjoyed last summer. Soon the whole flock seemed to be hopefully excited, the mothers calling their lambs, the lambs replying in tones wonderfully human, their fondly quavering calls interrupted now and then by hastily snatched mouthfuls of withered grass. Amid all this seeming babel of baas as they streamed over the hills every mother and child recognised each other's voice. In case a tired lamb, half asleep in the smothering dust, should fail to answer, its mother would come running back through the flock toward the spot whence its last response was heard, and refused to be comforted until she found it, the one of a thousand, though to our eyes and ears all seemed alike.

The flock travelled at the rate of about a mile an hour, outspread in the form of an irregular triangle, about a hundred yards wide at the base and a hundred and fifty yards long, with a crooked, ever changing point made up of the strongest foragers, called the 'leaders,' which, with the most active of those scattered along the ragged sides of the 'main body,' hastily explored nooks in the rocks and bushes for grass and leaves; the lambs and feeble old mothers dawdling in the rear were called the 'tail end'.

About noon the heat was hard to bear; the poor sheep panted pitifully and tried to stop in the shade of every tree they came to, while we gazed with eager longing through the dim burning glare toward the snowy mountains and streams, though not one was in sight. The landscape is only wavering foothills roughened here and there with bushes and trees and outcropping masses of slate. The trees, mostly the blue oak (*Quercus Douglasii*), are about thirty to forty feet high with pale blue-green leaves and white bark, sparsely planted on the thinnest soil or in crevices of rocks beyond the reach of grass fires. The slates in many places rise abruptly through the tawny grass in sharp lichen-covered slabs like tombstones in deserted burying grounds. With the exception of the oak and four or five species of manzanita and ceanothus, the vegetation of the foothills is mostly the same as that of the plains. I saw this region in the early spring, when it was a charming landscape garden full of birds and bees and flowers. Now the scorching weather makes everything dreary. The ground is full of cracks, lizards glide about on the rocks and ants in amazing numbers, whose tiny sparks of life only burn the brighter with the heat, fairly quiver with unquenchable energy as they run in long lines to fight and gather food. How it comes that they do not dry to a crisp in a few seconds exposure to such sun-fire is marvellous. A few rattlesnakes lie coiled in out of the way places, but are seldom seen. Magpies and crows, usually so noisy, are silent now, standing in mixed flocks on the ground beneath the best shade trees, with bills wide open and wings drooped, too breathless to speak; the quails also are trying to keep in the shade about the few tepid alkaline waterholes; cottontail rabbits are running from shade to shade among the ceanothus brush and occasionally the long-eared hare is seen cantering gracefully across the wider openings.

After a short noon rest in a grove, the poor dust-choked flock was again driven ahead over the brushy hills, but the dim roadway we had been following faded away just where it was most needed, compelling us to stop to look about us and get our bearings. The Chinaman seemed to think we were lost, and chattered in pidgin English concerning the abundance of 'litty stick' (chaparral), while the Indian silently scanned the billowy ridges and gulches for openings. Pushing through the thorny jungle, we at length discovered a road trending toward Coulterville, which we followed until an hour before sunset, when we reached a dry ranch and camped for the night.

Camping in the foothills with a flock of sheep is simple and easy but far from pleasant. The sheep were allowed to pick what they could find in the neighbourhood until after sunset, watched by the shepherd, while the others gathered wood, made a fire, cooked, unpacked and fed the horses, etc. About dusk the weary sheep were gathered on the highest open spot near camp where they willingly bunched close together and after each mother had found her lamb and suckled it, all lay down and required no attention until morning.

Supper was announced by the call, 'Grub!' Each with a tin plate helped himself direct from the pots and pans while chatting about such camp studies as sheep-feed, mines, coyotes, bears, or adventures during the memorable gold days of pay dirt. The Indian kept in the background, saying never a word, as if he belonged to another species. The meal finished, the dogs were fed, the smokers smoked by the fire, and under the influences of fullness and tobacco the calm that settled on their faces seemed almost divine, something like the mellow meditative glow potrayed on the countenances of saints. Then suddenly, as if awakening from a dream, each with a sigh or a grunt knocked the ashes out of his pipe, yawned, gazed at the fire a few moments, said, 'Well, I believe I'll turn in,' and straightway vanished beneath his blankets. The fire smouldered and flickered an hour or two longer; the stars shone brighter; coons, coyotes and owls stirred the silence here and there, while crickets and hylas made a cheerful, continuous music, so fitting and full that it seemed a part of the very body of the night. The only discordance came from a snoring sleeper and the coughing sheep with dust in their throats. In the starlight the flock looked like a big grey blanket.

4 June. The camp was astir at daybreak; coffee, bacon and beans formed the breakfast, followed by quick dish-washing and packing. A general bleating began about sunrise. As soon as a mother ewe arose, her lamb came bounding and bunting for its breakfast and after the thousand youngsters had been suckled the flock began to nibble and spread. The restless wethers with ravenous appetites were the first to move but dared not go far from the main body. Billy and the Indian and the Chinaman kept them headed along the weary road, and allowed them to pick up what little they could find on a breadth of about a quarter of a mile. But as several flocks had already gone ahead of us, scarce a leaf, green or dry, was left; therefore the starving flock had to be hurried on over the bare, hot hills to the nearest of the green pastures, about twenty or thirty miles from here.

The pack-animals were led by Don Quixote, a heavy rifle over his shoulder intended for bears and wolves. This day has been as hot and dusty as the first, leading over gently sloping brown hills with mostly the same vegetation, excepting the strange looking Sabine pine (*Pinus Sabiniana*), which here forms small groves or is scattered among the blue oaks. The trunk divides at a height of fifteen or twenty feet into two or more stems, outleaning or nearly upright with many straggling branches and long grey needles, casting but little shade. In general appearance this tree looks more like a palm than a pine. The cones are about six or seven inches long, about five in diameter, very heavy, and last long after they fall so that the ground beneath the trees is covered with them. They make fine resiny, light giving campfires, next to ears of Indian corn the most beautiful fuel I've ever seen. The nuts, the Don tells me, are gathered in large quantities by the Digger Indians for food. They are about as large and hard-shelled as hazelnuts – food and fire fit for the gods from the same fruit.

5 June. This morning a few hours after setting out with the crawling sheep cloud, we gained the summit of the first well-defined bench on the mountain flank at Pino Blanco. The Sabine pines interest me greatly. They are so airy and strangely palm-like I was eager to sketch them and was in a fever of excitement without accomplishing much. I managed to halt long enough however to make a tolerably fair sketch of Pino Blanco peak from the southwest side, where there is a small field and vineyard irrigated by a stream that makes a pretty fall on its way down a gorge by the roadside.

After gaining the open summit of this first bench, feeling the natural exhilaration due to the slight elevation of a thousand feet or so and the hopes excited concerning the outlook to be obtained, a magnificent section of the Merced Valley at what is called Horseshoe Bend came full in sight – a glorious wilderness that seemed to be calling with a thousand songful voices. Bold, down-sweeping slopes, feathered with pines and clumps of manzanita with sunny, open spaces between them, make up most of the foreground; the middle and background present fold beyond fold of finely modelled hills and ridges rising into mountain-like masses in the distance, all covered with a shaggy growth of chaparral, mostly adenostoma, planted so marvellously close and even that it looks like soft, rich plush without a single tree or bare spot. As far as the eye can reach it extends, a heaving, swelling sea of green as regular and continuous as that produced by the heaths of Scotland. The sculpture of the landscape is as striking in its main lines as in its lavish richness of detail; a grand congregation of massive heights with the river shining between, each carved into smooth, graceful folds without leaving a single rocky angle exposed, as if the delicate fluting and ridging fashioned out of metamorphic slates had been carefully sandpapered. The whole landscape showed design, like man's noblest sculptures. How wonderful the power of its beauty! Gazing awestricken, I might have left everything for it. Glad, endless work would then be mine tracing the forces that have brought forth its features, its rocks and plants and animals and glorious weather. Beauty beyond thought everywhere, beneath, above, made and being made forever. I gazed and gazed and longed and admired until the dusty sheep and packs were far out of sight, made hurried notes and a sketch, though there was no need of either, for the colours and lines and expression of this divine landscape countenance are so burned into mind and heart they surely can never grow dim.

The evening of this charmed day is cool, calm, cloudless and full of a kind of lightning I have never seen before – white glowing cloud shaped masses down among the trees and bushes, like quick throbbing fire-flies in the Wisconsin meadows rather than the so called 'wild fire'. The spreading hairs of the horses' tails and sparks from our blankets show how highly charged the air is.

6 June. We are now on what may be called the second bench or plateau of the range, after making many small ups and downs over belts of hill waves, with of course, corresponding changes in the vegetation. In open spots many of the lowland compositae are still to be found and some of the Mariposa tulips and other conspicuous members of the lily family; but the characteristic blue oak of the foothills is left below and its place is taken by a fine large species (*Quercus Californica*) with deeply lobed deciduous leaves, picturesquely divided trunk, and broad, massy, finely lobed and modelled head. Here also at a height of about twenty five hundred feet we come to the edge of the great coniferous forest, made up mostly of yellow pine with just a few sugar pines. We are now in the mountains and they are in us, kindling enthusiasm, making every nerve quiver, filling every pore and cell of us. Our flesh and bone tabernacle seems transparent as glass to the beauty about us, as if truly an inseparable part of it, thrilling with the air and trees, streams and rocks, in the waves of the sun – a part of all nature, neither old nor young, sick nor well, but immortal. Just now I can hardly conceive of any bodily condition dependent on food or breath any more than the ground or the sky. How glorious a conversion, so complete and wholesome it is, scarce memory enough of old bondage days left as a standpoint to view it from! In this newness of life we seem to have been so always.

Through a meadow opening in the pine woods I see snowy peaks about the headwaters of the Merced above Yosemite. How near they seem and how clear their outlines on the blue air, or rather *in* the blue air; for they seem to be saturated with it. How consuming strong the invitation they extend! Shall I be allowed to go to them? Night and day I'll pray that I may, but it seems too good to be true. Someone worthy will go, able for the Godful work, yet as far as I can I must drift about these lovemonument mountains, glad to be a servant of servants in so holy a wilderness.

Found a lovely lily (*Calochortus albus*) in a shady adenostoma thicket near Coulterville, in company with *Adiantum Chilense*. It is white with a faint purplish tinge inside at the base of the petals, a most impressive plant, pure as a snow crystal, one of the plant saints that all must love and be made so much the purer by it every time it is seen. It puts the roughest mountaineer on his good behaviour. With this plant the whole world would seem rich though none other existed. It is not easy to keep on with the camp cloud while such plant people are standing preaching by the wayside.

During the afternoon we passed a fine meadow bounded by stately pines, mostly the arrowy yellow pine, with here and there a noble sugar pine, its feathery arms outspread above the spires of its companion species in marked contrast; a glorious tree, its cones fifteen to twenty inches long, swinging like tassels at the ends of the branches with superb ornamental effect. Saw some logs of this species at the Greeley Mill. They are round and regular as if turned in a lathe, excepting the butt cuts, which have a few buttressing projections. The fragrance of the sugary sap is delicious and scents the mill and lumber yard. How beautiful the ground beneath this pine thickly strewn with slender needles and grand cones and the piles of cone scales, seed-wings and shells around the instep of each tree where the squirrels have been feasting! They get the seeds by cutting off the scales at the base in regular order, following their spiral arrangement, and the two seeds at the base of each scale, a hundred or two in a cone, must make a good meal. The yellow pine cones and those of most other species and genera are held upside down on the ground by the Douglas squirrel and turned around gradually until stripped, while he sits usually with his back to a tree, probably for safety. Strange to say, he never seems to get himself smeared with gum, not even his paws or whiskers – and how cleanly and beautiful in colour the cone-litter kitchen-middens he makes.

We are now approaching the region of clouds and cool streams. Magnificent white cumuli appeared about noon above the Yosemite region – floating fountains refreshing the glorious wilderness – sky mountains in whose pearly hills and dales the streams take their rise – blessing with cooling shadows and rain. No rock landscape is more varied in sculpture, none more delicately modelled than these landscapes of the sky; domes and peaks rising, swelling, white as finest marble and firmly outlined, a most impressive manifestation of world building. Every rain cloud, however fleeting, leaves its mark, not only on trees and flowers whose pulses are quickened and on the replenished streams and lakes, but also on the rocks are its marks engraved whether we can see them or not.

I have been examining the curious and influential shrub *Adenostoma fasciculata*, first noticed about Horseshoe Bend. It is very abundant on the lower slopes of the second plateau near Coulterville, forming a dense, almost impenetrable growth that looks dark in the distance. It belongs to the rose family, is about six or eight feet high, has small white flowers in racemes eight to twelve inches long, round needle-like leaves, and reddish bark that becomes shreddy when old. It grows on sunbeaten slopes and like the grass is often swept away by running fires, but is quickly renewed from the roots. Any trees that may have established themselves in its midst are at length killed by these fires and this no doubt is the secret of the unbroken character of its broad belts. A few manzanitas, which also rise again from the root after consuming fires, make out to dwell with it, also a few bush compositae – baccharis and linosyris and some liliaceous plants, mostly calochortus and brodiaea, with deepset bulbs safe from fire. A multitude of birds and 'wee, sleekit, cow'rin', tim'rous beasties' find good homes in its deepest thickets, and the open bays and lanes that fringe the margins of its main belts offer shelter and food to the deer when winter storms drive them down from their high mountain pastures. A most admirable plant! It is now in bloom, and I like to wear its pretty fragrant racemes in my buttonhole.

Azalea occidentalis, another charming shrub, grows beside cool streams hereabouts and much higher in the Yosemite region. We found it this evening in bloom a few miles above Greeley's Mill, where we are camped for the night. It is closely related to the rhododendrons, is very showy and fragrant, and everybody must like it not only for itself but for the shady alders and willows, ferny meadows, and living water associated with it.

Another conifer was met today – incense cedar (*Libocedrus decurrens*), a large tree with warm yellow green foliage in flat plumes like those of arborvitae, bark cinnamon-coloured, and as the boles of the old trees are without limbs they make striking pillars in the woods where the sun chances to shine on them – a worthy companion of the kingly sugar and yellow pines. I feel strangely attracted to this tree. The brown close-grained wood, as well as the small scale-like leaves, is fragrant, and the flat overlapping plumes make fine beds, and must shed the rain well. It would be delightful to be stormbound beneath one of these noble, hospitable, inviting old trees, its broad sheltering arms bent down like a tent, incense rising from the fire made from its dry fallen branches, and a hearty wind chanting overhead. But the weather is calm tonight, and our camp is only a sheep camp. We are near the North Fork of the Merced. The night wind is telling the wonders of the upper mountains, their snow fountains and gardens, forests and groves; even their topography is in its tones. And the stars, the everlasting sky lilies, how bright they are now that we have climbed above the lowland dust! The horizon is bounded and adorned by a spiry wall of pines, every tree harmoniously related to every other; definite symbols, divine hieroglyphics written with sunbeams. Would I could understand them! The stream flowing past the camp through ferns and lilies and alders makes sweet music to the ear, but the pines marshalled around the edge of the sky make a yet sweeter music to the eye. Divine beauty all. Here I could stay tethered forever with just bread and water, nor would I be lonely; loved friends and neighbours, as love for everything increased, would seem all the nearer however many the miles and mountains between us.

7 June. The sheep were sick last night, and many of them are still far from well, hardly able to leave camp, coughing, groaning, looking wretched and pitiful, all from eating the leaves of the blessed azalea. So at least say the shepherd and the Don. Having had but little grass since they left the plains, they are starving, and so eat anything green they can get. 'Sheep men' call azalea 'sheep-poison', and wonder what the Creator was thinking about when he made it – so desperately does sheep business blind and degrade, though supposed to have a refining influence in the good old days we read of. The California sheep-owner is in haste to get rich, and often does, now that pasturage costs nothing, while the climate is so favourable that no winter food supply, shelter pens, or barns are required. Therefore large flocks may be kept at slight expense and large profits realised, the money invested doubling, it is claimed, every other year. This quickly acquired wealth usually creates desire for more. Then indeed the wool is drawn close down over the poor fellow's eyes, dimming or shutting out almost everything worth seeing.

As for the shepherd, his case is still worse, especially in winter when he lives alone in a cabin. For, though stimulated at times by hopes of one day owning a flock and getting rich like his boss, he at the same time is likely to be degraded by the life he leads, and seldom reaches the dignity or advantage – or disadvantage – of ownership. The degradation in his case has for cause one not far to seek. He is solitary most of the year, and solitude to most people seems hard to bear. He seldom has much good mental work or recreation in the way of books. Coming into his dingy hovel cabin at night, stupidly weary, he finds nothing to balance and level his life with the universe. No, after his dull drag all day after the sheep, he must get his supper; he is likely to slight this task and try to satisfy his hunger with whatever comes handy. Perhaps no bread is baked; then he just makes a few grimy flapjacks in his unwashed frying-pan, boils a handful of tea, and perhaps fries a few strips of rusty bacon. Usually there are dried peaches or apples in the cabin, but he hates to be bothered with the cooking of them, just swallows the bacon and flapjacks, and depends on the genial stupefaction of tobacco for the rest. Then to bed, often without removing the clothing worn during the day. Of course his health suffers, reacting on his mind; and seeing nobody for weeks or months, he finally becomes semi insane or wholly so.

The shepherd in Scotland seldom thinks of being anything but a shepherd. He has probably descended from a race of shepherds and inherited a love and aptitude for the business almost as marked as that of his collie. He has but a small flock to look after, sees his family and neighbours, has time for reading in fine weather and often carries books to the fields with which he may converse with kings. The oriental shepherd, we read, called his sheep by name; they knew his voice and followed him. The flocks must have been small and easily managed, allowing piping on the hills and ample leisure for reading and thinking. But whatever the blessings of sheep culture in other times and countries, the California shepherd, as far as I've seen or heard, is never quite sane for any considerable time. Of all Nature's voices baa is about all he hears. Even the howls and ki-yis of coyotes might be blessings if well heard, but he hears them only through a blur of mutton and wool, and they do him no good.

The sick sheep are getting well and the shepherd is discoursing on the various poisons lurking in these high pastures – azalea, kalmia, alkali. After crossing the North Fork of the Merced we turned to the left toward Pilot Peak and made a considerable ascent on a rocky, brush-covered ridge to Brown's Flat, where for the first time since leaving the plains the flock is enjoying plenty of green grass. Mr Delaney intends to seek a permanent camp somewhere in the neighbourhood, to last several weeks.

Before noon we passed Bower Cave, a delightful marble palace, not dark and dripping but filled with sunshine, which pours into it through its wide-open mouth facing the south. It has a fine, deep, clear little lake with mossy banks embowered with broad-leaved maples, all under ground, wholly unlike anything I have seen in the cave line even in Kentucky, where a large part of the State is honeycombed with caves. This curious specimen of subterranean scenery is located on a belt of marble that is said to extend from the north end of the range to the extreme south. Many other caves occur on the belt, but none like this as far as I have learned, combining as it does sunny outdoor brightness and vegetation with the crystalline beauty of the underworld. It is claimed by a Frenchman, who has fenced and locked it, placed a boat on the lakelet and seats on the mossy bank under the maple trees, and charges a dollar admission fee. Being on one of the ways to the Yosemite Valley, a good many tourists visit it during the travel months of summer, regarding it as an interesting addition to their Yosemite wonders.

Poison oak or poison ivy (*Rhus diversiloba*), both as a bush and a scrambler up trees and rocks, is common throughout the foothill region up to a height of at least three thousand feet above the sea. It is somewhat troublesome to most travellers, inflaming the skin and eyes, but blends harmoniously with its companion plants, and many a charming flower leans confidingly upon it for protection and shade. I have oftentimes found the curious twining lily (*Stropholirion Californicum*) climbing its branches, showing no fear but rather congenial companionship. Sheep eat it without apparent ill effects; so do horses to some extent, though not fond of it, and to many persons it is harmless. Like most other things not apparently useful to man, it has few friends, and the blind question, 'Why was it made?' goes on and on with never a guess that first of all it might have been made for itself.

Brown's Flat is a shallow fertile valley on the top of the divide between the North Fork of the Merced and Bull Creek, commanding magnificent views in every direction. Here the adventurous pioneer David Brown made his headquarters for many years, dividing his time between gold-hunting and bear-hunting. Where could lonely hunter find a better solitude? Game in the woods, gold in the rocks, health and exhilaration in the air, while the colours and cloud furniture of the sky are ever inspiring through all sorts of weather. Though sternly practical, like most pioneers, old David seems to have been uncommonly fond of scenery. Mr Delaney, who knew him well, tells me that he dearly loved to climb to the summit of a commanding ridge to gaze abroad over the forest to the snow-clad peaks and sources of the rivers, and over the foreground valleys and gulches to note where miners were at work or claims were abandoned, judging by smoke from cabins and camp-fires, the sounds of axes, etc.; and when a rifle-shot was heard, to guess who was the hunter, whether Indian or some poacher on his wide domain. His dog Sandy accompanied him everywhere, and well the little hairy mountaineer knew and loved his master and his master's aims. In deer-hunting he had but little to do, trotting behind his master as he slowly made his way through the wood, careful not to step heavily on dry twigs, scanning open spots in the chaparral, where the game loves to feed in the early morning and towards sunset; peering cautiously over ridges as new outlooks were reached, and along the meadowy borders of streams. But when bears were hunted, little Sandy became more important, and it was as a bear hunter that Brown became famous. His hunting method, as described by Mr Delaney, who had passed many a night with him in his lonely cabin and learned his stories, was simply to go slowly and silently through the best bear pastures, with his dog and rifle and a few pounds of flour, until he found a fresh track and then follow it to the death, paying no heed to the time required. Wherever the bear went he followed, led by little Sandy, who had a keen nose and never lost the track, however rocky the ground. When high open points were reached, the likeliest places were carefully scanned. The time of year enabled the hunter to determine approximately where the bear would be found – in the spring and early summer on open spots about the banks of streams and springy places eating grass and clover and lupines, or in dry meadows feasting on strawberries; toward the end of summer, on dry ridges, feasting on manzanita berries, sitting on his haunches, pulling down the laden branches with his paws and pressing them together so as to get good compact mouthfuls however much mixed with twigs and leaves; in the Indian summer, beneath the pines, chewing the cones cut off by the squirrels, or occasionally climbing a tree to gnaw and break off the fruitful branches. In late autumn, when acorns are ripe, Bruin's favourite feeding grounds are groves of the California oak in park-like canyon flats. Always the cunning hunter knew where to look, and seldom came upon Bruin unawares. When the hot scent showed the dangerous game was nigh, a long halt was made, and the intricacies of the topography and vegetation leisurely scanned to catch a glimpse of the shaggy wanderer, or to at least determine where he was most likely to be.

'Whenever', said the hunter, 'I saw a bear before it saw me I had no trouble in killing it. I just studied the lay of the land and got to leeward of it no matter how far around I had to go, and then worked up to within a few hundred yards or so, at the foot of a tree that I could easily climb, but too small for the bear to climb. Then I looked well to the condition of my rifle, took off my boots so as to climb well if necessary, and waited until the bear turned its side in clear view when I could make a sure or at least a good shot. In case it showed fight I climbed out of reach. But bears are slow and awkward with their eyes, and being to leeward of them they could not scent me, and I often got in a second shot before they noticed the smoke. Usually, however, they run when wounded and hide in the brush. I let them run a good safe time before I ventured to follow them and Sandy was pretty sure to find them dead. If not, he barked and drew their attention and occasionally rushed in for a distracting bite, so that I was able to get to a safe distance for a final shot. Oh, yes, bear hunting is safe enough when followed in a safe way, though like every other business it has its accidents, and little doggie and I have had some close calls. Bears like to keep out of the way of men as a general thing, but if an old, lean, hungry mother with cubs met a man on her own ground she would, in my opinion, try to catch and eat him. This would be only fair play anyhow, for we eat them, but nobody hereabout has been used for bear grub that I know of.'

Brown had left his mountain home ere we arrived, but a considerable number of Digger Indians still linger in their cedar bark huts on the edge of the flat. They were attracted in the first place by the white hunter whom they had learned to respect, and to whom they looked for guidance and protection against their enemies the Pah Utes, who sometimes made raids across from the east side of the range to plunder the stores of the comparatively feeble Diggers and steal their wives.

CHAPTER TWO

In Camp on the North Fork of the Merced

8 JUNE. The sheep, now grassy and good-natured, slowly nibbled their way down into the valley of the north fork of the Merced at the foot of Pilot Peak Ridge to the place selected by the Don for our first central camp, a picturesque hopper-shaped hollow formed by converging hill slopes at a bend of the river. Here racks for dishes and provisions were made in the shade of the riverbank trees, and beds of fern fronds, cedar plumes, and various flowers, each to the taste of its owner, and a corral back on the open flat for the wool.

9 June. How deep our sleep last night in the mountain's heart, beneath the trees and stars, hushed by solemn-sounding waterfalls and many small soothing voices in sweet accord whispering peace! And our first pure mountain day, warm, calm, cloudless – how immeasurable it seems, how serenely wild! I can scarcely remember its beginning. Along the river, over the hills, in the ground, in the sky, spring work is going on with joyful

enthusiasm, new life, new beauty, unfolding, unrolling in glorious exuberant extravagance – new birds in their nests, new winged creatures in the air, and new leaves, new flowers, spreading, shining, rejoicing everywhere.

The trees about the camp stand close, giving ample shade for ferns and lilies, while back from the bank most of the sunshine reaches the ground, calling up the grasses and flowers in glorious array, tall bromus waving like bamboos, starry compositae, monardella, Mariposa tulips, lupines, gilias, violets, glad children of light. Soon every fern frond will be unrolled, great beds of common pteris and woodwardia along the river, wreaths and rosettes of pellaea and cheilanthes on sunny rocks. Some of the woodwardia fronds are already six feet high.

A handsome little shrub, *Chamoebatia foliolosa*, belonging to the rose family, spreads a yellow-green mantle beneath the sugar pines for miles without a break, not mixed or roughened with other plants. Only here and there a Washington lily may be seen nodding above its even surface, or a bunch or two of tall bromus as if for ornament. This fine carpet shrub begins to appear at, say, twenty five hundred or three thousand feet above sea level, is about knee high or less, has brown branches, and the largest stems are only about half an inch in diameter. The leaves, light yellow-green, thrice pinnate and finely cut, give them a rich ferny appearance, and they are dotted with minute glands that secrete wax with a peculiar pleasant odour that blends finely with the spicy fragrance of the pines. The flowers are white, five eighths of an inch in diameter and look like those of the strawberry. Am delighted with this little bush. It is the only true carpet shrub of this part of the Sierra. The manzanita, rhamnus, and most of the species of ceanothus make shaggy rugs and border fringes rather than carpets or mantles.

The sheep do not take kindly to their new pastures, perhaps from being too closely hemmed in by the hills. They are never fully at rest. Last night they were frightened, probably by bears or coyotes prowling and planning for a share of the grand mass of mutton.

10 June. Very warm. We get water for the camp from a rock basin at the foot of a picturesque cascading reach of the river where it is well stirred and made lively without being beaten into dusty foam. The rock here is black metamorphic slate, worn into smooth knobs in the stream channels, contrasting with the fine grey and white cascading water as it glides and glances and falls in lace-like sheets and braided overfolding currents. Tufts of sedge growing on the rock knobs that rise above the surface produce a charming effect, the long elastic leaves arching over in every direction, the tips of the longest drooping into the current, which dividing against the projecting rocks makes still finer lines, uniting with the sedges to see how beautiful the happy stream can be made. Nor is this all, for the giant saxifrage also is growing on some of the knob rock islets, firmly anchored and displaying their broad, round, umbrella-like leaves in showy groups by themselves, or above the sedge tufts. The flowers of this species (*Saxifraga peltata*) are purple, and form tall glandular racemes that are in bloom before the appearance of the leaves. The fleshy root stocks grip the rock in cracks and hollows, and thus enable the plant to hold on against occasional floods – a marked species employed by Nature to make yet more beautiful the most interesting portions of these cool clear streams. Near camp the trees arch over from bank to bank, making a leafy tunnel full of soft subdued light, through which the young river sings and shines like a happy living creature.

Heard a few peals of thunder from the upper Sierra and saw firm white bossy cumuli rising back of the pines. This was about noon.

11 June. On one of the eastern branches of the river discovered some charming cascades with a pool at the foot of each of them. White dashing water, a few bushes and tufts of carex on ledges leaning over with fine effect, and large orange lilies assembled in superb groups on fertile soil beds beside the pools.

There are no large meadows or grassy plains near camp to supply lasting pasture for our thousands of busy nibblers. The main dependence is ceanothus brush on the hills and tufted grass patches here and there, with lupines and pea vines among the flowers on sunny open spaces. Large areas have already been stripped bare, or nearly so, compelling the poor hungry wool bundles to scatter far and wide, keeping the shepherds and dogs at the top of their speed to hold them within bounds. Mr Delaney has gone back to the plains, taking the Indian and Chinaman with him, leaving instruction to keep the flock here or hereabouts until his return, which he promised would not be long delayed.

How fine the weather is! Nothing more celestial can I conceive. How gently the winds blow! Scarce can these tranquil air currents be called winds. They seem the very breath of Nature, whispering peace to every living thing. Down in the camp dell there is no swaying of treetops; most of the time not a leaf moves. I don't remember having seen a single lily swinging on its stalk, though they are so tall the least breeze would rock them. What grand bells these lilies have! Some of them big enough for children's bonnets. I have been sketching them, and would fain draw every leaf of their wide shining whorls and every curved and spotted petal. More beautiful, better kept gardens cannot be imagined. The species is *Lilium pardalinum*, five to six feet high, leaf whorls a foot wide, flowers about six inches wide, bright orange, purple spotted in the throat, segments revolute – a majestic plant.

12 June. A slight sprinkle of rain – large drops far apart, falling with hearty pat and plash on leaves and stones and into the mouths of the flowers. Cumuli rising to the eastward. How beautiful their pearly bosses! How well they harmonise with the upswelling rocks beneath them. Mountains of the sky, solid-looking, finely sculptured, their richly varied topography wonderfully defined. Never before have I seen clouds so substantial looking in form and texture. Nearly every day toward noon they rise with visible swelling motion as if new worlds were being created. And how fondly they brood and hover over the gardens and forests with their cooling shadows and showers, keeping every petal and leaf in glad health and heart. One may fancy the clouds themselves are plants, springing up in the sky-fields at the call of the sun, growing in beauty until they reach their prime, scattering rain and hail like berries and seeds, then wilting and dying.

The mountain live oak, common here and a thousand feet or so higher, is like the live oak of Florida, not only in general appearance, foliage, bark, and wide-branching habit, but in its tough, knotty, unwedgeable wood. Standing alone with plenty of elbow room, the largest trees are about seven to eight feet in diameter near the ground, sixty feet high and as wide or wider across the head. The leaves are small and undivided, mostly without teeth or wavy edging, though on young shoots some are sharply serrated, both kinds being found on the same tree. The cups of the medium-sized acorns are shallow, thick walled and covered with a golden dust of minute hairs. Some of the trees have hardly any main trunk, dividing near the ground into large wide-spreading limbs, and these, dividing again and again, terminate in long, drooping, cord-like branchlets, many of which reach nearly to the ground, while a dense canopy of short, shining, leafy branchlets forms a round head which looks something like cumulus cloud when the sunshine is pouring over it.

A marked plant is the bush poppy (*Dendromecon rigidum*), found on the hot hillsides near camp, the only woody member of the order I have yet met in all my walks. Its flowers are bright orange yellow, an inch to two inches wide, fruit pods three or four inches long, slender and curving – height of bushes about four feet, made up of many slim, straight branches, radiating from the root – a companion of the manzanita and other sun loving chaparral shrubs.

13 June. Another glorious Sierra day in which one seems to be dissolved and absorbed and sent pulsing onward we know not where. Life seems neither long nor short, and we take no more heed to save time or make haste than do the trees and stars. This is true freedom, a good practical sort of immortality. Yonder rises another white skyland. How sharply the yellow pine spires and the palm-like crowns of the sugar pines are outlined on its smooth white domes. And hark! the grand thunder billows booming, rolling from ridge to ridge, followed by the faithful shower.

A good many herbaceous plants come thus far up the mountains from the plains and are now in flower, two months later than their lowland relatives. Saw a few columbines today. Most of the ferns are in their prime – rock ferns on the sunny hillsides, cheilanthes, pellaea, gymnogramme; woodwardia, aspidium, woodsia along the stream banks, and the common *Pteris aquilina* on sandy flats. This last, however common, is here making shows of strong, exuberant, abounding beauty to set the botanist wild with admiration. I measured some scarce full grown that are more than seven feet high. Though the commonest and most widely distributed of all the ferns, I might almost say that I never saw it before. The broad-shouldered fronds held high on smooth stout stalks growing close together, overleaning and overlapping, make a complete ceiling, beneath which one may walk erect over several acres without being seen, as if beneath a roof. And how soft and lovely the light streaming through this living ceiling, revealing the arching branching ribs and veins of the fronds as the framework of countless panes of pale green and yellow plant glass nicely fitted together – a fairyland created out of the commonest fern-stuff.

The smaller animals wander about as if in a tropical forest. I saw the entire flock of sheep vanish at one side of a patch and reappear a hundred yards farther on at the other, their progress betrayed only by the jerking and trembling of the fronds; and strange to say very few of the stout woody stalks were broken. I sat a long time beneath the tallest fronds and never enjoyed anything in the way of a bower of wild leaves more strangely impressive. Only spread a fern frond over a man's head and worldly cares are cast out, and freedom and beauty and peace come in. The waving of a pine tree on the top of a mountain – a magic wand in Nature's hand – every devout mountaineer knows its power; but the marvellous beauty value of what the Scotch call 'a breckan in a still dell', what poet has sung this? It would seem impossible that any one, however incrusted with care, could escape the Godful influence of these sacred fern forests. Yet this very day I saw a shepherd pass through one of the finest of them without betraying more feeling than his sheep. 'What do you think of these grand ferns?' I asked. 'Oh, they're only d——d big brakes,' he replied.

Lizards of every temper, style, and colour dwell here, seemingly as happy and companionable as the birds and squirrels. Lowly, gentle fellow mortals, enjoying God's sunshine, and doing the best they can in getting a living, I like to watch them at their work and play. They bear acquaintance well, and one likes them the better the longer one looks into their beautiful, innocent eyes. They are easily tamed and one soon learns to love them, as they dart about on the hot rocks, swift as dragonflies. The eye can hardly follow them; but they never make long sustained runs, usually only about ten or twelve feet, then a sudden stop and as sudden a start again; going all their journeys by quick, jerking impulses. These many stops I find are necessary as rests, for they are short-winded and when pursued steadily are soon out of breath, pant pitifully and are easily caught. Their bodies are more than half tail, but these tails are well managed, never heavily dragged nor curved up as if hard to carry; on the contrary, they seem to follow the body lightly of their own will. Some are coloured like the sky, bright as bluebirds, others grey like the lichened rocks on which they hunt and bask. Even the horned toad of the plains is a mild, harmless creature and so are the snake-like species which glide in curves with true snake motion, while their small, undeveloped limbs drag as useless appendages. One specimen fourteen inches long which I observed closely made no use whatever of its tender, sprouting limbs, but glided with all the soft, sly ease and grace of a snake. Here comes a little, grey, dusty fellow who seems to know and trust me, running about my feet and looking up cunningly into my face. Carlo is watching, makes a quick pounce on him, for the fun of the thing I suppose; but Liz has shot away from his paws like an arrow, and is safe in the recesses of a clump of chaparral. Gentle saurians, dragons, descendants of an ancient and mighty race, Heaven bless you all and make your virtues known! for few of us know as yet that scales may cover fellow creatures as gentle and lovable as feathers, or hair, or cloth.

Mastodons and elephants used to live here no great geological time ago, as shown by their bones, often discovered by miners in washing gold-gravel. And bears of at least two species are here now, besides the California lion or panther, and wild cats, wolves, foxes, snakes, scorpions, wasps, tarantulas; but one is almost tempted at times to regard a small savage black ant as the master existence of this vast mountain world. These fearless, restless, wandering imps, though only about a quarter of an inch long, are fonder of fighting and biting than any beast I know. They attack every living thing around their homes, often without cause as far as I can see. Their bodies are mostly jaws curved like ice hooks, and to get work for these weapons seems to be their chief aim and pleasure. Most of their colonies are established in living oaks somewhat decayed or hollowed, in which they can conveniently build their cells. These are chosen probably because of their strength as opposed to the attacks of animals and storms. They work both day and night, creep into dark caves, climb the highest trees, wander and hunt through cool ravines as well as on hot, unshaded ridges, and extend their highways and byways over everything but water and sky. From the foothills to a mile above the level of the sea nothing can stir without their knowledge; and alarms are spread in an incredibly short time, without any howl or cry that we can hear. I can't understand the need of their ferocious courage; there seems to be no common sense in it. Sometimes, no doubt, they fight in defence of their homes but they fight anywhere and always wherever they can find anything to bite. As soon as a vulnerable spot is discovered on man or beast, they stand on their heads and sink their jaws, and though torn limb from limb, they will yet hold on and die biting deeper. When I contemplate this fierce creature so widely distributed and strongly intrenched, I see that much remains to be done ere the world is brought under the rule of universal peace and love.

On my way to camp a few minutes ago, I passed a dead pine nearly ten feet in diameter. It has been enveloped in fire from top to bottom so that now it looks like a grand black pillar set up as a monument. In this noble shaft a colony of large jet black ants have established themselves, laboriously cutting tunnels and cells through the wood, whether sound or decayed. The entire trunk seems to have been honeycombed, judging by the size of the talus of gnawed chips like sawdust piled up around its base. They are more intelligent looking than their small, belligerent, strong-scented brethren and have better manners, though quick to fight when required. Their towns are carved in fallen trunks as well as in those left standing, but never in sound, living trees or in the ground. When you happen to sit down to rest or take notes near a colony, some wandering hunter is sure to find you and come cautiously forward to discover the nature of the intruder and what ought to be done. If you are not too near the town and keep perfectly still he may run across your feet a few times, over your legs and hands and face, up your trousers, as if taking your measure and getting comprehensive views, then go in peace without raising an alarm. If, however, a tempting spot is offered or some suspicious movement excites him, a bite follows, and such a bite! I fancy that a bear or wolf bite is not to be compared with it. A quick electric flame of pain flashes along the outraged nerves, and you discover for the first time how great is the capacity for sensation you are possessed of. A shriek, a grab for the animal, and a bewildered stare follow this bite of bites as one comes back to consciousness from sudden eclipse. Fortunately, if careful, one need not be bitten oftener than once or twice in a lifetime. This wonderful electric species is about three fourths of an inch long. Bears are fond of them, and tear and gnaw their home logs to pieces, and roughly devour the eggs, larvae, parent ants, and the rotten or sound wood of the cells, all in one spicy acid hash. The Digger Indians also are fond of the larvae and even of the perfect ants, so I have been told by old mountaineers. They bite off and reject the head and eat the tickly acid body with keen relish. Thus are the poor biters bitten, like every other biter, big or little, in the world's great family.

There is also a fine, active, intelligent looking red species, intermediate in size between the above. They dwell in the ground and build large piles of seed husks, leaves, straw, etc., over their nests. Their food seems to be mostly insects and plant leaves, seeds and sap. How many mouths Nature has to fill, how many neighbours we have, how little we know about them and how seldom we get in each other's way! Then to think of the infinite numbers of smaller fellow mortals, invisibly small, compared with which the smallest ants are as mastodons.

14 June. The pool basins below the falls and cascades hereabouts, formed by the heavy down-plunging currents, are kept nicely clean and clear of detritus. The heavier parts of the material swept over the falls are heaped up a short distance in front of the basins in the form of a dam, thus tending, together with erosion, to increase their size. Sudden changes, however, are effected during the spring floods, when the snow is melting and the upper tributaries are roaring loud from 'bank to brae'. Then boulders that have fallen into the channels and which the ordinary summer and winter currents were unable to move, are suddenly swept forward as by a mighty besom, hurled over the falls into these pools and piled up in a new dam together with part of the old one, while some of the smaller boulders are carried farther down stream and variously lodged according to size and shape, all seeking rest where the force of the current is less than the resistance they are able to offer. But the greatest changes made in these relations of fall, pool, and dam are caused, not by the ordinary spring floods, but by extraordinary ones that occur at irregular intervals. The testimony of trees growing on flood boulder deposits shows that a century or more has passed since the last master flood came to awaken everything movable to go swirling and dancing on wonderful journeys. These floods may occur during the summer, when heavy thunder showers, called 'cloud bursts', fall on wide, steeply inclined stream basins furrowed by converging channels which suddenly gather the waters together into the main trunk in booming torrents of enormous transporting power, though short lived.

One of these ancient flood boulders stands firm in the middle of the stream channel, just below the lower edge of the pool dam at the foot of the fall nearest our camp. It is a nearly cubical mass of granite about eight feet high, plushed with mosses over the top and down the sides to ordinary high-water mark. When I climbed on top of it today and lay down to rest, it seemed the most romantic spot I had yet found – the one big stone with its mossy level top and smooth sides standing square and firm and solitary, like an altar, the fall in front of it bathing it lightly with the finest of the spray, just enough to keep its moss cover fresh; the clear green pool beneath, with its foam-bells and its half circle of lilies leaning forward like a band of admirers, and flowering dogwood and alder trees leaning over all in sun sifted arches. How soothingly, restfully cool it is beneath that leafy, translucent ceiling, and how delightful the water music – the deep bass tones of the fall, the clashing, ringing spray, and infinite variety of small low tones of the current gliding past the side of the boulder island, and glinting against a thousand smaller stones down the ferny channel! All this shut in; every one of these influences acting at short range as if in a quiet room. The place seemed holy, where one might hope to see God.

After dark, when the camp was at rest, I groped my way back to the altar boulder and passed the night on it – above the water, beneath the leaves and stars – everything still more impressive than by day, the fall seen dimly white, singing Nature's old love song with solemn enthusiasm, while the stars peering through the leaf roof seemed to join in the white water's song. Precious night, precious day to abide in me forever. Thanks be to God for this immortal gift.

15 June. Another reviving morning. Down the long mountain slopes the sunbeams pour, gilding the awakening pines, cheering every needle, filling every living thing with joy. Robins are singing in the alder and maple groves, the same old song that has cheered and sweetened countless seasons over almost all of our blessed continent. In this mountain hollow they seem as much at home as in farmers' orchards. Bullock's oriole and the Louisiana tanager are here also, with many warblers and other little mountain troubadours, most of them now busy about their nests.

Discovered another magnificent specimen of the goldcup oak six feet in diameter, a Douglas spruce seven feet and a twining lily (*Stropholirion*), with stem eight feet long, and sixty rose-coloured flowers.

Sugar pine cones are cylindrical, slightly tapered at the end and rounded at the base. Found one today nearly twenty four inches long and six in diameter, the scales being open. Another specimen nineteen inches long; the average length of full grown cones on trees favourably situated is nearly eighteen inches. On the lower edge of the belt at a height of about twenty five hundred feet above sea they are smaller, say a foot to fifteen inches long, and at a height of seven thousand feet or more near the upper limits of its growth in the Yosemite region they are about the same size. This noble tree is an inexhaustible study and source of pleasure. I never weary of gazing at its grand tassel cones, its perfectly round bole one hundred feet or more without a limb, the fine purplish colour of its bark, and its magnificent outsweeping, down-curving feathery arms forming a crown always bold and striking and exhilarating. In habit and general port it looks somewhat like a palm, but no palm that I have yet seen displays such majesty of form and behaviour either when poised silent and thoughtful in sunshine, or wide awake waving in storm winds with every needle quivering. When young it is very straight and regular in form like most other conifers; but at the age of fifty to one hundred years it begins to acquire individuality, so that no two are alike in their prime or old age. Every tree calls for special admiration. I have been making many sketches and regret that I cannot draw every needle. It is said to reach a height of three hundred feet, though the tallest I have measured falls short of this stature sixty feet or more. The diameter of the largest near the ground is about ten feet, though I've heard of some twelve feet thick or even fifteen. The diameter is held to a great height, the taper being almost imperceptibly gradual. Its companion, the yellow pine, is almost as large. The long silvery foliage of the younger specimens forms magnificent cylindrical brushes on the top shoots and the ends of the upturned branches, and when the wind sways the needles all one way at a certain angle every tree becomes a tower of white quivering sun-fire. Well may this shining species be called the silver pine. The needles are sometimes more than a foot long, almost as long as those of the long-leaf pine of Florida. But though in size the yellow pine almost equals the sugar pine, and in rugged enduring strength seems to surpass it, it is far less marked in general habit and expression, with its regular conventional spire and its comparatively small cones clustered stiffly among the needles. Were there no sugar pine, then would this be the king of the world's eighty or ninety species, the brightest of the bright, waving, worshipping multitude. Were they mere mechanical sculptures, what noble objects they would still be! How much more throbbing, thrilling, overflowing, full of life in every fibre and cell, grand glowing silver rods – the very gods of the plant kingdom, living their sublime century lives in sight of Heaven, watched and loved and admired from generation to generation! And how many other radiant resiny sun trees are here and higher up – libocedrus, Douglas spruce, silver fir, sequoia. How rich our inheritance in these blessed mountains, the tree pastures into which our eyes are turned!

Now comes sundown. The west is all a glory of colour transfiguring everything. Far up the Pilot Peak Ridge the radiant host of trees stand hushed and thoughtful, receiving the Sun's goodnight, as solemn and impressive a leave-taking as if sun and trees were to meet no more. The daylight fades, the colour spell is broken, and the forest breathes free in the night breeze beneath the stars.

16 June. One of the Indians from Brown's Flat got right into the middle of the camp this morning, unobserved. I was seated on a stone, looking over my notes and sketches and happening to look up, was startled to see him standing grim and silent within a few steps of me, as motionless and weather-stained as an old tree-stump that had stood there for centuries. All Indians seem to have learned this wonderful way of walking unseen – making themselves invisible like certain spiders I have been observing here, which, in case of alarm, caused for example by a bird alighting on the bush their webs are spread upon, immediately bounce themselves up and down on their elastic threads so rapidly that only a blur is visible. The wild Indian power of escaping observation, even where there is little or no cover to hide in, was probably slowly acquired in hard hunting and fighting lessons while trying to approach game, take enemies by surprise, or get safely away when compelled to retreat. And this experience transmitted through many generations seems at length to have become what is vaguely called instinct.

How smooth and changeless seems the surface of the mountains about us! Scarce a track is to be found beyond the range of the sheep except on small open spots on the sides of the streams, or where the forest carpets are thin or wanting. On the smoothest of these open strips and patches deer tracks may be seen, and the great suggestive footprints of bears, which, with those of the many small animals, are scarce enough to answer as a kind of light ornamental stitching or embroidery. Along the main ridges and larger branches of the river Indian trails may be traced, but they are not nearly as distinct as one would expect to find them. How many centuries Indians have roamed these woods nobody knows, probably a great many, extending far beyond the time that Columbus touched our shores, and it seems strange that heavier marks have not been made. Indians walk softly and hurt the landscape hardly more than the birds and squirrels, and their brush and bark huts last hardly longer than those of wood rats, while their more enduring monuments, excepting those wrought on the forests by the fires they made to improve their hunting grounds, vanish in a few centuries.

How different are most of those of the white man, especially on the lower gold region – roads blasted in the solid rock, wild streams dammed and tamed and turned out of their channels and led along the sides of canyons and valleys to work in mines like slaves. Crossing from ridge to ridge, high in the air, on long straddling trestles as if flowing on stilts, or down and up across valleys and hills imprisoned in iron pipes to strike and wash away hills and miles of the skin of the mountain's face, riddling, stripping every gold gully and flat. These are the white man's marks made in a few feverish years, to say nothing of mills, fields, villages, scattered hundreds of miles along the flank of the range. Long will it be ere these marks are effaced, though Nature is doing what she can, replanting, gardening, sweeping away old dams and flumes, levelling gravel and bouider piles, patiently trying to heal every raw scar. The main gold storm is over. Calm enough are the grey old miners scratching a bare living in waste diggings here and there. Thundering underground blasting is still going on to feed the pounding quartz mills, but their influence on the landscape is light as compared with that of the pick and shovel storms waged a few years ago. Fortunately for Sierra scenery the gold-bearing slates are mostly restricted to the foothills. The region about our camp is still wild, and higher lies the snow about as trackless as the sky.

Only a few hills and domes of cloudland were built yesterday and none at all today. The light is peculiarly white and thin, though pleasantly warm. The serenity of this mountain weather in the spring, just when Nature's pulses are beating highest, is one of its greatest charms. There is only a moderate breeze from the summits of the range at night, and a slight breathing from the sea and the lowland hills and plains during the day, or stillness so complete no leaf stirs. The trees hereabouts have but little wind history to tell.

Sheep, like people, are ungovernable when hungry. Excepting my guarded lily gardens, almost every leaf that these hoofed locusts can reach within a radius of a mile or two from camp has been devoured. Even the bushes are stripped bare and in spite of dogs and shepherds the sheep scatter to all points of the compass and vanish in dust. I fear some are lost, for one of the sixteen black ones is missing.

17 June. Counted the wool bundles this morning as they bounced through the narrow corral gate. About three hundred are missing, and as the shepherd could not go to seek them, I had to go. I tied a crust of bread to my belt, and with Carlo set out for the upper slopes of the Pilot Peak Ridge and had a good day, notwithstanding the care of seeking the silly runaways. I went out for wool and did not come back shorn. A peculiar light circled around the horizon, white and thin like that often seen over the auroral corona, blending into the blue of the upper sky. The only clouds were a few faint flossy pencillings like combed silk. I pushed direct to the boundary of the usual range of the flock, and around it until I found the outgoing trail of the wanderers. It led far up the ridge into an open place surrounded by a hedge-like growth of ceanothus chaparral. Carlo knew what I was about, and eagerly followed the scent until we came up to them, huddled in a timid, silent bunch. They had evidently been here all night and all the forenoon, afraid to go out to feed. Having escaped restraint, they were, like some people we know of, afraid of their freedom, did not know what to do with it, and seemed glad to get back into the old familiar bondage.

18 June. Another inspiring morning, nothing better in any world can be conceived. No description of Heaven that I have ever heard or read of seems half so fine. At noon the clouds occupied about five per cent of the sky, white filmy touches drawn delicately on the azure.

The high ridges and hilltops beyond the woolly locusts are now gay with monardella, clarkia, coreopsis, and tall tufted grasses, some of them tall enough to wave like pines. The lupines, of which there are many ill-defined species, are now mostly out of flower, and many of the compositae are beginning to fade, their radiant corollas vanishing in fluffy pappus like stars in mist.

We had another visitor from Brown's Flat today, an old Indian woman with a basket on her back. Like our first caller from the village, she got fairly into camp and was standing in plain view when discovered. How long she had been quietly looking on, I cannot say. Even the dogs failed to notice her stealthy approach. She was on her way, I suppose, to some wild garden, probably for lupine and starchy saxifrage leaves and rootstocks. Her dress was calico rags, far from clean. In every way she seemed sadly unlike Nature's neat well-dressed animals, though living like them on the bounty of the wilderness. Strange that mankind alone is dirty. Had she been clad in fur, or cloth woven of grass or shreddy bark, like the juniper and libocedrus mats, she might then have seemed a rightful part of the wilderness; like a good wolf at least, or bear. But from no point of view that I have found are such debased fellow beings a whit more natural than the glaring tailored tourists we saw that frightened the birds and squirrels.

19 June. Pure sunshine all day. How beautiful a rock is made by leafy shadows! Those of the live oak are particularly clear and distinct, and beyond all art in grace and delicacy, now still as if painted on stone, now gliding softly as if afraid of noise, now dancing, waltzing in swift, merry swirls, or jumping on and off sunny rocks in quick dashes like wave embroidery on seashore cliffs. How true and substantial is this shadow beauty, and with what sublime extravagance is beauty thus multiplied! The big orange lilies are now arrayed in all their glory of leaf and flower. Noble plants, in perfect health, Nature's darlings.

20 June. Some of the silly sheep got caught fast in a tangle of chaparral this morning, like flies in a spider's web and had to be helped out. Carlo found them and tried to drive them from the trap by the easiest way. How far above sheep are intelligent dogs! No friend and helper can be more affectionate and constant than Carlo. The noble St Bernard is an honour to his race.

The air is distinctly fragrant with balsam and resin and mint – every breath of it a gift we may well thank God for. Who could ever guess that so rough a wilderness should yet be so fine, so full of good things. One seems to be in a majestic domed pavilion in which a grand play is being acted with scenery and music and incense – all the furniture and action so interesting we are in no danger of being called on to endure one dull moment. God himself seems to be always doing his best here, working like a man in a glow of enthusiasm.

21 June. Sauntered along the riverbank to my lily gardens. The perfection of beauty in these lilies of the wilderness is a never ending source of admiration and wonder. Their rhizomes are set in black mould accumulated in hollows of the metamorphic slates beside the pools, where they are well watered without being subjected to flood action. Every leaf in the level whorls around the tall polished stalks is as finely finished as the petals, and the light and heat required are measured for them and tempered in passing through the branches of overleaning trees. However strong the winds from the noon rain-storms, they are securely sheltered. Beautiful hypnum carpets bordered with ferns are spread beneath them, violets too, and a few daisies. Everything around them sweet and fresh like themselves.

Cloudland today is only a solitary white mountain; but it is so enriched with sunshine and shade, the tones of colour on its big domed head and bossy outbulging ridges, and in the hollows and ravines between them, are ineffably fine.

22 June Unusually cloudy. Besides the periodical shower-bearing cumuli there is a thin, diffused, fog-like cloud overhead. About seventy five per cent in all.

23 June. Oh, these vast, calm, measureless mountain days, inciting at once to work and rest! Days in whose light everything seems equally divine, opening a thousand windows to show us God. Nevermore, however weary, should one faint by the way who gains the blessings of one mountain day; whatever his fate, long life, short life, stormy or calm, he is rich forever.

24 June. Our regular allowance of clouds and thunder. Shepherd Billy is in a peck of trouble about the sheep; he declares that they are possessed with more of the evil one than any other flock from the beginning of the invention of mutton and wool to the last batch of it. No matter how many are missing, he will not, he says, go a step to seek them, because, as he reasons, while getting back one wanderer he would probably lose ten. Therefore runaway hunting must be Carlo's and mine. Billy's little dog Jack is also giving trouble by leaving camp every night to visit his neighbours up the mountain at Brown's Flat. He is a common-looking cur of no particular breed, but tremendously enterprising in love and war. He has cut all the ropes and leather straps he has been tied with, until his master in desperation, after climbing the brushy mountain again and again to drag him back, fastened him with a pole attached to his collar under his chin at one end, and to a stout sapling at the other. But the pole gave good leverage, and by constant twisting during the night, the fastening at the sapling end was chaffed off, and he set out on his usual journey, dragging the pole through the brush, and reached the Indian settlement in safety. His master followed, and making no allowance, gave him a beating, and swore in bad terms that next evening he would 'fix that infatuated pup' by anchoring him unmercifully to the heavy cast iron lid of our Dutch oven, weighing about as much as the dog. It was linked directly to his collar close up under the chin, so that the poor fellow seemed unable to stir. He stood quite discouraged until after dark, unable to look about him, or even to lie down unless he stretched himself out with his front feet across the lid, and his head close down between his paws. Before morning, however, Jack was heard far up the height howling Excelsior, cast iron anchor to the contrary notwithstanding. He must have walked, or rather climbed, erect on his hind legs, clasping the heavy lid like a shield against his breast, a formidable ironclad condition in which to meet his rivals. Next night, dog, pot lid and all, were tied up in an old bean sack, and thus at last angry Billy gained the victory. Just before leaving home, Jack was bitten in the lower jaw by a rattlesnake, and for a week or so his head and neck were swollen to more than double the normal size; nevertheless he ran about as brisk and lively as ever, and is now completely recovered. The only treatment he got was fresh milk – a gallon or two at a time forcibly poured down his sore, poisoned throat.

25 June. Though only a sheep camp, this grand mountain hollow is home, sweet home, every day growing sweeter, and I shall be sorry to leave it. The lily gardens are safe as yet from the trampling flock. Poor, dusty, raggedy, famishing creatures, I heartily pity them. Many a mile they must go every day to gather their fifteen or twenty tons of chaparral and grass.

26 June. Nuttall's flowering dogwood makes a fine show when in bloom. The whole tree is then snowy white. The involucres are six to eight inches wide. Along the streams it is a good-sized tree thirty to fifty feet high, with a broad head when not crowded by companions. Its showy involucres attract a crowd of moths, butterflies, and other winged people about it for their own, and I suppose, the tree's advantage. It likes plenty of cool water, and is a great drinker like the alder, willow and cottonwood, and flourishes best on stream banks, though it often wanders far from streams in damp shady glens beneath the pines, where it is much smaller. When the leaves ripen in the autumn, they become more beautiful than the flowers, displaying charming tones of red, purple and lavender. Another species grows in abundance as a chaparral shrub on the shady sides of the hills, probably *Cornus sessilis*. The leaves are eaten by the sheep. – Heard a few lightning strokes in the distance, with rumbling, mumbling reverberations.

27 June. The beaked hazel (*Corylus rostrata*, var. *Californica*) is common on cool slopes up toward the summit of the Pilot Peak Ridge. There is something peculiarly attractive in the hazel, like the oaks and heaths of the cool countries of our forefathers, and through them our love for these plants has, I suppose, been transmitted. This species is four or five feet high, leaves soft and hairy, grateful to the touch, and the delicious nuts are eagerly gathered by Indians and squirrels. The sky as usual adorned with white noon clouds.

28 June. Warm, mellow summer. The glowing sunbeams make every nerve tingle. The new needles of the pines and firs are nearly full grown and shine gloriously. Lizards are glinting about on the hot rocks; some that live near the camp are more than half tame. They seem attentive to every movement on our part, as if curious to simply look on without suspicion of harm, turning their heads to look back, and making a variety of pretty gestures. Gentle, guileless creatures with beautiful eyes, I shall be sorry to leave them when we leave camp.

29 June. I have been making the acquaintance of a very interesting little bird that flits about the falls and rapids of the main branches of the river. It is not a water bird in structure, though it gets its living in the water, and never leaves the streams. It is not web-footed, yet it dives fearlessly into deep swirling rapids, evidently to feed at the bottom, using its wings to swim with under water just as ducks and loons do. Sometimes it wades about in shallow places, thrusting its head under from time to time in a jerking, nodding, frisky way that is sure to attract attention. It is about the size of a robin, has short crisp wings serviceable for flying either in water or air, and a tail of moderate size slanted upward, giving it, with its nodding, bobbing manners, a wrennish look. Its colour is plain bluish ash, with a tinge of brown on the head and shoulders. It flies from fall to fall, rapid to rapid, with a solid whirr of wing beats like those of a quail, follows the windings of the stream, and usually alights on some rock jutting up out of the current, or on some stranded snag, or rarely on the dry limb of an overhanging tree, perching like regular tree birds when it suits its convenience. It has the oddest, daintiest mincing manners imaginable; and the little fellow can sing too, a sweet, thrushy, fluty song, rather low, not the least boisterous, and much less keen and accentuated than from its vigorous briskness one would be led to look for. What a romantic life this little bird leads on the most beautiful portions of the streams, in a genial climate with shade and cool water and spray to temper the summer heat. No wonder it is a fine singer, considering the stream songs it hears day and night. Every breath the little poet draws is part of a song, for all the air about the rapids and falls is beaten into music, and its first lessons must begin before it is born by the thrilling and quivering of the eggs in unison with the tones of the falls. I have not yet found its nest, but it must be near the streams, for it never leaves them.

30 June. Half cloudy, half sunny, clouds lustrous white. The tall pines crowded along the top of the Pilot Peak Ridge look like six-inch miniatures exquisitely outlined on the satiny sky. Average cloudiness for the day about twenty five per cent. No rain. And so this memorable month ends, a stream of beauty unmeasured, no more to be sectioned off by almanac arithmetic than sun radiance or the currents of seas and rivers – a peaceful, joyful stream of beauty. Every morning arising from the death of sleep, the happy plants and all our fellow animal creatures great and small, and even the rocks, seemed to be shouting, 'Awake, awake, rejoice, rejoice, come love us and join in our song. Come! Come!' Looking back through the stillness and romantic enchanting beauty and peace of the camp grove, this June seems the greatest of all the months of my life, the most truly, divinely free, boundless like eternity, immortal. Everything in it seems equally divine – one smooth, pure, wild glow of Heaven's love, never to be blotted or blurred by anything past or to come.

1 July. Summer is ripe. Flocks of seeds are already out of their cups and pods seeking their predestined places. Some will strike root and grow up beside their parents, others flying on the wings of the wind far from them, among strangers. Most of the young birds are full feathered and out of their nests, though still looked after by both father and mother, protected and fed and to some extent educated. How beautiful the home life of birds! No wonder we all love them.

I like to watch the squirrels. There are two species here, the large California grey and the Douglas. The latter is the brightest of all the squirrels I have ever seen, a hot spark of life, making every tree tingle with his prickly toes, a condensed nugget of fresh mountain vigour and valour, as free from disease as a sunbeam. One cannot think of such an animal ever being weary or sick. He seems to think the mountains belong to him and at first tried to drive away the whole flock of sheep as well as the shepherd and dogs. How he scolds and what faces he makes, all eyes, teeth and whiskers! If not so comically small, he would indeed be a dreadful fellow. I should like to know more about his bringing up, his life in the home knot-hole, as well as in the treetops, throughout all seasons. Strange that I have not yet found a nest full of young ones. The Douglas is nearly allied to the red squirrel of the Atlantic slope, and may have been distributed to this side of the continent by way of the great unbroken forests of the north.

The California grey is one of the most beautiful and, next to the Douglas, the most interesting of our hairy neighbours. Compared with the Douglas he is twice as large, but far less lively and influential as a worker in the woods and he manages to make his way through leaves and branches with less stir than his small brother. I have never heard him bark at anything except our dogs. When in search of food he glides silently from branch to branch, examining last year's cones to see whether some few seeds may not be left between the scales, or gleans fallen ones among the leaves on the ground, since none of the present season's crop is yet available. His tail floats now behind him, now above him, level or gracefully curled like a wisp of cirrus cloud, every hair in its place, clean and shining and radiant as thistledown in spite of rough, gummy work. His whole body seems about as unsubstantial as his tail. The little Douglas is fiery, peppery, full of brag and fight and show, with movements so quick and keen they almost sting the onlooker, and the harlequin gyrating show he makes of himself turns one giddy to see. The grey is shy, and oftentimes stealthy in his movements, as if half expecting an enemy in every tree and bush and back of every log, wishing only to be let alone apparently, and manifesting no desire to be seen or admired or feared. The Indians hunt this species for food, a good cause for caution, not to mention other enemies – hawks, snakes, wild cats. In woods where food is abundant they wear paths through sheltering thickets and over prostrate trees to some favourite pool where in hot and dry weather they drink at nearly the same hour every day. These pools are said to be narrowly watched, especially by the boys, who lie in ambush with bow and arrow and kill without noise. But, in spite of enemies, squirrels are happy fellows, forest favourites, types of tireless life. Of all Nature's wild beasts they seem to me the wildest. May we come to know each other better.

The chaparral-covered hill slope to the south of the camp, besides furnishing nesting places for countless merry birds, is the home and hiding place of the curious wood rat (*Neotoma*), a handsome, interesting animal, always attracting attention wherever seen. It is more like a squirrel than a rat, is much larger, has delicate, thick, soft fur of a bluish slate colour, white on the belly; ears large, thin and translucent; eyes soft, full and liquid; claws slender, sharp as needles; and as his limbs are strong, he can climb about as well as a squirrel. No rat or squirrel has so innocent a look, is so easily approached or expresses such confidence in one's good intentions. He seems too fine for the thorny thickets he inhabits and his hut also is as unlike himself as may be, though softly furnished inside. No other animal inhabitant of these mountains builds houses so large and striking in appearance. The traveller coming suddenly upon a group of them for the first time will not be likely to forget them. They are built of all kinds of sticks, old rotten pieces picked up anywhere, and green prickly twigs bitten from the nearest bushes, the whole mixed with miscellaneous odds and ends of everything movable, such as bits of cloddy earth, stones, bones and deerhorn, piled up in a conical mass as if it were got ready for burning. Some of these curious cabins are six feet high and as wide as the base, and a dozen or more of them are occasionally grouped together, less perhaps for the sake of society than for advantages of food and shelter. Coming through the dense shaggy thickets of some lonely hillside, the solitary explorer happening into one of these strange villages is startled at the sight, and may fancy himself in an Indian settlement, and begin to wonder what kind of reception he is likely to get. But no savage face will he see, perhaps not a single inhabitant, or at most two or three seated on top of their wigwams, looking at the stranger with the mildest of wild eyes and allowing a near approach. In the centre of the rough spiky hut a soft nest is made of the inner fibres of bark chewed to tow, and lined with feathers and the down of various seeds, such as willow and milkweed. The delicate creature in its prickly, thick-walled home suggests a tender flower in a thorny involucre. Some of the nests are built in trees thirty or forty feet from the ground and even in garrets, as if seeking the company and protection of man, like swallows and linnets, though accustomed to the wildest solitude. Among housekeepers Neotoma has the reputation of a thief, because he carries away everything transportable to his queer hut – knives, forks, combs, nails, tin cups and spectacles – merely however to strengthen his fortifications, I guess. His food at home, as far as I have learned, is nearly the same as that of the squirrels – nuts, berries, seeds and sometimes the bark and tender shoots of the various species of ceanothus.

2 July. Warm, sunny day, thrilling plant and animals and rocks alike, making sap and blood flow fast and making every particle of the crystal mountains throb and swirl and dance in glad accord like stardust. No dullness anywhere visible or thinkable. No stagnation, no death. Everything kept in joyful rhythmic motion in the pulses of Nature's big heart.

Pearl cumuli over the higher mountains – clouds, not with a silver lining, but all silver. The brightest, crispest, rockiest looking clouds, most varied in features and keenest in outline I ever saw at any time of year in any country. The daily building and unbuilding of these snowy cloud ranges – the highest Sierra – is a prime marvel to me and I gaze at the stupendous white domes, miles high, with ever fresh admiration. But in the midst of these sky and mountain affairs a change of diet is pulling us down. We have been out of bread a few days, and begin to miss it more than seems reasonable, for we have plenty of meat and sugar and tea. Strange we should feel food-poor in so rich a wilderness. The Indians put us to shame, so do the squirrels – starchy roots and seeds and bark in abundance, yet the failure of the meal sack disturbs our bodily balance and threatens our best enjoyments.

3 July. Warm. Breeze just enough to sift through the woods and waft fragrance from their thousand fountains. The pine and fir cones are growing well, resin and balsam dripping from every tree, and seeds are ripening fast, promising a fine harvest. The squirrels will have bread. They eat all kinds of nuts long before they are ripe and yet never seem to suffer in stomach.

CHAPTER THREE

A Bread Famine

4 JULY. The air beyond the flock range, full of the essences of the woods, is growing sweeter and more fragrant from day to day, like ripening fruit.

Mr Delaney is expected to arrive soon from the lowlands with a new stock of provisions and as the flock is to be moved to fresh pastures we shall all be well fed. In the meantime our stock of beans as well as flour has failed – everything but mutton, sugar and tea. The shepherd is somewhat demoralised and seems to care but little what becomes of his flock. He says that since the boss has failed to feed him he is not rightly bound to feed the sheep and swears that no decent white man can climb these steep mountains on mutton alone. 'It's not fittin' grub for a white man really white. For dogs and coyotes and Indians it's different. Good grub, good sheep. That's what I say.' Such was Billy's Fourth of July oration.

5 July. The clouds of noon on the High Sierra seem yet more marvellously, indescribably beautiful from day to day as one becomes more wakeful to see them. The smoke of the gunpowder burned yesterday on the lowlands and the eloquence of the orators has probably settled or been blown away by this

time. Here every day is a holiday. a jubilee ever sounding with serene
enthusiasm, without wear or waste or cloying weariness. Everything rejoicing.
Not a single cell or crystal unvisited or forgotten.

6 July. Mr Delaney has not arrived, and the bread famine is sore. We must
eat mutton a while longer, though it seems hard to get accustomed to it. I
have heard of Texas pioneers living without bread or anything made from the
cereals for months without suffering, using the breast meat of wild turkeys for
bread. Of this kind they had plenty in the good old days when life, though
considered less safe, was fussed over the less. The trappers and fur traders of
early days in the Rocky Mountain regions lived on bison and beaver meat for
months. Salmon eaters too, there are among both Indians and whites who
seem to suffer little or not at all from the want of bread. Just at this moment
mutton seems the least desirable of food, though of good quality. We pick out
the leanest bits, and down they go against heavy disgust, causing nausea and
an effort to reject the offensive stuff. Tea makes matters worse, if possible.
The stomach begins to assert itself as an independent creature with a will of its
own. We should boil lupine leaves, clover, starchy petioles and saxifrage
rootstocks like the Indians. We try to ignore our gastric troubles, rise and
gaze about us, turn our eyes to the mountains and climb doggedly up through
brush and rocks into the heart of the scenery. A stifled calm comes on, and
the day's duties and even enjoyments are languidly got through with. We
chew a few leaves of ceanothus by way of luncheon and smell or chew the
spicy monardella for the dull headache and stomach ache that now lightens,
now comes muffling down upon us and into us like fog. At night more
mutton, flesh to flesh, down with it, not too much and there are the stars
shining through the cedar plumes and branches above our beds.

7 July. Rather weak and sickish this morning and all about a piece of bread.
Can scarce command attention to my best studies, as if one couldn't take a
few days' saunter in the Godful woods without maintaining a base on a
wheatfield and grist mill. Like caged parrots we want a cracker, any of the
hundred kinds – the remainder biscuit of a voyage around the world would
answer well enough, nor would the wholesomeness of saleratus biscuit be
questioned. Bread without flesh is a good diet, as on many botanical excursions I have proved. Tea also may easily be ignored. Just bread and water and
delightful toil is all I need – not unreasonably much, yet one ought to be
trained and tempered to enjoy life in these brave wilds in full independence
of any particular kind of nourishment. That this may be accomplished is
manifest, as far as bodily welfare is concerned, in the lives of people of other
climes. The Eskimo, for example, gets a living far north of the wheat line,
from oily seals and whales. Meat, berries, bitter weeds and blubber, or only
the last, for months at a time; and yet these people all around the frozen
shores of our continent are said to be hearty, jolly, stout and brave. We hear,
too, of fish eaters, carnivorous as spiders, yet well enough as far as stomachs
are concerned, while we are so ridiculously helpless, making wry faces over
our fare, looking sheepish in digestive distress amid rumbling, grumbling
sounds that might well pass for smothered baas. We have a large supply of
sugar, and this evening it occurred to me that these belligerent stomachs

might possibly, like complaining children, be coaxed with candy. Accordingly the frying pan was cleansed and a lot of sugar cooked in it to a sort of wax, but this stuff only made matters worse.

Man seems to be the only animal whose food soils him making necessary much washing and shield-like bibs and napkins. Moles living in the earth and eating slimy worms are yet as clean as seals or fishes, whose lives are one perpetual wash. And, as we have seen, the squirrels in these resiny woods keep themselves clean in some mysterious way; not a hair is sticky, though they handle the gummy cones, and glide about apparently without care. The birds, too, are clean, though they seem to make a good deal of fuss washing and cleaning their feathers. Certain flies and ants I see are in a fix, entangled and sealed up in the sugar wax we threw away, like some of their ancestors in amber. Our stomachs, like tired muscles, are sore with long squirming. Once I was very hungry in the Bonaventure graveyard near Savannah, Georgia, having fasted for several days; then the empty stomach seemed to chafe in much the same way as now and a somewhat similar tenderness and aching was produced, hard to bear, though the pain was not acute. We dream of bread, a sure sign we need it. Like the Indians, we ought to know how to get the starch out of fern and saxifrage stalks, lily bulbs, pine bark, etc. Our education has been sadly neglected for many generations. Wild rice would be good. I noticed a leersia in wet meadow edges, but the seeds are small. Acorns are not ripe, nor pine nuts, nor filberts. The inner bark of pine or spruce might be tried. Drank tea until half intoxicated. Man seems to crave a stimulant when anything extraordinary is going on and this is the only one I use. Billy chews great quantities of tobacco, which I suppose helps to stupefy and moderate his misery. We look and listen for the Don every hour. How beautiful upon the mountains his big feet would be.

In the warm, hospitable Sierra, shepherds and mountain men in general, as far as I have seen, are easily satisfied as to food supplies and bedding. Most of them heartily content to 'rough it', ignoring Nature's fineness as bothersome or unmanly. The shepherd's bed is often only the bare ground and a pair of blankets, with a stone, a piece of wood or a pack-saddle for a pillow. In choosing the spot, he shows less care than the dogs, for they usually deliberate before making up their minds in so important an affair, going from place to place, scraping away loose sticks and pebbles and trying for comfort by making many changes, while the shepherd casts himself down anywhere, seemingly the least skilled of all rest seekers. His food too, even when he has all he wants, is usually far from delicate, either in kind or cooking. Beans, bread of any sort, bacon, mutton, dried peaches and sometimes potatoes and onions, make up his bill of fare, the two latter articles being regarded as luxuries on account of their weight as compared with the nourishment they contain; a half sack or so of each may be put into the pack in setting out from the home ranch and in a few days they are done. Beans are the main standby, portable, wholesome and capable of going far, besides being easily cooked, although curiously enough a great deal of mystery is supposed to lie about the bean pot. No two cooks quite agree on the methods of making beans do their best, and after petting and coaxing and nursing the savoury mess – well oiled and mellowed with bacon boiled into the heart of it – the proud cook will ask, after dishing out a quart or two for trial, 'Well, how do you like *my* beans?' as if by no possibility could they be like any other beans cooked in the same way, but must needs possess some special virtue of which he alone is master. Molasses, sugar, or pepper may be used to give desired flavours; or the first water may be poured off and a spoonful or two of ashes or soda added to dissolve or soften the skins more fully, according to various tastes and notions. But, like casks of wine, no two potfuls are exactly alike to every palate. Some are supposed to be spoiled by the moon, by some unlucky day, by the beans having been grown on soil not suitable; or the whole year may be to blame as not favourable for beans.

Coffee too, has its marvels in the camp kitchen but not so many and not so inscrutable as those that beset the bean pot. A low complacent grunt follows a mouthful drawn in with a gurgle and the remark cast forth aimlessly, 'That's good coffee.' Then another gurgling sip and repetition of the judgment, '*Yes sir*, that *is* good coffee.' As to tea, there are but two kinds, weak and strong, the stronger the better. The only remark heard is, 'That tea's weak,' otherwise it is good enough and not worth mentioning. If it has been boiled an hour or two or smoked on a pitchy fire, no matter – who cares for a little tannin or creosote? They make the black beverage all the stronger and more attractive to tobacco tanned palates.

Sheep-camp bread, like most California camp bread, is baked in Dutch ovens, some of it in the form of yeast powder biscuit, an unwholesome sticky compound leading straight to dyspepsia. The greater part, however, is fermented with sour dough, a handful from each batch being saved and put away in the mouth of the flour sack to inoculate the next. The oven is simply a cast iron pot, about five inches deep and from twelve to eighteen inches wide. After the batch has been mixed and kneaded in a tin pan, the oven is slightly heated and rubbed with a piece of tallow or pork rind. The dough is then placed in it, pressed out against the sides, and left to rise. When ready for baking a shovelful of coals is spread out by the side of the fire and the oven set upon them, while another shovelful is placed on top of the lid, which is raised from time to time to see that the requisite amount of heat is being kept up. With care good bread may be made in this way, though it is liable to be burned or to be sour, or raised too much, and the weight of the oven is a serious objection.

At last Don Delaney comes doon the lang glen – hunger vanishes, we turn our eyes to the mountains, and tomorrow we go climbing toward cloudland.

Never while anything is left of me shall this first camp be forgotten. It has fairly grown into me, not merely as memory pictures, but as part and parcel of mind and body alike. The deep hopper-like hollow, with its majestic trees through which all the wonderful nights the stars poured their beauty. The flowery wildness of the high steep slope toward Brown's Flat, and its bloom-fragrance descending at the close of the still days. The embowered river-reaches with their multitude of voices making melody, the stately flow and rush and glad exulting onsweeping currents caressing the dipping sedge-leaves and bushes and mossy stones, swirling in pools, dividing against little flowery islands, breaking grey and white here and there, ever rejoicing, yet with deep solemn undertones recalling the ocean – the brave little bird ever beside them, singing with sweet human tones among the waltzing foam-bells, and like a blessed evangel explaining God's love. And the Pilot Peak Ridge, its long withdrawing slopes gracefully modelled and braided, reaching from climate to climate, feathered with trees that are the kings of their race, their ranks nobly marshalled to view, spire above spire, crown above crown, waving their long, leafy arms, tossing their cones like ringing bells – blessed sun-fed mountaineers rejoicing in their strength, every tree tuneful, a harp for the winds and the sun. The hazel and buckthorn pastures of the deer, the sun-beaten brows purple and yellow with mint and goldenrods, carpeted with chamoebatia, humming with bees. And the dawns and sunrises and sundowns of these mountain days – the rose light creeping higher among the stars, changing to daffodil yellow, the level beams bursting forth, streaming across the ridges, touching pine after pine, awakening and warming all the mighty host to do gladly their shining day's work. The great sun-gold noons, the alabaster cloud mountains, the landscape beaming with consciousness like the face of a god. The sunsets, when the trees stood hushed awaiting their goodnight blessings. Divine, enduring, unwastable health.

CHAPTER FOUR

To the High Mountains

8 JULY. Now away we go toward the topmost mountains. Many still, small voices, as well as the noon thunder, are calling, 'Come higher'. Farewell, blessed dell, woods, gardens, streams, birds, squirrels, lizards and a thousand others. Farewell. Farewell.

Up through the woods, the hoofed locusts streamed beneath a cloud of brown dust. Scarcely were they driven a hundred yards from the old corral ere they seemed to know that at last they were going to new pastures, and rushed wildly ahead, crowding through gaps in the brush, jumping, tumbling like exulting, hurrahing flood waters escaping through a broken dam. A man on each flank kept shouting advice to the leaders, who in their famishing condition were behaving like Gadarene swine; two other drivers were busy with stragglers, helping them out of brush tangles; the Indian, calm, alert, silently watched for wanderers likely to be overlooked; the two dogs ran here and there, at a loss to know what was best to be done, while the Don, soon far in the rear, was trying to keep in sight of his troublesome wealth.

As soon as the boundary of the old eaten out range was passed the hungry horde suddenly became calm, like a mountain stream in a meadow. Thence-forward they were allowed to eat their way as slowly as they wished, care being taken only to keep them headed toward the summit of the Merced and

Tuolumne divide. Soon the two thousand flattened paunches were bulged out with sweetpea vines and grass and the gaunt, desperate creatures, more like wolves than sheep became bland and governable, while the howling drivers changed to gentle shepherds, and sauntered in peace.

Toward sundown we reached Hazel Green, a charming spot on the summit of the dividing ridge between the basins of the Merced and Tuolumne, where there is a small brook flowing through hazel and dogwood thickets beneath magnificent silver firs and pines. Here we are camped for the night, our big fire, heaped high with resiny logs and branches, is blazing like a sunrise, gladly giving back the light slowly sifted from the sunbeams of centuries of summers; and in the glow of that old sunlight how impressively surrounding objects are brought forward in relief against the outer darkness! Grasses, larkspurs, columbines, lilies, hazel bushes, and the great trees form a circle around the fire like thoughtful spectators, gazing and listening with human-like enthusiasm. The night breeze is cool, for all day we have been climbing into the upper sky, the home of the cloud mountains we so long have admired. How sweet and keen the air! Every breath a blessing. Here the sugar pine reaches its fullest development in size and beauty and number of individuals, filling every swell and hollow and down-plunging ravine almost to the exclusion of other species. A few yellow pines are still to be found as companions, and in the coolest places silver firs; but noble as these are, the sugar pine is king, and spreads long protecting arms above them while they rock and wave in sign of recognition.

We have now reached a height of six thousand feet. In the forenoon we passed along a flat part of the dividing ridge that is planted with manzanita (*Arctostaphylos*), some specimens the largest I have seen. I measured one, the bole of which is four feet in diameter and only eighteen inches high from the ground, where it dissolves into many widespreading branches forming a broad round head about ten or twelve feet high, covered with clusters of small narrow-throated pink bells. The leaves are pale green, glandular, and set on edge by a twist of the petiole. The branches seem naked; for the chocolate-coloured bark is very smooth and thin, and is shed off in flakes that curl when dry. The wood is red, close-grained, hard, and heavy. I wonder how old these curious tree bushes are, probably as old as the great pines. Indians and bears and birds and fat grubs feast on the berries, which look like small apples, often rosy on one side, green on the other. The Indians are said to make a kind of beer or cider out of them. There are many species. This one, *Arctostaphylos pungens*, is common hereabouts. No need have they to fear the wind, so low they are and steadfastly rooted. Even the fires that sweep the woods seldom destroy them utterly, for they rise again from the root and some of the dry ridges they grow on are seldom touched by fire. I must try to know them better.

I miss my river songs tonight. Here Hazel Creek at its topmost springs has a voice like a bird. The wind tones in the great trees overhead are strangely impressive, all the more because not a leaf stirs below them. But it grows late and I must to bed. The camp is silent; everybody asleep. It seems extravagant to spend hours so precious in sleep. 'He giveth his beloved sleep.' Pity the poor beloved needs it, weak, weary, forspent; oh, the pity of it, to sleep in the midst of eternal, beautiful motion instead of gazing forever, like the stars.

9 July. Exhilarated with the mountain air, I feel like shouting this morning with excess of wild animal joy. The Indian lay down away from the fire last night without blankets, having nothing on, by way of clothing, but a pair of blue overalls and a calico shirt wet with sweat. The night air is chilly at this elevation, and we gave him some horse blankets, but he didn't seem to care for them. A fine thing to be independent of clothing where it is so hard to carry. When food is scarce, he can live on whatever comes in his way – a few berries, roots, bird eggs, grasshoppers, black ants, fat wasp or bumblebee larvae, without feeling that he is doing anything worth mention, so I have been told.

Our course today was along the broad top of the main ridge to a hollow beyond Crane Flat. It is scarce at all rocky, and is covered with the noblest pines and spruces I have yet seen. Sugar pines from six to eight feet in diameter are not uncommon, with a height of two hundred feet or even more. The silver firs (*Abies concolour* and *A. magnifica*) are exceedingly beautiful, especially the *magnifica*, which becomes more abundant the higher we go. It is of great size, one of the most notable in every way of the giant conifers of the Sierra. I saw specimens that measured seven feet in diameter and over two hundred feet in height, while the average size for what might be called full grown mature trees can hardly be less than one hundred and eighty or two hundred feet high and five or six feet in diameter; and with these noble dimensions there is a symmetry and perfection of finish not to be seen in any other tree, hereabout at least. The branches are whorled in fives mostly, and stand out from the tall, straight, exquisitely tapered bole in level collars, each branch regularly pinnated like the fronds of ferns, and densely clad with leaves all around the branchlets, thus giving them a singularly rich and sumptuous appearance. The extreme top of the tree is a thick blunt shoot pointing straight to the zenith like an admonishing finger. The cones stand erect like casks on the upper branches. They are about six inches long, three in diameter, blunt velvety, and cylindrical in form, and very rich and precious looking. The seeds are about three quarters of an inch long, dark reddish brown with brilliant iridescent purple wings, and when ripe, the cone falls to pieces, and the seeds thus set free at a height of one hundred and fifty to two hundred feet have a good send off and may fly considerable distances in a good breeze; and it is when a good breeze is blowing that most of them are shaken free to fly.

The other species, *Abies concolour*, attains nearly as great a height and thickness as the *magnifica*, but the branches do not form such regular whorls, nor are they so exactly pinnated or richly leaf-clad. Instead of growing all around the branchlets, the leaves are mostly arranged in two flat horizontal rows. The cones and seeds are like those of the *magnifica* in form but less than half as large. The bark of the *magnifica* is reddish purple and closely furrowed, that of the *concolour* grey and widely furrowed. A noble pair.

At Crane Flat we climbed a thousand feet or more in a distance of about two miles, the forest growing more dense and the silvery *magnifica* fir forming a still greater portion of the whole. Crane Flat is a meadow with a wide sandy border lying on the top of the divide. It is often visited by blue cranes to rest and feed on their long journeys, hence the name. It is about half a mile long, draining into the Merced, sedgy in the middle with a margin bright with lilies, columbines, larkspurs, lupines, castilleia then an outer zone of dry, gently sloping ground starred with a multitude of small flowers – eunanus, mimulus, gilia, with rosettes of spraguea and tufts of several species of eriogonum and the brilliant zauschneria. The noble forest wall about it is made up of the two silver firs and the yellow and sugar pines, which here seem to reach their highest pitch of beauty and grandeur; for the elevation, six thousand feet or a little more, is not too great for the sugar and yellow pines or too low for the *magnifica* fir, while the *concolour* seems to find this elevation the best possible. About a mile from the north end of the flat there is a grove of *Sequoia gigantea*, the king of all the conifers. Furthermore, the Douglas spruce (*Pseudotsuga Douglasii*) and *Libocedrus decurrens*, and a few two-leaved pines, occur here and there, forming a small part of the forest. Three pines, two silver firs, one Douglas spruce, one sequoia – all of them, except the two-leaved pine, colossal trees – are found here together, an assemblage of conifers unrivalled on the globe.

We passed a number of charming garden-like meadows lying on top of the divide or hanging like ribbons down its sides, imbedded in the glorious forest. Some are taken up chiefly with the tall white-flowered *Veratrum Californicum*, with boat-shaped leaves about a foot long, eight or ten inches wide and veined like those of cypripedium – a robust, hearty, liliaceous plant, fond of water and determined to be seen. Columbine and larkspur grow on the dryer edges of the meadows, with a tall handsome lupine standing waist-deep in long grasses and sedges. Castilleias, too, of several species make a bright show with beds of violets at their feet. But the glory of these forest meadows is a lily (*L. parvum*). The tallest are from seven to eight feet high with magnificent racemes of ten to twenty or more small orange-coloured flowers; they stand out free in open ground, with just enough grass and other companion plants about them to fringe their feet, and show them off to best advantage. This is a grand addition to my lily acquaintances – a true mountaineer, reaching prime vigour and beauty at a height of seven thousand feet or thereabouts. It varies, I find, very much in size even in the same meadow, not only with the soil, but with age. I saw a specimen that had only one flower, and another within a stone's throw had twenty five. And to think that the sheep should be allowed in these lily meadows! After how many centuries of Nature's care planting and watering them, tucking the bulbs in snugly below winter frost, shading the tender shoots with clouds drawn above them like curtains, pouring refreshing rain, making them perfect in beauty, and keeping them safe by a thousand miracles; yet, strange to say, allowing the trampling of devastating sheep. One might reasonably look for a wall of fire to fence such gardens. So extravagant is nature with her choicest treasures, spending plant beauty as she spends sunshine, pouring it forth into land and sea, garden and desert. And so the beauty of lilies falls on angels and men, bears and squirrels, wolves and sheep, birds and bees, but as far as I have seen, man alone, and the animals he tames, destroy these gardens. Awkward, lumbering bears, the Don tells me, love to wallow in them in hot weather, and deer with their sharp feet cross them again and again, sauntering and feeding, yet never a lily have I seen spoiled by them. Rather, like gardeners, they seem to cultivate them, pressing and dibbling as required. Anyhow not a leaf or petal seems misplaced.

The trees round about them seem as perfect in beauty and form as the lilies, their boughs whorled like lily leaves in exact order. This evening, as usual, the glow of our campfire is working enchantment on everything within reach of its rays. Lying beneath the firs, it is glorious to see them dipping their spires in the starry sky, the sky like one vast lily meadow in bloom! How can I close my eyes on so precious a night?

10 July. A Douglas squirrel, peppery, pungent autocrat of the woods, is barking overhead this morning and the small forest birds, so seldom seen when one travels noisily, are out on sunny branches along the edge of the meadow getting warm, taking a sun bath and dew bath – a fine sight. How charming the sprightly confident looks and ways of these little feathered people of the trees! They seem sure of dainty, wholesome breakfasts, and where are so many breakfasts to come from? How helpless should we find ourselves should we try to set a table for them of such buds, seeds, insects, etc., as would keep them in the pure wild health they enjoy! Not a headache or any other ache amongst them, I guess. As for the irrepressible Douglas squirrels, one never thinks of their breakfasts or the possibility of hunger, sickness or death; rather they seem like stars above chance or change, even though we may see them at times busy gathering burrs, working hard for a living.

On through the forest ever higher we go, a cloud of dust dimming the way, thousands of feet, trampling leaves and flowers, but in this mighty wilderness they seem but a feeble band, and a thousand gardens will escape their blighting touch. They cannot hurt the trees, though some of the seedlings suffer, and should the woolly locusts be greatly multiplied, as on account of dollar value they are likely to be, then the forests too, may in time be destroyed. Only the sky will then be safe, though hid from view by dust and smoke, incense of a bad sacrifice. Poor, helpless, hungry sheep, in great part misbegotten, without good right to be, semi-manufactured, made less by God than man, born out of time and place, yet their voices are strangely human and call out one's pity.

Our way is still along the Merced and Tuolumne divide, the streams on our right going to swell the songful Yosemite River, those on our left to the songful Tuolumne, slipping through sunny carex and lily meadows and breaking into song down a thousand ravines almost as soon as they are born. A more tuneful set of streams surely nowhere exists, or more sparkling crystal pure, now gliding with tinkling whisper, now with merry dimpling rush, in and out through sunshine and shade, shimmering in pools, uniting their currents, bouncing, dancing from form to form over cliffs and inclines, ever more beautiful the farther they go until they pour into the main glacial rivers.

All day I have been gazing in growing admiration at the noble groups of the magnificent silver fir which more and more is taking the ground to itself. The woods above Crane Flat still continue comparatively open, letting in the sunshine on the brown needle-strewn ground. Not only are the individual trees admirable in symmetry and superb in foliage and port, but half a dozen or more, often form temple groves in which the trees are so nicely graded in size and position as to seem one. Here indeed, is the tree-lover's paradise. The dullest eye in the world must surely be quickened by such trees as these.

Fortunately the sheep need little attention, as they are driven slowly and allowed to nip and nibble as they like. Since leaving Hazel Green we have been following the Yosemite trail; visitors to the famous valley coming by way of Coulterville and Chinese Camp pass this way – the two trails uniting at Crane Flat – and enter the valley on the north side. Another trail enters on the south side by way of Mariposa. The tourists we saw were in parties of from three or four to fifteen or twenty, mounted on mules or small mustang ponies. A strange show they made, winding single file through the solemn woods in gaudy attire, scaring the wild creatures, and one might fancy that even the great pines would be disturbed and groan aghast. But what may we say of ourselves and the flock?

We are now camped at Tamarack Flat, within four or five miles of the lower end of Yosemite. Here is another fine meadow embosomed in the woods, with a deep, clear stream gliding through it, its banks rounded and bevelled with a thatch of dipping sedges. The flat is named after the two leaved pine (*Pinus contorta*, var. *Murrayana*), common here, especially around the cool margin of the meadow. On rocky ground it is a rough, thickset tree, about forty to sixty feet high and one to three feet in diameter, bark thin and gummy, branches rather naked, tassels, leaves and cones small. But in damp, rich soil it grows close and slender, and reaches a height at times of nearly a hundred feet. Specimens only six inches in diameter at the ground are often fifty or sixty feet in height, as slender and sharp in outline as arrows, like the true tamarack (larch) of the Eastern States; hence the name, though it is a pine.

11 July. The Don has gone ahead on one of the pack animals to spy out the land to the north of Yosemite in search of the best point for a central camp. Much higher than this we cannot now go, for the upper pastures, said to be better than any hereabouts, are still buried in heavy winter snow. Glad I am that camp is to be fixed in the Yosemite region, for many a glorious ramble I'll have along the top of the walls, and then what landscapes I shall find with their new mountains and canyons, forests and gardens, lakes and streams and falls.

We are now about seven thousand feet above the sea and the nights are so cool we have to pile coats and extra clothing on top of our blankets. Tamarack Creek is icy cold, delicious, exhilarating champagne water. It is flowing bank full in the meadow with silent speed, but only a few hundred yards below our camp the ground is bare grey granite strewn with boulders, large spaces being without a single tree or only a small one here and there anchored in narrow seams and cracks. The boulders, many of them very large, are not in piles or scattered like rubbish among loose crumbling debris as if weathered out of the solid as boulders of disintegration; they mostly occur singly, and are lying on a clean pavement on which the sunshine falls in a glare that contrasts with the shimmer of light and shade we have been accustomed to in the leafy woods. And strange to say, these boulders lying so still and deserted, with no moving force near them, no boulder carrier anywhere in sight, were nevertheless brought from a distance, as difference in colour and composition shows, quarried and carried and laid down here each in its place; nor have they stirred, most of them, through calm and storm since first they arrived. They look lonely here, strangers in a strange land – huge blocks, angular mountain chips, the largest twenty or thirty feet in diameter, the chips that Nature has made in modelling her landscapes, fashioning the forms of her mountains and valleys. And with what tool were they quarried and carried? On the pavement we find its marks. The most resisting unweathered portion of the surface is scored and striated in a rigidly parallel way, indicating that the region has been overswept by a glacier from the north-eastward, grinding down the general mass of the mountains, scoring and polishing, producing a strange, raw, wiped appearance, and dropping whatever boulders it chanced to be carrying at the time it was melted at the close of the Glacial Period. A fine discovery this. As for the forests we have been passing through, they are probably growing on deposits of soil most of which has been laid down by this same ice agent in the form of moraines of different sorts, now in great part disintegrated and outspread by post-glacial weathering.

Out of the grassy meadow and down over this ice-planed granite runs the glad young Tamarack Creek, rejoicing, exulting, chanting, dancing in white, glowing, irised falls and cascades on its way to the Merced Canyon, a few miles below Yosemite, falling more than three thousand feet in a distance of about two miles.

All the Merced streams are wonderful singers, and Yosemite is the centre where the main tributaries meet. From a point about half a mile from our camp we can see into the lower end of the famous valley, with its wonderful cliffs and groves, a grand page of mountain manuscript that I would gladly give my life to be able to read. How vast it seems, how short human life when we happen to think of it, and how little we may learn, however hard we try! Yet why bewail our poor inevitable ignorance? Some of the external beauty is always in sight, enough to keep every fibre of us tingling, and this we are able to gloriously enjoy though the methods of its creation may lie beyond our ken. Sing on, brave Tamarack Creek, fresh from your snowy fountains, plash and swirl and dance to your fate in the sea; bathing, cheering every living thing along your way.

Have greatly enjoyed all this huge day, sauntering and seeing, steeping in the mountain influences, sketching, noting, pressing flowers, drinking ozone and Tamarack water. Found the white fragrant Washington lily, the finest of all the Sierra lilies. Its bulbs are buried in shaggy chaparral tangles, I suppose for safety from pawing bears; and its magnificent panicles sway and rock over the top of the rough snow-pressed bushes, while big, bold, blunt-nosed bees drone and mumble in its polleny bells. A lovely flower, worth going hungry and footsore endless miles to see. The whole world seems richer now that I have found this plant in so noble a landscape.

A log house serves to mark a claim to the Tamarack meadow, which may become valuable as a station in case travel to Yosemite should greatly increase. Belated parties occasionally stop here. A white man with an Indian woman is holding possession of the place.

Sauntered up the meadow about sundown, out of sight of camp and sheep and all human mark, into the deep peace of the solemn old woods, everything glowing with Heaven's unquenchable enthusiasm.

12 July. The Don has returned, and again we go on pilgrimage. 'Looking over the Yosemite Creek country', he said, 'from the tops of the hills you see nothing but rocks and patches of trees; but when you go down into the rocky desert you find no end of small grassy banks and meadows, and so the country is not half so lean as it looks. There we'll go and stay until the snow is melted from the upper country.'

I was glad to hear that the high snow made a stay in the Yosemite region necessary, for I am anxious to see as much of it as posssible. What fine times I shall have sketching, studying plants and rocks, and scrambling about the brink of the great valley alone, out of sight and sound of camp!

We saw another party of Yosemite tourists today. Somehow most of these travellers seem to care but little for the glorious objects about them, though enough to spend time and money and endure long rides to see the famous valley. And when they are fairly within the mighty walls of the temple and hear the psalms of the falls, they will forget themselves and become devout. Blessed indeed, should be every pilgrim in these holy mountains!

We moved slowly eastward along the Mono Trail, and early in the afternoon unpacked and camped on the bank of Cascade Creek. The Mono Trail crosses the range by the Bloody Canyon Pass to gold mines near the north end of Mono Lake. These mines were reported to be rich when first discovered, and a grand rush took place, making a trail necessary. A few small bridges were built over streams where fording was not practicable on account of the softness of the bottom, sections of fallen trees cut out and lanes made through thickets wide enough to allow the passage of bulky packs; but over the greater part of the way scarce a stone or shovelful of earth has been moved.

The woods we passed through are composed almost wholly of *Abies magnifica*, the companion species, *concolor*, being mostly left behind on account of altitude, while the increasing elevation seems grateful to the charming *magnifica*. No words can do anything like justice to this noble tree. At one place many had fallen during some heavy wind storm, owing to the loose sandy character of the soil, which offered no secure anchorage. The soil is mostly decomposed and disintegrated moraine material.

The sheep are lying down on a bare rocky spot such as they like, chewing the cud in grassy peace. Cooking is going on, appetites growing keener every day. No lowlander can appreciate the mountain appetite, and the facility with which heavy food called 'grub' is disposed of. Eating, walking, resting, seem alike delightful, and one feels inclined to shout lustily on rising in the morning like a crowing cock. Sleep and digestion as clear as the air. Fine spicy plush boughs for bedding we shall have tonight, and a glorious lullaby from this cascading creek. Never was stream more fittingly named, for as far as I have traced it above and below our camp it is one continuous bouncing, dancing, white bloom of cascades. And at the very last unwearied it finishes its wild course in a grand leap of three hundred feet or more to the bottom of the main Yosemite canyon near the fall of Tamarack Creek, a few miles below the foot of the valley. These falls almost rival some of the far famed Yosemite falls. Never shall I forget these glad cascade songs, the low booming, the roaring, the keen, silvery clashing of the cool water rushing exulting from form to form beneath irised spray; or in the deep still night seen white in the darkness, and its multitude of voices sounding still more impressively sublime. Here I find the little water ouzel as much at home as any linnet in a leafy grove, seeming to take the greater delight the more boisterous the stream. The dizzy precipices, the swift dashing energy displayed, and the thunder tones of the sheer falls are awe-inspiring, but there is nothing awful about this little bird. Its song is sweet and low, and all its gestures, as it flits about amid the loud uproar, bespeak strength and peace and joy. Contemplating these darlings of Nature coming forth from spray sprinkled nests on the brink of savage streams, Samson's riddle comes to mind, 'Out of the strong cometh forth sweetness'. A yet finer bloom is this little bird than the foam bells in eddying pools. Gentle bird, a precious message you bring me. We may miss the meaning of the torrent, but thy sweet voice, only love is in it.

13 July. Our course all day has been eastward over the rim of Yosemite Creek basin and down about half-way to the bottom, where we have encamped on a sheet of glacier-polished granite, a firm foundation for beds. Saw the tracks of a very large bear on the trail, and the Don talked of bears in general. I said I should like to see the maker of these immense tracks as he marched along, and follow him for days, without disturbing him, to learn something of the life of this master beast of the wilderness. Lambs, the Don told me, born in the lowland, that never saw or heard a bear, snort and run in terror when they catch the scent, showing how fully they have inherited a knowledge of their enemy. Hogs, mules, horses and cattle are afraid of bears, and are seized with ungovernable terror when they approach, particularly hogs and mules. Hogs are frequently driven to pastures in the foothills of the Coast Range and Sierra where acorns are abundant and are herded in droves of hundreds like sheep. When a bear comes to the range they promptly leave it, emigrating in a body, usually in the night time, the keepers being powerless to prevent; they thus show more sense than sheep, that simply scatter in the rocks and brush and await their fate. Mules flee like the wind with or without riders when they see a bear, and, if picketed, sometimes break their necks in trying to break their ropes, though I have not heard of bears killing mules or horses. Of hogs they are said to be particularly fond, bolting small ones, bones and all, without choice of parts. In particular, Mr Delaney assured me that all kinds of bears in the Sierra are very shy, and that hunters found far greater difficulty in getting within gunshot of them than of deer or indeed any other animal in the Sierra and if I was anxious to see much of them I should have to wait and watch with endless Indian patience and pay no attention to anything else.

Night is coming on, the grey rock waves are growing dim in the twilight.

How raw and young this region appears! Had the ice sheet that swept over it vanished but yesterday, its traces on the more resisting portions about our camp could hardly be more distinct than they now are. The horses and sheep and all of us, indeed, slipped on the smoothest places.

14 July. How deathlike is sleep in this mountain air, and quick the awakening into newness of life! A calm dawn, yellow and purple, then floods of sungold, making everything tingle and glow.

In an hour or two we came to Yosemite Creek, the stream that makes the greatest of all the Yosemite falls. It is about forty feet wide at the Mono Trail crossing, and now about four feet in average depth, flowing about three miles an hour. The distance to the verge of the Yosemite wall, where it makes its tremendous plunge, is only about two miles from here. Calm, beautiful, and nearly silent, it glides with stately gestures, a dense growth of the slender two-leaved pine along its banks, and a fringe of willow, purple spirea, sedges, daisies, lilies and columbines. Some of the sedges and willow boughs dip into the current, and just outside of the close ranks of trees there is a sunny flat of washed gravelly sand which seems to have been deposited by some ancient flood. It is covered with millions of erethrea, eriogonum, and oxytheca, with more flowers than leaves, forming an even growth, slightly dimpled and ruffled here and there by rosettes of *Spraguea umbellata*. Back of this flowery strip there is a wavy upsloping plain of solid granite, so smoothly ice-polished in many places that it glistens in the sun like glass. In shallow hollows there are patches of trees, mostly the rough form of the two-leaved pine, rather scrawny looking where there is little or no soil. Also a few junipers (*Juniperus occidentalis*), short and stout, with bright cinnamon-coloured bark and grey foliage, standing alone mostly, on the sun-beaten pavement, safe from fire, clinging by slight joints – a sturdy storm-enduring mountaineer of a tree, living on sunshine and snow, maintaining tough health on this diet for perhaps more than a thousand years.

Up towards the head of the basin I see groups of domes rising above the wavelike ridges, and some picturesque castellated masses, and dark strips and patches of silver fir, indicating deposits of fertile soil. Would that I could command the time to study them! What rich excursions one could make in this well-defined basin! Its glacial inscriptions and sculptures, how marvellous they seem, how noble the studies they offer! I tremble with excitement in the dawn of these glorious mountain sublimities, but I can only gaze and wonder, and, like a child, gather here and there a lily, half hoping I may be able to study and learn in years to come.

The drivers and dogs had a lively, laborious time getting the sheep across the creek, the second large stream thus far that they have been compelled to cross without a bridge; the first being the north fork of the Merced near Bower Cave. Men and dogs, shouting and barking, drove the timid, water-fearing creatures in a close crowd against the bank, but not one of the flock would launch away. While thus jammed, the Don and the shepherd rushed through the frightened crowd to stampede those in front, but this would only cause a break backward, and away they would scamper through the stream bank trees and scatter over the rocky pavement. Then with the aid of the dogs the runaways would again be gathered and made to face the stream, and again the compacted mass would break away, amid wild shouting and barking that might well have disturbed the stream itself and marred the music of its falls, to which visitors no doubt from all quarters of the globe were listening. 'Hold them there! Now hold them there!' shouted the Don; 'The front ranks will soon tire of the pressure, and be glad to take to the water, then all will jump in and cross in a hurry.' But they did nothing of the kind; they only avoided the pressure by breaking back in scores and hundreds, leaving the beauty of the banks sadly trampled.

If only one could be got to cross over, all would make haste to follow; but that one could not be found. A lamb was caught, carried across, and tied to a bush on the opposite bank, where it cried piteously for its mother. But though greatly concerned, the mother only called it back. That play on maternal affection failed, and we began to fear that we should be forced to make a long roundabout drive and cross the widespread tributaries of the creek in succession. This would require several days, but it had its advantages, for I was eager to see the sources of so famous a stream. Don Quixote, however, determined that they must ford just here, and immediately began a sort of siege by cutting down slender pines on the bank and building a corral barely large enough to hold the flock when well pressed together. And as the stream would form one side of the corral he believed that they could easily be forced into the water.

In a few hours the enclosure was completed, and the silly animals were driven in and rammed hard against the brink of the ford. Then the Don, forcing a way through the compacted mass, pitched a few of the terrified unfortunates into the stream by main strength; but instead of crossing over, they swam about close to the bank, making desperate attempts to get back into the flock. Then a dozen or more were shoved off, and the Don, tall like a crane and a good natural wader, jumped in after them, seized a struggling wether, and dragged it to the opposite shore. But no sooner did he let it go than it jumped into the stream and swam back to its frightened companions in the corral, thus manifesting sheep nature as unchangeable as gravitation. Pan with his pipes would have had no better luck, I fear. We were now pretty well baffled. The silly creatures would suffer any sort of death rather than cross that stream. Calling a council, the dripping Don declared that starvation was now the only likely scheme to try, and that we might as well camp here in comfort and let the besieged flock grow hungry and cool and come to their senses, if they had any. In a few minutes after being thus let alone, an adventurer in the foremost rank plunged in and swam bravely to the farther shore. Then suddenly all rushed in pell-mell together, trampling one another under water, while we vainly tried to hold them back. The Don jumped into the thickest of the gasping gurgling, drowning mass, and shoved them right and left as if each sheep was a piece of floating timber. The current also served to drift them apart; a long bent column was soon formed and in a few minutes all were over and began baaing and feeding as if nothing out of the common had happened. That none were drowned seems wonderful. I fully expected that hundreds would gain the romantic fate of being swept into Yosemite over the highest waterfall in the world.

As the day was far spent we camped a little way back from the ford and let the dripping flock scatter and feed until sundown. The wool is dry now, and calm, cud-chewing peace has fallen on all the comfortable band, leaving no trace of the watery battle. I have seen fish driven out of the water with less ado than was made in driving these animals into it. Sheepbrain must surely be poor stuff. Compare today's exhibition with the performances of deer swimming quietly across broad and rapid rivers, and from island to island in seas and lakes; or with dogs, or even with the squirrels that, as the story goes, cross the Mississippi River on selected chips, with tails for sails comfortably trimmed to the breeze. A sheep can hardly be called an animal; an entire flock is required to make one foolish individual.

CHAPTER FIVE

The Yosemite

15 JULY. Followed the Mono Trail up the eastern rim of the basin nearly to its summit, then turned off southward to a small shallow valley that extends to the edge of the Yosemite, which we reached about noon, and encamped. After luncheon I made haste to high ground, and from the top of the ridge on the west side of Indian Canyon gained the noblest view of the summit peaks I have ever yet enjoyed. Nearly all the upper basin of the Merced was displayed, with its sublime domes and canyons, dark upsweeping forests, and glorious array of white peaks deep in the sky, every feature glowing, radiating beauty that pours into our flesh and bones like heat rays from fire. Sunshine over all; no breath of wind to stir the brooding calm. Never before had I seen so glorious a landscape, so boundless an affluence of sublime mountain beauty. The most extravagant description I might give of this view to any one who has not seen similar landscapes with his own eyes would not so much as hint its grandeur and the spiritual glow that covered it. I shouted and gesticulated in a wild burst of ecstasy, much to the astonishment of St Bernard Carlo, who came running up to me, manifesting in his intelligent eyes a puzzled concern that was very ludicrous, which had the effect of bringing me to my senses. A brown bear, too, it would seem, had been a spectator of the show I had made of myself, for I had gone but a few yards when I started one from a thicket of brush. He evidently considered me dangerous, for he ran away very fast, tumbling over the tops of the tangled manzanita bushes in his haste. Carlo drew back, with his ears depressed as if afraid, and kept looking me in the face, as if expecting me to pursue and shoot, for he had seen many a bear battle in his day.

Following the ridge, which made a gradual descent to the south, I came at length to the brow of that massive cliff that stands between Indian Canyon and Yosemite Falls, and here the far-famed valley came suddenly into view throughout almost its whole extent. The noble walls – sculptured into endless variety of domes and gables, spires and battlements and plain mural precipices – all atremble with the thunder tones of the falling water. The level bottom seemed to be dressed like a garden – sunny meadows here and there, and groves of pine and oak; the river of Mercy sweeping in majesty through the midst of them and flashing back the sunbeams. The great Tissiack, or Half-Dome, rising at the upper end of the valley to a height of nearly a mile, is nobly proportioned and lifelike, the most impressive of all the rocks, holding the eye in devout admiration, calling it back again and again from falls or meadows, or even the mountains beyond – marvellous cliffs, marvellous in sheer dizzy depth and sculpture, types of endurance. Thousands of years have they stood in the sky exposed to rain, snow, frost, earthquake and avalanche, yet they still wear the bloom of youth.

I rambled along the valley rim to the westward; most of it is rounded off on the very brink, so that it is not easy to find places where one may look clear down the face of the wall to the bottom. When such places were found and I had cautiously set my feet and drawn my body erect, I could not help fearing a little that the rock might split off and let me down, and what a down! – more than three thousand feet. Still my limbs did not tremble, nor did I feel the least uncertainty as to the reliance to be placed on them. My only fear was that a flake of the granite, which in some places showed joints more or less open and running parallel with the face of the cliff, might give way. After withdrawing from such places, excited with the view I had got, I would say to myself, 'Now don't go out on the verge again'. But in the face of Yosemite scenery cautious remonstrance is vain; under its spell one's body seems to go where it likes with a will over which we seem to have scarce any control.

After a mile or so of this memorable cliff work I approached Yosemite Creek, admiring its easy, graceful, confident gestures as it comes bravely forward in its narrow channel, singing the last of its mountain songs on its way to its fate – a few rods more over the shining granite, then down half a mile in showy foam to another world, to be lost in the Merced, where climate, vegetation, inhabitants, all are different. Emerging from its last gorge, it glides in wide lace-like rapids down a smooth incline into a pool where it seems to rest and compose its grey, agitated waters before taking the grand plunge, then slowly slipping over the lip of the pool basin, it descends another glossy slope with rapidly accelerated speed to the brink of the tremendous cliff, and with sublime, fateful confidence springs out free in the air.

I took off my shoes and stockings and worked my way cautiously down alongside the rushing flood, keeping my feet and hands pressed firmly on the polished rock. The booming, roaring water, rushing past close to my head, was very exciting. I had expected that the sloping apron would terminate with the perpendicular wall of the valley, and that from the foot of it, where it is less steeply inclined, I should be able to lean far enough out to see the forms and behaviour of the fall all the way down to the bottom. But I found that there was yet another small brow over which I could not see, and which appeared to be too steep for mortal feet. Scanning it keenly, I discovered a narrow shelf about three inches wide on the very brink, just wide enough for a rest for one's heels. But there seemed to be no way of reaching it over so steep a brow. At length, after careful scrutiny of the surface, I found an irregular edge of a flake of the rock some distance back from the margin of the torrent. If I was to get down to the brink at all that rough edge, which might offer slight finger holds, was the only way. But the slope beside it looked dangerously smooth and steep, and the swift roaring flood beneath, overhead, and beside me was very nerve trying. I therefore concluded not to venture farther, but did nevertheless. Tufts of artemisia were growing in clefts of the rock near by, and I filled my mouth with the bitter leaves, hoping they might help to prevent giddiness. Then, with a caution not known in ordinary circumstances, I crept down safely to the little ledge, got my heels well planted on it, then shuffled in a horizontal direction twenty or thirty feet until close to the outplunging current, which, by the time it had descended thus far, was already white. Here I obtained a perfectly free view down into the heart of the snowy, chanting throng of comet-like streamers, into which the body of the fall soon separates.

While perched on that narrow niche I was not distinctly conscious of danger. The tremendous grandeur of the fall in form and sound and motion, acting at close range, smothered the sense of fear, and in such places one's body takes keen care for safety on its own account. How long I remained down there, or how I returned, I can hardly tell. Anyhow I had a glorious time, and got back to camp about dark, enjoying triumphant exhilaration soon followed by dull weariness. Hereafter I'll try to keep from such extravagant, nerve straining places. Yet such a day is well worth venturing for. My first view of the High Sierra, first view looking down into Yosemite, the death song of Yosemite Creek, and its flight over the vast cliff, each one of these is of itself enough for a great lifelong landscape fortune – a most memorable day of days – enjoyment enough to kill if that were possible.

16 July. My enjoyments yesterday afternoon, especially at the head of the fall, were too great for good sleep. Kept starting up last night in a nervous tremor, half awake, fancying that the foundation of the mountain we were camped on had given way and was falling into Yosemite Valley. In vain I roused myself to make a new beginning for sound sleep. The nerve strain had been too great, and again and again I dreamed I was rushing through the air above a glorious avalanche of water and rocks. One time, springing to my feet, I said, 'This time it is real – all must die, and where could mountaineer find a more glorious death!'

Left camp soon after sunrise for an all day ramble eastward. Crossed the head of Indian Basin, forested with *Abies magnifica*, underbrush mostly *Ceanothus cordulatus* and manzanita, a mixture not easily trampled over or penetrated, for the ceanothus is thorny and grows in dense snow-pressed masses, and the manzanita has exceedingly crooked, stubborn branches. From the head of the canyon continued on past North Dome into the basin of Dome or Porcupine Creek. Here are fine meadows embedded in the woods, gay with *Lilium parvum* and its companions; the elevation, about eight thousand feet, seems to be best suited for it – saw specimens that were a foot or two higher than my head. Had more magnificent views of the upper mountains, and of the great South Dome, said to be the grandest rock in the world. Well it may be, since it is of such noble dimensions and sculpture. A wonderfully impressive monument, its lines exquisite in fineness, and though sublime in size, is finished like the finest work of art, and seems to be alive.

17 July. A new camp was made today in a magnificent silver fir grove at the head of a small stream that flows into Yosemite by way of Indian Canyon. Here we intend to stay several weeks – a fine location from which to make excursions about the great valley and its fountains. Glorious days I'll have sketching, pressing plants, studying the wonderful topography and the wild animals, our happy fellow mortals and neighbours. But the vast mountains in the distance, shall I ever know them, shall I be allowed to enter into their midst and dwell with them?

We were pelted about noon by a short, heavy rain-storm, sublime thunder reverberating among the mountains and canyons – some strokes near, crashing, ringing in the tense crisp air with startling keenness, while the distant peaks loomed gloriously through the cloud fringes and sheets of rain. Now the storm is past, and the fresh washed air is full of the essences of the flower gardens and groves. Winter storms in Yosemite must be glorious. May I see them!

Have got my bed made in our new camp – plushy sumptuous, and deliciously fragrant, most of it *magnifica* fir plumes, of course, with a variety of sweet flowers in the pillow. Hope to sleep tonight without tottering nerve dreams. Watched a deer eating ceanothus leaves and twigs.

18 July. Slept pretty well; the valley walls did not seem to fall, though I still fancied myself at the brink, alongside the white, plunging flood, especially when half asleep. Strange the danger of that adventure should be more troublesome now that I am in the bosom of the peaceful woods, a mile or more from the fall, than it was while I was on the brink of it.

Bears seem to be common here, judging by their tracks. About noon we had another rain-storm with keen startling thunder, the metallic, ringing, clashing, clanging notes gradually fading into low bass rolling and muttering in the distance. For a few minutes the rain came in a grand torrent like a waterfall, then hail; some of the hailstones an inch in diameter, hard, icy, and irregular in form, like those oftentimes seen in Wisconsin. Carlo watched them with intelligent astonishment as they came pelting and thrashing through the quivering branches of the trees. The cloud scenery sublime. Afternoon calm, sunful, and clear, with delicious freshness and fragrance from the firs and flowers and steaming ground.

19 July. Watching the daybreak and sunrise. The pale rose and purple sky changing softly to daffodil yellow and white, sunbeams pouring through the passes between the peaks and over the Yosemite domes, making their edges burn; the silver firs in the middle ground catching the glow on the spiry tops, and our camp grove fills and thrills with the glorious light. Everything awakening alert and joyful; the birds begin to stir and innumerable insect people. Deer quietly withdraw into leafy hiding places in the chaparral; the dew vanishes, flowers spread their petals, every pulse beats high, every life cell rejoices, the very rocks seem to thrill with life. The whole landscape glows like a human face in a glory of enthusiasm, and the blue sky, pale around the horizon, bends peacefully down over all like one vast flower.

About noon, as usual, big bossy cumuli began to grow above the forest, and the rainstorm pouring from them is the most imposing I have yet seen. The silvery zigzag lightning lances are longer than usual and the thunder gloriously impressive, keen, crashing, intensely concentrated, speaking with such tremendous energy it would seem that an entire mountain is being shattered at every stroke, but probably only a few trees are being shattered, many of which I have seen on my walks hereabouts strewing the ground. At last the clear ringing strokes are succeeded by deep low tones that grow gradually fainter as they roll afar into the recesses of the echoing mountains, where they seem to be welcomed home. Then another and another peal, or rather crashing, splintering stroke, follows in quick succession, perchance splitting some giant pine or fir from top to bottom into long rails and slivers, and scattering them to all points of the compass. Now comes the rain, with corresponding extravagant grandeur, covering the ground high and low with a sheet of flowing water, a transparent film fitted like a skin upon the rugged anatomy of the landscape, making the rocks glitter and glow, gathering in the ravines, flooding the streams, and making them shout and boom in reply to the thunder.

How interesting to trace the history of a single raindrop! It is not long, geologically speaking, as we have seen, since the first raindrops fell on the newborn leafless Sierra landscapes. How different the lot of these falling now! Happy the showers that fall on so fair a wilderness – scarce a single drop can fail to find a beautiful spot – on the tops of the peaks, on the shining glacier pavements, on the great smooth domes, on forests and gardens and brushy moraines, plashing, glinting, pattering, laving. Some go to the high snowy fountains to swell their well-saved stores; some into the lakes, washing the mountain windows, patting their smooth glassy levels, making dimples and bubbles and spray; some into the waterfalls and cascades, as if eager to join in their dance and song and beat their foam yet finer; good luck and good work for the happy mountain raindrops, each one of them a high waterfall in itself, descending from the cliffs and hollows of the clouds to the cliffs and hollows of the rocks, out of the sky-thunder into the thunder of the falling rivers. Some, falling on meadows and bogs, creep silently out of sight to the grass roots, hiding softly as in a nest, slipping, oozing hither, thither, seeking and finding their appointed work. Some, descending through the spires of the woods, sift spray through the shining needles, whispering peace and good cheer to each one of them. Some drops with happy aim glint on the sides of crystals – quartz, hornblende, garnet, zircon, tourmaline, feldspar – patter on grains of gold and heavy way-worn nuggets; some, with blunt plap-plap and low bass drumming, fall on the broad leaves of veratrum, saxifrage, cypripedium. Some happy drops fall straight into the cups of flowers, kissing the lips of lilies. How far they have to go, how many cups to fill, great and small, cells too small to be seen, cups holding half a drop as well as lake basins between the hills, each replenished with equal care, every drop in all the blessed throng a silvery newborn star with lake and river, garden and grove, valley and mountain, all that the landscape holds reflected in its crystal depths, God's messenger, angel of love sent on its way with majesty and pomp and display of power that make man's greatest shows ridiculous.

Now the storm is over, the sky is clear, the last rolling thunder-wave is spent on the peaks, and where are the raindrops now – what has become of all the shining throng? In winged vapour rising some are already hastening back to the sky, some have gone into the plants, creeping through invisible doors into the round rooms of cells, some are locked in crystals of ice, some in rock crystals, some in porous moraines to keep their small springs flowing, some have gone journeying on in the rivers to join the larger raindrop of the ocean. From form to form, beauty to beauty, ever changing, never resting, all are speeding on with love's enthusiasm, singing with the stars the eternal song of creation.

20 July. Fine calm morning; air tense and clear; not the slightest breeze astir; everything shining, the rocks with wet crystals, the plants with dew, each receiving its portion of irised dewdrops and sunshine like living creatures getting their breakfast, their dew manna coming down from the starry sky like swarms of smaller stars. How wondrous fine are the particles in showers of dew, thousands required for a single drop, growing in the dark as silently as the grass! What pains are taken to keep this wilderness in health – showers of snow, showers of rain, showers of dew, floods of light, floods of invisible vapour, clouds, winds, all sorts of weather, interaction of plant on plant and animal on animal, beyond thought! How fine Nature's methods! How deeply with beauty is beauty overlaid! The ground covered with crystals, the crystals with mosses and lichens and low-spreading grasses and flowers, these with larger plants leaf over leaf with ever changing colour and form, the broad palms of the firs outspread over these, the azure dome over all like a bell-flower, and star above star.

Yonder stands the South Dome, its crown high above our camp, though its base is four thousand feet below us; a most noble rock, it seems full of thought, clothed with living light, no sense of dead stone about it, all spiritualised, neither heavy looking nor light, steadfast in serene strength like a god.

Our shepherd is a queer character and hard to place in this wilderness. His bed is a hollow made in red dry rot punky dust beside a log which forms a portion of the south wall of the corral. Here he lies with his wonderful everlasting clothing on, wrapped in a red blanket, breathing not only the dust of the decayed wood but also that of the corral, as if determined to take ammoniacal snuff all night after chewing tobacco all day. Following the sheep he carries a heavy six-shooter swung from his belt on one side and his luncheon on the other. The ancient cloth in which the meat, fresh from the frying pan, is tied serves as a filter through which the clear fat and gravy juices drip down on his right hip and leg in clustering stalactites. This oleaginous formation is soon broken up however, and diffused and rubbed evenly into his scanty apparel, by sitting down, rolling over, crossing his legs while resting on logs, making shirt and trousers watertight and shiny. His trousers, in particular, have become so adhesive with the mixed fat and resin that pine needles, thin flakes and fibres of bark, hair, mica scales and minute grains of quartz, hornblende, etc., feathers, seed wings, moth and butterfly wings, legs and antennae of innumerable insects, or even whole insects such as the small beetles, moths and mosquitoes, with flower petals, pollen dust and indeed bits of all plants, animals and minerals of the region adhere to them and are safely embedded, so that though far from being a naturalist he collects fragmentary specimens of everything and becomes richer than he knows. His specimens are kept passably fresh too, by the purity of the air and the resiny bituminous beds into which they are pressed. Man is a microcosm, at least our shepherd is, or rather his trousers. These precious overalls are never taken off, and nobody knows how old they are, though one may guess by their thickness and concentric structure. Instead of wearing thin they wear thick, and in their stratification have no small geological significance.

Besides herding the sheep, Billy is the butcher, while I have agreed to wash the few iron and tin utensils and make the bread. Then, these small duties done, by the time the sun is fairly above the mountain tops I am beyond the flock, free to rove and revel in the wilderness all the big immortal days.

Sketching on the North Dome. It commands views of nearly all the valley besides a few of the high mountains. I would fain draw everything in sight – rock, tree, and leaf. But little can I do beyond mere outlines – marks with meanings like words, readable only to myself – yet I sharpen my pencils and work on as if others might possibly be benefited. Whether these picture-sheets are to vanish like fallen leaves or go to friends like letters, matters not much; for little can they tell to those who have not themselves seen similar wilderness, and like a language have learned it. No pain here, no dull empty hours, no fear of the past, no fear of the future. These blessed mountains are so compactly filled with God's beauty, no petty personal hope or experience has room to be. Drinking this champagne water is pure pleasure, so is breathing the living air, and every movement of limbs is pleasure, while the body seems to feel beauty when exposed to it as it feels the campfire or sunshine, entering not by the eyes alone, but equally through all one's flesh like radiant heat, making a passionate ecstatic pleasure glow not explainable. One's body then seems homogeneous throughout, sound as a crystal.

Perched like a fly on this Yosemite dome, I gaze and sketch and bask, oftentimes settling down into dumb admiration without definite hope of ever learning much, yet with the longing, unresting effort that lies at the door of hope, humbly prostrate before the vast display of God's power, and eager to offer self-denial and renunciation with eternal toil to learn any lesson in the divine manuscript.

It is easier to feel than to realise, or in any way explain, Yosemite grandeur. The magnitudes of the rocks and trees and streams are so delicately har-monised they are mostly hidden. Sheer precipices three thousand feet high are fringed with tall trees growing close like grass on the brow of a lowland hill, and extending along the feet of these precipices a ribbon of meadow a mile wide and seven or eight long, that seems like a strip a farmer might mow in less than a day. Waterfalls, five hundred to one or two thousand feet high, are so subordinated to the mighty cliffs over which they pour that they seem like wisps of smoke, gentle as floating clouds, though their voices fill the valley and make the rocks tremble. The mountains too, along the eastern sky, and the domes in front of them, and the succession of smooth rounded waves between, swelling higher, higher, with dark woods in their hollows, serene in massive exuberant bulk and beauty, tend yet more to hide the grandeur of the Yosemite temple and make it appear as a subdued subordinate feature of the vast harmonious landscape. Thus every attempt to appreciate any one feature is beaten down by the overwhelming influence of all the others. And, as if this were not enough, lo! in the sky arises another mountain range with topography as rugged and substantial-looking as the one beneath it – snowy peaks and domes and shadowy Yosemite valley – another version of the snowy Sierra, a new creation heralded by a thunderstorm. How fiercely, devoutly wild is Nature in the midst of her beauty-loving tenderness! – painting lilies, watering them, caressing them with gentle hand, going from flower to flower like a gardener while building rock mountains and cloud mountains full of lightning and rain. Gladly we run for shelter beneath an overhanging cliff and examine the reassuring ferns and mosses, gentle love tokens growing in cracks and chinks. Daisies too, and ivesias, confiding wild children of light, too small to fear. To these one's heart goes home, and the voices of the storm become gentle. Now the sun breaks forth and fragrant steam arises. The birds are out singing on the edges of the groves. The west is flaming in gold and purple, ready for the ceremony of the sunset, and back I go to camp with my notes and pictures, the best of them printed in my mind as dreams. A fruitful day, without measured beginning or ending. A terrestrial eternity. A gift of good God.

Wrote to my mother and a few friends, mountain hints to each. They seem as near as if within voice-reach or touch. The deeper the solitude the less the sense of loneliness, and the nearer our friends. Now bread and tea, fir bed and goodnight to Carlo, a look at the sky lilies, and death sleep until the dawn of another Sierra tomorrow.

21 July. Sketching on the Dome – no rain; clouds at noon about quarter filled the sky, casting shadows with fine effect on the white mountains at the heads of the streams, and a soothing cover over the gardens during the warm hours.

Saw a common house fly and a grasshopper and a brown bear. The fly and grasshopper paid me a merry visit on the top of the Dome, and I paid a visit to the bear in the middle of a small garden meadow between the Dome and the camp where he was standing alert among the flowers as if willing to be seen to advantage. I had not gone more than half a mile from camp this morning, when Carlo, who was trotting on a few yards ahead of me, came to a sudden, cautious standstill. Down went tail and ears, and forward went his knowing nose, while he seemed to be saying, 'Ha, what's this? A bear, I guess'. Then a cautious advance of a few steps, setting his feet down softly like a hunting cat, and questioning the air as to the scent he had caught until all doubt vanished. Then he came back to me, looked me in the face, and with his speaking eyes reported a bear near by; then led on softly, careful, like an experienced hunter, not to make the slightest noise, and frequently looking back as if whispering, 'Yes, it's a bear; come and I'll show you'. Presently we came to where the sunbeams were streaming through between the purple shafts of the firs, which showed that we were nearing an open spot, and here Carlo came behind me, evidently sure that the bear was very near. So I crept to a low ridge of moraine boulders on the edge of a narrow garden meadow, and in this meadow I felt pretty sure the bear must be. I was anxious to get a good look at the sturdy mountaineer without alarming him; so drawing myself up noiselessly back of one of the largest of the trees I peered past its bulging buttresses, exposing only a part of my head, and there stood neighbour Bruin within a stone's throw, his hips covered by tall grass and flowers, and his front feet on the trunk of a fir that had fallen out into the meadow, which raised his head so high that he seemed to be standing erect. He had not yet seen me, but was looking and listening attentively, showing that in some way he was aware of our approach. I watched his gestures and tried to make the most of my opportunity to learn what I could about him, fearing he would catch sight of me and run away. For I had been told that this sort of bear, the cinnamon, always ran from his bad brother man, never showing fight unless wounded or in defence of young. He made a telling picture standing alert in the sunny forest garden. How well he played his part, harmonising in bulk and colour and shaggy hair with the trunks of the trees and lush vegetation, as natural a feature as any other in the landscape. After examination at leisure, noting the sharp muzzle thrust inquiringly forward, the long shaggy hair on his broad chest, the stiff, erect ears nearly buried in hair, and the slow, heavy way he moved his head, I thought I should like to see his gait in running, so I made a sudden rush at him, shouting and swinging my hat to frighten him, expecting to see him make haste to get away. But to my dismay he did not run or show any sign of running. On the contrary, he stood his ground ready to fight and defend himself, lowered his head, thrust it forward, and looked sharply and fiercely at me. Then I suddenly began to fear that upon me would fall the work of running; but I was afraid to run, and therefore, like the bear, held my ground. We stood staring at each other in solemn silence within a dozen yards or thereabouts, while I fervently hoped that the power of the human eye over wild beasts would prove as great as it is said to be. How long our awfully strenuous interview lasted, I don't know; but at length in the slow fullness of time he pulled his huge paws down off the log, and with magnificent deliberation turned and walked leisurely up the meadow, stopping frequently to look back over his shoulder to see whether I was pursuing him, then moving on again, evidently neither fearing me very much nor trusting me. He was probably about five hundred pounds in weight, a broad, rusty bundle of ungovernable wildness, a happy fellow whose lines have fallen in pleasant places. The flowery glade in which I saw him so well, framed like a picture, is one of the best of all I have yet discovered, a conservatory of Nature's precious plant people. Tall lilies were swinging their bells over that bear's back, with geraniums, larkspurs, columbines, and daisies brushing against his sides. A place for angels, one would say, instead of bears.

In the great canyons Bruin reigns supreme. Happy fellow, whom no famine can reach while one of his thousand kinds of food is spared him. His bread is sure at all seasons, ranged on the mountain shelves like stores in a pantry. From one to the other, up or down he climbs, tasting and enjoying each in turn in different climates, as if he had journeyed thousands of miles to other countries north or south to enjoy their varied productions. I should like to know my hairy brothers better – though after this particular Yosemite bear, my very neighbour, had sauntered out of sight this morning, I reluctantly went back to camp for the Don's rifle to shoot him, if necessary, in defence of the flock. Fortunately I couldn't find him, and after tracking him a mile or two towards Mount Hoffman I bade him Godspeed and gladly returned to my work on the Yosemite Dome.

The house fly also seemed at home and buzzed about me as I sat sketching, and enjoying my bear interview now it was over. I wonder what draws house flies so far up the mountains, heavy gross feeders as they are, sensitive to cold, and fond of domestic ease. How have they been distributed from continent to continent, across seas and deserts and mountain chains, usually so influential in determining boundaries of species both of plants and animals. Beetles and butterflies are sometimes restricted to small areas. Each mountain in a range, and even the different zones of a mountain, may have its own peculiar species. But the house fly seems to be everywhere. I wonder if any island in mid-ocean is flyless. The bluebottle is abundant in these Yosemite woods, ever ready with his marvellous store of eggs to make all dead flesh fly. Bumblebees are here, and are well fed on boundless stores of nectar and pollen. The honeybee, though abundant in the foothills, has not yet got so high. It is only a few years since the first swarm was brought to California. A queer fellow and a jolly fellow is the grasshopper. Up the mountains he comes on excursions, how high I don't know, but at least as far and high as Yosemite tourists. I was much interested with the hearty enjoyment of the one that danced and sang for me on the Dome this afternoon. He seemed brimful of glad, hilarious energy, manifested by springing into the air to a height of twenty or thirty feet, then diving and springing up again and making a sharp musical rattle just as the lowest point in the descent was reached. Up and down a dozen times or so he danced and sang, then alighted to rest, then up and at it again. The curves he described in the air in diving and rattling resembled those made by cords hanging loosely and attached at the same height at the ends, the loops nearly covering each other. Braver, heartier, keener, carefree enjoyment of life I have never seen or heard in any creature, great or small. The life of this comic redlegs, the mountain's merriest child, seems to be made up of pure, condensed gaiety. The Douglas squirrel is the only living creature that I can compare him with in exuberant, rollicking, irrepressible jollity. Wonderful that these sublime mountains are so loudly cheered and brightened by a creature so queer. Nature in him seems to be snapping her fingers in the face of all earthly dejection and melancholy with a boyish hip hip hurrah. How the sound is made I do not understand. When he was on the ground he made not the slightest noise, nor when he was simply flying from place to place, but only when diving in curves, the motion seeming to be required for the sound; for the more vigorous the diving the more energetic the corresponding outbursts of jolly rattling. I tried to observe him closely while he was resting in the intervals of his performances; but he would not allow a near approach, always getting his jumping legs ready to spring for immediate flight, and keeping his eyes on me. A fine sermon the little fellow danced for me on the Dome, a likely place to look for sermons in stones, but not for grasshopper sermons. A large and imposing pulpit for so small a preacher. No danger of weakness in the knees of the world while Nature can spring such a rattle as this. Even the bear did not express for me the mountain's wild health and strength and happiness so tellingly as did this comical little hopper. No cloud of care in his day, no winter of discontent in sight. To him every day is a holiday; and when at length his sun sets, I fancy he will cuddle down on the forest floor and die like the leaves and flowers, and like them leave no unsightly remains calling for burial.

Sundown, and I must to camp. Goodnight, friends three – brown bear, rugged boulder of energy in groves and gardens fair as Eden; restless, fussy fly with gauzy wings stirring the air around all the world; and grasshopper, crisp, electric spark of joy enlivening the massy sublimity of the mountains like the laugh of a child. Thank you, thank you all three for your quickening company. Heaven guide every wing and leg. Goodnight friends three, goodnight.

22 July. A fine specimen of the black-tailed deer went bounding past camp this morning. A buck with wide spread of antlers, showing admirable vigour and grace. Wonderful the beauty, strength, and graceful movements of animals in wilderness, cared for by Nature only, when our experience with domestic animals would lead us to fear that all the so-called neglected wild beasts would degenerate. Yet the upshot of Nature's method of breeding and teaching seems to lead to excellence of every sort. Deer, like all wild animals, are as clean as plants. The beauties of their gestures and attitudes, alert or in repose, surprise yet more than their bounding exuberant strength. Every movement and posture is graceful, the very poetry of manners and motion. Mother Nature is too often spoken of as in reality no mother at all. Yet how wisely, sternly, tenderly she loves and looks after her children in all sorts of weather and wildernesses. The more I see of deer the more I admire them as mountaineers. They make their way into the heart of the roughest solitudes with smooth reserve of strength, through dense belts of brush and forest encumbered with fallen trees and boulder piles, across canyons, roaring streams, and snowfields, ever showing forth beauty and courage. Over nearly all the continent the deer find homes. In the Florida savannas and hummocks, in the Canada woods, in the far north, roaming over mossy tundras, swimming lakes and rivers and arms of the sea from island to island washed with waves, or climbing rocky mountains, everywhere healthy and able, adding beauty to every landscape – a truly admirable creature and great credit to Nature.

Have been sketching a silver fir that stands on a granite ridge a few hundred yards to the eastward of camp – a fine tree with a particular snowstorm story to tell. It is about one hundred feet high, growing on bare rock, thrusting its roots into a weathered joint less than an inch wide, and bulging out to form a base to bear its weight. The storm came from the north while it was young and broke it down nearly to the ground, as is shown by the old, dead, weather-beaten top leaning out from the living trunk built up from a new shoot below the break. The annual rings of the trunk that have overgrown the dead sapling tell the year of the storm. Wonderful that a side branch forming a portion of one of the level collars that encircle the trunk of this species (*Abies magnifica*) should bend upward, grow erect, and take the place of the lost axis to form a new tree.

Many others, pines as well as firs, bear testimony to the crushing severity of this particular storm. Trees, some of them fifty to seventy five feet high, were bent to the ground and buried like grass, whole groves vanishing as if the forest had been cleared away, leaving not a branch or needle visible until the spring thaw. Then the more elastic undamaged saplings rose again, aided by the wind, some reaching a nearly erect attitude, others remaining more or less bent, while those with broken backs endeavoured to specialise a side branch below the break and make a leader of it to form a new axis of development. It is as if a man, whose back was broken or nearly so and who was compelled to go bent, should find a branch backbone sprouting straight up from below the break and should gradually develop new arms and shoulders and head, while the old damaged portion of his body died.

Grand white cloud mountains and domes created about noon as usual, ridges and ranges of endless variety, as if Nature dearly loved this sort of work, doing it again and again nearly every day with infinite industry, and producing beauty that never palls. A few zigzags of lightning, five minutes shower, then a gradual wilting and clearing.

23 July. Another midday cloudland, displaying power and beauty that one never wearies in beholding, but hopelessly unsketchable and untellable. What can poor mortals say about clouds? While a description of their huge glowing domes and ridges, shadowy gulfs and canyons, and feather-edged ravines is being tried, they vanish, leaving no visible ruins. Nevertheless, these fleeting sky mountains are as substantial and significant as the more lasting upheavals of granite beneath them. Both alike are built up and die, and in God's calendar difference of duration is nothing. We can only dream about them in wondering, worshipping admiration, happier than we dare tell even to friends who see farthest in sympathy, glad to know that not a crystal or vapour particle of them, hard or soft, is lost; that they sink and vanish only to rise again and again in higher and higher beauty. As to our own work, duty, influence, etc., concerning which so much fussy pother is made, it will not fail of its due effect, though, like a lichen on a stone, we keep silent.

24 July. Clouds at noon occupying about half the sky gave half an hour of heavy rain to wash one of the cleanest landscapes in the world. How well it is washed! The sea is hardly less dusty than the ice-burnished pavements and ridges, domes and canyons, and summit peaks plashed with snow like waves with foam. How fresh the woods are and calm after the last films of clouds have been wiped from the sky! A few minutes ago every tree was excited, bowing to the roaring storm, waving, swirling, tossing their branches in glorious enthusiasm like worship. But though to the outer ear these trees are now silent, their songs never cease. Every hidden cell is throbbing with music and life, every fibre thrilling like harp strings, while incense is ever flowing from the balsam bells and leaves. No wonder the hills and groves were God's first temples, and the more they are cut down and hewn into cathedrals and churches, the farther off and dimmer seems the Lord himself. The same may be said of stone temples. Yonder, to the eastward of our camp grove, stands one of Nature's cathedrals, hewn from the living rock, almost conventional in form, about two thousand feet high, nobly adorned with spires and pinnacles, thrilling under floods of sunshine as if alive like a grove-temple, and well named 'Cathedral Peak'. Even Shepherd Billy turns at times to this wonderful mountain building, though apparently deaf to all stone sermons. Snow that refused to melt in fire would hardly be more wonderful than unchanging dullness in the rays of God's beauty. I have been trying to get him to walk to the brink of Yosemite for a view, offering to watch the sheep for a day, while he should enjoy what tourists come from all over the world to see. But though within a mile of the famous valley, he will not go to it even out of mere curiosity. 'What', says he, 'is Yosemite but a canyon – a lot of rocks – a hole in the ground – a place dangerous about falling into – a d —— d good place to keep away from'. 'But think of the waterfalls, Billy – just think of that, and the sound it makes. You can hear it now like the roar of the sea.' Thus I pressed Yosemite upon him like a missionary offering the gospel, but he would have none of it. 'I should be afraid to look over so high a wall', he said. 'It would make my head swim. There is nothing worth seeing anywhere, only rocks, and I see plenty of them here. Tourists that spend their money to see rocks and falls are fools, that's all. You can't humbug me. I've been in this country too long for that.' Such souls, I suppose, are asleep, or smothered and befogged beneath mean pleasures and cares.

25 July. Another cloudland. Some clouds have an over-ripe decaying look, watery and bedraggled and drawn out into wind-torn shreds and patches, giving the sky a littered appearance; not so these Sierra summer midday clouds. All are beautiful with smooth definite outlines and curves like those of glacier-polished domes. They begin to grow about eleven o'clock, and seem so wonderfully near and clear from this high camp one is tempted to try to climb them and trace the streams that pour like cataracts from their shadowy fountains. The rain to which they give birth is often very heavy, a sort of waterfall as imposing as if pouring from rock mountains. Never in all my travels have I found anything more truly novel and interesting than these midday mountains of the sky, their fine tones of colour, majestic visible growth, and ever-changing scenery and general effects, though mostly as well let alone as far as description goes. I oftentimes think of Shelley's cloud poem, 'I sift the snow on the mountains below'.

CHAPTER SIX

Mount Hoffman and Lake Tenaya

26 JULY. Ramble to the summit of Mount Hoffman, eleven thousand feet high, the highest point in life's journey my feet have yet touched. And what glorious landscapes are about me, new plants, new animals, new crystals, and multitudes of new mountains far higher than Hoffman, towering in glorious array along the axis of the range, serene, majestic, snow-laden, sun-drenched, vast domes and ridges shining below them, forests, lakes, and meadows in the hollows, the pure blue bell-flower sky brooding them all – a glory day of admission into a new realm of wonders as if Nature had wooingly whispered, 'Come higher'. What questions I asked, and how little I know of all the vast show, and how eagerly, tremulously hopeful of some day knowing more, learning the meaning of these divine symbols crowded together on this wondrous page.

Mount Hoffman is the highest part of a ridge or spur about fourteen miles from the axis of the main range, perhaps a remnant brought into relief and isolated by unequal denudation. The southern slopes shed their waters into Yosemite Valley by Tenaya and Dome Creeks, the northern in part into the Tuolumne River, but mostly into the Merced by Yosemite Creek. The rock is mostly granite, with some small piles and crests rising here and there in picturesque pillared and castellated remnants of red metamorphic slates. Both the granite and slates are divided by joints, making them separable into blocks like the stones of artificial masonry, suggesting the Scripture 'He hath builded the mountains'. Great banks of snow and ice are piled in hollows on the cool precipitous north side forming the highest perennial sources of Yosemite Creek. The southern slopes are much more gradual and accessible. Narrow slot-like gorges extend across the summit at right angles, which look like lanes, formed evidently by the erosion of less resisting beds. They are usually called 'devil's slides', though they lie far above the region usually haunted by the devil; for though we read that he once climbed an exceeding high mountain, he cannot be much of a mountaineer, for his tracks are seldom seen above the timber line.

The broad grey summit is barren and desolate-looking in general views, wasted by ages of gnawing storms; but looking at the surface in detail, one finds it covered by thousands and millions of charming plants with leaves and flowers so small they form no mass of colour visible at a distance of a few hundred yards. Beds of azure daisies smile confidingly in moist hollows, and along the banks of small rills, with several species of eriogonum, silky-leaved ivesia, pentstemon, orthocarpus, and patches of *Primula suffruticosa*, a beautiful shrubby species. Here also I found bryanthus, a charming heathwort

245

covered with purple flowers and dark green foliage like heather, and three trees new to me – a hemlock and two pines. The hemlock (*Tsuga Mertensiana*) is the most beautiful conifer I have ever seen; the branches and also the main axis droop in a singularly graceful way, and the dense foliage covers the delicate, sensitive, swaying branchlets all around. It is now in full bloom, and the flowers, together with thousands of last season's cones still clinging to the drooping sprays, display wonderful wealth of colour, brown and purple and blue. Gladly I climbed the first tree I found to revel in the midst of it. How the touch of the flowers makes one's flesh tingle! The pistillate are dark, rich purple, and almost translucent, the staminate blue – a vivid, pure tone of blue like the mountain sky – the most uncommonly beautiful of all the Sierra tree flowers I have seen. How wonderful that, with all its delicate feminine grace and beauty of form and dress and behaviour, this lovely tree up here, exposed to the wildest blasts, has already endured the storms of centuries of winters!

The two pines also are brave storm-enduring trees, the mountain pine (*Pinus monticola*) and the dwarf pine (*Pinus albicaulis*). The mountain pine is closely related to the sugar pine, though the cones are only about four to six inches long. The largest trees are from five to six feet in diameter at four feet above the ground, the bark rich brown, Only a few storm-beaten adventurers approach the summit of the mountain. The dwarf or white-bark pine is the species that forms the timber line, where it is so completely dwarfed that one may walk over the top of a bed of it as over snow-pressed chaparral.

How boundless the day seems as we revel in these storm-beaten sky gardens amid so vast a congregation of onlooking mountains! Strange and admirable it is that the more savage and chilly and storm-chafed the mountains, the finer the glow on their faces and the finer the plants they bear. The myriads of flowers tingeing the mountain top do not seem to have grown out of the dry, rough gravel of disintegration, but rather they appear as visitors, a cloud of witnesses to Nature's love in what we in our timid ignorance and unbelief call howling desert. The surface of the ground, so dull and forbidding at first sight, besides being rich in plants, shines and sparkles with crystals: mica, hornblende, feldspar, quartz, tourmaline. The radiance in some places is so great as to be fairly dazzling, keen lance rays of every colour flashing, sparkling in glorious abundance, joining the plants in their fine, brave beauty work – every crystal, every flower a window opening into heaven, a mirror reflecting the Creator.

From garden to garden, ridge to ridge, I drifted enchanted, now on my knees gazing into the face of a daisy, now climbing again and again among the purple and azure flowers of the hemlocks, now down into the treasuries of the snow, or gazing afar over domes and peaks, lakes and woods, and the billowy glaciated fields of the upper Tuolumne, and trying to sketch them. In the midst of such beauty, pierced with its rays, one's body is all one tingling palate. Who wouldn't be a mountaineer! Up here all the world's prizes seem nothing.

The largest of the many glacier lakes in sight, and the one with the finest shore scenery, is Tenaya, about a mile long, with an imposing mountain dipping its feet into it on the south side, Cathedral Peak a few miles above its head, many smooth swelling rock-waves and domes on the north, and in the distance southward a multitude of snowy peaks, the fountain-heads of rivers. Lake Hoffman lies shimmering beneath my feet, mountain pines around its shining rim. To the northward the picturesque basin of Yosemite Creek glitters with lakelets and pools; but the eye is soon drawn away from these bright mirror wells, however attractive, to revel in the glorious congregation of peaks on the axis of the range in their robes of snow and light.

Carlo caught an unfortunate woodchuck when it was running from a grassy spot to its boulder pile home – one of the hardiest of the mountain animals. I tried hard to save him, but in vain. After telling Carlo that he must be careful not to kill anything, I caught sight, for the first time, of the curious pika, or little chief hare, that cuts large quantities of lupines and other plants and lays them out to dry in the sun for hay, which it stores in underground barns to last through the long, snowy winter. Coming upon these plants freshly cut and lying in handfuls here and there on the rocks has a startling effect of busy life on the lonely mountain top. These little haymakers, endowed with brain stuff something like our own – God up here looking after them – what lessons they teach, how they widen our sympathy!

An eagle soaring above a sheer cliff, where I suppose its nest is, makes another striking show of life, and helps to bring to mind the other people of the so-called solitude – deer in the forest caring for their young; the strong, well-clad, well-fed bears; the lively throng of squirrels; the blessed birds, great and small, stirring and sweetening the groves; and the clouds of happy insects filling the sky with joyous hum as part and parcel of the down-pouring sunshine. All these come to mind, as well as the plant people, and the glad streams singing their way to the sea. But most impressive of all is the vast glowing countenance of the wilderness in awful, infinite repose.

Toward sunset, enjoyed a fine run to camp, down the long south slopes, across ridges and ravines, gardens and avalanche gaps, through the firs and chaparral, enjoying wild excitement and excess of strength, and so ends a day that will never end.

27 July. Up and away to Lake Tenaya – another big day, enough for a lifetime. The rocks, the air, everything speaking with audible voice or silent; joyful, wonderful, enchanting, banishing weariness and sense of time. No longing for anything now or hereafter as we go home into the mountain's heart. The level sunbeams are touching the fir tops, every leaf shining with dew. Am holding an easterly course, the deep canyon of Tenaya Creek on the right hand, Mount Hoffman on the left, and the lake straight ahead about ten miles distant, the summit of Mount Hoffman about three thousand feet above me, Tenaya Creek four thousand feet below and separated from the shallow, irregular valley, along which most of the way lies, by smooth domes and wave-ridges. Many mossy emerald bogs, meadows and gardens in rocky hollows to wade and saunter through – and what fine plants they give me, what joyful streams I have to cross, and how many views are displayed of the Hoffman and Cathedral Peak masonry, and what a wondrous breadth of shining granite pavement to walk over for the first time about the shores of the lake! On I sauntered in freedom complete; body without weight as far as I was aware; now wading through starry parnassia bogs, now through gardens shoulder deep in larkspur and lilies, grasses and rushes, shaking off showers of dew; crossing piles of crystalline moraine boulders, bright mirror pavements, and cool, cheery streams going to Yosemite; crossing bryanthus carpets and the scoured pathways of avalanches, and thickets of snow-pressed ceanothus; then down a broad, majestic stairway into the ice-sculptured lake basin.

The snow on the high mountains is melting fast, and the streams are singing bank-full, swaying softly through the level meadows and bogs, quivering with sun-spangles, swirling in potholes, resting in deep pools, leaping, shouting in wild, exulting energy over rough boulder dams, joyful, beautiful in all their forms. No Sierra landscape that I have seen holds anything truly dead or dull, or any trace of what in manufactories is called rubbish or waste; everything is perfectly clean and pure and full of divine lessons. This quick, inevitable interest attaching to everything seems marvellous until the hand of God becomes visible; then it seems reasonable that what interests Him may well interest us. When we try to pick out anything by itself, we find it hitched to everything else in the universe. One fancies a heart like our own must be beating in every crystal and cell, and we feel like stopping to speak to the plants and animals as friendly fellow mountaineers. Nature as a poet, an enthusiastic workingman, becomes more and more visible the farther and higher we go; for the mountains are fountains – beginning places, however related to sources beyond mortal ken.

I found three kinds of meadows: (1) Those contained in basins not yet filled with earth enough to make a dry surface. They are planted with several species of carex, and have their margins diversified with robust flowering plants such as veratrum, larkspur and lupine, etc. (2) Those contained in the same sort of basins, once lakes like the first, but so situated in relation to the streams that flow through them and beds of transportable sand, gravel, etc., that they are now high and dry and well drained. This dry condition and corresponding difference in their vegetation may be caused by no superiority of position, or power of transporting filling material in the streams that belong to them, but simply by the basin being shallow and therefore sooner filled. They are planted with grasses, mostly fine, silky, and rather short-leaved, *Calamagrostis* and *Agrostis* being the principal genera. They form delightfully smooth, level sods in which one finds two or three species of gentian and as many of purple and yellow orthocarpus, violet, vaccinium, kalmia, bryanthus, and lonicera. (3) Meadows hanging on ridge and mountain slopes, not in basins at all, but made and held in place by masses of boulders and fallen trees, which, forming dams one above another in close succession on small, outspread, channelless streams, have collected soil enough for the growth of grasses, carices and many flowering plants, and being kept well watered, without being subject to currents sufficiently strong to carry them away, a hanging or sloping meadow is the result. Their surfaces are seldom so smooth as the others, being roughened more or less by the projecting tops of the dam rocks or logs; but at a little distance this roughness is not noticed and the effect is very striking – bright green, fluent, down-sweeping flowery ribbons on grey slopes. The broad shallow streams these meadows belong to are mostly derived from banks of snow and because the soil is well drained in some places, while in others the dam rocks are packed close and caulked with bits of wood and leaves, making boggy patches; the vegetation, of course, is correspondingly varied. I saw patches of willow, bryanthus, and a fine show of lilieg on some of them, not forming a margin, but scattered about among the carex and grass. Most of these meadows are now in their prime. How wonderful must be the temper of the elastic leaves of grasses and sedges to make curves so perfect and fine. Tempered a little harder, they would stand erect, stiff and bristly, like strips of metal; a little softer, and every leaf would lie flat. And what fine painting and tinting there is on the glumes and pales, stamens and feathery pistils. Butterflies coloured like the flowers waver above them in wonderful profusion, and many other beautiful winged people, numbered and known and loved only by the Lord, are waltzing together high overhead, seemingly in pure play and hilarious enjoyment of their little sparks of life. How wonderful they are! How do they get a living, and endure the weather? How are their little bodies, with muscles, nerves, organs, kept warm and jolly in such admirable exuberant health? Regarded only as mechanical inventions, how wonderful they are! Compared with these, Godlike man's greatest machines are as nothing.

Most of the sandy gardens on moraines are in prime beauty like the meadows, though some on the north sides of rocks and beneath groves of sapling pines have not yet bloomed. On sunny sheets of crystal soil along the slopes of the Hoffman Mountains, I saw extensive patches of ivesia and purple gilia with scarce a green leaf, making fine clouds of colour. Ribes bushes, vaccinium and kalmia, now in flower, make beautiful rugs and borders along the banks of the streams. Shaggy beds of dwarf oak (*Quercus chrysolepis*, var. *vaccinifolia*) over which one may walk are common on rocky moraines, yet this is the same species as the large live oak seen near Brown's Flat. The most beautiful of the shrubs is the purple-flowered bryanthus, here making glorious carpets at an elevation of nine thousand feet.

The principal tree for the first mile or two from camp is the magnificent silver fir, which reaches perfection here both in size and form of individual trees, and in the mode of grouping in groves with open spaces between. So trim and tasteful are these silvery, spiry groves one would fancy they must have been placed in position by some master landscape gardener, their regularity seeming almost conventional. But Nature is the only gardener able to do work so fine. A few noble specimens two hundred feet high occupy central positions in the groups with younger trees around them; and outside of these another circle of yet smaller ones, the whole arranged like tastefully symmetrical bouquets, every tree fitting nicely the place assigned to it as if made especially for it; small roses and eriogonums are usually found blooming on the open spaces about the groves, forming charming pleasure grounds. Higher, the firs gradually become smaller and less perfect, many showing double summits, indicating storm stress. Still, where good moraine soil is found, even on the rim of the lake basin, specimens one hundred and fifty feet in height and five feet in diameter occur nearly nine thousand feet above the sea. The saplings I find, are mostly bent with the crushing weight of the winter snow, which at this elevation must be at least eight or ten feet deep, judging by marks on the trees; and this depth of compacted snow is heavy enough to bend and bury young trees twenty or thirty feet in height and hold them down for four or five months. Some are broken; the others spring up when the snow melts and at length attain a size that enables them to withstand the snow pressure. Yet even in trees five feet thick the traces of this early discipline are still plainly to be seen in their curved insteps, and frequently in old dried saplings protruding from the trunk, partially overgrown by the new axis developed from a branch below the break. Yet through all this stress the forest is maintained in marvellous beauty.

Beyond the silver firs I find the two-leaved pine (*Pinus contorta*, var. *Murrayana*) forms the bulk of the forest up to an elevation of ten thousand feet or more – the highest timber-belt of the Sierra. I saw a specimen nearly five feet in diameter growing on deep, well watered soil at an elevation of about nine thousand feet. The form of this species varies very much with position, exposure and soil, etc. On stream banks, where it is closely planted, it is very slender; some specimens seventy five feet high do not exceed five inches in diameter at the ground, but the ordinary form, as far as I have seen, is well proportioned. The average diameter when full grown at this elevation is about twelve or fourteen inches, height forty or fifty feet, the straggling branches bent up at the end, the bark thin and bedraggled with amber-coloured resin. The pistillate flowers form little crimson rosettes a fourth of an inch in diameter on the ends of the branchlets, mostly hidden in the leaf tassels; the staminate are about three eighths of an inch in diameter, sulphur-yellow, in showy clusters, giving a remarkably rich effect – a brave, hardy mountaineer pine, growing cheerily on rough beds of avalanche boulders and joints of rock pavements, as well as in fertile hollows, standing up to the waist in snow every winter for centuries, facing a thousand storms and blooming every year in colours as bright as those worn by the sun-drenched trees of the tropics.

A still hardier mountaineer is the Sierra juniper (*Juniperus occidentalis*), growing mostly on domes and ridges and glacier pavements. A thickset, sturdy, picturesque highlander, seemingly content to live for more than a score of centuries on sunshine and snow; a truly wonderful fellow, dogged endurance expressed in every feature, lasting about as long as the granite he stands on. Some are nearly as broad as high. I saw one on the shore of the lake nearly ten feet in diameter, and many six to eight feet. The bark, cinnamon-coloured, flakes off in long ribbon-like strips with a satiny lustre. Surely the most enduring of all tree mountaineers, it never seems to die a natural death, or even to fall after it has been killed. If protected from accidents, it would perhaps be immortal. I saw some that had withstood an avalanche from snowy Mount Hoffman cheerily putting out new branches, as if repeating, like Grip, 'Never say die'. Some were simply standing on the pavement where no fissure more than half an inch wide offered a hold for its roots. The common height for these rock dwellers is from ten to twenty feet; most of the old ones have broken tops, and are mere stumps, with a few tufted branches, forming picturesque brown pillars on bare pavements, with plenty of elbow room and a clear view in every direction. On good moraine soil it reaches a height of from forty to sixty feet, with dense grey foliage. The rings of the trunk are very thin, eighty to an inch of diameter in some specimens I examined. Those ten feet in diameter must be very old – thousands of years. Wish I could live, like these junipers, on sunshine and snow, and stand beside them on the shore of Lake Tenaya for a thousand years. How much I should see, and how delightful it would be! Everything in the mountains would find me and come to me, and everything from the heavens like light.

The lake was named for one of the chiefs of the Yosemite tribe. Old Tenaya is said to have been a good Indian to his tribe. When a company of soldiers followed his band into Yosemite to punish them for cattle stealing and other crimes, they fled to this lake by a trail that leads out of the upper end of the valley, early in the spring, while the snow was still deep; but being pursued, they lost heart and surrendered. A fine monument the old man has in this bright lake, and likely to last a long time, though lakes die as well as Indians, being gradually filled with detritus carried in by the feeding streams, and to some extent also by snow avalanches and rain and wind. A considerable portion of the Tenaya basin is already changed into a forested flat and meadow at the upper end, where the main tributary enters from Cathedral Peak. Two other tributaries come from the Hoffman Range. The outlet flows westward through Tenaya Canyon to join the Merced River in Yosemite. Scarce a handful of loose soil is to be seen on the north shore. All is bare, shining granite, suggesting the Indian name of the lake, Pywiack, meaning shining rock. The basin seems to have been slowly excavated by the ancient glaciers, a marvellous work requiring countless thousands of years. On the south side an imposing mountain rises from the water's edge to a height of three thousand feet or more, feathered with hemlock and pine; and huge shining domes on the east, over the tops of which the grinding, wasting, moulding glacier must have swept as the wind does today.

28 July. No cloud mountains, only curly cirrus wisps scarce perceptible, and the want of thunder to strike the noon hour seems strange, as if the Sierra clock had stopped. Have been studying the *Magnifica* fir – measured one near two hundred and forty feet high, the tallest I have yet seen. This species is the most symmetrical of all conifers, but though gigantic in size it seldom lives more than four or five hundred years. Most of the trees die from the attacks of a fungus at the age of two or three centuries. This dry-rot fungus perhaps enters the trunk by way of the stumps of limbs broken off by the snow that loads the broad palmate branches. The younger specimens are marvels of symmetry, straight and erect as a plumb line, their branches in regular level whorls of five mostly, each branch as exact in its divisions as a fern frond, and thickly covered by the leaves, making a rich plush over all the tree, excepting only the trunk and a small portion of the main limbs. The leaves turn upward, especially on the branchlets, and are stiff and sharp, pointed on all the upper portion of the tree. They remain on the tree about eight or ten years, and as the growth is rapid it is not rare to find the leaves still in place on the upper part of the axis where it is three to four inches in diameter, wide apart of course, and their spiral arrangement beautifully displayed. The leaf scars are conspicuous for twenty years or more, but there is a good deal of variation in different trees as to the thickness and sharpness of the leaves.

After the excursion to Mount Hoffman I had seen a complete cross section of the Sierra forest, and I find that *Abies magnifica* is the most symmetrical tree of all the noble coniferous company. The cones are grand affairs, superb in form, size, and colour, cylindrical, stand erect on the upper branches like casks, and are from five to eight inches in length by three or four in diameter, greenish grey, and covered with fine down which has a silvery lustre in the sunshine, and their brilliance is augmented by beads of transparent balsam which seems to have been poured over each cone, bringing to mind the old ceremonies of anointing with oil. If possible, the inside of the cone is more beautiful than the outside; the scales, bracts, and seed wings are tinted with the loveliest rosy purple with a bright lustrous iridescence; the seeds, three fourths of an inch long, are dark brown. When the cones are ripe the scales and bracts fall off, setting the seeds free to fly to their predestined places, while the dead spike-like axes are left on the branches for many years to mark the positions of the vanished cones, excepting those cut off when green by the Douglas squirrel. How he gets his teeth under the broad bases of the sessile cones, I don't know. Climbing these trees on a sunny day to visit the growing cones and to gaze over the tops of the forest is one of my best enjoyments.

29 July. Bright, cool, exhilarating. Clouds about five per cent. Another glorious day of rambling, sketching, and universal enjoyment.

30 July. Clouds, twenty per cent, but the regular shower did not reach us, though thunder was heard a few miles off striking the noon hour. Ants, flies and mosquitoes seem to enjoy this fine climate. A few house flies have discovered our camp. The Sierra mosquitoes are courageous and of good size, some of them measuring nearly an inch from tip of sting to tip of folded wings. Though less abundant than in most wildernesses, they occasionally make quite a hum and stir, and pay but little attention to time or place. They sting anywhere, any time of day, wherever they can find anything worth while, until they are themselves stung by frost. The large, jet-black ants are only ticklish and troublesome when one is lying down under the trees. Noticed a borer drilling a silver fir. Ovipositor about an inch and a half in length, polished and straight like a needle. When not in use, it is folded back in a sheath, which extends straight behind like the legs of a crane in flying. This drilling, I suppose, is to save nest building, and the after care of feeding the young. Who would guess that in the brain of a fly so much knowledge could find lodgment? How do they know that their eggs will hatch in such holes, or, after they hatch, that the soft, helpless grubs will find the right sort of nourishment in silver fir sap? This domestic arrangement calls to mind the curious family of gallflies. Each species seems to know what kind of plant will respond to the irritation or stimulus of the puncture it makes and the eggs it lays, in forming a growth that not only answers for a nest and home but also provides food for the young. Probably these gallflies make mistakes at times like anybody else; but when they do, there is simply a failure of that particular brood, while enough to perpetuate the species do find the proper plants and nourishment. Many mistakes of this kind might be made without being discovered by us. Once a pair of wrens made the mistake of building a nest in the sleeve of a workman's coat, which was called for at sundown, much to the consternation and discomfiture of the birds. Still the marvel remains that any of the children of such small people as gnats and mosquitoes should escape their own and their parents' mistakes, as well as the vicissitudes of the weather and hosts of enemies, and come forth in full vigour and perfection to enjoy the sunny world. When we think of the small creatures that are visible, we are led to think of many that are smaller still and lead us on and on into infinite mystery.

31 July. Another glorious day, the air is delicious to the lungs as nectar to the tongue; indeed the body seems one palate, and tingles equally throughout. Cloudiness about five per cent, but our ordinary shower has not yet reached us, though I hear thunder in the distance.

The cheery little chipmunk, so common about Brown's Flat, is common here also, and perhaps other species. In their light, airy habits they recall the familiar species of the Eastern States, which we admired in the oak openings of Wisconsin as they skimmed along the zigzag rail fences. These Sierra chipmunks are more arboreal and squirrel-like. I first noticed them on the lower edge of the coniferous belt, where the Sabine and yellow pines meet – exceedingly interesting little fellows, full of odd, funny ways, and without being true squirrels, have most of their accomplishments without their aggressive quarrelsomeness. I never weary watching them as they frisk about in the bushes gathering seeds and berries, like song sparrows poising daintily on slender twigs, and making even less stir than most birds of the same size. Few of the Sierra animals interest me more; they are so able, gentle, confiding, and beautiful, they take one's heart, and get themselves adopted as darlings. Though weighing hardly more than field mice, they are laborious collectors of seeds, nuts, and cones, and are therefore well fed, but never in the least swollen with fat or lazily full. On the contrary, of their frisky, birdlike liveliness there is no end. They have a great variety of notes corresponding with their movements, some sweet and liquid, like water dripping with tinkling sounds into pools. They seem dearly to love teasing a dog, coming frequently almost within reach, then frisking away with lively chipping, like sparrows, beating time to their music with their tails, which at each chip describe half circles from side to side. Not even the Douglas squirrel is surer-footed or more fearless. I have seen them running about on sheer precipices of the Yosemite walls seemingly holding on with as little effort as flies, and as unconscious of danger, where, if the slightest slip were made, they would have fallen two or three thousand feet. How fine it would be could we mountaineers climb these tremendous cliffs with the same sure grip! The venture I made the other day for a view of the Yosemite Fall and which tried my nerves so sorely, this little Tamias would have made for an ear of grass.

The woodchuck (*Arctomys monax*) of the bleak mountain tops is a very different sort of mountaineer – the most bovine of rodents, a heavy eater, fat, aldermanic in bulk and fairly bloated, in his high pastures, like a cow in a clover field. One woodchuck would outweigh a hundred chipmunks and yet he is by no means a dull animal. In the midst of what we regard as storm-beaten desolation he pipes and whistles right cheerily, and enjoys long life in his skyland homes. His burrow is made in disintegrated rocks or beneath large boulders. Coming out of his den in the cold hoarfrost mornings, he takes a sun-bath on some favourite flat-topped rock, then goes to breakfast in garden hollows, eats grass and flowers until comfortably swollen, then goes a-visiting to fight and play. How long a woodchuck lives in this bracing air I don't know, but some of them are rusty and grey like lichen-covered boulders.

1 August. A grand cloudland and five minute shower, refreshing the blessed wilderness, already so fragrant and fresh, steeping the black meadow mould and dead leaves like tea.

The waycup, or flicker, so familiar to every boy in the old Middle West States, is one of the most common of the woodpeckers hereabouts, and makes one feel at home. I can see no difference in plumage or habits from the Eastern species, though the climate here is so different – a fine, brave, confiding, beautiful bird. The robin too, is here, with all his familiar notes and gestures, tripping daintily on open garden spots and high meadows. Over all America he seems to be at home, moving from the plains to the mountains and from north to south, back and forth, up and down, with the march of the seasons and food supply. How admirable the constitution and temper of this brave singer, keeping in cheery health over so vast and varied a range! Oftentimes, as I wander through these solemn woods, awe-stricken and silent, I hear the reassuring voice of this fellow wanderer ringing out, sweet and clear, 'Fear not! fear not!'

The mountain quail (*Oreortyx ricta*) I often meet in my walks – a small brown partridge with a very long, slender, ornamental crest worn jauntily like a feather in a boy's cap, giving it a very marked appearance. This species is considerably larger than the valley quail, so common on the hot foothills. They seldom alight in trees, but love to wander in flocks of from five or six to twenty through the ceanothus and manzanita thickets and over open, dry meadows and rocks of the ridges where the forest is less dense or wanting, uttering a low clucking sound to enable them to keep together. When disturbed they rise with a strong birr of wingbeats, and scatter as if exploded to a distance of a quarter of a mile or so. After the danger is past they call one another together with a loud piping note – Nature's beautiful mountain chickens. I have not yet found their nests. The young of this season are already hatched and away – new broods of happy wanderers half as large as their parents. I wonder how they live through the long winters, when the ground is snow-covered ten feet deep. They must go down towards the lower edge of the forest, like the deer, though I have not heard of them there.

The blue, or dusky, grouse is also common here. They like the deepest and closest fir woods, and when disturbed, burst from the branches of the trees with a strong, loud whirr of wingbeats, and vanish in a wavering, silent slide, without moving a feather – a stout, beautiful bird about the size of the prairie chicken of the old west, spending most of the time in the trees, excepting the breeding season, when it keeps to the ground. The young are now able to fly.

When scattered by man or dog, they keep still until the danger is supposed to be passed, then the mother calls them together. The chicks can hear the call a distance of several hundred yards, though it is not loud. Should the young be unable to fly, the mother feigns desperate lameness or death to draw one away, throwing herself at one's feet within two or three yards, rolling over on her back, kicking and gasping, so as to deceive man or beast. They are said to stay all the year in the woods hereabouts, taking shelter in dense tufted branches of fir and yellow pine during snowstorms, and feeding on the young buds of these trees. Their legs are feathered down to their toes, and I have never heard of their suffering in any sort of weather. Able to live on pine and fir buds, they are forever independent in the matter of food, which troubles so many of us and controls our movements. Gladly, if I could, I would live forever on pine buds, however full of turpentine and pitch, for the sake of this grand independence. Just to think of our sufferings last month merely for grist-mill flour. Man sems to have more difficulty in gaining food than any other of the Lord's creatures. For many in towns it is a consuming, lifelong struggle; for others, the danger of coming to want is so great, the deadly habit of endless hoarding for the future is formed, which smothers all real life, and is continued long after every reasonable need has been over-supplied.

On Mount Hoffman I saw a curious dove-coloured bird that seemed half woodpecker, half magpie, or crow. It screams something like a crow, but flies like a woodpecker, and has a long, straight bill, with which I saw it opening the cones of the mountain and white-barked pines. It seems to keep to the heights, though no doubt it comes down for shelter during winter, if not for food. So far as food is concerned, these bird-mountaineers, I guess, can glean nuts enough, even in winter, from the different kinds of conifers; for always there are a few that have been unable to fly out of the cones and remain for hungry winter gleaners.

CHAPTER SEVEN

A Strange Experience

2 AUGUST. Clouds and showers, about the same as yesterday. Sketching all day on the North Dome until four or five o'clock in the afternoon, when, as I was busily employed thinking only of the glorious Yosemite landscape, trying to draw every tree and every line and feature of the rocks, I was suddenly and without warning, possessed with the notion that my friend, Professor J. D. Butler, of the State University of Wisconsin, was below me in the valley, and I jumped up full of the idea of meeting him, with almost as much startling excitement as if he had suddenly touched me to make me look up. Leaving my work without the slightest deliberation, I ran down the western slope of the Dome and along the brink of the valley wall, looking for a way to the

bottom, until I came to a side canyon which, judging by its apparently continuous growth of trees and bushes, I thought might afford a practical way into the valley, and immediately began to make the descent, late as it was, as if drawn irresistibly. But after a little, common sense stopped me and explained that it would be long after dark ere I could possibly reach the hotel, that the visitors would be asleep, that nobody would know me, that I had no money in my pockets, and moreover was without a coat. I therefore compelled myself to stop, and finally succeeded in reasoning myself out of the notion of seeking my friend in the dark, whose presence I only felt in a strange, telepathic way. I succeeded in dragging myself back through the woods to camp, never for a moment wavering however, in my determination to go down to him next morning. This I think is the most unexplainable notion that ever struck me. Had someone whispered in my ear while I sat on the Dome, where I had spent so many days, that Professor Butler was in the valley, I could not have been more surprised and startled. When I was leaving the university, he said, 'Now, John, I want to hold you in sight and watch your career. Promise to write me at least once a year'. I received a letter from him in July, at our first camp in the Hollow, written in May, in which he said that he might possibly visit California some time this summer, and therefore hoped to meet me. But inasmuch as he named no meeting place, and gave no directions as to the course he would probably follow, and as I should be in the wilderness all summer, I had not the slightest hope of seeing him, and all thought of the matter had vanished from my mind until this afternoon, when he seemed to be wafted bodily almost against my face. Well, tomorrow I shall see; for, reasonable or unreasonable, I feel I must go.

3 August. Had a wonderful day. Found Professor Butler as the compass needle finds the pole. So last evening's telepathy, transcendental revelation, or whatever else it may be called, was true; for strange to say, he had just entered the valley by way of the Coulterville Trail and was coming up the valley past El Capitan when his presence struck me. Had he then looked toward the North Dome with a good glass when it first came in sight, he might have seen me jump up from my work and run toward him. This seems the one well-defined marvel of my life of the kind called supernatural; for, absorbed in glad Nature, spirit rappings, second sight, ghost stories, etc., have never interested me since boyhood, seeming comparatively useless and infinitely less wonderful than Nature's open, harmonious, songful, sunny, everyday beauty.

This morning, when I thought of having to appear among tourists at a hotel, I was troubled because I had no suitable clothes and at best am desperately bashful and shy. I was determined to go however, to see my old friend after two years among strangers; got on a clean pair of overalls, a cashmere shirt, and a sort of jacket – the best my camp wardrobe afforded – tied my notebook on my belt and strode away on my strange journey, followed by Carlo. I made my way through the gap discovered last evening, which proved to be Indian Canyon. There was no trail in it, and the rocks and brush were so rough that Carlo frequently called me back to help him down precipitous places. Emerging from the canyon shadows, I found a man making hay on one of the meadows and asked him whether Professor Butler was in the valley. 'I don't know,' he replied; 'but you can easily find out at the hotel. There are but few visitors in the valley just now. A small party came in yesterday afternoon, and I heard someone called Professor Butler, or Butterfield, or some name like that.'

In front of the gloomy hotel I found a tourist party adjusting their fishing tackle. They all stared at me in silent wonderment, as if I had been seen dropping down through the trees from the clouds, mostly, I suppose, on account of my strange garb. Inquiring for the office, I was told it was locked, and that the landlord was away, but I might find the landlady, Mrs Hutchings, in the parlour. I entered in a sad state of embarrassment, and after I had waited in the big, empty room and knocked at several doors the landlady at length appeared, and in reply to my question said she rather thought Professor Butler *was* in the valley, but to make sure, she would bring the register from the office. Among the names of the last arivals I soon discovered the Professor's familiar handwriting, at the sight of which bashfulness vanished; and having learned that his party had gone up the valley – probably to the Vernal and Nevada Falls – I pushed on in glad pursuit, my heart now sure of its prey. In less than an hour I reached the head of the Nevada Canyon at the Vernal Fall, and just outside of the spray discovered a distinguished-looking gentleman, who, like everybody else I have seen today, regarded me curiously as I approached. When I made bold to inquire if he knew where Professor Butler was, he seemed yet more curious to know what could possibly have happened that required a messenger for the Professor, and instead of answering my question he asked with military sharpness, 'Who wants him?' 'I want him,' I replied with equal sharpness. 'Why? Do *you* know him?' 'Yes,' I said. 'Do *you* know him?' Astonished that any one in the mountains could possibly know Professor Butler and find him as soon as he had reached the valley, he came down to meet the strange mountaineer on equal terms, and courteously replied, 'Yes, I know Professor Butler very well. I am General Alvord, and we were fellow students in Rutland, Vermont, long ago, when we were both young.' 'But where is he now?' I persisted, cutting short his story. 'He has gone beyond the falls with a companion, to try to climb that big rock, the top of which you see from here.' His guide now volunteered the information that it was the Liberty Cap Professor Butler and his companion had gone to climb, and that if I waited at the head of the fall I should be sure to find them on their way down. I therefore climbed the ladders alongside the Vernal Fall, and was pushing forward, determined to go to the top of Liberty Cap rock in my hurry, rather than wait, if I should not meet my friend sooner. So heart-hungry at times may one be to see a friend in the flesh, however happily full and carefree one's life may be. I had gone but a short distance however, above the brow of the Vernal Fall when I caught sight of him in the brush and rocks, half erect, groping his way, his sleeves rolled up, vest open, hat in his hand, evidently very hot and tired. When he saw me coming he sat down on a boulder to wipe the perspiration from his brow and neck, and taking me for one of the valley guides, he inquired the way to the fall ladders. I pointed out the path marked with little piles of stones, on seeing which he called his companion, saying that the way was found; but he did not yet recognize me. Then I stood directly in front of him, looked him in the face, and held out my hand. He thought I was offering to assist him in rising. 'Never mind,' he said. Then I said, 'Professor Butler, don't you know me?' 'I think not,' he replied; but catching my eye, sudden recognition followed, and astonishment that I should have found him just when he was lost in the brush and did not know that I was within hundreds of miles of him. 'John Muir, John Muir, where have you come from?' Then I told him the story of my feeling his presence when he entered the valley last evening, when he was four or five miles distant, as I sat sketching on the North Dome. This, of course, only made him wonder the more. Below the foot of the Vernal Fall the guide was waiting with his saddle-horse, and I walked along the trail, chatting all the way back to the hotel, talking of school days, friends in Madison, of the students, how each had prospered, ever and anon gazing at the stupendous rocks about us, now growing indistinct in the gloaming, and again quoting from the poets – a rare ramble.

It was late ere we reached the hotel, and General Alvord was waiting the Professor's arrival for dinner. When I was introduced he seemed yet more astonished than the Professor at my descent from cloudland and going straight to my friend without knowing in any ordinary way that he was even in California. They had come on direct from the East, had not yet visited any of their friends in the state, and considered themselves undiscoverable. As we sat at dinner, the General leaned back in his chair, and looking down the table, thus introduced me to the dozen guests or so, including the staring fisherman mentioned above: 'This man, you know, came down out of these huge, trackless mountains, you know, to find his friend Professor Butler here, the very day he arrived; and how did he know he was here? He just felt him, he says. This is the queerest case of Scotch farsightedness I ever heard of,' etc., etc. While my friend quoted Shakespeare: 'More things in heaven and earth, Horatio, than are dreamt of in your philosophy,' 'As the sun, ere he has risen, sometimes paints his image in the firmament, e'en so the shadows of events precede the events, and in today already walks tomorrow.'

Had a long conversation, after dinner, over Madison days. The Professor wants me to promise to go with him, sometime, on a camping trip in the Hawaiian Islands, while I tried to get him to go back with me to camp in the high Sierra. But he says, 'Not now'. He must not leave the General; and I was surprised to learn they are to leave the valley tomorrow or next day. I'm glad I'm not great enough to be missed in the busy world.

4 August. It seemed strange to sleep in a paltry hotel chamber after the spacious magnificence and luxury of the starry sky and silver fir grove. Bade farewell to my friend and the General. The old soldier was very kind, and an interesting talker. He told me long stories of the Florida Seminole war, in which he took part, and invited me to visit him in Omaha. Calling Carlo, I scrambled home through the Indian Canyon gate, rejoicing, pitying the poor Professor and General, bound by clocks, almanacs, orders and duties, and compelled to dwell with lowland care and dust and din, where Nature is covered and her voice smothered, while the poor, insignificant wanderer enjoys the freedom and glory of God's wilderness.

Apart from the human interest of my visit today, I greatly enjoyed Yosemite, which I had visited only once before, having spent eight days last spring in rambling amid its rocks and waters. Wherever we go in the mountains, or indeed in any of God's wild fields, we find more than we seek. Descending four thousand feet in a few hours, we enter a new world – climate, plants, sounds, inhabitants, and scenery all new or changed. Near camp the goldcup oak forms sheets of chaparral, on top of which we may make our beds. Going down the Indian Canyon we observe this little bush changing by regular gradations to a large bush, to a small tree, and then larger, until on the rocky taluses near the bottom of the valley we find it developed into a broad, wide-spreading, gnarled, picturesque tree from four to eight feet in diameter, and forty or fifty feet high. Innumerable are the forms of water displayed. Every gliding reach, cascade, and fall has characters of its own. Had a good view of the Vernal and Nevada, two of the main falls of the valley, less than a mile apart, and offering striking differences in voice, form and colour. The Vernal, four hundred feet high and about seventy five or eighty feet wide, drops smoothly over a round-lipped precipice and forms a superb apron of embroidery, green and white, slightly folded and fluted, maintaining this form nearly to the bottom, where it is suddenly veiled in quick-flying billows of spray and mist, in which the afternoon sunbeams play with ravishing beauty of rainbow colours. The Nevada is white from its first appearance as it leaps out into the freedom of the air. At the head it presents a twisted appearance, by an overfolding of the current from striking on the side of its channel just before the first free outbounding leap is made. About two thirds of the way down, the hurrying throng of comet-shaped masses glance on an inclined part of the face of the precipice and are beaten into yet whiter foam, greatly expanded, and sent bounding outward, making an indescribably glorious show, especially when the afternoon sunshine is pouring into it. In this fall – one of the most wonderful in the world – the water does not seem to be under the dominion of ordinary laws, but rather as if it were a living creature, full of the strength of the mountains and their huge, wild joy.

From beneath heavy throbbing blasts of spray the broken river is seen emerging in ragged boulder-chafed strips. These are speedily gathered into a roaring torrent, showing that the young river is still gloriously alive. On it goes, shouting, roaring, exulting in its strength, passes through a gorge with sublime display of energy, then suddenly expands on a gently inclined pavement, down which it rushes in thin sheets and folds of lacework into a quiet pool – 'Emerald Pool', as it is called – a stopping place, a period separating two grand sentences. Resting here long enough to part with its foam-bells and grey mixtures of air, it glides quietly to the verge of the Vernal precipice in a broad sheet and makes its new display in the Vernal Fall; then more rapids and rock tossings down the canyon, shaded by live oak, Douglas spruce, fir, maple, and dogwood. It receives the Illilouette tributary, and makes a long sweep out into the level, sun-filled valley to join the other streams which, like itself, have danced and sung their way down from snowy heights to form the main Merced – the river of Mercy. But of this there is no end, and life, when one thinks of it, is so short. Never mind, one day in the midst of these divine glories is well worth living and toiling and starving for.

Before parting with Professor Butler he gave me a book, and I gave him one of my pencil sketches for his little son Henry, who is a favourite of mine. He used to make many visits to my room when I was a student. Never shall I forget his patriotic speeches for the Union, mounted on a tall stool, when he was only six years old.

It seems strange that visitors to Yosemite should be so little influenced by its novel grandeur, as if their eyes were bandaged and their ears stopped. Most of those I saw yesterday were looking down as if wholly unconscious of anything going on about them, while the sublime rocks were trembling with the tones of the mighty chanting congregation of waters gathered from all the mountains round about, making music that might draw angels out of heaven. Yet respectable-looking, even wise-looking people were fixing bits of worms on bent pieces of wire to catch trout. Sport they called it. Should churchgoers try to pass the time fishing in baptismal fonts while dull sermons were being preached, the so-called sport might not be so bad; but to play in the Yosemite temple, seeking pleasure in the pain of fishes struggling for their lives, while God himself is preaching his sublimest water and stone sermons!

Now I'm back at the campfire, and cannot help thinking about my recognition of my friend's presence in the valley while he was four or five miles away, and while I had no means of knowing that he was not thousands of miles away. It seems supernatural, but only because it is not understood. Anyhow, it seems silly to make so much of it, while the natural and common is more truly marvellous and mysterious than the so-called supernatural. Indeed most of the miracles we hear of are infinitely less wonderful than the commonest of natural phenomena, when fairly seen. Perhaps the invisible rays that struck me while I sat at work on the Dome are something like those which attract and repel people at first sight, concerning which so much nonsense has been written. The worst apparent effect of these mysterious odd things is blindness to all that is divinely common. Hawthorne, I fancy, could weave one of his weird romances out of this little telepathic episode, the one strange marvel of my life, probably replacing my good old Professor by an attractive woman.

5 August. We were awakened this morning before daybreak by the furious barking of Carlo and Jack and the sound of stampeding sheep. Billy fled from his punk bed to the fire, and refused to stir into the darkness to try to gather the scattered flock, or ascertain the nature of the disturbance. It was a bear attack, as we afterward learned, and I suppose little was gained by attempting to do anything before daylight. Nevertheless, being anxious to know what was up, Carlo and I groped our way through the woods, guided by the rustling sound made by fragments of the flock, not fearing the bear, for I knew that the runaways would go from their enemy as far as possible and Carlo's nose was also to be depended upon. About half a mile east of the corral we overtook twenty or thirty of the flock and succeeded in driving them back; then turning to the westward, we traced another band of fugitives and got them back to the flock. After daybreak I discovered the remains of a sheep carcass, still warm, showing that Bruin must have been enjoying his early mutton breakfast while I was seeking the runaways. He had eaten about half of it. Six dead sheep lay in the corral, evidently smothered by the crowding and piling up of the flock against the side of the corral wall when the bear entered. Making a wide circuit of the camp, Carlo and I discovered a third band of fugitives and drove them back to camp. We also discovered another dead sheep half eaten, showing there had been two of the shaggy freebooters at this early breakfast. They were easily traced. They had each caught a sheep, jumped over the corral fence with them, carrying them as a cat carries a mouse, laid them at the foot of fir trees a hundred yards or so back from the corral, and eaten their fill. After breakfast I set out to seek more of the lost, and found seventy five at a considerable distance from camp. In the afternoon I succeeded, with Carlo's help, in getting them back to the flock. I don't know whether all are together again or not. I shall make a big fire this evening and keep watch.

When I asked Billy why he made his bed against the corral in rotten wood, when so many better places offered, he replied that he 'wished to be as near the sheep as possible in case bears should attack them'. Now that the bears have come, he has moved his bed to the far side of the camp, and seems afraid that he may be mistaken for a sheep.

This has been mostly a sheep day, and of course studies have been interrupted. Nevertheless, the walk through the gloom of the woods before the dawn was worth while, and I have learned something about these noble bears. Their tracks are very telling, and so are their breakfasts. Scarce a trace of clouds today, and of course our ordinary midday thunder is wanting.

6 August. Enjoyed the grand illumination of the camp grove, last night, from the fire we made to frighten the bears – compensation for loss of sleep and sheep. The noble pillars of verdure, vividly aglow, seemed to shoot into the sky like the flames that lighted them. Nevertheless, one of the bears paid us another visit, as if more attracted than repelled by the fire, climbed into the corral, killed a sheep and made off with it without being seen, while still another was lost by trampling and suffocation against the side of the corral. Now that our mutton has been tasted, I suppose it will be difficult to put a stop to the ravages of these freebooters.

The Don arrived today from the lowlands with provisions and a letter. On learning the losses he had sustained, he determined to move the flock at once to the Upper Tuolumne region, saying that the bears would be sure to visit the camp every night as long as we stayed, and that no fire or noise we might make would avail to frighten them. No clouds save a few thin, lustrous touches on the eastern horizon. Thunder heard in the distance.

CHAPTER EIGHT

The Mono Trail

7 AUGUST. Early this morning bade goodbye to the bears and blessed silver fir camp, and moved slowly eastward along the Mono Trail. At sundown camped for the night on one of the many small flowery meadows so greatly enjoyed on my excursion to Lake Tenaya. The dusty, noisy flock seems outrageously foreign and out of place in these nature gardens, more so than bears among sheep. The harm they do goes to the heart, but glorious hope lifts above all the dust and din and bids me look forward to a good time coming, when money enough will be earned to enable me to go walking where I like in pure wildness, with what I can carry on my back, and when the bread sack is empty, run down to the nearest point on the breadline for more. Nor will these run-downs be blanks, for, whether up or down, every step and jump on these blessed mountains is full of fine lessons.

8 August. Camp at the west end of Lake Tenaya. Arriving early, I took a walk on the glacier-polished pavements along the north shore, and climbed the magnificent mountain rock at the east end of the lake, now shining in the late afternoon light. Almost every yard of its surface shows the scoring and polishing action of a great glacier that enveloped it and swept heavily over its summit, though it is about two thousand feet high above the lake and ten thousand above sea level. This majestic, ancient ice-flood came from the eastward, as the scoring and crushing of the surface shows. Even below the waters of the lake the rock in some places is still grooved and polished; the lapping of the waves and their disintegrating action have not as yet obliterated even the superficial marks of glaciation. In climbing the steepest polished places I had to take off shoes and stockings. A fine region this for study of glacial action in mountain-making. I found many charming plants: arctic daisies, phlox, white spiraea, bryanthus, and rock ferns – pellaea, cheilanthes, allosorus – fringing weathered seams all the way up to the summit; and sturdy junipers, grand old grey and brown monuments, stood bravely erect on fissured spots here and there, telling storm and avalanche stories of hundreds of winters. The view of the lake from the top is, I think, the best of all. There is another rock, more striking in form than this, standing isolated at the head of the lake, but it is not more than half as high. It is a knob or knot of burnished granite, perhaps about a thousand feet high, apparently as flawless and strong in structure as a wave-worn pebble, and probably owes its existence to the superior resistance it offered to the action of the overflowing ice-flood.

Made sketch of the lake, and sauntered back to camp, my iron-shod shoes clanking on the pavements disturbing the chipmunks and birds. After dark went out to the shore – not a breath of air astir, the lake a perfect mirror reflecting the sky and mountains with their stars and trees and wonderful sculpture, all their grandeur refined and doubled – a marvellously impressive picture, that seemed to belong more to heaven than earth.

9 August. I went ahead of the flock, and crossed over the divide between the Merced and Tuolumne Basins. The gap between the east end of the Hoffman spur and the mass of mountain rocks about Cathedral Peak, though roughened by ridges and waving folds, seems to be one of the channels of a broad ancient glacier that came from the mountains on the summit of the range. In crossing this divide the ice-river made an ascent of about five hundred feet from the Tuolumne Meadows. This entire region must have been overswept by ice.

From the top of the divide, and also from the big Tuolumne Meadows, the wonderful mountain called Cathedral Peak is in sight. From every point of view it shows marked individuality. It is a majestic temple of one stone, hewn from the living rock, and adorned with spires and pinnacles in regular cathedral style. The dwarf pines on the roof look like mosses. I hope some time to climb to it to say my prayers and hear the stone sermons.

The big Tuolumne Meadows are flowery lawns, lying along the south fork of the Tuolumne River at a height of about eighty five hundred to nine thousand feet above the sea, partially separated by forests and bars of glaciated granite. Here the mountains seem to have been cleared away or set back, so that wide open views may be had in every direction. The upper end of the series lies at the base of Mount Lyell, the lower below the east end of the Hoffman Range, so the length must be about ten or twelve miles. They vary in width from a quarter of a mile to perhaps three quarters, and a good many branch meadows put out along the banks of the tributary streams. This is the most spacious and delightful high pleasure ground I have yet seen. The air is keen and bracing, yet warm during the day; and though lying high in the sky, the surrounding mountains are so much higher, one feels protected as if in a grand hall. Mounts Dana and Gibbs, massive red mountains, perhaps thirteen thousand feet high or more, bound the view on the east, the Cathedral and Unicorn Peaks, with many nameless peaks, on the south, the Hoffman Range on the west, and a number of peaks unnamed, as far as I know, on the north. One of these last is much like the Cathedral. The grass of the meadows is mostly fine and silky, with exceedingly slender leaves, making a close sod, above which the panicles of minute purple flowers seem to float in airy, misty lightness, while the sod is enriched with at least three species of gentian and as many or more of orthocarpus, potentilla, ivesia, solidago, pentstemon, with their gay colours – purple, blue, yellow and red – all of which I may know better ere long. A central camp will probably be made in this region, from which I hope to make long excursions into the surrounding mountains.

On the return trip I met the flock about three miles east of Lake Tenaya. Here we camped for the night near a small lake lying on top of the divide in a clump of the two-leaved pine. We are now about nine thousand feet above the sea. Small lakes abound in all sorts of situations – on ridges, along mountain sides, and in piles of moraine boulders, most of them mere pools. Only in those canyons of the larger streams at the foot of declivities, where the down thrust of the glaciers was heaviest, do we find lakes of considerable size and depth. How grateful a task it would be to trace them all and study them! How pure their waters are, clear as crystal in polished stone basins! None of them, so far as I have seen, have fishes, I suppose on account of falls making them inaccessible. Yet one would think their eggs might get into these lakes by some chance or other; on ducks' feet, for example, or in their mouths, or in their crops, as some plant seeds are distributed. Nature has so many ways of doing such things. How did the frogs, found in all the bogs and pools and lakes, however high, manage to get up these mountains? Surely not by jumping. Such excursions through miles of dry bush and boulders would be very hard on frogs. Perhaps their stringy gelatinous spawn is occasionally entangled or glued on the feet of water birds. Anyhow, they are here and in hearty health and voice. I like their cheery tronk and crink. They take the place of songbirds at a pinch.

10 August. Another of those charming exhilarating days that make the blood dance and excite nerve currents that render one unweariable and well nigh immortal. Had another view of the broad ice-ploughed divide, and gazed again and again at the Sierra temple and the great red mountains east of the meadows.

We are camped near the Soda Springs on the north side of the river. A hard time we had getting the sheep across. They were driven into a horseshoe bend and fairly crowded off the bank. They seemed willing to suffer death rather than risk getting wet, though they swim well enough when they have to. Why sheep should be so unreasonably afraid of water, I don't know, but they do fear it as soon as they are born and perhaps before. I once saw a lamb only a few hours old approach a shallow stream about two feet wide and an inch deep, after it had walked only about a hundred yards on its life journey. All the flock to which it belonged had crossed this inch-deep stream, and as the mother and her lamb were the last to cross, I had a good opportunity to observe them. As soon as the flock was out of the way, the anxious mother crossed over and called the youngster. It walked cautiously to the brink, gazed at the water, bleated piteously, and refused to venture. The patient mother went back to it again and again to encourage it, but long without avail. Like the pilgrim on Jordan's stormy bank it feared to launch away. At length, gathering its trembling inexperienced legs for the mighty effort, throwing up its head as if it knew all about drowning, and was anxious to keep its nose above water, it made the tremendous leap, and landed in the middle of the inch-deep stream. It seemed astonished to find that, instead of sinking over head and ears, only its toes were wet, gazed at the shining water a few seconds, and then sprang to the shore safe and dry through the dreadful adventure. All kinds of wild sheep are mountain animals, and their descendants' dread of water is not easily accounted for.

11 August. Fine shining weather, with a ten minutes noon thunderstorm and rain. Rambling all day getting acquainted with the region north of the river. Found a small lake and many charming glacier meadows embosomed in an extensive forest of the two-leaved pine. The forest is growing on broad, almost continuous deposits of moraine material, is remarkably even in its growth, and the trees are much closer together than in any of the fir or pine woods farther down the range. The evenness of the growth would seem to indicate that the trees are all of the same age or nearly so. This regularity has probably been in great part the result of fire. I saw several large patches and strips of dead bleached spars, the ground beneath them covered with a young even growth. Fire can run in these woods, not only because the thin bark of the trees is dripping with resin, but because the growth is close, and the comparatively rich soil produces good crops of tall broad-leaved grasses on which fire can travel, even when the weather is calm. Besides these fire-killed patches there are a good many fallen uprooted trees here and there, some with the bark and needles still on, as if they had lately been blown down in some thunderstorm blast. Saw a large black-tailed deer, a buck with antlers like the upturned roots of a fallen pine.

After a long ramble through the dense encumbered woods I emerged upon a smooth meadow full of sunshine like a lake of light, about a mile and a half long, a quarter to half a mile wide, and bounded by tall arrowy pines. The sod, like that of all the glacier meadows hereabouts, is made of silky agrostis and calamagrostis chiefly; their panicles of purple flowers and purple stems, exceedingly light and airy, seem to float above the green plush of leaves like a thin misty cloud, while the sod is brightened by several species of gentian, potentilla, ivesia, orthocarpus, and their corresponding bees and butterflies. All the glacier meadows are beautiful, but few are so perfect as this one. Compared with it the most carefully levelled, licked, snipped artificial lawns of pleasure grounds are coarse things. I should like to live here always. It is so calm and withdrawn while open to the universe in full communion with everything good. To the north of this glorious meadow I discovered the camp of some Indian hunters. Their fire was still burning, but they had not yet returned from the chase.

From meadow to meadow, every one beautiful beyond telling, and from lake to lake through groves and belts of arrowy trees, I held my way northward toward Mount Conness, finding telling beauty everywhere, while the encompassing mountains were calling 'Come'. Hope I may climb them all.

12 August. The sky scenery has changed but little so far with the change in elevation. Clouds about five per cent. Glorious pearly cumuli tinted with purple of ineffable fineness of tone. Moved camp to the side of the glacier meadow mentioned above. To let sheep trample so divinely fine a place seems barbarous. Fortunately they prefer the succulent broad-leaved triticum and other woodland grasses to the silky species of the meadows, and therefore seldom bite them or set foot on them.

The shepherd and the Don cannot agree about methods of herding. Billy sets his dog Jack on the sheep far too often, so the Don thinks; and after some dispute today, in which the shepherd loudly claimed the right to dog the sheep as often as he pleased, he started for the plains. Now I suppose the care of the sheep will fall on me, though Mr Delaney promises to do the herding himself for a while, then return to the lowlands and bring another shepherd, so as to leave me free to rove as I like.

Had another rich ramble. Pushed northward beyond the forests to the head of the general basin, where traces of glacial action are strikingly clear and interesting. The recesses among the peaks look like quarries, so raw and fresh are the moraine chips and boulders that strew the ground in Nature's glacial workshops.

Soon after my return to camp we received a visit from an Indian, probably one of the hunters whose camp I had discovered. He came from Mono, he said, with others of his tribe, to hunt deer. One that he had killed a short distance from here he was carrying on his back, its legs tied together in an ornamental bunch on his forehead. Throwing down his burden, he gazed stolidly for a few minutes in silent Indian fashion, then cut off eight or ten pounds of venison for us, and begged a 'lill' (little) of everything he saw or could think of – flour, bread, sugar, tobacco, whiskey and needles, etc. We gave a fair price for the meat in flour and sugar and added a few needles. A strangely dirty and irregular life these dark-eyed, dark-haired, half happy savages lead in this clean wilderness – starvation and abundance, death-like calm, indolence, and admirable, indefatigable action succeeding each other in stormy rhythm like winter and summer. Two things they have that civilised toilers might well envy them – pure air and pure water. These go far to cover and cure the grossness of their lives. Their food is mostly good berries, pine nuts, clover, lily bulbs, wild sheep, antelope, deer, grouse, sage hens, and the larvae of ants, wasps, bees, and other insects.

13 August. Day all sunshine, dawn and evening purple, noon gold, no clouds, air motionless. Mr Delaney arrived with two shepherds, one of them an Indian. On his way up from the plains he left some provisions at the Portuguese camp on Porcupine Creek near our old Yosemite camp, and I set out this morning with one of the pack animals to fetch them. Arrived at the Porcupine camp at noon, and might have returned to the Tuolumne late in the evening, but concluded to stay overnight with the Portuguese shepherds at their pressing invitation. They had sad stories to tell of losses from the Yosemite bears, and were so discouraged they seemed on the point of leaving the mountains; for the bears came every night and helped themselves to one or several of the flock in spite of all their efforts to keep them off.

I spent the afternoon in a grand ramble along the Yosemite walls. From the highest of the rocks called the Three Brothers, I enjoyed a magnificent view comprehending all the upper half of the floor of the valley and nearly all the rocks of the walls on both sides and at the head, with snowy peaks in the background. Saw also the Vernal and Nevada Falls, a truly glorious picture – rocky strength and permanence combined with beauty of plants frail and fine and evanescent; water descending in thunder, and the same water gliding through meadows and groves in gentlest beauty. This standpoint is about eight thousand feet above the sea, or four thousand feet above the floor of the valley, and every tree, though looking small and feathery, stands in admirable clearness, and the shadows they cast are as distinct in outline as if seen at a distance of a few yards. They appeared even more so. No words will ever describe the exquisite beauty and charm of this mountain park – Nature's landscape garden at once tenderly beautiful and sublime. No wonder it draws nature-lovers from all over the world.

Glacial action even on this lofty summit is plainly displayed. Not only has all the lovely valley now smiling in sunshine been filled to the brim with ice, but it has been deeply overflowed.

I visited our old Yosemite camp ground on the head of Indian Creek, and found it fairly patted and smoothed down with bear tracks. The bears had eaten all the sheep that were smothered in the corral, and some of the grand animals must have died, for Mr Delaney, before leaving camp, put a large quantity of poison in the carcasses. All sheep men carry strychnine to kill coyotes, bears, and panthers, though neither coyotes nor panthers are at all numerous in the upper mountains. The little dog-like wolves are far more numerous in the foothill region and on the plains, where they find a better supply of food – saw only one panther track above eight thousand feet.

On my return after sunset to the Portuguese camp I found the shepherds greatly excited over the behaviour of the bears that have learned to like mutton. 'They are getting worse and worse', they lamented. Not willing to wait decently until after dark for their suppers, they come and kill and eat their fill in broad daylight. The evening before my arrival, when the two shepherds were leisurely driving the flock toward camp half an hour before sunset, a hungry bear came out of the chaparral within a few yards of them and shuffled deliberately toward the flock. 'Portuguese Joe', who always carried a gun loaded with buckshot, fired excitedly, threw down his gun, fled to the nearest suitable tree, and climbed to a safe height without waiting to see the effect of his shot. His companion also ran, but said that he saw the bear rise on his hind legs and throw out its arms as if feeling for somebody, and then go into the brush as if wounded.

At another of their camps in this neighbourhood, a bear with two cubs attacked the flock before sunset, just as they were approaching the corral. Joe promptly climbed a tree out of danger, while Antone, rebuking his companion for cowardice in abandoning his charge, said that he was not going to let bears 'eat up his sheeps' in daylight, and rushed towards the bears, shouting and setting his dog on them. The frightened cubs climbed a tree, but the mother ran to meet the shepherd and seemed anxious to fight. Antone stood astonished for a moment, eyeing the oncoming bear, then turned and fled, closely pursued. Unable to reach a suitable tree for climbing, he ran to the camp and scrambled up to the roof of the little cabin; the bear followed, but did not climb to the roof – only stood glaring up at him for a few minutes, threatening him and holding him in mortal terror, then went to her cubs, called them down, went to the flock, caught a sheep for supper, and vanished in the brush. As soon as the bear left the cabin, the trembling Antone begged Joe to show him a good safe tree, up which he climbed like a sailor climbing a mast, and remained as long as he could hold on, the tree being almost branchless. After these disastrous experiences the two shepherds chopped and gathered large piles of dry wood and made a ring of fire around the corral every night, while one with a gun kept watch from a comfortable stage built on a neighbouring pine that commanded a view of the corral. This evening the show made by the circle of fire was very fine, bringing out the surrounding trees in most impressive relief, and making the thousands of sheep eyes glow like a glorious bed of diamonds.

14 August. Up to the time I went to bed last night all was quiet, though we expected the shaggy freebooters every minute. They did not come till near midnight, when a pair walked boldly to the corral between two of the great fires, climbed in, killed two sheep and smothered ten, while the frightened watcher in the tree did not fire a single shot, saying that he was afraid he might kill some of the sheep, for the bears got into the corral before he got a good clear view of them. I told the shepherds they should at once move the flock to another camp. 'Oh, no use, no use,' they lamented; 'where we go, the bears go too. See my poor dead sheeps – soon all dead. No use try another camp. We go down to the plains.' And as I afterwards learned, they were driven out of the mountains a month before the usual time. Were bears much more numerous and destructive, the sheep would be kept away altogether.

It seems strange that bears, so fond of all sorts of flesh, running the risks of guns and fires and poison, should never attack men except in defence of their young. How easily and safely a bear could pick us up as we lie asleep! Only wolves and tigers seem to have learned to hunt man for food, and perhaps sharks and crocodiles. Mosquitoes and other insects would, I suppose, devour a helpless man in some parts of the world, and so might lions, leopards, wolves, hyenas and panthers at times if pressed by hunger – but under ordinary circumstances perhaps, only the tiger among land animals may be said to be a man eater – unless we add man himself.

Clouds as usual about five per cent. Another glorious Sierra day, warm, crisp, fragrant, and clear. Many of the flowering plants have gone to seed, but many others are unfolding their petals every day, and the firs and pines are more fragrant than ever. Their seeds are nearly ripe, and will soon be flying in the merriest flocks that ever spread a wing.

On the way back to our Tuolumne camp, I enjoyed the scenery if possible more than when it first came to view. Every feature already seems familiar as if I had lived here always. I never weary gazing at the wonderful Cathedral. It has more individual character than any other rock or mountain I ever saw, excepting perhaps the Yosemite South Dome. The forests, too, seem kindly familiar, and the lakes and meadows and glad singing streams. I should like to dwell with them forever. Here with bread and water I should be content. Even if not allowed to roam and climb, tethered to a stake or tree in some meadow or grove, even then I should be content forever. Bathed in such beauty, watching the expressions ever varying on the faces of the mountains, watching the stars, which here have a glory that the lowlander never dreams of, watching the circling seasons, listening to the songs of the waters and winds and birds, would be endless pleasure. And what glorious cloudlands I should see, storms and calms – a new heaven and a new earth every day, aye and new inhabitants. And how many visitors I should have. I feel sure I should not have one dull moment. And why should this appear extravagant? It is only common sense, a sign of health, genuine, natural, all awake health. One would be at an endless Godful play, and what speeches and music and acting and scenery and lights! – sun, moon, stars, auroras. Creation just beginning, the morning stars 'still singing together and all the sons of God shouting for joy'.

CHAPTER NINE

Bloody Canyon and Mono Lake

21 AUGUST. Have just returned from a fine wild excursion across the range to Mono Lake, by way of the Mono or Bloody Canyon Pass. Mr Delaney has been good to me all summer, lending a helping, sympathising hand at every opportunity, as if my wild notions and rambles and studies were his own. He is one of those remarkable California men who have been overflowed and denuded and remodelled by the excitements of the gold fields, like the Sierra landscapes by grinding ice, bringing the harder bosses and ridges of character into relief – a tall, lean, big-boned, big-hearted Irishman, educated for a priest in Maynooth College – lots of good in him, shining out now and then in this mountain light. Recognising my love of wild places, he told me one evening that I ought to go through Bloody Canyon, for he was sure I should find it wild enough. He had not been there himself, he said, but had heard many of his mining friends speak of it as the wildest of all the Sierra passes. Of course I was glad to go. It lies just to the east of our camp and swoops down from the summit of the range to the edge of the Mono Desert, making a descent of about four thousand feet in a distance of about four miles. It was known and travelled as a pass by wild animals and the Indians long before its discovery by white men in the gold year of 1858, as is shown by old trails which come together at the head of it. The name may have been suggested by the red colour of the metamorphic slates in which the canyon abounds, or by the bloodstains on the rocks from the unfortunate animals that were compelled to slide and shuffle over the sharp-angled boulders.

Early in the morning I tied my notebook and some bread to my belt, and strode away full of eager hope, feeling that I was going to have a glorious revel. The glacier meadows that lay along my way served to soothe my morning speed, for the sod was full of blue gentians and daisies, kalmia and dwarf vaccinium, calling for recognition as old friends, and I had to stop many times to examine the shining rocks over which the ancient glacier had passed with tremendous pressure, polishing them so well that they reflected the sunlight like glass in some places, while fine striae, seen clearly through a lens, indicated the direction in which the ice had flowed. On some of the sloping polished pavements abrupt steps occur, showing that occasionally large masses of the rock had given way before the glacial pressure, as well as small particles; moraines, too, some scattered, others regular like long curving embankments and dams, occur here and there, giving the general surface of the region a young, new-made appearance. I watched the gradual dwarfing of the pines as I ascended, and the corresponding dwarfing of nearly all the rest of the vegetation. On the slopes of Mammoth Mountain, to the south of the pass, I saw many gaps in the woods reaching from the upper edge of the timber-line down to the level meadows, where avalanches of snow had descended, sweeping away every tree in their paths as well as the soil they were growing in, leaving the bedrock bare. The trees are nearly all uprooted, but a few that had been extremely well anchored in clefts of the rock were broken off near the ground. It seems strange at first sight that trees that had been allowed to grow for a century or more undisturbed should in their old age be thus swished away at a stroke. Such avalanches can only occur under rare conditions of weather and snowfall. No doubt on some positions of the mountain slopes the inclination and smoothness of the surface is such that avalanches must occur every winter, or even after every heavy snowstorm, and of course no trees or even bushes can grow in their channels. I noticed a few clean-swept slopes of this kind. The uprooted trees that had grown in the pathway of what might be called 'century avalanches' were piled in windrows, and tucked snugly against the wall-trees of the gaps, heads downward, excepting a few that were carried out into the open ground of the meadows, where the heads of the avalanches had stopped. Young pines, mostly the two-leaved and the white-barked, are already springing up in these cleared gaps. It would be interesting to ascertain the age of these saplings, for thus we should gain a fair approximation to the year that the great avalanches occurred. Perhaps most or all of them occurred the same winter. How glad I should be if free to pursue such studies!

Near the summit at the head of the pass I found a species of dwarf willow lying perfectly flat on the ground, making a nice, soft, silky grey carpet, not a single stem or branch more than three inches high; but the catkins, which are now nearly ripe, stand erect and make a close, nearly regular grey growth, being larger than all the rest of the plants. Some of these interesting dwarfs have only one catkin – willow bushes reduced to their lowest terms. I found patches of dwarf vaccinium also forming smooth carpets, closely pressed to the ground or against the sides of stones, and covered with round pink flowers in lavish abundance as if they had fallen from the sky like hail. A little higher, almost at the very head of the pass, I found the blue arctic daisy and purple-flowered bryanthus, the mountain's own darlings, gentle mountaineers face to face with the sky, kept safe and warm by a thousand miracles, seeming always the finer and purer the wilder and stormier their homes. The trees, tough and resiny, seem unable to go a step farther; but up and up, far above the tree line, these tender plants climb, cheerily spreading their grey and pink carpets right up to the very edges of the snow banks in deep hollows and shadows. Here, too, is the familiar robin, tripping on the flowery lawns, bravely singing the same cheery song I first heard when a boy in Wisconsin newly arrived from old Scotland. In this fine company sauntering enchanted, taking no heed of time, I at length entered the gate of the pass, and the huge rocks began to close around me in all their mysterious impressiveness. Just then I was startled by a lot of queer, hairy, muffled creatures coming shuffling, shambling, wallowing towards me as if they had no bones in their bodies. Had I discovered them while they were yet a good way off, I should have tried to avoid them. What a picture they made contrasted with the others I had just been admiring.

When I came up to them, I found that they were only a band of Indians from Mono on their way to Yosemite for a load of acorns. They were wrapped in blankets made of the skins of sage-rabbits. The dirt on some of the faces seemed almost old enough and thick enough to have a geological significance; some were strangely blurred and divided into sections by seams and wrinkles that looked like cleavage joints, and had a worn abraded look as if they had lain exposed to the weather for ages. I tried to pass them without stopping, but they wouldn't let me; forming a dismal circle about me, I was closely besieged while they begged whiskey or tobacco, and it was hard to convince them that I hadn't any. How glad I was to get away from the grey grim crowd and see them vanish down the trail! Yet it seems sad to feel such desperate repulsion from one's fellow beings, however degraded. To prefer the society of squirrels and woodchucks to that of our own species must surely be unnatural. So with a fresh breeze and a hill or mountain between us I must wish them Godspeed and try to pray and sing with Burns, 'It's coming yet, for a' that, that man to man, the warld o'er, shall brothers be for a' that'.

How the day passed I hardly know. By the map I have come only about ten or twelve miles, though the sun is already low in the west, showing how long I must have lingered, observing, sketching, taking notes among the glaciated rocks and moraines and Alpine flower beds.

At sundown the sombre crags and peaks were inspired with the ineffable beauty of the alpenglow, and a solemn, awful stillness hushed everything in the landscape. Then I crept into a hollow by the side of a small lake near the head of the canyon, smoothed a sheltered spot, and gathered a few pine tassels for a bed. After the short twilight began to fade I kindled a sunny fire, made a tin cupful of tea, and lay down to watch the stars. Soon the night-wind began to flow from the snowy peaks overhead, at first only a gentle breathing, then gaining strength, in less than an hour rumbled in massive volume something like a boisterous stream in a boulder-choked channel, roaring and moaning down the canyon as if the work it had to do was tremendously important and fateful; and mingled with these storm tones were those of the waterfalls on the north side of the canyon, now sounding distinctly, now smothered by the heavier cataracts of air, making a glorious psalm of savage wildness. My fire squirmed and struggled as if ill at ease, for though in a sheltered nook, detached masses of icy wind often fell like icebergs on top of it, scattering sparks and coals, so that I had to keep well back to avoid being burned. But the big resiny roots and knots of the dwarf pine could neither be beaten out nor blown away, and the flames, now rushing up in long lances, now flattened and twisted on the rocky ground, roared as if trying to tell the storm stories of the trees they belonged to, as the light given out was telling the story of the sunshine they had gathered in centuries of summers.

The stars shone clear in the strip of sky between the huge dark cliffs; and as I lay recalling the lessons of the day, suddenly the full moon looked down over the canyon wall, her face apparently filled with eager concern, which had a startling effect, as if she had left her place in the sky and had come down to gaze on me alone, like a person entering one's bedroom. It was hard to realise that she was in her place in the sky, and was looking abroad on half the globe, land and sea, mountains, plains, lakes, rivers, oceans, ships, cities with their myriads of inhabitants sleeping and waking, sick and well. No, she seemed to be just on the rim of Bloody Canyon and looking only at me. This was indeed getting near to Nature. I remember watching the harvest moon rising above the oak trees in Wisconsin apparently as big as a cartwheel and not farther than half a mile distant. With these exceptions I might say I never before had seen the moon, and this night she seemed so full of life and so near, the effect was marvellously impressive and made me forget the Indians, the great black rocks above me, and the wild uproar of the winds and waters making their way down the huge jagged gorge. Of course I slept but little and gladly welcomed the dawn over the Mono Desert. By the time I had made a cupful of tea the sunbeams were pouring through the canyon, and I set forth, gazing eagerly at the tremendous walls of red slates savagely hacked and scarred and apparently ready to fall in avalanches great enough to choke the pass and fill up the chain of lakelets. But soon its beauties came to view, and I bounded lightly from rock to rock, admiring the polished bosses shining in the slant sunshine with glorious effect in the general roughness of moraines and avalanche taluses, even toward the head of the canyon near the highest fountains of the ice. Here, too, are most of the lowly plant people seen yesterday on the other side of the divide now opening their beautiful eyes. None could fail to glory in Nature's tender care for them in so wild a place. The little ouzel is flitting from rock to rock along the rapid swirling Canyon Creek, diving for breakfast in icy pools, and merrily singing as if the huge rugged avalanche-swept gorge was the most delightful of all its mountain homes. Besides a high fall on the north wall of the canyon, apparently coming direct from the sky, there are many narrow cascades, bright silvery ribbons zigzagging down the red cliffs, tracing the diagonal cleavage joints of the metamorphic slates, now contracted and out of sight, now leaping from ledge to ledge in filmy sheets through which the sunbeams sift. And on the main Canyon Creek, to which all these are tributary, is a series of small falls, cascades and rapids extending all the way down to the foot of the canyon, interrupted only by the lakes in which the tossed and beaten waters rest. One of the finest of the cascades is outspread on the face of a precipice, its waters separated into ribbon-like strips, and woven into a diamond-like pattern by tracing the cleavage joints of the rocks, while tufts of bryanthus, grass, sedge and saxifrage form beautiful fringes. Who could imagine beauty so fine in so savage a place? Gardens blooming in all sorts of nooks and hollows – at the head alpine eriogonums, erigerons, saxifrages, gentians, cowania, bush primula; in the middle region larkspur, columbine, orthocarpus, castilleia, harebell, epilobium, violets, mints, yarrow; near the foot sunflowers, lilies, brier rose, iris, lonicera, clematis.

One of the smallest of the cascades, which I name the Bower Cascade, is in the lower region of the pass, where the vegetation is snowy and luxuriant. Wild rose and dogwood form dense masses overarching the stream, and out of this bower the creek, grown strong with many indashing tributaries, leaps forth into the light, and descends in a fluted curve thick-sown with crisp flashing spray. At the foot of the canyon there is a lake formed in part at least by the damming of the stream by a terminal moraine. The three other lakes in the canyon are in basins eroded from the solid rock, where the pressure of the glacier was greatest, and the most resisting portions of the basin rims are beautifully, tellingly polished. Below Moraine Lake at the foot of the canyon there are several old lake basins lying between the large lateral moraines which extend out into the desert. These basins are now completely filled up by the material carried in by the streams, and changed to dry sandy flats covered mostly by grass and artemisia and sun-loving flowers. All these lower lake basins were evidently formed by terminal moraine dams deposited where the receding glacier had lingered during short periods of less waste, or greater snowfall, or both.

Looking up the canyon from the warm sunny edge of the Mono plain my morning ramble seems a dream, so great is the change in the vegetation and climate. The lilies on the bank of Moraine Lake are higher than my head, and the sunshine is hot enough for palms. Yet the snow round the arctic gardens at the summit of the pass is plainly visible, only about four miles away, and between lie specimen zones of all the principal climates of the globe. In little more than an hour one may swoop down from winter to summer, from an Arctic to a torrid region, through as great changes of climate as one would encounter in travelling from Labrador to Florida.

The Indians I had met near the head of the canyon had camped at the foot of it the night before they made the ascent, and I found their fire still smoking on the side of a small tributary stream near Moraine Lake; and on the edge of what is called the Mono Desert, four or five miles from the lake, I came to a patch of elymus, or wild rye, growing in magnificent waving clumps six or eight feet high, bearing heads six to eight inches long. The crop was ripe, and Indian women were gathering the grain in baskets by bending down large handfuls, beating out the seed, and fanning it in the wind. The grains are about five eighths of an inch long, dark-coloured and sweet. I fancy the bread made from it must be as good as wheat bread. A fine squirrelish employment this wild grain gathering seems, and the women were evidently enjoying it, laughing and chattering and looking almost natural, though most Indians I have seen are not a whit more natural in their lives than we civilised whites. Perhaps if I knew them better I should like them better. The worst thing about them is their uncleanliness. Nothing truly wild is unclean. Down on the shore of Mono Lake I saw a number of their flimsy huts on the banks of streams that dash swiftly into that dead sea – mere brush tents where they lie and eat at their ease. Some of the men were feasting on buffalo berries, lying beneath the tall bushes now red with fruit. The berries are rather insipid, but they must needs be wholesome, since for days and weeks the Indians, it is said, eat nothing else. In the season they in like manner depend chiefly on the fat larvae of a fly that breeds in the saltwater of the lake, or on the big fat corrugated caterpillars of a species of silkworm that feeds on the leaves of the yellow pine. Occasionally a grand rabbit-drive is organised and hundreds are slain with clubs on the lake shore, chased and frightened into a dense crowd by dogs, boys, girls, men and women, and rings of sage brush fire, when of course they are quickly killed. The skins are made into blankets. In the autumn the more enterprising of the hunters bring in a good many deer, and rarely a wild sheep from the high peaks. Antelopes used to be abundant on the desert at the base of the interior mountain ranges. Sage hens, grouse, and squirrels help to vary their wild diet of worms; pine nuts also from the small interesting *Pinus monophylla*, and good bread and good mush are made from acorns and wild rye. Strange to say, they seem to like the lake larvae best of all. Long windrows are washed up on the shore, which they gather and dry like grain for winter use. It is said that wars, on account of encroachments on each other's worm grounds, are of common occurrence among the various tribes and families. Each claims a certain marked portion of the shore. The pine nuts are delicious – large quantities are gathered every autumn. The tribes of the west flank of the range trade acorns for worms and pine nuts. The squaws carry immense loads on their backs across the rough passes and down the range, making journeys of about forty or fifty miles each way.

The desert around the lake is surprisingly flowery. In many places among the sage bushes I saw mentzelia, abronia, aster, bigelovia, and gilia, all of which seemed to enjoy the hot sunshine. The abronia, in particular, is a delicate, fragrant, and most charming plant.

Opposite the mouth of the canyon a range of volcanic cones extends southward from the lake, rising abruptly out of the desert like a chain of mountains. The largest of the cones are about twenty five hundred feet high above the lake level, have well-formed craters, and all of them are evidently comparatively recent additions to the landscape. At a distance of a few miles they look like heaps of loose ashes that have never been blest by either rain or snow, but, for a' that and a' that, yellow pines are climbing their grey slopes, trying to clothe them and give beauty for ashes. A country of wonderful contrasts. Hot deserts bounded by snow laden mountains – cinders and ashes scattered on glacier polished pavements – frost and fire working together in the making of beauty. In the lake are several volcanic islands, which show that the waters were once mingled with fire.

Glad to get back to the green side of the mountains, though I have greatly enjoyed the grey east side and hope to see more of it. Reading these grand mountain manuscripts displayed through every vicissitude of heat and cold, calm and storm, upheaving volcanoes and down-grinding glaciers, we see that everything in Nature called destruction must be creation – a change from beauty to beauty.

Our glacier meadow camp north of the Soda Springs seems more beautiful every day. The grass covers all the ground though the leaves are thread-like in fineness, and in walking on the sod it seems like a plush carpet of marvellous richness and softness, and the purple panicles brushing against one's feet are not felt. This is a typical glacier meadow, occupying the basin of a vanished lake, very definitely bounded by walls of the arrowy two-leaved pines drawn up in a handsome orderly array like soldiers on parade. There are many other meadows of the same kind hereabouts embedded in the woods. The main big meadows along the river are the same in general and extend with but little interruption for ten or twelve miles, but none I have seen are so finely finished and perfect as this one. It is richer in flowering plants than the prairies of

Wisconsin and Illinois were when in all their wild glory. The showy flowers are mostly three species of gentian, a purple and yellow orthocarpus, a golden-rod or two, a small blue pentstemon almost like a gentian, potentilla, ivesia, pedicularis, white violet, kalmia, and bryanthus. There are no coarse weedy plants. Through this flowery lawn flows a stream silently gliding, swirling, slipping as if careful not to make the slightest noise. It is only about three feet wide in most places, widening here and there into pools six or eight feet in diameter with no apparent current, the banks bossily rounded by the down-curving mossy sod, grass panicles over-leaning like miniature pine trees, and rugs of bryanthus spreading here and there over sunken boulders. At the foot of the meadow the stream, rich with the juices of the plants it has refreshed, sings merrily down over shelving rock ledges on its way to the Tuolumne River. The sublime, massive Mount Dana and its companions, green, red and white, loom impressively above the pines along the eastern horizon; a range or spur of grey rugged granite crags and mountains on the north; the curiously crested and battlemented Mount Hoffman on the west; and the Cathedral Range on the south with its grand Cathedral Peak, Cathedral Spires, Unicorn Peak, and several others, grey and pointed or massively rounded.

CHAPTER TEN

The Tuolumne Camp

22 AUGUST. Clouds none, cool west wind, slight hoarfrost on the meadows. Carlo is missing; have been seeking him all day. In the thick woods between camp and the river, among tall grass and fallen pines, I discovered a baby fawn. At first it seemed inclined to come to me; but when I tried to catch it, and got within a rod or two, it turned and walked softly away, choosing its steps like a cautious, stealthy, hunting cat. Then, as if suddenly called or alarmed, it began to buck and run like a grown deer, jumping high above the fallen trunks, and was soon out of sight. Possibly its mother may have called it, but I did not hear her. I don't think fawns ever leave the home thicket or follow their mothers until they are called or frightened. I am distressed about Carlo. There are several other camps and dogs not many miles from here, and I still hope to find him. He never left me before. Panthers are very rare here, and I don't think any of these cats would dare touch him. He knows bears too well to be caught by them, and as for Indians, they don't want him.

23 August. Cool, bright day, hinting Indian summer. Mr Delaney has gone to the Smith Ranch, on the Tuolumne below Hetch-Hetchy Valley, thirty-five or forty miles from here, so I'll be alone for a week or more – not really alone, for Carlo has come back. He was at a camp a few miles to the northwestward. He looked sheepish and ashamed when I asked him where he had been and why he had gone away without leave. He is now trying to get me to caress him and show signs of forgiveness. A wondrous wise dog. A great load is off my mind. I could not have left the mountains without him. He seems very glad to get back to me.

Rose and crimson sunset, and soon after the stars appeared the moon rose in most impressive majesty over the top of Mount Dana. I sauntered up the meadow in the white light. The jet-black tree shadows were so wonderfully distinct and substantial looking, I often stepped high in crossing them, taking them for black charred logs.

24 August. Another charming day, warm and calm soon after sunrise, clouds only about one per cent – faint, silky cirrus wisps, scarcely visible. Slight frost, Indian summerish, the mountains growing softer in outline and dreamy looking, their rough angles melted off, apparently. Sky at evening with fine, dark, subdued purple, almost like the evening purple of the San Joaquin plains in settled weather. The moon is now gazing over the summit of Dana. Glorious exhilarating air. I wonder if in all the world there is another mountain range of equal height blessed with weather so fine, and so openly kind and hospitable and approachable.

25 August. Cool as usual in the morning, quickly changing to the ordinary serene generous warmth and brightness. Toward evening the west wind was cool and sent us to the campfire. Of all Nature's flowery carpeted mountain halls none can be finer than this glacier meadow. Bees and butterflies seem as abundant as ever. The birds are still here, showing no sign of leaving for winter quarters though the frost must bring them in mind. For my part I should like to stay here all winter or all my life or even all eternity.

26 August. Frost this morning; all the meadow grass and some of the pine needles sparkling with irised crystals – flowers of light. Large picturesque clouds, craggy like rocks, are piled on Mount Dana, reddish in colour like the mountain itself; the sky for a few degrees around the horizon is pale purple, into which the pines dip their spires with fine effect. Spent the day as usual looking about me, watching the changing lights, the ripening autumn colours of the grass, seeds, late-blooming gentians, asters, goldenrods; parting the meadow grass here and there and looking down into the underworld of mosses and liverworts; watching the busy ants and beetles and other small people at work and play like squirrels and bears in a forest; studying the formation of lakes and meadows, moraines, mountain sculpture; making small beginnings in these directions, charmed by the serene beauty of everything.

The day has been extra cloudy, though bright on the whole, for the clouds were brighter than common. Clouds about fifteen per cent, which in Switzerland would be considered extra clear. Probably more free sunshine falls on this majestic range than on any other in the world I've ever seen or heard of. It has the brightest weather, brightest glacier-polished rocks, the greatest abundance of irised spray from its glorious waterfalls, the brightest forests of silver firs and silver pines, more starshine, moonshine, and perhaps more crystalshine than any other mountain chain, and its countless mirror lakes, having more light poured into them, glow and spangle most. And how glorious the shining after the short summer showers and after frosty nights when the morning sunbeams are pouring through the crystals on the grass and pine needles, and how ineffably spiritually fine is the morning glow on the mountain tops and the alpenglow of evening. Well may the Sierra be named, not the Snowy Range, but the Range of Light.

27 August. Clouds only five per cent – mostly white and pink cumuli over the Hoffman spur towards evening – frosty morning. Crystals grow in marvellous beauty and perfection of form these still nights, every one built as carefully as the grandest holiest temple, as if planned to endure forever.

Contemplating the lace-like fabric of streams outspread over the mountains, we are reminded that everything is flowing – going somewhere, animals and so-called lifeless rocks as well as water. Thus the snow flows fast or slow in grand beauty-making glaciers and avalanches; the air in majestic floods carrying minerals, plant leaves, seeds, spores, with streams of music and fragrance; water streams carrying rocks both in solution and in the form of mud particles, sand, pebbles, and boulders. Rocks flow from volcanoes like water from springs, and animals flock together and flow in currents modified by stepping, leaping, gliding, flying and swimming, etc. While the stars go streaming through space pulsed on and on forever like blood globules in Nature's warm heart.

28 August. The dawn a glorious song of colour. Sky absolutely cloudless. A fine crop of hoarfrost. Warm after ten o'clock. The gentians don't mind the first frost though their petals seem so delicate; they close every night as if going to sleep, and awake fresh as ever in the morning sun glory. The grass is a shade browner since last week, but there are no nipped wilted plants of any sort as far as I have seen. Butterflies and the grand host of smaller flies are benumbed every night, but they hover and dance in the sunbeams over the meadows before noon with no apparent lack of playful, joyful life. Soon they must all fall like petals in an orchard, dry and wrinkled, not a wing of all the mighty host left to tingle the air. Nevertheless new myriads will arise in the spring, rejoicing, exulting, as if laughing cold death to scorn.

29 August. Clouds about five per cent, slight frost. Bland serene Indian summer weather. Have been gazing all day at the mountains, watching the changing lights. More and more plainly are they clothed with light as a garment, white tinged with pale purple, palest during the midday hours, richest in the morning and evening. Everything seems consciously peaceful, thoughtful, faithfully waiting God's will.

30 August. This day just like yesterday. A few clouds motionless and apparently with no work to do beyond looking beautiful. Frost enough for crystal building – glorious fields of ice diamonds destined to last but a night. How lavish is Nature building, pulling down, creating, destroying, chasing every material particle from form to form, ever changing, ever beautiful.

Mr Delaney arrived this morning. Felt not a trace of loneliness while he was gone. On the contrary, I never enjoyed grander company. The whole wilderness seems to be alive and familiar, full of humanity. The very stones seem talkative, sympathetic, brotherly. No wonder when we consider that we all have the same Father and Mother.

31 August. Clouds five per cent. Silky cirrus wisps and fringes so fine they almost escape notice. Frost enough for another crop of crystals on the meadows but none on the forests. The gentians, goldenrods and asters don't seem to feel it; neither petals nor leaves are touched though they seem so tender. Every day opens and closes like a flower, noiseless, effortless. Divine peace glows on all the majestic landscape like the silent enthusiastic joy that sometimes transfigures a noble human face.

1 September. Clouds five per cent – motionless, of no particular colour – ornaments with no hint of rain or snow in them. Day all calm – another grand throb of Nature's heart, ripening late flowers and seeds for next summer, full of life and the thoughts and plans of life to come, and full of ripe and ready death beautiful as life, telling divine wisdom and goodness and immortality. Have been up Mount Dana, making haste to see as much as I can now that the time of departure is drawing nigh. The views from the summit reach far and wide, eastward over the Mono Lake and Desert; mountains beyond mountains looking strangely barren and grey and bare like heaps of ashes dumped from the sky. The lake, eight or ten miles in diameter, shines like a burnished disc of silver, no trees about its grey, ashy, cindery shores. Looking westward, the glorious forests are seen sweeping over countless ridges and hills, girdling domes and subordinate mountains, fringing in long curving lines the dividing ridges, and filling every hollow where the glaciers have spread soil beds however rocky or smooth. Looking northward and southward along the axis of the range, you see the glorious array of high mountains, crags and peaks and snow, the fountain-heads of rivers that are flowing west to the sea through the famous Golden Gate, and east to hot salt lakes and deserts to evaporate and hurry back into the sky. Innumerable lakes are shining like eyes beneath heavy rock brows, bare or tree fringed, or embedded in black forests. Meadow openings in the woods seem as numerous as the lakes or perhaps more so. Far up the moraine-covered slopes and among crumbling rocks I found many delicate hardy plants, some of them still in flower. The best gains of this trip were the lessons of unity and interrelation of all the features of the landscape revealed in general views. The lakes and meadows are located just where the ancient glaciers bore heaviest at the foot of the steepest parts of their channels, and of course their longest diameters are approximately parallel with each other and with the belts of forests growing in long curving lines on the lateral and medial moraines, and in broad out-spreading fields on the terminal beds deposited toward the end of the ice period when the glaciers were receding. The domes, ridges, and spurs also show the influence of glacial action in their forms, which approximately seem to be the forms of greatest strength with reference to the stress of over-sweeping, past-sweeping, down-grinding ice-streams; survivals of the most resisting masses, or those most favourably situated. How interesting everything is! Every rock, mountain, stream, plant, lake, lawn, forest, garden, bird, beast, insect seems to call and invite us to come and learn something of its history and relationship. But shall the poor ignorant scholar be allowed to try the lessons they offer? It seems too great and good to be true. Soon I'll be going to the lowlands. The bread camp must soon be removed. If I had a few sacks of flour, an axe, and some matches, I would build a cabin of pine logs, pile up plenty of firewood about it and stay all winter to see the grand fertile snowstorms, watch the birds and animals that winter thus high, how they live, how the forests look snowladen or buried, and how the avalanches look and sound on their way down the mountains. But now I'll have to go, for there is nothing to spare in the way of provisions. I'll surely be back, however, surely I'll be back. No other place has ever so overwhelmingly attracted me as this hospitable, Godful wilderness.

2 September. A grand, red, rosy, crimson day – a perfect glory of a day. What it means I don't know. It is the first marked change from tranquil sunshine with purple mornings and evenings and still, white noons. There is nothing like a storm, however. The average cloudiness only about eight per cent, and there is no sighing in the woods to betoken a big weather change. The sky was red in the morning and evening, the colour not diffused like the ordinary purple glow, but loaded upon separate well-defined clouds that remained motionless, as if anchored around the jagged mountain-fenced horizon. A deep red cap, bluffy around its sides, lingered a long time on Mount Dana and Mount Gibbs, drooping so low as to hide most of their bases, but leaving Dana's round summit free, which seemed to float separate and alone over the crimson cloud. Mammoth Mountain, to the south of Gibbs and Bloody Canyon, striped and spotted with snow banks and clumps of dwarf pine, was also favoured with a glorious crimson cap, in the making of which there was no trace of economy – a huge bossy pile coloured with a perfect passion of crimson that seemed important enough to be sent off to burn among the stars in majestic independence. One is constantly reminded of the infinite lavishness and fertility of Nature – inexhaustible abundance amid what seems enormous wastage. And yet when we look into any of her operations that lie within reach of our minds, we learn that no particle of her material is wasted or worn out. It is eternally flowing from use to use, beauty to yet higher beauty; and we soon cease to lament waste and death, and rather rejoice and exult in the imperishable, unspendable wealth of the universe, and faithfully watch and wait the reappearance of everything that melts and fades and dies about us, feeling sure that its next appearance will be better and more beautiful than the last.

I watched the growth of these red lands of the sky as eagerly as if new mountain ranges were being built. Soon the group of snowy peaks in whose recesses lie the highest fountains of the Tuolumne, Merced, and North Fork of the San Joaquin were decorated with majestic coloured clouds like those already described, but more complicated, to correspond with the grand fountain-heads of the rivers they overshadowed. The Sierra Cathedral, to the south of camp, was overshadowed like Sinai. Never before noticed so fine a union of rock and cloud in form and colour and substance, drawing earth and sky together as one; and so human is it, every feature and tint of colour goes to one's heart and we shout, exulting in wild enthusiasm as if all the divine show were our own. More and more, in a place like this, we feel ourselves part of wild Nature, kin to everything. Spent most of the day high up on the north rim of the valley, commanding views of the clouds in all their red glory spreading their wonderful light over all the basin, while the rocks and trees and small Alpine plants at my feet seemed hushed and thoughtful, as if they also were conscious spectators of the glorious new cloud world.

Here and there, as I plodded farther and higher, I came to small garden patches and ferneries just where one would naturally decide that no plant-creature could possibly live. But, as in the region about the head of Mono Pass and the top of Dana, it was in the wildest, highest places that the most beautiful and tender and enthusiastic plant-people were found. Again and again, as I lingered over these charming plants, I said, How came you here? How do you live through the winter? Our roots, they explained, reach far down the joints of the summer-warmed rocks, and beneath our fine snow mantle killing frosts cannot reach us, while we sleep away the dark half of the year dreaming of spring.

Ever since I was allowed entrance into these mountains I have been looking for cassiope, said to be the most beautiful and best loved of the heathworts, but, strange to say, I have not yet found it. On my high mountain walks I keep muttering, 'Cassiope, cassiope'. This name, as Calvinists say, is driven in upon me, notwithstanding the glorious host of plants that come about me uncalled as soon as I show myself. Cassiope seems the highest name of all the small mountain-heath people, and as if conscious of her worth, keeps out of my way. I must find her soon, if at all this year.

4 September. All the vast sky dome is clear, filled only with mellow Indian summer light. The pine and hemlock and fir cones are nearly ripe and are falling fast from morning to night, cut off and gathered by the busy squirrels. Almost all the plants have matured their seeds, their summer work done; and the summer crop of birds and deer will soon be able to follow their parents to the foothills and plains at the approach of winter, when the snow begins to fly.

5 September. No clouds. Weather cool, calm, bright as if no great thing was yet ready to be done. Have been sketching the North Tuolumne Church. The sunset gloriously coloured.

6 September. Still another perfectly cloudless day, purple evening and morning, all the middle hours one mass of pure serene sunshine. Soon after sunrise the air grew warm, and there was no wind. One naturally halted to see what Nature intended to do. There is a suggestion of real Indian summer in the hushed brooding, faintly hazy weather. The yellow atmosphere, though thin, is still plainly of the same general character as that of eastern Indian summer. The peculiar mellowness is perhaps in part caused by myriads of ripe spores adrift in the sky.

Mr Delaney now keeps up a solemn talk about the need of getting away from these high mountains, telling sad stories of flocks that perished in storms that broke suddenly into the midst of fine innocent weather like this we are now enjoying. 'In no case', said he, 'will I venture to stay so high and far back in the mountains as we now are later than the middle of this month, no matter how warm and sunny it may be'. He would move the flock slowly at first, a few miles a day until the Yosemite Creek basin was reached and crossed, then while lingering in the heavy pine woods should the weather threaten he could hurry down to the foothills, where the snow never falls deep enough to smother a sheep. Of course I am anxious to see as much of the wilderness as possible in the few days left me, and I say again – may the good time come when I can stay as long as I like with plenty of bread, far and free from trampling flocks, though I may well be thankful for this generous foodful inspiring summer. Anyhow we never know where we must go nor what guides we are to get – men, storms, guardian angels, or sheep. Perhaps almost everybody in the least natural is guarded more than he is ever aware of. All the wilderness seems to be full of tricks and plans to drive and draw us up into God's Light.

Have been busy planning, and baking bread for at least one more good wild excursion among the high peaks, and surely none however hopefully aiming at fortune or fame, ever felt so gloriously happily excited by the outlook.

7 September. Left camp at daybreak and made direct for Cathedral Peak, intending to strike eastward and southward from that point among the peaks and ridges at the heads of Tuolumne, Merced, and San Joaquin Rivers. Down through the pine woods I made my way, across the Tuolumne River and meadows, and up the heavily timbered slope forming the south boundary of the upper Tuolumne basin, along the east side of Cathedral Peak, and up to its topmost spire, which I reached at noon, having loitered by the way to study the fine trees – two-leaved pine, mountain pine, albicaulis pine, silver fir, and the most charming, most graceful of all the evergreens, the mountain hemlock. High, cool, late flowering meadows also detained me, and lakelets and avalanche tracks and huge quarries of moraine rocks above the forests.

All the way up from the Big Meadows to the base of the Cathedral the ground is covered with moraine material, the left lateral moraine of the great glacier that must have completely filled this upper Tuolumne basin. Higher there are several small terminal moraines of residual glaciers shoved forward at right angles against the grand simple lateral of the main Tuolumne Glacier. A fine place to study mountain sculpture and soil making. The view from the Cathedral Spires is very fine and telling in every direction. Innumerable peaks, ridges, domes, meadows, lakes and woods; the forests extending in long curving lines and broad fields wherever the glaciers have left soil for them to grow on, while the sides of the highest mountains show a straggling dwarf growth clinging to rifts in the rocks apparently independent of soil. The dark heath-like growth on the Cathedral roof I found to be dwarf snow-pressed albicaulis pine, about three or four feet high, but very old looking. Many of them are bearing cones, and the noisy Clarke crow is eating the seeds, using his long bill like a woodpecker in digging them out of the cones. A good many flowers are still in bloom about the base of the peak, and even on the roof among the little pines, especially a woody yellow-flowered eriogonum and a handsome aster. The body of the Cathedral is nearly square, and the roof slopes are wonderfully regular and symmetrical, the ridge trending northeast and southwest. This direction has apparently been determined by structure joints in the granite. The gable on the northeast end is magnificent in size and simplicity, and at its base there is a big snow bank protected by the shadow of the building. The front is adorned with many pinnacles and a tall spire of curious workmanship. Here too the joints in the rock are seen to have played an important part in determining their forms and size and general arrangement. The Cathedral is said to be about eleven thousand feet above the sea, but the height of the building itself above the level of the ridge it stands on is about fifteen hundred feet. A mile or so to the westward there is a handsome lake, and the glacier-polished granite about it is shining so brightly it is not easy in some places to trace the line between the rock and water, both shining alike. Of this lake with its silvery basin and bits of meadow and groves I have a fine view from the spires; also of Lake Tenaya, Cloud's Rest and the South Dome of Yosemite, Mount Starr King, Mount Hoffman, the Merced peaks, and the vast multitude of snowy mountain peaks extending far north and south along the axis of the range. No feature, however, of all the noble landscape as seen from here seems more wonderful than the Cathedral itself, a temple displaying Nature's best masonry and sermons in stones. How often I have gazed at it from the tops of hills and ridges, and through openings in the forests on my many short excursions, devoutly wondering, admiring, longing! This I may say is the first time I have been at church in California, led here at last, every door graciously opened for the poor lonely worshipper. In our best times everything turns into religion, all the world seems a church and the mountains altars. And lo, here at last in front of the Cathedral is blessed cassiope, ringing her thousands of sweet-toned bells, the sweetest church music I ever enjoyed. Listening, admiring, until late in the afternoon I compelled myself to hasten away eastward back of rough, sharp, spiry, splintery peaks, all of them granite like the Cathedral, sparkling with crystals – feldspar, quartz, hornblende, mica, tourmaline. Had a rather difficult walk and creep across an immense snow and ice cliff which gradually increased in steepness as I advanced until it was almost impassable. Slipped on a dangerous place, but managed to stop by digging my heels into the thawing surface just on the brink of a yawning ice gulf. Camped beside a little pool and a group of crinkled dwarf pines; and as I sit by the fire trying to write notes the shallow pool seems fathomless with the infinite stary heavens in it, while the onlooking rocks and trees, tiny shrubs and daisies and sedges, brought forward in the fireglow, seem full of thought as if about to speak aloud and tell all their wild stories. A marvellously impressive meeting in which every one has something worthwhile to tell. And beyond the firebeams out in the solemn darkness, how impressive is the music of a choir of rills singing their way down from the snow to the river! And when we call to mind that thousands of these rejoicing rills are assembled in each one of the main streams, we wonder the less that our Sierra rivers are songful all the way to the sea.

About sundown saw a flock of dun greyish sparrows going to roost in crevices of a crag above the big snowfield. Charming little mountaineers! Found a species of sedge in flower within eight or ten feet of a snowbank. Judging by the looks of the ground, it can hardly have been out in the sunshine much longer than a week, and it is likely to be buried again in fresh snow in a month or so, thus making a winter about ten months long, while spring, summer and autumn are crowded and hurried into two months. How delightful it is to be alone here! How wild everything is – wild as the sky and as pure! Never shall I forget this big, divine day – the Cathedral and its thousands of cassiope bells, and the landscapes around them, and this camp in the grey crags above the woods, with its stars and streams and snow.

8 September. Day of climbing, scrambling, sliding on the peaks around the highest source of the Tuolumne and Merced. Climbed three of the most commanding of the mountains, whose names I don't know; crossed streams and huge beds of ice and snow more than I could keep count of. Neither could I keep count of the lakes scattered on table-lands and in the cirques of the peaks, and in chains in the canyons, linked together by the streams – a tremendously wild grey wilderness of hacked, shattered crags, ridges and peaks, a few clouds drifting over and through the midst of them as if looking for work. In general views all the immense round landscape seems raw and lifeless as a quarry, yet the most charming flowers were found rejoicing in countless nooks and garden-like patches everywhere. I must have done three or four days' climbing work in this one. Limbs perfectly tireless until near sundown, when I descended into the main upper Tuolumne valley at the foot of Mount Lyell, the camp still eight or ten miles distant. Going up through the pine woods past the Soda Springs Dome in the dark, where there is much fallen timber, and when all the excitement of seeing things was wanting, I was tired. Arrived at the main camp at nine o'clock, and soon was sleeping sound as death.

CHAPTER ELEVEN

Back to the Lowlands

9 SEPTEMBER. Weariness rested away and I feel eager and ready for another excursion a month or two long in the same wonderful wilderness. Now, however, I must turn toward the lowlands, praying and hoping Heaven will shove me back again.

The most telling thing learned in these mountain excursions is the influence of cleavage joints on the features sculptured from the general mass of the range. Evidently the denudation has been enormous, while the inevitable outcome is subtle balanced beauty. Comprehended in general views, the features of the wildest landscape seem to be as harmoniously related as the features of a human face. Indeed, they look human and radiate spiritual beauty, divine thought, however covered and concealed by rock and snow.

Mr Delaney has hardly had time to ask me how I enjoyed my trip, though he has facilitated and encouraged my plans all summer, and declares I'll be famous some day, a kind guess that seems strange and incredible to a wandering wilderness-lover with never a thought or dream of fame while humbly trying to trace and learn and enjoy Nature's lessons.

The camp stuff is now packed on the horses, and the flock is headed for the home ranch. Away we go, down through the pines, leaving the lovely lawn where we have camped so long. I wonder if I'll ever see it again. The sod is so tough and close it is scarcely at all injured by the sheep. Fortunately they are not fond of silky glacier meadow grass. The day is perfectly clear, not a cloud or the faintest hint of a cloud is visible, and there is no wind. I wonder if in all the world, at a height of nine thousand feet, weather so steadily, faithfully calm and bright and hospitable may anywhere else be found. We are going away fearing destructive storms, though it is difficult to conceive weather changes so great.

Though the water is now low in the river, the usual difficulty occurred in getting the flock across it. Every sheep seemed to be invincibly determined to die any sort of dry death rather than wet its feet. Carlo has learned the sheep business as perfectly as the best shepherd, and it is interesting to watch his intelligent efforts to push or frighten the silly creatures into the water. They had to be fairly crowded and shoved over the bank; and when at last one crossed because it could not push its way back, the whole flock suddenly plunged in headlong together, as if the river was the only desirable part of the world. Aside from mere money profit one would rather herd wolves than sheep. As soon as they clambered up the opposite bank, they began baaing and feeding as if nothing unusual had happened. We crossed the meadows and drove slowly up the south rim of the valley through the same woods I had passed on my way to Cathedral Peak, and camped for the night by the side of a small pond on top of the big lateral moraine.

10 September. In the morning at daybreak not one of the two thousand sheep was in sight. Examining the tracks, we discovered that they had been scattered, perhaps by a bear. In a few hours all were found and gathered into one flock again. Had fine view of a deer. How graceful and perfect in every way it seemed as compared with the silly, dusty, tousled sheep! From the high ground hereabouts had another grand view to the northward – a heaving, swelling set of domes and round-backed ridges fringed with pines, and bounded by innumerable sharp-pointed peaks, grey and barren-looking, though so full of beautiful life. Another day of the calm, cloudless kind, purple in the morning and evening. The evening glow has been very marked for the last two or three weeks. Perhaps the 'zodiacal light'.

11 September. Cloudless. Slight frost. Calm. Fairly started downhill, and now are camped at the west end meadows of Lake Tenaya – a charming place. Lake smooth as glass, mirroring its miles of glacier-polished pavements and bold mountain walls. Find aster still in flower. Here is about the upper limit of the dwarf form of the goldcup oak – eight thousand feet above sea level – reaching about two thousand feet higher than the California black oak (*Quercus Californica*). Lovely evening, the lake reflections after dark marvellously impressive.

12 September. Cloudless day, all pure sungold. Among the magnificent silver firs once more, within two miles of the brink of Yosemite, at the famous Portuguese bear camp. Chaparral of goldcup oak, manzanita, and ceanothus abundant hereabouts, wanting about the Tuolumne meadows, although the elevation is but little higher there. The two-leaved pine, though far more abundant about the Tuolumne meadow region, reaches its greatest size on stream sides hereabouts and around meadows that are rather boggy. All the best dry ground is taken by the magnificent silver fir, which here reaches its greatest size and forms a well-defined belt. A glorious tree. Have fine bed of its boughs tonight.

13 September. Camp this evening at Yosemite Creek, close to the stream, on a little sand flat near our old camp ground. The vegetation is already brown and yellow and dry; the creek almost dry also. The slender form of the two-leaved pine on its banks is, I think, the handsomest I have anywhere seen. It might easily pass at first sight for a distinct species, though surely only a variety (*Murrayana*), due to crowded and rapid growth on good soil. The yellow pine is as variable, or perhaps more so. The form here and a thousand feet higher, on crumbling rocks, is broad branching, with closely furrowed, reddish bark, large cones, and long leaves. It is one of the hardiest of pines, and has wonderful vitality. The tassels of long, stout needles shining silvery in the sun, when the wind is blowing them all in the same direction, is one of the most splendid spectacles these glorious Sierra forests have to show. This variety of *Pinus ponderosa* is regarded as a distinct species, *Pinus Jeffreyi*, by some botanists. The basin of this famous Yosemite stream is extremely rocky – seems fairly to be paved with domes like a street with big cobblestones. I wonder if I shall ever be allowed to explore it. It draws me so strongly, I would make any sacrifice to try to read its lessons. I thank God for this glimpse of it. The charms of these mountains are beyond all common reason, unexplainable and mysterious as life itself.

14 September. Nearly all day in magnificent fir forest, the top branches laden with superb erect grey cones shining with beads of pure balsam. The squirrels are cutting them off at a great rate. Bump, bump, I hear them falling, soon to be gathered and stored for winter bread. Those that chance to be left by the industrious harvesters drop the scales and bracts when fully ripe, and it is fine to see the purple-winged seeds flying in swirling, merry looking flocks seeking their fortunes. The bole and dead limbs of nearly every tree in the main forest belt are ornamented by conspicuous tufts and strips of a yellow lichen.

Camped for the night at Cascade Creek, near the Mono Trail crossing. Manzanita berries now ripe. Cloudiness today about ten per cent. The sunset very rich, flaming purple and crimson showing gloriously through the aisles of the woods.

15 September. The weather pure gold, cloudiness about five per cent, white cirrus flecks and pencillings around the horizon. Move two or three miles and camp at Tamarack Flat. Wandering in the woods here back of the pines which bound the meadows, I found very noble specimens of the magnificent silver fir, the tallest about two hundred and forty feet high and five feet in diameter four feet from the ground.

16 September. Crawled slowly four or five miles today through the glorious forest to Crane Flat, where we are camped for the night. The forests we so admired in summer seem still more beautiful and sublime in this mellow autumn light. Lovely starry night, the tall, spiring treetops relieved in jet black against the sky. I linger by the fire, loath to go to bed.

17 September. Left camp early. Ran over the Tuolomne divide and down a few miles to a grove of sequoias that I had heard of, directed by the Don. They occupy an area of perhaps less than a hundred acres. Some of the trees are noble, colossal old giants, surrounded by magnificent sugar pines and Douglas spruces. The perfect specimens not burned or broken are singularly regular and symmetrical, though not at all conventional, showing infinite variety in general unity and harmony; the noble shafts with rich purplish brown fluted bark, free of limbs for one hundred and fifty feet or so, ornamented here and there with leafy rosettes; main branches of the oldest trees very large, crooked and rugged, zigzagging stiffly outward seemingly lawless, yet unexpectedly stooping just at the right distance from the trunk and dissolving in dense bossy masses of branchlets, thus making a regular though greatly varied outline – a cylinder of leafy, outbulging spray masses, terminating in a noble dome, that may be recognised while yet far off upheaved against the sky above the dark bed of pines and firs and spruces, the king of all conifers, not only in size but in sublime majesty of behaviour and port. I found a black, charred stump about thirty feet in diameter and eighty or ninety feet high – a venerable, impressive old monument of a tree that in its prime may have been the monarch of the grove; seedlings and saplings growing up here and there, thrifty and hopeful, giving no hint of the dying out of the species. Not any unfavourable change of climate, but only fire, threatens the existence of these noblest of God's trees. Sorry I was not able to get a count of the old monument's annual rings.

Camp this evening at Hazel Green, on the broad back of the dividing ridge near our old camp ground when we were on the way up the mountains in the spring. This ridge has the finest sugar pine groves and finest manzanita and ceanothus thickets I have yet found on all this wonderful summer journey.

18 September. Made a long descent on the south side of the divide to Brown's Flat, the grand forests now left above us, though the sugar pine still flourishes fairly well, and with the yellow pine, libocedrus, and Douglas spruce, makes forests that would be considered most wonderful in any other part of the world.

The Indians here, with great concern, pointed to an old garden patch on the flat and told us to keep away from it. Perhaps some of their tribe are buried here.

19 September. Camped this evening at Smith's Mill, on the first broad mountain bench or plateau reached in ascending the range, where pines grow large enough for good lumber. Here wheat, apples, peaches and grapes grow, and we were treated to wine and apples. The wine I didn't like, but Mr Delaney and the Indian driver and the shepherd seemed to think the stuff divine. Compared to sparkling Sierra water fresh from the heavens, it seemed a dull, muddy, stupid drink. But the apples, best of fruits, how delicious they were – fit for gods or men.

On the way down from Brown's Flat we stopped at Bower Cave, and I spent an hour in it – one of the most novel and interesting of all Nature's underground mansions. Plenty of sunlight pours into it through the leaves of the four maple trees growing in its mouth, illuminating its clear, calm pool and marble chambers – a charming place, ravishingly beautiful, but the accessible parts of the walls sadly disfigured with names of vandals.

20 September. The weather still golden and calm, but hot. We are now in the foothills, and all the conifers are left behind except the grey Sabine pine. Camped at the Dutch Boy's Ranch, where there are extensive barley fields now showing nothing save dusty stubble.

21 September. A terrible hot, dusty, sunburned day, and as nothing was to be gained by loitering where the flock could find nothing to eat save thorny twigs and chaparral, we made a long drive, and before sundown reached the home ranch on the yellow San Joaquin plain.

22 September. The sheep were let out of the corral one by one, this morning, and counted, and strange to say, after all their adventurous wanderings in bewildering rocks and brush and streams, scattered by bears, poisoned by azalea, kalmia, alkali, all are accounted for. Of the two thousand and fifty that left the corral in the spring lean and weak, two thousand and twenty-five have returned fat and strong. The losses are: ten killed by bears, one by a rattle-snake, one that had to be killed after it had broken its leg on a boulder slope, and one that ran away in blind terror on being accidentally separated from the flock – thirteen all told. Of the other twelve doomed never to return, three were sold to ranchmen and nine were made camp mutton.

Here ends my forever memorable first High Sierra excursion. I have crossed the Range of Light, surely the brightest and best of all the Lord has built; and rejoicing in its glory, I gladly, gratefully, hopefully pray I may see it again.

A DWARF PINE.

THE MOUNTAINS OF CALIFORNIA

The Mountains
of California

First published by Century, New York and Fisher Unwin, London 1894

WATER-OUZEL DIVING AND FEEDING.

Contents

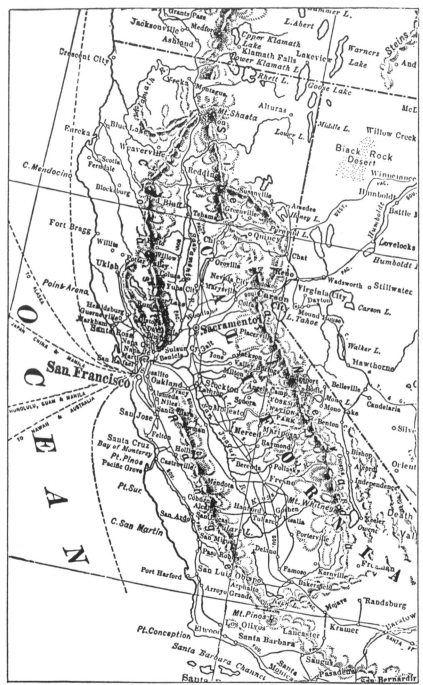

MAP OF THE SIERRA NEVADA

CHAPTER ONE

The Sierra Nevada

GO WHERE you may within the bounds of California, mountains are ever in sight, charming and glorifying every landscape. Yet so simple and massive is the topography of the State in general views, that the main central portion displays only one valley, and two chains of mountains which seem almost perfectly regular in trend and height: the Coast Range on the west side, the Sierra Nevada on the east. These two ranges coming together in curves on the north and south enclose a magnificent basin, with a level floor more than 400 miles long, and from 35 to 60 miles wide. This is the grand Central Valley of California, the waters of which have only one outlet to the sea through the Golden Gate. But with this general simplicity of features there is great complexity of hidden detail. The Coast Range, rising as a grand green barrier against the ocean, from 2,000 to 8,000ft. high is composed of innumerable forest-crowned spurs, ridges, and rolling hill-waves which inclose a multitude of smaller valleys; some looking out through long, forest-lined vistas to the sea; others, with but few trees, to the Central Valley; while a thousand others yet smaller are embosomed and concealed in mild, round-browed hills, each with its own climate, soil, and productions.

Making your way through the mazes of the Coast Range to the summit of any of the inner peaks or passes opposite San Francisco, in the clear spring-time, the grandest and most telling of all California landscapes is outspread before you. At your feet lies the great Central Valley glowing golden in the sunshine, extending north and south farther than the eye can reach, one smooth, flowery, lake-like bed of fertile soil. Along its eastern margin rises the mighty Sierra, miles in height, reposing like a smooth cumulous cloud in the sunny sky, and so gloriously coloured, and so luminous, it seems to be not clothed with light, but wholly composed of it, like the wall of some celestial city. Along the top, and extending a good way down, you see a pale, pearl-grey belt of snow; and below it a belt of blue and dark purple, marking the extension of the forests; and along the base of the range a broad belt of rose-purple and yellow, where lie the miner's gold-fields and the foot-hill gardens. All these coloured belts blending smoothly make a wall of light ineffably fine, and as beautiful as a rainbow, yet firm as adamant.

When I first enjoyed this superb view, one glowing April day, from the summit of the Pacheco Pass, the Central Valley, but little trampled or ploughed as yet, was one furred, rich sheet of golden compositae, and the luminous wall of the mountains shone in all its glory. Then it seemed to me the Sierra should be called not the Nevada, or Snowy Range, but the Range of Light. And after ten years spent in the heart of it, rejoicing and wondering, bathing in its glorious floods of light, seeing the sunbursts of morning among the icy peaks, the noonday radiance on the trees and rocks and snow, the flush of the alpenglow, and a thousand dashing waterfalls with their marvellous abundance of irised spray, it still seems to be above all others the Range of Light, the most divinely beautiful of all the mountain-chains I have ever seen.

The Sierra is about 500 miles long, 70 miles wide, and from 7,000 to nearly 15,000ft. high. In general views no mark of man is visible on it, nor anything to suggest the richness of the life it cherishes, or the depth and grandeur of its sculpture. None of its magnificent forest-crowned ridges rises much above the general level to publish its wealth. No great valley or lake is seen, or river, or group of well-marked features of any kind, standing out in distinct pictures. Even the summit-peaks, so clear and high in the sky, seem comparatively smooth and featureless. Nevertheless, glaciers are still at work in the shadows of the peaks, and thousands of lakes and meadows shine and bloom beneath them, and the whole range is furrowed with canyons to a depth of from 2,000 to 5,000ft., in which once flowed majestic glaciers, and in which now flow and sing a band of beautiful rivers.

Though of such stupendous depth, these famous canyons are not raw, gloomy, jagged-walled gorges, savage and inaccessible. With rough passages here and there they still make delightful pathways for the mountaineer, conducting from the fertile lowlands to the highest icy fountains, as a kind of mountain streets full of charming life and light, graded and sculptured by the ancient glaciers, and presenting, throughout all their courses, a rich variety of novel and attractive scenery, the most attractive that has yet been discovered in the mountain-ranges of the world.

In many places, especially in the middle region of the western flank of the range, the main canyons widen into spacious valleys or parks, diversified like artificial landscape-gardens, with charming groves and meadows, and thickets of blooming bushes, while the lofty, retiring walls, infinitely varied in form and sculpture, are fringed with ferns, flowering-plants of many species, oaks, and evergreens, which find anchorage on a thousand narrow steps and benches; while the whole is enlivened and made glorious with rejoicing streams that come dancing and foaming over the sunny brows of the cliffs to join the shining river that flows in tranquil beauty down the middle of each one of them.

The walls of these park valleys of the Yosemite kind are made up of rocks mountains in size, partly separated from each other by narrow gorges and side-canyons; and they are so sheer in front, and so compactly built together on a level floor, that, comprehensively seen, the parks they enclose look like immense halls of temples lighted from above. Every rock seems to glow with life. Some lean back in majestic repose; others, absolutely sheer, or nearly so, for thousands of feet, advance their brows in thoughtful attitudes beyond their companions, giving welcome to storms and calms alike, seemingly conscious yet heedless of everything going on about them, awful in stern majesty, types of permanence, yet associated with beauty of the frailest and most fleeting forms; their feet set in pine-groves and gay emerald meadows, their brows in the sky; bathed in light, bathed in floods of singing water, while snow-clouds, avalanches, and the winds shine and surge and wreathe about them as the years go by, as if into these mountain mansions Nature had taken pains to gather her choicest treasures to draw her lovers into close and confiding communion with her.

Here, too, in the middle region of deepest canyons are the grandest forest-trees, the Sequoia, king of conifers, the noble sugar and yellow pines, Douglas spruce, libocedrus, and the silver firs, each a giant of its kind, assembled together in one and the same forest, surpassing all other coniferous forests in the world, both in the number of its species and in the size and beauty of its trees. The winds flow in melody through their colossal spires, and they are vocal everywhere with the songs of birds and running water. Miles of fragrant ceanothus and manzanita bushes bloom beneath them, and lily gardens and meadows, and damp, ferny glens in endless variety of fragrance and colour, compelling the admiration of every observer. Sweeping on over ridge and valley, these noble trees extend a continuous belt from end to end of the range, only slightly interrupted by sheer-walled canyons at intervals of about fifteen and twenty miles. Here the great burly brown bears delight to roam, harmonizing with the brown boles of the trees beneath which they feed. Deer, also, dwell here, and find food and shelter in ceanothus tangles, with a multitude of smaller people. Above this region of giants, the trees grow smaller until the utmost limit of the timber line is reached on the stormy mountain-slopes at a height of from ten to twelve thousand feet above the sea, where the dwarf pine is so lowly and hard beset by storms and heavy snow, it is pressed into flat tangles, over the tops of which we may easily walk. Below the main forest belt the trees likewise diminish in size, frost and burning drouth repressing and blasting alike.

The rose-purple zone along the base of the range comprehends nearly all the famous gold region of California. And here it was that miners from every country under the sun assembled in a wild, torrent-like rush to seek their fortunes. On the banks of every river, ravine, and gully they have left their marks. Every gravel- and boulder-bed has been desperately riddled over and over again. But in this region the pick and shovel, once wielded with savage enthusiasm, have been laid away, and only quartz-mining is now being carried on to any considerable extent. The zone in general is made up of low, tawny, waving foot-hills, roughened here and there with brush and trees, and out-cropping masses of slate, coloured grey and red with lichens. The smaller masses of slate, rising abruptly from the dry, grassy sod in leaning slabs, look like ancient tombstones in a deserted burying-ground. In early spring, say from February to April, the whole of this foot-hill belt is a paradise of bees and flowers. Refreshing rains then fall freely, birds are busy building their nests, and the sunshine is balmy and delightful. But by the end of May the soil, plants, and sky seem to have been baked in an oven. Most of the plants crumble to dust beneath the foot, and the ground is full of cracks; while the thirsty traveller gazes with eager longing through the burning glare to the snowy summits looming like hazy clouds in the distance.

The trees, mostly *Quercus Douglasii* and *Pinus Sabiniana,* thirty to forty feet high, with thin, pale-green foliage, stand far apart and cast but little shade. Lizards glide about on the rocks enjoying a constitution that no drouth can dry, and ants in amazing numbers, whose tiny sparks of life seem to burn the brighter with the increasing heat, ramble industriously in long trains in search of food. Crows, ravens, magpies – friends in distress – gather on the ground beneath the best shade-trees, panting with drooping wings and bills wide open, scarce a note from any of them during the midday hours. Quails, too, seek the shade during the heat of the day about tepid pools in the channels of the larger mid-river streams. Rabbits scurry from thicket to thicket among the ceanothus bushes, and occasionally a long-eared hare is seen cantering gracefully across the wider openings. The nights are calm and dewless during the summer, and a thousand voices proclaim the abundance of life, notwithstanding the desolating effect of dry sunshine on the plants and larger animals. The hylas make a delightfully pure and tranquil music after sunset; and coyotes, the little, despised dogs of the wilderness, brave, hardy fellows, looking like withered wisps of hay, bark in chorus for hours. Mining-towns, most of them dead, and a few living ones with bright bits of cultivation about them, occur at long intervals along the belt, and cottages covered with climbing roses, in the midst of orange and peach orchards, and sweet-scented hay-fields in fertile flats where water for irrigation may be had. But they are mostly far apart, and make scarce any mark in general views.

Every winter the High Sierra and the middle forest region get snow in glorious abundance, and even the foot-hills are at times whitened. Then all the range looks like a vast bevelled wall of purest marble. The rough places are then made smooth, the death and decay of the year is covered gently and kindly, and the ground seems as clean as the sky. And though silent in its flight from the clouds, and when it is taking its place on rock, or tree, or grassy meadow, how soon the gentle snow finds a voice! Slipping from the heights, gathering in avalanches, it booms and roars like thunder, and makes a glorious show as it sweeps down the mountain-side, arrayed in long, silken streamers and wreathing, swirling films of crystal dust.

The north half of the range is mostly covered with floods of lava, and dotted with volcanoes and craters, some of them recent and perfect in form, others in various stages of decay. The south half is composed of granite nearly from base to summit, while a considerable number of peaks, in the middle of the range, are capped with metamorphic slates, among which are Mounts Dana and Gibbs to the east of Yosemite Valley. Mount Whitney, the culminating point of the range near its southern extremity, lifts its helmet-shaped crest to a height of nearly 14,700ft. Mount Shasta, a colossal volcanic cone, rises to a height of 14,440ft. at the northern extremity, and forms a noble landmark for all the surrounding region within a radius of a hundred miles. Residual masses of volcanic rocks occur throughout most of the granitic southern portion also, and a considerable number of old volcanoes on the flanks, especially along the eastern base of the range near Mono Lake and southward. But it is only to the northward that the entire range, from base to summit, is covered with lava.

From the summit of Mount Whitney only granite is seen. Innumerable peaks and spires but little lower than its own storm-beaten crags rise in groups like forest-trees, in full view, segregated by canyons of tremendous depth and ruggedness. On Shasta nearly every feature in the vast view speaks of the old volcanic fires. Far to the northward, in Oregon, the icy volcanoes of Mount Pitt and the Three Sisters rise above the dark evergreen woods. Southward innumerable smaller craters and cones are distributed along the axis of the range and on each flank. Of these, Lassen's Butte is the highest, being nearly 11,000ft. above sea-level. Miles of its flanks are reeking and bubbling with hot springs, many of them so boisterous and sulphurous they seem ever ready to become spouting geysers like those of the Yellowstone.

The Cinder Cone near marks the most recent volcanic eruption in the Sierra. It is a symmetrical truncated cone about 700ft. high, covered with grey cinders and ashes, and has a regular unchanged crater on its summit, in which a few small two-leaved pines are growing. These show that the age of the cone is not less than eighty years. It stands between two lakes, which a short time ago were one. Before the cone was built, a flood of rough vesicular lava was poured into the lake, cutting it in two, and, overflowing its banks, the fiery flood advanced into the pine-woods, overwhelming the trees in its way, the charred ends of some of which may still be seen projecting from beneath the snout of the lava-stream where it came to rest. Later still there was an eruption of ashes and loose obsidian cinders, probably from the same vent, which, besides forming the Cinder Cone, scattered a heavy shower over the surrounding woods for miles to a depth of from six inches to several feet.

The history of this last Sierra eruption is also preserved in the traditions of the Pitt River Indians. They tell of a fearful time of darkness, when the sky was black with ashes and smoke that threatened every living thing with death, and that when at length the sun appeared once more it was red like blood.

Less recent craters in great numbers roughen the adjacent region; some of them with lakes in their throats, others overgrown with trees and flowers, Nature in these old hearths and firesides having literally given beauty for ashes. On the northwest side of Mount Shasta there is a subordinate cone about 3,000ft. below the summit, which has been active subsequent to the breaking up of the main ice-cap that once covered the mountain, as is shown by its comparatively unwasted crater and the streams of unglaciated lava radiating from it. The main summit is about a mile and a half in diameter, bounded by small crumbling peaks and ridges, among which we seek in vain for the outlines of the ancient crater.

These ruinous masses, and the deep glacial grooves that flute the sides of the mountain, show that it has been considerably lowered and wasted by ice; how much we have no sure means of knowing. Just below the extreme summit hot sulphurous gases and vapour issue from irregular fissures, mixed with spray derived from melting snow, the last feeble expression of the mighty force that built the mountain. Not in one great convulsion was Shasta given birth. The crags of the summit and the sections exposed by the glaciers down the sides display enough of its internal framework to prove that comparatively long periods of quiescence intervened between many distinct eruptions, during which the cooling lavas ceased to flow, and became permanent additions to the bulk of the growing mountain. With alternate haste and deliberation eruption succeeded eruption till the old volcano surpassed even its present sublime height.

Standing on the icy top of this, the grandest of all the fire-mountains of the Sierra, we can hardly fail to look forward to its next eruption. Gardens, vineyards, homes have been planted confidingly on the flanks of volcanoes which, after remaining steadfast for ages, have suddenly blazed into violent action, and poured forth overwhelming floods of fire. It is known that more than a thousand years of cool calm have intervened between violent eruptions. Like gigantic geysers spouting molten rock instead of water, volcanoes work and rest, and we have no sure means of knowing whether they are dead when still, or only sleeping.

Along the western base of the range a telling series of sedimentary rocks containing the early history of the Sierra are now being studied. But leaving for the present these first chapters, we see that only a very short geological time ago, just before the coming on of that winter of winters called the glacial period, a vast deluge of molten rocks poured from many a chasm and crater on the flanks and summit of the range, filling lake basins and river channels, and obliterating nearly every existing feature on the northern portion. At length these all-destroying floods ceased to flow. But while the great volcanic cones built up along the axis still burned and smoked, the whole Sierra passed under the domain of ice and snow. Then over the bald, featureless, fire-blackened mountains, glaciers began to crawl, covering them from the summits to the sea with a mantle of ice; and then with infinite deliberation the work went on of sculpturing the range anew. These mighty agents of erosion, halting never through unnumbered centuries, crushed and ground the flinty lavas and granites beneath their crystal folds, wasting and building until in the fullness of time the Sierra was born again, brought to light nearly as we behold it today, with glaciers and snow-crushed pines at the top of the range, wheat-fields and orange-groves at the foot of it.

This change from icy darkness and death to life and beauty was slow, as we count time, and is still going on, north and south, over all the world wherever glaciers exist, whether in the form of distinct rivers, as in Switzerland, Norway, the mountains of Asia, and the Pacific Coast; or in continuous mantling folds, as in portions of Alaska, Greenland, Franz-Joseph-Land, Nova Zembla, Spitzbergen, and the lands about the South Pole. But in no country, as far as I know, may these majestic changes be studied to better advantage than in the plains and mountains of California.

Toward the close of the glacial period, when the snow-clouds became less fertile and the melting waste of sunshine became greater, the lower folds of the ice-sheet in California, discharging fleets of icebergs into the sea, began to shallow and recede from the lowlands, and then move slowly up the flanks of the Sierra in compliance with the changes of climate. The great white mantle on the mountains broke up into a series of glaciers more or less distinct and river-like, with many tributaries, and these again were melted and divided into still smaller glaciers, until now only a few of the smallest residual topmost branches of the grand system exist on the cool slopes of the summit peaks.

Plants and animals, biding their time, closely followed the retiring ice, bestowing quick and joyous animation on the new-born landscapes. Pine-trees marched up the sun-warmed moraines in long, hopeful files, taking the ground and establishing themselves as soon as it was ready for them; brown-spiked sedges fringed the shores of the new-born lakes; young rivers roared in the abandoned channels of the glaciers; flowers bloomed around the feet of the great burnished domes – while with quick fertility mellow beds of soil, settling and warming, offered food to multitudes of Nature's waiting children, great and small, animals as well as plants; mice, squirrels, marmots, deer, bears, elephants, etc. The ground burst into bloom with magical rapidity, and the young forests into bird-song: life in every form warming and sweetening and growing richer as the years passed away over the mighty Sierra so lately suggestive of death and consummate desolation only.

It is hard without long and loving study to realize the magnitude of the work done on these mountains during the last glacial period by glaciers, which are only streams of closely compacted snow-crystals. Careful study of the phenomena presented goes to show that the pre-glacial condition of the range was comparatively simple: one vast wave of stone in which a thousand mountains, domes, canyons, ridges, etc., lay concealed. And in the development of these Nature chose for a tool not the earthquake or lightning to rend and split asunder, not the stormy torrent or eroding rain, but the tender snow-flowers noiselessly falling through unnumbered centuries, the offspring of the sun and sea. Labouring harmoniously in united strength they crushed and ground and wore away the rocks in their march, making vast beds of soil, and at the same time developed and fashioned the landscapes into the delightful variety of hill and dale and lordly mountain that mortals call beauty. Perhaps more than a mile in average depth has the range been thus degraded during the last glacial period – a quantity of mechanical work almost inconceivably great. And our admiration must be excited again and again as we toil and study and learn that this vast job of rockwork, so far-reaching in its influences, was done by agents so fragile and small as are these flowers of the mountain clouds. Strong only by force of numbers, they carried away entire mountains, particle by particle, block by block, and cast them into the sea: sculptured, fashioned, modelled all the range, and developed its predestined beauty. All these new Sierra landscapes were evidently predestined, for the physical structure of the rocks on which the features of the scenery depend was acquired while they lay at least a mile deep below the pre-glacial surface. And it was while these features were taking form in the depths of the range, the particles of the rocks marching to their appointed places in the dark with reference to the coming beauty, that the particles of icy vapour in the sky marching to the same music assembled to bring them to the light. Then, after their grand task was done, these bands of snow-flowers, these mighty glaciers, were melted and removed as if of no more importance than dew destined to last but an hour. Few, however, of Nature's agents have left monuments so noble and enduring as they. The great granite domes a mile high, the canyons as deep, the noble peaks, the Yosemite valleys, these, and indeed nearly all other features of the Sierra scenery, are glacier monuments.

Contemplating the works of these flowers of the sky, one may easily fancy them endowed with life: messengers sent down to work in the mountain mines on errands of divine love. Silently flying through the darkened air, swirling, glinting, to their appointed places, they seem to have taken counsel together, saying, 'Come, we are feeble; let us help one another. We are many, and together we will be strong. Marching in close, deep ranks, let us roll away the stones from these mountain sepulchres, and set the landscapes free. Let us uncover these clustering domes. Here let us carve a lake basin; there, a Yosemite Valley; here, a channel for a river with fluted steps and brows for the plunge of songful cataracts. Yonder let us spread broad sheets of soil, that man and beast may be fed; and here pile trains of boulders for pines and giant Sequoias. Here make ground for a meadow; there, for a garden and grove, making it smooth and fine for small daisies and violets and beds of heathy bryanthus, spicing it well with crystals, garnet feldspar, and zircon.' Thus and so on it has oftentimes seemed to me sang and planned and laboured the hearty snow-flower crusaders; and nothing that I can write can possibly exaggerate the grandeur and beauty of their work. Like morning mist they have vanished in sunshine, all save the few small companies that still linger on the coolest mountainsides, and, as residual glaciers, are still busily at work completing the last of the lake basins, the last beds of soil, and the sculpture of some of the highest peaks.

CHAPTER TWO

The Glaciers

OF THE small residual glaciers mentioned in the preceding chapter, I have found sixty-five in that portion of the range lying between latitude 36° 30' and 39°. They occur singly or in small groups on the north sides of the peaks of the High Sierra, sheltered beneath broad frosty shadows, in amphitheatres of their own making, where the snow, shooting down from the surrounding heights in avalanches, is most abundant. Over two thirds of the entire number lie between latitude 37° and 38°, and form the highest fountains of the San Joaquin, Merced, Tuolumne, and Owen's rivers.

The glaciers of Switzerland, like those of the Sierra, are mere wasting remnants of mighty ice-floods that once filled the great valleys and poured into the sea. So, also, are those of Norway, Asia, and South America. Even the grand continuous mantles of ice that still cover Greenland, Spitzbergen, Nova Zembla, Franz-Joseph-Land, parts of Alaska, and the south polar region are shallowing and shrinking. Every glacier in the world is smaller than it once was. All the world is growing warmer, or the crop of snow-flowers is diminishing. But in contemplating the condition of the glaciers of the world, we must bear in mind while trying to account for the changes going on that the same sunshine that wastes them builds them. Every glacier records the expenditure of an enormous amount of sun-heat in lifting the vapour for the snow of which it is made from the ocean to the mountains, as Tyndall strikingly shows.

The numbers of glaciers in the Alps, according to the Schlagintweit brothers, is 1,100, of which 100 may be regarded as primary, and the total area of ice, snow, and *névé* is estimated at 1,177 square miles, or an average for each glacier of little more than one square mile. On the same authority, the average height above sea-level at which they melt is about 7,414ft. The Grindelweld glacier descends below 4,000ft., and one of the Mont Blanc glaciers reaches nearly as low a point. One of the largest of the Himalaya glaciers on the head waters of the Ganges does not, according to Captain Hodgson, descend below 12,914ft. The largest of the Sierra glaciers on Mount Shasta descends to within 9,500ft. of the level of the sea, which, as far as I have observed, is the lowest point reached by any glacier within the bounds of California, the average height of all being not far from 11,000ft.

The changes that have taken place in the glacial conditions of the Sierra from the time of greatest extension is well illustrated by the series of glaciers of every size and form extending along the mountains of the coast to Alaska. A general exploration of this instructive region shows that to the north of California, through Oregon and Washington, groups of active glaciers still exist on all the high volcanic cones of the Cascade Range – Mount Pitt, the Three Sisters, Mounts Jefferson, Hood, St Helens, Adams, Rainier, Baker, and others – some of them of considerable size, though none of them approach the sea. Of these mountains Rainier, in Washington, is the highest and iciest. Its dome-like summit, between 14,000 and 15,000ft. high, is capped with ice, and eight glaciers, seven to twelve miles long, radiate from it as a centre, and form the sources of the principal streams of the State. The lowest-descending of this fine group flows through beautiful forests to within 3,500ft. of the sea-level, and sends forth a river laden with glacier mud and sand. On through British Colombia and south-eastern Alaska the broad, sustained mountain-chain, extending along the coast, is generally glacier-bearing. The upper branches of nearly all the main canyons and fiords are occupied by glaciers, which gradually increase in size, and descend lower until the high region between Mount Fairweather and Mount St Elias is reached, where a considerable number discharge into the waters of the ocean. This is pre-eminently the ice-land of Alaska and of the entire Pacific Coast.

Northward from here the glaciers gradually diminish in size and thickness, and melt at higher levels. In Prince William Sound and Cook's Inlet many fine glaciers are displayed, pouring from the surrounding mountains; but to the north of latitude 62° few, if any, glaciers remain, the ground being mostly low and the snowfall light. Between latitude 56° and 60° there are probably more than 5,000 glaciers, not counting the smallest. Hundreds of the largest size descend through the forests to the level of the sea, or near it, though as far as my own observations have reached, after a pretty thorough examination of the region, not more than twenty-five discharge icebergs into the sea. All the long high-walled fiords into which these great glaciers of the first class flow are of course crowded with icebergs of every conceivable form, which are

detached with thundering noise at intervals of a few minutes from an imposing ice-wall that is thrust forward into deep water. But these Pacific Coast
icebergs are small as compared with those of Greenland and the Antarctic
region, and only a few of them escape from the intricate system of channels,
with which this portion of the coast is fringed, into the open sea. Nearly all of
them are swashed and drifted by wind and tide back and forth in the fiords
until finally melted by the ocean water, the sunshine, the warm winds, and the
copious rains of summer. Only one glacier on the coast, observed by Prof.
Russell, discharges its bergs directly into the open sea, at Icy Cape, opposite
Mount St Elias. The southernmost of the glaciers that reach the sea occupies a
narrow, picturesque fiord about twenty miles to the northwest of the mouth of
the Stikeen River, in latitude 56° 50'. The fiord is called by the natives 'Hutli',
or Thunder Bay, from the noise made by the discharge of the icebergs. About
one degree farther north there are four of these complete glaciers, discharging at the heads of the long arms of Holkam Bay. At the head of the Tahkoo
Inlet, still farther north, there is one; and at the head and around the sides of
Glacier Bay, trending in a general northerly direction from Cross Sound in
latitude 58° to 59°, there are seven of these complete glaciers pouring bergs
into the bay and its branches, and keeping up an eternal thundering. The
largest of this group, the Muir, has upward of 200 tributaries, and a width
below the confluence of the main tributaries of about twenty-five miles.
Between the west side of this icy bay and the ocean all the ground, high and
low, excepting the peaks of the Fairweather Range, is covered with a mantle
of ice from 1,000 to probably 3,000ft. thick, which discharges by many distinct
mouths.

This fragmentary ice-sheet, and the immense glaciers about Mount St
Elias, together with the multitude of separate river-like glaciers that load the
slopes of the coast mountains, evidently once formed part of a continuous ice-
sheet that flowed over all the region hereabouts, and only a comparatively
short time ago extended as far southward as the mouth of the Strait of Juan de
Fuca, probably farther. All the islands of the Alexander Archipelago, as well
as the headlands and promontories of the mainland, display telling traces of
this great mantle that are still fresh and unmistakable. They all have the forms
of the greatest strength with reference to the action of a vast rigid press of
oversweeping ice from the north and north-west, and their surfaces have a
smooth, rounded, overrubbed appearance, generally free from angles. The
intricate labyrinth of canals, channels, straits, passages, sounds, narrows,
etc., between the islands, and extending into the mainland, of course manifest
in their forms and trends and general characteristics the same subordination
to the grinding action of universal glaciation as to their origin, and differ from
the islands and banks of the fiords only in being portions of the pre-glacial
margin of the continent more deeply eroded, and therefore covered by the
ocean waters which flowed into them as the ice was melted out of them. The
formation and extension of fiords in this manner is still going on, and may be
witnessed in many places in Glacier Bay, Yakutat Bay, and adjacent regions.
That the domain of the sea is being extended over the land by the wearing
away of its shores, is well known, but in these icy regions of Alaska, and even

as far south as Vancouver Island, the coast rocks have been so short a time exposed to wave-action they are but little wasted as yet. In these regions the extension of the sea effected by its own action in post-glacial time is scarcely appreciable as compared with that effected by ice-action.

Traces of the vanished glaciers made during the period of greater extension abound on the Sierra as far south as latitude 36°. Even the polished rock surfaces, the most evanescent of glacial records, are still found in a wonderfully perfect state of preservation on the upper half of the middle portion of the range, and form the most striking of all the glacial phenomena. They occur in large irregular patches in the summit and middle regions, and though they have been subjected to the action of the weather with its corroding storms for thousands of years, their mechanical excellence is such that they still reflect the sunbeams like glass, and attract the attention of every observer. The attention of the mountaineer is seldom arrested by moraines, however regular and high they may be, or by canyons, however deep, or by rocks, however noble in form and sculpture; but he stoops and rubs his hands admiringly on the shining surfaces and tries hard to account for their mysterious smoothness. He has seen the snow descending in avalanches, but concludes this cannot be the work of snow, for he finds it where no avalanches occur. Nor can water have done it, for he sees this smoothness glowing on the sides and tops of the highest domes. Only the winds of all the agents he knows seem capable of flowing in the directions indicated by the scoring. Indians, usually so little curious about geological phenomena, have come to me occasionally and asked me, 'What makeum the ground so smooth at Lake Tenaya?' Even horses and dogs gaze wonderingly at the strange brightness of the ground, and smell the polished spaces and place their feet cautiously on them when they come to them for the first time, as if afraid of sinking. The most perfect of the polished pavements and walls lie at an elevation of from 7,000 to 9,000ft. above the sea, where the rock is compact silicious granite. Small dim patches may be found as low as 3,000ft. on the driest and most enduring portions of sheer walls with a southern exposure, and on compact swelling bosses partially protected from rain by a covering of large boulders. On the north half of the range the striated and polished surfaces are less common, not only because this part of the chain is lower, but because the surface rocks are chiefly porous lavas subject to comparatively rapid waste. The ancient moraines also, though well preserved on most of the south half of the range, are nearly obliterated to the northward, but their material is found scattered and disintegrated.

A similar blurred condition of the superficial records of glacial action obtains throughout most of Oregon, Washington, British Columbia, and Alaska, due in great part to the action of excessive moisture. Even in southeastern Alaska, where the most extensive glaciers on the continent are, the more evanescent of the traces of their former greater extension, though comparatively recent, are more obscure than those of the ancient California glaciers where the climate is drier and the rocks more resisting.

These general views of the glaciers of the Pacific Coast will enable my readers to see something of the changes that have taken place in

California, and will throw light on the residual glaciers of the High Sierra.

Prior to the autumn of 1871 the glaciers of the Sierra were unknown. In October of that year I discovered the Black Mountain Glacier in a shadowy amphitheatre between Black and Red Mountains, two of the peaks of the Merced group. This group is the highest portion of a spur that straggles out from the main axis of the range in the direction of Yosemite Valley. At the time of this interesting discovery I was exploring the *névé* amphitheatres of the group, and tracing the courses of the ancient glaciers that once poured from its ample fountains through the Illilouette Basin and the Yosemite Valley, not expecting to find any active glaciers so far south in the land of sunshine.

Beginning on the northwestern extremity of the group, I explored the chief tributary basins in succession, their moraines, roches moutonnées, and splendid glacier pavements, taking them in regular succession without any reference to the time consumed in their study. The monuments of the tributary that poured its ice from between Red and Black Mountains I found to be the most interesting of them all; and when I saw its magnificent moraines extending in majestic curves from the spacious amphitheatre between the mountains, I was exhilarated with the work that lay before me. It was one of the golden days of the Sierra Indian summer, when the rich sunshine glorifies every landscape however rocky and cold, and suggests anything rather than glaciers. The path of the vanished glacier was warm now, and shone in many places as if washed with silver. The tall pines growing on the moraines stood transfigured in the glowing light, the poplar groves on the levels of the basin were masses of orange-yellow, and the late-blooming goldenrods added gold to gold. Pushing on over my rosy glacial highway, I passed lake after lake set in solid basins of granite, and many a thicket and meadow watered by a stream that issues from the amphitheatre and links the lakes together; now wading through plushy bogs knee-deep in yellow and purple sphagnum; now passing over bare rock. The main lateral moraines that bounded the view on either hand are from 100 to nearly 200ft. high, and about as regular as artificial embankments, and covered with a superb growth of Silver Fir and Pine. But this garden and forest luxuriance was speedily left behind. The trees were dwarfed as I ascended; patches of the alpine bryanthus and cassiope began to appear, and arctic willows pressed into flat carpets by the winter snow. The lakelets, which a few miles down the valley were so richly embroidered with flowery meadows, had here, at an elevation of 10,000ft., only small brown mats of carex, leaving bare rocks around more than half their shores. Yet amid this alpine suppression the mountain pine bravely tossed his storm-beaten branches on the ledges and buttresses of Red Mountain, some specimens being over 100ft. high, and 24ft. in circumference, seemingly as fresh and vigorous as the giants of the lower zones.

Evening came on just as I got fairly within the portal of the main amphitheatre. It is about a mile wide, and a little less than two miles long. The crumbling spurs and battlements of Red Mountain bound it on the north, the sombre, rudely sculptured precipices of Black Mountain on the south, and a hacked, splintery *col*, curving around from mountain to mountain, shuts it in on the east.

I chose a camping-ground on the brink of one of the lakes where a thicket of hemlock spruce sheltered me from the night wind. Then, after making a tin-cupful of tea, I sat by my camp-fire reflecting on the grandeur and significance of the glacial records I had seen. As the night advanced the mighty rock walls of my mountain mansion seemed to come nearer, while the starry sky in glorious brightness stretched across like a ceiling from wall to wall, and fitted closely down into all the spiky irregularities of the summits. Then, after a long fire-side rest and a glance at my note-book, I cut a few leafy branches for a bed, and fell into the clear, death-like sleep of the tired mountaineer.

Early next morning I set out to trace the grand old glacier that had done so much for the beauty of the Yosemite region back to its farthest fountains, enjoying the charm that every explorer feels in Nature's untrodden wildernesses. The voices of the mountains were still asleep. The wind scarce stirred the pine-needles. The sun was up, but it was yet too cold for the birds and the few burrowing animals that dwell here. Only the stream, cascading from pool to pool, seemed to be wholly awake. Yet the spirit of the opening day called to action. The sunbeams came streaming gloriously through the jagged openings of the *col,* glancing on the burnished pavements and lighting the silvery lakes, while every sun-touched rock burned white on its edges like melting iron in a furnace. Passing round the north shore of my camp lake I followed the central stream past many cascades from lakelet to lakelet. The scenery became more rigidly arctic, the dwarf pines and hemlocks disappeared, and the stream was bordered with icicles. As the sun rose higher rocks were loosened on shattered portions of the cliffs, and came down in rattling avalanches, echoing wildly from crag to crag.

The main lateral moraines that extend from the jaws of the amphitheatre into the Illilouette Basin are continued in straggling masses along the walls of the amphitheatre, while separate boulders, hundreds of tons in weight, are left stranded here and there out in the middle of the channel. Here, also, I observed a series of small terminal moraines ranged along the south wall of the amphitheatre, corresponding in size and form with the shadows cast by the highest portions. The meaning of this correspondence between moraines and shadows was afterward made plain. Tracing the stream back to the last of its chain of lakelets, I noticed a deposit of fine grey mud on the bottom except where the force of the entering current had prevented it settling. It looked like the mud worn from a grindstone, and I at once suspected its glacial origin, for the stream that was carrying it came gurgling out of the base of a raw moraine that seemed in process of formation. Not a plant or weather-stain was visible on its rough, unsettled surface. It is from 60 to over 100ft. high, and plunges forward at an angle of 38°. Cautiously picking my way, I gained the top of the moraine and was delighted to see a small but well characterized glacier swooping down from the gloomy precipices of Black Mountain in a finely graduated curve to the moraine on which I stood. The compact ice appeared on all the lower portions of the glacier, though grey with dirt and stones embedded in it. Farther up the ice disappeared beneath coarse granulated snow. The surface of the glacier was further characterized by dirt bands and the outcropping edges of the blue veins, showing the laminated structure of the ice. The uppermost crevasse, or 'bergschrund', where the *névé* was attached to the mountain, was from 12 to 14ft. wide, and was bridged in a few places by the remains of snow avalanches. Creeping along the edge of the schrund, holding on with benumbed fingers, I discovered clear sections where the bedded structure was beautifully revealed. The surface snow, though sprinkled with stones shot down from the cliffs, was in some places almost pure, gradually becoming crystalline and changing to whitish porous ice of different shades of colour, and this again changing at a depth of 20 or 30ft. to blue ice, some of the ribbon-like bands of which were nearly pure, and blended with the paler bands in the most gradual and delicate manner imaginable. A series of rugged zigzags enabled me to make my way down into the weird under-world of the crevasse. Its chambered hollows were hung with a multitude of clustered icicles, amid which pale, subdued light pulsed and shimmered with indescribable loveliness. Water dripped and tinkled overhead, and from far below came strange, solemn murmurings from currents that were feeling their way through veins and fissures in the dark. The chambers of a glacier are perfectly enchanting, notwithstanding one feels out of place in their frosty beauty. I was soon cold in my shirt-sleeves, and the leaning wall threatened to engulf me; yet it was hard to leave the delicious music of the water and the lovely light. Coming again to the surface, I noticed boulders of every size on their journeys to the terminal moraine – journeys of more than a hundred years, without a single stop, night or day, winter or summer.

The sun gave birth to a network of sweet-voiced rills that ran gracefully down the glacier, curling and swirling in their shining channels, and cutting clear sections through the porous surface-ice into the solid blue, where the structure of the glacier was beautifully illustrated.

The series of small terminal moraines which I had observed in the morning, along the south wall of the amphitheatre, correspond in every way with the moraine of this glacier, and their distribution with reference to shadows was now understood. When the climatic changes came on that caused the melting and retreat of the main glacier that filled the amphitheatre, a series of residual glaciers were left in the cliff shadows, under the protection of which they lingered, until they formed the moraines we are studying. Then, as the snow became still less abundant, all of them vanished in succession, except the one just described; and the cause of its longer life is sufficiently apparent in the greater area of snow-basin it drains, and its more perfect protection from wasting sunshine. How much longer this little glacier will last depends, of course, on the amount of snow it receives from year to year, as compared with melting waste.

After this discovery, I made excursions over all the High Sierra, pushing my explorations summer after summer, and discovered that what at first sight in the distance looked like extensive snow-fields, were in great part glaciers, busily at work completing the sculpture of the summit-peaks so grandly blocked out by their giant predecessors.

On 21 August, I set a series of stakes in the Maclure Glacier, near Mount Lyell, and found its rate of motion to be little more than an inch a day in the middle, showing a great contrast to the Muir Glacier in Alaska, which, near the front, flows at a rate of from five to ten feet in twenty-four hours.

Mount Shasta has three glaciers, but Mount Whitney, although it is the highest mountain in the range, does not now cherish a single glacier. Small patches of lasting snow and ice occur on its northern slopes, but they are shallow, and present no well marked evidence of glacial motion. Its sides, however, are scored and polished in many places by the action of its ancient glaciers that flowed east and west as tributaries of the great glaciers that once filled the valleys of the Kern and Owen's rivers.

CHAPTER THREE

The Snow

THE FIRST snow that whitens the Sierra, usually falls about the end of October or early in November, to a depth of a few inches, after months of the most charming Indian summer weather imaginable. But in a few days, this light covering mostly melts from the slopes exposed to the sun and causes but little apprehension on the part of mountaineers who may be lingering among the high peaks at this time. The first general winter storm that yields snow that is to form a lasting portion of the season's supply, seldom breaks on the mountains before the end of November. Then, warned by the sky, cautious mountaineers, together with the wild sheep, deer, and most of the birds and bears, make haste to the lowlands or foot-hills; and burrowing marmots, mountain beavers, wood-rats, and such people go into winter quarters, some of them not again to see the light of day until the general awakening and resurrection of the spring in June or July. The first heavy fall is usually from about two to four feet in depth. Then, with intervals of splendid sunshine, storm succeeds storm, heaping snow on snow, until thirty to fifty feet has fallen. But on account of its settling and compacting, and the almost constant waste from melting and evaporation, the average depth actually found at any time seldom exceeds ten feet in the forest region, or fifteen feet along the slopes of the summit peaks.

Even during the coldest weather evaporation never wholly ceases, and the sunshine that abounds between the storms is sufficiently powerful to melt the surface more or less through all the winter months. Waste from melting also goes on to some extent on the bottom from heat stored up in the rocks, and given off slowly to the snow in contact with them, as is shown by the rising of the streams on all the higher regions after the first snowfall, and their steady sustained flow all winter.

The greater portion of the snow deposited around the lofty summits of the range falls in small crisp flakes and broken crystals, or, when accompanied by strong winds and low temperatures, the crystals, instead of being locked together in their fall to form tufted flakes, are beaten and broken into meal and fine dust. But down in the forest region the greater portion comes gently to the ground, light and feathery, some of the flakes in mild weather being nearly an inch in diameter, and it is evenly distributed and kept from drifting to any great extent by the shelter afforded by the large trees. Every tree during the progress of gentle storms is loaded with fairy bloom at the coldest and darkest time of year, bending the branches, and hushing every singing needle. But as soon as the storm is over, and the sun shines, the snow at once begins to shift and settle and fall from the branches in miniature avalanches, and the white forest soon becomes green again. The snow on the ground also settles and thaws every bright day, and freezes at night, until it becomes coarsely granulated, and loses every trace of its rayed crystalline structure, and then a man may walk firmly over its frozen surface as if on ice. The forest region up to an elevation of 7,000ft. is usually in great part free from snow in June, but at this time the higher regions are still heavy-laden, and are not touched by spring weather to any considerable extent before the middle or end of July.

One of the most striking effects of the snow on the mountains is the burial of the rivers and small lakes.

> As the snaw fa's in the river
> A moment white, then lost forever,

sang Burns, in illustrating the fleeting character of human pleasure. The first snowflakes that fall into the Sierra rivers vanish thus suddenly; but in great storms, when the temperature is low, the abundance of snow at length chills the water nearly to the freezing-point, and then, of course, it ceases to melt and consume the snow so suddenly. The falling flakes and crystals form cloud-like masses of blue sludge, which are swept forward with the current and carried down to warmer climates many miles distant, while some are lodged against logs and rocks and projecting points of the banks, and last for days, piled high above the level of the water, and show white again, instead of being at once 'lost forever,' while the rivers themselves are at length lost for months during the snowy period. The snow is first built out from the banks in bossy, over-curling drifts, compacting and cementing until the streams are spanned. They then flow in the dark beneath a continuous covering across the snowy zone, which is about thirty miles wide. All the Sierra rivers and their tributaries in these high regions are thus lost every winter, as if another glacial period had come on. Not a drop of running water is to be seen excepting at a few points where large falls occur, though the rush and rumble of the heavier currents may still be heard. Toward spring, when the weather is warm during the day and frosty at night, repeated thawing and feezing and new layers of snow render the bridging-masses dense and firm, so that one may safely walk across the streams, or even lead a horse across them without danger of falling through. In June the thinnest parts of the winter ceiling, and those most exposed to sunshine, begin to give way, forming dark, rugged-edged, pit-like sinks, at the bottom of which the rushing water may be seen. At the end of June only here and there may the mountaineer find a secure snow-bridge. The most lasting of the winter bridges, thawing from below as well as from above, because of warm currents of air passing through the tunnels, are strikingly arched and sculptured; and by the occasional freezing of the oozing, dripping water of the ceiling they become brightly and picturesquely icy. In some of the reaches, where there is a free margin, we may walk through them. Small skylights appearing here and there, these tunnels are not very dark. The roaring river fills all the arching way with impressively loud reverberating music, which is sweetened at times by the ouzel, a bird that is not afraid to go wherever a stream may go, and to sing wherever a stream sings.

All the small alpine pools and lakelets are in like manner obliterated from the winter landscapes, either by being first frozen and then covered by snow, or by being filled in by avalanches. The first avalanche of the season shot into a lake basin may perhaps find the surface frozen. Then there is a grand crashing of breaking ice and dashing of waves mingled with the low, deep booming of the avalanche. Detached masses of the invading snow, mixed with fragments of ice, drift about in sludgy, island-like heaps, while the main body of it forms a talus with its base wholly or in part resting on the bottom of the basin, as controlled by its depth and the size of the avalanche. The next avalanche, of course, encroaches still farther, and so on with each in succession until the entire basin may be filled and its water sponged up or displaced. This huge mass of sludge, more or less mixed with sand, stones, and perhaps timber, is frozen to a considerable depth, and much sun-heat is required to thaw it. Some of these unfortunate lakelets are not clear of ice and snow until near the end of the summer. Others are never quite free, opening only on the side opposite the entrance of the avalanches. Some show only a narrow crescent of water lying between the shore and sheer bluffs of icy compacted snow, masses of which breaking off float in front like icebergs in a miniature Arctic Ocean, while the avalanche heaps leaning back against the mountains look like small glaciers. The frontal cliffs are in some instances quite picturesque, and with the berg-dotted waters in front of them lighted with sunshine are exceedingly beautiful. It often happens that while one side of a lake basin is hopelessly snow-buried and frozen, the other, enjoying sunshine, is adorned with beautiful flower-gardens. Some of the smaller lakes are extinguished in an instant by a heavy avalanche either of rocks or snow. The rolling, sliding, ponderous mass entering on one side sweeps across the bottom and up the opposite side, displacing the water and even scraping the basin clean, and shoving the accumulated rocks and sediments up the farther bank and taking full possession. The dislodged water is in part absorbed, but most of it is sent around the front of the avalanche and down the channel of the outlet, roaring and hurrying as if frightened and glad to escape.

SNOW—BANNERS

The most magnificent storm phenomenon I ever saw, surpassing in showy grandeur the most imposing effects of clouds, floods or avalanches, was the peaks of the High Sierra, back of Yosemite Valley, decorated with snow-banners. Many of the starry snow-flowers, out of which these banners are made, fall before they are ripe, while most of those that do attain perfect development as six-rayed crystals glint and chafe against one another in their fall through the frosty air, and are broken into fragments. This dry fragmentary snow is still further prepared for the formation of banners by the action of the wind. For, instead of finding rest at once, like the snow which falls into the tranquil depths of the forests, it is rolled over and over, beaten against rock-ridges, and swirled in pits and hollows, like boulders, pebbles and sand in the pot-holes of a river, until finally the delicate angles of the crystals are worn off, and the whole mass is reduced to dust. And whenever storm-winds find this prepared snow-dust in a loose condition on exposed slopes, where there is a free upward sweep to leeward, it is tossed back into the sky, and borne onward from peak to peak in the form of banners or cloudy drifts, according to the velocity of the wind and the conformation of the slopes up or around which it is driven. While thus flying through the air, a small portion makes good its escape, and remains in the sky as vapour. But far the greater part, after being driven into the sky again and again, is at length locked fast in bossy drifts, or in the wombs of glaciers, some of it to remain silent and rigid for centuries before it is finally melted and sent singing down the mountain-sides to the sea.

Yet, notwithstanding the abundance of winter snow-dust in the mountains, and the frequency of high winds, and the length of time the dust remains loose and exposed to their action, the occurrence of well-formed banners is, for causes we shall hereafter note, comparatively rare. I have seen only one display of this kind that seemed in every way perfect. This was in the winter of 1873, when the snow-laden summits were swept by a wild 'norther'. I happened at the time to be wintering in Yosemite Valley, that sublime Sierra temple where every day one may see the grandest sights. Yet even here the wild gala-day of the north wind seemed surpassingly glorious. I was awakened in the morning by the rocking of my cabin and the beating of pine-burs on the roof. Detached torrents and avalanches from the main wind-flood overhead were rushing wildly down the narrow side canyons, and over the precipitous walls, with loud resounding roar, rousing the pines to enthusiastic action, and making the whole valley vibrate as though it were an instrument being played.

But afar on the lofty exposed peaks of the range standing so high in the sky, the storm was expressing itself in still grander characters, which I was soon to see in all their glory. I had long been anxious to study some points in the structure of the ice-cone that is formed every winter at the foot of the upper Yosemite fall, but the blinding spray by which it is invested had hitherto prevented me from making a sufficiently near approach. This morning the entire body of the fall was torn into gauzy shreds, and blown horizontally along the face of the cliff, leaving the cone dry; and while making my way to the top of an overlooking ledge to seize so favourable an opportunity to examine the interior of the cone, the peaks of the Merced group came in sight over the shoulder of the South Dome, each waving a resplendent banner against the blue sky, as regular in form, and as firm in texture, as if woven of fine silk. So rare and splendid a phenomenon, of course, overbore all other considerations, and I at once let the ice-cone go, and began to force my way out of the valley to some dome or ridge sufficiently lofty to command a general view of the main summits, feeling assured that I should find them bannered still more gloriously; nor was I in the least disappointed. Indian Canyon, through which I climbed, was choked with snow that had been shot down in avalanches from the high cliffs on either side, rendering the ascent difficult; but inspired by the roaring storm, the tedious wallowing brought no fatigue, and in four hours I gained the top of a ridge above the valley, 8,000ft. high. And there in bold relief, like a clear painting, appeared a most imposing scene. Innumerable peaks, black and sharp, rose grandly into the dark blue sky, their bases set in solid white, their sides streaked and splashed with snow, like ocean rocks with foam; and from every summit, all free and unconfused, was streaming a beautiful silky silvery banner, from half a mile to a mile in length, slender at the point of attachment, then widening gradually as it extended from the peak until it was about 1,000 or 1,500ft. in breadth, as near as I could estimate. The cluster of peaks called the 'Crown of the Sierra,' at the head of the Merced and Tuolumne rivers – Mounts Dana, Gibbs, Conness, Lyell, Maclure, Ritter, with their nameless compeers – each had its own refulgent banner, waving with a clearly visible motion in the sunglow, and there was not a single cloud in the sky to mar their simple grandeur. Fancy yourself standing on this Yosemite ridge looking eastward. You notice a strange garish glitter in the air. The gale drives wildly overhead with a fierce, tempestuous roar, but its violence is not felt, for you are looking through a sheltered opening in the woods as through a window. There, in the immediate foreground of your picture, rises a majestic forest of Silver Fir blooming in eternal freshness, the foliage yellow-green, and the snow beneath the trees strewn with their beautiful plumes, plucked off by the wind. Beyond, and extending over all the middle ground, are sombre swaths of pine, interrupted by huge swelling ridges and domes; and just beyond the dark forest you see the monarchs of the High Sierra waving their magnificent banners. They are twenty miles away, but you would not wish them nearer, for every feature is distinct, and the whole glorious show is seen in its right proportions. After this general view, mark how sharply the dark snowless ribs and buttresses and summits of the peaks are defined, excepting the portions veiled by the banners, and how delicately their sides are streaked with snow, where it has come to rest in narrow flutings and gorges. Mark, too, how grandly the banners wave as the wind is deflected against their sides, and how trimly each is attached to the very summit of its peak, like a streamer at a masthead; how smooth and silky they are in texture, and how finely their fading fringes are pencilled on the azure sky. See how dense and opaque they are at the point of attachment, and how filmy and translucent toward the end, so that the peaks back of them are seen dimly, as though you were looking through ground glass. Yet again observe how some of the longest, belonging to the loftiest summits, stream perfectly free all the way across intervening notches and passes from peak to peak, while others overlap and partly hide each other. And consider how keenly every particle of this wondrous cloth of snow is flashing out jets of light. These are the main features of the beautiful and terrible picture as seen from the forest window; and it would still be surpassingly glorious were the fore- and middle-grounds obliterated altogether, leaving only the black peaks, the white banners and the blue sky.

Glancing now in a general way at the formation of snow-banners, we find that the main causes of the wondrous beauty and perfection of those we have been contemplating were the favourable direction and great force of the wind, the abundance of snow-dust, and the peculiar conformation of the slopes of the peaks. It is essential not only that the wind should move with great velocity and steadiness to supply a sufficiently copious and continuous stream of snow-dust, but that it should come from the north. No perfect banner is ever hung on the Sierra peaks by a south wind. Had the gale that day blown from the south, leaving other conditions unchanged, only a dull, confused, fog-like drift would have been produced; for the snow, instead of being spouted up over the tops of the peaks in concentrated currents to be drawn out as streamers, would have been shed off around the sides, and piled down into the glacier wombs. The cause of the concentrated action of the north wind is found in the peculiar form of the north sides of the peaks, where the amphitheatres of the residual glaciers are. In general the south sides are convex and irregular, while the north sides are concave both in their vertical and horizontal sections; the wind in ascending these curves converges towards the summits, carrying the snow in concentrating currents with it, shooting it almost straight up into the air above the peaks, from which it is then carried away in a horizontal direction.

This difference in form between the north and south sides of the peaks was almost wholly produced by the difference in the kind and quantity of the glaciation to which they have been subjected, the north sides having been hollowed by residual shadow-glaciers of a form that never existed on the sun-beaten sides.

It appears, therefore, that shadows in great part determine not only the forms of lofty icy mountains, but also those of the snow-banners that the wild winds hang on them.

CHAPTER FOUR

A Near View of the High Sierra

EARLY ONE bright morning in the middle of an Indian summer, while the glacier meadows were still crisp with frost crystals, I set out from the foot of Mount Lyell, on my way down to Yosemite Valley, to replenish my exhausted store of bread and tea. I had spent the past summer, as many preceding ones, exploring the glaciers that lie on the head waters of the San Joaquin, Tuolumne, Merced and Owen's rivers; measuring and studying their movements, trends, crevasses, moraines, etc., and the part they had played during the period of their greater extension in the creation and development of the landscapes of this alpine wonderland. The time for this kind of work was nearly over for the year, and I began to look forward with delight to the approaching winter with its wondrous storms, when I would be warmly snowbound in my Yosemite cabin with plenty of bread and books; but a tinge of regret came on when I considered that possibly I might not see this favourite region again until the next summer, excepting distant views from the heights about the Yosemite walls.

To artists, few portions of the High Sierra are, strictly speaking, picturesque. The whole massive uplift of the range is one great picture, not clearly divisible into smaller ones; differing much in this respect from the older, and what may be called, riper mountains of the Coast Range. All the landscapes of the Sierra, as we have seen, were born again, remodelled from base to summit by the developing ice-floods of the last glacial winter. But all these new landscapes were not brought forth simultaneously; some of the highest, where the ice lingered longest, are tens of centuries younger than those of the warmer regions below them. In general, the younger the mountain-landscapes – younger, I mean, with reference to the time of their emergence from the ice of the glacial period – the less separable are they into artistic bits capable of being made into warm, sympathetic, lovable pictures with appreciable humanity in them.

Here, however, on the head waters of the Tuolumne, is a group of wild peaks on which the geologist may say that the sun has but just begun to shine, which is yet in a high degree picturesque, and in its main features so regular and evenly balanced as almost to appear conventional – one sombre cluster of snow-laden peaks with grey pine-fringed granite bosses braided around its base, the whole surging free into the sky from the head of a magnificent valley, whose lofty walls are bevelled away on both sides so as to embrace it all without admitting anything not strictly belonging to it. The foreground was now aflame with autumn colours, brown and purple and gold, ripe in the mellow sunshine; contrasting brightly with the deep, cobalt blue of the sky, and the black and grey, and pure, spiritual white of the rocks and glaciers. Down through the midst, the young Tuolumne was seen pouring from its crystal fountains, now resting in glassy pools as if changing back again into ice, now leaping in white cascades as if turning to snow; gliding right and left between granite bosses, then sweeping on through the smooth, meadowy levels of the valley, swaying pensively from side to side with calm, stately gestures past dipping willows and sedges, and around groves of arrowy pine; and throughout its whole eventful course, whether flowing fast or slow, singing loud or low, ever filling the landscape with spiritual animation, and manifesting the grandeur of its sources in every movement and tone.

Pursuing my lonely way down the valley, I turned again and again to gaze on the glorious picture, throwing up my arms to enclose it as in a frame. After long ages of growth in the darkness beneath the glaciers, through sunshine and storms, it seemed now to be ready and waiting for the elected artist, like yellow wheat for the reaper; and I could not help wishing that I might carry colours and brushes with me on my travels, and learn to paint. In the meantime I had to be content with photographs on my mind and sketches in my note-books. At length, after I had rounded a precipitous headland that puts out from the west wall of the valley, every peak vanished from sight, and I pushed rapidly along the frozen meadows, over the divide between the waters of the Merced and Tuolumne, and down through the forests that clothe the slopes of Clouds' Rest, arriving in Yosemite in due time – which, with me is *any* time. And, strange to say, among the first people I met here were two artists who, with letters of introduction, were awaiting my return. They enquired whether in the course of my explorations in the adjacent mountains I had ever come upon a landscape suitable for a large painting; whereupon I began a description of the one that had so lately excited my admiration. Then, as I went on further and further into details, their faces began to glow, and I offered to guide them to it, while they declared that they would gladly follow, far or near, whithersoever I could spare the time to lead them.

Since storms might come breaking down through the fine weather at any time, burying the colours in snow, and cutting off the artists' retreat, I advised getting ready at once.

I led them out of the valley by the Vernal and Nevada Falls, thence over the main dividing ridge to the Big Tuolumne Meadows, by the old Mono trail, and thence along the upper Tuolumne River to its head. This was my companions' first excursion into the High Sierra, and as I was almost always alone in my mountaineering, the way that the fresh beauty was reflected in their faces made for me a novel and interesting study. They naturally were affected most of all by the colours – the intense azure of the sky, the purplish greys of the granite, the red and browns of dry meadows, and the translucent purple and crimson of huckleberry bogs; the flaming yellow of aspen groves, the silvery flashing of the streams, and the bright green and blue of the glacier lakes. But the general expression of the scenery – rocky and savage – seemed sadly disappointing; and as they threaded the forest from ridge to ridge, eagerly scanning the landscapes as they were unfolded, they said: 'All this is huge and sublime, but we see nothing as yet at all available for effective pictures. Art is long, and art is limited, you know; and here are foregrounds, middle-grounds, backgrounds, all alike; bare rock-waves, woods, groves, diminutive flecks of meadow, and strips of glittering water.' 'Never mind,' I replied, 'only bide a wee, and I will show you something you will like'.

At length, toward the end of the second day, the Sierra Crown began to come into view, and when we had fairly rounded the projecting headland before mentioned, the whole picture stood revealed in the flush of the alpenglow. Their enthusiasm was excited beyond bounds, and the more impulsive of the two, a young Scotchman, dashed ahead, shouting and gesticulating and tossing his arms in the air like a madman. Here, at last, was a typical alpine landscape.

After feasting awhile on the view, I proceeded to make camp in a sheltered grove a little way back from the meadow, where pine-boughs could be obtained for beds, and where there was plenty of dry wood for fires, while the artists ran here and there, along the river-bends and up the sides of the canyon, choosing foregrounds for sketches. After dark, when our tea was made and a rousing fire had been built, we began to make our plans. They decided to remain several days, at the least, while I concluded to make an excursion in the mean time to the untouched summit of Ritter.

It was now about the middle of October, the springtime of snow-flowers. The first winter-clouds had already bloomed, and the peaks were strewn with fresh crystals, without, however, affecting the climbing to any dangerous extent. And as the weather was still profoundly calm, and the distance to the foot of the mountain only a little more than a day, I felt that I was running no great risk of being storm-bound.

Mount Ritter is king of the mountains of the middle portion of the High Sierra, as Shasta of the north and Whitney of the south sections. Moreover, as far as I know, it had never been climbed. I had explored the adjacent wilderness summer after summer, but my studies thus far had never drawn me to the top of it. Its height above sea-level is about 13,300ft., and it is fenced round by steeply inclined glaciers, and canyons of tremendous depth and ruggedness, which render it almost inaccessible. But difficulties of this kind only exhilarate the mountaineer.

Next morning, the artists went heartily to their work and I to mine. Former experiences had given good reason to know that passionate storms, invisible as yet, might be brooding in the calm sun-gold; therefore, before bidding farewell, I warned the artists not to be alarmed should I fail to appear before a week or ten days, and advised them, in case a snow-storm should set in, to keep up big fires and shelter themselves as best they could, and on no account to become frightened and attempt to seek their way back to Yosemite alone through the drifts.

My general plan was simply this: to scale the canyon wall, cross over to the eastern flank of the range, and then make my way southward to the northern spurs of Mount Ritter in compliance with the intervening topography; for to push on directly southward from camp through the innumerable peaks and pinnacles that adorn this portion of the axis of the range, however interesting, would take too much time, besides being extremely difficult and dangerous at this time of year.

All my first day was pure pleasure; simply mountaineering indulgence, crossing the dry pathways of the ancient glaciers, tracing happy streams, and learning the habits of the birds and marmots in the groves and rocks. Before I had gone a mile from camp, I came to the foot of a white cascade that beats its way down a rugged gorge in the canyon wall, from a height of about nine hundred feet, and pours its throbbing waters into the Tuolumne. I was acquainted with its fountains, which, fortunately, lay in my course. What a fine travelling companion it proved to be, what songs it sang, and how passionately it told the mountain's own joy! Gladly I climbed along its dashing border, absorbing its divine music, and bathing from time to time in waftings of irised spray. Climbing higher, higher, new beauty came streaming on the sight: painted meadows, late-blooming gardens, peaks of rare architecture, lakes here and there, shining like silver, and glimpses of the forested middle region and the yellow lowlands far in the west. Beyond the range I saw the so-called Mono Desert, lying dreamily silent in thick purple light – a desert of heavy sun-glare beheld from a desert of ice-burnished granite. Here the waters divide, shouting in glorious enthusiasm, and falling eastward to vanish in the volcanic sands and dry sky of the Great Basin, or westward to the Great Valley of California, and thence through the Bay of San Francisco and the Golden Gate to the sea.

Passing a little way down over the summit until I had reached an elevation of about 10,000ft. I pushed on southward toward a group of savage peaks that stand guard about Ritter on the north and west, groping my way, and dealing instinctively with every obstacle as it presented itself. Here a huge gorge would be found cutting across my path, along the dizzy edge of which I scrambled until some less precipitous point was discovered where I might safely venture to the bottom and then, selecting some feasible portion of the opposite wall, reascend with the same slow caution. Massive, flat-topped spurs alternate with the gorges, plunging abruptly from the shoulders of the snowy peaks, and planting their feet in the warm desert. These were every-where marked and adorned with characteristic sculptures of the ancient glaciers that swept over this entire region like one vast ice-wind, and the polished surfaces produced by the ponderous flood are still so perfectly preserved that in many places the sunlight reflected from them is about as trying to the eyes as sheets of snow.

God's glacial-mills grind slowly, but they have been kept in motion long enough in California to grind sufficient soil for a glorious abundance of life, though most of the grist has been carried to the lowlands, leaving these high regions comparatively lean and bare; while the post-glacial agents of erosion have not yet furnished sufficient available food over the general surface for more than a few tufts of the hardiest plants, chiefly carices and eriogonæ. And it is interesting to learn in this connection that the sparseness and repressed character of the vegetation at this height is caused more by want of soil than by harshness of climate; for, here and there, in sheltered hollows (counter-sunk beneath the general surface) into which a few rods of well-ground moraine chips have been dumped, we find groves of spruce and pine thirty to forty feet high, trimmed around the edges with willow and huckleberry bushes, and oftentimes still further by an outer ring of tall grasses, bright with lupines, larkspurs, and showy columbines, suggesting a climate by no means repressingly severe. All the streams, too, and the pools at this elevation are furnished with little gardens wherever soil can be made to lie, which, though making scarce any show at a distance, constitute charming surprises to the appreciative observer. In these bits of leafiness a few birds find grateful homes. Having no acquaintance with man, they fear no ill, and flock curiously about the stranger, almost allowing themselves to be taken in the hand. In so wild and so beautiful a region was spent my first day, every sight and sound inspiring, leading one far out of himself, yet feeding and building up his individuality.

Now came the solemn, silent evening. Long, blue, spiky shadows crept out across the snow-fields, while a rosy glow, at first scarce discernible, gradually deepened and suffused every mountain-top, flushing the glaciers and the harsh crags above them. This was the alpenglow, to me one of the most impressive of all the terrestrial manifestations of God. At the touch of this divine light, the mountains seemed to kindle to a rapt, religious conscious-ness, and stood hushed and waiting like devout worshippers. Just before the alpenglow began to fade, two crimson clouds came streaming across the summit like wings of flame, rendering the sublime scene yet more impressive; then came darkness and the stars.

Icy Ritter was still miles away, but I could proceed no farther that night. I found a good camp-ground on the rim of a glacier basin about 11,000ft. above the sea. A small lake nestles in the bottom of it, from which I got water for my tea, and a stormbeaten thicket near by furnished abundance of resiny fire-wood. Sombre peaks, hacked and shattered, circled half-way around the horizon, wearing a savage aspect in the gloaming, and a waterfall chanted solemnly across the lake on its way down from the foot of a glacier. The fall and the lake and the glacier were almost equally bare; while the scraggy pines anchored in the rock-fissures were so dwarfed and shorn by storm-winds that you might walk over their tops. In tone and aspect the scene was one of the most desolate I ever beheld. But the darkest scriptures of the mountains are illumined with bright passages of love that never fail to make themselves felt when one is alone.

I made my bed in a nook of the pine-thicket, where the branches were pressed and crinkled overhead like a roof, and bent down around the sides. These are the best bedchambers the high mountains afford – snug as squirrel-nests, well ventilated, full of spicy odours, and with plenty of wind-played needles to sing one asleep. I little expected company, but creeping in through a low side-door, I found five or six birds nestling among the tassels. The night-wind began to blow soon after dark; at first only a gentle breathing, but increasing toward midnight to a rough gale that fell upon my leafy roof in ragged surges like a cascade, bearing wild sounds from the crags overhead. The waterfall sang in chorus, filling the old ice-fountain with its solemn roar, and seeming to increase in power as the night advanced – fit voice for such a landscape. I had to creep out many times to the fire during the night, for it was biting cold and I had no blankets. Gladly I welcomed the morning star.

The dawn in the dry, wavering air of the desert was glorious. Everything encouraged my undertaking and betokened success. There was no cloud in the sky, no storm-tone in the wind. Breakfast of bread and tea was soon made. I fastened a hard, durable crust to my belt by way of provision, in case I should be compelled to pass a night on the mountain-top; then, securing the remainder of my little stock against wolves and wood-rats, I set forth free and hopeful.

How glorious a greeting the sun gives the mountains! To behold this alone is worth the pains of any excursion a thousand times over. The highest peaks burned like islands in a sea of liquid shade. Then the lower peaks and spires caught the glow, and long lances of light, streaming through many a notch and pass, fell thick on the frozen meadows. The majestic form of Ritter was full in sight, and I pushed rapidly on over rounded rock-bosses and pavements, my iron-shod shoes making a clanking sound, suddenly hushed now and then in rugs of bryanthus, and sedgy lake-margins soft as moss. Here, too, in this so-called 'land of desolation', I met cassiope, growing in fringes among the battered rocks. Her blossoms had faded long ago, but they were still clinging with happy memories to the evergreen sprays, and still so beautiful as to thrill every fibre of one's being. Winter and summer, you may hear her voice, the low, sweet melody of her purple bells. No evangel among the mountain plants speaks Nature's love more plainly than cassiope. Where she dwells, the redemption of the coldest solitude is complete. The very rocks and glaciers seem to feel her presence, and become imbued with her own fountain sweet-ness. All things were warming and awakening. Frozen rills began to flow, the marmots came out of their nests in boulder-piles and climbed sunny rocks to bask, and the dun-headed sparrows were flitting about seeking their break-fasts. The lakes seen from every ridge-top were brilliantly rippled and spangled, shimmering like the thickets of the low dwarf pines. The rocks, too, seemed responsive to the vital heat – rock-crystals and snow-crystals thrilling alike. I strode on exhilarated, as if never more to feel fatigue, limbs moving of themselves, every sense unfolding like the thawing flowers, to take part in the new day harmony.

All along my course thus far, excepting when down in the canyons, the landscapes were mostly open to me, and expansive, at least on one side. On the left were the purple plains of Mono, reposing dreamily and warm; on the right, the near peaks springing keenly into the thin sky with more and more impressive sublimity. But these larger views were at length lost. Rugged spurs, and moraines, and huge, projecting buttresses began to shut me in. Every feature became more rigidly alpine, without, however, producing any chilling effect; for going to the mountains is like going home. We always find that the strangest objects in these fountain wilds are in some degree familiar, and we look upon them with a vague sense of having seen them before.

On the southern shore of a frozen lake, I encountered an extensive field of hard, granular snow, up which I scampered in fine tone, intending to follow it to its head, and cross the rocky spur against which it leans, hoping thus to come direct upon the base of the main Ritter peak. The surface was pitted with oval hollows, made by stones and drifted pine-needles that had melted themselves into the mass by the radiation of absorbed sun-heat. These afforded good footholds, but the surface curved more and more steeply at the head, and the pits became shallower and less abundant, until I found myself in danger of being shed off like avalanching snow. I persisted, however, creeping on all fours, and shuffling up the smoothest places on my back, as I had often done on burnished granite, until, after slipping several times, I was compelled to retrace my course to the bottom, and make my way around the west end of the lake, and thence up to the summit of the divide between the head waters of Rush Creek and the northernmost tributaries of the San Joaquin.

Arriving on the summit of this dividing crest, one of the most exciting pieces of pure wilderness was disclosed that I ever discovered in all my mountaineering. There, immediately in front, loomed the majestic mass of

Mount Ritter, with a glacier swooping down its face nearly to my feet, then curving westward and pouring its frozen flood into a dark blue lake, whose shores were bound with precipices of crystalline snow; while a deep chasm drawn between the divide and the glacier separated the massive picture from everything else. I could see only the one sublime mountain, the one glacier, the one lake; the whole veiled with one blue shadow – rock, ice and water close together without a single leaf or sign of life. After gazing spellbound, I began instinctively to scrutinize every notch and gorge and weathered buttress of the mountain, with reference to making the ascent. The entire front above the glacier appeared as one tremendous precipice, slightly receding at the top, and bristling with spires and pinnacles set above one another in formidable array. Massive lichen-stained battlements stood forward here and there, hacked at the top with angular notches, and separated by frosty gullies and recesses that have been veiled in shadow ever since their creation; while to right and left, as far as I could see, were huge, crumbling buttresses, offering no hope to the climber. The head of the glacier sends up a few finger-like branches through narrow *couloirs*; but these seemed too steep and short to be available, especially as I had no axe with which to cut steps, and the numerous narrow-throated gullies down which stones and snow are avalanched seemed hopelessly steep, besides being interrupted by vertical cliffs; while the whole front was rendered still more terribly forbidding by the chill shadow and the gloomy blackness of the rocks.

Descending the divide in a hesitating mood, I picked my way across the yawning chasm at the foot, and climbed out upon the glacier. There were no meadows now to cheer with their brave colours, nor could I hear the dun-headed sparrows, whose cheery notes so often relieve the silence of our highest mountains. The only sounds were the gurgling of small rills down in the veins and crevasses of the glacier, and now and then the rattling report of falling stones, with the echoes they shot out into the crisp air.

I could not distinctly hope to reach the summit from this side, yet I moved on across the glacier as if driven by fate. Contending with myself, the season is too far spent, I said, and even should I be successful, I might be storm-bound on the mountain; and in the cloud-darkness, with the cliffs and crevasses covered with snow, how could I escape? No; I must wait till next summer. I would only approach the mountain now, and inspect it, creep about its flanks, learn what I could of its history, holding myself ready to flee on the approach of the first storm-cloud. But we little know until tried how much of the uncontrollable there is in us, urging across glaciers and torrents, and up dangerous heights, let the judgment forbid as it may.

I succeeded in gaining the foot of the cliff on the eastern extremity of the glacier, and there discovered the mouth of a narrow avalanche gully, through which I began to climb, intending to follow it as far as possible, and at least obtain some fine wild views for my pains. Its general course is oblique to the plane of the mountain-face, and the metamorphic slates of which the mountain is built are cut by cleavage planes in such a way that they weather off in angular blocks, giving rise to irregular steps that greatly facilitate climbing on the sheer places. I thus made my way into a wilderness of crumbling spires and battlements, built together in bewildering combinations, and glazed in many places with a thin coating of ice, which I had to hammer off with stones. The situation was becoming gradually more perilous; but, having passed several dangerous spots, I dared not think of descending; for, so steep was the entire ascent, one would inevitably fall to the glacier in case a single mis-step were made. Knowing, therefore, the tried danger beneath, I became all the more anxious concerning the developments to be made above, and began to be conscious of a vague foreboding of what actually befell; not that I was given to fear, but rather because my instincts, usually so positive and true, seemed vitiated in some way, and were leading me astray. At length, after attaining an elevation of about 12,800ft., I found myself at the foot of a sheer drop in the bed of the avalanche channel I was tracing, which seemed absolutely to bar further progress. It was only about forty-five or fifty feet high, and somewhat roughened by fissures and projections; but these seemed so slight and insecure, as footholds, that I tried hard to avoid the precipice altogether, by scaling the wall of the channel on either side. But, though less steep, the walls were smoother than the obstructing rock, and repeated efforts only showed that I must either go right ahead or turn back. The tried dangers beneath seemed even greater than that of the cliff in front; therefore, after scanning its face again and again, I began to scale it, picking my holds with intense caution. After gaining a point about half-way to the top, I was suddenly brought to a dead stop, with arms outspread, clinging close to the face of the rock, unable to move hand or foot either up or down. My doom appeared fixed. I *must* fall. There would be a moment of bewilderment, and then a lifeless rumble down the one general precipice to the glacier below.

When this final danger flashed upon me, I became nerve-shaken for the first time since setting foot on the mountains, and my mind seemed to fill with a stifling smoke. But this terrible eclipse lasted only a moment, when life blazed forth again with preternatural clearness. I seemed suddenly to become possessed of a new sense. The other self, bygone experiences, instinct, or Guardian Angel – call it what you will – came forward and assumed control. Then my trembling muscles became firm again, every rift and flaw in the rock was seen as through a microscope, and my limbs moved with a positiveness and precision with which I seemed to have nothing at all to do. Had I been borne aloft upon wings, my deliverance could not have been more complete.

Above this memorable spot, the face of the mountain is still more savagely hacked and torn. It is a maze of yawning chasms and gullies, in the angles of which rise beetling crags and piles of detached boulders that seem to have been gotten ready to be launched below. But the strange influx of strength I had received seemed inexhaustible. I found a way without effort, and soon stood upon the topmost crag in the blessed light.

How truly glorious the landscape circled around this noble summit! – giant mountains, valleys innumerable, glaciers and meadows, rivers and lakes, with the wide blue sky bent tenderly over them all. But in my first hour of freedom from that terrible shadow, the sunlight in which I was laving seemed all in all.

Looking southward along the axis of the range, the eye is first caught by a row of exceedingly sharp and slender spires, which rise openly to a height of about a thousand feet, above a series of short, residual glaciers that lean back against their bases; their fantastic sculpture and the unrelieved sharpness with which they spring out of the ice rendering them peculiarly wild and striking. These are 'The Minarets.' Beyond them you behold a sublime wilderness of mountains, their snowy summits towering together in crowded abundance, peak beyond peak, swelling higher, higher as they sweep on southward, until the culminating point of the range is reached on Mount Whitney, near the head of the Kern River, at an elevation of nearly 14,700ft. above the level of the sea.

Westward, the general flank of the range is seen flowing sublimely away from the sharp summits, in smooth undulations; a sea of huge grey granite waves dotted with lakes and meadows, and fluted with stupendous canyons that grow steadily deeper as they recede in the distance. Below this grey region lies the dark forest zone, broken here and there by upswelling ridges and domes; and yet beyond lies a yellow, hazy belt, marking the broad plain of the San Joaquin, bounded on its farther side by the blue mountains of the coast.

Turning now to the northward, there in the immediate foreground is the glorious Sierra Crown, with Cathedral Peak, a temple of marvellous architecture, a few degrees to the left of it; the grey, massive form of Mammouth Mountain to the right; while Mounts Ord, Gibbs, Dana, Conness, Tower Peak, Castle Peak, Silver Mountain, and a host of noble companions, as yet nameless, make a sublime show along the axis of the range.

Eastward, the whole region seems a land of desolation covered with beautiful light. The torrid volcanic basin of Mono, with its one bare lake fourteen miles long; Owen's Valley and the broad lava table-land at its head, dotted with craters, and the massive Inyo Range, rivaling even the Sierra in height; these are spread, map-like, beneath you, with countless ranges beyond, passing and overlapping one another into the horizon.

At a distance of less than 3,000ft. below the summit of Mount Ritter you may find tributaries of the San Joaquin and Owen's rivers, bursting forth from the ice and snow of the glaciers that load its flanks; while a little to the north of here are found the highest affluents of the Tuolumne and Merced. Thus, the fountains of four of the principal rivers of California are within a radius of four or five miles.

Lakes are seen gleaming in all sorts of places – round, or oval, or square, like very mirrors; others narrow and sinuous, drawn close around the peaks like silver zones, the highest reflecting only rocks, snow, and the sky. But neither these nor the glaciers, nor the bits of brown meadow and moorland that occur here and there, are large enough to make any marked impression upon the mighty wilderness of mountains. The eye, rejoicing in its freedom, roves about the vast expanse, yet returns again and again to the fountain peaks. Perhaps some of the multitude excites special attention, some gigantic castle with turret and battlement, or some Gothic cathedral more abundantly spired than Milan's. But, generally, when looking for the first time from an all-embracing standpoint like this, the inexperienced observer is oppressed by the incomprehensible grandeur, variety, and abundance of the mountains rising shoulder to shoulder beyond the reach of vision; and it is only after they have been studied one by one, long and lovingly, that their far-reaching harmonies become manifest. Then, penetrate the wilderness where you may, the main telling features, to which all the surrounding topography is subordinate, are quickly perceived, and the most complicated clusters of peaks stand revealed harmoniously correlated and fashioned like works of art – eloquent monuments of the ancient ice-rivers that brought them into relief from the general mass of the range. The canyons, too, some of them a mile deep, mazing wildly through the mighty host of mountains, however lawless and ungovernable at first sight they appear, are at length recognized as the necessary effects of causes which followed each other in harmonious sequence – Nature's poems carved on tables of stone – the simplest the most emphatic of her glacial compositions.

Could we have been here to observe during the glacial period, we should have overlooked a wrinkled ocean of ice as continuous as that now covering the landscapes of Greenland: filling every valley and canyon with only the tops of the fountain peaks rising darkly above the rock-encumbered ice-waves like islets in a stormy sea – those islets the only hints of the glorious landscapes now smiling in the sun. Standing here in the deep, brooding silence all the wilderness seems motionless, as if the work of creation were done. But in the midst of this outer steadfastness we know there is incessant motion and change. Ever and anon, avalanches are falling from yonder peaks. These cliff-bound glaciers, seemingly wedged and immovable, are flowing like water and grinding the rocks beneath them. The lakes are lapping their granite shores and wearing them away, and every one of these rills and young rivers is fretting the air into music, and carrying the mountains to the plains. Here are the roots of all the life of the valleys, and here more simply than elsewhere is the eternal flux of nature manifested. Ice changing to water, lakes to meadows, and mountains to plains. And while we thus contemplate Nature's methods of landscape creation, and, reading the records she has carved on the rocks, reconstruct, however imperfectly, the landscapes of the past, we also learn that as these we now behold have succeeded those of the pre-glacial age, so they in turn are withering and vanishing to be succeeded by others yet unborn.

But in the midst of these fine lessons and landscapes, I had to remember that the sun was wheeling far to the west, while a new way down the mountain had to be discovered to some point on the timber line where I could have a fire; for I had not even burdened myself with a coat. I first scanned the western spurs, hoping some way might appear through which I might reach the northern glacier, and cross its snout; or pass around the lake into which it flows, and thus strike my morning track. This route was soon sufficiently unfolded to show that, if practicable at all, it would require so much time that reaching camp that night would be out of the question. I therefore scrambled back eastward, descending the southern slopes obliquely at the same time. Here the crags seemed less formidable, and the head of a glacier that flows northeast came in sight, which I determined to follow as far as possible, hoping thus to make my way to the foot of the peak on the east side, and thence across the intervening canyons and ridges to camp.

The inclination of the glacier is quite moderate at the head, and, as the sun had softened the *névé*, I made safe and rapid progress, running and sliding, and keeping up a sharp outlook for crevasses. About half a mile from the head, there is an ice-cascade, where the glacier pours over a sharp declivity and is shattered into massive blocks separated by deep, blue fissures. To thread my way through the slippery mazes of this crevassed portion seems impossible, and I endeavoured to avoid it by climbing off to the shoulder of the mountain. But the slopes rapidly steepened and at length fell away in sheer precipices, compelling a return to the ice. Fortunately, the day had been warm enough to loosen the ice-crystals so as to admit of hollows being dug in the rotten portions of the blocks, thus enabling me to pick my way with far less difficulty than I had anticipated. Continuing down over the snout, and along the left lateral moraine, was only a confident saunter, showing that the ascent of the mountain by way of this glacier is easy, provided one is armed with an axe to cut steps here and there.

The lower end of the glacier was beautifully waved and barred by the outcropping edges of the bedded ice-layers which represent the annual snow-falls, and to some extent the irregularities of structure caused by the weathering of the walls of crevasses, and by separate snowfalls which have been followed by rain, hail, thawing and freezing, etc. Small rills were gliding and swirling over the melting surface with a smooth, oily appearance, in channels of pure ice – their quick, compliant movements contrasting most impressively with the rigid, invisible flow of the glacier itself, on whose back they all were riding.

Night drew near before I reached the eastern base of the mountain, and my camp lay many a rugged mile to the north; but ultimate success was assured. It was now only a matter of endurance and ordinary mountain-craft. The sunset was, if possible, yet more beautiful than that of the day before. The Mono landscape seemed to be fairly saturated with warm, purple light. The peaks marshalled along the summit were in shadow, but through every notch and pass streamed vivid sun-fire, soothing and irradiating their rough, black angles, while companies of small, luminous clouds hovered above them like very angels of light.

Darkness came on, but I found my way by the trends of the canyons and the peaks projected against the sky. All excitement died with the light, and then I was weary. But the joyful sound of the waterfall across the lake was heard at last, and soon the stars were seen reflected in the lake itself. Taking my bearings from these, I discovered the little pine thicket in which my nest was, and then I had a rest such as only a tired mountaineer may enjoy. After lying loose and lost for a while, I made a sunrise fire, went down to the lake, dashed water on my head, and dipped a cupful for tea. The revival brought about by bread and tea was as complete as the exhaustion from excessive enjoyment and toil. Then I crept beneath the pine-tassels to bed. The wind was frosty and the fire burned low, but my sleep was none the less sound, and the evening constellations had swept far to the west before I awoke.

After thawing and resting in the morning sunshine, I sauntered home – that is, back to the Tuolumne camp, – bearing away toward a cluster of peaks that hold the fountain snows of one of the north tributaries of Rush Creek. Here I discovered a group of beautiful glacier lakes, nestled together in a grand amphitheatre. Toward evening I crossed the divide separating the Mono waters from those of the Tuolumne, and entered the glacier basin that now holds the fountain snows of the stream that forms the upper Tuolumne cascades. This stream I traced down through its many dells and gorges, meadows and bogs, reaching the brink of the main Tuolumne at dusk.

A loud whoop for the artists was answered again and again. Their camp-fire came in sight, and half an hour afterward I was with them. They seemed unreasonably glad to see me. I had been absent only three days; nevertheless, though the weather was fine, they had already been weighing chances as to whether I would ever return, and trying to decide whether they should wait longer or begin to seek their way back to the lowlands. Now their curious troubles were over. They packed their precious sketches, and next morning we set out homeward bound, and in two days entered the Yosemite Valley from the north by way of Indian Canyon.

CHAPTER FIVE

The Passes

THE SUSTAINED grandeur of the High Sierra is strikingly illustrated by the great height of the passes. Between latitude 36° 20′ and 38° the lowest pass, gap, gorge, or notch of any kind cutting across the axis of the range, as far as I have discovered, exceeds 9,000ft. in height above the level of the sea; while the average height of all that are in use, either by Indians or whites, is perhaps not less than 11,000ft., and not one of these is a carriage-pass.

Farther north a carriage-road has been constructed through what is known as the Sonora Pass, on the head waters of the Stanislaus and Walker's rivers, the summit of which is about 10,000ft. above the sea. Substantial wagon-roads have also been built through the Carson and Johnson passes, near the head of Lake Tahoe, over which immense quantities of freight were hauled from California to the mining regions of Nevada, before the construction of the Central Pacific Railroad.

Still farther north a considerable number of comparatively low passes occur, some of which are accessible to wheeled vehicles, and through these rugged defiles during the exciting years of the gold period long emigrant-trains with foot-sore cattle wearily toiled. After the toil-worn adventurers had escaped a thousand dangers and had crawled thousands of miles across the plains the snowy Sierra at last loomed in sight, the eastern wall of the land of gold. And as with shaded eyes they gazed through the tremulous haze of the desert, with what joy must they have descried the pass through which they were to enter the better land of their hopes and dreams!

Between the Sonora Pass and the southern extremity of the High Sierra, a distance of nearly 160 miles, there are only five passes through which trails conduct from one side of the range to the other. These are barely practicable for animals; a pass in these regions meaning simply any notch or canyon through which one may, by the exercise of unlimited patience, make out to lead a mule, or a sure-footed mustang; animals that can slide or jump as well as walk. Only three of the five passes may be said to be in use, viz: the Kearsarge, Mono, and Virginia Creek; the tracks leading through the others being only obscure Indian trails, not graded in the least, and scarcely traceable by white men; for much of the way is over solid rock and earthquake avalanche taluses, where the unshod ponies of the Indians leave no appreciable sign. Only skilled mountaineers are able to detect the marks that serve to guide the Indians, such as slight abrasions of the looser rocks, the displacement of stones here and there, and bent bushes and weeds. A general knowledge of the topography is, then, the main guide, enabling one to determine where the trail ought to go – *must* go. One of these Indian trails crosses the range by a nameless pass between the head waters of the south and middle forks of the San Joaquin, the other between the north and middle forks of the same river, just to the south of 'The Minarets'; this last being about 9,000ft. high, is the lowest of the five. The Kearsarge is the highest, crossing the summit near the head of the south fork of Kings River, about eight miles to the north of Mount Tyndall, through the midst of the most stupendous rock-scenery. The summit of this pass is over 12,000ft. above sea-level; nevertheless, it is one of the safest of the five, and is used every summer, from July to October or November, by hunters, prospectors, and stock-owners, and to some extent by enterprising pleasure-seekers also. For, besides the surpassing grandeur of the scenery about the summit, the trail, in ascending the western flank of the range, conducts through a grove of the giant Sequoias, and through the magnificent Yosemite Valley of the south fork of King's River. This is, perhaps, the highest travelled pass on the North American continent.

The Mono Pass lies to the east of Yosemite Valley, at the head of one of the tributaries of the south fork of the Tuolumne. This is the best known and most extensively travelled of all that exist in the High Sierra. A trail was made through it about the time of the Mono gold excitement, in the year 1858, by adventurous miners and prospectors – men who would build a trail down the throat of darkest Erebus on the way to gold. Though more than a thousand feet lower than the Kearsarge, it is scarcely less sublime in rock-scenery, while in snowy, falling water it far surpasses it. Being so favourably situated for the stream of Yosemite travel, the more adventurous tourists cross over through this glorious gateway to the volcanic region around Mono Lake. It has therefore gained a name and fame above every other pass in the range. According to the few barometrical observations made upon it, its highest point is 10,765ft. above the sea. The other pass of the five we have been considering is somewhat lower, and crosses the axis of the range a few miles to the north of the Mono Pass, at the head of the southernmost tributary of Walker's River. It is used chiefly by roaming bands of the Pah Ute Indians and 'sheepmen'.

But, leaving wheels and animals out of the question, the free mountaineer with a sack of bread on his shoulders and an axe to cut steps in ice and frozen snow can make his way across the range almost everywhere, and at any time of the year when the weather is calm. To him nearly every notch between the peaks is a pass, though much patient step-cutting is at times required up and down steeply inclined glaciers, with cautious climbing over precipices that at first sight would seem hopelessly inaccessible.

In pursuing my studies, I have crossed from side to side of the range at intervals of a few miles all along the highest portion of the chain, with far less real danger than one would naturally count on. And what fine wildness was thus revealed – storms and avalanches, lakes and waterfalls, gardens and meadows, and interesting animals – only those will ever know who give the freest and most buoyant portion of their lives to climbing and seeing for themselves.

To the timid traveller, fresh from the sedimentary levels of the lowlands, these highways, however picturesque and grand, seem terribly forbidding – cold, dead, gloomy gashes in the bones of the mountains, and of all Nature's ways the ones to be most cautiously avoided. Yet they are full of the finest and most telling examples of Nature's love; and though hard to travel, none are safer. For they lead through regions that lie far above the ordinary haunts of the devil, and of the pestilence that walks in darkness. True, there are innumerable places where the careless step will be the last step; and a rock falling from the cliffs may crush without warning like lightning from the sky; but what then? Accidents in the mountains are less common than in the lowlands, and these mountain mansions are decent, delightful, even divine, places to die in, compared with the doleful chambers of civilization. Few places in this world are more dangerous than home. Fear not, therefore, to try the mountain-passes. They will kill care, save you from deadly apathy, set you free, and call forth every faculty into vigorous, enthusiastic action. Even the sick should try these so-called dangerous passes, because for every unfortunate they kill, they cure a thousand.

All the passes make their steepest ascents on the eastern flank. On this side the average rise is not far from a thousand feet to the mile, while on the west it is about two hundred feet. Another marked difference between the eastern and western portions of the passes is that the former begin at the very foot of the range, while the latter can hardly be said to begin lower than an elevation of from seven to ten thousand feet. Approaching the range from the grey levels of Mono and Owen's Valley on the east, the traveller sees before him the steep, short passes in full view, fenced in by rugged spurs that come plunging down from the shoulders of the peaks on either side, the courses of the more direct being disclosed from top to bottom without interruption. But from the west one sees nothing of the way he may be seeking until near the summit, after days have been spent in threading the forests growing on the main dividing ridges between the river canyons.

It is interesting to observe how surely the alp-crossing animals of every kind fall into the same trails. The more rugged and inaccessible the general character of the topography of any particular region, the more surely will the trails of white men, Indians, bears, wild sheep, etc., be found converging into the best passes. The Indians of the western slope venture cautiously over the passes in settled weather to attend dances, and obtain loads of pine-nuts and the larvae of a small fly that breeds in Mono and Owen's lakes, which, when dried, forms an important article of food; while the Pah Utes cross over from the east to hunt the deer and obtain supplies of acorns; and it is truly astonishing to see what immense loads the haggard old squaws make out to carry bare-footed through these rough passes, oftentimes for a distance of sixty or seventy miles. They are always accompanied by the men, who stride on, unburdened and erect, a little in advance, kindly stooping at difficult places to pile stepping-stones for their patient, pack-animal wives, just as they would prepare the way for their ponies.

Bears evince great sagacity as mountaineers, but although they are tireless and enterprising travellers they seldom cross the range. I have several times tracked them through the Mono Pass, but only in late years, after cattle and sheep had passed that way, when they doubtless were following to feed on the stragglers and on those that had been killed by falling over the rocks. Even the wild sheep, the best mountaineers of all, choose regular passes in making journeys across the summits. Deer seldom cross the range in either direction. I have never yet observed a single specimen of the mule-deer of the Great Basin west of the summit, and rarely one of the black-tailed species on the eastern slope, notwithstanding many of the latter ascend the range nearly to the summit every summer, to feed in the wild gardens and bring forth their young.

The glaciers are the pass-makers, and it is by them that the courses of all mountaineers are pre-destined. Without exception every pass in the Sierra was created by them without the slightest aid or predetermining guidance from any of the cataclysmic agents. I have seen elaborate statements of the amount of drilling and blasting accomplished in the construction of the railroad across the Sierra, above Donner Lake; but for every pound of rock moved in this way, the glaciers which descended east and west through this same pass, crushed and carried away more than a hundred tons.

The so-called practicable road-passes are simply those portions of the range more degraded by glacial action than the adjacent portions, and degraded in such a way as to leave the summits rounded, instead of sharp; while the peaks, from the superior strength and hardness of their rocks, or from more favourable position, having suffered less degradation, are left towering above the passes as if they had been heaved into the sky by some force acting from beneath.

The scenery of all the passes, especially at the head, is of the wildest and grandest description – lofty peaks massed together and laden around their bases with ice and snow; chains of glacier lakes; cascading streams in endless variety, with glorious views, westward over a sea of rocks and woods, and eastward over strange ashy plains, volcanoes, and the dry, dead-looking ranges of the Great Basin. Every pass, however, possesses treasures of beauty all its own.

Having thus in a general way indicated the height, leading features, and distribution of the principal passes, I will now endeavour to describe the Mono Pass in particular, which may, I think, be regarded as a fair example of the higher alpine passes in general.

The main portion of the Mono Pass is formed by Bloody Canyon, which begins at the summit of the range, and runs in a general east–northeasterly direction to the edge of the Mono Plain.

The first white men who forced a way through its sombre depths were, as we have seen, eager gold-seekers. But the canyon was known and travelled as a pass by the Indians and mountain animals long before its discovery by white men, as is shown by the numerous tributary trails which come into it from every direction. Its name accords well with the character of the 'early times' in California, and may perhaps have been suggested by the predominant colour of the metamorphic slates in which it is in great part eroded; or more probably by blood-stains made by the unfortunate animals which were compelled to slip and shuffle awkwardly over its rough, cutting rocks. I have never known an animal, either mule or horse, to make its way through the canyon, either in going up or down, without losing more or less blood from wounds on the legs. Occasionally one is killed outright – falling headlong and rolling over precipices like a boulder. But such accidents are rarer than from the terrible appearance of the trail one would be led to expect; the more experienced when driven loose find their way over the dangerous places with a caution and sagacity that is truly wonderful. During the gold excitement it was at times a matter of considerable pecuniary importance to force a way through the canyon with pack-trains early in the spring while it was yet heavily blocked with snow; and then the mules with their loads had sometimes to be let down over the steepest drifts and avalanche beds by means of ropes.

A good bridle-path leads from Yosemite through many a grove and meadow up to the head of the canyon, a distance of about thirty miles. Here the scenery undergoes a sudden and startling condensation. Mountains, red, grey and black, rise close at hand on the right, whitened around their bases with banks of enduring snow; on the left swells the huge red mass of Mount Gibbs, while in front the eye wanders down the shadowy canyon, and out on the warm plain of Mono, where the lake is seen gleaming like a burnished metallic disk, with clusters of lofty volcanic cones to the south of it.

When at length we enter the mountain gateway, the sombre rocks seem aware of our presence, and seem to come thronging closer about us. Happily the ouzel and the old familiar robin are here to sing us welcome, and azure daisies beam with trustfulness and sympathy, enabling us to feel something of Nature's love even here, beneath the gaze of her coldest rocks.

The effect of this expressive outspokenness on the part of the canyon-rocks is greatly enhanced by the quiet aspect of the alpine meadows through which we pass just before entering the narrow gateway. The forests in which they lie, and the mountain-tops rising beyond them, seem quiet and tranquil. We catch their restful spirit, yield to the soothing influences of the sunshine, and saunter dreamily on through flowers and bees, scarce touched by a definite thought; then suddenly we find ourselves in the shadowy canyon, closeted with Nature in one of her wildest strongholds.

After the first bewildering impression begins to wear off, we perceive that it is not altogether terrible; for besides the reassuring birds and flowers we discover a chain of shining lakelets hanging down from the very summit of the pass, and linked together by a silvery stream. The highest are set in bleak, rough bowls, scantily fringed with brown and yellow sedges. Winter storms blow snow through the canyon in blinding drifts, and avalanches shoot from the heights. Then are these sparkling tarns filled and buried, leaving not a hint of their existence. In June and July they begin to blink and thaw out like sleepy eyes, the carices thrust up their short brown spikes, the daisies bloom in turn, and the most profoundly buried of them all is at length warmed and summered as if winter were only a dream.

Red Lake is the lowest of the chain, and also the largest. It seems rather dull and forbidding at first sight, lying motionless in its deep, dark bed. The canyon wall rises sheer from the water's edge on the south, but on the opposite side there is sufficient space and sunshine for a sedgy daisy garden, the centre of which is brilliantly lighted with lilies, castilleias, larkspurs, and columbines, sheltered from the wind by leafy willows, and forming a most joyful outburst of plant-life keenly emphasized by the chill baldness of the onlooking cliffs.

After indulging here in a dozing, shimmering lake-rest, the happy stream sets forth again, warbling and trilling like an ouzel, ever delightfully confiding, no matter how dark the way; leaping, gliding, hither, thither, clear or foaming: manifesting the beauty of its wildness in every sound and gesture.

One of its most beautiful developments is the Diamond Cascade, situated a short distance below Red Lake. Here the tense, crystalline water is first dashed into coarse, granular spray mixed with dusty foam, and then divided into a diamond pattern by following the diagonal cleavage-joints that intersect the face of the precipice over which it pours. Viewed in front, it resembles a strip of embroidery of definite pattern, varying through the seasons with the temperature and the volume of water. Scarce a flower may be seen along its snowy border. A few bent pines look on from a distance, and small fringes of cassiope and rock-ferns are growing in fissures near the head, but these are so lowly and undemonstrative that only the attentive observer will be likely to notice them.

On the north wall of the canyon, a little below the Diamond Cascade, a glittering side stream makes its appearance, seeming to leap directly out of the sky. It first resembles a crinkled ribbon of silver hanging loosely down the wall, but grows wider as it descends, and dashes the dull rock with foam. A long rough talus curves up against this part of the cliff, overgrown with snow-pressed willows, in which the fall disappears with many an eager surge and swirl and plashing leap, finally beating its way down to its confluence with the main canyon stream.

Below this point the climate is no longer arctic. Butterflies become larger and more abundant, grasses with imposing spread of panicle wave above your shoulders, and the summery drone of the bumblebee thickens the air. The dwarf pine, the tree-mountaineer that climbs highest and braves the coldest blasts, is found scattered in stormbeaten clumps from the summit of the pass about half-way down the canyon. Here it is succeeded by the hardy two-leaved pine, which is speedily joined by the taller yellow and mountain pines. These, with the burly juniper, and shimmering aspen, rapidly grow larger as the sunshine becomes richer, forming groves that block the view; or they stand more apart here and there in picturesque groups, that make beautiful and obvious harmony with the rocks and with one another. Blooming underbrush becomes abundant – azalea, spiræa, and the brier-rose weaving fringes for the streams, and shaggy rugs to relieve the stern, unflinching rock-bosses.

Through this delightful wilderness, Canyon Creek roves without any constraining channel, throbbing and wavering; now in sunshine, now in thoughtful shade; falling, swirling, flashing from side to side in weariless exuberance of energy. A glorious milky way of cascades is thus developed, of which Bower Cascade, though one of the smallest, is perhaps the most beautiful of them all. It is situated in the lower region of the pass, just where the sunshine begins to mellow between the cold and warm climates. Here the glad creek, grown strong with tribute gathered from many a snowy fountain on the heights, sings richer strains, and becomes more human and lovable at every step. Now you may by its side find the rose and homely yarrow, and small meadows full of bees and clover. At the head of a low-browed rock, luxuriant dogwood bushes and willows arch over from bank to bank, embowering the stream with their leafy branches; and drooping plumes, kept in motion by the current, fringe the brow of the cascade in front. From this leafy covert the stream leaps out into the light in a fluted curve thick sown with sparkling crystals, and falls into a pool filled with brown boulders, out of which it creeps grey with foam-bells and disappears in a tangle of verdure like that from which it came.

Hence, to the foot of the canyon, the metamorphic slates give place to granite, whose nobler sculpture calls forth expressions of corresponding beauty from the stream in passing over it – bright trills of rapids, booming notes of falls, solemn hushes of smooth-gliding sheets, all chanting and blending in glorious harmony. When, at length, its impetuous alpine life is done it slips through a meadow with scarce an audible whisper, and falls asleep in Moraine Lake.

This water-bed is one of the finest I ever saw. Evergreens wave soothingly about it, and the breath of flowers floats over it like incense. Here our blessed stream rests from its rocky wanderings, all its mountaineering done – no more foaming rock-leaping, no more wild, exulting song. It falls into a smooth, glassy sleep, stirred only by the night-wind, which, coming down the canyon, makes it croon and mutter in ripples along its broidered shores.

Leaving the lake, it glides quietly through the rushes, destined never more to touch the living rock. Henceforth its path lies through ancient moraines and reaches of ashy sage-plain, which nowhere afford rocks suitable for the development of cascades or sheer falls. Yet this beauty of maturity, though less striking, is of a still higher order, enticing us lovingly on through gentian meadows and groves of rustling aspen to Lake Mono, where, spirit-like, our happy stream vanishes in vapour, and floats free again in the sky.

Bloody Canyon, like every other in the Sierra, was recently occupied by a glacier, which derived its fountain snows from the adjacent summits, and descended into Mono Lake, at a time when its waters stood at a much higher level than now. The principal characters in which the history of the ancient glacies is preserved are displayed here in marvellous freshness and simplicity, furnishing the student with extraordinary advantages for the acquisition of knowledge of this sort. The most striking passages are polished and striated surfaces, which in many places reflect the rays of the sun like smooth water. The dam of Red Lake is an elegantly modelled rib of metamorphic slate, brought into relief because of its superior strength, and because of the greater intensity of the glacial erosion of the rock immediately above it, caused by a steeply inclined tributary glacier, which entered the main trunk with a heavy down-thrust at the head of the lake.

Moraine Lake furnishes an equally interesting example of a basin formed wholly, or in part, by a terminal moraine dam curved across the path of a stream between two lateral moraines.

At Moraine Lake the canyon proper terminates although apparently continued by the two lateral moraines of the vanished glacier. These moraines are about 300ft. high, and extend unbrokenly from the sides of the canyon into the plain, a distance of about five miles, curving and tapering in beautiful lines. Their sunward sides are gardens, their shady sides are groves; the former devoted chiefly to eriogonæ, compositæ, and graminæ; a square rod containing five or six profusely flowered eriogonums of several species, about the same number of bahia and linosyris, and a few grass tufts; each species being planted trimly apart, with bare gravel between, as if cultivated artificially.

My first visit to Bloody Canyon was made in the summer of 1869, under circumstances well calculated to heighten the impressions that are the peculiar offspring of the mountains. I came from the blooming tangles of Florida, and waded out into the plant-gold of the great valley of California, when its flora was as yet untrodden. Never before had I beheld congregations of social flowers half so extensive or half so glorious. Golden compositæ covered all the ground from the Coast Range to the Sierra like a stratum of curdled sunshine, in which I revelled for weeks, watching the rising and setting of their innumerable suns; then I gave myself up to be borne forward on the crest of the summer wave that sweeps annually up the Sierra and spends itself on the snowy summits.

At the Big Tuolumne Meadows I remained more than a month, sketching, botanizing, and climbing among the surrounding mountains. The mountaineer with whom I then happened to be camping was one of those remarkable men one so frequently meets in California, the hard angles and bosses of whose characters have been brought into relief by the grinding excitements of the gold period, until they resemble glacial landscapes. But at this late day, my friend's activities had subsided, and his craving for rest caused him to become a gentle shepherd and literally to lie down with the lamb.

Recognizing the unsatisfiable longings of my Scotch Highland instincts, he threw out some hints concerning Bloody Canyon, and advised me to explore it. 'I have never seen it myself,' he said, 'for I never was so unfortunate as to pass that way. But I have heard many a strange story about it, and I warrant you will at least find it wild enough.'

Then of course I made haste to see it. Early next morning I made up a bundle of bread, tied my note-book to my belt, and strode away in the bracing air, full of eager, indefinite hope. The plushy lawns that lay in my path served to soothe my morning haste. The sod in many places was starred with daisies and blue gentians, over which I lingered. I traced the paths of the ancient glaciers over many a shining pavement, and marked the gaps in the upper forests that told the power of the winter avalanches. Climbing higher, I saw for the first time the gradual dwarfing of the pines in compliance with climate, and on the summit discovered creeping mats of the arctic willow overgrown with silky catkins, and patches of the dwarf vaccinium with its round flowers sprinkled in the grass like purple hail; while in every direction the landscape stretched sublimely away in fresh wildness – a manuscript written by the hand of Nature alone.

At length, as I entered the pass, the huge rocks began to close around in all their wild, mysterious impressiveness, when suddenly, as I was gazing eagerly about me, a drove of grey hairy beings came in sight, lumbering toward me with a kind of boneless, wallowing motion like bears.

I never turn back, though often so inclined, and in this particular instance, amid such surroundings, everything seemed singularly unfavourable for the calm acceptance of so grim a company. Suppressing my fears, I soon discovered that although as hairy as bears and as crooked as summit pines, the strange creatures were sufficiently erect to belong to our own species. They proved to be nothing more formidable than Mono Indians dressed in the skins of sage-rabbits. Both the men and the women begged persistently for whisky and tobacco, and seemed so accustomed to denials that I found it impossible to convince them that I had none to give. Excepting the names of these two products of civilization, they seemed to understand not a word of English; but I afterward learned that they were on their way to Yosemite Valley to feast awhile on trout and procure a load of acorns to carry back through the pass to their huts on the shore of Mono Lake.

Occasionally a good countenance may be seen among the Mono Indians, but these, the first specimens I had seen, were most ugly, and some of them altogether hideous. The dirt on their faces was fairly stratified, and seemed so ancient and so undisturbed it might also possess a geological significance. The older faces were, moreover, strangely blurred and divided into sections by furrows that looked like the cleavage-joints of rocks, suggesting exposure on the mountains in a cast-away condition for ages. Somehow they seemed to have no right place in the landscape, and I was glad to see them fading out of sight down the pass.

Then came evening, and the sombre cliffs were inspired with the ineffable beauty of the alpenglow. A solemn calm fell upon everything. All the lower portion of the canyon was in gloaming shadow, and I crept into a hollow near one of the upper lakelets to smooth the ground in a sheltered nook for a bed. When the short twilight faded, I kindled a sunny fire, made a cup of tea, and lay down to rest and look at the stars. Soon the night-wind began to flow and pour in torrents among the jagged peaks, mingling strange tones with those of the waterfalls sounding far below; and as I drifted toward sleep I began to experience an uncomfortable feeling of nearness to the furred Monos. Then the full moon looked down over the edge of the canyon wall, her countenance seemingly filled with intense concern, and apparently so near as to produce a startling effect as if she had entered my bedroom, forgetting all the world, to gaze on me alone.

The night was full of strange sounds, and I gladly welcomed the morning. Breakfast was soon done, and I set forth in the exhilarating freshness of the new day, rejoicing in the abundance of pure wildness so close about me. The stupendous rocks, hacked and scarred with centuries of storms, stood sharply out in the thin early light, while down in the bottom of the canyon grooved and polished bosses heaved and glistened like swelling sea-waves, telling a grand old story of the ancient glacier that poured its crushing floods above them.

Here for the first time I met the arctic daisies in all their perfection of purity and spirituality – gentle mountaineers face to face with the stormy sky, kept safe and warm by a thousand miracles. I leaped lightly from rock to rock, glorying in the eternal freshness and sufficiency of Nature, and in the ineffable tenderness with which she nurtures her mountain darlings in the very fountains of storms. Fresh beauty appeared at every step, delicate rock-ferns, and groups of the fairest flowers. Now another lake came to view, now a waterfall. Never fell light in brighter spangles, never fell water in whiter foam. I seemed to float through the canyon enchanted, feeling nothing of its roughness, and was out in the Mono levels before I was aware.

Looking back from the shore of Moraine Lake, my morning ramble seemed all a dream. There curved Bloody Canyon, a mere glacial furrow 2,000ft. deep, with smooth rocks projecting from the sides and braided together in the middle, like bulging, swelling muscles. Here the lilies were higher than my head, and the sunshine was warm enough for palms. Yet the snow around the arctic willows was plainly visible only four miles away, and between were narrow specimen zones of all the principal climates of the globe.

On the bank of a small brook that comes gurgling down the side of the left lateral moraine, I found a camp fire still burning, which no doubt belonged to the grey Indians I had met on the summit, and I listened instinctively and moved cautiously forward, half expecting to see some of their grim faces peering out of the bushes.

Passing on toward the open plain, I noticed three well-defined terminal moraines curved gracefully across the canyon stream, and joined by long splices to the two noble laterals. These mark the halting-places of the vanished glacier when it was retreating into its summit shadows on the breaking-up of the glacial winter.

Five miles below the foot of Moraine Lake, just where the lateral moraines lose themselves in the plain, there was a field of wild rye, growing in magnificent waving bunches six to eight feet high, bearing heads from six to twelve inches long. Rubbing out some of the grains, I found them about five eighths of an inch long, dark-coloured, and sweet. Indian women were gathering it in baskets, bending down large handfuls, beating it out, and fanning it in the wind. They were quite picturesque, coming through the rye, as one caught glimpses of them here and there, in winding lanes and openings, with splendid tufts arching above their heads, while their incessant chat and laughter showed their heedless joy.

Like the rye-field, I found the so-called desert of Mono blooming in a high state of natural cultivation with the wild rose, cherry, aster, and the delicate abronia; also innumerable gilias, phloxes, poppies, and bush-compositæ. I observed their gestures and the various expressions of their corollas, enquiring how they could be so fresh and beautiful out in this volcanic desert. They told as happy a life as any plant-company I ever met, and seemed to enjoy even the hot sand and the wind.

But the vegetation of the pass has been in great part destroyed, and the same may be said of all the more accessible passes throughout the range. Immense numbers of starving sheep and cattle have been driven through them into Nevada, trampling the wild gardens and meadows almost out of existence. The lofty walls are untouched by any foot, and the falls sing on unchanged; but the sight of crushed flowers and stripped, bitten bushes goes far toward destroying the charm of wildness.

The canyon should be seen in winter. A good, strong traveller, who knows the way and the weather, might easily make a safe excursion through it from Yosemite Valley on snow-shoes during some tranquil time, when the storms are hushed. The lakes and falls would be buried then; but so, also, would be the traces of destructive feet, while the views of the mountains in their winter garb, and the ride at lightning speed down the pass between the snowy walls, would be truly glorious.

CHAPTER SIX

The Glacier Lakes

AMONG THE many unlooked-for treasures that are bound up and hidden away in the depths of Sierra solitudes, none more surely charm and surprise all kinds of travellers than the glacier lakes. The forests and the glaciers and the snowy fountains of the streams advertise their wealth in a more or less telling manner even in the distance, but nothing is seen of the lakes until we have climbed above them. All the upper branches of the rivers are fairly laden with lakes, like orchard trees with fruit. They lie embosomed in the deep woods, down in the groovy bottoms of canyons, high on bald table-lands, and around the feet of the icy peaks, mirroring back their wild beauty over and over again. Some conception of their lavish abundance may be made from the fact that, from one standpoint on the summit of Red Mountain, a day's journey to the east of Yosemite Valley, no fewer than forty-two are displayed within a radius of ten miles. The whole number in the Sierra can hardly be less than fifteen hundred, not counting the smaller pools and tarns, which are innumerable. Perhaps two thirds or more lie on the western flank of the range, and all are restricted to the alpine and subalpine regions. At the close of the last glacial period, the middle and foot-hill regions also abounded in lakes, all of which have long since vanished as completely as the magnificent ancient glaciers that brought them into existence.

Though the eastern flank of the range is excessively steep, we find lakes pretty regularly distributed throughout even the most precipitous portions. They are mostly found in the upper branches of the canyons, and in the glacial amphitheatres around the peaks.

Occasionally long, narrow specimens occur upon the steep sides of dividing ridges, their basins swung lengthwise like hammocks, and very rarely one is found lying so exactly on the summit of the range at the head of some pass that its waters are discharged down both flanks when the snow is melting fast. But, however situated, they soon cease to form surprises to the studious mountaineer; for, like all the love-work of Nature, they are harmoniously related to one another, and to all the other features of the mountains. It is easy, therefore, to find the bright lake-eyes in the roughest and most ungovernable-looking topography of any landscape countenance. Even in the lower regions, where they have been closed for many a century, their rocky orbits are still discernible, filled in with the detritus of flood and avalanche. A beautiful system of grouping in correspondence with the glacial fountains is soon perceived; also their extension in the direction of the trends of the ancient glaciers; and in general their dependence as to form, size, and position upon the character of the rocks in which their basins have been eroded, and the quantity and direction of application of the glacial force expended upon each basin.

In the upper canyons we usually find them in pretty regular succession, strung together like beads on the bright ribbons of their feeding-streams, which pour, white and grey with foam and spray, from one to the other, their perfect mirror stillness making impressive contrasts with the grand blare and glare of the connecting cataracts. In Lake Hollow, on the north side of the Hoffman spur, immediately above the great Tuolumne canyon, there are ten lovely lakelets lying near together in one general hollow, like eggs in a nest. Seen from above, in a general view, feathered with Hemlock Spruce, and fringed with sedge, they seem to me the most singularly beautiful and interestingly located lake-cluster I have ever yet discovered.

Lake Tahoe, 22 miles long by about 10 wide, and from 500 to over 1,600ft. in depth, is the largest of all the Sierra lakes. It lies just beyond the northern limit of the higher portion of the range between the main axis and a spur that puts out on the east side from near the head of the Carson River. Its forested shores go curving in and out around many an emerald bay and pine-crowned promontory, and its waters are everywhere as keenly pure as any to be found among the highest mountains.

Donner Lake, rendered memorable by the terrible fate of the Donner party, is about three miles long, and lies about ten miles to the north of Tahoe, at the head of one of the tributaries of the Truckee. A few miles farther north lies Lake Independence, about the same size as Donner. But far the greater number of the lakes lie much higher and are quite small, few of them exceeding a mile in length, most of them less than half a mile.

Along the lower edge of the lake-belt, the smallest have disappeared by the filling-in of their basins, leaving only those of considerable size. But all along the upper freshly glaciated margin of the lake-bearing zone, every hollow, however small, lying within reach of any portion of the close network of streams, contains a bright, brimming pool; so that the landscape viewed from the mountain-tops seems to be sown broadcast with them. Many of the larger lakes are encircled with smaller ones like central gems girdled with sparkling brilliants. In general, however, there is no marked dividing line as to size. In order, therefore, to prevent confusion, I would state here that in giving numbers, I include none less than 500 yards in circumference.

In the basin of the Merced River, I counted 131, of which 111 are upon the tributaries that fall so grandly into Yosemite Valley. Pohono Creek, which forms the fall of that name, takes its rise in a beautiful lake, lying beneath the shadow of a lofty granite spur that puts out from Buena Vista peak. This is now the only lake left in the whole Pohono Basin. The Illilouette has sixteen, the Nevada no fewer than sixty-seven, the Tenaya eight, Hoffmann Creek five, and Yosemite Creek fourteen. There are but two other lake-bearing affluents of the Merced, viz, the South Fork with fifteen, and Cascade Creek with five, both of which unite with the main trunk below Yosemite.

The Merced River, as a whole, is remarkably like an elm-tree, and it requires but little effort on the part of the imagination to picture it standing upright, with all its lakes hanging upon its spreading branches, the topmost eighty miles in height. Now add all the other lake-bearing rivers of the Sierra, each in its place, and you will have a truly glorious spectacle – an avenue the length and width of the range; the long, slender, grey shafts of the main trunks, the milky way of arching branches, and the silvery lakes, all clearly defined and shining on the sky. How excitedly such an addition to the scenery would be gazed at! Yet these lakeful rivers are still more excitingly beautiful and impressive in their natural positions to those who have the eyes to see them as they lie embedded in their meadows and forests and glacier-sculptured rocks.

When a mountain lake is born – when, like a young eye, it first opens to the light – it is an irregular, expressionless crescent, enclosed in banks of rock and ice – bare, glaciated rock on the lower side, the rugged snout of a glacier on the upper. In this condition it remains for many a year, until at length, toward the end of some auspicious cluster of seasons, the glacier recedes beyond the upper margin of the basin, leaving it open from shore to shore for the first time, thousands of years after its conception beneath the glacier that excavated its basin. The landscape, cold and bare, is reflected in its pure depths; the winds ruffle its glassy surface, and the sun fills it with throbbing spangles, while its waves begin to lap and murmur around its leafless shores – sun-spangles during the day and reflected stars at night its only flowers, the winds and the snow its only visitors. Meanwhile the glacier continues to recede, and numerous rills, still younger than the lake itself, bring down glacier-mud, sand-grains, and pebbles, giving rise to margin-rings and plats of soil. To these fresh soil-beds come many a waiting plant. First, a hardy carex with arching leaves and a spike of brown flowers; then, as the seasons grow warmer, and the soil-beds deeper and wider, other sedges take their appointed places, and these are joined by blue gentians, daisies, dodecatheons, violets, honeyworts, and many a lowly moss. Shrubs also hasten in time to the new gardens – kalmia with its glossy leaves and purple flowers, the arctic willow, making soft woven carpets, together with the heathy bryanthus and cassiope, the fairest and dearest of them all. Insects now enrich the air, frogs pipe cheerily in the shallows, soon followed by the ouzel, which is the first bird to visit a glacier lake, as the sedge is the first of plants.

So the young lake grows in beauty, becoming more and more humanly lovable from century to century. Groves of aspen spring up, and hardy pines, and the hemlock spruce, until it is richly overshadowed and embowered. But while its shores are being enriched, the soil-beds creep out with incessant growth, contracting its area, while the lighter mud-particles deposited on the bottom cause it to grow constantly shallower, until at length the last remnant of the lake vanishes – closed forever in ripe and natural old age. And now its feeding-stream goes winding on without halting through the new gardens and groves that have taken its place.

The length of the life of any lake depends ordinarily upon the capacity of its basin, as compared with the carrying power of the streams that flow into it, the character of the rocks over which these streams flow, and the relative position of the lake toward other lakes. In a series whose basins lie in the same canyon, and are fed by one and the same main stream, the uppermost will, of course, vanish first unless some other lake-filling agent comes in to modify the result; because at first it receives nearly all of the sediments that the stream brings down, only the finest of the mud-particles being carried through the highest of the series to the next below. Then the next higher, and the next would be successively filled, and the lowest would be the last to vanish. But this simplicity as to duration is broken in upon in various ways, chiefly through the action of side-streams that enter the lower lakes direct. For, notwithstanding many of these side tributaries are quite short, and, during late summer, feeble, they all become powerful torrents in springtime when the snow is melting, and carry not only sand and pine-needles, but large trunks and boulders, tons in weight, sweeping them down their steeply inclined channels and into the lake basins with astounding energy. Many of these side affluents also have the advantage of access to the main lateral moraines of the vanished glacier that occupied the canyon, and upon these they draw for lake-filling material, while the main trunk stream flows mostly over clean glacier pavements, where but little moraine matter is ever left for them to carry. Thus a small rapid stream with abundance of loose transportable material within its reach may fill up an extensive basin in a few centuries while a large perennial trunk stream, flowing over clean, enduring pavements, though ordinarily a hundred times larger, may not fill a smaller basin in thousands of years.

The comparative influence of great and small streams as lake-fillers is strikingly illustrated in Yosemite Valley, through which the Merced flows. The bottom of the valley is now composed of level meadow-lands and dry, sloping soil-beds planted with oak and pine, but it was once a lake stretching from wall to wall and nearly from one end of the valley to the other, forming one of the most beautiful cliff-bound sheets of water that ever existed in the Sierra. And though never perhaps seen by human eye, it was but yesterday, geologically speaking, since it disappeared, and the traces of its existence are still so fresh, it may easily be restored to the eye of imagination and viewed in all its grandeur, about as truly and vividly as if actually before us. Now we find that the detritus which fills this magnificent basin was not brought down from the distant mountains by the main streams that converge here to form the river, however powerful and available for the purpose at first sight they appear; but almost wholly by the small local tributaries, such as those of Indian Canyon, the Sentinel, and the Three Brothers, and by a few small residual glaciers which lingered in the shadows of the walls long after the main trunk glacier had receded beyond the head of the valley.

Had the glaciers that once covered the range been melted at once, leaving the entire surface bare from top to bottom simultaneously, then of course all the lakes would have come into existence at the same time, and the highest, other circumstances being equal, would, as we have seen, be the first to vanish. But because they melted gradually from the foot of the range upward, the lower lakes were the first to see the light and the first to be obliterated. Therefore, instead of finding the lakes of the present day at the foot of the range, we find them at the top. Most of the lower lakes vanished thousands of years before those now brightening the alpine landscapes were born. And in general, owing to the deliberation of the upward retreat of the glaciers, the lowest of the existing lakes are also the oldest, a gradual transition being apparent throughout the entire belt, from the older, forested, meadow-rimmed and contracted forms all the way up to those that are new born, lying bare and meadowless among the highest peaks.

A few small lakes unfortunately situated are extinguished suddenly by a single swoop of an avalanche, carrying down immense numbers of trees, together with the soil they were growing upon. Others are obliterated by land-slips, earthquake taluses, etc., but these lake-deaths compared with those resulting from the deliberate and incessant deposition of sediments, may be termed accidental. Their fate is like that of trees struck by lightning.

The lake-line is of course still rising, its present elevation being about 8,000ft. above sea-level; somewhat higher than this toward the southern extremity of the range, lower toward the northern, on account of the difference in time of the withdrawal of the glaciers, due to difference in climate. Specimens occur here and there considerably below this limit, in basins specially protected from in-washing detritus, or exceptional in size. These, however, are not sufficiently numerous to make any marked irregularity in the line. The highest I have yet found lies at an elevation of about 12,000ft., in a glacier womb, at the foot of one of the highest of the summit peaks, a few miles to the north of Mount Ritter. The basins of perhaps twenty-five or thirty are still in process of formation beneath the few lingering glaciers, but by the time they are born, an equal or greater number will probably have died. Since the beginning of the close of the ice-period the whole number in the range has perhaps never been greater than at present.

A rough approximation to the average duration of these mountain lakes may be made from data already suggested, but I cannot stop here to present the subject in detail. I must also forego, in the meantime, the pleasure of a full discussion of the interesting question of lake–basin formation, for which fine, clear, demonstrative material abounds in these mountains. In addition to what has been already given on the subject, I will only make this one statement. Every lake in the Sierra is a glacier lake. Their basins were not merely remodelled and scoured out by this mighty agent, but in the first place were eroded from the solid.

I must now make haste to give some nearer views of representative specimens lying at different elevations on the main lake-belt, confining myself to descriptions of the features most characteristic of each.

SHADOW LAKE

This is a fine specimen of the oldest and lowest of the existing lakes. It lies about eight miles above Yosemite Valley, on the main branch of the Merced, at an elevation of about 7,350ft. above the sea; and is everywhere so securely cliff-bound that without artificial trails only wild animals can get down to its rocky shores from any direction. Its original length was about a mile and a half; now it is only half a mile in length by about a fourth of a mile in width, and over the lowest portion of the basin ninety-eight feet deep. Its crystal waters are clasped around on the north and south by majestic granite walls sculptured in true Yosemitic style into domes, gables, and battlemented headlands, which on the south come plunging down sheer into deep water, from a height of from 1,500 to 2,000ft. The South Lyell glacier eroded this magnificent basin out of solid porphyritic granite while forcing its way westward from the summit fountains towards Yosemite, and the exposed rocks around the shores, and the projecting bosses of the walls, ground and burnished beneath the vast ice-flood, still glow with silvery radiance, notwithstanding the innumerable corroding storms that have fallen upon them. The general conformation of the basin, as well as the moraines laid along the top of the walls, and the grooves and scratches on the bottom and sides, indicate in the most unmistakable manner the direction pursued by this mighty ice-river, its great depth, and the tremendous energy it exerted in thrusting itself into and out of the basin; bearing down with superior pressure upon this portion of its channel, because of the greater declivity, consequently eroding it deeper than the other portions about it, and producing the lake-bowl as the necessary result.

With these magnificent ice-characters so vividly before us it is not easy to realize that the old glacier that made them vanished tens of centuries ago; for, excepting the vegetation that has sprung up, and the changes effected by an earthquake that hurled rock-avalanches from the weaker headlands, the basin as a whole presents the same appearance that it did when first brought to light. The lake itself, however, has undergone marked changes; one sees at a glance that it is growing old. More than two thirds of its original area is now dry land, covered with meadow-grasses and groves of pine and fir, and the level bed of alluvium stretching across from wall to wall at the head is evidently growing out along its lakeward margin, and will at length close the lake forever.

Every lover of fine wildness would delight to saunter on a summer day through the flowery groves now occupying the filled-up portion of the basin. The curving shore is clearly traced by a ribbon of white sand upon which the ripples play; then comes a belt of broad-leafed sedges, interrupted here and there by impenetrable tangles of willows; beyond this there are groves of trembling aspen; then a dark, shadowy belt of two-leaved pine, with here and there a round carex meadow ensconced nest-like in its midst; and lastly, a narrow outer margin of majestic silver fir 200ft. high. The ground beneath the trees is covered with a luxuriant crop of grasses, chiefly triticum, bromus, and calamagrostis, with purple spikes and panicles arching to one's shoulders; while the open meadow patches glow throughout the summer with showy flowers – heleniums, goldenrods, erigerons, lupines, castilleias, and lilies, and form favourite hiding- and feeding-grounds for bears and deer.

The rugged south wall is feathered darkly along the top with an imposing array of spirey silver firs, while the rifted precipices all the way down to the water's edge are adorned with picturesque old junipers, their cinnamon-coloured bark showing finely upon the neutral grey of the granite. These, with a few venturesome dwarf pines and spruces, lean out over fissured ribs and tablets, or stand erect back in shadowy niches, in an indescribably wild and fearless manner. Moreover, the white-flowered Douglas spiræa and dwarf evergreen oak form graceful fringes along the narrower seams, wherever the slightest hold can be effected. Rock-ferns, too, are here, such as allosorus, pellæa, and cheilanthes, making handsome rosettes on the drier fissures; and the delicate maidenhair, cistoperis, and woodsia hide back in mossy grottoes, moistened by some trickling rill; and then the orange wall-flower holds up its showy panicles here and there in the sunshine, and bahia makes bosses of gold. But, notwithstanding all this plant beauty, the general impression in looking across the lake is of stern, unflinching rockiness; the ferns and flowers are scarcely seen, and not one fiftieth of the whole surface is screened with plant life.

The sunnier north wall is more varied in sculpture, but the general tone is the same. A few headlands, flat-topped and soil-covered, support clumps of cedar and pine; and up-curving tangles of chinquapin and live-oak, growing on rough earthquake taluses, girdle their bases. Small streams come cascading down between them, their foaming margins brightened with gay primulas, gilias, and mimuluses. And close along the shore on this side there is a strip of rocky meadow enamelled with buttercups, daises, and white violets, and the purple-topped grasses out on its bevelled border dip their leaves into the water.

The lower edge of the basin is a dam-like swell of solid granite, heavily abraded by the old glacier, but scarce at all cut into as yet by the outflowing stream, though it has flowed on unceasingly since the lake came into existence.

As soon as the stream is fairly over the lake-lip it breaks into cascades, never for a moment halting, and scarce abating one jot of its glad energy, until it reaches the next filled-up basin, a mile below. Then swirling and curving drowsily through meadow and grove, it breaks forth anew into grey rapids and falls, leaping and gliding in glorious exuberance of wild bound and dance down into another and yet another filled-up lake basin. Then, after a long rest in the levels of Little Yosemite, it makes its grandest display in the famous Nevada Fall. Out of the clouds of spray at the foot of the fall the battered, roaring river gropes its way, makes another mile of cascades and rapids, rests a moment in Emerald Pool, then plunges over the grand cliff of the Vernal Fall, and goes thundering and chafing down a boulder-choked gorge of tremendous depth and wildness into the tranquil reaches of the old Yosemite lake basin.

The colour-beauty about Shadow Lake during the Indian summer is much richer than one could hope to find in so young and so glacial a wilderness. Almost every leaf is tinted then, and the goldenrods are in bloom; but most of the colour is given by the ripe grasses, willows, and aspens. At the foot of the lake you stand in a trembling aspen grove, every leaf painted like a butterfly, and away to right and left round the shores sweeps a curving ribbon of meadow, red and brown dotted with pale yellow, shading off here and there into hazy purple. The walls, too, are dashed with bits of bright colour that gleam out on the neutral granite grey. But neither the walls, nor the margin meadow, nor yet the gay, fluttering grove in which you stand, nor the lake itself, flashing with spangles, can long hold your attention; for at the head of the lake there is a gorgeous mass of orange-yellow, belonging to the main aspen belt of the basin, which seems the very fountain whence all the colour below it had flowed, and here your eye is filled and fixed. This glorious mass is about thirty feet high, and extends across the basin nearly from wall to wall. Rich bosses of willow flame in front of it, and from the base of these the brown meadow comes forward to the water's edge, the whole being relieved against the unyielding green of the coniferæ, while thick sun-gold is poured over all.

During these blessed colour-days no cloud darkens the sky, the winds are gentle, and the landscape rests, hushed everywhere, and indescribably impressive. A few ducks are usually seen sailing on the lake, apparently more for pleasure than anything else, and the ouzels at the head of the rapids sing always; while robins, grosbeaks, and the Douglas squirrels are busy in the groves, making delightful company, and intensifying the feeling of grateful sequestration without ruffling the deep, hushed calm and peace.

This autumnal mellowness usually lasts until the end of November. Then come days of quite another kind. The winter clouds grow, and bloom, and shed their starry crystals on every leaf and rock, and all the colours vanish like a sunset. The deer gather and hasten down their well-known trails, fearful of being snow-bound. Storm succeeds storm, heaping snow on the cliffs and meadows, and bending the slender pines to the ground in wide arches, one over the other, clustering and interlacing like lodged wheat. Avalanches rush and boom from the shelving heights, piling immense heaps upon the frozen lake, and all the summer glory is buried and lost. Yet in the midst of this hearty winter the sun shines warm at times, calling the Douglas squirrel to frisk in the snowy pines and seek out his hidden stores; and the weather is never so severe as to drive away the grouse and little nut-hatches and chickadees.

Toward May, the lake begins to open. The hot sun sends down innumerable streams over the cliffs, streaking them round and round with foam. The snow slowly vanishes, and the meadows show tintings of green. Then spring comes on apace; flowers and flies enrich the air and the sod, and the deer come back to the upper groves like birds to an old nest.

I first discovered this charming lake in the autumn of 1872, while on my way to the glaciers at the head of the river. It was rejoicing then in its gayest colours, untrodden, hidden in the glorious wildness like unmined gold. Year after year I walked its shores without discovering any other trace of humanity than the remains of an Indian camp-fire, and the thigh bones of a deer that had been broken to get at the marrow. It lies out of the regular ways of Indians, who love to hunt in more accessible fields adjacent to trails. Their knowledge of deer-haunts had probably enticed them here some hunger-time when they wished to make sure of a feast; for hunting in this lake-hollow is like hunting in a fenced park. I had told the beauty of Shadow Lake only to a few friends, fearing it might come to be trampled and 'improved' like Yosemite. On my last visit, as I was sauntering along the shore on the strip of sand between the water and sod, reading the tracks of the wild animals that live here, I was startled by a human track, which I at once saw belonged to some shepherd; for each step was turned out 35° or 40° from the general course pursued, and was also run over in an uncertain sprawling fashion at the heel, while a row of round dots on the right indicated the staff that shepherds carry. None but a shepherd could make such a track, and after tracing it a few minutes I began to fear that he might be seeking pasturage; for what else could he be seeking? Returning from the glaciers shortly afterward, my worst fears were realized. A trail had been made down the mountain-side from the north, and all the gardens and meadows were destroyed by a horde of hoofed locusts, as if swept by a fire. The money-changers were in the temple.

ORANGE LAKE

Besides these larger canyon lakes, fed by the main canyon streams, there are many smaller ones lying aloft on the top of rock benches, entirely independent of the general drainage channels, and of course drawing their supplies from a very limited area. Notwithstanding they are mostly small and shallow, owing to their immunity from avalanche detritus, and the inwashings of powerful streams, they often endure longer than others many times larger but less favourably situated. When very shallow they become dry toward the end of summer; but because their basins are ground out of seamless stone they suffer no loss save from evaporation alone; and the great depth of snow that falls, lasting into June, makes their dry season short in any case.

Orange Lake is a fair illustration of this bench form. It lies in the middle of a beautiful glacial pavement near the lower margin of the lake-line, about a mile and a half to the northwest of Shadow Lake. It is only about 100 yards in circumference. Next the water there is a girdle of carices with wide over-arching leaves, then in regular order a shaggy ruff of huckleberry bushes, a zone of willows with here and there a bush of the Mountain Ash, then a zone of aspens with a few pines around the outside. These zones are of course concentric, and together form a wall beyond which the naked ice-burnished granite stretches away in every direction, leaving it conspicuously relieved, like a bunch of palms in a desert.

In autumn, when the colours are ripe, the whole circular grove, at a little distance, looks like a big handful of flowers set in a cup to be kept fresh – a tuft of goldenrods. Its feeding-streams are exceedingly beautiful, notwithstanding their inconstancy and extreme shallowness. They have no channel whatever, and consequently are left free to spread in thin sheets upon the shining granite and wander at will. In many places the current is less than a fourth of an inch deep, and flows with so little friction it is scarcely visible. Sometimes there is not a single foam-bell, or drifting pine-needle, or irregularity of any sort to manifest its motion. Yet when observed narrowly it is seen to form a web of gliding lacework exquisitely woven, giving beautiful reflections from its minute curving ripples and eddies, and differing from the water-laces of large cascades in being everywhere transparent. In spring, when the snow is melting, the lake-bowl is brimming full, and sends forth quite a large stream that slips glassily for 200 yards or so, until it comes to an almost vertical precipice 800ft. high, down which it plunges in a fine cataract; then it gathers its scattered waters and goes smoothly over folds of gently dipping granite to its confluence with the main canyon stream. During the greater portion of the year, however, not a single water sound will you hear either at head or foot of the lake, not even the whispered lappings of ripple-waves along the shore; for the winds are fenced out. But the deep mountain silence is sweetened now and then by birds that stop here to rest and drink on their way across the canyon.

LAKE STARR KING

A beautiful variety of the bench-top lakes occurs just where the great lateral moraines of the main glaciers have been shoved forward in outswelling concentric rings by small residual tributary glaciers. Instead of being encompassed by a narrow ring of trees like Orange Lake, these lie embosomed in dense moraine woods, so dense that in seeking them you may pass them by again and again, although you may know nearly where they lie concealed.

Lake Starr King, lying to the north of the cone of that name, above the Little Yosemite Valley, is a fine specimen of this variety. The ouzels pass it by, and so do the ducks; they could hardly get into it if they would, without plumping straight down inside the circling trees.

Yet these isolated gems, lying like fallen fruit detached from the branches, are not altogether without inhabitants and joyous, animating visitors. Of course fishes cannot get into them, and this is generally true of nearly every glacier lake in the range, but they are all well stocked with happy frogs. How did the frogs get into them in the first place? Perhaps their sticky spawn was carried in on the feet of ducks or other birds, else their progenitors must have made some exciting excursions through the woods and up the sides of the canyons. Down in the still, pure depths of these hidden lakelets you may also find the larvæ of innumerable insects and a great variety of beetles, while the air above them is thick with humming wings, through the midst of which fly-catchers are constantly darting. And in autumn, when the huckleberries are ripe, bands of robins and grosbeaks come to feast, forming altogether delightful little byworlds for the naturalist.

Pushing our way upward toward the axis of the range, we find lakes in greater and greater abundance, and more youthful in aspect. At an elevation of about 9,000ft. above sea-level they seem to have arrived at middle age – that is, their basins seem to be about half-filled with alluvium. Broad sheets of meadow-land are seen extending into them, imperfect and boggy in many places and more nearly level than those of the older lakes below them, and the vegetation of their shores is of course more alpine. Kalmia, ledum, and cassiope fringe the meadow rocks, while the luxuriant, waving groves, so characteristic of the lower lakes, are represented only by clumps of the dwarf pine and hemlock spruce. These, however, are oftentimes very pictur-esquely grouped on rocky headlands around the outer rim of the meadows, or with still more striking effect crown some rocky islet.

Moreover, from causes that we cannot stop here to explain, the cliffs about these middle-aged lakes are seldom of the massive Yosemite type, but are more broken, and less sheer, and they usually stand back, leaving the shores comparatively free; while the few precipitous rocks that do come forward and plunge directly into deep water are seldom more than three or four hundred feet high.

I have never yet met ducks in any of the lakes of this kind, but the ouzel is never wanting where the feeding-streams are perennial. Wild sheep and deer may occasionally be seen on the meadows, and very rarely a bear. One might camp on the rugged shores of these bright fountains for weeks, without meeting any animal larger than the marmots that burrow beneath glacier boulders along the edges of the meadows.

The highest and youngest of all the lakes lie nestled in glacier wombs. At first sight, they seem pictures of pure bloodless desolation, miniature arctic seas, bound in perpetual ice and snow, and overshadowed by harsh, gloomy, crumbling precipices. Their waters are keen ultramarine blue in the deepest parts, lively grass-green toward the shore shallows and around the edges of the small bergs usually floating about in them. A few hardy sedges, frost-pinched every night, are occasionally found making soft sods along the sun-touched portions of their shores, and when their northern banks slope openly to the south, and are soil-covered, no matter how coarsely, they are sure to be brightened with flowers. One lake in particular now comes to mind which illustrates the floweriness of the sun-touched banks of these icy gems. Close up under the shadow of the Sierra Matterhorn, on the eastern slope of the range, lies one of the iciest of these glacier lakes at an elevation of about 12,000ft. A short, ragged-edged glacier crawls into it from the south, and on the opposite side it is embanked and dammed by a series of concentric terminal moraines, made by the glacier when it entirely filled the basin. Half a mile below lies a second lake, at a height of 11,500ft., about as cold and as pure as a snow-crystal. The waters of the first come gurgling down into it over and through the moraine dam, while a second stream pours into it direct from a glacier that lies to the southeast. Sheer precipices of crystalline snow rise out of deep water on the south, keeping perpetual winter on that side, but there is a fine summery spot on the other, notwithstanding the lake is only about 300 yards wide. Here, on 25 August 1873, I found a charming company of flowers, not pinched, crouching dwarfs, scarce able to look up, but warm and juicy, standing erect in rich cheery colour and bloom. On a narrow strip of shingle, close to the water's edge, there were a few tufts of carex gone to seed; and a little way back up the rocky bank at the foot of a crumbling wall so inclined as to absorb and radiate as well as reflect a considerable quantity of sun-heat, was the garden, containing a thrifty thicket of cowania covered with large yellow flowers; several bushes of the alpine ribes with berries nearly ripe and wildly acid; a few handsome grasses belonging to two distinct species, and one goldenrod; a few hairy lupines and radiant spragueas, whose blue and rose-coloured flowers were set off to fine advantage amid green carices; and along a narrow seam in the very warmest angle of the wall a perfectly gorgeous fringe of *Epilobium obcordatum* with flowers an inch wide, crowded together in lavish profusion, and coloured as royal a purple as ever was worn by any high-bred plant of the tropics; and best of all, and greatest of all, a noble thistle in full bloom, standing erect, head and shoulders above his companions, and thrusting out his lances in sturdy vigour as if growing on a Scottish brae. All this brave warm bloom among the raw stones, right in the face of the onlooking glaciers.

As far as I have been able to find out, these upper lakes are snow-buried in winter to a depth of about thirty-five or forty feet, and those most exposed to avalanches, to a depth of even a hundred feet or more. These last are, of course, nearly lost to the landscape. Some remain buried for years, when the snowfall is exceptionally great, and many open only on one side late in the season. The snow of the closed side is composed of coarse granules compacted and frozen into a firm, faintly stratified mass, like the *névé* of a glacier. The lapping waves of the open portion gradually undermine and cause it to break off in large masses like icebergs, which gives rise to a precipitous front like the discharging wall of a glacier entering the sea. The play of the lights among the crystal angles of these snow-cliffs, the pearly white of the out-swelling bosses, the bergs drifting in front, aglow in the sun and edged with green water, and the deep blue disk of the lake itself extending to your feet – this forms a picture that enriches all your afterlife, and is never forgotten. But however perfect the season and the day, the cold incompleteness of these young lakes is always keenly felt. We approach them with a kind of mean caution, and steal unconfidingly around their crystal shores, dashed and ill at ease, as if expecting to hear some forbidding voice. But the love-songs of the ouzels and the love-looks of the daisies gradually reassure us, and manifest the warm fountain humanity that pervades the coldest and most solitary of them all.

CHAPTER SEVEN

The Glacier Meadows

AFTER THE lakes on the High Sierra come the glacier meadows. They are smooth, level, silky lawns, lying embedded in the upper forests, on the floors of the valleys, and along the broad backs of the main dividing ridges, at a height of about 8,000 to 9,500ft. above the sea.

They are nearly as level as the lakes whose places they have taken, and present a dry, even surface free from rock-heaps, mossy bogginess, and the frowsy roughness of rank, coarse-leaved, weedy, and shrubby vegetation. The sod is close and fine, and so complete that you cannot see the ground; and at the same time so brightly enamelled with flowers and butterflies that it may well be called a garden-meadow, or meadow-garden; for the plushy sod is in many places so crowded with gentians, daises, ivesias, and various species of orthocarpus that the grass is scarcely noticeable, while in others the flowers are only pricked in here and there singly, or in small ornamental rosettes.

The most influential of the grasses composing the sod is a delicate calamagrostis with fine filiform leaves, and loose, airy panicles that seem to float above the flowery lawn like a purple mist. But, write as I may, I cannot give anything like an adequate idea of the exquisite beauty of these mountain carpets as they lie smoothly outspread in the savage wilderness. What words are fine enough to picture them? to what shall we liken them? The flowery levels of the prairies of the old West, the luxuriant savannahs of the South, and the finest of cultivated meadows are coarse in comparison. One may at first sight compare them with the carefully tended lawns of pleasure-grounds; for they are as free from weeds as they, and as smooth, but here the likeness ends; for these wild lawns, with all their exquisite fineness, have no trace of that painful, licked, snipped, repressed appearance that pleasure-ground lawns are apt to have even when viewed at a distance. And, not to mention the flowers with which they are brightened, their grasses are very much finer both in colour and texture, and instead of lying flat and motionless, matted together like a dead green cloth, they respond to the touches of every breeze, rejoicing in pure wildness, blooming and fruiting in the vital light.

Glacier meadows abound throughout all the alpine and subalpine regions of the Sierra in still greater numbers than the lakes. Probably from 2,500 to 3,000 exist between latitude 36° 30′ and 30°, distributed, of course, like the lakes, in concordance with all the other glacial features of the landscape.

On the head waters of the rivers there are what are called 'Big Meadows,' usually about from five to ten miles long. These occupy the basins of the ancient ice-seas, where many tributary glaciers came together to form the grand trunks. Most, however, are quite small, averaging perhaps but little more than three fourths of a mile in length.

One of the very finest of the thousands I have enjoyed lies hidden in an extensive forest of the two-leavèd pine, on the edge of the basin of the ancient Tuolumne Mer de Glace, about eight miles to the west of Mount Dana.

Imagine yourself at the Tuolumne Soda Springs on the bank of the river, a day's journey above Yosemite Valley. You set off northward through a forest that stretches away indefinitely before you, seemingly unbroken by openings of any kind. As soon as you are fairly into the woods, the grey mountain-peaks, with their snowy gorges and hollows, are lost to view. The ground is littered with fallen trunks that lie crossed and recrossed like storm-lodged wheat; and besides this close forest of pines, the rich moraine soil supports a luxuriant growth of ribbon-leaved grasses – bromus, triticum, calamagrostis, agrostis, etc., which rear their handsome spikes and panicles above your waist. Making your way through the fertile wilderness – finding lively bits of interest now and then in the squirrels and Clark crows, and perchance in a deer or bear – after a lapse of an hour or two vertical bars of sunshine are seen ahead between the brown shafts of the pines, showing that you are approaching an open space, and then you suddenly emerge from the forest shadows upon a delightful purple lawn lying smooth and free in the light like a lake. This is a glacier meadow. It is about a mile and a half long by a quarter of a mile wide. The trees come pressing forward all around in close serried ranks, planting their feet exactly on its margin, and holding themselves erect, strict and orderly like soldiers on parade; thus bounding the meadow with exquisite precision, yet with free curving lines such as Nature alone can draw. With inexpressible delight you wade out into the grassy sun-lake, feeling yourself contained in one of Nature's most sacred chambers, withdrawn from the sterner influences of the mountains, secure from all intrusion, secure from yourself, free in the universal beauty. And notwithstanding the scene is so impressively spiritual, and you seem dissolved in it, yet everything about you is beating with warm, terrestrial, human love and life delightfully substantial and familiar. The resiny pines are types of health and steadfastness; the robins feeding on the sod belong to the same species you have known since childhood; and surely these daisies, larkspurs and goldenrods are the very friend-flowers of the old home garden. Bees hum as in a harvest noon, butterflies waver above the flowers, and like them you lave in the vital sunshine, too richly and homogeneously joy-filled to be capable of partial thought. You are all eye, sifted through and through with light and beauty. Sauntering along the brook that meanders silently through the meadow from the east, special flowers call you back to discriminating consciousness. The sod comes curving down to the water's edge, forming bossy outswelling banks, and in some places overlapping countersunk boulders and forming bridges. Here you find mats of the curious dwarf willow scarce an inch high, yet sending up a multitude of grey silky catkins, illumined here and there with the purple cups and bells of bryanthus and vaccinium.

Go where you may, you everywhere find the lawn divinely beautiful, as if Nature had fingered and adjusted every plant this very day. The floating grass panicles are scarcely felt in brushing through their midst, so fine are they, and none of the flowers have tall or rigid stalks. In the brightest places you find three species of gentians with different shades of blue, daisies pure as the sky, silky leaved ivesias with warm yellow flowers, several species of orthocarpus with blunt, bossy spikes, red and purple and yellow; the alpine goldenrod, pentstemon and clover, fragrant and honeyful, with their colours massed and blended. Parting the grasses and looking more closely you may trace the branching of their shining stems, and note the marvellous beauty of their mist of flowers, the glumes and pales exquisitely pencilled, the yellow dangling stamens, and feathery pistils. Beneath the lowest leaves you discover a fairy realm of mosses – hypnum, dicranum, polytrichum and many others – their precious spore-cups poised daintily on polished shafts, curiously hooded, or open, showing the richly ornate peristomas worn like royal crowns. Creeping liverworts are here also in abundance, and several rare species of fungi, exceedingly small, and frail, and delicate, as if made only for beauty. Caterpillars, black beetles and ants roam the wilds of this lower world, making their way through miniature groves and thickets like bears in a thick wood.

And how rich, too, is the life of the sunny air! Every leaf and flower seems to have its winged representative overhead. Dragon-flies shoot in vigorous zigzags through the dancing swarms, and a rich profusion of butterflies – the leguminosæ of insects – make a fine addition to the general show. Many of these last are comparatively small at this elevation, and as yet almost un-known to science; but every now and then a familiar vanessa or papilio comes sailing past. Humming-birds, too, are quite common here, and the robin is always found along the margin of the stream, or out in the shallowest portions of the sod, and sometimes the grouse and mountain quail, with their broods of precious fluffy chickens. Swallows skim the grassy lake from end to end, fly-catchers come and go in fitful flights from the tops of dead spars, while woodpeckers swing across from side to side in graceful festoon curves – birds, insects and flowers all in their own way telling a deep summer joy.

The influences of pure nature seem to be so little known as yet, that it is generally supposed that complete pleasure of this kind, permeating one's very flesh and bones, unfits the student for scientific pursuits in which cool judge-ment and observation are required. But the effect is just the opposite. Instead of producing a dissipated condition, the mind is fertilized and stimulated and developed like sun-fed plants. All that we have seen here enables us to see with surer vision the fountains among the summit-peaks to the east whence flowed the glaciers that ground soil for the surrounding forest; and down at the foot of the meadow the moraine which formed the dam which gave rise to the lake that occupied this basin before the meadow was made; and around the margin the stones that were shoved back and piled up into a rude wall by the expansion of the lake ice during long bygone winters; and along the sides of the streams the slight hollows of the meadow which mark those portions of the old lake that were the last to vanish.

I would fain ask my readers to linger awhile in this fertile wilderness, to trace its history from its earliest glacial beginnings, and learn what we may of its wild inhabitants and visitors. How happy the birds are all summer and some of them all winter; how the pouched marmots drive tunnels under the snow, and how fine and brave a life the slandered coyote lives here, and the deer and bears! But, knowing well the difference between reading and seeing, I will only ask attention to some brief sketches of its varying aspects as they are presented throughout the more marked seasons of the year.

The summer life we have been depicting lasts with but little abatement until October, when the night frosts begin to sting, bronzing the grasses, and ripening the leaves of the creeping heathworts along the banks of the stream to reddish purple and crimson; while the flowers disappear, all save the goldenrods and a few daisies, that continue to bloom on unscathed until the beginning of snowy winter. In still nights the grass panicles and every leaf and stalk are laden with frost crystals, through which the morning sunbeams sift in ravishing splendour, transforming each to a precious diamond radiating the colours of the rainbow. The brook shallows are plaited across and across with slender lances of ice, but both these and the grass crystals are melted before midday, and, notwithstanding the great elevation of the meadow, the afternoons are still warm enough to revive the chilled butterflies and call them out to enjoy the late-flowering goldenrods. The divine alpenglow flushes the surrounding forest every evening, followed by a crystal night with hosts of lily stars, whose size and brilliancy cannot be conceived by those who have never risen above the lowlands.

Thus come and go the bright sun-days of autumn, not a cloud in the sky, week after week until near December. Then comes a sudden change. Clouds of a peculiar aspect with a slow, crawling gait gather and grow in the azure, throwing out satiny fringes, and becoming gradually darker until every lake-like rift and opening is closed and the whole bent firmament is obscured in equal structureless gloom. Then comes the snow, for the clouds are ripe, the meadows of the sky are in bloom, and shed their radiant blossoms like an orchard in the spring. Lightly, lightly they lodge in the brown grasses and in the tasselled needles of the pines, falling hour after hour, day after day, silently, lovingly – all the winds hushed – glancing and circling hither, thither, glinting against one another, rays interlocking in flakes as large as daisies; and then the dry grasses, and the trees, and the stones are all equally abloom again. Thunder-showers occur here during the summer months, and impressive it is to watch the coming of the big transparent drops, each a small world in itself – one unbroken ocean without islands hurling free through the air like planets through space. But still more impressive to me is the coming of the snow-flowers – falling stars, winter daisies – giving bloom to all the ground alike. Raindrops blossom brilliantly in the rainbow, and change to flowers in the sod, but snow comes in full flower direct from the dark, frozen sky.

The later snow-storms are oftentimes accompanied by winds that break up the crystals, when the temperature is low, into single petals and irregular dusty fragments; but there is comparatively little drifting on the meadow, so securely is it embosomed in the woods. From December to May, storm succeeds storm, until the snow is about fifteen or twenty feet deep, but the surface is always as smooth as the breast of a bird.

Hushed now is the life that so late was beating warmly. Most of the birds have gone down below the snow-line, the plants sleep, and all the fly-wings are folded. Yet the sun beams gloriously many a cloudless day in midwinter, casting long lance shadows athwart the dazzling expanse. In June small flecks of the dead, decaying sod begin to appear, gradually widening and uniting with one another, covered with creeping rags of water during the day, and ice by night, looking as hopeless and unvital as crushed rocks just emerging from the darkness of the glacial period. Walk the meadow now! Scarce the memory of a flower will you find. The ground seems twice dead. Nevertheless, the annual resurrection is drawing near. The life-giving sun pours his floods, the last snow-wreath melts, myriads of growing points push eagerly through the steaming mold, the birds come back, new wings fill the air, and fervid summer life comes surging on, seemingly yet more glorious than before.

This is a perfect meadow, and under favourable circumstances exists without manifesting any marked changes for centuries. Nevertheless, soon or late it must inevitably grow old and vanish. During the calm Indian summer, scarce a sand-grain moves around its banks, but in flood-times and storm-times, soil is washed forward upon it and laid in successive sheets around its gently sloping rim, and is gradually extended to the centre, making it drier. Through a considerable period the meadow vegetation is not greatly affected thereby, for it gradually rises with the rising ground, keeping on the surface like water-plants rising on the swell of waves. But at length the elevation of the meadowland goes on so far as to produce too dry a soil for the specific meadow-plants, when, of course, they have to give up their places to others fitted for the new conditions. The most characteristic of the newcomers at this elevation above the sea are principally sun-loving gilias, eriogonæ, and compositæ, and finally forest-trees. Henceforward the obscuring changes are so manifold that the original lake-meadow can be unveiled and seen only by the geologist.

Generally speaking, glacier lakes vanish more slowly than the meadows that succeed them, because, unless very shallow, a greater quantity of material is required to fill up their basins and obliterate them than is required to render the surface of the meadow too high and dry for meadow vegetation. Furthermore, owing to the weathering to which the adjacent rocks are subjected, material of the finer sort, susceptible of transportation by rains and ordinary floods, is more abundant during the meadow period than during the lake period. Yet doubtless many a fine meadow favourably situated exists in almost prime beauty for thousands of years, the process of extinction being exceedingly slow, as we reckon time. This is especially the case with meadows circumstanced like the one we have described – embosomed in deep woods, with the ground rising gently away from it all around, the network of tree-roots in which all the ground is clasped preventing any rapid torrential washing. But, in exceptional cases, beautiful lawns formed with great deliberation are overwhelmed and obliterated at once by the action of land-slips, earthquake avalanches, or extraordinary floods, just as lakes are.

In those glacier meadows that take the places of shallow lakes which have been fed by feeble streams, glacier mud and fine vegetable humus enter largely into the composition of the soil; and on account of the shallowness of this soil, and the seamless, water-tight, undrained condition of the rock-basins, they are usually wet, and therefore occupied by tall grasses and sedges, whose coarse appearance offers a striking contrast to that of the delicate lawn-making kind described above. These shallow-soiled meadows are oftentimes still further roughened and diversified by partially buried moraines and swelling bosses of the bed-rock, which, with the trees and shrubs growing upon them, produce a striking effect as they stand in relief like islands in the grassy level, or sweep across in rugged curves from one forest wall to the other.

Throughout the upper meadow region, wherever water is sufficiently abundant and low in temperature, in basins secure from flood-washing, hand-some bogs are formed with a deep growth of brown and yellow sphagnum picturesquely ruffled with patches of kalmia and ledum which ripen masses of beautiful colour in the autumn. Between these cool, spongy bogs and the dry, flowery meadows there are many interesting varieties which are graduated into one another by the varied conditions already alluded to, forming a series of delightful studies.

HANGING MEADOWS

Another very well-marked and interesting kind of meadow, differing greatly both in origin and appearance from the lake-meadows, is found lying aslant upon moraine-covered hillsides trending in the direction of greatest declivity, waving up and down over rock heaps and ledges, like rich green ribbons brilliantly illumined with tall flowers. They occur both in the alpine and subalpine regions in considerable numbers, and never fail to make telling features in the landscape. They are often a mile or more in length, but never very wide – usually from thirty to fifty yards. When the mountain or canyon side on which they lie dips at the required angle, and other conditions are at the same time favourable, they extend from above the timber line to the bottom of a canyon or lake basin, descending in fine, fluent lines like cas-cades, breaking here and there into a kind of spray on large boulders, or dividing and flowing around on either side of some projecting islet. Some-times a noisy stream goes brawling down through them, and again, scarcely a drop of water is in sight. They owe their existence, however, to streams, whether visible or invisible, the wildest specimens being found where some perennial fountain, as a glacier or snowbank or moraine spring, sends down its waters across a rough sheet of soil in a dissipated web of feeble, oozing rivulets. These conditions give rise to a meadowy vegetation, whose extending roots still more obstruct the free flow of the waters, and tend to dissipate them out over a yet wider area. Thus the moraine soil and the necessary moisture requisite for the better class of meadow plants are at times combined about as perfectly as if smoothly outspread on a level surface. Where the soil happens to be composed of the finer qualities of glacial detritus and the water is not in excess, the nearest approach is made by the vegetation to that of the lake-meadow. But where, as is more commonly the case, the soil is coarse and bouldery, the vegetation is correspondingly rank. Tall, wide-leaved grasses take their places along the sides, and rushes and nodding carices in the wetter portions, mingled with the most beautiful and imposing flowers – orange lilies and larkspurs seven or eight feet high, lupines, senecios, aliums, painted-cups, many species of mimulus and pentstemon, the ample boat-leaved *veratrum alba,* and the magnificent alpine columbine, with spurs an inch and a half long. At an elevation of from seven to nine thousand feet showy flowers frequently form the bulk of the vegetation; then the hanging meadows become hanging gardens.

In rare instances we find an alpine basin the bottom of which is a perfect meadow, and the sides nearly all the way round, rising in gentle curves, are covered with moraine soil, which, being saturated with melting snow from encircling fountains, gives rise to an almost continuous girdle of down-curving meadow vegetation that blends gracefully into the level meadow at the bottom, thus forming a grand, smooth, soft, meadow-lined mountain nest. It is in meadows of this sort that the mountain beaver (*Haplodon*) loves to make his home, excavating snug chambers beneath the sod, digging canals, turning the underground waters from channel to channel to suit his convenience, and feeding the vegetation.

Another kind of meadow or bog occurs on densely timbered hillsides where small perennial streams have been dammed at short intervals by fallen trees. Still another kind is found hanging down smooth, flat precipices, while corresponding leaning meadows rise to meet them.

There are also three kinds of small pot-hole meadows one of which is found along the banks of the main streams, another on the summits of rocky ridges, and the third on glacier pavements, all of them interesting in origin and brimful of plant beauty.

CHAPTER EIGHT

The Forests

THE CONIFEROUS forests of the Sierra are the grandest and most beautiful in the world, and grow in a delightful climate on the most interesting and accessible of mountain-ranges, yet strange to say they are not well known. More than sixty years ago David Douglas, an enthusiastic botanist and tree lover, wandered alone through fine sections of the sugar pine and silver fir woods wild with delight. A few years later, other botanists made short journeys from the coast into the lower woods. Then came the wonderful multitude of miners into the foot-hill zone, mostly blind with gold-dust, soon followed by 'sheepmen,' who, with wool over their eyes, chased their flocks through all the forest belts from one end of the range to the other. Then the Yosemite Valley was discovered, and thousands of admiring tourists passed through sections of the lower and middle zones on their way to that wonderful park, and gained fine glimpses of the sugar pines and silver firs along the edges of dusty trails and roads. But few indeed, strong and free with eyes undimmed with care, have gone far enough and lived long enough with the trees to gain anything like a loving conception of their grandeur and significance as manifested in the harmonies of their distribution and varying aspects throughout the seasons, as they stand arrayed in their winter garb rejoicing in storms, putting forth their fresh leaves in the spring while steaming with resiny fragrance, receiving the thunder-showers of summer, or reposing heavy-laden with ripe cones in the rich sungold of autumn. For knowledge of this kind one must dwell with the trees and grow with them, without any reference to time in the almanac sense.

The distribution of the general forest in belts is readily perceived. These, as we have seen, extend in regular order from one extremity of the range to the other; and however dense and sombre they may appear in general views, neither on the rocky heights nor down in the leafiest hollows will you find anything to remind you of the dank, malarial selvas of the Amazon and Orinoco, with their 'boundless contiguity of shade,' the monotonous uniformity of the Deodar forests of the Himalaya, the Black Forest of Europe, or the dense dark woods of Douglas spruce where rolls the Oregon. The giant pines, and firs, and Sequoias hold their arms open to the sunlight, rising above one another on the mountain benches, marshalled in glorious array, giving forth the utmost expression of grandeur and beauty with inexhaustible variety and harmony.

The inviting openness of the Sierra woods is one of their most distinguishing characteristics. The trees of all the species stand more or less apart in groves, or in small, irregular groups, enabling one to find a way nearly everywhere, along sunny colonnades and through openings that have a smooth, park-like surface, strewn with brown needles and burs. Now you cross a wild garden, now a meadow, now a ferny, willowy stream; and ever and anon you emerge from all the groves and flowers upon some granite pavement or high, bare ridge commanding superb views above the waving sea of evergreens far and near.

One would experience but little difficulty in riding on horseback through the successive belts all the way up to the storm-beaten fringes of the icy peaks. The deep canyons, however, that extend from the axis of the range, cut the belts more or less completely into sections, and prevent the mounted traveller from tracing them lengthwise.

This simple arrangement in zones and sections brings the forest, as a whole, within the comprehension of every observer. The different species are ever found occupying the same relative positions to one another, as controlled by soil, climate and the comparative vigour of each species in taking and holding the ground; and so appreciable are these relations, one need never be at a loss in determining, within a few hundred feet, the elevation above sea-level by the trees alone; for, notwithstanding some of the species range upward for several thousand feet, and all pass one another more or less, yet even those possessing the greatest vertical range are available in this connection, in as much as they take on new forms corresponding with the variations in altitude.

Crossing the treeless plains of the Sacramento and San Joaquin from the west and reaching the Sierra foot-hills, you enter the lower fringe of the forest, composed of small oaks and pines, growing so far apart that not one twentieth of the surface of the ground is in shade at clear noonday. After advancing fifteen or twenty miles, and making an ascent of from two to three thousand feet, you reach the lower margin of the main pine belt, composed of the gigantic sugar pine, yellow pine, incense cedar and Sequoia. Next you come to the magnificent silver fir belt, and lastly to the upper pine belt, which sweeps up the rocky acclivities of the summit peaks in a dwarfed, wavering fringe to a height of from ten to twelve thousand feet.

This general order of distribution, with reference to climate dependent on elevation, is perceived at once, but there are other harmonies, as far-reaching in this connection, that become manifest only after patient observation and study. Perhaps the most interesting of these is the arrangement of the forests in long, curving bands, braided together into lace-like patterns, and outspread in charming variety. The key to this beautiful harmony is the ancient glaciers; where they flowed the trees followed, tracing their wavering courses along canyons, over ridges, and over high, rolling plateaus. The Cedars of Lebanon, says Hooker, are growing upon one of the moraines of an ancient glacier. All the forests of the Sierra are growing upon moraines. But moraines vanish like the glaciers that make them. Every storm that falls upon them wastes them, cutting gaps, disintegrating boulders, and carrying away their decaying material into new formations, until at length they are no longer recognizable by any save students, who trace their transitional forms down from the fresh moraines still in process of formation, through those that are more and more ancient, and more and more obscured by vegetation and all kinds of post-glacial weathering.

Had the ice-sheet that once covered all the range been melted simultaneously from the foot-hills to the summits, the flanks would, of course, have been left almost bare of soil, and these noble forests would be wanting. Many groves and thickets would undoubtedly have grown up on lake and avalanche beds, and many a fair flower and shrub would have found food and a dwelling-place in weathered nooks and crevices, but the Sierra as a whole would have been a bare, rocky desert.

It appears, therefore, that the Sierra forests in general indicate the extent and positions of the ancient moraines as well as they do lines of climate. For forests, properly speaking, cannot exist without soil; and, since the moraines have been deposited upon the solid rock, and only upon elected places, leaving a considerable portion of the old glacial surface bare, we find luxuriant forests of pine and fir abruptly terminated by scored and polished pavements on which not even a moss is growing, though soil alone is required to fit them for the growth of trees 200ft. in height.

THE NUT PINE
(*Pinus Sabiniana*)

The nut pine, the first conifer met in ascending the range from the west, grows only on the torrid foot-hills, seeming to delight in the most ardent sun-heat, like a palm; springing up here and there singly, or in scattered groups of five or six, among scrubby white oaks and thickets of ceanothus and manzanita; its extreme upper limit being about 4,000ft. above the sea, its lower about from 500 to 800ft.

This tree is remarkable for its airy, widespread, tropical appearance, which suggests a region of palms, rather than cool, resiny pine woods. No one would take it at first sight to be a conifer of any kind, it is so loose in habit and so widely branched, and its foliage is so thin and grey. Full-grown specimens are from forty to fifty feet in height, and from two to three feet in diameter. The trunk usually divides into three or four main branches, about fifteen and twenty feet from the ground, which, after bearing away from one another, shoot straight up and form separate summits; while the crooked subordinate branches aspire, and radiate, and droop in ornamental sprays. The slender, greyish-green needles are from eight to twelve inches long, loosely tasselled, and inclined to droop in handsome curves, contrasting with the stiff, dark-coloured trunk and branches in a very striking manner. No other tree of my acquaintance, so substantial in body, is in its foliage so thin and so pervious to the light. The sunbeams sift through even the leafiest trees with scarcely any interruption, and the weary, heated traveller finds but little protection in their shade.

The generous crop of nutritious nuts which the nut pine yields makes it a favourite with Indians, bears and squirrels. The cones are most beautiful, measuring from five to eight inches in length, and not much less in thickness, rich chocolate-brown in colour, and protected by strong, down-curving hooks which terminate the scales. Nevertheless, the little Douglas squirrel can open them. Indians gathering the ripe nuts make a striking picture. The men climb the trees like bears and beat off the cones with sticks, or recklessly cut off the more fruitful branches with hatchets, while the squaws gather the big, generous cones, and roast them until the scales open sufficiently to allow the hard-shelled seeds to be beaten out. Then, in the cool evenings, men, women, and children, with their capacity for dirt greatly increased by the soft resin with which they are all bedraggled, form circles around camp-fires, on the bank of the nearest stream, and lie in easy independence cracking nuts and laughing and chattering, as heedless of the future as the squirrels.

PINUS TUBERCULATA

This curious little pine is found at an elevation of from 1,500 to 3,000ft., growing in close, willowy groves. It is exceedingly slender and graceful in habit, although trees that chance to stand alone outside the groves sweep forth long, curved branches, producing a striking contrast to the ordinary grove form. The foliage is of the same peculiar grey-green colour as that of the nut pine, and is worn about as loosely, so that the body of the tree is scarcely obscured by it.

At the age of seven or eight years it begins to bear cones, not on branches, but on the main axis, and, as they never fall off, the trunk is soon picturesquely dotted with them. The branches also become fruitful after they attain sufficient size. The average size of the older trees is about thirty or forty feet in height, and twelve to fourteen inches in diameter. The cones are about four inches long, exceedingly hard, and covered with a sort of silicious varnish and gum, rendering them impervious to moisture, evidently with a view to the careful preservation of the seeds.

No other conifer in the range is so closely restricted to special localities. It is usually found apart, standing deep in chaparral on sunny hill- and canyonsides where there is but little depth of soil, and, where found at all, it is quite plentiful; but the ordinary traveller, following carriage-roads and trails, may ascend the range many times without meeting it.

While exploring the lower portion of the Merced Canyon I found a lonely miner seeking his fortune in a quartz vein on a wild mountain-side planted with this singular tree. He told me that he called it the hickory pine, because of the whiteness and toughness of the wood. It is so little known, however, that it can hardly be said to have a common name. Most mountaineers refer to it as 'that queer little pine-tree covered all over with burs.' In my studies of this species I found a very interesting and significant group of facts, whose relations will be seen almost as soon as stated:

1. All the trees in the groves I examined, however unequal in size, are of the same age.

2. Those groves are all planted on dry hillsides covered with chaparral, and therefore are liable to be swept by fire.

3. There are no seedlings or saplings in or about the living groves, but there is always a fine, hopeful crop springing up on the ground once occupied by any grove that has been destroyed by the burning of the chaparral.

4. The cones never fall off and never discharge their seeds until the tree or branch to which they belong dies.

A full discussion of the bearing of these facts upon one another would perhaps be out of place here, but I may at least call attention to the admirable adaptation of the tree to the fire-swept regions where alone it is found. After a grove has been destroyed, the ground is at once sown lavishly with all the seeds ripened during its whole life, which seemed to have been carefully held in store with reference to such a calamity. Then a young grove immediately springs up, giving beauty for ashes.

SUGAR PINE
(Pinus Lambertiana)

This is the noblest pine yet discovered, surpassing all others not merely in size but also in kingly beauty and majesty.

It towers sublimely from every ridge and canyon of the range, at an elevation of from three to seven thousand feet above the sea, attaining most perfect development at a height of about 5,000ft.

Full-grown specimens are commonly about 220ft. high, and from six to eight feet in diameter near the ground, though some grand old patriarch is occasionally met that has enjoyed five or six centuries of storms, and attained a thickness of ten or even twelve feet, living on undecayed, sweet and fresh in every fibre.

In southern Oregon, where it was first discovered by David Douglas, on the head waters of the Umpqua, it attains still grander dimensions, one specimen having been measured that was 245ft. high, and over eighteen feet in diameter three feet from the ground. The discoverer was the Douglas for whom the noble Douglas spruce is named, and many other plants which will keep his memory sweet and fresh as long as trees and flowers are loved. His first visit to the Pacific Coast was made in the year 1825. The Oregon Indians watched him with curiosity as he wandered in the woods collecting specimens, and, unlike the fur-gathering strangers they had hitherto known, caring nothing about trade. And when at length they came to know him better, and saw that from year to year the growing things of the woods and prairies were his only objects of pursuit, they called him 'The Man of Grass,' a title of which he was proud. During his first summer on the waters of the Columbia he made Fort Vancouver his headquarters, making excursions from this Hudson Bay post in every direction. On one of his long trips he saw in an Indian's pouch some of the seeds of a new species of pine which he learned were obtained from a very large tree far to the southward of the Columbia. At the end of the next summer, returning to Fort Vancouver, after the setting in of the winter rains, bearing in mind the big pine he had heard of, he set out on an excursion up the Willamette Valley in search of it; and how he fared, and what dangers and hardships he endured, are best told in his own journal, from which I quote as follows:

26 October 1826. Weather dull. Cold and cloudy. When my friends in England are made acquainted with my travels I fear they will think I have told them nothing but my miseries. ... I quitted my camp early in the morning to survey the neighbouring country, leaving my guide to take charge of the horses until my return in the evening. About an hour's walk from the camp I met an Indian, who on perceiving me instantly strung his bow, placed on his left arm a sleeve of raccoon skin and stood on the defensive. Being quite sure that conduct was prompted by fear and not by hostile intentions, the poor fellow having probably never seen such a being as myself before, I laid my gun at my feet on the ground and waved my hand for him to come to me, which he did slowly and with great caution. I then made him place his bow and quiver of arrows beside my gun, and striking a light gave him a smoke out of my own pipe and a present of a few beads. With my pencil I made a rough sketch of the cone and pine tree which I wanted to obtain, and drew his attention to it, when he instantly pointed with his hand to the hills fifteen or twenty miles distant towards the south; and when I expressed my intention of going thither, cheerfully set out to accompany me. At midday I reached my long-wished-for pines, and lost no time in examining them and endeavouring to collect specimens and seeds. New and strange things seldom fail to make strong impressions, and are therefore frequently over-rated; so that, lest I should never see my friends in England to inform them verbally of this most beautiful and immensely grand tree, I shall here state the dimensions of the largest I could find among several that had been blown down by the wind. At 3ft. from the ground its circumference is 57ft. 9in.; at 134ft., 17ft. 5 in.; the extreme length 245ft. . . . As it was impossible either to climb the tree or hew it down, I endeavoured to knock off the cones by firing at them with ball, when the report of my gun brought eight Indians, all of them painted with red earth, armed with bows, arrows, bone-tipped spears and flint-knives. They appeared anything but friendly. I explained to them what I wanted, and they seemed satisfied and sat down to smoke; but presently I saw one of them string his bow, and another sharpen his flint knife with a pair of wooden pincers and suspend it on the wrist of his right hand. Further testimony of their intentions was unnecessary. To save myself by flight was impossible, so without hesitation I stepped back about five paces, cocked my gun, drew one of the pistols out of my belt, and holding it in my left hand and the gun in my right, showed myself determined to fight for my life. As much as possible I endeavoured to preserve my coolness, and thus we stood looking at one another without making any movement or uttering a word for perhaps ten minutes, when one at last, who seemed to be the leader, gave a sign that they wished for some tobacco; this I signified that they should have if they fetched a quantity of cones. They went off immediately in search of them, and no sooner were they all out of sight than I picked up my three cones and some twigs of the trees and made the quickest possible retreat, hurrying back to the camp, which I reached before dusk. . . . I now write lying on the grass with my gun cocked beside me, and penning these lines by the light of my Columbian candle, namely, an ignited piece of rosin-wood.

This grand pine discovered under such exciting circumstances Douglas named in honour of his friend Dr Lambert of London.

The trunk is a smooth, round, delicately tapered shaft, mostly without limbs, and coloured rich purplish-brown, usually enlivened with tufts of yellow lichen. At the top of this magnificent bole, long, curving branches sweep gracefully outward and downward, sometimes forming a palm-like crown, but far more nobly impressive than any palm crown I ever beheld. The needles are about three inches long, finely tempered and arranged in rather close tassels at the ends of slender branchlets that clothe the long, out-sweeping limbs. How well they sing in the wind, and how strikingly harmonious an effect is made by the immense cylindrical cones that depend loosely from the ends of the main branches! No one knows what Nature can do in the way of pine-burs until he has seen those of the sugar pine. They are commonly from fifteen to eighteen inches long, and three in diameter; green, shaded with dark purple on their sunward sides. They are ripe in September and October. Then the flat scales open and the seeds take wing, but the empty cones become still more beautiful and effective, for their diameter is nearly doubled by the spreading of the scales, and their colour changes to a warm yellowish-brown; while they remain swinging on the tree all the following winter and summer, and continue effectively beautiful even on the ground many years after they fall. The wood is deliciously fragrant, and fine in grain and texture; it is of a rich cream-yellow, as if formed of condensed sunbeams. *Retinospora obtusa, Siebold,* the glory of Eastern forests, is called 'Fu-si-no-ki' (tree of the sun) by the Japanese; the sugar pine is the sun-tree of the

Sierra. Unfortunately it is greatly prized by the lumbermen, and in accessible places is always the first tree in the woods to feel their steel. But the regular lumbermen, with their saw-mills, have been less generally destructive thus far than the shingle-makers. The wood splits freely, and there is a constant demand for the shingles. And because an axe, and saw, and frow are all the capital required for the business, many of that drifting, unsteady class of men so large in California engage in it for a few months in the year. When prospectors, hunters, ranch hands, etc., touch their 'bottom dollar' and find themselves out of employment, they say, 'Well, I can at least go to the sugar pines and make shingles.' A few posts are set in the ground, and a single length cut from the first tree felled produces boards enough for the walls and roof of a cabin; all the rest the lumberman makes is for sale, and he is speedily independent. No gardener or haymaker is more sweetly perfumed than these rough mountaineers while engaged in this business, but the havoc they make is most deplorable.

The sugar, from which the common name is derived, is to my taste the better of sweets – better than maple sugar. It exudes from the heartwood, where wounds have been made, either by forest fires, or the axe, in the shape of irregular, crisp, candy-like kernels, which are crowded together in masses of considerable size, like clusters of resin-beads. When fresh, it is perfectly white and delicious, but, because most of the wounds on which it is found have been made by fire, the exuding sap is stained on the charred surface, and the hardened sugar becomes brown. Indians are fond of it, but on account of its laxative properties only small quantities may be eaten. Bears, so fond of sweet things in general, seem never to taste it; at least I have failed to find any trace of their teeth in this connection.

No lover of trees will ever forget his first meeting with the sugar pine nor will he afterward need a poet to call him to 'listen what the pine–tree saith.' In most pine–trees there is a sameness of expression, which, to most people, is apt to become monotonous; for the typical spiry form, however beautiful, affords but little scope for appreciable individual character. The sugar pine is as free from conventionalities of form and motion as any oak. No two are alike, even to the most inattentive observer; and, notwithstanding they are ever tossing out their immense arms in what might seem most extravagant gestures, there is a majesty and repose about them that precludes all possibility of the grotesque, or even picturesque, in their general expression. They are the priests of pines, and seem ever to be addressing the surrounding forest. The yellow pine is found growing with them on warm hillsides, and the white silver fir on cool northern slopes; but, noble as these are, the sugar pine is easily king, and spreads his arms above them in blessing while they rock and wave in sign of recognition. The main branches are sometimes found to be forty feet in length, yet persistently simple, seldom dividing at all, excepting near the end; but anything like a bare cable appearance is prevented by the small, tasselled branchlets that extend all around them; and when these superb limbs sweep out symmetrically on all sides, a crown sixty or seventy feet wide is formed, which, gracefully poised on the summit of the noble shaft, and filled with sunshine, is one of the most glorious forest objects conceivable. Commonly, however, there is a great preponderance of limbs toward the east, away from the direction of the prevailing winds.

No other pine seems to me so unfamiliar and self-contained. In approaching it, we feel as if in the presence of a superior being, and begin to walk with a light step, holding our breath. Then, perchance, while we gaze awe-stricken, along comes a merry squirrel, chattering and laughing, to break the spell, running up the trunk with no ceremony, and gnawing off the cones as if they were made only for him; while the carpenter-woodpecker hammers away at the bark, drilling holes in which to store his winter supply of acorns.

Although so wild and unconventional when full-grown, the sugar pine is a remarkably proper tree in youth. The old is the most original and independent in appearance of all the Sierra evergreens; the young is the most regular – a strict follower of coniferous fashions – slim, erect, with leafy, supple branches kept exactly in place, each tapering in outline and terminating in a spiry point. The successive transitional forms presented between the cautious neatness of youth and bold freedom of maturity offer a delightful study. At the age of fifty or sixty years, the shy, fashionable form begins to be broken up. Specialized branches push out in the most unthought-of places, and bend with the great cones, at once marking individual character, and this being constantly augmented from year to year by the varying action of the sunlight, winds, snow-storms, etc., the individuality of the tree is never again lost in the general forest.

The most constant companion of this species is the yellow pine, and a worthy companion it is. The Douglas spruce, libocedrus, Sequoia, and the white silver fir are also more or less associated with it; but on many deep-soiled mountain-sides, at an elevation of about 5,000ft. above the sea, it forms the bulk of the forest, filling every swell and hollow and down-plunging ravine. The majestic crowns, approaching each other in bold curves, make a glorious canopy through which the tempered sunbeams pour, silvering the needles, and gilding the massive boles, and flowery, park-like ground, into a scene of enchantment.

On the most sunny slopes the white-flowered fragrant chamoebatia is spread like a carpet, brightened during early summer with the crimson sarcodes, the wild rose, and innumerable violets and gilias. Not even in the shadiest nooks will you find any rank, untidy weeds or unwholesome darkness. On the north sides of ridges the boles are more slender, and the ground is mostly occupied by an underbrush of hazel, ceanothus, and flowering dogwood, but never so densely as to prevent the traveller from sauntering where he will; while the crowning branches are never impenetrable to the rays of the sun, and never so interblended as to lose their individuality.

View the forest from beneath or from some commanding ridge-top; each tree presents a study in itself, and proclaims the surpassing grandeur of the species.

YELLOW, OR SILVER PINE
(Pinus ponderosa)

The silver, or yellow, pine, as it is commonly called, ranks second among the pines of the Sierra as a lumber tree, and almost rivals the sugar pine in stature and nobleness of port. Because of its superior powers of enduring variations of climate and soil, it has a more extensive range than any other conifer growing on the Sierra. On the western slope it is first met at an elevation of about 2,000ft., and extends nearly to the upper limit of the timber line. Thence, crossing the range by the lowest passes, it descends to the eastern base, and pushes out for a considerable distance into the hot volcanic plains, growing bravely upon well-watered moraines, gravelly lake basins, arctic ridges and torrid lava-beds; planting itself upon the lips of craters, flourishing vigorously even there, and tossing ripe cones among the ashes and cinders of Nature's hearths.

The average size of full-grown trees on the western slope, where it is associated with the sugar pine, is a little less than 200ft. in height and from five to six feet in diameter, though specimens may easily be found that are considerably larger. I measured one, growing at an elevation of 4,000ft. in the valley of the Merced, that is a few inches over eight feet in diameter, and 220ft. high.

Where there is plenty of free sunshine and other conditions are favourable, it presents a striking contrast in form to the sugar pine, being a symmetrical spire, formed of a straight round trunk, clad with innumerable branches that are divided over and over again. About one half of the trunk is commonly branchless, but where it grows at all close, three fourths or more become naked; the tree presenting then a more slender and elegant shaft than any other tree in the woods. The bark is mostly arranged in massive plates, some of them measuring four or five feet in length by eighteen inches in width, with a thickness of three or four inches, forming a quite marked and distinguishing feature. The needles are of a fine, warm, yellow-green colour, six to eight inches long, firm and elastic, and crowded in handsome, radiant tassels on the upturning ends of the branches. The cones are about three or four inches long, and two and a half wide, growing in close, sessile clusters among the leaves.

The species attains its noblest form in filled-up lake basins, especially in those of the older yosemites, and so prominent a part does it form of their groves that it may well be called the Yosemite pine. Ripe specimens favourably situated are almost always 200ft. or more in height, and the branches clothe the trunk nearly to the ground.

The Jeffrey variety attains its finest development in the northern portion of the range, in the wide basins of the McCloud and Pitt rivers, where it forms magnificent forests scarcely invaded by any other tree. It differs from the ordinary form in size, being only about half as tall, and in its redder and more closely furrowed bark, greyish-green foliage, less divided branches, and larger cones; but intermediate forms come in which make a clear separation impossible, although some botanists regard it as a distinct species. It is this variety that climbs storm-swept ridges, and wanders out among the volcanoes of the Great Basin. Whether exposed to extremes of heat or cold, it is dwarfed like every other tree, and becomes all knots and angles, wholly unlike the majestic forms we have been sketching. Old specimens, bearing cones about as big as pineapples, may sometimes be found clinging to rifted rocks at an elevation of seven or eight thousand feet, whose highest branches scarce reach above one's shoulders.

I have oftentimes feasted on the beauty of these noble trees when they were towering in all their winter grandeur, laden with snow – one mass of bloom; in summer, too, when the brown, staminate clusters hang thick among the shimmering needles, and the big purple burs are ripening in the mellow light; but it is during cloudless wind-storms that these colossal pines are most impressively beautiful. Then they bow like willows, their leaves streaming forward all in one direction, and, when the sun shines upon them at the required angle, entire groves glow as if every leaf were burnished silver. The fall of tropic light on the royal crown of a palm is a truly glorious spectacle, the fervid sun-flood breaking upon the glossy leaves in long lance-rays, like mountain water among boulders. But to me there is something more impressive in the fall of light upon these silver pines. It seems beaten to the finest dust, and is shed off in myriads of minute sparkles that seem to come from the very heart of the trees, as if, like rain falling upon fertile soil, it had been absorbed, to reappear in flowers of light.

This species also gives forth the finest music to the wind. After listening to it in all kinds of winds, night and day, season after season, I think I could approximate to my position on the mountains by this pine-music alone. If you would catch the tones of separate needles, climb a tree. They are well tempered, and give forth no uncertain sound, each standing out, with no interference excepting during heavy gales; then you may detect the click of one needle upon another, readily distinguishable from their free, wing-like hum. Some idea of their temper may be drawn from the fact that, notwithstanding they are so long, the vibrations that give rise to the peculiar shimmering of the light are made at the rate of about two hundred and fifty per minute.

When a sugar pine and one of this species equal in size are observed together, the latter is seen to be far more simple in manners, more lithely graceful, and its beauty is of a kind more easily appreciated; but then, it is, on the other hand, much less dignified and original in demeanour. The silver pine seems eager to shoot aloft. Even while it is drowsing in autumn sun-gold, you may still detect a skyward aspiration. But the sugar pine seems too unconsciously noble, and too complete in every way, to leave room for even a heavenward care.

DOUGLAS SPRUCE
(*Pseudotsuga Douglasii*)

This tree is the king of the spruces, as the sugar pine is king of pines. It is by far the most majestic spruce I ever beheld in any forest, and one of the largest and longest lived of the giants that flourish throughout the main pine belt, often attaining a height of nearly 200ft, and a diameter of six or seven. Where the growth is not too close, the strong, spreading branches come more than halfway down the trunk, and these are hung with innumerable slender, swaying sprays, that are handsomely feathered with the short leaves which radiate at right angles all around them. This vigorous spruce is ever beautiful, welcoming the mountain winds and the snow as well as the mellow summer light, and maintaining its youthful freshness undiminished from century to century through a thousand storms.

It makes its finest appearance in the months of June and July. The rich brown buds with which its sprays are tipped swell and break about this time, revealing the young leaves, which at first are bright yellow, making the tree appear as if covered with gay blossoms; while the pendulous bracted cones with their shell-like scales are a constant adornment.

The young trees are mostly gathered into beautiful family groups, each sapling exquisitely symmetrical. The primary branches are whorled regularly around the axis, generally in fives, while each is draped with long, feathery sprays, that descend in curves as free and as finely drawn as those of falling water.

In Oregon and Washington, it grows in dense forests, growing tall and mast-like to a height of 300ft., and is greatly prized as a lumber tree. But in the Sierra it is scattered among other trees, or forms small groves, seldom ascending higher than 5,500ft., and never making what would be called a forest. It is not particular in its choice of soil – wet or dry, smooth or rocky, it makes out to live well on them all. Two of the largest specimens I have measured are in Yosemite Valley, one of which is more than eight feet in diameter, and is growing upon the terminal moraine of the residual glacier that occupied the South Fork Canyon; the other is nearly as large, growing upon angular blocks of granite that have been shaken from the precipitous front of the Liberty Cap near the Nevada Fall. No other tree seems so capable of adapting itself to earthquake taluses, and many of these rough boulder-slopes are occupied by it almost exclusively, especially in yosemite gorges moistened by the spray of waterfalls.

INCENSE CEDAR
(Libocedrus decurrens)

The incense cedar is another of the giants quite generally distributed throughout this portion of the forest, without exclusively occupying any considerable area, or even making extensive groves. It ascends to about 5,000ft. on the warmer hillsides, and reaches the climate most congenial to it at about from 3,000 to 4,000ft., growing vigorously at this elevation on all kinds of soil, and in particular it is capable of enduring more moisture about its roots than any of its companions, excepting only the Sequoia.

The largest specimens are about 150ft. high, and seven feet in diameter. The bark is brown, of a singularly rich tone very attractive to artists, and the foliage is tinted with a warmer yellow than that of any other evergreen in the woods. Casting your eye over the general forest from some ridge-top, the colour alone of its spiry summits is sufficient to identify it in any company.

In youth, say up to the age of seventy or eighty years, no other tree forms so strictly tapered a cone from top to bottom. The branches swoop outward and downward in bold curves, excepting the younger ones near the top, which aspire, while the lowest droop to the ground, and all spread out in flat, ferny plumes, beautifully fronded, and imbricated upon one another. As it becomes older, it grows strikingly irregular and picturesque. Large special branches put out at right angles from the trunk, form big, stubborn elbows, and then shoot up parallel with the axis. Very old trees are usually dead at the top, the main axis protruding above ample masses of green plumes, grey and lichen-covered, and drilled full of acorn holes by the woodpeckers. The plumes are exceedingly beautiful; no waving fern-frond in shady dell is more un-reservedly beautiful in form and texture, or half so inspiring in colour and spicy fragrance. In its prime, the whole tree is thatched with them, so that they shed off rain and snow like a roof, making fine mansions for storm-bound birds and mountaineers. But if you would see the *Libocedrus* in all its glory, you must go to the woods in winter. Then it is laden with myriads of four-sided staminate cones about the size of wheat grains – winter wheat – producing a golden tinge, and forming a noble illustration of Nature's im-mortal vigour and virility. The fertile cones are about three fourths of an inch long, borne on the outside of the plumy branchlets, where they serve to enrich still more the surpassing beauty of this grand winter-blooming goldenrod.

WHITE SILVER FIR
(*Abies concolor*)

We come now to the most regularly planted of all the main forest belts, composed almost exclusively of two noble firs – *A. concolor* and *A. magnifica*. It extends with no marked interruption for 450 miles, at an elevation of from 5,000 to nearly 9,000ft. above the sea. In its youth *A. concolor* is a charmingly symmetrical tree with branches regularly whorled in level collars around its whitish-grey axis, which terminates in a strong, hopeful shoot. The leaves are in two horizontal rows, along branchlets that commonly are less than eight years old, forming handsome plumes, pinnated like the fronds of ferns. The cones are greyish-green when ripe, cylindrical, about from three to four inches long by one and a half to two inches wide, and stand upright on the upper branches.

Full-grown trees, favourably situated as to soil and exposure, are about 200ft. high, and five or six feet in diameter near the ground, though larger specimens are by no means rare.

As old age creeps on, the bark becomes rougher and greyer, the branches lose their exact regularity, many are snow-bent or broken off, and the main axis often becomes double or otherwise irregular from accidents to the ter-minal bud or shoot; but throughout all the vicissitudes of its life on the mountains, come what may, the noble grandeur of the species is patent to every eye.

MAGNIFICENT SILVER FIR, OR RED FIR
(*Abies magnifica*)

This is the most charmingly symmetrical of all the giants of the Sierra woods, far surpassing its companion species in this respect, and easily distinguished from it by the purplish-red bark, which is also more closely furrowed than that of the white, and by its larger cones, more regularly whorled and fronded branches, and by its leaves, which are shorter, and grow all around the branchlets and point upward.

In size, these two silver firs are about equal, the *magnifica* perhaps a little the taller. Specimens from 200 to 250ft. high are not rare on well-ground moraine soil, at an elevation of from 7,500 to 8,500ft. above sea-level. The largest that I measured stands back three miles from the brink of the north wall of Yosemite Valley. Fifteen years ago it was 240ft. high, with a diameter of a little more than five feet.

Happy the man with the freedom and the love to climb one of these superb trees in full flower and fruit. How admirable the forest-work of Nature is then seen to be, as one makes his way up through the midst of the broad, fronded branches, all arranged in exquisite order around the trunk, like the whorled leaves of lilies, and each branch and branchlet about as strictly pinnate as the most symmetrical fern-frond. The staminate cones are seen growing straight downward from the under side of the young branches in lavish profusion, making fine purple clusters amid the greyish-green foliage. On the topmost branches the fertile cones are set firmly on end like small casks. They are about six inches long, three wide, covered with a fine grey down, and streaked with crystal balsam that seems to have been poured upon each cone from above.

Both the silver firs live 250 years or more when the conditions about them are at all favourable. Some venerable patriarch may often be seen, heavily storm-marked, towering in severe majesty above the rising generation, with a protecting grove of saplings pressing close around his feet, each dressed with such loving care that not a leaf seems wanting. Other companies are made up of trees near the prime of life, exquisitely harmonized to one another in form and gesture, as if Nature had culled them one by one with nice discrimination from all the rest of the woods.

It is from this tree, called red fir by the lumberman, that mountaineers always cut boughs to sleep on when they are so fortunate as to be within its limits. Two rows of the plushy branches overlapping along the middle, and a crescent of smaller plumes mixed with ferns and flowers for a pillow, form the very best bed imaginable. The essences of the pressed leaves seem to fill every pore of one's body, the sounds of falling water make a soothing hush, while the spaces between the grand spires afford noble openings through which to gaze dreamily into the starry sky. Even in the matter of sensuous ease, any combination of cloth, steel springs, and feathers seems vulgar in comparison.

The fir woods are delightful sauntering-grounds at any time of year, but most so in autumn. Then the noble trees are hushed in the hazy light, and drip with balsam; the cones are ripe, and the seeds, with their ample purple wings, mottle the air like flocks of butterflies; while deer feeding in the flowery openings between the groves, and birds and squirrels in the branches, make a pleasant stir which enriches the deep, brooding calm of the wilderness, and gives a peculiar impressiveness to every tree. No wonder the enthusiastic Douglas went wild with joy when he first discovered this species. Even in the Sierra, where so many noble evergreens challenge admiration, we linger among these colossal firs with fresh love, and extol their beauty again and again, as if no other in the world could henceforth claim our regard.

It is in these woods the great granite domes rise that are so striking and characteristic a feature of the Sierra. And here too we find the best of the garden meadows. They lie level on the tops of the dividing ridges, or sloping on the sides of them, embedded in the magnificent forest. Some of these meadows are in great part occupied by *Veratrum alba,* which here grows rank and tall, with boat-shaped leaves thirteen inches long and twelve inches wide, ribbed like those of cypripedium. Columbine grows on the drier margins with tall larkspurs and lupines waist-deep in grasses and sedges; several species of castilleia also make a bright show in beds of blue and white violets and daisies. But the glory of these forest meadows is a lily – *L. parvum.* The flowers are orange-coloured and quite small, the smallest I ever saw of the true lilies; but it is showy nevertheless, for it is seven to eight feet high and waves magnificent racemes of ten to twenty flowers or more over one's head, while it stands out in the open ground with just enough grass and other plants about it to make a fringe for its feet and show it off to best advantage.

A dry spot a little way back from the margin of a silver fir lily garden makes a glorious camp-ground, especially where the slope is toward the east and opens a view of the distant peaks along the summit of the range. The tall lilies are brought forward in all their glory by the light of your blazing camp-fire, relieved against the outer darkness, and the nearest of the trees with their whorled branches tower above you like larger lilies, and the sky seen through the garden opening seems one vast meadow of white lily stars.

In the morning everything is joyous and bright, the delicious purple of the dawn changes softly to daffodil yellow and white; while the sunbeams pouring through the passes between the peaks give a margin of gold to each of them. Then the spires of the firs in the hollows of the middle region catch the glow, and your camp grove is filled with light. The birds begin to stir, seeking sunny branches on the edge of the meadow for sun-baths after the cold night, and looking for their breakfasts, every one of them as fresh as a lily and as charmingly arrayed. Innumerable insects begin to dance, the deer withdraw from the open glades and ridge-tops to their leafy hiding-places in the chaparral, the flowers open and straighten their petals as the dew vanishes, every pulse beats high, every life-cell rejoices, the very rocks seem to tingle with life, and God is felt brooding over everything great and small.

BIG TREE
(*Sequoia gigantea*)

Between the heavy pine and silver fir belts we find the Big Tree, the king of all the conifers in the world, 'the noblest of a noble race.' It extends in a widely interrupted belt from a small grove on the middle fork of the American River to the head of Deer Creek, a distance of about 260 miles, the northern limit being near the thirty-ninth parallel, the southern a little below the thirty-sixth, and the elevation of the belt above the sea varies from about 5,000 to 8,000ft. From the American River grove to the forest on King's River the species occurs only in small isolated groups so sparsely distributed along the belt that three of the gaps in it are from forty to sixty miles wide. But from Kings River southward the Sequoia is not restricted to mere groves, but extends across the broad rugged basins of the Kaweah and Tule rivers in noble forests, a distance of nearly seventy miles, the continuity of this part of the belt being broken only by deep canyons. The Fresno, the largest of the northern groves, occupies an area of three or four square miles, a short distance to the southward of the famous Mariposa Grove. Along the bevelled rim of the canyon of the south fork of Kings River there is a majestic forest of Sequoia about six miles long by two wide. This is the northernmost assemblage of Big Trees that may fairly be called a forest. Descending the precipitous divide between the Kings River and Kaweah you enter the grand forests that form the main continuous portion of the belt. Advancing southward the giants become more and more irrepressibly exuberant, heaving their massive crowns into the sky from every ridge and slope, and waving onward in graceful compliance with the complicated topography of the region. The finest of the Kaweah section of the belt is on the broad ridge between Marble Creek and the middle fork, and extends from the granite headlands overlooking the hot plains to within a few miles of the cool glacial fountains of the summit peaks. The extreme upper limit of the belt is reached between the middle and south forks of the Kaweah at an elevation of 8,400ft. But the finest block of Big Tree forest in the entire belt is on the north fork of Tule River. In the northern groves there are comparatively few young trees or saplings. But here for every old, storm-stricken giant there are many in all the glory of prime vigour, and for each of these a crowd of eager, hopeful young trees and saplings growing heartily on moraines, rocky ledges, along watercourses, and in the moist alluvium of meadows, seemingly in hot pursuit of eternal life.

But though the area occupied by the species increases so much from north to south there is no marked increase in the size of the trees. A height of 275ft. and a diameter near the ground of about twenty feet is perhaps about the average size of full-grown trees favourably situated; specimens twenty-five feet in diameter are not very rare, and a few are nearly 300ft. high. In the Calaveras Grove there are four trees over 300ft. in height, the tallest of which by careful measurement is 325ft. The largest I have yet met in the course of my explorations is a majestic old scarred monument in the Kings River forest. It is 35ft. 8in. in diameter inside the bark four feet from the ground. Under the most favourable conditions these giants probably live 5,000 years or more, though few of even the larger trees are more than half as old. I never saw a Big Tree that had died a natural death; barring accidents they seem to be immortal, being exempt from all the diseases that afflict and kill other trees. Unless destroyed by man, they live on indefinitely until burned, smashed by lightning, or cast down by storms, or by the giving way of the ground on which they stand. The age of one that was felled in the Calaveras Grove, for the sake of having its stump for a dancing-floor, was about 1,300 years, and its diameter, measured across the stump, 24ft. inside the bark. Another that was cut down in the Kings River forest was about the same size, but nearly a thousand years older (2,200 years), though not a very old-looking tree. It was felled to procure a section for exhibition, and thus an opportunity was given to count its annual rings of growth. The colossal scarred monument in the Kings River forest mentioned above is burned half through, and I spent a day in making an estimate of its age, clearing away the charred surface with an axe and carefully counting the annual rings with the aid of a pocket-lens. The wood-rings in the section I laid bare were so involved and contorted in some places that I was not able to determine its age exactly, but I counted over 4,000 rings, which showed that this tree was in its prime, swaying in the Sierra winds, when Christ walked the earth. No other tree in the world, as far as I know, has looked down on so many centuries as the Sequoia, or opens such impressive and suggestive views into history.

So exquisitely harmonious and finely balanced are even the very mightiest of these monarchs of the woods in all their proportions and circumstances there never is anything overgrown or monstrous-looking about them. On coming in sight of them for the first time, you are likely to say, 'Oh, see what beautiful, noble-looking trees are towering there among the firs and pines!' – their grandeur being in the mean time in great part invisible, but to the living eye it will be manifested sooner or later, stealing slowly on the senses, like the grandeur of Niagara, or the lofty Yosemite domes. Their great size is hidden from the inexperienced observer as long as they are seen at a distance in one harmonious view. When, however, you approach them and walk round them, you begin to wonder at their colossal size and seek a measuring-rod. These giants bulge considerably at the base, but not more than is required for beauty and safety; and the only reason that this bulging seems in some cases excessive is that only a comparatively small section of the shaft is seen at once in near views. One that I measured in the Kings River forest was 25ft. in diameter at the ground, and 10ft. in diameter 200ft. above the ground, showing that the taper of the trunk as a whole is charmingly fine. And when you stand back far enough to see the massive columns from the swelling instep to the lofty summit dissolving in a dome of verdure, you rejoice in the unrivalled display of combined grandeur and beauty. About 100ft. or more of the trunk is usually branchless, but its massive simplicity is relieved by the bark furrows, which instead of making an irregular network run evenly parallel, like the fluting of an architectural column, and to some extent by tufts of slender sprays that wave lightly in the winds and cast flecks of shade, seeming to have been pinned on here and there for the sake of beauty only. The young trees have slender simple branches down to the ground, put on with strict regularity, sharply aspiring at the top, horizontal about half-way down, and drooping in handsome curves at the base. By the time the sapling is 500 or 600 years old this spiry, feathery, juvenile habit merges into the firm, rounded dome form of middle age, which in turn takes on the eccentric picturesqueness of old age. No other tree in the Sierra forest has foliage so densely massed or presents outlines so firmly drawn and so steadily subordinate to a special type. A knotty ungovernable-looking branch five to eight feet thick may be seen pushing out abruptly from the smooth trunk, as if sure to throw the regular curve into confusion, but as soon as the general outline is reached it stops short and dissolves in spreading bosses of law-abiding sprays, just as if every tree were growing beneath some huge, invisible bell-glass, against whose sides every branch was being pressed and moulded, yet somehow indulging in so many small departures from the regular form that there is still an appearance of freedom.

The foliage of the saplings is dark bluish-green in colour, while the older trees ripen to a warm brownish-yellow tint like libocedrus. The bark is rich cinnamon-brown, purplish in young trees and in shady portions of the old, while the ground is covered with brown leaves and burs forming colour-masses of extraordinary richness, not to mention the flowers and underbrush that rejoice about them in their seasons. Walk the Sequoia woods at any time of year and you will say they are the most beautiful and majestic on earth. Beautiful and impressive contrasts meet you everywhere: the colours of tree and flower, rock and sky, light and shade, strength and frailty, endurance and evanescence, tangles of supple hazel-bushes, tree-pillars about as rigid as granite domes, roses and violets, the smallest of their kind, blooming around the feet of the giants, and rugs of the lowly chamæbatia where the sunbeams fall. Then in winter the trees themselves break forth in bloom, myriads of small four-sided staminate cones crowd the ends of the slender sprays, colouring the whole tree, and when ripe dusting the air and the ground with golden pollen. The fertile cones are bright grass-green, measuring about two inches in length by one and a half in thickness, and are made up of about forty firm rhomboidal scales densely packed, with from five to eight seeds at the base of each. A single cone, therefore, contains from 200 to 300 seeds, which are about a fourth of an inch long by three sixteenths wide, including a thin, flat margin that makes them go glancing and wavering in their fall like a boy's kite. The fruitfulness of Sequoia may be illustrated by two specimen branches one and a half and two inches in diameter on which I counted 480 cones. No other Sierra conifer produces nearly so many seeds. Millions are ripened annually by a single tree, and in a fruitful year the product of one of the northern groves would be enough to plant all the mountain-ranges of the world. Nature takes care, however, that not one seed in a million shall germinate at all, and of those that do perhaps not one in ten thousand is suffered to live through the many vicissitudes of storm, drought, fire and snow-crushing that beset their youth.

The Douglas squirrel is the happy harvester of most of the Sequoia cones. Out of every hundred perhaps ninety fall to his share, and unless cut off by his ivory sickle they shake out their seeds and remain on the tree for many years. Watching the squirrels at their harvest work in the Indian summer is one of the most delightful diversions imaginable. The woods are calm and the ripe colours are blazing in all their glory; the cone-laden trees stand motionless in the warm, hazy air, and you may see the crimson-crested woodcock, the prince of Sierra woodpeckers, drilling some dead limb or fallen trunk with his bill, and ever and anon filling the glens with his happy cackle. The humming-bird, too, dwells in these noble woods, and may oftentimes be seen glancing among the flowers or resting wing-weary on some leafless twig; here also are the familiar robin of the orchards, and the brown and grizzly bears so obviously fitted for these majestic solitudes; and the Douglas squirrel, making more hilarious, exuberant, vital stir than all the bears, birds, and humming wings together.

As soon as any accident happens to the crown of these Sequoias, such as being stricken off by lightning or broken by storms, then the branches beneath the wound, no matter how situated, seem to be excited like a colony of bees that have lost their queen, and become anxious to repair the damage. Limbs that have grown outward for centuries at right angles to the trunk begin to turn upward to assist in making a new crown, each speedily assuming the special form of true summits. Even in the case of mere stumps, burned half through, some mere ornamental tuft will try to go aloft and do its best as a leader in forming a new head.

Groups of two or three of these grand trees are often found standing close together, the seeds from which they sprang having probably grown on ground cleared for their reception by the fall of a large tree of a former generation. These patches of fresh, mellow soil beside the upturned roots of the fallen giant may be from forty to sixty feet wide, and they are speedily occupied by seedlings. Out of these seedling-thickets perhaps two or three may become trees, forming those close groups called 'three graces,' 'loving couples,' etc. For even supposing that the trees should stand twenty or thirty feet apart while young, by the time they are full-grown their trunks will touch and crowd against each other and even appear as one in some cases.

It is generally believed that this grand Sequoia was once far more widely distributed over the Sierra; but after long and careful study I have come to the conclusion that it never was, at least since the close of the glacial period, because a diligent search along the margins of the groves, and in the gaps between, fails to reveal a single trace of its previous existence beyond its present bounds. Notwithstanding, I feel confident that if every Sequoia in the range were to die to-day, numerous monuments of their existence would remain, of so imperishable a nature as to be available for the student more than ten thousand years hence.

In the first place we might notice that no species of coniferous tree in the range keeps its individuals so well together as Sequoia; a mile is perhaps the greatest distance of any straggler from the main body, and all of those stragglers that have come under my observation are young, instead of old monumental trees, relics of a more extended growth.

Again, Sequoia trunks frequently endure for centuries after they fall. I have a specimen block, cut from a fallen trunk, which is hardly distinguishable from specimens cut from living trees, although the old trunk-fragment from which it was derived has lain in the damp forest more than 380 years, probably thrice as long. The time measure in the case is simply this: when the ponderous trunk to which the old vestige belonged fell, it sunk itself into the ground, thus making a long, straight ditch, and in the middle of this ditch a silver fir is growing that is now four feet in diameter and 380 years old, as determined by cutting it half through and counting the rings, thus demonstrating that the remnant of the trunk that made the ditch has lain on the ground *more* than 380 years. For it is evident that to find the whole time, we must add to the 380 years the time that the vanished portion of the trunk lay in the ditch before being burned out of the way, plus the time that passed before the seed from which the monumental fir sprang fell into the prepared soil and took root. Now, because Sequoia trunks are never wholly consumed in one forest fire, and those fires recur only at considerable intervals, and because Sequoia ditches after being cleared are often left unplanted for centuries, it becomes evident that the trunk remnant in question may probably have lain a thousand years or more. And this instance is by no means a rare one.

But admitting that upon those areas supposed to have been once covered with Sequoia every tree may have fallen, and every trunk may have been burned or buried, leaving not a remnant, many of the ditches made by the fall of the ponderous trunks, and the bowls made by their upturning roots, would remain patent for thousands of years after the last vestige of the trunks that made them had vanished. Much of this ditch-writing would no doubt be quickly effaced by the flood-action of overflowing streams and rain-washing; but no inconsiderable portion would remain enduringly engraved on ridge-tops beyond such destructive action; for, where all the conditions are favourable, it is almost imperishable. *Now these historic ditches and root bowls occur in all the present Sequoia groves and forests, but as far as I have observed, not the faintest vestige of one presents itself outside of them.*

We therefore conclude that the area covered by Sequoia has not been diminished during the last eight or ten thousand years, and probably not at all in post-glacial times.

Is the species verging to extinction? What are its relations to climate, soil and associated trees?

All the phenomena bearing on these questions also throw light, as we shall endeavour to show, upon the peculiar distribution of the species, and sustain the conclusion already arrived at on the question of extension.

In the northern groups, as we have seen, there are few young trees or saplings growing up around the failing old ones to perpetuate the race, and in as much as those aged Sequoias, so nearly childless, are the only ones commonly known, the species, to most observers, seems doomed to speedy extinction, as being nothing more than an expiring remnant, vanquished in the so-called struggle for life by pines and firs that have driven it into its last strongholds in moist glens where climate is exceptionally favourable. But the language of the majestic continuous forests of the south creates a very different impression. No tree of all the forest is more enduringly established in concordance with climate and soil. It grows heartily everywhere – on moraines, rocky ledges, along watercourses, and in the deep, moist alluvium of meadows, with a multitude of seedlings and saplings crowding up around the aged, seemingly abundantly able to maintain the forest in prime vigour. For every old storm-stricken tree, there is one or more in all the glory of prime; and for each of these many young trees and crowds of exuberant saplings. So that if all the trees of any section of the main Sequoia forest were ranged together according to age, a very promising curve would be presented, all the way up from last year's seedlings to giants, and with the young and middle-aged portion of the curve many times longer than the old portion. Even as far north as the Fresno, I counted 536 saplings and seedlings growing promisingly upon a piece of rough avalanche soil not exceeding two acres in area. This soil bed is about seven years old, and has been seeded almost simultaneously by pines, firs, libocedrus and Sequoia, presenting a simple and instructive illustration of the struggle for life among the rival species; and it was interesting to note that the conditions thus far affecting them have enabled the young Sequoias to gain a marked advantage.

In every instance like the above I have observed that the seedling Sequoia is capable of growing on both drier and wetter soil than its rivals, but requires more sunshine than they; the latter fact being clearly shown wherever a sugar pine or fir is growing in close contact with a Sequoia of about equal age and size, and equally exposed to the sun; the branches of the latter in such cases are always less leafy. Toward the south, however, where the Sequoia becomes *more* exuberant and numerous, the rival trees become *less* so; and where they mix with Sequoias, they mostly grow up beneath them, like slender grasses among stalks of Indian corn. Upon a bed of sandy flood-soil I counted ninety-four Sequoias, from one to twelve feet high, on a patch of ground once occupied by four large sugar pines which lay crumbling beneath them – an instance of conditions which have enabled Sequoias to crowd out the pines.

I also noted eighty-six vigorous saplings upon a piece of fresh ground prepared for their reception by fire. Thus fire, the great destroyer of Sequoia, also furnishes bare virgin ground, one of the conditions essential for its growth from the seed. Fresh ground is, however, furnished in sufficient quantities for the constant renewal of the forests without fire, viz., by the fall of old trees. The soil is thus upturned and mellowed, and many trees are planted for every one that falls. Land-slips and floods also give rise to bare virgin ground; and a tree now and then owes its existence to a burrowing wolf or squirrel, but the most regular supply of fresh soil is furnished by the fall of aged trees.

The climatic changes in progress in the Sierra, bearing on the tenure of tree life, are entirely misapprehended, especially as to the time and the means employed by Nature in effecting them. It is constantly asserted in a vague way that the Sierra was vastly wetter than now, and that the increasing drought will of itself extinguish Sequoia, leaving its ground to other trees supposed capable of flourishing in a drier climate. But that Sequoia can and does grow on as dry ground as any of its present rivals, is manifest in a thousand places. 'Why, then,' it will be asked, 'are Sequoias always found in greatest abundance in well-watered places where streams are exceptionally abundant?' Simply because a growth of Sequoias creates those streams. The thirsty mountaineer knows well that in every Sequoia grove he will find running water, but it is a mistake to suppose that the water is the cause of the grove being there; on the contrary, the grove is the cause of the water being there. Drain off the water and the trees will remain, but cut off the trees, and the streams will vanish. Never was cause more completely mistaken for effect than in the case of these related phenomena of Sequoia woods and perennial streams, and I confess that at first I shared in the blunder.

When attention is called to the method of Sequoia stream-making, it will be apprehended at once. The roots of this immense tree fill the ground, forming a thick sponge that absorbs and holds back the rains and melting snows, only allowing them to ooze and flow gently. Indeed, every fallen leaf and rootlet, as well as long clasping root, and prostrate trunk, may be regarded as a dam hoarding the bounty of storm-clouds, and dispensing it as blessings all through the summer, instead of allowing it to go headlong in short-lived floods. Evaporation is also checked by the dense foliage to a greater extent than by any other Sierra tree, and the air is entangled in masses and broad sheets that are quickly saturated; while thirsty winds are not allowed to go sponging and licking along the ground.

So great is the retention of water in many places in the main belt, that bogs and meadows are created by the killing of the trees. A single trunk falling across a stream in the woods forms a dam 200ft. long, and from ten to thirty feet high, giving rise to a pond which kills the trees within its reach. These dead trees fall in turn, thus making a clearing, while sediments gradually accumulate changing the pond into a bog, or meadow, for a growth of carices and sphagnum. In some instances a series of small bogs or meadows rise above one another on a hillside, which are gradually merged into one another, forming sloping bogs, or meadows, which make striking features of Sequoia woods, and since all the trees that have fallen into them have been preserved, they contain records of the generations that have passed since they began to form.

Since, then, it is a fact that thousands of Sequoias are growing thriftily on what is termed dry ground, and even clinging like mountain pines to rifts in granite precipices; and since it has also been shown that the extra moisture found in connection with the denser growths is an effect of their presence, instead of a cause of their presence, then the notions as to the former extension of the species and its near approach to extinction, based upon its supposed dependence on greater moisture, are seen to be erroneous.

The decrease in the rain- and snowfall since the close of the glacial period in the Sierra is much less than is commonly guessed. The highest post-glacial watermarks are well preserved in all the upper river channels, and they are not greatly higher than the spring floodmarks of the present; showing conclusively that no extraordinary decrease has taken place in the volume of the upper tributaries of post-glacial Sierra streams since they came into existence. But in the meantime, eliminating all this complicated question of climatic change, the plain fact remains that *the present rain- and snowfall is abundantly sufficient for the luxuriant growth of Sequoia forests.* Indeed, all my observations tend to show that in a prolonged drought the sugar pines and firs would perish before the Sequoia, not alone because of the greater longevity of individual trees, but because the species can endure more drought, and make the most of whatever moisture falls.

Again, if the restriction and irregular distribution of the species can be interpreted as a result of the desiccation of the range, then instead of increasing as it does in individuals toward the south where the rainfall is less, it should diminish.

If, then, the peculiar distribution of Sequoia has not been governed by superior conditions of soil as to fertility or moisture, by what has it been governed?

In the course of my studies I observed that the northern groves, the only ones I was at first acquainted with, were located on just those portions of the general forest soil-belt that were first laid bare toward the close of the glacial period when the ice-sheet began to break up into individual glaciers. And while searching the wide basin of the San Joaquin, and trying to account for the absence of Sequoia where every condition seemed favourable for its growth, it occurred to me that this remarkable gap in the Sequoia belt is located exactly in the basin of the vast ancient *mer de glace* of the San Joaquin and Kings River basins, which poured its frozen floods to the plain, fed by the snows that fell on more than fifty miles of the summit. I then perceived that the next great gap in the belt to the northward, forty miles wide, extending between the Calaveras and Tuolumne groves, occurs in the basin of the great ancient *mer de glace* of the Tuolumne and Stanislaus basins, and that the smaller gap between the Merced and Mariposa groves occurs in the basin of the smaller glacier of the Merced. *The wider the ancient glacier, the wider the corresponding gap in the Sequoia belt.*

Finally, pursuing my investigations across the basins of the Kaweah and Tule, I discovered that the Sequoia belt attained its greatest development just where, owing to the topographical peculiarities of the region, the ground had been most perfectly protected from the main ice-rivers that continued to pour past from the summit fountains long after the smaller local glaciers had been melted.

Taking now a general view of the belt, beginning at the south, we see that the majestic ancient glaciers were shed off right and left down the valleys of Kern and Kings Rivers by the lofty protective spurs outspread embracingly above the warm Sequoia-filled basins of the Kaweah and Tule. Then, next northward, occurs the wide Sequoia-less channel, or basin, of the ancient San Joaquin and Kings River *mer de glace*; then the warm, protected spots of Fresno and Mariposa groves; then the Sequoia-less channel of the ancient Merced glacier; next the warm, sheltered ground of the Merced and Tuolumne groves; then the Sequoia-less channel of the grand ancient *mer de glace* of the Tuolumne and Stanislaus; then the warm old ground of the Calaveras and Stanislaus groves. It appears, therefore, that just where, at a certain period in the history of the Sierra, the glaciers were not, there the Sequoia is, and just where the glaciers were, there the Sequoia is not.

What the other conditions may have been that enabled Sequoia to establish itself upon these oldest and warmest portions of the main glacial soil-belt, I cannot say. I might venture to state, however, in this connection, that since the Sequoia forests present a more and more ancient aspect as they extend southward, I am inclined to think that the species was distributed from the south, while the sugar pine, its great rival in the northern groves, seems to have come around the head of the Sacramento valley and down the Sierra from the north; consequently, when the Sierra soil-beds were first thrown open to pre-emption on the melting of the ice-sheet, the Sequoia may have established itself along the available portions of the south half of the range prior to the arrival of the sugar pine, while the sugar pine took possession of the north half prior to the arrival of Sequoia.

But however much uncertainty may attach to this branch of the question, there are no obscuring shadows upon the grand general relationship we have pointed out between the present distribution of Sequoia and the ancient glaciers of the Sierra. And when we bear in mind that all the present forests of the Sierra are young, growing on moraine soil recently deposited, and that the flank of the range itself, with all its landscapes, is new-born, recently sculptured, and brought to the light of day from beneath the ice mantle of the glacial winter, then a thousand lawless mysteries disappear, and broad harmonies take their places.

But although all the observed phenomena bearing on the post-glacial history of this colossal tree point to the conclusion that it never was more widely distributed on the Sierra since the close of the glacial epoch; that its present forests are scarcely past prime, if, indeed, they have reached prime; that the post-glacial day of the species is probably not half done; yet, when from a wider outlook the vast antiquity of the genus is considered, and its ancient richness in species and individuals; comparing our Sierra Giant and *Sequoia sempervirens* of the Coast Range, the only other living species of Sequoia, with the twelve fossil species already discovered and described by Heer and Lesquereux, some of which seemed to have flourished over vast areas in the Arctic regions and in Europe and our own territories, during tertiary and cretaceous times – then indeed it becomes plain that our two surviving species, restricted to narrow belts within the limits of California, are mere remnants of the genus, both as to species and individuals, and that they probably are verging to extinction. But the verge of a period beginning in cretaceous times may have a breadth of tens of thousands of years, not to mention the possible existence of conditions calculated to multiply and re-extend both species and individuals. This, however, is a branch of the question into which I do not now purpose to enter.

In studying the fate of our forest king, we have thus far considered the action of purely natural causes only; but, unfortunately, *man* is in the woods, and waste and pure destruction are making rapid headway. If the importance of forests were at all understood, even from an economic standpoint, their preservation would call forth the most watchful attention of government. Only of late years by means of forest reservations has the simplest groundwork for available legislation been laid, while in many of the finest groves every species of destruction is still moving on with accelerated speed.

In the course of my explorations I found no fewer than five mills located on or near the lower edge of the Sequoia belt, all of which were cutting considerable quantities of Big Tree lumber. Most of the Fresno group are doomed to feed the mills recently erected near them, and a company of lumbermen are now cutting the magnificent forest on Kings River. In these milling operations waste far exceeds use, for after the choice young manageable trees on any given spot have been felled, the woods are fired to clear the ground of limbs and refuse with reference to further operations, and, of course, most of the seedlings and saplings are destroyed.

These mill ravages, however, are small as compared with the comprehensive destruction caused by 'sheepmen'. Incredible numbers of sheep are driven to the mountain pastures every summer, and their course is ever marked by desolation. Every wild garden is trodden down, the shrubs are stripped of leaves as if devoured by locusts, and the woods are burned. Running fires are set everywhere, with a view to clearing the ground of prostrate trunks, to facilitate the movements of the flocks and improve the pastures. The entire forest belt is thus swept and devastated from one extremity of the range to the other, and, with the exception of the resinous *Pinus contorta,* Sequoia suffers most of all. Indians burn off the underbrush in certain localities to facilitate deer-hunting, mountaineers and lumbermen carelessly allow their camp-fires to run; but the fires of the sheepmen, or *muttoneers,* form more than ninety per cent of all destructive fires that range the Sierra forests.

It appears, therefore, that notwithstanding our forest king might live on gloriously in Nature's keeping, it is rapidly vanishing before the fire and steel of man; and unless protective measures be speedily invented and applied, in a few decades, at the farthest, all that will be left of *Sequoia gigantea* will be a few hacked and scarred monuments.

TWO-LEAVED, OR TAMARACK, PINE
(*Pinus contorta,* Var. *Marrayana*)

This species forms the bulk of the alpine forests, extending along the range, above the fir zone, up to a height of from 8,000 to 9,500ft. above the sea, growing in beautiful order upon moraines that are scarcely changed as yet by post-glacial weathering. Compared with the giants of the lower zones, this is a small tree, seldom attaining a height of a hundred feet. The largest specimen I ever measured was ninety feet in height, and a little over six in diameter four feet from the ground. The average height of mature trees throughout the entire belt is probably not far from fifty or sixty feet, with a diameter of two feet. It is a well-proportioned, rather handsome little pine, with greyish-brown bark, and crooked, much-divided branches, which cover the greater portion of the trunk, not so densely, however, as to prevent its being seen. The lower limbs curve downward, gradually take a horizontal position about half-way up the trunk, then aspire more and more toward the summit, thus forming a sharp, conical top. The foliage is short and rigid, two leaves in a fascicle, arranged in comparatively long, cylindrical tassels at the ends of the tough, up-curving branchlets. The cones are about two inches long, growing in stiff clusters among the needles, without making any striking effect, except while very young, when they are of a vivid crimson colour, and the whole tree appears to be dotted with brilliant flowers. The sterile cones are still more showy, on account of their great abundance, often giving a reddish-yellow tinge to the whole mass of the foliage, and filling the air with pollen.

No other pine on the range is so regularly planted as this one. Moraine forests sweep along the sides of the high, rocky valleys for miles without interruption; still, strictly speaking, they are not dense, for flecks of sunshine and flowers find their way into the darkest places, where the trees grow tallest and thickest. Tall, nutritious grasses are specially abundant beneath them, growing over all the ground, in sunshine and shade, over extensive areas like a farmer's crop, and serving as pasture for the multitude of sheep that are driven from the arid plains every summer as soon as the snow is melted.

The two-leaved pine, more than any other, is subject to destruction by fire. The thin bark is streaked and sprinkled with resin, as though it had been showered down upon it like rain, so that even the green trees catch fire readily, and during strong winds whole forests are destroyed, the flames leaping from tree to tree, forming one continuous belt of roaring fire that goes surging and racing onward above the bending woods, like the grass-fires of a prairie. During the calm, dry season of Indian summer, the fire creeps quietly along the ground, feeding on the dry needles and burs; then, arriving at the foot of a tree, the resiny bark is ignited, and the heated air ascends in a powerful current, increasing in velocity, and dragging the flames swiftly upward; then the leaves catch fire, and an immense column of flame, beautifully spired on the edges, and tinted a rose-purple hue, rushes aloft thirty or forty feet above the top of the tree, forming a grand spectacle, especially on a dark night. It lasts, however, only a few seconds, vanishing with magical rapidity, to be succeeded by others along the fire-line at irregular intervals for weeks at a time – tree after tree flashing and darkening, leaving the trunks and branches hardly scarred. The heat, however, is sufficient to kill the trees, and in a few years the bark shrivels and falls off. Belts miles in extent are thus killed and left standing with the branches on, peeled and rigid, appearing grey in the distance, like misty clouds. Later the branches drop off, leaving a forest of bleached spars. At length the roots decay, and the forlorn trunks are blown down during some storm, and piled one upon another encumbering the ground until they are consumed by the next fire, and leave it ready for a fresh crop.

The endurance of the species is shown by its wandering occasionally out over the lava plains with the yellow pine, and climbing moraineless mountain -sides with the dwarf pine, clinging to any chance support in rifts and crevices of storm-beaten rocks – always, however, showing the effects of such hardships in every feature.

Down in sheltered lake hollows, on beds of rich alluvium, it varies so far from the common form as frequently to be taken for a distinct species. Here it grows in dense sods, like grasses, from forty to eighty feet high, bending all together to the breeze and whirling in eddying gusts more lithely than any other tree in the woods. I have frequently found specimens fifty feet high less than five inches in diameter. Being thus slender, and at the same time well clad with leafy boughs, it is oftentimes bent to the ground when laden with soft snow, forming beautiful arches in endless variety, some of which last until the melting of the snow in spring.

MOUNTAIN PINE
(*Pinus monticola*)

The mountain pine is king of the alpine woods, brave, hardy, and long-lived, towering grandly above its companions, and becoming stronger and more imposing just where other species begin to crouch and disappear. At its best it is usually about ninety feet high and five or six in diameter, though a specimen is often met considerably larger than this. The trunk is as massive and as suggestive of enduring strength as that of an oak. About two thirds of the trunk is commonly free of limbs, but close, fringy tufts of sprays occur all the way down, like those which adorn the colossal shafts of Sequoia. The bark is deep reddish-brown upon trees that occupy exposed situations near its upper limit, and furrowed rather deeply, the main furrows running nearly parallel with each other, and connected by conspicuous cross furrows, which, with one exception, are, as far as I have noticed, peculiar to this species.

The cones are from four to eight inches long; slender, cylindrical and somewhat curved, resembling those of the common white pine of the Atlantic coast. They grow in clusters of about from three to six or seven, becoming pendulous as they increase in weight, chiefly by the bending of the branches.

This species is nearly related to the sugar pine, and, though not half so tall, it constantly suggests its noble relative in the way that it extends its long arms and in general habit. The mountain pine is first met on the upper margin of the fir zone, growing singly in a subdued, inconspicuous form, in what appear as chance situations, without making much impression on the general forest. Continuing up through the two-leaved pines in the same scattered growth, it begins to show its character, and at an elevation of about 10,000ft. attains its noblest development near the middle of the range, tossing its tough arms in the frosty air, welcoming storms and feeding on them, and reaching the grand old age of 1,000 years.

JUNIPER, OR RED CEDAR
(Juniperus occidentalis)

The Juniper is pre-eminently a rock tree, occupying the baldest domes and pavements, where there is scarcely a handful of soil, at a height of from 7,000 to 9,500ft. In such situations the trunk is frequently over eight feet in diameter, and not much more in height. The top is almost always dead in old trees, and great stubborn limbs push out horizontally that are mostly broken and bare at the ends, but densely covered and embedded here and there with bossy mounds of grey foliage. Some are mere weathered stumps, as broad as long, decorated with a few leafy sprays, reminding one of the crumbling towers of some ancient castle scantily draped with ivy. Only upon the head waters of the Carson have I found this species established on good moraine soil. Here it flourishes with the silver and two-leaved pines, in great beauty and luxuriance, attaining a height of from forty to sixty feet, and manifesting but little of that rocky angularity so characteristic a feature throughout the greater portion of its range. Two of the largest, growing at the head of Hope Valley, measured twenty-nine feet three inches and twenty-five feet six inches in circumference, respectively, four feet from the ground. The bark is of a bright cinnamon colour, and, in thrifty trees, beautifully braided and reticulated, flaking off in thin, lustrous ribbons that are sometimes used by Indians for tent-matting. Its fine colour and odd picturesqueness always catch an artist's eye, but to me the Juniper seems a singularly dull and taciturn tree, never speaking to one's heart. I have spent many a day and night in its company, in all kinds of weather, and have ever found it silent, cold and rigid, like a column of ice. Its broad stumpiness, of course, precludes all possibility of waving, or even shaking; but it is not this rocky steadfastness that constitutes its silence. In calm, sun-days the sugar pine preaches the grandeur of the mountains like an apostle without moving a leaf.

On level rocks it dies standing, and wastes insensibly out of existence like granite, the wind exerting about as little control over it alive or dead as it does over a glacier boulder. Some are undoubtedly over 2,000 years old. All the trees of the alpine woods suffer, more or less, from avalanches, the two-leaved pine most of all. Gaps two or three hundred yards wide, extending from the upper limit of the tree-line to the bottoms of valleys and lake basins, are of common occurrence in all the upper forests, resembling the clearing of settlers in the old backwoods. Scarcely a tree is spared, even the soil is scraped away, while the thousands of uprooted pines and spruces are piled upon one another heads downward, and tucked snugly in along the sides of the clearing in two windrows, like lateral moraines. The pines lie with branches wilted and drooping like weeds. Not so the burly junipers. After braving in silence the storms of perhaps a dozen or twenty centuries, they seem in this, their last calamity, to become somewhat communicative, making sign of a very unwilling acceptance of their fate, holding themselves well up from the ground on knees and elbows, seemingly ill at ease, and anxious, like stubborn wrestlers, to rise again.

HEMLOCK SPRUCE
(Tsuga Pattoniana)

The hemlock spruce is the most singularly beautiful of all the California coniferæ. So slender is its axis at the top, that it bends over and droops like the stalk of a nodding lily. The branches droop also, and divide into innumerable slender, waving sprays, which are arranged in a varied, eloquent harmony that is wholly indescribable. Its cones are purple, and hang free, in the form of little tassels two inches long from all the sprays from top to bottom. Though exquisitely delicate and feminine in expression, it grows best where the snow lies deepest, far up in the region of storms, at an elevation of from 9,000 to 9,500ft., on frosty northern slopes; but it is capable of growing considerably higher, say 10,500ft. The tallest specimens, growing in sheltered hollows somewhat beneath the heaviest wind-currents, are from eighty to a hundred feet high, and from two to four feet in diameter. The very largest specimen I ever found was nineteen feet seven inches in circumference four feet from the ground, growing on the edge of Lake Hollow, at an elevation of 9,250ft. above the level of the sea. At the age of twenty or thirty years it becomes fruitful, and hangs out its beautiful purple cones at the ends of the slender sprays, where they swing free in the breeze, and contrast delightfully with the cool green foliage. They are translucent when young, and their beauty is delicious. After they are fully ripe, they spread their shell-like scales and allow the brown-winged seeds to fly in the mellow air, while the empty cones remain to beautify the tree until the coming of a fresh crop.

The staminate cones of all the coniferæ are beautiful, growing in bright clusters, yellow, and rose, and crimson. Those of the hemlock spruce are the most beautiful of all, forming little conelets of blue flowers, each on a slender stem.

Under all conditions, sheltered or stormbeaten, well-fed or ill-fed, this tree is singularly graceful in habit. Even at its highest limit upon exposed ridge-tops, though compelled to crouch in dense thickets, huddled close together, as if for mutual protection, it still manages to throw out its sprays in irrepressible loveliness; while on well-ground moraine soil it develops a perfectly tropical luxuriance of foliage and fruit, and is the very loveliest tree in the forest; poised in thin white sunshine, clad with branches from head to foot, yet not in the faintest degree heavy or bunchy, it towers in unassuming majesty, drooping as if unaffected with the aspiring tendencies of its race, loving the ground while transparently conscious of heaven and joyously receptive of its blessings, reaching out its branches like sensitive tentacles, feeling the light and revelling in it. No other of our alpine conifers so finely veils its strength. Its delicate branches yield to the mountains' gentlest breath; yet is it strong to meet the wildest onsets of the gale – strong not in resistance, but compliance, bowing, snow-laden, to the ground, gracefully accepting burial month after month in the darkness beneath the heavy mantle of winter.

When the first soft snow begins to fall, the flakes lodge in the leaves, weighing down the branches against the trunk. Then the axis bends yet lower and lower, until the slender top touches the ground, thus forming a fine ornamental arch. The snow still falls lavishly, and the whole tree is at length buried, to sleep and rest in its beautiful grave as though dead. Entire groves of young trees, from ten to forty feet high, are thus buried every winter like slender grasses. But, like the violets and daisies which the heaviest snows crush not, they are safe. It is as though this were only Nature's method of putting her darlings to sleep instead of leaving them exposed to the biting storms of winter.

Thus warmly wrapped they await the summer resurrection. The snow becomes soft in the sunshine, and freezes at night, making the mass hard and compact, like ice, so that during the months of April and May you can ride a horse over the prostrate groves without catching sight of a single leaf. At length the down-pouring sunshine sets them free. First the elastic tops of the arches begin to appear, then one branch after another, each springing loose with a gentle rustling sound, and at length the whole tree, with the assistance of the winds, gradually unbends and rises and settles back into its place in the warm air, as dry and feathery and fresh as young ferns just out of the coil.

Some of the finest groves I have yet found are on the southern slopes of Lassen's Butte. There are also many charming companies on the head waters of the Tuolumne, Merced and San Joaquin, and in general, the species is so far from being rare that you can scarcely fail to find groves of considerable extent in crossing the range, choose what pass you may. The mountain pine grows beside it, and more frequently the two-leaved species; but there are many beautiful groups, numbering 1,000 individuals, or more, without a single intruder.

I wish I had space to write more of the surpassing beauty of this favourite spruce. Every tree-lover is sure to regard it with special admiration; apathetic mountaineers, even, seeking only game or gold, stop to gaze on first meeting it, and mutter to themselves: 'That's a mighty pretty tree,' some of them adding 'd——d pretty!' In autumn, when its cones are ripe, the little striped tamias, and the Douglas squirrel, and the Clark crow make a happy stir in its groves. The deer love to lie down beneath its spreading branches; bright streams from the snow that is always near ripple through its groves, and bryanthus spreads precious carpets in its shade. But the best words only hint its charms. Come to the mountains and see.

DWARF PINE
(*Pinus albicaulis*)

This species forms the extreme edge of the timber line throughout nearly the whole extent of the range on both flanks. It is first met growing in company with *Pinus contorta*, var. *Murrayana*, on the upper margin of the belt, as an erect tree from fifteen to thirty feet high and from one to two feet in thickness; thence it goes straggling up the flanks of the summit peaks, upon moraines or crumbling ledges, wherever it can obtain a foothold, to an elevation of from 10,000 to 12,000ft., where it dwarfs to a mass of crumpled, prostrate branches, covered with slender, upright shoots, each tipped with a short, close-packed tassel of leaves. The bark is smooth and purplish, in some places almost white. The fertile cones grow in rigid clusters upon the upper branches, dark chocolate in colour while young, and bear beautiful pearly seeds about the size of peas, most of which are eaten by two species of tamias and the notable Clark crow. The staminate cones occur in clusters, about an inch wide, down among the leaves, and, as they are coloured bright rose-purple, they give rise to a lively, flowery appearance little looked for in such a tree.

Pines are commonly regarded as sky-loving trees that must necessarily aspire or die. This species forms a marked exception, creeping lowly, in compliance with the most rigorous demands of climate, yet enduring bravely to a more advanced age than many of its lofty relatives in the sun-lands below. Seen from a distance, it would never be taken for a tree of any kind. Yonder, for example, is Cathedral Peak, some three miles away, with a scattered growth of this pine creeping like mosses over the roof and around the bevelled edges of the north gable, nowhere giving any hint of an ascending axis. When approached quite near it still appears matted and heathy, and is so low that one experiences no great difficulty in walking over the top of it. Yet it is seldom absolutely prostrate, at its lowest usually attaining a height of three or four feet, with a main trunk, and branches outspread and intertangled above it, as if in ascending they had been checked by a ceiling, against which they had grown and been compelled to spread horizontally. The winter snow is indeed such a ceiling, lasting half the year; while the pressed, shorn surface is made yet smoother by violent winds, armed with cutting sand-grains, that beat down any shoot that offers to rise much above the general level, and carve the dead trunks and branches in beautiful patterns.

During stormy nights I have often camped snugly beneath the interlacing arches of this little pine. The needles, which have accumulated for centuries, make fine beds, a fact well known to other mountaineers, such as deer and wild sheep, who paw out oval hollows and lie beneath the larger trees in safe and comfortable concealment.

The longevity of this lowly dwarf is far greater than would be guessed. Here, for example, is a specimen, growing at an elevation of 10,700ft., which seems as though it might be plucked up by the roots, for it is only three and a half inches in diameter, and its topmost tassel is hardly three feet above the ground. Cutting it half through and counting the annual rings with the aid of a lens, we find its age to be no less than 255 years. Here is another telling specimen about the same height, 426 years old, whose trunk is only six inches in diameter; and one of its supple branchlets, hardly an eighth of an inch in diameter inside the bark, is seventy-five years old, and so filled with oily balsam, and so well seasoned by storms, that we may tie it in knots like a whip-cord.

WHITE PINE
(*Pinus flexilis*)

This species is widely distributed throughout the Rocky Mountains, and over all the higher of the many ranges of the Great Basin, between the Wahsatch Mountains and the Sierra, where it is known as white pine. In the Sierra it is sparsely scattered along the eastern flank, from Bloody Canyon southward nearly to the extremity of the range, opposite the village of Lone Pine, nowhere forming any appreciable portion of the general forest. From its peculiar position, in loose, straggling parties, it seems to have been derived from the Basin ranges to the eastward, where it is abundant.

It is a larger tree than the dwarf pine. At an elevation of about 9,000ft. above the sea, it often attains a height of forty or fifty feet, and a diameter of from three to five feet. The cones open freely when ripe, and are twice as large as those of the *albicaulis,* and the foliage and branches are more open, having a tendency to sweep out in free, wild curves, like those of the Mountain Pine, to which it is closely allied. It is seldom found lower than 9,000ft. above sea-level, but from this elevation it pushes upward over the roughest ledges to the extreme limit of tree-growth, where, in its dwarfed, storm-crushed condition, it is more like the white-barked species.

Throughout Utah and Nevada it is one of the principal timber-trees, great quantities being cut every year for the mines. The famous White Pine Mining District, White Pine City and the White Pine Mountains have derived their names from it.

NEEDLE PINE
(*Pinus aristata*)

This species is restricted in the Sierra to the southern portion of the range, about the head waters of Kings and Kern rivers, where it forms extensive forests, and in some places accompanies the dwarf pine to the extreme limit of tree-growth.

It is first met at an elevation of between 9,000 and 10,000ft., and runs up to 11,000 without seeming to suffer greatly from the climate or the leanness of the soil. It is a much finer tree than the dwarf pine. Instead of growing in clumps and low, heathy mats, it manages in some way to maintain an erect position, and usually stands single. Wherever the young trees are at all sheltered, they grow up straight and arrowy, with delicately tapered bole, and ascending branches terminated with glossy, bottle-brush tassels. At middle age, certain limbs are specialized and pushed far out for the bearing of cones, after the manner of the sugar pine; and in old age these branches droop and cast about in every direction, giving rise to very picturesque effects. The trunk becomes deep brown and rough, like that of the mountain pine, while the young cones are of a strange, dull, blackish-blue colour, clustered on the upper branches. When ripe they are from three to four inches long, yellowish brown, resembling in every way those of the mountain pine. Excepting the sugar pine, no tree on the mountains is so capable of individual expression, while in grace of form and movement it constantly reminds one of the hemlock spruce.

The largest specimen I measured was a little over five feet in diameter and ninety feet in height, but this is more than twice the ordinary size.

This species is common throughout the Rocky Mountains and most of the short ranges of the Great Basin, where it is called the fox-tail pine, from its long dense leaf-tassels. On the Hot Creek, White Pine and Golden Gate ranges it is quite abundant. About a foot or eighteen inches of the ends of the branches is densely packed with stiff outstanding needles which radiate like an electric fox or squirrel's tail. The needles have a glossy polish, and the sunshine sifting through them makes them burn with silvery lustre, while their number and elastic temper tell delightfully in the winds. This tree is here still more original and picturesque than in the Sierra, far surpassing not only its companion conifers in this respect, but also the most noted of the lowland oaks. Some stand firmly erect, feathered with radiant tassels down to the ground, forming slender tapering towers of shining verdure; others, with two or three specialized branches pushed out at right angles to the trunk and densely clad with tasselled sprays, take the form of beautiful ornamental crosses. Again in the same woods you find trees that are made up of several boles united near the ground, spreading at the sides in a plane parallel to the axis of the mountain, with the elegant tassels hung in charming order between them, making a harp held against the main wind lines where they are most effective in playing the grand storm harmonies. And besides these there are many variable arching forms, alone or in groups, with innumerable tassels drooping beneath the arches or radiant above them, and many lowly giants of no particular form that have braved the storms of a thousand years. But whether old or young, sheltered or exposed to the wildest gales, this tree is ever found irrepressibly and extravagantly picturesque, and offers a richer and more varied series of forms to the artist than any other conifer I know of.

NUT PINE
(*Pinus monophylla*)

The nut pine covers or rather dots the eastern flank of the Sierra, to which it is mostly restricted, in greyish, bush-like patches, from the margin of the sage-plains to an elevation of from 7,000 to 8,000ft.

A more contentedly fruitful and unaspiring conifer could not be conceived. All the species we have been sketching make departures more or less distant from the typical spire form, but none goes so far as this. Without any apparent exigency of climate or soil, it remains near the ground, throwing out crooked, divergent branches like an orchard apple-tree, and seldom pushes a single shoot higher than fifteen or twenty feet above the ground.

The average thickness of the trunk is, perhaps, about ten or twelve inches. The leaves are mostly undivided, like round awls, instead of being separated, like those of other pines, into twos and threes and fives. The cones are green while growing, and are usually found over all the tree, forming quite a marked feature as seen against the bluish-grey foliage. They are quite small, only about two inches in length, and give no promise of edible nuts; but when we come to open them, we find that about half the entire bulk of the cone is made up of sweet, nutritious seeds, the kernels of which are nearly as large as those of hazel-nuts.

This is undoubtedly the most important food-tree on the Sierra, and furnishes the Mono, Carson and Walker River Indians with more and better nuts than all the other species taken together. It is the Indians' own tree, and many a white man have they killed for cutting it down.

In its development Nature seems to have aimed at the formation of as great a fruit-bearing surface as possible. Being so low and accessible, the cones are readily beaten off with poles, and the nuts procured by roasting them until the scales open. In bountiful seasons a single Indian will gather thirty or forty bushels of them – a fine squirrelish employment.

Of all the conifers along the eastern base of the Sierra, and on all the many mountain groups and short ranges of the Great Basin, this foodful little pine is the commonest tree, and the most important. Nearly every mountain is planted with it to a height of from 8,000 to 9,000ft. above the sea. Some are covered from base to summit by this one species, with only a sparse growth of juniper on the lower slopes to break the continuity of its curious woods, which, though dark-looking at a distance, are almost shadeless, and have none of the damp, leafy glens and hollows so characteristic of other pine woods. Tens of thousands of acres occur in continuous belts. Indeed, viewed comprehensively the entire Basin seems to be pretty evenly divided into level plains dotted with sage-bushes and mountain-chains covered with Nut Pines. No slope is too rough, none too dry, for these bountiful orchards of the red man.

The value of this species to Nevada is not easily overestimated. It furnishes charcoal and timber for the mines, and, with the juniper, supplies the ranches with fuel and rough fencing. In fruitful seasons the nut crop is perhaps greater than the California wheat crop, which exerts so much influence throughout the food markets of the world. When the crop is ripe, the Indians make ready the long beating poles; bags, baskets, mats and sacks are collected; the women out at service among the settlers, washing or drudging, assemble at the family huts; the men leave their ranch work; old and young, all are mounted on ponies and start in great glee to the nut lands, forming curiously picturesque cavalcades; flaming scarfs and calico skirts stream loosely over the knotty ponies, two squaws usually astride of each, with baby midgets bandaged in baskets slung on their backs or balanced on the saddle-bow; while nut-baskets and water-jars project from each side, and the long beating-poles make angles in every direction. Arriving at some well-known central point where grass and water are found, the squaws with baskets, the men with poles ascend the ridges to the laden trees, followed by the children. Then the beating begins right merrily, the burs fly in every direction, rolling down the slopes, lodging here and there against rocks and sage-bushes, chased and gathered by the women and children with fine natural gladness. Smoke-columns speedily mark the joyful scene of their labours as the roasting-fires are kindled, and, at night, assembled in gay circles garrulous as jays, they begin the first nut feast of the season.

The nuts are about half an inch long and a quarter of an inch in diameter, pointed at the top, round at the base, light brown in general colour, and, like many other pine seeds, handsomely dotted with purple, like birds' eggs. The shells are thin and may be crushed between the thumb and finger. The kernels are white, becoming brown by roasting, and are sweet to every palate, being eaten by birds, squirrels, dogs, horses and men. Perhaps less than one bushel in a thousand of the whole crop is ever gathered. Still, besides supplying their own wants, in times of plenty the Indians bring large quantities to market; then they are eaten around nearly every fireside in the State, and are even fed to horses occasionally instead of barley.

Of other trees growing on the Sierra, but forming a very small part of the general forest, we may briefly notice the following:

Chamæcyparis Lawsoniana is a magnificent tree in the coast ranges, but small in the Sierra. It is found only well to the northward along the banks of cool streams on the upper Sacramento toward Mount Shasta. Only a few trees of this species, as far as I have seen, have as yet gained a place in the Sierra woods. It has evidently been derived from the coast range by way of the tangle of connecting mountains at the head of the Sacramento Valley.

In shady dells and on cool stream banks of the northern Sierra we also find the yew (*Taxus brevifolia*).

The interesting nutmeg tree (*Torreya Californica*) is sparsely distributed along the western flank of the range at an elevation of about 4,000ft., mostly in gulches and canyons. It is a small, prickly leaved, glossy evergreen, like a conifer, from twenty to fifty feet high, and one to two feet in diameter. The fruit resembles a green-gage plum, and contains one seed, about the size of an acorn, and like a nutmeg, hence the common name. The wood is fine-grained and of a beautiful, creamy yellow colour like box, sweet-scented when dry, though the green leaves emit a disagreeable odour.

Betula occidentalis, the only birch, is a small, slender tree restricted to the eastern flank of the range along stream-sides below the pine-belt, especially in Owen's Valley.

Alder, maple, and Nuttall's flowering dogwood make beautiful bowers over swift, cool streams at an elevation of from 3,000 to 5,000ft., mixed more or less' with willows and cottonwood; and above these in lake basins the aspen forms fine ornamental groves, and lets its light shine gloriously in the autumn months.

The chestnut oak (*Quercus densiflora*) seems to have come from the coast range around the head of the Sacramento Valley, like the *Chamæcyparis,* but as it extends southward along the lower edge of the main pine-belt it grows smaller until it finally dwarfs to a mere chaparral bush. In the coast mountains it is a fine, tall, rather slender tree, about from sixty to seventy-five feet high, growing with the grand *Sequoia sempervirens,* or redwood. But unfortunately it is too good to live, and is now being rapidly destroyed for tan-bark.

Besides the common Douglas oak and the grand *Quercus Wislizeni* of the foot-hills, and several small ones that make dense growths of chaparral, there are two mountain-oaks that grow with the pines up to an elevation of about 5,000ft. above the sea, and greatly enhance the beauty of the Yosemite parks. These are the mountain live oak and the Kellogg oak, named in honour of the admirable botanical pioneer of California. Kellogg's Oak (*Quercus Kelloggii*) is a firm, bright, beautiful tree, reaching a height of sixty feet, four to seven feet in diameter, with wide-spreading branches, and growing at an elevation of from 3,000 to 5,000ft. in sunny valleys and flats among the evergreens, and higher in a dwarfed state. In the cliff-bound parks about 4,000ft. above the sea it is so abundant and effective it might fairly be called the Yosemite oak. The leaves make beautiful masses of purple in the spring, and yellow in ripe autumn; while its acorns are eagerly gathered by Indians, squirrels and woodpeckers. The mountain live oak (*Q. Chrysolepis*) is a tough, rugged mountaineer of a tree, growing bravely and attaining noble dimensions on the roughest earthquake taluses in deep canyons and Yosemite valleys. The trunk is usually short, dividing near the ground into great wide-spreading limbs, and these again into a multitude of slender sprays, many of them cord-like and drooping to the ground, like those of the great white oak of the lowlands (*Q. lobata*). The top of the tree where there is plenty of space is broad and bossy, with a dense covering of shining leaves, making delightful canopies, the complicated system of grey, interlacing, arching branches as seen from beneath being exceedingly rich and picturesque. No other tree that I know dwarfs so regularly and completely as this under changes of climate due to changes in elevation. At the foot of a canyon 4,000ft. above the sea you may find magnificent specimens of this oak fifty feet high, with craggy, bulging trunks, five to seven feet in diameter, and at the head of the canyon, 2,500ft. higher, a dense, soft, low, shrubby growth of the same species, while all the way up the canyon between these extremes of size and habit a perfect gradation may be traced. The largest I have seen was fifty feet high, eight feet in diameter, and about seventy-five feet in spread. The trunk was all knots and buttresses, grey like granite, and about as angular and irregular as the boulders on which it was growing – a type of steadfast, unwedgeable strength.

CHAPTER NINE

The Douglas Squirrel

(Sciurus Douglasii)

THE DOUGLAS SQUIRREL is by far the most interesting and influential of the California sciuridæ, surpassing every other species in force of character, numbers, and extent of range, and in the amount of influence he brings to bear upon the health and distribution of the vast forests he inhabits.

Go where you will throughout the noble woods of the Sierra Nevada, among the giant pines and spruces of the lower zones, up through the towering silver firs to the storm-bent thickets of the summit peaks, you everywhere find this little squirrel the master-existence. Though only a few inches long, so intense is his fiery vigour and restlessness, he stirs every grove with wild life, and makes himself more important than even the huge bears that shuffle through the tangled underbrush beneath him. Every wind is fretted by his voice, almost every bole and branch feels the sting of his sharp feet. How much the growth of the trees is stimulated by this means it is not easy to learn, but his action in manipulating their seeds is more appreciable. Nature has made him master forester and committed most of her coniferous crops to his paws. Probably over fifty per cent of all the cones ripened on the Sierra are cut off and handled by the Douglas alone, and of those of the Big Trees perhaps ninety per cent pass through his hands: the greater portion is of course stored away for food to last during the winter and spring, but some of them are tucked separately into loosely covered holes, where some of the seeds germinate and become trees. But the Sierra is only one of the many provinces over which he holds sway, for his dominion extends over all the Redwood Belt of the Coast Mountains, and far northward throughout the majestic forests of Oregon, Washington and British Columbia. I make haste to mention these facts, to show upon how substantial a foundation the importance I ascribe to him rests.

The Douglas is closely allied to the red squirrel or chickaree of the eastern woods. Ours may be a lineal descendant of this species, distributed westward to the Pacific by way of the Great Lakes and the Rocky Mountains, and thence southward along our forested ranges. This view is suggested by the fact that our species becomes redder and more chickaree-like in general, the farther it is traced back along the course indicated above. But whatever their relationship, and the evolutionary forces that have acted upon them, the Douglas is now the larger and more beautiful animal.

From the nose to the root of the tail he measures about eight inches; and his tail, which he so effectively uses in interpreting his feelings, is about six inches in length. He wears dark bluish-grey over the back and half-way down the sides, bright buff on the belly, with a stripe of dark grey, nearly black, separating the upper and under colours; this dividing stripe, however, is not very sharply defined. He has long black whiskers, which gives him a rather fierce look when observed closely, strong claws, sharp as fish-hooks, and the brightest of bright eyes, full of telling speculation.

A Kings River Indian told me that they call him 'Pillillooeet,' which, rapidly pronounced with the first syllable heavily accented, is not unlike the lusty exclamation he utters on his way up a tree when excited. Most mountaineers in California call him the pine squirrel; and when I asked an old trapper whether he knew our little forester, he replied with brightening countenance: 'Oh, yes, of course I know him; everybody knows him. When I'm huntin' in the woods, I often find out where the deer are by his barkin' at 'em. I call 'em Lightnin' Squirrels, because they're so mighty quick and peert.'

All the true squirrels are more or less birdlike in speech and movements; but the Douglas is pre-eminently so, possessing, as he does, every attribute peculiarly squirrelish enthusiastically concentrated. He is the squirrel of squirrels, flashing from branch to branch of his favourite evergreens crisp and glossy and undiseased as a sunbeam. Give him wings and he would outfly any bird in the woods. His big grey cousin is a looser animal, seemingly light enough to float on the wind; yet when leaping from limb to limb, or out of one tree-top to another, he sometimes halts to gather strength, as if making efforts concerning the upshot of which he does not always feel exactly confident. But the Douglas, with his denser body, leaps and glides in hidden strength, seemingly as independent of common muscles as a mountain stream. He threads the tasselled branches of the pines, stirring their needles like a rustling breeze; now shooting across openings in arrowy lines; now launching in curves, glinting deftly from side to side in sudden zigzags, and swirling in giddy loops and spirals around the knotty trunks; getting into what seem to be the most impossible situations without sense of danger; now on his haunches, now on his head; yet ever graceful, and punctuating his most irrepressible outbursts of energy with little dots and dashes of perfect repose. He is, without exception, the wildest animal I ever saw – a fiery, sputtering little bolt of life, luxuriating in quick oxygen and the woods' best juices. One can hardly think of such a creature being dependent, like the rest of us, on climate and food. But, after all, it requires no long acquaintance to learn he is human, for he works for a living. His busiest time is in the Indian summer. Then he gathers burs and hazelnuts like a plodding farmer, working continuously every day for hours; saying not a word; cutting off the ripe cones at the top of his speed, as if employed by the job, and examining every branch in regular order, as if careful that not one should escape him; then, descending, he stores them away beneath logs and stumps, in anticipation of the pinching hunger days of winter. He seems himself a kind of coniferous fruit – both fruit and flower. The resiny essences of the pines pervade every pore of his body, and eating his flesh is like chewing gum.

One never tires of this bright chip of nature – this brave little voice crying in the wilderness – of observing his many works and ways, and listening to his curious language. His musical, piny gossip is as savoury to the ear as balsam to the palate; and, though he has not exactly the gift of song, some of his notes are as sweet as those of a linnet – almost flute-like in softness, while others prick and tingle like thistles. He is the mocking-bird of squirrels, pouring forth mixed chatter and song like a perennial fountain; barking like a dog, screaming like a hawk, chirping like a blackbird or a sparrow; while in bluff, audacious noisiness he is a very jay.

In descending the trunk of a tree with the intention of alighting on the ground, he preserves a cautious silence, mindful, perhaps, of foxes and wildcats; but while rocking safely at home in the pine-tops there is no end to his capers and noise; and woe to the grey squirrel or chipmunk that ventures to set foot on his favourite tree! No matter how slyly they trace the furrows of the bark, they are speedily discovered, and kicked down-stairs with comic vehemence, while a torrent of angry notes comes rushing from his whiskered lips that sounds remarkably like swearing. He will even attempt at times to drive away dogs and men, especially if he has had no previous knowledge of them. Seeing a man for the first time, he approaches nearer and nearer, until within a few feet; then, with an angry outburst, he makes a sudden rush, all teeth and eyes, as if about to eat you up. But, finding that the big, forked animal doesn't scare, he prudently beats a retreat, and sets himself up to reconnoitre on some overhanging branch, scrutinizing every movement you make with ludicrous solemnity. Gathering courage, he ventures down the trunk again, churring and chirping, and jerking nervously up and down in curious loops, eyeing you all the time, as if showing off and demanding your admiration. Finally, growing calmer, he settles down in a comfortable posture on some horizontal branch commanding a good view, and beats time with his tail to a steady 'Chee-up! chee-up!' or, when somewhat less excited, 'Pee-ah!' with the first syllable keenly accented, and the second drawn out like the scream of a hawk – repeating this slowly and more emphatically at first, then gradually faster, until a rate of about 150 words a minute is reached; usually sitting all the time on his haunches, with paws resting on his breast, which pulses visibly with each word. It is remarkable, too, that, though articulating distinctly, he keeps his mouth shut most of the time, and speaks through his nose. I have occasionally observed him even eating Sequoia seeds and nibbling a troublesome flea, without ceasing or in any way confusing his 'Pee-ah! pee-ah!' for a single moment.

While ascending trees all his claws come into play, but in descending the weight of his body is sustained chiefly by those of the hind feet; still in neither case do his movements suggest effort, though if you are near enough you may see the bulging strength of his short, bear-like arms, and note his sinewy fists clinched in the bark.

Whether going up or down, he carries his tail extended at full length in line with his body, unless it be required for gestures. But while running along horizontal limbs or fallen trunks, it is frequently folded forward over the back, with the airy tip daintily upcurled. In cool weather it keeps him warm. Then, after he has finished his meal, you may see him crouched close on some level limb with his tail-robe neatly spread and reaching forward to his ears, the electric, outstanding hairs quivering in the breeze like pine-needles. But in wet or very cold weather he stays in his nest, and while curled up there his comforter is long enough to come forward around his nose. It is seldom so cold, however, as to prevent his going out to his stores when hungry.

Once as I lay storm-bound on the upper edge of the timber line on Mount Shasta, the thermometer nearly at zero and the sky thick with driving snow, a Douglas came bravely out several times from one of the lower hollows of a dwarf pine near my camp, faced the wind without seeming to feel it much, frisked lightly about over the mealy snow, and dug his way down to some hidden seeds with wonderful precision, as if to his eyes the thick snow-covering were glass.

No other of the Sierra animals of my acquaintance is better fed, not even the deer, amid abundance of sweet herbs and shrubs, or the mountain sheep, or omniverous bears. His food consists of grass-seeds, berries, hazel-nuts, chinquapins and the nuts and seeds of all the coniferous trees without exception – pine, fir, spruce, libocedrus, juniper and Sequoia – he is fond of them all, and they all agree with him, green or ripe. No cone is too large for him to manage, none so small as to be beneath his notice. The smaller ones, such as those of the hemlock, and the Douglas spruce, and the two-leaved pine, he cuts off and eats on a branch of the tree, without allowing them to fall; beginning at the bottom of the cone and cutting away the scales to expose the seeds; not gnawing by guess, like a bear, but turning them round and round in regular order, in compliance with their spiral arrangement.

When thus employed, his location in the tree is betrayed by a dribble of scales, shells and seed-wings, and, every few minutes, by the fall of the stripped axis of the cone. Then of course he is ready for another, and if you are watching you may catch a glimpse of him as he glides silently out to the end of a branch and see him examining the cone-clusters until he finds one to his mind; then, leaning over, pull back the springy needles out of his way, grasp the cone with his paws to prevent its falling, snip it off in an incredibly short time, seize it with jaws grotesquely stretched, and return to his chosen seat near the trunk. But the immense size of the cones of the sugar pine – from fifteen to twenty inches in length – and those of the Jeffrey variety of the yellow pine compel him to adopt a quite different method. He cuts them off without attempting to hold them, then goes down and drags them from where they have chanced to fall up to the bare, swelling ground around the instep of the tree, where he demolishes them in the same methodical way, beginning at the bottom and following the scale-spirals to the top.

From a single sugar pine cone he gets from two to four hundred seeds about half the size of a hazelnut, so that in a few minutes he can procure enough to last a week. He seems, however, to prefer those of the two silver firs above all others; perhaps because they are most easily obtained, as the scales drop off when ripe without needing to be cut. Both species are filled with an exceedingly pungent, aromatic oil, which spices all his flesh, and is of itself sufficient to account for his lightning energy.

You may easily know this little workman by his chips. On sunny hillsides around the principal trees they lie in big piles – bushels and basketfuls of them, all fresh and clean, making the most beautiful kitchen-middens imaginable. The brown and yellow scales and nut-shells are as abundant and as delicately pencilled and tinted as the shells along the sea-shore; while the beautiful red and purple seed-wings mingled with them would lead one to fancy that innumerable butterflies had there met their fate.

He feasts on all the species long before they are ripe, but is wise enough to wait until they are matured before he gathers them into his barns. This is in October and November which with him are the two busiest months of the year. All kinds of burs, big and little, are now cut off and showered down alike, and the ground is speedily covered with them. A constant thudding and bumping is kept up; some of the larger cones chancing to fall on old logs make the forest re-echo with the sound. Other nut-eaters less industrious know well what is going on, and hasten to carry away the cones as they fall. But however busy the harvester may be, he is not slow to descry the pilferers below, and instantly leaves his work to drive them away. The little striped tamias is a thorn in his flesh, stealing persistently, punish him as he may. The large grey squirrel gives trouble also, although the Douglas has been accused of stealing from him. Generally, however, just the opposite is the case.

The excellence of the Sierra evergreens is well known to nurserymen throughout the world, conseqently there is considerable demand for the seeds. The greater portion of the supply has hitherto been procured by chopping down the trees in the more accessible sections of the forest alongside of bridle-paths that cross the range. Sequoia seeds at first brought from twenty to thirty dollars per pound, and therefore were eagerly sought after. Some of the smaller fruitful trees were cut down in the groves not protected by government, especially those of Fresno and Kings River. Most of the Sequoias, however, are of so gigantic a size that the seedsmen have to look for the greater portion of their supplies to the Douglas, who soon learns he is no match for these freebooters. He is wise enough, however, to cease working the instant he perceives them, and never fails to embrace every opportunity to recover his burs whenever they happen to be stored in any place accessible to him, and the busy seedsman often finds on returning to camp that the little Douglas has exhaustively spoiled the spoiler. I know one seed-gatherer who, whenever he robs the squirrels, scatters wheat or barley beneath the trees as conscience-money.

The want of appreciable life remarked by so many travellers in the Sierra forests is never felt at this time of year. Banish all the humming insects and the birds and quadrupeds, leaving only Sir Douglas, and the most solitary of our so-called solitudes would still throb with ardent life. But if you should go impatiently even into the most populous of the groves on purpose to meet him, and walk about looking up among the branches, you would see very little of him. But lie down at the foot of one of the trees and straightway he will come. For, in the midst of the ordinary forest sounds, the falling of burs, piping of quails, the screaming of the Clark crow, and the rustling of deer and bears among the chaparral, he is quick to detect your strange footsteps, and will hasten to make a good, close inspection of you as soon as you are still. First, you may hear him sounding a few notes of curious inquiry, but more likely the first intimation of his approach will be the prickly sounds of his feet as he descends the tree overhead, just before he makes his savage onrush to frighten you and proclaim your presence to every squirrel and bird in the neighbourhood. If you remain perfectly motionless, he will come nearer and nearer, and probably set your flesh a-tingle by frisking across your body. Once, while I was seated at the foot of a hemlock spruce in one of the most inaccessible of the San Joaquin yosemites engaged in sketching, a reckless fellow came up behind me, passed under my bended arm, and jumped on my paper. And one warm afternoon, while an old friend of mine was reading out in the shade of his cabin, one of his Douglas neighbours jumped from the gable upon his head, and then with admirable assurance ran down over his shoulder and on to the book he held in his hand.

Our Douglas enjoys a large social circle; for, besides his numerous relatives, *Sciurus fossor, Tamias quadrivitatus, T. Townsendii, Spermophilus Beecheyi, S. Douglasii,* he maintains intimate relations with the nut-eating birds, particularly the Clark crow (*Picicorvus columbianus*) and the numerous woodpeckers and jays. The two spermophiles are astonishingly abundant in the lowlands and lower foot-hills, but more and more sparingly distributed up through the Douglas domains – seldom venturing higher than six or seven thousand feet above the level of the sea. The grey sciurus ranges but little higher than this. The little striped tamias alone is associated with him everywhere. In the lower and middle zones, where they all meet, they are tolerably harmonious – a happy family, though very amusing skirmishes may occasionally be witnessed. Wherever the ancient glaciers have spread forest soil there you find our wee hero, most abundant where depth of soil and genial climate have given rise to a corresponding luxuriance in the trees, but following every kind of growth up the curving moraines to the highest glacial fountains.

Though I cannot of course expect all my readers to sympathize fully in my admiration of this little animal, few, I hope, will think this sketch of his life too long. I cannot begin to tell here how much he has cheered my lonely wanderings during all the years I have been pursuing my studies in these glorious wilds; or how much unmistakable humanity I have found in him. Take this for example: one calm, creamy Indian summer morning, when the nuts were ripe, I was camped in the upper pine-woods of the south fork of the San Joaquin, where the squirrels seemed to be about as plentiful as the ripe burs. They were taking an early breakfast before going to their regular harvest-work. While I was busy with my own breakfast I heard the thudding fall of two or three heavy cones from a yellow pine near me. I stole noiselessly forward within about twenty feet of the base of it to observe. In a few moments down came the Douglas. The breakfast-burs he had cut off had rolled on the gently sloping ground into a clump of ceanothus bushes, but he seemed to know exactly where they were, for he found them at once, apparently without searching for them. They were more than twice as heavy as himself, but after turning them into the right position for getting a good hold with his long sickle-teeth he managed to drag them up to the foot of the tree from which he had cut them, moving backward. Then seating himself comfortably, he held them on end, bottom up, and demolished them at his ease. A good deal of nibbling had to be done before he got anything to eat, because the lower scales are barren, but when he had patiently worked his way up to the fertile ones he found two sweet nuts at the base of each, shaped like trimmed hams, and spotted purple like birds' eggs. And notwithstanding these cones were dripping with soft balsam, and covered with prickles, and so strongly put together that a boy would be puzzled to cut them open with a jack-knife, he accomplished his meal with easy dignity and cleanliness, making less effort apparently than a man would in eating soft cookery from a plate.

Breakfast done, I whistled a tune for him before he went to work, curious to see how he would be affected by it. He had not seen me all this while; but the instant I began to whistle he darted up the tree nearest to him, and came out on a small dead limb opposite me, and composed himself to listen. I sang and whistled more than a dozen airs, and as the music changed his eyes sparkled, and he turned his head quickly from side to side, but made no other response. Other squirrels, hearing the strange sounds, came around on all sides, also chipmunks and birds. One of the birds, a handsome, speckle-breasted thrush, seemed even more interested than the squirrels. After listening for awhile on one of the lower dead sprays of a pine, he came swooping forward within a few feet of my face, and remained fluttering in the air for half a minute or so, sustaining himself with whirring wing-beats, like a humming-bird in front of a flower, while I could look into his eyes and see his innocent wonder.

By this time my performance must have lasted nearly half an hour. I sang or whistled 'Bonnie Doon,' 'Lass o' Gowrie,' 'O'er the Water to Charlie,' 'Bonnie Woods o' Cragie Lee,' etc., all of which seemed to be listened to with bright interest, my first Douglas sitting patiently through it all, with his telling eyes fixed upon me until I ventured to give the 'Old Hundredth,' when he screamed his Indian name, Pillillooeet, turned tail, and darted with ludicrous haste up the tree out of sight, his voice and actions in the case leaving a somewhat profane impression, as if he had said, 'I'll be hanged if you get me to hear anything so solemn and unpiny.' This acted as a signal for the general dispersal of the whole hairy tribe, though the birds seemed willing to wait further developments, music being naturally more in their line.

What there can be in that grand old church-tune that is so offensive to birds and squirrels I can't imagine. A year or two after this High Sierra concert, I was sitting one fine day on a hill in the Coast Range where the common ground squirrels were abundant. They were very shy on account of being hunted so much; but after I had been silent and motionless for half an hour or so they began to venture out of their holes and to feed on the seeds of the grasses and thistles around me as if I were no more to be feared than a tree-stump. Then it occurred to me that this was a good opportunity to find out whether they also disliked 'Old Hundredth.' Therefore I began to whistle as nearly as I could remember the same familiar airs that had pleased the mountaineers of the Sierra. They at once stopped eating, stood erect, and listened patiently until I came to 'Old Hundredth,' when with ludicrous haste every one of them rushed to their holes and bolted in, their feet twinkling in the air for a moment as they vanished.

No one who makes the acquaintance of our forester will fail to admire him; but he is far too self-reliant and warlike ever to be taken for a darling.

How long the life of a Douglas squirrel may be, I don't know. The young seem to sprout from knot-holes, perfect from the first, and as enduring as their own trees. It is difficult, indeed, to realize that so condensed a piece of sun-fire should ever become dim or die at all. He is seldom killed by hunters, for he is too small to encourage much of their attention, and when pursued in settled regions becomes excessively shy, and keeps close in the furrows of the highest trunks, many of which are of the same colour as himself. Indian boys, however, lie in wait with unbounded patience to shoot them with arrows. In the lower and middle zones a few fall a prey to rattlesnakes. Occasionally he is pursued by hawks and wildcats, etc. But, upon the whole, he dwells safely in the deep bosom of the woods, the most highly favoured of all his happy tribe. May his tribe increase!

CHAPTER TEN

A Wind-Storm in the Forests

THE MOUNTAIN winds, like the dew and rain, sunshine and snow, are measured and bestowed with love on the forests to develop their strength and beauty. However restricted the scope of other forest influences, that of the winds is universal. The snow bends and trims the upper forests every winter, the lightning strikes a single tree here and there, while avalanches mow down thousands at a swoop as a gardener trims out a bed of flowers. But the winds go to every tree, fingering every leaf and branch and furrowed bole; not one is forgotten; the mountain pine towering with outstretched arms on the rugged buttresses of the icy peaks, the lowliest and most retiring tenant of the dells; they seek and find them all, caressing them tenderly, bending them in lusty exercise, stimulating their growth, plucking off a leaf or limb as required, or removing an entire tree or grove, now whispering and cooing through the branches like a sleepy child, now roaring like the ocean; the winds blessing the forests, the forests the winds, with ineffable beauty and harmony as the sure result.

After one has seen pines six feet in diameter bending like grasses before a mountain gale, and ever and anon some giant falling with a crash that shakes the hills, it seems astonishing that any, save the lowest thickset trees, could ever have found a period sufficiently stormless to establish themselves; or, once established, that they should not, sooner or later, have been blown down. But when the storm is over, and we behold the same forests tranquil again, towering fresh and unscathed in erect majesty, and consider what centuries of storms have fallen upon them since they were first planted – hail, to break the tender seedlings; lightning to scorch and shatter; snow, winds and avalanches, to crush and overwhelm – while the manifest result of all this wild storm-culture is the glorious perfection we behold; then faith in Nature's forestry is established, and we cease to deplore the violence of her most destructive gales, or of any other storm-implement whatsoever.

There are two trees in the Sierra forests that are never blown down, so long as they continue in sound health. These are the juniper and the dwarf pine of the summit peaks. Their stiff, crooked roots grip the storm-beaten ledges like eagles' claws, while their lithe, cord-like branches bend round compliantly, offering but slight holds for winds, however violent. The other alpine conifers – the needle pine, mountain pine, two-leaved pine and hemlock spruce – are never thinned out by this agent to any destructive extent, on account of their admirable toughness and the closeness of their growth. In general the same is true of the giants of the lower zones. The kingly sugar pine, towering aloft to a height of more than 200ft., offers a fine mark to storm-winds; but it is not densely foliaged, and its long, horizontal arms swing round compliantly in the blast, like tresses of green, fluent algae in a brook; while the silver firs in most places keep their ranks well together in united strength. The yellow or silver pine is more frequently overturned than any other tree on the Sierra, because its leaves and branches form a larger mass in proportion to its height, while in many places it is planted sparsely, leaving open lanes through which storms may enter with full force. Furthermore, because it is distributed along the lower portion of the range, which was the first to be left bare on the breaking up of the ice-sheet at the close of the glacial winter, the soil it is growing upon has been longer exposed to post-glacial weathering, and consequently is in a more crumbling, decayed condition than the fresher soils farther up the range, and therefore offers a less secure anchorage for the roots.

While exploring the forest zones of Mount Shasta, I discovered the path of a hurricane strewn with thousands of pines of this species. Great and small had been uprooted or wrenched off by sheer force, making a clean gap, like that made by a snow avalanche. But hurricanes capable of doing this class of work are rare in the Sierra, and when we have explored the forests from one extremity of the range to the other, we are compelled to believe that they are the most beautiful on the face of the earth, however we may regard the agents that have made them so.

There is always something deeply exciting, not only in the sounds of winds in the woods, which exert more or less influence over every mind, but in their varied waterlike flow as manifested by the movements of the trees, especially those of the conifers. By no other trees are they rendered so extensively and impressively visible, not even by the lordly tropic palms or tree-ferns responsive to the gentlest breeze. The waving of a forest of the giant Sequoias is indescribably impressive and sublime, but the pines seem to me the best interpreters of winds. They are mighty waving goldenrods, ever in tune, singing and writing wind-music all their long century lives. Little, however, of this noble tree-waving and tree-music will you see or hear in the strictly alpine portion of the forests. The burly juniper, whose girth sometimes more than equals its height, is about as rigid as the rocks on which it grows. The slender lash-like sprays of the dwarf pine stream out in wavering ripples, but the tallest and slenderest are far too unyielding to wave even in the heaviest gales. They only shake in quick, short vibrations. The hemlock spruce, however, and the mountain pine, and some of the tallest thickets of the two-leaved species bow in storms with considerable scope and gracefulness. But it is only in the lower and middle zones that the meeting of winds and woods is to be seen in all its grandeur.

One of the most beautiful and exhilarating storms I ever enjoyed in the Sierra occurred in December, 1874, when I happened to be exploring one of the tributary valleys of the Yuba River. The sky and the ground and the trees had been thoroughly rain-washed and were dry again. The day was intensely pure, one of those incomparable bits of California winter, warm and balmy and full of white sparkling sunshine, redolent of all the purest influences of the spring, and at the same time enlivened with one of the most bracing wind-storms conceivable. Instead of camping out, as I usually do, I then chanced to be stopping at the house of a friend. But when the storm began to sound, I lost no time in pushing out into the woods to enjoy it. For on such occasions Nature has always something rare to show us, and the danger to life and limb is hardly greater than one would experience crouching deprecatingly beneath a roof.

It was still early morning when I found myself fairly adrift. Delicious sunshine came pouring over the hills, lighting the tops of the pines, and setting free a steam of summery fragrance that contrasted strangely with the wild tones of the storm. The air was mottled with pine-tassels and bright green plumes, that went flashing past in the sunlight like birds pursued. But there was not the slightest dustiness, nothing less pure than leaves, and ripe pollen, and flecks of withered bracken and moss. I heard trees falling for hours at the rate of one every two or three minutes; some uprooted, partly on account of the loose, water-soaked condition of the ground; others broken straight across, where some weakness caused by fire had determined the spot. The gestures of the various trees made a delightful study. Young sugar pines, light and feathery as squirrel-tails, were bowing almost to the ground; while the grand old patriarchs, whose massive boles had been tried in a hundred storms, waved solemnly above them, their long, arching branches streaming fluently on the gale, and every needle thrilling and ringing and shedding off keen lances of light like a diamond. The Douglas spruces, with long sprays drawn out in level tresses, and needles massed in a grey, shimmering glow, presented a most striking appearance as they stood in bold relief along the hilltops. The madroños in the dells, with their red bark and large glossy leaves tilted every way, reflected the sunshine in throbbing spangles like those one so often sees on the rippled surface of a glacier lake. But the silver pines were now the most impressively beautiful of all. Colossal spires 200ft. in height waved like supple goldenrods chanting and bowing low as if in worship, while the whole mass of their long, tremulous foliage was kindled into one con-tinuous blaze of white sun-fire. The force of the gale was such that the most steadfast monarch of them all rocked down to its roots with a motion plainly perceptible when one leaned against it. Nature was holding high festival, and every fibre of the most rigid giants thrilled with glad excitement.

I drifted on through the midst of this passionate music and motion, across many a glen, from ridge to ridge; often halting in the lee of a rock for shelter, or to gaze and listen. Even when the grand anthem had swelled to its highest pitch, I could distinctly hear the varying tones of individual trees – spruce, and fir, and pine, and leafless oak – and even the infinitely gentle rustle of the withered grasses at my feet. Each was expressing itself in its own way – singing its own song, and making its own peculiar gestures – manifesting a richness of variety to be found in no other forest I have yet seen. The coniferous woods of Canada, and the Carolinas, and Florida, are made up of trees that resemble one another about as nearly as blades of grass, and grow close together in much the same way. Coniferous trees, in general, seldom possess individual character, such as is manifest among oaks and elms. But the California forests are made up of a greater number of distinct species than any other in the world. And in them we find, not only a marked differentiation into special groups, but also a marked individuality in almost every tree, giving rise to storm effects indescribably glorious.

Toward midday, after a long, tingling scramble through copses of hazel and ceanothus, I gained the summit of the highest ridge in the neighbourhood; and then it occurred to me that it would be a fine thing to climb one of the trees to obtain a wider outlook and get my ear close to the Æolian music of its topmost needles. But under the circumstances the choice of a tree was a serious matter. One whose instep was not very strong seemed in danger of being blown down, or of being struck by others in case they should fall; another was branchless to a considerable height above the ground, and at the same time too large to be grasped with arms and legs in climbing; while others were not favourably situated for clear views. After cautiously casting about, I made choice of the tallest of a group of Douglas spruces that were growing close together like a tuft of grass, no one of which seemed likely to fall unless all the rest fell with it. Though comparatively young, they were about 100ft. high, and their lithe, brushy tops were rocking and swirling in wild ecstasy. Being accustomed to climb trees in making botanical studies, I experienced no difficulty in reaching the top of this one, and never before did I enjoy so noble an exhilaration of motion. The slender tops fairly flapped and swished in the passionate torrent, bending and swirling backward and forward, round and round, tracing indescribable combinations of vertical and horizontal curves, while I clung with muscles firm braced, like a bobo-link on a reed.

In its widest sweeps my tree-top described an arc from twenty to thirty degrees, but I felt sure of its elastic temper, having seen others of the same species still more severely tried – bent almost to the ground indeed, in heavy snows – without breaking a fibre. I was therefore safe, and free to take the wind into my pulses and enjoy the excited forest from my superb outlook. The view from here must be extremely beautiful in any weather. Now my eye roved over the piny hills and dales as over fields of waving grain, and felt the light running in ripples and broad swelling undulations across the valleys from ridge to ridge, as the shining foliage was stirred by corresponding waves of air. Oftentimes these waves of reflected light would break up suddenly into a kind of beaten foam, and again, after chasing one another in regular order, they would seem to bend forward in concentric curves, and disappear on some hillside, like sea-waves on a shelving shore. The quantity of light reflected from the bent needles was so great as to make whole groves appear as if covered with snow, while the black shadows beneath the trees greatly enhanced the effect of the silvery splendour.

Excepting only the shadows there was nothing sombre in all this wild sea of pines. On the contrary, notwithstanding this was the winter season, the colours were remarkably beautiful. The shafts of the pine and libocedrus were brown and purple, and most of the foliage was well tinged with yellow; the laurel groves, with the pale undersides of their leaves turned upward, made masses of grey, and then there was many a dash of chocolate colour from clumps of manzanita, and jet of vivid crimson from the bark of the madroños, while the ground on the hillsides, appearing here and there through openings between the groves, displayed masses of pale purple and brown.

The sounds of the storm corresponded gloriously with this wild exuberance of light and motion. The profound bass of the naked branches and boles booming like waterfalls; the quick, tense vibrations of the pine-needles, now rising to a shrill, whistling hiss, now falling to a silky murmur; the rustling of laurel groves in the dells, and the keen metallic click of leaf on leaf – all this was heard in easy analysis when the attention was calmly bent.

The varied gestures of the multitude were seen to fine advantage, so that one could recognize the different species at a distance of several miles by this means alone, as well as by their forms and colours, and the way they reflected the light. All seemed strong and comfortable, as if really enjoying the storm, while responding to its most enthusiastic greetings. We hear much nowadays concerning the universal struggle for existence, but no struggle in the common meaning of the word was manifest here; no recognition of danger by any tree; no deprecation; but rather an invincible gladness as remote from exultation as from fear.

I kept my lofty perch for hours, frequently closing my eyes to enjoy the music by itself, or to feast quietly on the delicious fragrance that was streaming past. The fragrance of the woods was less marked than that produced during warm rain, when so many balsamic buds and leaves are steeped like tea; but, from the chafing of resiny branches against each other, and the incessant attrition of myriads of needles, the gale was spiced to a very tonic degree. And besides the fragrance from these local sources there were traces of scents brought from afar. For this wind came first from the sea, rubbing against its fresh, briny waves, then distilled through the redwoods, threading rich ferny gulches, and spreading itself in broad undulating currents over many a flower-enamelled ridge of the coast mountains, then across the golden plains, up the purple foot-hills, and into these piny woods with the varied incense gathered by the way.

Winds are advertisements of all they touch, however much or little we may be able to read them; telling their wanderings even by their scents alone.

Mariners detect the flowery perfume of land-winds far at sea, and sea-winds carry the fragrance of dulse and tangle far inland, where it is quickly recognized, though mingled with the scents of a thousand land-flowers. As an illustration of this, I may tell here that I breathed sea-air on the Firth of Forth, in Scotland, while a boy; then was taken to Wisconsin, where I remained nineteen years; then, without in all this time having breathed one breath of the sea, I walked quietly, alone, from the middle of the Mississippi Valley to the Gulf of Mexico, on a botanical excursion, and while in Florida, far from the coast, my attention wholly bent on the splendid tropical vegetation about me, I suddenly recognized a sea-breeze, as it came sifting through the palmettos and blooming vine-tangles, which at once awakened and set free a thousand dormant associations, and made me a boy again in Scotland, as if all the intervening years had been annihilated.

Most people like to look at mountain rivers, and bear them in mind; but few care to look at the winds, though far more beautiful and sublime, and though they become at times about as visible as flowing water. When the north winds in winter are making upward sweeps over the curving summits of the High Sierra, the fact is sometimes published with flying snow-banners a mile long. Those portions of the winds thus embodied can scarce be wholly invisible, even to the darkest imagination. And when we look around over an agitated forest, we may see something of the wind that stirs it, by its effects upon the trees. Yonder it descends in a rush of water-like ripples, and sweeps over the bending pines from hill to hill. Nearer, we see detached plumes and leaves, now speeding by on level currents, now whirling in eddies, or, escaping over the edges of the whirls, soaring aloft on grand, upswelling domes of air, or tossing on flame-like crests. Smooth, deep currents, cascades, falls and swirling eddies, sing around every tree and leaf, and over all the varied topography of the region with telling changes of form, like mountain rivers conforming to the features of their channels.

After tracing the Sierra streams from their fountains to the plains, marking where they bloom white in falls, glide in crystal plumes, surge grey and foam-filled in boulder-choked gorges, and slip through the woods in long, tranquil reaches – after thus learning their language and forms in detail, we may at length hear them chanting all together in one grand anthem, and comprehend them all in clear inner vision, covering the range like lace. But even this spectacle is far less sublime and not a whit more substantial than what we may behold of these storm-streams of air in the mountain woods.

We all travel the milky way together, trees and men; but it never occurred to me until this storm-day, while swinging in the wind, that trees are travellers, in the ordinary sense. They make many journeys, not extensive ones, it is true; but our own little journeys, away and back again, are only little more than tree-wavings – many of them not so much.

When the storm began to abate, I dismounted and sauntered down through the calming woods. The storm-tones died away, and, turning toward the east, I beheld the countless hosts of the forests hushed and tranquil, towering above one another on the slopes of the hills like a devout audience. The setting sun filled them with amber light, and seemed to say, while they listened, 'My peace I give unto you.'

As I gazed on the impressive scene, all the so-called ruin of the storm was forgotten, and never before did these noble woods appear so fresh, so joyous, so immortal.

CHAPTER ELEVEN

The River Floods

THE SIERRA rivers are flooded every spring by the melting of the snow as regularly as the famous old Nile. They begin to rise in May, and in June high-water mark is reached. But because the melting does not go on rapidly over all the fountains, high and low, simultaneously, and the melted snow is not reinforced at this time of year by rain, the spring floods are seldom very violent or destructive. The thousand falls, however, and the cascades in the canyons are then in full bloom, and sing songs from one end of the range to the other. Of course the snow on the lower tributaries of the rivers is first melted, then that on the higher fountains most exposed to sunshine, and about a month later the cooler, shadowy fountains send down their treasures, thus allowing the main trunk streams nearly six weeks to get their waters hurried through the foot-hills and across the lowlands to the sea. Therefore very violent spring floods are avoided, and will be as long as the shading, restraining forests last. The rivers of the north half of the range are still less subject to sudden floods, because their upper fountains in great part lie protected from the changes of the weather beneath thick folds of lava, just as many of the rivers of Alaska lie beneath folds of ice, coming to the light farther down the range in large springs, while those of the high Sierra lie on the surface of solid granite, exposed to every change of temperature. More than ninety per cent of the water derived from the snow and ice of Mount Shasta is at once absorbed and drained away beneath the porous lava folds of the mountain, where mumbling and groping in the dark they at length find larger fissures and tunnel-like caves from which they emerge, filtered and cool, in the form of large springs, some of them so large they give birth to rivers that set out on their journeys beneath the sun without any visible intermediate period of childhood. Thus the Shasta River issues from a large lake-like spring in Shasta Valley, and about two-thirds of the volume of the McCloud River gushes forth suddenly from the face of a lava bluff in a roaring spring seventy-five yards wide.

These spring rivers of the north are of course shorter than those of the south whose tributaries extend up to the tops of the mountains. Fall River, an important tributary of the Pitt or Upper Sacramento, is only about ten miles long, and is all falls, cascades and springs from its head to its confluence with the Pitt. Bountiful springs, charmingly embowered, issue from the rocks at one end of it, a snowy fall a hundred and eighty feet high thunders at the other, and a rush of crystal rapids sing and dance between. Of course such streams are but little affected by the weather. Sheltered from evaporation their flow is nearly as full in the autumn as in the time of general spring floods. While those of the High Sierra diminish to less than the hundredth part of their springtime prime, shallowing in autumn to a series of silent pools among the rocks and hollows of their channels, connected by feeble, creeping threads of water, like the sluggish sentences of a tired writer, connected by a drizzle of 'ands' and 'buts'. Strange to say, the greatest floods occur in winter, when one would suppose all the wild waters would be muffled and chained in frost and snow. The same long, all-day storms of the so-called Rainy Season in California, that give rain to the lowlands, give dry frosty snow to the mountains. But at rare intervals warm rains and warm winds invade the mountains and push back the snow line from 2,000ft. to 8,000, or even higher, and then come the big floods.

I was usually driven down out of the High Sierra about the end of November, but the winter of 1874 and 1875 was so warm and calm that I was tempted to seek general views of the geology and topography of the basin of Feather River in January. And I had just completed a hasty survey of the region, and made my way down to winter quarters, when one of the grandest flood-storms that I ever saw broke on the mountains. I was then in the edge of the main forest belt at a small foot-hill town called Knoxville, on the divide between the waters of the Feather and Yuba Rivers. The cause of this notable flood was simply a sudden and copious fall of warm wind and rain on the basins of these rivers at a time when they contained a considerable quantity of snow. The rain was so heavy and long-sustained that it was, of itself, sufficient to make a good wild flood, while the snow which the warm wind and rain melted on the upper and middle regions of the basins was sufficient to make another flood equal to that of the rain. Now these two distinct harvests of flood waters were gathered simultaneously and poured out on the plain in one magnificent avalanche. The basins of the Yuba and Feather, like many others of the Sierra, are admirably adapted to the growth of floods of this kind. Their many tributaries radiate far and wide, comprehending extensive areas, and the tributaries are steeply inclined, while the trunks are comparatively level. While the flood-storm was in progress the thermometer at Knoxville ranged between 44° and 50°; and when warm wind and warm rain fall simultaneously on snow contained in basins like these, both the rain and that portion of the snow which the rain and wind melt are at first sponged up and held back until the combined mass becomes sludge, which at length, suddenly dissolving, slips and descends all together to the trunk channel; and since the deeper the stream the faster it flows, the flooded portion of the current above overtakes the slower foot-hill portion below it, and all sweeping forward together with a high, overcurling front, debouches on the open plain with a violence and suddenness that at first seem wholly unaccountable. The destructiveness of the lower portion of this particular flood was somewhat augmented by mining gravel in the river channels, and by levees which gave way after having at first

restrained and held back the accumulating waters. These exaggerating conditions did not, however, greatly influence the general result, the main effect
having been caused by the rare combination of flood factors indicated above.
It is a pity that but few people meet and enjoy storms so noble as this in their
homes in the mountains, for, spending themselves in the open levels of the
plains, they are likely to be remembered more by the bridges and houses they
carry away than by their beauty or the thousand blessings they bring to the
fields and gardens of Nature.

On the morning of the flood, January 19th, all the Feather and Yuba
landscapes were covered with running water, muddy torrents filled every
gulch and ravine, and the sky was thick with rain. The pines had long been
sleeping in sunshine; they were now awake, roaring and waving with the
beating storm, and the winds sweeping along the curves of hill and dale,
streaming through the woods, surging and gurgling on the tops of rocky
ridges, made the wildest of wild storm melody.

It was easy to see that only a small part of the rain reached the ground in
the form of drops. Most of it was thrashed into dusty spray like that into
which small waterfalls are divided when they dash on shelving rocks. Never
have I seen water coming from the sky in denser or more passionate streams.
The wind chased the spray forward in choking drifts, and compelled me again
and again to seek shelter in the dell copses and back of large trees to rest and
catch my breath. Wherever I went, on ridges or in hollows, enthusiastic water
still flashed and gurgled about my ankles, recalling a wild winter flood in
Yosemite when a hundred waterfalls came booming and chanting together
and filled the grand valley with a sea-like roar.

After drifting an hour or two in the lower woods, I set out for the summit of
a hill 900ft. high, with a view to getting as near the heart of the storm as
possible. In order to reach it I had to cross Dry Creek, a tributary of the Yuba
that goes crawling along the base of the hill on the northwest. It was now a
booming river as large as the Tuolumne at ordinary stages, its current brown
with mining-mud washed down from many a 'claim,' and mottled with sluice-
boxes, fence-rails and logs that had long lain above its reach. A slim foot-
bridge stretched across it, now scarcely above the swollen current. Here I was
glad to linger, gazing and listening, while the storm was in its richest mood –
the grey rain-flood above, the brown river-flood beneath. The language of the
river was scarcely less enchanting than that of the wind and rain; the sublime
overboom of the main bouncing, exulting current, the swash and gurgle of the
eddies, the keen dash and clash of heavy waves breaking against rocks, and
the smooth, downy hush of shallow currents feeling their way through the
willow thickets of the margin. And amid all this varied throng of sounds I
heard the smothered bumping and rumbling of boulders on the bottom as
they were shoving and rolling forward against one another in a wild rush,
after having lain still for probably 100 years or more.

The glad creek rose high above its banks and wandered from its channel out
over many a briery sand-flat and meadow. Alders and willows waist-deep
were bearing up against the current with nervous trembling gestures, as if
afraid of being carried away, while supple branches bending confidingly,

dipped lightly and rose again, as if stroking the wild waters in play. Leaving the bridge and passing on through the storm-thrashed woods, all the ground seemed to be moving. Pine-tassels, flakes of bark, soil, leaves and broken branches were being swept forward, and many a rock-fragment, weathered from exposed ledges, was now receiving its first rounding and polishing in the wild streams of the storm. On they rushed through every gulch and hollow, leaping, gliding, working with a will, and rejoicing like living creatures.

Nor was the flood confined to the ground. Every tree had a water system of its own spreading far and wide like miniature Amazons and Mississippis.

Toward midday, cloud, wind and rain reached their highest development. The storm was in full bloom, and formed, from my commanding outlook on the hilltop, one of the most glorious views I ever beheld. As far as the eye could reach, above, beneath, around, wind-driven rain filled the air like one vast waterfall. Detached clouds swept imposingly up the valley, as if they were endowed with independent motion and had special work to do in replenishing the mountain wells, now rising above the pine-tops, now descending into their midst, fondling their arrowy spires and soothing every branch and leaf with gentleness in the midst of all the savage sound and motion. Others keeping near the ground glided behind separate groves, and brought them forward into relief with admirable distinctness; or, passing in front, eclipsed whole groves in succession, pine after pine melting in their grey fringes and bursting forth again seemingly clearer than before.

The forms of storms are in great part measured, and controlled by the topography of the regions where they rise and over which they pass. When, therefore, we attempt to study them from the valleys, or from gaps and openings of the forest, we are confounded by a multitude of separate and apparently antagonistic impressions. The bottom of the storm is broken up into innumerable waves and currents that surge against the hillsides like sea-waves against a shore, and these, reacting on the nether surface of the storm, erode immense cavernous hollows and canyons, and sweep forward the resulting detritus in long trains, like the moraines of glaciers. But, as we ascend, these partial, confusing effects disappear and the phenomena are beheld united and harmonious.

The longer I gazed into the storm, the more plainly visible it became. The drifting cloud detritus gave it a kind of visible body, which explained many perplexing phenomena, and published its movements in plain terms, while the texture of the falling mass of rain rounded it out and rendered it more complete. Because raindrops differ in size they fall at different velocities and overtake and clash against one another, producing mist and spray. They also, of course, yield unequal compliance to the force of the wind, which gives rise to a still greater degree of interference, and passionate gusts sweep off clouds of spray from the groves like that torn from wave-tops in a gale. All these factors of irregularity in density, colour and texture of the general rain mass tend to make it the more appreciable and telling. It is then seen as one grand flood rushing over bank and brae, bending the pines like weeds, curving this way and that, whirling in huge eddies in hollows and dells, while the main current pours grandly over all, like ocean currents over the landscapes that lie hidden at the bottom of the sea.

I watched the gestures of the pines while the storm was at its height, and it was easy to see that they were not distressed. Several large sugar pines stood near the thicket in which I was sheltered, bowing solemnly and tossing their long arms as if interpreting the very words of the storm while accepting its wildest onsets with passionate exhilaration. The lions were feeding. Those who have observed sunflowers feasting on sunshine during the golden days of Indian summer know that none of their gestures express thankfulness. Their celestial food is too heartily given, too heartily taken to leave room for thanks. The pines were evidently accepting the benefactions of the storm in the same whole-souled manner; and when I looked down among the budding hazels, and still lower to the young violets and fern-tufts on the rocks, I noticed the same divine methods of giving and taking, and the same exquisite adaptations of what seems an outbreak of violent and uncontrollable force to the purposes of beautiful and delicate life. Calms like sleep come upon landscapes, just as they do on people and trees, and storms awaken them in the same way. In the dry midsummer of the lower portion of the range the withered hills and valleys seem to lie as empty and expressionless as dead shells on a shore. Even the highest mountains may be found occasionally dull and uncommunicative as if in some way they had lost countenance and shrunk to less than half their real stature. But when the lightnings crash and echo in the canyons, and the clouds come down wreathing and crowning their bald snowy heads, every feature beams with expression and they rise again in all their imposing majesty.

Storms are fine speakers, and tell all they know, but their voices of lightning, torrent and rushing wind are much less numerous than the nameless still, small voices too low for human ears; and because we are poor listeners we fail to catch much that is fairly within reach. Our best rains are heard mostly on roofs, and winds in chimneys; and when by choice or compulsion we are pushed into the heart of a storm, the confusion made by cumbersome equipments and nervous haste and mean fear, prevent our hearing any other than the loudest expressions. Yet we may draw enjoyment from storm sounds that are beyond hearing, and storm movements we cannot see. The sublime whirl of planets around their suns is as silent as raindrops oozing in the dark among the roots of plants. In this great storm, as in every other, there were tones and gestures inexpressibly gentle manifested in the midst of what is called violence and fury, but easily recognized by all who look and listen for them. The rain brought out the colours of the woods with delightful freshness, the rich brown of the bark of the trees and the fallen burs and leaves and dead ferns; the greys of rocks and lichens; the light purple of swelling buds, and the warm yellow greens of the libocedrus and mosses. The air was steaming with delightful fragrance, not rising and wafting past in separate masses, but diffused through all the atmosphere. Pine woods are always fragrant, but most so in spring when the young tassels are opening and in warm weather when the various gums and balsams are softened by the sun. The wind was now chafing their innumerable needles and the warm rain was steeping them.

Monardella grows here in large beds in the openings, and there is plenty of laurel in dells and manzanita on the hillsides, and the rosy, fragrant chamœbatia carpets the ground almost everywhere. These, with the gums and balsams of the woods, form the main local fragrance-fountains of the storm. The ascending clouds of aroma wind-rolled and rain-washed became pure like light and travelled with the wind as part of it. Toward the middle of the afternoon the main flood cloud lifted along its western border revealing a beautiful section of the Sacramento Valley some twenty or thirty miles away, brilliantly sun-lighted and glistering with rain-sheets as if paved with silver. Soon afterward a jagged bluff-like cloud with a sheer face appeared over the valley of the Yuba, dark-coloured and roughened with numerous furrows like some huge lava-table. The blue Coast Range was seen stretching along the sky like a bevelled wall, and the sombre, craggy Marysville Buttes rose impressively out of the flooded plain like islands out of the sea. Then the rain began to abate and I sauntered down through the dripping bushes revelling in the universal vigour and freshness that inspired all the life about me. How clean and unworn and immortal the woods seemed to be! – the lofty cedars in full bloom laden with golden pollen and their washed plumes shining; the pines rocking gently and settling back into rest, and the evening sunbeams spangling on the broad leaves of the madroños, their tracery of yellow boughs relieved against dusky thickets of chestnut oak; liverworts, lycopodiums, ferns were exulting in glorious revival, and every moss that had ever lived seemed to be coming crowding back from the dead to clothe each trunk and stone in living green. The steaming ground seemed fairly to throb and tingle with life; smilax, fritillaria, saxifrage and young violets were pushing up as if already conscious of the summer glory, and innumerable green and yellow buds were peeping and smiling everywhere.

As for the birds and squirrels, not a wing or tail of them was to be seen while the storm was blowing. Squirrels dislike wet weather more than cats do; therefore they were at home rocking in their dry nests. The birds were hiding in the dells out of the wind, some of the strongest of them pecking at acorns and manzanita berries, but most were perched on low twigs, their breast feathers puffed out and keeping one another company through the hard time as best they could.

When I arrived at the village about sundown, the good people bestirred themselves, pitying my bedraggled condition as if I were some benumbed castaway snatched from the sea, while I, in turn, warm with excitement and reeking like the ground, pitied them for being dry and defrauded of all the glory that Nature had spread round about them that day.

CHAPTER TWELVE

Sierra Thunder-Storms

THE WEATHER of spring and summer in the middle region of the Sierra is usually well flecked with rains and light dustings of snow, most of which are far too obviously joyful and life-giving to be regarded as storms; and in the picturesque beauty and clearness of outlines of their clouds they offer striking contrasts to those boundless, all-embracing cloud-mantles of the storms of winter. The smallest and most perfectly individualized specimens present a richly modelled cumulous cloud rising above the dark woods, about 11 am, swelling with a visible motion straight up into the calm, sunny sky to a height of 12,000 to 14,000ft. above the sea, its white, pearly bosses relieved by grey and pale purple shadows in the hollows, and showing outlines as keenly defined as those of the glacier-polished domes. In less than an hour it attains full development and stands poised in the blazing sunshine like some colossal mountain, as beautiful in form and finish as if it were to become a permanent addition to the landscape. Presently a thunderbolt crashes through the crisp air, ringing like steel on steel, sharp and clear, its startling detonation breaking into a spray of echoes against the cliffs and canyon walls. Then down comes a cataract of rain. The big drops sift through the pine-needles, plash and patter on the granite pavements, and pour down the sides of ridges and domes in a network of grey, bubbling rills. In a few minutes the cloud withers to a mesh of dim filaments and disappears, leaving the sky perfectly clear and bright, every dust-particle wiped and washed out of it. Everything is refreshed and invigorated, a steam of fragrance rises, and the storm is finished – one cloud, one lightning-stroke and one dash of rain. This is the Sierra mid-summer thunder-storm reduced to its lowest terms. But some of them attain much larger proportions, and assume a grandeur and energy of expression hardly surpassed by those bred in the depths of winter, producing those sudden floods called 'cloud-bursts,' which are local, and to a considerable extent periodical, for they appear nearly every day about the same time for weeks, usually about eleven o'clock, and lasting from five minutes to an hour or two. One soon becomes so accustomed to see them that the noon sky seems empty and abandoned without them, as if Nature were forgetting something. When the glorious pearl and alabaster clouds of these noonday storms are being built I never give attention to anything else. No mountain or mountain-range, however divinely clothed with light, has a more enduring charm than those fleeting mountains of the sky – floating fountains bearing water for every well, the angels of the streams and lakes; brooding in the deep azure, or sweeping softly along the ground over ridge and dome, over meadow, over forest, over garden and grove; lingering with cooling shadows, refreshing every flower, and soothing rugged rock-brows with a gentleness of touch and gesture wholly divine.

The most beautiful and imposing of the summer storms rise just above the upper edge of the silver fir zone, and all are so beautiful that it is not easy to choose any one for particular description. The one that I remember best fell on the mountains near Yosemite Valley, 19 July, 1869, while I was encamped in the silver fir woods. A range of bossy cumuli took possession of the sky, huge domes and peaks rising one beyond another with deep canyons between them, bending this way and that in long curves and reaches, interrupted here and there with white upboiling masses that looked like the spray of waterfalls. Zigzag lances of lightning followed each other in quick succession, and the thunder was so gloriously loud and massive it seemed as if surely an entire mountain was being shattered at every stroke. Only the trees were touched, however, so far as I could see – a few firs 200ft. high, perhaps, and five to six feet in diameter, were split into long rails and slivers from top to bottom and scattered to all points of the compass. Then came the rain in a hearty flood, covering the ground and making it shine with a continuous sheet of water that, like a transparent film or skin, fitted closely down over all the rugged anatomy of the landscape.

It is not long, geologically speaking, since the first raindrop fell on the present landscapes of the Sierra; and in the few tens of thousands of years of stormy cultivation they have been blest with, how beautiful they have become! The first rains fell on raw, crumbling moraines and rocks without a plant. Now scarcely a drop can fail to find a beautiful mark: on the tops of the peaks, on the smooth glacier pavements, on the curves of the domes, on moraines full of crystals, on the thousand forms of yosemitic sculpture with their tender beauty of balmy, flowery vegetation, laving, plashing, glinting, pattering; some falling softly on meadows, creeping out of sight, seeking and finding every thirsty rootlet, some through the spires of the woods, sifting in dust through the needles, and whispering good cheer to each of them; some falling with blunt tapping sounds, drumming on the broad leaves of veratrum, cypripedium, saxifrage; some falling straight into fragrant corollas, kissing the lips of lilies, glinting on the sides of crystals, on shining grains of gold; some falling into the fountains of snow to swell their well-saved stores; some into the lakes and rivers, patting the smooth, glassy levels, making dimples and bells and spray, washing the mountain windows, washing the wandering winds; some plashing into the heart of snowy falls and cascades as if eager to join in the dance and the song and beat the foam yet finer. Good work and happy work for the merry mountain raindrops, each one of them a brave fall in itself, rushing from the cliffs and hollows of the clouds into the cliffs and hollows of the mountains; away from the thunder of the sky into the thunder of the roaring rivers. And how far they have to go, and how many cups to fill – cassiope-cups, holding half a drop, and lake basins between the hills, each replenished with equal care – every drop God's messenger sent on its way with glorious pomp and display of power – silvery new-born stars with lake and river, mountain and valley – all that the landscape holds – reflected in their crystal depths.

CHAPTER THIRTEEN

The Water-Ouzel

THE WATERFALLS of the Sierra are frequented by only one bird – the Ouzel or Water Thrush (*Cinclus Mexicanus*, Sw.). He is a singularly joyous and lovable little fellow, about the size of a robin, clad in a plain waterproof suit of bluish grey, with a tinge of chocolate on the head and shoulders. In form he is about as smoothly plump and compact as a pebble that has been whirled in a pot-hole, the flowing contour of his body being interrupted only by his strong feet and bill, the crisp wing-tips, and the up-slanted wren-like tail.

Among all the countless waterfalls I have met in the course of ten years' exploration in the Sierra, whether among the icy peaks, or warm foot-hills, or in the profound yosemitic canyons of the middle region, not one was found without its ouzel. No canyon is too cold for this little bird, none too lonely, provided it be rich in falling water. Find a fall, or cascade, or rushing rapid, anywhere upon a clear stream, and there you will surely find its complementary ouzel, flitting about in the spray, diving in foaming eddies, whirling like a leaf among beaten foam-bells; ever vigorous and enthusiastic, yet self-contained, and neither seeking nor shunning your company.

If disturbed while dipping about in the margin shallows, he either sets off with a rapid whir to some other feeding-ground up or down the stream, or alights on some half-submerged rock or snag out in the current, and immediately begins to nod and curtsey like a wren, turning his head from side to side with many other odd dainty movements that never fail to fix the attention of the observer.

He is the mountain streams' own darling, the humming-bird of blooming waters, loving rocky ripple-slopes and sheets of foam as a bee loves flowers, as a lark loves sunshine and meadows. Among all the mountain birds, none has cheered me so much in my lonely wanderings – none so unfailingly. For both in winter and summer he sings, sweetly, cheerily, independent alike of sunshine and of love, requiring no other inspiration than the stream on which he dwells. While water sings, so must he, in heat or cold, calm or storm, ever attuning his voice in sure accord; low in the drought of summer and the drought of winter, but never silent.

During the golden days of Indian summer, after most of the snow has been melted, and the mountain streams have become feeble – a succession of silent pools, linked together by shallow, transparent currents and strips of silvery lacework – then the song of the ouzel is at its lowest ebb. But as soon as the winter clouds have bloomed, and the mountain treasuries are once more replenished with snow, the voices of the streams and ouzels increase in strength and richness until the flood season of early summer. Then the torrents chant their noblest anthems, and then is the flood-time of our songster's melody. As for weather, dark days and sun days are the same to him. The voices of most song-birds, however joyous, suffer a long winter eclipse; but the ouzel sings on through all the seasons and every kind of storm. Indeed no storm can be more violent than those of the waterfalls in the midst of which he delights to dwell. However dark and boisterous the weather, snowing, blowing, or cloudy, all the same he sings, and with never a note of sadness. No need of spring sunshine to thaw *his* song, for it never freezes. Never shall you hear anything wintry from *his* warm breast; no pinched cheeping, no wavering notes between sorrow and joy; his mellow, fluty voice is ever tuned to downright gladness, as free from dejection as cock-crowing.

It is pitiful to see wee frost-pinched sparrows on cold mornings in the mountain groves shaking the snow from their feathers, and hopping about as if anxious to be cheery, then hastening back to their hidings out of the wind, puffing out their breast-feathers over their toes, and subsiding among the leaves, cold and breakfastless, while the snow continues to fall, and there is no sign of clearing. But the ouzel never calls forth a single touch of pity; not because he is strong to endure, but rather because he seems to live a charmed life beyond the reach of every influence that makes endurance necessary.

One wild winter morning, when Yosemite Valley was swept its length from west to east by a cordial snow-storm, I sallied forth to see what I might learn and enjoy. A sort of grey, gloaming-like darkness filled the valley, the huge walls were out of sight, all ordinary sounds were smothered, and even the loudest booming of the falls was at times buried beneath the roar of the heavy-laden blast. The loose snow was already over five feet deep on the meadows, making extended walks impossible without the aid of snow-shoes. I found no great difficulty, however, in making my way to a certain ripple on the river where one of my ouzels lived. He was at home, busily gleaning his breakfast among the pebbles of a shallow portion of the margin, apparently unaware of anything extraordinary in the weather. Presently he flew out to a stone against which the icy current was beating, and turning his back to the wind, sang as delightfully as a lark in springtime.

After spending an hour or two with my favourite, I made my way across the valley, boring and wallowing through the drifts, to learn as definitely as possible how the other birds were spending their time. The Yosemite birds are easily found during the winter because all of them excepting the ouzel are restricted to the sunny north side of the valley, the south side being constantly eclipsed by the great frosty shadow of the wall. And because the Indian Canyon groves, from their peculiar exposure, are the warmest, the birds congregate there, more especially in severe weather.

I found most of the robins cowering on the lee side of the larger branches where the snow could not fall upon them, while two or three of the more enterprising were making desperate efforts to reach the mistletoe berries by clinging nervously to the underside of the snow-crowned masses, back downward, like woodpeckers. Every now and then they would dislodge some of the loose fringes of the snow-crown, which would come sifting down on them and send them screaming back to camp, where they would subside among their companions with a shiver, muttering in low, querulous chatter like hungry children.

Some of the sparrows were busy at the feet of the larger trees gleaning seeds and benumbed insects, joined now and then by a robin weary of his unsuccessful attempts upon the snow-covered berries. The brave woodpeckers were clinging to the snowless sides of the larger boles and overarching branches of the camp trees, making short flights from side to side of the grove, pecking now and then at the acorns they had stored in the bark, and chattering aimlessly as if unable to keep still, yet evidently putting in the time in a very dull way, like storm-bound travellers at a country tavern. The hardy nut-hatches were threading the open furrows of the trunks in their usual industrious manner, and uttering their quaint notes, evidently less distressed than their neighbours. The Steller jays were of course making more noisy stir than all the other birds combined; ever coming and going with loud bluster, screaming as if each had a lump of melting sludge in his throat, and taking good care to improve the favourable opportunity afforded by the storm to steal from the acorn stores of the woodpeckers. I also noticed one solitary grey eagle braving the storm on the top of a tall pine-stump just outside the main grove. He was standing bolt upright with his back to the wind, a tuft of snow piled on his square shoulders, a monument of passive endurance. Thus every snow-bound bird seemed more or less uncomfortable if not in positive distress. The storm was reflected in every gesture, and not one cheerful note, not to say song, came from a single bill; their cowering, joyless endurance offering a striking contrast to the spontaneous, irrepressible gladness of the Ouzel, who could no more help exhaling sweet song than a rose sweet fragrance. He *must* sing though the heavens fall. I remember noticing the distress of a pair of robins during the violent earthquake of the year 1872, when the pines of the Valley, with strange movements, flapped and waved their branches, and beetling rock-brows came thundering down to the meadows in tremendous avalanches. It did not occur to me in the midst of the excitement of other observations to look for the ouzels, but I doubt not they were singing straight on through it all, regarding the terrible rock-thunder as fearlessly as they do the booming of the waterfalls.

What may be regarded as the separate songs of the ouzel are exceedingly difficult of description, because they are so variable and at the same time so confluent. Though I have been acqiainted with my favourite ten years, and during most of this time have heard him sing nearly every day, I still detect notes and strains that seem new to me. Nearly all of his music is sweet and tender, lapsing from his round breast like water over the smooth lip of a pool, then breaking farther on into a sparkling foam of melodious notes, which glow with subdued enthusiasm, yet without expressing much of the strong, gushing ecstasy of the bobolink or skylark.

The more striking strains are perfect arabesques of melody, composed of a few full, round, mellow notes, embroidered with delicate trills which fade and melt in long slender cadences. In a general way his music is that of the streams refined and spiritualized. The deep booming notes of the falls are in it, the trills of rapids, the gurgling of margin eddies, the low whispering of level reaches, and the sweet tinkle of separate drops oozing from the ends of mosses and falling into tranquil pools.

The ouzel never sings in chorus with other birds, nor with his kind, but only with the streams. And like flowers that bloom beneath the surface of the ground, some of our favourite's best song-blossoms never rise above the surface of the heavier music of the water. I have often observe him singing in the midst of beaten spray, his music completely buried beneath the water's roar; yet I know he was surely singing by his gestures and the movements of his bill.

His food, as far as I have noticed, consists of all kinds of water insects, which in summer are chiefly procured along shallow margins. Here he wades about ducking his head under water and deftly turning over pebbles and fallen leaves with his bill, seldom choosing to go into deep water where he has to use his wings in diving.

He seems to be especially fond of the larvæ of mosquitos, found in abundance attached to the bottom of smooth rock channels where the current is shallow. When feeding in such places he wades up-stream, and often while his head is under water the swift current is deflected upward along the glossy curves of his neck and shoulders, in the form of a clear, crystalline shell, which fairly encloses him like a bell-glass, the shell being broken and re-formed as he lifts and dips his head; while ever and anon he sidles out to where the too powerful current carries him off his feet; then he dexterously rises on the wing and goes gleaning again in shallower places.

But during the winter, when the stream-banks are embossed in snow, and the streams themselves are chilled nearly to the freezing-point, so that the snow falling into them in stormy weather is not wholly dissolved, but forms a thin, blue sludge, thus rendering the current opaque – then he seeks the deeper portions of the main rivers, where he may dive to clear water beneath the sludge. Or he repairs to some open lake or mill-pond, at the bottom of which he feeds in safety.

When thus compelled to betake himself to a lake, he does not plunge into it at once like a duck, but always alights in the first place upon some rock or fallen pine along the shore. Then flying out thirty or forty yards, more or less, according to the character of the bottom, he alights with a dainty glint on the surface, swims about, looks down, finally makes up his mind, and disappears with a sharp stroke of his wings. After feeding for two or three minutes he suddenly re-appears, showers the water from his wings with one vigorous shake, and rises abruptly into the air as if pushed up from beneath, comes back to his perch, sings a few minutes, and goes out to dive again; thus coming and going, singing and diving at the same place for hours.

The ouzel is usually found singly; rarely in pairs, excepting during the breeding season, and *very* rarely in threes or fours. I once observed three thus spending a winter morning in company, upon a small glacier lake, on the Upper Merced, about 7,500ft. above the level of the sea. A storm had occurred during the night, but the morning sun shone unclouded, and the shadowy lake, gleaming darkly in its setting of fresh snow, lay smooth and motionless as a mirror. My camp chanced to be within a few feet of the water's edge, opposite a fallen pine, some of the branches of which leaned out over the lake. Here my three dearly welcome visitors took up their station, and at once began to embroider the frosty air with their delicious melody, doubly delightful to me that particular morning, as I had been somewhat apprehensive of danger in breaking my way down through the snow-choked canyons to the lowlands.

The portion of the lake bottom selected for a feeding-ground lies at a depth of fifteen or twenty feet below the surface, and is covered with a short growth of algae and other aquatic plants – facts I had previously determined while sailing over it on a raft. After alighting on the glassy surface, they occasionally indulged in a little play, chasing one another round about in small circles; then all three would suddenly dive together, and then come ashore and sing.

The ouzel seldom swims more than a few yards on the surface, for, not being web-footed, he makes rather slow progress, but by means of his strong, crisp wings he swims, or rather flies, with celerity under the surface, often to considerable distances. But it is in withstanding the force of heavy rapids that his strength of wing in this respect is most strikingly manifested. The following may be regarded as a fair illustration of his power of sub-aquatic flight. One stormy morning in winter when the Merced River was blue and green with unmelted snow, I observed one of my ouzels perched on a snag out in the midst of a swift-rushing rapid, singing cheerily, as if everything was just to his mind; and while I stood on the bank admiring him, he suddenly plunged into the sludgy current, leaving his song abruptly broken off. After feeding a minute or two at the bottom, and when one would suppose that he must inevitably be swept far down-stream, he emerged just where he went down, alighted on the same snag, showered the water-beads from his feathers, and continued his unfinished song, seemingly in tranquil ease as if it had suffered no interruption.

The ouzel alone of all birds dares to enter a white torrent. And though strictly terrestrial in structure, no other is so inseparably related to water, not even the duck, or the bold ocean albatross, or the stormy-petrel. For ducks go ashore as soon as they finish feeding in undisturbed places, and very often make long flights overland from lake to lake or field to field. The same is true of most other aquatic birds. But the ouzel, born on the brink of a stream, or on a snag or boulder in the midst of it, seldom leaves it for a single moment. For, notwithstanding he is often on the wing, he never flies overland, but whirs with rapid, quail-like beat above the stream, tracing all its windings. Even when the stream is quite small, say from five to ten feet wide, he seldom shortens his flight by crossing a bend, however abrupt it may be; and even when disturbed by meeting some one on the bank, he prefers to fly over one's head, to dodging out over the ground. When, therefore, his flight along a crooked stream is viewed endwise, it appears most strikingly wavered – a description on the air of every curve with lightning-like rapidity.

The vertical curves and angles of the most precipitous torrents he traces with the same rigid fidelity, swooping down the inclines of cascades, dropping sheer over dizzy falls amid the spray, and ascending with the same fearlessness and ease, seldom seeking to lessen the steepness of the acclivity by beginning to ascend before reaching the base of the fall. No matter though it may be several hundred feet in height he holds straight on, as if about to dash headlong into the throng of booming rockets, then darts abruptly upward, and, after alighting at the top of the precipice to rest a moment, proceeds to feed and sing. His flight is solid and impetuous, without any intermission of wing-beats – one homogeneous buzz like that of a laden bee on its way home. And while thus buzzing freely from fall to fall, he is frequently heard giving utterance to a long outdrawn train of unmodulated notes, in no way connected with his song, but corresponding closely with his flight in sustained vigour.

Were the flights of all the ouzels in the Sierra traced on a chart, they would indicate the direction of the flow of the entire system of ancient glaciers, from about the period of the breaking up of the ice-sheet until near the close of the glacial winter; because the streams which the ouzels so rigidly follow are, with the unimportant exceptions of a few side tributaries, all flowing in channels eroded for them out of the solid flank of the range by the vanished glaciers – the streams tracing the ancient glaciers, the ouzels tracing the streams. Nor do we find so complete compliance to glacial conditions in the life of any other mountain bird, or animal of any kind. Bears frequently accept the pathways laid down by glaciers as the easiest to travel; but they often leave them and cross over from canyon to canyon. So also, most of the birds trace the moraines to some extent, because the forests are growing on them. But they wander far, crossing the canyons from grove to grove, and draw exceedingly angular and complicated courses.

The ouzel's nest is one of the most extraordinary pieces of bird architecture I ever saw, odd and novel in design, perfectly fresh and beautiful, and in every way worthy of the genius of the little builder. It is about a foot in diameter, round and bossy in outline, with a neatly arched opening near the bottom, somewhat like an old-fashioned brick oven, or Hottentot's hut. It is built almost exclusively of green and yellow mosses, chiefly the beautiful fronded hypnum that covers the rocks and old drift-logs in the vicinity of waterfalls. These are deftly interwoven, and felted together into a charming little hut; and so situated that many of the outer mosses continue to flourish as if they had not been plucked. A few fine, silky-stemmed grasses are occasionally found interwoven with the mosses, but, with the exception of a thin layer lining the floor, their presence seems accidental, as they are of a species found growing with the mosses and are probably plucked with them. The site chosen for this curious mansion is usually some little rock-shelf within reach of the lighter particles of the spray of a waterfall, so that its walls are kept green and growing, at least during the time of high water.

No harsh lines are presented by any portion of the nest as seen in place, but when removed from its shelf, the back and bottom, and sometimes a portion of the top, is found quite sharply angular, because it is made to conform to the surface of the rock upon which and against which it is built, the little architect always taking advantage of slight crevices and protuberances that may chance to offer, to render his structure stable by means of a kind of gripping and dovetailing.

In choosing a building-spot, concealment does not seem to be taken into consideration; yet notwithstanding the nest is large and guilelessly exposed to view, it is far from being easily detected, chiefly because it swells forward like any other bulging moss-cushion growing naturally in such situations. This is more especially the case where the nest is kept fresh by being well sprinkled. Sometimes these romantic little huts have their beauty enhanced by rock-ferns and grasses that spring up around the mossy walls, or in front of the door-sill, dripping with crystal beads.

Furthermore, at certain hours of the day, when the sunshine is poured down at the required angle, the whole mass of the spray enveloping the fairy establishment is brilliantly irised; and it is through so glorious a rainbow atmosphere as this that some of our blessed ouzels obtain their first peep at the world.

Ouzels seem so completely part and parcel of the streams they inhabit, they scarce suggest any other origin than the streams themselves; and one might almost be pardoned in fancying they come direct from the living waters, like flowers from the ground. At least, from whatever cause, it never occurred to me to look for their nests until more than a year after I had made the acquaintance of the birds themselves, although I found one the very day on which I began the search. In making my way from Yosemite to the glaciers at the heads of the Merced and Tuolumne rivers, I camped in a particularly wild and romantic portion of the Nevada canyon where in previous excursions I had never failed to enjoy the company of my favourites, who were attracted here, no doubt, by the safe nesting-places in the shelving rocks, and by the abundance of food and falling water. The river, for miles above and below, consists of a succession of small falls from ten to sixty feet in height, con-nected by flat, plume-like cascades that go flashing from fall to fall, free and almost channelless, over waving folds of glacier-polished granite.

On the south side of one of the falls, that portion of the precipice which is bathed by the spray presents a series of little shelves and tablets caused by the development of planes of cleavage in the granite, and by the consequent fall of masses through the action of the water. 'Now here,' said I, 'of all places, is the most charming spot for an ouzel's nest.' Then carefully scanning the fretted face of the precipice through the spray, I at length noticed a yellowish moss-cushion, growing on the edge of a level tablet within five or six feet of the outer folds of the fall. But apart from the fact of its being situated where one acquainted with the lives of ouzels would fancy an ouzel's nest ought to be, there was nothing in its appearance visible at first sight, to distinguish it from other bosses of rock-moss similarly situated with reference to perennial spray; and it was not until I had scrutinized it again and again, and had removed my shoes and stockings and crept along the face of the rock within eight or ten feet of it, that I could decide certainly whether it was a nest or a natural growth.

In these moss huts three or four eggs are laid, white foam-like bubbles; and well may the little birds hatched from them sing water songs, for they hear them all their lives, and even before they are born.

I have often observed the young just out of the nest making their odd gestures, and seeming in every way as much at home as their experienced parents, like young bees on their first excursions to the flower fields. No amount of familiarity with people and their ways seems to change them in the least. To all appearance their behaviour is just the same on seeing a man for the first time, as when they have seen him frequently.

On the lower reaches of the rivers where mills are built, they sing on through the din of the machinery, and all the noisy confusion of dogs, cattle and workmen. On one occasion, while a wood-chopper was at work on the river-bank, I observed one cheerily singing within reach of the flying chips. Nor does any kind of unwanted disturbance put him in bad humour, or frighten him out of calm self-possession. In passing through a narrow gorge, I once drove one ahead of me from rapid to rapid, disturbing him four times in quick succession where he could not very well fly past me on account of the narrowness of the channel. Most birds under similar circumstances fancy themselves pursued, and become suspiciously uneasy; but, instead of growing nervous about it, he made his usual dippings, and sang one of his most tranquil strains. When observed within a few yards their eyes are seen to express remarkable gentleness and intelligence; but they seldom allow so near a view unless one wears clothing of about the same colour as the rocks and trees, and knows how to sit still. On one occasion, while rambling along the shore of a mountain lake, where the birds, at least those born that season, had never seen a man, I sat down to rest on a large stone close to the water's edge, upon which it seemed the ouzels and sandpipers were in the habit of alighting when they came to feed on that part of the shore, and some of the other birds also, when they came down to wash or drink. In a few minutes, along came a whirring ouzel and alighted on the stone beside me, within reach of my hand. Then suddenly observing me, he stooped nervously as if about to fly on the instant, but as I remained as motionless as the stone, he gained confidence, and looked me steadily in the face for about a minute, then flew quietly to the outlet and began to sing. Next came a sandpiper and gazed at me with much the same guileless expression of eye as the ouzel. Lastly, down with a swoop came a Steller's jay out of a fir-tree, probably with the intention of moistening his noisy throat. But instead of sitting confidingly as my other visitors had done, he rushed off at once, nearly tumbling heels over head into the lake in his suspicious confusion, and with loud screams roused the neighbourhood.

Love for song-birds, with their sweet human voices, appears to be more common and unfailing than love for flowers. Everyone loves flowers to some extent, at least in life's fresh morning, attracted by them as instinctively as humming-birds and bees. Even the young Digger Indians have sufficient love for the brightest of those found growing on the mountains to gather them and braid them as decorations for the hair. And I was glad to discover, through the few Indians that could be induced to talk on the subject, that they have names for the wild rose and the lily, and other conspicuous flowers, whether available as food or otherwise. Most men, however, whether savage or civilized, become apathetic toward all plants that have no other apparent use than the use of beauty. But fortunately one's first instinctive love of song-birds is never wholly obliterated, no matter what the influences upon our lives may be. I have often been delighted to see a pure, spiritual glow come into the countenances of hard business-men and old miners, when a song-bird chanced to alight near them. Nevertheless, the little mouthful of meat that swells out the breasts of some song-birds is too often the cause of their death. Larks and robins in particular are brought to market in hundreds. But fortunately the ouzel has no enemy so eager to eat his little body as to follow him into the mountain solitudes. I never knew him to be chased even by hawks.

An acquaintance of mine, a sort of foot-hill mountaineer, had a pet cat, a great, dozy, overgrown creature, about as broad-shouldered as a lynx. During the winter, while the snow lay deep, the mountaineer sat in his lonely cabin among the pines smoking his pipe and wearing the dull time away. Tom was his sole companion, sharing his bed, and sitting beside him on a stool with much the same drowsy expression of eye as his master. The good-natured bachelor was content with his hard fare of soda-bread and bacon, but Tom, the only creature in the world acknowledging dependence on him, must needs be provided with fresh meat. Accordingly he bestirred himself to contrive squirrel-traps, and waded the snowy woods with his gun, making sad havoc among the few winter birds, sparing neither robin, sparrow, nor tiny nut-hatch, and the pleasure of seeing Tom eat and grow fat was his great reward.

One cold afternoon, while hunting along the river-bank, he noticed a plain-feathered little bird skipping about in the shallows, and immediately raised his gun. But just then the confiding songster began to sing, and after listening to his summery melody the charmed hunter turned away, saying, 'Bless your little heart, I can't shoot you, not even for Tom.'

Even so far north as icy Alaska, I have found my glad singer. When I was exploring the glaciers between Mount Fairweather and the Stikeen River, one cold day in November, after trying in vain to force a way through the innumerable icebergs of Sum Dum Bay to the great glaciers at the head of it, I was weary and baffled and sat resting in my canoe convinced at last that I would have to leave this part of my work for another year. Then I began to plan my escape to open water before the young ice which was beginning to form should shut me in. While I thus lingered drifting with the bergs, in the midst of these gloomy forebodings and all the terrible glacial desolation and grandeur, I suddenly heard the well-known whir of an ouzel's wings, and, looking up, saw my little comforter coming straight across the ice from the shore. In a second or two he was with me, flying three times round my head with a happy salute, as if saying, 'Cheer up, old friend; you see I'm here, and all's well.' Then he flew back to the shore, alighted on the topmost jag of a stranded iceberg, and began to nod and bow as though he were on one of his favourite boulders in the midst of a sunny Sierra cascade.

The species is distributed all along the mountain-ranges of the Pacific Coast from Alaska to Mexico, and east to the Rocky Mountains. Nevertheless, it is as yet comparatively little known. Audubon and Wilson did not meet it. Swainson was, I believe, the first naturalist to describe a specimen from Mexico. Specimens were shortly afterward procured by Drummond near the sources of the Athabasca River, between the fifty-fourth and fifty-sixth parallels; and it has been collected by nearly all of the numerous exploring expeditions undertaken of late through our Western States and Territories; for it never fails to engage the attention of naturalists in a very particular manner.

Such, then, is our little cinclus, beloved of every one who is so fortunate as to know him. Tracing on strong wing every curve of the most precipitous torrents from one extremity of the Sierra to the other; not fearing to follow them through their darkest gorges and coldest snow-tunnels; acquainted with every waterfall, echoing their divine music; and throughout the whole of their beautiful lives interpreting all that we in our unbelief call terrible in the utterances of torrents and storms, as only varied expressions of God's eternal love.

CHAPTER FOURTEEN

The Wild Sheep

(Ovis montana)

THE WILD sheep ranks highest among the animal mountaineers of the Sierra. Possessed of keen sight and scent, and strong limbs, he dwells secure amid the loftiest summits, leaping unscathed from crag to crag, up and down the fronts of giddy precipices, crossing foaming torrents and slopes of frozen snow, exposed to the wildest storms, yet maintaining a brave, warm life, and developing from generation to generation in perfect strength and beauty.

Nearly all the lofty mountain-chains of the globe are inhabited by wild sheep, most of which, on account of the remote and all but inaccessible regions where they dwell, are imperfectly known as yet. They are classified by different naturalists under from five to ten distinct species or varieties, the best known being the burrhel of the Himalaya (*Ovis burrhel,* Blyth); the argali; the large wild sheep of central and northeastern Asia (*O. ammon,* Linn., or *Caprovis argali*); the Corsican mouflon (*O. musimon,* Pal.); the aoudad of the mountains of northern Africa (*Ammotragus tragelaphus*); and the Rocky Mountain bighorn (*O. montana,* Cuv.). To this last-named species belongs the wild sheep of the Sierra. Its range, according to the late Professor Baird of the Smithsonian Institution, extends 'from the region of the upper Missouri and Yellowstone to the Rocky Mountains and the high grounds adjacent to them on the eastern slope, and as far south as the Rio Grande. Westward it extends to the coast ranges of Washington, Oregon and California, and follows the highlands some distance into Mexico.'[1] Throughout the vast region bounded on the east by the Wahsatch Mountains and on the west by the Sierra there are more than a hundred subordinate ranges and

---

[1] Pacific Railroad Survey, Vol. VIII, page 678.

mountain groups, trending north and south, range beyond range, with summits rising from eight to twelve thousand feet above the level of the sea, probably all of which, according to my own observations, is, or has been, inhabited by this species.

Compared with the argali, which, considering its size and the vast extent of its range, is probably the most important of all the wild sheep, our species is about the same size, but the horns are less twisted and less divergent. The more important characteristics are, however, essentially the same, some of the best naturalists maintaining that the two are only varied forms of one species. In accordance with this view, Cuvier conjectures that since central Asia seems to be the region where the sheep first appeared, and from which it has been distributed, the argali may have been distributed over this continent from Asia by crossing Bering Strait on ice. This conjecture is not so ill founded as at first sight would appear; for the Strait is only about fifty miles wide, is interrupted by three islands, and is jammed with ice nearly every winter. Furthermore the argali is abundant on the mountains adjacent to the Strait at East Cape, where it is well known to the Tschuckchi hunters and where I have seen many of their horns.

On account of the extreme variability of the sheep under culture, it is generally supposed that the innumerable domestic breeds have all been derived from the few wild species; but the whole question is involved in obscurity. According to Darwin, sheep have been domesticated from a very ancient period, the remains of a small breed, differing from any now known, having been found in the famous Swiss lake-dwellings.

Compared with the best-known domestic breeds, we find that our wild species is much larger, and, instead of an all-wool garment, wears a thick overcoat of hair like that of the deer, and an under-covering of fine wool. The hair, though rather coarse, is comfortably soft and spongy, and lies smooth, as if carefully tended with comb and brush. The predominant colour during most of the year is brownish-grey, varying to bluish-grey in the autumn; the belly and a large, conspicuous patch on the buttocks are white; and the tail, which is very short, like that of a deer, is black, with a yellowish border. The wool is white, and grows in beautiful spirals down out of sight among the shining hair, like delicate climbing vines among stalks of corn.

The horns of the male are of immense size, measuring in their greater diameter from five to six and a half inches, and from two and a half to three feet in length around the curve. They are yellowish-white in colour, and ridged transversely, like those of the domestic ram. Their cross-section near the base is somewhat triangular in outline, and flattened toward the tip. Rising boldly from the top of the head, they curve gently backward and outward, then forward and outward, until about three fourths of a circle is described, and until the flattened, blunt tips are about two feet or two and a half feet apart. Those of the female are flattened throughout their entire length, are less curved than those of the male, and much smaller, measuring less than a foot along the curve.

A ram and ewe that I obtained near the Modoc lava-beds, to the northeast of Mount Shasta, measured as follows:

	Ram		Ewe	
	ft.	in.	ft.	in.
Height at shoulders..............................	3	6	3	0
Girth around shoulders	3	11	3	3¾
Length from nose to root of tail	5	10¼	4	3½
Length of ears	0	4¾	0	5
Length of tail.................................	0	4½	0	4½
Length of horns around curve	2	9	0	11½
Distance across from tip to tip of horns	2	5½		
Circumference of horns at base..................	1	4	0	6

The measurements of a male obtained in the Rocky Mountains by Audubon vary but little as compared with the above. The weight of his specimen was 344 pounds,[1] which is, perhaps, about an average for full-grown males. The females are about a third lighter.

Besides these differences in size, colour, hair, etc., as noted above, we may observe that the domestic sheep, in a general way, is expressionless, like a dull bundle of something only half alive, while the wild is as elegant and graceful as a deer, every movement manifesting admirable strength and character. The tame is timid; the wild is bold. The tame is always more or less ruffled and dirty; while the wild is as smooth and clean as the flowers of his mountain pastures.

The earliest mention that I have been able to find of the wild sheep in America is by Father Picolo, a Catholic missionary at Monterey, in the year 1797, who, after describing it, oddly enough, as 'a kind of deer with a sheep-like head, and about as large as a calf one or two years old,' naturally hurries on to remark: 'I have eaten of these beasts; their flesh is very tender and delicious.' Mackenzie, in his northern travels, heard the species spoken of by the Indians as 'white buffaloes.' And Lewis and Clark tell us that, in a time of great scarcity on the head waters of the Missouri, they saw plenty of wild sheep, but they were 'too shy to be shot.'

A few of the more energetic of the Pah Ute Indians hunt the wild sheep every season among the more accessible sections of the High Sierra, in the neighbourhood of passes, where, from having been pursued, they have become extremely wary; but in the rugged wilderness of peaks and canyons, where the foaming tributaries of the San Joaquin and King's rivers take their rise, they fear no hunter save the wolf, and are more guileless and approachable than their tame kindred.

While engaged in the work of exploring high regions where they delight to roam I have been greatly interested in studying their habits. In the months of November and December, and probably during a considerable portion of midwinter, they all flock together, male and female, old and young. I once found a complete band of this kind numbering upward of fifty, which, on being alarmed, went bounding away across a jagged lava-bed at admirable speed, led by a majestic old ram, with the lambs safe in the middle of the flock.

[1] Audubon and Bachman's 'Quadrupeds of North America.'

In spring and summer, the full-grown rams form separate bands of from three to twenty, and are usually found feeding along the edges of glacier meadows, or resting among the castle-like crags of the high summits; and whether quietly feeding, or scaling the wild cliffs, their noble forms and the power and beauty of their movements never fail to strike the beholder with lively admiration.

Their resting-places seem to be chosen with reference to sunshine and a wide outlook, and most of all to safety. Their feeding-grounds are among the most beautiful of the wild gardens, bright with daisies and gentians and mats of purple bryanthus, lying hidden away on rocky headlands and canyon sides, where sunshine is abundant, or down in the shady glacier valleys, along the banks of the streams and lakes, where the plushy sod is greenest. Here they feast all summer, the happy wanderers, perhaps relishing the beauty as well as the taste of the lovely flora on which they feed.

When the winter storms set in, loading their highland pastures with snow, then, like the birds, they gather and go to lower climates, usually descending the eastern flank of the range to the rough, volcanic table-lands and treeless ranges of the Great Basin adjacent to the Sierra. They never make haste, however, and seem to have no dread of storms, many of the strongest only going down leisurely to bare, wind-swept ridges, to feed on bushes and dry bunch-grass, and then returning up into the snow. Once I was snow-bound on Mount Shasta for three days, a little below the timber line. It was a dark and stormy time, well calculated to test the skill and endurance of mountaineers. The snow-laden gale drove on night and day in hissing, blinding floods, and when at length it began to abate, I found that a small band of wild sheep had weathered the storm in the lee of a clump of dwarf pines a few yards above my storm-nest, where the snow was eight or ten feet deep. I was warm back of a rock, with blankets, bread and fire. My brave companions lay in the snow, without food, and with only the partial shelter of the short trees, yet they made no sign of suffering or faint-heartedness.

In the months of May and June, the wild sheep bring forth their young in solitary and almost inaccessible crags, far above the nesting-rocks of the eagle. I have frequently come upon the beds of the ewes and lambs at an elevation of from 12,000 to 13,000ft. above sea-level. These beds are simply oval-shaped hollows, pawed out among loose, disintegrating rock-chips and sand, upon some sunny spot commanding a good outlook, and partially sheltered from the winds that sweep those lofty peaks almost without inter-mission. Such is the cradle of the little mountaineer, aloft in the very sky; rocked in storms, curtained in clouds, sleeping in thin, icy air; but, wrapped in his hairy coat, and nourished by a strong, warm mother, defended from the talons of the eagle and the teeth of the sly coyote, the bonny lamb grows apace. He soon learns to nibble the tufted rock-grasses and leaves of the white spiræa; his horns begin to shoot, and before summer is done he is strong and agile, and goes forth with the flock, watched by the same divine love that tends the more helpless human lamb in its cradle by the fireside.

Nothing is more commonly remarked by noisy, dusty trail-travellers in the Sierra than the want of animal life – no song-birds, no deer, no squirrels, no game of any kind, they say. But if such could only go away quietly into the wilderness, sauntering afoot and alone with natural deliberation, they would soon learn that these mountain mansions are not without inhabitants, many of whom, confiding and gentle, would not try to shun their acquaintance.

In the fall of 1873 I was tracing the South Fork of the San Joaquin up its wild canyon to its farthest glacier fountains. It was the season of alpine Indian summer. The sun beamed lovingly; the squirrels were nutting in the pine-trees, butterflies hovered about the last of the goldenrods, the willow and maple thickets were yellow, the meadows brown, and the whole sunny, mellow landscape glowed like a countenance in the deepest and sweetest repose. On my way over the glacier-polished rocks along the river, I came to an expanded portion of the canyon, about two miles long and half a mile wide, which formed a level park enclosed with picturesque granite walls like those of Yosemite Valley. Down through the middle of it poured the beautiful river shining and spangling in the golden light, yellow groves on its banks, and strips of brown meadow; while the whole park was astir with wild life, some of which even the noisiest and least observing of travellers must have seen had they been with me. Deer, with their supple, well-grown fawns, bounded from thicket to thicket as I advanced; grouse kept rising from the brown grass with a great whirring of wings, and, alighting on the lower branches of the pines and poplars, allowed a near approach, as if curious to see me. Farther on, a broad-shouldered wildcat showed himself, coming out of a grove, and crossing the river on a flood-jamb of logs, halting for a moment to look back. The bird-like tamias frisked about my feet everywhere among the pine-needles and seedy grass-tufts; cranes waded the shallows of the river-bends, the kingfisher rattled from perch to perch, and the blessed ouzel sang amid the spray of every cascade. Where may lonely wanderer find a more interesting family of mountain-dwellers, earth-born companions and fellow-mortals? It was afternoon when I joined them, and the glorious land-scape began to fade in the gloaming before I awoke from their enchantment. Then I sought a camp-ground on the river-bank, made a cupful of tea, and lay down to sleep on a smooth place among the yellow leaves of an aspen grove. Next day I discovered yet grander landscapes and grander life. Following the river over huge, swelling rock-bosses through a majestic canyon, and past innumerable cascades, the scenery in general became gradually wilder and more alpine. The sugar pine and silver firs gave place to the hardier cedar and hemlock spruce. The canyon walls became more rugged and bare, and gentians and arctic daisies became more abundant in the gardens and strips of meadow along the streams. Toward the middle of the afternoon I came to another valley, strikingly wild and original in all its features, and perhaps never before touched by human foot. As regards area of level bottom-land, it is one of the very smallest of the Yosemite type, but its walls are sublime, rising to a height of from 2,000 to 4,000ft. above the river. At the head of the valley the main canyon forks, as is found to be the case in all yosemites. The formation of this one is due chiefly to the action of two great glaciers, whose fountains lay to the eastward, on the flanks of Mounts Humphrey and Emerson and a cluster of nameless peaks farther south.

The grey, boulder-chafed river was singing loudly through the valley, but above its massy roar I heard the booming of a waterfall, which drew me eagerly on; and just as I emerged from the tangled groves and brier-thickets at the head of the valley, the main fork of the river came in sight, falling fresh from its glacier fountains in a snowy cascade, between granite walls 2,000ft. high. The steep incline down which the glad waters thundered seemed to bar all farther progress. It was not long, however, before I discovered a crooked seam in the rock, by which I was enabled to climb to the edge of a terrace that crosses the canyon, and divides the cataract nearly in the middle. Here I sat down to take breath and make some entries in my note-book, taking advantage, at the same time, of my elevated position above the trees to gaze back over the valley into the heart of the noble landscape, little knowing the while what neighbours were near.

After spending a few minutes in this way, I chanced to look across the fall, and there stood three sheep quietly observing me. Never did the sudden appearance of a mountain, or fall, or human friend more forcibly seize and rivet my attention. Anxiety to observe accurately held me perfectly still. Eagerly I marked the flowing undulations of their firm, braided muscles, their strong legs, ears, eyes, heads, their graceful rounded necks, the colour of their hair, and the bold, upsweeping curves of their noble horns. When they moved I watched every gesture, while they, in no wise disconcerted either by my attention or by the tumultuous roar of the water, advanced deliberately alongside the rapids, between the two divisons of the cataract, turning now and then to look at me. Presently they came to a steep, ice-burnished acclivity, which they ascended by a succession of quick, short, stiff-legged leaps, reaching the top without a struggle. This was the most startling feat of mountaineering I had ever witnessed, and, considering only the mechanics of the thing, my astonishment could hardly have been greater had they displayed wings and taken to flight. 'Sure-footed' mules on such ground would have fallen and rolled like loosened boulders. Many a time, where the slopes are far lower, I have been compelled to take off my shoes and stockings, tie them to my belt, and creep barefooted, with the utmost caution. No wonder then, that I watched the progress of these animal mountaineers with keen sympathy, and exulted in the boundless sufficiency of wild nature displayed in their invention, construction, and keeping. A few minutes later I caught sight of a dozen more in one band, near the foot of the upper fall. They were standing on the same side of the river with me, only twenty-five or thirty yards away, looking as unworn and perfect as if created on the spot. It appeared by their tracks, which I had seen in the Little Yosemite, and by their present position, that when I came up the canyon they were all feeding together down in the valley, and in their haste to reach high ground, where they could look about them to ascertain the nature of the strange disturbance, they were divided, three ascending on one side of the river, the rest on the other.

The main band, headed by an experienced chief, now began to cross the wild rapids between the two divisions of the cascade. This was another exciting feat; for, among all the varied experiences of mountaineers, the crossing of boisterous, rock-dashed torrents is found to be one of the most trying to the nerves. Yet these fine fellows walked fearlessly to the brink, and jumped from boulder to boulder, holding themselves in an easy poise above the whirling, confusing current, as if they were doing nothing extraordinary.

In the immediate foreground of this rare picture there was a fold of ice-burnished granite, traversed by a few bold lines in which rock-ferns and tufts of bryanthus were growing, the grey canyon walls on the sides, nobly sculptured and adorned with brown cedars and pines; lofty peaks in the distance, and in the middle ground the snowy fall, the voice and soul of the landscape; fringing bushes beating time to its thunder-tones, the brave sheep in front of it, their grey forms slightly obscured in the spray, yet standing out in good, heavy relief against the close white water, with their huge horns rising like the upturned roots of dead pine-trees, while the evening sunbeams streaming up the canyon coloured all the picture a rosy purple and made it glorious. After crossing the river, the dauntless climbers, led by their chief, at once began to scale the canyon wall, turning now right, now left, in long, single file, keeping well apart out of one another's way, and leaping in regular succession from crag to crag, now ascending slippery dome-curves, now walking leisurely along the edges of precipices, stopping at times to gaze down at me from some flat-topped rock, with heads held aslant, as if curious to learn what I thought about it, or whether I was likely to follow them. After reaching the top of the wall, which, at this place, is somewhere between 1,500 and 2,000ft. high, they were still visible against the sky as they lingered, looking down in groups of twos or threes.

Throughout the entire ascent they did not make a single awkward step, or an unsuccessful effort of any kind. I have frequently seen tame sheep in mountains jump upon a sloping rock-surface, hold on tremulously a few seconds, and fall back baffled and irresolute. But in the most trying situations, where the slightest want or inaccuracy would have been fatal, these always seemed to move in comfortable reliance on their strength and skill, the limits of which they never appeared to know. Moreover, each one of the flock, while following the guidance of the most experienced, climbed with intelligent independence as a perfect individual, capable of separate existence whenever it should wish or be compelled to withdraw from the little clan. The domestic sheep, on the contrary, is only a fraction of an animal, a whole flock being required to form an individual, just as numerous flowerets are required to make one complete sunflower.

Those shepherds who, in summer, drive their flocks to the mountain pastures, and, while watching them night and day, have seen them frightened by bears and storms, and scattered like wind-driven chaff, will, in some measure, be able to appreciate the self-reliance and strength and noble individuality of Nature's sheep.

Like the Alp-climbing ibex of Europe, our mountaineer is said to plunge headlong down the faces of sheer precipices, and alight on his big horns. I know only two hunters who claim to have actually witnessed this feat; I never was so fortunate. They describe the act as a diving head-foremost. The horns are so large at the base that they cover the upper portion of the head down nearly to a level with the eyes, and the skull is exceedingly strong. I struck an old, bleached specimen on Mount Ritter a dozen blows with my ice-axe without breaking it. Such skulls would not fracture very readily by the wildest rock-diving, but other bones could hardly be expected to hold together in such a performance; and the mechanical difficulties in the way of controlling their movements, after striking upon an irregular surface, are, in themselves, sufficient to show this boulder-like method of progression to be impossible, even in the absence of all other evidence on the subject; moreover, the ewes follow wherever the rams may lead, although their horns are mere spikes. I have found many pairs of the horns of the old rams considerably battered, doubtless a result of fighting. I was particularly interested in the question, after witnessing the performances of this San Joaquin band upon the glaciated rocks at the foot of the falls; and as soon as I procured specimens and examined their feet, all the mystery disappeared. The secret, considered in connection with exceptionally strong muscles, is simply this: the wide posterior portion of the bottom of the foot, instead of wearing down and becoming flat and hard, like the feet of tame sheep and horses, bulges out in a soft, rubber-like pad or cushion, which not only grips and holds well on smooth rocks, but fits into small cavities, and down upon or against slight protuberances. Even the hardest portions of the edge of the hoof are comparatively soft and elastic; furthermore, the toes admit of an extraordinary amount of both lateral and vertical movement, allowing the foot to accommodate itself still more perfectly to the irregularities of rock surfaces, while at the same time increasing the gripping power.

At the base of Sheep Rock, one of the winter strongholds of the Shasta flocks, there lives a stock-raiser who has the advantage of observing the movements of wild sheep every winter; and, in the course of a conversation with him on the subject of their diving habits, he pointed to the front of a lava headland about 150ft. high, which is only eight or ten degrees out of the perpendicular. 'There,' said he, 'I followed a band of them fellows to the back of that rock yonder, and expected to capture them all, for I thought I had a dead thing on them. I got behind them on a narrow bench that runs along the face of the wall near the top and comes to an end where they couldn't get away without falling and being killed; but they jumped off, and landed all right, as if that were the regular thing with them.'

'What!' said I, 'jumped 150ft. perpendicular! Did you see them do it?'

'No,' he replied, 'I didn't see them going down, for I was behind them; but I saw them go off over the brink, and then I went below and found their tracks where they struck on the loose rubbish at the bottom. They just *sailed right off*, and landed on their feet right side up. That is the kind of animal *they* is – beats anything else that goes on four legs.'

On another occasion, a flock that was pursued by hunters retreated to another portion of this same cliff where it is still higher, and, on being followed, they were seen jumping down in perfect order, one behind another, by two men who happened to be chopping where they had a fair view of them and could watch their progress from top to bottom of the precipice. Both ewes and rams made the frightful descent without evincing any extraordinary concern, hugging the rock closely, and controlling the velocity of their half falling, half leaping movements by striking at short intervals and holding back with their cushioned, rubber feet upon small ledges and roughened inclines until near the bottom, when they 'sailed off' into the free air and alighted on their feet, but with their bodies so nearly in a vertical position that they appeared to be diving.

It appears, therefore, that the methods of this wild mountaineering become clearly comprehensible as soon as we make ourselves acquainted with the rocks, and the kind of feet and muscles brought to bear upon them.

The Modoc and Pah Ute Indians are, or rather have been, the most successful hunters of the wild sheep in the regions that have come under my own observation. I have seen large numbers of heads and horns in the caves of Mount Shasta and the Modoc lava-beds, where the Indians had been feasting in stormy weather; also in the canyons of the Sierra opposite Owen's Valley; while the heavy obsidian arrow-heads found on some of the highest peaks show that this warfare has long been going on.

In the more accessible ranges that stretch across the desert regions of western Utah and Nevada, considerable numbers of Indians used to hunt in company like packs of wolves, and being perfectly acquainted with the topography of their hunting-grounds, and with the habits and instincts of the game, they were pretty successful. On the tops of nearly every one of the Nevada mountains that I have visited, I found small, nest-like enclosures built of stones, in which, as I afterward learned, one or more Indians would lie in wait while their companions scoured the ridges below, knowing that the alarmed sheep would surely run to the summit, and when they could be made to approach with the wind they were shot at short range.

Still larger bands of Indians used to make extensive hunts upon some dominant mountain much frequented by the sheep, such as Mount Grant on the Wassuck Range to the west of Walker Lake. On some particular spot, favourably situated with reference to the well-known trails of the sheep, they built a high-walled corral, with long guiding wings diverging from the gateway; and into this enclosure they sometimes succeeded in driving the noble game. Great numbers of Indians were of course required, more, indeed, than they could usually muster, counting in squaws, children and all; they were compelled, therefore, to build rows of dummy hunters out of stones, along the ridge-tops which they wished to prevent the sheep from crossing. And, without discrediting the sagacity of the game, these dummies were found effective; for, with a few live Indians moving about excitedly among them, they could hardly be distinguished at a little distance from men, by any one not in the secret. The whole ridge-top then seemed to be alive with hunters.

The only animal that may fairly be regarded as a companion or rival of the sheep is the so-called Rocky Mountain goat (*Aplocerus montana,* Rich.), which, as its name indicates, is more antelope than goat. He, too, is a brave and hardy climber, fearlessly crossing the wildest summits, and braving the severest storms, but he is shaggy, short-legged, and much less dignified in demeanour than the sheep. His jet-black horns are only about five or six inches in length, and the long, white hair with which he is covered obscures the expression of his limbs. I have never yet seen a single specimen in the

Sierra, though possibly a few flocks may have lived on Mount Shasta a comparatively short time ago.

The ranges of these two mountaineers are pretty distinct, and they see but little of each other; the sheep being restricted mostly to the dry, inland mountains; the goat or chamois to the wet, snowy glacier-laden mountains of the northwest coast of the continent in Oregon, Washington, British Columbia and Alaska. Probably more than 200 dwell on the icy, volcanic cone of Mount Rainier; and while I was exploring the glaciers of Alaska I saw flocks of these admirable mountaineers nearly every day, and often followed their trails through the mazes of bewildering crevasses, in which they are excellent guides.

Three species of deer are found in California – the black-tailed, white-tailed and mule deer. The first mentioned (*Cervus Columbianus*) is by far the most abundant, and occasionally meets the sheep during the summer on high glacier meadows, and along the edge of the timber line; but being a forest animal, seeking shelter and rearing its young in dense thickets, it seldom visits the wild sheep in its higher homes. The antelope, though not a mountaineer, is occasionally met in winter by the sheep while feeding along the edges of the sage-plains and bare volcanic hills to the east of the Sierra. So also is the mule deer, which is almost restricted in its range to this eastern region. The white-tailed species belongs to the coast ranges.

Perhaps no wild animal in the world is without enemies, but highlanders, as a class, have fewer than lowlanders. The wily panther, slipping and crouching among long grass and bushes, pounces upon the antelope and deer, but seldom crosses the bald, craggy thresholds of the sheep. Neither can the bears be regarded as enemies; for, though they seek to vary their every-day diet of nuts and berries by an occasional meal of mutton, they prefer to hunt tame and helpless flocks. Eagles and coyotes, no doubt, capture an unprotected lamb at times, or some unfortunate beset in deep, soft snow, but these cases are little more than accidents. So, also, a few perish in long-continued snow-storms, though, in all my mountaineering, I have not found more than five or six that seemed to have met their fate in this way. A little band of three were discovered snow-bound in Bloody Canyon a few years ago, and were killed with an axe by mountaineers, who chanced to be crossing the range in winter.

Man is the most dangerous enemy of all, but even from him our brave mountain-dweller has little to fear in the remote solitudes of the High Sierra. The golden plains of the Sacramento and San Joaquin were lately thronged with bands of elk and antelope, but, being fertile and accessible, they were required for human pastures. So, also, are many of the feeding-grounds of the deer – hill, valley, forest and meadow – but it will be long before man will care to take the highland castles of the sheep. And when we consider here how rapidly entire species of noble animals, such as the elk, moose and buffalo, are being pushed to the very verge of extinction, all lovers of wildness will rejoice with me in the rocky security of *Ovis montana,* the bravest of all the Sierra mountaineers.

CHAPTER FIFTEEN

In The Sierra Foot-Hills

MURPHY'S CAMP is a curious old mining-town in Calaveras County, at an elevation of 2,400ft. above the sea, situated like a nest in the centre of a rough, gravelly region, rich in gold. Granites, slates, lavas, limestone, iron ores, quartz veins, auriferous gravels, remnants of dead fire-rivers and dead water-rivers are developed here side by side within a radius of a few miles, and placed invitingly open before the student like a book, while the people and the region beyond the camp furnish mines of study of never-failing interest and variety.

When I discovered this curious place, I was tracing the channels of the ancient pre-glacial rivers, instructive sections of which have been laid bare here and in the adjacent regions by the miners. Rivers, according to the poets, 'go on forever'; but those of the Sierra are young as yet and have scarcely learned the way down to the sea; while at least one generation of them have died and vanished together with most of the basins they drained. All that remains of them to tell their history is a series of interrupted fragments of channels, mostly choked with gravel, and buried beneath broad, thick sheets of lava. These are known as the 'Dead Rivers of California,' and the gravel deposited in them is comprehensively called the 'Blue Lead.' In some places the channels of the present rivers trend in the same direction, or nearly so, as those of the ancient rivers; but, in general, there is little correspondence between them, the entire drainage having been changed, or, rather, made new. Many of the hills of the ancient landscapes have become hollows, and the old hollows have become hills. Therefore the fragmentary channels, with their loads of auriferous gravel, occur in all ·kinds of unthought-of places, trending obliquely, or even at right angles to the present drainage, across the tops of lofty ridges or far beneath them, presenting impressive illustrations of the magnitude of the changes accomplished since those ancient streams were annihilated. The last volcanic period preceding the regeneration of the Sierra landscapes seems to have come on over all the range· almost simultaneously, like the glacial period, notwithstanding lavas of different age occur together in many places, indicating numerous periods of activity in the Sierra fire-fountains. The most important of the ancient river-channels in this region is a section that extends from the south side of the town beneath Coyote Creek and the ridge beyond it to the Canyon of the Stanislaus; but on account of its depth below the general surface of the present valleys the rich gold gravels it is known to contain cannot be easily worked on a large scale. Their extraordinary richness may be inferred from the fact that many claims were profitably worked in them by sinking shafts to a depth of 200ft. or more, and hoisting the dirt by a windlass. Should the dip of this ancient channel be such as to make the Stanislaus Canyon available as a dump, then the grand deposit might be worked by the hydraulic method, and although a long, expensive tunnel would be required, the scheme might still prove profitable, for there is 'millions in it.'

The importance of these ancient gravels as gold fountains is well known to miners. Even the superficial placers of the present streams have derived much of their gold from them. According to all accounts, the Murphy placers have been very rich – 'terrific rich,' as they say here. The hills have been cut and scalped, and every gorge and gulch and valley torn to pieces and disembowelled, expressing a fierce and desperate energy hard to understand. Still, any kind of effort-making is better than inaction, and there is something sublime in seeing men working in dead earnest at anything, pursuing an object with glacier-like energy and persistence. Many a brave fellow has recorded a most eventful chapter of life on these Calaveras rocks. But most of the pioneer miners are sleeping now, their wild day done, while the few survivors linger languidly in the washed-out gulches or sleepy village like harried bees around the ruins of their hive. 'We have no industry left *now*,' they told me, 'and no men; everybody and everything hereabouts has gone to decay. We are only bummers – out of the game, a thin scatterin' of poor, dilapidated cusses, compared with what we used to be in the grand old gold-days. We were giants then, and you can look around here and see our tracks.' But although these lingering pioneers are perhaps more exhausted than the mines, and about as dead as the dead rivers, they are yet a rare and interesting set of men, with much gold mixed with the rough, rocky gravel of their characters; and they manifest a breeding and intelligence little looked for in such surroundings as theirs. As the heavy, long-continued grinding of the glaciers brought out the features of the Sierra, so the intense experiences of the gold period have brought out the features of these old miners, forming a richness and variety of character little known as yet. The sketches of Bret Harte, Hayes and Miller have not exhausted this field by any means. It is interesting to note the extremes possible in one and the same character: harshness and gentleness, manliness and childishness, apathy and fierce endeavour. Men who, twenty years ago, would not cease their shovelling to save their lives, now play in the streets with children. Their long, Micawber-like waiting after the exhaustion of the placers has brought on an exaggerated form of dotage. I heard a group of brawny pioneers in the street eagerly discussing the quantity of tail required for a boy's kite; and one greybeard undertook the sport of flying it, volunteering the information that he was a boy, 'always was a boy, and d—n a man who was not a boy inside, however ancient outside!' Mines, morals, politics, the immortality of the soul, etc., were discussed beneath shade-trees and in saloons, the time for each being governed apparently by the temperature. Contact with Nature, and the habits of observation acquired in gold-seeking, had made them all, to some extent, collectors, and, like wood-rats, they had gathered all kinds of odd specimens into their cabins, and now required me to examine them. They were themselves the oddest and most interesting specimens. One of them offered to show me around the old diggings, giving me fair warning before setting out that I might not like him, 'because,' said he, 'people say I'm eccentric. I notice everything, and gather beetles and snakes and anything that's queer; and so some don't like me, and call me eccentric. I'm always trying to find out things. Now, there's a weed; the Indians eat it for greens. What do you call those long-bodied flies with big heads?' 'Dragon-flies,' I suggested. 'Well, their jaws work sidewise, instead of up and down, and grasshoppers' jaws work the same way, and therefore I think they are the same species. I always notice everything like that, and just because I do, they say I'm eccentric,' etc.

Anxious that I should miss none of the wonders of their old gold-field, the good people had much to say about the marvellous beauty of Cave City Cave, and advised me to explore it. This I was very glad to do, and finding a guide who knew the way to the mouth of it, I set out from Murphy the next morning.

The most beautiful and extensive of the mountain caves of California occur in a belt of metamorphic limestone that is pretty generally developed along the western flank of the Sierra from the McCloud River on the north to the Kaweah on the south, a distance of over 400 miles, at an elevation of from 2,000 to 7,000ft. above the sea. Besides this regular belt of caves, the California landscapes are diversified by long imposing ranks of sea-caves, rugged and variable in architecture, carved in the coast headlands and preci- pices by centuries of wave-dashing; and innumerable lava-caves, great and small, originating in the unequal flowing and hardening of the lava sheets in which they occur, fine illustrations of which are presented in the famous Modoc Lava Beds, and around the base of icy Shasta. In this comprehensive glance we may also notice the shallow wind-worn caves in stratified sand- stones along the margins of the plains; and the cave-like recesses in the Sierra slates and granites, where bears and other mountaineers find shelter during the fall of sudden storms. In general, however, the grand massive uplift of the Sierra, as far as it has been laid bare to observation, is about as solid and caveless as a boulder.

Fresh beauty opens one's eyes wherever it is really seen, but the very abundance and completeness of the common beauty that besets our steps prevents its being absorbed and appreciated. It is a good thing, therefore, to make short excursions now and then to the bottom of the sea among dulse and coral, or up among the clouds on mountain-tops, or in balloons, or even to creep like worms into dark holes and caverns underground, not only to learn something of what is going on in those out-of-the-way places, but to see better what the sun sees on our return to common every-day beauty.

Our way from Murphy's to the cave lay across a series of picturesque, moory ridges in the chaparral region between the brown foot-hills and the forests, a flowery stretch of rolling hill-waves breaking here and there into a kind of rocky foam on the higher summits, and sinking into delightful bosky hollows embowered with vines. The day was a fine specimen of California summer, pure sunshine, unshaded most of the time by a single cloud. As the sun rose higher, the heated air began to flow in tremulous waves from every southern slope. The sea-breeze that usually comes up the foot-hills at this season, with cooling on its wings, was scarcely perceptible. The birds were assembled beneath leafy shade, or made short, languid flights in search of food, all save the majestic buzzard; with broad wings outspread he sailed the warm air unwearily from ridge to ridge, seeming to enjoy the fervid sunshine like a butterfly. Squirrels, too, whose spicy ardour no heat or cold may abate, were nutting among the pines, and the innumerable hosts of the insect kingdom were throbbing and wavering unwearied as sunbeams.

This brushy, berry-bearing region used to be a deer and bear pasture, but since the disturbances of the gold period these fine animals have almost wholly disappeared. Here, also, once roamed the mastodon and elephant, whose bones are found entombed in the river gravels and beneath thick folds of lava. Toward noon, as we were riding slowly over bank and brae, basking in the unfeverish sun-heat, we witnessed the upheaval of a new mountain-range, a Sierra of clouds abounding in landscapes as truly sublime and beautiful – if only we have a mind to think so and eyes to see – as the more ancient rocky Sierra beneath it, with its forests and waterfalls; reminding us that, as there is a lower world of caves, so, also, there is an upper world of clouds. Huge, bossy, cumuli developed with astonishing rapidity from mere buds, swelling with visible motion into colossal mountains, and piling higher, higher, in long massive ranges, peak beyond peak, dome over dome, with many a picturesque valley and shadowy cave between; while the dark firs and pines of the upper benches of the Sierra were projected against their pearl bosses with exquisite clearness of outline. These cloud mountains vanished in the azure as quickly as they were developed, leaving no detritus; but they were not a whit less real or interesting on this account. The more enduring hills over which we rode were vanishing as surely as they, only not so fast, a difference which is great or small according to the standpoint from which it is contemplated.

At the bottom of every dell we found little homesteads embosomed in wild brush and vines wherever the recession of the hills left patches of arable ground. These secluded flats are settled mostly by Italians and Germans, who plant a few vegetables and grape-vines at odd times, while their main business is mining and prospecting. In spite of all the natural beauty of these dell cabins, they can hardly be called homes. They are only a better kind of camp, gladly abandoned whenever the hoped-for gold harvest has been gathered. There is an air of profound unrest and melancholy about the best of them. Their beauty is thrust upon them by exuberant Nature, apart from which they are only a few logs and boards rudely jointed and without either ceiling or floor, a rough fireplace with corresponding cooking utensils, a shelf-bed and stool. The ground about them is strewn with battered prospecting pans, picks, sluice-boxes and quartz specimens from many a ledge, indicating the trend of their owners' hard lives.

The ride from Murphy's to the cave is scarcely two hours long, but we lingered among quartz-ledges and banks of dead river gravel until long after noon. At length emerging from a narrow-throated gorge, a small house came in sight set in a thicket of fig-trees at the base of a limestone hill. 'That,' said my guide, pointing to the house, 'is Cave City, and the cave is in that grey hill.' Arriving at the one house of this one-house city, we were boisterously welcomed by three drunken men who had come to town to hold a spree. The mistress of the house tried to keep order, and in reply to our enquiries told us that the cave guide was then in the cave with a party of ladies. 'And must we wait until he returns?' we asked. No, that was unnecessary; we might take candles and go into the cave alone, provided we shouted from time to time so as to be found by the guide, and were careful not to fall over the rocks or into the dark pools. Accordingly taking a trail from the house, we were led around the base of the hill to the mouth of the cave, a small inconspicuous archway, mossy around the edges and shaped like the door of a water-ouzel's nest, with no appreciable hint or advertisement of the grandeur of the many crystal chambers within. Lighting our candles, which seemed to have no illuminating power in the thick darkness, we groped our way onward as best we could along narrow lanes and alleys, from chamber to chamber, around rustic columns and heaps of fallen rocks, stopping to rest now and then in particularly beautiful places – fairy alcoves furnished with admirable variety of shelves and tables, and round bossy stools covered with sparkling crystals. Some of the corridors were muddy, and in plodding along these we seemed to be in the streets of some prairie village in spring time. Then we would come to handsome marble stairways conducting right and left into upper chambers ranged above one another three or four stories high, floors, ceilings and walls lavishly decorated with innumerable crystalline forms. After thus wandering exploringly, and alone for a mile or so, fairly enchanted, a murmur of voices and a gleam of light betrayed the approach of the guide and his party, from whom, when they came up, we received a most hearty and natural stare, as we stood half concealed in a side recess among stalagmites. I ventured to ask the dripping, crouching company how they had enjoyed their saunter, anxious to learn how the strange sunless scenery of the underworld had impressed them. 'Ah, it's nice! It's splendid!' they all replied and echoed. 'The Bridal Chamber back here is just glorious! This morning we came down from the Calaveras Big Tree Grove, and the trees are nothing to it.' After making this curious comparison they hastened sunward, the guide promising to join us shortly on the bank of a deep pool, where we were to wait for him. This is a charming little lakelet of unknown depth, never yet stirred by a breeze, and its eternal calm excites the imagination even more profoundly than the silvery lakes of the glaciers rimmed with meadows and snow and reflecting sublime mountains.

Our guide, a jolly, rollicking Italian, led us into the heart of the hill, up and down, right and left, from chamber to chamber more and more magnificent, all a-glitter like a glacier cave with icicle-like stalactites and stalagmites combined in forms of indescribable beauty. We were shown one large room that was occasionally used as a dancing-hall; another that was used as a chapel, with natural pulpit and crosses and pews, sermons in every stone, where a priest had said mass. Mass-saying is not so generally developed in connection with natural wonders as dancing. One of the first conceits excited by the giant Sequoias was to cut one of them down and dance on its stump. We have also seen dancing in the spray of Niagara; dancing in the famous

Bower Cave about Coulterville; and nowhere have I seen so much dancing as in Yosemite. A dance on the inaccessible South Dome would likely follow the making of an easy way to the top of it.

It was delightful to witness here the infinite deliberation of Nature, and the simplicity of her methods in the production of such mighty results, such perfect repose combined with restless enthusiastic energy. Though cold and bloodless as a landscape of polar ice, building was going on in the dark with incessant activity. The archways and ceilings were everywhere hung with down-growing crystals, like inverted groves of leafless saplings, some of them large, others delicately attenuated, each tipped with a single drop of water, like the terminal bud of a pine-tree. The only appreciable sounds were the dripping and tinkling of water falling into pools or faintly plashing on the crystal floors.

In some places the crystal decorations are arranged in graceful flowing folds deeply plicated like stiff silken drapery. In others straight lines of the ordinary stalactite forms are combined with reference to size and tone in a regularly graduated system like the strings of a harp with musical tones corresponding thereto; and on these stone harps we played by striking the crystal strings with a stick. The delicious liquid tones they gave forth seemed perfectly divine as they sweetly whispered and wavered through the majestic halls and died away in faintest cadence – the music of fairy-land. Here we lingered and revelled, rejoicing to find so much music in stony silence, so much splendour in darkness, so many mansions in the depths of the mountains, buildings ever in process of construction, yet ever finished, developing from perfection to perfection, profusion without overabundance; every particle visible or invisible in glorious motion, marching to the music of the spheres in a region regarded as the abode of eternal stillness and death.

The outer chambers of mountain caves are frequently selected as homes by wild beasts. In the Sierra, however, they seem to prefer homes and hiding-places in chaparral and beneath shelving precipices, as I have never seen their tracks in any of the caves. This is the more remarkable because notwithstanding the darkness and oozing water there is nothing uncomfortably cellar-like or sepulchral about them.

When we emerged into the bright landscapes of the sun everything looked brighter, and we felt our faith in Nature's beauty strengthened, and saw more clearly that beauty is universal and immortal, above, beneath, on land and sea, mountain and plain, in heat and cold, light and darkness.

CHAPTER SIXTEEN

The Bee-Pastures

WHEN CALIFORNIA was wild, it was one sweet bee-garden throughout its entire length, north and south, and all the way across from the snowy Sierra to the ocean.

Wherever a bee might fly within the bounds of this virgin wilderness – through the redwood forests, along the banks of the rivers, along the bluffs and headlands fronting the sea, over valley and plain, park and grove, and deep, leafy glen, or far up the piny slopes of the mountains – throughout every belt and section of climate up to the timber line, bee-flowers bloomed in lavish abundance. Here they grew more or less apart in special sheets and patches of no great size, there in broad, flowing folds hundreds of miles in length – zones of polleny forests, zones of flowery chaparral, stream-tangles of rubus and wild rose, sheets of golden compositæ, beds of violets, beds of mint, beds of bryanthus and clover, and so on, certain species blooming somewhere all the year round.

But of late years ploughs and sheep have made sad havoc in these glorious pastures, destroying tens of thousands of the flowery acres like a fire, and banishing many species of the best honey-plants to rocky cliffs and fence-corners, while, on the other hand, cultivation thus far has given no adequate compensation, at least in kind; only acres of alfalfa for miles of the richest wild pasture, ornamental roses and honeysuckles around cottage doors for cascades of wild roses in the dells, and small, square orchards and orange-groves for broad mountain-belts of chaparral.

The Great Central Plain of California, during the months of March, April and May, was one smooth, continuous bed of honey-bloom, so marvellously rich that, in walking from one end of it to the other, a distance of more than 400 miles, your foot would press about a hundred flowers at every step. Mints, gilias, nemophilias, castilleias and innumerable compositæ were so crowded together that, had ninety-nine per cent of them been taken away, the plain would still have seemed to any but Californians extravagantly flowery. The radiant, honeyful corollas, touching and overlapping, and rising above one another, glowed in the living light like a sunset sky – one sheet of purple and gold, with the bright Sacramento pouring through the midst of it from the north, the San Joaquin from the south, and their many tributaries sweeping in at right angles from the mountains, dividing the plain into sections fringed with trees.

Along the rivers there is a strip of bottom-land, countersunk beneath the general level, and wider toward the foot-hills, where magnificent oaks, from three to eight feet in diameter, cast grateful masses of shade over the open, prairie-like levels. And close along the water's edge there was a fine jungle of tropical luxuriance, composed of wild-rose and bramble bushes and a great variety of climbing vines, wreathing and interlacing the branches and trunks of willows and alders, and swinging across from summit to summit in heavy festoons. Here the wild bees revelled in fresh bloom long after the flowers of the drier plain had withered and gone to seed. And in midsummer, when the 'blackberries' were ripe, the Indians came from the mountains to feast – men, women and babies in long, noisy trains, often joined by the farmers of the neighbourhood, who gathered this wild fruit with commendable appreciation of its superior flavour, while their home orchards were full of ripe peaches, apricots, nectarines and figs, and their vineyards were laden with grapes. But, though these luxuriant, shaggy river-beds were thus distinct from the smooth, treeless plain, they made no heavy dividing lines in general views. The whole appeared as one continuous sheet of bloom bounded only by the mountains.

When I first saw this central garden, the most extensive and regular of all the bee-pastures of the State, it seemed all one sheet of plant gold, hazy and vanishing in the distance, distinct as a new map along the foot-hills at my feet.

Descending the eastern slopes of the Coast Range through beds of gilias and lupines, and around many a breezy hillock and bush-crowned headland, I at length waded out into the midst of it. All the ground was covered, not with grass and green leaves, but with radiant corollas, about ankle-deep next the foot-hills, knee-deep or more five or six miles out. Here were bahia, madia, madaria, burrielia, chrysopsis, corethrogyne, grindelia, etc., growing in close social congregations of various shades of yellow, blending finely with the purples of clarkia, orthocarpus, and œnothera, whose delicate petals were drinking the vital sunbeams without giving back any sparkling glow.

Because so long a period of extreme drought succeeds the rainy season, most of the vegetation is composed of annuals, which spring up simultaneously, and bloom together at about the same height above the ground, the general surface being but slightly ruffled by the taller phacelias, pentstemons and groups of *Salvia carduacea,* the king of the mints.

Sauntering in any direction, hundreds of these happy sun-plants brushed against my feet at every step, and closed over them as if I were wading in liquid gold. The air was sweet with fragrance, the larks sang their blessed songs, rising on the wing as I advanced, then sinking out of sight in the polleny sod, while myriads of wild bees stirred the lower air with their monotonous hum – monotonous, yet forever fresh and sweet as everyday sunshine. Hares and spermophiles showed themselves in considerable numbers in shallow places, and small bands of antelopes were almost constantly in sight, gazing curiously from some slight elevation, and then bounding swiftly away with unrivalled grace of motion. Yet I could discover no crushed flowers to mark their track, nor, indeed, any destructive action of any wild foot or tooth whatever.

The great yellow days circled by uncounted, while I drifted toward the north, observing the countless forms of life thronging about me, lying down almost anywhere on the approach of night. And what glorious botanical beds I had! Often-times on awaking I would find several new species leaning over me and looking me full in the face, so that my studies would begin before rising.

About the first of May I turned eastward, crossing the San Joaquin River between the mouths of the Tuolumne and Merced, and by the time I had reached the Sierra foot-hills most of the vegetation had gone to seed and become as dry as hay.

All the seasons of the great plain are warm or temperate, and bee-flowers are never wholly wanting; but the grand springtime – the annual resurrection – is governed by the rains, which usually set in about the middle of November or the beginning of December. Then the seeds, that for six months have lain on the ground dry and fresh as if they had been gathered into barns, at once unfold their treasured life. The general brown and purple of the ground, and the dead vegetation of the preceding year, give place to the green of mosses and liverworts and myriads of young leaves. Then one species after another comes into flower, gradually overspreading the green with yellow and purple, which lasts until May.

The 'rainy season' is by no means a gloomy, soggy period of constant cloudiness and rain. Perhaps nowhere else in North America, perhaps in the world, are the months of December, January, February and March so full of bland, plant-building sunshine. Referring to my notes of the winter and spring of 1868–69, every day of which I spent out of doors, on that section of the plain lying between the Tuolumne and Merced Rivers, I find that the first rain of the season fell on December 18th. January had only six rainy days – that is, days on which rain fell; February three, March five, April three and May three, completing the so-called rainy season, which was about an average one. The ordinary rain-storm of this region is seldom very cold or violent. The winds, which in settled weather come from the northwest, veer round into the opposite direction, the sky fills gradually and evenly with one general cloud, from which the rain falls steadily, often for days in succession, at a temperature of about 45° or 50°.

More than seventy-five per cent of all the rain of this season came from the northwest, down the coast over southeastern Alaska, British Columbia, Washington and Oregon, though the local winds of these circular storms blow from the southeast. One magnificent local storm from the northwest fell on March 21. A massive, round-browed cloud came swelling and thundering over the flowery plain in most imposing majesty, its bossy front burning white and purple in the full blaze of the sun, while warm rain poured from its ample fountains like a cataract, beating down flowers and bees, and flooding the dry watercourses as suddenly as those of Nevada are flooded by the so-called 'cloud-bursts.' But in less than half an hour not a trace of the heavy, mountain-like cloud-structure was left in the sky, and the bees were on the wing, as if nothing more gratefully refreshing could have been sent them.

By the end of January four species of plants were in flower, and five or six mosses had already adjusted their hoods and were in the prime of life; but the flowers were not sufficiently numerous as yet to affect greatly the general green of the young leaves. Violets made their appearance in the first week of February, and toward the end of this month the warmer portions of the plain were already golden with myriads of the flowers of rayed compositæ.

This was the full springtime. The sunshine grew warmer and richer, new plants bloomed every day; the air became more tuneful with humming wings, and sweeter with the fragrance of the opening flowers. Ants and ground squirrels were getting ready for their summer work, rubbing their benumbed limbs, and sunning themselves on the husk-piles before their doors, and spiders were busy mending their old webs, or weaving new ones.

In March, the vegetation was more than doubled in depth and colour; claytonia, calandrinia, a large white gilia and two nemophilas were in bloom, together with a host of yellow compositæ, tall enough now to bend in the wind and show wavering ripples of shade.

In April, plant-life, as a whole, reached its greatest height, and the plain, over all its varied surface, was mantled with a close, furred plush of purple and golden corollas. By the end of this month, most of the species had ripened their seeds, but undecayed, still seemed to be in bloom from the numerous corolla-like involucres and whorls of chaffy scales of the compositæ. In May, the bees found in flower only a few deep-set liliaceous plants and eriogonums.

June, July, August and September is the season of rest and sleep – a winter of dry heat – followed in October by a second outburst of bloom at the very driest time of the year. Then, after the shrunken mass of leaves and stalks of the dead vegetation crinkle and turn to dust beneath the foot, as if it had been baked in an oven, *Hemizonia virgata,* a slender, unobtrusive little plant, from six inches to three feet high, suddenly makes its appearance in patches miles in extent, like a resurrection of the bloom of April. I have counted upward of 3,000 flowers, five eighths of an inch in diameter on a single plant. Both its leaves and stems are so slender as to be nearly invisible, at a distance of a few yards, amid so showy a multitude of flowers. The ray and disk flowers are both yellow, the stamens purple, and the texture of the rays is rich and velvety, like the petals of garden pansies. The prevailing wind turns all the heads round to the southeast, so that in facing northwestward we have the flowers looking us in the face. In my estimation, this little plant, the last born of the brilliant host of compositæ that glorify the plain, is the most interesting of all. It remains in flower until November, uniting with two or three species of wiry eriogonums, which continue the floral chain around December to the spring flowers of January. Thus, although the main bloom and honey season is only about three months long, the floral circle, however thin around some of the hot, rainless months, is never completely broken.

How long the various species of wild bees have lived in this honey-garden, nobody knows; probably ever since the main body of the present flora gained possession of the land, toward the close of the glacial period. The first brown honey-bees brought to California are said to have arrived in San Francisco in March, 1853. A bee-keeper by the name of Shelton purchased a lot, consisting of twelve swarms, from someone at Aspinwall, who had brought them from New York. When landed at San Francisco, all the hives contained live bees, but they finally dwindled to one hive, which was taken to San José. The little immigrants flourished and multiplied in the bountiful pastures of the Santa Clara Valley, sending off three swarms the first season. The owner was killed shortly afterward, and in settling up his estate, two of the swarms were sold at auction for $105 and $110 respectively. Other importations were made, from time to time, by way of the Isthmus, and, though great pains were taken to ensure success, about one half usually died on the way. Four swarms were brought safely across the plains in 1859, the hives being placed in the rear end of a wagon, which was stopped in the afternoon to allow the bees to fly and feed in the floweriest places that were within reach until dark, when the hives were closed.

In 1855, two years after the time of the first arrivals from New York, a single swarm was brought over from San José, and let fly in the Great Central Plain. Bee-culture, however, has never gained much attention here, notwithstanding the extraordinary abundance of honey-bloom, and the high price of honey during the early years. A few hives are found here and there among settlers who chanced to have learned something about the business before coming to the State. But sheep, cattle, grain and fruit raising are the chief industries, as they require less skill and care, while the profits thus far have been greater. In 1856 honey sold here at from one and a half to two dollars per pound. Twelve years later the price had fallen to twelve and a half cents. In 1868 I sat down to dinner with a band of ravenous sheep-shearers at a ranch on the San Joaquin, where fifteen or twenty hives were kept, and our host advised us not to spare the large pan of honey he had placed on the table, as it was the cheapest article he had to offer. In all my walks, however, I have never come upon a regular bee-ranch in the Central Valley like those so common and so skilfully managed in the southern counties of the State. The few pounds of honey and wax produced are consumed at home, and are scarcely taken into account among the coarser products of the farm. The swarms that escape from their careless owners have a weary, perplexing time of it in seeking suitable homes. Most of them make their way to the foot-hills of the mountains, or to the trees that line the banks of the rivers, where some hollow log or trunk may be found. A friend of mine, while out hunting on the San Joaquin, came upon an old coon trap, hidden among some tall grass, near the edge of the river, upon which he sat down to rest. Shortly afterward his attention was attracted to a crowd of angry bees that were flying excitedly about his head, when he discovered that he was sitting upon their hive, which was found to contain more than 200 pounds of honey. Out in the broad, swampy delta of the Sacramento and San Joaquin Rivers, the little wanderers have been known to build their combs in a bunch of rushes, or stiff, wiry grass, only slightly protected from the weather, and in danger every spring of being carried away by floods. They have the advantage, however, of a vast extent of fresh pasture, accessible only to themselves.

The present condition of the Grand Central Garden is very different from that we have sketched. About twenty years ago, when the gold placers had been pretty thoroughly exhausted, the attention of fortune-seekers – not home-seekers – was, in great part, turned away from the mines to the fertile plains, and many began experiments in a kind of restless, wild agriculture. A load of lumber would be hauled to some spot on the free wilderness, where water could be easily found, and a rude box-cabin built. Then a gang-plough was procured, and a dozen mustang ponies, worth ten or fifteen dollars apiece, and with these hundreds of acres were stirred as easily as if the land had been under cultivation for years, tough, perennial roots being almost wholly absent. Thus a ranch was established, and from these bare wooden huts, as centres of desolation, the wild flora vanished in ever-widening circles. But the arch destroyers are the shepherds, with their flocks of hoofed locusts, sweeping over the ground like a fire, and trampling down every rod that escapes the plough as completely as if the whole plain were a cottage garden-plot without a fence. But notwithstanding these destroyers, a thousand swarms of bees may be pastured here for every one now gathering honey. The greater portion is still covered every season with a repressed growth of bee-flowers, for most of the species are annuals, and many of them are not relished by sheep or cattle, while the rapidity of their growth enables them to develop and mature their seeds before any foot has time to crush them. The ground is, therefore, kept sweet, and the race is perpetuated, though only as a suggestive shadow of the magnificence of its wildness.

The time will undoubtedly come when the entire area of this noble valley will be tilled like a garden, when the fertilizing waters of the mountains, now flowing to the sea, will be distributed to every acre, giving rise to prosperous towns, wealth, arts, etc. Then, I suppose, there will be few left, even among botanists, to deplore the vanished primeval flora. In the mean time, the pure waste going on – the wanton destruction of the innocents – is a sad sight to see, and the sun may well be pitied in being compelled to look on.

The bee-pastures of the Coast Ranges last longer and are more varied than those of the great plain, on account of differences of soil and climate, moisture, and shade, etc. Some of the mountains are upward of 4,000ft. in height, and small streams, springs, oozy bogs, etc., occur in great abundance and variety in the wooded regions, while open parks, flooded with sunshine, and hill-girt valleys lying at different elevations, each with its own peculiar climate and exposure, possess the required conditions for the development of species and families of plants widely varied.

Next the plain there is, first, a series of smooth hills, planted with a rich and showy vegetation that differs but little from that of the plain itself – as if the edge of the plain had been lifted and bent into flowing folds, with all its flowers in place, only toned down a little as to their luxuriance, and a few new species introduced, such as the hill lupines, mints and gilias. The colours show finely when thus held to view on the slopes, patches of red, purple, blue, yellow and white, blending around the edges, the whole appearing at a little distance like a map coloured in sections.

Above this lies the park and chaparral region, with oaks, mostly evergreen, planted wide apart, and blooming shrubs from three to ten feet high; manzanita and ceanothus of several species, mixed with rhamnus, cercis, pickeringia, cherry, amelanchier, and adenostoma, in shaggy, interlocking thickets, and many species of hosackia, clover, monardella, castilleia, etc., in the openings.

The main ranges send out spurs somewhat parallel to their axes, enclosing level valleys, many of them quite extensive, and containing a great profusion of sun-loving bee-flowers in their wild state; but these are, in great part, already lost to the bees by cultivation.

Nearer the coast are the giant forests of the redwoods, extending from near the Oregon line to Santa Cruz. Beneath the cool, deep shade of these majestic trees the ground is occupied by ferns, chiefly woodwardia and aspidiums, with only a few flowering plants – oxalis, trientalis, erythronium, fritillaria, smilax and other shade-lovers. But all along the redwood belt there are sunny openings on hill-slopes looking to the south, where the giant trees stand back, and give the ground to the small sunflowers and the bees. Around the lofty redwood walls of these little bee-acres there is usually a fringe of chestnut oak, laurel, and madroño, the last of which is a surpassingly beautiful tree, and a great favourite with the bees. The trunks of the largest specimens are seven or eight feet thick, and about fifty feet high; the bark red and chocolate coloured, the leaves plain, large and glossy, like those of *Magnolia grandiflora,* while the flowers are yellowish-white, and urn-shaped, in well-proportioned panicles, from five to ten inches long. When in full bloom, a single tree seems to be visited at times by a whole hive of bees at once, and the deep hum of such a multitude makes the listener guess that more than the ordinary work of honey-winning must be going on.

How perfectly enchanting and care-obliterating are these withdrawn gardens of the woods – long vistas opening to the sea – sunshine sifting and pouring upon the flowery ground in a tremulous, shifting mosaic, as the light-ways in the leafy wall open and close with the swaying breeze – shining leaves and flowers, birds and bees, mingling together in springtime harmony, and soothing fragrance exhaling from a thousand thousand fountains! In these balmy, dissolving days, when the deep heart-beats of Nature are felt thrilling rocks and trees and everything alike, common business and friends are happily forgotten, and even the natural honey-work of bees, and the care of birds for their young, and mothers for their children, seem slightly out of place.

To the northward, in Humboldt and the adjacent counties, whole hillsides are covered with rhododendron, making a glorious melody of bee-bloom in the spring. And the Western azalea, hardly less flowery, grows in massy thickets three to eight feet high around the edges of groves and woods as far south as San Luis Obispo, usually accompanied by manzanita; while the valleys, with their varying moisture and shade, yield a rich variety of the smaller honey-flowers, such as mentha, lycopus, micromeria, audibertia, trichostema and other mints; with vaccinium, wild strawberry, geranium, calais and goldenrod; and in the cool glens along the stream-banks, where the shade of trees is not too deep, spiræa, dog-wood, heteromeles and calycanthus, and many species of rubus form interlacing tangles, some portion of which continues in bloom for months.

Though the coast region was the first to be invaded and settled by white men, it has suffered less from a bee point of view than either of the other main divisons, chiefly, no doubt, because of the unevenness of the surface, and because it is owned and protected instead of lying exposed to the flocks of the wandering 'sheepmen.' These remarks apply more particularly to the north half of the coast. Farther south there is less moisture, less forest shade, and the honey flora is less varied.

The Sierra region is the largest of the three main divisions of the bee-lands of the State, and the most regularly varied in its subdivisions, owing to their gradual rise from the level of the Central Plain to the alpine summits. The foot-hill region is about as dry and sunful, from the end of May until the setting in of the winter rains, as the plain. There are no shady forests, no damp glens, at all like those lying at the same elevations in the Coast Mountains. The social compositæ of the plain, with a few added species, form the bulk of the herbaceous portion of the vegetation up to a height of 1,500ft. or more, shaded lightly here and there with oaks and Sabine Pines, and interrupted by patches of ceanothus and buckeye. Above this, and just below the forest region, there is a dark, heath-like belt of chaparral, composed almost exclusively of *Adenostoma fasciculata,* a bush belonging to the rose family, from five to eight feet high, with small, round leaves in fascicles, and bearing a multitude of small white flowers in panicles on the ends of the upper branches. Where it occurs at all, it usually covers all the ground with a close, impenetrable growth, scarcely broken for miles.

Up through the forest region, to a height of about 9,000ft. above sea-level, there are ragged patches of manzanita, and five or six species of ceanothus, called deer-brush or California lilac. These are the most important of all the honey-bearing bushes of the Sierra. *Chamœbatia foliolosa,* a little shrub about a foot high, with flowers like the strawberry, makes handsome carpets beneath the pines, and seems to be a favourite with the bees; while pines themselves furnish unlimited quantities of pollen and honey-dew. The product of a single tree, ripening its pollen at the right time of year, would be sufficient for the wants of a whole hive. Along the streams there is a rich growth of lilies, larkspurs, pedicularis, castilleias and clover. The alpine region contains the flowery glacier meadows, and countless small gardens in all sorts of places full of potentilla of several species, spraguea, ivesia, epilobium and goldenrod, with beds of bryanthus and the charming cassiope covered with sweet bells. Even the tops of the mountains are blessed with flowers – dwarf phlox, polemonium, ribes, hulsea, etc. I have seen wild bees and butterflies feeding at a height of 13,000ft. above the sea. Many, however, that go up these dangerous heights never come down again. Some, undoubtedly, perish in storms, and I have found thousands lying dead or benumbed on the suface of the glaciers, to which they had perhaps been attracted by the white glare, taking them for beds of bloom.

From swarms that escaped their owners in the lowlands, the honey-bee is now generally distributed throughout the whole length of the Sierra, up to an elevation of 8,000ft. above sea-level. At this height they flourish without care, though the snow every winter is deep. Even higher than this several bee-trees have been cut which contained over 200 pounds of honey.

The destructive action of sheep has not been so general on the mountain pastures as on those of the great plain, but in many places it has been more complete, owing to the more friable character of the soil, and its sloping position. The slant digging and down-raking action of hoofs on the steeper slopes of moraines has uprooted and buried many of the tender plants from year to year, without allowing them time to mature their seeds. The shrubs, too, are badly bitten, especially the various species of ceanothus. Fortunately, neither sheep nor cattle care to feed on the manzanita, spiræa, or adenostoma; and these fine honey-bushes are too stiff and tall, or grow in places too rough and inaccessible, to be trodden under foot. Also the canyon walls and gorges, which form so considerable a part of the area of the range, while inaccessible to domestic sheep, are well fringed with honey-shrubs, and contain thousands of lovely bee-gardens, lying hid in narrow side-canyons and recesses fenced with avalanche taluses, and on the top of flat, projecting headlands, where only bees would think to look for them.

But, on the other hand, a great portion of the woody plants that escape the feet and teeth of the sheep are destroyed by the shepherds by means of running fires, which are set everywhere during the dry autumn for the purposes of burning off the old fallen trunks and underbrush, with a view to improving the pastures, and making more open ways for the flocks. These destructive sheep-fires sweep through nearly the entire forest belt of the range, from one extremity to the other, consuming not only the underbrush, but the young trees and seedlings on which the permanence of the forests depends; thus setting in motion a long train of evils which will certainly reach far beyond bees and bee-keepers.

The plough has not yet invaded the forest region to any appreciable extent, neither has it accomplished much in the foot-hills. Thousands of bee-ranches might be established along the margin of the plain, and up to a height of 4,000ft., wherever water could be obtained. The climate at this elevation admits of the making of permanent homes, and by moving the hives to higher pastures as the lower pass out of bloom, the annual yield of honey would be nearly doubled. The foot-hill pastures, as we have seen, fail about the end of May, those of the chaparral belt and lower forests are in full bloom in June, those of the upper and alpine region in July, August and September. In Scotland, after the best of the Lowland bloom is past, the bees are carried in carts to the Highlands, and set free on the heather hills. In France, too, and in Poland, they are carried from pasture to pasture among orchards and fields in the same way, and along the rivers in barges to collect the honey of the delightful vegetation of the banks. In Egypt they are taken far up the Nile, and floated slowly home again, gathering the honey-harvest of the various fields on the way, timing their movements in accord with the seasons. Were similar methods pursued in California the productive season would last nearly all the year.

The average elevation of the north half of the Sierra is, as we have seen, considerably less than that of the south half, and small streams, with the bank and meadow gardens dependent upon them, are less abundant. Around the head waters of the Yuba, Feather and Pitt rivers, the extensive table-lands of lava are sparsely planted with pines, through which the sunshine reaches the ground with little interruption. Here flourishes a scattered, tufted growth of golden applopappus, linosyris, bahia, wyetheia, arnica, artemisia and similar plants; with manzanita, cherry, plum and thorn in ragged patches on the cooler hill-slopes. At the extremities of the Great Central Plain, the Sierra and Coast Ranges curve around and lock together in a labyrinth of mountains and valleys, throughout which their floras are mingled, making at the north, with its temperate climate and copious rainfall, a perfect paradise for bees, though, strange to say, scarcely a single regular bee-ranch has yet been established in it.

Of all the upper flower fields of the Sierra, Shasta is the most honeyful, and may yet surpass in fame the celebrated honey hills of Hybla and hearthy Hymettus. Regarding this noble mountain from a bee point of view, encircled by its many climates, and sweeping aloft from the torrid plain into the frosty azure, we find the first 5,000ft. from the summit generally snow-clad, and therefore about as honeyless as the sea. The base of this arctic region is girdled by a belt of crumbling lava measuring about 1,000ft. in vertical breadth, and is mostly free from snow in summer. Beautiful lichens enliven the faces of the cliffs with their bright colours, and in some of the warmer nooks there are a few tufts of alpine daisies, wall-flowers and pentstemons; but, notwithstanding these bloom freely in the late summer, the zone as a whole is almost as honeyless as the icy summit, and its lower edge may be taken as the honey-line. Immediately below this comes the forest zone, covered with a rich growth of conifers, chiefly silver firs, rich in pollen and honey-dew, and diversified with countless garden openings, many of them less than a hundred yards across. Next, in orderly succession, comes the great bee zone. Its area far surpasses that of the icy summit and both the other zones combined, for it goes sweeping majestically around the entire mountain, with a breadth of six or seven miles and a circumference of nearly a hundred miles.

Shasta, as we have already seen, is a fire-mountain created by a succession of eruptions of ashes and molten lava, which, flowing over the lips of its several craters, grew outward and upward like the trunk of a knotty exogenous tree. Then followed a strange contrast. The glacial winter came on, loading the cooling mountain with ice, which flowed slowly outward in every direction, radiating from the summit in the form of one vast conical glacier – a down-crawling mantle of ice upon a fountain of smouldering fire, crushing and grinding for centuries its brown, flinty lavas with incessant activity, and thus degrading and remodelling the entire mountain. When, at length, the glacial period began to draw near its close, the ice-mantle was gradually melted off around the bottom, and, in receding and breaking into its present fragmentary condition, irregular rings and heaps of moraine matter were stored upon its flanks. The glacial erosion of most of the Shasta lavas produces detritus, composed of rough, sub-angular boulders of moderate size and of porous gravel and sand, which yields freely to the transporting power of running water. Magnificent floods from the ample fountains of ice and snow working with sublime energy upon this prepared glacial detritus, sorted it out and carried down immense quantities from the higher slopes, and reformed it in smooth, delta-like beds around the base; and it is these flood-beds joined together that now form the main honey-zone of the old volcano.

Thus, by forces seemingly antagonistic and destructive, has Mother Nature accomplished her beneficent designs – now a flood of fire, now a flood of ice, now a flood of water; and at length an outburst of organic life, a milky way of snowy petals and wings, girdling the rugged mountain like a cloud, as if the vivifying sunbeams beating against its sides had broken into a foam of plant-bloom and bees, as sea-waves break and bloom on a rock shore.

In this flowery wilderness the bees rove and revel, rejoicing in the bounty of the sun, clambering eagerly through bramble and hucklebloom, ringing the myriad bells of the manzanita, now humming aloft among polleny willows and firs, now down on the ashy ground among gilias and buttercups, and anon plunging deep into snowy banks of cherry and buckthorn. They consider the lilies and roll into them, and, like lilies, they toil not, for they are impelled by sun-power, as water-wheels by water-power; and when the one has plenty of high-pressure water, the other plenty of sunshine, they hum and quiver alike. Sauntering in the Shasta bee-lands in the sun-days of summer, one may readily infer the time of day from the comparative energy of bee-movements alone – drowsy and moderate in the cool of the morning, increasing in energy with the ascending sun, and, at high noon, thrilling and quivering in wild ecstasy, then gradually declining again to the stillness of night. In my excursions among the glaciers I occasionally meet bees that are hungry, like mountaineers who venture too far and remain too long above the bread-line; then they droop and wither like autumn leaves. The Shasta bees are perhaps better fed than any others in the Sierra. Their field-work is one perpetual feast; but, however exhilarating the sunshine or bountiful the supply of flowers, they are always dainty feeders. Humming-moths and humming-birds seldom set foot upon a flower, but poise on the wing in front of it, and reach forward as if they were sucking through straws. But bees, though as dainty as they, hug their favourite flowers with profound cordiality, and push their blunt, polleny faces against them, like babies on their mother's bosom. And fondly, too, with eternal love, does Mother Nature clasp her small bee-babies, and suckle them, multitudes at once, on her warm Shasta breast.

Besides the common honey-bee there are many other species here – fine mossy, burly fellows, who were nourished on the mountains thousands of sunny seasons before the advent of the domestic species. Among these are the bumblebees, mason-bees, carpenter-bees and leaf-cutters. Butterflies, too, and moths of every size and pattern; some broad-winged like bats, flapping slowly, and sailing in easy curves; others like small, flying violets, shaking about loosely in short, crooked flights close to the flowers, feasting luxuriously night and day. Great numbers of deer also delight to dwell in the brushy portions of the bee-pastures.

Bears, too, roam the sweet wilderness, their blunt, shaggy forms harmonizing well with the trees and tangled bushes, and with the bees, also, notwithstanding the disparity in size. They are fond of all good things, and enjoy them to the utmost, with but little troublesome discrimination – flowers and leaves as well as berries, and the bees themselves as well as their honey. Though the California bears have as yet had but little experience with honey-bees, they often succeed in reaching their bountiful stores, and it seems doubtful whether bees themselves enjoy honey with so great a relish. By means of their powerful teeth and claws they can gnaw and tear open almost any hive conveniently accessible. Most honey-bees, however, in search of a home are wise enough to make choice of a hollow in a living tree, a considerable distance above the ground, when such places are to be had; then they are pretty secure, for though the smaller black and brown bears climb well, they are unable to break into strong hives while compelled to exert themselves to keep from falling, and at the same time to endure the stings of the fighting bees without having their paws free to rub them off. But woe to the black bumblebees discovered in their mossy nests in the ground! With a few strokes of their huge paws the bears uncover the entire establishment, and, before time is given for a general buzz, bees old and young, larvae, honey, stings, nest and all are taken in one ravishing mouthful.

Not the least influential of the agents concerned in the superior sweetness of the Shasta flora are its storms – storms I mean that are strictly local, bred and born on the mountain. The magical rapidity with which they are grown on the mountain-top, and bestow their charity in rain and snow, never fails to astonish the inexperienced lowlander. Often in calm, glowing days, while the bees are still on the wing, a storm-cloud may be seen far above in the pure ether, swelling its pearl bosses, and growing silently, like a plant. Presently a clear, ringing discharge of thunder is heard, followed by a rush of wind that comes sounding over the bending woods like the roar of the ocean, mingling rain-drops, snow-flowers, honey-flowers and bees in wild storm harmony.

Still more impressive are the warm, reviving days of spring in the mountain pastures. The blood of the plants throbbing beneath the life-giving sunshine seems to be heard and felt. Plant growth goes on before our eyes, and every tree in the woods and every bush and flower is seen as a hive of restless industry. The deeps of the sky are mottled with singing wings of every tone and colour; clouds of brilliant chrysididæ dancing and swirling in exquisite rhythm, golden-barred vespidæ, dragon-flies, butterflies, grating cicadas and jolly, rattling grasshoppers, fairly enamelling the light.

On bright, crisp mornings a striking optical effect may frequently be observed from the shadows of the higher mountains while the sunbeams are pouring past overhead. Then every insect, no matter what may be its own proper colour, burns white in the light. Gauzy-winged hymenoptera, moths, jet-black beetles, all are transfigured alike in pure, spiritual white, like snowflakes.

In Southern California, where bee-culture has had so much skilful attention of late years, the pasturage is not more abundant, or more advantageously varied as to the number of its honey-plants and their distribution over mountain and plain, than that of many other portions of the State where the industrial currents flow in other channels. The famous white sage (*Audibertia*), belonging to the mint family, flourishes here in all its glory, blooming in May, and yielding great quantities of clear, pale honey, which is greatly prized in every market it has yet reached. This species grows chiefly in the valleys and low hills. The black sage on the mountains is part of a dense, thorny chaparral, which is composed chiefly of adenostoma, ceanothus, manzanita and cherry – not differing greatly from that of the southern portion of the Sierra, but more dense and continuous, and taller, and remaining longer in bloom. Streamside gardens, so charming a feature of both the Sierra and Coast Mountains, are less numerous in Southern California, but they are exceedingly rich in honey-flowers, wherever found – melilotus, columbine, collinsia, verbena, zauschneria, wild rose, honeysuckle, philadelphus and lilies rising from the warm, moist dells in a very storm of exuberance. Wild buckwheat of many species is developed in abundance over the dry, sandy valleys and lower slopes of the mountains, toward the end of summer, and is, at this time, the main dependence of the bees, reinforced here and there by orange groves, alfalfa fields and small home gardens.

The main honey months, in ordinary seasons, are April, May, June, July and August; while the other months are usually flowery enough to yield sufficient for the bees.

According to Mr J. T. Gordon, President of the Los Angeles County Bee-keepers' Association, the first bees introduced into the county were a single hive, which cost $150 in San Francisco, and arrived in September, 1854.[1] In April, of the following year, this hive sent out two swarms, which were sold for $100 each. From this small beginning the bees gradually multiplied to about 3,000 swarms in the year 1873. In 1876 it was estimated that there were between 15,000 and 20,000 hives in the county, producing an annual yield of about 100 pounds to the hive – in some exceptional cases, a much greater yield.

In San Diego County, at the beginning of the season of 1878, there were about 24,000 hives, and the shipments from the one port of San Diego for the same year, from July 17 to November 10, were 1071 barrels, 15,544 cases, and nearly 90 tons. The largest bee-ranches have about a thousand hives, and are carefully and skilfully managed, every scientific appliance of merit being brought into use. There are few bee-keepers, however, who own half as many as this, or who give their undivided attention to the business. Orange culture, at present, is heavily overshadowing every other business.

A good many of the so-called bee-ranches of Los Angeles and San Diego counties are still of the rudest pioneer kind imaginable. A man unsuccessful in everything else hears the interesting story of the profits and comforts of bee-keeping, and concludes to try it; he buys a few colonies, or gets them from some overstocked ranch on shares, takes them back to the foot of some canyon, where the pasturage is fresh, squats on the land, with, or without, the permission of the owner, sets up his hives, makes a box-cabin for himself, scarcely bigger than a bee-hive, and awaits his fortune.

Bees suffer sadly from famine during the dry years which occasionally occur in the southern and middle portions of the State. If the rainfall amounts only to three or four inches, instead of from twelve to twenty, as in ordinary seasons, then sheep and cattle die in thousands, and so do these small, winged cattle, unless they are carefully fed, or removed to other pastures. The year 1877 will long be remembered as exceptionally rainless and distressing. Scarcely a flower bloomed on the dry valleys away from the stream-sides, and not a single grain-field depending upon rain was reaped. The seed only sprouted, came up a little way, and withered. Horses, cattle and sheep grew thinner day by day, nibbling at bushes and weeds, along the shallowing edges of streams, many of which were dried up altogether, for the first time since the settlement of the country.

In the course of a trip I made during the summer of that year through Monterey, San Luis Obispo, Santa Barbara, Ventura and Los Angeles counties, the deplorable effects of the drought were everywhere visible – leafless fields, dead and dying cattle, dead bees and half-dead people with

---

[1] Fifteen hives of Italian bees were introduced into Los Angeles County in 1855, and in 1876 they had increased to 500. The marked superiority claimed for them over the common species is now attracting considerable attention.

dusty, doleful faces. Even the birds and squirrels were in distress, though their suffering was less painfully apparent than that of the poor cattle. These were falling one by one in slow, sure starvation along the banks of the hot, sluggish streams, while thousands of buzzards correspondingly fat were sailing above them, or standing gorged on the ground beneath the trees, waiting with easy faith for fresh carcasses. The quails, prudently considering the hard times, abandoned all thought of pairing. They were too poor to marry, and so continued in flocks all through the year without attempting to rear young. The ground-squirrels, though an exceptionally industrious and enterprising race, as every farmer knows, were hard pushed for a living; not a fresh leaf or seed was to be found save in the trees, whose bossy masses of dark green foliage presented a striking contrast to the ashen baldness of the ground beneath them. The squirrels, leaving their accustomed feeding-grounds, betook themselves to the leafy oaks to gnaw out the acorn stores of the provident woodpeckers, but the latter kept up a vigilant watch upon their movements. I noticed four woodpeckers in league against one squirrel, driving the poor fellow out of an oak that they claimed. He dodged round the knotty trunk from side to side, as nimbly as he could in his famished condition, only to find a sharp bill everywhere. But the fate of the bees that year seemed the saddest of all. In different portions of Los Angeles and San Diego counties, from one half to three fourths of them died of sheer starvation. Not less than 18,000 colonies perished in these two counties alone, while in the adjacent counties the death-rate was hardly less.

Even the colonies nearest to the mountains suffered this year, for the smaller vegetation on the foot-hills was affected by the drought almost as severely as that of the valleys and plains, and even the hardy, deep-rooted chaparral, the surest dependence of the bees, bloomed sparingly, while much of it was beyond reach. Every swarm could have been saved, however, by promptly supplying them with food when their own stores began to fail, and before they became enfeebled and discouraged; or by cutting roads back into the mountains, and taking them into the heart of the flowery chaparral. The Santa Lucia, San Rafael, San Gabriel, San Jacinto and San Bernardino ranges are almost untouched as yet save by the wild bees. Some idea of their resources, and of the advantages and disadvantages they offer to bee-keepers, may be formed from an excursion that I made into the San Gabriel Range about the beginning of August of 'the dry year.' This range, containing most of the characteristic features of the other ranges just mentioned, overlooks the Los Angeles vineyards and orange groves from the north, and is more rigidly inaccessible in the ordinary meaning of the word than any other that I ever attempted to penetrate. The slopes are exceptionally steep and insecure to the foot, and they are covered with thorny bushes from five to ten feet high. With the exception of little spots not visible in general views, the entire surface is covered with them, massed in close hedge growth, sweeping gracefully down into every gorge and hollow, and swelling over every ridge and summit in shaggy, ungovernable exuberance, offering more honey to the acre for half the year than the most crowded cloverfield. But when beheld from the open San Gabriel Valley, beaten with dry sunshine, all that was seen of the range seemed to wear a forbidding aspect. From base to summit all seemed grey, barren, silent, its glorious chaparral appearing like dry moss creeping over its dull, wrinkled ridges and hollows.

Setting out from Pasadena, I reached the foot of the range about sundown; and being weary and heated with my walk across the shadeless valley, concluded to camp for the night. After resting a few moments, I began to look about among the flood-boulders of Eaton Creek for a camp-ground, when I came upon a strange, dark-looking man who had been chopping cord-wood. He seemed surprised at seeing me, so I sat down with him on the live-oak log he had been cutting, and made haste to give a reason for my appearance in his solitude, explaining that I was anxious to find out something about the mountains, and meant to make my way up Eaton Creek next morning. Then he kindly invited me to camp with him, and led me to his little cabin, situated at the foot of the mountains, where a small spring oozes out of a bank overgrown with wild-rose bushes. After supper, when the daylight was gone, he explained that he was out of candles; so we sat in the dark, while he gave me a sketch of his life in a mixture of Spanish and English. He was born in Mexico, his father Irish, his mother Spanish. He had been a miner, rancher, prospector, hunter, etc., rambling always, and wearing his life away in mere waste; but now he was going to settle down. His past life, he said, was of 'no account,' but the future was promising. He was going to 'make money and marry a Spanish woman.' People mine here for water as for gold. He had been running a tunnel into a spur of the mountain back of his cabin. 'My prospect is good,' he said, 'and if I chance to strike a good, strong flow, I'll soon be worth $5,000 or $10,000. For that flat out there,' referring to a small irregular patch of bouldery detritus, two or three acres in size, that had been deposited by Eaton Creek during some flood season – 'that flat is large enough for a nice orange-grove, and the bank behind the cabin will do for a vineyard, and after watering my own trees and vines I will have some water left to sell to my neighbours below me, down the valley. And then,' he continued, 'I can keep bees, and make money that way, too, for the mountains above here are just full of honey in the summer-time, and one of my neighbours down here says that he will let me have a whole lot of hives, on shares, to start with. You see I've a good thing; I'm all right now.' All this prospective affluence in the sunken, boulder-choked flood-bed of a mountain-stream! Leaving the bees out of the count, most fortune-seekers would as soon think of settling on the summit of Mount Shasta. Next morning, wishing my hopeful entertainer good luck, I set out on my shaggy excursion.

About half an hour's walk above the cabin, I came to 'The Fall,' famous throughout the valley settlements as the finest yet discovered in the San Gabriel Mountains. It is a charming little thing, with a low, sweet voice, singing like a bird, as it pours from a notch in a short ledge, some thirty-five or forty feet into a round mirror-pool. The face of the cliff back of it, and on both sides, is smoothly covered and embossed with mosses, against which the white water shines out in showy relief, like a silver instrument in a velvet case. Hither come the San Gabriel lads and lassies, to gather ferns and dabble away their hot holidays in the cool water, glad to escape from their commonplace palm-gardens and orange-groves. The delicate maidenhair grows on fissured rocks within reach of the spray, while broad-leaved maples and sycamores cast soft, mellow shade over a rich profusion of bee-flowers, growing among boulders in front of the pool – the fall, the flowers, the bees, the ferny rocks and leafy shade forming a charming little poem of wildness, the last of a series extending down the flowery slopes of Mount San Antonio through the rugged, foam-beaten bosses of the main Eaton Canyon.

From the base of the fall I followed the ridge that forms the western rim of the Eaton basin to the summit of one of the principal peaks, which is about 5,000ft. above sea-level. Then, turning eastward, I crossed the middle of the basin, forcing a way over its many subordinate ridges and across its eastern rim, having to contend almost everywhere with the floweriest and most impenetrable growth of honey-bushes I had ever encountered since first my mountaineering began. Most of the Shasta chaparral is leafy nearly to the ground; here the main stems are naked for three or four feet, and interspiked with dead twigs, forming a stiff *chevaux de frise* through which even the bears make their way with difficulty. I was compelled to creep for miles on all fours, and in following the bear-trails often found tufts of hair on the bushes where they had forced themselves through.

For 100ft. or so above the fall the ascent was made possible only by tough cushions of club-moss that clung to the rock. Above this the ridge weathers away to a thin knife-blade for a few hundred yards, and thence to the summit of the range it carries a bristly mane of chaparral. Here and there small openings occur on rocky places, commanding fine views across the cultivated valley to the ocean. These I found by the tracks were favourite outlooks and resting-places for the wild animals – bears, wolves, foxes, wildcats, etc. – which abound here, and would have to be taken into account in the establishment of bee-ranches. In the deepest thickets I found wood-rat villages – groups of huts four to six feet high, built of sticks and leaves in rough, tapering piles, like musk-rat cabins. I noticed a good many bees, too, most of them wild. The tame honey-bees seemed languid and wing-weary, as if they had come all the way up from the flowerless valley.

After reaching the summit I had time to make only a hasty survey of the basin, now glowing in the sunset gold, before hastening down into one of the tributary canyons in search of water. Emerging from a particularly tedious breadth of chaparral, I found myself free and erect in a beautiful park-like grove of mountain live oak, where the ground was planted with aspidiums and brier-roses, while the glossy foliage made a close canopy overhead, leaving the grey dividing trunks bare to show the beauty of their interlacing arches. The bottom of the canyon was dry where I first reached it, but a bunch of scarlet mimulus indicated water at no great distance, and I soon discovered about a bucketful in a hollow of the rock. This, however, was full of dead bees, wasps, beetles and leaves, well steeped and simmered, and would, therefore, require boiling and filtering through fresh charcoal before it could be made available. Tracing the dry channel about a mile farther down to its junction with a larger tributary canyon, I at length discovered a lot of boulder pools, clear as crystal, brimming full, and linked together by glistening streamlets just strong enough to sing audibly. Flowers in full bloom adorned their margins, lilies ten feet high, larkspur, columbines and luxuriant ferns, leaning and overarching in lavish abundance, while a noble old live oak spread its rugged arms over all. Here I camped, making my bed on smooth cobblestones.

Next day, in the channel of a tributary that heads on Mount San Antonio, I passed about fifteen or twenty gardens like the one in which I slept – lilies in every one of them, in the full pomp of bloom. My third camp was made near the middle of the general basin, at the head of a long system of cascades from ten to 200ft. high, one following the other in close succession down a rocky, inaccessible canyon, making a total descent of nearly 1,700ft. Above the cascades the main stream passes through a series of open, sunny levels, the largest of which are about an acre in size, where the wild bees and their companions were feasting on a showy growth of zauschneria, painted cups and monardella; and grey squirrels were busy harvesting the burs of the Douglas spruce, the only conifer I met in the basin.

The eastern slopes of the basin are in every way similar to those we have described, and the same may be said of other portions of the range. From the highest summit, far as the eye could reach, the landscape was one vast bee-pasture, a rolling wilderness of honey-bloom, scarcely broken by bits of forest or the rocky outcrops of hilltops and ridges.

Behind the San Bernardino Range lies the wild 'sage-brush country,' bounded on the east by the Colorado River, and extending in a general northerly direction to Nevada and along the eastern base of the Sierra beyond Mono Lake.

The greater portion of this immense region, including Owen's Valley, Death Valley and the Sink of the Mohave, the area of which is nearly one fifth that of the entire State, is usually regarded as a desert, not because of any lack in the soil, but for want of rain, and rivers available for irrigation. Very little of it, however, is desert in the eyes of a bee.

Looking now over all the available pastures of California, it appears that the business of bee-keeping is still in its infancy. Even in the more enterprising of the southern counties, where so vigorous a beginning has been made, less than a tenth of their honey resources have as yet been developed; while in the Great Plain, the Coast Ranges, the Sierra Nevada and the northern region about Mount Shasta, the business can hardly be said to exist at all. What the limits of its developments in the future may be, with the advantages of cheaper transportation and the invention of better methods in general, it is not easy to guess. Nor, on the other hand, are we able to measure the influence on bee interests likely to follow the destruction of the forests, now rapidly falling before fire and the axe. As to the sheep evil, that can hardly become greater than it is at the present day. In short, notwithstanding the wide-spread deterioration and destruction of every kind already effected, California, with her incomparable climate and flora, is still, as far as I know, the best of all the bee-lands of the world.

OUR NATIONAL PARKS

Our National Parks

First published by Houghton Mifflin Co., Boston, 1901

YOSEMITE BIRDS, SNOW-BOUND AT THE FOOT OF INDIAN CAÑON.

Contents

VIEW IN THE SIERRA FOREST.

CHAPTER ONE

The Wild Parks and Forest Reservations of the West

'Keep not standing fix'd and rooted,
  Briskly venture, briskly roam;
Head and hand, where'er thou foot it,
  And stout heart are still at home.
In each land the sun does visit
  We are gay, whate'er betide:
To give room for wandering is it
  That the world was made so wide.'

THE TENDENCY nowadays to wander in wildernesses is delightful to see. Thousands of tired, nerve-shaken, over-civilized people are beginning to find out that going to the mountains is going home; that wildness is a necessity; and that mountain parks and reservations are useful not only as fountains of timber and irrigating rivers, but as fountains of life. Awakening from the stupefying effects of the vice of over-industry and the deadly apathy of luxury, they are trying as best they can to mix and enrich their own little ongoings with those of Nature, and to get rid of rust and disease. Briskly venturing and roaming, some are washing off sins and cobweb cares of the devil's spinning in all-day storms on mountains; sauntering in rosiny pinewoods or in gentian meadows, brushing through chaparral, bending down and parting sweet, flowery sprays; tracing rivers to their sources, getting in touch with the nerves of Mother Earth; jumping from rock to rock, feeling the life of them, learning the songs of them, panting in whole-souled exercise, and rejoicing in deep, long-drawn breaths of pure wildness. This is fine and natural and full of promise. So also is the growing interest in the care and preservation of forests and wild places in general, and in the half wild parks and gardens of towns. Even the scenery habit in its most artificial forms, mixed with spectacles, silliness, and kodaks; its devotees arrayed more gorgeously than scarlet tanagers, frightening the wild game with red umbrellas – even this is encouraging, and may well be regarded as a hopeful sign of the times.

All the Western mountains are still rich in wildness, and by means of good roads are being brought nearer civilization every year. To the sane and free it will hardly seem necessary to cross the continent in search of wild beauty, however easy the way, for they find it in abundance wherever they chance to be. Like Thoreau they see forests in orchards and patches of huckleberry brush, and oceans in ponds and drops of dew. Few in these hot, dim, strenuous times are quite sane or free; choked with care like clocks full of dust, laboriously doing so much good and making so much money – or so little – they are no longer good for themselves.

When, like a merchant taking a list of his goods, we take stock of our wildness, we are glad to see how much of even the most destructible kind is still unspoiled. Looking at our continent as scenery when it was all wild, lying between beautiful seas, the starry sky above it, the starry rocks beneath it, to compare its sides, the East and the West, would be like comparing the sides of a rainbow. But it is no longer equally beautiful. The rainbows of today are, I suppose, as bright as those that first spanned the sky; and some of our landscapes are growing more beautiful from year to year, nothwithstanding the clearing, trampling work of civilization. New plants and animals are enriching woods and gardens, and many landscapes wholly new, with divine sculpture and architecture, are just now coming to the light of day as the mantling folds of creative glaciers are being withdrawn, and life in a thousand cheerful, beautiful forms is pushing into them, and new-born rivers are beginning to sing and shine in them. The old rivers, too, are growing longer, like healthy trees, gaining new branches and lakes as the residual glaciers at their highest sources on the mountains recede, while the rootlike branches in their flat deltas are at the same time spreading farther and wider into the seas and making new lands.

Under the control of the vast mysterious forces of the interior of the earth all the continents and islands are slowly rising or sinking. Most of the mountains are diminishing in size under the wearing action of the weather, though a few are increasing in height and girth, especially the volcanic ones, as fresh floods of molten rocks are piled on their summits and spread in successive layers, like the wood-rings of trees, on their sides. New mountains, also, are being created from time to time as islands in lakes and seas, or as subordinate cones on the slopes of old ones, thus in some measure balancing the waste of old beauty with new. Man, too, is making many far-reaching changes. This most influential half animal, half angel is rapidly multiplying and spreading, covering the seas and lakes with ships, the land with huts, hotels, cathedrals, and clustered city shops and homes, so that soon, it would seem, we may have to go farther than Nansen to find a good sound solitude. None of Nature's landscapes are ugly so long as they are wild; and much, we can say comfortingly, must always be in great part wild, particularly the sea and the sky, the floods of light from the stars, and the warm, unspoilable heart of the earth, infinitely beautiful, though only dimly visible to the eye of imagination. The geysers, too, spouting from the hot underworld; the steady, long-lasting glaciers on the mountains, obedient only to the sun; Yosemite domes and the tremendous grandeur of rocky canyons and mountains in general – these must always be wild, for man can change them and mar them hardly more than can the butterflies that hover above them. But the continent's outer beauty is fast passing away, especially the plant part of it, the most destructible and most universally charming of all.

Only thirty years ago, the great Central Valley of California, five hundred miles long and fifty miles wide, was one bed of golden and purple flowers. Now it is ploughed and pastured out of existence, gone forever – scarce a memory of it left in fence corners and along the bluffs of the streams. The gardens of the Sierra, also, and the noble forests in both the reserved and unreserved portions are sadly hacked and trampled, notwithstanding the ruggedness of the topography – all excepting those of the parks guarded by a few soldiers. In the noblest forests of the world, the ground, once divinely beautiful, is desolate and repulsive, like a face ravaged by disease. This is true also of many other Pacific Coast and Rocky Mountain valleys and forests. The same fate, sooner or later, is awaiting them all, unless awakening public opinion comes forward to stop it. Even the great deserts in Arizona, Nevada, Utah and New Mexico, which offer so little to attract settlers, and which a few years ago pioneers were afraid of, as places of desolation and death, are now taken as pastures at the rate of one or two square miles per cow, and of course their plant treasures are passing away – the delicate abronias, phloxes, gilias, etc. Only a few of the bitter, thorny, unbitable shrubs are left, and the sturdy cactuses that defend themselves with bayonets and spears.

Most of the wild plant wealth of the East also has vanished – gone into dusty history. Only vestiges of its glorious prairie and woodland wealth remain to bless humanity in boggy, rocky, unploughable places. Fortunately, some of these are purely wild, and go far to keep Nature's love visible. White water-lilies, with rootstocks deep and safe in mud, still send up every summer a Milky Way of starry, fragrant flowers around a thousand lakes, and many a tuft of wild grass waves its panicles on mossy rocks, beyond reach of trampling feet, in company with saxifrages, bluebells, and ferns. Even in the midst of farmers' fields, precious sphagnum bogs, too soft for the feet of cattle, are preserved with their charming plants unchanged – chiogenes, andromeda, kalmia, linnæa, arethusa, etc. Calypso borealis still hides in the arbor vitæ swamps of Canada, and away to the southward there are a few unspoiled swamps, big ones, where miasma, snakes, and alligators, like guardian angels, defend their treasures and keep them as pure as paradise. And beside a' that and a' that, the East is blessed with good winters and blossoming clouds that shed white flowers over all the land, covering every scar and making the saddest landscape divine at least once a year.

The most extensive, least spoiled, and most unspoilable of the gardens of the continent are the vast tundras of Alaska. In summer they extend smooth, even, undulating, continuous beds of flowers and leaves from about lat. 62° to the shores of the Arctic Ocean; and in winter sheets of snowflowers make all the country shine, one mass of white radiance like a star. Nor are these Arctic plant people the pitiful frost-pinched unfortunates they are guessed to be by those who have never seen them. Though lowly in stature, keeping near the frozen ground as if loving it, they are bright and cheery, and speak Nature's love as plainly as their big relatives of the South. Tenderly happed and tucked in beneath downy snow to sleep through the long, white winter, they make haste to bloom in the spring without trying to grow tall, though some rise high enough to ripple and wave in the wind, and display masses of colour – yellow, purple and blue – so rich that they look like beds of rainbows, and are visible miles and miles away.

As early as June one may find the showy geum glaciale in flower, and the dwarf willows putting forth myriads of fuzzy catkins, to be followed quickly, especially on the dryer ground, by mertensia, eritrichium, polemonium, oxytropis, astragalus, lathyrus, lupinus, myosotis, dodecatheon, arnica, chrysanthemum, nardosmia, saussurea, senecio, erigeron, matrecaria, caltha, valeriana, stellaria, tofieldia, polygonum, papaver, phlox, lychnis, cheiranthus, linnæa, and a host of drabas, saxifrages and heathworts, with bright stars and bells in glorious profusion, particularly cassiope, andromeda, ledum, pyrola, and vaccinium – cassiope the most abundant and beautiful of them all. Many grasses also grow here, and wave fine purple spikes and panicles over the other flowers – poa, aira, calamagrostis, alopecurus, trisetum, elymus, festuca, glyceria, etc. Even ferns are found thus far north, carefully and comfortably unrolling their precious fronds – aspidium, cystopteris, and woodsia, all growing on a sumptuous bed of mosses and lichens; not the scaly lichens seen on rails and trees and fallen logs to the southward, but massive, roundheaded, finely coloured plants like corals, wonderfully beautiful, worth going round the world to see. I should like to mention all the plant friends I found in a summer's wanderings in this cool reserve, but I fear few would care to read their names, although everybody, I am sure, would love them could they see them blooming and rejoicing at home.

On my last visit to the region about Kotzebue Sound, near the middle of September 1881, the weather was so fine and mellow that it suggested the Indian summer of the Eastern States. The winds were hushed, the tundra glowed in creamy golden sunshine, and the colours of the ripe foliage of the heathworts, willows and birch – red, purple and yellow, in pure bright tones – were enriched with those of berries which were scattered everywhere, as if they had been showered from the clouds like hail. When I was back a mile or two from the shore, revelling in this colour-glory, and thinking how fine it would be could I cut a square of the tundra sod of conventional picture size, frame it, and hang it among the paintings on my study walls at home, saying to myself, 'Such a Nature painting taken at random from any part of the thousand-mile bog would make the other pictures look dim and coarse,' I heard merry shouting, and, looking round, saw a band of Eskimos – men, women and children, loose and hairy like wild animals – running towards me. I could not guess at first what they were seeking, for they seldom leave the shore; but soon they told me, as they threw themselves down, sprawling and laughing, on the mellow bog, and began to feast on the berries. A lively picture they made, and a pleasant one, as they frightened the whirring ptarmigans, and surprised their oily stomachs with the beautiful acid berries of many kinds, and filled sealskin bags with them to carry away for festive days in winter.

Nowhere else on my travels have I seen so much warm-blooded, rejoicing life as in this grand Arctic reservation, by so many regarded as desolate. Not only are there whales in abundance along the shores, and innumerable seals, walruses and white bears, but on the tundras great herds of fat reindeer and wild sheep, foxes, hares, mice, piping marmots, and birds. Perhaps more birds are born here than in any other region of equal extent on the continent. Not only do strong-winged hawks, eagles and water-fowl, to whom the length of the continent is merely a pleasant excursion, come up here every summer in great numbers, but also many short-winged warblers, thrushes and finches, repairing hither to rear their young in safety, reinforce the plant bloom with their plumage, and sweeten the wilderness with song; flying all the way, some of them, from Florida, Mexico and Central America. In coming north they are coming home, for they were born here, and they go south only to spend the winter months, as New Englanders go to Florida. Sweet-voiced troubadours, they sing in orange groves and vine-clad magnolia woods in winter, in thickets of dwarf birch and alder in summer, and sing and chatter more or less all the way back and forth, keeping the whole country glad. Oftentimes, in New England, just as the last snow-patches are melting and the sap in the maples begins to flow, the blessed wanderers may be heard about orchards and the edges of fields where they have stopped to glean a scanty meal, not tarrying long, knowing they have far to go. Tracing the footsteps of spring, they arrive in their tundra homes in June or July, and set out on their return journey in September, or as soon as their families are able to fly well.

This is Nature's own reservation, and every lover of wildness will rejoice with me that by kindly frost it is so well defended. The discovery lately made that it is sprinkled with gold may cause some alarm; for the strangely exciting stuff makes the timid bold enough for anything, and the lazy destructively industrious. Thousands at least half insane are now pushing their way into it, some by the southern passes over the mountains, perchance the first mountains they have ever seen – sprawling, struggling, gasping for breath, as, laden with awkward, merciless burdens of provisions and tools, they climb over rough-angled boulders and cross thin miry bogs. Some are going by the mountains and rivers to the eastward through Canada, tracing the old romantic ways of the Hudson Bay traders; others by Bering Sea and the Yukon, sailing all the way, getting glimpses perhaps of the famous fur-seals, the ice-floes, and the innumerable islands and bars of the great Alaska river. In spite of frowning hardships and the frozen ground, the Klondike gold will increase the crusading crowds for years to come, but comparatively little harm will be done. Holes will be burned and dug into the hard ground here and there, and into the quartz-ribbed mountains and hills; ragged towns like beaver and muskrat villages will be built, and mills and locomotives will make rumbling, screeching, disenchanting noises; but the miner's pick will not be followed far by the plough, at least not until Nature is ready to unlock the frozen soil-beds with her slow-turning climate key. On the other hand, the roads of the pioneer miners will lead many a lover of wildness into the heart of the reserve, who without them would never see it.

In the meantime, the wildest health and pleasure grounds accessible and available to tourists seeking escape from care and dust and early death are the parks and reservations of the West. There are four national parks,[1] – the Yellowstone, Yosemite, General Grant and Sequoia – all within easy reach, and thirty forest reservations, a magnificent realm of woods, most of which, by railroads and trails and open ridges, is also fairly accessible, not only to the

---

[1] There are now five parks and thirty-eight reservations.

determined traveller rejoicing in difficulties, but to those (may their tribe increase) who, not tired, not sick, just naturally take wing every summer in search of wildness. The forty million acres of these reserves are in the main unspoiled as yet, though sadly wasted and threatened on their more open margins by the axe and fire of the lumberman and prospector, and by hoofed locusts, which, like the winged ones, devour every leaf within reach, while the shepherds and owners set fires with the intention of making a blade of grass grow in the place of every tree, but with the result of killing both the grass and the trees.

In the million acre Black Hills Reserve of South Dakota, the easternmost of the great forest reserves, made for the sake of the farmers and miners, there are delightful, riviving sauntering-grounds in open parks of yellow pine, planted well apart, allowing plenty of sunshine to warm the ground. This tree is one of the most variable and most widely distributed of American pines. It grows sturdily on all kinds of soil and rocks, and, protected by a mail of thick bark, defies frost and fire and disease alike, daring every danger in firm, calm beauty and strength. It occurs here mostly on the outer hills and slopes where no other tree can grow. The ground beneath it is yellow most of the summer with showy Wythia, arnica, applopappus, solidago, and other sun-loving plants, which, though they form no heavy entangling growth, yet give abundance of colour and make all the woods a garden. Beyond the yellow pine woods there lies a world of rocks of wildest architecture, broken, splintery, and spiky, not very high, but the strangest in form and style of grouping imaginable. Countless towers and spires, pinnacles and slender domed columns, are crowded together, and feathered with sharp-pointed Engelmann spruces, making curiously mixed forests – half trees, half rocks. Level gardens here and there in the midst of them offer charming surprises, and so do the many small lakes with lilies on their meadowy borders, and bluebells, anemones, daisies, castilleias, comandras, etc., together forming landscapes delightfully novel, and made still wilder by many interesting animals – elk, deer, beavers, wolves, squirrels and birds. Not very long ago this was the richest of all the red man's hunting-grounds hereabout. After the season's buffalo hunts were over – as described by Parkman, who, with a picturesque cavalcade of Sioux savages, passed through these famous hills in 1846 – every winter deficiency was here made good, and hunger was unknown until, in spite of most determined, fighting, killing opposition, the white gold-hunters entered the fat game reserve and spoiled it. The Indians are dead now, and so are most of the hardly less striking free trappers of the early romantic Rocky Mountain times. Arrows, bullets, scalping-knives, need no longer be feared; and all the wilderness is peacefully open.

The Rocky Mountain reserves are the Teton, Yellowstone, Lewis and Clark, Bitter Root, Priest River and Flathead, comprehending more than twelve million acres of mostly unclaimed, rough, forest-covered mountains in which the great rivers of the country take their rise. The commonest tree in most of them is the brave, indomitable, and altogether admirable Pinus contorta, widely distributed in all kinds of climate and soil, growing cheerily in frosty Alaska, breathing the damp salt air of the sea as well as the dry biting blasts of the Arctic interior, and making itself at home on the most dangerous flame-swept slopes and ridges of the Rocky Mountains in immeasurable abundance and variety of forms. Thousands of acres of this species are destroyed by running fires nearly every summer, but a new growth springs quickly from the ashes. It is generally small, and yields few sawlogs of commercial value, but is of incalculable importance to the farmer and miner; supplying fencing, mine timbers, and firewood, holding the porous soil on steep slopes, preventing landslips and avalanches, and giving kindly, nourishing shelter to animals and the widely outspread sources of the life-giving rivers. The other trees are mostly spruce, mountain pine, cedar, juniper, larch, and balsam fir; some of them, especially on the western slopes of the mountains, attaining grand size and furnishing abundance of fine timber.

Perhaps the least known of all this grand group of reserves is the Bitter Root, of more than four million acres. It is the wildest, shaggiest block of forest wildness in the Rocky Mountains, full of happy, healthy, storm-loving trees, full of streams that dance and sing in glorious array, and full of Nature's animals – elk, deer, wild sheep, bears, cats and innumerable smaller people.

In calm Indian summer, when the heavy winds are hushed, the vast forests covering hill and dale, rising and falling over the rough topography and vanishing in the distance, seem lifeless. No moving thing is seen as we climb the peaks, and only the low, mellow murmur of falling water is heard, which seems to thicken the silence. Nevertheless, how many hearts with warm red blood in them are beating under cover of the woods, and how many teeth and eyes are shining! A multitude of animal people, intimately related to us, but of whose lives we know almost nothing, are as busy about their own affairs as we are about ours: beavers are building and mending dams and huts for winter, and storing them with food; bears are studying winter quarters as they stand thoughtful in open spaces, while the gentle breeze ruffles the long hair on their backs; elk and deer, assembling on the heights, are considering cold pastures where they will be farthest away from the wolves; squirrels and marmots are busily laying up provisions and lining their nests against coming frost and snow foreseen; and countless thousands of birds are forming parties and gathering their young about them for flight to the southlands; while butterflies and bees, apparently with no thought of hard times to come, are hovering about the late-blooming goldenrods, and, with countless other insect folk, are dancing and humming right merrily in the sunbeams and shaking all the air into music.

Wander here a whole summer, if you can. Thousands of God's wild blessings will search you and soak you as if you were a sponge, and the big days will go by uncounted. If you are business-tangled, and so burdened with duty that only weeks can be got out of the heavy-laden year, then go to the Flathead Reserve; for it is easily and quickly reached by the Great Northern Railroad. Get off the track at Belton Station, and in a few minutes you will find yourself in the midst of what you are sure to say is the best care-killing scenery on the continent – beautiful lakes derived straight from glaciers, lofty mountains steeped in lovely nemophila-blue skies and clad with forests and glaciers, mossy, ferny waterfalls in their hollows, nameless and numberless, and meadowy gardens abounding in the best of everything. When you are calm enough for discriminating observation, you will find the king of the larches, one of the best of the Western giants, beautiful, picturesque, and regal in port, easily the grandest of all the larches in the world. It grows to a height of one hundred and fifty to two hundred feet, with a diameter at the ground of five to eight feet, throwing out its branches into the light as no other tree does. To those who before have seen only the European larch or the Lyall species of the eastern Rocky Mountains, or the little tamarack or hackmatack of the Eastern States and Canada, this Western king must be a revelation.

Associated with this grand tree in the making of the Flathead forests is the large and beautiful mountain pine, or Western white pine (Pinus monticola), the invincible contorta or lodge-pole pine, and spruce and cedar. The forest floor is covered with the richest beds of Linnæa borealis I ever saw, thick fragrant carpets, enriched with shining mosses here and there, and with clintonia, pyrola, moneses, and vaccinium, weaving hundred-mile beds of bloom that would have made blessed old Linnæus weep for joy.

Lake McDonald, full of brisk trout, is in the heart of this forest, and Avalanche Lake is ten miles above McDonald, at the feet of a group of glacier-laden mountains. Give a month at least to this precious reserve. The time will not be taken from the sum of your life. Instead of shortening, it will indefinitely lengthen it and make you truly immortal. Nevermore will time seem short or long, and cares will never again fall heavily on you, but gently and kindly as gifts from heaven.

The vast Pacific Coast reverses in Washington and Oregon – the Cascade, Washington, Mount Rainier, Olympic, Bull Run and Ashland, named in order of size – include more than 12,500,000 acres of magnificent forests of beautiful and gigantic trees. They extend over the wild, unexplored Olympic Mountains and both flanks of the Cascade Range, the wet and the dry. On the east side of the Cascades the woods are sunny and open, and contain principally yellow pine, of moderate size, but of great value as a cover for the irrigating streams that flow into the dry interior, where agriculture on a grand scale is being carried on. Along the moist, balmy, foggy, west flank of the mountains, facing the sea, the woods reach their highest development, and, excepting the California redwoods, are the heaviest on the continent. They are made up mostly of the Douglas spruce (Pseudotsuga taxifolia), with the giant arbor vitæ, or cedar, and several species of fir and hemlock in varying abundance, forming a forest kingdom unlike any other, in which limb meets limb, touching and overlapping in bright, lively, triumphant exuberance, two hundred and fifty, three hundred, and even four hundred feet above the shady, mossy ground. Over all the other species the Douglas spruce reigns supreme. It is not only a large tree, the tallest in America next to the redwood, but a very beautiful one, with bright green drooping foliage, handsome pendent cones, and a shaft exquisitely straight and round and regular. Forming extensive forests by itself in many places, it lifts its spiry tops into the sky close together with as even a growth as a well-tilled field of grain. No ground has been better tilled for wheat than these Cascade Mountains for trees: they were ploughed by mighty glaciers, and harrowed and mellowed and outspread by the broad streams that flowed from the ice-ploughs as they were withdrawn at the close of the glacial period.

In proportion to its weight when dry, Douglas spruce timber is perhaps stronger than that of any other large conifer in the country, and being tough, durable, and elastic, it is admirably suited for ship-building, piles, and heavy timbers in general; but its hardness and liability to warp when it is cut into boards render it unfit for fine work. In the lumber markets of California it is called 'Oregon pine'. When lumbering is going on in the best Douglas woods, especially about Puget Sound, many of the long, slender boles are saved for spars; and so superior is their quality that they are called for in almost every shipyard in the world, and it is interesting to follow their fortunes. Felled and peeled and dragged to tide-water, they are raised again as yards and masts for ships, given iron roots and canvas foliage, decorated with flags, and sent to sea, where in glad motion they go cheerily over the ocean prairie in every latitude and longitude, singing and bowing responsive to the same winds that waved them when they were in the woods. After standing in one place for centuries they thus go round the world like tourists, meeting many a friend from the old home forest; some travelling like themselves, some standing head downward in muddy harbours, holding up the platforms of wharves, and others doing all kinds of hard timber work, showy or hidden.

This wonderful tree also grows far northward in British Columbia, and southward along the coast and middle regions of Oregon and California; flourishing with the redwood wherever it can find an opening, and with the sugar pine, yellow pine, and libocedrus in the Sierra. It extends into the San Gabriel, San Bernardino and San Jacinto Mountains of southern California. It also grows well on the Wasatch Mountains, where it is called 'red pine', and on many parts of the Rocky Mountains and short interior ranges of the Great Basin. But though thus widely distributed, only in Oregon, Washington and some parts of British Columbia does it reach perfect development.

To one who looks from some high standpoint over its vast breadth, the forest on the west side of the Cascades seems all one dim, dark, monotonous field, broken only by the white volcanic cones along the summit of the range. Back in the untrodden wilderness a deep furred carpet of brown and yellow mosses covers the ground like a garment, pressing about the feet of the trees, and rising in rich bosses softly and kindly over every rock and mouldering trunk, leaving no spot uncared for; and dotting small prairies, and fringing the meadows and the banks of streams not seen in general views, we find, besides the great conifers, a considerable number of hardwood trees – oak, ash, maple, alder, wild apple, cherry, arbutus, Nuttall's flowering dogwood, and in some places chestnut. In a few favoured spots the broad-leaved maple grows to a height of a hundred feet in forests by itself, sending out large limbs in magnificent interlacing arches covered with mosses and ferns, thus forming lofty sky-gardens, and rendering the underwoods delightfully cool. No finer forest ceiling is to be found than these maple arches, while the floor, ornamented with tall ferns and rubus vines, and cast into hillocks by the bulging, moss-covered roots of the trees, matches it well.

Passing from beneath the heavy shadows of the woods, almost anywhere one steps into lovely gardens of lilies, orchids, heathworts, and wild roses. Along the lower slopes, especially in Oregon, where the woods are less dense, there are miles of rhododendron, making glorious masses of purple in the spring, while all about the streams and the lakes and the beaver meadows there is a rich tangle of hazel, plum, cherry, crab-apple, cornel, gaultheria and rubus, with myriads of flowers and abundance of other more delicate bloomers, such as erythronium, brodiæa, fritillaria, calochortus, clintonia, and the lovely hider of the north, calypso. Beside all these bloomers there are wonderful ferneries about the many misty waterfalls, some of the fronds ten feet high, others the most delicate of their tribe, the maidenhair fringing the rocks within reach of the lightest dust of the spray, while the shading trees on the cliffs above them, leaning over, look like eager listeners anxious to catch every tone of the restless waters. In the autumn berries of every colour and flavour abound, enough for birds, bears and everybody, particularly about the stream-sides and meadows where sunshine reaches the ground: huckleberries, red, blue, and black, some growing close to the ground others on bushes ten feet high; gaultheria berries, called 'sal-al' by the Indians; salmon berries, an inch in diameter, growing in dense prickly tangles, the flowers, like wild roses, still more beautiful than the fruit; raspberries, gooseberries, currants, blackberries and strawberries. The underbrush and meadow fringes are in great part made up of these berry bushes and vines; but in the depths of the woods there is not much underbrush of any kind – only a thin growth of rubus, huckleberry and vine-maple.

Notwithstanding the outcry against the reservations last winter in Washington, that uncounted farms, towns and villages were included in them, and that all business was threatened or blocked, nearly all the mountains in which the reserves lie are still covered with virgin forests. Though lumbering has long been carried on with tremendous energy along their boundaries, and home-seekers have explored the woods for openings available for farms, however small, one may wander in the heart of the reserves for weeks without meeting a human being, Indian or white man, or any conspicuous trace of one. Indians used to ascend the main streams on their way to the mountains for wild goats, whose wool furnished them clothing. But with food in abundance on the coast there was little to draw them into the woods, and the monuments they have left there are scarcely more conspicuous than those of birds and squirrels; far less so than those of the beavers, which have dammed streams and made clearings that will endure for centuries. Nor is there much in these woods to attract cattle-keepers. Some of the first settlers made farms on the small bits of prairie and in the comparatively open Cowlitz and Chehalis valleys of Washington; but before the gold period most of the immigrants from the Eastern States settled in the fertile and open Willamette Valley of Oregon. Even now, when the search for tillable land is so keen, excepting the bottom-lands of the rivers around Puget Sound, there are few cleared spots in all western Washington. On every meadow or opening of any sort someone will be found keeping cattle, raising hops, or cultivating patches of grain, but these spots are few and far between. All the larger spaces were taken long ago; therefore most of the newcomers build their cabins where the beavers built theirs. They keep a few cows, laboriously widen their little meadow openings by hacking, girdling and burning the rim of the close-pressing forest, and scratch and plant among the huge blackened logs and stumps, girdling and killing themselves in killing the trees.

Most of the farm lands of Washington and Oregon, excepting the valleys of the Willamette and Rogue Rivers, lie on the east side of the mountains. The forests on the eastern slopes of the Cascades fail altogether ere the foot of the range is reached, stayed by drought as suddenly as on the west side they are stopped by the sea; showing strikingly how dependent are these forest giants on the generous rains and fogs so often complained of in the coast climate. The lower portions of the reserves are solemnly soaked and poulticed in rain and fog during the winter months, and there is a sad dearth of sunshine, but with a little knowledge of woodcraft anyone may enjoy an excursion into these woods even in the rainy season. The big, grey days are exhilarating, and the colours of leaf and branch and mossy bole are then at their best. The mighty trees getting their food are seen to be wide-awake, every needle thrilling in the welcome nourishing storms, chanting and bowing low in glorious harmony, while every raindrop and snowflake is seen as a beneficent messenger from the sky. The snow that falls on the lower woods is mostly soft, coming through the trees in downy tufts, loading their branches, and bending them down against the trunks until they look like arrows, while a strange muffled silence prevails, making everything impressively solemn. But these lowland snowstorms and their effects quickly vanish. The snow melts in a day or two, sometimes in a few hours, the bent branches spring up again, and all the forest work is left to the fog and the rain. At the same time, dry snow is falling on the upper forests and mountain tops. Day after day, often for weeks, the big clouds give their flowers without ceasing, as if knowing how important is the work they have to do. The glinting, swirling swarms thicken the blast, and the trees and rocks are covered to a depth of ten to twenty feet. Then the mountaineer, snug in a grove with bread and fire, has nothing to do but gaze and listen and enjoy. Ever and anon the deep, low roar of the storm is broken by the booming of avalanches, as the snow slips from the overladen heights and rushes down the long white slopes to fill the fountain hollows. All the smaller streams are hushed and buried, and the young groves of spruce and fir near the edge of the timber-line are gently bowed to the ground and put to sleep, not again to see the light of day or stir branch or leaf until the spring.

These grand reservations should draw thousands of admiring visitors at least in summer, yet they are neglected as if of no account, and spoilers are allowed to ruin them as fast as they like.[1] A few peeled spars cut here were set up in London, Philadelphia and Chicago, where they excited wondering attention; but the countless hosts of living trees rejoicing at home on the

---

[1] The outlook over forest affairs is now encouraging. Popular interest, more practical than sentimental in whatever touches the welfare of the country's forests, is growing rapidly, and a hopeful beginning has been made by the Government in real protection for the reservations as well as for the parks. From 1 July 1900, there have been 9 superintendents, 39 supervisors, and from 330 to 445 rangers of reservations.

mountains are scarce considered at all. Most travellers here are content with
what they can see from car windows or the verandas of hotels, and in going
from place to place cling to their precious trains and stages like wrecked
sailors to rafts. When an excursion into the woods is proposed, all sorts of
dangers are imagined – snakes, bears, Indians. Yet it is far safer to wander in
God's woods than to travel on black highways or to stay at home. The snake
danger is so slight it is hardly worth mentioning. Bears are a peaceable
people, and mind their own business, instead of going about like the devil
seeking whom they may devour. Poor fellows, they have been poisoned,
trapped and shot at until they have lost confidence in brother man, and it is
not now easy to make their acquaintance. As to Indians, most of them are
dead or civilized into useless innocence. No American wilderness that I know
of is so dangerous as a city home 'with all the modern improvements'. One
should go to the woods for safety, if for nothing else. Lewis and Clark, in their
famous trip across the continent in 1804–1805, did not lose a single
man by Indians or animals, though all the West was then wild. Captain Clark
was bitten on the hand as he lay asleep. That was one bite among more
than a hundred men while travelling nine thousand miles. Loggers are far
more likely to be met than Indians or bears in the reserves or about their
boundaries, brown weather-tanned men with faces furrowed like bark, tired-
looking, moving slowly, swaying like the trees they chop. A little of everything in the woods is fastened to their clothing, rosiny and smeared with balsam,
and rubbed into it, so that their scanty outer garments grow thicker with use
and never wear out. Many a forest giant have these old woodmen felled, but,
round-shouldered and stooping, they too are leaning over and tottering to
their fall. Others, however, stand ready to take their places, stout young
fellows, erect as saplings; and always the foes of trees outnumber their
friends. Far up the white peaks one can hardly fail to meet the wild goat, or
American chamois – an admirable mountaineer, familiar with woods and
glaciers as well as rocks – and in leafy thickets deer will be found; while
gliding about unseen there are many sleek furred animals enjoying their
beautiful lives, and birds also, notwithstanding few are noticed in hasty walks.
The ousel sweetens the glens and gorges where the streams flow fastest, and
every grove has its singers, however silent it seems – thrushes, linnets,
warblers; humming-birds glint about the fringing bloom of the meadows and
peaks, and the lakes are stirred into lively pictures by water-fowl.

The Mount Rainier Forest Reserve should be made a national park and
guarded while yet its bloom is on;[1] for if in the making of the West Nature had
what we call parks in mind – places for rest, inspiration and prayers – this
Rainier region must surely be one of them. In the centre of it there is a lonely
mountain capped with ice; from the ice-cap glaciers radiate in every direction,
and young rivers from the glaciers; while its flanks, sweeping down in beautiful curves, are clad with forests and gardens, and filled with birds and animals.

[1] This was done shortly after the above was written. 'One of the most important measures taken during the past year in
connection with forest reservations was the action of Congress in withdrawing from the Mount Rainier Forest Reserve a portion
of the region immediately surrounding Mount Rainier and setting it apart as a national park.' (*Report of Commissioner of General
Land Office*, for the year ended June 1899.) But the park as it now stands is far too small.

Specimens of the best of Nature's treasures have been lovingly gathered here and arranged in simple symmetrical beauty within regular bounds.

Of all the fire-mountains which, like beacons, once blazed along the Pacific Coast, Mount Rainier is the noblest in form, has the most interesting forest cover, and, with perhaps the exception of Shasta, is the highest and most flowery. Its massive white dome rises out of its forests, like a world by itself, to a height of fourteen thousand to fifteen thousand feet. The forests reach to a height of a little over six thousand feet, and above the forests there is a zone of the loveliest flowers, fifty miles in circuit and nearly two miles wide, so closely planted and luxuriant that it seems as if Nature, glad to make an open space between woods so dense and ice so deep, were economizing the precious ground, and trying to see how many of her darlings she can get together in one mountain wreath – daisies, anemones, geraniums, columbines, erythroniums, larkspur, etc., among which we wade knee-deep and waist-deep, the bright corollas in myriads touching petal to petal. Picturesque detached groups of the spiry abies lasiocarpa stand like islands along the lower margin of the garden zone, while on the upper margin there are extensive beds of bryanthus, cassiope, kalmia and other heathworts, and higher still saxifrages and drabas, more and more lowly, reach up to the edge of the ice. Altogether this is the richest subalpine garden I ever found, a perfect floral elysium. The icy dome needs none of man's care, but unless the reserve is guarded the flower bloom will soon be killed, and nothing of the forests will be left but black stump monuments.

The Sierra of California is the most openly beautiful and useful of all the forest reserves, and the largest excepting the Cascade Reserve of Oregon and the Bitter Root of Montana and Idaho. It embraces over four million acres of the grandest scenery and grandest trees on the continent, and its forests are planted just where they do the most good, not only for beauty, but for farming in the great San Joaquin Valley beneath them. It extends southward from the Yosemite National Park to the end of the range, a distance of nearly two hundred miles. No other coniferous forest in the world contains so many species or so many large and beautiful trees – Sequoia gigantea, king of conifers, 'the noblest of a noble race', as Sir Joseph Hooker well says; the sugar pine, king of all the world's pines, living or extinct; the yellow pine, next in rank, which here reaches most perfect development, forming noble towers of verdure two hundred feet high; the mountain pine, which braves the coldest blasts far up the mountains on grim, rocky slopes; and five others, flourishing each in its place, making eight species of pine in one forest, which is still further enriched by the great Douglas spruce, libocedrus, two species of silver fir, large trees and exquisitely beautiful, the Paton hemlock, the most graceful of evergreens, the curious tumion, oaks of many species, maples, alders, poplars and flowering dogwood, all fringed with flowery underbrush, manzanita, ceanothus, wild rose, cherry, chestnut, and rhododendron. Wandering at random through these friendly, approachable woods, one comes here and there to the loveliest lily gardens, some of the lilies ten feet high, and the smoothest gentian meadows, and Yosemite valleys known only to mountaineers. Once I spent a night by a camp-fire on Mount Shasta with

Asa Gray and Sir Joseph Hooker, and, knowing that they were acquainted with all the great forests of the world, I asked whether they knew any coniferous forest that rivalled that of the Sierra. They unhesitatingly said; 'No. In the beauty and grandeur of individual trees, and in number and variety of species, the Sierra forests surpass all others.'

This Sierra Reserve, proclaimed by the President of the United States in September 1893, is worth the most thoughtful care of the government for its own sake, without considering its value as the fountain of the rivers on which the fertility of the great San Joaquin Valley depends. Yet it gets no care at all. In the fog of tariff, silver and annexation politics it is left wholly unguarded, though the management of the adjacent national parks by a few soldiers shows how well and how easily it can be preserved. In the meantime, lumbermen are allowed to spoil it at their will, and sheep in uncountable ravenous hordes to trample it and devour every green leaf within reach; while the shepherds, like destroying angels, set innumerable fires, which burn not only the undergrowth of seedlings on which the permanence of the forest depends, but countless thousands of the venerable giants. If every citizen could take one walk through this reserve, there would be no more trouble about its care; for only in darkness does vandalism flourish.[1]

The reserves of southern California – the San Gabriel, San Bernardino, San Jacinto and Trabuco – though not large, only about two million acres together, are perhaps the best appreciated. Their slopes are covered with a close, almost impenetrable growth of flowery bushes, beginning on the sides of the fertile coast valleys and the dry interior plains. Their higher ridges, however, and mountains are open, and fairly well forested with sugar pine, yellow pine, Douglas spruce, libocedrus and white fir. As timber fountains they amount to little, but as bird and bee pastures, cover for the precious streams that irrigate the lowlands, and quickly available retreats from dust and heat and care, their value is incalculable. Good roads have been graded into them, by which in a few hours lowlanders can get well up into the sky and find refuge in hospitable camps and club-houses, where, while breathing reviving ozone, they may absorb the beauty about them, and look comfortably down on the busy towns and the most beautiful orange groves ever planted since gardening began.

The Grand Canyon Reserve of Arizona, of nearly two million acres, or the most interesting part of it, as well as the Rainier region, should be made into a national park, on account of their supreme grandeur and beauty. Setting out from Flagstaff, a station on the Atchison, Topeka and Santa Fé Railroad, on the way to the canyon you pass through beautiful forests of yellow pine – like those of the Black Hills, but more extensive – and curious dwarf forests of nut pine and juniper, the spaces between the miniature trees planted with many interesting species of eriogonum, yucca and cactus. After riding or walking seventy-five miles through these pleasure-grounds, the San Francisco and other mountains, abounding in flowery parklike openings and smooth shallow valleys with long vistas which in fineness of finish and arrangement suggest the

[1] See note, p. 469.

work of a consummate landscape artist, watching you all the way, you come to the most tremendous canyon in the world. It is abruptly countersunk in the forest plateau, so that you see nothing of it until you are suddenly stopped on its brink, with its immeasurable wealth of divinely coloured and sculptured buildings before you and beneath you. No matter how far you have wandered hitherto, or how many famous gorges and valleys you have seen, this one, the Grand Canyon of the Colorado, will seem as novel to you, as unearthly in the colour and grandeur and quantity of its architecture, as if you had found it after death, on some other star; so incomparably lovely and grand and supreme is it above all the other canyons in our fire-moulded, earthquake-shaken, rain-washed, wave-washed, river and glacier sculptured world. It is about six thousand feet deep where you first see it, and from rim to rim ten to fifteen miles wide. Instead of being dependent for interest upon waterfalls, depth, wall sculpture and beauty of parklike floor, like most other great canyons, it has no waterfalls in sight, and no appreciable floor spaces. The big river has just room enough to flow and roar obscurely, here and there groping its way as best it can, like a weary, murmuring, overladen traveller trying to escape from the tremendous, bewildering labyrinthic abyss, while its roar serves only to deepen the silence. Instead of being filled with air, the vast space between the walls is crowded with Nature's grandest buildings – a sublime city of them, painted in every colour, and adorned with richly fretted cornice and battlement spire and tower in endless variety of style and architecture. Every architectural invention of man has been anticipated, and far more, in this grandest of God's terrestrial cities.

CHAPTER TWO

The Yellowstone National Park

OF THE four national parks of the West, the Yellowstone is far the largest. It is a big, wholesome wilderness on the broad summit of the Rocky Mountains, favoured with abundance of rain and snow – a place of fountains where the greatest of the American rivers take their rise. The central portion is a densely forested and comparatively level volcanic plateau with an average elevation of about eight thousand feet above the sea, surrounded by an imposing host of mountains belonging to the subordinate Gallatin, Wind River, Teton, Absaroka and snowy ranges. Unnumbered lakes shine in it, united by a famous band of streams that rush up out of hot lava beds, or fall from the frosty peaks in channels rocky and bare, mossy and bosky, to the main rivers, singing cheerily on through every difficulty, cunningly dividing and finding their way east and west to the two far-off seas.

Glacier meadows and beaver meadows are outspread with charming effect along the banks of the streams, parklike expanses in the woods, and innumerable small gardens in rocky recesses of the mountains, some of them containing more petals than leaves, while the whole wilderness is enlivened with happy animals.

Beside the treasures common to most mountain regions that are wild and blessed with a kind climate, the park is full of exciting wonders. The wildest geysers in the world, in bright, triumphant bands, are dancing and singing in it amid thousands of boiling springs, beautiful and awful, their basins arrayed in gorgeous colours like gigantic flowers; and hot paint-pots, mud springs, mud volcanoes, mush and broth cauldrons whose contents are of every colour and consistency, plash and heave and roar in bewildering abundance. In the adjacent mountains, beneath the living trees the edges of petrified forests are exposed to view, like specimens on the shelves of a museum, standing on ledges tier above tier where they grew, solemnly silent in rigid crystalline beauty after swaying in the winds thousands of centuries ago, opening marvellous views back into the years and climates and life of the past. Here, too, are hills of sparkling crystals, hills of sulphur, hills of glass, hills of cinders and ashes, mountains of every style of architecture, icy or forested, mountains covered with honey-bloom sweet as Hymettus, mountains boiled soft like potatoes and coloured like a sunset sky. A' that and a' that, and twice as muckle's a' that, Nature has on show in the Yellowstone Park. Therefore it is called Wonderland, and thousands of tourists and travellers stream into it every summer, and wander about in it enchanted.

Fortunately, almost as soon as it was discovered it was dedicated and set apart for the benefit of the people, a piece of legislation that shines benignly amid the common dust-and-ashes history of the public domain, for which the world must thank Professor Hayden above all others; for he led the first scientific exploring party into it, described it, and with admirable enthusiasm urged Congress to preserve it. As delineated in the year 1872, the park contained about 3,344 square miles. On 30 March 1891 it was to all intents and purposes enlarged by the Yellowstone National Park Timber Reserve, and in December 1897, by the Teton Forest Reserve; thus nearly doubling its original area, and extending the southern boundary far enough to take in the sublime Teton range and the famous pasture-lands of the big Rocky Mountain game animals. The withdrawal of this large tract from the public domain did no harm to anyone; for its height, 6,000 to over 13,000 feet above the sea, and its thick mantle of volcanic rocks, prevent its ever being available for agriculture or mining, while on the other hand its geographical position, reviving climate, and wonderful scenery combine to make it a grand health, pleasure and study resort – a gathering-place for travellers from all the world.

The national parks are not only withdrawn from sale and entry like the forest reservations, but are efficiently managed and guarded by small troops of United States cavalry, directed by the Secretary of the Interior. Under this care the forests are flourishing, protected from both axe and fire; and so, of course, are the shaggy beds of underbrush and the herbaceous vegetation. The so-called curiosities, also, are preserved, and the furred and feathered tribes, many of which, in danger of extinction a short time ago, are now increasing in numbers – a refreshing thing to see amid the blind, ruthless destruction that is going on in the adjacent regions. In pleasing contrast to the noisy, ever changing management, or mismanagement, of blundering, plundering, money-making vote-sellers who receive their places from boss politicians as purchased goods, the soldiers do their duty so quietly that the traveller is scarce aware of their presence.

This is the coolest and highest of the parks. Frosts occur every month of the year. Nevertheless, the tenderest tourist finds it warm enough in summer. The air is electric and full of ozone, healing, reviving, exhilarating, kept pure by frost and fire, while the scenery is wild enough to awaken the dead. It is a glorious place to grow in and rest in; camping on the shores of the lakes, in the warm openings of the woods golden with sunflowers, on the banks of the streams, by the snowy waterfalls, beside the exciting wonders or away from them in the scallops of the mountain walls sheltered from every wind, on smooth silky lawns enamelled with gentians, up in the fountain hollows of the ancient glaciers between the peaks, where cool pools and brooks and gardens of precious plants charmingly embowered are never wanting, and good rough rocks with every variety of cliff and scaur are invitingly near for outlooks and exercise.

From these lovely dens you may make excursions whenever you like into the middle of the park, where the geysers and hot springs are reeking and spouting in their beautiful basins, displaying an exuberance of colour and strange motion and energy admirably calculated to surprise and frighten, charm and shake up the least sensitive out of apathy into newness of life.

However orderly your excursions or aimless, again and again amid the calmest, stillest scenery you will be brought to a standstill hushed and awe-stricken before phenomena wholly new to you. Boiling springs and huge deep pools of purest green and azure water, thousands of them, are plashing and heaving in these high, cool mountains as if a fierce furnace fire were burning beneath each one of them; and a hundred geysers, white torrents of boiling water and steam, like inverted waterfalls, are ever and anon rushing up out of the hot, black underworld. Some of these ponderous geyser columns are as large as sequoias – five to sixty feet in diameter, one hundred and fifty to three hundred feet high – and are sustained at this great height with tremendous energy for a few minutes, or perhaps nearly an hour, standing rigid and erect, hissing, throbbing, booming, as if thunderstorms were raging beneath their roots, their sides roughened or fluted like the furrowed boles of trees, their tops dissolving in feathery branches, while the irised spray, like misty bloom is at times blown aside, revealing the massive shafts shining against a background of pine-covered hills. Some of them lean more or less, as if storm-bent, and instead of being round are flat or fan-shaped, issuing from irregular slits in silex pavements with radiate structure, the sunbeams sifting through them in ravishing splendour. Some are broad and round-headed like oaks; others are low and bunchy, branching near the ground like bushes; and a few are hollow in the centre like big daisies or water-lilies. No frost cools them, snow never covers them nor lodges in their branches; winter and summer they welcome alike; all of them, of whatever form or size, faithfully rising and sinking in fairy rhythmic dance night and day, in all sorts of weather, at

varying periods of minutes, hours, or weeks growing up rapidly, uncontrollable as fate, tossing their pearly branches in the wind, bursting into bloom
and vanishing like the frailest flowers – plants of which Nature raises hundreds or thousands of crops a year with no apparent exhaustion of the fiery
soil.

The so-called geyser basins, in which this rare sort of vegetation is growing,
are mostly open valleys on the central plateau that were eroded by glaciers
after the greater volcanic fires had ceased to burn. Looking down over the
forests as you approach them from the surrounding heights, you see a multitude of white columns, broad, reeking masses, and irregular jets and puffs of
misty vapour ascending from the bottom of the valley, or entangled like
smoke among the neighbouring trees, suggesting the factories of some busy
town or the camp-fires of an army. These mark the position of each mush-pot,
paint-pot, hot spring and geyser, or gusher, as the Icelandic words mean. And
when you saunter into the midst of them over the bright sinter pavements,
and see how pure and white and pearly grey they are in the shade of the
mountains, and how radiant in the sunshine, you are fairly enchanted. So
numerous they are and varied, Nature seems to have gathered them from all
the world as specimens of her rarest fountains, to show in one place what she
can do. Over four thousand hot springs have been counted in the park, and a
hundred geysers; how many more there are nobody knows.

These valleys at the heads of the great rivers may be regarded as laboratories and kitchens, in which, amid a thousand retorts and pots, we may see
Nature at work as chemist or cook, cunningly compounding an infinite variety
of mineral messes; cooking whole mountains; boiling and steaming flinty
rocks to smooth paste and mush – yellow, brown, red, pink, lavender, grey
and creamy white – making the most beautiful mud in the world; and distilling
the most ethereal essences. Many of these pots and cauldrons have been
boiling thousands of years. Pots of sulphurous mush, stringy and lumpy, and
pots of broth as black as ink, are tossed and stirred with constant care, and
thin transparent essences, too pure and fine to be called water, are kept
simmering gently in beautiful sinter cups and bowls that grow ever more
beautiful the longer they are used. In some of the spring basins, the waters,
though still warm, are perfectly calm, and shine blandly in a sod of overleaning grass and flowers, as if they were thoroughly cooked at last, and set
aside to settle and cool. Others are wildly boiling over as if running to waste,
thousands of tons of the precious liquids being thrown into the air to fall in
scalding floods on the clean coral floor of the establishment, keeping onlookers at a distance. Instead of holding liquid pale green or azure water,
other pots and craters are filled with scalding mud, which is tossed up from
three or four feet to thirty feet, in sticky, rank-smelling masses, with gasping,
belching, thudding sounds, plastering the branches of neighbouring trees;
every flask, retort, hot spring and geyser has something special in it, no two
being the same in temperature, colour or composition.

In these natural laboratories one needs stout faith to feel at ease. The
ground sounds hollow underfoot, and the awful subterranean thunder shakes
one's mind as the ground is shaken, especially at night in the pale moonlight,

or when the sky is overcast with storm-clouds. In the solemn gloom, the geysers, dimly visible, look like monstrous dancing ghosts, and their wild songs and the earthquake thunder replying to the storms overhead seem doubly terrible, as if divine government were at an end. But the trembling hills keep their places. The sky clears, the rosy dawn is reassuring, and up comes the sun like a god, pouring his faithful beams across the mountains and forest, lighting each peak and tree and ghastly geyser alike, and shining into the eyes of the reeking springs, clothing them with rainbow light, and dissolving the seeming chaos of darkness into varied forms of harmony. The ordinary work of the world goes on. Gladly we see the flies dancing in the sunbeams, birds feeding their young, squirrels gathering nuts, and hear the blessed ouzel singing confidingly in the shallows of the river – most faithful evangel, calming every fear, reducing everything to love.

The variously tinted sinter and travertine formations, outspread like pavements over large areas of the geyser valleys, lining the spring basins and throats of the craters, and forming beautiful coral-like rims and curbs about them, always excite admiring attention; so also does the play of the waters from which they are deposited. The various minerals in them are rich in colours, and these are greatly heightened by a smooth, silky growth of brilliantly coloured confervæ which lines many of the pools and channels and terraces. No bed of flower-bloom is more exquisite than these myriads of minute plants, visible only in mass, growing in the hot waters. Most of the spring borders are low and daintily scalloped, crenelated, and beaded with sinter pearls. Some of the geyser craters are massive and picturesque, like ruined castles or old burned-out sequoia stumps, and are adorned on a grand scale with outbulging, cauliflower-like formations. From these as centres the silex pavements slope gently away in thin, crusty, overlapping layers, slightly interrupted in some places by low terraces. Or, as in the case of the Mammoth Hot Springs, at the north end of the park, where the building waters issue from the side of a steep hill, the deposits form a succession of higher and broader terraces of white travertine tinged with purple, like the famous Pink Terrace at Rotomahana, New Zealand, draped in front with clustering stalactites, each terrace having a pool of indescribably beautiful water upon it in a basin with a raised rim that glistens with confervæ – the whole, when viewed at a distance of a mile or two, looking like a broad, massive cascade pouring over shelving rocks in snowy purpled foam.

The stones of this divine masonry, invisible particles of lime or silex, mined in quarries no eye has seen, go to their appointed places in gentle, tinkling, transparent currents or through the dashing turmoil of floods, as surely guided as the sap of plants streaming into bole and branch, leaf and flower. And thus from century to century this beauty-work has gone on and is going on.

Passing through many a mile of pine and spruce woods, toward the centre of the park you come to the famous Yellowstone Lake. It is about twenty miles long and fifteen wide, and lies at a height of nearly 8,000 feet above the level of the sea, amid dense black forests and snowy mountains. Around its winding, wavering shores, closely forested and picturesquely varied with promontories and bays, the distance is more than 100 miles. It is not very deep, only from 200 to 300 feet, and contains less water than the celebrated Lake Tahoe of the California Sierra, which is nearly the same size, lies at a height of 6,400 feet, and is over 1,600 feet deep. But no other lake in North America of equal area lies so high as the Yellowstone, or gives birth to so noble a river. The terraces around its shores show that at the close of the glacial period its surface was about 160 feet higher than it is now, and its area nearly twice as great.

It is full of trout, and a vast multitude of birds – swans, pelicans, geese, ducks, cranes, herons, curlews, plovers, snipe – feed in it and upon its shores; and many forest animals come out of the woods, and wade a little way in shallow, sandy places to drink and look about them, and cool themselves in the free flowing breezes.

In calm weather it is a magnificent mirror for the woods and mountains and sky, now pattered with hail and rain, now roughened with sudden storms that send waves to fringe the shores and wash its border of gravel and sand. The Absaroka Mountains and the Wind River Plateau on the east and south pour their gathered waters into it, and the river issues from the north side in a broad, smooth, stately current, silently gliding with such serene majesty that one fancies it knows the vast journey of four thousand miles that lies before it, and the work it has to do. For the first twenty miles its course is in a level, sunny valley lightly fringed with trees, through which it flows in silvery reaches stirred into spangles here and there by ducks and leaping trout, making no sound save a low whispering among the pebbles and the dipping willows and sedges of its banks. Then suddenly, as if preparing for hard work, it rushes eagerly, impetuously forward rejoicing in its strength, breaks into foam-bloom, and goes thundering down into the Grand Canyon in two magnificent falls, one hundred and three hundred feet high.

The canyon is so tremendously wild and impressive that even these great falls cannot hold your attention. It is about twenty miles long and a thousand feet deep – a weird, unearthly-looking gorge of jagged, fantastic architecture, and most brilliantly coloured. Here the Washburn range, forming the northern rim of the Yellowstone basin, made up mostly of beds of rhyolite decomposed by the action of thermal waters, has been cut through and laid open to view by the river; and a famous section it has made. It is not the depth or the shape of the canyon, nor the waterfall, nor the green and grey river chanting its brave song as it goes foaming on its way, that most impresses the observer, but the colours of the decomposed volcanic rocks. With few exceptions, the traveller in strange lands finds that, however much the scenery and vegetation in different countries may change, Mother Earth is ever familiar and the same. But here the very ground is changed, as if belonging to some other world. The walls of the canyon from top to bottom burn in a perfect glory of colour, confounding and dazzling when the sun is shining – white, yellow, green, blue, vermilion and various other shades of red indefinitely blending. All the earth hereabouts seems to be paint. Millions of tons of it lie in sight, exposed to wind and weather as if of no account, yet marvellously fresh and bright, fast colours not to be washed out or bleached out by either sunshine or storms. The effect is so novel and awful, we imagine that even a river might be afraid to enter such a place. But the rich and gentle beauty of the vegetation is reassuring. The lovely linnæa borealis hangs her twin bells over the brink of the cliffs, forests and gardens extend their treasures in smiling confidence on either side, nuts and berries ripen well whatever may be going on below; blind fears vanish, and the grand gorge seems a kindly, beautiful part of the general harmony, full of peace and joy and goodwill.

The park is easy of access. Locomotives drag you to its northern boundary at Cinnabar, and horses and guides do the rest. From Cinnabar you will be whirled in coaches along the foaming Gardiner River to Mammoth Hot Springs; thence through woods and meadows, gulches and ravines along branches of the Upper Gallatin, Madison and Firehole Rivers to the main geyser basins; thence over the Continental Divide and back again, up and down through dense pine, spruce, and fir woods to the magnificent Yellowstone Lake, along its northern shore to the outlet, down the river to the falls and Grand Canyon, and thence back through the woods to Mammoth Hot Springs and Cinnabar; stopping here and there at the so-called points of interest among the geysers, springs, paint-pots, mud volcanoes, etc., where you will be allowed a few minutes or hours to saunter over the sinter pavements, watch the play of a few of the geysers, and peer into some of the most beautiful and terrible of the craters and pools. These wonders you will enjoy, and also the views of the mountains, especially the Gallatin and Absaroka ranges, the long, willowy glacier and beaver meadows, the beds of violets, gentians, phloxes, asters, phacelias, goldenrods, eriogonums, and many other flowers, some species giving colour to whole meadows and hillsides. And you will enjoy your short views of the great lake and river and canyon. No scalping Indians will you see. The Blackfeet and Bannocks that once roamed here are gone; so are the old beaver-catchers, the Coulters and Bridgers, with all their attractive buckskin and romance. There are several bands of buffaloes in the park, but you will not thus cheaply in tourist fashion see them nor many of the other large animals hidden in the wilderness. The song-birds, too, keep mostly out of sight of the rushing tourist, though off the roads thrushes, warblers, orioles, grosbeaks, etc., keep the air sweet and merry. Perhaps in passing rapids and falls you may catch glimpses of the water-ouzel, but in the whirling noise you will not hear his song. Fortunately, no road noise frightens the Douglas squirrel, and his merry play and gossip will amuse you all through the woods. Here and there a deer may be seen crossing the road, or a bear. Most likely, however, the only bears you will see are the half tame ones that go to the hotels every night for dinner-table scraps – yeast-powder biscuit, Chicago canned stuff, mixed pickles, and beefsteaks that have proved too tough for the tourists.

Among the gains of a coach trip are the acquaintances made and the fresh views into human nature; for the wilderness is a shrewd touchstone, even thus lightly approached, and brings many a curious trait to view. Setting out, the driver cracks his whip, and the four horses go off at half gallop, half trot, in trained, showy style, until out of sight of the hotel. The coach is crowded, old and young side by side, blooming and fading, full of hope and fun and care.

Some look at the scenery or the horses, and all ask questions, an odd mixed lot of them: 'Where is the umbrella? What is the name of that blue flower over there? Are you sure the little bag is aboard? Is that hollow yonder a crater? How is your throat this morning? How high did you say the geysers spout? How does the elevation affect your head? Is that a geyser reeking over there in the rocks, or only a hot spring?' A long ascent is made, the solemn mountains come to view, small cares are quenched, and all become natural and silent, save perhaps some unfortunate expounder who has been reading guidebook geology, and rumbles forth foggy subsidences and upheavals until he is in danger of being heaved overboard. The driver will give you the names of the peaks and meadows and streams as you come to them, call attention to the glass road, tell how hard it was to build how the obsidian cliffs naturally pushed the surveyor's lines to the right, and the industrious beavers, by flooding the valley in front of the cliff, pushed them to the left.

Geysers, however, are the main objects, and as soon as they come in sight other wonders are forgotten. All gather around the crater of the one that is expected to play first. During the eruptions of the smaller geysers, such as the Beehive and Old Faithful, though a little frightened at first, all welcome the glorious show with enthusiasm, and shout, 'Oh, how wonderful, beautiful, splendid majestic!' Some venture near enough to stroke the column with a stick, as if it were a stone pillar or a tree, so firm and substantial and permanent it seems. While tourists wait around a large geyser, such as the Castle or the Giant, there is a chatter of small talk in anything but solemn mood; and during the intervals between the preliminary splashes and up-heavals some adventurer occasionally looks down the throat of the crater, admiring the silex formations and wondering whether Hades is as beautiful. But when, with awful uproar as if avalanches were falling and storms thundering in the depths, the tremendous outburst begins, all run away to a safe distance, and look on, awe-stricken and silent, in devout, worshipping wonder.

The largest and one of the most wonderfully beautiful of the springs is the Prismatic, which the guide will be sure to show you. With a circumference of 300 yards, it is more like a lake than a spring. The water is pure deep blue in the centre, fading to green on the edges, and its basin and the slightly terraced pavement about it are astonishingly bright and varied in colour. This one of the multitude of Yellowstone fountains is of itself object enough for a trip across the continent. No wonder that so many fine myths have originated in springs; that so many fountains were held sacred in the youth of the world, and had miraculous virtues ascribed to them. Even in these cold, doubting, questioning, scientific times many of the Yellowstone fountains seem able to work miracles. Near the Prismatic Spring is the great Excelsior Geyser, which is said to throw a column of boiling water 60 to 70 feet in diameter to a height of from 50 to 300 feet, at irregular periods. This is the greatest of all the geysers yet discovered anywhere. The Firehole River, which sweeps past it, is, at ordinary stages, a stream about 100 yards wide and 3 feet deep; but when the geyser is in eruption, so great is the quantity of water discharged that the volume of the river is doubled, and it is rendered too hot and rapid to be forded.

Geysers are found in many other volcanic regions – in Iceland, New Zealand, Japan, the Himalayas, the Eastern Archipelago, South America, the Azores and elsewhere; but only in Iceland, New Zealand and this Rocky Mountain park do they display their grandest forms, and of these three famous regions the Yellowstone is easily first, both in the number and in the size of its geysers. The greatest height of the column of the Great Geyser of Iceland actually measured was 212 feet, and of the Strokhr 162 feet.

In New Zealand, the Te Pueia at Lake Taupo, the Waikite at Rotorna, and two others are said to lift their waters occasionally to a height of 100 feet, while the celebrated Te Tarata at Rotomahana sometimes lifts a boiling column 20 feet in diameter to a height of 60 feet. But all these are far surpassed by the Excelsior. Few tourists, however, will see the Excelsior in action, or a thousand other interesting features of the park that lie beyond the wagon-roads and the hotels. The regular trips – from three to five days – are too short. Nothing can be done well at a speed of forty miles a day. The multitude of mixed, novel impressions rapidly piled on one another make only a dreamy, bewildering, swirling blur, most of which is unrememberable. Far more time should be taken. Walk away quietly in any direction and taste the freedom of the mountaineer. Camp out among the grass and gentians of glacier meadows, in craggy garden nooks full of Nature's darlings. Climb the mountains and get their good tidings. Nature's peace will flow into you as sunshine flows into trees. The winds will blow their own freshness into you, and the storms their energy, while cares will drop off like autumn leaves. As age comes on, one source of enjoyment after another is closed, but Nature's sources never fail. Like a generous host, she offers here brimming cups in endless variety, served in a grand hall, the sky its ceiling, the mountains its walls, decorated with glorious paintings and enlivened with bands of music ever playing. The petty discomforts that beset the awkward guest, the unskilled camper, are quickly forgotten, while all that is precious remains. Fears vanish as soon as one is fairly free in the wilderness.

Most of the dangers that haunt the unseasoned citizen are imaginery; the real ones are perhaps too few rather than too many for his good. The bears that always seem to spring up thick as trees, in fighting, devouring attitudes before the frightened tourist whenever a camping trip is proposed, are gentle now, finding they are no longer likely to be shot; and rattlesnakes, the other big irrational dread of over-civilized people, are scarce here, for most of the park lies above the snake-line. Poor creatures, loved only by their Maker, they are timid and bashful, as mountaineers know; and though perhaps not possessed of much of that charity that suffers long and is kind, seldom, either by mistake or by mishap, do harm to anyone. Certainly they cause not the hundredth part of the pain and death that follow the footsteps of the admired Rocky Mountain trapper. Nevertheless, again and again, in season and out of season, the question comes up, 'What are rattlesnakes good for?' As if nothing that does not obviously make for the benefit of man had any right to exist; as if our ways were God's ways. Long ago, an Indian to whom a French traveller put this old question replied that their tails were good for toothache, and their heads for fever. Anyhow, they are all, head and tail, good for themselves, and we need not begrudge them their share of life.

Fear nothing. No town park you have been accustomed to saunter in is so free from danger as the Yellowstone. It is a hard place to leave. Even its names in your guidebook are attractive, and should draw you far from wagon-roads – all save the early ones, derived from the infernal regions: Hell Roaring River, Hell Broth Springs, The Devil's Caldron, etc. Indeed, the whole region was at first called Coulter's Hell, from the fiery brimstone stories told by trapper Coulter, who left the Lewis and Clark expedition and wandered through the park, in the year 1807, with a band of Bannock Indians. The later names, many of which we owe to Mr. Arnold Hague of the U.S. Geological Survey, are so telling and exhilarating that they set our pulses dancing and make us begin to enjoy the pleasures of excursions ere they are commenced. Three River Peak, Two Ocean Pass, Continental Divide, are capital geographical descriptions, suggesting thousands of miles of rejoicing streams and all that belongs to them. Big Horn Pass, Bison Peak, Big Game Ridge, bring brave mountain animals to mind. Birch Hill, Garnet Hills, Amethyst Mountain, Storm Peak, Electric Peak, Roaring Mountain, are bright, bracing names. Wapiti, Beaver, Tern and Swan lakes, conjure up fine pictures, and so also do Osprey and Ouzel falls. Antelope Creek, Otter, Mink, and Grayling creeks, Geode, Jasper, Opal, Carnelian, and Chalcedony creeks, are lively and sparkling names that help the streams to shine; and Azalea, Stellaria, Arnica, Aster, and Phlox creeks, what pictures these bring up! Violet, Morning Mist, Hygeia, Beryl, Vermilion, and Indigo springs, and many beside, give us visions of fountains more beautifully arrayed than Solomon in all his purple and golden glory. All these and a host of others call you to camp. You may be a little cold some nights, on mountain tops above the timber-line, but you will see the stars, and by and by you can sleep enough in your town bed, or at least in your grave. Keep awake while you may in mountain mansions so rare.

If you are not very strong, try to climb Electric Peak when a big bossy, well-charged thunder-cloud is on it, to breathe the ozone set free, and get yourself kindly shaken and shocked. You are sure to be lost in wonder and praise, and every hair of your head will stand up and hum and sing like an enthusiastic congregation.

After this reviving experience, you should take a look into a few of the tertiary volumes of the grand geological library of the park, and see how God writes history. No technical knowledge is required; only a calm day and a calm mind. Perhaps nowhere else in the Rocky Mountains have the volcanic forces been so busy. More than ten thousand square miles hereabouts have been covered to a depth of at least five thousand feet with material spouted from chasms and craters during the tertiary period, forming broad sheets of basalt, andesite, rhyolite, etc., and marvellous masses of ashes, sand, cinders and stones now consolidated into conglomerates, charged with the remains of plants and animals that lived in the calm, genial periods that separated the volcanic outbursts.

Perhaps the most interesting and telling of these rocks, to the hasty tourist, are those that make up the mass of Amethyst Mountain. On its north side it presents a section two thousand feet high of roughly stratified beds of sand, ashes and conglomerates coarse and fine, forming the untrimmed edges of a wonderful set of volumes lying on their sides – books a million years old, well bound, miles in size, with full-page illustrations. On the ledges of this one section we see trunks and stumps of fifteen or twenty ancient forests ranged one above another, standing where they grew, or prostrate and broken like the pillars of ruined temples in desert sands – a forest fifteen or twenty stories high, the roots of each spread above the tops of the next beneath it, telling wonderful tales of the bygone centuries, with their winters and summers, growth and death, fire, ice and flood.

There were giants in those days. The largest of the standing opal and agate stumps and prostrate sections of the trunks are from two or three to fifty feet in height or length, and from five to ten feet in diameter; and so perfect is the petrification that the annual rings and ducts are clearer and more easily counted than those of living trees, centuries of burial having brightened the records instead of blurring them. They show that the winters of the tertiary period gave as decided a check to vegetable growth as do those of the present time. Some trees favourably located grew rapidly, increasing twenty inches in diameter in as many years, while others of the same species, on poorer soil or overshadowed, increased only two or three inches in the same time.

Among the roots and stumps on the old forest floors we find the remains of ferns and bushes, and the seeds and leaves of trees like those now growing on the southern Alleghanies – such as magnolia, sassafras, laurel, linden, persimmon, ash, alder, dogwood. Studying the lowest of these forests, the soil it grew on the the deposits it is buried in, we see that it was rich in species, and flourished in a genial, sunny climate. When its stately trees were in their glory, volcanic fires broke forth from chasms and craters, like larger geysers, spouting ashes, cinders, stones, and mud, which fell on the doomed forest like hail and snow; sifting, hurtling through the leaves and branches, choking the streams, covering the ground, crushing bushes and ferns, rapidly deepening, packing around the trees and breaking them, rising higher until the topmost boughs of the giants were buried, leaving not a leaf or twig in sight, so complete was the desolation. At last the volcanic storm began to abate, the fiery soil settled; mud floods and boulder floods passed over it, enriching it, cooling it; rains fell and mellow sunshine, and it became fertile and ready for another crop. Birds, and the winds, and roaming animals brought seeds from more fortunate woods, and a new forest grew up on the top of the buried one. Centuries of genial growing seasons passed. The seedling trees became giants, and with strong outreaching banches spread a leafy canopy over the grey land.

The sleeping subterranean fires again awake and shake the mountains, and every leaf trembles. The old craters, with perhaps new ones, are opened, and immense quantities of ashes, pumice, and cinders are again thrown into the sky. The sun, shorn of his beams, glows like a dull red ball, until hidden in sulphurous clouds. Volcanic snow, hail, and floods fall on the new forest, burying it alive, like the one beneath its roots. Then come another noisy band of mud floods and boulder floods, mixing, settling, enriching the new ground, more seeds, quickening sunshine and showers; and a third noble magnolia forest is carefully raised on the top of the second. And so on. Forest was planted above forest and destroyed, as if Nature were ever repenting, undoing the work she had so industriously done, and burying it.

Of course this destruction was creation, progress in the march of beauty through death. How quickly these old monuments excite and hold the imagination! We see the old stone stumps budding and blossoming and waving in the wind as magnificent trees, standing shoulder to shoulder, branches interlacing in grand varied round-headed forests; see the sunshine of morning and evening gilding their mossy trunks, and at high noon spangling on the thick glossy leaves of the magnolia, filtering through translucent canopies of linden and ash, and falling in mellow patches on the ferny floor; see the shining after rain, breathe the exhaling fragrance, and hear the winds and birds and the murmur of brooks and insects. We watch them from season to season; see the swelling buds when the sap begins to flow in the spring, the opening leaves and blossoms, the ripening of summer fruits, the colours of autumn, and the maze of leafless branches and sprays in winter; and we see the sudden oncome of the storms that overwhelmed them.

One calm morning at sunrise I saw the oaks and pines in Yosemite Valley shaken by an earthquake, their tops swishing back and forth, and every branch and needle shuddering as if in distress like the frightened screaming birds. One may imagine the trembling, rocking, tumultuous waving of those ancient Yellowstone woods, and the terror of their inhabitants when the first foreboding shocks were felt, the sky grew dark, and rock-laden floods began to roar. But though they were close pressed and buried, cut off from sun and wind, all their happy leaf-fluttering and waving done, other currents coursed through them, fondling and thrilling every fibre, and beautiful wood was replaced by beautiful stone. Now their rocky sepulchres are partly open, and show forth the natural beauty of death.

After the forest times and fire times had passed away, and the volcanic furnaces were banked and held in abeyance, another great change occurred. The glacial winter came on. The sky was again darkened, not with dust and ashes, but with snow which fell in glorious abundance, piling deeper, deeper, slipping from the overladen heights in booming avalanches, compacting into glaciers, that flowed over all the landscape, wiping off forests, grinding, sculpturing, fashioning the comparatively featureless lava beds into the beautiful rhythm of hill and dale and ranges of mountains we behold to-day; forming basins for lakes, channels for streams, new soils for forests, gardens, and meadows. While this ice-work was going on, the slumbering volcanic fires were boiling the subterranean waters, and with curious chemistry decomposing the rocks, making beauty in the darkness; these forces, seemingly antagonistic, working harmoniously together. How wild their meetings on the surface were we may imagine. When the glacier period began, geysers and hot springs were playing in grander volume, it may be, than those of today. The glaciers flowed over them while they spouted and thundered, carrying away their fine sinter and travertine structures, and shortening their mysterious channels.

The soils made in the down-grinding required to bring the present features of the landscape into relief are possibly no better than were some of the old volcanic soils that were carried away, and which, as we have seen, nourished magnificent forests, but the glacial landscapes are incomparably more beautiful than the old volcanic ones were. The glacial winter has passed away, like the ancient summers and fire periods, though in the chronology of the geologist all these times are recent. Only small residual glaciers on the cool northern slopes of the highest mountains are left of the vast all-embracing ice-mantle, as solfataras and geysers are all that are left of the ancient volcanoes.

Now the post-glacial agents are at work on the grand old palimpsest of the park region, inscribing new characters; but still in its main telling features it remains distinctly glacial. The moraine soils are being levelled, sorted, refined, re-formed, and covered with vegetation; the polished pavements and scoring and other superficial glacial inscriptions on the crumbling lavas are being rapidly obliterated; gorges are being cut in the decomposed rhyolites and loose conglomerates, and turrets and pinnacles seem to be springing up like growing trees; while the geysers are depositing miles of sinter and travertine. Nevertheless, the ice-work is scarce blurred as yet. These later effects are only spots and wrinkles on the grand glacial countenance of the park.

Perhaps you have already said that you have seen enough for a lifetime. But before you go away you should spend at least one day and a night on a mountain top, for a last general, calming, settling view. Mount Washburn is a good one for the purpose, because it stands in the middle of the park, is unencumbered with other peaks, and is so easy of access that the climb to its summit is only a saunter. First your eye goes roving around the mountain rim amid the hundreds of peaks: some with plain flowing skirts, others abruptly precipitous and defended by sheer battlemented escarpments; flat-topped or round; heaving like sea-waves or spired and turreted like Gothic cathedrals; streaked with snow in the ravines, and darkened with files of adventurous trees climbing the ridges. The nearer peaks are perchance clad in sapphire blue, others far off in creamy white. In the broad glare of noon they seem to shrink and crouch to less than half their real stature, and grow dull and uncommunicative – mere dead, draggled heaps of waste ashes and stone, giving no hint of the multitude of animals enjoying life in their fastnesses, or of the bright bloom-bordered streams and lakes. But when storms blow they awake and rise, wearing robes of cloud and mist in majestic speaking attitudes like gods. In the colour glory of morning and evening they become still more impressive; steeped in the divine light of the alpenglow their earthiness disappears, and, blending with the heavens, they seem neither high nor low.

Over all the central plateau, which from here seems level, and over the foothills and lower slopes of the mountains, the forest extends like a black uniform bed of weeds, interrupted only by lakes and meadows and small burned spots called parks – all of them, except the Yellowstone Lake, being mere dots and spangles in general views, made conspicuous by their colour and brightness. About eighty-five per cent of the entire area of the park is covered with trees, mostly the indomitable lodge-pole pine (*Pinus contorta*, var. *Murrayana*), with a few patches and sprinklings of Douglas spruce, Engelmann spruce, silver fir (*Abies lasiocarpa*), Pinus flexilis, and a few alders, aspens and birches. The Douglas spruce is found only on the lowest portions, the silver fir on the highest, and the Engelmann spruce on the dampest places, best defended from fire. Some fine specimens of the flexilis pine are growing on the margins of openings – wide-branching, sturdy trees, as broad as high, with trunks five feet in diameter, leafy and shady, laden with purple cones and rose-coloured flowers. The Engelmann spruce and sub-alpine silver fir are beautiful and notable trees – tall, spiry, hardy, frost and snow defying, and widely distributed over the West, wherever there is a mountain to climb or a cold moraine slope to cover. But neither of these is a good firefighter. With rather thin bark, and scattering their seeds every year as soon as they are ripe, they are quickly driven out of fire-swept regions. When the glaciers were melting, these hardy mountaineering trees were probably among the first to arrive on the new moraine soil beds; but as the plateau became drier and fires began to run, they were driven up the mountains, and into the wet spots and islands where we now find them leaving nearly all the park to the lodge-pole pine, which, though as thin-skinned as they and as easily killed by fire, takes pains to store up its seeds in firmly closed cones, and holds them from three to nine years, so that, let the fire come when it may, it is ready to die and ready to live again in a new generation. For when the killing fires have devoured the leaves and thin resinous bark, many of the cones, only scorched, open as soon as the smoke clears away; the hoarded store of seeds is sown broadcast on the cleared ground, and a new growth immediately springs up triumphant out of the ashes. Therefore, this tree not only holds its ground, but extends its conquests farther after every fire. Thus the evenness and closeness of its growth are accounted for. In one part of the forest that I examined, the growth was about as close as a cane-brake. The trees were from four to eight inches in diameter, one hundred feet high, and one hundred and seventy-five years old. The lower limbs die young and drop off for want of light. Life with these close-planted trees is a race for light, more light, and so they push straight for the sky. Mowing off ten feet from the top of the forest would make it look like a crowded mass of telegraph-poles; for only the sunny tops are leafy. A sapling ten years old, growing in the sunshine, has as many leaves as a crowded tree one or two hundred years old. As fires are multiplied and the mountains become drier, this wonderful lodge-pole pine bids fair to obtain possession of nearly all the forest ground in the West.

How still the woods seem from here, yet how lively a stir the hidden animals are making; digging, gnawing, biting, eyes shining, at work and play, getting food, rearing young, roving through the underbrush, climbing the rocks, wading solitary marshes, tracing the banks of the lakes and streams! Insect swarms are dancing in the sunbeams, burrowing in the ground, diving, swimming – a cloud of witnesses telling Nature's joy. The plants are as busy as the animals, every cell in a swirl of enjoyment, humming like a hive, singing the old new song of creation. A few columns and puffs of steam are seen rising above the treetops, some near, but most of them far off, indicating geysers and hot springs, gentle-looking and noiseless as downy clouds, softly hinting the reaction going on between the surface and the hot interior. From here you see them better than when you are standing beside them, frightened and confused, regarding them as lawless cataclysms. The shocks and out-bursts of earthquakes, volcanoes, geysers, storms, the pounding of waves, the uprush of sap in plants, each and all tell the orderly love-beats of Nature's heart.

Turning to the eastward, you have the Grand Canyon and reaches of the river in full view; and yonder to the southward lies the great lake, the largest and most important of all the high fountains of the Missouri-Mississippi, and the last to be discovered.

In the year 1541, when De Soto, with a romantic band of adventurers, was seeking gold and glory and the fountain of youth, he found the Mississippi a few hundred miles above its mouth, and made his grave beneath its floods. La Salle, in 1682, after discovering the Ohio, one of the largest and most beautiful branches of the Mississippi, traced the latter to the sea from the mouth of the Illinois, through adventures and privations not easily realized now. About the same time Joliet and Father Marquette reach the 'Father of Waters' by way of the Wisconsin, but more than a century passed ere its highest sources in these mountains were seen. The advancing stream of civilization has ever followed its guidance toward the west, but none of the thousand tribes of Indians living on its banks could tell the explorer whence it came. From those romantic De Soto and La Salle days to these times of locomotives and tourists, how much has the greater river seen and done! Great as it now is, and still growing longer through the ground of its delta and the basins of receding glaciers at its head, it was immensely broader toward the close of the glacial period, when the ice-mantle of the mountains was melting: then with its three hundred thousand miles of branches outspread over the plains and valleys of the continent, laden with fertile mud, it made the biggest and most generous bed of soil in the world.

Think of this mighty stream springing in the first place in vapour from the sea, flying on the wind, alighting on the mountains in hail and snow and rain, lingering in many a fountain feeding the trees and grass; then gathering its scattered waters, gliding from its noble lake, and going back home to the sea, singing all the way! On it sweeps, through the gates of the mountains, across the vast prairies and plains, through many a wild, gloomy forest, cane-brake, and sunny savanna; from glaciers and snowbanks and pine woods to warm groves of magnolia and palm; geysers dancing at its head keeping time with the sea-waves at its mouth; roaring and grey in rapids, booming in broad, bossy falls, murmuring, gleaming in long, silvery reaches, swaying now hither, now thither, whirling, bending in huge doubling, eddying folds, serene, majestic, ungovernable, overflowing all its metes and bounds, fright-ening the dwellers upon its banks; building, wasting, uprooting, planting; engulfing old islands and making new ones, taking away fields and towns as if in sport, carrying canoes and ships of commerce in the midst of its spoils and drift, fertilizing the continent as one vast farm. Then, its work done, it gladly vanishes in its ocean home, welcomed by the waiting waves.

Thus naturally, standing here in the midst of its fountains, we trace the fortunes of the great river. And how much more comes to mind as we overlook this wonderful wilderness! Fountains of the Columbia and Colorado lie before us, interlaced with those of the Yellowstone and Missouri, and fine it would be to go with them to the Pacific; but the sun is already in the west, and soon our day will be done.

Yonder is Amethyst Mountain, and other mountains hardly less rich in old forests, which now seem to spring up again in their glory; and you see the storms that buried them – the ashes and torrents laden with boulders and mud, the centuries of sunshine, and the dark, lurid nights. You see again the vast floods of lava, red-hot and white-hot, pouring out from gigantic geysers, usurping the basins of lakes and streams, absorbing or driving away their hissing, screaming waters, flowing around hills and ridges, submerging every subordinate feature. Then you see the snow and glaciers taking possession of the land, making new landscapes. How admirable it is that, after passing through so many vicissitudes of frost and fire and flood, the physiognomy and even the complexion of the landscape should still be so divinely fine!

Thus reviewing the eventful past, we see Nature working with enthusiasm like a man, blowing her volcanic forges like a blacksmith blowing his smithy fires, shoving glaciers over the landscapes like a carpenter shoving his planes, clearing, ploughing, harrowing, irrigating, planting, and sowing broadcast like a farmer and gardener, doing rough work and fine work, planting sequoias and pines, rosebushes and daisies; working in gems, filling every crack and hollow with them; distilling fine essences; painting plants and shells, clouds, mountains, all the earth and heavens, like an artist – ever working toward beauty higher and higher. Where may the mind find more stimulating, quickening pasturage? A thousand Yellowstone wonders are calling, 'Look up and down and round about you!' And a multitude of still, small voices may be heard directing you to look through all this transient, shifting show of things called 'substantial' into the truly substantial spiritual world whose forms flesh and wood, rock and water, air and sunshine, only veil and conceal, and to learn that here is heaven and the dwelling-place of the angels.

The sun is setting; long, violet shadows are growing out over the woods from the mountains along the western rim of the park; the Absaroka range is baptized in the divine light of the alpenglow, and its rocks and trees are transfigured. Next to the light of the dawn on high mountain tops, the alpenglow is the most impressive of all the terrestrial manifestations of God.

Now comes the gloaming. The alpenglow is fading into earthy, murky gloom, but do not let your town habits draw you away to the hotel. Stay on this good fire-mountain and spend the night among the stars. Watch their glorious bloom until the dawn, and get one more baptism of light. Then, with fresh heart, go down to your work, and whatever your fate, under ignorance or knowledge you may afterward chance to suffer, remember these fine, wild views, and look back with joy to your wa in the blessed old Yellowstone Wonderland.

CHAPTER THREE

The Yosemite National Park

OF ALL the mountain ranges I have climbed, I like the Sierra Nevada the best. Though extremely rugged, with its main features on the grandest scale in height and depth, it is nevertheless easy of access and hospitable; and its marvellous beauty, displayed in striking and alluring forms, wooes the admiring wanderer on and on, higher and higher, charmed and enchanted. Benevolent, solemn, fateful, pervaded with divine light, every landscape glows like a countenance hallowed in eternal repose; and every one of its living creatures, clad in flesh and leaves, and every crystal of its rocks, whether on the surface shining in the sun or buried miles deep in what we call darkness, is throbbing and pulsing with the heartbeats of God. All the world lies warm in one heart, yet the Sierra seems to get more light than other mountains. The weather is mostly sunshine embellished with magnificent storms, and nearly everything shines from base to summit – the rocks, streams, lakes, glaciers, irised falls, and the forests of silver fir and silver pine. And how bright is the shining after summer showers and dewy nights, and after frosty nights in spring and autumn, when the morning sunbeams are pouring through the crystals on the bushes and grass, and in winter through the snow-laden trees!

The average cloudiness for the whole year is perhaps less than ten hundredths. Scarcely a day of all the summer is dark, though there is no lack of magnificent thundering cumuli. They rise in the warm midday hours, mostly over the middle region, in June and July, like new mountain ranges, higher Sierras, mightily augmenting the grandeur of the scenery while giving rain to the forests and gardens and bringing forth their fragrance. The wonderful weather and beauty inspire everybody to be up and doing. Every summer day is a workday to be confidently counted on, the short dashes of rain forming, not interruptions, but rests. The big blessed storm days of winter, when the whole range stands white, are not a whit less inspiring and kind. Well may the Sierra be called the Range of Light, not the Snowy Range; for only in winter is it white, while all the year it is bright.

Of this glorious range the Yosemite National Park is a central section, thirty-six miles in length and forty-eight miles in breadth. The famous Yosemite Valley lies in the heart of it, and it includes the head waters of the Tuolumne and Merced Rivers, two of the most songful streams in the world;

innumerable lakes and waterfalls and smooth silky lawns; the noblest forests, the loftiest granite domes, the deepest ice-sculptured canyons, the brightest crystalline pavements, and snowy mountains soaring into the sky twelve and thirteen thousand feet, arrayed in open ranks and spiry pinnacled groups partially separated by tremendous canyons and amphitheatres; gardens on their sunny brows, avalanches thundering down their long white slopes, cataracts roaring grey and foaming in the crooked rugged gorges, and glaciers in their shadowy recesses working in silence, slowly completing their sculpture; new-born lakes at their feet, blue and green, free or encumbered with drifting icebergs like miniature Arctic Oceans, shining, sparkling, calm as stars.

Nowhere will you see the majestic operations of nature more clearly revealed beside the frailest, most gentle and peaceful things. Nearly all the park is a profound solitude. Yet it is full of charming company, full of God's thoughts, a place of peace and safety amid the most exalted grandeur and eager enthusiastic action, a new song, a place of beginnings abounding in first lessons on life, mount-building, eternal, invincible, unbreakable order; with sermons in stones, storms, trees, flowers, and animals brimful of humanity. During the last glacial period, just past, the former features of the range were rubbed off as a chalk sketch from a blackboard, and a new beginning was made. Hence the wonderful clearness and freshness of the rocky pages.

But to get all this into words is a hopeless task. The leanest sketch of each feature would need a whole chapter. Nor would any amount of space, however industriously scribbled, be of much avail. To defrauded town toilers, parks in magazine articles are like pictures of bread to the hungry. I can write only hints to incite good wanderers to come to the feast.

While this glorious park embraces big, generous samples of the very best of the Sierra treasures, it is, fortunately, at the same time, the most accessible portion. It lies opposite San Francisco, at a distance of about one hundred and forty miles. Railroads connected with all the continent reach into the foothills, and three good carriage roads, from Big Oak Flat, Coulterville, and Raymond, run into Yosemite Valley. Another, called the Tioga road, runs from Crocker's Station on the Yosemite Big Oak Flat road near the Tuolumne Big Tree Grove, right across the park to the summit of the range by way of Lake Tenaya, the Big Tuolumne Meadows, and Mount Dana. These roads, with many trails that radiate from Yosemite Valley, bring most of the park within reach of everybody, well or half well.

The three main natural divisions of the park, the lower, middle, and alpine regions, are fairly well defined in altitude, topographical features, and vegetation. The lower, with an average elevation of about five thousand feet, is the region of the great forests, made up of sugar pine, the largest and most beautiful of all the pines in the world; the silvery yellow pine, the next in rank; Douglas spruce, libocedrus, the white and red silver firs, and the Sequoia gigantea, or 'big tree', the king of conifers, the noblest of a noble race. On warm slopes next the foothills there are a few Sabine nut pines; oaks make beautiful groves in the canyon valleys; and poplar, alder, maple, laurel, and Nuttall's flowering dogwood shade the banks of the streams. Many of the pines are more than two hundred feet high, but they are not crowded together. The sunbeams streaming through their feathery arches brighten the ground, and you walk beneath the radiant ceiling in devout subdued mood, as if you were in a grand cathedral with mellow light sifting through coloured windows, while the flowery pillared aisles open enchanting vistas in every direction. Scarcely a peak or ridge in the whole region rises bare above the forests, though they are thinly planted in some places where the soil is shallow. From the cool breezy heights you look abroad over a boundless waving sea of evergreens, covering hill and ridge and smooth-flowing slope as far as the eye can reach, and filling every hollow and down-plunging ravine in glorious triumphant exuberance.

Perhaps the best general view of the pine forests of the park, and one of the best in the range, is obtained from the top of the Merced and Tuolumne divide near Hazel Green. On the long, smooth, finely folded slopes of the main ridge, at a height of five to six thousand feet above the sea, they reach most perfect development and are marshalled to view in magnificent towering ranks, their colossal spires and domes and broad palmlike crowns, deep in the kind sky, rising above one another – a multitude of giants in perfect health and beauty – sun-fed mountaineers rejoicing in their strength, chanting with the winds, in accord with the falling waters. The ground is mostly open and inviting to walkers. The fragrant chamæbatia is outspread in rich carpets miles in extent; the manzanita, in orchard-like groves, covered with pink bell-shaped flowers in the spring, grows in openings facing the sun, hazel and buckthorn in the dells; warm brows are purple with mint, yellow with sun-flowers and violets; and tall lilies ring their bells around the borders of meadows and along the ferny, mossy banks of the streams. Never was mountain forest more lavishly furnished.

Hazel Green is a good place quietly to camp and study, to get acquainted with the trees and birds, to drink the reviving water and weather, and to watch the changing lights of the big charmed days. The rose light of the dawn, creeping higher among the stars, changes to daffodil yellow; then come the level enthusiastic sunbeams pouring across the feathery ridges, touching pine after pine, spruce and fir, libocedrus and lordly sequoia, searching every recess, until all are awakened and warmed. In the white noon they shine in silvery splendour, every needle and cell in bole and branch thrilling and tingling with ardent life; and the whole landscape glows with consciousness, like the face of a god. The hours go by uncounted. The evening flames with purple and gold. The breeze that has been blowing from the lowlands dies away, and far and near the mighty host of trees baptized in the purple flood stand hushed and thoughtful, awaiting the sun's blessing and farewell – as impressive a ceremony as if it were never to rise again. When the daylight fades, the night breeze from the snowy summits begins to blow, and the trees, waving and rustling beneath the stars, breathe free again.

It is hard to leave such camps and woods; nevertheless, to the large majority of travellers the middle region of the park is still more interesting, for it has the most striking features of all the Sierra scenery – the deepest sections of the famous canyons, of which the Yosemite Valley, Hetch-Hetchy

Valley, and many smaller ones are wider portions, with level parklike floors and walls of immense height and grandeur of sculpture. This middle region holds also the greater number of the beautiful glacier lakes and glacier meadows, the great granite domes, and the most brilliant and most extensive of the glacier pavements. And though in large part it is severely rocky and bare, it is still rich in trees. The magnificent silver fir (*Abies magnifica*), which ranks with the giants, forms a continuous belt across the park above the pines at an elevation of from seven to nine thousand feet, and north and south of the park boundaries to the extremities of the range, only slightly interrupted by the main canyons. The two-leaved or tamarack pine makes another less regular belt along the upper margin of the region, while between these two belts, and mingling with them, in groves or scattered, are the mountain hemlock, the most graceful of evergreens; the noble mountain pine; the Jeffrey form of the yellow pine, with big cones and long needles; and the brown, burly, sturdy Western juniper. All these, except the juniper, which grows on bald rocks, have plenty of flowery brush about them, and gardens in open spaces.

Here, too, lies the broad, shining, heavily sculptured region of primeval granite, which best tells the story of the glacial period on the Pacific side of the continent. No other mountain chain on the globe, as far as I know, is so rich as the Sierra in bold, striking, well-preserved glacial monuments, easily understood by anybody capable of patient observation. Every feature is more or less glacial, and this park portion of the range is the brightest and clearest of all. Not a peak, ridge, dome, canyon, lake basin, garden, forest or stream but in some way explains the past existence and modes of action of flowing, grinding, sculpturing, soil-making, scenery-making ice. For, notwithstanding the post-glacial agents – air, rain, frost, rivers, earthquakes, avalanches – have been at work upon the greater part of the range for tens of thousands of stormy years, engraving their own characters over those of the ice, the latter are so heavily emphasized and enduring they still rise in sublime relief, clear and legible through every after inscription. The streams have traced only shallow wrinkles as yet, and avalanche, wind, rain, and melting snow have made blurs and scars, but the change effected on the face of the landscape is not greater than is made on the face of a mountaineer by a single year of weathering.

Of all the glacial phenomena presented here, the most striking and attractive to travellers are the polished pavements, because they are so beautiful, and their beauty is of so rare a kind – unlike any part of the loose earthy lowlands where people dwell and earn their bread. They are simply flat or gently undulating areas of solid resisting granite, the unchanged surface over which the ancient glaciers flowed. They are found in the most perfect condition at an elevation of from eight to nine thousand feet above sea level. Some are miles in extent, only slightly blurred or scarred by spots that have at least yielded to the weather; while the best preserved portions are brilliantly polished, and reflect the sunbeams as calm water or glass, shining as if rubbed and burnished every day, notwithstanding they have been exposed to plashing, corroding rains, dew, frost and melting sloppy snows for thousands of years.

The attention of hunters and prospectors, who see so much in their wild journeys, is seldom attracted by moraines, however regular and artificial-looking; or rocks, however boldly sculptured; or canyons, however deep and sheer-walled. But when they come to these pavements, they go down on their knees and rub their hands admiringly on the glistening surface, and try hard to account for its mysterious smoothness and brightness. They may have seen the winter avalanches come down the mountains, through the woods, sweeping away the trees and scouring the ground; but they conclude that this cannot be the work of avalanches, because the striæ show that the agent, whatever it was, flowed along and around and over the top of high ridges and domes, and also filled the deep canyons. Neither can they see how water could be the agent, for the strange polish is found thousands of feet above the reach of any conceivable flood. Only the winds seem capable of moving over the face of the country in the directions indicated by the lines and grooves.

The pavements are particularly fine around Lake Tenaya, and have suggested the Indian name Py-we-ack, the Lake of the Shining Rocks. Indians seldom trouble themselves with geological questions, but a Mono Indian once came to me and asked if I could tell him what made the rocks so smooth at Tenaya. Even dogs and horses, on their first journeys into this region, study geology to the extent of gazing wonderingly at the strange brightness of the ground, and pawing it and smelling it, as if afraid of falling or sinking.

In the production of this admirable hard finish, the glaciers in many places exerted a pressure of more than a hundred tons to the square foot, planing down granite, slate, and quartz alike, showing their structure, and making beautiful mosaics where large feldspar crystals form the greater part of the rock. On such pavements the sunshine is at times dazzling, as if the surface were of burnished silver.

Here, also, are the brightest of the Sierra landscapes in general. The regions lying at the same elevation to the north and south were perhaps subjected to as long and intense a glaciation; but because the rocks are less resisting, their polished surfaces have mostly given way to the weather, leaving here and there only small imperfect patches on the most enduring portions of canyon walls protected from the action of rain and snow, and on hard bosses kept comparatively dry by boulders. The short, steeply inclined canyons of the east flank of the range are in some places brightly polished, but they are far less magnificent than those of the broad west flank.

One of the best general views of the middle region of the park is to be had from the top of a majestic dome which long ago I named the Glacier Monument. It is situated a few miles to the north of Cathedral Peak, and rises to a height of about fifteen hundred feet above its base and ten thousand above the sea. At first sight it seems sternly inaccessible, but a good climber will find that it may be scaled on the south side. Approaching it from this side you pass through a dense bryanthus-fringed grove of mountain hemlock, catching glimpses now and then of the colossal dome towering to an immense height above the dark evergreens; and when at last you have made your way across woods, wading through azalea and ledum thickets, you step abruptly out of the tree shadows and mossy leafy softness upon a bare porphyry pavement, and behold the dome unveiled in all its grandeur. Fancy a nicely proportioned monument, eight or ten feet high, hewn from one stone, standing in a pleasure ground; magnify it to a height of fifteen hundred feet, retaining its simplicity of form and fineness, and cover its surface with crystals; then you may gain an idea of the sublimity and beauty of this ice-burnished dome, one of many adorning this wonderful park.

In making the ascent, one finds that the curve of the base rapidly steepens, until one is in danger of slipping; but feldspar crystals, two or three inches long, that have been weathered into relief, afford slight footholds. The summit is in part burnished, like the sides and base, the striæ and scratches indicating that the mighty Tuolumne Glacier, two or three thousand feet deep, overwhelmed it while it stood firm like a boulder at the bottom of a river. The pressure it withstood must have been enormous. Had it been less solidly built, it would have been ground and crushed into moraine fragments, like the general mass of the mountain flank in which at first it lay imbedded; for it is only a hard residual knob or knot with a concentric structure of superior strength, brought into relief by the removal of the less resisting rock about it – an illustration in stone of the survival of the strongest and most favourably situated.

Hardly less wonderful, when we contemplate the storms it has encountered since first it saw the light, is its present unwasted condition. The whole quantity of postglacial wear and tear it has suffered has not diminished its stature a single inch, as may be readily shown by measuring from the level of the unchanged polished portions of the surface. Indeed, the average post-glacial denudation of the entire region, measured in the same way, is found to be less than two inches – a mighty contrast to that of the ice; for the glacial denudation here has been not less than a mile; that is, in developing the present landscapes, an amount of rock a mile in average thickness has been silently carried away by flowing ice during the last glacial period.

A few erratic boulders nicely poised on the rounded summit of the monu-ment tell an interesting story. They came from a mountain on the crest of the range, about twelve miles to the eastward, floating like chips on the frozen sea, and were stranded here when the top of the monument emerged to the light of day, while the companions of these boulders, whose positions chanced to be over the slopes where they could not find rest, were carried farther on by the shallowing current.

The general view from the summit consists of a sublime assemblage of iceborn mountains and rocks and long wavering ridges, lakes and streams and meadows, moraines in wide-sweeping belts, and beds covered and dotted with forests and groves – hundreds of square miles of them composed in wild harmony. The snowy mountains on the axis of the range, mostly sharp-peaked and crested, rise in noble array along the sky to the eastward and northward; the grey-pillared Hoffman spur and the Yosemite domes and a countless number of others to the westward; Cathedral Peak with its many spires and companion peaks and domes to the southward; and a smooth billowy multitude of rocks, from fifty feet or less to a thousand feet high, which from their peculiar form seem to be rolling on westward, fill most of the middle ground. Immediately beneath you are the Big Tuolumne Meadows, with an ample swath of dark pine woods on either side, enlivened by the young river, that is seen sparkling and shimmering as it sways from side to side, tracing as best it can its broad glacial channel.

The ancient Tuolumne Glacier, lavishly-flooded by many a noble affluent from the snow-laden flanks of Mounts Dana, Gibbs, Lyell, Maclure, and others nameless as yet, poured its majestic overflowing current, four or five miles wide, directly against the high outstanding mass of Mount Hoffman, which divided and deflected it right and left, just as a river is divided against an island that stands in the middle of its channel. Two distinct glaciers were thus formed, one of which flowed through the Big Tuolumne Canyon and Hetch-Hetchy Valley, while the other swept upward five hundred feet in a broad current across the divide between the basins of the Tuolumne and Merced into the Tenaya basin, and thence down through the Tenaya Canyon and Yosemite Valley.

The maplike distinctness and freshness of this glacial landscape cannot fail to excite the attention of every observer, no matter how little of its scientific significance he may at first recognize. These bald, glossy, westward-leaning rocks in the open middle ground, with their rounded backs and shoulders toward the glacier fountains of the summit mountains and their split angular fronts looking in the opposite direction, every one of them displaying the form of greatest strength with reference to physical structure and glacial action, show the tremendous force with which through unnumbered centuries the ice flood swept over them, and also the direction of the flow; while the mountains, with their sharp summits and abraded sides, indicate the height to which the glacier rose; and the moraines, curving and swaying in beautiful lines, mark the boundaries of the main trunk and its tributaries as they existed toward the close of the glacial winter. None of the commercial highways of the sea or land, marked with buoys and lamps, fences and guideboards, is so unmistakably indicated as are these channels of the vanished Tuolumne glaciers.

The action of flowing ice, whether in the form of river-like glaciers or broad mantling folds, is but little understood as compared with that of other sculpturing agents. Rivers work openly where people dwell, and so do the rain, and the sea thundering on all the shores of the world; and the universal ocean of air, though unseen, speaks aloud in a thousand voices and explains its modes of working and its power. But glaciers, back in their cold solitudes, work apart from men, exerting their tremendous energies in silence and darkness. Coming in vapour from the sea, flying invisible on the wind, descending in snow, changing to ice, white, spiritlike, they brood outspread over the predestined landscapes, working on unwearied through unmeasured ages, until in the fullness of time the mountains and valleys are brought forth, channels furrowed for the rivers, basins made for meadows and lakes, and soil beds spread for the forests and fields that man and beast may be fed. Then vanishing like clouds, they melt into streams and go singing back home to the sea.

To an observer upon this adamantine old monument in the midst of such scenery, getting glimpses of the thoughts of God, the day seems endless, the sun stands still. Much faithless fuss is made over the passage in the Bible telling of the standing still of the sun for Joshua. Here you may learn that the miracle occurs for every devout mountaineer, for everybody doing anything worth doing, seeing anything worth seeing. One day is as a thousand years, a thousand years as one day, and while yet in the flesh you enjoy immortality.

From the monument you will find any easy way down through the woods and along the Big Tuolumne Meadows to Mount Dana, the summit of which commands a grand telling view of the alpine region. The scenery all the way is inspiring, and you saunter on without knowing that you are climbing. The spacious sunny meadows, through the midst of which the bright river glides, extend with but little interruption ten miles to the eastward, dark woods rising on either side to the limit of tree growth, and above the woods a picturesque line of grey peaks and spires dotted with snow banks; while, on the axis of the Sierra, Mount Dana and his noble compeers repose in massive sublimity, their vast size and simple flowing contours contrasting in the most striking manner with the clustering spires and thin-pinnacled crests crisply outlined on the horizon to the north and south of them.

Tracing the silky lawns, gradually ascending, gazing at the sublime scenery more and more openly unfolded, noting the avalanche gaps in the upper forests, lingering over beds of blue gentians and purple-flowered bryanthus and cassiope, and dwarf willows an inch high in close-felted grey carpets, brightened here and there with kalmia and soft creeping mats of vaccinium sprinkled with pink bells that seem to have been showered down from the sky like hail – thus beguiled and enchanted, you reach the base of the mountain wholly unconscious of the miles you have walked. And so on to the summit. For all the way up the long red slate slopes, that in the distance seemed barren, you find little garden beds and tufts of dwarf phlox, ivesia, and blue arctic daisies that go straight to your heart, blessed fellow mountaineers kept safe and warm by a thousand miracles. You are now more than thirteen thousand feet above the sea, and to the north and south you behold a sublime wilderness of mountains in glorious array, their snowy summits towering together in crowded, bewildering abundance, shoulder to shoulder, peak beyond peak. To the east lies the Great Basin, barren-looking and silent, apparently a land of pure desolation, rich only in beautiful light. Mono Lake, fourteen miles long, is outspread below you at a depth of nearly seven thousand feet, its shores of volcanic ashes and sand, treeless and sunburned; a group of volcanic cones, with well-formed, unwasted craters rises to the south of the lake; while up from its eastern shore innumerable mountains with soft flowing outlines extend range beyond range, grey, and pale purple, and blue – the farthest gradually fading on the glowing horizon. Westward you look down and over the countless moraines, glacier meadows, and grand sea of domes and rock waves of the upper Tuolumne basin, the Cathedral and Hoffman mountains with their wavering lines and zones of forest, the wonderful region to the north of the Tuolumne Canyon, and across the dark belt of silver firs to the pale mountains of the coast.

In the icy fountains of the Mount Lyell and Ritter groups of peaks, to the south of Dana, three of the most important of the Sierra rivers – the Tuolumne, Merced and San Joaquin – take their rise, their highest tributaries being within a few miles of one another as they rush forth on their adventurous courses from beneath snow banks and glaciers.

Of the small shrinking glaciers of the Sierra, remnants of the majestic system that sculptured the range, I have seen sixty-five. About twenty-five of them are in the park, and eight are in sight from Mount Dana.

The glacier lakes are sprinkled over all the alpine and subalpine regions, gleaming like eyes beneath heavy rock brows, tree-fringed or bare, embosomed in the woods, or lying in open basins with green and purple meadows around them; but the greater number are in the cool shadowy hollows of the summit mountains not far from the glaciers, the highest lying at an elevation of from eleven to nearly twelve thousand feet above the sea. The whole number in the Sierra, not counting the smallest, can hardly be less than fifteen hundred, of which about two hundred and fifty are in the park. From one standpoint, on Red Mountain, I counted forty-two, most of them within a radius of ten miles. The glacier meadows, which are spread over the filled-up basins of vanished lakes and form one of the most charming features of the scenery, are still more numerous than the lakes.

An observer stationed here, in the glacial period, would have overlooked a wrinkled mantle of ice as continuous as that which now covers the continent of Greenland; and of all the vast landscape now shining in the sun, he would have seen only the tops of the summit peaks, rising darkly like storm-beaten islands, lifeless and hopeless, above rock-encumbered ice waves. If among the agents that nature has employed in making these mountains there be one that above all others deserves the name of Destroyer, it is the glacier. But we quickly learn that destruction is creation. During the dreary centuries through which the Sierra lay in darkness, crushed beneath the ice folds of the glacial winter, there was a steady invincible advance toward the warm life and beauty of today; and it is just where the glaciers crushed most destructively that the greatest amount of beauty is made manifest. But as these landscapes have succeeded the preglacial landscapes, so they in turn are giving place to others already planned and foreseen. The granite domes and pavements, apparently imperishable, we take as symbols of permanence, while these crumbling peaks, down whose frosty gullies avalanches are ever falling, are symbols of change and decay. Yet all alike, fast or slow, are surely vanishing away.

Nature is ever at work building and pulling down, creating and destroying, keeping everything whirling and flowing, allowing no rest but in rhythmical motion, chasing everything in endless song out of one beautiful form into another.

CHAPTER FOUR

The Forests of the Yosemite Park

THE CONIFEROUS forests of the Yosemite Park, and of the Sierra in general, surpass all others of their kind in America or indeed in the world, not only in the size and beauty of the trees, but in the number of species assembled together, and the grandeur of the mountains they are growing on. Leaving the workaday lowlands, and wandering into the heart of the mountains, we find a new world, and stand beside the majestic pines and firs and sequoias silent and awestricken, as if in the presence of superior beings new arrived from some other star, so calm and bright and godlike they are.

Going to the woods is going home; for I suppose we came from the woods originally. But in some of nature's forests the adventurous traveller seems a feeble, unwelcome creature; wild beasts and the weather trying to kill him, the rank, tangled vegetation, armed with spears and stinging needles, barring his way and making life a hard struggle. Here everything is hospitable and kind, as if planned for your pleasure, ministering to every want of body and soul. Even the storms are friendly and seem to regard you as a brother, their beauty and tremendous fateful earnestness charming alike. But the weather is mostly sunshine, both winter and summer, and the clear sunny brightness of the park is one of its most striking characteristics. Even the heaviest portions of the main forest belt, where the trees are tallest and stand closest, are not in the least gloomy. The sunshine falls in glory through the colossal spires and crowns, each a symbol of health and strength, the noble shafts faithfully upright like the pillars of temples, upholding a roof of infinite leafy interlacing arches and fretted skylights. The more open portions are like spacious parks, carpeted with small shrubs, or only with the fallen needles sprinkled here and there with flowers. In some places, where the ground is level or slopes gently, the trees are assembled in groves, and the flowers and underbrush in trim beds and thickets as in landscape gardens or the lovingly planted grounds of homes; or they are drawn up in orderly rows around meadows and lakes and along the brows of canyons. But in general the forests are distributed in wide belts in accordance with climate and the comparative strength of each kind in gaining and holding possession of the ground, while anything like monotonous uniformity is prevented by the grandly varied topography, and by the arrangement of the best soilbeds in intricate patterns like embroidery; for these soilbeds are the moraines of ancient glaciers more or less modified by weathering and stream action, and the trees trace them over the hills and ridges, and far up the sides of the mountains, rising with even growth on levels, and towering above one another on the long rich slopes prepared for them by the vanished glaciers.

Had the Sierra forests been cheaply accessible, the most valuable of them commercially would ere thus have fallen a prey to the lumberman. Thus far the redwood of the Coast Mountains and the Douglas spruce of Oregon and Washington have been more available for lumber than the pine of the Sierra. It cost less to go a thousand miles up the coast for timber, where the trees came down to the shores of navigable rivers and bays, than fifty miles up the mountains. Nevertheless, the superior value of the sugar pine for many purposes has tempted capitalists to expend large sums on flumes and railroads to reach the best forests, though perhaps none of these enterprises has paid. Fortunately, the lately established system of parks and reservations has put a stop to any great extension of the business hereabouts in its most destructive forms. And as the Yosemite Park region has escaped the millmen, and the all-devouring hordes of hoofed locusts have been banished, it is still in the main a pure wilderness, unbroken by axe clearings except on the lower margin, where a few settlers have opened spots beside hay meadows for their cabins and gardens. But these are mere dots of cultivation, in no appreciable degree disturbing the grand solitude. Twenty or thirty years ago a good many trees were felled for their seeds; traces of this destructive method of seed-collecting are still visible along the trails; but these as well as the shingle-makers' ruins are being rapidly overgrown, the gardens and beds of underbrush once devastated by sheep are blooming again in all their wild glory, and the park is a paradise that makes even the loss of Eden seem insignificant.

On the way to Yosemite Valley, you get some grand views over the forests of the Merced and Tuolumne basins and glimpses of some of the finest trees by the roadside without leaving your seat in the stage. But to learn how they live and behave in pure wildness, to see them in their varying aspects through the seasons and weather, rejoicing in the great storms, in the spiritual mountain light, putting forth their new leaves and flowers when all the streams are in flood and the birds are singing, and sending away their seeds in the thoughtful Indian summer when all the landscape is glowing in deep calm enthusiasm – for this you must love them and live with them, as free from schemes and cares and time as the trees themselves.

And surely nobody will find anything hard in this. Even the blind must enjoy these woods, drinking their fragrance, listening to the music of the winds in their groves, and fingering their flowers and plumes and cones and richly furrowed boles. The kind of study required is as easy and natural as breathing. Without any great knowledge of botany or wood-craft, in a single season you may learn the name and something more of nearly every kind of tree in the park.

With few exceptions all the Sierra trees are growing in the park – nine species of pine, two of silver fir, one each of Douglas spruce, libocedrus, hemlock, juniper and sequoia – sixteen conifers in all, and about the same number of round-headed trees, oaks, maples, poplars, laurel, alder, dogwood, tumion, etc.

The first of the conifers you meet in going up the range from the west is the digger nut-pine (*Pinus Sabiniana*), a remarkably open, airy, wide-branched tree, forty to sixty feet high, with long, sparse, greyish green foliage and large cones. At a height of fifteen to thirty feet from the ground the trunk usually divides into several main branches, which, after bearing away from one another, shoot straight up and form separate heads as if the axis of the tree had been broken, while the secondary branches divide again and again into rather slender sprays loosely tasseled, with leaves eight to twelve inches long. The yellow and purple flowers are about an inch long, the staminate in showy clusters. The big, rough, burly cones, five to eight or ten inches in length and five or six in diameter, are rich brown in colour when ripe, and full of hard-shelled nuts that are greatly prized by Indians and squirrels. This strange-looking pine, enjoying hot sunshine like a palm, is sparsely distributed along the driest part of the Sierra among small oaks and chaparral, and with its grey mist of foliage, strong trunk and branches, and big cones seen in relief on the glowing sky, forms the most striking feature of the foothill vegetation.

Pinus attenuata is a small, slender, arrowy tree, and pale green leaves in threes, clustered flowers half an inch long, brownish yellow and crimson, and cones whorled in conspicuous clusters around the branches and also around the trunk. The cones never fall off or open until the tree dies. They are about four inches long, exceedingly strong and solid, and varnished with hard resin forming a waterproof and almost worm and squirrel proof package, in which the seeds are kept fresh and safe during the lifetime of the tree. Sometimes one of the trunk cones is overgrown and imbedded in the heart wood like a knot, but nearly all are pushed out and kept on the surface by the pressure of the successive layers of wood against the base.

This admirable little tree grows on bushy, sunbeaten slopes, which from their position and the inflammable character of the vegetation are most frequently fire-swept. These grounds it is able to hold against all comers, however big and strong, by saving its seeds until death, when all it has produced are scattered over the bare cleared ground, and a new generation quickly springs out of the ashes. Thus the curious fact that all the trees of extensive groves and belts are of the same age is accounted for, and their slender habit; for the lavish abundance of seed sown at the same time makes a crowded growth, and the seedlings with an even start rush up in a hurried race for light and life.

Only a few of the attenuata and Sabiniana pines are within the boundaries of the park, the former on the side of the Merced Canyon, the latter on the walls of Hetch-Hetchy Valley and in the canyon below it.

The nut-pine (*Pinus monophylla*) is a small, hardy, contented-looking tree, about fifteen or twenty feet high and a foot in diameter. In its youth the close radiating and aspiring branches form a handsome broad-based pyramid, but when fully grown it becomes round-topped, knotty, and irregular, throwing out crooked divergent limbs like an apple tree. The leaves are pale greyish green, about an inch and a half long, and instead of being divided into clusters they are single, round, sharp-pointed, and rigid like spikes, amid which in the spring the red flowers glow brightly. The cones are only about two inches in length and breadth, but nearly half of their bulk is made up of sweet nuts.

This fruitful little pine grows on the dry east side of the park, along the margin of the Mono sage plain, and is the commonest tree of the short mountain ranges of the Great Basin. Tens of thousands of acres are covered with it, forming bountiful orchards for the Red-man. Being so low and accessible, the cones are easily beaten off with poles, and the nuts procured by roasting until the scales open. To the tribes of the desert and sage plains these seeds are the staff of life. They are eaten either raw or parched, or in the form of mush or cakes after being pounded into meal. The time of nut harvest in the autumn is the Indian's merriest time of all the year. An industrious squirrelish family can gather fifty or sixty bushels in a single month before the snow comes, and then their bread for the winter is sure.

The white pine (*Pinus flexilis*) is widely distributed through the Rocky Mountains and the ranges of the Great Basin, where in many places it grows to a good size, and is an important timber tree where none better is to be found. In the park it is sparsely scattered along the eastern flank of the range from Mono Pass southward, above the nut-pine, at an elevation of from eight to ten thousand feet, dwarfing to a tangled bush near the timber-line, but under favourable conditions attaining a height of forty or fifty feet, with a diameter of three to five. The long branches show a tendency to sweep out in bold curves, like those of the mountain and sugar pines to which it is closely related. The needles are in clusters of five, closely packed on the ends of the branchlets. The cones are about five inches long – the smaller ones nearly oval, the larger cylindrical. But the most interesting feature of the tree is its bloom, the vivid red pistillate flowers glowing among the leaves like coals of fire.

The dwarfed pine or white-barked pine (*Pinus albicaulis*) is sure to interest every observer on account of its curious low matted habit, and the great height on the snowy mountains at which it bravely grows. It forms the extreme edge of the timber-line on both flanks of the summit mountains – if so lowly a tree can be called timber – at an elevation of ten to twelve thousand feet above the level of the sea. Where it is first met on the lower limit of its range it may be thirty or forty feet high, but farther up the rocky wind-swept slopes, where the snow lies deep and heavy for six months of the year, it makes shaggy clumps and beds, crinkled and pressed flat, over which you can easily walk. Nevertheless in this crushed, down-pressed, felted condition it clings hardily to life, puts forth fresh leaves every spring on the ends of its tasselled branchlets, blooms bravely in the lashing blasts with abundance of gay red and purple flowers, matures its seeds in the short summers, and often outlives the favoured giants of the sun lands far below. One of the trees that I examined was only about three feet high, with a stem six inches in diameter at the ground, and branches that spread out horizontally as if they had grown up against a ceiling; yet it was four hundred and twenty-six years old, and one of its supple branchlets, about an eighth of an inch in diameter inside the bark, was seventy-five years old, and so tough that I tied it into knots. At the age of this dwarf many of the sugar and yellow pines and sequoias are seven feet in diameter and over two hundred feet high.

In detached clumps never touched by fire the fallen needles of centuries of growth make fine elastic mattresses for the weary mountaineer, while the tasselled branchlets spread a roof over him, and the dead roots, half

resin, usually found in abundance, make capital camp-fires, unquenchable
in thickest storms of rain or snow. Seen from a distance the belts and patches
darkening the mountain sides look like mosses on a roof, and bring to mind
Dr Johnson's remarks on the trees of Scotland. His guide, anxious for
the honour of Mull, was still talking of its woods and pointing them out. 'Sir',
said Johnson, 'I saw at Tobermory what they called a wood, which I
unluckily took for heath. If you show me what I shall take for furze, it will be
something'.

The mountain pine (*Pinus monticola*) is far the largest of the Sierra tree
mountaineers. Climbing nearly as high as the dwarf albicaulis, it is still a giant
in size, bold and strong, standing erect on the storm-beaten peaks and ridges,
tossing its cone-laden branches in the rough winds, living a thousand years,
and reaching its greatest size – ninety to a hundred feet in height, six to eight
in diameter – just where other trees, its companions, are dwarfed. But it is not
able to endure burial in snow so long as the albicaulis and flexilis. Therefore,
on the upper limit of its range it is found on slopes which, from their steepness
or exposure, are least snowy. Its soft graceful beauty in youth, and its leaves,
cones, and outsweeping feathery branches constantly remind you of the sugar
pine, to which it is closely allied. An admirable tree, growing nobler in form
and size the colder and balder the mountains about it.

The giants of the main forest in the favoured middle region are the sequoia,
sugar pine, yellow pine, libocedrus, Douglas spruce, and the two silver firs.
The park sequoias are restricted to two small groves, a few miles apart, on the
Tuolumne and Merced divide, about seventeen miles from Yosemite Valley.
The Big Oak Flat road to the valley runs through the Tuolumne Grove, the
Coulterville through the Merced. The more famous and better known
Mariposa Grove, belonging to the state, lies near the southwest corner of the
park, a few miles above Wawona.

The sugar pine (*Pinus Lambertiana*) is first met in the park in open, sunny,
flowery woods, at an elevation of about thirty-five hundred feet above the
sea, attains full development at a height between five and six thousand feet,
and vanishes at the level of eight thousand feet. In many places, especially on
the northern slopes of the main ridges between the rivers, it forms the bulk of
the forest, but mostly it is intimately associated with its noble companions,
above which it towers in glorious majesty on every hill, ridge, and plateau
from one extremity of the range to the other, a distance of five hundred miles
– the largest, noblest, and most beautiful of all the seventy or eighty species of
pine trees in the world, and of all the confiers second only to King Sequoia.

A good many are from two hundred to two hundred and twenty feet in
height, with a diameter at four feet from the ground of six to eight feet, and
occasionally a grand patriarch, seven or eight hundred years old, is found that
is ten or even twelve feet in diameter and two hundred and forty feet high,
with a magnificent crown seventy feet wide. David Douglas, who discovered
'this most beautiful and immensely grand tree' in the fall of 1826 in southern
Oregon, says that the largest of several that had been blown down, 'at three
feet from the ground was fifty-seven feet nine inches in circumference'
(or fully eighteen feet in diameter); 'at one hundred and thirty-four feet,

seventeen feet five inches; extreme length, two hundred and forty-five feet'. Probably for *fifty-seven* we should read *thirty-seven* for the base measurement, which would make it correspond with the other dimensions; for none of this species with anything like so great a girth has since been seen. A girth of even thirty feet is uncommon. A fallen specimen that I measured was nine feet three inches in diameter inside the bark at four feet from the ground, and six feet in diameter at a hundred feet from the ground. A comparatively young tree, three hundred and thirty years old, that had been cut down, measured seven feet across the stump, was three feet three inches in diameter at a height of one hundred and fifty feet, and two hundred and ten feet in length.

The trunk is a round, delicately tapered shaft with finely furrowed purplish-brown bark, usually free of limbs for a hundred feet or more. The top is furnished with long and comparatively slender branches, which sweep gracefully downward and outward, feathered with short tasselled branchlets, and divided only at the ends, forming a palmlike crown fifty to seventy-five feet wide, but without the monotonous uniformity of palm crowns or of the spires of most conifers. The old trees are as tellingly varied and picturesque as oaks. No two are alike, and we are tempted to stop and admire everyone we come to, whether as it stands silent in the calm balsam-scented sunshine or waving in accord with enthusiastic storms. The leaves are about three or four inches long, in clusters of five, finely tempered, bright lively green, and radiant. The flowers are but little larger than those of the dwarf pine, and far less showy. The immense cylindrical cones, fifteen to twenty or even twenty-four inches long and three in diameter, hang singly or in clusters, like ornamental tassels, at the ends of the long branches, green, flushed with purple on the sunward side. Like those of almost all the pines they ripen in the autumn of the second season from the flower, and the seeds of all that have escaped the Indians, bears, and squirrels take wing and fly to their places. Then the cones become still more effective as ornaments, for by the spreading of the scales the diameter is nearly doubled, and the colour changes to a rich brown. They remain on the tree the following winter and summer; therefore few fertile trees are ever found without them. Nor even after they fall is the beauty work of these grand cones done, for they make a fine show on the flowery, needle-strewn ground. The wood is pale yellow, fine in texture, and deliciously fragrant. The sugar, which gives name to the tree, exudes from the heart wood on wounds made by fire or the axe, and forms irregular crisp white candy-like masses. To the taste of most people it is as good as maple sugar, though it cannot be eaten in large quantities.

No traveller, whether a tree lover or not, will ever forget his first walk in a sugar-pine forest. The majestic crowns approaching one another make a glorious canopy, through the feathery arches of which the sunbeams pour, silvering the needles and gilding the stately columns and the ground into a scene of enchantment.

The yellow pine (*Pinus ponderosa*) is surpassed in size and nobleness of port only by its kingly companion. Full-grown trees in the main forest where it is associated with the sugar pine, are about one hundred and seventy-five feet high, with a diameter of five to six feet, though much larger specimens may easily be found. The largest I ever measured was a little over eight feet in diameter four feet above the ground, and two hundred and twenty feet high. Where there is plenty of sunshine and other conditions are favourable, it is a massive symmetrical spire, formed of a strong straight shaft clad with innumerable branches, which are divided again and again into stout branchlets laden with bright shining needles and green or purple cones. Where the growth is at all close half or more of the trunk is branchless. The species attains its greatest size and most majestic form in open groves on the deep, well-drained soil of lake basins at an elevation of about four thousand feet. There nearly all the old trees are over two hundred feet high, and the heavy, leafy, much-divided branches sumptuously clothe the trunk almost to the ground. Such trees are easily climbed, and in going up the winding stairs of knotty limbs to the top you will gain a most telling and memorable idea of the height, the richness and intricacy of the branches, and the marvellous abundance and beauty of the long shining elastic foliage. In tranquil weather, you will see the firm outstanding needles in calm content, shimmering and throwing off keen minute rays of light like lances of ice; but when heavy winds are blowing, the strong towers bend and wave in the blast with eager wide-awake enthusiasm, and every tree in the grove glows and flashes in one mass of white sunfire.

Both the yellow and sugar pines grow rapidly on good soil where they are not crowded. At the age of a hundred years they are about two feet in diameter and a hundred or more high. They are then very handsome, though very unlike: the sugar pine, lithe, feathery, closely clad with ascending branches; the yellow, open, showing its axis from the ground to the top, its whorled branches but little divided as yet, spreading and turning up at the ends with magnificent tassels of long stout bright needles, the terminal shoot with its leaves being often three or four feet long and a foot and a half wide, the most hopeful looking and the handsomest tree-top in the woods. But instead of increasing, like its companion, in wildness and individuality of form with age, it becomes more evenly and compactly spiry. The bark is usually very thick, four to six inches at the ground, and arranged in large plates, some of them on the lower part of the trunk four or five feet long and twelve to eighteen inches wide, forming a strong defence against fire. The leaves are in threes, and from three inches to a foot long. The flowers appear in May: the staminate pink or brown, in conspicuous clusters two or three inches wide; the pistillate crimson, a fourth of an inch wide, and mostly hidden among the leaves on the tips of the branchlets. The cones vary from about three to ten inches in length, two to five in width, and grow in sessile outstanding clusters near the ends of the upturned branchlets.

Being able to endure fire and hunger and many climates this grand tree is widely distributed: eastward from the coast across the broad Rocky Mountain ranges to the Black Hills of Dakota, a distance of more than a thouand miles, and southward from British Columbia, near latitude 51°, to Mexico, about fifteen hundred miles. South of the Columbia River it meets the sugar pine, and accompanies it all the way down along the Coast and Cascade mountains and the Sierra and southern ranges to the mountains of the peninsula of

Lower California, where they find their southmost homes together. Pinus ponderosa is extremely variable, and much bother it gives botanists who try to catch and confine the unmanageable proteus in two or a dozen species – Jeffreyi, deflexa, apacheca latifolia, etc. But in all its wanderings, in every form, it manifests noble strength. Clad in thick bark like a warrior in mail, it extends its bright ranks over all the high ranges of the wild side of the continent: flourishes in the drenching fog and rain of the northern coast at the level of the sea, in the snow-laden blasts of the mountains, and the white glaring sunshine of the interior plateaus and plains, on the borders of mirage-haunted deserts, volcanoes, and lava beds, waving its bright plumes in the hot winds undaunted, blooming every year for centuries, and tossing big ripe cones among the cinders and ashes of nature's hearths.

The Douglas spruce grows with the great pines, especially on the cool north sides of ridges and canyons, and is here nearly as large as the yellow pine, but less abundant. The wood is strong and tough, the bark thick and deeply furrowed, and on vigorous, quick-growing trees the stout, spreading branches are covered with innumerable slender, swaying sprays, handsomely clothed with short leaves. The flowers are about three fourths of an inch in length, red or greenish, not so showy as the pendulous bracted cones. But in June and July, when the young bright yellow leaves appear, the entire tree seems to be covered with bloom.

It is this grand tree that forms the famous forests of western Oregon, Washington, and the adjacent coast regions of British Columbia, where it attains its greatest size and is most abundant, making almost pure forests over thousands of square miles, dark and close and almost inaccessible, many of the trees towering with straight, imperceptibly tapered shafts to a height of three hundred feet, their heads together shutting out the light – one of the largest, most widely distributed, and most important of all the Western giants.

The incense cedar (*Libocedrus decurrens*), when full grown, is a magnificent tree, one hundred and twenty to nearly two hundred feet high, five to eight and occasionally twelve feet in diameter, with cinnamon-coloured bark and warm yellow-green foliage, and in general appearance like an abour vitæ. It is distributed through the main forest from an elevation of three to six thousand feet, and in sheltered portions of canyons on the warm sides to seven thousand five hundred. In midwinter, when most trees are asleep, it puts forth its flowers. The pistillate are pale green and inconspicuous; but the staminate are yellow, about one fourth of an inch long, and are produced in myriads, tingeing all the branches with gold, and making the tree as it stands in the snow look like a gigantic goldenrod. Though scattered rather sparsely amongst its companions in the open woods, it is seldom out of sight, and its bright brown shafts and warm masses of plumy foliage make a striking feature of the landscape. While young and growing fast in an open situation no other tree of its size in the park forms so exactly tapered a pyramid. The branches, outspread in flat plumes and beautifully fronded, sweep gracefully downward and outward, except those near the top, which aspire; the lowest droop to the ground, overlapping one another, shedding off rain and snow, and making fine tents for storm-bound mountaineers and birds. In old age it becomes irregular and picturesque, mostly from accidents: running fires, heavy wet snow breaking the branches, lightning shattering the top, compelling it to try to make new summits out of side branches, etc. Still it frequently lives more than a thousand years, invincibly beautiful, and worthy of its place beside the Douglas spruce and the great pines.

This unrivalled forest is still further enriched by two majestic silver firs, Abies magnifica and Abies concolour, bands of which come down from the main fir belt by cool shady ridges and glens. Abies magnifica is the noblest of its race, growing on moraines, at an elevation of seven thousand to eight thousand five hundred feet above the sea, to a height of two hundred or two hundred and fifty feet, and five to seven in diameter; and with these noble dimensions there is a richness and symmetry and perfection of finish not to be found in any other tree in the Sierra. The branches are whorled, in fives mostly, and stand out from the straight red purple bole in level or, on old trees, in drooping collars, every branch regularly pinnated like fern fronds, and clad with silvery needles, making broad plumes singularly rich and sumptuous.

The flowers are in their prime about the middle of June: the staminate red, growing on the underside of the branchlets in crowded profusion, giving a rich colour to nearly all the tree; the pistillate greenish yellow tinged with pink, standing erect on the upper side of the topmost branches; while the tufts of young leaves, about as brightly coloured as those of the Douglas spruce, push out their fragrant brown buds a few weeks later, making another grand show.

The cones mature in a single season from the flowers. When full grown they are about six to eight inches long, three or four in diameter, blunt, massive, cylindrical, greenish grey in colour, covered with a fine silvery down, and beaded with transparent balsam, very rich and precious-looking, standing erect like casks on the topmost branches. If possible, the inside of the cone is still more beautiful. The scales and bracts are tinged with red, and the seed wings are purple with bright iridescence.

Abies concolour, the white silver fir, grows best about two thousand feet lower than the magnifica. It is nearly as large, but the branches are less regularly pinnated and whorled, the leaves are longer, and instead of standing out around the branchlets or turning up and clasping them they are mostly arranged in two horizontal or ascending rows, and the cones are less than half as large. The bark of the magnifica is reddish purple and closely furrowed, that of the concolour is grey and widely furrowed – a noble pair, rivalled only by the Abies grandis, amabilis, and nobilis of the forests of Oregon, Washington, and the Northern California Coast Range. But none of these northern species form pure forests that in extent and beauty approach those of the Sierra.

The seeds of the conifers are curiously formed and coloured, white, brown, purple, plain or spotted like birds' eggs, and excepting the juniper they are all handsomely and ingeniously winged with reference to their distribution. They are a sort of cunningly devised flying machine – one-winged birds, birds with but one feather – and they take but one flight, all save those which, after flying from the cone-nest in calm weather, chance to alight on branches where they have to wait for a wind. And though these seed wings are intended for only a moment's use, they are as thoughtfully coloured and fashioned as the wings of birds, and require from one to two seasons to grow. Those of the pine, fir, hemlock and spruce are curved in such manner that, in being dragged through the air by the seeds, they are made to revolve, whirling the seeds in a close spiral, and sustaining them long enough to allow the winds to carry them to considerable distances – a style of flying full of quick merry motion, strikingly contrasted to the sober dignified sailing of seeds on tufts of feathery pappus. Surely no merrier adventurers ever set out to seek their fortunes. Only in the fir woods are large flocks seen; for, unlike the cones of the pine, spruce, hemlock, etc., which let the seeds escape slowly, one or two at a time, by spreading the scales, the fir cones when ripe fall to pieces, and let nearly all go at once in favourable weather. All along the Sierra for hundreds of miles, on dry breezy autumn days, the sunny spaces in the woods among the colossal spires are in a whirl with these shining purple-winged wanderers, notwithstanding the harvesting squirrels have been working at the top of their speed for weeks trying to cut off every cone before the seeds were ready to swarm and fly. Sequoia seeds have flat wings, and glint and glance in their flight like a boy's kite. The dispersal of juniper seeds is effected by the plum and cherry plan of hiring birds at the cost of their board, and thus obtaining the use of a pair of extra good wings.

Above the great fir belt, and below the ragged beds and fringes of the dwarf pine, stretch the broad dark forests of Pinus contorta, var. Murrayana, usually called tamarack pine. On broad fields of moraine material it forms nearly pure forests at an elevation of about eight or nine thousand feet above the sea, where it is a small, well proportioned tree, fifty or sixty feet high and one or two in diameter, with thin grey bark, crooked much-divided straggling branches, short needles in clusters of two, bright yellow and crimson flowers, and small prickly cones. The very largest I ever measured was ninety feet in height, and a little over six feet in diameter four feet above the ground. On moist well-drained soil in sheltered hollows along streamsides it grows tall and slender with ascending branches, making graceful arrowy spires fifty to seventy-five feet high, with stems only five or six inches thick.

The most extensive forest of this pine in the park lies to the north of the Big Tuolumne Meadows – a famous deer pasture and hunting ground of the Mono Indians. For miles over wide moraine beds there is an even, nearly pure growth, broken only by glacier meadows, around which the trees stand in trim array, their sharp spires showing to fine advantage both in green flowery summer and white winter. On account of the closeness of its growth in many places, and the thinness and gumminess of its bark, it is easily killed by running fires, which work widespread destruction on its ranks; but a new generation rises quickly from the ashes, for all or a part of its seeds are held in reserve for a year or two or many years, and when the tree is killed the cones open and the seeds are scattered over the burned ground like those of the attenuata.

Next to the mountain hemlock and the dwarf pine this species best endures burial in heavy show, while in braving hunger and cold on rocky ridgetops it is not surpassed by any. It is distributed from Alaska to Southern California, and inland across the Rocky Mountains, taking many forms in accordance with demands of climate, soil, rivals and enemies; growing patiently in bogs and on sand dunes beside the sea where it is pelted with salt scud, on high snowy mountains and down in the throats of extinct volcanoes; springing up with invincible vigour after every devastating fire and extending its conquests farther.

The sturdy storm-enduring red cedar (*Juniperus occidentalis*) delights to dwell on the tops of granite domes and ridges and glacier pavements of the upper pine belt, at an elevation of seven to ten thousand feet, where it can get plenty of sunshine and snow and elbow-room without encountering quick-growing overshadowing rivals. They never make anything like a forest, seldom come together even in groves, but stand out separate and independent in the wind, clinging by slight joints to the rock, living chiefly on snow and thin air, and maintaining tough health on this diet for two thousand years or more, every feature and gesture expressing steadfast dogged endurance. The largest are usually about six or eight feet in diameter, and fifteen or twenty in height. A very few are ten feet in diameter, and on isolated moraine heaps forty to sixty feet in height. Many are mere stumps, as broad as high, broken by avalanches and lightning, picturesquely tufted with dense grey scalelike foliage, and giving no hint of dying. The staminate flowers are like those of the libocedrus, but smaller; the pistillate are inconspicuous. The wood is red, fine-grained, and fragrant; the bark bright cinnamon and red, and in thrifty trees is strikingly braided and reticulated, flaking off in thin lustrous ribbons, which the Indians used to weave into matting and coarse cloth. These brown unshakable pillars, standing solitary on polished pavements with bossy masses of foliage in their arms, are exceedingly picturesque, and never fail to catch the eye of the artist. They seem sole survivors of some ancient race, wholly unacquainted with their neighbours.

I have spent a good deal of time, trying to determine their age, but on account of dry rot which honeycombs most of the old ones, I never got a complete count of the largest. Some are undoubtedly more than two thousand years old; for though on good moraine soil they grow about as fast as oaks, on bare pavements and smoothly glaciated overswept granite ridges in the dome region they grow extremely slowly. One on the Starr King ridge, only two feet eleven inches in diameter, was eleven hundred and forty years old. Another on the same ridge, only one foot seven and a half inches in diameter, had reached the age of eight hundred and thirty-four years. The first fifteen inches from the bark of a medium-sized tree – six feet in diameter – on the north Tenaya pavement had eight hundred and fifty-nine layers of wood, or fifty-seven to the inch. Beyond this the count was stopped by dry rot and scars of old wounds. The largest I examined was thirty-three feet in girth, or nearly ten in diameter; and though I failed to get anything like a complete count, I learned enough from this and many other specimens to convince me that most of the trees eight to ten feet thick standing on pavements are more than twenty centuries of age rather than less. Barring accidents, for all I can see, they would live forever. When killed, they waste out of existence about as slowly as granite. Even when overthrown by avalanches, after standing so long, they refuse to lie at rest, leaning stubbornly on their big elbows as if anxious to rise, and while a single root holds to the rock putting forth fresh leaves with a grim never-say-die and never-lie-down expression.

As the juniper is the most stubborn and unshakable of trees, the mountain hemlock (*Tsuga Mertensiana*) is the most graceful and pliant and sensitive, responding to the slightest touches of the wind. Until it reaches a height of fifty or sixty feet it is sumptuously clothed down to the ground with drooping branches, which are divided into countless delicate waving sprays, grouped and arranged in most indescribably beautiful ways and profusely sprinkled with handsome brown cones. The flowers also are peculiarly beautiful and effective: the pistillate very dark rich purple; the staminate blue of so fine and pure a tone that the best azure of the high sky seems to be condensed in them.

Though apparently the most delicate and feminine of all the mountain trees, it grows best where the snow lies deepest, at an elevation of from nine thousand to nine thousand and five hundred feet, in hollows on the northern slopes of mountains and ridges. But under all circumstances and conditions of weather and soil, sheltered from the main currents of the winds or in blank exposure to them, well fed or starved, it is always singularly graceful in habit. Even at its highest limit in the park, ten thousand five hundred feet above the sea on exposed ridgetops, where it crouches and huddles close together in low thickets like those of the dwarf pine, it still contrives to put forth its sprays and branches in forms of irrepressible beauty, while on moist well-drained moraines it displays a perfectly tropical luxuriance of foliage, flower, and fruit.

In the first winter storms the snow is often-times soft, and lodges in the dense leafy branches, pressing them down against the trunk, and the slender drooping axis bends lower and lower as the load increases, until the top touches the ground and an ornamental arch is made. Then, as storm succeeds storm and snow is heaped on snow, the whole tree is at last buried, not again to see the light or move leaf or limb until set free by the spring thaws in June or July. Not the young saplings only are thus carefully covered and put to sleep in the whitest of white beds for five or six months of the year, but trees thirty and forty feet high. From April to May, when the snow is compacted, you may ride over the prostrate groves without seeing a single branch or leaf of them. In the autumn they are full of merry life, when Clark crows, squirrels and chipmunks are gathering the abundant crop of seeds while the deer rest beneath the thick concealing branches. The finest grove in the park is near Mount Conness, and the trail from the Tuolumne soda springs to the mountain runs through it. Many of the trees in this grove are three to four or five feet in diameter and about a hundred feet high.

The mountain hemlock is widely distributed from near the south extremity of the High Sierra northward along the Cascade Mountains of Oregon and Washington and the coast ranges of British Columbia to Alaska, where it was first discovered in 1827. Its northmost limit, so far as I have observed, is in the icy fiords of Prince William's Sound in latitude 61°, where it forms pure forests at the level of the sea, growing tall and majestic on the banks of the great glaciers, waving in accord with the mountain winds and the thunder of the falling icebergs. Here as in the Sierra it is ineffably beautiful, the very loveliest evergreen in America.

Of the round-headed dicotyledonous trees in the park the most influential are the black and goldcup oaks. They occur in some parts of the main forest belt, scattered among the big pines like a heavier chaparral, but form extensive groves and reach perfect development only in the Yosemite valleys and flats of the main canyons. The California black oak (*Quercus Californica*) is one of the largest and most beautiful of the Western oaks, attaining under favourable conditions a height of sixty to a hundred feet, with a trunk three to seven feet in diameter, wide-spreading picturesque branches, and smooth lively green foliage handsomely scalloped, purple in the spring, yellow and red in autumn. It grows best in sunny open groves on ground covered with ferns, chokecherry, brier rose, rubus, mints, goldenrods, etc. Few, if any, of the famous oak groves of Europe, however extensive, surpass these in the size and strength and bright, airy beauty of the trees, the colour and fragrance of the vegetation beneath them, the quality of the light that fills their leafy arches, and in the grandeur of the surrounding scenery. The finest grove in the park is in one of the little Yosemite valleys of the Tuolumne Canyon, a few miles above Hetch-Hetchy.

The mountain live-oak, or goldcup oak (*Quercus chrysolepis*), forms extensive groves on earthquake and avalanche taluses and terraces in canyons and Yosemite valleys, from about three to five thousand feet above the sea. In tough, sturdy, unwedgeable strength this is the oak of oaks. In general appearance it resembles the great live-oak of the Southern states. It has pale grey bark, a short, uneven, heavily buttressed trunk which usually divides a few feet above the ground into strong wide-reaching limbs, forming noble arches, and ending in an intricate maze of small branches and sprays, the outer ones frequently drooping in long tresses to the ground like those of the weeping willow, covered with small simple polished leaves, making a canopy broad and bossy, on which the sunshine falls in glorious brightness. The acorn cups are shallow, thick-walled, and covered with yellow fuzzy dust. The flowers appear in May and June with a profusion of pollened tresses, followed by the bronze-coloured young leaves.

No tree in the park is a better measure of altitude. In canyons, at an elevation of four thousand feet, you may easily find a tree six or eight feet in diameter; and at the head of a side canyon, three thousand feet higher, up which you can climb in less than two hours, you find the knotty giant dwarfed to a slender shrub, with leaves like those of huckleberry bushes, still bearing acorns, and seemingly contented, forming dense patches of chaparral, on the top of which you may make your bed and sleep softly like a Highlander in heather. About a thousand feet higher it is still smaller, making fringes about a foot high around boulders and along seams in pavements and the brows of canyons, giving hand-holds here and there on cliffs hard to climb. The largest I have measured were from twenty-five to twenty-seven feet in girth, fifty to sixty feet high, and the spread of the limbs was about double the height.

The principal riverside trees are poplar, alder, willow, broad-leaved maple and Nuttall's flowering dogwood. The poplar (*Populus trichocarpa*), often called balm of Gilead from the gum on its buds, is a tall, stately tree, towering above its companions and gracefully embowering the banks of the main streams at an elevation of about four thousand feet. Its abundant foliage turns bright yellow in the fall, and the Indian-summer sunshine sifts through it in delightful tones over the slow-gliding waters when they are at their lowest ebb.

The flowering dogwood is brighter still in these brooding days, for every branch of its broad head is then a brilliant crimson flame. In the spring, when the streams are in flood, it is the whitest of trees, white as a snow bank with its magnificent flowers four to eight inches in width, making a wonderful show, and drawing swarms of moths and butterflies.

The broad-leaved maple is usually found in the coolest boulder-choked canyons, where the streams are grey and white with foam, over which it spreads its branches in beautiful arches from bank to bank, forming leafy tunnels full of soft green light and spray – favourite homes of the water ousel. Around the glacier lakes, two or three thousand feet higher, the common aspen grows in fringing lines and groves which are brilliantly coloured in autumn, reminding you of the colour glory of the Eastern woods.

Scattered here and there or in groves the botanist will find a few other trees, mostly small – the mountain mahogany, cherry, chestnut-oak, laurel and nutmeg. The California nutmeg (*Tumion Californicum*) is a handsome evergreen, belonging to the yew family, with pale bark, prickly leaves, fruit like a greengage plum and seed like a nutmeg. One of the best groves of it in the park is at the Cascades below Yosemite.

But the noble oaks and all these rock-shading, stream-embowering trees are as nothing amid the vast abounding billowy forests of conifers. During my first years in the Sierra I was ever calling on everybody within reach to admire them, but I found no one half warm enough until Emerson came. I had read his essays, and felt sure that of all men he would best interpret the sayings of these noble mountains and trees. Nor was my faith weakened when I met him in Yosemite. He seemed as serene as a Sequoia, his head in the empyrean; and forgetting his age, plans, duties, ties of every sort, I proposed an immeasurable camping trip back in the heart of the mountains. He seemed anxious to go, but considerately mentioned his party. I said: 'Never mind. The mountains are calling; run away, and let plans and parties and dragging lowland duties all "gang tapsal-teerie". We'll go up a canyon singing your own song, "Good-bye, proud world! I'm going home", in divine earnest. Up there lies a new heaven and a new earth; let us go to the show'. But alas, it was too late – too near the sundown of his life. The shadows were growing long, and he leaned on his friends. His party, full of indoor philosophy, failed to see the natural beauty and fullness of promise of my wild plan, and laughed at it in good-natured ignorance, as if it were necessarily amusing to imagine that Boston people might be led to accept Sierra manifestations of God at the price of rough camping. Anyhow, they would have none of it, and held Mr Emerson to the hotels and trails.

After spending only five tourist days in Yosemite he was led away, but I saw him two days more; for I was kindly invited to go with the party as far as the mariposa big trees. I told Mr Emerson that I would gladly go to the sequoias with him, if he would camp in the grove. He consented heartily, and I felt sure that we would have at least one good wild memorable night around a sequoia camp-fire. Next day we rode through the magnificent forests of the Merced basin, and I kept calling his attention to the sugar pines, quoting his wood-notes, 'Come listen what the pine tree saith', etc., pointing out the noblest as kings and high priests, the most eloquent and commanding preachers of all the mountain forests, stretching forth their century-old arms in benediction over the worshipping congregations crowded about them. He gazed in devout admiration, saying but little, while his fine smile faded away.

Early in the afternoon, when we reached Clark's Station, I was surprised to see the party dismount. And when I asked if we were not going up into the grove to camp they said: 'No; it would never do to lie out in the night air. Mr Emerson might take cold; and you know, Mr Muir, that would be a dreadful thing'. In vain I urged, that only in homes and hotels were colds caught, that nobody ever was known to take cold camping in these woods, that there was not a single cough or sneeze in all the Sierra. Then I pictured the big climate-changing, inspiring fire I would make, praised the beauty and fragrance of sequoia flame, told how the great trees would stand about us transfigured in the purple light, while the stars looked down between the great domes; ending by urging them to come on and make an immortal Emerson night of it. But the house habit was not to be overcome, nor the strange dread of pure night air, though it is only cooled day air with a little dew in it. So the carpet dust and unknowable reeks were preferred. And to think of this being a Boston choice! Sad commentary on culture and the glorious transcendentalism.

Accustomed to reach whatever place I started for, I was going up the mountain alone to camp, and wait the coming of the party next day. But since Emerson was so soon to vanish, I concluded to stop with him. He hardly spoke a word all the evening, yet it was a great pleasure simply to be near him, warming in the light of his face as at a fire. In the morning we rode up the trail through a noble forest of pine and fire into the famous Mariposa Grove, and stayed an hour or two, mostly in ordinary tourist fashion – looking at the biggest giants, measuring them with a tape line, riding through prostrate fire-bored trunks, etc., though Mr Emerson was alone occasionally, sauntering about as if under a spell. As we walked through a fine group, he quoted, 'There were giants in those days', recognizing the antiquity of the race. To commemorate his visit, Mr Galen Clark, the guardian of the grove, selected the finest of the unnamed trees and requested him to give it a name. He named it Samoset, after the New England sachem, as the best that occurred to him.

The poor bit of measured time was soon spent, and while the saddles were being adjusted I again urged Emerson to stay. 'You are yourself a Sequoia,' I said. 'Stop and get acquainted with your big brethren'. But he was past his prime, and was now as a child in the hands of his affectionate but sadly civilized friends, who seemed as full of old-fashioned conformity as of bold intellectual independence. It was the afternoon of the day and the afternoon of his life, and his course was now westward down all the mountains into the sunset. The party mounted and rode away in wondrous contentment, apparently, tracing the trail through ceanothus and dogwood bushes, around the bases of the big trees, up the slope of the sequoia basin, and over the divide. I followed to the edge of the grove. Emerson lingered in the rear of the train, and when he reached the top of the ridge, after all the rest of the party were over and out of sight, he turned his horse, took off his hat and waved me a last good-bye. I felt lonely, so sure had I been that Emerson of all men would be the quickest to see the mountains and sing them. Gazing awhile on the spot where he vanished, I sauntered back into the heart of the grove, made a bed of sequoia plumes and ferns by the side of a stream, gathered a store of firewood, and then walked about until sundown. The birds, robins, thrushes, warblers, etc., that had kept out of sight, came about me, now that all was quiet, and made cheer. After sundown I built a great fire, and as usual had it all to myself. And though lonesome for the first time in these forests, I quickly took heart again – the trees had not gone to Boston, nor the birds; and as I sat by the fire, Emerson was still with me in spirit, though I never again saw him in the flesh. He sent books and wrote, cheering me on; advised me not to stay too long in solitude. Soon he hoped that my guardian angel would intimate that my probation was at a close. Then I was to roll up my herbariums, sketches and poems (though I never knew I had any poems), and come to his house; and when I tired of him and his humble surroundings, he would show me to better people.

But there remained many a forest to wander through, many a mountain and glacier to cross, before I was to see his Wachusett and Monadnock, Boston and Concord. It was seventeen years after our parting on the Wawona ridge that I stood beside his grave under a pine tree on the hill above Sleepy Hollow. He had gone to higher Sierras, and, as I fancied, was again waving his hand in friendly recognition.

CHAPTER FIVE

The Wild Gardens of the Yosemite Park

WHEN CALIFORNIA was wild, it was the floweriest part of the continent. And perhaps it is so still, nothwithstanding the lowland flora has in great part vanished before the farmers' flocks and ploughs. So exuberant was the bloom of the main valley of the state, it would still have been extravagantly rich had ninety-nine out of every hundred of its crowded flowers been taken away – far flowerier than the beautiful prairies of Illinois and Wisconsin, or the savannas of the Southern states. In the early spring it was a smooth, evenly planted sheet of purple and gold, one mass of bloom more than four hundred miles long, with scarce a green leaf in sight.

Still more interesting is the rich and wonderfully varied flora of the mountains. Going up the Sierra across the Yosemite Park to the Summit peaks, thirteen thousand feet high, you find as much variety in the vegetation as in the scenery. Change succeeds change with bewildering rapidity, for in a few days you pass through as many climates and floras, ranged one above another, as you would in walking along the lowlands to the Arctic Ocean.

And to the variety due to climate there is added that caused by the topographical features of the different regions. Again, the vegetation is profoundly varied by the peculiar distribution of the soil and moisture. Broad and deep moraines, ancient and well weathered, are spread over the lower regions, rough and comparatively recent and unweathered moraines over the middle and upper regions, alternating with bare ridges and domes and glacier-polished pavements, the highest in the icy recesses of the peaks, raw and shifting, some of them being still in process of formation, and of course scarcely planted as yet.

Besides these main soilbeds there are many others comparatively small, reformations of both glacial and weather soils, sifted, sorted out, and deposited by running water and the wind on gentle slopes and in all sorts of hollows, potholes, valleys, lake basins, etc. – some in dry and breezy situations, others sheltered and kept moist by lakes, streams, and waftings of waterfall spray, making comfortable homes for plants widely varied. In general, glaciers give soil to high and low places almost alike, while water currents are dispensers of special blessings, constantly tending to make the ridges poorer and the valleys richer. Glaciers mingle all kinds of material together, mud particles and boulders fifty feet in diameter: water, whether in oozing currents or passionate torrents, discriminates both in the size and shape of the material it carries. Glacier mud is the finest meal ground for any use in the Park, and its transportation into lakes and as foundations for flowery garden meadows was the first work that the young rivers were called on to do. Bogs occur only in shallow alpine basins where the climate is cool enough for sphagnum, and where the surrounding topographical conditions are such that they are safe, even in the most copious rains and thaws, from the action of flood currents capable of carrying rough gravel and sand, but where the water supply is nevertheless constant. The mosses dying from year to year gradually give rise to those rich spongy peat-beds in which so many of our best alpine plants delight to dwell. The strong winds that occasionally sweep the High Sierra play a more important part in the distribution of special soil-beds than is at first sight recognized, carrying forward considerable quantities of sand and gravel, flakes of mica, etc., and depositing them in fields and beds beautifully ruffled and embroidered and adapted to the wants of some of the hardiest and handsomest of the alpine shrubs and flowers. The more resisting of the smooth, solid, glacier-polished domes and ridges can hardly be said to have any soil at all, while others beginning to give way to the weather are thinly sprinkled with coarse angular gravel. Some of them are full of crystals, which as the surface of the rock is decomposed are set free, covering the summits and rolling down the sides in minute avalanches, giving rise to zones and beds of crystalline soil. In some instances the various crystals occur only here and there, sprinkled in the grey gravel like daisies in a sod; but in others half or more is made up of crystals, and the glow of the imbedded or loosely strewn gems and their coloured gleams and glintings at different times of the day when the sun is shining might well exhilarate the flowers that grow among them, and console them for being so completely outshone.

These radiant sheets and belts and dome-encircling rings of crystals are the most beautiful of all the Sierra soil-beds, while the huge taluses ranged along the walls of the great canyons are the deepest and roughest. Instead of being slowly weathered and accumulated from the cliffs overhead like common taluses, they were all formed suddenly and simultaneously by an earthquake that occurred at least three centuries ago. Though thus hurled into existence at a single effort, they are the least changeable and destructible of all the soil formations in the range. Excepting those which were launched directly into the channels of rivers, scarcely one of their wedged and interlocked boulders has been moved since the day of their creation, and though mostly made up of huge angular blocks of granite, many of them from ten to fifty feet cube, trees and shrubs make out to live and thrive on them, and even delicate herbaceous plants – draperia, collomia, zauschneria, etc. – soothing their rugged features with gardens and groves. In general views of the Park scarce a hint is given of its floral wealth. Only by patiently, lovingly sauntering about in it will you discover that it is all more or less flowery, the forests as well as the open spaces, and the mountain tops and rugged slopes around the glaciers as well as the sunny meadows.

Even the majestic canyon cliffs, seemingly absolutely flawless for thousands of feet and necessarily doomed to eternal sterility, are cheered with happy flowers on invisible niches and ledges wherever the slightest grip for a root can be found; as if Nature, like an enthusiastic gardener, could not resist the temptation to plant flowers everywhere. On high, dry rocky summits and plateaus, most of the plants are so small they make but little show even when in bloom. But in the opener parts of the main forests, the meadows, stream banks, and the level floors of Yosemite valleys the vegetation is exceedingly rich in flowers, some of the lilies and larkspurs being from eight to ten feet high. And on the upper meadows there are miles of blue gentians and daisies, white and blue violets; and great breadths of rosy purple heathworts covering rocky moraines with a marvellous abundance of bloom, enlivened by humming-birds, butterflies and a host of other insects as beautiful as flowers. In the lower and middle regions, also, many of the most extensive beds of bloom are in great part made by shrubs – adenostoma, manzanita, ceanothus, chamæbatia, cherry, rose, rubus, spiræa, shad, laurel, azalea, honeysuckle, calycanthus, ribes, philadelphus, and many others, the sunny spaces about them bright and fragrant with mints, lupines, geraniums, lilies, daisies, goldenrods, castilleias, gilias, pentstemons, etc.

Adenostoma fasciculatum is a handsome, hardy, heathlike shrub belonging to the rose family, flourishing on dry ground below the pine belt, and often covering areas of twenty or thirty square miles of rolling sun-beaten hills and dales with a dense, dark green, almost impenetrable chaparral, which in the distance looks like Scotch heather. It is about six to eight feet high, has slender elastic branches, red shreddy bark, needle-shaped leaves, and small white flowers in panicles about a foot long, making glorious sheets of fragrant bloom in the spring. To running fires it offers no resistance, vanishing with the few other flowery shrubs and vines and liliaceous plants that grow with it about as fast as dry grass, leaving nothing but ashes. But with wonderful vigour it rises again and again in fresh beauty from the root, and calls back to its hospitable mansions the multitude of wild animals that had to flee for their lives.

As soon as you enter the pine woods you meet the charming little chamæbatia foliolosa, one of the handsomest of the Park shrubs, next in fineness and beauty to the heathworts of the alpine regions. Like adenostoma it belongs to the rose family, is from twelve to eighteen inches high, has brown bark, slender branches, white flowers like those of the strawberry, and thrice-pinnate glandular, yellow-green leaves, finely cut and fernlike, as if unusual pains had been taken in fashioning them. Where there is plenty of sunshine at an elevation of three thousand to six thousand feet, it makes a close, continuous growth, leaf touching leaf over hundreds of acres, spreading a handsome mantle beneath the yellow and sugar pines. Here and there a lily rises above it, an arching bunch of tall bromus, and at wide intervals a rosebush or clump of ceanothus or manzanita, but there are no rough weeds mixed with it – no roughness of any sort.

Perhaps the most widely distributed of all the Park shrubs and of the Sierra in general, certainly the most strikingly characteristic, are the many species of manzanita (*Arctostaphylos*). Though one species, the uva-ursa, or bearberry – the kinikinic of the Western Indians – extends around the world, the greater part of them are Californian. They are mostly from four to ten feet high, round-headed, with innumerable branches, brown or red bark, pale green leaves set on edge, and a rich profusion of small, pink, narrow-thoated, urn-shaped flowers like those of arbutus. The branches are knotty, zigzaggy and about as rigid as bones, and the bark is so thin and smooth, both trunk and branches seem to be naked, looking as if they had been peeled, polished and painted red. The wood also is red, hard and heavy.

These grand bushes seldom fail to engage the attention of the traveller and hold it, especially if he has to pass through closely planted fields of them such as grow on moraine slopes at an elevation of about seven thousand feet, and in canyons choked with earthquake boulders; for they make the most uncompromisingly stubborn of all chaparral. Even bears take pains to go around the stoutest patches if possible, and when compelled to force a passage leave tufts of hair and broken branches to mark their way, while less skilful mountaineers under like circumstances sometimes lose most of their clothing and all their temper.

The manzanitas like sunny ground. On warm ridges and sandy flats at the foot of sun-beaten canyon cliffs, some of the tallest specimens have well-defined trunks six inches to a foot or more thick, and stand apart in orchard-like growths which in bloomtime are among the finest garden sights in the

Park. The largest I ever saw had a round, slightly fluted trunk nearly four feet in diameter, which at a height of only eighteen inches from the ground dissolved into a wilderness of branches, rising and spreading to a height and width of about twelve feet. In spring every bush over all the mountains is covered with rosy flowers, in autumn with fruit. The red pleasantly acid berries, about the size of peas, are like little apples, and the hungry mountaineer is glad to eat them, though half their bulk is made up of hard seeds. Indians, bears, coyotes, foxes, birds and other mountain people live on them for months.

Associated with manzanita there are six or seven species of ceanothus, flowery, fragrant, and altogether delightful shrubs, growing in glorious abundance in the forests on sunny or half-shaded ground, up to an elevation of about nine thousand feet above the sea. In the sugar-pine woods the most beautiful species is C. integerrimus, often called California lilac, or deer brush. It is five or six feet high, smooth, slender, willowy, with bright foliage and abundance of blue flowers in close, showy panicles. Two species, prostatus and procumbens, spread handsome blue-flowered mats and rugs on warm ridges beneath the pines, and offer delightful beds to the tired mountaineers. The commonest species, C. cordulatus, is mostly restricted to the silver fir belt. It is white-flowered and thorny, and makes extensive thickets of tangled chaparral, far too dense to wade through, and too deep and loose to walk on, though it is pressed flat every winter by ten or fifteen feet of snow.

Above these thorny beds, sometimes mixed with them, a very wild, red-fruited cherry grows in magnificent tangles, fragrant and white as snow when in bloom. The fruit is small and rather bitter, not so good as the black, puckery chokecherry that grows in the canyons, but thrushes, robins, chipmunks like it. Below the cherry tangles, chinquapin and goldcup oak spread generous mantles of chaparral, and with hazel and ribes thickets in adjacent glens help to clothe and adorn the rocky wilderness, and produce food for the many mouths Nature has to fill. Azalea occidentalis is the glory of cool streams and meadows. It is from two to five feet high, has bright green leaves and a rich profusion of large, fragrant white and yellow flowers, which are in prime beauty in June, July and August, according to the elevation (from three thousand to six thousand feet). Only the purple-flowered rhododendron of the redwood forests rivals or surpasses it in superb abounding bloom.

Back a little way from the azalea-bordered streams, a small wild rose makes thickets, often several acres in extent, deliciously fragrant on dewy mornings and after showers, the fragrance mingled with the music of birds nesting in them. And not far from these rose gardens rubus nutkanus covers the ground with broad velvety leaves and pure white flowers as large as those of its neighbour the rose, and finer in texture; followed at the end of summer by soft red berries good for bird and beast and man also. This is the commonest and the most beautiful of the whole blessed flowery fruity genus.

The glory of the alpine region in bloomtime are the heathworts, cassiope, bryanthus, kalmia and vaccinium, enriched here and there by the alpine honeysuckle, Lonicera conjugialis, and by the purple-flowered primula suffruticosa, the only primrose discovered in California, and the only shrubby species in the genus. The lowly, hardy, adventurous cassiope has exceedingly slender creeping branches, scalelike leaves, and pale pink or white waxen bell flowers. Few plants, large or small, so well endure hard weather and rough ground over so great a range. In July it spreads a wavering, interrupted belt of the loveliest bloom around glacier lakes and meadows and across wild moory expanses, between roaring streams, all along the Sierra, and northward beneath cold skies by way of the mountain chains of Oregon, Washington, British Columbia and Alaska, to the Arctic regions; gradually descending, until at the north end of the continent it reaches the level of the sea; blooming as profusely and at about the same time on mossy frozen tundras as on the High Sierra moraines.

Bryanthus, the companion of cassiope, accompanies it as far north as southeastern Alaska, where together they weave thick plushy beds on rounded mountain tops above the glaciers. It grows mostly at slightly lower elevations; the upper margin of what may be called the bryanthus belt in the Sierra uniting with and overlapping the lower margin of the cassiope. The wide bell-shaped flowers are bright purple, about three fourths of an inch in diameter, hundreds to the square yard, the young branches, mostly erect, being covered with them. No Highlander in heather enjoys more luxurious rest than the Sierra mountaineer in a bed of blooming bryanthus. And imagine the show on calm dewy mornings, when there is a radiant globe in the throat of every flower, and smaller gems on the needle-shaped leaves, the sunbeams pouring through them.

In the same wild, cold region the tiny vaccinium myrtillus, mixed with kalmia and dwarf willows, spreads thinner carpets, the downpressed matted leaves profusely sprinkled with pink bells; and on higher sandy slopes you will find several alpine species of eriogonum with gorgeous bossy masses of yellow bloom, and the lovely Arctic daisy with many blessed companions; charming plants, gentle mountaineers, Nature's darlings, which seem always the finer the higher and stormier their homes.

Many interesting ferns are distributed over the Park from the foothills to a little above the timber line. The greater number are rock ferns, pellæa, cheilanthes, polypodium, adiantum, woodsia, cryptogramme, etc., with small tufted fronds, lining glens and gorges and fringing the cliffs and moraines. The most important of the larger species are woodwardia, aspidium, asplenium, and the common pteris. Woodwardia radicans is a superb fern five to eight feet high, growing in vaselike clumps where the ground is level, and on slopes in a regular thatch, frond over frond, like shingles on a roof. Its range in the Park is from the western boundary up to about five thousand feet, mostly on benches of the north walls of canyons watered by small outspread streams. It is far more abundant in the Coast Mountains beneath the noble redwoods, where it attains a height of ten to twelve feet. The aspidiums are mostly restricted to the moist parts of the lower forests, asplenium filix-fœ-mina to marshy streams. The hardy, broad-shouldered pteris aquilina, the commonest of ferns, grows tall and graceful on sunny flats and hillsides, at elevations between three thousand and six thousand feet. Those who know it only in the Eastern states can form no fair conception of its stately beauty in the sunshine of the Sierra. On the level sandy floors of Yosemite valleys it often attains a height of six to eight feet in fields thirty or forty acres in extent, the magnificent fronds outspread in a nearly horizontal position, forming a ceiling beneath which one may walk erect in delightful mellow shade. No other fern does so much for the colour glory of autumn, with its browns and reds and yellows changing and interblending. Even after lying dead all winter beneath the snow it spreads a lively brown mantle over the desolate ground, until the young fronds with a noble display of faith and hope come rolling up into the light through the midst of the beautiful ruins. A few weeks suffice for their development, then, gracefully poised each in its place, they manage themselves in every exigency of weather as if they had passed through a long course of training. I have seen solemn old sugar pines thrown into momentary confusion by the sudden onset of a storm, tossing their arms excitedly as if scarce awake, and wondering what had happened, but I never noticed surprise or embarrassment in the behaviour of this noble pteris.

Of five species of pellæa in the Park, the handsome andromedæfolia, growing in brushy foothills with adiantum emarginatum, is the largest. P. breweri, the hardiest and at the same time the most fragile of the genus, grows in dense tufts among rocks on storm-beaten mountain sides along the upper margin of the fern line. It is a charming little fern, four or five inches high, has shining bronze-coloured stalks which are about as brittle as glass, and pale green pinnate fronds. Its companions on the lower part of its range are cryptogramme acrostichoides and phegopteris alpestris, the latter soft and tender, not at all like a rock fern, though it grows on rocks where the snow lies longest. P. bridgesii, with blue-green, narrow, simply pinnate fronds, is about the same size as breweri and ranks next to it as a mountaineer, growing in fissures and around boulders on glacier pavements. About a thousand feet lower we find the smaller and more abundant P. densa, on ledges and boulder-strewn fissured pavements, watered until late in summer by oozing currents from snow-banks or thin outspread streams from moraines, growing in close sods – its little bright green triangular tripinnate fronds, about an inch in length, as innumerable as leaves of grass. P. ornithopus has twice or thrice pinnate fronds, is dull in colour, and dwells on hot rocky hillsides among chaparral.

Three species of cheilanthes – Californica, gracillima and myriophylla, with beautiful two to four pinnate fronds, an inch to five inches long, adorn the stupendous walls of the canyons, however dry and sheer. The exceedingly delicate and interesting Californica is rare, the others abundant at from three thousand to seven thousand feet elevation, and are often accompanied by the little gold fern, gymnogramme triangularis, and rarely by the curious little botrychium simplex, the smallest of which are less than an inch high.

The finest of all the rock ferns is *Adiantum pedatum*, lover of waterfalls and the lightest waftings of irised spray. No other Sierra fern is so constant a companion of white spray-covered streams, or tells so well their wild thundering music. The homes it loves best are cave-like hollows beside the main falls, where it can float its plumes on their dewy breath, safely sheltered from the heavy spray-laden blasts. Many of these moss-lined chambers, so cool, so moist, and brightly coloured with rainbow light, contain thousands of these happy ferns, clinging to the emerald walls by the slightest holds, reaching out the most wonderfully delicate fingered fronds on dark glossy stalks, sensitive, tremulous, all alive, in an attitude of eager attention; throbbing in unison with every motion and tone of the resounding waters, compliant to their faintest impulses, moving each division of the frond separately at times as if fingering the music, playing on invisible keys.

Considering the lilies as you go up the mountains, the first you come to is L. pardalinum, with large orange-yellow, purple-spotted flowers big enough for babies' bonnets. It is seldom found higher than thirty-five hundred feet above the sea, grows in magnificent groups of fifty to a hundred or more, in romantic waterfall dells in the pine woods shaded by overarching maple and willow, alder and dogwood, with bushes in front of the embowering trees for a border, and ferns and sedges in front of the bushes; while the bed of black humus in which the bulbs are set is carpeted with mosses and liverworts. These richly furnished lily gardens are the pride of the falls on the lower tributaries of the Tuolumne and Merced Rivers, falls not like those of Yosemite valleys – coming from the sky with rock-shaking thunder tones – but small, with low, kind voices cheerily singing in calm leafy bowers, self-contained, keeping their snowy skirts well about them, yet furnishing plenty of spray for the lilies.

The Washington lily (*L. Washingtonianum*) is white, deliciously fragrant, moderate in size, with three to ten flowered racemes. The largest I ever measured was eight feet high, the raceme two feet long, with fifty-two flowers, fifteen of them open; the others had faded or were still in the bud. This famous lily is distributed over the sunny portions of the sugar-pine woods, never in large garden companies like pardalinum, but widely scattered, standing up to the waist in dense ceanothus and manzanita chaparral, waving its lovely flowers above the blooming wilderness of brush, and giving their fragrance to the breeze. These stony, thorny jungles are about the last places in the mountains in which one would look for lilies. But though they toil not nor spin, like other people under adverse circumstances, they have to do the best they can. Because their large bulbs are good to eat they are dug up by Indians and bears; therefore, like hunted animals, they seek refuge in the chaparral, where among the boulders and tough tangled roots they are comparatively safe. This is the favourite Sierra lily, and it is now growing in all the best parks and gardens of the world.

The showiest gardens in the Park lie embedded in the silver fir forests on the top of the main dividing ridges or hang like gaily coloured scarfs down their sides. Their wet places are in great part taken up by veratrum, a robust broad-leaved plant determined to be seen, and habenaria and spiranthes; the drier parts by tall columbines, larkspurs, castilleias, lupines, hosackias, erigerons, valerian, etc., standing deep in grass, with violets here and there around the borders. But the finest feature of these forest gardens is lilium parvum. It varies greatly in size, the tallest being from six to nine feet high, with splendid racemes of ten to fifty small orange-coloured flowers, which rock and wave with great dignity above the other flowers in the infrequent winds that fall over the protecting wall of trees. Though rather frail-looking it is strong, reaching prime vigour and beauty eight thousand feet above the sea, and in some places venturing as high as eleven thousand.

Calochortus, or Mariposa tulip, is a unique genus of many species confined to the California side of the continent; charming plants, somewhat resembling the tulips of Europe, but far finer. The richest calochortus region lies below the western boundary of the Park; still five or six species are included. C. Nuttallii is common on moraines in the forests of the two-leaved pine; and C. cæruleus and nudus, very slender, lowly species, may be found in moist garden spots near Yosemite. C. albus, with pure white flowers, growing in shady places among the foothill shrubs, is, I think, the very loveliest of all the lily family – a spotless soul, plant saint, that everyone must love and so be made better. It puts the wildest mountaineer on his good behaviour. With this plant the whole world would seem rich though none other existed. Next after calochortus, broadiæa is the most interesting genus. Nearly all the many species have beautiful showy heads of blue, lilac, and yellow flowers, enriching the gardens of the lower pine region. Other liliaceous plants likely to attract attention are the blue-flowered camassia, the bulbs of which are prized as food by Indians; fritillaria, smilacina, chloragalum, and the twining climbing stropholirion.

The common orchidaceous plants are corallorhiza, goodyera, spiranthes, and habenaria. Cypripedium montanum, the only moccasin flower I have seen in the Park, is a handsome, thoughtful-looking plant living beside cool brooks. The large oval lip is white, delicately veined with purple; the other petals and sepals purple, strap-shaped, and elegantly curved and twisted.

To tourists the most attractive of all the flowers of the forest is the snow plant (*Sarcodes sanguinea*). It is a bright red, fleshy, succulent pillar that pushes up through the dead needles in the pine and fir woods like a gigantic asparagus shoot. The first intimation of its coming is a loosening and upbulging of the brown stratum of decomposed needles on the forest floor, in the cracks of which you notice fiery gleams; presently a blunt dome-shaped head an inch or two in diameter appears, covered with closely imbricated scales and bracts. In a week or so it grows to a height of six to twelve inches. Then the long fringed bracts spread and curl aside, allowing the twenty or thirty five-lobed bell-shaped flowers to open and look straight out from the fleshy axis. It is said to grow up through the snow; on the contrary it always waits until the ground is warm, though with other early flowers it is occasionally buried or half buried for a day or two by spring storms. The entire plant – flowers, bracts, stem, scales and roots – is red. But notwithstanding its glowing colour and beautiful flowers, it is singularly unsympathetic and cold. Everybody admires it as a wonderful curiosity, but nobody loves it. Without fragrance, rooted in decaying vegetable matter, it stands beneath the pines and firs lonely, silent, and about as rigid as a graveyard monument.

Down in the main canyons adjoining the azalea and rose gardens there are fine beds of herbaceous plants – tall mints and sunflowers, iris, œnothera, broadiæa, and bright beds of erythræa on the ferny meadows. Bolandera, sedum, and airy, feathery, purple-flowered heuchera adorn mossy nooks near falls, the shading trees wreathed and festooned with wild grapevines and clematis; while lightly shaded flats are covered with gilia and eunanus of many species, hosackia, arnica, chænactis, gayophytum, gnaphalium, monardella, etc.

Thousands of the most interesting gardens in the Park are never seen, for they are small and lie far up on ledges and terraces of the sheer canyon walls, wherever a strip of soil, however narrow and shallow, can rest. The birds, winds and down-washing rains have planted them with all sorts of hardy mountain flowers, and where there is sufficient moisture they flourish in profusion. Many of them are watered by little streams that seem lost on the tremendous precipices, clinging to the face of the rock in lacelike strips, and dripping from ledge to ledge, too silent to be called falls, pathless wanderers from the upper meadows, which for centuries have been seeking a way down to the rivers they belong to, without having worn as yet any appreciable channel, mostly evaporated or given to the plants they meet before reaching the foot of the cliffs. To these unnoticed streams the finest of the cliff gardens owe their luxuriance and freshness of beauty. In the larger ones ferns and showy flowers flourish in wonderful profusion – woodwardia, columbine, collomia, castilleia, draperia, geranium, erythræa, pink and scarlet mimulus, hosackia, saxifrage, sunflowers and daisies, with azalea, spiræa and calycanthus, a few specimens of each that seem to have been culled from the large gardens above and beneath them. Even lilies are occasionally found in these irrigated cliff gardens, swinging their bells over the giddy precipices, seemingly as happy as their relatives down in the waterfall dells. Most of the cliff gardens, however, are dependent on summer showers, and though from the shallowness of the soil beds they are often dry, they still display a surprising number of bright flowers – scarlet zauschneria, purple bush pentstemon, mints, gilias, and bosses of glowing golden bahia. Nor is there any lack of commoner plants; the homely yarrow is often found in them, and sweet clover and honeysuckle for the bees.

In the upper canyons, where the walls are inclined at so low an angle that they are loaded with moraine material, through which perennial streams percolate in broad diffused currents, there are long wavering garden beds, that seem to be descending through the forest like cascades, their fluent lines suggesting motion, swaying from side to side of the forested banks, surging up here and there over island-like boulder piles, or dividing and flowing around them. In some of these floral cascades the vegetation is chiefly sedges and grasses ruffled with willows; in others, showy flowers like those of the lily gardens on the main divides. Another curious and picturesque series of wall gardens are made by thin streams that ooze slowly from moraines and slip gently over smooth glaciated slopes. From particles of sand and mud they carry, a pair of lobe-shaped sheets of soil an inch or two thick are gradually formed, one of them hanging down from the brow of the slope, the other leaning up from the foot of it, like stalactite and stalagmite, the soil being held together by the flowery, moisture-loving plants growing in it.

Along the rocky parts of the canyon bottoms between lake basins, where the streams flow fast over glacier-polished granite, there are rows of pothole gardens full of ferns, daisies, goldenrods, and other common plants of the neighbourhood nicely arranged like bouquets, and standing out in telling relief on the bare shining rock banks. And all the way up the canyons to the Summit mountains, wherever there is soil of any sort, there is no lack of flowers, however short the summer may be. Within eight or ten feet of a snow bank lingering beneath a shadow, you may see belated ferns unrolling their fronds in September, and sedges hurrying up their brown spikes on ground that has been free from snow only eight or ten days, and likely to be covered again within a few weeks; the winter in the coolest of these shadow gardens being about eleven months long, while spring, summer and autumn are hurried and crowded into one month. Again, under favourable conditions, alpine gardens three or four thousand feet higher than the last are in their prime in June. Between the Summit peaks at the head of the canyons surprising effects are produced where the sunshine falls direct on rocky slopes and reverberates among boulders. Toward the end of August, in one of these natural hothouses on the north shore of a glacier lake 11,500 feet above the sea, I found a luxuriant growth of hairy lupines, thistles, goldenrods, shrubby potentilla, spraguea and the mountain epilobium with thousands of purple flowers an inch wide, while the opposite shore, at a distance of only three hundred yards, was bound in heavy avalanche snow – flowery summer on one side, winter on the other. And I know a bench garden on the north wall of Yosemite in which a few flowers are in bloom all winter; the massive rocks about it storing up sunshine enough in summer to melt the snow about as fast as it falls. When tired of the confinement of my cabin I used to camp out in it in January, and never failed to find flowers, and butterflies also, except during snowstorms and a few days after.

From Yosemite one can easily walk in a day to the top of Mount Hoffman, a massive grey mountain that rises in the centre of the Park, with easy slopes adorned with castellated piles and crests on the south side, rugged precipices banked with perpetual snow on the north. Most of the broad summit is comparatively level and smooth, and covered with crystals of quartz, mica, hornblende, feldspar, garnet, zircon, tourmaline, etc., weathered out and strewn loosely as if sown broadcast; their radiance so dazzling in some places as to fairly hide the multitude of small flowers that grow among them; myriads of keen lance rays infinitely fine, white or coloured, making an almost continuous glow over all the ground, with here and there throbbing, spangling lilies of light, on the larger gems. At first sight only these crystal sunflowers are noticed, but looking closely you discover minute gilias, ivesias, eunanus, phloxes, etc., in thousands, showing more petals than leaves; and larger plants in hollows and on the borders of rills – lupines, potentillas, daisies, harebells, mountain columbine, astragalus, fringed with heathworts. You wander about from garden to garden enchanted, as if walking among stars, gathering the brightest gems, each and all apparently doing their best with eager enthusiasm, as if everything depended on faithful shining; and considering the flowers basking in the glorious light, many of them looking like swarms of small moths and butterflies that were resting after long dances in the sunbeams. Now your attention is called to colonies of woodchucks and pikas, the mounds in front of their burrows glittering like heaps of jewellery – romantic ground to live in or die in. Now you look abroad over the vast round landscape bounded by the down-curving sky, nearly all the Park in it displayed like a map – forests, meadows, lakes, rock waves and snowy mountains. Northward lies the basin of Yosemite Creek, paved with bright domes and lakes like larger crystals; eastward, the meadowy, billowy Tuolumne region and the Summit peaks in glorious array; southward, Yosemite; and westward, the boundless forests. On no other mountain that I know of are you more likely to linger. It is a magnificent camp ground. Clumps of dwarf pine furnish rosiny roots and branches for fuel, and the rills pure water. Around your camp fire the flowers seem to be looking eagerly at the light, and the crystals shine unweariedly, making fine company as you lie at rest in the very heart of the vast, serene, majestic night.

The finest of the glacier meadow gardens lie at an elevation of about nine thousand feet, embedded in the upper pine forests like lakes of light. They are smooth and level, a mile or two long, and the rich, well-drained ground is completely covered with a soft, silky, plushy sod enamelled with flowers, not one of which is in the least weedy or coarse. In some places the sod is so crowded with showy flowers that the grasses are scarce noticed, in others they are rather sparingly scattered; while every leaf and flower seems to have its winged representative in the swarms of happy flower-like insects that enliven the air above them.

With the winter snowstorms wings and petals are folded, and for more than half the year the meadows are snow-buried ten or fifteen feet deep. In June they begin to thaw out, small patches of the dead sloppy sod appear, gradually increasing in size until they are free and warm again, face to face with the sky; myriads of growing points push through the steaming mould, frogs sing cheeringly, soon joined by the birds, and the merry insects come back as if suddenly raised from the dead. Soon the ground is green with mosses and liverworts and dotted with small fungi, making the first crop of the season. Then the grass leaves weave a new sod, and the exceedingly slender panicles rise above it like a purple mist, speedily followed by potentilla, ivesia, bossy orthocarpus, yellow and purple, and a few pentstemons. Later come the daisies and goldenrods, asters and gentians. Of the last there are three species, small and fine, with varying tones of blue, and in glorious abundance, colouring extensive patches where the sod is shallowest. Through the midst flows a stream only two or three feet wide, silently gliding as if careful not to disturb the hushed calm of the solitude, its banks embossed by the common sod bent down to the water's edge, and trimmed with mosses and violets; slender grass panicles lean over like miniature pine trees, and here and there on the driest places small mats of heathworts are neatly spread, enriching without roughening the bossy down-curling sod. In spring and summer the weather is mostly crisp, exhilarating sunshine, though magnificent mountain ranges of cumuli are often upheaved about noon, their shady hollows tinged with purple ineffably fine, their snowy sun-beaten bosses glowing against the sky, casting cooling shadows for an hour or two, then dissolving in a quick washing rain. But for days in succession there are no clouds at all, or only faint wisps and pencillings scarcely discernible.

Toward the end of August the sunshine grows hazy, announcing the coming of Indian summer, the outlines of the landscapes are softened and mellowed, and more and more plainly are the mountains clothed with light, white tinged with pale purple, richest in the morning and evening. The warm, brooding days are full of life and thoughts of life to come, ripening seeds with next summer in them or a hundred summers. The nights are unspeakably impressive and calm; frost crystals of wondrous beauty grow on the grass – each carefully planned and finished as if intended to endure forever. The sod becomes yellow and brown, but the late asters and gentians, carefully closing their flowers at night, do not seem to feel the frost; no nipped, wilted plants of any kind are to be seen; even the early snowstorms fail to blight them. At last the precious seeds are ripe, all the work of the season is done, and the sighing pines tell the coming of winter and rest.

Ascending the range you find that many of the higher meadows slope considerably, from the amount of loose material washed into their basins; and sedges and rushes are mixed with the grasses or take their places, though all are still more or less flowery and bordered with heathworts, sibbaldea, and dwarf willows. Here and there you come to small bogs, the wettest smooth and adorned with parnassia and buttercups, others tussocky and ruffled like bits of Arctic tundra, their mosses and lichens interwoven with dwarf shrubs. On boulder piles the red iridescent oxyria abounds, and on sandy, gravelly slopes several species of shrubby, yellow-flowered eriogonum, some of the plants, less than a foot high, being very old, a century or more, as is shown by the rings made by the annual whorls of leaves on the big roots. Above these flower-dotted slopes the grey, savage wilderness of crags and peaks seems lifeless and bare. Yet all the way up to the tops of the highest mountains, commonly supposed to be covered with eternal snow, there are bright garden spots crowded with flowers, their warm colours calling to mind the sparks and jets of fire on polar volcanoes rising above a world of ice. The principal mountain-top plants are phloxes, drabas, saxifrages, silene, cymopterus, hulsea, and polemonium, growing in detached stripes and mats – the highest steaks and splashes of the summer wave as it breaks against those wintry heights. The most beautiful are the phloxes (douglasii and cæspitosum), and the red-flowered silene, with innumerable flowers hiding the leaves. Though herbaceous plants, like the trees and shrubs, are dwarfed as they ascend, two of these mountain dwellers, hulsea algida and polemonium confertum, are notable exceptions. The yellow-flowered hulsea is eight to twelve inches high, stout, erect – the leaves, three to six inches long, secreting a rosiny, fragrant gum, standing up boldly on the grim lichen-stained crags, and never looking in the least tired or discouraged. Both the ray and disk flowers are yellow; the heads are nearly two inches wide, and are eagerly sought for by roving bee mountaineers. The polemonium is quite as luxuriant and tropical-looking as its companion, about the same height, glandular, fragrant, its blue flowers closely packed in eight or ten heads, twenty to forty in a head. It is never far from hulsea, growing at elevations of between eleven and thirteen thousand feet wherever a little hollow or crevice favourably situated with a handful of wind-driven soil can be found.

From these frosty Arctic sky gardens you may descend in one straight swoop to the abronia, mentzelia, and œnothera gardens of Mono, where the sunshine is warm enough for palms.

But the greatest of all the gardens is the belt of forest trees, profusely covered in the spring with blue and purple, red and yellow blossoms, each tree with a gigantic panicle of flowers fifty to a hundred feet long. Yet strange to say they are seldom noticed. Few travel through the woods when they are in bloom, the flowers of some of the showiest species opening before the snow is off the ground. Nevertheless, one would think the news of such gigantic flowers would quickly spread, and travellers from all the world would make haste to the show. Eager inquiries are made for the bloomtime of rhododendron-covered mountains and for the bloomtime of Yosemite streams, that they may be enjoyed in their prime; but the far grander outburst of tree bloom covering a thousand mountains – who inquires about that? That the pistillate flowers of the pines and firs should escape the eyes of careless lookers is less to be wondered at, since they mostly grow aloft on the topmost branches, and can hardly be seen from the foot of the trees. Yet even these make a magnificent show from the top of an overlooking ridge when the sunbeams are pouring through them. But the far more numerous staminate flowers of the pines in large rosy clusters, and those of the silver firs in countless thousands on the under side of the branches, cannot be hid, stand where you may. The mountain hemlock also is gloriously coloured with a profusion of lovely blue and purple flowers, a spectacle to gods and men. A single pine or hemlock or silver fir in the prime of its beauty about the middle of June is well worth the pains of the longest journey; how much more broad forests of them thousands of miles long!

One of the best ways to see tree flowers is to climb one of the tallest trees and to get into close tingling touch with them, and then look abroad. Speaking of the benefits of tree climbing, Thoreau says: 'I found my account in climbing a tree once. It was a tall white pine, on the top of a hill; and though I got well pitched, I was well paid for it, for I discovered new mountains in the horizon which I had never seen before. I might have walked about the foot of the tree for threescore years and ten, and yet I certainly should never have seen them. But, above all, I disovered around me – it was near the middle of June – on the ends of the topmost branches, a few minute and delicate red conelike blossoms, the fertile flower of the white pine looking heavenward. I carried straightway to the village the topmost spire, and showed it to stranger jurymen who walked the streets – for it was court week – and to farmers and lumbermen and woodchoppers and hunters, and not one had ever seen the like before, but they wondered as at a star dropped down'.

The same marvellous blindness prevails here, although the blossoms are a thousandfold more abundant and telling. Once when I was collecting flowers of the red silver fir near a summer tourist resort on the mountains above Lake Tahoe, I carried a handful of flowery branches to the boarding house, where they quickly attracted a wondering, admiring crowd of men, women, and children. 'Oh, where did you get these?' they cried. 'How pretty they are – mighty handsome – just too lovely for anything – where do they grow?' 'On the commonest trees about you', I replied. 'You are now standing beside one of them, and it is in full bloom; look up.' And I pointed to a blossom-laden abies magnifica, about a hundred and twenty feet high, in front of the house, used as a hitching post. And seeing its beauty for the first time, their wonder could hardly have been greater or more sincere had their silver fir hitching post blossomed for them at that moment as suddenly as Aaron's rod.

The mountain hemlock extends an almost continuous belt along the Sierra and northern ranges to Prince William's Sound, accompanied part of the way by the pines; our two silver firs, to Mount Shasta, thence the fir belt is continued through Oregon, Washington, and British Columbia by four other species, abies nobilis, grandis, amabilis and lasiocarpa; while the magnificent Sitka spruce, with large, bright, purple flowers, adorns the coast region from California to Cook's Inlet and Kodiak. All these, interblending, form one flowery belt – one garden blooming in June, rocking its myriad spires in the hearty weather, bowing and swirling, enjoying clouds and the winds and filling them with balsam; covering thousands of miles of the wildest mountains, clothing the long slopes by the sea, crowning bluffs and headlands and innumerable islands, and, fringing the banks of the glaciers, one wild wavering belt of the noblest flowers in the world, worth a lifetime of love work to know it.

CHAPTER SIX

Among the Animals of the Yosemite

THE SIERRA bear, brown or grey, the sequoia of the animals, tramps over all the park, though few travellers have the pleasure of seeing him. On he fares through the majestic forests and canyons, facing all sorts of weather, rejoicing in his strength, everywhere at home, harmonizing with the trees and rocks and shaggy chaparral. Happy fellow! his lines have fallen in pleasant places – lily gardens in silver-fir forests, miles of bushes in endless variety and exuberance of bloom over hill-waves and valleys and along the banks of streams, canyons full of music and waterfalls, parks fair as Eden – places in which one might expect to meet angels rather than bears.

In this happy land no famine comes nigh him. All the year round his bread is sure, for some of the thousand kinds that he likes are always in season and accessible, ranged on the shelves of the mountains like stores in a pantry. From one to another, from climate to climate, up and down he climbs, feasting on each in turn – enjoying as great variety as if he travelled to far-off countries north and south. To him almost everything is food except granite. Every tree helps to feed him, every bush and herb, with fruits and flowers, leaves and bark; and all the animals he can catch – badgers, gophers, ground squirrels, lizards, snakes, etc., and ants, bees, wasps, old and young, together with their eggs and larvæ and nests. Craunched and hashed, down all go to his marvellous stomach, and vanish as if cast into a fire. What digestion! A sheep or a wounded deer or a pig he eats warm, about as quickly as a boy eats a buttered muffin; or should the meat be a month old, it still is welcomed with tremendous relish. After so gross a meal as this, perhaps the next will be strawberries and clover, or raspberries with mushrooms and nuts, or puckery acorns and chokecherries. And as if fearing that anything eatable in all his dominions should escape being eaten, he breaks into cabins to look after sugar, dried apples, bacon, etc. Occasionally he eats the mountaineer's bed; but when he has had a full meal of more tempting dainties he usually leaves it undisturbed, though he has been known to drag it up through a hole in the roof, carry it to the foot of a tree, and lie down on it to enjoy a siesta. Eating everything, never is he himself eaten except by man, and only man is an enemy to be feared. 'B'ar meat', said a hunter from whom I was seeking information, 'b'ar meat is the best meat in the mountains; their skins make the best beds, and their grease the best butter. Biscuit shortened with b'ar grease goes as far as beans; a man will walk all day on a couple of them biscuit'.

In my first interview with a Sierra bear we were frightened and embarrassed, both of us, but the bear's behaviour was better than mine. When I discovered him, he was standing in a narrow strip of meadow, and I was concealed behind a tree on the side of it. After studying his appearance as he stood at rest, I rushed toward him to frighten him, that I might study his gait in running. But, contrary to all I had heard about the shyness of bears, he did not run at all; and when I stopped short within a few steps of him, as he held his ground in a fighting attitude, my mistake was monstrously plain. I was then put on my good behaviour, and never afterward forgot the right manners of the wilderness.

This happened on my first Sierra excursion in the forest to the north of Yosemite Valley. I was eager to meet the animals, and many of them came to me as if willing to show themselves and make my acquaintance; but the bears kept out of my way.

An old mountaineer, in reply to my questions, told me that bears were very shy, all save grim old grizzlies, and that I might travel the mountains for years without seeing one, unless I gave my mind to them and practiced the stealthy ways of hunters. Nevertheless, it was only a few weeks after I had received this information that I met the one mentioned above, and obtained instruction at first-hand.

I was encamped in the woods about a mile back of the rim of Yosemite, beside a stream that falls into the valley by the way of Indian Canyon. Nearly every day for weeks I went to the top of the North Dome to sketch; for it commands a general view of the valley, and I was anxious to draw every tree and rock and waterfall. Carlo, a St Bernard dog, was my companion – a fine, intelligent fellow that belonged to a hunter who was compelled to remain all summer on the hot plains, and who loaned him to me for the season for the sake of having him in the mountains, where he would be so much better off. Carlo knew bears through long experience, and he it was who led me to my first interview, though he seemed as much surprised as the bear at my unhunter-like behaviour. One morning in June, just as the sunbeams began to stream through the trees, I set out for a day's sketching on the dome; and before we had gone half a mile from camp Carlo sniffed the air and looked cautiously ahead, lowered his bushy tail, drooped his ears, and began to step softly like a cat, turning every few yards and looking me in the face with a telling expression, saying plainly enough, 'There is a bear a little way ahead'. I walked carefully in the indicated direction, until I approached a small flowery meadow that I was familiar with, then crawled to the foot of a tree on its margin, bearing in mind what I had been told about the shyness of bears. Looking out cautiously over the instep of the tree, I saw a big, burly cinnamon bear about thirty yards off, half erect, his paws resting on the trunk of a fir that had fallen into the meadow, his hips almost buried in grass and flowers. He was listening attentively and trying to catch the scent, showing that in some way he was aware of our approach. I watched his gestures, and tried to make the most of my opportunity to learn what I could about him, fearing he would not stay long. He made a fine picture, standing alert in the sunny garden walled in by the most beautiful firs in the world.

After examining him at leisure, noting the sharp muzzle thrust inquiringly forward, the long shaggy hair on his broad chest, the stiff ears nearly buried in hair, and the slow, heavy way in which he moved his head, I foolishly made a rush on him, throwing up my arms and shouting to frighten him, to see him run. He did not mind the demonstration much; only pushed his head farther forward, and looked at me sharply as if asking, 'What now? If you want to fight, I'm ready'. Then I began to fear that on me would fall the work of running. But I was afraid to run, lest he should be encouraged to pursue me; therefore I held my ground, staring him in the face within a dozen yards or so, putting on as bold a look as I could, and hoping the influence of the human eye would be as great as it is said to be. Under these strained relations the interview seemed to last a long time. Finally, the bear, seeing how still I was, calmly withdrew his huge paws from the log, gave me a piercing look, as if warning me not to follow him, turned, and walked slowly up the middle of the meadow into the forest; stopping every few steps and looking back to make sure that I was not tryng to take him at a disadvantage in a rear attack. I was glad to part with him, and greatly enjoyed the vanishing view as he waded through the lilies and columbines.

Thenceforth I always tried to give bears respectful notice of my approach, and they usually kept well out my way. Though they often came around my camp in the night, only once afterward, as far as I know, was I very near one of them in daylight. This time it was a grizzly I met; and as luck would have it, I was even nearer to him than I had been to the big cinnamon. Though not a large specimen, he seemed formidable enough at a distance of less than a dozen yards. His shaggy coat was well grizzled, his head almost white. When I first caught sight of him he was eating acorns under a Kellogg oak, at a distance of perhaps seventy-five yards, and I tried to slip past without disturbing him. But he had either heard my steps on the gravel or caught my scent, for he came straight toward me, stopping every rod or so to look and listen: and as I was afraid to be seen running, I crawled on my hands and knees a little way to one side and hid behind a libocedrus, hoping he would pass me unnoticed. He soon came up opposite me, and stood looking ahead, while I looked at him, peering past the bulging trunk of the tree. At last, turning his head, he caught sight of mine, stared sharply a minute or two, and then, with fine dignity, disappeared in a manzanita-covered earthquake talus.

Considering how heavy and broad-footed bears are, it is wonderful how little harm they do in the wilderness. Even in the well-watered gardens of the middle region, where the flowers grow tallest, and where during warm weather the bears wallow and roll, no evidence of destruction is visible. On the contrary, under nature's direction, the massive beasts act as gardeners. On the forest floor, carpeted with needles and brush, and on the tough sod of glacier meadows, bears make no mark; but around the sandy margin of lakes their mangificent tracks form grand lines of embroidery. Their well-worn trails extend along the main canyons on either side, and though dusty in some places make no scar on the landscape. They bite and break off the branches of some of the pines and oaks to get the nuts, but this pruning is so light that few mountaineers ever notice it; and though they interfere with the orderly lichen-veiled decay of fallen trees, tearing them to pieces to reach the colonies of ants that inhabit them, the scattered ruins are quickly pressed back into harmony by snow and rain and over-leaning vegetation.

The number of bears that make the Park their home may be guessed by the number that have been killed by the two best hunters, Duncan and old David Brown. Duncan began to be known as a bear-killer about the year 1865. He was then roaming the woods, hunting and prospecting on the south fork of the Merced. A friend told me that he killed his first bear near his cabin at Wawona; that after mustering courage to fire he fled, without waiting to learn the effect of his shot. Going back in a few hours he found poor Bruin dead, and gained courage to try again. Duncan confessed to me, when we made an excursion together in 1875, that he was at first mortally afraid of bears, but after killing a half dozen he began to keep count of his victims, and became ambitious to be known as a great bear-hunter. In nine years he had killed forty-nine, keeping count by notches cut on one of the timbers of his cabin on the shore of Crescent Lake, near the south boundary of the Park. He said the more he knew about bears, the more he respected them and the less he feared them. But at the same time he grew more and more cautious, and never fired until he had every advantage, no matter how long he had to wait and how far he had to go before he got the bear just right as to the direction of the wind, the distance, and the way of escape in case of accident; making allowance also for the character of the animal, old or young, cinnamon or grizzly. For old grizzlies, he said, he had no use whatever, and he was mighty careful to avoid their acquaintance. He wanted to kill an even hundred; then he was going to confine himself to safer game. There was not much money in bears, anyhow, and a round hundred was enough for glory.

I have not seen or heard of him lately, and do not know how his bloody count stands. On my excursions, I occasionally passed his cabin. It was full of meat and skins hung in bundles from the rafters, and the ground about it was strewn with bones and hair – infinitely less tidy than a bear's den. He went as hunter and guide with a geological survey party for a year or two, and was very proud of the scientific knowledge he picked up. His admiring fellow mountaineers, he said, gave him credit for knowing not only the botanical names of all the trees and bushes, but also the 'botanical names of the bears'.

The most famous hunter of the region was David Brown, an old pioneer, who early in the gold period established his main camp in a little forest glade on the north fork of the Merced, which is still called, 'Brown's Flat'. No finer solitude for a hunter and prospector could be found; the climate is delightful all the year, and the scenery of both earth and sky is a perpetual feast. Though he was not much of a 'scenery fellow', his friends say that he knew a pretty place when he saw it as well as anyone, and liked mightily to get on the top of a commanding ridge to 'look off'.

When out of provisions, he would take down his old-fashioned long-barrelled rifle from its deerhorn rest over the fireplace and set out in search of game. Seldom did he have to go far for venison, because the deer liked the wooded slopes of Pilot Peak ridge, with its open spots where they could rest and look about them, and enjoy the breeze from the sea in warm weather, free from troublesome flies, while they found hiding-places and fine aromatic food in the deer-brush chaparral. A small, wise dog was his only companion, and well the little mountaineer understood the object of every hunt, whether deer or bears, or only grouse hidden in the fir-tops. In deerhunting Sandy had little to do, trotting behind his master as he walked noiselessly through the fragrant woods, careful not to step heavily on dry twigs, scanning open spots in the chaparral where the deer feed in the early morning and toward sunset, peering over ridges and swells as new outlooks were reached, and along alder and willow fringed flats and streams, until he found a young buck, killed it, tied its legs together, threw it on his shoulder, and so back to camp. But when bears were hunted, Sandy played an important part as leader, and several times saved his master's life; and it was as a bear-hunter that David Brown became famous. His method, as I had it from a friend who had passed many an evening in his cabin listening to his long stories of adventure, was simply to take a few pounds of flour and his rifle, and go slowly and silently over hill and valley in the loneliest part of the wilderness, until little Sandy came upon the fresh track of a bear, then follow it to the death, paying no heed to time. Wherever the bear went he went, however rough the ground, led by Sandy, who looked back from time to time to see how his master was coming on, and regulated his pace accordingly, never growing weary or allowing any other track to divert him. When high ground was reached a halt was made, to scan the openings in every direction, and perchance Bruin would be discovered sitting upright on his haunches, eating manzanita berries; pulling down the fruit-laden branches with his paws and pressing them together, so as to get substantial mouthfuls, however mixed with leaves and twigs. The time of year enabled the hunter to determine approximately where the game would be found: in spring and early summer, in lush grass and clover meadows and in berry tangles along the banks of streams, or on pea-vine and lupine clad slopes; in late summer and autumn, beneath the pines, eating the cones cut off by the squirrels, and in oak groves at the bottom of canyons, munching acorns, manzanita berries, and cherries; and after snow had fallen, in alluvial bottoms, feeding on ants and yellow-jacket wasps. These food places were always cautiously approached, so as to avoid the chance of sudden encounters.

'Whenever', said the hunter, 'I saw a bear before he saw me, I had no trouble in killing him. I just took lots of time to learn what he was up to and how long he would be likely to stay, and to study the direction of the wind and the lay of the land. Then I worked round to leeward of him, no matter how far I had to go; crawled and dodged to within a hundred yards, near the foot of a tree that I could climb, but which was too small for a bear to climb. There I looked well to the priming of my rifle, took off my boots so as to climb quickly if necessary, and, with my rifle in rest and Sandy behind me, waited until my bear stood right, when I made a sure, or at least a good shot back of the fore leg. In case he showed fight, I got up the tree I had in mind, before he could reach me. But bears are slow and awkward with their eyes, and being to windward they could not scent me, and often I got in a second shot before they saw the smoke. Usually, however, they tried to get away when they were hurt, and I let them go a good safe while before I ventured into the brush after them. Then Sandy was pretty sure to find them dead; if not, he barked bold as a lion to draw attention, or rushed in and nipped them behind, enabling me to get to a safe distance and watch a chance for a finishing shot'.

'Oh yes, bear-hunting is a mighty interesting business, and safe enough if followed just right, though, like every other business, especially the wild kind, it has its accidents, and Sandy and I have had close calls at times. Bears are nobody's fools, and they know enough to let men alone as a general thing, unless they are wounded, or cornered, or have cubs. In my opinion, a hungry old mother would catch and eat a man, if she could; which is only fair play, anyhow, for we eat them. But nobody, as far as I know, has been eaten up in these rich mountains. Why they never tackle a fellow when he is lying asleep I never could understand. They could gobble us mighty handy, but I suppose it's nature to respect a sleeping man'.

Sheep-owners and their shepherds have killed a great many bears, mostly by poison and traps of various sorts. Bears are fond of mutton, and levy heavy toll on every flock driven into the mountains. They usually come to the corral at night, climb in, kill a sheep with a stroke of the paw, carry it off a little distance, eat about half of it, and return the next night for the other half; and so on all summer, or until they are themselves killed. It is not, however, by direct killing, but by suffocation through crowding against the corral wall in fright, that the greatest losses are incurred. From ten to fifteen sheep are found dead, smothered in the corral, after every attack; or the walls are broken, and the flock is scattered far and wide. A flock may escape the attention of these marauders for a week or two in the spring; but after their first taste of the fine mountain-fed meat the visits are persistently kept up, in spite of all precautions. Once I spent a night with two Portuguese shepherds, who were greatly troubled with bears, from two to four or five visiting them almost every night. Their camp was near the middle of the Park, and the wicked bears, they said, were getting worse and worse. Not waiting now until dark, they came out of the brush in broad daylight, and boldly carried off as many sheep as they liked. One evening, before sundown, a bear, followed by two cubs, came for an early supper, as the flock was being slowly driven toward the camp. Joe, the elder of the shepherds, warned by many exciting experiences, promptly climbed a tall tamarack pine, and left the freebooters to help themselves; while Antone, calling him a coward, and declaring that he was not going to let bears eat up his sheep before his face, set the dogs on them, and rushed toward them with a great noise and a stick. The frightened cubs ran up a tree, and the mother ran to meet the shepherd and dogs. Antone stood astonished for a moment, eyeing the oncoming bear; then fled faster than Joe had, closely pursued. He scrambled to the roof of their little cabin, the only refuge quickly available; and fortunately, the bear, anxious about her young, did not climb after him – only held him in mortal terror a few minutes, glaring and threatening, then hastened back to her cubs, called them down, went to the frightened, huddled flock, killed a sheep, and feasted in peace. Antone piteously entreated cautious Joe to show him a good safe tree, up which he climbed like a sailor climbing a mast, and held on as long as he could with legs crossed, the slim pine recommended by Joe being nearly branchless. 'So you, too, are a bear coward as well as Joe', I said, after hearing the story. 'Oh, I tell you', he replied, with grand solemnity, 'bear face close by look awful; she just as soon eat me as not. She do so as eef all my sheeps b'long every one to her own self. I run to bear no more. I take tree every time'.

After this the shepherds corraled the flock about an hour before sundown, chopped large quantities of dry wood and made a circle of fires around the corral every night, and one with a gun kept watch on a stage built in pine by the side of the cabin, while the other slept. But after the first night or two this fire fence did no good, for the robbers seemed to regard the light as an advantage, after becoming used to it.

On the night I spent at their camp the show made by the wall of fire when it was blazing in its prime was magnificent – the illumined trees round about relieved against solid darkness, and the two thousand sheep lying down in one grey mass, sprinkled with gloriously brilliant gems, the effect of the firelight in their eyes. It was nearly midnight when a pair of the freebooters arrived. They walked boldly through a gap in the fire circle, killed two sheep, carried them out, and vanished in the dark woods, leaving ten dead in a pile, trampled down and smothered against the corral fence; while the scared watcher in the tree did not fire a single shot, saying he was afraid he would hit some of the sheep, as the bears got among them before he could get a good sight.

In the morning I asked the shepherds why they did not move the flock to a new pasture. 'Oh, no use!' cried Antone. 'Look my dead sheeps. We move three four time before, all the same bear come by the track. No use. To-morrow we go home below. Look my dead sheeps. Soon all dead.'

Thus were they driven out of the mountains more than a month before the usual time. After Uncle Sam's soldiers, bears are the most effective forest police, but some of the shepherds are very successful in killing them. Altogether, by hunters, mountaineers, Indians, and sheepmen, probably five or six hundred have been killed within the bounds of the Park, during the last thirty years. But they are not in danger of extinction. Now that the Park is guarded by soldiers, not only has the vegetation in great part come back to the desolate ground, but all the wild animals are increasing in numbers. No guns are allowed in the Park except under certain restrictions, and after a permit has been obtained from the officer in charge. This has stopped the barbarous slaughter of bears, and especially of deer, by shepherds, hunters, and hunting tourists, who, it would seem, can find no pleasure without blood.

The Sierra deer – the blacktail – spend the winters in the brushy and exceedingly rough region just below the main timber-belt, and are less accessible to hunters there than when they are passing through the comparatively open forests to and from their summer pastures near the summits of the range. They go up the mountains early in the spring as the snow melts, not waiting for it all to disappear; reaching the High Sierra about the first of June, and the coolest recesses at the base of the peaks a month or so later. I have tracked them for miles over compacted snow from three to ten feet deep.

Deer are capital mountaineers, making their way into the heart of the roughest mountains; seeking not only pasturage, but a cool climate, and safe hidden places in which to bring forth their young. They are not supreme as rock climbing animals; they take second rank, yielding the first to the mountain sheep, which dwell above them on the highest crags and peaks. Still, the two meet frequently; for the deer climbs all the peaks save the lofty summits above the glaciers, crossing piles of angular boulders, roaring swollen streams, and sheer-walled canyons by fords and passes that would try the nerves of the hardiest mountaineers – climbing with graceful ease and reserve of strength that cannot fail to arouse admiration. Everywhere some species of deer seems to be at home – on rough or smooth ground, lowlands or highlands, in swamps and barrens and the densest woods, in varying climates, hot or cold, over all the continent; maintaining glorious health, never making an awkward step. Standing, lying down, walking, feeding, running even for life, it is always invincibly graceful, and adds beauty and animation to every landscape – a charming animal, and a great credit to nature.

I never see one of the common, blacktail deer, the only species in the Park, without fresh admiration; and since I never carry a gun I see them well: lying beneath a juniper or dwarf pine, among the brown needles on the brink of some cliff or the end of a ridge commanding a wide outlook; feeding in sunny openings among chaparral, daintily selecting aromatic leaves and twigs; leading their fawns out of my way, or making them lie down and hide; bounding past through the forest, or curiously advancing and retreating again and again.

One morning when I was eating breakfast in a little garden spot on the Kaweah, hedged around with chaparral, I noticed a deer's head thrust through the bushes, the big beautiful eyes gazing at me. I kept still, and the deer ventured forward a step, then snorted and withdrew. In a few minutes she returned, and came into the open garden, stepping with infinite grace, followed by two others. After showing themselves for a moment, they bounded over the hedge with sharp, timid snorts and vanished. But curiosity brought them back with still another, and all four came into my garden, and, satisfied that I meant them no ill, began to feed, actually eating breakfast with me, like tame, gentle sheep around a shepherd – rare company, and the most graceful in movements and attitudes. I eagerly watched them while they fed on ceanothus and wild cherry, daintily culling single leaves here and there from the side of the hedge, turning now and then to snip a few leaves of mint from the midst of the garden flowers. Grass they did not eat at all. No wonder the contents of the deer's stomach are eaten by the Indians.

While exploring the upper canyon of the north fork of the San Joaquin, one evening, the sky threatening rain, I searched for a dry bed, and made choice of a big juniper that had been pushed down by a snow avalanche, but was resting stubbornly on its knees high enough to let me lie under its broad trunk. Just below my shelter there was another juniper on the very brink of a precipice, and, examining it, I found a deer-bed beneath it, completely protected and concealed by drooping branches – a fine refuge and lookout as well as resting-place. About an hour before dark I heard the clear, sharp snorting of a deer, and looking down on the brushy, rocky canyon bottom, discovered an anxious doe that no doubt had her fawns concealed near by. She bounded over the chaparral and up the further slope of the wall, often stopping to look back and listen – a fine picture of vivid, eager alertness. I sat perfectly still, and as my shirt was coloured like the juniper bark I was not easily seen. After a little she came cautiously toward me, sniffing the air and grazing, and her movements, as she descended the canyon side over boulder piles and brush and fallen timber, were admirably strong and beautiful; she never strained or made apparent efforts, although jumping high here and there. As she drew night she sniffed anxiously, trying the air in different directions until she caught my scent; then bounded off, and vanished behind a small grove of firs. Soon she came back with the same caution and insatiable curiosity – coming and going five or six times. While I sat admiring her, a Douglas squirrel, evidently excited by her noisy alarms, climbed a boulder beneath me, and witnessed her performances as attentively as I did, while a frisky chipmunk, too restless or hungry for such shows, busied himself about his supper in a thicket of shadbushes, the fruit of which was then ripe, glancing about on the slender twigs lightly as a sparrow.

Toward the end of the Indian summer, when the young are strong, the deer begin to gather in little bands of from six to fifteen or twenty, and on the approach of the first snowstorm they set out on their march down the mountains to their winter quarters; lingering usually on warm hillsides and spurs eight or ten miles below the summits, as if loath to leave. About the end of November, a heavy, far-reaching storm drives them down in haste along the dividing ridges between the rivers, led by old experienced bucks whose knowledge of the topography is wonderful.

It is when the deer are coming down that the Indians set out on their grand fall hunt. Too lazy to go into the recesses of the mountains away from trails, they wait for the deer to come out, and then waylay them. This plan also has the advantage of finding them in bands. Great preparations are made. Old guns are mended, bullets moulded, and the hunters wash themselves and fast to some extent, to insure good luck, as they say. Men and women, old and young, set forth together. Central camps are made on the well-known highways of the deer, which are soon red with blood. Each hunter comes in laden, old crones as well as maidens smiling on the luckiest. All grow fat and merry. Boys, each armed with an antlered head, play at buck-fighting, and plague the industrious women, who are busily preparing the meat for transportation, by stealing up behind them and throwing fresh hides over them. But the Indians are passing away here as everywhere, and their red camps on the mountains are fewer every year.

There are panthers, foxes, badgers, porcupines, and coyotes in the Park, but not in large numbers. I have seen coyotes well back in the range at the head of the Tuolumne Meadows as early as 1 June, before the snow was gone, feeding on marmots; but they are far more numerous on the inhabited lowlands around ranches, where they enjoy life on chickens, turkeys, quail eggs, ground squirrels, hares, etc., and all kinds of fruit. Few wild sheep, I fear, are left here-abouts; for, though safe on the high peaks, they are driven down the eastern slope of the mountains when the deer are driven down the western, to ridges and outlying spurs where the snow does not fall to a great depth, and there they are within reach of the cattlemen's rifles.

The two squirrels of the Park, the Douglas and the California grey, keep all the woods lively. The former is far more abundant and more widely distributed, being found all the way up from the foothills to the dwarf pines on the Summit peaks. He is the most influential of the Sierra animals, though small, and the brightest of all the squirrels I know – a squirrel of squirrels, quick mountain vigour and valour condensed, purely wild, and as free from disease as a sunbeam. One cannot think of such an animal ever being weary or sick. He claims all the woods, and is inclined to drive away even men as intruders. How he scolds, and what faces he makes! If not so comically small he would be a dreadful fellow. The grey, sciurus fossor, is the handsomest, I think, of all the large American squirrels. He is something like the Eastern grey, but is brighter and clearer in colour, and more lithe and slender. He dwells in the oak and pine woods up to a height of about five thousand feet above the sea, is rather common in Yosemite Valley, Hetch-Hetchy, Kings River Canyon, and indeed in all the main canyons and Yosemites, but does not like the high fir-covered ridges. Compared with the Douglas, the grey is more than twice as large; nevertheless, he manages to make his way through the trees with less stir than his small, peppery neighbour, and is much less influential in every way. In the spring, before the pine-nuts and hazel-nuts are ripe, he examines last year's cones for the few seeds that may be left in them between the half open scales, and gleans fallen nuts and seeds on the ground among the leaves, after making sure that no enemy is nigh. His fine tail floats, now behind, now above him, level or gracefully curled, light and radiant as dry thistledown. His body seems hardly more substantial than his tail. The

Douglas is a firm, emphatic bolt of life, fiery, pungent, full of brag and show and fight, and his movements have none of the elegant deliberation of the grey. They are so quick and keen they almost sting the onlooker, and the acrobatic harlequin gyrating show he makes of himself turns one giddy to see. The grey is shy and oftentimes stealthy, as if half expecting to find an enemy in every tree and bush and behind every log; he seems to wish to be let alone, and manifests no desire to be seen, or admired, or feared. He is hunted by the Indians, and this of itself is cause enough for caution. The Douglas is less attractive for game, and probably increasing in numbers in spite of every enemy. He goes his ways bold as a lion, up and down and across, round and round, the happiest, merriest of all the hairy tribe, and at the same time tremendously earnest and solemn, sunshine incarnate, making every tree tingle with his electric toes. If you prick him, you cannot think he will bleed. He seems above the chance and change that beset common mortals, though in busily gathering burs and nuts he shows that he has to work for a living, like the rest of us. I never found a dead Douglas. He gets into the world and out of it without being noticed; only in prime is he seen, like some little plants that are visible only when in bloom.

The little striped tamias quadrivittatus is one of the most amiable and delightful of all the mountain tree-climbers. A brighter, cheerier chipmunk does not exist. He is smarter, more arboreal and squirrel-like, than the familiar Eastern species, and is distributed as widely on the Sierra as the Douglas. Every forest, however dense or open, every hilltop and canyon, however brushy or bare, is cheered and enlivened by this happy little animal. You are likely to notice him first on the lower edge of the coniferous belt, where the Sabine and yellow pines meet; and thence upward, go where you may, you will find him every day, even in winter, unless the weather is stormy. He is an exceedingly interesting little fellow, full of odd, quaint ways, confiding, thinking no evil; and without being a squirrel – a true shadow-tail – he lives the life of a squirrel, and has almost all squirrelish accomplishments without aggressive quarrelsomeness.

I never weary of watching him as he frisks about the bushes, gathering seeds and berries; poising on slender twigs of wild cherry, shad, chinquapin, buckthorn, bramble; skimming along prostrate trunks or over the grassy, needle-strewn forest floor; darting from boulder to boulder on glacial pavements and the tops of the great domes. When the seeds of the conifers are ripe, he climbs the trees and cuts off the cones for a winter store, working diligently, though not with the tremendous lightning energy of the Douglas, who frequently drives him out of the best trees. Then he lies in wait, and picks up a share of the burs cut off by his domineering cousin, and stores them beneath logs and in hollows. Few of the Sierra animals are so well liked as this little airy, fluffy half squirrel, half spermophile. So gentle, confiding, and busily cheery and happy, he takes one's heart and keeps his place among the bestloved of the mountain darlings. A diligent collector of seeds, nuts, and berries, of course he is well fed, though never in the least dumpy with fat. On the contrary, he looks like a mere fluff of fur, weighing but little more than a field mouse, and of his frisky, birdlike liveliness without haste there is no end.

Douglas can bark with his mouth closed, but little quad always opens his when he talks or sings. He has a considerable variety of notes which correspond with his movements, some of them sweet and liquid, like water dripping into a pool with tinkling sound. His eyes are black and animated, shining like dew. He seems dearly to like teasing a dog, venturing within a few feet of it, then frisking away with a lively chipping and low squirrelish churring; beating time to his music, such as it is, with his tail, which at each chip and churr describes a half circle. Not even Douglas is surer footed or takes greater risks. I have seen him running about on sheer Yosemite cliffs, holding on with as little effort as a fly and as little thought of danger, in places where, if he had made the least slip, he would have fallen thousands of feet. How fine it would be could mountaineers move about on precipices with the same sure grip!

Before the pine-nuts are ripe, grass seeds and those of the many species of ceanothus, with strawberries, raspberries, and the soft red thimbleberries of Rubus nutkanus, form the bulk of his food, and a neater eater is not to be found in the mountains. Bees powdered with pollen, poking their blunt noses into the bells of flowers, are comparatively clumsy and boorish. Frisking along some fallen pine or fir, when the grass seeds are ripe, he looks about him, considering which of the tufts he sees is likely to have the best, runs out to it, selects what he thinks is sure to be a good head, cuts it off, carries it to the top of the log, sits upright and nibbles out the grain without getting awns in his mouth, turning the head round, holding it and fingering it as if playing on a flute; then skips for another and another, bringing them to the same dining-log.

The woodchuck (*Arctomys monax*) dwells on high bleak ridges and boulder piles; and a very different sort of mountaineer is he – bulky, fat, aldermanic and fairly bloated at times by hearty indulgence in the lush pastures of his airy home. And yet he is by no means a dull animal. In the midst of what we regard as storm-beaten desolation, high in the frosty air, beside the glaciers he pipes and whistles right cheerily and lives to a good old age. If you are as early a riser as he is, you may oftentimes see him come blinking out of his burrow to meet the first beams of the morning and take a sunbath on some favourite flat-topped boulder. Afterward, well warmed, he goes to breakfast in one of his garden hollows, eats heartily like a cow in clover until comfortably swollen, then goes a-visiting, and plays and loves and fights.

In the spring of 1875, when I was exploring the peaks and glaciers about the head of the middle fork of the San Joaquin, I had crossed the range from the head of Owen River, and one morning, passing around a frozen lake where the snow was perhaps ten feet deep, I was surprised to find the fresh track of a woodchuck plainly marked, the sun having softened the surface. What could the animal be thinking of, coming out so early while all the ground was snow-buried? The steady trend of his track showed he had a definite aim, and fortunately it was toward a mountain thirteen thousand feet high that I meant to climb. So I followed to see if I could find out what he was up to. From the base of the mountain the track pointed straight up, and I knew by the melting snow that I was not far behind him. I lost the track on a crumbling ridge, partly projecting through the snow, but soon discovered it again. Well toward the summit of the mountain, in an open spot on the south side, nearly inclosed by disintregrating pinnacles among which the sun heat reverberated, making an isolated patch of warm climate, I found a nice garden, full of rock cress, phlox, silene, draba, etc., and a few grasses; and in this garden I overtook the wanderer, enjoying a fine fresh meal, perhaps the first of the season. How did he know the way to this one garden spot, so high and far off, and what told him that it was in bloom while yet the snow was ten feet deep over his den? For this it would seem he would need more botanical, topographical, and climatological knowledge than most mountaineers are possessed of.

The shy, curious mountain beaver, haplodon, lives on the heights, not far from the woodchuck. He digs canals and controls the flow of small streams under the sod. And it is startling when one is camped on the edge of a sloping meadow near the homes of these industrious mountaineers, to be awakened in the still night by the sound of water rushing and gurgling under one's head in a newly formed canal. Pouched gophers also have a way of awakening nervous campers that is quite as exciting as the Haplodon's plan; that is, by a series of firm upward pushes when they are driving tunnels and shoving up the dirt. One naturally cries out, 'Who's there?' and then discovering the cause, 'All right. Go on. Good-night', and goes to sleep again.

The haymaking pika, bob-tailed spermophile, and wood-rat are also among the most interesting of the Sierra animals. The last neotoma is scarcely at all like the common rat, is nearly twice as large, has a delicate, soft, brownish fur, white on the belly, large ears thin and translucent, eyes full and liquid and mild in expression, nose blunt and squirrelish, slender claws sharp as needles, and as his limbs are strong he can climb about as well as a squirrel; while no rat or squirrel has so innocent a look, is so easily approached, or in general expresses so much confidence in one's good intentions. He seems too fine for the thorny thickets he inhabits, and his big, rough hut is as unlike himself as possible. No other animal in these mountains makes nests so large and striking in appearance as his. They are built of all kinds of sticks (broken branches, and old rotten mossgrown chunks and green twigs, smooth or thorny, cut from the nearest bushes), mixed with miscellaneous rubbish and curious odds and ends – bits of cloddy earth, stones, bones, bits of deer-horn, etc.: the whole simply piled in conical masses on the ground in chaparral thickets. Some of these cabins are five or six feet high, and occasionally a dozen or more are grouped together; less, perhaps, for society's sake than for advantages of food and shelter.

Coming through deep, stiff chaparral in the heart of the wilderness, heated and weary in forcing a way, the solitary explorer, happening into one of these curious neotoma villages, is startled at the strange sight, and may imagine he is in an Indian village, and feel anxious as to the reception he will get in a place so wild. At first, perhaps, not a single inhabitant will be seen, or at most only two or three seated on the tops of their huts as at the doors, observing the stranger with the mildest of mild eyes. The nest in the centre of the cabin is made of grass and films of bark chewed to tow, and lined with feathers and the down of various seeds. The thick, rough walls seem to be built for defence against enemies – fox, coyote, etc. – as well as for shelter, and the delicate creatures in their big, rude homes, suggest tender flowers, like those of salvia carduacea, defended by thorny involucres.

Sometimes the home is built in the forks of an oak, twenty or thirty feet from the ground, and even in garrets. Among housekeepers who have these bushmen as neighbours or guests they are regarded as thieves, because they carry away and pile together everything transportable (knives, forks, tin cups, spoons, spectacles, combs, nails, kindling-wood, etc., as well as eatables of all sorts), to strengthen their fortifications or to shine among rivals. Once, far back in the High Sierra, they stole my snow-goggles, the lid of my teapot, and my aneroid barometer; and one stormy night, when encamped under a prostrate cedar, I was awakened by a gritting sound on the granite, and by the light of my fire I discovered a handsome neotoma beside me, dragging away my ice-hatchet, pulling with might and main by a buckskin string on the handle. I threw bits of bark at him and made a noise to frighten him, but he stood scolding and chattering back at me, his fine eyes shining with an air of injured innocence.

A great variety of lizards enliven the warm portions of the Park. Some of them are more than a foot in length, others but little larger than grasshoppers. A few are snaky and repulsive at first sight, but most of the species are handsome and attractive, and bear acquaintance well; we like them better the further we see into their charming lives. Small fellow mortals, gentle and guileless, they are easily tamed, and have beautiful eyes, expressing the clearest innocence, so that, in spite of prejudices brought from cool, lizardless countries, one must soon learn to like them. Even the horned toad of the plains and foothills, called horrid, is mild and gentle, with charming eyes, and so are the snakelike species found in the underbrush of the lower forests. These glide in curves with all the ease and grace of snakes, while their small, undeveloped limbs drag for the most part as useless appendages. One specimen that I measured was fourteen inches long, and as far as I saw it made no use whatever of its diminutive limbs.

Most of them glint and dart on the sunny rocks and across open spaces from bush to bush, swift as dragonflies and humming-birds, and about as brilliantly coloured. They never make a long-sustained run, whatever their object, but dart direct as arrows for a distance of ten or twenty feet, then suddenly stop, and as suddenly start again. These stops are necessary as rests, for they are short-winded, and when pursued steadily are soon run out of breath, pant pitifully, and may easily be caught where no retreat in bush or rock is quickly available.

If you stay with them a week or two and behave well, these gentle saurians, descendants of an ancient race of giants, will soon know and trust you, come to your feet, play, and watch your every motion with cunning curiosity. You will surely learn to like them, not only the bright ones, gorgeous as the rainbow, but the little ones, grey as lichened granite, and scarcely bigger than grasshoppers; and they will teach you that scales may cover as fine a nature as hair or feathers or anything tailored.

There are many snakes in the canyons and lower forests, but they are mostly handsome and harmless. Of all the tourists and travellers who have visited Yosemite and the adjacent mountains, not one has been bitten by a snake of any sort, while thousands have been charmed by them. Some of them vie with the lizards in beauty of colour and dress patterns. Only the rattlesnake is venomous, and he carefully keeps his venom to himself as far as man is concerned, unless his life is threatened.

Before I learned to respect rattlesnakes I killed two, the first on the San Joaquin plain. He was coiled comfortably around a tuft of bunch-grass, and I discovered him when he was between my feet as I was stepping over him. He held his head down and did not attempt to strike, although in danger of being trampled. At that time, thirty years ago, I imagined that rattlesnakes should be killed wherever found. I had no weapon of any sort, and on the smooth plain there was not a stick or a stone within miles; so I crushed him by jumping on him, as the deer are said to do. Looking me in the face he saw I meant mischief, and quickly cast himself into a coil, ready to strike in defence. I knew he could not strike when travelling, therefore I threw handfuls of dirt and grass sods at him, to tease him out of coil. He held his ground a few minutes, threatening and striking, and then started off to get rid of me. I ran foward and jumped on him; but he drew back his head so quickly my heel missed, and he also missed his stroke at me. Persecuted, tormented, again and again he tried to get away, bravely striking out to protect himself; but at last my heel came squarely down, sorely wounding him, and a few more brutal stampings crushed him. I felt degraded by the killing business, further from heaven, and I made up my mind to try to be at least as fair and charitable as the snakes themselves, and to kill no more save in self-defence.

The second killing might also, I think have been avoided, and I have always felt somewhat sore and guilty about it. I had built a little cabin in Yosemite, and for convenience in getting water, and for the sake of music and society, I led a small stream from Yosemite Creek into it. Running along the side of the wall it was not in the way, and it had just fall enough to ripple and sing in low, sweet tones, making delightful company, especially at night when I was lying awake. Then a few frogs came in and made merry with the stream – and one snake, I suppose to catch the frogs.

Returning from my long walks, I usually brought home a large handful of plants, partly for study, partly for ornament, and set them in a corner of the cabin, with their stems in the stream to keep them fresh. One day, when I picked up a handful that had begun to fade, I uncovered a large coiled rattler that had been hiding behind the flowers. Thus suddenly brought to light face to face with the rightful owner of the place, the poor reptile was desperately embarrassed, evidently realizing that he had no right in the cabin. It was not only fear that he showed, but a good deal of downright bashfulness and embarrassment, like that of a more than half honest person caught under suspicious circumstances behind a door. Instead of striking or threatening to strike, though coiled and ready, he slowly drew his head down as far as he could, with awkward, confused kinks in his neck and a shamefaced expression, as if wishing the ground would open and hide him. I have looked into the eyes of so many wild animals that I feel sure I did not mistake the feelings of this unfortunate snake. I did not want to kill him, but I had many visitors, some of them children, and I oftentimes came in late at night; so I judged he must die.

Since then I have seen perhaps a hundred or more in these mountains, but I have never intentionally disturbed them, nor have they disturbed me to any great extent, even by accident, though in danger of being stepped on. Once, while I was on my knees kindling a fire, one glided under the arch made by my arm. He was only going away from the ground I had selected for a camp, and there was not the slightest danger, because I kept still and allowed him to go in peace. The only time I felt myself in serious danger was when I was coming out of the Tuolumne Canyon by a steep side canyon toward the head of Yosemite Creek. On an earthquake talus, a boulder in my way presented a front so high that I could just reach the upper edge of it while standing on the next below it. Drawing myself up, as soon as my head was above the flat top of it I caught sight of a coiled rattler. My hands had alarmed him, and he was ready for me; but even with this provocation, and when my head came in sight within a foot of him, he did not strike. The last time I sauntered through the big canyon I saw about two a day. One was not coiled, but neatly folded in a narrow space between two cobblestones on the side of the river, his head below the level of them, ready to shoot up like a Jack-in-the-box for frogs or birds. My foot spanned the space above within an inch or two of his head, but he only held it lower. In making my way through a particularly tedious tangle of buckthorn, I parted the branches on the side of an open spot and threw my bundle of bread into it; and when, with my arms free, I was pushing through after it, I saw a small rattlesnake dragging his tail from beneath my bundle. When he caught sight of me he eyed me angrily, and with an air of righteous indignation seemed to be asking why I had thrown that stuff on him. He was so small that I was inclined to slight him, but he struck out so angrily that I drew back, and approached the opening from the other side. But he had been listening, and when I looked through the brush I found him confronting me, still with a come-in-if-you-dare expression. In vain I tried to explain that I only wanted my bread; he stoutly held the ground in front of it; so I went back a dozen rods and kept still for half an hour, and when I returned he had gone.

One evening, near sundown, in a very rough, boulder-choked portion of the canyon, I searched long for a level spot for a bed, and at last was glad to find a patch of flood-sand on the riverbank, and a lot of driftwood close by for a campfire. But when I threw down my bundle, I found two snakes in possession of the ground. I might have passed the night even in this snake den without danger, for I never knew a single instance of their coming into camp in the night; but fearing that, in so small a space, some late comers, not aware of my presence, might get stepped on when I was replenishing the fire, to avoid possible crowding I encamped on one of the earthquake boulders.

There are two species of crotalus in the Park, and when I was exploring the basin of Yosemite Creek I thought I had discovered a new one. I saw a snake with curious divided appendages on its head. Going nearer, I found that the strange headgear was only the feet of a frog. Cutting a switch, I struck the snake lightly until he disgorged the poor frog, or rather allowed it to back out. On its return to the light from one of the very darkest of death valleys, it blinked a moment with a sort of dazed look, then plunged into a stream, apparently happy and well.

Frogs abound in all the bogs, marshes, pools and lakes, however cold and high and isolated. How did they manage to get up these high mountains? Surely not by jumping. Long and dry excursions through weary miles of boulders and brush would be trying to frogs. Most likely their stringy spawn is carried on the feet of ducks, cranes, and other waterbirds. Anyhow, they are most thoroughly distributed, and flourish famously. What a cheery, hearty set they are, and how bravely their krink and tronk concerts enliven the rocky wilderness!

None of the high-lying mountain lakes or branches of the rivers above sheer falls had fish of any sort until stocked by the agency of man. In the High Sierra, the only river in which trout exist naturally is the middle fork of Kings River. There are no sheer falls on this stream; some of the rapids, however, are so swift and rough, even at the lowest stage of water, that it is surprising any fish can climb them. I found trout in abundance in this fork up to seventy-five hundred feet. They also run quite high on the Kern. On the Merced they get no higher than Yosemite Valley, four thousand feet, all the forks of the river being barred there by sheer falls, and on the main Tuolumne they are stopped by a fall below Hetch-Hetchy, still lower than Yosemite. Though these upper waters are inaccessible to the fish, one would suppose their eggs might have been planted there by some means. Nature has so many ways of doing such things. In this case she waited for the agency of man, and now many of these hitherto fishless lakes and streams are full of fine trout, stocked by individual enterprise, Walton clubs, etc., in great part under the auspices of the United States Fish Commission. A few trout carried into Hetch-Hetchy in a common water-bucket have multiplied wonderfully fast. Lake Tenaya, at an elevation of over eight thousand feet, was stocked eight years ago by Mr Murphy, who carried a few trout from Yosemite. Many of the small streams of the eastern slope have also been stocked with trout transported over the passes in tin cans on the backs of mules. Soon, it would seem, all the streams of the range will be enriched by these lively fish, and will become the means of drawing thousands of visitors into the mountains. Catching trout with a bit of bent wire is a rather trivial business, but fortunately people fish better than they know. In most cases it is the man who is caught. Trout-fishing regarded as bait for catching men, for the saving of both body and soul, is important, and deserves all the expense and care bestowed on it.

CHAPTER SEVEN

Among the Birds of the Yosemite

TRAVELLERS in the Sierra forests usually complain of the want of life. 'The trees', they say, 'are fine, but the empty stillness is deadly; there are no animals to be seen, no birds. We have not heard a song in all the woods'. And no wonder! They go in large parties with mules and horses; they make a great noise; they are dressed in outlandish, unnatural colours; every animal shuns them. Even the frightened pines would run away if they could. But Nature-lovers, devout, silent, open-eyed, looking and listening with love, find no lack of inhabitants in these mountain mansions, and they come to them gladly. Not to mention the large animals or the small insect people, every waterfall has its ouzel and every tree its squirrel or tamias or bird: tiny nuthatch threading the furrows of the bark, cheerily whispering to itself as it deftly pries off loose scales and examines the curled edges of lichens; or Clarke crow or jay examining the cones; or some singer – oriole, tanager, warbler – resting, feeding, attending to domestic affairs. Hawks and eagles sail over-head, grouse walk in happy flocks below, and song sparrows sing in every bed of chaparral. There is no crowding, to be sure. Unlike the low Eastern trees, those of the Sierra in the main forest belt average nearly two hundred feet in height, and of course many birds are required to make much show in them, and many voices to fill them. Nevertheless, the whole range, from foothills to snowy summits, is shaken into song every summer; and though low and thin in winter, the music never ceases.

The sage cock (*Centrocercus urophasianus*) is the largest of the Sierra game-birds and the king of American grouse. It is an admirably strong, hardy, handsome, independent bird, able with comfort to bid defiance to heat, cold, drought, hunger, and all sorts of storms, living on whatever seeds or insects chance to come in its way, or simply on the leaves of sage-brush, everywhere abundant on its desert range. In winter, when the temperature is oftentimes below zero, and heavy snowstorms are blowing, he sits beneath a sage bush and allows himself to be covered, poking his head now and then through the snow to feed on the leaves of his shelter. Not even the Arctic ptarmigan is hardier in braving frost and snow and wintry darkness. When in full plumage he is a beautiful bird, with a long, firm, sharp-pointed tail, which in walking is slightly raised and swings sidewise back and forth with each step. The male is handsomely marked with black and white on the neck, back, and wings, weighs five or six pounds, and measures about thirty inches in length. The female is clad mostly in plain brown, and is not so large. They occasionally wander from the sage plains into the open nut-pine and juniper woods, but never enter the main coniferous forest. It is only in the broad, dry, half-desert

544

sage plains that they are quite at home, where the weather is blazing hot in summer, cold in winter. If anyone passes through a flock, all squat on the grey ground and hold their heads low, hoping to escape observation; but when approached within a rod or so, they rise with a magnificent burst of wing-beats, looking about as big as turkeys and making a noise like a whirlwind.

On the 28 June, at the head of Owens Valley, I caught one of the young that was then just able to fly. It was seven inches long, of a uniform grey colour, blunt-billed, and when captured cried lustily in a shrill piping voice, clear in tone as a boy's small willow whistle. I have seen flocks of from ten to thirty or forty on the east margin of the Park, where the Mono Desert meets the grey foothills of the Sierra; but since cattle have been pastured there they are becoming rarer every year.

Another magnificent bird, the blue or dusky grouse, next in size to the sage cock, is found all through the main forest belt, though not in great numbers. They like best the heaviest silver-fir woods near garden and meadow openings, where there is but little underbrush to cover the approach of enemies. When a flock of these brave birds, sauntering and feeding on the sunny, flowery levels of some hidden meadow or Yosemite valley far back in the heart of the mountains, see a man for the first time in their lives, they rise with hurried notes of surprise and excitement and alight on the lowest branches of the trees, wondering what the wanderer may be, and showing great eagerness to get a good view of the strange vertical animal. Knowing nothing of guns, they allow you to approach within a half dozen paces, then quietly hop a few branches higher or fly to the next tree without a thought of concealment, so that you may observe them as long as you like, near enough to see the fine shading of their plumage, the feathers on their toes, and the innocent wonderment in their beautiful wild eyes. But in the neighbourhood of roads and trails they soon become shy, and when disturbed fly into the highest, leafiest trees, and suddenly become invisible, so well do they know how to hide and keep still and make use of their protective colouring. Nor can they be easily dislodged ere they are ready to go. In vain the hunter goes round and round some tall pine or fir into which he has perhaps seen a dozen enter, gazing up through the branches, straining his eyes while his gun is held ready; not a feather can he see unless his eyes have been sharpened by long experience and knowledge of the blue grouse's habits. Then, perhaps, when he is thinking that the tree must be hollow and that the birds have all gone inside, they burst forth with a startling whir of wing-beats, and after gaining full speed go skating swiftly away through the forest arches in a long, silent, wavering slide, with wings held steady.

During the summer they are most of the time on the ground, feeding on insects, seeds, berries, etc., around the margins of open spots and rocky moraines, playing and sauntering, taking sun baths and sand baths, and drinking at little pools and rills during the heat of the day. In winter they live mostly in the trees, depending on buds for food, sheltering beneath dense overlapping branches at night and during storms on the leeside of the trunk, sunning themselves on the southside limbs in fine weather, and sometimes diving into the mealy snow to flutter and wallow, apparently for exercise and fun.

I have seen young broods running beneath the firs in June at a height of eight thousand feet above the sea. On the approach of danger, the mother with a peculiar cry warns the helpless midgets to scatter and hide beneath leaves and twigs, and even in plain open places it is almost impossible to discover them. In the meantime the mother feigns lameness, throws herself at your feet, kicks and gasps and flutters, to draw your attention from the chicks. The young are generally able to fly about the middle of July; but even after they can fly well they are usually advised to run and hide and lie still, no matter how closely approached, while the mother goes on with her loving, lying acting, apparently as desperately concerned for their safety as when they were featherless infants. Sometimes, however, after carefully studying the circumstances, she tells them to take wing; and up and away in a blurry birr and whir they scatter to all points of the compass, as if blown up with gunpowder, dropping cunningly out of sight three or four hundred yards off, and keeping quiet until called, after the danger is supposed to be past. If you walk on a little way without manifesting any inclination to hunt them, you may sit down at the foot of a tree near enough to see and hear the happy reunion. One touch of nature makes the whole world kin; and it is truly wonderful how love-telling the small voices of these birds are, and how far they reach through the woods into one another's hearts and into ours. The tones are so perfectly human and so full of anxious affection, few mountaineers can fail to be touched by them.

They are cared for until full grown. On the 20 August, as I was passing along the margin of a garden spot on the head-waters of the San Joaquin, a grouse rose from the ruins of an old juniper that had been uprooted and brought down by an avalanche from a cliff overhead. She threw herself at my feet, limped and fluttered and gasped, showing, as I thought, that she had a nest and was raising a second brood. Looking for the eggs, I was surprised to see a strong-winged flock nearly as large as the mother fly up around me.

Instead of seeking a warmer climate when the winter storms set in, these hardy birds stay all the year in the High Sierra forests, and I have never known them to suffer in any sort of weather. Able to live on the buds of pine, spruce, and fir, they are forever independent in the matter of food supply, which gives so many of us trouble, dragging us here and there away from our best work. How gladly I would live on pine buds, however pitchy, for the sake of this grand independence! With all his superior resources, man makes more distracting difficulty concerning food than any other of the family.

The mountain quail, or plumed partridge (*Oreortyx pictus plumiferus*) is common in all the upper portions of the Park, though nowhere in numbers. He ranges considerably higher than the grouse in summer, but is unable to endure the heavy storms of winter. When his food is buried, he descends the range to the brushy foothills, at a height of from two thousand to three thousand feet above the sea; but like every true mountaineer, he is quick to follow the spring back into the highest mountains. I think he is the very handsomest and most interesting of all the American partridges, larger and handsomer than the famous Bob White, or even the fine California valley quail, or the Massena partridge of Arizona and Mexico. That he is not so regarded, is because as a lonely mountaineer he is not half known.

His plumage is delicately shaded, brown above, white and rich chestnut below and on the sides, with many dainty markings of black and white and grey here and there, while his beautiful head plume, three or four inches long, nearly straight, composed of two feathers closely folded so as to appear as one, is worn jauntily slanted backward like a single feather in a boy's cap, giving him a very marked appearance. They wander over the lonely mountains in family flocks of from six to fifteen, beneath ceanothus, manzanita, and wild cherry thickets, and over dry sandy flats, glacier meadows, rocky ridges, and beds of bryanthus around glacier lakes, especially in autumn, when the berries of the upper gardens are ripe, uttering low clucking notes to enable them to keep together. When they are so suddenly disturbed that they are afraid they cannot escape the danger by running into thickets, they rise with a fine hearty whir and scatter in the brush over an area of half a square mile or so, a few of them diving into leafy trees. But as soon as the danger is past, the parents with a clear piping note call them together again. By the end of July the young are two thirds grown and fly well, though only dire necessity can compel them to try their wings. In gait, gestures, habits, and general behaviour they are like domestic chickens, but infinitely finer, searching for insects and seeds, looking to this side and that, scratching among fallen leaves, jumping up to pull down grass heads, and clucking and muttering in low tones.

Once when I was seated at the foot of a tree on the head-waters of the Merced, sketching, I heard a flock up the valley behind me, and by their voices gradually sounding nearer I knew that they were feeding toward me. I kept still, hoping to see them. Soon one came within three or four feet of me, without noticing me any more than if I were a stump or a bulging part of the trunk against which I was leaning, my clothing being brown, nearly like the bark. Presently along came another and another, and it was delightful to get so near a view of these handsome chickens perfectly undisturbed, observe their manners, and hear their low peaceful notes. At last one of them caught my eye, gazed in silent wonder for a moment, then uttered a peculiar cry, which was followed by a lot of hurried muttered notes that sounded like speech. The others, of course, saw me as soon as the alarm was sounded, and joined the wonder talk, gazing and chattering, astonished but not frightened. Then all with one accord ran back with the news to the rest of the flock. 'What is it? What is it? Oh, you never saw the like', they seemed to be saying. 'Not a deer, or a wolf, or a bear; come see, come see.' 'Where? Where?' 'Down there by that tree.' Then they approached cautiously, past the tree, stretching their necks, and looking up in turn as if knowing from the story told them just where I was. For fifteen or twenty minutes they kept coming and going, venturing within a few feet of me, and discussing the wonder in charming chatter. Their curiosity at last satisfied, they began to scatter and feed again, going back in the direction they had come from; while I, loath to part with them, followed noiselessly, crawling beneath the bushes, keeping them in sight for an hour or two, learning their habits, and finding out what seeds and berries they liked best.

The valley quail is not a mountaineer, and seldom enters the Park except at a few of the lowest places on the western boundary. It belongs to the brushy foothills and plains, orchards and wheatfields, and is a hundred times more numerous than the mountain quail. It is a beautiful bird, about the size of the Bob White, and has a handsome crest of four or five feathers an inch long, recurved, standing nearly erect at times or drooping forward. The loud calls of these quails in the spring – Pe-check-ah, Pe-check-a, Hoy, Hoy – are heard far and near over all the lowlands. They have vastly increased in numbers since the settlement of the country, notwithstanding the immense numbers killed every season by boys and pot-hunters as well as the regular leggined sportsmen from the towns; for man's destructive action is more than counter-balanced by increased supply of food from cultivation, and by the destruction of their enemies – coyotes, skunks, foxes, hawks, owls, etc. – which not only kill the old birds, but plunder their nests. Where coyotes and skunks abound, scarce one pair in a hundred is successful in raising a brood. So well aware are these birds of the protection afforded by man, even now that the number of their wild enemies has been greatly diminished, that they prefer to nest near houses, notwithstanding they are so shy. Four or five pairs rear their young around our cottage every spring. One year a pair nested in a straw pile within four or five feet of the stable door, and did not leave the eggs when the men led the horses back and forth within a foot or two. For many seasons a pair nested in a tuft of pampas grass in the garden; another pair in an ivy vine on the cottage roof, and when the young were hatched, it was interesting to see the parents getting the fluffy dots down. They were greatly excited, and their anxious calls and directions to their many babes attracted our attention. They had no great difficulty in persuading the young birds to pitch themselves from the main roof to the porch roof among the ivy, but to get them safely down from the latter to the ground, a distance of ten feet, was most distressing. It seemed impossible the frail soft things could avoid being killed. The anxious parents led them to a point above a spiræa bush, that reached nearly to the eaves, which they seemed to know would break the fall. Anyhow they led their chicks to this point, and with infinite coaxing and encouragement got them to tumble themselves off. Down they rolled and sifted through the soft leaves and panicles to the pavement, and, strange to say, all got away unhurt except one that lay as if dead for a few minutes. When it revived, the joyful parents, with their brood fairly launched on the journey of life, proudly led them down the cottage hill, through the garden, and along an osage orange hedge into the cherry orchard. These charming birds even enter towns and villages, where the gardens are of good size and guns are forbidden, some-times going several miles to feed, and returning every evening to their roots in ivy or brushy trees and shrubs.

Geese occasionally visit the Park, but never stay long. Sometimes on their way across the range, a flock wanders into Hetch Hetchy or Yosemite to rest or get something to eat, and if shot at, are often sorely bewildered in seeking a way out. I have seen them rise from the meadow or river, wheel round in a spiral until a height of four or five hundred feet was reached, then form ranks and try to fly over the wall. But Yosemite magnitudes seem to be as deceptive to geese as to men, for they would suddenly find themselves against the cliffs not a fourth of the way to the top. Then turning in confusion, and screaming at the strange heights, they would try the opposite side, and so on until exhausted they were compelled to rest, and only after discovering the river canyon could they make their escape. Large, harrow-shaped flocks may often be seen crossing the range in the spring, at a height of at least fourteen thousand feet. Think of the strength of wing required to sustain so heavy a bird in air so thin. At this elevation it is but little over half as dense as at the sea level. Yet they hold bravely on in beautifully dressed ranks, and have breath enough to spare for loud honking. After the crest of the Sierra is passed it is only a smooth slide down the sky to the waters of Mono, where they may rest as long as they like.

Ducks of five or six species, among which are the mallard and wood duck, go far up into the heart of the mountains in the spring, and of course come down in the fall with the families they have reared. A few, as if loath to leave the mountains, pass the winter in the lower valleys of the Park at a height of three thousand to four thousand feet, where the main streams are never wholly frozen over, and snow never falls to a great depth or lies long. In summer they are found up to a height of eleven thousand feet on all the lakes and branches of the rivers except the smallest, and those beside the glaciers incumbered with drifting ice and snow. I found mallards and wood ducks at Lake Tenaya, 1 June, before the ice-covering was half melted, and a flock of young ones in Bloody Canyon Lake, 20 June. They are usually met in pairs, never in large flocks. No place is too wild or rocky or solitary for these brave swimmers, no stream too rapid. In the roaring, resounding canyon torrents, they seem as much at home as in the tranquil reaches and lakes of the broad glacial valleys. Abandoning themselves to the wild play of the waters, they go drifting confidingly through blinding, thrashing spray, dancing on boulder-dashed waves, tossing in beautiful security on rougher water than is usually encountered by sea birds when storms are blowing.

A mother duck with her family of ten little ones, waltzing round and round in a pot-hole ornamented with foam bells, huge rocks leaning over them, cascades above and below and beside them, made one of the most interesting bird pictures I ever saw.

I have never found the great northern diver in the Park lakes. Most of them are inaccessible to him. He might plump down into them, but would hardly be able to get out of them, since, with his small wings and heavy body, a wide expanse of elbow room is required in rising. Now and then one may be seen in the lower Sierra lakes to the northward about Lassens Butte and Shasta, at a height of four thousand to five thousand feet, making the loneliest places lonelier with the wildest of wild cries.

Plovers are found along the sandy shores of nearly all the mountain lakes, tripping daintily on the water's edge, picking up insects; and it is interesting to learn how few of these familiar birds are required to make a solitude cheerful.

Sandhill cranes are sometimes found in comparatively small marshes, mere dots in the mighty forest. In such spots, at an elevation of from six thousand to eight thousand feet above the sea, they are occasionally met in pairs as early as the end of May, while the snow is still deep in the surrounding fir and sugar-pine woods. And on sunny days in autumn, large flocks may be seen sailing at a great height above the forests, shaking the crisp air into rolling waves with their hearty koor-r-r, koor-r-r, uck-uck, soaring in circles for hours together on their majestic wings, seeming to float without effort like clouds, eying the wrinkled landscape outspread like a map mottled with lakes and glaciers and meadows and streaked with shadowy canyons and streams, and surveying every frog marsh and sandy flat within a hundred miles.

Eagles and hawks are oftentimes seen above the ridges and domes. The greatest height at which I have observed them was about twelve thousand feet, over the summits of Mount Hoffman, in the middle region of the Park. A few pairs had their nests on the cliffs of this mountain, and could be seen every day in summer, hunting marmots, mountain beavers, pikas, etc. A pair of golden eagles have made their home in Yosemite ever since I went there thirty years ago. Their nest is on the Nevada Fall Cliff, opposite the Liberty Cap. Their screams are rather pleasant to hear in the vast gulfs between the granite cliffs, and they help the owls in keeping the echoes busy.

But of all the birds of the High Sierra, the strangest, noisiest, and most notable is the Clarke crow (*Nucifraga columbiana*). He is a foot long and nearly two feet in extent of wing, ashy grey in general colour, with black wings, white tail, and a strong, sharp bill, with which he digs into the pine cones for the seeds on which he mainly subsists. He is quick, boisterous, jerky, and irregular in his movements and speech, and makes a tremendously loud and showy advertisement of himself – swooping and diving in deep curves across gorges and valleys from ridge to ridge, alighting on dead spars, looking warily about him, and leaving his dry springy perches, trembling from the vigour of his kick as he launches himself for a new flight, screaming from time to time loud enough to be heard more than a mile in still weather. He dwells far back on the high stormbeaten margin of the forest, where the mountain pine, juniper, and hemlock grow wide apart on glacier pavements and domes and rough crumbling ridges, and the dwarf pine makes a low crinkled growth along the flanks of the Summit peaks. In so open a region, of course, he is well seen. Everybody notices him, and nobody at first knows what to make of him. One guesses he must be a woodpecker; another a crow or some sort of jay, another a magpie. He seems to be a pretty thoroughly mixed and fermented compound of all these birds, has all their strength, cunning, shyness, thievishness, and wary, suspicious curiosity combined and condensed. He flies like a woodpecker, hammers dead limbs for insects, digs big holes in pine cones to get at the seeds, cracks nuts held between his toes, cries like a crow or Stellar jay – but in a far louder, harsher, and more forbidding tone of voice – and besides his crow caws and screams, has a great variety of small chatter talk, mostly uttered in a fault-finding tone. Like the magpie, he steals articles that can be of no use to him. Once when I made my camp in a grove at Cathedral Lake, I chanced to leave a cake of soap on the shore where I had been washing, and a few minutes afterward I saw my soap flying past me through the grove, pushed by a Clarke crow.

In winter, when the snow is deep, the cones of the mountain pines are empty, and the juniper, hemlock, and dwarf pine orchard buried, he comes down to glean seeds in the yellow pine forests, startling the grouse with his loud screams. But even in winter, in calm weather, he stays in his high mountain home, defying the bitter frost. Once I lay snowbound through a three days' storm at the timber-line on Mount Shasta; and while the roaring snow-laden blast swept by, one of these brave birds came to my camp, and began hammering at the cones on the topmost branches of half-buried pines, without showing the slightest distress. I have seen Clarke crows feeding their young as early as 19 June, at a height of more than ten thousand feet, when nearly the whole landscape was snow-covered.

They are excessively shy, and keep away from the traveller as long as they think they are observed; but when one goes on without seeming to notice them, or sits down and keeps still, their curiosity speedily gets the better of their caution, and they come flying from tree to tree, nearer and nearer, and watch every motion. Few, I am afraid, will ever learn to like this bird, he is so suspicious and self-reliant, and his voice is so harsh that to most ears the scream of the eagle will seem melodious compared with it. Yet the mountaineer who has battled and suffered and struggled must admire his strength and endurance – the way he faces the mountain weather, cleaves the icy blasts, cares for his young, and digs a living from the stern wilderness.

Higher yet than Nucifraga dwells the little dun-headed sparrow (*Leucosticte tephrocotis*). From early spring to late autumn he is to be found only on the snowy, icy peaks at the head of the glacier cirques and canyons. His feeding grounds in spring are the snow sheets between the peaks, and in midsummer and autumn the glaciers. Many bold insects go mountaineering almost as soon as they are born, ascending the highest summits on the mild breezes that blow in from the sea every day during steady weather; but comparatively few of these adventurers find their way down or see a flower bed again. Getting tired and chilly, they alight on the snow fields and glaciers, attracted perhaps by the glare, take cold, and die. There they lie as if on a white cloth purposely outspread for them, and the dun sparrows find them a rich and varied repast requiring no pursuit – bees and butterflies on ice, and many spicy beetles, a perpetual feast on tables big for guests so small, and in vast banqueting halls ventilated by cool breezes that ruffle the feathers of the fairy brownies. Happy fellows, no rivals come to dispute possession with them. No other birds, not even hawks, as far as I have noticed, live so high. They see people so seldom, they flutter around the explorer with the liveliest curiosity, and come down a little way, sometimes nearly a mile, to meet him and conduct him into their icy homes.

When I was exploring the Merced group, climbing up the grand canyon between the Merced and Red mountains into the fountain amphitheatre of an ancient glacier, just as I was approaching the small active glacier that leans back in the shadow of Merced Mountain, a flock of twenty or thirty of these little birds, the first I had seen, came down the canyon to meet me, flying low, straight toward me as if they meant to fly in my face. Instead of attacking me or passing by, they circled round my head, chirping and fluttering for a minute or two, then turned and escorted me up the canyon, alighting on the nearest rocks on either hand, and flying ahead a few yards at a time to keep even with me.

I have not discovered their winter quarters. Probably they are in the desert ranges to the eastward, for I never saw any of them in Yosemite, the winter refuge of so many of the mountain birds.

Humming-birds are among the best and most conspicuous of the mountaineers, flashing their ruby throats in countless wild gardens far up the higher slopes, where they would be least expected. All one has to do to enjoy the company of these mountain-loving midgets is to display a showy blanket or handkerchief.

The arctic bluebird is another delightful mountaineer, singing a wild, cheery song and 'carrying the sky on his back' over all the grey ridges and domes of the subalpine region.

A fine, hearty, good-natured lot of woodpeckers dwell in the Park, and keep it lively all the year round. Among the most notable of these are the magnificent log cock (*Ceophlœus pileatus*), the prince of Sierra woodpeckers, and only second in rank as far as I know, of all the woodpeckers of the world; the Lewis woodpecker, large, black, glossy, that flaps and flies like a crow, does but little hammering, and feeds in great part on wild cherries and berries; and the carpenter, who stores up great quantities of acorns in the bark of trees for winter use. The last-named species is a beautiful bird, and far more common than the others. In the woods of the West he represents the Eastern red-head. Bright, cheerful, industrious, not in the least shy, the carpenters give delightful animation to the open Sierra forests at a height of from three thousand to fifty-five hundred feet, especially in autumn, when the acorns are ripe. Then no squirrel works harder at his pine-nut harvest than these woodpeckers at their acorn harvest, drilling holes in the thick, corky bark of the yellow pine and incense cedar, in which to store the crop for winter use – a hole for each acorn, so nicely adjusted as to size that when the acorn, point foremost, is driven in, it fits so well that it cannot be drawn out without digging around it. Each acorn is thus carefully stored in a dry bin, perfectly protected from the weather – a most laborious method of stowing away a crop, a granary for each kernel. Yet the birds seem never to weary at the work, but go on so diligently that they seem determined to save every acorn in the grove. They are never seen eating acorns at the time they are storing them, and it is commonly believed that they never eat them or intend to eat them, but that the wise birds store them and protect them from the depredations of squirrels and jays, solely for the sake of the worms they are supposed to contain. And because these worms are too small for use at the time the acorns drop, they are shut up like lean calves and steers, each in a separate stall with abundance of food, to grow big and fat by the time they will be most wanted, that is, in winter, when insects are scarce and stall-fed worms most valuable. So these woodpeckers are supposed to be a sort of cattle-raisers, each with a drove of thousands, rivalling the ants that raise grain and keep herds of plant lice for milk cows. Needless to say the story is not true, though some naturalists, even, believe it. When Emerson was in the Park, having heard the worm story and seen the great pines plugged full of acorns, he asked (just to pump me, I suppose), 'Why do the woodpeckers take the trouble to put acorns into the bark of the trees?' 'For the same reason', I replied, 'that bees store honey and squirrels nuts.' 'But they tell me, Mr Muir, that woodpeckers don't eat acorns.' 'Yes they do', I said, 'I have seen them eating them. During snowstorms they seem to eat little besides acorns. I have repeatedly interrupted them at their meals, and seen the perfectly sound, half-eaten acorns. They eat them in the shell as some people eat eggs'. 'But what about the worms?' 'I suppose', I said, 'that when they come to a wormy one they eat both worm and acorn. Anyhow, they eat the sound ones when they can't find anything they like better, and from the time they store them until they are used they guard them, and woe to the squirrel or jay caught stealing'. Indians, in times of scarcity, frequently resort to these stores and chop them out with hatchets; a bushel or more may be gathered from a single cedar or pine.

The common robin, with all his familiar notes and gestures, is found nearly everywhere throughout the Park – in shady dells beneath dogwoods and maples, along the flowery banks of the streams, tripping daintily about the margins of meadows in the fir and pine woods, and far beyond on the shores of glacier lakes and the slopes of the peaks. How admirable the constitution and temper of this cheery, graceful bird, keeping glad health over so vast and varied a range. In all America he is at home, flying from plains to mountains, up and down, north and south, away and back, with the seasons and supply of food. Oftentimes in the High Sierra, as you wander through the solemn woods, awestricken and silent, you will hear the reassuring voice of this fellow wanderer ringing out sweet and clear as if saying, 'Fear not, fear not. Only love is here'. In the severest solitudes he seems as happy as in gardens and apple orchards.

The robins enter the Park as soon as the snow melts, and go on up the mountains, gradually higher, with the opening flowers, until the topmost glacier meadows are reached in June and July. After the short summer is done, they descend like most other summer visitors in concord with the weather, keeping out of the first heavy snows as much as possible, while lingering among the frost-nipped wild cherries on the slopes just below the glacier meadows. Thence they go to the lower slopes of the forest region, compelled to make haste at times by heavy all-day storms, picking up seeds or benumbed insects by the way; and at last all, save a few that winter in Yosemite valleys, arrive in the vineyards and orchards and stubble-fields of the lowlands in November, picking up fallen fruit and grain, and awakening old-time memories among the white-headed pioneers, who cannot fail to recognize the influence of so homelike a bird. They are then in flocks of hundreds, and make their way into the gardens of towns as well as into the parks and fields and orchards about the bay of San Francisco, where many of the wanderers are shot for sport and the morsel of meat on their breasts. Man then seems a beast of prey. Not even genuine piety can make the robin-killer quite respectable. Saturday is the great slaughter day in the bay region. Then the city pot-hunters, with a rag-tag of boys, go forth to kill, kept in countenance by a sprinkling of regular sportsmen arrayed in self-conscious majesty and leggins, leading dogs and carrying hammerless, breech-loading guns of famous makers. Over the fine landscapes the killing goes forward with shameful enthusiasm. After escaping countless dangers, thousands fall, big bagfuls are gathered, many are left wounded to die slowly, no Red Cross Society to help them. Next day, Sunday, the blood and leggins vanish from the most devout of the bird-butchers, who go to church, carrying gold-headed canes instead of guns. After hymns, prayers and sermon they go home to feast, to put God's song birds to use, put them in their dinners instead of in their hearts, eat them, and suck the pitiful little drumsticks. It is only race living on race, to be sure, but Christians singing Divine Love need not be driven to such straits while wheat and apples grow and the shops are full of dead cattle. Song birds for food! Compared with this, making kindlings of pianos and violins would be pious economy.

The larks come in large flocks from the hills and mountains in the autumn, and are slaughtered as ruthlessly as the robins. Fortunately, most of our song birds keep back in leafy hidings, and are comparatively inaccessible.

The water ouzel, in his rocky home amid foaming waters, seldom sees a gun, and of all the singers I like him the best. He is a plainly dressed little bird, about the size of a robin, with short, crisp, but rather broad wings, and a tail of moderate length, slanted up, giving him, with his nodding, bobbing manners, a wrennish look. He is usually seen fluttering about in the spray of falls and the rapid cascading portions of the main branches of the rivers. These are his favourite haunts; but he is often seen also on comparatively level reaches and occasionally on the shores of mountain lakes, especially at the beginning of winter, when heavy snowfalls have blurred the streams with sludge. Though not a water-bird in structure, he gets his living in the water, and is never seen away from the immediate margin of streams. He dives fearlessly into rough, boiling eddies and rapids to feed at the bottom, flying under water seemingly as easily as in the air. Sometimes he wades in shallow places, thrusting his head under from time to time in a nodding, frisky way that is sure to attract attention. His flight is a solid whir of wing-beats like that of a partridge, and in going from place to place along his favourite string of rapids he follows the windings of the stream, and usually alights on some rock or snag on the bank or out in the current, or rarely on the dry limb of an overhanging tree, perching like a tree bird when it suits his convenience. He has the oddest, neatest manners imaginable, and all his geatures as he flits about in the wild, dashing waters bespeak the utmost cheerfulness and confidence. He sings both winter and summer, in all sorts of weather – a sweet, fluty melody, rather low, and much less keen and accentuated than from the brisk vigour of his movements one would be led to expect.

How romantic and beautiful is the life of this brave little singer on the wild mountain streams, building his round bossy nest of moss by the side of a rapid or fall, where it is sprinkled and kept fesh and green by the spray! No wonder he sings well, since all the air about him is music; every breath he draws is part of a song, and he gets his first music lessons before he is born; for the eggs vibrate in time with the tones of the waterfalls. Bird and stream are inseparable, songful and wild, gentle and strong – the bird ever in danger in the midst of the stream's mad whirlpools, yet seemingly immortal. And so I might go on, writing words, words, words; but to what purpose? Go see him and love him, and through him as through a window look into Nature's warm heart.

CHAPTER EIGHT

The Fountains and Streams of the Yosemite National Park

'Come let's to the fields, the meads, and the mountains,
The forests invite us, the streams and the fountains'.
Carlyle, *Translations*, vol. iii.

THE joyful, songful streams of the Sierra are among the most famous and interesting in the world, and draw the admiring traveller on and on through their wonderful canyons, year after year, unwearied. After long wanderings with them, tracing them to their fountains, learning their history and the forms they take in their wild works and way throughout the different seasons of the year, we may then view them together in one magnificent show, outspread over all the range like embroidery, their silvery branches interlacing on a thousand mountains, singing their way home to the sea: the small rills, with hard roads to travel, dropping from ledge to ledge, pool to pool, like chains of sweet-toned bells, slipping gently over beds of pebbles and sand, resting in lakes, shining, spangling, shimmering, lapping the shores with whispering ripples, and shaking over-leaning bushes and grass; the larger streams and rivers in the canyons displaying noble purity and beauty with ungovernable energy, rushing down smooth inclines in wide foamy sheets fold over fold, springing up here and there in magnificent whirls, scattering crisp clashing spray for the sunbeams to iris, bursting with hoarse reverberating roar through rugged gorges and boulder dams, booming in falls, gliding, glancing with cool soothing murmuring, through long forested reaches richly embowered – filling the grand canyons with glorious song, and giving life to all the landscape.

The present rivers of the Sierra are still young, and have made but little mark as yet on the grand canyons prepared for them by the ancient glaciers. Only a very short geological time ago they all lay buried beneath the glaciers they drained, singing in low smothered or silvery ringing tones in crystal channels, while the summer weather melted the ice and snow of the surface or gave showers. At first only in warm weather was any part of these buried rivers displayed in the light of day; for as soon as frost prevailed the surface rills vanished, though the streams beneath the ice and in the body of it flowed on all the year.

When, toward the close of the glacial period, the ice mantle began to shrink and recede from the lowlands, the lower portions of the rivers were developed, issuing from cavelike openings on the melting margin and growing longer as the ice withdrew; while for many a century the tributaries and upper portions of the trunks remained covered. In the fullness of time these also were set free in the sunshine, to take their places in the newborn landscapes; each tributary with its smaller branches being gradually developed like the main trunks, as the climatic changes went on. At first all of them were muddy with glacial detritus, and they became clear only after the glaciers they drained had receded beyond lake basins in which the sediments were dropped.

This early history is clearly explained by the present rivers of southeastern Alaska. Of those draining glaciers that discharge into arms of the sea, only the rills on the surface of the ice, and upboiling, eddying, turbid currents in the tide water in front of the terminal ice wall, are visible. Where glaciers, in the first stage of decadence, have receded from the shore, short sections of the trunks of the rivers that are to take their places may be seen rushing out from caverns and tunnels in the melting front – rough, roaring, detritus-laden torrents, foaming and tumbling over outspread terminal moraines to the sea, perhaps without a single bush or flower to brighten their raw, shifting banks. Again, in some of the warmer canyons and valleys from which the trunk glaciers have been melted, the main trunks of the rivers are well developed, and their banks planted with fine forests, while their upper branches, lying high on the snowy mountains, are still buried beneath shrinking residual glaciers; illustrating every stage of development, from icy darkness to light, and from muddiness to crystal clearness.

Now that the hard grinding sculpture work of the glacial period is done, the whole bright band of Sierra rivers run clear all the year, except when the snow is melting fast in the warm spring weather, and during extraordinary winter floods and the heavy thunderstorms of summer called cloud-bursts. Even then they are not muddy above the foothill mining region, unless the moraines have been loosened and the vegetation destroyed by sheep; for the rocks of the upper basins are clean, and the most able streams find but little to carry save the spoils of the forests – trees, branches, flakes of bark, cones, leaves, pollen dust, etc. – with scales of mica, sand grains, and boulders, which are rolled along the bottom of the steep parts of the main channels. Short sections of a few of the highest tributaries heading in glaciers are of course turbid with finely ground rock mud, but this is dropped in the first lakes they enter.

On the northern part of the range, mantled with porous fissured volcanic rocks, the fountain waters sink and flow below the surface for considerable distances, groping their way in the dark like the draining streams of glaciers, and at last bursting forth in big generous springs, filtered and cool and exquisitely clear. Some of the largest look like lakes, their waters welling straight up from the bottom of deep rock basins in quiet massive volume giving rise to young rivers. Others issue from horizontal clefts in sheer bluffs, with loud tumultuous roaring that may be heard half a mile or more. Magnificent examples of these great northern spring fountains, twenty or thirty feet deep and ten to nearly a hundred yards wide, abound on the main branches of the Feather, Pitt, McCloud, and Fall Rivers.

The springs of the Yosemite Park, and the High Sierra in general, though many times more numerous, are comparatively small, oozing from moraines and snowbanks in thin, flat irregular currents which remain on the surface or near it, the rocks of the south half of the range being mostly flawless impervious granite; and since granite is but slightly soluble, the streams are particularly pure. Nevertheless, though they are all clear, and in the upper and main central forest regions delightfully lively and cool, they vary somewhat in colour and taste as well as temperature, on account of differences, however slight, in exposure, and in the rocks and vegetation with which they come in contact. Some are more exposed than others to winds and sunshine in their falls and thin plumelike cascades; the amount of dashing, mixing, and airing the waters of each receive varies considerably; and there is always more or less variety in the kind and quantity of the vegetation they flow through, and in the time they lie in shady or sunny lakes and bogs.

The water of one of the branches of the north fork of Owens River, near the southeastern boundary of the Park, at an elevation of ninety-five hundred feet above the sea, is the best I ever found. It is not only delightfully cool and bright, but brisk, sparkling, exhilarating, and so positively delicious to the taste that a party of friends I led to it twenty-five years ago still praise it, and refer to it as 'that wonderful champagne water'; though, comparatively, the finest wine is a coarse and vulgar drink. The party camped about a week in a pine grove on the edge of a little round sedgy meadow through which the stream ran bank full, and drank its icy water on frosty mornings, before breakfast, and at night about as eagerly as in the heat of the day; lying down and taking massy draughts direct from the brimming flood, lest the touch of a cup might disturb its celestial flavour. On one of my excursions I took pains to trace this stream to its head-springs. It is mostly derived from snow that lies in heavy drifts and avalanche heaps on or near the axis of the range. It flows first in flat sheets over coarse sand or shingle derived from a granite ridge and the metamorphic slates of Red Mountain. Then, gathering its many small branches, it runs through beds of moraine material, and a series of lakelets and meadows and frosty juicy bogs bordered with heathworts and linked together by short bouldery reaches. Below these, growing strong with tribute drawn from many a snowy fountain on either side, the glad stream goes dashing and swirling through clumps of the white-barked pine, and tangled willow and alder thickets enriched by the fragrant herbaceous vegetation usually found about them. And just above the level camp meadow it is chafed and churned and beaten white over and over again in crossing a talus of big earthquake boulders, giving it a very thorough airing. But to what the peculiar indefinable excellence of this water is due I don't know; for other streams in adjacent canyons are aired in about the same way, and draw traces of minerals and plant essences from similar sources. The best mineral water yet discovered in the Park flows from the Tuolumne soda springs, on the north side of the Big

Meadow. Mountaineers like it and ascribe every healing virtue to it, but in no way can any of these waters be compared with the Owens River champagne.

It is a curious fact that the waters of some of the Sierra lakes and streams are invisible, or nearly so, under certain weather conditions. This is noticed by mountaineers, hunters, and prospectors, wide-awake, sharp-eyed observers, little likely to be fooled by fine whims. One of these mountain men, whom I had nursed while a broken leg was mending, always gratefully reported the wonders he found. Once, returning from a trip on the head waters of the Tuolumne, he came running eagerly, crying: 'Muir, I've found the queerest lake in the mountains! It's high up where nothing grows; and when it isn't shiny you can't see it, and you walk right into it as if there was nothing there. The first you know of that lake you are in it, and get tripped up by the water, and hear the splash.' The waters of Illilouette Creek are nearly invisible in the autumn; so that, in following the channel, jumping from boulder to boulder after a shower, you will frequently drag your feet in the apparently surfaceless pools.

Excepting a few low, warm slopes, fountain snow usually covers all the Yosemite Park from November or December to May, most of it until June or July, while on the coolest parts of the north slopes of the mountains, at a height of eleven to thirteen thousand feet, it is perpetual. It seldom lies at a greater depth than two or three feet on the lower margin, ten feet over the middle forested region, or fifteen to twenty feet in the shadowy canyons and cirques among the peaks of the Summit, except where it is drifted, or piled in avalanche heaps at the foot of long converging slopes to form perennial fountains.

The first crop of snow crystals that whitens the mountains and refreshes the streams usually falls in September or October, in the midst of charming Indian summer weather, often while the goldenrods and gentians are in their prime; but these Indian summer snows, like some of the late ones that bury the June gardens, vanish in a day or two, and garden work goes on with accelerated speed. The grand winter storms that load the mountains with enduring fountain snow seldom set in before the end of November. The fertile clouds, descending, glide about and hover in brooding silence, as if thoughtfully examining the forests and streams with reference to the work before them; then small flakes or single crystals appear, glinting and swirling in zigzags and spirals; and soon the thronging feathery masses fill the sky and make darkness like night, hurrying wandering mountaineers to their winter quarters. The first fall is usually about two to four feet deep. Then, with intervals of bright weather, not very cold, storm succeeds storm, heaping snow on snow, until from thirty to fifty or sixty feet has fallen; but on account of heavy settling and compacting, and the waste from evaporation and melting, the depth in the middle region, as stated above, rarely exceeds ten feet. Evaporation never wholly ceases, even in the coldest weather, and the sunshine between storms melts the surface more or less. Waste from melting also goes on at the bottom from summer heat stored in the rocks, as is shown by the rise of the streams after the first general storm, and their steady sustained flow all winter.

In the deep sugar pine and silver fir woods, up to a height of eight thousand feet, most of the snow lies where it falls, in one smooth universal fountain, until set free in the streams. But in the lighter forests of the two-leaved pine, and on the bleak slopes above the timber line, there is much wild drifting during storms accompanied by high winds, and for a day or two after they have fallen, when the temperature is low, and the snow dry and dusty. Then the trees, bending in the darkening blast, roar like feeding lions; the frozen lakes are buried; so also are the streams, which now flow in dark tunnels, as if another glacial period had come. On high ridges, where the winds have a free sweep, magnificent overcurling cornices are formed, which, with the avalanche piles, last as fountains almost all summer; and when an exceptionally high wind is blowing from the north, the snow, rolled, drifted, and ground to dust, is driven up the converging northern slopes of the peaks and sent flying for miles in the form of bright wavering banners, displayed in wonderful clearness and beauty against the sky.

The greatest storms, however, are usually followed by a deep, peculiar silence, especially profound and solemn in the forests; and the noble trees stand hushed and motionless, as if under a spell, until the morning sunbeams begin to sift through their laden spires. Then the snow, shifting and falling from the top branches, strikes the lower ones in succession, and dislodges bossy masses all the way down. Thus each tree is enveloped in a hollow conical avalanche of fairy fineness, silvery white, irised on the outside; while the relieved branches spring up and wave with startling effect in the general stillness, as if moving of their own volition. These beautiful tree avalanches, hundreds of which may be seen falling at once on fine mornings after storms, pile their snow in raised rings around corresponding hollows beneath the trees, making the forest mantle somewhat irregular, but without greatly influencing its duration and the flow of the streams.

The large storm avalanches are most abundant on the summit peaks of the range. They descend the broad, steep slopes, as well as narrow gorges and couloirs, with grand roaring and booming, and glide in graceful curves out on the glaciers they so bountifully feed.

Down in the main canyons of the middle region broad masses are launched over the brows of cliffs three or four thousand feet high, which, worn to dust by friction in falling so far through the air, oftentimes hang for a minute or two in front of the tremendous precipices like gauzy half-transparent veils, gloriously beautiful when the sun is shining through them. Most of the canyon avalanches, however, flow in regular channels, like the cascades of tributary streams. When the snow first gives way on the upper slopes of their basins a dull muffled rush and rumble is heard, which, increasing with heavy deliberation, seems to draw rapidly nearer with appalling intensity of tone. Presently the wild flood comes in sight, bounding out over bosses and sheer places, leaping from bench to bench, spreading and narrowing and throwing off clouds of whirling diamond dust like a majestic foamy cataract. Compared with cascades and falls, avalanches are short-lived, and the sharp clashing sounds so common in dashing water are usually wanting; but in their deep thunder tones and pearly purple-tinged whiteness, and in dress, gait, gestures and general behaviour, they are much alike.

Besides these common storm avalanches there are two other kinds, the annual and the century, which still further enrich the scenery, though their influence on fountains is comparatively small. Annual avalanches are composed of heavy compacted snow which has been subjected to frequent alternations of frost and thaw. They are developed on canyon and mountain sides, the greater number of them, at elevations of from nine to ten thousand feet, where the slopes are so inclined that the dry snows of winter accumulate and hold fast until the spring thaws sap their foundations and make them slippery. Then away in grand style go the ponderous icy masses, adorned with crystalline spray without any cloudy snow dust; some of the largest descending more than a mile with even, sustained energy and directness like thunderbolts. The grand century avalanches, that mow wide swaths through the upper forests, occur on shady mountain sides about ten to twelve thousand feet high, where, under ordinary conditions, the snow accumulated from winter to winter lies at rest for many years, allowing trees fifty to a hundred feet high to grow undisturbed on the slopes below them. On their way through the forests they usually make a clean sweep, stripping off the soil as well as the trees, clearing paths two or three hundred yards wide from the timber line to the glacier meadows, and piling the uprooted trees, head downward, in windrows along the sides like lateral moraines. Scars and broken branches on the standing trees bordering the gaps record the side depth of the overwhelming flood; and when we come to count the annual wood rings of the uprooted trees, we learn that some of these colossal avalanches occur only once in about a century, or even at still wider intervals.

Few mountaineers go far enough, during the snowy months, to see many avalanches, and fewer still know the thrilling exhilaration of riding on them. In all my wild mountaineering I have enjoyed only one avalanche ride; and the start was so sudden, and the end came so soon, I thought but little of the danger that goes with this sort of travel, though one thinks fast at such times. One calm, bright morning in Yosemite, after a hearty storm had given three or four feet of fresh snow to the mountains, being eager to see as many avalanches as possible, and gain wide views of the peaks and forests arrayed in their new robes, before the sunshine had time to change or rearrange them, I set out early to climb by a side canyon to the top of a commanding ridge a little over three thousand feet above the valley. On account of the looseness of the snow that blocked the canyon I knew the climb would be trying, and estimated it might require three or four hours. But it proved far more difficult than I had foreseen. Most of the way I sank waist-deep, in some places almost out of sight; and after spending the day to within half an hour of sundown in this loose, baffling snow work, I was still several hundred feet below the summit. Then my hopes were reduced to getting up in time for the sunset, and a quick, sparkling home-going beneath the stars. But I was not to get top views of any sort that day; for deep trampling near the canyon head, where the snow was strained, started an avalanche, and I was swished back down to the foot of the canyon as if by enchantment. The plodding, wallowing ascent of about a mile had taken all day, the undoing descent perhaps a minute. When the snow suddenly gave way, I instinctively threw myself on my back and spread my arms, to try to keep from sinking. Fortunately, though the grade of the canyon was steep, it was not interrupted by step levels or precipices big enough to cause outbounding or free plunging. On no part of the rush was I buried. I was only moderately imbedded on the surface or a little below it, and covered with a hissing back-streaming veil of dusty snow particles; and as the whole mass beneath or about me joined in the flight I felt no friction, though tossed here and there, and lurched from side to side. And when the torrent swedged and came to rest, I found myself on the top of the crumpled pile, without a single bruise or scar. Hawthorne says that steam has spiritualized travel, notwithstanding the smoke, friction, smells and clatter of boat and rail riding. This flight in a milky way of snow flowers was the most spiritual of all my travels; and, after many years, the mere thought of it is still an exhilaration.

In the spring, after all the avalanches are down and the snow is melting fast, it is glorious to hear the streams sing out on the mountains. Every fountain swelling, countless rills hurry together to the rivers at the call of the sun – beginning to run and sing soon after sunrise, increasing until toward sundown, then gradually failing through the cold frosty hours of the night. Thus the volume of the upper rivers, even in flood time, is nearly doubled during the day, rising and falling as regularly as the tides of the sea. At the height of flood, in the warmest June weather, they seem fairly to shout for joy, and clash their upleaping waters together like clapping of hands; racing down the canyons with white manes flying in glorious exuberance of strength, compelling huge sleeping boulders to wake up and join in the dance and song to swell their chorus.

Then the plants also are in flood; the hidden sap singing into leaf and flower, responding as faithfully to the call of the sun as the streams from the snow, gathering along the outspread roots like rills in their channels on the mountains, rushing up the stems of herb and tree, swirling in their myriad cells like streams in potholes, spreading along the branches and breaking into foamy bloom, while fragrance, like a finer music, rises and flows with the winds.

About the same may be said of the spring gladness of blood when the red streams surge and sing in accord with the swelling plants and rivers, inclining animals and everybody to travel in hurrahing crowds like floods, while exhilarating melody in colour and fragrance, form and motion, flows to the heart through all the quickening senses.

In early summer the streams are in bright prime, running crystal clear, deep and full, but not overflowing their banks – about as deep through the night as the day, the variation so marked in spring being now too slight to be noticed. Nearly all the weather is cloudless sunshine, and everything is at its brightest – lake, river, garden and forest, with all their warm throbbing life. Most of the plants are in full leaf and flower; the blessed ouzels have built their mossy huts, and are now singing their sweetest songs on spray-sprinkled ledges beside the waterfalls.

In tranquil, mellow autumn, when the year's work is about done, when the fruits are ripe, birds and seeds out of their nests, and all the landscape is glowing like a benevolent countenance at rest, then the streams are at their lowest ebb – their wild rejoicing soothed to thoughtful calm. All the smaller tributaries whose branches do not reach back to the perennial fountains of the summit peaks shrink to whispering, tinkling currents. The snow of their basins gone, they are now fed only by small moraine springs, whose waters are mostly evaporated in passing over warm pavements, and in feeling their way from pool to pool through the midst of boulders and sand. Even the main streams are so low they may be easily forded, and their grand falls and cascades, now gentle and approachable, have waned to sheets and webs of embroidery, falling fold over fold in new and ever changing beauty.

Two of the most songful of the rivers, the Tuolumne and Merced, water nearly all the Park, spreading their branches far and wide, like broad-headed oaks; and the highest branches of each draw their sources from one and the same fountain on Mount Lyell, at an elevation of about thirteen thousand feet above the sea. The crest of the mountain, against which the head of the glacier rests, is worn to a thin blade full of joints, through which a part of the glacial water flows southward, giving rise to the highest trickling affluents of the Merced; while the main drainage, flowing northward, gives rise to those of the Tuolumne. After diverging for a distance of ten or twelve miles, these twin rivers flow in a general westerly direction, descending rapidly for the first thirty miles, and rushing in glorious apron cascades and falls from one Yosemite valley to another. Below the Yosemites they descend in grey rapids and swirling, swaying reaches, through the chaparral-clad canyons of the foothills and across the golden California plain, to their confluence with the San Joaquin, where, after all their long wanderings, they are only about ten miles apart.

The main canyons are from fifty to seventy miles long, and from two to four thousand feet deep, carved in the solid flank of the range. Though rough in some places and hard to travel, they are the most delightful of roads, leading through the grandest scenery, full of life and motion, and offering most telling lessons in earth sculpture. The walls, far from being unbroken, featureless cliffs, seem like ranges of separate mountains, so deep and varied is their sculpture; rising in lordly domes, towers, round-browed outstanding headlands, and clustering spires, with dark, shadowy side canyons between. But, however wonderful in height and mass and fineness of finish, no anomalous curiosities are presented, no 'freaks of nature'. All stand related in delicate rhythm, a grand glacial rock song.

Among the most interesting and influential of the secondary features of canyon scenery are the great avalanche taluses that lean against the walls at intervals of a mile or two. In the middle Yosemite region they are usually from three to five hundred feet high, and are made up of huge, angular, well-preserved, unshifting boulders, overgrown with grey lichens, trees, shrubs, and delicate flowering plants. Some of the largest of the boulders are forty or fifty feet cube, weighing from five to ten thousand tons; and where the cleavage joints of the granite are exceptionally wide apart a few blocks may be found nearly a hundred feet in diameter. These wonderful boulder piles are distributed throughout all the canyons of the range, completely choking them in some of the narrower portions, and no mountaineer will be likely to forget the savage roughness of the roads they make. Even the swift, overbearing rivers, accustomed to sweep everything out of their way, are in some places bridled and held in check by them. Foaming, roaring, in glorious majesty of flood, rushing off long rumbling trains of ponderous blocks without apparent effort, they are not able to move the largest, which, withstanding all assaults for centuries, are left at rest in the channels like islands, with gardens on their tops, fringed with foam below, with flowers above.

On some points concerning the origin of these taluses I was long in doubt. Plainly enough they were derived from the cliffs above them, the size of each talus being approximately measured by a scar on the wall, the rough angular surface of which contrasts with the rounded, glaciated, unfractured parts. I saw also that, instead of being slowly accumulated material, weathered off, boulder by boulder, in the ordinary way, almost every talus had been formed suddenly, in a single avalanche, and had not been increased in size during the last three or four centuries; for trees three or four hundred years old were growing on them, some standing at the top close to the wall, without a bruise or broken branch, showing that scarcely a single boulder had fallen among them since they were planted. Furthermore, all the taluses throughout the range seemed, by the trees and lichens growing on them, to be of the same age. All the phenomena pointed straight to a grand ancient earthquake. But I left the question open for years, and went on from canyon to canyon, observing again and again; measuring the heights of taluses throughout the range on both flanks, and the variations in the angles of their surface slopes; studying the way their boulders were assorted and related and brought to rest, and the cleavage joints of the cliffs from whence they were derived, cautious about making up my mind. Only after I had seen one made did all doubt as to their formation vanish.

In Yosemite Valley, one morning about two o'clock, I was aroused by an earthquake; and though I had never before enjoyed a storm of this sort, the strange, wild thrilling motion and rumbling could not be mistaken, and I ran out of my cabin, near the Sentinal Rock, both glad and frightened, shouting, 'A noble earthquake!' feeling sure I was going to learn something. The shocks were so violent and varied, and succeeded one another so closely, one had to balance in walking as if on the deck of a ship among the waves, and it seemed impossible the high cliffs should escape being shattered. In particular, I feared that the sheer-fronted Sentinel Rock, which rises to a height of three thousand feet, would be shaken down, and I took shelter back of a big pine, hoping I might be protected from outbounding boulders, should any come so far. I was now convinced that an earthquake had been the maker of the taluses, and positive proof soon came. It was a calm moonlight night, and no sound was heard for the first minute or two save a low muffled and underground rumbling and a slight rustling of the agitated trees, as if, in wrestling with the mountains, Nature were holding her breath. Then, suddenly, out of the strange silence and strange motion there came a tremendous roar. The

Eagle Rock, a short distance up the valley, had given way, and I saw it falling in thousands of the great boulders I had been studying so long, pouring to the valley floor in a free curve luminous from friction, making a terribly sublime and beautiful spectacle – an arc of fire fifteen hundred feet span, as true in form and as steady as a rainbow, in the midst of the stupendous roaring rock storm. The sound was inconceivably deep and broad and earnest, as if the whole earth, like a living creature, had at last found a voice and were calling to her sister planets. It seemed to me that if all the thunder I ever heard were condensed into one roar it would not equal this rock roar at the birth of a mountain talus. Think, then, of the roar that arose to heaven when all the thousands of ancient canyon taluses throughout the length and breadth of the range were simultaneously given birth.

The main storm was soon over, and, eager to see the new-born talus, I ran up the valley in the moonlight and climbed it before the huge blocks, after their wild fiery flight, had come to complete rest. They were slowly settling into their places, chafing, grating against one another, groaning, and whispering; but no motion was visible except in a stream of small fragments pattering down the face of the cliff at the head of the talus. A cloud of dust particles, the smallest of the boulders, floated out across the whole breadth of the valley and formed a ceiling that lasted until after sunrise; and the air was loaded with the odour of crushed Douglas spruces, from a grove that had been mowed down and mashed like weeds.

Sauntering about to see what other changes had been made, I found the Indians in the middle of the valley, terribly frightened, of course, fearing the angry spirits of the rocks were trying to kill them. The few whites wintering in the valley were assembled in front of the old Hutchings Hotel, comparing notes and meditating flight to steadier ground, seemingly as sorely frightened as the Indians. It is always interesting to see people in dead earnest, from whatever cause, and earthquakes make everybody earnest. Shortly after sunrise, a low blunt muffled rumbling, like distant thunder, was followed by another series of shocks, which, though not nearly so severe as the first, made the cliffs and domes tremble like jelly, and the big pines and oaks thrill and swish and wave their branches with startling effect. Then the groups of talkers were suddenly hushed, and the solemnity on their faces was sublime. One in particular of these winter neighbours, a rather thoughtful, speculative man, with whom I had often conversed, was a firm believer in the cataclysmic origin of the valley; and I now jokingly remarked that his wild tumble-down-and-engulfment hypothesis might soon be proved, since these underground rumblings and shakings might be the forerunners of another Yosemite-making cataclysm, which would perhaps double the depth of the valley by swallowing the floor, leaving the ends of the wagon roads and trails three or four thousand feet in the air. Just then came the second series of shocks, and it was fine to see how awfully silent and solemn he became. His belief in the existence of a mysterious abyss, into which the suspended floor of the valley and all the domes and battlements of the walls might at any moment go roaring down, mightily troubled him. To cheer and tease him into another view of the case, I said: 'Come, cheer up; smile a little and clap your hands, now that kind Mother Earth is trotting us on her knee to amuse us and make us good.' But the well-meant joke seemed irreverent and utterly failed, as if only prayerful terror could rightly belong to the wild beauty-making business. Even after all the heavier shocks were over, I could do nothing to reassure him. On the contrary, he handed me the keys of his little store, and, with a companion of like mind, fled to the lowlands. In about a month he returned; but a sharp shock occurred that very day, which sent him flying again.

The rocks trembled more or less every day for over two months, and I kept a bucket of water on my table to learn what I could of the movements. The blunt thunder-tones in the depths of the mountains were usually followed by sudden jarring, horizontal thrusts from the northward, often succeeded by twisting, upjolting movements. Judging by its effects, this Yosemite, or Inyo earthquake, as it is sometimes called, was gentle as compared with the one that gave rise to the grand talus system of the range and did so much for the canyon scenery. Nature, usually so deliberate in her operations, then created, as we have seen, a new set of features, simply by giving the mountains a shake – changing not only the high peaks and cliffs, but the streams. As soon as these rock avalanches fell every stream began to sing new songs; for in many places thousands of boulders were hurled into their channels, roughening and half damming them, compelling the waters to surge and roar in rapids where before they were gliding smoothly. Some of the streams were completely dammed, driftwood, leaves, etc., filling the interstices between the boulders, thus giving rise to lakes and level reaches; and these, again, after being gradually filled in, to smooth meadows, through which the streams now silently meander; while at the same time some of the taluses took the places of old meadows and groves. Thus rough places were made smooth, and smooth places rough. But on the whole, by what at first sight seemed pure confusion and ruin, the landscapes were enriched; for gradually every talus, however big the boulders composing it, was covered with groves and gardens, and made a finely proportioned and ornamental base for the sheer cliffs. In this beauty work, every boulder is prepared and measured and put in its place more thoughtfully than are the stones of temples. If for a moment you are inclined to regard these taluses as mere draggled, chaotic dumps, climb to the top of one of them, tie your mountain shoes firmly over the instep, and with braced nerves run down without any haggling, puttering hesitation, boldly jumping from boulder to boulder with even speed. You will then find your feet playing a tune, and quickly discover the music and poetry of rock piles – a fine lesson; and all nature's wildness tells the same story. Storms of every sort, torrents, earthquakes, cataclysms, 'convulsions of nature', etc., however mysterious and lawless at first sight they may seem, are only harmonious notes in the song of creation, varied expressions of God's love.

CHAPTER NINE

The Sequoia and General Grant National Parks

THE Big Tree (*Sequoia gigantea*) is Nature's forest masterpiece, and, so far as I know, the greatest of living things. It belongs to an ancient stock, as its remains in old rocks show, and has a strange air of other days about it, a thoroughbred look inherited from the long ago – the auld lang syne of trees. Once the genus was common, and with many species flourished in the now desolate Arctic regions, in the interior of North America, and in Europe, but in long, eventful wanderings from climate to climate only two species have survived the hardships they had to encounter, the gigantea and sempervirens, the former now restricted to the western slopes of the Sierra, the other to the Coast Mountains, and both to California, excepting a few groves of redwood which extend into Oregon. The Pacific Coast in general is the paradise of conifers. Here nearly all of them are giants, and display a beauty and magnificence unknown elsewhere. The climate is mild, the ground never freezes, and moisture and sunshine abound all the year. Nevertheless it is not easy to account for the colossal size of the Sequoias. The largest are about three hundred feet high and thirty feet in diameter. Who of all the dwellers of the plains and prairies and fertile home forests of round-headed oak and maple, hickory and elm, ever dreamed that earth could bear such growths – trees that the familiar pines and firs seem to know nothing about, lonely, silent, serene, with a physiognomy almost godlike; and so old, thousands of them still living had already counted their years by tens of centuries when Columbus set sail from Spain and were in the vigour of youth or middle age when the star led the Chaldean sages to the infant Saviour's cradle! As far as man is concerned they are the same yesterday, today and forever, emblems of permanence.

No description can give any adequate idea of their singular majesty, much less of their beauty. Excepting the sugar pine, most of their neighbours with pointed tops seem to be forever shouting Excelsior, while the big tree, though soaring above them all, seems satisfied, its rounded head, poised lightly as a cloud, giving no impression of trying to go higher. Only in youth does it show like other conifers a heavenward yearning, keenly aspiring with a long quick-growing top. Indeed the whole tree for the first century or two, or until a hundred to a hundred and fifty feet high, is arrowhead in form, and, compared with the solemn rigidity of age, is as sensitive to the wind as a squirrel tail. The lower branches are gradually dropped as it grows older, and the upper ones thinned out until comparatively few are left. These, however, are developed to great size, divide again and again, and terminate in bossy rounded masses of leafy branchlets, while the head becomes dome-shaped.

Then poised in fullness of strength and beauty, stern and solemn in mien, it glows with eager, enthusiastic life, quivering to the tip of every leaf and branch and far-reaching root, calm as a granite dome, the first to feel the touch of the rosy beams of the morning, the last to bid the sun good-night.

Perfect specimens, unhurt by running fires or lightning, are singularly regular and symmetrical in general form, though not at all conventional, showing infinite variety in sure unity and harmony of plan. The immensely strong, stately shafts, with rich purplish brown bark, are free of limbs for a hundred and fifty feet or so, though dense tufts of sprays occur here and there, producing an ornamental effect, while long parallel furrows give a fluted columnar appearance. It shoots forth its limbs with equal boldness in every direction, showing no weather side. On the old trees the main branches are crooked and rugged, and strike rigidly outward mostly at right angles from the trunk, but there is always a certain measured restraint in their reach which keeps them within bounds. No other Sierra tree has foliage so densely massed or outline so finely, firmly drawn and so obediently subordinate to an ideal type. A particularly knotty, angular, ungovernable-looking branch, five to eight feet in diameter and perhaps a thousand years old, may occasionally be seen pushing out from the trunk as if determined to break across the bounds of the regular curve, but like all the others, as soon as the general outline is approached the huge limb dissolves into massy bosses of branchlets and sprays, as if the tree were growing beneath an invisible bell glass against the sides of which the branches were moulded, while many small, varied departures from the ideal form give the impression of freedom to grow as they like.

Except in picturesque old age, after being struck by lightning and broken by a thousand snowstorms, this regularity of form is one of the big tree's most distinguishing characteristics. Another is the simple sculptural beauty of the trunk and its great thickness as compared with its height and the width of the branches, many of them being from eight to ten feet in diameter at a height to two hundred feet from the ground, and seeming more like finely modeled and sculptured architectural columns than the stems of trees, while the great strong limbs are like rafters supporting the magnificent dome head.

The root system corresponds in magnitude with the other dimensions of the tree, forming a flat far-reaching spongy network two hundred feet or more in width without any taproot, and the instep is so grand and fine, so suggestive of endless strength, it is long ere the eye is released to look above it. The natural swell of the roots, though at first sight excessive, gives rise to buttresses no greater than are required for beauty as well as strength, as at once appears when you stand back far enough to see the whole tree in its true proportions. The fineness of the taper of the trunk is shown by its thickness at great heights – a diameter of ten feet at a height of two hundred being, as we have seen, not uncommon. Indeed the boles of but few trees hold their thickness as well as Sequoia. Resolute, consummate, determined in form, always beheld with wondering admiration, the big tree always seems unfamiliar, standing alone, unrelated, with peculiar physiognomy, awfully solemn and earnest. Nevertheless, there is nothing alien in its looks. The madrona, clad in thin, smooth, red and yellow bark and big glossy leaves, seems, in the dark coniferous forests of Washington and Vancouver Island, like some lost wanderer from the magnolia groves of the South, while the Sequoia, with all its strangeness, seems more at home than any of its neighbours, holding the best right to the ground as the oldest, strongest inhabitant. One soon becomes acquainted with new species of pine and fir and spruce as with friendly people, shaking their outstretched branches like shaking hands, and fondling their beautiful little ones; while the venerable aboriginal Sequoia, ancient of other days, keeps you at a distance, taking no notice of you, speaking only to the winds, thinking only of the sky, looking as strange in aspect and behaviour among the neighbouring trees as would the mastodon or hairy elephant among the homely bears and deer. Only the Sierra juniper is at all like it, standing rigid and unconquerable on glacial pavements for thousands of years, grim, rusty, silent, uncommunicative, with an air of antiquity about as pronounced as that so characteristic of Sequoia.

The bark of full grown trees is from one to two feet thick, rich cinnamon brown, purplish on young trees and shady parts of the old, forming magnificent masses of colour with the underbrush and beds of flowers. Toward the end of winter the trees themselves bloom while the snow is still eight or ten feet deep. The pistillate flowers are about three eighths of an inch long, pale green, and grow in countless thousands on the ends of the sprays. The staminate are still more abundant, pale yellow, a fourth of an inch long; and when the golden pollen is ripe they colour the whole tree and dust the air and the ground far and near.

The cones are bright grass-green in colour, about two and a half inches long, one and a half wide, and are made up of thirty or forty strong, closely packed, rhomboidal scales with four to eight seeds at the base of each. The seeds are extremely small and light, being only from an eighth to a fourth of an inch long and wide, including a filmy surrounding wing, which causes them to glint and waver in falling and enables the wind to carry them considerable distances from the tree.

The faint lisp of snowflakes as they alight is one of the smallest sounds a mortal can hear. The sound of falling Sequoia seeds, even when they happen to strike on flat leaves or flakes of bark, is about as faint. Very different is the bumping and thudding of the falling cones. Most of them are cut off by the Douglas squirrel and stored for the sake of the seeds, small as they are. In the calm Indian summer these busy harvesters with ivory sickles go to work early in the morning, as soon as breakfast is over, and nearly all day the ripe cones fall in a steady pattering, bumping shower. Unless harvested in this way they discharge their seeds and remain on the trees for many years. In fruitful seasons the trees are fairly laden. On two small specimen branches one and a half and two inches in diameter I counted four hundred and eighty cones. No other California conifer produces nearly so many seeds, excepting perhaps its relative, the redwood of the Coast Mountains. Millions are ripened annually by a single tree, and the product of one of the main groves in a fruitful year would suffice to plant all the mountain ranges of the world.

The dense tufted sprays make snug nesting places for birds, and in some of the loftiest, leafiest towers of verdure thousands of generations have been reared, the great solemn trees shedding off flocks of merry singers every year from nests, like the flocks of winged seeds from the cones.

The big tree keeps its youth far longer than any of its neighbours. Most silver firs are old in their second or third century, pines in their fourth or fifth, while the big tree growing beside them is still in the bloom of its youth, juvenile in every feature at the age of old pines, and cannot be said to attain anything like prime size and beauty before its fifteen hundredth year, or under favourable circumstances become old before its three thousandth. Many, no doubt, are much older than this. On one of the Kings River giants, thirty-five feet and eight inches in diameter exclusive of bark, I counted upwards of four thousand annual wood-rings, in which there was no trace of decay after all these centuries of mountain weather. There is no absolute limit to the existence of any tree. Their death is due to accidents, not, as of animals, to the wearing out of organs. Only the leaves die of old age, their fall is foretold in their structure; but the leaves are renewed every year and so also are the other essential organs – wood, roots, bark, buds. Most of the Sierra trees die of disease. Thus the magnificent silver firs are devoured by fungi, and comparatively few of them live to see their three hundredth birth year. But nothing hurts the big tree. I never saw one that was sick or showed the slightest sign of decay. It lives on through indefinite thousands of years until burned, blown down, undermined, or shattered by some tremendous lightning stroke. No ordinary bolt ever seriously hurts Sequoia. In all my walks I have seen only one that was thus killed outright. Lightning, though rare in the California lowlands, is common on the Sierra. Almost every day in June and July small thunderstorms refresh the main forest belt. Clouds like snowy mountains of marvellous beauty grow rapidly in the calm sky about midday and cast cooling shadows and showers that seldom last more than an hour. Nevertheless these brief, kind storms wound or kill a good many trees. I have seen silver firs two hundred feet high split into long peeled rails and slivers down to the roots, leaving not even a stump, the rails radiating like the spokes of a wheel from a hole in the ground where the tree stood. But the Sequoia, instead of being split and slivered, usually has forty or fifty feet of its brash knotty top smashed off in short chunks about the size of cord-wood, the beautiful rosy red ruins covering the ground in a circle a hundred feet wide or more. I never saw any that had been cut down to the ground or even to below the branches except one in the Stanislaus Grove, about twelve feet in diameter, the greater part of which was smashed to fragments, leaving only a leafless stump about seventy-feet high. It is a curious fact that all the very old Sequoias have lost their heads by lightning. 'All things come to him who waits.' But of all living things Sequoia is perhaps the only one able to wait long enough to make sure of being struck by lightning. Thousands of years it stands ready and waiting, offering its head to every passing cloud as if inviting its fate, praying for heaven's fire as a blessing; and when at last the old head is off, another of the same shape immediately begins to grow on. Every bud and branch seems excited, like bees that have lost their queen, and tries hard to repair the damage. Branches that for many centuries have been growing out horizontally at once turn upward and all their branchlets arrange themselves with reference to a new top of the same peculiar curve as the old one. Even the small subordinate branches half-way down the trunk do their best to push up to the top and help in this curious head-making.

The great age of these noble trees is even more wonderful than their huge size, standing bravely up, millennium in, millennium out, to all that fortune may bring them, triumphant over tempest and fire and time, fruitful and beautiful, giving food and shelter to multitudes of small fleeting creatures dependent on their bounty. Other trees may claim to be about as large or as old: Australian gums, Senegal baobabs, Mexican taxodiums, English yews, and venerable Lebanon cedars, trees of renown, some of which are from ten to thirty feet in diameter. We read of oaks that are supposed to have existed ever since the creation, but strange to say I can find no definite accounts of the age of any of these trees, but only estimates based on tradition and assumed average rates of growth. No other known tree approaches the Sequoia in grandeur, height and thickness being considered, and none as far as I know has looked down on so many centuries or opens such impressive and suggestive views into history. The majestic monument of the Kings River Forest is, as we have seen, fully four thousand years old, and measuring the rings of annual growth we find it was no less than twenty-seven feet in diameter at the beginning of the Christian era, while many observations lead me to expect the discovery of others ten or twenty centuries older. As to those of moderate age, there are thousands, mere youths as yet, that –

> 'Saw the light that shone
>   On Mahomet's uplifted crescent,
> On many a royal gilded throne
>   And deed forgotten in the present,
>   . . . saw the age of sacred trees
>   And Druid groves and mystic larches,
> And saw from forest domes like these
>   The builder bring his Gothic arches'.

Great trees and groves used to be venerated as sacred monuments and halls of council and worship. But soon after the discovery of the Calaveras Grove one of the grandest trees was cut down for the sake of a stump! The laborious vandals had seen 'the biggest tree in the world', then, forsooth, they must try to see the biggest stump and dance on it.

The growth in height for the first two centuries is usually at the rate of eight to ten inches a year. Of course all very large trees are old, but those equal in size may vary greatly in age on account of variations in soil, closeness or openness of growth, etc. Thus a tree about ten feet in diameter that grew on the side of a meadow was, according to my own count of woodrings, only two hundred and fifty-nine years old at the time it was felled, while another in the same grove, of almost exactly the same size but less favourably situated, was fourteen hundred and forty years old. The Calaveras tree cut for a dance floor was twenty-four feet in diameter and only thirteen hundred years old, another about the same size was a thousand years older.

The following Sequoia notes and measurements are copied from my notebooks:

Diameter.		Height in Feet.	Age: Years.
Feet.	Inches.		
0	1 3–4	10	7
0	5	24	20
0	5	25	41
0	6	25	66
0	6	28 1–2	39
0	8	25	29
0	11	45	71
1	0	60	71
3	2	156	260
6	0	192	240
7	3	195	339
7	3	255	506
7	6	240	493
7	7	207	424
9	0	243	259
9	3	222	280
10	6		1440
12			1825[1]
15			2150[2]
24			1300
25			2300
35	8 inside bark		over 4000

[1] 6 feet in diameter at height of 200 feet. [2] 7 feet in diameter at height of 200 feet.

Little, however, is to be learned in confused, hurried tourist trips, spending only a poor noisy hour in a branded grove with a guide. You should go looking and listening alone on long walks through the wild forests and groves in all the seasons of the year. In the spring the winds are balmy and sweet, blowing up and down over great beds of chaparral and through the woods now rich in softening balsam and rosin and the scent of steaming earth. The sky is mostly sunshine, oftentimes tempered by magnificent clouds, the breath of the sea built up into new mountain ranges, warm during the day, cool at night, good flower-opening weather. The young cones of the big trees are showing in clusters, their flower time already past, and here and there you may see the sprouting of their tiny seeds of the previous autumn, taking their first feeble hold of the ground and unpacking their tender whorls of cotyledon leaves. Then you will naturally be led on to consider their wonderful growth up and up through the mountain weather, now buried in snow bent and crinkled, now straightening in summer sunshine like uncoiling ferns, shooting eagerly aloft in youth's joyful prime, and towering serene and satisfied through countless years of calm and storm, the greatest of plants and all but immortal.

Under the huge trees up come the small plant people, putting forth fresh leaves and blossoming in such profusion that the hills and valleys would still seem gloriously rich and glad were all the grand trees away. By the side of melting snowbanks rise the crimson sarcodes, round-topped and massive as the Sequoias themselves, and beds of blue violets and larger yellow ones with leaves curiously lobed; azalea and saxifrage, daisies and lilies on the mossy banks of the streams; and a little way back of them, beneath the trees and on sunny spots on the hills around the groves, wild rose and rubus, spiræa and ribes, mitella, tiarella, campanula, monardella, forget-me-not, etc., many of them as worthy of lore immortality as the famous Scotch daisy, wanting only a Burns to sing them home to all hearts.

In the midst of this glad plant work the birds are busy nesting, some singing at their work, some silent, others, especially the big pileated woodpeckers, about as noisy as backwoodsmen building their cabins. Then every bower in the groves is a bridal bower, the winds murmur softly overhead, the streams sing with the birds, while from far-off waterfalls and thunder-clouds come deep rolling organ notes.

In summer the days go by in almost constant brightness, cloudless sunshine pouring over the forest roof, while in the shady depths there is the subdued light of perpetual morning. The new leaves and cones are growing fast and make a grand show, seeds are ripening, young birds learning to fly, and with myriads of insects glad as birds keep the air whirling, joy in every wing-beat, their humming and singing blending with the gentle ah-ing of the winds; while at evening every thicket and grove is enchanted by the tranquil chirping of the blessed hylas, the sweetest and most peaceful of sounds, telling the very heart-joy of earth as it rolls through the heavens.

In the autumn the sighing of the winds is softer than ever, the gentle ah-ah-ing filling the sky with a fine universal mist of music, the birds have little to say, and there is no appreciable stir or rustling among the trees save that caused by the harvesting squirrels. Most of the seeds are ripe and away, those of the trees mottling the sunny air, glinting, glancing through the midst of the merry insect people, rocks and trees, everything alike drenched in gold light, heaven's colours coming down to the meadows and groves, making every leaf a romance, air, earth and water in peace beyond thought, the great brooding days opening and closing in divine psalms of colour.

Winter comes suddenly, arrayed in storms, though to mountaineers silky streamers on the peaks and the tones of the wind give sufficient warning. You hear strange whisperings among the tree-tops, as if the giants were taking counsel together. One after another, nodding and swaying, calling and reply-ing, spreads the news, until all with one accord break forth into glorious song, welcoming the first grand snowstorm of the year, and looming up in the dim clouds and snowdrifts like lighthouse towers in flying scud and spray. Study-ing the behaviour of the giants from some friendly shelter, you will see that even in the glow of their wildest enthusiasm, when the storm roars loudest, they never lose their god-like composure, never toss their arms or bow or wave like the pines, but only slowly, solemnly nod and sway, standing erect, making no sign of strife, none of rest, neither in alliance nor at war with the winds, too calmly, unconsciously noble and strong to strive with or bid defiance to anything. Owing to the density of the leafy branchlets and great breadth of head the big tree carries a much heavier load of snow than any of its neighbours, and after a storm, when the sky clears, the laden trees are a glorious spectacle, worth any amount of cold camping to see. Every bossy limb and crown is solid white, and the immense height of the giants becomes visible as the eye travels the white steps of the colossal tower, each relieved by a mass of blue shadow.

In midwinter the forest depths are as fresh and pure as the crevasses and caves of glaciers. Grouse, nuthatches, a few woodpeckers, and other hardy birds dwell in the groves all winter, and the squirrels may be seen every clear day frisking about, lively as ever, tunnelling to their stores, never coming up empty-mouthed, diving in the loose snow about as quickly as ducks in water, while storms and sunshine sing to each other.

One of the noblest and most beautiful of the late winter sights is the blossoming of the big tree like gigantic goldenrods and the sowing of their pollen over all the forest and the snow-covered ground – a most glorious view of Nature's immortal virility and flower-love.

One of my own best excursions among the Sequoias was made in the autumn of 1875, when I explored the then unknown or little known Sequoia region south of the Mariposa Grove for comprehensive views of the belt, and to learn what I could of the peculiar distribution of the species and its history in general. In particular I was anxious to try to find out whether it had ever been more widely distributed since the glacial period; what conditions favourable or otherwise were affecting it; what were its relations to climate, topography, soil and the other trees growing with it, etc.; and whether, as was generally supposed, the species was nearing extinction. I was already acquainted in a general way with the northern groves, but excepting some passing glimpses gained on excursions into the high Sierra about the headwaters of Kings and Kern Rivers I had seen nothing of the south end of the belt.

Nearly all my mountaineering has been done on foot, carrying as little as possible, depending on camp-fires for warmth, that so I might be light and free to go wherever my studies might lead. On this Sequoia trip, which promised to be long, I was persuaded to take a small wild mule with me to carry provisions and a pair of blankets. The friendly owner of the animal, having noticed that I sometimes looked tired when I came down from the peaks to replenish my bread sack, assured me that his 'little Brownie mule' was just what I wanted, tough as a knot, perfectly untirable, low and narrow, just right for squeezing through brush, able to climb like a chipmunk, jump from boulder to boulder like a wild sheep, and go anywhere a man could go. But tough as he was and accomplished as a climber, many a time in the course of our journey when he was jaded and hungry, wedged fast in rocks or struggling in chaparral like a fly in a spiderweb, his troubles were sad to see, and I wished he would leave me and find his way home alone.

We set out from Yosemite about the end of August, and our first camp was made in the well-known Mariposa Grove. Here and in the adjacent pine woods I spent nearly a week, carefully examining the boundaries of the grove for traces of its greater extension without finding any. Then I struck out into the majestic trackless forest to the southeastward, hoping to find new groves or traces of old ones in the dense silver fir and pine woods about the head of Big Creek, where soil and climate seemed most favourable to their growth, but not a single tree or old monument of any sort came to light until I climbed the high rock called Wamellow by the Indians. Here I obtained telling views of the fertile forest-filled basin of the upper Fresno. Innumerable spires of the noble yellow pine were displayed rising above one another on the braided slopes, and yet nobler sugar pines with superb arms outstretched in the rich autumn light, while away toward the southwest, on the verge of the glowing horizon, I discovered the majestic dome-like crowns of big trees towering high over all, singly and in close grove congregations. There is something wonderfully attractive in this king tree, even when beheld from afar, that draws us to it with indescribable enthusiasm; its superior height and massive smoothly rounded outlines proclaiming its character in any company; and when one of the oldest attains full stature on some commanding ridge it seems the very god of the woods. I ran back to camp, packed Brownie, steered over the divide and down into the heart of the Fresno Grove. Then choosing a camp on the side of a brook where the grass was good, I made a cup of tea, and set off free among the brown giants, glorying in the abundance of new work about me. One of the first special things that caught my attention was an extensive landslip. The ground on the side of a stream had given way to a depth of about fifty feet and with all its trees had been launched into the bottom of the stream ravine. Most of the trees – pines, firs, incense cedar and Sequoia – were still standing erect and uninjured, as if unconscious that anything out of the common had happened. Tracing the ravine alongside the avalanche, I saw many trees whose roots had been laid bare, and in one instance discovered a Sequoia about fifteen feet in diameter growing above an old prostrate trunk that seemed to belong to a former generation. This slip had occurred seven or eight years ago, and I was glad to find that not only were most of the big trees uninjured, but that many companies of hopeful seedlings and saplings were growing confidently on the fresh soil along the broken front of the avalanche. These young trees were already eight or ten feet high, and were shooting up vigorously, as if sure of eternal life, though young pines, firs and libocedrus were running a race with them for the sunshine with an even start. Farther down the ravine I counted five hundred and thirty-six promising young Sequoias on a bed of rough bouldery soil not exceeding two acres in extent.

The Fresno big trees covered an area of about four square miles, and while wandering about surveying the boundaries of the grove, anxious to see every tree, I came suddenly on a handsome log cabin, richly embowered and so fresh and unweathered it was still redolent of gum and balsam like a newly felled tree. Strolling forward, wondering who could have built it, I found an old, weary-eyed, speculative, grey-haired man on a bark stool by the door, reading a book. The discovery of his hermitage by a stranger seemed to surprise him, but when I explained that I was only a tree-lover sauntering along the mountains to study Sequoia, he bade me welcome, made me bring my mule down to a little slanting meadow before his door and camp with him, promising to show me his pet trees and many curious things bearing on my studies.

After supper, as the evening shadows were falling, the good hermit sketched his life in the mines, which in the main was like that of most other pioneer gold-hunters – a succession of intense experiences full of big ups and downs like the mountain topography. Since "49' he had wandered over most of the Sierra, sinking innumerable prospect holes like a sailor making soundings, digging new channels for streams, sifting gold-sprinkled boulder and gravel beds with unquenchable energy, life's noon the meanwhile passing unnoticed into late afternoon shadows. Then, health and gold gone, the game played and lost, like a wounded deer creeping into this forest solitude, he awaits the sundown call. How sad the undertones of many a life here, now the noise of the first big gold battles has died away! How many interesting wrecks lie drifted and stranded in hidden nooks of the gold region! Perhaps no other range contains the remains of so many rare and interesting men. The name of my hermit friend is John A. Nelder, a fine kind man, who in going into the woods has at last gone home; for he loves nature truly, and realizes that these last shadowy days with scarce a glint of gold in them are the best of all. Birds, squirrels, plants get loving, natural recognition, and delightful it was to see how sensitively he responds to the silent influences of the woods. His eyes brightened as he gazed on the trees that stand guard around his little home; squirrels and mountain quail come to his call to be fed, and he tenderly stroked the little snowbent sapling Sequoias, hoping they yet might grow straight to the sky and rule the grove. One of the greatest of his trees stands a little way back of his cabin, and he proudly led me to it, bidding me admire its colossal proportions and measure it to see if in all the forest there could be another so grand. It proved to be only twenty-six feet in diameter, and he seemed distressed to learn that the Mariposa Grizzly Giant was larger. I tried to comfort him by observing that his was the taller, finer formed, and perhaps the more favourably situated. Then he led me to some noble ruins, remnants of gigantic trunks of trees that he supposed must have been larger than any now standing, and though they had lain on the damp ground exposed to fire and the weather for centuries, the wood was perfectly sound. Sequoia timber is not only beautiful in colour, rose red when fresh, and as easily worked as pine, but it is almost absolutely unperishable. Build a house of big tree logs on granite and that house will last about as long as its foundation. Indeed fire seems to be the only agent that has any appreciable effect on it. From one of these ancient trunk remnants I cut a specimen of the wood, which neither in colour, strength nor soundness could be distinguished from specimens cut from living trees, although it had certainly lain on the damp forest floor for more than three hundred and eighty years, probably more than thrice as long. The time in this instance was determined as follows: When the tree from which the specimen was derived fell it sunk itself into the ground, making a ditch about two hundred feet long and five or six feet deep; and in the middle of this ditch, where a part of the fallen trunk had been burned, a silver fir four feet in diameter and three hundred and eighty years old was growing, showing that the Sequoia trunk had lain on the ground three hundred and eighty years plus the unknown time that it lay before the part whose place had been taken by the fir was burned out of the way, and that which had elapsed ere the seed from which the monumental fir sprang fell into the prepared soil and took root. Now because Sequoia trunks are never wholly consumed in one forest fire and these fires recur only at considerable intervals, and because Sequoia ditches, after being cleared, are often left unplanted for centuries, it becomes evident that the trunk remnant in question may have been on the ground a thousand years or more. Similar vestiges are common, and together with the rootbowls and long straight ditches of the fallen monarchs, throw a sure light back on the post-glacial history of the species, bearing on its distribution. One of the most interesting features of this grove is the apparent ease and strength and comfortable independence in which the trees occupy their place in the general forest. Seedlings, saplings, young and middle-aged trees are grouped promisingly around the old patriarchs, betraying no sign of approach to extinction. On the contrary, all seem to be saying, 'Everything is to our mind and we mean to live forever'. But, sad to tell, a lumber company was building a large mill and flume near by, assuring widespread destruction.

In the cones and sometimes in the lower portion of the trunk and roots there is a dark gritty substance which dissolves readily in water and yields a magnificent purple colour. It is a strong astringent, and is said to be used by the Indians as a big medicine. Mr Nelder showed me specimens of ink he had made from it, which I tried and found good, flowing freely and holding its colour well. Indeed everything about the tree seems constant. With these interesting trees, forming the largest of the northern groves, I stopped only a week, for I had far to go before the fall of the snow. The hermit seemed to cling to me and tried to make me promise to winter with him after the season's work was done. Brownie had to be got home, however, and other work awaited me, therefore I could only promise to stop a day or two on my way back to Yosemite and give him the forest news.

The next two weeks were spent in the wide basin of the San Joaquin, climbing innumerable ridges and surveying the far-extending sea of pines and firs. But not a single Sequoia crown appeared among them all, nor any trace of a fallen trunk, until I had crossed the south divide of the basin, opposite Dinky Creek, one of the northmost tributaries of Kings River. On this stream there is a small grove, said to have been discovered a few years before my visit by two hunters in pursuit of a wounded bear. Just as I was fording one of the branches of Dinky Creek I met a shepherd, and when I asked him whether he knew anything about the big trees of the neighbourhood he replied, 'I know all about them, for I visited them only a few days ago and pastured my sheep in the grove'. He was fresh from the East, and as this was his first summer in the Sierra I was curious to learn what impression the Sequoias had made on him. When I asked whether it was true that the big trees were really so big as people say, he warmly replied, 'Oh, yes sir, you bet. They're whales. I never used to believe half I heard about the awful size of California trees, but they're monsters and no mistake. One of them over here, they tell me, is the biggest tree in the whole world, and I guess it is, for it's forty foot through and as many good long paces around'. He was very earnest, and in fullness of faith offered to guide me to the grove that I might not miss seeing this biggest tree. A fair measurement four feet from the ground, above the main swell of the roots, showed a diameter of only thirty-two feet, much to the young man's disgust. 'Only thirty-two feet', he lamented, 'only thirty-two, and I always thought it was forty!' Then with a sigh of relief, 'No matter, that's a big tree, anyway; no fool of a tree, sir, that you can cut a plank out of thirty feet broad, straight-edged, no bark, all good wood, sound and solid. It would make the brag white pine planks from old Maine look like laths'. A good many other fine specimens are distributed along three small branches of the creek, and I noticed several thrifty moderate-sized Sequoias growing on a granite ledge, apparently as independent of deep soil as the pines and firs, clinging to seams and fissures and sending their roots far abroad in search of moisture.

The creek is very clear and beautiful, gliding through tangles of shrubs and flower beds, gay bee and butterfly pastures, the grove's own stream, pure Sequoia water, flowing all the year, every drop filtered through moss and leaves and the myriad spongy rootlets of the giant trees. One of the most interesting features of the grove is a small waterfall with a flowery, ferny, clear brimming pool at the foot of it. How cheerily it sings the songs of the wilderness, and how sweet its tones! You seem to taste as well as hear them, while only the subdued roar of the river in the deep canyon reaches up into the grove, sounding like the sea and the winds. So charming a fall and pool in the heart of so glorious a forest good pagans would have consecrated to some lovely nymph.

Hence down into the main Kings River canyon, a mile deep, I led and dragged and shoved my patient, much-enduring mule through miles and miles of gardens and brush, fording innumerable streams, crossing savage rock slopes and taluses, scrambling, sliding through gulches and gorges, then up into the grand Sequoia forests of the south side, cheered by the royal crowns displayed on the narrow horizon. In a day and a half we reached the Sequoia woods in the neighbourhood of the old Thomas' Mill Flat. Thence striking off northeastward I found a magnificent forest nearly six miles long by two in width, composed mostly of big trees, with outlying groves as far east as Boulder Creek. Here five or six days were spent, and it was delightful to learn from countless trees, old and young, how comfortably they were settled down in concordance with climate and soil and their noble neighbours.

Imbedded in these majestic woods there are numerous meadows, around the sides of which the big trees press close together in beautiful lines, showing their grandeur openly from the ground to their domed heads in the sky. The young trees are still more numerous and exuberant than in the Fresno and Dinky groves, standing apart in beautiful family groups, or crowding around the old giants. For every venerable lightning-stricken tree, there is one or more in all the glory of prime, and for each of these, many young trees and crowds of saplings. The young trees express the grandeur of their race in a way indefinable by any words at my command. When they are five or six feet in diameter and a hundred and fifty feet high, they seem like mere baby saplings as many inches in diameter, their juvenile habit and gestures completely veiling their real size, even to those who, from long experience, are able to make fair approximation in their measurements of common trees. One morning I noticed three airy, spiry, quick-growing babies on the side of a meadow, the largest of which I took to be about eight inches in diameter. On measuring it, I found to my astonishment it was five feet six inches in diameter, and about a hundred and forty feet high.

On a bed of sandy ground fifteen yards square, which had been occupied by four sugar pines, I counted ninety-four promising seedlings, an instance of Sequoia gaining ground from its neighbours. Here also I noted eighty-six young Sequoias from one to fifty feet high on less than half an acre of ground that had been cleared and prepared for their reception by fire. This was a small bay burned into dense chaparral, showing that fire, the great destroyer of tree life, is sometimes followed by conditions favourable for new growths. Sufficient fresh soil, however, is furnished for the constant renewal of the forest by the fall of old trees without the help of any other agent – burrowing animals, fire, flood, landslip, etc. – for the ground is thus turned and stirred as well as cleared, and in every roomy, shady hollow beside the walls of upturned roots many hopeful seedlings spring up.

The largest, and as far as I know the oldest, of all the Kings River trees that I saw is the majestic stump, already referred to, about a hundred and forty feet high, which above the swell of the roots is thirty-five feet and eight inches inside the bark, and over four thousand years old. It was burned nearly half through at the base, and I spent a day in chopping off the charred surface, cutting into the heart, and counting the woodrings with the aid of a lens. I made out a little over four thousand without difficulty or doubt, but I was unable to get a complete count, owing to confusion in the rings where wounds had been healed over. Judging by what is left of it, this was a fine, tall, symmetrical tree nearly forty feet in diameter before it lost its bark. In the last sixteen hundred and seventy-two years the increase in diameter was ten feet. A short distance south of this forest lies a beautiful grove, now mostly included in the General Grant National Park. I found many shake-makers at work in it, access to these magnificent woods having been made easy by the old mill wagon road. The Park is only two miles square, and the largest of its many fine trees is the General Grant, so named before the date of my first visit, twenty-eight years ago, and said to be the largest tree in the world, though above the craggy bulging base the diameter is less than thirty feet. The Sanger Lumber Company own nearly all the Kings River groves outside the Park, and for many years the mills have been spreading desolation without any advantage.

One of the shake-makers directed me to an 'old snag biggeren Grant'. It proved to be a huge black charred stump thirty-two feet in diameter, the next in size to the grand monument mentioned above.

I found a scattered growth of big trees extending across the main divide to within a short distance of Hyde's Mill, on a tributary of Dry Creek. The mountain ridge on the south side of the stream was covered from base to summit with a most superb growth of big trees. What a picture it made! In all my wide forest wanderings I had seen none so sublime. Every tree of all the mighty host seemed perfect in beauty and strength, and their majestic domed heads, rising above one another on the mountain slope, were most imposingly displayed, like a range of bossy upswelling cumulus clouds on a calm sky.

In this glorious forest the mill was busy, forming a sore, sad centre of destruction, though small as yet, so immensely heavy was the growth. Only the smaller and most accessible of the trees were being cut. The logs, from three to ten or twelve feet in diameter, were dragged or rolled with long strings of oxen into a chute and sent flying down the steep mountain side to the mill flat, where the largest of them were blasted into manageable dimensions for the saws. And as the timber is very brash, by this blasting and careless felling on uneven ground, half or three fourths of the timber was wasted.

I spent several days exploring the ridge and counting the annual wood rings on a large number of stumps in the clearings, then replenished my bread sack and pushed on southward. All the way across the broad rough basins of the Kaweah and Tule Rivers, Sequoia ruled supreme, forming an almost continuous belt for sixty or seventy miles, waving up and down in huge massy mountain billows in compliance with the grand glacier-ploughed topography.

Day after day, from grove to grove, canyon to canyon, I made a long, wavering way, terribly rough in some places for Brownie, but cheery for me, for big trees were seldom out of sight. We crossed the rugged, picturesque basins of Redwood Creek, the North Fork of the Kaweah, and Marble Fork gloriously forested, and full of beautiful cascades and falls, sheer and slanting, infinitely varied with broad curly foam fleeces and strips of embroidery in which the sunbeams revel. Thence we climbed into the noble forest on the Marble and Middle Fork Divide. After a general exploration of the Kaweah basin, this part of the Sequoia belt seemed to me the finest, and I then named it 'the Giant Forest'. It extends, a magnificent growth of giants grouped in pure temple groves, ranged in colonnades along the sides of meadows, or scattered among the other trees, from the granite headlands overlooking the hot foothills and plains of the San Joaquin back to within a few miles of the old glacier fountains at an elevation of 5,000 to 8,400 feet above the sea.

When I entered this sublime wilderness the day was nearly done, the trees with rosy, glowing countenances seemed to be hushed and thoughtful, as if waiting in conscious religious dependence on the sun, and one naturally walked softly and awe-stricken among them. I wandered on, meeting nobler trees where all are noble, subdued in the general calm, as if in some vast hall pervaded by the deepest sanctities and solemnities that sway human souls. At sundown the trees seemed to cease their worship and breathe free. I heard the birds going home. I too sought a home for the night on the edge of a level meadow where there is a long, open view between the evenly ranked trees standing guard along its sides. Then after a good place was found for poor Brownie, who had had a hard, weary day sliding and scrambling across the Marble Canyon, I made my bed and supper and lay on my back looking up to the stars through pillared arches finer far than the pious heart of man, telling its love, ever reared. Then I took a walk up the meadow to see the trees in the pale light. They seemed still more marvellously massive and tall than by day, heaving their colossal heads into the depths of the sky, among the stars, some of which appeared to be sparkling on their branches like flowers. I built a big fire that vividly illumined the huge brown boles of the nearest trees and the little plants and cones and fallen leaves at their feet, keeping up the show until I fell asleep to dream of boundless forests and trail-building for Brownie.

Joyous birds welcomed the dawn; and the squirrels, now their food cones were ripe and had to be quickly gathered and stored for winter, began their work before sunrise. My tea-and-bread-crumb breakfast was soon done, and leaving jaded Brownie to feed and rest I sauntered forth to my studies. In every direction Sequoia ruled the woods. Most of the other big conifers were present here and there, but not as rivals or companions. They only served to thicken and enrich the general wilderness. Trees of every age cover craggy ridges as well as the deep moraine-soiled slopes, and plant their magnificent shafts along every brookside and meadow. Bogs and meadows are rare or entirely wanting in the isolated groves north of Kings River; here there is a beautiful series of them lying on the broad top of the main dividing ridge, imbedded in the very heart of the mammoth woods as if for ornament, their smooth, plushy bosoms kept bright and fertile by streams and sunshine.

Resting awhile on one of the most beautiful of them when the sun was high, it seemed impossible that any other forest picture in the world could rival it. There lay the grassy, flowery lawn, three fourths of a mile long, smoothly outspread, basking in mellow autumn light, coloured brown and yellow and purple, streaked with lines of green along the streams, and ruffled here and there with patches of ledum and scarlet vaccinium. Around the margin there is first a fringe of azalea and willow bushes, coloured orange yellow, enlivened with vivid dashes of red cornel, as if painted. Then up spring the mighty walls of verdure three hundred feet high, the brown fluted pillars so thick and tall and strong they seem fit to uphold the sky; the dense foliage, swelling forward in rounded bosses on the upper half, variously shaded and tinted, that of the young trees dark green, of the old yellowish. An aged lightning-smitten patriarch standing a little forward beyond the general line with knotty arms outspread was covered with grey and yellow lichens and surrounded by a group of saplings whose slender spires seemed to lack not a single leaf or spray in their wondrous perfection. Such was the Kaweah meadow picture that golden afternoon, and as I gazed every colour seemed to deepen and glow as if the progress of the fresh sun-work were visible from hour to hour, while every tree seemed religious and conscious of the presence of God. A free man revels in a scene like this and time goes by unmeasured. I stood fixed in silent wonder or sauntered about shifting my points of view, studying the physiogonomy of separate trees, and going out to the different colour patches to see how they were put on and what they were made of, giving free expression to my joy, exulting in Nature's wild immortal vigour and beauty, never dreaming any other human being was near. Suddenly the spell was broken by dull bumping, thudding sounds, and a man and horse came in sight at the farther end of the meadow, where they seemed sadly out of place. A good big bear or mastodon or megatherium would have been more in keeping with the old mammoth forest. Nevertheless, it is always pleasant to meet one of our own species after solitary rambles, and I stepped out where I could be seen and shouted, when the rider reined in his galloping mustang and waited my approach. He seemed too much surprised to speak until, laughing in his puzzled face, I was glad to meet a fellow mountaineer in so lonely a place. Then he abruptly asked, 'What are you doing? How did you get here?' I explained that I came across the canyons from Yosemite and was only looking at the trees. 'Oh then, I know', he said, greatly to my surprise, 'you must be John Muir'. He was herding a band of horses that had been driven up a rough trail from the lowlands to feed on these forest meadows. A few handfuls of crumb detritus was all that was left in my bread sack, so I told him that I was nearly out of provision and asked whether he could spare me a little flour. 'Oh yes, of course you can have anything I've got', he said. 'Just take my track and it will lead you to my camp in a big hollow log on the side of a meadow two or three miles from here. I must ride after some strayed horses, but I'll be back before night; in the mean time make yourself at home.' He galloped away to the northward, I returned to my own camp, saddled Brownie, and by the middle of the afternoon discovered his noble den in a fallen Sequoia hollowed by fire – a spacious loghouse of one log, carbon-lined, centuries old yet sweet and fresh, weather proof, earthquake proof, likely to outlast the most durable stone castle, and commanding views of garden and grove grander far than the richest king every enjoyed. Brownie found plenty of grass and I found bread, which I ate with views from the big round, ever-open door. Soon the good Samaritan mountaineer came in, and I enjoyed a famous rest listening to his observations on trees, animals, adventures, etc., while he was busily preparing supper. In answer to inquiries concerning the distribution of the big trees he gave a good deal of particular information of the forest we were in, and he had heard that the species extended a long way south, he knew not how far. I wandered about for several days within a radius of six or seven miles of the camp, surveying boundaries, measuring trees, and climbing the highest points for general views. From the south side of the divide I saw telling ranks of Sequoia-crowned headlands stretching far into the hazy distance, and plunging vaguely down into profound canyon depths foreshadowing weeks of good work. I had now been out on the trip more than a month, and I began to fear my studies would be interrupted by snow, for winter was drawing nigh. 'Where there isn't a way make a way', is easily said when no way at the time is needed, but to the Sierra explorer with a mule travelling across the canyon lines of drainage the brave old phrase becomes heavy with meaning. There are ways across the Sierra graded by glaciers, well marked, and followed by men and beasts and birds, and one of them even by locomotives; but none natural or artificial along the range, and the explorer who would thus travel at right angles to the glacial ways must traverse canyons and ridges extending side by side in endless succession, roughened by side gorges and gulches and stubborn chaparral, and defended by innumerable sheer-fronted precipices. My own ways are easily made in any direction, but Brownie, though one of the toughest and most skilful of his race, was oftentimes discouraged for want of hands, and caused endless work. Wild at first, he was tame enough now; and when turned loose he not only refused to run away, but as his troubles increased came to depend on me in such a pitiful, touching way, I became attached to him and helped him as if he were a good-natured boy in distress, and then the labour grew lighter. Bidding good-bye to the kind Sequoia cave-dweller, we vanished again in the wilderness, drifting slowly southward, Sequoias on every ridge-top beckoning and pointing the way.

In the forest between the Middle and East forks of the Kaweah, I met a great fire, and as fire is the master scourge and controller of the distribution of trees, I stopped to watch it and learn what I could of its works and ways with the giants. It came racing up the steep chaparral-covered slopes of the East Fork canyon with passionate enthusiasm in a broad cataract of flames, now bending down low to feed on the green bushes, devouring acres of them at a breath, now towering high in the air as if looking abroad to choose a way, then stooping to feed again, the lurid flapping surges and the smoke and terrible rushing and roaring hiding all that is gentle and orderly in the work. But as soon as the deep forest was reached the ungovernable flood became calm like a torrent entering a lake, creeping and spreading beneath the trees where the ground was level or sloped gently, slowly nibbling the cake of compressed needles and scales with flames an inch high, rising here and there to a foot or two on dry twigs and clumps of small bushes and brome grass. Only at considerable intervals were fierce bonfires lighted, where heavy branches broken off by snow had accumulated, or around some venerable giant whose head had been stricken off by lightning.

I tethered Brownie on the edge of a little meadow beside a stream a good safe way off, and then cautiously chose a camp for myself in a big stout hollow trunk not likely to be crushed by the fall of burning trees, and made a bed of ferns and boughs in it. The night, however, and the strange wild fireworks were too beautiful and exciting to allow much sleep. There was no danger of being chased and hemmed in, for in the main forest belt of the Sierra, even when swift winds are blowing, fires seldom or never sweep over the trees in broad all-embracing sheets as they do in the dense Rocky Mountain woods and in those of the Cascade Mountains of Oregon and Washington. Here they creep from tree to tree with tranquil deliberation, allowing close observation, though caution is required in venturing around the burning giants to avoid falling limbs and knots and fragments from dead shattered tops. Though the day was best for study, I sauntered about night after night, learning what I could and admiring the wonderful show vividly displayed in the lonely dark-ness, the ground-fire advancing in long crooked lines gently grazing and smoking on the close-pressed leaves, springing up in thousands of little jets of pure flame on dry tassels and twigs, and tall spires and flat sheets with jagged flapping edges dancing here and there on grass tufts and bushes, big bonfires blazing in perfect storms of energy where heavy branches mixed with small ones lay smashed together in hundred cord piles, big red arches between spreading root-swells and trees growing close together, huge fire-mantled trunks on the hill slopes glowing like bars of hot iron, violet-coloured fire running up the tall trees, tracing the furrows of the bark in quick quivering rills, and lighting magnificent torches on dry shattered tops, and ever and anon, with a tremendous roar and burst of light, young trees clad in

1 (previous page), 2 (left) Two views of the 'Grizzly Giant" Sequoia in Mariposa Grove, Yosemite National Park, one of the big trees that so inspired Muir.
Photos: Yosemite National Park Research Library; John Cleare

3 (above) President Theodore Roosevelt (centre), John Muir (fourth from right), other notables and (presumably) bodyguards, pose at the base of the Grizzly Giant in May 1903.
Photo: Joseph LeConte (Yosemite National Park Research Library)

4 John Muir addresses Sierra Club members on the Hetch Hetchy trail, c.1909. *Photo: George King*

5 (above) A view from Yosemite Valley to Half Dome. *Photo: John Cleare*

6 (left) The High Sierra: an aerial view to the south from above Tuolomne Meadows to the Cathedral Range. Daff Dome is in foreground with Fairview Dome (9731ft) in the middle distance and on the skyline (*l to r*) Unicorn Peak, Cockscomb Peak, Echo Ridge (11,040ft), and Cathedral Peak with the prominent Eichorn's Pinnacle on its right.
Photo: John Cleare

7 (above) John Muir at home in Martinez, California (c.1903) with his wife, Louie (Louisa), and daughters Wanda (left) and Helen. 8 (below) Muir with his daughters and another in Kings Canyon (c.1903). *Photos: © Muir-Hanna Trust, Holt-Atherton Special Collections, University of the Pacific Libraries*

low-descending feathery branches vanishing in one flame two or three hundred feet high.

One of the most impressive and beautiful sights was made by the great fallen trunks lying on the hillsides all red and glowing like colossal iron bars fresh from a furnace, two hundred feet long some of them, and ten to twenty feet thick. After repeated burnings have consumed the bark and sapwood, the sound charred surface, being full of cracks and sprinkled with leaves, is quickly overspread with a pure, rich, furred, ruby glow almost flameless and smokeless, producing a marvellous effect in the night. Another grand and interesting sight are the fires on the tops of the largest living trees flaming above the green branches at a height of perhaps two hundred feet, entirely cut off from the ground-fires, and looking like signal beacons on watch towers. From one standpoint I sometimes saw a dozen or more, those in the distance looking like great stars above the forest roof. At first I could not imagine how these Sequoia lamps were lighted, but the very first night, strolling about waiting and watching, I saw the thing done again and again. The thick, fibrous bark of old trees is divided by deep, nearly continuous furrows, the sides of which are bearded with the bristling ends of fibres broken by the growth swelling of the trunk, and when the fire comes creeping around the feet of the trees, it runs up these bristly furrows in lovely pale blue quivering, bickering rills of flame with a low, earnest whispering sound to the lightning-shattered top of the trunk, which, in the dry Indian summer, with perhaps leaves and twigs and squirrel-gnawed cone-scales and seed-wings lodged in it, is readily ignited. These lamp-lighting rills, the most beautiful fire streams I ever saw, last only a minute or two, but the big lamps burn with varying brightness for days and weeks, throwing off sparks like the spray of a fountain, while ever and anon a shower of red coals comes sifting down through the branches, followed at times with startling effect by a big burned-off chunk weighing perhaps half a ton.

The immense bonfires where fifty or a hundred cords of peeled, split, smashed wood has been piled around some old giant by a single stroke of lightning is another grand sight in the night. The light is so great I found I could read common print three hundred yards from them, and the illumination of the circle of onlooking trees is indescribably impressive. Other big fires, roaring and booming like waterfalls, were blazing on the upper sides of trees on hillslopes, against which limbs broken off by heavy snow had rolled, while branches high overhead, tossed and shaken by the ascending air current, seemed to be writhing in pain. Perhaps the most startling phenomenon of all was the quick death of childlike Sequoias only a century or two of age. In the midst of the other comparatively slow and steady fire work one of these tall, beautiful saplings, leafy and branchy, would be seen blazing up suddenly, all in one heaving, booming, passionate flame reaching from the ground to the top of the tree and fifty to a hundred feet or more above it, with a smoke column bending forward and streaming away on the upper, free-flowing wind. To burn these green trees a strong fire of dry wood beneath them is required, to send up a current of air hot enough to distill inflammable gases from the leaves and sprays; then instead of the lower limbs gradually catching fire and igniting the next and next in succession, the whole tree seems to explode almost simultaneously, and with awful roaring and throbbing a round, tapering flame shoots up two or three hundred feet, and in a second or two is quenched, leaving the green spire a black, dead, mast, bristled and roughened with down-curling boughs. Nearly all the trees that have been burned down are lying with their heads uphill, because they are burned far more deeply on the upper side, on account of broken limbs rolling down against them to make hot fires, while only leaves and twigs accumulate on the lower side and are quickly consumed without injury to the tree. But green, resinless Sequoia wood burns very slowly, and many successive fires are required to burn down a large tree. Fires can run only at intervals of several years, and when the ordinary amount of firewood that has rolled against the gigantic trunk is consumed, only a shallow scar is made, which is slowly deepened by recurring fires until far beyond the centre of gravity, and when at last the tree falls, it of course falls uphill. The healing folds of wood layers on some of the deeply burned trees show that centuries have elapsed since the last wounds were made.

When a great Sequoia falls, its head is smashed into fragments about as small as those made by lightning, which are mostly devoured by the first running, hunting fire that finds them, while the trunk is slowly wasted away by centuries of fire and weather. One of the most interesting fire actions on the trunk is the boring of those great tunnel-like hollows through which horsemen may gallop. All of these famous hollows are burned out of the solid wood, for no Sequoia is ever hollowed by decay. When the tree falls the brash trunk is often broken straight across into sections as if sawed; into these joints the fire creeps, and, on account of the great size of the broken ends, burns for weeks or even months without being much influenced by the weather. After the great glowing ends fronting each other have burned so far apart that their rims cease to burn, the fire continues to work on in the centres, and the ends become deeply concave. Then heat being radiated from side to side, the burning goes on in each section of the trunk independent of the other, until the diameter of the bore is so great that the heat radiated across from side to side is not sufficient to keep them burning. It appears, therefore, that only very large trees can receive the fire-auger and have any shell rim left.

Fire attacks the large trees only at the ground consuming the fallen leaves and humus at their feet, doing them but little harm unless considerable quantities of fallen limbs happen to be piled about them, their thick mail of spongy, unpitchy, almost unburnable bark affording strong protection. Therefore the oldest and most perfect unscarred trees are found on ground that is nearly level, while those growing on hillsides, against which falling branches roll, are always deeply scarred on the upper side, and as we have seen are sometimes burned down. The saddest thing of all was to see the hopeful seedlings, many of them crinkled and bent with the pressure of winter snow, yet bravely aspiring at the top, helplessly perishing, and young trees, perfect spires of verdure and naturally immortal, suddenly changed to dead masts. Yet the sun looked cheerily down the openings in the forest roof, turning the black smoke to a beautiful brown, as if all was for the best.

Beneath the smoke-clouds of the suffering forest we again pushed south-ward, descending a side-gorge of the East Fork canyon and climbing another into new forests and groves not a whit less noble. Brownie, the meanwhile, had been resting, while I was weary and sleepy with almost ceaseless wander-ings, giving only an hour or two each night or day to sleep in my log home. Way-making here seemed to become more and more difficult, 'impossible', in common phrase, for four-legged travellers. Two or three miles was all the day's work as far as distance was concerned. Nevertheless, just before sun-down we found a charming camp ground with plenty of grass, and a forest to study that had felt no fire for many a year. The camp hollow was evidently a favourite home of bears. On many of the trees, at a height of six or eight feet, their autographs were inscribed in strong, free, flowing strokes on the soft bark where they had stood up like cats to stretch their limbs. Using both hands, every claw a pen, the handsome curved lines of their writing take the form of remarkably regular interlacing pointed arches, producing a truly ornamental effect. I looked and listened, half expecting to see some of the writers alarmed and withdrawing from the unwanted disturbance. Brownie also looked and listened, for mules fear bears instinctively and have a very keen nose for them. When I turned him loose, instead of going to the best grass, he kept cautiously near the camp-fire for protection, but was careful not to step on me. The great starry night passed away in deep peace and the rosy morning sunbeams were searching the grove ere I awoke from a long, blessed sleep.

The breadth of the Sequoia belt here is about the same as on the north side of the river, extending, rather thin and scattered in some places, among the noble pines from near the main forest belt of the range well back towards the frosty peaks, where most of the trees are growing on moraines but little changed as yet.

Two days' scramble above Bear Hollow I enjoyed an interesting interview with deer. Soon after sunrise a little company of four came to my camp in a wild garden imbedded in chaparral, and after much cautious observation quietly began to eat breakfast with me. Keeping perfectly still I soon had their confidence, and they came so near I found no difficulty, while admiring their graceful manners and gestures, in determining what plants they were eating, thus gaining a far finer knowledge and sympathy than comes by killing and hunting.

Indian summer gold with scarce a whisper of winter in it was painting the glad wilderness in richer and yet richer colours as we scrambled across the South canyon into the basin of the Tule. Here the big tree forests are still more extensive, and furnished abundance of work in tracing boundaries and gloriously crowned ridges up and down, back and forth, exploring, studying, admiring, while the great measureless days passed on and away uncounted. But in the calm of the camp-fire the end of the season seemed near. Brownie too often brought snowstorms to mind. He became doubly jaded, though I never rode him, and always left him in camp to feed and rest while I explored. The invincible bread business also troubled me again; the last mealy crumbs were consumed, and grass was becoming scarce even in the roughest rock-piles, naturally inaccessible to sheep. One afternoon, as I gazed over the rolling bossy Sequoia billows stretching interminably southward, seeking a way and counting how far I might go without food, a rifle shot rang out sharp and clear. Marking the direction I pushed gladly on, hoping to find some hunter who could spare a little food. Within a few hundred rods I struck the track of a shod horse, which led to the camp of two Indian shepherds. One of them was cooking supper when I arrived. Glancing curiously at me he saw that I was hungry, and gave me some mutton and bread, and said encouragingly as he pointed to the west, 'Putty soon Indian come, heap speak English'. Toward sundown two thousand sheep beneath a cloud of dust came streaming through the grand Sequoias to a meadow below the camp, and presently the English-speaking shepherd came in, to whom I explained my wants and what I was doing. Like most white men, he could not conceive how anything other than gold could be the object of such rambles as mine, and asked repeatedly whether I had discovered any mines. I tried to make him talk about trees and the wild animals, but unfortunately he proved to be a tame Indian from the Tule Reservation, had been to school, claimed to be civilized, and spoke contemptuously of 'wild Indians', and so of course his inherited instincts were blurred or lost. The big trees, he said, grew far south, for he had seen them in crossing the mountains from Porterville to Lone Pine. In the morning he kindly gave me a few pounds of flour, and assured me that I would get plenty more at a sawmill on the South Fork if I reached it before it was shut down for the season.

Of all the Tule basin forest the section on the North Fork seemed the finest, surpassing, I think, even the Giant Forest of the Kaweah. Southward from here, though the width and general continuity of the belt is well sustained, I thought I could detect a slight falling off in the height of the trees and in closeness of growth. All the basin was swept by swarms of hoofed locusts, the southern part over and over again, until not a leaf within reach was left on the wettest bogs, the outer edges of the thorniest chaparral beds, or even on the young conifers, which, unless under the stress of dire famine, sheep never touch. Of course Brownie suffered, though I made diligent search for grassy sheep-proof spots. Turning him loose one evening on the side of a carex bog, he dolefully prospected the desolate neighbourhood without finding anything that even a starving mule could eat. Then, utterly discouraged, he stole up behind me while I was bent over on my knees making a fire for tea, and in a pitiful mixture of bray and neigh, begged for help. It was a mighty touching prayer, and I answered it as well as I could with half of what was left of a cake made from the last of the flour given me by the Indians, hastily passing it over my shoulder, and saying, 'Yes, poor fellow, I know, but soon you'll have plenty. Tomorrow down we go to alfalfa and barley', speaking to him as if he were human, as through stress of trouble plainly he was. After eating his portion of bread he seemed content, for he said no more, but patiently turned away to gnaw leafless ceanothus stubs. Such clinging, confiding dependence after all our scrambles and adventures together was very touching, and I felt conscience-stricken for having led him so far in so rough and desolate a country. 'Man', says Lord Bacon, 'is the god of the dog'. So, also, he is of the mule and many other dependent fellow mortals.

Next morning I turned westward, determined to force a way straight to pasture, letting Sequoia wait. Fortunately ere we had struggled down through half a mile of chaparral we heard a mill whistle, for which we gladly made a bee line. At the sawmill we both got a good meal, then taking the dusty lumber road pursued our way to the lowlands. The nearest good pasture I counted might be thirty or forty miles away. But scarcely had we gone ten when I noticed a little log cabin a hundred yards or so back from the road, and a tall man straight as a pine standing in front of it observing us as we came plodding down through the dust. Seeing no sign of grass or hay, I was going past without stopping, when he shouted, 'Travelin'?' Then drawing nearer, 'Where have you come from? I didn't notice you go up'. I replied I had come through the woods from the north, looking at the trees. 'Oh, then, you must be John Muir. Halt, you're tired; come and rest and I'll cook for you.' Then I explained that I was tracing the Sequoia belt, that on account of sheep my mule was starving, and therefore must push on to the lowlands. 'No, no', he said, 'that corral over there is full of hay and grain. Turn your mule into it. I don't own it, but the fellow who does is hauling lumber, and it will be all right. He's a white man. Come and rest. How tired you must be! The big trees don't go much farther south, nohow. I know the country up there, have hunted all over it. Come and rest, and let your little doggone rat of a mule rest. How in heavens did you get him across the canyons – roll him? or carry him? He's poor, but he'll get fat, and I'll give you a horse and go with you up the mountains, and while you're looking at the trees I'll go hunting. It will be a short job, for the end of the big trees is not far'. Of course I stopped. No true invitation is ever declined. He had been hungry and tired himself many a time in the Rocky Mountains as well as in the Sierra. Now he owned a band of cattle and lived alone. His cabin was about eight by ten feet, the door at one end, a fireplace at the other, and a bed on one side fastened to the logs. Leading me in without a word of mean apology, he made me lie down on the bed, then reached under it, brought forth a sack of apples and advised me to keep 'chawing' at them until he got supper ready. Finer, braver hospitality I never found in all this good world so often called selfish.

Next day with hearty, easy alacrity the mountaineer procured horses, prepared and packed provisions, and got everything ready for an early start the following morning. Well mounted, we pushed rapidly up the South Fork of the river and soon after noon were among the giants once more. On the divide between the Tule and Deer Creek a central camp was made, and the mountaineer spent his time in deer-hunting, while with provisions for two or three days I explored the woods, and in accordance with what I had been told soon reached the southern extremity of the belt on the South Fork of Deer Creek. To make sure, I searched the woods a considerable distance south of the last Deer Creek grove, passed over into the basin of the Kern, and climbed several high points commanding extensive views over the sugar pine woods, without seeing a single Sequoia crown in all the wide expanse to the southward. On the way back to camp, however, I was greatly interested in a grove I discovered on the east side of the Kern River divide, opposite the North Fork of Deer Creek. The height of the pass where the species crossed over is about 7,000 feet, and I heard of still another grove whose waters drain into the upper Kern opposite the Middle Fork of the Tule.

It appears, therefore, that though the Sequoia belt is two hundred and sixty miles long, most of the trees are on a section to the south of Kings River only about seventy miles in length. But though the area occupied by the species increases so much to the southward, there is but little difference in the size of the trees. A diameter of twenty feet and height of two hundred and seventy-five is perhaps about the average for anything like mature and favourably situated trees. Specimens twenty-five feet in diameter are not rare, and a good many approach a height of three hundred feet. Occasionally one meets a specimen thirty feet in diameter, and rarely one that is larger. The majestic stump on Kings River is the largest I saw and measured on the entire trip. Careful search around the boundaries of the forests and groves and in the gaps of the belt failed to discover any trace of the former existence of the species beyond its present limits. On the contrary, it seems to be slightly extending its boundaries; for the outstanding stragglers, occasionally met a mile or two from the main bodies, are young instead of old monumental trees. Ancient ruins and the ditches and root-bowls the big trunks make in falling were found in all the groves, but none outside of them. We may therefore conclude that the area covered by the species has not been diminished during the last eight or ten thousand years, and probably not at all in post-glacial times. For admitting that upon those areas supposed to have been once covered by Sequoia every tree may have fallen, and that fire and the weather had left not a vestige of them, many of the ditches made by the fall of the ponderous trunks, weighing five hundred to nearly a thousand tons, and the bowls made by their upturned roots would remain visible for thousands of years after the last remnants of the trees had vanished. Some of these records would doubtless be effaced in a comparatively short time by the inwashing of sediments, but no inconsiderable part of them would remain enduringly engraved on flat ridge tops, almost wholly free from such action.

In the northern groves, the only ones that at first came under the observation of students, there are but few seedlings and young trees to take the places of the old ones. Therefore the species was regarded as doomed to speedy extinction, as being only an expiring remnant vanquished in the so-called struggle for life, and shoved into its last strongholds in moist glens where conditions are exceptionally favourable. But the majestic continuous forests of the south end of the belt create a very different impression. Here, as we have seen, no tree in the forest is more enduringly established. Nevertheless it is oftentimes vaguely said that the Sierra climate is drying out, and that this oncoming, constantly increasing drought will of itself surely extinguish King Sequoia, though sections of wood-rings show that there has been no appreciable change of climate during the last forty centuries. Furthermore, that Sequoia can grow and is growing on as dry ground as any of its neighbours or rivals, we have seen proved over and over again. 'Why, then', it will be asked, 'are the big tree groves always found on well-watered spots?' Simply because big trees give rise to streams. It is a mistake to suppose that the water is the cause of the groves being there. On the contrary, the groves are the cause of the water being there. The roots of this immense tree fill the ground, forming a sponge which boards the bounty of the clouds and sends it forth in clear perennial streams instead of allowing it to rush headlong in short-lived destructive floods. Evaporation is also checked, and the air kept still in the shady Sequoia depths, while thirsty robber winds are shut out.

Since, then, it appears that Sequoia can and does grow on as dry ground as its neighbours and that the greater moisture found with it is an effect rather than a cause of its presence, the notions as to the former greater extension of the species and its near approach to extinction, based on its supposed dependence on greater moisture, are seen to be erroneous. Indeed, all my observations go to show that in cases of prolonged drought the sugar pines and firs would die before Sequoia. Again, if the restricted and irregular distribution of the species be interpreted as the result of the desiccation of the range, then, instead of increasing in individuals toward the south, where the rainfall is less, it should diminish.

If, then, its peculiar distribution has not been governed by superior conditions of soil and moisture, by what has it been governed? Several years before I made this trip, I noticed that the northern groves were located on those parts of the Sierra soil-belt that were first laid bare and opened to preemption when the ice-sheet began to break up into individual glaciers. And when I was examining the basin of the San Joaquin and trying to account for the absence of Sequoia, when every condition seemed favourable for its growth, it occurred to me that this remarkable gap in the belt is located in the channel of the great ancient glacier of the San Joaquin and Kings River basins, which poured its frozen floods to the plain, fed by the snows that fell on more than fifty miles of the summit peaks of the range. Constantly brooding on the question, I next perceived that the great gap in the belt to the northward, forty miles wide, between the Stanislaus and Tuolumne groves, occurs in the channel of the great Stanislaus and Tuolumne glacier, and that the smaller gap between the Merced and Mariposa groves occurs in the channel of the smaller Merced glacier. The wider the ancient glacier, the wider the gap in the Sequoia belt, while the groves and forests attain their greatest development in the Kaweah and Tule River basins, just where, owing to topographical conditions, the region was first cleared and warmed, while protected from the main ice-rivers, that flowed past to right and left down the Kings and Kern valleys. In general, where the ground on the belt was first cleared of ice, there the Sequoia now is, and where at the same elevation and time the ancient glaciers lingered, there the Sequoia is not. What the other conditions may have been which enabled the Sequoia to establish itself upon these oldest and warmest parts of the main soil-belt I cannot say. I might venture to state, however, that since the Sequoia forests present a more and more ancient and long established aspect to the southward, the species was probably distributed from the south toward the close of the glacial period, before the arrival of other trees. About this branch of the question, however, there is at present much fog, but the general relationship we have pointed out between the distribution of the big tree and the ancient glacial system is clear. And when we bear in mind that all the existing forests

of the Sierra are growing on comparatively fresh morraine soil, and that the
range itself has been recently sculptured and brought to light from beneath
the ice-mantle of the glacial winter, then many lawless mysteries vanish, and
harmonies take their places.

But nothwithstanding all the observed phenomena bearing on the post-
glacial history of this colossal tree, point to the conclusion that it never was
more widely distributed on the Sierra since the close of the glacial epoch; that
its present forests are scarcely past prime; if, indeed, they have reached
prime; that the post-glacial day of the species is probably not half done; yet,
when from a wider outlook the vast antiquity of the genus is considered,
and its ancient richness in species and individuals, comparing our Sierra
giant and Sequoia sempervirens of the coast, the only other living species,
with the many fossil species already discovered, and described by Heer and
Lesquereux, some of which flourished over large areas around the Arctic
Circle, and in Europe and our own territories, during tertiary and cretaceous
times – then, indeed, it becomes plain that our two surviving species,
restricted to narrow belts within the limits of California, are mere remnants of
the genus both as to species and individuals, and that they probably are
verging to extinction. But the verge of a period beginning in cretaceous times
may have a breadth of tens of thousands of years, not to mention the possible
existence of conditions calculated to multiply and re-extend both species and
individuals. No unfavourable change of climate, so far as I can see, no
disease, but only fire and the axe and the ravages of flocks and herds threaten
the existence of these noblest of God's trees. In Nature's keeping they are
safe, but through man's agency destruction is making rapid progress, while in
the work of protection only a beginning has been made. The Mariposa Grove
belongs to and is guarded by the State; the General Grant and Sequoia
National Parks, established ten years ago, are efficiently guarded by a troop
of cavalry under the direction of the Secretary of the Interior; so also are the
small Tuolumne and Merced Groves, which are included in the Yosemite
National Park, while a few scattered patches and fringes, scarce at all
protected, though belonging to the national government, are in the Sierra
Forest Reservation.

Perhaps more than half of all the big trees have been sold, and are now in
the hands of speculators and mill men. Even the beautiful little Calaveras
Grove of ninety trees, so historicaly interesting from its being the first discovered, is now owned, together with the much larger South or Stanislaus
Grove, by a lumber company.

Far the largest and most important section of protected big trees is in the
grand Sequoia National Park, now easily accessible by stage from Visalia. It
contains seven townships and extends across the whole breadth of the magnificent Kaweah basin. But large as it is, it should be made much larger. Its
natural eastern boundary is the High Sierra, and the northern and southern
boundaries, the Kings and Kern Rivers, thus including the sublime scenery on
the headwaters of these rivers and perhaps nine tenths of all the big trees in
existence. Private claims cut and blotch both of the Sequoia parks as well
as all the best of the forests, every one of which the government should

gradually extinguish by purchase, as it readily may, for none of these holdings are of much value to their owners. Thus as far as possible the grand blunder of selling would be corrected. The value of these forests in storing and dispensing the bounty of the mountain clouds is infinitely greater than lumber or sheep. To the dwellers of the plain, dependent on irrigation, the big tree, leaving all its higher uses out of the count, is a tree of life, a never-failing spring, sending living water to the lowlands all through the hot, rainless summer. For every grove cut down a stream is dried up. Therefore, all California is crying, 'Save the trees of the fountains', nor, judging by the signs of the times, is it likely that the cry will cease until the salvation of all that is left of Sequoia gigantea is sure.

CHAPTER TEN

The American Forests

THE FORESTS of America, however slighted by man, must have been a great delight to God; for they were the best he ever planted. The whole continent was a garden, and from the beginning it seemed to be favoured above all the other wild parks and gardens of the globe. To prepare the ground, it was rolled and sifted in seas with infinite loving deliberation and forethought, lifted into the light, submerged and warmed over and over again, pressed and crumpled into folds and ridges, mountains, and hills, subsoiled with heaving volcanic fires, ploughed and ground and sculptured into scenery and soil with glaciers and rivers – every feature growing and changing from beauty to beauty, higher and higher. And in the fullness of time it was planted in groves, and belts, and broad, exuberant, mantling forests, with the largest, most varied, most fruitful, and most beautiful trees in the world. Bright seas made its border, with wave embroidery and icebergs; grey deserts were outspread in the middle of it, mossy tundras on the north, savannas on the south, and blooming prairies and plains; while lakes and rivers shone through all the vast forests and openings, and happy birds and beasts gave delightful animation. Everywhere, everywhere over all the blessed continent, there were beauty and melody and kindly, wholesome, foodful abundance.

These forests were composed of about five hundred species of trees, all of them in some way useful to man, ranging in size from twenty-five feet in height and less than one foot in diameter at the ground to four hundred feet in height and more than twenty feet in diameter – lordly monarchs proclaiming the gospel of beauty like apostles. For many a century after the ice-ploughs were melted, nature fed them and dressed them every day – working like a man, a loving, devoted, painstaking gardener; fingering every leaf and flower and mossy furrowed bole; bending, trimming, modelling, balancing; painting them with the loveliest colours; bringing over them now clouds with cooling shadows and showers, now sunshine; fanning them with gentle winds and rustling their leaves; exercising them in every fibre with storms, and pruning them; loading them with flowers and fruit, loading them with snow, and ever making them more beautiful as the years rolled by. Wide-branching oak and elm in endless variety, walnut and maple, chestnut and beech, ilex and locust, touching limb to limb, spread a leafy translucent canopy along the coast of the Atlantic over the wrinkled folds and ridges of the Alleghanies – a green billowy sea in summer, golden and purple in autumn, pearly grey like a steadfast frozen mist of interlacing branches and sprays in leafless, restful winter.

To the southward stretch dark, level-topped cypresses in knobby, tangled swamps, grassy savannas in the midst of them like lakes of light, groves of gay, sparkling spice-trees, magnolias and palms, glossy-leaved and blooming and shining continually. To the northward, over Maine and Ottawa, rose hosts of spiry, rosiny evergreens – white pine and spruce, hemlock and cedar, shoulder to shoulder, laden with purple cones, their myriad needles sparkling and shimmering, covering hills and swamps, rocky headlands and domes, ever bravely aspiring and seeking the sky; the ground in their shade now snow-clad and frozen, now mossy and flowery; beaver meadows here and there, full of lilies and grass; lakes gleaming like eyes, and a silvery embroidery of rivers and creeks watering and brightening all the vast glad wilderness.

Thence westward were oak and elm, hickory and tupelo, gum and liriodendron, sassafras and ash, linden and laurel, spreading on ever wider in glorious exuberance over the great fertile basin of the Mississippi, over damp level bottoms, low dimpling hollows, and round dotting hills, embosoming sunny prairies and cheery park openings, half sunshine, half shade; while a dark wilderness of pines covered the region around the Great Lakes. Thence still westward swept the forests to right and left around grassy plains and deserts a thousand miles wide: irrepressible hosts of spruce and pine, aspen and willow, nut-pine and juniper, cactus and yucca, caring nothing for drought, extending undaunted from mountain to mountain, over mesa and desert, to join the darkening multitudes of pines that covered the high Rocky ranges and the glorious forests along the coast of the moist and balmy Pacific, where new species of pine, giant cedars and spruces, silver firs and Sequoias, kings of their race, growing close together like grass in a meadow, poised their brave domes and spires in the sky, three hundred feet above the ferns and the lilies that enameled the ground; towering serene through the long centuries, preaching God's forestry fresh from heaven.

Here the forests reached their highest development. Hence they went wavering northward over icy Alaska, brave spruce and fir, poplar and birch, by the coasts and the rivers, to within sight of the Arctic Ocean. American forests! the glory of the world! Surveyed thus from the east to the west, from the north to the south, they are rich beyond thought, immortal, immeasurable, enough and to spare for every feeding, sheltering beast and bird, insect and son of Adam; and nobody need have cared had there been no pines in Norway, no cedars and deodars on Lebanon and the Himalayas, no vine-clad selvas in the basin of the Amazon. With such variety, harmony, and triumphant exuberance, even nature, it would seem, might have rested content with the forests of North America, and planted no more.

So they appeared a few centuries ago when they were rejoicing in wildness. The Indians with stone axes could do them no more harm than could gnawing beavers and browsing moose. Even the fires of the Indians and the fierce shattering lightning seemed to work together only for good in clearing spots here and there for smooth garden prairies, and openings for sunflowers seeking the light. But when the steel axe of the white man rang out on the startled air their doom was sealed. Every tree heard the bodeful sound, and pillars of smoke gave the sign in the sky. I suppose we need not go mourning the buffaloes. In the nature of things they had to give place to better cattle, though the change might have been made without barbarous wickedness. Likewise many of nature's five hundred kinds of wild trees had to make way for orchards and cornfields. In the settlement and civilization of the country, bread more than timber or beauty was wanted; and in the blindness of hunger, the early settlers, claiming Heaven as their guide, regarded God's trees as only a larger kind of pernicious weeds, extremely hard to get rid of. Accordingly, with no eye to the future, these pious destroyers waged interminable forest wars; chips flew thick and fast; trees in their beauty fell crashing by millions, smashed to confusion, and the smoke of their burning has been rising to heaven more than two hundred years. After the Atlantic coast from Maine to Georgia had been mostly cleared and scorched into melancholy ruins, the overflowing multitude of bread and money seekers poured over the Alleghanies into the fertile middle West, spreading ruthless devastation ever wider and farther over the rich valley of the Mississippi and the vast shadowy pine region about the Great Lakes. Thence still westward, the invading horde of destroyers called settlers made its fiery way over the broad Rocky Mountains, felling and burning more fiercely than ever, until at last it has reached the wild side of the continent, and entered the last of the great aboriginal forests on the shores of the Pacific.

Surely, then, it should not be wondered at that lovers of their country, bewailing its baldness, are now crying aloud, 'Save what is left of the forests!' Clearing has surely now gone far enough; soon timber will be scarce, and not a grove will be left to rest in or pray in. The remnant protected will yield plenty of timber, a perennial harvest for every right use, without further diminution of its area, and will continue to cover the springs of the rivers that rise in the mountains and give irrigating waters to the dry valleys at their feet, prevent wasting floods and be a blessing to everybody forever.

Every other civilized nation in the world has been compelled to care for its forests, and so must we if waste and destruction are not to go on to the bitter end, leaving America as barren as Palestine or Spain. In its calmer moments, in the midst of bewildering hunger and war and restless over-industry, Prussia has learned that the forest plays an important part in human progress, and that the advance in civilization only makes it more indispensable. It has, therefore, as shown by Mr Pinchot, refused to deliver its forests to more or less speedy destruction by permitting them to pass into private ownership.

But the state woodlands are not allowed to lie idle. On the contrary, they are made to produce as much timber as is possible without spoiling them. In the administration of its forests, the state righteously considers itself bound to treat them as a trust for the nation as a whole, and to keep in view the common good of the people for all time.

In France no government forests have been sold since 1870. On the other hand, about one half of the fifty million francs spent on forestry has been given to engineering works, to make the replanting of denuded areas possible. The disappearance of the forests in the first place, it is claimed, may be traced in most cases directly to mountain pasturage. The provisions of the Code concerning private woodlands are substantially these: no private owner may clear his woodlands without giving notice to the government at least four months in advance, and the forest service may forbid the clearing on the following grounds – to maintain the soil on mountains, to defend the soil against erosion and flooding by rivers or torrents, to insure the existence of springs or watercourses, to protect the dunes and seashore, etc. A proprietor who has cleared his forest without permission is subject to heavy fine, and in addition may be made to replant the cleared area.

In Switzerland, after many laws like our own had been found wanting, the Swiss forest school was established in 1865, and soon after the federal forest law was enacted, which is binding over nearly two thirds of the country. Under its provisions, the cantons must appoint and pay the number of suitably educated foresters required for the fulfilment of the forest law; and in the organization of a normally stocked forest, the object of first importance must be the cutting each year of an amount of timber equal to the total annual increase, and no more.

The Russian government passed a law in 1888, declaring that clearing is forbidden in protected forests, and is allowed in others 'only when its effects will not be to disturb the suitable relations which should exist between forest and agricultural lands'.

Even Japan is ahead of us in the management of her forests. They cover an area of about twenty-nine million acres. The feudal lords valued the woodlands, and enacted vigorous protective laws; and when, in the latest civil war, the Mikado government destroyed the feudal system, it declared the forests that had belonged to the feudal lords to be the property of the state, promulgated a forest law binding on the whole kingdom, and founded a school of forestry in Tokyo. The forest service does not rest satisfied with the present proportion of woodland, but looks to planting the best forest trees it can find in any country, if likely to be useful and to thrive in Japan.

In India systematic forest management was begun about forty years ago, under difficulties – presented by the character of the country, the prevalence of running fires, opposition from lumbermen, settlers, etc. – not unlike those which confront us now. Of the total area of government forests, perhaps seventy million acres, fifty-five million acres have been brought under the control of the forestry department – a larger area than that of all our national parks and reservations. The chief aims of the administration are effective protection of the forests from fire, an efficient system of regeneration, and cheap transportation of the forest products; the results so far have been most beneficial and encouraging.

It seems, therefore, that almost every civilized nation can give us a lesson on the management and care of forests. So far our government has done nothing effective with its forests, though the best in the world, but is like a rich and foolish spendthrift who has inherited a magnificent estate in perfect order, and then has left his fields and meadows, forests and parks, to be sold and plundered and wasted at will, depending on their inexhaustible abundance. Now it is plain that the forests are not inexhaustible, and that quick measures must be taken if ruin is to be avoided. Year by year the remnant is growing smaller before the axe and fire, while the laws in existence provide neither for the protection of the timber from destruction nor for its use where it is most needed.

As is shown by Mr E. A. Bowers, formerly Inspector of the Public Land Service, the foundation of our protective policy, which has never protected, is an act passed 1 March 1817, which authorized the Secretary of the Navy to reserve lands producing live-oak and cedar, for the sole purpose of supplying timber for the navy of the United States. An extension of this law by the passage of the act of 2 March 1831, provided that if any person should cut live-oak or red cedar trees or *other timber* from the lands of the United States for any other purpose than the construction of the navy, such person should pay a fine not less than triple the value of the timber cut, and be imprisoned for a period not exceeding twelve months. Upon this old law, as Mr Bowers points out, having the construction of a wooden navy in view, the United States government has today chiefly to rely in protecting its timber through-out the arid regions of the West, where none of the naval timber which the law had in mind is to be found.

By the act of 3 June 1878, timber can be taken from public lands not subject to entry under any existing laws except for minerals, by *bona fide* residents of the Rocky Mountain states and territories and the Dakotas. Under the timber and stone act, of the same date, land in the Pacific States and Nevada, valuable mainly for timber, and unfit for cultivation if the timber is removed, can be purchased for two dollars and a half an acre, under certain restrictions. By the act of 3 March 1875, all land-grant and right-of-way railroads are authorized to take timber from the public lands adjacent to their lines for construction purposes; and they have taken it with a vengeance, destroying a hundred times more than they have used, mostly by allowing fires to run in the woods. The settlement laws, under which a settler may enter lands valuable for timber as well as for agriculture, furnish another means of obtaining title to public timber.

With the exception of the timber culture act, under which, in consideration of planting a few acres of seedlings, settlers on the treeless plains got 160 acres each, the above is the only legislation aiming to protect and promote the planting of forests. In no other way than under some of these laws can a citizen of the United States make any use of the public forests. To show the results of the timber-planting act, it need only be stated that of the thirty-eight million acres entered under it, less than one million acres have been patented.

This means that less than fifty thousand acres have been planted with stunted, woebegone, almost hopeless sprouts of trees, while at the same time the government has allowed millions of acres of the grandest forest trees to be stolen or destroyed, or sold for nothing. Under the act of 3 June 1878, settlers in Colorado and the Territories were allowed to cut timber for mining and educational purposes from mineral land, which in the practical West means both cutting and burning anywhere and everywhere, for any purpose, on any sort of public land. Thus, the prospector, the miner, and mining and railroad companies are allowed by law to take all the timber they like for their mines and roads, and the forbidden settler, if there are no mineral lands near his farm or stock-ranch, or none that he knows of, can hardly be expected to forbear taking what he needs wherever he can find it. Timber is as necessary as bread, and no scheme of management failing to recognize and properly provide for this want can possibly be maintained. In any case, it will be hard to teach the pioneers that it is wrong to steal government timber. Taking from the government is with them the same as taking from nature, and their consciences flinch no more in cutting timber from the wild forests than in drawing water from a lake or river. As for reservation and protection of forests, it seems as silly and needless to them as protection and reservation of the ocean would be, both appearing to be boundless and inexhaustible.

The special land agents employed by the General Land Office to protect the public domain from timber depredations are supposed to collect testimony to sustain prosecution and to superintend such prosecution on behalf of the government, which is represented by the district attorneys. But timber thieves of the Western class are seldom convicted, for the good reason that most of the jurors who try such cases are themselves as guilty as those on trial. The effect of the present confused, discriminating and unjust system has been to place almost the whole population in opposition to the government; and as conclusive of its futility, as shown by Mr Bowers, we need only state that during the seven years from 1881 to 1887 inclusive, the value of the timber reported stolen from the government lands was $36,719,935, and the amount recovered was $478,073, while the cost of the services of special agents alone was $455,000, to which must be added the expense of the trials. Thus for nearly thirty-seven million dollars' worth of timber the government got less than nothing; and the value of that consumed by running fires during the same period, without benefit even to thieves, was probably over two hundred millions of dollars. Land commissioners and Secretaries of the Interior have repeatedly called attention to this ruinous state of affairs, and asked Congress to enact the requisite legislation for reasonable reform. But, busied with tariffs, etc., Congress has given no heed to these or other appeals, and our forests, the most valuable and the most destructible of all the natural resources of the country, are being robbed and burned more rapidly than ever. The annual appropriation for so-called 'protection service' is hardly sufficient to keep twenty-five timber agents in the field, and as far as any efficient protection of timber is concerned these agents themselves might as well be timber.[1]

---

[1] A change for the better, compelled by public opinion, is now going on – 1901.

That a change from robbery and ruin to a permanent rational policy is urgently needed nobody with the slightest knowledge of American forests will deny. In the East and along the northern Pacific coast, where the rainfall is abundant, comparatively few care keenly what becomes of the trees so long as fuel and lumber are not noticeably dear. But in the Rocky Mountains and California and Arizona, where the forests are inflammable, and where the fertility of the lowlands depends upon irrigation, public opinion is growing stronger every year in favour of permanent protection by the federal government of all the forests that cover the sources of the streams. Even lumbermen in these regions, long accustomed to steal, are now willing and anxious to buy lumber for their mills under cover of law: some possibly from a late second growth of honesty, but most, especially the small mill-owners, simply because it no longer pays to steal where all may not only steal, but also destroy, and in particular because it costs about as much to steal timber for one mill as for ten, and, therefore, the ordinary lumberman can no longer compete with the large corporations. Many of the miners find that timber is already becoming scarce and dear on the denuded hills around their mills, and they, too, are asking for protection of forests, at least against fire. The slow-going, unthrifty farmers, also, are beginning to realize that when the timber is stripped from the mountains the irrigating streams dry up in summer, and are destructive in winter; that soil, scenery, and everything slips off with the trees: so of course they are coming into the ranks of tree-friends.

Of all the magnificent coniferous forests around the Great Lakes, once the property of the United States, scarcely any belong to it now. They have disappeared in lumber and smoke, mostly smoke, and the government got not one cent for them; only the land they were growing on was considered valuable, and two and a half dollars an acre was charged for it. Here and there in the Southern States there are still considerable areas of timbered government land, but these are comparatively unimportant. Only the forests of the West are significant in size and value, and these, although still great, are rapidly vanishing. Last summer, of the unrivalled redwood forests of the Pacific Coast Range, the United States Forestry Commission could not find a single quarter-section that remained in the hands of the government.[1]

Under the timber and stone act of 1878, which might well have been called the 'dust and ashes act', any citizen of the United States could take up one hundred and sixty acres of timber land, and by paying two dollars and a half an acre for it obtain title. There was some virtuous effort made with a view to limit the operations of the act by requiring that the purchaser should make affidavit that he was entering the land exclusively for his own use, and by not allowing any association to enter more than one hundred and sixty acres. Nevertheless, under this act wealthy corporations have fraudulently obtained title to from ten thousand to twenty thousand acres or more. The plan was usually as follows: a mill company, desirous of getting title to a large body of redwood or sugar pine land, first blurred the eyes and ears of the land agents,

[1] The State of California recently appropriated two hundred and fifty thousand dollars to buy a block of redwood land near Santa Cruz for a state park. A much larger national park should be made in Humboldt or Mendocino county.

and then hired men to enter the land they wanted, and immediately deed it to the company after a nominal compliance with the law; false swearing in the wilderness against the government being held of no account. In one case which came under the observation of Mr Bowers, it was the practice of a lumber company to hire the entire crew of every vessel which might happen to touch at any port in the redwood belt, to enter one hundred and sixty acres each and immediately deed the land to the company, in consideration of the company's paying all expenses and giving the jolly sailors fifty dollars apiece for their trouble.

By such methods have our magnificent redwoods and much of the sugar pine forests of the Sierra Nevada been absorbed by foreign and resident capitalists. Uncle Sam is not often called a fool in business matters, yet he has sold millions of acres of timber land at two dollars and a half an acre on which a single tree was worth more than a hundred dollars. But this priceless land has been patented, and nothing can be done now about the crazy bargain. According to the everlasting law of righteousness, even the fraudulent buyers at less than one per cent of its value are making little or nothing, on account of fierce competition. The trees are felled, and about half of each giant is left on the ground to be converted into smoke and ashes; the better half is sawed into choice lumber and sold to citizens of the United States or to foreigners: thus robbing the country of its glory and impoverishing it without right benefit to anybody – a bad, black business from beginning to end.

The redwood is one of the few conifers that sprout from the stump and roots, and it declares itself willing to begin immediately to repair the damage of the lumberman and also that of the forest-burner. As soon as a redwood is cut down or burned it sends up a crowd of eager, hopeful shoots, which, if allowed to grow, would in a few decades attain a height of a hundred feet, and the strongest of them would finally become giants as great as the original tree. Gigantic second and third growth trees are found in the redwoods, forming magnificent temple-like circles around charred ruins more than a thousand years old. But not one denuded acre in a hundred is allowed to raise a new forest growth. On the contrary, all the brains, religion, and superstition of the neighbourhood are brought into play to prevent a new growth. The sprouts from the roots and stumps are cut off again and again, with zealous concern as to the best time and method of making death sure. In the clearings of one of the largest mills on the coast we found thirty men at work, last summer, cutting off redwood shoots 'in the dark of the moon', claiming that all the stumps and roots cleared at this auspicious time would send up no more shoots. Anyhow, these vigorous, almost immortal trees are killed at last, and black stumps are now their only monuments over most of the chopped and burned areas.

The redwood is the glory of the Coast Range. it extends along the western slope, in a nearly continuous belt about ten miles wide, from beyond the Oregon boundary to the south of Santa Cruz, a distance of nearly four hundred miles, and in massive sustained grandeur and closeness of growth surpasses all the other timber woods of the world. Trees from ten to fifteen feet in diameter and three hundred feet high are not uncommon, and a few attain a height of three hundred and fifty feet or even four hundred, with a diameter at the base of fifteen to twenty feet or more, while the ground beneath them is a garden of fresh, exuberant ferns, lilies, gaultheria, and rhododendron. This grand tree, Sequoia sempervirens, is surpassed in size only by its near relative, Sequoia gigantea, or big tree, of the Sierra Nevada, if, indeed, it is surpassed. The sempervirens is certainly the taller of the two. The gigantea attains a greater girth, and is heavier, more noble in port, and more sublimely beautiful. These two Sequoias are all that are known to exist in the world, though in former geological times the genus was common and had many species. The redwood is restricted to the Coast Range, and the big tree to the Sierra.

As timber the redwood is too good to live. The largest sawmills ever built are busy along its seaward border, 'with all the modern improvements', but so immense is the yield per acre it will be long ere the supply is exhausted. The big tree is also, to some extent, being made into lumber. It is far less abundant than the redwood, and is, fortunately, less accessible, extending along the western flank of the Sierra in a partially interrupted belt, about two hundred and fifty miles long, at a height of from four to eight thousand feet above the sea. The enormous logs, too heavy to handle are blasted into manageable dimensions with gunpowder. A large portion of the best timber is thus shattered and destroyed, and, with the huge, knotty tops, is left in ruins for tremendous fires that kill every tree within their range, great and small. Still, the species is not in danger of extinction. It has been planted and is flourishing over a great part of Europe, and magnificent sections of the aboriginal forests have been reserved as national and State parks – the Mariposa Sequoia Grove, near Yosemite, managed by the State of California,and the General Grant and Sequoia national parks on the Kings, Kaweah, and Tule Rivers, efficiently guarded by a small troop of United States cavalry under the direction of the Secretary of the Interior. But there is not a single specimen of the redwood in any national park. Only by gift or purchase, so far as I know, can the government get back into its possession a single acre of this wonderful forest.

The legitimate demands on the forests that have passed into private ownership, as well as those in the hands of the government, are increasing every year with the rapid settlement and upbuilding of the country, but the methods of lumbering are as yet grossly wasteful. In most mills only the best portions of the best trees are used, while the ruins are left on the ground to feed great fires, which kill much of what is left of the less desirable timber, together with the seedlings, on which the permanence of the forest depends. Thus every mill is a centre of destruction far more severe from waste and fire than from use. The same thing is true of the mines, which consume and destroy indirectly immense quantities of timber with their innumerable fires, accidental or set to make open ways, and often without regard to how far they run. The prospector deliberately sets fires to clear off the woods just where they are densest, to lay the rocks bare and make the discovery of mines easier. Sheep-owners and their shepherds also set fires everywhere through the woods in the fall to facilitate the march of their countless flocks the next summer, and perhaps in some places to improve the pasturage. The axe is not yet at the root of every tree, but the sheep is, or was before the national parks were established and guarded by the military, the only effective and reliable arm of the government free from the blight of politics. Not only do the shepherds, at the driest time of the year, set fire to everything that will burn, but the sheep consume every green leaf, not sparing even the young conifers, when they are in a starving condition from crowding, and they rake and dibble the loose soil of the mountain sides for the spring floods to wash away, and thus at last leave the ground barren.

Of all the destroyers that infest the woods, the shake-maker seems the happiest. Twenty or thirty years ago, shakes, a kind of long, board-like shingles split with a mallet and a frow, were in great demand for covering barns and sheds, and many are used still in preference to common shingles, especially those made from the sugar pine, which do not warp or crack in the hottest sunshine. Drifting adventurers in California, after harvest and threshing are over, oftentimes meet to discuss their plans for the winter, and their talk is interesting. Once, in a company of this kind, I heard a man say, as he peacefully smoked his pipe: 'Boys, as soon as this job's done I'm goin' into the duck business. There's big money in it, and your grub costs nothing. Tule Joe made five hundred dollars last winter on mallard and teal. Shot 'em on the Joaquin, tied 'em in dozens by the neck, and shipped 'em to San Francisco. And when he was tired wading in the sloughs and touched with rheumatiz, he just knocked off on ducks, and went to the Contra Costa hills for dove and quail. It's a mighty good business, and you're your own boss, and the whole thing's fun.'

Another of the company, a bushy-bearded fellow, with a trace of brag in his voice, drawled out: 'Bird business is well enough for some, but bear is my game, with a deer and a California lion thrown in now and then for change. There's always market for bear grease, and sometimes you can sell the hams. They're good as hog hams any day. And you are your own boss in my business too, if the bears ain't too big and too many for you. Old grizzlies I despise – they want cannon to kill 'em; but the blacks and browns are beauties for grease, and when once I get 'em just right, and draw a bead on 'em, I fetch 'em every time.' Another said he was going to catch up a lot of mustangs as soon as the rains set in, hitch them to a gang-plough, and go to farming on the San Joaquin plains for wheat. But most preferred the shake business, until something more profitable and as sure could be found, with equal comfort and independence.

With a cheap mustang or mule to carry a pair of blankets, a sack of flour, a few pounds of coffee, and an axe, a frow, and a cross-cut saw, the shake-maker ascends the mountains to the pine belt where it is most accessible, usually by some mine or mill road. Then he strikes off into the virgin woods, where the sugar pine, king of all the hundred species of pines in the world in size and beauty, towers on the open sunny slopes of the Sierra in the fullness of its glory. Selecting a favourable spot for a cabin near a meadow with a stream, he unpacks his animal and stakes it out on the meadow. Then he chops into one after another of the pines, until he finds one that he feels sure will split feely, cuts this down, saws off a section four feet long, splits it, and from this first cut, perhaps seven feet in diameter, he gets shakes enough for a cabin and its furniture – walls, roof, door, bedstead, table and stool. Besides his labour, only a few pounds of nails are required. Sapling poles form the frame of the airy building, usually about six feet by eight in size, on which the shakes are nailed, with the edges overlapping. A few bolts from the same section that the shakes were made from are split into square sticks and built up to form a chimney, the inside and interspaces being plastered and filled in with mud. Thus, with abundance of fuel, shelter and comfort by his own fireside are secured. Then he goes to work sawing and splitting for the market, tying the shakes in bundles of fifty or a hundred. They are four feet long, four inches wide, and about one fourth of an inch thick. The first few thousands he sells or trades at the nearest mill or store, getting provisions in exchange. Then he advertises, in whatever way he can, that he has excellent sugar pine shakes for sale, easy of access and cheap.

Only the lower, perfectly clear, free-splitting portions of the giant pines are used – perhaps ten to twenty feet from a tree two hundred and fifty in height; all the rest is left a mass of ruins, to rot or to feed the forest fires, while thousands are hacked deeply and rejected in proving the grain. Over nearly all of the more accessible slopes of the Sierra and Cascade mountains in southern Oregon, at a height of from three to six thousand feet above the sea, and for a distance of about six hundred miles, this waste and confusion extends. Happy robbers! dwelling in the most beautiful woods, in the most salubrious climate, breathing delightful odours both day and night, drinking cool living water – roses and lilies at their feet in the spring, shedding fragrance and ringing bells as if cheering them on in their desolating work. There is none to say them nay. They buy no land, pay no taxes, dwell in a paradise with no forbidding angel either from Washington or from heaven. Every one of the frail shake shanties is a centre of destruction, and the extent of the ravages wrought in this quiet way is in the aggregate enormous.

It is not generally known that, notwithstanding the immense quantities of timber cut every year for foreign and home markets and mines, from five to ten times as much is destroyed as is used, chiefly by running forest fires that only the federal government can stop. Travellers through the West in summer are not likely to forget the firework displayed along the various railway tracks. Thoreau, when contemplating the destruction of the forests on the east side of the continent, said that soon the country would be so bald that every man would have to grow whiskers to hide its nakedness, but he thanked God that at least the sky was safe. Had he gone West he would have found out that the sky was not safe; for all through the summer months, over most of the mountain regions, the smoke of mill and forest fires is so thick and black that no sunbeam can pierce it. The whole sky, with clouds, sun, moon and stars, is simply blotted out. There is no real sky and no scenery. Not a mountain is left in the landscape. At least none is in sight from the lowlands, and they all might as well be on the moon, as far as scenery is concerned.

The half-dozen transcontinental railroad companies advertise the beauties of their lines in gorgeous many-coloured folders, each claiming its as the 'scenic route'. 'The route of superior desolation' – the smoke, dust and ashes route – would be a more truthful description. Every train rolls on through dismal smoke and barbarous, melancholy ruins; and the companies might well cry in their advertisements: 'Come! travel our way. Ours is the blackest. It is the only genuine Erebus route. The sky is black and the ground is black, and on either side there is a continous border of black stumps and logs and blasted trees appealing to heaven for help as if still half alive, and their mute eloquence is most interestingly touching. The blackness is perfect. On account of the superior skill of our workmen, advantages of climate, and the kind of trees, the charring is generally deeper along our line, and the ashes are deeper, and the confusion and desolation displayed can never be rivalled. No other route on this continent so fully illustrates the abomination of desolation'. Such a claim would be reasonable, as each seems the worst, whatever route you chance to take.

Of course a way had to be cleared through the woods. But the felled timber is not worked up into firewood for the engines and into lumber for the company's use; it is left lying in vulgar confusion, and is fired from time to time by sparks from locomotives or by the workmen camping along the line. The fires, whether accidental or set, are allowed to run into the woods as far as they may, thus assuring comprehensive destruction. The directors of a line that guarded against fires, and cleared a clean gap edged with living trees, and fringed and mantled with the grass and flowers and beautiful seedlings that are ever ready and willing to spring up, might justly boast of the beauty of their road; for nature is always ready to heal every scar. But there is no such road on the western side of the continent. Last summer, in the Rocky Mountains, I saw six fires started by sparks from a locomotive within a distance of three miles, and nobody was in sight to prevent them from spreading. They might run into the adjacent forests and burn the timber from hundreds of square miles; not a man in the State could care to spend an hour in fighting them, as long as his own fences and buildings were not threatened.

Notwithstanding all the waste and use which have been going on unchecked like a storm for more than two centuries, it is not yet too late – though it is high time – for the government to begin a rational administration of its forests. About seventy million acres it still owns – enough for all the country, if wisely used. These residual forests are generally on mountain slopes, just where they are doing the most good, and where their removal would be followed by the greatest number of evils; the lands they cover are too rocky and high for agriculture, and can never be made as valuable for any other crop as for the present crop of trees. It has been shown over and over again that if these mountains were to be stripped of their trees and underbrush, and kept bare and sodless by hordes of sheep and the innumerable fires the shepherds set, besides those of the millmen, prospectors, shake-makers, and all sorts of adventurers, both lowlands and mountains would speedily become little better than deserts, compared with their present beneficent fertility. During heavy rainfalls and while the winter accumulations of snow were melting, the larger streams would swell into destructive torrents, cutting deep, rugged-edged gullies, carrying away the fertile humus and soil as well as sand and rocks, filling up and overflowing their lower channels, and covering the lowland fields with raw detritus. Drought and barrenness would follow.

In their natural condition, or under wise management, keeping out destructive sheep, preventing fires, selecting the trees that should be cut for lumber, and preserving the young ones and the shrubs and sod of herbaceous vegetation, these forests would be a never failing fountain of wealth and beauty. The cool shades of the forest give rise to moist beds and currents of air, and the sod of grasses and the various flowering plants and shrubs thus fostered, together with the network and sponge of tree roots, absorb and hold back the rain and the waters from melting snow, compelling them to ooze and percolate and flow gently through the soil in streams that never dry. All the pine needles and rootlets and blades of grass, and the fallen, decaying trunks of trees, are dams, storing the bounty of the clouds and dispensing it in perennial life-giving streams, instead of allowing it to gather suddenly and rush headlong in short-lived devastating floods. Everybody on the dry side of the continent is beginning to find this out, and, in view of the waste going on, is growing more and more anxious for government protection. The outcries we hear against forest reservations come mostly from thieves who are wealthy and steal timber by wholesale. They have so long been allowed to steal and destroy in peace that any impediment to forest robbery is denounced as a cruel and irreligious interference with 'vested rights', likely to endanger the repose of all ungodly welfare.

Gold, gold, gold! How strong a voice that metal has!

'O wae for the siller, it is sae preva'lin'!'

Even in Congress a sizable chuck of gold, carefully concealed, will outtalk and outfight all the nation on a subject like forestry, well smothered in ignorance, and in which the money interests of only a few are conspicuously involved. Under these circumstances, the bawling, blethering oratorical stuff drowns the voice of God himself. Yet the dawn of a new day in forestry is breaking. Honest citizens see that only the rights of the government are being trampled, not those of the settlers. Only what belongs to all alike is reserved, and every acre that is left should be held together under the federal government as a basis for a general policy of administration for the public good. The people will not always be deceived by selfish opposition, whether from lumber and mining corporations or from sheepmen and prospectors, however cunningly brought forward underneath fables and gold.

Emerson says that things refuse to be mismanaged long. An exception would seem to be found in the case of our forests, which have been mismanaged rather long, and now come desperately near being like smashed eggs and spilt milk. Still, in the long run the world does not move backward. The wonderful advance made in the last few years, in creating four national parks in the West, and thirty forest reservations, embracing nearly forty million acres; and in the planting of the borders of streets and highways and spacious parks in all the great cities, to satisfy the natural taste and hunger for landscape beauty and righteousness that God has put, in some measure, into every human being and animal, shows the trend of awakening public opinion. The making of the far-famed New York Central Park was opposed by even good men, with misguided pluck, perseverance, and ingenuity; but straight right won its way, and now that park is appreciated. So we confidently believe it will be with our great national parks and forest reservations. There will be a period of indifference on the part of the rich, sleepy with wealth, and of the toiling millions, sleepy with poverty, most of whom never saw a forest; a period of screaming protest and objection from the plunderers, who are as unconscionable and enterprising as Satan. But light is surely coming, and the friends of destruction will preach and bewail in vain.

The United States government has always been proud of the welcome it has extended to good men of every nation, seeking freedom and homes and bread. Let them be welcomed still as nature welcomes them, to the woods as well as to the prairies and plains. No place is too good for good men, and still there is room. They are invited to heaven, and may well be allowed in America. Every place is made better by them. Let them be as free to pick gold and gems from the hills, to cut and hew, dig and plant, for homes and bread, as the birds are to pick berries from the wild bushes, and moss and leaves for nests. The ground will be glad to feed them, and the pines will come down from the mountains for their homes as willingly as the cedars came from Lebanon for Solomon's temple. Nor will the woods be the worse for this use, or their benign influences be diminished any more than the sun is diminished by shining. Mere destroyers, however, tree-killers, wool and mutton men, spreading death and confusion in the fairest groves and gardens ever planted – let the government hasten to cast them out and make an end of them. For it must be told again and gain, and be burningly borne in mind, that just now, while protective measures are being deliberated languidly, destruction and use are speeding on faster and further every day. The axe and saw are insanely busy, chips are flying thick as snowflakes, and every summer thousands of acres of priceless forests, with their underbrush, soil, springs, climate, scenery and religion, are vanishing away in clouds of smoke, while, except in the national parks, not one forest guard is employed.

All sorts of local laws and regulations have been tried and found wanting, and the costly lessons of our own experience, as well as that of every civilized nation, show conclusively that the fate of the remnant of our forests is in the hands of the federal government, and that if the remnant is to be saved at all, it must be saved quickly.

Any fool can destroy trees. They cannot run away; and if they could, they would still be destroyed – chased and hunted down as long as fun or a dollar could be got out of their bark hides, branching horns, or magnificent bole backbones. Few that fell trees plant them; nor would planting avail much towards getting back anything like the noble primeval forests. During a man's life only saplings can be grown, in the place of the old trees – tens of centuries old – that have been destroyed. It took more than three thousand years to make some of the trees in these Western woods – trees that are still standing in perfect strength and beauty, waving and singing in the mighty forests of the Sierra. Through all the wonderful, eventful centuries since Christ's time – and long before that – God has cared for these trees, saved them from drought, disease, avalanches and a thousand straining, levelling tempests and floods; but he cannot save them from fools – only Uncle Sam can do that.

A WIND-STORM IN THE CALIFORNIA FORESTS.
(AFTER A SKETCH BY THE AUTHOR.)

THE YOSEMITE

The Yosemite

First published by The Century Co., New York, 1912

LAKE TENAYA, ONE OF THE YOSEMITE FOUNTAINS.

Contents

CHAPTER ONE

The Approach to the Valley

WHEN I set out on the long excursion that finally led to California I wandered afoot and alone, from Indiana to the Gulf of Mexico, with a plant-press on my back, holding a generally southward course, like the birds when they are going from summer to winter. From the west coast of Florida I crossed the gulf to Cuba, enjoyed the rich tropical flora there for a few months, intending to go thence to the north end of South America, make my way through the woods to the headwaters of the Amazon, and float down that grand river to the ocean. But I was unable to find a ship bound for South America – fortunately perhaps, for I had incredibly little money for so long a trip and had not yet fully recovered from a fever caught in the Florida swamps. Therefore I decided to visit California for a year or two to see its wonderful flora and the famous Yosemite Valley. All the world was before me and every day was a holiday, so it did not seem important to which one of the world's wildernesses I first should wander.

Arriving by the Panama steamer, I stopped one day in San Francisco and then inquired for the nearest way out of town. 'But where do you want to go?' asked the man to whom I had applied for this important information. 'To any place that is wild,' I said. This reply startled him. He seemed to fear I might be crazy and therefore the sooner I was out of town the better, so he directed me to the Oakland ferry.

So on the first of April, 1868, I set out afoot for Yosemite. It was the bloom-time of the year over the lowlands and coast ranges; the landscapes of the Santa Clara Valley were fairly drenched with sunshine, all the air was quivering with the songs of the meadow-larks, and the hills were so covered with flowers that they seemed to be painted. Slow indeed was my progress through these glorious gardens, the first of the California flora I had seen. Cattle and cultivation were making few scars as yet, and I wandered enchanted in long wavering curves, knowing by my pocket map that Yosemite Valley lay to the east and that I should surely find it.

THE SIERRA FROM THE WEST

Looking eastward from the summit of the Pacheco Pass one shining morning, a landscape was displayed that after all my wanderings still appears as the most beautiful I have ever beheld. At my feet lay the Great Central Valley of California, level and flowery, like a lake of pure sunshine, forty or fifty miles wide, five hundred miles long, one rich furred garden of yellow *Compositae*. And from the eastern boundary of this vast golden flower-bed rose the mighty

Sierra, miles in height, and so gloriously coloured and so radiant, it seemed not clothed with light, but wholly composed of it, like the wall of some celestial city. Along the top and extending a good way down, was a rich pearl-grey belt of snow; below it a belt of blue and dark purple, marking the extension of the forests; and stretching along the base of the range a broad belt of rose-purple; all these colours, from the blue sky to the yellow valley smoothly blending as they do in a rainbow, making a wall of light ineffably fine. Then it seemed to me that the Sierra should be called, not the Nevada or Snowy Range, but the Range of Light. And after ten years of wandering and wondering in the heart of it, rejoicing in its glorious floods of light, the white beams of the morning streaming through the passes, the noonday radiance on the crystal rocks, the flush of the alpenglow, and the irised spray of countless waterfalls, it still seems above all others the Range of Light.

In general views no mark of man is visible upon it; nor anything to suggest the wonderful depth and grandeur of its sculpture. None of its magnificent forest-crowned ridges seems to rise much above the general level to publish its wealth. No great valley or river is seen, or group of well-marked features of any kind standing out as distinct pictures. Even the summit peaks, mar-shalled in glorious array so high in the sky, seem comparatively regular in form. Nevertheless the whole range five hundred miles long is furrowed with canyons 2,000 to 5,000ft. deep, in which once flowed majestic glaciers, and in which now flow and sing the bright rejoicing rivers.

CHARACTERISTICS OF THE CANYONS

Though of such stupendous depth, these canyons are not gloomy gorges, savage and inaccessible. With rough passages here and there they are flowery pathways conducting to the snowy, ice fountains; mountain streets full of life and light, graded and sculptured by the ancient glaciers, and presenting throughout all their courses a rich variety of novel and attractive scenery – the most attractive that has yet been discovered in the mountain ranges of the world. In many places, especially in the middle region of the western flank, the main canyons widen into spacious valleys or parks diversified like land-scape gardens with meadows and groves and thickets of blooming bushes, while the lofty walls, infinitely varied in form, are fringed with ferns, flower-ing plants, shrubs of many species, and tall evergreens and oaks that find footholds on small benches and tables, all enlivened and made glorious with rejoicing streams that come chanting in chorus over the cliffs and through side canyons in falls of every conceivable form, to join the river that flows in tranquil, shining beauty down the middle of each one of them.

THE INCOMPARABLE YOSEMITE

The most famous and accessible of these canyon valleys, and also the one that presents their most striking and sublime features on the grandest scale, is the Yosemite, situated in the basin of the Merced River at an elevation of 4000 feet above the level of the sea. It is about seven miles long, half a mile to a mile wide, and nearly a mile deep in the solid granite flank of the range. The walls are made up of rocks, mountains in size, partly separated from each other by side canyons, and they are so sheer in front, and so compactly and harmoniously arranged on a level floor, that the Valley, comprehensively seen, looks like an immense hall or temple lighted from above.

But no temple made with hands can compare with Yosemite. Every rock in its walls seems to glow with life. Some lean back in majestic repose; others, absolutely sheer or nearly so for thousands of feet, advance beyond their companions in thoughtful attitudes, giving welcome to storms and calms alike, seemingly aware, yet heedless, of everything going on about them. Awful in stern, immovable majesty, how softly these rocks are adorned, and how fine and reassuring the company they keep: their feet among beautiful groves and meadows, their brows in the sky, a thousand flowers leaning confidingly against their feet, bathed in floods of water, floods of light, while the snow and waterfalls, the winds and avalanches and clouds shine and sing and wreathe about them as the years go by, and myriads of small winged creatures – birds, bees, butterflies – give glad animation and help to make all the air into music. Down through the middle of the Valley flows the crystal Merced, River of Mercy, peacefully quiet, reflecting lilies and trees and the onlooking rocks; things frail and fleeting and types of endurance meeting here and blending in countless forms, as if into this one mountain mansion Nature had gathered her choicest treasures, to draw her lovers into close and confiding communion with her.

THE APPROACH TO THE VALLEY

Sauntering up the foothills to Yosemite by any of the old trails or roads in use before the railway was built from the town of Merced up the river to the boundary of Yosemite Park, richer and wilder become the forests and streams. At an elevation of 6,000ft. above the level of the sea the silver firs are 200ft. high, with branches whorled around the colossal shafts in regular order, and every branch beautifully primate like a fern frond. The Douglas spruce, the yellow and sugar pines and brown-barked Libocedrus here reach their finest developments of beauty and grandeur. The majestic Sequoia is here, too, the king of conifers, the noblest of all the noble race. These colossal trees are as wonderful in fineness of beauty and proportion as in stature – an assemblage of conifers surpassing all that have ever yet been discovered in the forests of the world. Here indeed is the tree-lover's paradise; the woods, dry and wholesome, letting in the light in shimmering masses of half sunshine, half shade; the night air as well as the day air indescribably spicy and exhilarating; plushy fir-boughs for campers' beds, and cascades to sing us to sleep. On the highest ridges, over which these old Yosemite ways passed, the silver fir (*Abies magnifica*) forms the bulk of the woods, pressing forward in glorious array to the very brink of the Valley walls on both sides, and beyond the Valley to a height of from 8,000 to 9,000ft. above the level of the sea. Thus it appears that Yosemite, presenting such stupendous faces of bare granite, is nevertheless imbedded in magnificent forests, and the main species of pine, fir, spruce and libocedrus are also found in the Valley itself, but there are no 'big trees' (*Sequoia gigantea*) in the Valley or about the rim of it. The nearest are about ten and twenty miles beyond the lower end of the valley on small tributaries of the Merced and Tuolumne Rivers.

THE FIRST VIEW: THE BRIDAL VEIL

From the margin of these glorious forests the first general view of the Valley used to be gained – a revelation in landscape affairs that enriches one's life forever. Entering the Valley, gazing overwhelmed with the multitude of grand objects about us, perhaps the first to fix our attention will be the Bridal Veil, a beautiful waterfall on our right. Its brow, where it first leaps free from the cliff, is about 900ft. above us; and as it sways and sings in the wind, clad in gauzy, sun-sifted spray, half falling, half floating, it seems infinitely gentle and fine; but the hymns it sings tell the solemn fateful power hidden beneath its soft clothing.

The Bridal Veil shoots free from the upper edge of the cliff by the velocity the stream has acquired in descending a long slope above the head of the fall. Looking from the top of the rock-avalanche talus on the west-side, about one hundred feet above the foot of the fall, the under surface of the water arch is seen to be finely grooved and striated; and the sky is seen through the arch between rock and water, making a novel and beautiful effect.

Under ordinary weather conditions the fall strikes on flat-topped slabs, forming a kind of ledge about two-thirds of the way down from the top, and as the fall sways back and forth with great variety of motions among those flat-topped pillars, kissing and plashing notes as well as thunder-like detonations are produced, like those of the Yosemite Fall, though on a smaller scale.

The rainbows of the Veil, or rather the spray- and foam-bows, are superb, because the waters are dashed among angular blocks of granite at the foot, producing abundance of spray of the best quality for iris effects, and also for a luxuriant growth of grass and maiden-hair on the side of the talus, which lower down is planted with oak, laurel and willows.

GENERAL FEATURES OF THE VALLEY

On the other side of the Valley, almost immediately opposite the Bridal Veil, there is another fine fall, considerably wider than the Veil when the snow is melting fast and more than 1,000ft. in height, measured from the brow of the cliff where it first springs out into the air to the head of the rocky talus on which it strikes and is broken up into ragged cascades. It is called the Ribbon Fall or Virgin's Tears. During the spring floods it is a magnificent object, but the suffocating blasts of spray that fill the recess in the wall which it occupies prevent a near approach. In autumn, however, when its feeble current falls in a shower, it may then pass for tears with the sentimental onlooker fresh from a visit to the Bridal Veil.

Just beyond this glorious flood the El Capitan Rock, regarded by many as the most sublime feature of the Valley, is seen through the pine groves, standing forward beyond the general line of the wall in most imposing grandeur, a type of permanence. It is 3,300ft. high, a plain, severely simple, glacier-sculptured face of granite, the end of one of the most compact and enduring of the mountain ridges, unrivalled in height and breadth and flawless strength.

Across the Valley from here, next to the Bridal Veil, are the picturesque Cathedral Rocks, nearly 2,700ft. high, making a noble display of fine yet massive sculpture. They are closely related to El Capitan, having been eroded from the same mountain ridge by the great Yosemite Glacier when the Valley was in process of formation.

Next to the Cathedral Rocks on the south side towers the Sentinel Rock to a height of more than 3,000ft., a telling monument of the glacial period.

Almost immediately opposite the Sentinel are the Three Brothers, an immense mountain mass with three gables fronting the Valley, one above another, the topmost gable nearly 4,000ft. high. They were named for three brothers, sons of old Tenaya, the Yosemite chief, captured here during the Indian War, at the time of the discovery of the Valley in 1852.

Sauntering up the Valley, through meadow and grove, in the company of these majestic rocks, which seem to follow us as we advance, gazing, admiring, looking for new wonders ahead where all about us is so wonderful, the thunder of the Yosemite Fall is heard, and when we arrive in front of the Sentinel Rock it is revealed in all its glory from base to summit, half a mile in height, and seeming to spring out into the Valley sunshine direct from the sky. But even this fall, perhaps the most wonderful of its kind in the world, cannot at first hold our attention, for now the wide upper portion of the Valley is displayed to view, with the finely modelled North Dome, the Royal Arches and Washington Column on our left; Glacier Point, with its massive, magnificent sculpture on the right; and in the middle, directly in front, looms Tissiack or Half Dome, the most beautiful and most sublime of all the wonderful Yosemite rocks, rising in serene majesty from flowery groves and meadows to a height of 4,750ft..

THE UPPER CANYONS

Here the Valley divides into three branches, the Tenaya, Nevada, and Illilouette Canyons, extending back into the fountains of the High Sierra, with scenery every way worthy the relation they bear to Yosemite.

In the south branch, a mile or two from the main Valley, is the Illilouette Fall, 600ft. high, one of the most beautiful of all the Yosemite choir, but to most people inaccessible as yet on account of its rough, steep, boulder-choked canyon. Its principal fountains of ice and snow lie in the beautiful and interesting mountains of the Merced group, while its broad open basin between its fountain mountains and canyon is noted for the beauty of its lakes and forests and magnificent moraines.

Returning to the Valley, and going up the north branch of the Tenaya Canyon, we pass between the North Dome and Half Dome, and in less than an hour come to Mirror Lake, the Dome Cascades, and Tenaya Fall. Beyond the Fall, on the north side of the canyon, is the sublime El Capitan-like rock called Mount Watkins; on the south the vast granite wave of Clouds' Rest, a mile in height; and between them the fine Tenaya Cascade with silvery plumes outspread on smooth glacier-polished folds of granite, making a vertical descent in all of about 700ft.

Just beyond the Dome Cascades, on the shoulder of Mount Watkins, there is an old trail once used by Indians on their way across the range to Mono, but in the canyon above this point there is no trail of any sort. Between Mount Watkins and Clouds' Rest the canyon is accessible only to mountaineers, and it is so dangerous that I hesitate to advise even good climbers, anxious to test their nerve and skill, to attempt to pass through it. Beyond the Cascades no great difficulty will be encountered. A succession of charming lily gardens and meadows occurs in filled-up lake basins among the rock-waves in the bottom of the canyon, and everywhere the surface of the granite has a smooth-wiped appearance, and in many places reflects the sunbeams like glass, a phenomenon due to glacial action, the canyon having been the channel of one of the main tributaries of the ancient Yosemite Glacier.

About ten miles above the Valley we come to the beautiful Tenaya Lake, and here the canyon terminates. A mile or two above the lake stands the grand Sierra Cathedral, a building of one stone, hewn from the living rock, with sides, roof, gable, spire and ornamental pinnacles, fashioned and finished symmetrically like a work of art, and set on a well-graded plateau about 9,000ft. high, as if Nature in making so fine a building had also been careful that it should be finely seen. From every direction its peculiar form and graceful, majestic beauty of expression never fail to charm. Its height from its base to the ridge of the roof is about 2,500ft., and among the pinnacles that adorn the front grand views may be gained of the upper basins of the Merced and Tuolumne Rivers.

Passing the Cathedral we descend into the delightful, spacious Tuolumne Valley, from which excursions may be made to Mounts Dana, Lyell, Ritter, Conness, and Mono Lake, and to the many curious peaks that rise above the meadows on the south, and to the Big Tuolumne Canyon, with its glorious abundance of rocks and falling, gliding, tossing water. For all these the beautiful meadows near the Soda Springs form a delightful centre.

NATURAL FEATURES NEAR THE VALLEY

Returning now to Yosemite and ascending the middle or Nevada branch of the Valley, occupied by the main Merced River, we come within a few miles to the Vernal and Nevada Falls, 400 and 600ft. high, pouring their white, rejoicing waters in the midst of the most novel and sublime rock scenery to be found in all the world. Tracing the river beyond the head of the Nevada Fall we are led into the Little Yosemite, a valley like the great Yosemite in form, sculpture and vegetation. It is about three miles long, with walls 1,500 to 2,000ft. high, cascades coming over them, and the river flowing through the meadows and groves of the level bottom in tranquil, richly-embowered reaches.

Beyond this Little Yosemite in the main canyon, there are three other little yosemites, the highest situated a few miles below the base of Mount Lyell, at an elevation of about 7,800ft. above the sea. To describe these, with all their wealth of Yosemite furniture, and the wilderness of lofty peaks above them, the home of the avalanche and treasury of the fountain snow, would take us far beyond the bounds of a single book. Nor can we here consider the formation of these mountain landscapes – how the crystal rocks were brought to light by glaciers made up of crystal snow, making beauty whose influence is so mysterious on every one who sees it.

Of the small glacier lakes so characteristic of these upper regions, there are no fewer than sixty-seven in the basin of the middle branch, besides countless smaller pools. In the basin of the Illilouette there are sixteen, in the Tenaya basin and its branches thirteen, in the Yosemite Creek basin fourteen, and in the Pohono or Bridal Veil one, making a grand total of one hundred and eleven lakes whose waters come to sing at Yosemite. So glorious is the background of the great Valley, so harmonious its relations to its widespreading fountains.

The same harmony prevails in all the other features of the adjacent landscapes. Climbing out of the Valley by the subordinate canyons, we find the ground rising from the brink of the walls: on the south side to the fountains of the Bridal Veil Creek, the basin of which is noted for the beauty of its meadows and its superb forests of silver fir; on the north side through the basin of the Yosemite Creek to the dividing ridge along the Tuolumne Canyon and the fountains of the Hoffman Range.

DOWN THE YOSEMITE CREEK

In general views the Yosemite Creek basin seems to be paved with domes and smooth, whaleback masses of granite in every stage of development – some showing only their crowns; others rising high and free above the girdling forests, singly or in groups. Others are developed only on one side, forming bold outstanding bosses usually well fringed with shrubs and trees, and presenting the polished surfaces given them by the glacier that brought them into relief. On the upper portion of the basin broad moraine beds have been deposited and on these fine, thrifty forests are growing. Lakes and meadows and small spongy bogs may be found hiding here and there in the woods or back in the fountain recesses of Mount Hoffman, while a thousand gardens are planted along the banks of the streams.

All the wide, fan-shaped upper portion of the basin is covered with a network of small rills that go cheerily on their way to their grand fall in the Valley, now flowing on smooth pavements in sheets thin as glass, now diving under willows and laving their red roots, oozing through green, plushy bogs, plashing over small falls and dancing down slanting cascades, calming again, gliding through patches of smooth glacier meadows with sod of alpine agrostis mixed with blue and white violets and daisies, breaking, tossing among rough boulders and fallen trees, resting in calm pools, flowing together until, all united, they go to their fate with stately, tranquil gestures like a full-grown river. At the crossing of the Mono Trail, about two miles above the head of the Yosemite Fall, the stream is nearly forty feet wide, and when the snow is melting rapidly in the spring it is about four feet deep, with a current of two and a half miles an hour. This is about the volume of water that forms the Fall in May and June when there had been much snow the preceeding winter; but it varies greatly from month to month. The snow rapidly vanishes from the open portion of the basin, which faces southward, and only a few of the tributaries reach back to perennial snow and ice fountains in the shadowy amphitheatres on the precipitous northern slopes of Mount Hoffman. The total descent made by the stream from its highest sources to its confluence with the Merced in the Valley is about 6,000ft., while the distance is only about ten miles, an average fall of 600ft. per mile. The last mile of its course lies between the sides of sunken domes and swelling folds of the granite that are clustered and pressed together like a mass of bossy cumulus clouds. Through this shining way Yosemite Creek goes to its fate, swaying and swirling with easy, graceful gestures and singing the last of its mountain songs before it reaches the dizzy edge of Yosemite to fall 2,600ft. into another world, where climate, vegetation, inhabitants, all are different. Emerging from this last canyon the stream glides, in flat, lace-like folds, down a smooth incline into a small pool where it seems to rest and compose itself before taking the grand plunge. Then calmly, as if leaving a lake, it slips over the polished lip of the pool down another incline and out over the brow of the precipice in a magnificent curve thick-sown with rainbow spray.

THE YOSEMITE FALL

Long ago before I had traced this fine stream to its head back of Mount Hoffman, I was eager to reach the extreme verge to see how it behaved in flying so far through the air; but after enjoying this view and getting safely away I have never advised any one to follow my steps. The last incline down which the stream journeys so gracefully is so steep and smooth one must slip cautiously forward on hands and feet alongside the rushing water, which so near one's head is very exciting. But to gain a perfect view one must go yet farther, over a curving brow to a slight shelf on the extreme brink. This shelf, formed by the flaking off of a fold of granite, is about three inches wide, just wide enough for a safe rest for one's heels. To me it seemed nerve-trying to slip to this narrow foothold and poise on the edge of such a precipice so close to the confusing whirl of the waters; and after casting longing glances over the shining brow of the fall and listening to its sublime psalm, I concluded not to attempt to go nearer, but, nevertheless, against reasonable judgment, I did. Noticing some tufts of artemisia in a cleft of rock, I filled my mouth with the leaves, hoping their bitter taste might help to keep caution keen and prevent giddiness. In spite of myself I reached the little ledge, got my heels well set, and worked sidewise twenty or thirty feet to a point close to the out-plunging current. Here the view is perfectly free down into the heart of the bright irised throng of comet-like streamers into which the whole ponderous volume of the fall separates, two or three hundred feet below the brow. So glorious a display of pure wildness, acting at close range while cut off from all the world beside, is terribly impressive. A less nerve-trying view may be obtained from a fissured portion of the edge of the cliff about forty yards to the eastward of the fall. Seen from this point towards noon, in the spring, the rainbow on its brow seems to be broken up and mingled with the rushing comets until all the fall is stained with iris colours, leaving no white water visible. This is the best of the safe views from above, the huge steadfast rocks, the flying waters, and the rainbow light forming one of the most glorious pictures conceivable.

The Yosemite Fall is separated into an upper and a lower fall with a series of falls and cascades between them, but when viewed in front from the bottom of the Valley they all appear as one.

So grandly does this magnificent fall display itself from the floor of the Valley, few visitors take the trouble to climb the walls to gain nearer views, unable to realize how vastly more impressive it is near by than at a distance of one or two miles.

A WONDERFUL ASCENT

The views developed in a walk up the zigzags of the trail leading to the foot of the Upper Fall are about as varied and impressive as those displayed along the favourite Glacier Point Trail. One rises as if on wings. The groves, meadows, fern-flats and reaches of the river gain new interest, as if never seen before; all the views changing in a most striking manner as we go higher from point to point. The foreground also changes every few rods in the most surprising manner, although the earthquake talus and the level bench on the face of the wall over which the trail passes seem monotonous and commonplace as seen from the bottom of the Valley. Up we climb with glad exhilaration, through shaggy fringes of laurel, ceanothus, glossy-leaved manzanita and live-oak, from shadow to shadow across bars and patches of sunshine, the leafy openings making charming frames for the Valley pictures beheld through them, and for the glimpses of the high peaks that appear in the distance. The higher we go the farther we seem to be from the summit of the vast granite wall. Here we pass a projecting buttress whose grooved and rounded surface tells a plain story of the time when the Valley, now filled with sunshine, was filled with ice, when the grand old Yosemite Glacier, flowing river-like from its distant fountains, swept through it, crushing, grinding, wearing its way ever deeper, developing and fashioning these sublime rocks. Again we cross a white, battered gully, the pathway of rock avalanches or snow avalanches. Farther on we come to a gentle stream slipping down the face of the cliff in lace-like strips, and dropping from ledge to ledge – too small to be called a fall – trickling, dripping, oozing, a pathless wanderer from one of the upland meadows lying a little way back of the Valley rim, seeking a way century after century to the depths of the Valley without any appreciable channel. Every morning after a cool night, evaporation being checked, it gathers strength and sings like a bird, but as the day advances and the sun strikes its thin currents outspread on the heated precipices, most of its waters vanish ere the bottom of the Valley is reached. Many a fine, hanging-garden aloft on breezy inaccessible heights owes to it its freshness and fullness of beauty; ferneries in shady nooks, filled with adiantum, woodwardia, woodsia, aspidium, pellaea, and cheilanthes, rosetted and tufted and ranged in lines, daintily overlapping, thatching the stupendous cliffs with softest beauty, some of the delicate fronds seeming to float on the warm moist air, without any connection with rock or stream. Nor is there any lack of coloured plants wherever they can find a place to cling to; lilies and mints, the showy cardinal mimulus, and glowing cushions of the golden bahia, enlivened with butterflies and bees and all the other small, happy humming creatures that belong to them.

After the highest point on the lower division of the trail is gained it leads up into the deep recess occupied by the great fall, the noblest display of falling water to be found in the Valley, or perhaps in the world. When it first comes in sight it seems almost within reach of one's hand, so great in the spring is its volume and velocity, yet it is still nearly a third of a mile away and appears to recede as we advance. The sculpture of the walls about it is on a scale of grandeur, according nobly with the fall – plain and massive, though elaborately finished, like all the other cliffs about the Valley.

In the afternoon an immense shadow is cast athwart the plateau in front of the fall, and over the chaparral bushes that clothe the slopes and benches of the walls to the eastward, creeping upward until the fall is wholly overcast, the contrast between the shaded and illumined sections being very striking in these near views.

Under this shadow, during the cool centuries immediately following the breaking-up of the Glacial Period, dwelt a small residual glacier, one of the few that lingered on this sun-beaten side of the Valley after the main trunk glacier had vanished. It sent down a long winding current through the narrow canyon on the west side of the fall, and must have formed a striking feature of the ancient scenery of the Valley; the lofty fall of ice and fall of water side by side, yet separate and distinct.

The coolness of the afternoon shadow and the abundant dewy spray make a fine climate for the plateau ferns and grasses, and for the beautiful azalea bushes that grow here in profusion and bloom in September, long after the warmer thickets down on the floor of the Valley have withered and gone to seed. Even close to the fall, and behind it at the base of the cliff, a few venturesome plants may be found undisturbed by the rock-shaking torrent.

The basin at the foot of the fall into which the current directly pours, when it is not swayed by the wind, is about ten feet and fifteen to twenty feet in diameter. That it is not much deeper is surprising, when the great height and force of the fall is considered. But the rock where the water strikes probably suffers less erosion than it would were the descent less than half as great, since the current is outspread, and much of its force is spent ere it reaches the bottom – being received on the air as upon an elastic cushion, and borne outward and dissipated over a surface more than fifty yards wide.

This surface, easily examined when the water is low, is intensely clean and fresh looking. It is the raw, quick flesh of the mountain wholly untouched by the weather. In summer droughts, when the snowfall of the preceding winter has been light, the fall is reduced to a mere shower of separate drops without any obscuring spray. Then we may safely go back of it and view the crystal shower from beneath, each drop wavering and pulsing as it makes its way through the air, and flashing off jets of coloured light of ravishing beauty. But all this is invisible from the bottom of the Valley, like a thousand other interesting things. One must labour for beauty as for bread, here as elsewhere.

THE GRANDEUR OF THE YOSEMITE FALL

During the time of the spring floods the best near view of the fall is obtained from Fern Ledge on the east side above the blinding spray at a height of about 400ft. above the base of the fall. A climb of about 1,400ft. from the Valley has to be made, and there is no trail, but to any one fond of climbing this will make the ascent all the more delightful. A narrow part of the ledge extends to the side of the fall and back of it, enabling us to approach it as closely as we wish. When the afternoon sunshine is streaming through the throng of comets, ever wasting, ever renewed, the marvellous fineness, firmness and variety of their forms are beautifully revealed. At the top of the fall they seem to burst forth in irregular spurts from some grand, throbbing mountain heart. Now and then one mighty throb sends forth a mass of solid water into the free air far beyond the others, which rushes alone to the bottom of the fall with long streaming tail, like combed silk, while the others, descending in clusters, gradually mingle and lose their identity. But they all rush past us with amazing velocity and display of power, though apparently drowsy and deliberate in their movements when observed from a distance of a mile or two. The heads of these comet-like masses are composed of nearly solid water, and are dense white in colour like pressed snow, from the friction they suffer in rushing through the air, the portion worn off forming the tail, between the white lustrous threads and films of which faint, greyish pencilings appear, while the outer, finer sprays of water-dust, whirling in sunny eddies, are pearly grey throughout. At the bottom of the fall there is but little distinction of form visible. It is mostly a hissing, clashing seething, upwhirling mass of scud and spray, through which the light sifts in grey and purple tones, while at times when the sun strikes at the required angle, the whole wild and apparently lawless, stormy, striving mass is changed to brilliant rainbow hues, manifesting finest harmony. The middle portion of the fall is the most openly beautiful; lower, the various forms into which the waters are wrought are more closely and voluminously veiled, while higher, towards the head, the current is comparatively simple and undivided. But even at the bottom, in the boiling clouds of spray, there is no confusion, while the rainbow light makes all divine, adding glorious beauty and peace to glorious power. This noble fall has far the richest, as well as the most powerful, voice of all the falls of the Valley, its tones varying from the sharp hiss and rustle of the wind in the glossy leaves of the live-oaks and the soft, sifting, hushing tones of the pines, to the loudest rush and roar of storm winds and thunder among the crags of the summit peaks. The low bass, booming, reverberating tones, heard under favourable circumstances five or six miles away, are formed by the dashing and exploding of heavy masses mixed with air upon two projecting ledges on the face of the cliff, the one on which we are standing and another about 200 feet above it. The torrent of massive comets is continuous at time of high water, while the explosive, booming notes are wildly intermittent, because, unless influenced by the wind, most of the heavier masses shoot out from the face of the precipice, and pass the ledges upon which at other times they are exploded. Occasionally the whole fall is swayed away from the front of the cliff, then suddenly dashed flat against it, or vibrated from side to side like a pendulum, giving rise to endless variety of forms and sounds.

THE NEVADA FALL

The Nevada Fall is 600ft. high and is usually ranked next to the Yosemite in general interest among the five main falls of the Valley. Coming through the Little Yosemite in tranquil reaches, the river is first broken into rapids on a moraine boulder-bar that crosses the lower end of the Valley. Thence it pursues its way to the head of the fall in a rough, solid rock channel, dashing on side angles, heaving in heavy surging masses against elbow knobs, and swirling and swashing in pot-holes without a moment's rest. Thus, already chafed and dashed to foam, overfolded and twisted, it plunges over the brink of the precipice as if glad to escape into the open air. But before it reaches the bottom it is pulverized yet finer by impinging upon a sloping portion of the cliff about half-way down, thus making it the whitest of all the falls of the Valley, and altogether one of the most wonderful in the world.

On the north side, close to its head, a slab of granite projects over the brink, forming a fine point for a view, over its throng of streamers and wild plunging, into its intensely white bosom, and, through the broad drifts of spray, to the river far below, gathering its spent waters and rushing on again down the canyon in glad exultation into Emerald Pool, where at length it grows calm and gets rest for what still lies before it. All the features of the view correspond with the waters in grandeur and wildness. The glacier-sculptured walls of the canyon on either hand, with the sublime mass of the Glacier Point Ridge in front, form a huge triangular pit-like basin, which, filled with the roaring of the falling river, seems as if it might be the hopper of one of the mills of the gods in which the mountains were being ground.

THE VERNAL FALL

The Vernal, about a mile below the Nevada, is 400ft. high, a staid, orderly, graceful, easy-going fall, proper and exact in every movement and gesture, with scarce a hint of the passionate enthusiasm of the Yosemite or of the impetuous Nevada, whose chafed and twisted waters hurrying over the cliff seem glad to escape into the open air, while its deep, booming, thunder-tones reverberate over the listening landscape. Nevertheless it is a favourite with most visitors, doubtless because it is more accessible than any other, more closely approached and better seen and heard. A good stairway ascends the cliff beside it and the level plateau at the head enables one to saunter safely along the edge of the river as it comes from Emerald Pool and to watch its waters, calmly bending over the brow of the precipice, in a sheet eighty feet wide, changing in colour from green to purplish grey and white until dashed on a boulder talus. Thence issuing from beneath its fine broad spray-clouds we see the tremendously adventurous river still unspent, beating its way down the wildest and deepest of all its canyons in grey roaring rapids, dear to the ouzel, and below the confluence of the Illilouette, sweeping around the shoulder of the Half Dome on its approach to the head of the tranquil levels of the Valley.

THE ILLILOUETTE FALL

The Illilouette in general appearance most resembles the Nevada. The volume of water is less than half as great, but it is about the same height (600ft.) and its waters received the same kind of preliminary tossing in a rocky, irregular channel. Therefore it is a very white and fine-grained fall. When it is in full springtime bloom it is partly divided by rocks that roughen the lip of the precipice, but this division amounts only to a kind of fluting and grooving of the column, which has a beautiful effect. It is not nearly so grand a fall as the upper Yosemite, or so symmetrical as the Vernal, or so airily graceful and simple as the Bridal Veil, nor does it ever display so tremendous an outgush of snowy magnificence as the Nevada; but in the exquisite fineness and richness of texture of its flowing folds it surpasses them all.

One of the finest effects of sunlight on falling water I ever saw in Yosemite or elsewhere I found on the brow of this beautiful fall. It was in the Indian summer, when the leaf colours were ripe and the great cliffs and domes were transfigured in the hazy golden air. I had scrambled up its rugged talus-dammed canyon, oftentimes stopping to take breath and look back to admire the wonderful views to be had there of the great Half Dome, and to enjoy the extreme purity of the water, which in the motionless pools on this stream is almost perfectly invisible; the coloured foliage of the maples, dogwoods, *Rubus* tangles, etc., and the late goldenrods and asters. The voice of the fall was now low, and the grand spring and summer floods had waned to sifting, drifting gauze and thin-broidered folds of linked and arrowy lace-work. When I reached the foot of the fall sunbeams were glinting across its head, leaving all the rest of it in shadow; and on its illumined brow a group of yellow spangles of singular form and beauty were playing, flashing up and dancing in large flame-shaped masses, wavering at times, then steadying, rising and falling in accord with the shifting forms of the water. But the colour of the dancing spangles changed not at all. Nothing in clouds or flowers, on bird-wings or the lips of shells, could rival it in fineness. It was the most divinely beautiful mass of rejoicing yellow light I ever beheld – one of Nature's precious gifts that perchance may come to us but once in a lifetime.

THE MINOR FALLS

There are many other comparatively small falls and cascades in the Valley. The most notable are the Yosemite Gorge Fall and Cascades, Tenaya Fall and Cascades, Royal Arch Falls, the two Sentinel Cascades and the falls of Cascade and Tamarack Creeks, a mile or two below the lower end of the Valley. These last are often visited. The others are seldom noticed or mentioned; although in almost any other country they would be visited and described as wonders.

The six intermediate falls in the gorge between the head of the Lower and the base of the Upper Yosemite Falls, separated by a few deep pools and strips of rapids, and three slender, tributary cascades on the west side form a series more strikingly varied and combined than any other in the Valley, yet very few of all the Valley visitors ever see them or hear of them. No available standpoint commands a view of them all. The best general view is obtained from the mouth of the gorge near the head of the Lower Fall. The two lowest of the series, together with one of the three tributary cascades, are visible from this standpoint, but in reaching it the last twenty or thirty feet of the descent is rather dangerous in time of high water, the shelving rocks being then slippery on account of spray, but if one should chance to slip when the water is low, only a bump or two and a harmless plash would be the penalty. No part of the gorge, however, is safe to any but cautious climbers.

Though the dark gorge hall of these rejoicing waters is never flushed by the purple light of morning or evening, it is warmed and cheered by the white light of noonday, which, falling into so much foam and spray of varying degrees of fineness, makes marvellous displays of rainbow colours. So filled, indeed, is it with this precious light, at favourable times it seems to take the place of common air. Laurel bushes shed fragrance into it from above and live-oaks, those fearless mountaineers, hold fast to angular seams and lean out over it with their fringing sprays and bright mirror leaves.

One bird, the ouzel, loves this gorge and flies through it merrily, or cheerily, rather, stopping to sing on foam-washed bosses where other birds could find no rest for their feet. I have even seen a grey squirrel down in the heart of it beside the wild rejoicing water.

One of my favourite night walks was along the rim of this wild gorge in times of high water when the moon was full, to see the lunar bows in the spray.

For about a mile above Mirror Lake the Tenaya Canyon is level, and richly planted with fir, Douglas spruce and libocedrus, forming a remarkably fine grove, at the head of which is the Tenaya Fall. Though seldom seen or described, this is, I think, the most picturesque of all the small falls. A considerable distance above it, Tenaya Creek comes hurrying down, white and foamy, over a flat pavement inclined at an angle of about eighteen degrees. In time of high water this sheet of rapids is nearly seventy feet wide, and is varied in a very striking way by three parallel furrows that extend in the direction of its flow. These furrows, worn by the action of the stream upon cleavage joints, vary in width, are slightly sinuous, and have large boulders firmly wedged in them here and there in narrow places, giving rise, of course, to a complicated series of wild dashes, doublings, and upleaping arches in the swift torrent. Just before it reaches the head of the fall the current is divided, the left division making a vertical drop of about eighty feet in a romantic, leafy, flowery, mossy nook, while the other forms a rugged cascade.

The Royal Arch Fall in time of high water is a magnificent object, forming a broad ornamental sheet in front of the arches. The two Sentinel Cascades, 3,000ft. high, are also grand spectacles when the snow is melting fast in the spring, but by the middle of summer they have diminshed to mere streaks scarce noticeable amid their sublime surroundings.

THE BEAUTY OF THE RAINBOWS

The Bridal Veil and Vernal Falls are famous for their rainbows; and special visits to them are often made when the sun shines into the spray at the most favourable angle. But amid the spray and foam and fine-ground mist ever rising from the various falls and cataracts there is an affluence and variety of iris bows scarcely known to visitors who stay only a day or two. Both day and night, winter and summer, this divine light may be seen wherever water is falling, dancing, singing; telling the heart-peace of Nature amid the wildest displays of her power. In the bright spring mornings the black-walled recess at the foot of the Lower Yosemite Fall is lavishly filled with irised spray; and not simply does this span the dashing foam, but the foam itself, the whole mass of it, beheld at a certain distance, seems to be coloured, and drifts and wavers from colour to colour, mingling with the foliage of the adjacent trees, without suggesting any relationship to the ordinary rainbow. This is perhaps the largest and most reservoir-like fountain of iris colours to be found in the Valley.

Lunar rainbows or spray bows also abound in the glorious affluence of dashing, rejoicing, hurrahing, enthusiastic spring floods, their colours as distinct as those of the sun and regularly and obviously banded, though less vivid. Fine specimens may be found any night at the foot of the Upper Yosemite Fall, glowing gloriously amid the gloomy shadows and thundering waters, whenever there is plenty of moonlight and spray. Even the secondary bow is at times distinctly visible.

The best point from which to observe them is on Fern Ledge. For some time after moonrise, at time of high water, the arc has a span of about five hundred feet, and is set upright; one end planted in the boiling spray at the bottom, the other in the edge of the fall, creeping lower, of course, and becoming less upright as the moon rises higher. This grand arc of colour, glowing in mild, shapely beauty in so weird and huge a chamber of night shadows, and amid the rush and roar and tumultuous dashing of this thunder-voiced fall, is one of the most impressive and most cheering of all the blessed mountain evangels.

Smaller bows may be seen in the gorge on the plateau between the Upper and Lower Falls. Once toward midnight, after spending a few hours with the wild beauty of the Upper Fall, I sauntered along the edge of the gorge, looking in here and there, wherever the footing felt safe, to see what I could learn of the night aspects of the smaller falls that dwell there. And down in an exceedingly black, pit-like portion of the gorge, at the foot of the highest of the intermediate falls, into which the moonbeams were pouring through a narrow opening, I saw a well-defined spray-bow, beautifully distinct in colours, spanning the pit from side to side, while pure white foam-waves beneath the beautiful bow were constantly springing up out of the dark into the moonlight like dancing ghosts.

AN UNEXPECTED ADVENTURE

A wild scene, but not a safe one, is made by the moon as it appears through the edge of the Yosemite Fall when one is behind it. Once, after enjoying the night-song of the waters and watching the formation of the coloured bow as the moon came round the domes and sent her beams into the wild uproar, I ventured out on the narrow bench that extends back of the fall from Fern Ledge and began to admire the dim-veiled grandeur of the view. I could see the fine gauzy threads of the fall's filmy border by having the light in front; and wishing to look at the moon through the meshes of some of the denser portions of the fall, I ventured to creep farther behind it while it was gently wind-swayed, without taking sufficient thought about the consequences of its swaying back to its natural position after the wind-pressure should be removed. The effect was enchanting: fine, savage music sounding above, beneath, around me; while the moon, apparently in the very midst of the rushing waters, seemed to be struggling to keep her place, on account of the ever-varying form and density of the water masses through which she was seen, now darkly veiled or eclipsed by a rush of thick-headed comets, now flashing out through openings between their tails. I was in fairyland between the dark wall and the wild throng of illumined waters, but suffered sudden disenchantment; for, like the witch-scene in Alloway Kirk, 'in an instant all was dark.' Down came a dash of spent comets, thin and harmless-looking in the distance, but they felt desperately solid and stony when they struck my shoulders, like a mixture of choking spray and gravel and big hailstones. Instinctively dropping on my knees, I gripped an angle of the rock, curled up like a young fern frond with my face pressed against my breast, and in this attitude submitted as best I could to my thundering bath. The heavier masses seemed to strike like cobblestones, and there was a confused noise of many waters about my ears – hissing, gurgling, clashing sounds that were not heard as music. The situation was quickly realized. How fast one's thoughts burn in such times of stress! I was weighing chances of escape. Would the column be swayed a few inches away from the wall, or would it come yet closer! The fall was in flood and not so lightly would its ponderous mass be swayed. My fate seemed to depend on a breath of the 'idle wind.' It was moved gently forward, the pounding ceased, and I was once more visited by glimpses of the moon. But fearing I might be caught at a disadvantage in making too hasty a retreat, I moved only a few feet along the bench to where a block of ice lay. I wedged myself between the ice and the wall, and lay face downwards, until the steadiness of the light gave encouragement to rise and get away. Somewhat nerve-shaken, drenched, and benumbed, I made out to build a fire, warmed myself, ran home, reached my cabin before daylight, got an hour or two of sleep and awoke sound and comfortable, better, not worse, for my hard midnight bath.

CLIMATE AND WEATHER

Owing to the westerly trend of the Valley and its vast depth there is a great difference between the climates of the north and south sides – greater than between many countries far apart; for the south wall is in shadow during the winter months, while the north is bathed in sunshine every clear day. Thus there is mild spring weather on one side of the Valley while winter rules the other. Far up the north-side cliffs many a nook may be found closely embraced by sun-beaten rock-bosses in which flowers bloom every month of the year. Even butterflies may be seen in these high winter gardens except when snow-storms are falling and a few days after they have ceased. Near the head of the lower Yosemite Fall in January I found the ant lions lying in wait in their warm sand-cups, rock ferns being unrolled, club mosses covered with fresh-growing points, the flowers of the laurel nearly open, and the honey-suckle rosetted with bright young leaves; every plant seemed to be thinking about summer. Even on the shadow-side of the Valley the frost is never very sharp. The lowest temperature I ever observed during four winters was 7° Fahrenheit. The first twenty-four days of January had an average temperature at 9 am of 32°, minimum 22°; at 3 pm the average was 40° 30', the minimum 32°. Along the top of the walls, 7,000 and 8,000ft. high, the temperature was, of course, much lower. But the difference in temperature between the north and south sides is due not so much to the winter sunshine as to the heat of the preceeding summer, stored up in the rocks, which rapidly melts the snow in contact with them. For though summer sun-heat is stored in the rocks of the south-side also, the amount is much less because the rays fall obliquely on the south wall even in summer and almost vertically on the north.

The upper branches of the Yosemite streams are buried every winter beneath a heavy mantle of snow, and set free in the spring in magnificent floods. Then, all the fountains, full and overflowing, every living thing breaks forth into singing, and the glad exulting streams, shining and falling in the warm sunny weather, shake everything into music, making all the mountain-world a song.

The great annual spring thaw usually begins in May in the forest region, and in June and July on the High Sierra, varying somewhat both in time and fullness with the weather and the depth of the snow. Toward the end of summer the streams are at their lowest ebb, few even of the strongest singing much above a whisper as they slip and ripple through gravel and boulder-beds from pool to pool in the hollows of their channels, and drop in pattering showers like rain, and slip down precipices and fall in sheets of embroidery, fold over fold. But, however low their singing, it is always ineffably fine in tone, in harmony with the restful time of the year.

The first snow of the season that comes to the help of the streams usually falls in September or October, sometimes even in the latter part of August, in the midst of yellow Indian summer, when the goldenrods and gentians of the glacier meadows are in their prime. This Indian-summer snow, however, soon melts, the chilled flowers spread their petals to the sun, and the gardens as well as the streams are refreshed as if only a warm shower had fallen. The snow-storms that load the mountains to form the main fountain supply for the year seldom set in before the middle or end of November.

WINTER BEAUTY OF THE VALLEY

When the first heavy storms stopped work on the high mountains, I made haste down to my Yosemite den, not to 'hole up' and sleep the white months away; I was out every day, and often all night, sleeping but little, studying the so-called wonders and common things ever on show, wading, climbing, sauntering among the blessed storms and calms, rejoicing in almost everything alike that I could see or hear: the glorious brightness of frosty mornings; the sunbeams pouring over the white domes and crags into the groves and waterfalls, kindling marvellous iris fires in the hoarfrost and spray; the great forests and mountains in their deep noon sleep; the good-night alpenglow; the stars; the solemn gazing moon, drawing the huge domes and headlands one by one glowing white out of the shadows hushed and breathless like an audience in awful enthusiasm, while the meadows at their feet sparkle with frost-stars like the sky; the sublime darkness of storm-nights, when all the lights are out; the clouds in whose depths the frail snow-flowers grow; the behaviour and many voices of the different kinds of storms, trees, birds, waterfalls, and snow-avalanches in the ever-changing weather.

Every clear, frosty morning loud sounds are heard booming and reverberating from side to side of the Valley at intervals of a few minutes, beginning soon after sunrise and continuing an hour or two like a thunder-storm. In my first winter in the Valley I could not make out the source of this noise. I thought of falling boulders, rock-blasting, etc. Not till I saw what looked like hoarfrost dropping from the side of the Fall was the problem explained. The strange thunder is made by the fall of sections of ice formed of spray that is frozen on the face of the cliff along the sides of the Upper Yosemite Fall – a sort of crystal plaster, a foot or two thick, cracked off by the sunbeams, awakening all the Valley like cock-crowing, announcing the finest weather, shouting aloud Nature's infinite industry and love of hard work in creating beauty.

EXPLORING AN ICE CONE

This frozen spray gives rise to one of the most interesting winter features of the Valley – a cone of ice at the foot of the fall, four or five hundred feet high. From the Fern Ledge standpoint its crater like throat is seen, down which the fall plunges with deep, gasping explosions of compressed air, and, after being well churned in the stormy interior, the water bursts forth through arched openings at its base, apparently scourged and weary and glad to escape, while belching spray, spouted up out of the throat past the descending current, is wafted away in irised drifts to the adjacent rocks and groves. It is built during the night and early hours of the morning; only in spells of exceptionally cold and cloudy weather is the work continued through the day. The greater part of the spray material falls in crystalline showers direct to its place, something like a small local snow-storm; but a considerable portion is first frozen on the face of the cliff along the sides of the fall and stays there until expanded and cracked off in irregular masses, some of them tons in weight, to be built into the walls of the cone; while in windy, frosty weather, when the fall is swayed from side to side, the cone is well drenched and the loose ice masses and spray-dust are all firmly welded and frozen together. Thus the finest of the downy wafts and curls of spray-dust, which in mild nights falls about as silently as dew, are held back until sunrise to make a store of heavy ice to reinforce the waterfall's thunder-tones.

While the cone is in process of formation, growing higher and wider in the frosty weather, it looks like a beautiful smooth, pure-white hill; but when it is wasting and breaking up in the spring its surface is strewn with leaves, pine branches, stones, sand, etc., that have been brought over the fall, making it look like a heap of avalanche detritus.

Anxious to learn what I could about the structure of this curious hill I often approached it in calm weather and tried to climb it, carrying an axe to cut steps. Once I nearly succeeded in gaining the summit. At the base I was met by a current of spray and wind that made seeing and breathing difficult. I pushed on backward, however, and soon gained the slope of the hill, where by creeping close to the surface most of the choking blast passed over me and I managed to crawl up but with little difficulty. Thus I made my way nearly to the summit, halting at times to peer up through the wild whirls of spray at the veiled grandeur of the fall, or to listen to the thunder beneath me; the whole hill was sounding as if it were a huge, bellowing drum. I hoped that by waiting until the fall was blown aslant I should be able to climb to the lip of the crater and get a view of the interior; but a suffocating blast, half air, half water, followed by the fall of an enormous mass of frozen spray from a spot high up on the wall, quickly discouraged me. The whole cone was jarred by the blow and some fragments of the mass sped past me dangerously near; so I beat a hasty retreat, chilled and drenched, and lay down on a sunny rock to dry.

Once during a wind-storm when I saw that the fall was frequently blown westward, leaving the cone dry, I ran up to Fern Lodge hoping to gain a clear view of the interior. I set out at noon. All the way up the storm notes were so loud about me that the voice of the fall was almost drowned by them. Notwithstanding the rocks and bushes everywhere were drenched by the wind-driven spray, I approached the brink of the precipice overlooking the mouth of the ice cone, but I was almost suffocated by the drenching, gusty spray, and was compelled to seek shelter. I searched for some hiding-place in the wall from whence I might run out at some opportune moment when the fall with its whirling spray and torn shreds of comet tails and trailing, tattered skirts was borne westward, as I had seen it carried several times before, leaving the cliffs on the east side and the ice hill bare in the sunlight. I had not long to wait, for, as if ordered so for my special accommodation, the mighty downrush of comets with their whirling drapery swung westward and remained aslant for nearly half an hour. The cone was admirably lighted and deserted by the water, which fell most of the time on the rocky western slopes mostly outside of the cone. The mouth into which the fall pours was, as near as I could guess, about one hundred feet in diameter north and south and about two hundred feet east and west, which is about the shape and size of the fall at its best in its normal condition at this season.

The crater-like opening was not a true oval, but more like a huge coarse mouth. I could see down the throat about one hundred feet or perhaps farther.

The fall precipice overhangs from a height of 400ft. above the base; therefore the water strikes some distance from the base of the cliff, allowing space for the accumulation of a considerable mass of ice between the fall and the wall.

CHAPTER TWO

Winter Storms and Spring Floods

THE BRIDAL Veil and the Upper Yosemite Falls, on account of their height and exposure, are greatly influenced by winds. The common summer winds that come up the river canyon from the plains are seldom very strong; but the north winds do some very wild work, worrying the falls and the forests, and hanging snow-banners on the comet-peaks. One wild winter morning I was awakened by a storm-wind that was playing with the falls as if they were mere wisps of mist and making the great pines bow and sing with glorious enthusiasm. The Valley had been visited a short time before by a series of fine snow-storms, and the floor and the cliffs and all the region round about were lavishly adorned with its best winter-jewellery, the air was full of fine snow-dust, and pine branches, tassels and empty cones were flying in an almost continuous flock.

Soon after sunrise, when I was seeking a place safe from flying branches, I saw the Lower Yosemite Fall thrashed and pulverized from top to bottom into one glorious mass of rainbow dust; while a thousand feet above it the main Upper Fall was suspended on the face of the cliff in the form of an inverted bow, all silvery white and fringed with short wavering strips. Then, suddenly assailed by a tremendous blast, the whole mass of the fall was blown into threads and ribbons, and driven back over the brow of the cliff whence it came, as if denied admission to the Valley. This kind of storm-work was continued about ten or fifteen minutes; then another change in the play of the huge exulting swirls and billows and upheaving domes of the gale allowed the baffled fall to gather and arrange its tattered waters, and sink down again in its place. As the day advanced, the gale gave no sign of dying, excepting brief lulls, the Valley was filled with its weariless roar, and the cloudless sky grew garish-white from myriads of minute, sparkling snow-spicules. In the afternoon, while I watched the Upper Fall from the shelter of a big pine tree, it was suddenly arrested in its descent at a point about half-way down, and was neither blown upward nor driven aside, but simply held stationary in mid-air, as if gravitation below that point in the path of its descent had ceased to act. The ponderous flood, weighing hundreds of tons, was sustained, hovering, hesitating, like a bunch of thistledown, while I counted one hundred and ninety. All this time the ordinary amount of water was coming over the cliff and accumulating in the air, swedging and widening and forming an irregular cone about seven hundred feet high, tapering to the top of the wall, the whole standing still, resting on the invisible arm of the North Wind. At length, as if commanded to go on again, scores of arrowy comets shot forth from the bottom of the suspended mass as if escaping from separate outlets.

The brow of El Capitan was decked with long snow-streamers like hair, Clouds' Rest was fairly enveloped in drifting gossamer films, and the Half Dome loomed up in the garish light like a majestic, living creature clad in the same gauzy, wind-woven drapery, while upward currents meeting at times overhead made it smoke like a volcano.

AN EXTRAORDINARY STORM AND FLOOD

Glorious as are these rocks and waters arrayed in storm robes, or chanting rejoicing in every-day dress, they are still more glorious when rare weather conditions meet to make them sing with floods. Only once during all the years I have lived in the Valley have I seen it in full flood bloom. In 1871 the early winter weather was delightful; the days all sunshine, the nights all starry and calm, calling forth fine crops of frost-crystals on the pines and withered ferns and grasses for the morning sunbeams to sift through. In the afternoon of 16 December, when I was sauntering on the meadows, I noticed a massive crimson cloud growing in solitary grandeur above the Cathedral Rocks, its form scarcely less striking than its colour. It had a picturesque, bulging base like an old Sequoia, a smooth, tapering stem, and a bossy, down-curling crown like a mushroom; all its parts were coloured alike, making one mass of translucent crimson. Wondering what the meaning of that strange, lonely red cloud might be, I was up betimes next morning looking at the weather, but all seemed tranquil as yet. Towards noon grey clouds with a close, curly grain like bird's-eye maple began to grow, and late at night rain fell, which soon changed to snow. Next morning the snow on the meadows was about ten inches deep, and it was still falling in a fine, cordial storm. During the night of the 18th heavy rain fell on the snow, but as the temperature was 34°, the snow-line was only a few hundred feet above the bottom of the Valley, and one had only to climb a little higher than the tops of the pines to get out of the rain-storm into the snow-storm. The streams, instead of being increased in volume by the storm, were diminished, because the snow sponged up part of their waters and choked the smaller tributaries. But about midnight the temperature suddenly rose to 42°, carrying the snow-line far beyond the Valley walls, and next morning Yosemite was rejoicing in a glorious flood. The comparatively warm rain falling on the snow was at first absorbed and held back, and so also was that portion of the snow that the rain melted, and all that was melted by the warm wind, until the whole mass of snow was saturated and became sludgy, and at length slipped and rushed simultaneously from a thousand slopes in wildest extravagance, heaping and swelling flood over flood, and plunging into the Valley in stupendous avalanches.

Awakened by the roar, I looked out and at once recognized the extraordinary character of the storm. The rain was still pouring in torrent abundance and the wind at gale speed was doing all it could with the flood-making rain.

The section of the north wall visible from my cabin was fairly streaked with new falls – wild roaring singers that seemed strangely out of place. Eager to get into the midst of the show, I snatched a piece of bread for breakfast and ran out. The mountain waters, suddenly liberated, seemed to be holding a grand jubilee. The two Sentinel Cascades rivalled the great falls at ordinary stages, and across the Valley by the Three Brothers I caught glimpses of more falls than I could readily count; while the whole Valley throbbed and trembled, and was filled with an awful, massive, solemn, sea-like roar. After gazing a while enchanted with the network of new falls that were adorning and transfiguring every rock in sight, I tried to reach the upper meadows, where the Valley is widest, that I might be able to see the walls on both sides, and thus gain general views. But the river was over its banks and the meadows were flooded, forming an almost continuous lake dotted with blue sludgy islands, while innumerable streams roared like lions across my path and were sweeping forward rocks and logs with tremendous energy over ground where tiny gilias had been growing but a short time before. Climbing into the talus slopes, where these savage torrents were broken among earthquake boulders, I managed to cross them, and force my way up the Valley to Hutchings' Bridge, where I crossed the river and waded to the middle of the upper meadow. Here most of the new falls were in sight, probably the most glorious assemblage of waterfalls ever displayed from any one standpoint. On that portion of the south wall between Hutchings' and the Sentinel there were ten falls plunging and booming from a height of nearly three thousand feet, the smallest of which might have been heard miles away. In the neighbourhood of Glacier Point there were six; between the Three Brothers and Yosemite Fall, nine; between Yosemite and Royal Arch Falls, ten; from Washington Column to Mount Watkins, ten; on the slopes of Half Dome and Clouds' Rest, facing Mirror Lake and Tenaya Canyon, eight; on the shoulder of Half Dome, facing the Valley, three; fifty-six new falls occupying the upper end of the Valley, besides a countless host of silvery threads gleaming everywhere. In all the Valley there must have been upwards of a hundred. As if celebrating some great event, falls and cascades in Yosemite costume were coming down everywhere from fountain basins, far and near; and, though newcomers, they behaved and sang as if they had lived here always.

All summer-visitors will remember the comet forms of the Yosemite Fall and the laces of the Bridal Veil and Nevada. In the falls of this winter jubilee the lace forms predominated, but there was no lack of thunder-toned comets. The lower portion of one of the Sentinel Cascades was composed of two main white torrents with the space between them filled in with chained and beaded gauze of intricate pattern, through the singing threads of which the purplish-grey rock could be dimly seen. The series above Glacier Point was still more complicated in structure, displaying every form that one could imagine water might be dashed and combed and woven into. Those on the north wall between Washington Column and the Royal Arch Fall were so nearly related they formed an almost continuous sheet, and these again were but slightly separated from those about Indian Canyon. The group about the Three Brothers and El Capitan, owing to the topography and cleavage of the cliffs back of them, was more broken and irregular. The Tissiack Cascades were comparatively small, yet sufficient to give that noblest of mountain rocks a glorious voice. In the midst of all this extravagant rejoicing the great Yosemite Fall was scarce heard until about three o'clock in the afternoon. Then I was startled by a sudden thundering crash as if a rock avalanche had come to the help of the roaring waters. This was the flood-wave of Yosemite Creek, which had just arrived, delayed by the distance it had to travel, and by the choking snows of its widespread fountains. Now, with volume ten-fold increased beyond its springtime fullness, it took its place as leader of the glorious choir.

And the winds, too, were singing in wild accord, playing on every tree and rock, surging against the huge brows and domes and outstanding battlements, deflected hither and thither and broken into a thousand cascading, roaring currents in the canyons, and low bass, drumming swirls in the hollows. And these again, reacting on the clouds, eroded immense cavernous spaces in their grey depths and swept forward the resulting detritus in ragged trains like the moraines of glaciers. These cloud movements in turn published the work of the winds, giving them a visible body, and enabling us to trace them. As if endowed with independent motion, a detached cloud would rise hastily to the very top of the wall as if on some important errand, examining the faces of the cliffs, and then perhaps as suddenly descend to sweep imposingly along the meadows, trailing its draggled fringes through the pines, fondling its waving spires with infinite gentleness, or, gliding behind a grove or a single tree, bringing it into striking relief, as it bowed and waved in solemn rhythm. Sometimes, as the busy clouds drooped and condensed or dissolved to misty gauze, half of the Valley would be suddenly veiled, leaving here and there some lofty headland cut off from all visible connection with the walls, looming alone, dim, spectral, as if belonging to the sky – visitors, like the new falls, come to take part in the glorious festival. Thus for two days and nights in measureless extravagance the storm went on, and mostly without spectators, at least of a terrestrial kind. I saw nobody out – bird, bear, squirrel, or man. Tourists had vanished months before, and the hotel people and labourers were out of sight, careful about getting cold, and satisfied with views from windows. The bears, I suppose, were in their canyon-boulder dens, the squirrels in their knot-hole nests, the grouse in close fir groves, and the small singers in the Indian Canyon chaparral, trying to keep warm and dry. Strange to say, I did not see even the water-ouzels, though they must have greatly enjoyed the storm.

This was the most sublime waterfall flood I ever saw – clouds, winds, rocks, waters, throbbing together as one. And then to contemplate what was going on simultaneously with all this in other mountain temples; the Big Tuolumne Canyon – how the white waters and the winds were singing there! And in Hetch Hetchy Valley and the great Kings River Yosemite, and in all the other Sierra canyons and valleys from Shasta to the southernmost fountains of the Kern, thousands of rejoicing flood waterfalls chanting together in jubilee dress.

CHAPTER THREE

Snow-storms

As HAS already been stated, the first of the great snow-storms that replenish the Yosemite fountains seldom sets in before the end of November. Then, warned by the sky, wide-awake mountaineers, together with the deer and most of the birds, make haste to the lowlands or foothills; and burrowing marmots, mountain beavers, wood-rats, and other small mountain people, go into winter quarters, some of them not again to see the light of day until the general awakening and resurrection of the spring in June or July. The fertile clouds, drooping and condensing in brooding silence, seem to be thoughtfully examining the forests and streams with reference to the work that lies before them. At length, all their plans perfected, tufted flakes and single starry crystals come in sight, solemnly swirling and glinting to their blessed appointed places; and soon the busy throng fills the sky and makes darkness like night. The first heavy fall is usually from about two to four feet in depth; then with intervals of days or weeks of bright weather storm succeeds storm, heaping snow on snow, until thirty to fifty feet has fallen. But on account of its settling and compacting, and waste from melting and evaporation, the average depth actually found at any time seldom exceeds ten feet in the forest regions, or fifteen feet along the slopes of the summit peaks. After snow-storms come avalanches, varying greatly in form, size, behaviour and in the songs they sing; some on the smooth slopes of the mountains are short and broad; others long and river-like in the side canyons of Yosemites and in the main canyons, flowing in regular channels and booming like waterfalls, while countless smaller ones fall everywhere from laden trees and rocks and lofty canyon walls. Most delightful it is to stand in the middle of Yosemite on still clear mornings after snow-storms and watch the throng of avalanches as they come down, rejoicing, to their places, whispering, thrilling like birds, or booming and roaring like thunder. The noble yellow pines stand hushed and motionless as if under a spell until the morning sunshine begins to sift through their laden spires; then the dense masses on the ends of the leafy branches begin to shift and fall, those from the upper branches striking the lower ones in succession, enveloping each tree in a hollow conical avalanche of fairy fineness; while the relieved branches spring up and wave with startling effect in the general stillness, as if each tree was moving of its own volition. Hundreds of broad cloud-shaped masses may also be seen, leaping over the brows of the cliffs from great heights, descending at first with regular avalanche speed until, worn into dust by friction, they float in front of the precipices like irised clouds. Those which descend from the brow of El Capitan are particularly fine; but most of the great Yosemite avalanches flow in regular channels like cascades and waterfalls. When the snow first gives way on the upper slopes of their basins, a dull rushing, rumbling sound is heard which rapidly increases and seems to draw nearer with appalling intensity of tone. Presently the white flood comes bounding into sight over bosses and sheer places, leaping from bench to bench, spreading and narrowing and throwing off clouds of whirling dust like the spray of foaming cataracts. Compared with waterfalls and cascades, avalanches are short-lived, few of them lasting more than a minute or two, and the sharp, clashing sounds so common in falling water are mostly wanting; but in their low massy thundertones and purple-tinged whiteness, and in their dress, gait, gestures and general behaviour, they are much alike.

AVALANCHES

Besides these common after-storm avalanches that are to be found not only in the Yosemite but in all the deep, sheer-walled canyons of the Range there are two other important kinds, which may be called annual and century avalanches, which still further enrich the scenery. The only place about the Valley where one may be sure to see the annual kind is on the north slope of Clouds' Rest. They are composed of heavy, compacted snow, which has been subjected to frequent alternations of freezing and thawing. They are developed on canyon and mountain-sides at an elevation of from nine to ten thousand feet, where the slopes are inclined at an angle too low to shed off the dry winter snow, and which accumulates until the spring thaws sap their foundations and make them slippery; then away in grand style go the ponderous icy masses without any fine snow-dust. Those of Clouds' Rest descend like thunderbolts for more than a mile.

The great century avalanches and the kind that mow wide swaths through the upper forests occur on mountain-sides about ten or twelve thousand feet high, where under ordinary weather conditions the snow accumulated from winter to winter lies at rest for many years, allowing trees, fifty to a hundred feet high, to grow undisturbed on the slopes beneath them. On their way down through the woods they seldom fail to make a perfectly clean sweep, stripping off the soil as well as the tree, clearing paths two or three hundred yards wide from the timber line to the glacier meadows or lakes, and piling their uprooted trees, head downward, in rows along the sides of the gaps like lateral moraines. Scars and broken branches of the trees standing on the sides of the gaps record the depth of the overwhelming flood; and when we come to count the annual wood-rings on the up-rooted trees we learn that some of these immense avalanches occur only once in a century or even at still wider intervals.

A RIDE ON AN AVALANCHE

Few Yosemite visitors ever see snow avalanches and fewer still know the exhilaration of riding on them. In all my mountaineering I have enjoyed only one avalanche ride, and the start was so sudden and the end came so soon I had but little time to think of the danger that attends this sort of travel, though at such times one thinks fast. One fine Yosemite morning after a heavy snowfall, being eager to see as many avalanches as possible and wide views of the forest and summit peaks in their new white robes before the sunshine had time to change them, I set out early to climb by a side canyon to the top of a commanding ridge a little over three thousand feet above the Valley. On account of the looseness of the snow that blocked the canyon I knew the climb would require a long time, some three or four hours as I estimated; but it proved far more difficult than I had anticipated. Most of the way I sank waist deep, almost out of sight in some places. After spending the whole day to within half an hour or so of sundown, I was still several hundred feet below the summit. Then my hopes were reduced to getting up in time to see the sunset. But I was not to get summit views of any sort that day, for deep trampling near the canyon head, where the snow was strained, started an avalanche, and I was swished down to the foot of the canyon as if by enchantment. The wallowing ascent had taken nearly all day, the descent only about a minute. When the avalanche started I threw myself on my back and spread my arms to try to keep from sinking. Fortunately, though the grade of the canyon is very steep, it is not interrupted by precipices large enough to cause outbounding or free plunging. On no part of the rush was I buried. I was only moderately imbedded on the surface or at times a little below it, and covered with a veil of back-streaming dust particles; and as the whole mass beneath and about me joined in the flight there was no friction, though I was tossed here and there and lurched from side to side. When the avalanche swedged and came to rest I found myself on top of the crumpled pile without a bruise or scar. This was a fine experience. Hawthorne says somewhere that steam has spiritualized travel; though unspiritual smells, smoke, etc., still attend steam travel. This flight in what might be called a milky way of snow-stars was the most spiritual and exhilarating of all the modes of motion I have ever experienced. Elijah's flight in a chariot of fire could hardly have been more gloriously exciting.

THE STREAMS IN OTHER SEASONS

In the spring, after all the avalanches are down and the snow is melting fast, then all the Yosemite streams, from their fountains to their falls, sing their grandest songs. Countless rills make haste to the rivers, running and singing soon after sunrise, louder and louder with increasing volume until sundown; then they gradually fail through the frosty hours of the night. In this way the volume of the upper branches of the river is nearly doubled during the day, rising and falling as regularly as the tides of the sea. Then the Merced overflows its banks, flooding the meadows, sometimes almost from wall to wall in some places, beginning to rise towards sundown just when the streams on the fountains are beginning to diminish, the difference in time of the daily rise and fall being caused by the distance the upper flood streams have to travel before reaching the Valley. In the warmest weather they seem fairly to shout for joy and clash their upleaping waters together like clapping of hands; racing down the canyons with white manes flying in glorious exuberance of strength, compelling huge, sleeping boulders to wake up and join in their dance and song, to swell their exulting chorus.

In early summer, after the flood season, the Yosemite streams are in their prime, running crystal clear, deep and full but not overflowing their banks – about as deep through the night as the day, the difference in volume so marked in spring being now too slight to be noticed. Nearly all the weather is cloudless and everything is at its brightest – lake, river, garden and forest with all their life. Most of the plants are in full flower. The blessed ouzels have built their mossy huts and are now singing their best songs with the streams.

In tranquil, mellow autumn, when the year's work is about done and the fruits are ripe, birds and seeds out of their nests, and all the landscape is glowing like a benevolent countenance, then the streams are at their lowest ebb, with scarce a memory left of their wild spring floods. The small tributaries that do not reach back to the lasting snow fountains of the summit peaks shrink to whispering, tinkling currents. After the snow is gone from the basins, excepting occasional thunder-showers, they are now fed only by small springs whose waters are mostly evaporated in passing over miles of warm pavements, and in feeling their way slowly from pool to pool through the midst of boulders and sand. Even the main rivers are so low they may easily be forded, and their grand falls and cascades, now gentle and approachable, have waned to sheets of embroidery.

CHAPTER FOUR

Snow Banners

BUT IT is on the mountain tops, when they are laden with loose, dry snow and swept by a gale from the north, that the most magnificent storm scenery is displayed. The peaks along the axis of the Range are then decorated with resplendent banners, some of them more than a mile long, shining, streaming, waving with solemn exuberant enthusiasm as if celebrating some surpassingly glorious event.

The snow of which these banners are made falls on the High Sierra in most extravagant abundance, sometimes to a depth of fifteen or twenty feet, coming from the fertile clouds not in large tangled flakes such as one oftentimes sees in Yosemite, seldom even in complete crystals, for many of the starry blossoms fall before they are ripe, while most of those that attain perfect development as six-petalled flowers are more or less broken by glinting and chafing against one another on the way down to their work. This dry frosty snow is prepared for the grand banner-waving celebrations by the action of the wind. Instead of at once finding rest like that which falls into the tranquil depths of the forest, it is shoved and rolled and beaten against boulders and out-jutting rocks, swirled in pits and hollows like sand in river pot-holes, and ground into sparkling dust. And when storm winds find this snow-dust in a loose condition on the slopes above the timber-line they toss it back into the sky and sweep it onward from peak to peak in the form of smooth regular banners, or in cloudy drifts, according to the velocity and direction of the wind, and the confirmation of the slopes over which it is driven. While thus flying through the air a small portion escapes from the mountains to the sky as vapour; but far the greater part is at length locked fast in bossy overcurling cornices along the ridges, or in stratified sheets in the glacier cirques, some of it to replenish the small residual glaciers and remain silent and rigid for centuries before it is finally melted and sent singing down home to the sea.

But, though snow-dust and storm-winds abound on the mountains, regular shapely banners are, for causes we shall presently see, seldom produced. During the five winters that I spent in Yosemite I made many excursions to high points above the walls in all kinds of weather to see what was going on outside; from all my lofty outlooks I saw only one banner-storm that seemed in every way perfect. This was in the winter of 1873, when the snow-laden peaks were swept by a powerful norther. I was awakened early in the morning by a wild storm-wind and of course I had to make haste to the middle of the Valley to enjoy it. Rugged torrents and avalanches from the main wind-flood overhead were roaring down the side canyons and over the cliffs, arousing the rocks and the trees and the streams alike into glorious hurrahing enthusiasm, shaking the whole Valley into one huge song. Yet inconceivable as it must seem even to those who love all Nature's wildness, the storm was telling its story on the mountains in still grander characters.

A WONDERFUL WINTER SCENE

I had long been anxious to study some points in the structure of the ice-hill at the foot of the Upper Yosemite Fall, but, as I have already explained, blinding spray had hitherto prevented me from getting sufficiently near it. This morning the entire body of the Fall was oftentimes torn into gauzy strips and blown horizontally along the face of the cliff, leaving the ice-hill dry; and while making my way to the top of Fern Ledge to seize so favourable an opportunity to look down its throat, the peaks of the Merced group came in sight over the boulder of the South Dome, each waving a white glowing banner against the dark blue sky, as regular in form and firm and fine in texture as if it were made of silk. So rare and splendid a picture, of course, smothered everything else and I at once began to scramble and wallow up the snow-choked Indian Canyon to a ridge about 8,000ft. high, commanding a general view of the main summits along the axis of the Range, feeling assured I should find them bannered still more gloriously; nor was I in the least disappointed. I reached the top of the ridge in four or five hours, and through an opening in the woods the most imposing windstorm effect I ever beheld came full in sight; unnumbered mountains rising sharply into the cloudless sky, their bases solid white, their sides plashed with snow, like ocean rocks with foam, and on every summit a magnificent silvery banner, from two thousand to six thousand feet in height, slender at the point of attachment, and widening gradually until about a thousand or fifteen hundred feet in breadth, and as shapely and as substantial looking in texture as the banners of the finest silk, all streaming and waving free and clear in the sun-glow with nothing to blur the sublime picture they made.

Fancy yourself standing beside me on this Yosemite Ridge. There is a strange garish glitter in the air and the gale drives wildly overhead, but you feel nothing of its violence, for you are looking out through a sheltered opening in the woods, as through a meadow. In the immediate foreground there is a forest of silver firs, their foliage warm yellow-green, and the snow beneath them is strewn with their plumes, plucked off by the storm; and beyond a broad, ridgy, canyon-furrowed, dome-dotted middle ground, darkened here and there with belts of pines, you behold the lofty snow-laden mountains in glorious array, waving their banners with jubilant enthusiasm as if shouting aloud for joy. They are twenty miles away, but you would not wish them nearer, for every feature is distinct, and the whole wonderful show is seen in its right proportions, like a painting on the sky.

And now after this general view, mark how sharply the ribs and buttresses and summits of the mountains are defined, excepting the portions veiled by the banners; how gracefully and nobly the banners are waving in accord with the throbbing of the wind-flood; how trimly each is attached to the very summit of its peak like a streamer at a mast-head; how bright and glowing white they are, and how finely their fading fringes are pencilled on the sky! See how solid white and opaque they are at the point of attachment and how filmy and translucent toward the end, so that the parts of the peaks past which they are streaming look dim as if seen through a veil of ground glass. And see how some of the longest of the banners on the highest peaks are streaming perfectly free from peak to peak across intervening notches or passes, while others overlap and partly hide one another.

As to their formation, we find that the main causes of the wondrous beauty and perfection of those we are looking at are the favourable direction and force of the wind, the abundance of snow-dust, and the form of the north sides of the peaks. In general, the north sides are concave in both their horizontal and vertical sections, having been sculptured into this shape by the residual glaciers that lingered in the protecting northern shadows, while the sun-beaten south sides, having never been subjected to this kind of glaciation, are convex or irregular. It is essential, therefore, not only that the wind should move with great velocity and steadiness to supply a sufficiently copious and continuous stream of snow-dust, but that it should come from the north. No perfect banner is ever hung on the Sierra peaks by the south wind. Had the gale today blown from the south, leaving the other conditions unchanged, only swirling, interfering, cloudy drifts would have been produced; for the snow, instead of being spouted straight up and over the tops of the peaks in condensed currents to be drawn out as streamers, would have been driven over the convex southern slopes from peak to peak like white pearly fog.

It appears, therefore, that shadows in great part determine not only the forms of lofty ice mountains, but also those of the snow banners that the wild winds hang up on them.

EARTHQUAKE STORMS

The avalanche taluses, leaning against the walls at intervals of a mile or two, are among the most striking and interesting of the secondary features of the Valley. They are from about three to five hundred feet high, made up of huge, angular, well-preserved, unshifting boulders, and instead of being slowly weathered from the cliffs like ordinary taluses, they were all formed suddenly and simultaneously by a great earthquake that occurred at least three centuries ago. And though this hurled into existence in a few seconds or minutes, they are the least changeable of all the Sierra soil-beds. Excepting those which were launched directly into the channels of swift rivers, scarcely one of their wedged and interlacing boulders has moved since the day of their creation; and though mostly made up of huge blocks of granite, many of them from ten to fifty feet cube, weighing thousands of tons with only a few small chips, trees and shrubs make out to live and thrive on them and even delicate herbaceous plants – draperia, collomia, zauschneria, etc., soothing and colouring their wild rugged slopes with gardens and groves.

I was long in doubt on some points concerning the origin of these taluses. Plainly enough they were derived from the cliffs above them, because they are of the size of scars on the wall, the rough angular surface of which contrasts with the rounded, glaciated, unfractured parts. It was plain, too, that instead of being made up of material slowly and gradually weathered from the cliffs like ordinary taluses, almost every one of them had been formed suddenly in a single avalanche, and had not been increased in size during the last three or four centuries, for trees three or four hundred years old are growing on them, some standing at the top close to the wall without a bruise or broken branch, showing that scarcely a single boulder had ever fallen among them. Furthermore, all these taluses throughout the Range seemed by the trees and lichens growing on them to be of the same age. All the phenomena thus pointed straight to a grand ancient earthquake. But for years I left the question open, and went on from canyon to canyon, observing again and again; measuring the heights of taluses throughout the Range on both flanks, and the variations in the angles of their surface slopes; studying the way their boulders had been assorted and related and brought to rest, and their correspondence in size with the cleavage joints of the cliffs from whence they were derived, cautious about making up my mind. But at last all doubt as to their formation vanished.

At half-past two o'clock of a moonlit morning in March, I was awakened by a tremendous earthquake, and though I had never before enjoyed a storm of this sort, the strange thrilling motion could not be mistaken, and I ran out of my cabin, both glad and frightened, shouting, 'A noble earthquake! A noble earthquake!' feeling sure I was going to learn something. The shocks were so violent and varied, and succeeded one another so closely, that I had to balance myself carefully in walking as if on the deck of a ship among waves, and it seemed impossible that the high cliffs of the Valley could escape being shattered. In particular, I feared that the sheer-fronted Sentinel Rock, towering above my cabin, would be shaken down, and I took shelter back of a large yellow pine, hoping that it might protect me from at least the smaller outbounding boulders. For a minute or two the shocks became more and more violent – flashing horizontal thrusts mixed with a few twists and battering, explosive, upheaving jolts – as if Nature were wrecking her Yosemite temple, and getting ready to build a still better one.

I was now convinced before a single boulder had fallen that earthquakes were the talus-makers and positive proof soon came. It was a calm moonlight night, and no sound was heard for the first minute or so, save low, muffled, underground, bubbling rumblings, and the whispering and rustling of the agitated trees, as if Nature were holding her breath. Then, suddenly, out of the strange silence and strange motion there came a tremendous roar. The Eagle Rock on the south wall, about a half a mile up the Valley, gave way and I saw it falling in thousands of the great boulders I had so long been studying, pouring to the Valley floor in a free curve luminous from friction, making a terribly sublime spectacle – an arc of glowing, passionate fire, fifteen hundred feet span, as true in form and as serene in beauty as a rainbow in the midst of the stupendous, roaring rock-storm. The sound was so tremendously deep and broad and earnest, the whole earth like a living creature seemed to have at last found a voice and to be calling to her sister planets. In trying to tell something of the size of this awful sound it seems to me that if all the thunder of all the storms I had ever heard were condensed into one roar it would not equal this rock-roar at the birth of a mountain talus. Think, then, of the roar that arose to heaven at the simultaneous birth of all the thousands of ancient canyon-taluses throughout the length and breadth of the Range!

The first severe shocks were soon over, and eager to examine the new-born talus I ran up the Valley in the moonlight and climbed upon it before the huge blocks, after their fiery flight, had come to complete rest. They were slowly settling into their places, chafing, grating against one another, groaning, and whispering; but no motion was visible except in a stream of small fragments pattering down the face of the cliff. A cloud of dust particles, lighted by the moon, floated out across the whole breadth of the Valley, forming a ceiling that lasted until after sunrise, and the air was filled with the odour of crushed Douglas spruces from a grove that had been mowed down and mashed like weeds.

After the ground began to calm I ran across the meadow to the river to see in what direction it was flowing and was glad to find that *down* the Valley was still down. Its waters were muddy from portions of its banks having given way, but it was flowing around its curves and over its ripples and shallows with ordinary tones and gestures. The mud would soon be cleared away and the raw slips on the banks would be the only visible record of the shaking it suffered.

The Upper Yosemite Fall, glowing white in the moonlight, seemed to know nothing of the earthquake, manifesting no change in form or voice, as far as I could see or hear.

After a second startling shock, about half-past three o'clock, the ground continued to tremble gently, and smooth, hollow rumbling sounds, not always distinguishable from the rounded, bumping, explosive tones of the falls, came from deep in the mountains in a northern direction.

The few Indians fled from their huts to the middle of the Valley, fearing that angry spirits were trying to kill them; and, as I afterward learned, most of the Yosemite tribe, who were spending the winter at their village on Bull Creek forty miles away, were so terrified that they ran into the river and washed themselves – getting themselves clean enough to say their prayers, I suppose, or to die. I asked Dick, one of the Indians with whom I was acquainted, 'What made the ground shake and jump so much?' He only shook his head and said, 'No good. No good,' and looked appealingly to me to give him hope that his life was to be spared.

In the morning I found the few white settlers assembled in front of the old Hutchings Hotel comparing notes and meditating flight to the lowlands, seemingly as sorely frightened as the Indians. Shortly after sunrise a low, blunt, muffled rumbling, like distant thunder, was followed by another series of shocks, which, though not nearly so severe as the first, made the cliffs and domes tremble like jelly, and the big pines and oaks thrill and swish and wave their branches with startling effect. Then the talkers were suddenly hushed, and the solemnity on their faces was sublime. One in particular of these winter neighbours, a somewhat speculative thinker with whom I had often conversed, was a firm believer in the cataclysmic origin of the Valley; and I now jokingly remarked that his wild tumble-down-and-engulfment hypothesis might soon be proved, since these underground rumblings and shakings might be the forerunners of another Yosemite-making cataclysm, which would perhaps double the depth of the Valley by swallowing the floor, leaving the ends of the roads and trails dangling three or four thousand feet in the air. Just then came the third series of shocks, and it was fine to see how awfully silent and solemn he became. His belief in the existence of a mysterious abyss, into which the suspended floor of the Valley and all the domes and battlements of the walls might at any moment go roaring down, mightily troubled him. To diminish his fears and laugh him into something like reasonable faith, I said, 'Come, cheer up; smile a little and clap your hands, now that kind Mother Earth is trotting us on her knee to amuse us and make us good.' But the well-meant joke seemed irreverent and utterly failed, as if only prayerful terror could rightly belong to the wild beauty-making business. Even after all the heavier shocks were over I could do nothing to reassure him. On the contrary, he handed me the keys of his little store to keep, saying that with a companion of like mind he was going to the lowlands to stay until the fate of poor, trembling Yosemite was settled. In vain I rallied them on their fears, calling attention to the strength of the granite walls of our Valley home, the very best and solidest masonry in the world, and less likely to collapse and sink than the sedimentary lowlands to which they were looking for safety; and saying that in any case they sometime would have to die, and so grand a burial was not to be slighted. But they were too seriously panic-stricken to get comfort from anything I could say.

During the third severe shock the trees were so violently shaken that the birds flew out with frightened cries. In particular, I noticed two robins flying in terror from a leafless oak, the branches of which swished and quivered as if struck by a heavy battering-ram. Exceedingly interesting were the flashing and quivering of the elastic needles of the pines in the sunlight and the waving up and down of the branches while the trunks stood rigid. There was no swaying, waving or swivelling as in wind-storms, but quick, quivering jerks, and at times the heavy tasselled branches moved as if they had all been pressed down against the trunk and suddenly let go, to spring up and vibrate until they came to rest again. Only the owls seemed to be undisturbed. Before the rumbling echoes had died away a hollow-voiced owl began to hoot philosophical tranquillity from near the edge of the new talus as if nothing extraordinary had occurred, although, perhaps, he was curious to know what all the noise was about. His 'hoot-too-hoot-too-whoo' might have meant, 'what's a' the steer, klmmer?'.

It was long before the Valley found perfect rest. The rocks trembled more or less every day for over two months, and I kept a bucket of water on my table to learn what I could of the movements. The blunt thunder in the depths of the mountains was usually followed by sudden jarring, horizontal thrusts from the northward, often succeeded by twisting, upjolting movements. More than a month after the first great shock, when I was standing on a fallen tree up the Valley near Lamon's winter cabin, I heard a distinct bubbling thunder from the direction of Tenaya Canyon. Carlo, a large intelligent St Bernard dog standing beside me seemed greatly astonished, and looked intently in that direction with mouth open and uttered a low *Wouf!* as if saying, 'What's that?' He must have known that it was not thunder, though like it. The air was perfectly still, not the faintest breath of wind perceptible, and a fine, yellow, sunny hush pervaded everything in the midst of which came that subterranean thunder. Then, while we gazed and listened, came the corresponding shocks, distinct as if some mighty hand had shaken the ground. After the sharp horizontal jars died away, they were followed by a gentle rocking and undulating of the ground so distinct that Carlo looked at the log on which he was standing to see who was shaking it. It was the season of flooded meadows and the pools about me, calm as sheets of glass, were suddenly thrown into low ruffling waves.

Judging by its effects, this Yosemite, or Inyo earthquake, as it is sometimes called, was gentle as compared with the one that gave rise to the grand talus system of the Range and did so much for the canyon scenery. Nature, usually so deliberate in her operations, then created, as we have seen, a new set of features, simply by giving the mountains a shake – changing not only the high peaks and cliffs, but the streams. As soon as these rock avalanches fell, the streams began to sing new songs; for in many places thousands of boulders were hurled into their channels, roughening and half-damming them, compelling the waters to surge and roar in rapids where before they glided smoothly. Some of the streams were completely dammed; driftwood, leaves, etc., gradually filling the interstices between the boulders, thus giving rise to lakes and level reaches; and these again, after being gradually filled in, were changed to meadows, through which the streams are now silently meandering; while at the same time some of the taluses took the place of old meadows and groves. Thus rough places were made smooth, and smooth places rough. But, on the whole, by what at first sight seemed pure confounded confusion and ruin, the landscapes were enriched; for gradually every talus was covered with groves and gardens, and made a finely proportioned and ornamental base for the cliffs. In this work of beauty, every boulder is prepared and measured and put in its place more thoughtfully than are the stones of temples. If for a moment you are inclined to regard these taluses as mere draggled, chaotic dumps, climb to the top of one of them, and run down without any haggling, puttering hestitation, boldly jumping from boulder to boulder with even speed. You will then find your feet playing a tune, and quickly discover the music and poetry of these magnificent rock piles – a fine lesson; and all Nature's wildness tells the same story – the shocks and outbursts of earthquakes, volcanoes, geysers, roaring, thundering waves and floods, the silent uprush of sap in plants, storms of every sort – each and all the orderly beauty-making love-beats of Nature's heart.

CHAPTER FIVE

The Trees of the Valley

THE MOST influential of the Valley trees is the yellow pine (*Pinus ponderosa*). It attains its noblest dimensions on beds of water-washed, coarsely stratified moraine material, between the talus slopes and meadows, dry on the surface, well-watered below and where not too closely assembled in groves the branches reach nearly to the ground, forming grand spires 200 to 220ft. in height. The largest that I have measured is standing alone almost opposite the Sentinel Rock, or a little to the westward of it. It is a little over eight feet in diameter and about 220ft. high. Climbing these grand trees, especially when they are waving and singing in worship in wind-storms, is a glorious experience. Ascending from the lowest branch to the topmost is like stepping up stairs through a blaze of white light, every needle thrilling and shining as if with religious ecstasy.

Unfortunately there are but few sugar pines in the Valley, though in the King's yosemite they are in glorious abundance. The incense cedar (*Libocedrus decurrens*) with cinnamon-coloured bark and yellow-green foliage is one of the most interesting of the Yosemite trees. Some of them are 150ft. high, from six to ten feet in diameter, and they are never out of sight as you saunter among the yellow pines. Their bright brown shafts and towers of flat, frond-like branches make a striking feature of the landscapes throughout all the seasons. In midwinter, when most of the other trees are asleep, this cedar puts forth its flowers in millions – the pistillate pale green and inconspicuous, but the staminate bright yellow, tingeing all the branches and making the trees as they stand in the snow look like gigantic goldenrods. The branches, outspread in flat plumes and, beautifully fronded, sweep gracefully downward and outward, except those near the top, which aspire; the lowest, especially in youth and middle age, droop to the ground, overlapping one another, shedding off rain and snow like shingles, and making fine tents for birds and campers. This tree frequently lives more than a thousand years and is well worthy its place beside the great pines and the Douglas spruce.

The two largest specimens I know of the Douglas spruce, about eight feet in diameter, are growing out at the foot of the Liberty Gap near the Nevada Fall, and on the terminal moraine of the small residual glacier that lingered in the shady Illilouette Canyon.

After the conifers, the most important of the Yosemite trees are the oaks, two species; the California live-oak (*Quercus agrifolia*), with black trunks, reaching a thickness of from four to nearly seven feet, wide spreading branches and bright deeply-scalloped leaves. It occupies the greater part of the broad sandy flats of the upper end of the Valley, and is the species that yields the acorns so highly prized by the Indians and woodpeckers.

The other species is the mountain live-oak, or gold-cup oak (*Quercus chrysolepis*), a sturdy mountaineer of a tree, growing mostly on the earthquake taluses and benches of the sunny north wall of the Valley. In tough, unwedgeable, knotty strength, it is the oak of oaks, a magnificent tree.

The largest and most picturesque specimen in the Valley is near the foot of the Tenaya Fall, a romantic spot seldom seen on account of the rough trouble of getting to it. It is planted on three huge boulders and yet manages to draw sufficient moisture and food from this craggy soil to maintain itself in good health. It is twenty feet in circumference, measured above a large branch between three and four feet in diameter that has been broken off. The main knotty trunk seems to be made up of craggy granite boulders like those on which it stands, being about the same colour as the mossy, lichened boulders and about as rough. Two moss-lined caves near the ground open back into the trunk, one on the north side, the other on the west, forming picturesque, romantic seats. The largest of the main branches is eighteen feet and nine inches in circumference, and some of the long pendulous branchlets droop over the stream at the foot of the fall where it is grey with spray. The leaves are glossy yellow-green, ever in motion from the wind from the fall. It is a fine place to dream in, with falls, cascades, cool rocks lined with hypnum three inches thick; shaded with maple, dogwood, alder, willow; grand clumps of chain-ferns where no hand may touch them; light filtering through translucent leaves; oaks fifty feet high; lilies eight feet high in a filled lake basin near by, and the finest libocedrus groves and tallest ferns and goldenrods.

In the main river canyon below the Vernal Fall and on the shady south side of the Valley there are a few groves of the silver fir (*Abies concolor*), and superb forests of the magnificent species around the rim of the Valley.

On the tops of the domes is found the sturdy, storm-enduring red cedar (*Juniperus occidentalis*). It never makes anything like a forest here, but stands out separate and independent in the wind, clinging by slight joints to the rock, with scarce a handful of soil in sight of it, seeming to depend chiefly on snow and air for nourishment, and yet it has maintained tough health on this diet for two thousand years or more. The largest hereabouts are from five to six feet in diameter and fifty feet in height.

The principal river-side trees are poplar, alder, willow, broad-leaved maple, and Nuttall's flowering dogwood. The poplar (*Populus trichocarpa*), often called balm-of-Gilead from the gum on its buds, is a tall tree, towering above its companions and gracefully embowering the banks of the river. Its abundant foliage turns bright yellow in the fall, and the Indian-summer sunshine sifts through it in delightful tones over the slow-gliding waters when they are at their lowest ebb.

Some of the involucres of the flowering dogwood measure six to eight inches in diameter, and the whole tree when in flower looks as if covered with snow. In the spring when the streams are in flood it is the whitest of trees. In Indian summer the leaves become bright crimson, making a still grander show than the flowers.

The broad-leaved maple and mountain maple are found mostly in the cool canyons at the head of the Valley, spreading their branches in beautiful arches over the foaming streams.

Scattered here and there are a few other trees, mostly small – the mountain mahogany, cherry, chestnut-oak, and laurel. The California nutmeg (*Torreya californica*), a handsome evergreen, belonging to the yew family, forms small groves near the cascades a mile or two below the foot of the Valley.

CHAPTER SIX

The Forest Trees in General

FOR THE use of the ever-increasing number of Yosemite visitors who make extensive excursions into the mountains beyond the Valley, a sketch of the forest trees in general will probably be found useful. The different species are arranged in zones and sections, which brings the forest as a whole within the comprehension of every observer. These species are always found as controlled by the climates of different elevations, by soil and by the comparative strength of each species in taking and holding possession of the ground; and so appreciable are these relations the traveller need never be at a loss in determining within a few hundred feet his elevation above sea-level by the trees alone; for, notwithstanding some of the species range upward for several thousand feet and all pass one another more or less, yet even those species possessing the greatest vertical range are available in measuring the elevation; inasmuch as they take on new forms corresponding with variations and altitude. Entering the lower fringe of the forest composed of Douglas oaks and Sabine pines, the trees grow so far apart that not one-twentieth of the surface of the ground is in shade at noon. After advancing fifteen or twenty miles towards Yosemite and making an ascent of from two to three thousand feet you reach the lower margin of the main pine belt, composed of great sugar pine, yellow pine, incense cedar and Sequoia. Next you come to the magnificent silver-fir belt and lastly to the upper pine belt, which sweeps up to the feet of the summit peaks in a dwarfed fringe, to a height of from ten to twelve thousand feet. That this general order of distribution depends on climate as affected by height above the sea, is seen at once, but there are other harmonies that become manifest only after observation and study. One of the most interesting of these is the arrangement of the forest in long curving bands, braided together into lace-like patterns in some places and outspread in charming variety. The key to these striking arrangements is the system of ancient glaciers; where they flowed the trees followed, tracing their courses along the sides of canyons, over ridges, and high plateaus. The cedar of Lebanon, said Sir Joseph Hooker, occurs upon one of the moraines of an ancient glacier. All the forests of the Sierra are growing upon moraines, but moraines vanish like the glaciers that make them. Every storm that falls upon them wastes them, carrying away their decaying, disintegrating material into new formations, until they are no longer recognizable without tracing their transitional forms down from the range still in process of formation – in some places through those that are more and more ancient and more obscured by vegetation and all kinds of post-glacial weathering. It appears, therefore, that the Sierra forests indicate the extent and positions of ancient moraines as well as they do belts of climate.

One will have no difficulty in knowing the nut pine (*Pinus Sabiniana*), for it is the first conifer met in ascending the Range from the west, springing up here and there among Douglas oaks and thickets of ceanothus and manzanita; its extreme upper limit being about 4000ft. above the sea, its lower about from 500 to 800ft. It is remarkable for its loose, airy, wide-branching habit, and thin grey foliage. Full-grown specimens are from forty to fifty feet in height and from two to three feet in diameter. The trunk usually divides into three or four main branches about fifteen or twenty feet from the ground that, after bearing away from one another, shoot straight up and form separate summits. Their slender, greyish needles are from eight to twelve inches long, and inclined to droop, contrasting with the rigid, dark-coloured trunk and branches. No other tree of my acquaintance so substantial in its body has foliage so thin and pervious to the light. The cones are from five to eight inches long and about as large in thickness; rich chocolate-brown in colour and protected by strong, down-curving hooks which terminate the scales. Nevertheless the little Douglas squirrel can open them. Indians climb the trees like bears and beat off the cones or recklessly cut off the more fruitful branches with hatchets, while the squaws gather and roast them until the scales open sufficiently to allow the hard-shell seeds to be beaten out. The curious little *Pinus attenuata* is found at an elevation of from 1,500 to 3,000ft., growing in close groves and belts. It is exceedingly slender and graceful, although trees that chance to stand alone send out very long, curved branches, making a striking contrast to the ordinary grove form. The foliage is of the same peculiar grey-green colour as that of the nut pine, and is worn about as loosely, so that the body of the tree is scarcely obscured by it. At the age of seven or eight years it begins to bear cones in whorls on the main axis, and as they never fall off the trunk is soon picturesquely dotted with them. Branches also soon become fruitful. The average size of the tree is about thirty or forty feet in height and twelve to fourteen inches in diameter. The cones are about four inches long, and covered with a sort of varnish and gum, rendering them impervious to moisture.

No observer can fail to notice the admirable adaptation of this curious pine to the fire-swept regions where alone it is found. After a running fire has scorched and killed it the cones open and the ground beneath it is as one sown broadcast, with all the seeds ripened during its whole life. Then up spring a crowd of bright, hopeful seedlings, giving beauty for ashes in lavish abundance.

THE SUGAR PINE, KING OF PINE TREES

Of all the world's eighty or ninety species of pine trees, the Sugar Pine (*Pinus Lambertiana*) is king, surpassing all others, not merely in size but in lordly beauty and majesty. In the Yosemite region it grows at an elevation of from 3,000 to 7,000ft. above the sea and attains most perfect development at a height of about 5,000ft. The largest specimens are commonly about 220ft. high and from six to eight feet in diameter four feet from the ground, though some grand old patriarch may be met here and there that has enjoyed six or eight centuries of storms and attained a thickness of ten or even twelve feet, still sweet and fresh in every fibre. The trunk is a remarkably smooth, round, delicately-tapered shaft, straight and regular as if turned in a lathe, mostly without limbs, purplish brown in colour and usually enlivened with tufts of a yellow lichen. Toward the head of this magnificent column long branches sweep gracefully outward and downward, sometimes forming a palm-like crown, but far more impressive than any palm crown I ever beheld. The needles are about three inches long in fasicles of five, and arranged in rather close tassels at the ends of slender branchlets that clothe the long outsweeping limbs. How well they sing in the wind, and how strikingly harmonious an effect is made by the long cylindrical cones, depending loosely from the ends of the long branches! The cones are about fifteen to eighteen inches long, and three in diameter; green, shaded with dark purple on their sunward sides. They are ripe in September and October of the second year from the flower. Then the flat, thin scales open and the seeds take wing, but the empty cones become still more beautiful and effective as decorations, for their diameter is nearly doubled by the spreading of the scales, and their colour changes to yellowish brown while they remain, swinging on the tree all the following winter and summer, and continue effectively beautiful even on the ground many years after they fall. The wood is deliciously fragrant, fine in grain and texture and creamy yellow, as if formed of condensed sunbeams. The sugar from which the common name is derived is, I think, the best of sweets. It exudes from the heart-wood where wounds have been made by forest fires or the axe, and forms irregular, crisp, candy-like kernels of considerable size, something like clusters of resin beads. When fresh it is white, but because most of the wounds on which it is found have been made by fire the sap is stained and a hardened sugar becomes brown. Indians are fond of it, but on account of its laxative properties only small quantities may be eaten. No tree lover will ever forget his first meeting with the sugar pine. In most pine trees there is the sameness of expression which to most people is apt to become monotonous, for the typical spiral form of conifers, however beautiful, affords little scope for appreciable individual character. The sugar pine is as free from conventionalities as the most picturesque oaks. No two are alike, and though they toss out their immense arms in what might seem extravagant gestures they never lose their expression of serene majesty. They are the priests of pines and seem ever to be addressing the surrounding forest. The yellow pine is found growing with them on warm hillsides, and the silver fir on cool northern slopes; but, noble as these are, the sugar pine is easily king, and spreads his arms above them in blessing while they rock and wave in sign of recognition. The main branches are sometimes forty feet long, yet persistently simple, seldom dividing at all, excepting near the end; but anything like a bare cable appearance is prevented by the small, tasselled branchlets that extend all around them; and when these superb limbs sweep out symmetrically on all sides, a crown sixty or seventy feet wide is formed, which gracefully poised on the summit of the noble shaft, is a glorious object. Commonly, however, there is a preponderance of limbs toward the east, away from the direction of the prevailing winds.

Although so unconventional when full grown, the sugar pine is remarkably proper tree in youth – a strict follower of coniferous fashions – slim, erect, with leafy branches kept exactly in place, each tapering in outline and terminating in a spiry point. The successive forms between the cautious neatness of youth and the bold freedom of maturity offer a delightful study. At the age of fifty or sixty years, the shy, fashionable form begins to be broken up. Specialized branches push out and bend with the great cones, giving individual character, that becomes more marked from year to year. Its most constant companion is the yellow pine. The Douglas spruce, libocedrus, sequoia, and the silver fir are also more or less associated with it; but on many deep-soiled mountain-sides, at an elevation of about 5,000ft. above the sea, it forms the bulk of the forest, filling every swell and hollow and down-plunging ravine. The majestic crowns, approaching each other in bold curves, make a glorious canopy through which the tempered sunbeams pour, silvering the needles, and gilding the massive boles and the flowery, park-like ground into a scene of enchantment.

On the most sunny slopes the white-flowered, fragrant chamaebatia is spread like a carpet, brightened during early summer with the crimson sarcodes, the wild rose, and innumerable violes and gilias. Not even in the shadiest nooks will you find any rank, untidy weeds or unwholesome darkness. In the north sides of ridges the boles are more slender, and the ground is mostly occupied by an underbrush of hazel, ceanothus, and flowering dogwood, but not so densely as to prevent the traveller from sauntering where he will; while the crowning branches are never impenetrable to the rays of the sun, and never so interblended as to lose their individuality.

THE YELLOW OR SILVER PINE

The Silver Pine (*Pinus ponderosa*), or Yellow Pine, as it is commonly called, ranks second among the pines of the Sierra as a lumber tree, and almost rivals the sugar pine in stature and nobleness of port. Because of its superior powers of enduring variations of climate and soil, it has a more extensive range than any other conifer growing on the Sierra. On the western slope it is first met at an elevation of about 2,000ft., and extends nearly to the upper limit of the timber-line. Thence, crossing the range by the lowest passes, it descends to the eastern base, and pushes out for a considerable distance into the hot, volcanic plains, growing bravely upon well-watered moraines, gravelly lake basins, climbing old volcanoes and dropping ripe cones among ashes and cinders.

The average size of full-grown trees on the western slope, where it is associated with the sugar pine, is a little less than 200ft. in height and from five to six feet in diameter, though specimens considerably larger may easily be found. Where there is plenty of free sunshine and other conditions are favourable, it presents a striking contrast in form to the sugar pine, being a symmetrical spire, formed of a straight round trunk, clad with innumerable branches that are divided over and over again. Unlike the Yosemite form about one-half of the trunk is commonly branchless, but where it grows at all close three-fourths or more naked, presenting then a more slender and elegant shaft than any other tree in the woods. The bark is mostly arranged in massive plates, some of them measuring four or five feet in length by eighteen inches in width, with a thickness of three or four inches, forming a quite marked and distinguishing feature. The needles are of a fine, warm, yellow-green-colour, six to eight inches long, firm and elastic, and crowded in handsome, radiant tassels on the upturning ends of the branches. The cones are about three or four inches long, and two and a half wide, growing in close, sessile clusters among the leaves.

The species attains its noblest form in filled-up lake basins, especially in those of the older Yosemites, and as we have seen, so prominent a part does it form of their groves that it may well be called the Yosemite Pine.

The Jeffrey variety attains its finest development in the northern portion of the Range, in the wide basins of the McCloud and Pitt Rivers, where it forms magnificent forests scarcely invaded by any other tree. It differs from the ordinary form in size, being only about half as tall, in its redder and more closely-furrowed bark, greyish-green foliage, less divided branches, and much larger cones; but intermediate forms come in which make a clear separation impossible, although some botanists regard it as a distinct species. It is this variety of ponderosa that climbs storm-swept ridges above, and wanders out among the volcanoes of the Great Basin. Whether exposed to extremes of heat or cold, it is dwarfed like many other trees, and becomes all knots and angles, wholly unlike the majestic forms we have been sketching. Old specimens, bearing cones about as big as pineapples, may sometimes be found clinging to rifted rocks at an elevation of 7,000 or 8,000ft., whose highest branches scarce reach above one's shoulders.

I have often feasted on the beauty of these noble trees when they were towering in all their winter grandeur, laden with snow – one mass of bloom; in summer, too, when the brown, staminate clusters hang thick among the shimmering needles, and the big purple burrs are ripening in the mellow light, but it is during cloudless wind-storms that these colossal pines are most impressively beautiful. Then they bow like willows, their leaves streaming forward all in one direction, and, when the sun shines upon them at the required angle, entire groves glow as if every leaf were burnished silver. The fall of tropic light on the crown of a palm is a truly glorious spectacle, the fervid sun-flood breaking upon the glossy leaves in long lance-rays, at the foot of an enthusiastic cataract, like mountain water among boulders. But to me there is something more impressive in the fall of light upon these noble, silver pine pillars: it is beaten to the finest dust and shed off in myriads of minute sparkles that seem to radiate from the very heart of the tree, as if like rain, falling upon fertile soil, it had been absorbed to reappear in flowers of light. This species also gives forth the finest wind music. After listening to it in all kinds of winds, night and day, season after season, I think I could approximate to my position on the mountain by this pine music alone. If you would catch the tone of separate needles climb a tree in breezy weather. Every needle is carefully tempered and gives forth no uncertain sound, each standing out with no interference excepting during heavy gales; then you may detect the click of one needle from another, readily distinguishable from the free wind-like hum.

When a sugar pine and one of this species equal in size are observed together, the latter is seen to be more simple in manners, more lively and graceful, and its beauty is of a kind more easily appreciated; on the other hand it is less dignified and original in demeanour. The yellow pine seems ever eager to shoot aloft, higher and higher. Even while it is drowsing in autumn sun-gold you may still detect a skyward aspiration, but the sugar pine seems too unconsciously noble and too complete in every way to leave room for even a heavenward care.

THE DOUGLAS SPRUCE

The Douglas Spruce (*Pseudotsuga Douglasii*) is one of the largest and longest-lived of the giants that flourish throughout the main pine belt, often attaining a height of nearly 200ft., and a diameter of six or seven feet. Where the growth is not too close, the stout, spreading branches, covering more than half of the trunk, are hung with innumerable slender, drooping sprays, handsomely feathered with the short leaves which radiate at right angles all around them. This vigorous tree is ever beautiful, welcoming the mountain winds and the snow as well as the mellow summer light; and it maintains its youthful freshness undiminished from century to century through a thousand storms. It makes its finest appearance during the months of June and July, when the brown buds at the ends of the sprays swell and open, revealing the young leaves, which at first are bright yellow, making the tree appear as if covered with gay blossoms; while the pendulous bracted cones, three or four inches long, with their shell-like scales, are a constant adornment.

The young trees usually are assembled in family groups, each sapling exquisitely symmetrical. The primary branches are whorled regularly around the axis, generally in fives, while each is draped with long, feathery sprays that descend in lines as free and as finely drawn as those of falling water.

In Oregon and Washington it forms immense forests, growing tall and mast-like to a height of 300ft., and is greatly prized as a lumber tree. Here it is scattered among other trees, or forms small groves, seldom ascending higher than 5,500ft., and never making what would be called a forest. It is not particular in its choice of soil: wet or dry, smooth or rocky, it makes out to live well on them all. Two of the largest specimens, as we have seen, are in Yosemite; one of these, more than eight feet in diameter, is growing on a moraine; the other, nearly as large, on angular blocks of granite. No other tree in the Sierra seems so much at home on earthquake taluses and many of these huge boulder-slopes are almost exclusively occupied by it.

THE INCENSE CEDAR

Incense Cedar, (*Libocedrus decurrens*), already noticed among the Yosemite trees, is quite generally distributed throughout the pine belt without exclusively occupying any considerable area, or even making extensive groves. On the warmer mountain slopes it ascends to about 5,000ft., and reaches the climate most congenial to it at a height of about 4,000ft., growing vigorously at this elevation in all kinds of soil and, in particular, it is capable of enduring more moisture about its roots than any of its companions excepting only the sequoia.

Casting your eye over the general forest from some ridge-top you can identify it by the colour alone of its spiry summits, a warm yellow-green. In its youth up to the age of seventy or eighty years, none of its companions forms so strictly tapered a cone from top to bottom. As it becomes older it often-times grows strikingly irregular and picturesque. Large branches push out at right angles to the trunk, forming stubborn elbows and shoot up parallel with the axis. Very old trees are usually dead at the top. The flat fragrant plumes are exceedingly beautiful: no waving fern-frond is finer in form and texture. In its prime the whole tree is thatched with them, but if you would see the libocedrus in all its glory you must go to the woods in midwinter when it is laden with myriads of yellow flowers about the size of wheat grains, forming a noble illustration of nature's immortal virility and vigour. The mature cones, about three-fourths of an inch long, born on the ends of the plumy branchlets, serve to enrich still more the surpassing beauty of this winter-blooming tree-goldenrod.

THE SILVER FIRS

We come now to the most regularly planted and most clearly defined of the main forest belts, composed almost exclusively of two Silver Firs – *Abies concolor* and *Abies magnifica* – extending with but little interruption 450 miles at an elevation of from 5,000 to 9,000ft. above the sea. In its youth the silver fir is a charmingly symmetrical tree with its flat plumy branches arranged in regular whorls around the whitish-grey axis which terminates in a stout, hopeful shoot, pointing straight to the zenith, like an admonishing finger. The leaves are arranged in two horizontal rows along branchlets that commonly are less than eight years old, forming handsome plumes, pinnated like the fronds of ferns. The cones are a greyish-green when ripe, cylindrical, from three to four inches long, and one and a half to two inches wide, and stand upright on the upper horizontal branches. Full-grown trees in favourable situations are usually about 200ft. high and five or six feet in diameter. As old age creeps on, the rough bark becomes rougher and greyer, the branches loose their exact regularity of form. Many that are snow-bent are broken off and the axis often becomes double or otherwise irregular from accidents to the terminal bud or shoot. Nevertheless, throughout all the vicissitudes of its three or four centuries of life, come what may, the noble grandeur of these species, however obscured, is never lost.

The magnificent silver fir, or California red fir (*Abies magnifica*) is the most symmetrical of all the Sierra giants, far surpassing its companion species in this respect and easily distinguished from it by the purplish-red bark, which is also more closely-furrowed than that of the white, and by its larger cones, its more regularly whorled and fronded branches, and its shorter leaves, which grow all around the branches and point upward instead of being arranged in two horizontal rows. The branches are mostly whorled in fives, and stand out from the straight, red-purple bole in level, or in old trees in drooping, collars, every branch regularly pinnated like fern-fronds, making broad plumes, singularly rich and sumptuous-looking. The flowers are in their prime about the middle of June; the male red, growing on the underside of the branches in crowded profusion, giving a very rich colour to all the trees; the female greenish-yellow, tinged with pink, standing erect on the upper side of the topmost branches, while the tufts of young leaves, about as brightly coloured as those of the Douglas spruce, make another grand show, with cones mature in a single season from the flowers. When mature they are about six to eight inches long, three or four in diameter, covered with a fine grey down and streaked and beaded with transparent balsam, very rich and precious-looking, and stand erect like casts on the topmost branches. The inside of the cone is, if possible, still more beautiful. The scales and bracts are tinged with red and the seedlings are purple with bright iridescence. Both of the silver firs live between two and three centuries when the conditions about them are at all favourable. Some venerable patriarch may be seen heavily storm-marked, towering in severe majesty above the rising generation, with a protecting grove of hopeful saplings pressing close around his feet, each dressed with such loving care that not a leaf seems wanting. Other groups are made up of trees near the prime of life, nicely arranged as if Nature had carved them with discrimination from all the rest of the woods. It is from this tree, called red fir, by the lumbermen, that mountaineers cut boughs to sleep on when they are so fortunate as to be within its limits. Two or three rows of the sumptuous plushy-fronded branches, overlapping along the middle, and a crescent of smaller plumes mixed to one's taste with ferns and flowers for a pillow, form the very best bed imaginable. The essence of the pressed leaves seems to fill every pore of one's body. Falling water makes a soothing hush, while the spaces between the grand spires afford noble openings through which to gaze dreamily into the starry sky. The fir woods are fine sauntering-grounds at almost any time of the year, but finest in autumn when the noble trees are hushed in the hazy light and drip with balsam; and the flying, whirling seeds, escaping from the ripe cones, mottle the air like flocks of butterflies. Even in the richest part of these unrivalled forests where so many noble trees challenge admiration we linger fondly among the colossal firs and extol their beauty again and again, as if no other tree in the world could henceforth claim our love. It is in these woods the great granite domes arise that are so striking and characteristic a feature of the Sierra. Here, too, we find the best of the garden-meadows full of lilies. A dry spot a little way back from the margin of a silver fir lily-garden makes a glorious camp-ground, especially where the slope is toward the east with a view of the distant peaks along the summit of the Range. The tall lilies are brought forward most impressively like visitors by the light of your camp-fire and the nearest of the trees with their whorled branches tower above you like larger lilies and the sky seen through the garden-opening seems one vast meadow of white lily stars.

THE TWO-LEAVED PINE

The Two-Leaved Pine (*Pinus contorta*, var. *Murrayana*), above the silver fir zone, forms the bulk of the alpine forests up to a height of from 8,000 to 9,500ft. above the sea, growing in beautiful order on moraines scarcely changed as yet by post-glacial weathering. Compared with the giants of the lower regions this is a small tree, seldom exceeding a height of eighty or ninety feet. The largest I ever measured was ninety feet high and a little over six feet in diameter. The average height of mature trees throughout the entire belt is probably not far from fifty or sixty feet with a diameter of two feet. It is a well-proportioned, rather handsome tree with greyish-brown bark and crooked, much-divided branches which cover the greater part of the trunk, but not so densely as to prevent it being seen. The lower limbs, like those of most other conifers that grow in snowy regions, curve downward, gradually take a horizontal position about half-way up the trunk, then aspire more and more toward the summit. The short, rigid needles in fasicles of two are arranged in comparatively long cylindrical tassels at the ends of the tough up-curving branches. The cones are about two inches long, growing in clusters among the needles without any striking effect except while very young, when the flowers are of a vivid crimson colour and the whole tree appears to be dotted with brilliant flowers. The staminate flowers are still more showy on account of their great abundance, often giving a reddish-yellow tinge to the whole mass of foliage and filling the air with pollen. No other pine on the Range is so regularly planted as this one, covering moraines that extend along the sides of the high rocky valleys for miles without interruption. The thin bark is streaked and sprinkled with resin as though it had been showered upon the forest like rain

Therefore this tree more than any other is subject to destruction by fire. During strong winds extensive forests are destroyed, the flames leaping from tree to tree in continuous belts that go surging and racing onward above the bending wood like prairie-grass fires. During the calm season and Indian summer the fire creeps quietly along the ground, feeding on the needles and cones; arriving at the foot of a tree, the resin bark is ignited and the heated air ascends in a swift current, increasing in velocity and dragging the flames upward. Then the leaves catch, forming an immense column of fire, beautifully spired on the edges and tinted a rose-purple hue. It rushes aloft thirty or forty feet above the top of the tree, forming a grand spectacle, especially at night. It lasts, however, only a few seconds, vanishing with magical rapidity, to be succeeded by others along the fire-line at irregular intervals, tree after tree, upflashing and darting, leaving the trunks and branches scarcely scarred. The heat, however, is sufficient to kill the tree and in a few years the bark shrivels and falls off. Forests miles in extent are thus killed and left standing, with the branches on, but peeled and rigid, appearing grey in the distance like misty clouds. Later the branches drop off, leaving a forest of bleached spires. At length the roots decay and the forlorn grey trunks are blown down during some storm and piled one upon another, encumbering the ground until, dry and seasoned, they are consumed by another fire and leave the ground ready for a fresh crop.

In sheltered lake-hollows, on beds of alluvium, this pine varies so far from the common form that frequently it could be taken for a distinct species, growing in damp sods like grasses from forty to eighty feet high, bending all together to the breeze and whirling in eddying gusts more lively than any other tree in the woods. I frequently found species fifty feet high less than five inches in diameter. Being so slender and at the same time clad with leafy boughs, it is often bent and weighed down to the ground when laden with soft snow; thus forming fine ornamental arches, many of them to last until the melting of the snow in the spring.

THE MOUNTAIN PINE

The Mountain Pine (*Pinus monticola*) is the noblest tree of the alpine zone – hardy and long-lived, towering grandly above its companions and becoming stronger and more imposing just where other species begin to crouch and disappear. At its best it is usually about ninety feet high and five or six feet in diameter, though you may find specimens here and there considerably larger than this. It is as massive and as suggestive of enduring strength as an oak. About two-thirds of the trunk is commonly free of limbs, but close, fringy tufts of spray occur nearly all the way down to the ground. On trees that occupy exposed situations near its upper limit the bark is deep reddish-brown and rather deeply furrowed, the main furrows running nearly parallel to each other and connected on the old trees by conspicuous cross-furrows. The cones are from four to eight inches long, smooth, slender, cylindrical and somewhat curved. They grow in clusters of from three to six or seven and become pendulous as they increase in weight. This species is nearly related to the sugar pine and, though not half so tall, it suggests its noble relative in the way that it extends its long branches in general habit. It is first met on the upper margin of the silver fir zone, singly, in what appears as chance situations without making much impression on the general forest. Continuing up through the forests of the two-leaved pine it begins to show its distinguishing characteristic in the most marked way at an elevation of about 10,000ft., extending its tough, rather slender arms across the air, welcoming the storms and feeding on them and reaching sometimes to the grand old age of 1000 years.

THE WESTERN JUNIPER

The Juniper or Red Cedar (*Juniperus occidentalis*) is pre-eminently a rock tree, occupying the baldest domes and pavements in the upper silver fir and alpine zones, at a height of from 7,000 to 9,500ft. In such situations, rooted in narrow cracks or fissures, where there is scarcely a handful of soil, it is frequently over eight feet in diameter and not much more in height. The tops of old trees are almost always dead, and large stubborn-looking limbs push out horizontally, most of them broken and dead at the end, but densely covered, and imbedded here and there with tufts or mounds of grey-green scale-like foliage. Some trees are mere storm-beaten stumps about as broad as long, decorated with a few leafy sprays, reminding one of the crumbling towers of old castles, scantily draped with ivy. Its homes on bare, barren dome and ridge-top seem to have been chosen for safety against fire, for, on isolated mounds of sand and gravel free from grass and bushes on which fire could feed, it is often found growing tall and unscathed to a height of forty to sixty feet, with scarce a trace of the rocky angularity and broken limbs so characteristic a feature throughout the greater part of its range. It never makes anything like a forest, seldom even a grove. Usually it stands out separate and independent, clinging by slight joints to the rocks, living chiefly on snow and thin air and maintaining sound health on this diet for 2000 years or more. Every feature or every gesture it makes expresses steadfast, dogged endurance. The bark is of a bright cinnamon colour and is handsomely braided and reticulated on thrifty trees, flaking off in thin, shining ribbons that are sometimes used by the Indians for tent matting. Its fine colour and picturesqueness are appreciated by artists, but to me the juniper seems a singularly strange and taciturn tree. I have spent many a day and night in its company and always have found it silent and rigid. It seems to be a survivor of some ancient race, wholly unacquainted with its neighbours. Its broad stumpiness, of course, makes wind-waving or even shaking out of the question, but it is not this rocky rigidity that constitutes its silence. In calm sundays the sugar pine preaches like an enthusiastic apostle without moving a leaf. On level rocks the juniper dies standing and wastes insensibly out of existence like granite, the wind exerting about as little control over it, alive or dead, as it does over a glacier boulder.

I have spent a good deal of time trying to determine the age of these wonderful trees, but as all of the very old ones are honeycombed with dry rot I never was able to get a complete count of the largest. Some are undoubtedly more than 2000 years old, for though on deep moraine soil they grow about as fast as some of the pines, on bare pavements and smoothly glaciated, overswept ridges in the dome region they grow very slowly. One on the Starr King Ridge only two feet eleven inches in diameter was 1140 years old forty years ago. Another on the same ridge, only one foot seven and a half inches in diameter, had reached the age of 834 years. The first fifteen inches from the bark of the medium-size tree six feet in diameter, on the north Tenaya pavement, had 859 layers of wood. Beyond this the count was stopped by dry rot and scars. The largest I examined was thirty-three feet in girth, or nearly ten feet in diameter and, although I have failed to get anything like a complete count, I learned enough from this and many other specimens to convince me that most of the trees eight or ten feet thick, standing on pavements, are more than twenty centuries old rather than less. Barring accidents, for all I can see they would live forever; even when overthrown by avalanches, they refuse to lie at rest, lean stubbornly on their big branches as if anxious to rise, and while a single root holds to the rock, put forth fresh geaves with a grim never-say-die expression.

THE MOUNTAIN HEMLOCK

As the juniper is the most stubborn and unshakeable of trees in the Yosemite region, the Mountain Hemlock (*Tsuga Mertensiana*) is the most graceful and pliant and sensitive. Until it reaches a height of fifty or sixty feet it is sumptuously clothed down to the ground with drooping branches, which are divided again and again into delicate waving sprays, grouped and arranged in ways that are indescribably beautiful, and profusely adorned with small brown cones. The flowers also are peculiarly beautiful and effective; the female dark rich purple, the male blue, of so fine and pure a tone that the best azure of the mountain sky seems to be condensed in them. Though apparently the most delicate and feminine of all the mountain trees, it grows best where the snow lies deepest, at a height of from 9,000 to 9,500ft., in hollows on the northern slopes of mountains and ridges. But under all circumstances, sheltered from heavy winds or in bleak exposure to them, well fed or starved, even at its highest limit, 10,500ft. above the sea, on exposed ridge-tops where it has to crouch and huddle close in low thickets, it still contrives to put forth its sprays and branches in forms of invincible beauty, while on moist, well-drained moraines it displays a perfectly tropical luxuriance of foliage, flowers and fruit. The snow of the first winter storm is frequently soft, and lodges in the dense leafy branches, weighing them down against the trunk, and the slender, drooping axis, bending lower and lower as the load increases, at length reaches the ground, forming an ornamental arch. Then, as storm succeeds storm and snow is heaped on snow, the whole tree is at last buried, not again to see the light of day or move leaf or limb until set free by the spring thaws in June or July. Not only the young saplings are thus carefully covered and put to sleep in the whitest of white beds for five or six months of the year, but trees thirty feet high or more. From April to May, when the snow by repeated thawing and freezing is firmly compacted, you may ride over the prostrate groves without seeing a single branch or leaf of them. No other of our alpine conifers so finely veils its strength; poised in thin, white sunshine, clad with branches from head to foot, it towers in unassuming majesty, drooping as if unaffected with the aspiring tendencies of its race, loving the ground, conscious of heaven and joyously receptive of its blessings, reaching out its branches like sensitive tentacles, feeling the light and revelling in it. The largest specimen I ever found was nineteen feet seven inches in circumference. It was growing on the edge of Lake Hollow, north of Mount Hoffman, at an elevation of 9,250ft. above the level of the sea, and was probably about a hundred feet in height. Fine groves of mature trees, ninety to a hundred feet in height, are growing near the base of Mount Conness. It is widely distributed from near the south extremity of the high Sierra northward along the Cascade Mountains of Oregon and Washington and the coast ranges of British Columbia to Alaska, where it was first discovered in 1827. Its northernmost limit, so far as I have observed, is in the icy fiords of Prince William Sound in latitude 61°, where it forms pure forests at the level of the sea, growing tall and majestic on the banks of glaciers. There, as in the Yosemite region, it is ineffably beautiful, the very loveliest of all the American conifers.

THE WHITE-BARK PINE

The Dwarf Pine, or White-Bark Pine (*Pinus albicaulis*), forms the extreme edge of the timberline throughout nearly the whole extent of the Range on both flanks. It is first met growing with the two-leaved pine on the upper margin of the alpine belt, as an erect tree from fifteen to thirty feet high and from one to two feet in diameter; thence it goes straggling up the flanks of the summit peaks, upon moraines or crumbling ledges, wherever it can get a foothold, to an elevation of from 10,000 to 12,000ft., where it dwarfs to a mass of crumpled branches, covered with slender shoots, each tipped with a short, close-packed, leaf tassel. The bark is smooth and purplish, in some places almost white. The flowers are bright scarlet and rose-purple, giving a very flowery appearance little looked for in such a tree. The cones are about three inches long, an inch and a half in diameter, grow in rigid clusters, and are dark chocolate in colour while young, and bear beautiful pearly-white seeds about the size of peas, most of which are eaten by chipmunks and the Clarke's crows. Pines are commonly regarded as sky-living trees that must necessarily aspire or die. This species forms a marked exception, crouching and creeping in compliance with the most rigorous demands of climate; yet enduring bravely to a more advanced age than many of its lofty relatives in the sun-lands far below it. Seen from a distance it would never be taken for a tree of any kind. For example, on Cathedral Peak there is a scattered growth of this pine, creeping like mosses over the roof, nowhere giving hint of an ascending axis. While, approached quite near, it still appears matty and healthy, and one experiences no difficulty in walking over the top of it, yet it is seldom absolutely prostrate, usually attaining a height of three or four feet with a main trunk, and with branches outspread above it, as if in ascending they had been checked by a ceiling against which they had been compelled to spread horizontally. The winter snow *is* a sort of ceiling, lasting half the year; while the pressed surface is made yet smoother by violent winds armed with cutting sand-grains that bear down any shoot which offers to rise much above the general level, and that carve the dead trunks and branches in beautiful patterns.

During stormy nights I have often camped snugly beneath the interlacing arches of this little pine. The needles, which have accumulated for centuries, make fine beds, a fact well known to other mountaineers, such as deer and wild sheep, who paw out oval hollows and lie beneath the larger trees in safe and comfortable concealment. This lowly dwarf reaches a far greater age than would be guessed. A specimen that I examined, was growing at an elevation of 10,700ft., yet looked as though it might be plucked up by the roots, for it was only three and a half inches in diameter and its topmost tassel reached hardly three feet above the ground. Cutting it half through and counting the annual rings with the aid of a lens, I found its age to be no less than 255 years. Another specimen about the same height, with a trunk six inches in diameter, I found to be 426 years old, forty years ago; and one of its supple branchlets hardly an eighth of an inch in diameter inside the bark, was seventy-five years old, and so filled with oily balsam and seasoned by storms that I tied it in knots like a whip-cord.

THE NUT PINE

In going across the Range from the Tuolumne River Soda Springs to Mono Lake one makes the acquaintance of the curious little nut pine, (*Pinus monophylla*). It dots the eastern flank of the Sierra to which it is mostly restricted in greyish bush-like patches, from the margin of the sage-plains to an elevation of from 7,000 to 8,000ft. A more contented, fruitful and unaspiring conifer could not be conceived. All the species we have been sketching make departures more or less distant from the typical spire form, but none goes so far as this. Without any apparent cause it keeps near the ground, throwing out crooked, divergent branches like an orchard apple-tree, and seldom pushes a single shoot higher than fifteen or twenty feet above the ground.

The average thickness of the trunk is, perhaps, about ten or twelve inches. The leaves are mostly undivided, like round awls, instead of being separated, like those of other pines, into twos and threes and fives. The cones are green while growing, and are usually found over all the tree, forming quite a marked feature as seen against the bluish-grey foliage. They are quite small, only about two inches in length, and seem to have but little space for seeds; but when we come to open them, we find that about half the entire bulk of the cone is made up of sweet, nutritious nuts, nearly as large as hazel-nuts. This is undoubtedly the most important food-tree on the Sierra, and furnishes the Mona, Carson, and Walker River Indians with more and better nuts than all the other species taken together. It is the Indian's own tree, and many a white man have they killed for cutting it down. Being so low, the cones are readily beaten off with poles, and the nuts procured by roasting them until the scales open. In bountiful seasons a single Indian may gather thirty or forty bushels.

CHAPTER SEVEN

The Big Trees

BETWEEN THE heavy pine and silver fir zones towers the Big Tree (*Sequoia gigantea*), the king of all the conifers in the world, 'the noblest of the noble race.' The groves nearest Yosemite Valley are about twenty miles to the westward and southward and are called the Tuolumne, Merced and Mariposa groves. It extends, a widely interrupted belt, from a very small grove on the middle fork of the American River to the head of Deer Creek, a distance of about 260 miles, its northern limit being near the thirty ninth parallel, the southern a little below the thirty-sixth. The elevation of the belt above the sea varies from about 5,000 to 8,000ft. From the American River to Kings River the species occurs only in small isolated groups so sparsely distributed along the belt that three of the gaps in it are from forty to sixty miles wide. But from

Kings River southward the Sequoia is not restricted to mere groves but extends across the wide rugged basins of the Kaweah and Tule Rivers in noble forests, a distance of nearly seventy miles, the continuity of this part of the belt being broken only by the main canyons. The Fresno, the largest of the northern groves, has an area of three or four square miles, a short distance to the southward of the famous Mariposa grove. Along the south rim of the canyon of the south fork of Kings River there is a majestic Sequoia forest about six miles long by two miles wide. This is the northernmost group that may fairly be called a forest. Descending the divide between the Kings and Kaweah Rivers you come to the grand forests that form the main continuous portion of the belt. Southward the giants become more and more irrepressibly jubilant, heaving their massive crowns into the sky from every ridge and slope, waving onward in graceful compliance with the complicated topography of the region. The finest of the Kaweah section of the belt is on the broad ridge between Marble Creek and the middle fork, and is called the Giant Forest. It extends from the granite headlands, overlooking the hot San Joaquin plains, to within a few miles of the cool glacial fountains of the summit peaks. The extreme upper limit of the belt is reached between the middle and south forks of the Kaweah at a height of 8,400ft., but the finest block of big tree forests in the entire belt is on the north fork of Tule River, and is included in the Sequoia National Park.

In the northern groves there are comparatively few young trees or saplings. But here for every old storm-beaten giant there are many in their prime and for each of these a crowd of hopeful young trees and saplings, growing vigorously on moraines, rocky ledges, along water courses and meadows. But though the area occupied by the big tree increases so greatly from north to south, there is no marked increase in the size of the trees. The height of 275ft. or thereabouts and a diameter of about twenty feet, four feet from the ground is, perhaps, about the average size of what may be called full-grown trees, where they are favourably located. The specimens twenty-five feet in diameter are not very rare and a few are nearly three hundred feet high. In the Calaveras grove there are four trees over 300ft. in height, the tallest of which as measured by the Geological Survey is 325ft. The very largest that I have yet met in the course of my explorations is a majestic old fire-scarred monument in the Kings River forest. It is thirty-five feet and eight inches in diameter inside the bark, four feet above the ground. It is burned half through, and I spent a day in clearing away the charred surface with a sharp axe and counting the annual wood-rings with the aid of a pocket lens. I succeeded in laying bare a section all the way from the outside to the heart and counted a little over four thousand rings, showing that this tree was in its prime about twenty-seven feet in diameter at the beginning of the Christian era. No other tree in the world, as far as I know, has looked down on so many centuries as the Sequoia or opens so many impressive and suggestive views into history. Under the most favourable conditions these giants probably live 5000 years or more, though few of even the larger trees are half as old. The age of one that was felled in Calaveras grove, for the sake of having its stump for a dancing-floor, was about 1300 years, and its diameter measured across the stump twenty-four feet inside the bark. Another that was felled in the Kings River forest was about the same size but nearly a thousand years older (2200 years), though not a very old-looking tree.

So harmonious and finely balanced are even the mightiest of these monarchs in all their proportions that there is never anything overgrown or monstrous about them. Seeing them for the first time you are more impressed with their beauty than their size, their grandeur being a great part invisible; but sooner or later it becomes manifest to the loving eye, stealing slowly on the senses like the grandeur of Niagara or of the Yosemite Dome. When you approach them and walk around them you begin to wonder at their colossal size and try to measure them. They bulge considerably at the base, but not more than is required for beauty and safety and the only reason that this bulging seems in some cases excessive is that only a comparatively small section is seen in near views. One that I measured in the Kings River forest was twenty-five feet in diameter at the ground and ten feet in diameter 200ft. above the ground, showing the fineness of the taper of the trunk as a whole. No description can give anything like an adequate idea of their singular majesty, much less of their beauty. Except the sugar pine, most of their neigbours with pointed tops seem ever trying to go higher, while the big tree, soaring above them all, seems satisfied. Its grand domed head seems to be poised about as lightly as a cloud, giving no impression of seeking to rise higher. Only when it is young does it show like other conifers a heavenward yearning, sharply aspiring with a long quick-growing top. Indeed, the whole tree for the first century or two, or until it is a hundred or one hundred and fifty feet high, is arrowhead in form, and, compared with the solemn rigidity of age, seems as sensitive to the wind as a squirrel's tail. As it grows older, the lower branches are gradually dropped and the upper ones thinned out until comparatively few are left. These, however, are developed to a great size, divide again and again and terminate in bossy, rounded masses of leafy branchlets, while the head becomes dome-shaped, and is the first to feel the touch of the rosy beams of the morning, the last to bid the sun good night. Perfect specimens, unhurt by running fires or lightning, are singularly regular and symmetrical in general form, though not in the least conventionalized, for they show extraordinary variety in the unity and harmony of their general outline. The immensely strong, stately shafts are free of limbs for one hundred and fifty feet or so. The large limbs reach out with equal boldness in every direction, showing no weather side, and no other tree has foliage so densely massed, so finely moulded in outline and so perfectly subordinate to an ideal type. A particularly knotty, angular, ungovernable-looking branch, from five to seven or eight feet in diameter and perhaps a thousand years old, may occasionally be seen pushing out from the trunk as if determined to break across the bounds of the regular curve, but like all the others it dissolves in bosses of branchlets and sprays as soon as the general outline is approached. Except in picturesque old age, after being struck by lightning or broken by thousands of snow-storms, the regularity of forms is one of their most distinguishing characteristics. Another is the simple beauty of the trunk and its great thickness as compared with its height and the width of the branches, which makes them look more like finely modelled and sculptured architectural columns than the stems of trees, while the great limbs look like rafters, supporting the magnificent dome-head. But though so consummately beautiful, the big tree always seems unfamiliar, with peculiar physiognomy, awfully solemn and earnest; yet with all its strangeness it impresses us as being more at home than any of its neighbours, holding the best right to the ground as the oldest, strongest inhabitant. One soon becomes acquainted with new species of pine and fir and spruce as with friendly people, shaking their outstretched branches, like shaking hands and fondling their little ones, while the vulnerable aboriginal Sequoia, ancient of other days, keeps you at a distance, looking as strange in aspect and behaviour among its neighbour trees as would the mastodon among the homely bears and deers. Only the Sierra juniper is at all like it, standing rigid and unconquerable on glacier pavements for thousands of years, grim and silent, with an air of antiquity about as pronounced as that of the Sequoia.

The bark of the largest tree is from one to two feet thick, rich cinnamon brown, purplish on young trees, forming magnificent masses of colour with the underbrush. Toward the end of winter the trees are in bloom, while the snow is still eight or ten feet deep. The female flowers are about three-eighths of an inch long, pale green, and grow in countless thousands on the ends of sprays. The male are still more abundant, pale yellow, a fourth of an inch long and when the pollen is ripe they colour the whole tree and dust the air and the ground. The cones are bright grass-green in colour, about two and a half inches long, one and a half wide, made up of thirty or forty strong, closely-packed, rhomboidal scales, with four to eight seeds at the base of each. The seeds are wonderfully small and light, being only from an eighth to a fourth of an inch long and wide, including a filmy surrounding wing, which causes them to glint and waver in falling and enables the wind to carry them considerable distances. Unless harvested by the squirrels, the cones discharge their seed and remain on the tree for many years. In fruitful seasons the trees are fairly laden. On two small branches one and a half and two inches in diameter I counted 480 cones. No other California conifer produces nearly so many seeds, except, perhaps, the other Sequoia, the redwood of the Coast Mountains. Millions are ripened annually by a single tree, and in a fruitful year the product of one of the northern groves would be enough to plant all the mountain ranges in the world.

As soon as any accident happens to the crown, such as being smashed off by lightning, the branches beneath the wound, no matter how situated, seem to be excited, like a colony of bees that have lost their queen, and become anxious to repair the damage. Limbs that have grown outward for centuries at right angles to the trunk begin to turn upward to assist in making a new crown, each speedily assuming the special form of true summits. Even in the case of mere stumps, burned half through, some mere ornamental tuft will try to go aloft and do its best as a leader in forming a new head. Groups of two or three are often found standing close together, the seeds from which they sprang having probably grown on ground cleared for their reception by the fall of a large tree of a former generation. They are called 'loving couples,' 'three graces,' etc. When these trees are young they are seen to stand twenty or thirty feet apart, by the time they are full-grown their trunks will touch and crowd against each other and in some cases even appear as one.

It is generally believed that the Sequoia was once far more widely distributed over the Sierra; but after long and careful study I have come to the conclusion that it never was, at least since the close of the glacial period, because a diligent search along the margins of the groves, and in the gaps between fails to reveal a single trace of its previous existence beyond its present bounds. Notwithstanding, I feel confident that if every Sequoia in the Range were to die today, numerous monuments of their existence would remain, of so imperishable a nature as to be available for the student more than ten thousand years hence.

In the first place, no species of coniferous tree in the Range keeps its members so well together as the Sequoia; a mile is, perhaps, the greatest distance of any straggler from the main body, and all of those stragglers that have come under my observation are young, instead of old monumental trees, relics of a more extended growth.

Again, the great trunks of the Sequoia last for centuries after they fall. I have a specimen block of Sequoia wood, cut from a fallen tree, which is hardly distinguishable from a similar section cut from a living tree, although the one cut from the fallen trunk has certainly lain on the damp forest floor more than 380 years, probably thrice as long. The time-measure in the case is simply this: When the ponderous trunk to which the old vestige belonged fell, it sunk itself into the ground, thus making a long, straight ditch, and in the middle of this ditch a silver fir four feet in diameter and 380 years old was growing, as I determined by cutting it half through and counting the rings, thus demonstrating that the remnant of the trunk that made the ditch has lain on the ground *more* than 380 years. For it is evident that, to find the whole time, we must add to the 380 years the time that the vanished portion of the trunk lay in the ditch before being burned out of the way, plus the time that passed before the seed from which the monumental fir sprang fell into the prepared soil and took root. Now, because Sequoia trunks are never wholly consumed in one forest fire, and those fires recur only at considerable intervals, and because Sequoia ditches after being cleared are often left unplanted for centuries, it becomes evident that the trunk-remnant in question may proably have lain a thousand years or more. And this instance is by no means a rare one.

Again, admitting that upon those areas supposed to have been once covered with Sequoia forests, every tree may have fallen, and every trunk may have been burned or buried, leaving not a remnant, many of the ditches made by the fall of the ponderous trunks, and the bowls made by their upturning roots, would remain patent for thousands of years after the last vestige of the trunks that made them had vanished. Much of this ditch-writing would no doubt be quickly effaced by the flood-action of overflowing streams and rain-washing; but no inconsiderable portion would remain enduringly engraved on ridge-tops beyond such destructive action; for, where all the conditions are favourable, it is almost imperishable. Now these historic ditches and root-bowls occur in all the present Sequoia groves and forests, but, as far as I have observed, not the faintest vestige of one presents itself outside of them.

We therefore conclude that the area covered by Sequoia has not been diminished during the last eight or ten thousand years, and probably not at all in post-glacial time. Nevertheless, the questions may be asked: Is the species verging toward extinction? What are its relations to climate, soil, and associated trees?

All the phenomena bearing on these questions also throw light, as we shall endeavour to show, upon the peculiar distribution of the species, and sustain the conclusion already arrived at as to the question of former extension. In the northern groups, as we have seen, there are few young trees or saplings growing up around the old ones to perpetuate the race, and inasmuch as those aged Sequoias, so nearly childless, are the only ones commonly known, the species, to most observers, seems doomed to speedy extinction, as being nothing more than an expiring remnant, vanquished in the so-called struggle for life by pines and firs that have driven it into its last strongholds in moist glens where the climate is supposed to be exceptionally favourable. But the story told by the majestic continuous forests of the south creates a very different impression. No tree in the forest is more enduringly established in concordance with both climate and soil. It grows heartily everywhere – on moraines, rocky ledges, along watercourses, and in the deep, moist alluvium of meadows with; as we have seen, a multitude of seedlings and saplings crowding up around the aged, abundantly able to maintain the forest in prime vigour. So that if all the trees of any section of the main Sequoia forest were ranged together according to age, a very promising curve would be presented, all the way up from last year's seedlings to giants, and with the young and middle-aged portion of the curve many times longer than the old portion. Even as far north as the Fresno, I counted 536 saplings and seedlings, growing promisingly upon a landslip not exceeding two acres in area. This soil-bed was about seven years old, and had been seeded almost simultaneously by pines, firs, libocedrus, and Sequoia, presenting a simple and instructive illustration of the struggle for life among the rival species; and it was interesting to note that the conditions thus far affecting them have enabled the young Sequoias to gain a marked advantage. Toward the south where the Sequoia becomes most exuberant and numerous, the rival trees become less so; and where they mix with Sequoias they grow up beneath them like slender grasses among stalks of Indian corn. Upon a bed of sandy flood-soil I counted ninety-four Sequoias, from one to twelve feet high, on a patch of ground once occupied by four large sugar pines which lay crumbling beneath them – an instance of conditions which have enabled Sequoias to crowd out the pines. I also noted eighty-six vigorous saplings upon a piece of fresh ground prepared for their reception by fire. Thus fire, the great destroyer of the Sequoia, also furnishes the bare ground required for its growth from the seed. Fresh ground is, however, furnished in sufficient quantities for the renewal of the forests without the aid of fire – by the fall of old trees. The soil is thus upturned and mellowed, and many trees are planted for every one that falls.

It is constantly asserted in a vague way that the Sierra was vastly wetter than now, and that the increasing drought will of itself extinguish the Sequoia, leaving its ground to other trees supposed capable of flourishing in a drier climate. But that the Sequoia can and does grow on as dry ground as any of its present rivals is manifest in a thousand places. 'Why, then,' it will be asked, 'are Sequoias always found only in well-watered places?' Simply because a growth of Sequoias creates those streams. The thirsty mountaineer knows well that in every Sequoia grove he will find running water, but it is a mistake to suppose that the water is the cause of the grove being there; on the contrary, the grove is the cause of the water being there. Drain off the water and the trees will remain, but cut off the trees, and the streams will vanish. Never was cause more completely mistaken for effect than in the case of these related phenomena of Sequoia woods and perennial streams.

When attention is called to the method of Sequoia stream-making, it will be apprehended at once. The roots of this immense tree fill the ground, forming a thick sponge that absorbs and holds back the rain and melting snow, only allowing it to ooze and flow gently. Indeed, every fallen leaf and rootlet, as well as long clasping root, and prostrate trunk, may be regarded as a dam hoarding the bounty of storm-clouds, and dispensing it as blessings all through the summer, instead of allowing it to go headlong in short-lived floods.

Since, then, it is a fact that thousands of Sequoias are growing thriftily on what is termed dry ground, and even clinging like mountain pines to rifts in granite precipices, and since it has also been shown that the extra moisture found in connection with the denser growths is an effect of their presence, instead of a cause of their presence, then the notions as to the former extension of the species and its near approach to extinction, based upon its supposed dependence on greater moisture, are seen to be erroneous.

The decrease in the rain and snowfall since the close of the glacial period in the Sierra is much less than is commonly guessed. The highest post-glacial water-marks are well preserved in all the upper river channels, and they are not greatly higher than the spring flood-marks of the present; showing conclusively that no extraordinary decrease has taken place in the volume of the upper tributaries of post-glacial Sierra streams since they came into existence. But, in the meantime, eliminating all this complicated question of climatic change, the plain fact remains that the present rain and snowfall is abundantly sufficient for the luxuriant growth of Sequoia forests. Indeed, all my observations tend to show that in a prolonged drought the sugar pines and firs would perish before the Sequoia, not alone because of the greater longevity of individual trees, but because the species can endure more drought, and make the most of whatever moisture falls.

Again, if the restriction and irregular distribution of the species be interpreted as a result of the desiccation of the Range, then instead of increasing as it does in individuals toward the south where the rainfall is less, it should diminish. If, then, the peculiar distribution of Sequoia has not been governed by superior conditions of soil as to fertility or moisture, by what has it been governed?

In the course of my studies I observed that the northern groves, the only ones I was at first acquainted with, were located on just those portions of the general forest soil-belt that were first laid bare toward the close of the glacial period when the ice-sheet began to break up into individual glaciers. And while searching the wide basin of the San Joaquin, and trying to account for the absence of Sequoia where every condition seemed favourable for its growth, it occurred to me that this remarkable gap in the Sequoia belt fifty miles wide is located exactly in the basin of the vast, ancient *mer de glace* of the San Joaquin and Kings River basins which poured its frozen floods to the plain through this gap as its channel. I then perceived that the next great gap in the belt to the northward, forty miles wide, extending between the Calaveras and Tuolumne groves, occurs in the basin of the great ancient *mer de glace* of the Tuolumne and Stanislaus basins; and that the smaller gap between the Merced and Mariposa groves occurs in the basin of the smaller glacier of the Merced. The wider the ancient glacier, the wider the corresponding gap in the Sequoia belt.

Finally, pursuing my investigations across the basins of the Kaweah and Tule, I discovered that the Sequoia belt attained its greatest development just where, owing to the topographical peculiarities of the region, the ground had been best protected from the main ice-rivers that continued to pour past from the summit fountains long after the smaller local glaciers had been melted.

Taking now a general view of the belt, beginning at the south, we see that the majestic ancient glaciers were shed off right and left down the valleys of Kern and Kings Rivers by the lofty protective spurs outspread embracingly above the warm Sequoia-filled basins of the Kaweah and Tule. Then, next northward, occurs the wide Sequoia-less channel, or basin of the ancient San Joaquin and Kings River *mer de glace*; then the warm, protected spots of Fresno and Mariposa groves; then the Sequoia-less channel of the ancient Merced glacier; next the warm, sheltered ground of the Merced and Tuolumne groves; then the Sequoia-less channel of the grand ancient *mer de glace* of the Tuolumne and Stanislaus; then the warm old ground of the Calaveras and Stanislaus groves. It appears, therefore, that just where, at a certain period in the history of the Sierra, the glaciers were not, there the Sequoia is, and just where the glaciers were, there the Sequoia is not.

But although all the observed phenomena bearing on the post-glacial history of this colossal tree point to the conclusion that it never was more widely distributed on the Sierra since the close of the glacial epoch; that its present forests are scarcely past prime, if, indeed, they have reached prime; that the post-glacial day of the species is probably not half done; yet, when from a wider outlook the vast antiquity of the genus is considered, and its ancient richness in species and individuals – comparing our Sierra Giant and *Sequoia sempervirens* of the Coast Range, the only other living species of Sequoia, with the twelve fossil species already discovered and described by Heer and Lesquereux, some of which flourished over vast areas in the Arctic regions and in Europe and our own territories, during tertiary and cretaceous times – then, indeed, it becomes plain that our two surviving species, restricted to narrow belts within the limits of California, are mere remnants of the genus, both as to species and individuals, and that they may be verging to extinction. But the verge of a period beginning in cretaceous times may have a breadth of tens of thousands of years, not to mention the possible existence of conditions calculated to multiply and re-extend both species and individuals.

There is no absolute limit to the existence of any tree. Death is due to accidents, not, as that of animals, to the wearing out of organs. Only the leaves die of old age. Their fall is foretold in their structure; but the leaves are renewed every year, and so also are the essential organs – wood, roots, bark, buds. Most of the Sierra trees die of disease, insects, fungi, etc., but nothing hurts the big tree. I never saw one that was sick or showed the slightest sign of decay. Barring accidents, it seems to be immortal. It is a curious fact that all the very old Sequoias had lost their heads by lightning strokes. 'All things come to him who waits.' But of all the living things Sequoia is perhaps the only one able to wait long enough to make sure of being struck by lightning.

So far as I am able to see at present only fire and the axe threatens the existence of these noblest of God's trees. In Nature's keeping they are safe, but through the agency of man destruction is making rapid progress, while in the work of protection only a good beginning has been made. The Fresno grove, the Tuolumne, Merced and Mariposa groves are under the protection of the Federal Government in the Yosemite National Park. So are the General Grant and Sequoia National Parks; the latter, established twenty-one years ago, has an area of 240 square miles and is efficiently guarded by a troop of cavalry under the direction of the Secretary of the Interior; so also are the small General Grant National Park, established at the same time with an area of four square miles, and the Mariposa grove, about the same size and the small Merced and Tuolumne group. Perhaps more than half of all the big trees have been thoughtlessly sold and are now in the hands of speculators and mill men. It appears, therefore, that far the largest most important section of protected big trees is in the great Sequoia National Park, now easily accessible by rail to Lemon Cove and thence by a good stage road into the giant forest of the Kaweah and thence by trail to other parts of the park; but large as it is it should be made much larger. Its natural eastern boundary is the High Sierra and the northern and southern boundaries are the Kings and Kern Rivers. Thus could be included the sublime scenery on the headwaters of these rivers and perhaps nine-tenths of all the big trees in existence. All private claims within these bounds should be gradually extinguished by purchase by the Government. The big tree, leaving all its higher uses out of the count, is a tree of life to the dwellers of the plain dependent on irrigation, a never-failing spring, sending living waters to the lowland. For every grove cut down a stream is dried up. Therefore all California is crying, 'Save the trees of the fountains.' Nor, judging by the signs of the times, is it likely that the cry will cease until the salvation of all that is left of *Sequoia gigantea* is made sure.

CHAPTER EIGHT

The Flowers

YOSEMITE WAS all one glorious flower garden before ploughs and scythes and trampling, biting horses came to make its wide open spaces look like farmers' pasture fields. Nevertheless, countless flowers still bloom every year in glorious profusion on the grand talus slopes, wall benches and tablets, and in all the fine, cool side-canyons up to the rim of the Valley, and beyond, higher and higher, to the summits of the peaks. Even on the open floor and in easily-reached side-nooks many common flowering plants have survived and still make a brave show in the spring and early summer. Among these we may mention tall œnotheras, *Pentstemon lutea*, and *P. Douglasii* with fine blue and red flowers; spraguea, scarlet zauschneria, with its curious radiant rosettes characteristic of the sandy flats; mimulus, eunanus, blue and white violets, geranium, columbine, erythraea, larkspur, collomia, draperia, gilias, heleniums, bahia, goldenrods, daisies, honeysuckle; heuchera, bolandra, saxifrages, gentians; in cool canyon nooks and on Clouds' Rest and the base of Starr King Dome you may find *Primula suffrutescens*, the only wild primrose discovered in California, and the only known shrubby species in the genus. And there are several fine orchids, habenaria, and cypripedium, the latter very rare, once common in the Valley near the foot of Glacier Point, and in a bog on the rim of the Valley near a place called Gentry's Station, now abdandoned. It is a very beautiful species, the large oval lip white, delicately veined with purple; the other petals and the sepals purple, strap-shaped, and elegantly curled and twisted.

Of the lily family, fritillaria, smilacina, chlorogalum and several fine species of brodiæa, Ithuriel's spear, and others less prized are common, and the favourite calochortus, or Mariposa lily, a unique genus of many species, something like the tulips of Europe but far finer. Most of them grow on the warm foothills below the Valley, but two charming species, *C. cœruleus* and *C. nudus*, dwell in springy places on the Wawona road a few miles beyond the brink of the walls.

The snow plant (*Sarcodes sanguinea*) is more admired by tourists than any other in California. It is red, fleshy and watery and looks like a gigantic asparagus shoot. Soon after the snow is off the ground it rises through the dead needles and humus in the pine and fir woods like a bright glowing pillar of fire. In a week or so it grows to a height of eight or twelve inches with a diameter of an inch and a half or two inches; then its long fringed bracts curl aside, allowing the twenty- or thirty-five-lobed, bell-shaped flowers to open and look straight out from the axis. It is said to grow up through the snow; on the contrary, it always waits until the ground is warm, though with other early flowers it is occasionally buried or half-buried for a day or two by spring storms. The entire plant – flowers, bracts, stem, scales, and roots – is fiery red. Its colour should appeal to one's blood. Nevertheless, it is a singularly cold and unsympathetic plant. Everybody admires it as a wonderful curiosity, but nobody loves it as lilies, violets, roses, daisies are loved. Without fragrance, it stands beneath the pines and firs lonely and silent, as if unacquainted with any other plant in the world; never moving in the wildest storms; rigid as if lifeless, though covered with beautiful rosy flowers.

Far the most delightful and fragrant of the Valley flowers is the Washington lily, white, moderate in size, with from three- to ten-flowered racemes. I found one specimen in the lower end of the Valley at the foot of the Wawona grade that was eight feet high, the raceme two feet long, with fifty-two flowers, fifteen of them open; the others had faded or were still in the bud. This famous lily is distributed over the sunny portions of the sugar pine woods, never in large meadow-garden companies like the large and the small tiger lilies (*pardalinum* and *parvum*), but widely scattered, standing up to the waist in dense ceanothus and manzanita chaparral, waving its lovely flowers above the blooming wilderness of brush, and giving their fragrance to the breeze. It is now becoming scarce in the most accessible parts of its range on account of the high price paid for its bulbs by gardeners through whom it has been distributed far and wide over the flower-loving world. For, on account of its pure colour and delicate, delightful fragrance, all lily lovers at once adopted it as a favourite.

The principal shrubs are manzanita and ceanothus, several species of each, azalea, *Rubus nutkanus*, brier rose, choke-cherry, philadelphus, calycanthus, garrya, rhamnus, etc.

The manzanita never fails to attract particular attention. The species common in the Valley is usually about six or seven feet high, round-headed with innumerable branches, red or chocolate-colour bark, pale green leaves set on edge, and a rich profusion of small, pink, narrow-throated, urn-shaped flowers, like those of arbutus. The knotty, crooked, angular branches are about as rigid as bones, and the red bark is so thin and smooth on both trunk and branches, they look as if they had been peeled and polished and painted. In the spring large areas on the mountain up to a height of eight or nine thousand feet are brightened with the rosy flowers, and in autumn with their red fruit. The pleasantly acid berries, about the size of peas, look like little apples, and a hungry mountaineer is glad to eat them, though half their bulk is made up of hard seeds. Indians, bears, coyotes, foxes, birds and other mountain people live on them for weeks and months. The different species of ceanothus usually associated with manzanita are flowery fragrant and alto-gether delightful shrubs, growing in glorious abundance, not only in the Valley, but high up in the forest on sunny or half-shaded ground. In the sugar-pine woods the most beautiful species is *C. integerrimus*, often called Californian lilac, or deer brush. It is five or six feet high with slender branches, glossy foliage, and abundance of blue flowers in close, showy panicles. Two species, *C. prostratus* and *C. procumbens*, spread smooth, blue-flowered mats and rugs beneath the pines, and offer fine beds to tired mountaineers. The commonest species, *C. cordulatus*, is most common in the silver-fir woods. It is white-flowered and thorny, and makes dense thickets of tangled chaparral, difficult to wade through or to walk over. But it is pressed flat every winter by ten or fifteen feet of snow. The western azalea makes glorious beds of bloom along the river bank and meadows. In the Valley it is from two to five feet high, has fine green leaves, mostly hidden beneath its rich profusion of large, fragrant white and yellow flowers, which are in their prime in June, July and August, according to the elevation, ranging from 3,000 to 6,000ft. Near the azalea-bordered streams the small wild rose, resembling *R. blanda*, makes large thickets deliciously fragrant, especially on a dewy morning and after showers. Not far from these azalea and rose gardens, *Rubus nutkanus* covers the ground with broad, soft, velvety leaves, and pure-white flowers as large as those of its neighbour and relative, the rose, and much finer in texture, followed at the end of summer by soft red berries good for everybody. This is the commonest and the most beautiful of the whole blessed, flowery, fruity Rubus genus.

There are a great many interesting ferns in the Valley and about it. Naturally enough the greater number are rock ferns – pellæa, cheilanthes, polypodium, adiantum, woodsia, cryptogramma, etc., with small tufted fronds, lining cool glens and fringing the seams of the cliffs. The most important of the larger species are woodwardia, aspidium, asplenium, and, above all, the common pteris. *Woodwardia radicans* is a superb, broad-shouldered fern five to eight feet high, growing in vase-shaped clumps where the ground is nearly level and on some of the benches of the north wall of the Valley where it is watered by a broad trickling stream. It thatches the sloping rocks, frond overlapping frond like roof shingles. The broad-fronded, hardy *Pteris aquilina*, the commonest of ferns, covers large areas on the floor of the Valley. No other fern does so much for the colour glory of autumn, with its browns and reds and yellows, even after lying dead beneath the snow all winter. It spreads a rich brown mantle over the desolate ground in the spring before the grass has sprouted, and at the first touch of sun-heat its young fronds come rearing up full of faith and hope through the midst of the last year's ruins.

Of the five species of pellæa, *P. Breweri* is the hardiest as to enduring high altitudes and stormy weather and at the same time it is the most fragile of the genus. It grows in dense tufts in the clefts of storm-beaten rocks, high up on the mountain-side on the very edge of the fern line. It is a handsome little fern about four or five inches high, has pale-green pinnate fronds, and shining bronze-coloured stalks about as brittle as glass. Its companions on the lower part of its range are *Cryptogramma acrostichoides* and *Phegopteris alpestris*, the latter with soft, delicate fronds, not in the least like those of rock fern, though it grows on the rocks where the snow lies longest. *Pellæa Bridgesii*, with blue-green, narrow, simply-pinnate fronds, is about the same size as Breweri and ranks next to it as a moutaineer, growing in fissures, wet or dry, and around the edges of boulders that are resting on glacier pavements with no fissures whatever. About a thousand feet lower we find the smaller, more abundant *P. densa* on ledges and boulder-strewn, fissured pavements, watered until late in summer from oozing currents, derived from lingering snowbanks.

It is, or rather was, extremely abundant between the foot of the Nevada and the head of the Vernal Fall, but visitors with great industry have dug out almost every root, so that now one has to scramble in out-of-the-way places to find it. The three species of cheilanthes in the Valley – *C. californica, C. gracillima,* and *myriophylla,* with beautiful two-to-four-pinnate fronds, an inch to five inches long, adorn the stupendous walls however dry and sheer. The exceedingly delicate californica is so rare that I have found it only once. The others are abundant and are sometimes accompanied by the little gold fern, *Gymnogramme triangularis,* and rarely by the curious little *Botrychium simplex,* some of them less than an inch high. The finest of all the rock ferns is *Adiantum pedatum,* lover of waterfalls and the finest spray-dust. The homes it loves best are over-leaning, cave-like hollows, beside the larger falls, where it can wet its fingers with their dewy spray. Many of these moss-lined chambers contain thousands of these delightful ferns, clinging to mossy walls by the slightest hold, reaching out their delicate finger-fronds on dark, shining stalks, sensitive and tremulous, throbbing in unison with every movement and tone of the falling water, moving each division of the frond separately at times, as if fingering the music.

May and June are the main bloom-months of the year. Both the flowers and falls are then at their best. By the first of August the midsummer glories of the Valley are past their prime. The young birds are then out of their nests. Most of the plants have gone to seed; berries are ripe; autumn tints begin to kindle and burn over meadow and grove, and a soft mellow haze in the morning sunbeams heralds the approach of Indian summer. The shallow river is now at rest, its flood-work done. It is now but little more than a series of pools united by trickling, whispering currents that steal softly over brown pebbles and sand with scarce an audible murmur. Each pool has a character of its own and, though they are nearly currentless, the night air and tree shadows keep them cool. Their shores curve in and out in bay and promontory, giving the appearance of miniature lakes, their banks in most places embossed with brier and azalea, sedge and grass and fern; and above these in their glory of autumn colours a mingled growth of alder, willow, dogwood and balm-of-Gilead; mellow sunshine overhead, cool shadows beneath; light filtered and strained in passing through the ripe leaves like that which passes through coloured windows. The surface of the water is stirred, perhaps, by whirling water-beetles, or some startled trout, seeking shelter beneath fallen logs or roots. The falls, too, are quiet; no wind stirs, and the whole Valley floor is a mosaic of greens and purples, yellows and reds. Even the rocks seem strangely soft and mellow, as if they, too, had ripened.

CHAPTER NINE

The Birds

THE SONGS of the Yosemite winds and waterfalls are delightfully enriched with bird song, especially in the nesting time of spring and early summer. The most familiar and best known of all is the common robin, who may be seen every day, hopping about briskly on the meadows and uttering his cheery, enlivening call. The black-headed grosbeak, too, is here, with the Bullock oriole, and western tanager, brown song-sparrow, hermit thrush, the purple finch – a fine singer, with head and throat of a rosy-red hue – several species of warblers and vireos, kinglets, flycatchers, etc.

But the most wonderful singer of all the birds is the water-ouzel that dives into foaming rapids and feeds at the bottom, holding on in a wonderful way, living a charmed life.

Several species of humming-birds are always to be seen, darting and buzzing among the showy flowers. The little red-bellied, nuthatches, the chickadees, and little brown creepers, threading the furrows of the bark of the pines, searching for food in the crevices. The large Steller's jay makes merry in the pine-tops; flocks of beautiful green swallows skim over the streams, and the noisy Clarke's crow may oftentimes be seen on the highest points around the Valley; and in the deep woods beyond the walls you may frequently hear and see the dusky grouse and the pileated woodpecker, or woodcock almost as large as a pigeon. The junco or snow-bird builds its nest on the floor of the Valley among the ferns; several species of sparrow are common and the beautiful lazuli bunting, a common bird in the underbrush, flitting about among the azalea and ceanothus bushes and enlivening the groves with his brilliant colour; and on gravelly bars the spotted sandpiper is sometimes seen. Many woodpeckers dwell in the Valley; the familiar flicker, the Harris woodpecker and the species which so busily stores up acorns in the thick bark of the yellow pines.

The short, cold days of winter are also sweetened with the music and hopeful chatter of a considerable number of birds. No cheerier choir ever sang in snow. First and best of all is the water-ouzel, a dainty, dusky little bird about the size of a robin, that swings a sweet fluty song all winter and all summer, in storms and calms, sunshine and shadow, haunting the rapids and waterfalls with marvellous constancy, building his nest in the cleft of a rock bathed in spray. He is not web-footed, yet he dives fearlessly into foaming rapids, seeming to take the greater delight the more boisterous the stream, always as cheerful and calm as any linnet in a grove. All his gestures as he flits about amid the loud uproar of the falls bespeak the utmost simplicity and confidence – bird and stream one and inseparable. What a pair! yet they are well related. A finer bloom than the foam bell in an eddying pool is this little bird. We may miss the meaning of the loud-resounding torrent, but the flute-like voice of the bird – only love is in it.

A few robins, belated on their way down from the upper meadows, linger in the Valley and make out to spend the winter in comparative comfort, feeding on the mistletoe berries that grow on the oaks. In the depths of the great forests, on the high meadows, in the severest altitudes, they seem as much at home as in the fields and orchards about the busy habitations of man, ascending the Sierra as the snow melts, following the green footsteps of spring, until.in July or August the highest glacier meadows are reached on the summit of the Range. Then, after the short summer is over, and their work in cheering and sweetening these lofty wilds is done, they gradually make their way down again in accord with the weather, keeping below the snow-storms, lingering here and there to feed on huckleberries and frost-nipped wild cherries growing on the upper slopes. Thence down to the vineyards and orchards of the lowlands to spend the winter; entering the gardens of the great towns as well as parks and fields, where the blessed wanderers are too often slaughtered for food – surely a bad use to put so fine a musician to; better make stove wood of pianos to feed the kitchen fire.

The kingfisher winters in the Valley, and the flicker and, of course, the carpenter woodpecker, that lays up large stores of acorns in the bark of trees; wrens also, with a few brown and grey linnets, and flocks of the arctic bluebird, making lively pictures among the snow-laden mistletoe bushes. Flocks of pigeons are often seen, and about six species of ducks, as the river is never wholly frozen over. Among these are the mallard and the beautiful wood-duck, now less common on account of being so often shot at. Flocks of wandering geese used to visit the Valley in March and April, and perhaps do so still, driven down by hunger or stress of weather while on their way across the Range. When pursued by the hunters I have frequently seen them try to fly over the walls of the Valley until tired out and compelled to re-alight. Yosemite magnitudes seem to be as deceptive to geese as to men, for after circling to a considerable height and forming regular harrow-shaped ranks they would suddenly find themselves in danger of being dashed against the face of the cliff, much nearer the bottom than the top. Then turning in confusion with loud screams they would try again and again until exhausted and compelled to descend. I have occasionally observed large flocks on their travels crossing the summits of the Range at a height of 12,000 to 13,000ft. above the level of the sea, and even in so rare an atmosphere as this they seemed to be sustaining themselves without extra effort. Strong, however, as they are of wind and wing, they cannot fly over Yosemite walls, starting from the bottom.

A pair of golden eagles have lived in the Valley ever since I first visited it, hunting all winter along the northern cliffs and down the river canyon. Their nest is on a ledge of the cliff over which pours the Nevada Fall. Perched on the top of a dead spar, they were always interested observers of the geese when they were being shot at. I once noticed one of the geese compelled to leave the flock on account of being sorely wounded, although it still seemed to fly pretty well. Immediately the eagles pursued it and no doubt struck it down, although I did not see the result of the hunt. Anyhow, it flew past me up the Valley, closely pursued.

One wild, stormy winter morning after five feet of snow had fallen on the floor of the Valley and the flying flakes driven by a strong wind still thickened the air, making darkness like the approach of night, I sallied forth to see what I might learn and enjoy. It was impossible to go very far without the aid of snow-shoes, but I found no great difficulty in making my way to a part of the river where one of my ouzels lived. I found him at home busy about his breakfast, apparently unaware of anything uncomfortable in the weather. Presently he flew out to a stone against which the icy current was beating, and turning his back to the wind, sang as delightfully as a lark in springtime.

After spending an hour or two with my favourite, I made my way across the Valley, boring and wallowing through the loose snow, to learn as much as possible about the way the other birds were spending their time. In winter one can always find them because they are then restricted to the north side of the Valley, especially the Indian Canyon groves, which from their peculiar exposure are the warmest.

I found most of the robins cowering on the lee side of the larger branches of the trees, where the snow could not fall on them, while two or three of the more venturesome were making desperate efforts to get at the mistletoe berries by clinging to the underside of the snow-crowned masses, back downward, something like woodpeckers. Every now and then some of the loose snow was dislodged and sifted down on the hungry birds, sending them screaming back to their companions in the grove, shivering and muttering like cold, hungry children.

Some of the sparrows were busy scratching and pecking at the feet of the larger trees where the snow had been shed off, gleaning seeds and benumbed insects, joined now and then by a robin weary of his unsuccessful efforts to get at the snow-covered mistletoe berries. The brave woodpeckers were clinging to the snowless sides of the larger boles and overarching branches of the camp trees, making short flights from side to side of the grove, pecking now and then at the acorns they had stored in the bark, and chattering aimlessly as if unable to keep still, evidently putting in the time in a very dull way. The hardy nuthatches were threading the open furrows of the barks in their usual industrious manner and uttering their quaint notes, giving no evidence of distress. The Steller's jays were, of course, making more noise and stir than all the other birds combined; ever coming and going with loud bluster, screaming as if each had a lump of melting sludge in his throat, and taking good care to improve every opportunity afforded by the darkness and confusion of the storm to steal from the acorn stores of the woodpeckers. One of the golden eagles made an impressive picture as he stood bolt upright on the top of a tall pine-stump, braving the storm, with his back to the wind and a tuft of snow piled on his broad shoulders, a monument of passive endurance. Thus every storm-bound bird seemed more or less uncomfortable, if not in distress. The storm was reflected in every gesture, and not one cheerful note, not to say song, came from a single bill. Their cowering, joyless endurance offered striking contrasts to the spontaneous, irrepressible gladness of the ouzel, who could no more help giving out sweet song than a rose sweet fragrance. He must sing, though the heavens fall.

CHAPTER TEN

The South Dome

WITH THE exception of a few spires and pinnacles, the South Dome is the only rock about the Valley that is strictly inaccessible without artificial means, and its inaccessibility is expressed in severe terms. Nevertheless many a mountaineer, gazing admiringly, tried hard to invent a way to the top of its noble crown – all in vain, until in the year 1875, George Anderson, an indomitable Scotchman, undertook the adventure. The side facing Tenaya Canyon is an absolutely vertical precipice from the summit to a depth of about 1,600ft. and on the opposite side it is nearly vertical for about as great a depth. The southwest side presents a very steep and finely drawn curve from the top down a thousand feet or more, while on the northeast, where it is united with the Clouds' Rest Ridge, one may easily reach a point called the Saddle, about seven hundred feet below the summit. From the Saddle the Dome rises in a graceful curve a few degrees too steep for unaided climbing, besides being defended by overleaning ends of the concentric dome layers of the granite.

A year or two before Anderson gained the summit, John Conway, the master trail-builder of the Valley, and his little sons, who climbed smooth rocks like lizards, made a bold effort to reach the top by climbing barefooted up the grand curve with a rope which they fastened at irregular intervals by means of eye-bolts driven into joints of the rock. But finding that the upper part would require laborious drilling, they abandoned the attempt, glad to escape from the dangerous position they had reached, some 300ft. above the Saddle. Anderson began with Conway's old rope, which had been left in place, and resolutely drilled his way to the top, inserting eye-bolts five to six feet apart, and making his rope fast to each in succcession, resting his feet on the last bolt while he drilled a hole for the next above. Occasionally some irregularity in the curve, or slight foothold, would enable him to climb a few feet without a rope, which he would pass and begin drilling again, and thus the whole work was accomplished in a few days. From this slender beginning he proposed to construct a substantial stairway which he hoped to complete in time for the next year's travel, but while busy getting out timber for his stairway and dreaming of the wealth he hoped to gain from tolls, he was taken sick and died all alone in his little cabin.

On the 10th of November, after returning from a visit to Mount Shasta, a month or two after Anderson had gained the summit, I made haste to the Dome, not only for the pleasure of climbing, but to see what I might learn. The first winter stormclouds had blossomed and the mountains and all the high points about the Valley were mantled in fresh snow. I was, therefore, a little apprehensive of danger from the slipperiness of the rope and the rock.

Anderson himself tried to prevent me from making the attempt, refusing to believe that any one could climb his rope in the snow-muffled condition in which it then was. Moreover, the sky was overcast and solemn snow-clouds began to curl around the summit, and my late experiences on icy Shasta came to mind. But reflecting that I had matches in my pocket, and that a little fire-wood might be found, I concluded that in case of a storm the night could be spent on the Dome without suffering anything worth minding, no matter what the clouds might bring forth. I therefore pushed on and gained the top.

It was one of those brooding, changeful days that come between the Indian summer and winter, when the leaf colours have grown dim and the clouds come and go among the cliffs like living creatures looking for work: now hovering aloft, now caressing rugged rock-brows with great gentleness, or, wandering afar over the tops of the forests, touching the spires of fir and pine with their soft silken fringes as if trying to tell the glad news of the coming of snow.

The first view was perfectly glorious. A massive cloud of pure pearl luster, apparently as fixed and calm as the meadows and groves in the shadow beneath it, was arched across the Valley from wall to wall, one end resting on the grand abutment of El Capitan, the other on Cathedral Rock. A little later, as I stood on the tremendous verge overlooking Mirror Lake, a flock of smaller clouds, white as snow, came from the north, trailing their downy skirts over the dark forests, and entered the Valley with solemn god-like gestures through Indian Canyon and over the North Dome and Royal Arches, moving swiftly, yet with majestic deliberation. On they came, nearer and nearer, gathering and massing beneath my feet and filling the Tenaya Canyon. Then the sun shone free, lighting the pearly grey surface of the cloud-like sea and making it glow. Gazing, admiring, I was startled to see for the first time the rare optical phenomenon of the 'Spectre of the Brocken.' My shadow, clearly outlined, about half a mile long, lay upon this glorious white surface with startling effect. I walked back and forth, waved my arms and stuck all sorts of attitudes, to see every slightest movement enormously exaggerated. Considering that I have looked down so many times from mountain tops on seas of all sorts of clouds, it seems strange that I should have seen the 'Brocken Spectre' only this once. A grander surface and a grander standpoint, however, could hardly have been found in all the Sierra.

After this grand show the cloud-sea rose higher, wreathing the Dome, and for a short time submerging it, making darkness like night, and I began to think of looking for a camp ground in a cluster of dwarf pines. But soon the sun shone free again, the clouds, sinking lower and lower, gradually vanished, leaving the Valley with its Indian-summer colours apparently refreshed, while to the eastward the summit peaks, clad in new snow, towered along the horizon in glorious array.

Though apparently it is perfectly bald, there are four clumps of pines growing on the summit, representing three species, Pinus albicaulis, P. contorta and P. ponderosa, var. Jeffreyi – all three, of course, repressed and storm-beaten. The alpine spiræa grows here also and blossoms profusely with potentilla, erigeron, eriogonum, pentstemon, solidago, and an interesting species of onion, and four or five species of grasses and sedges. None of these differs in any respect from those of other summits of the same height, excepting the curious little narrow-leaved, waxen-bulbed onion, which I had not seen elsewhere.

Notwithstanding the enthusiastic eagerness of tourists to reach the crown of the Dome the views of the Valley from this lofty standpoint are less striking than from many other points comparatively low, chiefly on account of the foreshortening effect produced by looking down from so great a height. The North Dome is dwarfed almost beyond recognition, the grand sculpture of the Royal Arches is scarcely noticeable, and the whole range of walls on both sides seem comparatively low, especially when the Valley is flooded with noon sunshine; while the Dome itself, the most sublime feature of all the Yosemite views, is out of sight beneath one's feet. The view of Little Yosemite Valley is very fine, though inferior to one obtained from the base of the Starr King Cone, but the summit landscapes towards Mounts Ritter, Lyell, Dana, Conness and the Merced Group, are very effective and complete.

No one has attempted to carry out Anderson's plan of making the Dome accessible. For my part I should prefer leaving it in pure wildness, though, after all, no great damage could be done by tramping over it. The surface would be strewn with tin cans and bottles, but the winter gales would blow the rubbish away. Avalanches might strip off any sort of stairway or ladder that might be built. Blue jays and Clarke crows have trodden the Dome for many a day, and so have beetles and chipmunks, and Tissiack would hardly be more 'conquered' or spoiled should man be added to her list of visitors. His louder scream and heavier scrambling would not stir a line of her countenance.

When the sublime ice-floods of the glacial period poured down the flank of the Range over what is now Yosemite Valley, they were compelled to break through a dam of domes extending across from Mount Starr King to North Dome; and as the period began to draw near a close the shallowing ice-currents were divided and the South Dome was, perhaps, the first to emerge, burnished and shining like a mirror above the surface of the icy sea; and though it has sustained the wear and tear of the elements tens of thousands of years, it yet remains a telling monument of the action of the great glaciers that brought it to light. Its entire surface is still covered with glacial hieroglyphics whose interpretation is the reward of all who devoutly study them.

CHAPTER ELEVEN

The Ancient Yosemite Glaciers: How the Valley was Formed

ALL CALIFORNIA has been glaciated, the low plains and valleys as well as the mountains. Traces of an ice-sheet, thousands of feet in thickness, beneath whose heavy folds the present landscapes have been moulded, may be found everywhere, though glaciers now exist only among the peaks of the High

Sierra. No other mountain chain on this or any other of the continents that I
have seen is so rich as the Sierra in bold, striking, well-preserved glacial
monuments. Indeed, every feature is more or less tellingly glacial. Not a
peak, ridge, dome, canyon, yosemite, lake-basin, stream or forest will you
see that does not in some way explain the past existence and modes of action
of flowing, grinding, sculpturing, soil-making, scenery-making ice. For, notwithstanding the post-glacial agents – the air, rain, snow, frost, river,
avalanche, etc. – have been at work upon the greater portion of the Range for
tens of thousands of stormy years, each engraving its own characters more
and more deeply over those of the ice, the latter are so enduring and so
heavily emphasized, they still rise in sublime relief, clear and legible, through
every after-inscription. The landscapes of North Greenland, Antarctica, and
some of those of our own Alaska, are still being fashioned beneath a slow-
crawling mantle of ice, from a quarter of a mile to probably more than a mile
in thickness, presenting noble illustrations of the ancient condition of
California, when its sublime scenery lay hidden in process of formation. On
the Himalaya, the mountains of Norway and Switzerland, the Caucasus, and
on most of those of Alaska, their ice-mantle has been melted down into
separate glaciers that flow river-like through the valleys, illustrating a similar
past condition in the Sierra, when every canyon and valley was the channel of
an ice-stream, all of which may be easily traced back to their fountains, where
some sixty-five or seventy of their topmost residual branches still linger
beneath protecting mountain shadows.

The change from one to another of those glacial conditions was slow as we
count time. When the great cycle of snowy years, called the Glacial Period,
was nearly complete in California, the ice-mantle, wasting from season to
season faster than it was renewed, began to withdraw from the lowlands and
gradually became shallower everywhere. Then the highest of the Sierra domes
and dividing ridges, containing distinct glaciers between them, began to
appear above the icy sea. These first river-like glaciers remained united in one
continuous sheet toward the summit of the Range for many centuries. But as
the snow-fall diminished, and the climate became milder, this upper part of
the ice-sheet was also in turn separated into smaller distinct glaciers, and
these again into still smaller ones, while at the same time all were growing
shorter and shallower, though fluctuations of the climate now and then
occurred that brought their receding ends to a standstill, or even enabled
them to advance for a few tens or hundreds of years.

Meanwhile, hardy, home-seeking plants and animals, after long waiting,
flocked to their appointed places, pushing bravely on higher and higher, along
every sun-warmed slope, closely following the retreating ice, which, like
shreds of summer clouds, at length vanished from the new-born mountains,
leaving them in all their main, telling features, nearly as we find them now.

Tracing the way of glaciers, learning how Nature sculptures mountain-
waves in making scenery-beauty that so mysteriously influences every human
being, is glorious work.

The most striking and attractive of the glacial phenomena in the upper
Yosemite region are the polished glacier pavements, because they are so

beautiful, and their beauty is of so rare a kind, so unlike any portion of the loose, deeply weathered lowlands where people make homes and earn their bread. They are simply flat or gentle undulating areas of hard resisting granite, which present the unchanged surface upon which with enormous pressure the ancient glaciers flowed. They are found in most perfect condition in the subalpine region, at an elevation of from eight thousand to nine thousand feet. Some are miles in extent, only slightly interrupted by spots that have given way to the weather, while the best preserved portions reflect the sunbeams like calm water or glass, and shine as if polished afresh every day, notwithstanding they have been exposed to corroding rains, dew, frost, and snow measureless thousands of years.

The attention of wandering hunters and prospectors, who see so many mountain wonders, is seldom commanded by other glacial phenomena, moraines however regular and artificial-looking, canyons however deep or strangely modelled, rocks however high; but when they come to these shining pavements they stop and stare in wondering admiration, kneel again and again to examine the brightest spots, and try hard to account for their mysterious shining smoothness. They may have seen the winter avalanches of snow descending in awful majesty through the woods, scouring the rocks and sweeping away like weeds the trees that stood in their way, but conclude that this cannot be the work of avalanches, because the scratches and fine polished striæ show that the agent, whatever it was, moved along the sides of high rocks and ridges and up over the tops of them as well as down their slopes. Neither can they see how water may possibly have been the agent, for they find the same strange polish upon ridges and domes thousands of feet above the reach of any conceivable flood. Of all the agents of whose work they know anything, only the wind seems capable of moving across the face of the country in the directions indicated by the scratches and grooves. The Indian name of Lake Tenaya is 'Pyweak' – the lake of shining rocks. One of the Yosemite tribe, Indian Tom came to me and asked if I could tell him what had made the Tenaya rocks so smooth. Even dogs and horses, when first led up the mountains, study geology to this extent that they gaze wonderingly at the strange brightness of the ground and smell it, and place their feet cautiously upon it as if afraid of falling or sinking.

In the production of this admirable hard finish, the glaciers in many places flowed with a pressure of more than a thousand tons to the square yard, planing down granite, slate, and quartz alike, and bringing out the veins and crystals of the rocks with beautiful distinctness. Over large areas below like the sources of the Tuolumne and Merced the granite is porphyritic; feldspar crystals an inch or two in length in many places form the greater part of the rock, and these, when planed off level with the general surface, give rise to a beautiful mosaic on which the happy sunbeams plash and glow in passionate enthusiasm. Here lies the brightest of all the Sierra landscapes. The Range both to the north and south of this region was, perhaps, glaciated about as heavily, but because the rocks are less resisting, their polished surfaces have mostly given way to the weather, leaving only small imperfect patches. The lowest remnants of the old glacial surface occur at an elevation of from 3,000 to 5,000ft. above the sea-level, and twenty to thirty miles below the axis of the Range. The short, steeply inclined canyons of the eastern flank also contain enduring, brilliantly striated and polished rocks, but these are less magnificent than those of the broad western flank.

One of the best general views of the brightest and best of the Yosemite park landsapes that every Yosemite tourist should see, is to be had from the top of Fairview Dome, a lofty conoidal rock near Cathedral Peak that long ago I named the Tuolumne Glacier Monument, one of the most striking and best preserved of the domes. Its burnished crown is about 1,500ft. above the Tuolumne Meadows and 10,000 above the sea. At first sight it seems inaccessible, though a good climber will find it may be scaled on the south side. About half-way up you will find it so steep that there is danger of slipping, but feldspar crystals, two or three inches long, of which the rock is full, having offered greater resistance to atmospheric erosion than the mass of the rock in which they are imbedded, have been brought into slight relief in some places, roughening the surface here and there, and affording helping footholds.

The summit is burnished and scored like the sides and base, the scratches and striæ indicating that the mighty Tuolumne Glacier swept over it as if it were only a mere boulder in the bottom of its channel. The pressure it withstood must have been enormous. Had it been less solidly built it would have been carried away, ground into moraine fragments, like the adjacent rock in which it lay embedded; for, great as it is, it is only a hard residual knot like the Yosemite domes, brought into relief by the removal of less resisting rock about it; an illustration of the survival of the strongest and most favourably situated.

Hardly less wonderful is the resistance it has offered to the trying mountain weather since first its crown rose above the icy sea. The whole quantity of post-glacial wear and tear it has suffered has not degraded it a hundreth of an inch, as may readily be shown by the polished portions of the surface. A few erratic boulders, nicely poised on its crown, tell an interesting story. They came from the summit-peaks twelve miles away, drifting like chips on the frozen sea, and were stranded here when the top of the monument emerged from the ice, while their companions, whose positions chanced to be above the slopes of the sides where they could not find rest, were carried farther on by falling back on the shallowing ice current.

The general view from the summit consists of a sublime assemblage of ice-born rocks and mountains, long wavering ridges, meadows, lakes, and forest-covered moraines, hundreds of square miles of them. The lofty summit-peaks rise grandly along the sky to the east, the grey pillared slopes of the Hoffman Range toward the west, and a billowy sea of shining rocks like the Monument, some of them almost as high and which from their peculiar sculpture seem to be rolling westward in the middle ground, something like breaking waves. Immediately beneath you are the Big Tuolumne Meadows, smooth lawns with large breadths of woods on either side, and watered by the young Tuolumne River, rushing cool and clear from its many snow and ice-fountains. Nearly all the upper part of the basin of the Tuolumne Glacier is in sight, one of the greatest and most influential of all the Sierra ice-rivers. Lavishly flooded by many a noble affluent from the ice-laden flanks of Mounts Dana, Lyell, McClure, Gibbs, Conness, it poured its majestic outflowing current full against the end of the Hoffman Range, which divided and deflected it to right and left, just as a river of water is divided against an island in the middle of its channel. Two distinct glaciers were thus formed, one of which flowed through the great Tuolumne Canyon and Hetch Hetchy Valley, while the other swept upward in a deep current two miles wide across the divide, five hundred feet high between the basins of the Tuolumne and Merced, into the Tenaya Basin, and thence down through the Tenaya Canyon and Yosemite.

The map-like distinctness and freshness of this glacial landscape cannot fail to excite the attention of every beholder, no matter how little of its scientific significance may be recognized. These bald, westward-leaning rocks, with their rounded backs and shoulders toward the glacier fountains of the summit-mountains, and their split, angular fronts looking in the opposite direction, explain the tremendous grinding force with which the ice-flood passed over them, and also the direction of its flow. And the mountain peaks around the sides of the upper general Tuolumne Basin, with their sharp unglaciated summits and polished round sides, indicate the height to which the glaciers rose; while the numerous moraines, curving and swaying in beautiful lines, mark the boundaries of the main trunk and its tributaries as they existed toward the close of the glacial winter. None of the commercial highways of the land or sea, marked with buoys and lamps, fences and guide-boards, is so unmistakably indicated as are these broad, shining trails of the vanished Tuolumne Glacier and its far-reaching tributaries.

I should like now to offer some nearer views of a few characteristic specimens of these wonderful old ice-streams, though it is not easy to make a selection from so vast a system intimately interblended. The main branches of the Merced Glacier are, perhaps, best suited to our purpose, because their basins, full of telling inscriptions, are the ones most attractive and accessible to the Yosemite visitors who like to look beyond the valley walls. They number five, and may well be called Yosemite glaciers, since they were the agents Nature used in developing and fashioning the grand Valley. The names I have given them are, beginning with the northernmost, Yosemite Creek, Hoffman, Tenaya, South Lyell, and Illilouette Glaciers. These all converged in admirable poise around from northeast to southeast, welded themselves together into the main Yosemite Glacier, which, grinding gradually deeper, swept down through the Valley, receiving small tributaries on its way from the Indian, Sentinel and Pohono Canyons; and at length flowed out of the Valley, and on down the Range in a general westerly direction. At the time that the tributaries mentioned above were well defined as to their boundaries, the upper portion of the valley walls, and the highest rocks about them, such as the Domes, the uppermost of the Three Brothers and the Sentinel, rose above the surface of the ice. But during the Valley's earlier history, all its rocks, however lofty, were buried beneath a continuous sheet, which swept on above and about them like the wind, the upper portion of the current flowing steadily, while the lower portion went mazing and swedging down in the crooked and dome-blocked canyons toward the head of the Valley.

Every glacier of the Sierra fluctuated in width and depth and length, and consequently in degree of individuality, down to the latest glacial days. It must, therefore, be borne in mind that the following description of the Yosemite glaciers applies only to their separate condition, and to that phase of their separate condition that they presented toward the close of the glacial period after most of their work was finished, and all the more telling features of the Valley and the adjacent region were brought into relief.

The comparatively level, many-fountained Yosemite Creek Glacier was about fourteen miles in length by four or five in width, and from five hundred to a thousand feet deep. Its principal tributaries, drawing their sources from the northern spurs of the Hoffman Range, at first pursued a westerly course; then, uniting with each other, and a series of short affluents from the western rim of the basin, the trunk thus formed swept around to the southward in a magnificent curve, and poured its ice over the north wall of Yosemite in cascades about two miles wide. This broad and comparatively shallow glacier formed a sort of crawling, wrinkled ice-cloud, that gradually became more regular in shape and river-like as it grew older. Encircling peaks began to overshadow its highest fountains, rock islets rose here and there amid its ebbing currents, and its picturesque banks, adorned with domes and round-backed ridges, extended in massive grandeur down to the brink of the Yosemite walls.

In the meantime the chief Hoffman tributaries, slowly receding to the shelter of the shadows covering their fountains, continued to live and work independently, spreading soil, deepening lake-basins and giving finishing touches to the sculpture in general. At length these also vanished, and the whole basin is now full of light. Forests flourish luxuriantly upon its ample moraines, lakes and meadows shine and bloom amid its polished domes, and a thousand gardens adorn the banks of its streams

It is to the great width and even slope of the Yosemite Creek Glacier that we owe the unrivalled height and sheerness of the Yosemite Falls. For had the positions of the ice-fountains and the structure of the rocks been such as to cause down-thrusting concentration of the Glacier as it approached the Valley, then, instead of a high vertical fall we should have had a long slanting cascade, which after all would perhaps have been as beautiful and interesting, if we only had a mind to see it so.

The short, comparatively swift-flowing Hoffman Glacier, whose fountains extend along the south slopes of the Hoffman Range, offered a striking contrast to the one just described. The erosive energy of the latter was diffused over a wide field of sunken, boulder-like domes and ridges. The Hoffman Glacier, on the contrary, moved right ahead on a comparatively even surface, making a descent of nearly five thousand feet in five miles, steadily contracting and deepening its current, and finally united with the Tenaya Glacier as one of its most influential tributaries in the development and sculpture of the great Half Dome, North Dome and the rocks adjacent to them about the head of the Valley.

The story of its death is not unlike that of its companion already described, though the declivity of its channel, and its uniform exposure to sun-heat prevented any considerable portion of its current from becoming torpid, lingering only well up on the mountain slopes to finish their sculpture and encircle them with a zone of moraine soil for forests and gardens. Nowhere in all this wonderful region will you find more beautiful trees and shrubs and flowers covering the traces of ice.

The rugged Tenaya Glacier wildly crevassed here and there above the ridges it had to cross, instead of drawing its sources direct from the summit of the Range, formed, as we have seen, one of the outlets of the great Tuolumne Glacier, issuing from this noble fountain like a river from a lake, two miles wide, about fourteen miles long, and from 1,500 to 2,000ft. deep.

In leaving the Tuolumne region it crossed over the divide, as mentioned above, between the Tuolumne and Tenaya basins, making an ascent of five hundred feet. Hence, after contracting its wide current and receiving a strong affluent from the fountains about Cathedral Peak, it poured its massive flood over the northeastern rim of its basin in splendid cascades. Then, crushing heavily against the Clouds' Rest Ridge, it bore down upon the Yosemite domes with concentrated energy.

Toward the end of the ice period, while its Hoffman companion continued to grind rock-meal for coming plants, the main trunk became torpid, and vanished, exposing wide areas of rolling rock-waves and glistening pavements, on whose channelless surface water ran wild and free. And because the trunk vanished almost simultaneously throughout its whole extent, terminal moraines are found in its canyon channel; nor, since its walls are, in most places, too steeply inclined to admit of the deposition of moraine matter, do we find much of the two main laterals. The lowest of its residual glaciers lingered beneath the shadow of the Yosemite Half Dome; others along the base of Coliseum Peak above Lake Tenaya and along the precipitous wall extending from the lake to the Big Tuolumne Meadows. The latter, on account of the uniformity and continuity of their protecting shadows, formed moraines of considerable length and regularity that are liable to be mistaken for portions of the left lateral of the Tuolumne tributary glacier.

Spend all the time you can spare or steal on the tracks of this grand old glacier, charmed and enchanted by its magnificent canyon, lakes and cascades and resplendent glacier pavements.

The Nevada Glacier was longer and more symmetrical than the last, and the only one of the Merced system whose sources extended directly back to the main summits on the axis of the Range. Its numerous fountains were ranged side by side in three series, at an elevation of from 10,000 to 12,000ft. above the sea. The first, on the right side of the basin, extended from the Matterhorn to Cathedral Peak; that on the left through the Merced group, and these two parallel series were united by a third that extended around the head of the basin in a direction at right angles to the others.

The three ranges of high peaks and ridges that supplied the snow for these fountains, together with the Clouds' Rest Ridge, nearly inclose a rectangular basin, that was filled with a massive sea of ice, leaving an outlet toward the west through which flowed the main trunk glacier, three-fourths of a mile to a mile and a half wide, fifteen miles long, and from 1,000 to 1,500ft. deep, and entered Yosemite between the Half Dome and Mount Starr King.

Could we have visited Yosemite Valley at this period of its history, we should have found its ice cascades vastly more glorious than their tiny water representatives of the present day. One of the grandest of these was formed by that portion of the Nevada Glacier that poured over the shoulder of the Half Dome.

This glacier, as a whole, resembled an oak, with a gnarled swelling base and wide-spreading branches. Picturesque rocks of every conceivable form adorned its banks, among which glided the numerous tributaries, mottled with black and red and grey boulders, from the fountain peaks, while ever and anon, as the deliberate centuries passed away, dome after dome raised its burnished crown above the ice-flood to enrich the slowly opening landscapes.

The principal moraines occur in short irregular sections along the sides of the canyons, their fragmentary condition being due to interruptions caused by portions of the sides of the canyon walls being too steep for moraine matter to lie on, and to down-sweeping torrents and avalanches. The left lateral of the trunk may be traced about five miles from the mouth of the first main tributary to the Illilouette Canyon. The corresponding section of the right lateral, extending from Cathedral tributary to the Half Dome, is more complete because of the more favourable character of the north side of the canyon. A short side-glacier came in against it from the slopes of Clouds' Rest; but being fully exposed to the sun, it was melted long before the main trunk, allowing the latter to deposit this portion of its moraine undisturbed. Some conception of the size and appearance of this fine moraine may be gained by following the Clouds' Rest trail from Yosemite, which crosses it obliquely and conducts past several sections made by streams. Slate boulders may be seen that must have come from the Lyell group, twelve miles distant. But the bulk of the moraine is composed of porphyritic granite derived from Feldspar and Cathedral Valleys.

On the sides of the moraines we find a series of terraces, indicating fluctuations in the level of the glacier, caused by variations of snow-fall, temperature, etc., showing that the climate of the glacial period was diversified by cycles of milder or stormier seasons similar to those of post-glacial time.

After the depth of the main trunk diminished to about five hundred feet, the greater portion became torpid, as is shown by the moraines, and lay dying in its crooked channel like a wounded snake, maintaining for a time a feeble squirming motion in places of exceptional depth, or where the bottom of the canyon was more deeply inclined. The numerous fountain-wombs, however, continued fruitful long after the trunk had vanished, giving rise to an imposing array of short residual glaciers extending around the rim of the general basin a distance of nearly twenty-four miles. Most of these have but recently succumbed to the new climate, dying in turn as determined by elevation, size, and exposure, leaving only a few feeble survivors beneath the coolest shadows, which are now slowly completing the sculpture of one of the noblest of the Yosemite basins.

The comparatively shallow glacier that at this time filled the Illilouette

Basin, though once far from shallow, more resembled a lake than a river of ice, being nearly half as wide as it was long. Its greatest length was about ten miles, and its depth perhaps nowhere much exceeded 1,000ft. Its chief fountains, ranged along the west side of the Merced group, at an elevation of about 10,000ft., gave birth to fine tributaries that flowed in a westerly direction, and united in the centre of the basin. The broad trunk at first flowed northwestward, then curved to the northward, deflected by the lofty wall forming its western bank, and finally united with the grand Yosemite trunk, opposite Glacier Point.

All the phenomena relating to glacial action in this basin are remarkably simple and orderly, on account of the sheltered positions occupied by its ice-fountains, with reference to the disturbing effects of larger glaciers from the axis of the main Range earlier in the period. From the eastern base of the Starr King cone you may obtain a fine view of the principal moraines sweeping grandly out into the middle of the basin from the shoulders of the peaks, between which the ice-fountains lay. The right lateral of the tributary, which took its rise between Red and Merced Mountains, measures two hundred and fifty feet in height at its upper extremity, and displays three well-defined terraces, similar to those of the South Lyell Glacier. The comparative smoothness of the uppermost terrace shows that it is considerably more ancient than the others, many of the boulders of which it is composed having crumbled. A few miles to the westward, this moraine has an average slope of twenty-seven degrees, and an elevation above the bottom of the channel of six hundred and sixty feet. Near the middle of the main basin, just where the regularly formed medial and lateral moraines flatten out and disappear, there is a remarkably smooth field of gravel, planted with arctostaphylos, that looks at the distance of a mile like a delightful meadow. Stream sections show the gravel deposit to be composed of the same material as the moraines, but finer, and more water-worn from the action of converging torrents issuing from the tributary glaciers after the trunk was melted. The southern boundary of the basin is a strikingly perfect wall, grey on the top, and white down the sides and at the base with snow, in which many a crystal brook takes rise. The northern boundary is made up of smooth undulating masses of grey granite, that lift here and there into beautiful domes of which the Starr King cluster is the finest, while on the east tower the majestic fountain-peaks with wide canyons and *névé* amphitheatres between them, whose variegated rocks show out gloriously against the sky.

The ice-ploughs of this charming basin, ranged side by side in orderly gangs, furrowed the rocks with admirable uniformity, producing irrigating channels for a brood of wild streams, and abundance of rich soil adapted to every requirement of garden and grove. No other section of the Yosemite uplands is in so perfect a state of glacial cultivation. Its domes, and peaks, and swelling rock-waves, however majestic in themselves, are yet submissively subordinate to the garden centre. The other basins we have been describing are combinations of sculptured rocks, embellished with gardens and groves; the Illilouette is one grand garden and forest embellished with rocks, each of the five beautiful in its own way, and all as harmoniously related as are the five petals of a flower. After uniting in the Yosemite Valley, and expending the down-thrusting energy derived from their combined weight and the declivity of their channels, the grand trunk flowed on through and out of the Valley. In effecting its exit a considerable ascent was made, traces of which may still be seen on the abraded rocks at the lower end of the Valley, while the direction pursued after leaving the Valley is surely indicated by the immense lateral moraines extending from the ends of the walls at an elevation of from 1,500 to 1,800ft. The right lateral moraine was disturbed by a large tributary glacier that occupied the basin of Cascade Creek, causing considerable complication in its structure. The left is simple in form for several miles of its length, or to the point where a tributary came in from the southeast. But both are greatly obscured by the forests and underbrush growing upon them, and by the denuding action of rains and melting snows, etc. It is, therefore, the less to be wondered at that these moraines, made up of material derived from the distant fountain-mountains, and from the Valley itself, were not sooner recognized.

The ancient glacier systems of the Tuolumne, San Joaquin, Kern, and Kings River Basins were developed on a still grander scale and are so replete with interest that the most sketchy outline descriptions of each, with the works they have accomplished, would fill many a volume. Therefore I can do but little more than invite everybody who is free to go and see for himself.

The action of flowing ice, whether in the form of river-like glaciers or broad mantles, especially the part it played in sculpturing the earth, is as yet but little understood. Water rivers work openly where people dwell, and so does the rain, and the sea, thundering on all the shores of the world; and the universal ocean of air, though invisible, speaks aloud in a thousand voices, and explains its modes of working and its power. But glaciers, back in their white solitudes, work apart from men, exerting their tremendous energies in silence and darkness. Outspread, spirit-like, they brood above the predestined landscapes, work on unwearied through immeasureable ages, until, in the fullness of time, the mountains and valleys are brought forth, channels furrowed for rivers, basins made for lakes and meadows, and arms of the sea, soils spread for forests and fields; then they shrink and vanish like summer clouds.

CHAPTER TWELVE

How Best to Spend One's Yosemite Time

ONE-DAY EXCURSIONS NO. 1.

IF I were so time-poor as to have only one day to spend in Yosemite I should start at daybreak, say at three o'clock in midsummer, with a pocketful of any sort of dry breakfast stuff, for Glacier Point, Sentinel Dome, the head of Illilouette Fall, Nevada Fall, the top of Liberty Cap, Vernal Fall and the wild boulder-choked River Canyon. The trail leaves the Valley at the base of the Sentinel Rock, and as you slowly saunter from point to point along its many accommodating zigzags nearly all the Valley rocks and falls are seen in striking, ever-changing combinations. At an elevation of about five hundred feet a particularly fine, wide-sweeping view down the Valley is obtained, past the sheer face of the Sentinel and between the Cathedral Rocks and El Capitan. At a height of about 1,500ft. the great Half Dome comes full in sight, overshadowing every other feature of the Valley to the eastward. From Glacier Point you look down 3,000ft. over the edge of its sheer face to the meadows and groves and innumerable yellow pine spires, with the meandering river sparkling and spangling through the midst of them. Across the Valley a great telling view is presented of the Royal Arches, North Dome, Indian Canyon, Three Brothers and El Capitan, with the dome-paved basin of Yosemite Creek and Mount Hoffman in the background. To the eastward, the Half Dome close beside you looking higher and more wonderful than ever; southeastward the Starr King, girdled with silver firs, and the spacious garden-like basin of the Illilouette and its deeply sculptured fountain-peaks, called 'The Merced Group'; and beyond all, marshalled along the eastern horizon, the icy summits on the axis of the Range and broad swaths of forests growing on ancient moraines, while the Nevada, Vernal and Yosemite Falls are not only full in sight but are distinctly heard as if one were standing beside them in their spray.

The views from the summit of Sentinel Dome are still more extensive and telling. Eastward the crowds of peaks at the head of the Merced, Tuolumne and San Joaquin Rivers are presented in bewildering array; westward, the vast forests, yellow foothills and the broad San Joaquin plains and the Coast Ranges, hazy and dim in the distance.

From Glacier Point go down the trail into the lower end of the Illilouette basin, cross Illilouette Creek and follow it to the Fall where from an outjutting rock at its head you will get a fine view of its rejoicing waters and wild canyon and the Half Dome. Thence returning to the trail follow it to the head of the Nevada Fall. Linger here an hour or two, for not only have you glorious views of the wonderful fall, but of its wild, leaping, exulting rapids and, greater than all, the stupendous scenery into the heart of which the white passionate river goes wildly thundering, surpassing everything of its kind in the world. After an unmeasured hour or so of this glory, all your body aglow, nerve currents flashing through you never before felt, go to the top of the Liberty Cap, only a glad saunter now that your legs as well as head and heart are awake and rejoicing with everything. The Liberty Cap, a companion of the Half Dome, is sheer and inaccessible on three of its sides but on the east a gentle, ice-burnished, juniper-dotted slope extends to the summit where other wonderful views are displayed where all are wonderful: the south side and shoulders of Half Dome and Clouds' Rest, the beautiful Little Yosemite Valley and its many domes, the Starr King cluster of domes, Sentinel Dome, Glacier Point, and, perhaps the most tremendously impressive of all, the views of the hopper-shaped canyon of the river from the head of the Nevada Fall to the head of the Valley.

Returning to the trail you descend between the Nevada Fall and the Liberty Cap with fine side views of both the fall and the rock, pass on through clouds of spray and along the rapids to the head of the Vernal Fall, about a mile below the Nevada. Linger here if night is still distant, for views of this favourite fall and the stupendous rock scenery about it. Then descend a stairway by its side, follow a dim trail through its spray, and a plain one along the border of the boulder-dashed rapids and so back to the wide, tranquil Valley.

ONE-DAY EXCURSIONS NO. 2.

Another grand one-day excursion is to the Upper Yosemite Fall, the top of the highest of the Three Brothers, called Eagle Peak on the Geological Survey maps; the brow of El Capitan; the head of the Ribbon Fall; across the beautiful Ribbon Creek Basin; and back to the Valley by the Big Oak Flat wagon-road.

The trail leaves the Valley on the east side of the largest of the earthquake taluses immediately opposite the Sentinel Rock and as it passes within a few rods of the foot of the great fall, magnificent views are obtained as you approach it and pass through its spray, though when the snow is melting fast you will be well drenched. From the foot of the Fall the trail zigzags up a narrow canyon between the fall and a plain mural cliff that is burnished here and there by glacial action.

You should stop a while on a flat iron-fenced rock a little below the head of the fall beside the enthusiastic throng of starry comet-like waters to learn something of their strength, their marvellous variety of forms, and above all, their glorious music, gathered and composed from the snow-storms, hail-, rain- and wind-storms that have fallen on their glacier-sculptured, domey, ridgy basin. Refreshed and exhilarated, you follow your trail-way through silver fir and pine woods to Eagle Peak, where the most comprehensive of all the views to be had on the northwall heights are displayed. After an hour or two of gazing, dreaming, studying the tremendous topography, etc., trace the rim of the Valley to the grand El Capitan ridge and go down to its brow, where you will gain everlasting impressions of Nature's steadfastness and power combined with ineffable fineness of beauty.

Dragging yourself away, go to the head of the Ribbon Fall, thence across the beautiful Ribbon Creek Basin to the Big Oak Flat stage-road, and down its fine grades to the Valley, enjoying glorious Yosemite scenery all the way to the foot of El Capitan and your camp.

TWO-DAY EXCURSIONS NO. 1.

For a two-day trip I would go straight to Mount Hoffman, spend the night on the summit, next morning go down by May Lake to Tenaya Lake and return to the Valley by Clouds' Rest and the Nevada and Vernal Falls. As on the foregoing excursion, you leave the Valley by the Yosemite Falls trail and follow it to the Tioga wagon-road, a short distance east of Porcupine Flat.

From that point push straight up to the summit. Mount Hoffman is a mass of grey granite that rises almost in the centre of the Yosemite Park, about eight or ten miles in a straight line from the Valley. Its southern slopes are low and easily climbed, and adorned here and there with castle-like crumbling piles and long jagged crests that look like artificial masonry; but on the north side it is abruptly precipitous and banked with lasting snow. Most of the broad summit is comparatively level and thick sown with crystals, quartz, mica, hornblende, feldspar, granite, zircon, tourmaline, etc., weathered out and strewn closely and loosely as if they had been sown broadcast. Their radiance is fairly dazzling in sunlight, almost hiding the multitude of small flowers that grow among them. At first sight, only these radiant crystals are likely to be noticed, but looking closely you discover a multitude of very small gilias phloxes, mimulus, etc., many of them with more petals than leaves. On the borders of little streams larger plants flourish – lupines, daisies, asters, goldenrods, hairbell, mountain columbine, potentilla, astragalus and a few gentians; with charming heathworts – bryanthus, cassiope, kalmia, vaccinium in boulder-fringing rings or bank covers. You saunter among crystals and flowers as if you were walking among stars. From the summit nearly all the Yosemite Park is displayed like a map: forests, lakes, meadows, and snowy peaks. Northward lies Yosemite's wide basin with its domes and small lakes, shining like larger crystals; eastward the rocky, meadowy Tuolumne region, bounded by its snowy peaks in glorious array; southward Yosemite and westward the vast forest. On no other Yosemite mountain are you more likely to linger. You will find it a magnificent sky camp. Clumps of dwarf pine and mountain hemlock will furnish resin roots and branches for fuel and light, and the rills, sparkling water. Thousands of the little plant people will gaze at your camp-fire with the crystals and stars, companions and guardians as you lie at rest in the heart of the vast serene night.

The most telling of all the wide Hoffman views is the basin of the Tuolumne with its meadows, forests and hundreds of smooth rock-waves that appear to be coming rolling on towards you like high heaving waves ready to break, and beyond these the great mountains. But best of all are the dawn and the sunrise. No mountain top could be better placed for this most glorious of mountain views – to watch and see the deepening colours of the dawn and the sunbeams streaming through the snowy High Sierra passes, awakening the lakes and crystals, the chilled plant people and winged people, and making everything shine and sing in pure glory.

With your heart aglow, spangling Lake Tenaya and Lake May will beckon you away for walks on their ice-burnished shores. Leave Tenaya at the west and cross to the south side of the outlet, and gradually work your way up in an almost straight south direction to the summit of the divide between Tenaya Creek and the main upper Merced River or Nevada Creek and follow the divide to Clouds' Rest. After a glorious view from the crest of this lofty granite wave you will find a trail on its western end that will lead you down past Nevada and Vernal Falls to the Valley in good time, provided you left your Hoffman sky camp early.

TWO-DAY EXCURSIONS NO. 2.

Another grand two-day excursion is the same as the first of the one-day trips, as far as the head of Illilouette Fall. From there trace the beautiful stream up through the heart of its magnificent forests and gardens to the canyons between the Red and Merced Peaks, and pass the night where I camped forty-one years ago. Early next morning visit the small glacier on the north side of Merced Peak, the first of the sixty-five that I discovered in the Sierra.

Glacial phenomena in the Illilouette Basin are on the grandest scale, and in the course of my explorations I found that the canyon and moraines between the Merced and Red Mountains were the most interesting of them all. The path of the vanished glacier shone in many places as if washed with silver, and pushing up the canyon on this bright road I passed lake after lake in solid basins of granite and many a meadow along the canyon stream that links them together. The main lateral moraines that bound the view below the canyon are from a hundred to nearly two hundred feet high and wonderfully regular, like artificial embankments, covered with a magnificent growth of silver fir and pine. But this garden and forest luxuriance is speedily left behind, and patches of bryanthus, cassiope and arctic willows begin to appear. The small lakes which a few miles down the Valley are so richly bordered with flowery meadows have at an elevation of 10,000ft. only small brown mats of carex, leaving bare rocks around more than half their shores. Yet, strange to say, amid all this arctic repression the mountain pine on ledges and buttresses of Red Mountain seems to find the climate best suited to it. Some specimens that I have measured were over a hundred feet high and twenty-four feet in circumference, showing hardly a trace of severe storms, looking as fresh and vigorous as the giants of the lower zones. Evening came on just as I got fairly into the main canyon. It is about a mile wide and a little less than two miles long. The crumbling spurs of Red Mountain bound it on the north, the sombre cliffs of Merced Mountain on the south and a deeply-serrated, splintered ridge curving around from mountain to mountain shuts it in on the east. My camp was on the brink of one of the lakes in a thicket of mountain hemlock, partly sheltered from the wind. Early next morning I set out to trace the ancient glacier to its head. Passing around the north shore of my camp lake I followed the main stream from one lakelet to another. The dwarf pines and hemlocks disappeared and the stream was bordered with icicles. The main lateral moraines that extend from the mouth of the canyon are continued in straggling masses along the walls. Tracing the stream back to the highest of its little lakes, I noticed a deposit of fine grey mud, something like the mud worn from a grindstone. This suggested its glacial origin, for the stream that was carrying it issued from a raw-looking moraine that seemed to be in process of formation. It is from sixty to over a hundred feet high in front, with a slope of about thirty-eight degrees. Climbing to the top of it, I discovered a very small but well-characterized glacier swooping down from the shadowy cliffs of the mountain to its terminal moraine. The ice appeared on all the lower portion of the glacier; farther up it was covered with snow. The uppermost crevasse or 'bergeschrund' was from twelve to fourteen feet wide. The melting snow and ice formed a network of rills that ran gracefully down the surface of the glacier, merrily singing in their shining channels. After this discovery I made excursions over all the High Sierra and discovered that what at first sight looked like snowfields were in great part glaciers which were completing the sculpture of the summit peaks.

Rising early – which will be easy, as your bed will be rather cold and you will not be able to sleep much anyhow – after visiting the glacier, climb the Red Mountain and enjoy the magnificent views from the summit. I counted forty lakes from one standpoint on this mountain, and the views to the westward over the Illilouette Basin, the most superbly forested of all the basins whose waters drain into Yosemite, and those of the Yosemite rocks, especially the Half Dome and the upper part of the north wall, are very fine. But, of course, far the most imposing view is the vast array of snowy peaks along the axis of the Range. Then from the top of this peak, light and free and exhilarated with mountain air and mountain beauty, you should run lightly down the northern slope of the mountain, descend the canyon between Red and Grey Mountains, thence northward along the bases of Grey Mountain and Mount Clark and go down into the head of Little Yosemite, and thence down past the Nevada and Vernal Falls to the Valley, a truly glorious two-day trip!

A THREE-DAY EXCURSION

The best three-day excursion, as far as I can see, is the same as the first of the two-day trips until you reach Lake Tenaya. There instead of returning to the Valley, follow the Tioga road around the northwest side of the lake, over to the Tuolumne Meadows and up to the west base of Mount Dana. Leave the road there and make straight for the highest point on the timber line between Mounts Dana and Gibbs and camp there.

On the morning of the third day go to the top of Mount Dana in time for the glory of the dawn and the sunrise over the grey Mono Desert and the sublime forest of High Sierra peaks. When you leave the mountain go far enough down the north side for a view of the Dana Glacier, then make your way back to the Tioga road, follow it along the Tuolumne Meadows to the crossing of Budd Creek where you will find the Sunrise trail branching off up the mountain-side through the forest in a southwesterly direction past the west side of Cathedral Peak, which will lead you down to the Valley by the Vernal and Nevada Falls. If you are a good walker you can leave the trail where it begins to descend a steep slope in the silver fir woods, and bear off to the right and make straight for the top of Clouds' Rest. The walking is good and almost level and from the west end of Clouds' Rest take the Clouds' Rest trail which will lead direct to the Valley by the Nevada and Vernal Falls. To any one not desperately time-poor this trip should have four days instead of three; camping the second night at the Soda Springs; thence to Mount Dana and return to the Soda Springs, camping the third night there; thence by the Sunrise trail to Cathedral Peak, visiting the beautiful Cathedral lake which lies about a mile to the west of Cathedral Peak, eating your luncheon, and thence to Clouds' Rest and the Valley as above. This is one of the most interesting of all the comparatively short trips that can be made in the whole Yosemite region. Not only do you see all the grandest of the Yosemite rocks and waterfalls and the High Sierra with their glaciers, glacier lakes and glacier meadows, etc., but sections of the magnificent silver fir, two-leaved pine, and dwarf pine zones; with the principal alpine flowers and shrubs, especially sods of dwarf vaccinium covered with flowers and fruit though less than an inch high, broad mats of dwarf willow scarce an inch high with catkins that rise straight from the ground, and glorious beds of blue gentians – grandeur enough and beauty enough for a lifetime.

THE UPPER TUOLUMNE EXCURSION

We come now to the grandest of all the Yosemite excursions, one that requires at least two or three weeks. The best time to make it is from about the middle of July. The visitor entering the Yosemite in July has the advantage of seeing the falls not, perhaps, in their very flood prime but next thing to it; while the glacier-meadows will be in their glory and the snow on the mountains will be firm enough to make climbing safe. Long ago I made these Sierra trips, carrying only a sackful of bread with a little tea and sugar and was thus independent and free, but now that trails or carriage roads lead out of the Valley in almost every direction it is easy to take a pack animal, so that the luxury of a blanket and a supply of food can easily be had.

The best way to leave the Valley will be by the Yosemite Fall trail, camping the first night on the Tioga road opposite the east end of the Hoffman Range. Next morning climb Mount Hoffman; thence push on past Tenaya Lake into the Tuolumne Meadows and establish a central camp near the Soda Springs, from which glorious excursions can be made at your leisure. For here in this upper Tuolumne Valley is the widest, smoothest, most serenely spacious and in every way the most delightful summer pleasure-park in all the High Sierra. And since it is connected with Yosemite by two good trails, and a fairly good carriage road that passes between Yosemite and Mount Hoffman, it is also the most accessible. It is in the heart of the High Sierra east of Yosemite, 8,500 to 9,000ft. above the level of the sea. The grey, picturesque Cathedral Range bounds it on the south; a similar range or spur, the highest peak of which is Mount Conness, on the north; the noble Mounts Dana, Gibbs, Mammoth, Lyell, McClure and others on the axis of the Range on the east; a heaving, billowy crowd of glacier-polished rocks and Mount Hoffman on the west. Down through the open sunny meadow-levels of the Valley flows the Tuolumne River, fresh and cool from its many glacial fountains, the highest of which are the glaciers that lie on the north sides of Mount Lyell and Mount McClure.

Along the river a series of beautiful glacier-meadows extend with but little interruption, from the lower end of the Valley to its head, a distance of about twelve miles, forming charming sauntering-grounds from which the glorious mountains may be enjoyed as they look down in divine serenity over the dark forests that clothe their bases. Narrow strips of pine woods cross the meadow-carpet from side to side, and it is somewhat roughened here and there by moraine boulders and dead trees brought down from the heights by snow avalanches; but for miles and miles it is so smooth and level that a hundred horsemen may ride abreast over it.

The main lower portion of the meadows is about four miles long and from a quarter to half a mile wide; but the width of the Valley is, on an average, about eight miles. Tracing the river, we find that it forks a mile above the Soda Springs, the main fork turning southward to Mount Lyell, the other eastward to Mount Dana and Mount Gibbs. Along both forks strips of meadow extend almost to their heads. The most beautiful portions of the meadows are spread over lake basins, which have been filled up by deposits from the river. A few of these river-lakes still exist, but they are now shallow and are rapidly approaching extinction. The sod in most places is exceedingly fine and silky and free from weeds and bushes; while charming flowers abound, especially gentians, dwarf daisies, potentillas, and the pink bells of dwarf vaccinium. On the banks of the river and its tributaries cassiope and bryanthus may be found, where the sod curls over stream banks and around boulders. The principal grass of these meadows is a delicate calamagrostis with very slender filiform leaves, and when it is in flower the ground seems to be covered with faint purple mist, the stems of the panicles being so fine that they are almost invisible, and offer no appreciable resistance in walking through them. Along the edges of the meadows beneath the pines and throughout the greater part of the Valley tall ribbon-leaved grasses grow in abundance, chiefly bromus, triticum and agrostis.

In October the nights are frosty, and then the meadows at sunrise, when every leaf is laden with crystals, are a fine sight. The days are still warm and calm, and bees and butterflies continue to waver and hum about the late-blooming flowers until the coming of the snow, usually in November. Storm then follows storm in quick succession, burying the meadows to a depth of from ten to twenty feet, while magnificent avalanches descend through the forests from the laden heights, depositing huge piles of snow mixed with uprooted trees and boulders. In the open sunshine the snow usually lasts until the end of June but the new season's vegetation is not generally in bloom until late in July. Perhaps the best all round excursion-time after winters of average snowfall is from the middle of July to the middle or end of August. The snow is then melted from the woods and southern slopes of the mountains and the meadows and gardens are in their glory, while the weather is mostly all-reviving, exhilarating sunshine. The few clouds that rise now and then and the showers they yield are only enough to keep everything fresh and fragrant.

The groves about the Soda Springs are favourite camping-grounds on account of the cold, pleasant-tasting water charged with carbonic acid, and because of the views of the mountains across the meadow – the Glacier Monument, Cathedral Peak, Cathedral Spires, Unicorn Peak and a series of ornamental nameless companions, rising in striking forms and nearness above a dense forest growing on the left lateral moraine of the ancient Tuolumne Glacier, which, broad, deep, and far-reaching, exerted vast influence on the scenery of this portion of the Sierra. But there are fine camping-grounds all along the meadows, and one may move from grove to grove every day all summer, enjoying new homes and new beauty to satisfy every roving desire for change.

There are five main capital excursions to be made from here – to the summits of Mounts Dana, Lyell and Conness, and through the Bloody Canyon Pass to Mono Lake and the volcanoes, and down the Tuolumne Canyon, at least as far as the foot of the wonderful series of river cataracts. All of these excursions are sure to be made memorable with joyful health-giving experiences; but perhaps none of them will be remembered with keener delight than the days spent in sauntering on the broad velvet lawns by the river, sharing the sky with the mountains and trees, gaining something of their strength and peace.

The excursion to the top of Mount Dana is a very easy one; for though the mountain is 13,000ft. high, the ascent from the west side is so gentle and smooth that one may ride a mule to the very summit. Across many a busy stream, from meadow to meadow, lies your flowery way; mountains all about you, few of them hidden by irregular foregrounds. Gradually ascending, other mountains come in sight, peak rising above peak with their snow and ice in endless variety of grouping and sculpture. Now your attention is turned to the moraines, sweeping in beautiful curves from the hollows and canyons, now to the granite waves and pavements rising here and there above the heathy sod, polished a thousand years ago and still shining. Towards the base of the mountain you note the dwarfing of the trees, until at a height of about 11,000ft. you find patches of the tough, white-barked pine, pressed so flat by the ten or twenty feet of snow piled upon them every winter for centuries that you may walk over them as if walking on a shaggy rug. And, if curious about such things, you may discover specimens of this hardy tree-mountaineer not more than four feet high and about as many inches in diameter at the ground, that are from two hundred to four hundred years old, still holding bravely to life, making the most of their slender summers, shaking their tasselled needles in the breeze right cheerily, drinking the thin sunshine and maturing their fine purple cones as if they meant to live forever. The general view from the summit is one of the most extensive and sublime to be found in all the Range. To the eastward you gaze far out over the desert plains and mountains of the 'Great Basin', range beyond range extending with soft outlines, blue and purple in the distance. More than six thousand feet below you lies Lake Mono, ten miles in diameter from north to south, and fourteen from west to east, lying bare in the treeless desert like a disk of burnished metal, though at times it is swept by mountain stormwinds and streaked with foam. To the southward there is a well-defined range of pale-grey extinct volcanoes, and though the highest of them rises nearly two thousand feet above the lake, you can look down from here into their circular, cup-like craters, from which a comparatively short time ago ashes and cinders were showered over the surrounding sage plains and glacier-laden mountains.

To the westward the landscape is made up of exceedingly strong, grey, glaciated domes and ridge waves, most of them comparatively low, but the largest high enough to be called mountains; separated by canyons and darkened with lines and fields of forest, Cathedral Peak and Mount Hoffman in the distance; small lakes and innumerable meadows in the foreground. Northward and southward the great snowy mountains, marshalled along the axis of the Range, are seen in all their glory, crowded together in some places like trees in groves, making landscapes of wild, extravagant, bewildering magnificence, yet calm and silent as the sky.

Some eight glaciers are in sight. One of these is the Dana Glacier on the north side of the mountain, lying at the foot of a precipice about a thousand feet high, with a lovely pale-green lake a little below it. This is one of the many, small, shrunken remnants of the vast glacial system of the Sierra that once filled the hollows and valleys of the mountains and covered all the lower ridges below the immediate summit-fountains, flowing to right and left away from the axis of the Range, lavishly fed by the snows of the glacial period.

In the excursion to Mount Lyell the immediate base of the mountain is easily reached on meadow walks along the river. Turning to the southward above the forks of the river, you enter the narrow Lyell branch of the Valley, narrow enough and deep enought to be called a canyon. It is about eight miles long and from 2,000 to 3,000ft. deep. The flat meadow bottom is from about three hundred to two hundred yards wide, with gently curved margins about fifty yards wide from which rise the simple massive walls of grey granite at an angle of about thirty-three degrees, mostly timbered with a light growth of pine and streaked in many places with avalanche channels. Towards the upper end of the canyon the Sierra crown comes in sight, forming a finely balanced picture framed by the massive canyon walls. In the foreground, when the grass is in flower, you have the purple meadow willow-thickets on the river banks; in the middle distance huge swelling bosses of granite that form the base of the general mass of the mountain, with fringing lines of dark woods marking the lower curves, smoothly snow-clad except in the autumn.

If you wish to spend two days on the Lyell trip you will find a good camp-ground on the east side of the river, about a mile above a fine cascade that comes down over the canyon wall in telling style and makes good camp music. From here to the top of the mountains is usually an easy day's work. At one place near the summit careful climbing is necessary, but it is not so dangerous or difficult as to deter any one of ordinary skill, while the views are glorious. To the northward are Mammoth Mountain, Mount Gibbs, Dana, Warren, Conness and others, unnumbered and unnamed; to the southeast the indescribably wild and jagged range of Mount Ritter and the Minarets; southwestward stretches the dividing ridge between the north fork of the San Joaquin and the Merced, uniting with the Obelisk or Merced group of peaks that form the main fountains of the Illilouette branch of the Merced; and to the northwestward extends the Cathedral spur. These spurs like distinct ranges meet at your feet; therefore you look them mostly in the direction of their extension, and their peaks seem to be massed and crowded against one another, while immense amphitheatres, canyons and subordinate ridges with their wealth of lakes, glaciers, and snow-fields, maze and cluster between them. In making the ascent in June or October the glacier is easily crossed, for then its snow mantle is smooth or mostly melted off. But in midsummer the climbing is exceedingly tedious because the snow is then weathered into curious and beautiful blades, sharp and slender, and set on edge in a leaning position. They lean towards the head of the glacier and extend across from side to side in regular order in a direction at right angles to the direction of greatest declivity, the distance between the crests being about two or three feet, and the depth of the troughs between them about three feet. A more interesting problem than a walk over a glacier thus sculptured and adorned is seldom presented to the mountaineer.

The Lyell Glacier is about a mile wide and less than a mile long, but presents, nevertheless, all the essential characters of large, river-like glaciers – moraines, earth-bands, blue veins, crevasses, etc., while the streams that issue from it are, of course, turbid with rock-mud, showing its grinding action on its bed. And it is all the more interesting since it is the highest and most enduring remnant of the great Tuolumne Glacier, whose traces are still distinct fifty miles away, and whose influence on the landscape was so profound. The McClure Glacier, once a tributary of the Lyell, is smaller. Thirty-eight years ago I set a series of stakes in it to determine its rate of motion. Towards the end of summer in the middle of the glacier it was only a little over an inch in twenty-four hours.

The trip to Mono from the Soda Springs can be made in a day, but many days may profitably be spent near the shores of the lake, out on its islands and about the volcanoes.

In making the trip down the Big Tuolumne Canyon, animals may be led as far as a small, grassy, forested lake-basin that lies below the crossing of the Virginia Creek trail. And from this point any one accustomed to walking on earthquake boulders, carpeted with canyon chaparral, can easily go down as far as the big cascades and return to camp in one day. Many, however, are not able to do this, and it is better to go leisurely, prepared to camp anywhere, and enjoy the marvellous grandeur of the place.

The canyon begins near the lower end of the meadows and extends to the Hetch Hetchy Valley, a distance of about eighteen miles, though it will seem much longer to any one who scrambles through it. It is from twelve hundred to about five thousand feet deep, and is comparatively narrow, but there are several roomy, park-like openings in it, and throughout its whole extent Yosemite features are displayed on a grand scale – domes, El Capitan rocks, gables, Sentinels, Royal Arches, Glacier Points, Cathedral Spires, etc. There is even a Half Dome among its wealth of rock forms, though far less sublime than the Yosemite Half Dome. Its falls and cascades are innumerable. The sheer falls, except when the snow is melting in early spring, are quite small in volume as compared with those of Yosemite and Hetch Hetchy; though in any other country many of them would be regarded as wonders. But it is the cascades or sloping falls on the main river that are the crowning glory of the canyon, and these in volume, extent and variety surpass those of any other canyon in the Sierra. The most showy and interesting of them are mostly in the upper part of the canyon, above the point of entrance of Cathedral Creek and Hoffman Creek. For miles the river is one wild, exulting, on-rushing mass of snowy purple bloom, spreading over glacial waves of granite without any definite channel, gliding in magnificent silver plumes, dashing and foaming through huge boulder-dams, leaping high into the air in wheel-like whirls, displaying glorious enthusiasm, tossing from side to side, doubling, glinting, singing in exuberance of mountain energy.

Every one who is anything of a mountaineer should go on through the entire length of the canyon, coming out by Hetch Hetchy. There is not a dull step all the way. With wide variations, it is a Yosemite Valley from end to end.

Besides these main, far-reaching, much-seeing excursions from the main central camp, there are numberless, lovely little saunters and scrambles and a dozen or so not so very little. Among the best of these are to Lambert and Fair View Domes; to the topmost spires of Cathedral Peak, and to those of the North Church, around the base of which you pass on your way to Mount Conness; to one of the very loveliest of the glacier meadows imbedded in the pine woods about three miles north of the Soda Springs, where forty-two years ago I spent six weeks. It trends east and west, and you can find it easily by going past the base of Lambert's Dome to Dog Lake and thence up northward through the woods about a mile or so, to the shining rock-waves full of ice-burnished, feldspar crystals at the foot of the meadows; to Lake Tenaya; and, last but not least, a rather long and very hearty scramble down by the end of the meadow along the Tioga road toward Lake Tenaya to the crossing of Cathedral Creek, where you turn off and trace the creek down to its confluence with the Tuolumne. This is a genuine scramble much of the way but one of the most wonderfully telling in its glacial rock-forms and inscriptions.

If you stop and fish at every tempting lake and stream you come to, a whole month, or even two months, will not be too long for this grand High Sierra excursion. My own Sierra trip was ten years long.

OTHER TRIPS FROM THE VALLEY

Short carriage trips are usually made in the early morning to Mirror Lake to see its wonderful reflections of the Half Dome and Mount Watkins; and in the afternoon many ride down the Valley to see the Bridal Veil rainbows or up the river canyon to see those of the Vernal Fall; where standing in the spray, not minding getting drenched, you may see what are called round rainbows, when the two ends of the ordinary bow are lengthened and meet at your feet, forming a complete circle which is broken and united again and again as determined by the varying wafts of spray. A few ambitious scramblers climb to the top of the Sentinel Rock, others walk or ride down the Valley and up to the once-famous Inspiration Point for a last grand view; while a good many appreciative tourists, who have only a day or two, do no climbing or riding but spend their time sauntering on the meadows by the river, watching the falls, and the play of light and shade among the rocks from morning to night, perhaps gaining more than those who make haste up the trails in large noisy parties. Those who have unlimited time find something worth while all the year round on every accessible part of the vast, deeply sculptured walls. At least so I have found it after making the Valley my home for years.

Here are a few specimens of a few of my own short trips which walkers may find useful.

One, up the river canyon, across the bridge between the Vernal and Nevada Falls, through chaparral beds and boulders to the shoulder of Half Dome, along the top of the shoulder to the dome itself, down by a crumbling slot gully and close along the base of the tremendous split front (the most awfully impressive, sheer, precipice view I ever found in all my canyon wanderings), thence up the east shoulder and along the ridge to Clouds' Rest – a glorious sunset – then a grand starry run back home to my cabin; down through the junipers, down through the firs, now in black shadows, now in white light, past roaring Nevada and Vernal, glowering ghost-like beneath their huge frowning cliffs; down the dark, gloomy canyon, through the pines of the Valley, dreamily murmuring in their calm, breezy sleep – a fine wild little excursion for good legs and good eyes – so much sun- moon- and star- shine in it, and sublime, up-and-down rhythmical, glacial topography.

Another, to the head of Yosemite Fall by Indian Canyon; thence up the Yosemite Creek, tracing it all the way to its highest sources back of Mount Hoffman, then a wide sweep around the head of its dome-paved basin, passing its many little lakes and bogs, gardens and groves, trilling, warbling rills, and back by the Fall Canyon. This was one of my Sabbath walk, run-and-slide excursions long ago before any trail had been made on the north side of the Valley.

Another fine trip was up, bright and early, by Avalanche Canyon to Glacier Point along the rugged south wall, tracing all its far outs and ins to the head of the Bridal Veil Fall, thence back home, bright and late, by a brushy, bouldery slope between Cathedral rocks and Cathedral spires and along the level Valley floor. This was one of my long, bright-day and bright-night walks thirty or forty years ago when, like river and ocean currents, time flowed undivided, uncounted – a fine free, sauntery, scrambly, botanical, beauty-filled ramble. The walk up the Valley was made glorious by the marvellous brightness of the morning star. So great was her light, she made every tree cast a well-defined shadow on the smooth sandy ground.

Everybody who visits Yosemite wants to see the famous Big Trees. Before the railroad was constructed, all three of the stage-roads that entered the Valley passed through a grove of these trees by the way; namely, the Tuolumne, Merced and Mariposa groves. The Tuolumne grove was passed on the Big Oak Flat road, the Merced grove by the Coulterville road and the Mariposa grove by the Raymond and Wawona road. Now, to see any one of these groves, a special trip has to be made. Most visitors go to the Mariposa grove, the largest of the three. On this Sequoia trip you see not only the giant Big Trees but magnificent forests of silver fir, sugar pine, yellow pine, libocedrus and Douglas spruce. The trip need not require more than two days, spending a night in a good hotel at Wawona, a beautiful place on the south fork of the Merced River, and returning to the Valley or to El Portal, the terminus of the railroad. This extra trip by stage costs fifteen dollars. All the High Sierra excursions that I have sketched cost from a dollar a week to anything you like. None of mine when I was exploring the Sierra cost over a dollar a week, most of them less.

EARLY HISTORY OF THE VALLEY

In the wild gold years of 1849 and 1850, the Indian tribes along the western Sierra foothills became alarmed at the sudden invasion of their acorn orchard and game fields by miners, and soon began to make war upon them, in their usual murdering, plundering style. This continued until the United States Indian Commissioners succeeded in gathering them into reservations, some peacefully, others by burning their villages and stores of food. The Yosemite or Grizzly Bear tribe, fancying themselves secure in their deep mountain stronghold, were the most troublesome and defiant of all, and it was while the Mariposa battalion, under command of Major Savage, was trying to capture this warlike tribe and conduct them to the Fresno reservation that this deep mountain home, the Yosemite Valley, was discovered. From a camp on the south fork of the Merced, Major Savage sent Indian runners to the bands who were supposed to be hiding in the mountains, instructing them to tell the Indians that if they would come in and make treaty with the Commissioners they would be furnished with food and clothing and be protected, but if they did not come in he would make war upon them and kill them all. None of the Yosemite Indians responded to this general message, but when a special messenger was sent to the chief he appeared the next day. He came entirely alone and stood in dignified silence before one of the guards until invited to enter the camp. He was recognized by one of the friendly Indians as Tenaya, the old chief of the Grizzlies, and, after he had been supplied with food, Major Savage, with the aid of Indian interpreters, informed him of the wishes of the Commissioners. But the old chief was very suspicious of Savage and feared that he was taking this method of getting the tribe into his power for the purpose of revenging his personal wrong. Savage told him if he would go to the Commissioners and make peace with them as the other tribes had done there would be no more war. Tenaya inquired what was the object of taking all the Indians to the San Joaquin plain. 'My people,' said he, 'do not want anything from the Great Father you tell me about. The Great Spirit is our father and he has always supplied us with all we need. We do not want anything from white men. Our women are able to do our work. Go, then. Let us remain in the mountains where we were born, where the ashes of our fathers have been given to the wind. I have said enough.'

To this the Major answered abruptly in Indian style: 'If you and your people have all you desire, why do you steal our horses and mules? Why do you rob the miners' camps? Why do you murder the white men and plunder and burn their houses?'

Tenaya was silent for some time. He evidently understood what the Major had said, for he replied, 'My young men have sometimes taken horses and mules from the whites. This was wrong. It is not wrong to take the property of enemies who have wronged my people. My young people believed that the gold diggers were our enemies. We now know they are not and we shall be glad to live in peace with them. We will stay here and be friends. My people do not want to go to the plains. Some of the tribes who have gone there ar very bad. We cannot live with them. Here we can defend ourselves.'

To this Major Savage firmly said, 'Your people must go to the Commissioners. If they do not your young men will again steal horses and kill and plunder the whites. It was your people who robbed my stores, burned my houses and murdered my men. If they do not make a treaty, your whole tribe will be destroyed. Not one of them will be left alive.'

To this the old chief replied, 'It is useless to talk to you about who destroyed your property and killed your people. I am old and you can kill me if you will, but it is useless to lie to you who know more than all the Indians. Therefore I will not lie to you but if you will let me return to my people I will bring them in.' He was allowed to go. The next day he came back and said his people were on the way to our camp to go with the men sent by the Great Father, who was so good and rich.

Another day passed but no Indians from the deep Valley appeared. The old chief said that the snow was so deep and his village was so far down that it took a long time to climb out of it. After waiting still another day the expedition started for the Valley. When Tenaya was questioned as to the route and distance he said that the snow was so deep that the horses could not go through it. Old Tenaya was taken along as guide. When the party had gone about half-way to the Valley they met the Yosemites on their way to the camp on the south fork. There were only seventy-two of them and when the old chief was asked what had become of the rest of his band, he replied, 'This is all of my people that are willing to go with me to the plains. All the rest have gone with their wives and children over the mountains to the Mono and Tuolumne tribes.' Savage told Tenaya that he was not telling the truth, for Indians could not cross the mountains in the deep snow, and that he knew they must still be at his village or hiding somewhere near it. The tribe had been estimated to number over two hundred. Major Savage then said to him, 'You may return to camp with your people and I will take one of your young men with me to your village to see your people who will not come. They will come if I find them.' 'You will not find any of my people there,' said Tenaya; 'I do not know where they are. My tribe is small. Many of the people of my tribe have come from other tribes and if they go to the plains and are seen they will be killed by the friends of those with whom they have quarrelled. I was told that I was growing old and it was well that I should go, but that young and strong men can find plenty in the mountains: therefore, why should they go to the hot plains to be penned up like horses and cattle? My heart has been sore since that talk but I am now willing to go, for it is best for my people.'

Pushing ahead, taking turns in breaking a way through the snow, they arrived in sight of the great Valley early in the afternoon and, guided by one of Tenaya's Indians, descended by the same route as that followed by the Mariposa trail and the weary party went into camp on the river bank opposite El Capitan. After supper, seated around a big fire, the wonderful Valley became the topic of conversation and Dr Bunell suggested giving it a name.

Many were proposed, but after a vote had been taken the name Yosemite, proposed by Dr. Bunell, was adopted almost unanimously to perpetuate the name of the tribe who so long had made their home there. The Indian name of the valley, however, is Ahwahnee. The Indians had names for all the different rocks and streams of the Valley, but very few of them are now in use by the whites, Pohono, the Bridal Veil, being the principal one. The expedition remained only one day and two nights in the Valley, hurrying out on the approach of a storm and reached the southfork headquarters on the evening of the third day after starting out. Thus, in three days the round trip had been made to the Valley, most of it had been explored in a general way and some of its principal features had been named. But the Indians had fled up the Tenaya Canyon trail and none of them were seen, except an old woman unable to follow the fugitives.

A second expedition was made in the same year under command of Major Boling. When the Valley was entered no Indians were seen, but the many wigwams with smouldering fires showed that they had been hurriedly abandoned that very day. Later, five young Indians who had been left to watch the movements of the expedition were captured at the foot of the Three Brothers after a lively chase. Three of the five were sons of the old chief and the rock was named for them. All of these captives made good their escape within a few days, except the youngest son of Tenaya, who was shot by his guard while trying to escape. That same day the old chief was captured on the cliff on the east side of Indian Canyon by some of Boling's scouts. As Tenaya walked toward the camp his eye fell upon the dead body of his favourite son. Captain Boling through an interpreter, expressed his regret at the occurrence, but not a word did Tenaya utter in reply. Later, he made an attempt to escape but was caught as he was about to swim across the river. Tenaya expected to be shot for this attempt and when brought into the presence of Captain Boling he said in great emotion, 'Kill me, Sir Captain, yes, kill me as you killed my son, as you would kill my people if they were to come to you. You would kill all my tribe if you had the power. Yes, Sir America, you can now tell your warriors to kill the old chief. You have made my life dark with sorrow. You killed the child of my heart. Why not kill the father? But wait a little and when I am dead I will call my people to come and they shall hear me in their sleep and come to avenge the death of their chief and his son. Yes, Sir America, my spirit will make trouble for you and your people, as you have made trouble to me and my people. With the wizards I will follow the white people and make them fear me. You may kill me, Sir Captain, but you shall not live in peace. I will follow in your footsteps. I will not leave my home, but be with the spirits among the rocks, the waterfalls, in the rivers and in the winds; wherever you go I will be with you. You will not see me but you will fear the spirit of the old chief and grow cold. The Great Spirit has spoken. I am done.'

This expedition finally captured the remnants of the tribes at the head of Lake Tenaya and took them to the Fresno reservation, together with their chief, Tenaya. But after a short stay they were allowed to return to the Valley under restrictions. Tenaya promised faithfully to conform to everything required, joyfully left the hot and dry reservation, and with his family returned to his Yosemite home.

The following year a party of miners was attacked by the Indians in the Valley and two of them were killed. This led to another Yosemite expedition. A detachment of regular soldiers from Fort Miller under Lieutenant Moore, U.S.A., was at once dispatched to capture or punish the murderers. Lieutenant Moore entered the Valley in the night and surprised and captured a party of five Indians, but an alarm was given and Tenaya and his people fled from their huts and escaped to the Monos on the east side of the Range. On examination of the five prisoners in the morning it was discovered that each of them had some article of clothing that belonged to the murdered men. The bodies of the two miners were found and buried on the edge of the Bridal Veil meadow. When the captives were accused of the murder of the two white men they admitted that they had killed them to prevent the white men from coming to their Valley, declaring that it was their home and that white men had no right to come there without their consent. Lieutenant Moore told them through his interpreter that they had sold their lands to the Government, that it belonged to the white men now, and that they had agreed to live on the reservation provided for them. To this they replied that Tenaya had never consented to the sale of their Valley and had never received pay for it. The other chief, they said, had no right to sell their territory. The lieutenant being fully satisfied that he had captured the real murderers, promptly pronounced judgment and had them placed in line and shot. Lieutenant Moore pursued the fugitives to Mono but was not successful in finding any of them. After being hospitably entertained and protected by the Mono and Paute tribes they stole a number of stolen horses from their entertainers and made their way by a long, obscure route by the head of the north fork of the San Joaquin, reached their Yosemite home once more, but early one morning, after a feast of horse-flesh, a band of Monos surprised them in their huts, killing Tenaya and nearly all his tribe. Only a small remnant escaped down the river canyon. The Tenaya Canyon and Lake were named for the famous old chief.

Very few visits were made to the Valley before the summer of 1855, when Mr J. M. Hutchings, having heard of its wonderful scenery, collected a party and made the first regular tourist's visit to the Yosemite and in his California magazine described it in articles illustrated by a good artist, who was taken into the Valley by him for that purpose. This first party was followed by another from Mariposa the same year, consisting of sixteen or eighteen persons. The next year the regular pleasure travel began and a trail on the Mariposa side of the Valley was opened by Mann Brothers. This trail was afterwards purchased by the citizens of the county and made free to the public. The first house built in the Yosemite Valley was erected in the autumn of 1856 and was kept as a hotel the next year by G. A. Hite and later by J. J. Neal and S. M. Cunningham. It was situated directly opposite the Yosemite Fall. A little over half a mile farther up the Valley a canvas house was put up in 1858 by G. A. Hite. Next year a frame house was built and kept as a hotel by Mr Peck, afterward by Mr Longhurst and since 1864 by Mr Hutchings. All these hotels have vanishd except the frame house built in 1859, which has been changed beyond recognition. A large hotel built on the brink of the river in front of the old one is now the only hotel in the Valley. A large hotel built by the State and located farther up the Valley was burned. To provide for the overflow of visitors there are three camps with board floors, wood frame, and covered with canvas, well furnished, some of them with electric light. A large first-class hotel is very much needed.

Travel of late years has been rapidly increasing especially after the establishment, by Act of Congress in 1890, of the Yosemite National Park and the recession in 1905 of the original reservation to the Federal Government by the State. The greatest increase, of course, was caused by the construction of the Yosemite Valley railroad from Merced to the border of the Park, eight miles below the Valley.

It is eighty miles long, and the entire distance, except the first twenty-four miles from the town of Merced, is built through the precipitous Merced River Canyon. The roadbed was virtually blasted out of the solid rock for the entire distance in the canyon. Work was begun in September 1905, and the first train entered El Portal, the terminus, 15 April 1907. Many miles of the road cost as much as $100,000 per mile. Its business has increased from 4000 tourists in the first year it was operated to 15,000 in 1910.

CHAPTER THIRTEEN

Lamon

THE GOOD old pioneer, Lamon, was the first of all the early Yosemite settlers who cordially and unreservedly adopted the Valley as his home.

He was born in the Shenandoah Valley, Virginia 10 May 1817, emigrated to Illinois with his father, John Lamon, at the age of nineteen; afterwards went to Texas and settled on the Brazos, where he raised melons and hunted alligators for a living. 'Right interestin' business,' he said, 'especially the alligator part of it.' From the Brazos he went to the Comanche Indian country between Gonzales and Austin, twenty miles from his nearest neighbour. During the first summer, the only bread he had was the breast meat of wild turkeys. When the formidable Comanche Indians were on the war-path he left his cabin after dark and slept in the woods. From Texas he crossed the plains to California and worked in the Calaveras and Mariposa gold-fields.

He first heard Yosemite spoken of as a very beautiful mountain valley and after making two excursions in the summers of 1857 and 1858 to see the wonderful place he made up his mind to quit roving and make a permanent home in it. In April 1859, he moved into it, located a garden opposite Mount Half Dome, set out a lot of apple, pear and peach trees, planted potatoes, etc., that he had packed in on a 'contrary old mule,' and worked for his board in building a hotel which was afterwards purchased by Mr Hutchings. His neighbours thought he was very foolish in attempting to raise crops in so high and cold a valley, and warned him that he could raise nothing and sell nothing, and would surely starve.

For the first year or two lack of provisions compelled him to move out on the approach of winter, but in 1862 after he had succeeded in raising some fruit and vegetables he began to winter in the Valley.

The first winter he had no companions, not even a dog or cat, and one evening was greatly surprised to see two men coming up the Valley. They were very glad to see him, for they had come from Mariposa in search of him, a report having been spread that he had been killed by Indians. He assured his visitors that he felt safer in his Yosemite home, lying snug and squirrel-like in his 10 × 12 cabin than in Mariposa. When the avalanches began to slip, he wondered where all the wild roaring and booming came from, the flying snow prevented them from being seen. But, upon the whole, he wondered most at the brightness, gentleness and sunniness of the weather, and hopefully employed the calm days in clearing ground for an orchard and vegetable garden.

In the second winter he built a winter cabin under the Royal Arches, where he enjoyed more sunshine. But no matter how he praised the weather he could not induce any one to winter with him until 1864.

He liked to describe the great flood of 1867, the year before I reached California, when all the walls were striped with thundering waterfalls.

He was a fine, erect, whole-souled man, between six and seven feet high, with a broad, open face, bland and guileless as his pet oxen. No stranger to hunger and weariness, he knew well how to appreciate suffering of a like kind in others, and many there be, myself among the number, who can testify to his simple, unostentatious kindness that found expression in a thousand small deeds.

After gaining sufficient means to enjoy a long afternoon of life in comparative affluence and ease, he died in the autumn of 1876. He sleeps in a beautiful spot near Galen Clark and a monument hewn from a block of Yosemite granite marks his grave.

CHAPTER FOURTEEN

Galen Clark

GALEN CLARK was the best mountaineer I ever met, and one of the kindest and most amiable of all my mountain friends. I first met him at his Wawona ranch forty-three years ago on my first visit to Yosemite. I had entered the Valley with one companion by way of Coulterville, and returned by what was then known as the Mariposa trail. Both trails were buried in deep snow where the elevation was from 5,000 to 7,000ft. above sea-level in the sugar pine and silver fir regions. We had no great difficulty, however, in finding our way by the trends of the main features of the topography. Botanizing by the way, we made slow, plodding progress, and were again about out of provisions when we reached Clark's hospitable cabin at Wawona. He kindly furnished us with flour and a little sugar and tea, and my companion, who complained of the benumbing poverty of a strictly vegetarian diet, gladly accepted Mr Clark's offer of a piece of bear that had just been killed. After a short talk about bears and the forests and the way to the Big Trees, we pushed on up through the Wawona firs and sugar pines, and camped in the now-famous Mariposa grove.

Later, after making my home in the Yosemite Valley, I became well acquainted with Mr Clark, while he was guardian. He was elected again and again to this important office by different Boards of Commissioners on account of his efficiency and his real love of the Valley.

Although nearly all my mountaineering has been done without companions, I had the pleasure of having Galen Clark with me on three excursions. About thirty-five years ago I invited him to accompany me on a trip through the Big Tuolumne Canyon from Hetch Hetchy Valley. The canyon up to that time had not been explored, and knowing that the difference in the elevation of the river at the head of the canyon and in Hetch Hetchy was about 5,000ft., we expected to find some magnificent cataracts or falls; nor were we disappointed. When we were leaving Yosemite an ambitious young man begged leave to join us. I strongly advised him not to attempt such a long, hard trip, for it would undoubtedly prove very trying to an inexperienced climber. He assured us, however, that he was equal to anything, would gladly meet every difficulty as it came, and cause us no hindrance or trouble of any sort. So at last, after repeating our advice that he give up the trip, we consented to his joining us. We entered the canyon by way of Hetch Hetchy Valley, each carrying his own provisions, and making his own tea, porridge, bed, etc.

In the morning of the second day out from Hetch Hetchy we came to what is now known as 'Muir Gorge,' and Mr Clark without hesitation prepared to force a way through it, wading and jumping from one submerged boulder to another through the torrent, bracing and steadying himself with a long pole. Though the river was then rather low, the savage roaring, surging song it was singing was rather nerve-trying, especially to our inexperienced companion. With careful assistance, however, I managed to get him through but this hard trial, naturally enough, proved too much and he informed us, pale and trembling, that he could go no further. I gathered some wood at the upper throat of the gorge, made a fire for him and advised him to feel at home and make himself comfortable, hoped he would enjoy the grand scenery and the songs of the water-ouzels which haunted the gorge, and assured him that we would return some time in the night, though it might be late, as we wished to go on through the entire canyon if possible. We pushed our way through the dense chaparral and over the earthquake taluses with such speed that we reached the foot of the upper cataract while we had still an hour or so of daylight for the return trip. It was long after dark when we reached our adventurous, but nerve-shaken companion who, of course, was anxious and lonely, not being accustomed to solitude, however kindly and flowery and full of sweet bird-song and stream-song. Being tired we simply lay down in restful comfort on the river bank beside a good fire, instead of trying to go down the gorge in the dark or climb over its high shoulder to our blankets and provisions, which we had left in the morning in a tree at the foot of the gorge. I remember Mr Clark remarking that if he had his choice that night between provisions and blankets he would choose his blankets.

The next morning in about an hour we had crossed over the ridge though which the gorge is cut, reached our provisions, made tea, and had a good breakfast. As soon as we had returned to Yosemite I obtained fresh provisions, pushed off alone up to the head of Yosemite Creek basin, entered the canyon by a side canyon, and completed the exploration up to the Tuolumne Meadows.

It was on this first trip from Hetch Hetchy to the upper cataracts that I had convincing proofs of Mr Clark's daring and skill as a mountaineer, particularly in fording torrents, and in forcing his way through thick chaparral. I found it somewhat difficult to keep up with him in dense, tangled brush, though in jumping on boulder taluses and slippery cobble-beds I had no difficulty in leaving him behind.

After I had discovered the glaciers on Mount Lyell and Mount McClure, Mr Clark kindly made a second excursion with me to assist in establishing a line of stakes across the McClure glacier to measure its rate of flow. On this trip we also climbed Mount Lyell together, when the snow which covered the glacier was melted into upleaning, icy glades which were extremely difficult to cross, not being strong enough to support our weight, nor wide enough apart to enable us to stride across each blade as it was met. Here again I, being lighter, had no difficulty in keeping ahead of him. While resting after wearisome staggering and falling he stared at the marvellous ranks of leaning blades, and said, 'I think I have travelled all sorts of trails and canyons, through all kinds of brush and snow, but this gets me.'

Mr Clark at my urgent request joined my small party on a trip to the Kings River yosemite by way of the high mountains, most of the way without a trail. He joined us at the Mariposa Big Tree grove and intended to go all the way, but finding that, on account of the difficulties encountered, the time required was much greater than he expected, he turned back near the head of the north fork of the Kings River.

In cooking his mess of oatmeal porridge and making tea, his pot was always the first to boil and I used to wonder why, with all his skill in scrambling through brush in the easiest way, and preparing his meals, he was so utterly careless about his beds. He would lie down anywhere on any ground, rough or smooth, without taking pains even to remove cobbles or sharp-angled rocks protruding through the grass or gravel, saying that his own bones were as hard as any stones and could do him no harm.

His kindness to all Yosemite visitors and mountaineers was marvellously constant and uniform. He was not a good business man, and in building an extensive hotel and barns at Wawona, before the travel to Yosemite had been greatly developed, he borrowed money, mortgaged his property and lost it all.

Though not the first to see the Mariposa Big Tree grove, he was the first to explore it, after he had heard from a prospector, who had passed through the grove and who gave him the indefinite information, that there were some wonderful big trees up there on the top of the Wawona hill and that he believed they must be of the same kind that had become so famous and well-known in the Calaveras grove farther north. On this information, Galen Clark told me, he went up and thoroughly explored the grove, counting the trees and measuring the largest, and becoming familiar with it. He stated also that he had explored the forest to the southward and had discovered the much larger Fresno grove of about two square miles, six or seven miles distant from the Mariposa grove. Unfortunately most of the Fresno grove has been cut and flumed down to the railroad near Madera.

Mr Clark was truly and literally a gentle-man. I never heard him utter a hasty, angry, fault-finding word. His voice was uniformly pitched at a rather low tone, perfectly even, although glances of his eyes and slight intonations of his voice often indicated that something funny or mildly sarcastic was coming, but upon the whole he was serious and industrious, and, however deep and fun-provoking a story might be, he never indulged in boisterous laughter.

He was very fond of scenery and once told me after I became acquainted with him that he liked 'nothing in the world better than climbing to the top of a high ridge or mountain and looking off.' He preferred the mountain ridges and domes in the Yosemite regions on account of the wealth and beauty of the forests. Oftentimes he would take his rifle, a few pounds of bacon, a few pounds of flour, and a single blanket and go off hunting, for no other reason than to explore and get acquainted with the most beautiful points of view within a journey of a week or two from his Wawona home. On these trips he was always alone and could indulge in tranquil enjoyment of Nature to his heart's content. He said that on those trips, when he was a sufficient distance from home in a neigbourhood where he wished to linger, he always shot a deer, sometimes a grouse, and occasionally a bear. After diminishing the weight of a deer or bear by eating part of it, he carried as much as possible of the best of the meat to Wawona, and from his hospitable well-supplied cabin no weary wanderer ever went away hungry or unrested.

The value of the mountain air in prolonging life is well exemplified in Mr Clark's case. While working in the mines he contracted a severe cold that settled on his lungs and finally caused severe inflammation and bleeding, and none of his friends thought he would ever recover. The physicians told him he had but a short time to live. It was then that he repaired to the beautiful sugar pine woods at Wawona and took up a claim, including the fine meadows there, and building his cabin, began his life of wandering and exploring in the glorious mountains about him, usually going bareheaded. In a remarkably short time his lungs were healed.

He was one of the most sincere tree-lovers I ever knew. About twenty years before his death he made a choice of plot in the Yosemite cemetery on the north side of the Valley, not far from the Yosemite Fall, and selecting a dozen or so of seedling Sequoias in the Mariposa grove he brought them to the Valley and planted them around the spot he had chosen for his last rest. The ground there is gravelly and dry; by careful watering he finally nursed most of the seedlings into good, thrifty trees, and doubtless they will long shade the grave of their blessed lover and friend.

CHAPTER FIFTEEN

Hetch Hetchy Valley

YOSEMITE IS so wonderful that we are apt to regard it as an exceptional creation, the only valley of its kind in the world; but Nature is not so poor as to have only one of anything. Several other yosemites have been discovered in the Sierra that occupy the same relative positions on the Range and were formed by the same forces in the same kind of granite. One of these, the Hetch Hetchy Valley, is in the Yosemite National Park about twenty miles from Yosemite and is easily accessible to all sorts of travellers by a road and trail that leaves the Big Oak Flat road at Bronson Meadows a few miles below Crane Flat, and to mountaineers by way of Yosemite Creek basin and the head of the middle fork of the Tuolumne.

It is said to have been discovered by Joseph Screech, a hunter, in 1850, a year before the discovery of the great Yosemite. After my first visit to it in the autumn of 1871, I have always called it the 'Tuolumne Yosemite,' for it is a wonderfully exact counterpart of the Merced Yosemite, not only in its sublime rocks and waterfalls but in the gardens, groves and meadows of its flowery park-like floor. The floor of Yosemite is about 4,000ft. above the sea; the Hetch Hetchy floor about 3,700ft. And as the Merced River flows through Yosemite, so does the Tuolumne through Hetch Hetchy. The walls of both are of grey granite, rise abruptly from the floor, are sculptured in the same style and in both every rock is a glacier monument.

Standing boldly out from the south wall is a strikingly picturesque rock called by the Indians, Kolana, the outermost of a group 2,300ft. high, corresponding with the Cathedral Rocks of Yosemite both in relative position and form. On the opposite side of the Valley, facing Kolana, there is a counterpart of the El Capitan that rises sheer and plain to a height of 1,800ft., and over its massive brow flows a stream which makes the most graceful fall I have ever seen. From the edge of the cliff to the top of an earthquake talus it is perfectly free in the air for a thousand feet before it is broken into cascades among talus boulders. It is in all its glory in June, when the snow is melting fast, but fades and vanishes toward the end of summer. The only fall I know with which it may fairly be compared is the Yosemite Bridal Veil; but it excels even that favourite fall both in height and airy-fairy beauty and behaviour. Lowlanders are apt to suppose that mountain streams in their wild career over cliffs lose control of themselves and tumble in a noisy chaos of mist and spray. On the contrary, on no part of their travels are they more harmonious and self-controlled. Imagine yourself in Hetch Hetchy on a sunny day in June, standing waist-deep in grass and flowers (as I have often stood), while the great pines sway dreamily with scarcely perceptible motion. Looking northward across the Valley you see a plain, grey granite cliff rising abruptly out of the gardens and groves to a height of 1,800ft., and in front of it Tueeulala's silvery scarf burning with irised sun-fire. In the first white outburst at the head there is abundance of visible energy, but it is speedily hushed and concealed in divine repose and its tranquil progress to the base of the cliff is like that of a downy feather in a still room. Now observe the fineness and marvellous distinctness of the various sun-illumined fabrics into which the water is woven; they sift and float from form to form down the face of that grand grey rock in so leisurely and unconfused a manner that you can examine their texture, and patterns and tones of colour as you would a piece of embroidery held in the hand. Toward the top of the fall you see groups of booming, comet-like masses, their solid, white heads separate, their tails like combed silk interlacing among delicate grey and purple shadows, ever forming and dissolving, worn out by friction in their rush through the air. Most of these vanish a few hundred feet below the summit, changing to varied forms of cloud-like drapery. Near the bottom the width of the fall has increased from about twenty-five feet to a hundred feet. Here it is composed of yet finer tissues, and is still without a trace of disorder – air, water and sunlight woven into stuff that spirits might wear.

So fine a fall might well seem sufficient to glorify any valley; but here, as in Yosemite, Nature seems in nowise moderate, for a short distance to the eastward of Tueeulala booms and thunders the great Hetch Hetchy Fall, Wapama, so near that you have both of them in full view from the same standpoint. It is the counterpart of the Yosemite Fall, but has a much greater volume of water, is about 1,700ft. in height, and appears to be nearly vertical, though considerably inclined, and is dashed into huge outbounding bosses of foam on projecting shelves and knobs. No two falls could be more unlike – Tueeulala out in the open sunshine descending like thistledown; Wapama in a jagged, shadowy gorge roaring and thundering, pounding its way like an earthquake avalanche.

Besides this glorious pair there is a broad, massive fall on the main river a short distance above the head of the Valley. Its position is something like that of the Vernal in Yosemite, and its roar as it plunges into a surging trout-pool may be heard a long way, though it is only about twenty feet high. On Rancheria Creek, a large stream, corresponding in position with the Yosemite Tenaya Creek, there is a chain of cascades joined here and there with swift flashing plumes like the one between the Vernal and Nevada Falls, making magnificent shows as they go their glacier-sculptured way, sliding, leaping, hurrahing, covered with crisp clashing spray made glorious with sifting sunshine. And besides all these a few small streams come over the walls at wide intervals, leaping from ledge to ledge with birdlike song and watering many a hiden cliff-garden and fernery, but they are too unshowy to be noticed in so grand a place.

The correspondence between the Hetch Hetchy walls in their trends, sculpture, physical structure, and general arrangement of the main rock-masses and those of the Yosemite Valley has excited the wondering admiration of every observer. We have seen that the El Capitan and Cathedral rocks occupy the same relative positions in both valleys; so also do their Yosemite points and North Domes. Again, that part of the Yosemite north wall immediately to the east of the Yosemite Fall has two horizontal benches, about 500 and 1,500ft. above the floor, timbered with golden-cup oak. Two benches similarly situated and timbered occur on the same relative portion of the Hetch Hetchy north wall, to the east of Wapama Fall, and on no other. The Yosemite is bounded at the head by the great Half Dome. Hetch Hetchy is bounded in the same way, though its head rock is incomparably less wonderful and sublime in form.

The floor of the Valley is about three and a half miles long, and from a fourth to half a mile wide. The lower portion is mostly a level meadow about a mile long, with the trees restricted to the sides and the river banks, and partially separated from the main, upper, forested portion by a low bar of glacier-polished granite across which the river breaks in rapids.

The principal trees are the yellow and sugar pines, digger pine, incense cedar, Douglas spruce, silver fir, the California and golden-cup oaks, balsam cottonwood, Nuttall's flowering dogwood, alder, maple, laurel, tumion, etc. The most abundant and influential are the great yellow or silver pines like those of Yosemite, the tallest over two hundred feet in height, and the oaks assembled in magnificent groves with massive rugged trunks four to six feet in diameter, and broad, shady, wide-spreading heads. The shrubs forming conspicuous flowery clumps and tangles are manzanita, azalea, spiræa, brier-rose, several species of ceanothus, calycanthus, philadelphus, wild cherry, etc.; with abundance of showy and fragrant herbaceous plants growing about them or out in the open in beds by themselves – lilies, Mariposa tulips, brodiaeas, orchids, iris, spraguea, draperia, collomia, collinsia, castilleja, nemophila, larkspur, columbine, goldenrods, sunflowers, mints of many species, honeysuckle, etc. Many fine ferns dwell here also, especially the beautiful and interesting rockferns – pellaea, and cheilanthes of several species – fringing and rosetting dry rock-piles and ledges; woodwardia and asplenium on damp spots with fronds six or seven feet high; the delicate maidenhair in mossy nooks by the falls, and the sturdy, broad-shouldered pteris covering nearly all the dry ground beneath the oaks and pines.

It appears, therefore that Hetch Hetchy Valley, far from being a plain, common, rock-bound meadow, as many who have not seen it seem to suppose, is a grand landscape garden, one of Nature's rarest and most precious mountain temples. As in Yosemite, the sublime rocks of its walls seem to glow with life, whether leaning back in repose or standing erect in thoughtful attitudes, giving welcome to storms and calms alike, their brows in the sky, their feet set in the groves and gay flowery meadows, while birds, bees, and butterflies help the river and waterfalls to stir all the air into music – things frail and fleeting and types of permanence meeting here and blending, just as they do in Yosemite, to draw her lovers into close and confiding communion with her.

Sad to say, this most precious and sublime feature of the Yosemite National Park, one of the greatest of all our natural resources for the uplifting joy and peace and health of the people, is in danger of being dammed and made into a reservoir to help supply San Francisco with water and light, thus flooding it from wall to wall and burying its gardens and groves one or two hundred feet deep. This grossly destructive commercial scheme has long been planned and urged (though water as pure and abundant can be got from sources outside of the people's park, in a dozen different places), because of the comparative cheapness of the dam and of the territory which it is sought to divert from the great uses to which it was dedicated in the Act of 1890 establishing the Yosemite National Park.

The making of gardens and parks goes on with civilization all over the world, and they increase both in size and number as their value is recognized. Everybody needs beauty as well as bread, places to play in and pray in, where Nature may heal and cheer and give strength to body and soul alike. This natural beauty-hunger is made manifest in the little window-sill gardens of the poor, though perhaps only a geranium slip in a broken cup, as well as in the carefully tended rose and lily gardens of the rich, the thousands of spacious city parks and botanical gardens, and in our magnificent National parks – the Yellowstone, Yosemite, Sequoia, etc. – Nature's sublime wonderlands, the admiration and joy of the world. Nevertheless, like anything else worth while, from the very beginning, however well guarded, they have always been subject to attack by despoiling gainseekers and mischief-makers of every degree from Satan to Senators, eagerly trying to make everything immediately and selfishly commercial with schemes disguised in smug-smiling philanthropy, industriously, shampiously crying, 'Conservation, conservation, panutilization,' that man and beast may be fed and the dear Nation made great. Thus long ago a few enterprising merchants utilized the Jerusalem temple as a place of business instead of a place of prayer, changing money, buying and selling cattle and sheep and doves; and earlier still, the first forest reservation, including only one tree, was likewise despoiled. Ever since the establishment of the Yosemite National Park, strife has been going on around its borders and I suppose this will go on as part of the universal battle between right and wrong, however much its boundaries may be shorn, or its wild beauty destroyed.

The first application to the Government by the San Francisco Supervisors for the commercial use of Lake Eleanor and the Hetch Hetchy Valley was made in 1903, and on 22 December of that year it was denied by the Secretary of the Interior, Mr Hitchcock, who truthfully said:

'Presumably the Yosemite National Park was created such by law because of the natural objects of varying degrees of scenic importance located within its boundaries, inclusive alike of its beautiful small lakes, like Eleanor, and its majestic wonders, like Hetch Hetchy and Yosemite Valley. It is the aggregation of such natural scenic features that makes the Yosemite Park a wonderland which the Congress of the United States sought by law to reserve for all coming time as nearly as practicable in the condition fashioned by the hand of the Creator – a worthy object of National pride and a source of healthful pleasure and rest for the thousands of people who may annually sojourn there during the heated months.'

In 1907 when Mr Garfield became Secretary of the Interior the application was renewed and granted; but under his successor, Mr Fisher, the matter has been referred to a Commission, which as this volume goes to press still has it under consideration.

The most delightful and wonderful camp grounds in the Park are its three great valleys – Yosemite, Hetch Hetchy, and Upper Tuolumne; and they are also the most important places with reference to their positions relative to the other great features – the Merced and Tuolumne Canyons, and the High Sierra peaks and glaciers, etc., at the head of the rivers. The main part of the Tuolumne Valley is a spacious flowery lawn four or five miles long, surrounded by magnificent snowy mountains, slightly separated from other beautiful meadows, which together make a series about twelve miles in length, the highest reaching to the feet of Mount Dana, Mount Gibbs, Mount Lyell and Mount McClure. It is about 8500 feet above the sea, and forms the grand central High Sierra camp ground from which excursions are made to the noble mountains, domes, glaciers, etc,; across the Range to the Mono Lake and volcanoes and down the Tuolumne Canyon to Hetch Hetchy. Should Hetch Hetchy be submerged for a reservoir, as proposed, not only would it be utterly destroyed, but the sublime canyon way to the heart of the High Sierra would be hopelessly blocked and the great camping ground, as the watershed of a city drinking system, virtually would be closed to the public. So far as I have learned, few of all the thousands who have seen the park and seek rest and peace in it are in favour of this outrageous scheme.

One of my later visits to the Valley was made in the autumn of 1907 with the late William Keith, the artist. The leaf-colours were then ripe, and the great godlike rocks in repose seemed to glow with life. The artist, under their spell, wandered day after day along the river and through the groves and gardens, studying the wonderful scenery; and, after making about forty sketches, declared with enthusiasm that although its walls were less sublime in height, in picturesque beauty and charm Hetch Hetchy surpassed even Yosemite.

That any one would try to destroy such a place seems incredible; but sad experience shows that there are people good enough and bad enough for anything. The proponents of the dam scheme bring forward a lot of bad arguments to prove that the only righteous thing to do with the people's parks is to destroy them bit by bit as they are able. Their arguments are curiously like those of the devil, devised for the destruction of the first garden – so much of the very best Eden fruit going to waste; so much of the best Tuolumne water and Tuolumne scenery going to waste. Few of their statements are even partly true, and all are misleading.

Thus, Hetch Hetchy, they say, is a 'low-lying meadow'. On the contrary, it is a high-lying natural landscape garden.

'It is a common minor feature, like thousands of others.' On the contrary it is a very uncommon feature; after Yosemite, the rarest and in many ways the most important in the National Park.

'Damming and submerging it 175ft. deep would enhance its beauty by forming a crystal-clear lake.' Landscape gardens, places of recreation and worship, are never made beautiful by destroying and burying them. The beautiful sham lake, forsooth, would be only an eyesore, a dismal blot on the landscape, like many others to be seen in the Sierra. For, instead of keeping it at the same level all the year, allowing Nature centuries of time to make new shores, it would, of course, be full only a month or two in the spring, when the snow is melting fast; then it would be gradually drained, exposing the slimy sides of the basin and shallower parts of the bottom, with the gathered drift and waste, death and decay of the upper basins, caught here instead of being swept on to decent natural burial along the banks of the river or in the sea. Thus the Hetch Hetchy dam-lake would be only a rough imitation of a natural lake for a few of the spring months, an open sepulchre for the others.

'Hetch Hetchy water is the purest of all to be found in the Sierra, unpolluted, and forever unpollutable.' On the contrary, excepting that of the Merced below Yosemite, it is less pure than that of most of the other Sierra streams, because of the sewerage of camp grounds draining into it, especially of the Big Tuolumne Meadows camp ground, occupied by hundreds of tourists and mountainers, with their animals, for months every summer, soon to be followed by thousands from all the world.

These temple destroyers, devotees of ravaging commercialism, seem to have a perfect contempt for Nature, and, instead of lifting their eyes to the God of the mountains, lift them to the Almighty Dollar.

Dam Hetch Hetchy! As well as dam for water-tanks the people's cathedrals and churches, for no holier temple has ever been consecrated by the heart of man.

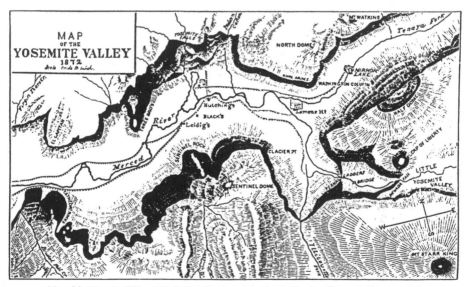

Map of the Yosemite Valley, 1872. Published in Samuel Kneeland's *Wonders of Yosemite* (Boston, 1873).

TRAVELS IN ALASKA

Travels in Alaska

First published by Houghton Mifflin Co., Boston, 1915

Contents

Part 1: The Trip of 1879

Part 2: The Trip of 1880

Part 3: The Trip of 1890

Part 1

The Trip of 1879

CHAPTER ONE

Puget Sound and British Columbia

AFTER ELEVEN years of study and exploration in the Sierra Nevada of California and the mountain-ranges of the Great Basin, studying in particular their glaciers, forests, and wild life, above all their ancient glaciers and the influence they exerted in sculpturing the rocks over which they passed with tremendous pressure, making new landscapes, scenery, and beauty which so mysteriously influence every human being, and to some extent all life, I was anxious to gain some knowledge of the regions to the northward, about Puget Sound and Alaska. With this grand object in view I left San Francisco in May, 1879, on the steamer Dakota, without any definite plan, as with the exception of a few of the Oregon peaks and their forests all the wild north was new to me.

To the mountaineer a sea voyage is a grand, inspiring, restful change. For forests and plains with their flowers and fruits we have new scenery, new life of every sort; water hills and dales in eternal visible motion for rock waves, types of permanence.

It was curious to note how suddenly the eager countenances of the passengers were darkened as soon as the good ship passed through the Golden Gate and began to heave on the waves of the open ocean. The crowded deck was speedily deserted on account of seasickness. It seemed strange that nearly every one afflicted should be more or less ashamed.

Next morning a strong wind was blowing, and the sea was grey and white, with long breaking waves, across which the Dakota was racing half-buried in spray. Very few passengers were on deck to enjoy the wild scenery. Every wave seemed to be making enthusiastic, eager haste to the shore, with long, irised tresses streaming from its tops, some of its outer fringes borne away in scud to refresh the wind, all the rolling, pitching, flying water exulting in the beauty of rainbow light. Gulls and albatrosses, strong, glad life in the midst of the stormy beauty, skimmed the waves against the wind, seemingly without effort, oftentimes flying nearly a mile without a single wing-beat, gracefully swaying from side to side and tracing the curves of the briny water hills with the finest precision, now and then just grazing the highest.

And yonder, glistening amid the irised spray, is a still more striking revelation of warm life in the so-called howling waste – a half-dozen whales, their broad backs like glaciated bosses of granite heaving aloft in near view, spouting lustily, drawing a long breath, and plunging down home in colossal health and comfort. A merry school of porpoises, a square mile of them, suddenly appear, tossing themselves into the air in abounding strength and hilarity, adding foam to the waves and making all the wilderness wilder. One cannot but feel sympathy with and be proud of these brave neighbours, fellow citizens in the commonwealth of the world, making a living like the rest of us. Our good ship also seemed like a thing of life, its great iron heart beating on through calm and storm, a truly noble spectacle. But think of the hearts of these whales, beating warm against the sea, day and night, through dark and light, on and on for centuries; how the red blood must rush and gurgle in and out, bucketfuls, barrelfuls at a beat!

The cloud colours of one of the four sunsets enjoyed on the voyage were remarkably pure and rich in tone. There was a well-defined range of cumuli a few degrees above the horizon, and a massive, dark-grey rain-cloud above it, from which depended long, bent fringes overlapping the lower cumuli and partially veiling them; and from time to time sunbeams poured through narrow openings and painted the exposed bosses and fringes in ripe yellow tones, which, with the reflections on the water, made magnificent pictures. The scenery of the ocean, however sublime in vast expanse, seems far less beautiful to us dry-shod animals than that of the land seen only in comparatively small patches; but when we contemplate the whole globe as one great dewdrop, striped and dotted with continents and islands, flying through space with other stars all singing and shining together as one, the whole universe appears as an infinite storm of beauty.

The California coast-hills and cliffs look bare and uninviting as seen from the ship, the magnificent forests keeping well back out of sight beyond the reach of the sea winds; those of Oregon and Washington are in some places clad with conifers nearly down to the shore; even the little detached islets, so marked a feature to the northward, are mostly tree-crowned. Up through the Straits of Juan de Fuca the forests, sheltered from the ocean gales and favoured with abundant rains, flourish in marvellous luxuriance on the glacier-sculptured mountains of the Olympic Range.

We arrived in Esquimault Harbour, three miles from Victoria, on the evening of the fourth day, and drove to the town through a magnificent forest of Douglas spruce – with an undergrowth in open spots of oak, madrone, hazel, dogwood, alder, spiræa, willow, and wild rose – and around many an upswelling *moutonné* rock, freshly glaciated and furred with yellow mosses and lichens.

Victoria, the capital of British Columbia, was in 1879 a small old-fashioned English town on the south end of Vancouver Island. It was said to contain about six thousand inhabitants. The government buildings and some of the business blocks were noticeable, but the attention of the traveller was more worthily attracted to the neat cottage homes found here, embowered in the freshest and floweriest climbing roses and honeysuckles conceivable. Californians may well be proud of their home roses loading sunny verandas, climbing to the tops of the roofs and falling over the gables in white and red cascades. But here, with so much bland fog and dew and gentle laving rain, a still finer development of some of the commonest garden plants is reached. English honeysuckle seems to have found here a most congenial home. Still more beautiful were the wild roses, blooming in wonderful luxuriance along the woodland paths, with corollas two and three inches wide. This rose and three species of spiræa fairly filled the air with fragrance after showers; and how brightly then did the red dogwood berries shine amid the green leaves beneath trees two hundred and fifty feet high.

Strange to say, all of this exuberant forest and flower vegetation was growing upon fresh moraine material scarcely at all moved or in any way modified by post-glacial agents. In the town gardens and orchards, peaches and apples fell upon glacier-polished rocks, and the streets were graded in moraine gravel; and I observed scratched and grooved rock bosses as unweathered and telling as those of the High Sierra of California eight thousand feet or more above sea-level. The Victoria Harbour is plainly glacial in origin, eroded from the solid; and the rock islets that rise here and there in it are unchanged to any appreciable extent by all the waves that have broken over them since first they came to light toward the close of the glacial period. The shores also of the harbour are strikingly grooved and scratched and in every way as glacial in all their characteristics as those of new-born glacial lakes. That the domain of the sea is being slowly extended over the land by incessant wave-action is well known; but in this freshly glaciated region the shores have been so short a time exposed to wave-action that they are scarcely at all wasted. The extension of the sea affected by its own action in post-glacial times is probably less than the millionth part of that affected by glacial action during the last glacier period. The direction of the flow of the ice-sheet to which all the main features of this wonderful region are due was in general southward.

From this quiet little English town I made many short excursions – up the coast to Nanaimo, to Burrard Inlet, now the terminus of the Canadian Pacific Railroad, to Puget Sound, up Frazer River to New Westminster and Yale at the head of navigation, charmed everywhere with the wild, new-born scenery. The most interesting of these and the most difficult to leave was the Puget Sound region, famous the world over for the wonderful forests of gigantic trees about its shores. It is an arm and many-fingered hand of the sea, reaching southward from the Straits of Juan de Fuca about a hundred miles into the heart of one of the noblest coniferous forests on the face of the globe. All its scenery is wonderful – broad river-like reaches sweeping in beautiful curves around bays and capes and jutting promontories, opening here and there into smooth, blue, lake-like expanses dotted with islands and feathered with tall, spiry evergreens, their beauty doubled on the bright mirror-water.

Sailing from Victoria, the Olympic Mountains are seen right ahead, rising in bold relief against the sky, with jagged crests and peaks from six to eight thousand feet high – small residual glaciers and ragged snow-fields beneath them in wide amphitheatres opening down through the forest-filled valleys. These valleys mark the courses of the Olympic glaciers at the period of their greatest extension, when they poured their tribute into that portion of the great northern ice-sheet that overswept Vancouver Island and filled the strait between it and the mainland.

On the way up to Olympia, then a hopeful little town situated at the end of one of the longest fingers of the Sound, one is often reminded of Lake Tahoe, the scenery of the widest expanses is so lake-like in the clearness and stillness of the water and the luxuriance of the surrounding forests. Doubling cape after cape, passing uncounted islands, new combinations break on the view in endless variety, sufficient to satisfy the lover of wild beauty through a whole life. When the clouds come down, blotting out everything, one feels as if at sea; again lifting a little, some islet may be seen standing alone with the tops of its trees dipping out of sight in grey misty fringes; then the ranks of spruce and cedar bounding the water's edge come to view; and when at length the whole sky is clear the colossal cone of Mount Rainier may be seen in spotless white, looking down over the dark woods from a distance of fifty or sixty miles, but so high and massive and so sharply outlined, it seems to be just back of a strip of woods only a few miles wide.

Mount Rainier, or Tahoma (the Indian name), is the noblest of the volcanic cones extending from Lassen Butte and Mount Shasta along the Cascade Range to Mount Baker. One of the most telling views of it hereabouts is obtained near Tacoma. From a bluff back of the town it was revealed in all its glory, laden with glaciers and snow down to the forested foothills around its finely curved base. Up to this time (1879) it had been ascended but once. From observations made on the summit with a single aneroid barometer, it was estimated to be about 14,500ft. high. Mount Baker, to the northward, is about 10,700ft. high, a noble mountain. So also are Mount Adams, Mount St Helens, and Mount Hood. The latter, overlooking the town of Portland, is perhaps the best known. Rainier, about the same height as Shasta, surpasses them all in massive icy grandeur – the most majestic solitary mountain I had ever yet beheld. How eagerly I gazed and longed to climb it and study its history only the mountaineer may know, but I was compelled to turn away and bide my time.

The species forming the bulk of the woods here is the Douglas spruce (*Pseudotsuga douglasii*), one of the greatest of the western giants. A specimen that I measured near Olympia was about three hundred feet in height and twelve feet in diameter four feet above the ground. It is a widely distributed tree, extending northward through British Columbia, southward through Oregon and California, and eastward to the Rocky Mountains. The timber is used for ship-building, spars, piles, and the framework of houses, bridges, etc. In the California lumber markets it is known as 'Oregon pine'. In Utah, where it is common on the Wahsatch Mountains, it is called 'red pine'. In California, on the western slope of the Sierra Nevada, it forms, in company with the yellow pine, sugar pine, and incense cedar, a pretty well-defined belt at a height of from three to six thousand feet above the sea; but it is only in Oregon and Washington, especially in this Puget Sound region, that it reaches its very grandest development – tall, straight, and strong, growing down close to tide-water.

All the towns of the Sound had a hopeful, thrifty aspect. Port Townsend, picturesquely located on a grassy bluff, was the port of clearance for vessels sailing to foreign parts. Seattle was famed for its coalmines, and claimed to be the coming town of the North Pacific Coast. So also did its rival, Tacoma, which had been selected as the terminus of the much-talked-of Northern Pacific Railway. Several coal-veins of astonishing thickness were discovered the winter before on the Carbon River, to the east of Tacoma, one of them said to be no less than twenty-one feet, another twenty feet, another fourteen, with many smaller ones, the aggregate thickness of all the veins being upwards of a hundred feet. Large deposits of magnetic iron ore and brown hematite, together with limestone, had been discovered in advantageous proximity to the coal, making a bright outlook for the Sound region in general in connection with its railroad hopes, its unrivalled timber resources, and its far-reaching geographical relations.

After spending a few weeks in the Puget Sound region with a friend from San Francisco, we engaged passage on the little mail steamer California, at Portland, Oregon, for Alaska. The sail down the broad lower reaches of the Columbia and across its foamy bar, around Cape Flattery, and up the Juan de Fuca Strait, was delightful; and after calling again at Victoria and Port Townsend we got fairly off for icy Alaska.

CHAPTER TWO

Alexander Archipelago and the Home I Found in Alaska

To the lover of pure wildness Alaska is one of the most wonderful countries in the world. No excursions that I know of may be made into any other American wilderness where so marvellous an abundance of noble, newborn scenery is so charmingly brought to view as on the trip through the Alexander Archipelago to Fort Wrangell and Sitka. Gazing from the deck of the steamer, one is borne smoothly over calm blue waters, through the midst of countless forest-clad islands. The ordinary discomforts of a sea voyage are not felt, for nearly all the whole long way is on inland waters that are about as waveless as rivers and lakes. So numerous are the islands that they seem to have been sown broadcast; long tapering vistas between the largest of them open in every direction.

Day after day in the fine weather we enjoyed, we seemed to float in true fairyland, each succeeding view seeming more and more beautiful, the one we chanced to have before us the most surprisingly beautiful of all. Never before this had I been embosomed in scenery so hopelessly beyond description. To sketch picturesque bits, definitely bounded, is comparatively easy – a lake in the woods, a glacier meadow, or a cascade in its dell; or even a grand master view of mountains beheld from some commanding outlook after climbing from height to height above the forests. These may be attempted, and more or less telling pictures made of them; but in these coast landscapes there is such indefinite, on-leading expansiveness, such a multitude of features without apparent redundance, their lines graduating delicately into one another in endless succession, while the whole is so fine, so tender, so ethereal, that all penwork seems hopelessly unavailing. Tracing shining ways through fiord and sound, past forests and waterfalls, islands and mountains and far azure headlands, it seems as if surely we must at length reach the very paradise of the poets, the abode of the blessed.

Some idea of the wealth of this scenery may be gained from the fact that the coast-line of Alaska is about twenty-six thousand miles long, more than twice as long as all the rest of the United States. The islands of the Alexander Archipelago, with the straits, channels, canals, sounds, passages, and fiords, form an intricate web of land and water embroidery sixty or seventy miles wide, fringing the lofty ice chain of coast mountains from Puget Sound to Cook Inlet; and, with infinite variety, the general pattern is harmonious throughout its whole extent of nearly a thousand miles. Here you glide into a narrow channel hemmed in by mountain walls, forested down to the water's edge, where there is no distant view, and your attention is concentrated on the objects close about you – the crowded spires of the spruces and hemlocks rising higher and higher on the steep green slopes; stripes of paler green where winter avalanches have cleared away the trees, allowing grasses and willows to spring up; zigzags of cascades appearing and disappearing among the bushes and trees; short, steep glens with brawling streams hidden beneath alder and dogwood, seen only where they emerge on the brown algæ of the shore; and retreating hollows, with lingering snow-banks marking the fountains of ancient glaciers. The steamer is often so near the shore that you may distinctly see the cones clustered on the tops of the trees, and the ferns and bushes at their feet.

But new scenes are brought to view with magical rapidity. Rounding some bossy cape, the eye is called away into far-reaching vistas, bounded on either hand by headlands in charming array, one dipping gracefully beyond another and growing fainter and more ethereal in the distance. The tranquil channel stretching river-like between, may be stirred here and there by the silvery plashing of upspringing salmon, or by flocks of white gulls floating like waterlilies among the sun spangles; while mellow, tempered sunshine is streaming over all, blending sky, land, and water in pale, misty blue. Then, while you are dreamily gazing into the depths of this leafy ocean lane, the little steamer, seeming hardly larger than a duck, turning into some passage not visible until the moment of entering it, glides into a wide expanse – a sound filled with islands, sprinkled and clustered in forms and compositions such as nature alone can invent; some of them so small the trees growing on them seem like single handfuls culled from the neighbouring woods and set in the water to keep them fresh, while here and there at wide intervals you may notice bare rocks just above the water, mere dots punctuating grand, outswelling sentences of islands.

The variety we find, both as to the contours and the collocation of the islands, is due chiefly to differences in the structure and composition of their rocks, and the unequal glacial denudation different portions of the coast were subjected to. This influence must have been especially heavy toward the end of the glacial period, when the main ice-sheet began to break up into separate glaciers. Moreover, the mountains of the larger islands nourished local glaciers, some of them of considerable size, which sculptured their summits and sides, forming in some cases wide cirques with canyons or valleys leading down from them into the channels and sounds. These causes have produced much of the bewildering variety of which nature is so fond, but none the less will the studious observer see the underlying harmony – the general trend of the islands in the direction of the flow of the main ice-mantle from the mountains of the Coast Range, more or less varied by subordinate foothill ridges and mountains. Furthermore, all the islands, great and small, as well as the headlands and promontories of the mainland, are seen to have a rounded, over-rubbed appearance produced by the over-sweeping ice-flood during the period of greatest glacial abundance.

The canals, channels, straits, passages, sounds, etc., are subordinate to the same glacial conditions in their forms, trends, and extent as those which determined the forms, trends, and distribution of the land-masses, their basins being the parts of the pre-glacial margin of the continent, eroded to varying depths below sea-level, and into which, of course, the ocean waters flowed as the ice was melted out of them. Had the general glacial denudation been much less, these ocean ways over which we are sailing would have been valleys and canyons and lakes; and the islands rounded hills and ridges, landscapes with undulating features like those found above sea-level wherever the rocks and glacial conditions are similar. In general, the island-bound channels are like rivers, not only in separate reaches as seen from the deck of a vessel, but continuously so for hundreds of miles in the case of the longest of them. The tide-currents, the fresh driftwood, the inflowing streams, and the luxuriant foliage of the out-leaning trees on the shores make this resemblance all the more complete. The largest islands look like part of the mainland in any view to be had of them from the ship, but far the greater number are small, and appreciable as islands, scores of them being less than a mile long. These the eye easily takes in and revels in their beauty with ever fresh delight. In their relations to each other the individual members of a group have evidently been derived from the same general rock-mass, yet they never seem broken or abridged in any way as to their contour lines, however abruptly they may dip their sides. Viewed one by one, they seem detached beauties, like extracts from a poem, while, from the completeness of their lines and the way that their trees are arranged, each seems a finished stanza in itself. Contemplating the arrangement of the trees on these small islands, a distinct impression is produced of their having been sorted and harmonized as to size like a well-balanced bouquet. On some of the smaller tufted islets a group of tapering spruces is planted in the middle, and two smaller groups that evidently correspond with each other are planted on the ends at about equal distances from the central group; or the whole appears as one group with marked fringing trees that match each other spreading around the sides, like flowers leaning outward against the rim of a vase. These harmonious tree relations are so constant that they evidently are the result of design, as much so as the arrangement of the feathers of birds or the scales of fishes.

Thus perfectly beautiful are these blessed evergreen islands, and their beauty is the beauty of youth, for though the freshness of their verdure must be ascribed to the bland moisture with which they are bathed from warm ocean-currents, the very existence of the islands, their features, finish, and peculiar distribution, are all immediately referable to ice-action during the great glacial winter just now drawing to a close.

We arrived at Wrangell 14 July, and after a short stop of a few hours went on to Sitka and returned on the 20th to Wrangell, the most inhospitable place at first sight I had ever seen. The little steamer that had been my home in the wonderful trip through the archipelago, after taking the mail, departed on her return to Portland, and as I watched her gliding out of sight in the dismal blurring rain, I felt strangely lonesome. The friend that had accompanied me thus far now left for his home in San Francisco, with two other interesting travellers who had made the trip for health and scenery, while my fellow passengers, the missionaries, went direct to the Presbyterian home in the old fort. There was nothing like a tavern or lodging-house in the village, nor could I find any place in the stumpy, rocky, boggy ground about it that looked dry enough to camp on until I could find a way into the wilderness to begin my studies. Every place within a mile or two of the town seemed strangely shelterless and inhospitable, for all the trees had long ago been felled for building-timber and firewood. At the worst, I thought, I could build a bark hut on a hill back of the village, where something like a forest loomed dimly through the draggled clouds.

I had already seen some of the high glacier-bearing mountains in distant views from the steamer, and was anxious to reach them. A few whites of the village, with whom I entered into conversation, warned me that the Indians were a bad lot, not to be trusted, that the woods were well-nigh impenetrable, and that I could go nowhere without a canoe. On the other hand, these natural difficulties made the grand wild country all the more attractive, and I determined to get into the heart of it somehow or other with a bag of hardtack, trusting to my usual good luck. My present difficulty was in finding a first base camp. My only hope was on the hill. When I was strolling past the old fort I happened to meet one of the missionaries, who kindly asked me where I was going to take up my quarters.

'I don't know', I replied. 'I have not been able to find quarters of any sort. The top of that little hill over there seems the only possible place.'

He then explained that every room in the mission house was full, but he thought I might obtain leave to spread my blanket in a carpenter-shop belonging to the mission. Thanking him, I ran down to the sloppy wharf for my bundle of baggage, laid it on the shop floor, and felt glad and snug among the dry sweet-smelling shavings.

The carpenter was at work on a new Presbyterian mission building, and when he came in I explained that Dr Jackson[1] had suggested that I might be allowed to sleep on the floor, and after I assured him that I would not touch

---

[1]Dr. Sheldon Jackson, 1834–1909, became Superintendent of Presbyterian Missions in Alaska in 1877, and United States General Agent of Education in 1885. [W. F. B.]

his tools or be in his way, he goodnaturedly gave me the freedom of the shop and also of his small private side room where I would find a wash-basin.

I was here only one night, however, for Mr Vanderbilt, a merchant, who with his family occupied the best house in the fort, hearing that one of the late arrivals, whose business none seemed to know, was compelled to sleep in the carpenter-shop, paid me a good-Samaritan visit and after a few explanatory words on my glacier and forest studies, with fine hospitality offered me a room and a place at his table. Here I found a real home, with freedom to go on all sorts of excursions as opportunity offered. Annie Vanderbilt, a little doctor of divinity two years old, ruled the household with love sermons and kept it warm.

Mr Vanderbilt introduced me to prospectors and traders and some of the most influential of the Indians. I visited the mission school and the home for Indian girls kept by Mrs MacFarland, and made short excursions to the nearby forests and streams, and studied the rate of growth of the different species of trees and their age, counting the annual rings on stumps in the large clearings made by the military when the fort was occupied, causing wondering speculation among the Wrangell folk, as was reported by Mr Vanderbilt.

'What can the fellow be up to?' they inquired. 'He seems to spend most of his time among stumps and weeds. I saw him the other day on his knees, looking at a stump as if he expected to find gold in it. He seems to have no serious object whatever.'

One night when a heavy rainstorm was blowing I unwittingly caused a lot of wondering excitement among the whites as well as the superstitious Indians. Being anxious to see how the Alaska trees behave in storms and hear the songs they sing, I stole quietly away through the grey drenching blast to the hill back of the town, without being observed. Night was falling when I set out and it was pitch dark when I reached the top. The glad, rejoicing storm in glorious voice was singing through the woods, noble compensation for mere body discomfort. But I wanted a fire, a big one, to see as well as hear how the storm and trees were behaving. After long, patient groping I found a little dry punk in a hollow trunk and carefully stored it beside my matchbox and an inch or two of candle in an inside pocket that the rain had not yet reached; then, wiping some dead twigs and whittling them into thin shavings, stored them with the punk. I then made a little conical bark hut about a foot high, and, carefully leaning over it and sheltering it as much as possible from the driving rain, I wiped and stored a lot of dead twigs, lighted the candle, and set it in the hut, carefully added pinches of punk and shavings, and at length got a little blaze, by the light of which I gradually added larger shavings, then twigs all set on end astride the inner flame, making the little hut higher and wider. Soon I had light enough to enable me to select the best dead branches and large sections of bark, which were set on end, gradually increasing the height and corresponding light of the hut fire. A considerable area was thus well lighted, from which I gathered abundance of wood, and kept adding to the fire until it had a strong, hot heart and sent up a pillar of flame thirty or forty feet high, illuminating a wide circle in spite of the rain, and casting a red glare into the flying clouds. Of all the thousands of camp-fires I have elsewhere built none was just like this one, rejoicing in triumphant strength and beauty in the heart of the rain-laden gale. It was wonderful – the illumined rain and clouds mingled together and the trees glowing against the jet background, the colours of the mossy, lichened trunks with sparkling streams pouring down the furrows of the bark, and the grey-bearded old patriarchs bowing low and chanting in passionate worship!

My fire was in all its glory about midnight, and, having made a bark shed to shelter me from the rain and partially dry my clothing, I had nothing to do but look and listen and join the trees in their hymns and prayers.

Neither the great white heart of the fire nor the quivering enthusiastic flames shooting aloft like auroral lances could be seen from the village on account of the trees in front of it and its being back a little way over the brow of the hill; but the light in the clouds made a great show, a portentous sign in the stormy heavens unlike anything ever before seen or heard of in Wrangell. Some wakeful Indians, happening to see it about midnight, in great alarm aroused the Collector of Customs and begged him to go to the missionaries and get them to pray away the frightful omen, and inquired anxiously whether white men had ever seen anything like that sky-fire, which instead of being quenched by the rain was burning brighter and brighter. The Collector said he had heard of such strange fires, and this one he thought might perhaps be what the white man called a 'volcano, or an *ignis fatuus*'. When Mr Young was called from his bed to pray, he, too, confoundedly astonished and at a loss for any sort of explanation, confessed that he had never seen anything like it in the sky or anywhere else in such cold wet weather, but that it was probably some sort of spontaneous combustion, 'that the white man called St. Elmo's fire, or Will-of-the-wisp'. These explanations, though not convincingly clear, perhaps served to veil their own astonishment and in some measure to diminish the superstitious fears of the natives; but from what I heard, the few whites who happened to see the strange light wondered about as wildly as the Indians.

I have enjoyed thousands of camp-fires in all sorts of weather and places, warm-hearted, short-flamed, friendly little beauties glowing in the dark on open spots in High Sierra gardens, daisies and lilies circled about them, gazing like enchanted children; and large fires in silver fir forests, with spires of flame towering like the trees about them, and sending up multitudes of starry sparks to enrich the sky; and still greater fires on the mountains in winter, changing camp climate to summer, and making the frosty snow look like beds of white flowers, and oftentimes mingling their swarms of swift-flying sparks with falling snow-crystals when the clouds were in bloom. But this Wrangell camp-fire, my first in Alaska, I shall always remember for its triumphant storm-defying grandeur, and the wondrous beauty of the psalm-singing, lichen-painted trees which it brought to light.

CHAPTER THREE

Wrangell Island and Alaska Summers

WRANGELL ISLAND is about fourteen miles long, separated from the mainland by a narrow channel or fiord, and trending in the direction of the flow of the ancient ice-sheet. Like all its neighbours, it is densely forested down to the water's edge with trees that never seem to have suffered from thirst or fire or the axe of the lumberman in all their long century lives. Beneath soft, shady clouds, with abundance of rain, they flourish in wonderful strength and beauty to a good old age, while the many warm days, half cloudy, half clear, and the little groups of pure sun-days enable them to ripen their cones and send myriads of seeds flying every autumn to insure the permanence of the forests and feed the multitude of animals.

The Wrangell village was a rough place. No mining hamlet in the placer gulches of California, nor any backwoods village I ever saw, approached it in picturesque, devil-may-care *abandon*. It was a lawless bedraggle of wooden huts and houses, built in crooked lines wrangling around the boggy shore of the island for a mile or so in the general form of the letter S, without the slightest subordination to the points of the compass or to building laws of any kind. Stumps and logs, like precious monuments, adorned its two streets, each stump and log, on account of the moist climate, moss-grown and tufted with grass and bushes, but muddy on the sides below the limit of the bogline. The ground in general was an oozy, mossy bog on a foundation of jagged rocks, full of concealed pitholes. This picturesque rock, bog and stump obstructions, however, were not so very much in the way, for there were no wagons or carriages there. There was not a horse on the island. The domestic animals were represented by chickens, a lonely cow, a few sheep, and hogs of a breed well calculated to deepen and complicate the mud of the streets.

Most of the permanent residents of Wrangell were engaged in trade. Some little trade was carried on in fish and furs, but most of the quickening business of the place was derived from the Cassiar gold-mines, some two hundred and fifty or three hundred miles inland, by way of the Stickeen River and Dease Lake. Two stern-wheel steamers plied on the river between Wrangell and Telegraph Creek at the head of navigation, a hundred and fifty miles from Wrangell, carrying freight and passengers and connecting with pack-trains for the mines. These placer mines, on tributaries of the Mackenzie River, were discovered in the year 1874. About eighteen hundred miners and prospectors were said to have passed through Wrangell that season of 1879, about half of them being Chinamen. Nearly a third of this whole number set out from here in the month of February, travelling on the Stickeen River, which usually remains safely frozen until toward the end of April. The main body of the miners, however, went up on the steamers in May and June. On account of the severe winters they were all compelled to leave the mines the end of September. Perhaps about two thirds of them passed the winter in Portland and Victoria and the towns of Puget Sound. The rest remained here in Wrangell, dozing away the long winter as best they could.

Indians, mostly of the Stickeen tribe, occupied the two ends of the town, the whites, of whom there were about forty or fifty, the middle portion; but there was no determinate line of demarcation, the dwellings of the Indians being mostly as large and solidly built of logs and planks as those of the whites. Some of them were adorned with tall totem poles.

The fort was a quadrangular stockade with a dozen block and frame buildings located upon rising ground just back of the business part of the town. It was built by our Government shortly after the purchase of Alaska, and was abandoned in 1872, reoccupied by the military in 1875, and finally abandoned and sold to private parties in 1877. In the fort and about it there were a few good, clean homes, which shone all the more brightly in their sombre surroundings. The ground occupied by the fort, by being carefully levelled and drained was dry, though formerly a portion of the general swamp, showing how easily the whole town could have been improved. But in spite of disorder and squalor, shaded with clouds, washed and wiped by rain and sea winds, it was triumphantly salubrious through all the seasons. And though the houses seemed to rest uneasily among the miry rocks and stumps, squirming at all angles as if they had been tossed and twisted by earthquake shocks, and showing but little more relation to one another than may be observed among moraine boulders, Wrangell was a tranquil place. I never heard a noisy brawl in the streets, or a clap of thunder, and the waves seldom spoke much above a whisper along the beach. In summer the rain comes straight down, steamy and tepid. The clouds are usually united, filling the sky, not racing along in threatening ranks suggesting energy of an overbearing destructive kind, but forming a bland, mild, laving bath. The cloudless days are calm, pearl-grey, and brooding in tone, inclining to rest and peace; the islands seem to drowse and float on the glassy water, and in the woods scarce a leaf stirs.

The very brightest of Wrangell days are not what Californians would call bright. The tempered sunshine sifting through the moist atmosphere makes no dazzling glare, and the town, like the landscape, rests beneath a hazy, hushing, Indian-summerish spell. On the longest days the sun rises about three o'clock, but it is daybreak at midnight. The cocks crowed when they woke, without reference to the dawn, for it is never quite dark; there were only a few full-grown roosters in Wrangell, half a dozen or so, to awaken the town and give it a civilized character. After sunrise a few languid smoke-columns might be seen, telling the first stir of the people. Soon an Indian or two might be noticed here and there at the doors of their barnlike cabins, and a merchant getting ready for trade; but scarcely a sound was heard, only a dull, muffled stir gradually deepening. There were only two white babies in the town, so far as I saw, and as for Indian babies, they woke and ate and made no crying sound. Later you might hear the croaking of ravens, and the strokes of an axe on firewood. About eight or nine o'clock the town was awake, Indians, mostly women and children, began to gather on the front platforms of the half-dozen stores, sitting carelessly on their blankets, every other face hideously blackened, a naked circle around the eyes, and perhaps a spot on the cheek-bone and the nose where the smut had been rubbed off. Some of the little children were also blackened, and none were over-clad, their light and airy costume consisting of a calico shirt reaching only to the waist. Boys eight or ten years old sometimes had an additional garment – a pair of castaway miner's overalls wide enough and ragged enough for extravagant ventilation. The larger girls and young women were arrayed in showy calico, and wore jaunty straw hats, gorgeously ribboned, and glowed among the blackened and blanketed old crones like scarlet tanagers in a flock of blackbirds. The women, seated on the steps and platform of the traders' shops, could hardly be called loafers, for they had berries to sell, basketfuls of huckleberries, large yellow salmon-berries, and bog raspberries that looked wondrous fresh and clean amid the surrounding squalor. After patiently waiting for purchasers until hungry, they ate what they could not sell, and went away to gather more.

Yonder you see a canoe gliding out from the shore, containing perhaps a man, a woman, and a child or two, all paddling together in natural, easy rhythm. They are going to catch a fish, no difficult matter, and when this is done their day's work is done. Another party puts out to capture bits of driftwood, for it is easier to procure fuel in this way than to drag it down from the outskirts of the woods through rocks and bushes. As the day advances, a fleet of canoes may be seen along the shore, all fashioned alike, high and long beak-like prows and sterns, with lines as fine as those of the breast of a duck. What the mustang is to the Mexican *vaquero*, the canoe is to these coast Indians. They skim along the shores to fish and hunt and trade, or merely to visit their neighbours, for they are sociable, and have family pride remarkably well developed, meeting often to inquire after each other's health, attend potlatches and dances, and gossip concerning coming marriages, births, deaths, etc. Others seem to sail for the pure pleasure of the thing, their canoes decorated with handfuls of the tall purple epilobium.

Yonder goes a whole family, grandparents and all, making a direct course for some favourite stream and camp-ground. They are going to gather berries, as the baskets tell. Never before in all my travels, north or south, had I found so lavish an abundance of berries as here. The woods and meadows are full of them, both on the lowlands and mountains – huckleberries of many species, salmon-berries, blackberries, raspberries, with service-berries on dry open places, and cranberries in the bogs, sufficient for every bird, beast, and human being in the territory and thousands of tons to spare. The huckleberries are especially abundant. A species that grows well up on the mountains is the best and largest, a half-inch and more in diameter and delicious in flavour. These grow on bushes three or four inches to a foot high. The berries of the commonest species are smaller and grow almost everywhere on the low grounds on bushes from three to six or seven feet high. This is the species on which the Indians depend most for food, gathering them in large quantities, beating them into a paste, pressing the paste into cakes about an inch thick, and drying them over a slow fire to enrich their winter stores. Salmon-berries and service-berries are preserved in the same way.

A little excursion to one of the best huckleberry-fields adjacent to Wrangell, under the direction of the Collector of Customs, to which I was invited, I greatly enjoyed. There were nine Indians in the party, mostly women and children going to gather huckleberries. As soon as we had arrived at the chosen camp-ground on the bank of a trout stream, all ran into the bushes and began eating berries before anything in the way of camp-making was done, laughing and chattering in natural animal enjoyment. The Collector went up the stream to examine a meadow at its head with reference to the quantity of hay it might yield for his cow, fishing by the way. All the Indians except the two eldest boys who joined the Collector, remained among the berries.

The fishermen had rather poor luck, owing, they said, to the sunny brightness of the day, a complaint seldom heard in this climate. They got good exercise, however, jumping from boulder to boulder in the brawling stream, running along slippery logs and through the bushes that fringe the bank, casting here and there into swirling pools at the foot of cascades, imitating the tempting little skips and whirls of flies so well known to fishing persons, but perhaps still better known to Indian boys. At the lake-basin the Collector, after he had surveyed his hay-meadow, went around it to the inlet of the lake with his brown pair of attendants to try their luck, while I botanised in the delightful flora which called to mind the cool sphagnum and carex bogs of Wisconsin and Canada. Here I found many of my old favourites the heathworts – kalmia, pyrola, chiogenes, huckleberry, cranberry, etc. On the margin of the meadow darling linnæa was in its glory; purple panicled grasses in full flower reached over my head, and some of the carices and ferns were almost as tall. Here, too, on the edge of the woods I found the wild apple tree, the first I had seen in Alaska. The Indians gather the fruit, small and sour as it is, to flavour their fat salmon. I never saw a richer bog and meadow growth anywhere. The principal forest-trees are hemlock, spruce, and Nootka cypress, with a few pines (*P. contorta*) on the margin of the meadow, some of them nearly a hundred feet high, draped with grey usnea, the bark also grey with scale lichens.

We met all the berry-pickers at the lake, excepting only a small girl and the camp-keeper. In their bright colours they made a lively picture among the quivering bushes, keeping up a low pleasant chanting as if the day and the place and the berries were according to their own hearts. The children carried small baskets, holding two or three quarts; the women two large ones swung over their shoulders. In the afternoon, when the baskets were full, all started back to the camp-ground, where the canoe was left. We parted at the lake, I choosing to follow quietly the stream through the woods. I was the first to arrive at camp. The rest of the party came in shortly afterwards, singing and humming like heavy-laden bees. It was interesting to note how kindly they held out handfuls of the best berries to the little girl, who welcomed them all in succession with smiles and merry words that I did not understand. But there was no mistaking the kindliness and serene good nature.

While I was at Wrangell the chiefs and head men of the Stickeen tribe got up a grand dinner and entertainment in honour of their distinguished visitors, three doctors of divinity and their wives, fellow passengers on the steamer with me, whose object was to organise the Presbyterian church. To both the dinner and dances I was invited, was adopted by the Stickeen tribe, and given an Indian name (Ancoutahan) said to mean adopted chief. I was inclined to regard this honour as being unlikely to have any practical value, but I was assured by Mr Vanderbilt, Mr Young and others that it would be a great safeguard while I was on my travels among the different tribes of the archipelago. For travellers without an Indian name might be killed and robbed without the offender being called to account as long as the crime was kept secret from the whites; but, being adopted by the Stickeens, no one belonging to the other tribes would dare attack me, knowing that the Stickeens would hold them responsible.

The dinner-tables were tastefully decorated with flowers, and the food and general arrangements were in good taste, but there was no trace of Indian dishes. It was mostly imported canned stuff served Boston fashion. After the dinner we assembled in Chief Shake's large block-house and were entertained with lively examples of their dances and amusements, carried on with great spirit, making a very novel barbarous durbar. The dances seemed to me wonderfully like those of the American Indians in general, a monotonous stamping accompanied by hand-clapping, head-jerking, and explosive grunts kept in time to grim drum-beats. The chief dancer and leader scattered great quantities of downy feathers like a snowstorm as blessings on everybody, while all chanted, 'Hee-ee-ah-ah, hee-ee-ah-ah', jumping up and down until all were bathed in perspiration.

After the dancing excellent imitations were given of the gait, gestures, and behaviour of several animals under different circumstances – walking, hunting, capturing, and devouring their prey, etc. While all were quietly seated, waiting to see what next was going to happen, the door of the big house was suddenly thrown open and in bounced a bear, so true to life in form and gestures we were all startled, though it was only a bear-skin nicely fitted on a man who was intimately acquainted with the animals and knew how to imitate them. The bear shuffled down into the middle of the floor and made the motion of jumping into a stream and catching a wooden salmon that was ready for him, carrying it out on to the bank, throwing his head around to listen and see if anyone was coming, then tearing it to pieces, jerking his head from side to side, looking and listening in fear of hunters' rifles. Besides the bear dance, there were porpoise and deer dances with one of the party imitating the animals by stuffed specimens with an Indian inside, and the movements were so accurately imitated that they seemed the real thing.

These animal plays were followed by serious speeches, interpreted by an Indian woman: 'Dear Brothers and Sisters, this is the way we used to dance. We liked it long ago when we were blind, we always danced this way, but now we are not blind. The Good Lord has taken pity upon us and sent his son, Jesus Christ, to tell us what to do. We have danced to-day only to show you how blind we were to like to dance in this foolish way. We will not dance any more.'

Another speech was interpreted as follows: ''Dear Brothers and Sisters,' the chief says, 'this is the way we used to dance and play. We do not wish to do so any more. We will give away all the dance dresses you have seen us wearing, though we value them very highly.' He says he feels much honoured to have so many white brothers and sisters at our dinner and plays.[1]

Several short explanatory remarks were made all through the exercises by Chief Shakes, presiding with grave dignity. The last of his speeches concluded thus: 'Dear Brothers and Sisters, we have been long, long in the dark. You have led us into strong guiding light and taught us the right way to live and the right way to die. I thank you for myself and all my people, and I give you my heart.'

At the close of the amusements there was a potlatch when robes made of the skins of deer, wild sheep, marmots, and sables were distributed, and many of the fantastic head-dresses that had been worn by Shamans. One of these fell to my share.

The floor of the house was strewn with fresh hemlock boughs, bunches of showy wild flowers adorned the walls, and the hearth was filled with huckleberry branches and epilobium. Altogether it was a wonderful show.

I have found southeastern Alaska a good, healthy country to live in. The climate of the islands and shores of the mainland is remarkably bland and temperate and free from extremes of either heat or cold throughout the year. It is rainy, however – so much so that hay-making will hardly ever be extensively engaged in here, whatever the future may show in the way of the development of mines, forests, and fisheries. This rainy weather, however, is of good quality, the best of the kind I ever experienced, mild in temperature, mostly gentle in its fall, filling the fountains of the rivers and keeping the whole land fresh and fruitful, while anything more delightful than the shining weather in the midst of the rain, the great round sun-days of July and August, may hardly be found anywhere, north or south. An Alaska summer day is a day without night. In the Far North, at Point Barrow, the sun does not set for weeks, and even here in southeastern Alaska it is only a few degrees below the horizon at its lowest point, and the topmost colours of the sunset blend with those of the sunrise, leaving no gap of darkness between. Midnight is only a low noon, the middle point of the gloaming. The thin clouds that are almost always present and then coloured yellow and red, making a striking advertisement of the sun's progress beneath the horizon. The day opens slowly. 'The low arc of light steals around to the northeastward with gradual increase of height and span and intensity of tone; and when at length the sun appears, it is without much of that stirring, impressive pomp, of flashing, awakening, triumphant energy, suggestive of the Bible imagery, a bride-groom coming out of his chamber and rejoicing like a strong man to run a race. The red clouds with yellow edges dissolve in hazy dimness; the islands, with greyish-white ruffs of mist about them, cast ill-defined shadows on the glistening waters, and the whole down-bending firmament becomes pearl-grey. For three or four hours after sunrise there is nothing especially impressive in the landscape. The sun, though seemingly unclouded, may almost be looked in the face, and the islands and mountains, with their wealth of woods and snow and varied beauty of architecture, seem comparatively sleepy and uncommunicative.

As the day advances toward high noon, the sunflood streaming through the damp atmosphere lights the water levels and the sky to glowing silver. Brightly play the ripples about the bushy edges of the islands and on the plume-shaped streaks between them, ruffled by gentle passing wind-currents. The warm air throbs and makes itself felt as a life-giving, energising ocean, embracing all the landscape, quickening the imagination, and bringing to mind the life and motion about us – the tides, the rivers, the flood of light streaming through the satiny sky; the marvellous abundance of fishes feeding in the lower ocean; the misty flocks of insects in the air; wild sheep and goats on a thousand grassy ridges; beaver and mink far back on many a running stream; Indians floating and basking along the shores; leaves and crystals drinking the sunbeams; and glaciers on the mountains, making valleys and basins for new rivers and lakes and fertile beds of soil.

Through the afternoon, all the way down to the sunset, the day grows in beauty. The light seems to thicken and become yet more generously fruitful without losing its soft mellow brightness. Everything seems to settle into conscious repose. The winds breathe gently or are wholly at rest. The few clouds visible are downy and luminous and combed out fine on the edges. Gulls here and there, winnowing the air on easy wing, are brought into striking relief; and every stroke of the paddles of Indian hunters in their canoes is told by a quick, glancing flash. Bird choirs in the grove are scarce heard as they sweeten the brooding stillness; and the sky, land, and water meet and blend in one inseparable scene of enchantment. Then comes the sunset with its purple and gold, not a narrow arch on the horizon, but oftentimes filling all the sky. The level cloud-bars usually present are fired on the edges, and the spaces of clear sky between them are greenish-yellow or pale amber, while the orderly flocks of small overlapping clouds, often seen higher up, are mostly touched with crimson like the out-leaning sprays of maple-groves in the beginning of an Eastern Indian Summer. Soft, mellow purple flushes the sky to the zenith and fills the air, fairly steeping and transfiguring the islands and making all the water look like wine. After the sun goes down, the glowing gold vanishes, but because it descends on a curve nearly in the same plane with the horizon, the glowing portion of the display lasts much longer than in more southern latitudes, while the upper colours with gradually lessening intensity of tone sweep around to the north, gradually increase to the eastward, and unite with those of the morning.

The most extravagantly coloured of all the sunsets I have yet seen in Alaska was one I enjoyed on the voyage from Portland to Wrangell, when we were in the midst of one of the most thickly islanded parts of the Alexander Archipelago. The day had been showery, but late in the afternoon the clouds melted away from the west, all save a few that settled down in narrow level bars near the horizon. The evening was calm and the sunset colours came on gradually, increasing in extent and richness of tone by slow degrees as if requiring more time than usual to ripen. At a height of about thirty degrees there was a heavy cloud-bank, deeply reddened on its lower edge and the projecting parts of its face. Below this were three horizontal belts of purple edged with gold, while a vividly defined, spreading fan of flame streamed upward across the purple bars and faded in a feather edge of dull red. But beautiful and impressive as was this painting on the sky, the most novel and exciting effect was in the body of the atmosphere itself, which, laden with moisture, became one mass of colour – a fine translucent purple haze in which the islands with softened outlines seemed to float, while a dense red ring lay around the base of each of them as a fitting border. The peaks, too, in the distance, and the snow-fields and glaciers and fleecy rolls of mist that lay in the hollows, were flushed with a deep, rosy alpenglow of ineffable loveliness. Everything near and far, even the ship, was comprehended in the glorious picture and the general colour effect. The mission divines we had aboard seemed then to be truly divine as they gazed transfigured in the celestial glory. So also seemed our bluff, storm-fighting old captain, and his tarry sailors and all.

About one third of the summer days I spent in the Wrangell region were cloudy with very little or no rain, one third decidedly rainy, and one third clear. According to a record kept here of a hundred and forty-seven days beginning 17 May of that year, there were sixty-five on which rain fell, forty-three cloudy with no rain, and thirty-nine clear. In June rain fell on eighteen days, in July eight days, in August fifteen days, in September twenty days. But on some of these days there was only a few minutes' rain, light showers scarce enough to count, while as a general thing the rain fell so gently and the temperature was so mild, very few of them could be called stormy or dismal; even the bleakest, most bedraggled of them all usually had a flush of late or early colour to cheer them, or some white illumination about the noon hours. I never before saw so much rain fall with so little noise. None of the summer winds make roaring storms, and thunder is seldom heard. I heard none at all. This wet, misty weather seems perfectly healthful. There is no mildew in the houses, as far as I have seen, or any tendency toward mouldiness in nooks hidden from the sun; and neither among the people nor the plants do we find anything flabby or dropsical.

In September clear days were rare, more than three fourths of them were either decidedly cloudy or rainy, and the rains of this month were, with one wild exception, only moderately heavy, and the clouds between showers drooped and crawled in a ragged, unsettled way without betraying hints of violence such as one often sees in the gestures of mountain storm-clouds.

July was the brightest month of the summer, with fourteen days of sunshine, six of them in uninterrupted succession, with a temperature at 7 am of about 60°, at 12 m, 70°. The average 7 am temperature for June was 54.3°; the average 7 am temperature for July was 55.3°; at 12 m the average temperature was 61.45°; the average 7 am temperature for August was 54.12°; 12 m, 61.48°; the average 7 am temperature for September was 52.14°; and 12 m, 56.12°.

The highest temperature observed here during the summer was seventy-six degrees. The most remarkable characteristic of this summer weather, even the brightest of it, is the velvet softness of the atmosphere. On the mountains of California, throughout the greater part of the year, the presence of an atmosphere is hardly recognized, and the thin, white, bodiless light of the morning comes to the peaks and glaciers as a pure spiritual essence, the most impressive of all the terrestrial manifestations of God. The clearest of Alaskan air is always appreciably substantial, so much so that it would seem as if one might test its quality by rubbing it between the thumb and finger. I never saw summer days so white and so full of subdued lustre.

The winter storms, up to the end of December when I left Wrangell, were mostly rain at a temperature of thirty-five or forty degrees, with strong winds which sometimes roughly lash the shores and carry scud far into the woods. The long nights are then gloomy enough and the value of snug homes with crackling yellow cedar fires may be finely appreciated. Snow falls frequently, but never to any great depth or to lie long. It is said that only once since the settlement of Fort Wrangell has the ground been covered to a depth of four feet. The mercury seldom falls more than five or six degrees below the freezing-point, unless the wind blows steadily from the mainland. Back from the coast, however, beyond the mountains, the winter months are very cold. On the Stickeen River at Glenora, less than a thousand feet above the level of the sea, a temperature of from thirty to forty degrees below zero is not uncommon.

CHAPTER FOUR

The Stickeen River

THE MOST interesting of the short excursions we made from Fort Wrangell was the one up the Stickeen River to the head of steam navigation. From Mount St. Elias the coast range extends in a broad, lofty chain beyond the southern boundary of the territory, gashed by stupendous canyons, each of which carries a lively river, though most of them are comparatively short, as their highest sources lie in the icy solitudes of the range within forty or fifty miles of the coast. A few, however, of these foaming, roaring streams – the Alsek, Chilcat, Chilcoot, Taku, Stickeen, and perhaps others – head beyond the range with some of the southwest branches of the Mackenzie and Yukon.

The largest side branches of the main-trunk canyons of all these mountain streams are still occupied by glaciers which descend in showy ranks, their massy, bulging snouts lying back a little distance in the shadows of the walls, or pushing forward among the cotton-woods that line the banks of the rivers, or even stretching all the way across the main canyons, compelling the rivers to find a channel beneath them.

The Stickeen was, perhaps, the best known of the rivers that cross the Coast Range, because it was the best way to the Mackenzie River Cassiar gold-mines. It is about three hundred and fifty miles long, and is navigable for small steamers a hundred and fifty miles to Glenora, and sometimes to Telegraph Creek, fifteen miles farther. It first pursues a westerly course through grassy plains darkened here and there with groves of spruce and pine; then, curving southward and receiving numerous tributaries from the north, it enters the Coast Range, and sweeps across it through a magnificent canyon three thousand to five thousand feet deep, and more than a hundred miles long. The majestic cliffs and mountains forming the canyon-walls display endless variety of form and sculpture, and are wonderfully adorned and enlivened with glaciers and waterfalls, while throughout almost its whole extent the floor is a flowery landscape garden, like Yosemite. The most striking features are the glaciers hanging over the cliffs, descending the side canyons and pushing forward to the river, greatly enhancing the wild beauty of all the others.

Gliding along the swift-flowing river, the views change with bewildering rapidity. Wonderful, too, are the changes dependent on the seasons and the weather. In spring, when the snow is melting fast, you enjoy the countless rejoicing waterfalls; the gentle breathing of warm winds; the colours of the young leaves and flowers when the bees are busy and wafts of fragrance are drifting hither and thither from miles of wild roses, clover, and honeysuckle; the swaths of birch and willow on the lower slopes following the melting of the winter avalanche snow-banks; the bossy cumuli swelling in white and purple piles above the highest peaks; grey rain-clouds wreathing the outstanding brows and battlements of the walls; and the breaking-forth of the sun after the rain; the shining of the leaves and streams and crystal architecture of the glaciers; the rising of fresh fragrance; the song of the happy birds; and the serene colour-grandeur of the morning and evening sky. In summer you find the groves and gardens in full dress; glaciers melting rapidly under sunshine and rain; waterfalls in all their glory; the river rejoicing in its strength; young birds trying their wings; bears enjoying salmon and berries; all the life of the canyon brimming full like the streams. In autumn comes rest, as if the year's work were done. The rich hazy sunshine streaming over the cliffs calls forth the last of the gentians and goldenrods; the groves and thickets and meadows bloom again as their leaves change to red and yellow petals; the rock also, and the glaciers, seem to bloom like the plants in the mellow golden light. And so goes the song, change succeeding change in sublime harmony through all the wonderful seasons and weather.

My first trip up the river was made in the spring with the missionary party soon after our arrival at Wrangell. We left Wrangell in the afternoon and anchored for the night above the river delta, and started up the river early next morning when the heights above the 'Big Stickeen' Glacier and the smooth domes and copings and arches of solid snow along the tops of the canyon walls were glowing in the early beams. We arrived before noon at the old trading-post called 'Buck's' in front of the Stickeen Glacier, and remained long enough to allow the few passengers who wished a nearer view to cross the river to the terminal moraine. The sunbeams streaming through the ice pinnacles along its terminal wall produced a wonderful glory of colour, and the broad, sparkling crystal prairie and the distant snowy fountains were wonderfully attractive and made me pray for opportunity to explore them.

Of the many glaciers, a hundred or more, that adorn the walls of the great Stickeen River Canyon, this is the largest. It draws its sources from snowy mountains within fifteen or twenty miles of the coast, pours through a comparatively narrow canyon about two miles in width in a magnificent cascade, and expands in a broad fan five or six miles in width, separated from the Stickeen River by its broad terminal moraine, fringed with spruces and willows. Around the beautifully drawn curve of the moraine the Stickeen River flows, having evidently been shoved by the glacier out of its direct course. On the opposite side of the canyon another somewhat smaller glacier, which now terminates four or five miles from the river, was once united front to front with the greater glacier, though at first both were tributaries of the main Stickeen Glacier which once filled the whole grand canyon. After the main trunk canyon was melted out, its side branches, drawing their sources from a height of three or four to five or six thousand feet, were cut off, and of course became separate glaciers, occupying cirques and branch canyons along the tops and sides of the walls. The Indians have a tradition that the river used to run through a tunnel under the united fronts of the two large tributary glaciers mentioned above, which entered the main canyon from either side; and that on one occasion an Indian, anxious to get rid of his wife, had her sent adrift in a canoe down through the ice tunnel, expecting that she would trouble him no more. But to his surprise she floated through under the ice in safety. All the evidence connected with the present appearance of these two glaciers indicates that they were united and formed a dam across the river after the smaller tributaries had been melted off and had receded to a greater or lesser height above the valley floor.

The big Stickeen Glacier is hardly out of sight ere you come upon another that pours a majestic crystal flood through the evergreens, while almost every hollow and tributary canyon contains a smaller one, the size, of course, varying with the extent of the area drained. Some are like mere snow-banks; others, with the blue ice apparent, depend in massive bulging curves and swells, and graduate into the river-like forms that maze through the lower forested regions and are so striking and beautiful that they are admired even by the passing miners with gold-dust in their eyes.

Thirty-five miles above the Big Stickeen Glacier is the 'Dirt Glacier', the second in size. Its outlet is a fine stream, abounding in trout. On the opposite side of the river there is a group of five glaciers, one of them descending to within a hundred feet of the river.

Near Glenora, on the northeastern flank of the main Coast Range, just below a narrow gorge called 'The Canyon', terraces first make their appearance, where great quantities of moraine material have been swept through the flood-choked gorge and of course outspread and deposited on the first open levels below. Here, too, occurs a marked change in climate and consequently in forests and general appearance of the face of the country. On account of destructive fires the woods are younger and are composed of smaller trees about a foot to eighteen inches in diameter and seventy-five feet high, mostly two-leaved pines which hold their seeds for several years after they are ripe. The woods here are without a trace of those deep accumulations of mosses, leaves, and decaying trunks which make so damp and unclearable a mass in the coast forests. Whole mountain-sides are covered with grey moss and lichens where the forest has been utterly destroyed. The river-bank cotton-woods are also smaller, and the birch and contorta pines mingle freely with the coast hemlock and spruce. The birch is common on the lower slopes and is very effective, its round, leafy, pale-green head contrasting with the dark, narrow spires of the conifers and giving a striking character to the forest. The 'tamarac pine' or black pine, as the variety of *P. contorta* is called here, is yellowish-green, in marked contrast with the dark lichen-draped spruce which grows above the pine at a height of about two thousand feet, in groves and belts where it has escaped fire and snow avalanches. There is another handsome spruce hereabouts, *Picea alba*, very slender and graceful in habit, drooping at the top like a mountain hemlock. I saw fine specimens a hundred and twenty-five feet high on deep bottom land a few miles below Glenora. The tops of some of them were almost covered with dense clusters of yellow and brown cones.

We reached the old Hudson's Bay trading-post at Glenora about one o'clock, and the captain informed me that he would stop here until the next morning, when he would make an early start for Wrangell.

At a distance of about seven or eight miles to the northeastward of the landing, there is an outstanding group of mountains crowning a spur from the main chain of the Coast Range, whose highest point rises about eight thousand feet above the level of the sea; and as Glenora is only a thousand feet above the sea, the height to be overcome in climbing this peak is about seven thousand feet. Though the time was short I determined to climb it, because of the advantageous position it occupied for general views of the peaks and glaciers of the east side of the great range.

Although it was now twenty minutes past three and the days were getting short, I thought that by rapid climbing I could reach the summit before sunset in time to get a general view and a few pencil sketches, and make my way back to the steamer in the night. Mr Young, one of the missionaries, asked permission to accompany me, saying that he was a good walker and climber and would not delay me or cause any trouble. I strongly advised him not to go, explaining that it involved a walk, coming and going of fourteen or sixteen miles, and a climb through brush and boulders of seven thousand feet, a fair day's work for a seasoned mountaineer to be done in less than half a day and part of a night. But he insisted that he was a strong walker, could do a mountaineer's day's work in half a day, and would not hinder me in any way.

'Well, I have warned you', I said, 'and will not assume responsibility for any trouble that may arise'.

He proved to be a stout walker, and we made rapid progress across a brushy timbered flat and up the mountain slopes, open in some places, and in others thatched with dwarf firs, resting a minute here and there to refresh ourselves with huckleberries, which grew in abundance in open spots. About

half an hour before sunset, when we were near a cluster of crumbling pinnacles that formed the summit, I had ceased to feel anxiety about the mountaineering strength and skill of my companion, and pushed rapidly on. In
passing around the shoulder of the highest pinnacle, where the rock was
rapidly disintegrating and the danger of slipping was great, I shouted in a
warning voice, 'Be very careful here, this is dangerous'.

Mr Young was perhaps a dozen or two yards behind me, but out of sight. I
afterwards reproached myself for not stopping and lending him a steadying
hand, and showing him the slight footsteps I had made by kicking out little
blocks of the crumbling surface, instead of simply warning him to be careful.
Only a few seconds after giving this warning, I was startled by a scream for
help, and hurrying back, found the missionary face downward, his arms
outstretched, clutching little crumbling knobs on the brink of a gully that
plunges down a thousand feet or more to a small residual glacier. I managed
to get below him, touched one of his feet, and tried to encourage him by
saying, 'I am below you. You are in no danger. You can't slip past me and I
will soon get you out of this.'

He then told me that both of his arms were dislocated. It was almost
impossible to find available footholds on the treacherous rock, and I was at
my wits' end to know how to get him rolled or dragged to a place where I
could get about him, find out how much he was hurt, and a way back down
the mountain. After narrowly scanning the cliff and making footholds, I
managed to roll and lift him a few yards to a place where the slope was less
steep, and there I attempted to set his arms. I found, however, that this was
impossible in such a place. I therefore tied his arms to his sides with my
suspenders and necktie, to prevent as much as possible inflammation from
movement. I then left him, telling him to lie still, that I would be back in a few
minutes, and that he was now safe from slipping. I hastily examined the
ground and saw no way of getting him down except by the steep glacier gully.
After scrambling to an outstanding point that commands a view of it from top
to bottom, to make sure that it was not interrupted by sheer precipices, I
concluded that with great care and the digging of slight footholds he could be
slid down to the glacier, where I could lay him on his back and perhaps be
able to set his arms. Accordingly, I cheered him up, telling him I had found a
way, but that it would require lots of time and patience. Digging a footstep in
the sand or crumbling rock five or six feet beneath him, I reached up, took
hold of him by one of his feet, and gently slid him down on his back, placed
his heels in the step, then descended another five or six feet, dug heel notches,
and slid him down to them. Thus the whole distance was made by a succession
of narrow steps at very short intervals, and the glacier was reached perhaps
about midnight. Here I took off one of my boots, tied a handkerchief around
his wrist for a good hold, placed my heel in his arm pit, and succeeded in
getting one of his arms in place, but my utmost strength was insufficient to
reduce the dislocation of the other. I therefore bound it closely to his side,
and asked him if in his exhausted and trembling condition he was still able to
walk.

'Yes', he bravely replied.

So, with a steadying arm around him and many stops for rest, I marched him slowly down in the starlight on the comparatively smooth, unfissured surface of the little glacier to the terminal moraine, a distance of perhaps a mile, crossed the moraine, bathed his head at one of the outlet streams, and after many rests reached a dry place and made a brush fire. I then went ahead looking for an open way through the bushes to where larger wood could be had, made a good lasting fire of resiny silver-fir roots, and a leafy bed beside it. I now told him I would run down the mountain, hasten back with help from the boat, and carry him down in comfort. But he would not hear of my leaving him.

'No, no', he said, 'I can walk down. Don't leave me.'

I reminded him of the roughness of the way, his nerve-shaken condition, and assured him I would not be gone long. But he insisted on trying, saying on no account whatever must I leave him. I therefore concluded to try to get him to the ship by short walks from one fire and resting-place to another. While he was resting I went ahead, looking for the best way through the brush and rocks, then returning, got him on his feet and made him lean on my shoulder while I steadied him to prevent his falling. This slow, staggering struggle from fire to fire lasted until long after sunrise. When at last we reached the ship and stood at the foot of the narrow single plank without side rails that reached from the bank to the deck at a considerable angle, I briefly explained to Mr Young's companions, who stood looking down at us, that he had been hurt in an accident, and requested one to assist me in getting him aboard. But strange to say, instead of coming down to help, they made haste to reproach him for having gone on a 'wild-goose chase' with Muir.

'These foolish adventures are well enough for Mr Muir', they said, 'but you, Mr Young, have a work to do; you have a family; you have a church, and you have no right to risk your life on treacherous peaks and precipices'.

The captain, Nat Lane, son of Senator Joseph Lane, had been swearing in angry impatience for being compelled to make so late a start and thus encounter a dangerous wind in a narrow gorge, and was threatening to put the missionaries ashore to seek their lost companion, while he went on down the river about his business. But when he heard my call for help, he hastened forward, and elbowed the divines away from the end of the gangplank, shouting in angry irreverence, 'Oh, blank! This is no time for preaching! Don't you see the man is hurt?'

He ran down to our help, and while I steadied my trembling companion from behind, the captain kindly led him up the plank into the saloon, and made him drink a large glass of brandy. Then, with a man holding down his shoulders, we succeeded in getting the bone into its socket, notwithstanding the inflammation and contraction of the muscles and ligaments. Mr Young was then put to bed, and he slept all the way back to Wrangell.

In his mission lectures in the East, Mr Young oftentimes told his story. I made no record of it in my notebook and never intended to write a word about it; but after a miserable, sensational caricature of the story had appeared in a respectable magazine, I thought it but fair to my brave companion that it should be told just as it happened.

CHAPTER FIVE

A Cruise in the Cassiar

SHORTLY AFTER our return to Wrangell the missionaries planned a grand mission excursion up the coast of the mainland to the Chilcat country, which I gladly joined, together with Mr Vanderbilt, his wife, and a friend from Oregon. The river steamer Cassiar was chartered, and we had her all to ourselves, ship and officers at our command to sail and stop where and when we would, and of course everybody felt important and hopeful. The main object of the missionaries was to ascertain the spiritual wants of the warlike Chilcat tribe, with a view to the establishment of a church and school in their principal village; the merchant and his party were bent on business and scenery; while my mind was on the mountains, glaciers, and forests.

This was toward the end of July, in the very brightest and best of Alaska summer weather, when the icy mountains towering in the pearly sky were displayed in all their glory, and the islands at their feet seemed to float and drowse on the shining mirror waters.

After we had passed through the Wrangell Narrows, the mountains of the mainland came in full view, gloriously arrayed in snow and ice, some of the largest and most river-like of the glaciers flowing through wide, high-walled valleys like Yosemite, their sources far back and concealed, others in plain sight, from their highest fountains to the level of the sea.

Cares of every kind were quickly forgotten, and though the Cassiar engines soon began to wheeze and sigh with doleful solemnity, suggesting coming trouble, we were too happy to mind them. Every face glowed with natural love of wild beauty. The islands were seen in long perspective, their forests dark green in the foreground, with varying tones of blue growing more and more tender in the distance; bays full of hazy shadows, graduating into open, silvery fields of light, and lofty headlands with fine arching insteps dipping their feet in the shining water. But every eye was turned to the mountains. Forgotten now were the Chilcats and missions while the word of God was being read in these majestic hieroglyphics blazoned along the sky. The earnest, childish wonderment with which this glorious page of Nature's Bible was contemplated was delightful to see. All evinced eager desire to learn.

'Is that a glacier', they asked, 'down in that canyon? And is it all solid ice?'

'Yes.'

'How deep is it?'

'Perhaps five hundred or a thousand feet.'

'You say it flows. How can hard ice flow?'

'It flows like water, though invisibly slow.'

'And where does it come from?'

'From snow that is heaped up every winter on the mountains.'

'And how, then, is the snow changed into ice?'

'It is welded by the pressure of its own weight.'

'Are these white masses we see in the hollows glaciers also?'

'Yes.'

'Are those bluish draggled masses hanging down from beneath the snow-fields what you call the snouts of the glaciers?'

'Yes.'

'What made the hollows they are in?'

'The glaciers themselves, just as travelling animals make their own tracks.'

'How long have they been there?'

'Numberless centuries', etc. I answered as best I could, keeping up a running commentary on the subject in general, while busily engaged in sketching and noting my own observations, preaching glacial gospel in a rambling way, while the Cassiar, slowly wheezing and creeping along the shore, shifted our position so that the icy canyons were opened to view and closed again in regular succession, like the leaves of a book.

About the middle of the afternoon we were directly opposite a noble group of glaciers some ten in number, flowing from a chain of crater-like snow fountains, guarded around their summits and well down their sides by jagged peaks and cols and curving mural ridges. From each of the larger clusters of fountains, a wide, sheer-walled canyon opens down to the sea. Three of the trunk glaciers descend to within a few feet of the sea-level. The largest of the three, probably about fifteen miles long, terminates in a magnificent valley like Yosemite, in an imposing wall of ice about two miles long, and from three to five hundred feet high, forming a barrier across the valley from wall to wall. It was to this glacier that the ships of the Alaska Ice Company resorted for the ice they carried to San Francisco and the Sandwich Islands, and, I believe, also to China and Japan. To load, they had only to sail up the fiord within a short distance of the front and drop anchor in the terminal moraine.

Another glacier, a few miles to the south of this one, receives two large tributaries about equal in size, and then flows down a forested valley to within a hundred feet or so of sea-level. The third of this low-descending group is four or five miles farther south, and, though less imposing than either of the two sketched above, is still a truly noble object, even as imperfectly seen from the channel, and would of itself be well worth a visit to Alaska to any lowlander so unfortunate as never to have seen a glacier.

The boilers of our little steamer were not made for sea water, but it was hoped that fresh water would be found at available points along our course where streams leap down the cliffs. In this particular we failed, however, and were compelled to use salt water an hour or two before reaching Cape Fanshawe, the supply of fifty tons of fresh water brought from Wrangell having then given out. To make matters worse, the captain and engineer were not in accord concerning the working of the engines. The captain repeatedly called for more steam, which the engineer refused to furnish, cautiously keeping the pressure low because the salt water foamed in the boilers and some of it passed over into the cylinders, causing heavy thumping at the end of each piston stroke, and threatening to knock out the cylinder-heads. At seven o'clock in the evening we had made only about seventy miles, which caused dissatisfaction, especially among the divines, who thereupon called a meeting in the cabin to consider what had better be done. In the discussions that followed much indignation and economy were brought to light. We had chartered the boat for sixty dollars per day, and the round trip was to have been made in four or five days. But at the present rate of speed it was found that the cost of the trip for each passenger would be five or ten dollars above the first estimate. Therefore, the majority ruled that we must return next day to Wrangell, the extra dollars outweighing the mountains and missions as if they had suddenly become dust in the balance.

Soon after the close of this economical meeting, we came to anchor in a beautiful bay, and as the long northern day had still hours of good light to offer, I gladly embraced the opportunity to go ashore to see the rocks and plants. One of the Indians, employed as a deck hand on the steamer, landed me at the mouth of a stream. The tide was low, exposing a luxuriant growth of algæ, which sent up a fine, fresh sea smell. The shingle was composed of slate, quartz, and granite, named in the order of abundance. The first land plant met was a tall grass, nine feet high, forming a meadow-like margin in front of the forest. Pushing my way well back into the forest, I found it composed almost entirely of spruce and two hemlocks (*Picea sitchensis, Tsuga heterophylla* and *T. mertensiana*) with a few specimens of yellow cypress. The ferns were developed in remarkable beauty and size – aspidiums, one of which is about six feet high, a woodsia, lomaria, and several species of polypodium. The underbrush is chiefly alder, rubus, ledum, three species of vaccinium, and *Echinopanax horrida*, the whole about from six to eight feet high, and in some places closely intertangled and hard to penetrate. On the opener spots beneath the trees the ground is covered to a depth of two or three feet with mosses of indescribable freshness and beauty, a few dwarf cornels often planted on their rich furred bosses, together with pyrola, coptis, and Solomon's-seal. The tallest of the trees are about a hundred and fifty feet high, with a diameter of about four or five feet, their branches mingling together and making a perfect shade. As the twilight began to fall, I sat down on the mossy instep of a spruce. Not a bush or tree was moving; every leaf seemed hushed in brooding repose. One bird, a thrush, embroidered the silence with cheery notes, making the solitude familiar and sweet, while the solemn monotone of the stream sifting through the woods seemed like the very voice of God, humanized, terrestrialized, and entering one's heart as to a home prepared for it. Go where we will, all the world over, we seem to have been there before.

The stream was bridged at short intervals with picturesque, moss-embossed logs, and the trees on its banks, leaning over from side to side, made high embowering arches. The log bridge I crossed was, I think, the most beautiful of the kind I ever saw. The massive log is plushed to a depth of six inches or more with mosses of three or four species, their different tones of yellow shading finely into each other, while their delicate fronded branches and foliage lie in exquisite order, inclining outward and down the sides in rich, furred, clasping sheets overlapping and felted together until the required thickness is attained. The pedicels and spore-cases give a purplish tinge, and the whole bridge is enriched with ferns and a row of small seedling trees and currant bushes with coloured leaves, every one of which seems to have been culled from the woods for this special use, so perfectly do they harmonise in size, shape, and colour with the mossy cover, the width of the span, and the luxuriant, brushy abutments.

Sauntering back to the beach, I found four or five Indian deck hands getting water, with whom I returned aboard the steamer, thanking the Lord for so noble an addition to my life as was this one big mountain, forest, and glacial day.

Next morning most of the company seemed uncomfortably conscience-stricken, and ready to do anything in the way of compensation for our broken excursion that would not cost too much. It was not found difficult, therefore, to convince the captain and disappointed passengers that instead of creeping back to Wrangell direct we should make an expiatory branch-excursion to the largest of the three low-descending glaciers we had passed. The Indian pilot, well acquainted with this part of the coast, declared himself willing to guide us. The water in these fiord channels is generally deep and safe, and though at wide intervals rocks rise abruptly here and there, lacking only a few feet in height to enable them to take rank as islands, the flat-bottomed Cassiar drew but little more water than a duck, so that even the most timid raised no objection on this score. The cylinder-heads of our engines were the main source of anxiety; provided they could be kept on all might yet be well. But in this matter there was evidently some distrust, the engineer having imprudently informed some of the passengers that in consequence of using salt water in his frothing boilers the cylinder-heads might fly off at any moment. To the glacier, however, it was at length decided we should venture.

Arriving opposite the mouth of its fiord, we steered straight inland between beautiful wooded shores, and the grand glacier came in sight in its granite valley, glowing in the early sunshine and extending a noble invitation to come and see. After we passed between the two mountain rocks that guard the gate of the fiord, the view that was unfolded fixed every eye in wondering admiration. No words can convey anything like an adequate conception of its sublime grandeur – the noble simplicity and fineness of the sculpture of the walls; their magnificent proportions; their cascades, gardens, and forest adornments; the placid fiord between them; the great white and blue ice wall, and the snow-laden mountains beyond. Still more important are words in telling the peculiar awe one experiences in entering these mansions of the icy North, notwithstanding it is only the natural effect of appreciable manifestations of the presence of God.

Standing in the gateway of this glorious temple, and regarding it only as a picture, its outlines may be easily traced, the water foreground of a pale-green colour, a smooth mirror sheet sweeping back five or six miles like one of the lower reaches of a great river, bounded at the head by a bevelled barrier wall of blueish-white ice four or five hundred feet high. A few snowy mountain-tops appear beyond it, and on either hand rise a series of majestic, pale-grey granite rocks from three to four thousand feet high, some of them thinly forested and striped with bushes and flowery grass on narrow shelves, especially about half-way up, others severely sheer and bare and built together into walls like those of Yosemite, extending far beyond the ice barrier, one immense brow appearing beyond another with their bases buried in the glacier. This is a Yosemite Valley in process of formation, the modelling and sculpture of the walls nearly completed and well planted, but no groves as yet or gardens or meadows on the raw and unfinished bottom. It is as if the explorer, in entering the Merced Yosemite, should find the walls nearly in their present condition, trees and flowers in the warm nooks and along the sunny portions of the moraine-covered brows, but the bottom of the valley still covered with water and beds of gravel and mud, and the grand glacier that formed it slowly receding but still filling the upper half of the valley.

Sailing directly up the edge of the low, outspread, water-washed terminal moraine, scarce noticeable in a general view, we seemed to be separated from the glacier only by a bed of gravel a hundred yards or so in width; but on so grand a scale are all the main features of the valley, we afterwards found the distance to be a mile or more.

The captain ordered the Indian deck hands to get out the canoe, take as many of us ashore as wished to go, and accompany us to the glacier in case we should need their help. Only three of the company, in the first place, availed themselves of this rare opportunity of meeting a glacier in the flesh – Mr Young, one of the doctors, and myself. Paddling to the nearest and driest-looking part of the moraine flat, we stepped ashore, but gladly wallowed back into the canoe; for the grey mineral mud, a paste made of fine-ground mountain meal kept unstable by the tides, at once began to take us in, swallowing us feet foremost with becoming glacial deliberation. Our next attempt, made nearer the middle of the valley, was successful, and we soon found ourselves on firm gravelly ground, and made haste to the huge ice wall, which seemed to recede as we advanced. The only difficulty we met was a network of icy streams, at the largest of which we halted, not willing to get wet in fording. The Indian attendant promptly carried us over on his back. When my turn came I told him I would ford, but he bowed his shoulders in so ludicrously persuasive a manner I thought I would try the queer mount, the only one of the kind I had enjoyed since boyhood days in playing leapfrog. Away staggered my perpendicular mule over the boulders into the brawling torrent, and in spite of top-heavy predictions to the contrary, crossed without a fall. After being ferried in this way over several more of these glacial streams, we at length reached the foot of the glacier wall. The doctor simply played tag on it, touched it gently as if it were a dangerous wild beast, and hurried back to the boat, taking the portage Indian with him for safety, little knowing what he was missing. Mr Young and I traced the glorious crystal wall, admiring its wonderful architecture, the play of light in the rifts and caverns, and the structure of the ice as displayed in the less fractured sections, finding fresh beauty everywhere and facts for study. We then tried to climb it, and by dint of patient zigzagging and doubling among the crevasses, and cutting steps here and there, we made our way up over the brow and back a mile or two to a height of about seven hundred feet. The whole front of the glacier is gashed and sculptured into a maze of shallow caves and crevasses, and a bewildering variety of novel architectural forms, clusters of glittering lance-tipped spires, gables, and obelisks, bold outstanding bastions and plain mural cliffs, adorned along the top with fretted cornice and battlement, while every gorge and crevasse, groove and hollow, was filled with light, shimmering and throbbing in pale-blue tones of ineffable tenderness and beauty. The day was warm, and back on the broad melting bosom of the glacier beyond the crevassed front, many streams were rejoicing, gurgling, ringing, singing, in frictionless channels worn down through the white disintegrated ice of the surface into the quick and living blue, in which they flowed with a grace of motion and flashing of light to be found only on the crystal hillocks and ravines of a glacier.

Along the sides of the glacier we saw the mighty flood grinding against the granite walls with tremendous pressure, rounding outswelling bosses, and deepening the retreating hollows into the forms they are destined to have when, in the fullness of appointed time, the huge ice tool shall be withdrawn by the sun. Every feature glowed with intention, reflecting the plans of God. Back a few miles from the front, the glacier is now probably but little more than a thousand feet deep; but when we examine the records on the walls, the rounded, grooved, striated, and polished features so surely glacial, we learn that in the earlier days of the ice age they were all over-swept, and that this glacier has flowed at a height of from three to four thousand feet above its present level, when it was at least a mile deep.

Standing here, with facts so fresh and telling and held up so vividly before us, every seeing observer, not to say geologist, must readily apprehend the earth-sculpturing, landscape-making action of flowing ice. And here, too, one learns that the world, though made, is yet being made; that this is still the morning of creation; that mountains long conceived are now being born, channels traced for coming rivers, basins hollowed for lakes; that moraine soil is being ground and outspread for coming plants, – coarse boulders and gravel for forests, finer soil for grasses and flowers – while the finest part of the grist, seen hastening out to sea in the draining streams, is being stored away in darkness and builded particle on particle, cementing and crystallizing, to make the mountains and valleys and plains of other predestined landscapes, to be followed by still others in endless rhythm and beauty.

Gladly would we have camped out on this grand old landscape mill to study its ways and works; but we had no bread and the captain was keeping the Cassiar whistle screaming for our return. Therefore, in mean haste, we threaded our way back through the crevasses and down the blue cliffs, snatched a few flowers from a warm spot on the edge of the ice, plashed across the moraine streams, and were paddled aboard, rejoicing in the possession of so blessed a day, and feeling that in very foundational truth we had been in one of God's own temples and had seen Him and heard Him working and preaching like a man.

Steaming solemnly out of the fiord and down the coast, the islands and mountains were again passed in review; the clouds that so often hide the mountaintops even in good weather were now floating high above them, and the transparent shadows they cast were scarce perceptible on the white glacier fountains. So abundant and novel are the objects of interest in a pure wilderness that unless you are pursuing special studies it matters little where you go, or how often to the same place. Wherever you chance to be always seems at the moment of all places the best; and you feel that there can be no happiness in this world or in any other for those who may not be happy here. The bright hours were spent in making notes and sketches and getting more of the wonderful region into memory. In particular a second view of the mountains made me raise my first estimate of their height. Some of them must be seven or eight thousand feet at the least. Also the glaciers seemed larger and more numerous. I counted nearly a hundred, large and small, between a point ten or fifteen miles to the north of Cape Fanshawe and the mouth of the Stickeen River. We made no more landings, however, until we had passed through the Wrangell Narrows and dropped anchor for the night in a small sequestered bay. This was about sunset, and I eagerly seized the opportunity to go ashore in the canoe and see what I could learn. It is here only a step from the marine algæ to terrestrial vegetation of almost tropical luxurance. Parting the alders and huckleberry bushes and the crooked stems of the prickly panax, I made my way into the woods, and lingered in the twilight doing nothing in particular, only measuring a few of the trees, listening to learn what birds and animals might be about, and gazing along the dusky aisles.

In the meantime another excursion was being invented, one of small size and price. We might have reached Fort Wrangell this evening instead of anchoring here; but the owners of the Cassiar would then receive only ten dollars fare from each person, while they had incurred considerable expense in fitting up the boat for this special trip, and had treated us well. No, under the circumstances, it would never do to return to Wrangell so meanly soon.

It was decided, therefore, that the Cassiar Company should have the benefit of another day's hire, in visiting the old deserted Stickeen village fourteen miles to the south of Wrangell.

'We shall have a good time', one of the most influential of the party said to me in a semi-apologetic tone, as if dimly recognizing my disappointment in not going on to Chilcat. 'We shall probably find stone axes and other curiosities. Chief Kadachan is going to guide us, and there are interesting old buildings and totem poles to be seen.'

It seemed strange, however, that so important a mission to the most influential of the Alaskan tribes should end in a deserted village. But divinity abounded nevertheless; the day was divine and there was plenty of natural religion in the newborn landscapes that were being baptized in sunshine, and sermons in the glacial boulders on the beach where we landed.

The site of the old village is on an outswelling strip of ground about two hundred yards long and fifty wide, sloping gently to the water with a strip of gravel and tall grass in front, dark woods back of it, and charming views over the water among the islands – a delightful place. The tide was low when we arrived, and I noticed that the exposed boulders on the beach – granite erratics that had been dropped by the melting ice toward the close of the glacial period – were piled in parallel rows at right angles to the shore-line, out of the way of the canoes that had belonged to the village.

Most of the party sauntered along the shore; for the ruins were overgrown with tall nettles, elder bushes, and prickly rubus vines through which it was difficult to force a way. In company with the most eager of the relic-seekers and two Indians, I pushed back among the dilapidated dwellings. They were deserted some sixty or seventy years before, and some of them were at least a hundred years old. So said our guide, Kadachan, and his word was corroborated by the venerable aspect of the ruins. Though the damp climate is destructive, many of the house timbers were still in a good state of preservation, particularly those hewn from the yellow cypress, or cedar as it is called here. The magnitude of the ruins and the excellence of the workmanship manifest in them was astonishing as belonging to Indians. For example, the first dwelling we visited was about forty feet square, with walls built of planks two feet wide and six inches thick. The ridgepole of yellow cypress was two feet in diameter, forty feet long, and as round and true as if it had been turned in a lathe; and, though lying in the damp weeds, it was still perfectly sound. The nibble marks of the stone adze were still visible, though crusted over with scale lichens in most places. The pillars that had supported the ridgepole were still standing in some of the ruins. They were all, as far as I observed, carved into life-size figures of men, women, and children, fishes, birds, and various other animals, such as the beaver, wolf, or bear. Each of the wall planks had evidently been hewn out of a whole log, and must have required sturdy deliberation as well as skill. Their geometrical truthfulness was admirable. With the same tools not one in a thousand of our skilled mechanics could do as good work. Compared with it the bravest work of civilized backwoodsmen is feeble and bungling. The completeness of form, finish, and proportion of these timbers suggested skill of a wild and positive kind, like that which guides the woodpecker in drilling round holes, and the bee in making its cells.

The carved totem-pole monuments are the most striking of the objects displayed here. The simplest of them consisted of a smooth, round post fifteen or twenty feet high and about eighteen inches in diameter, with the figure of some animal on top – a bear, porpoise, eagle, or raven, about life-size or larger. These were the totems of the families that occupied the houses in front of which they stood. Others supported the figure of a man or woman, life-size or larger, usually in a sitting posture, said to resemble the dead whose ashes were contained in a closed cavity in the pole. The largest were thirty or forty feet high, carved from top to bottom into human and animal totem figures, one above another, with their limbs grotesquely doubled and folded. Some of the most imposing were said to commemorate some event of an historical character. But a telling display of family pride seemed to have been the prevailing motive. All the figures were more or less rude, and some were broadly grotesque, but there was never any feebleness or obscurity in the expression. On the contrary, every feature showed grave force and decision; while the childish audacity displayed in the designs, combined with manly strength in their execution, was truly wonderful.

The coloured lichens and mosses gave them a venerable air, while the larger vegetation often found on such as were most decayed produced a picturesque effect. Here, for example, is a bear five or six feet long, reposing on top of his lichen-clad pillar, with paws comfortably folded, a tuft of grass growing in each ear and rubus bushes along his back. And yonder is an old chief poised on a taller pillar, apparently gazing out over the landscape in contemplative mood, a tuft of bushes leaning back with a jaunty air from the top of his weatherbeaten hat, and downy mosses about his massive lips. But no rudeness or grotesqueness that may appear, however combined with the decorations that nature has added, may possibly provoke mirth. The whole work is serious in aspect and brave and true in execution.

Similar monuments are made by other Thlinkit tribes. The erection of a totem pole is made a grand affair, and is often talked of for a year or two beforehand. A feast, to which many are invited, is held, and the joyous occasion is spent in eating, dancing, and the distribution of gifts. Some of the larger specimens cost a thousand dollars or more. From one to two hundred blankets, worth three dollars apiece, are paid to the genius who carves them, while the presents and feast usually cost twice as much, so that only the wealthy families can afford them. I talked with an old Indian who pointed out one of the carvings he had made in the Wrangell village, for which he told me had received forty blankets, a gun, a canoe, and other articles, all together worth about $170. Mr Swan, who has contributed much information concerning the British Columbian and Alaskan tribes, describes a totem pole that cost $2500. They are always planted firmly in the ground and stand fast, showing the sturdy erectness of their builders.

While I was busy with my pencil, I heard chopping going on at the north end of the village, followed by a heavy thud, as if a tree had fallen. It appeared that after digging about the old hearth in the first dwelling visited without finding anything of consequence, the archæological doctor called the steamer deck hands to one of the most interesting of the totems and directed them to cut it down, saw off the principal figure – a woman measuring three feet three inches across the shoulders – and convey it aboard the steamer, with a view to taking it on East to enrich some museum or other. This sacrilege came near causing trouble and would have cost us dear had the totem not chanced to belong to the Kadachan family, the representative of which is a member of the newly organized Presbyterian Church. Kadachan looked very seriously into the face of the reverend doctor and pushed home the pertinent question: 'How would you like to have an Indian go to a graveyard and break down and carry away a monument belonging to your family?'

However, the religious relations of the parties and a few trifling presents embedded in apologies served to hush and mend the matter.

Some time in the afternoon the steamer whistle called us together to finish our memorable trip. There was no trace of decay in the sky; a glorious sunset gilded the water and cleared away the shadows of our meditations among the ruins. We landed at the Wrangell wharf at dusk, pushed our way through a group of inquisitive Indians, across the two crooked streets, and up to our

homes in the fort. We had been away only three days, but they were so full of
novel scenes and impressions the time seemed indefinitely long, and our
broken Chilcat excursion, far from being a failure as it seemed to some, was
one of the most memorable of my life.

CHAPTER SIX

The Cassiar Trail

I MADE a second trip up the Stickeen in August and from the head of
navigation pushed inland for general views over dry grassy hills and plains on
the Cassiar trail.

Soon after leaving Telegraph Creek I met a merry trader who encouragingly assured me that I was going into the most wonderful region in the world,
that 'the scenery up the river was full of the very wildest freaks of nature,
surpassing all other sceneries either natural or artificial, on paper or in nature.
And give yourself no bothering care about provisions, for wild food grows in
prodigious abundance everywhere. A man was lost four days up there, but he
feasted on vegetables and berries and got back to camp in good condition. A
mess of wild parsnips and pepper, for example, will actually do you good.
And here's my advice – go slow and take the pleasures and sceneries as you
go.'

At the confluence of the first North Fork of the Stickeen I found a band of
Toltan or Stick Indians catching their winter supply of salmon in willow traps,
set where the fish are struggling in swift rapids on their way to the spawning-
grounds. A large supply had already been secured, and of course the Indians
were well fed and merry. They were camping in large booths made of poles
set on end in the ground, with many binding cross-pieces on which tons of
salmon were being dried. The heads were strung on separate poles and the
roes packed in willow baskets, all being well smoked from fires in the middle
of the floor. The largest of the booths near the bank of the river was about
forty feet square. Beds made of spruce and pine boughs were spread all
around the walls, on which some of the Indians lay asleep; some were
braiding ropes, others sitting and lounging, gossiping and courting, while a
little baby was swinging in a hammock. All seemed to be light-hearted and
jolly, with work enough and wit enough to maintain health and comfort. In
the winter they are said to dwell in substantial huts in the woods, where game,
especially caribou, is abundant. They are pale copper-coloured, have small
feet and hands, are not at all negroish in lips or cheeks like some of the coast
tribes, nor so thickset, short-necked, or heavy-featured in general. One of the
most striking of the geological features of this region are immense gravel
deposits displayed in sections on the walls of the river gorges. About two
miles above the North Fork confluence there is a bluff of basalt three hundred

and fifty feet high, and above this a bed of gravel four hundred feet thick, while beneath the basalt there is another bed at least fifty feet thick.

From 'Ward's', seventeen miles beyond Telegraph, and about fourteen hundred feet above sea-level, the trail ascends a gravel ridge to a pine-and-fir-covered plateau twenty-one hundred feet above the sea. Thence for three miles the trail leads through a forest of short, closely planted trees to the second North Fork of the Stickeen, where a still greater deposit of stratified gravel is displayed, a section at least six hundred feet thick resting on a red jaspery formation.

Nine hundred feet above the river there is a slightly dimpled plateau diversified with aspen and willow groves and mossy meadows. At 'Wilson's', one and a half miles from the river, the ground is carpeted with dwarf manzanita and the blessed *Linnæa borealis*, and forested with small pines, spruces, and aspens, the tallest fifty to sixty feet high.

From Wilson's to 'Caribou', fourteen miles, no water was visible, though the nearly level, mossy ground is swampy-looking. At 'Caribou Camp', two miles from the river, I saw two fine dogs, a Newfoundland and a spaniel. Their owner told me that he paid only twenty dollars for the team and was offered one hundred dollars for one of them a short time afterwards. The Newfoundland, he said, caught salmon on the ripples, and could be sent back for miles to fetch horses. The fine jet-black curly spaniel helped to carry the dishes from the table to the kitchen, went for water when ordered, took the pail and set it down at the stream-side, but could not be taught to dip it full. But their principal work was hauling camp-supplies on sleds up the river in winter. These two were said to be able to haul a load of a thousand pounds when the ice was in fairly good condition. They were fed on dried fish and oatmeal boiled together.

The timber hereabouts is mostly willow or poplar on the low ground, with here and there pine, birch, and spruce about fifty feet high. None seen much exceeded a foot in diameter. Thousand-acre patches have been destroyed by fire. Some of the green trees had been burned off at the root, the raised roots, packed in dry moss, being readily attacked from beneath. A range of mountains about five thousand to six thousand feet high trending nearly north and south for sixty miles is forested to the summit. Only a few cliff-faces and one of the highest points patched with snow are treeless. No part of this range as far as I could see is deeply sculptured, though the general denudation of the country must have been enormous as the gravel-beds show.

At the top of a smooth, flowery pass about four thousand feet above the sea, beautiful Dease Lake comes suddenly in sight, shining like a broad tranquil river between densely forested hills and mountains. It is about twenty-seven miles long, one to two miles wide, and its waters, tributary to the Mackenzie, flow into the Arctic Ocean by a very long, round-about, romantic way, the exploration of which in 1789 from Great Slave Lake to the Arctic Ocean must have been a glorious task for the heroic Scotchman, Alexander Mackenzie, whose name it bears.

Dease Creek, a fine rushing stream about forty miles long and forty or fifty feet wide, enters the lake from the west, drawing its sources from grassy mountain-ridges. Thibert Creek, about the same size, and McDames and Defot Creeks, with their many branches, head together in the same general range of mountains or on moor-like tablelands on the divide between the Mackenzie and Yukon and Stickeen. All these Mackenzie streams have proved rich in gold. The wing-dams, flumes, and sluice-boxes on the lower five or ten miles of their courses showed wonderful industry, and the quantity of glacial and perhaps preglacial gravel displayed was enormous. Some of the beds were not unlike those of the so-called Dead Rivers of California. Several ancient drift-filled channels on Thibert Creek, blue at bed rock, were exposed and had been worked. A considerable portion of the gold, though mostly coarse, had no doubt come from considerable distances, as boulders included in some of the deposits show. The deepest beds, though known to be rich, had not yet been worked to any great depth on account of expense. Diggings that yield less than five dollars a day to the man were considered worthless. Only three of the claims on Defot Creek, eighteen miles from the mouth of Thibert Creek, were then said to pay. One of the nuggets from this creek weighed forty pounds.

While wandering about the banks of these gold-besprinkled streams, looking at the plants and mines and miners, I was so fortunate as to meet an interesting French Canadian, an old *coureur de bois*, who after a few minutes' conversation invited me to accompany him to his gold-mine on the head of Defot Creek, near the summit of a smooth, grassy mountain-ridge which he assured me commanded extensive views of the region at the heads of Stickeen, Taku, Yukon, and Mackenzie tributaries. Although heavy-laden with flour and bacon, he strode lightly along the rough trails as if his load was only a natural balanced part of his body. Our way at first lay along Thibert Creek, now on gravel benches, now on bed rock, now close down on the bouldery edge of the stream. Above the mines the stream is clear and flows with a rapid current. Its banks are embossed with moss and grass and sedge well mixed with flowers – daisies, larkspurs, solidagos, parnassia, potentilla, strawberry, etc. Small strips of meadow occur here and there, and belts of slender arrowy fir and spruce with moss-clad roots grow close to the water's edge. The creek is about forty-five miles long, and the richest of its gold-bearing beds so far discovered were on the lower four miles of the creek; the higher four-or-five-dollars-a-day diggings were considered very poor on account of the high price of provisions and shortness of the season. After crossing many smaller streams with their strips of trees and meadows, bogs and bright wild gardens, we arrived at the Le Claire cabin about the middle of the afternoon. Before entering it he threw down his burden and made haste to show me his favourite flower, a blue forget-me-not, a specimen of which he found within a few rods of the cabin, and proudly handed it to me with the finest respect, and telling its many charms and lifelong associations, showed in every endearing look and touch and gesture that the tender little plant of the mountain wilderness was truly his best-loved darling.

After luncheon we set out for the highest point on the dividing ridge about a mile above the cabin, and sauntered and gazed until sundown, admiring the vast expanse of open rolling prairie-like highlands dotted with grooves and lakes, the fountain-heads of countless cool, glad streams.

Le Claire's simple, childlike love of nature, preserved undimmed through a hard wilderness life, was delightful to see. The grand landscapes with their lakes and streams, plants and animals, all were dear to him. In particular he was fond of the birds that nested near his cabin, watched the young, and in stormy weather helped their parents to feed and shelter them. Some species were so confiding they learned to perch on his shoulders and take crumbs from his hand.

A little before sunset snow began to fly, driven by a cold wind, and by the time we reached the cabin, though we had not far to go, everything looked wintry. At half-past nine we ate supper, while a good fire crackled cheerily in the ingle and a wintry wind blew hard. The little log cabin was only ten feet long, eight wide, and just high enough under the roof peak to allow one to stand upright. The bedstead was not wide enough for two, so Le Claire spread the blankets on the floor, and we gladly lay down after our long, happy walk, our heads under the bedstead, our feet against the opposite wall, and though comfortably tired, it was long ere we fell asleep, for Le Claire, finding me a good listener, told many stories of his adventurous life with Indians, bears and wolves, snow and hunger, and of his many camps in the Canadian woods, hidden like the nests and dens of wild animals; stories that have a singular interest to everybody, for they awaken inherited memories of the lang, lang syne when we were all wild. He had nine children, he told me, the youngest eight years of age, and several of his daughters were married. His home was in Victoria.

Next morning was cloudy and windy, snowy and cold, dreary December weather in August, and I gladly ran out to see what I might learn. A grey ragged-edged cloud capped the top of the divide, its snowy fringes drawn out by the wind. The flowers, though most of them were buried or partly so, were to some extent recognizable, the bluebells bent over, shining like eyes through the snow, and the gentians, too, with their corollas twisted shut; cassiope I could recognize under any disguise; and two species of dwarf willow with their seeds already ripe, one with comparatively small leaves, were growing in mere cracks and crevices of rock-ledges where the dry snow could not lie. Snowbirds and ptarmigan were flying briskly in the cold wind, and on the edge of a grove I saw a spruce from which a bear had stripped large sections of bark for food.

About nine o'clock the clouds lifted and I enjoyed another wide view from the summit of the ridge of the vast grassy fountain region with smooth rolling features. A few patches of forest broke the monotony of colour, and the many lakes, one of them about five miles long, were glowing like windows. Only the highest ridges were whitened with snow, while rifts in the clouds showed beautiful bits of yellow-green sky. The limit of tree growth is about five thousand feet.

Throughout all this region from Glenora to Cassiar the grasses grow luxuriantly in openings in the woods and on dry hillsides where the trees seem to have been destroyed by fire, and over all the broad prairies above the timber-line. A kind of bunch-grass in particular is often four or five feet high, and close enough to be mowed for hay. I never anywhere saw finer or more bountiful wild pasture. Here the caribou feed and grow fat, braving the intense winter cold, often forty to sixty degrees below zero. Winter and summer seem to be the only seasons here. What may fairly be called summer lasts only two or three months, winter nine or ten, for of pure well-defined spring or autumn there is scarcely a trace. Were it not for the long severe winters, this would be a capital stock country, equalling Texas and the prairies of the old West. From my outlook on the Defot ridge I saw thousands of square miles of this prairie-like region drained by tributaries of the Stickeen, Taku, Yukon, and Mackenzie Rivers.

Le Claire told me that the caribou, or reindeer, were very abundant on this ground. A flock of fifty or more was seen a short time before at the head of Defot Creek – fine, hardy, able animals like their near relatives the reindeer of the Arctic tundras. The Indians hereabouts, he said, hunted them with dogs, mostly in the autumn and winter. On my return trip I met several bands of these Indians on the march, going north to hunt. Some of the men and women were carrying puppies on top of their heavy loads of dried salmon, while the grown dogs had saddle-bags filled with odds and ends strapped on their backs. Small puppies, unable to carry more than five or six pounds, were thus made useful. I overtook another band going south, heavy laden with furs and skins to trade. An old woman, with short dress and leggings, was carrying a big load of furs and skins, on top of which was perched a little girl about three years old.

A brown, speckled marmot, one of Le Claire's friends, was getting ready for winter. The entrance of his burrow was a little to one side of the cabin door. A well-worn trail led to it through the grass and another to that of his companion, fifty feet away. He was a most amusing pet, always on hand at meal times for bread-crumbs and bits of bacon-rind, came when called, answering in a shrill whistle, moving like a squirrel with quick, nervous impulses, jerking his short flat tail. His fur clothing was neat and clean, fairly shining in the wintry light. The snowy weather that morning must have called winter to mind; for as soon as he got his breakfast, he ran to a tuft of dry grass, chewed it into fuzzy mouthfuls, and carried it to his nest, coming and going with admirable industry, forecast and confidence. None watching him as we did could fail to sympathize with him; and I fancy that in practical weather wisdom no government forecaster with all his advantages surpasses this little Alaska rodent, every hair and nerve a weather instrument.

I greatly enjoyed this little inland side trip – the wide views; the miners along the branches of the great river, busy as moles and beavers; young men dreaming and hoping to strike it rich and rush home to marry their girls faithfully waiting; others hoping to clear off weary farm mortgages, and brighten the lives of the anxious home folk; but most, I suppose, just struggling blindly for gold enough to make them indefinitely rich to spend their lives in aimless affluence, honour, and ease. I enjoyed getting acquainted with the trees, especially the beautiful spruce and silver fir; the flower gardens and great grassy caribou pastures; the cheery, able marmot mountaineer; and above all the friendship and kindness of Mr Le Claire, whom I shall never forget. Bidding goodbye, I sauntered back to the head of navigation on the Stickeen, happy and rich without a particle of obscuring gold-dust care.

CHAPTER SEVEN

Glenora Peak

ON THE trail to the steamboat-landing at the foot of Dease Lake, I met a Douglas squirrel, nearly as red and rusty in colour as his Eastern relative the chickaree. Except in colour he differs but little from the California Douglas squirrel. In voice, language, gestures, temperament, he is the same fiery, indomitable little king of the woods. Another darker and probably younger specimen met near the Caribou House, barked, chirruped, and showed off in fine style on a tree within a few feet of us.

'What does the little rascal mean?' said my companion, a man I had fallen in with on the trail. 'What is he making such a fuss about? I cannot frighten him.'

'Never mind,' I replied; 'just wait until I whistle "Old Hundred" and you will see him fly in disgust'. And so he did, just as his California brethren do. Strange that no squirrel or spermophile I yet have found ever seemed to have anything like enough of Scotch religion to enjoy this grand old tune.

The taverns along the Cassiar gold trail were the worst I had ever seen, rough shacks with dirt floors, dirt roofs, and rough meals. The meals are all alike – a potato, a slice of something like bacon, some grey stuff called bread, and a cup of muddy, semi-liquid coffee like that which the California miners call 'slickens' or 'slumgullion'. The bread was terrible and sinful. How the Lord's good wheat could be made into stuff so mysteriously bad is past finding out. The very de'il, it would seem, in wicked anger and ingenuity, has been the baker.

On our walk from Dease Lake to Telegraph Creek we had one of these rough luncheons at three o'clock in the afternoon of the first day, then walked on five miles to Ward's, where we were solemnly assured that we could not have a single bite of either supper or breakfast, but as a great favour we might sleep on his best grey bunk. We replied that, as we had lunched at the lake, supper would not be greatly missed, and as for breakfast we would start early and walk eight miles to the next road-house. We set out at half-past four, glad to escape into the fresh air, and reached the breakfast place at eight o'clock. The landlord was still abed, and when at length he came to the door, he scowled savagely at us as if our request for breakfast was preposterous and criminal beyond anything ever heard of in all goldful Alaska. A good many in those days were returning from the mines dead broke, and he probably regarded us as belonging to that disreputable class. Anyhow, we got nothing and had to tramp on.

As we approached the next house, three miles ahead, we saw the tavern-keeper keenly surveying us, and, as we afterwards learned, taking me for a certain judge whom for some cause he wished to avoid, he hurriedly locked his door and fled. Half a mile farther on we discovered him in a thicket a little way off the trail, explained our wants, marched him back to his house, and at length obtained a little sour bread, sour milk, and old salmon, our only lonely meal between the Lake and Telegraph Creek.

We arrived at Telegraph Creek, the end of my two-hundred-mile walk, about noon. After luncheon I went on down the river to Glenora in a fine canoe owned and manned by Kitty, a stout, intelligent-looking Indian woman, who charged her passengers a dollar for the fifteen-mile trip. Her crew was four Indian paddlers. In the rapids she also plied the paddle, with stout, telling strokes, and a keen-eyed old man, probably her husband, sat high in the stern and steered. All seemed exhilarated as we shot down through the narrow gorge on the rushing, roaring, throttled river, paddling all the more vigorously the faster the speed of the stream, to hold good steering way. The canoe danced lightly amid grey surges and spray as if alive and enthusiastically enjoying the adventure. Some of the passengers were pretty thoroughly drenched. In unskilful hands the frail dugout would surely have been wrecked or upset. Most of the season goods for the Cassiar gold camps were carried from Glenora to Telegraph Creek in canoes, the steamers not being able to overcome the rapids except during high water. Even then they had usually to line two of the rapids – that is, take a line ashore, make it fast to a tree on the bank, and pull up on the capstan. The freight canoes carried about three or four tons, for which fifteen dollars per ton was charged. Slow progress was made by poling along the bank out of the swiftest part of the current. In the rapids a tow line was taken ashore, only one of the crew remaining aboard to steer. The trip took a day unless a favouring wind was blowing, which often happened.

Next morning I set out from Glenora to climb Glenora Peak for the general view of the great Coast Range that I failed to obtain on my first ascent on account of the accident that befell Mr Young when we were within a minute or two of the top. It is hard to fail in reaching a mountain-top that one starts for, let the cause be what it may. This time I had no companion to care for, but the sky was threatening. I was assured by the local weather-prophets that the day would be rainy or snowy because the peaks in sight were muffled in clouds that seemed to be getting ready for work. I determined to go ahead, however, for storms of any kind are well worth while, and if driven back I could wait and try again.

With crackers in my pocket and a light rubber coat that a kind Hebrew passenger on the steamer Gertrude loaned me, I was ready for anything that might offer, my hopes for the grand view rising and falling as the clouds rose and fell. Anxiously I watched them as they trailed their draggled skirts across the glaciers and fountain peaks as if thoughtfully looking for the places where they could do the most good. From Glenora there is first a terrace of two hundred feet above the river covered mostly with bushes, yellow apocynum in the open spaces, together with carpets of dwarf manzanita, bunch-grass, and a few of the compositæ, galiums, etc. Then comes a flat stretch a mile wide, extending to the foothills, covered with birch, spruce, fir and poplar, now mostly killed by fire and the ground strewn with charred trunks. From this black forest the mountain rises in rather steep slopes covered with a luxuriant growth of bushes, grass, flowers and a few trees, chiefly spruce and fir, the firs gradually dwarfing into a beautiful chaparral, the most beautiful, I think, I have ever seen, the flat fan-shaped plumes thickly foliaged and imbricated by snow pressure, forming a smooth, handsome thatch which bears cones and thrives as if this repressed condition were its very best. It extends up an elevation of about fifty-five hundred feet. Only a few trees more than a foot in diameter and more than fifty feet high are found higher than four thousand feet above the sea. A few poplars and willows occur on moist places, gradually dwarfing like the conifers. Alder is the most generally distributed of the chaparral bushes, growing nearly everywhere; its crinkled stems an inch or two thick form a troublesome tangle to the mountaineer. The blue geranium, with leaves red and showy at this time of the year, is perhaps the most telling of the flowering plants. It grows up to five thousand feet or more. Larkspurs are common, with epilobium, senecio, erigeron, and a few solidagos. The harebell appears at about four thousand feet and extends to the summit, dwarfing in stature but maintaining the size of its handsome bells until they seem to be lying loose and detached on the ground as if like snow flowers they had fallen from the sky; and, though frail and delicate-looking, none of its companions is more enduring or rings out the praises of beauty-loving Nature in tones more appreciable to mortals, not forgetting even cassiope, who also is here and her companion, bryanthus, the loveliest and most widely distributed of the alpine shrubs. Then come crowberry, and two species of huckleberry, one of them from about six inches to a foot high with delicious berries, the other a most lavishly prolific and contented-looking dwarf, few of the bushes being more than two inches high, counting to the topmost leaf, yet each bearing from ten to twenty or more large berries. Perhaps more than half the bulk of the whole plant is fruit, the largest and finest-flavoured of all the huckleberries or blueberries I ever tasted, spreading fine feasts for the grouse and ptarmigan and many others of Nature's mountain people. I noticed three species of dwarf willows, one with narrow leaves, growing at the very summit of the mountain in cracks of the rocks, as well as on patches of soil, another with large, smooth leaves now turning yellow. The third species grows between the others as to elevation; its leaves, then orange-coloured, are strikingly pitted and reticulated. Another alpine shrub, a species of sericocarpus, covered with handsome heads of feathery achenia, beautiful dwarf echiverias with flocks of purple flowers pricked into their bright grass-green, cushion-like bosses of moss-like foliage, and a fine forget-me-not reach to the summit. I may also mention a large mertensia, a fine anemone, a veratrum, six feet high, a large blue daisy, growing up to three to four thousand feet, and at the summit a dwarf species, with dusky, hairy involucres, and a few ferns, aspidium, gymnogramma, and small rock cheilanthes, leaving scarce a foot of ground bare, though the mountain looks bald and brown in the distance like those of the desert ranges of the Great Basin in Utah and Nevada.

Charmed with these plant people, I had almost forgotten to watch the sky until I reached the top of the highest peak, when one of the greatest and most impressively sublime of all the mountain views I have ever enjoyed came full in sight – more than three hundred miles of closely packed peaks of the great Coast Range, sculptured in the boldest manner imaginable, their naked tops and dividing ridges dark in colour, their sides and the canyons, gorges and valleys between them loaded with glaciers and snow. From this standpoint I counted upwards of two hundred glaciers, while dark-centred luminous clouds with fringed edges hovered and crawled over them, now slowly descending, casting transparent shadows on the ice and snow, now rising high above them, lingering like loving angels guarding the crystal gifts they had bestowed. Although the range as seen from this Glenora mountain-top seems regular in its trend, as if the main axis were simple and continuous, it is, on the contrary, far from simple. In front of the highest ranks of peaks are others of the same form with their own glaciers, and lower peaks before these, and yet lower ones with their ridges and canyons, valleys and foothills. Alps rise beyond alps as far as the eye can reach, and clusters of higher peaks here and there closely crowded together; clusters, too, of needles and pinnacles innumerable like trees in groves. Everywhere the peaks seem comparatively slender and closely packed, as if Nature had here been trying to see how many noble well-dressed mountains could be crowded into one grand range.

The black rocks, too steep for snow to lie upon, were brought into sharp relief by white clouds and snow and glaciers, and these again were outlined and made tellingly plain by the rocks. The glaciers so grandly displayed are of every form, some crawling through gorge and valley like monster glittering serpents; others like broad cataracts pouring over cliffs into shadowy gulfs; others, with their main trunks winding through narrow canyons, display long, white finger-like tributaries descending from the summits of pinnacled ridges. Others lie back in fountain cirques walled in all around save at the lower edge, over which they pour in blue cascades. Snow, too, lay in folds and patches of every form on blunt, rounded ridges in curves, arrowy lines, dashes, and narrow ornamental flutings among the summit peaks and in broad radiating wings on smooth slopes. And on many a bulging headland and lower ridge there lay heavy, over-curling copings and smooth, white domes where wind-driven snow was pressed and wreathed and packed into every form and in every possible place and condition. I never before had seen so richly sculptured a range or so many awe-inspiring inaccessible mountains crowded together. If a line were drawn east and west from the peak on which I stood, and extended both ways to the horizon, cutting the whole round landscape in two equal parts, then all of the south half would be bounded by these icy peaks, which would seem to curve around half the horizon and about twenty degrees more, though extending in a general straight, or but moderately curved, line. The deepest and thickest and highest of all this wilderness of peaks lie to the southwest. They are probably from about nine to twelve thousand feet high, springing to this elevation from near the sea-level. The peak on which these observations were made is somewhere about seven thousand feet high, and from here I estimated the height of the range. The highest peak of all, or that seemed so to me, lies to the westward at an estimated distance of about one hundred and fifty to two hundred miles. Only its solid white summit was visible. Possibly it may be the topmost peak of St. Elias. Now look northward around the other half of the horizon, and instead of countless peaks crowding into the sky, you see a low brown region, heaving and swelling in gentle curves, apparently scarcely more waved than a rolling prairie. The so-called canyons of several forks of the upper Stickeen are visible, but even where best seen in the foreground and middle ground of the picture, they are like mere sunken gorges, making scarce perceptible marks on the landscape, while the tops of the highest mountain-swells show only small patches of snow and no glaciers.

Glenora Peak, on which I stood, is the highest point of a spur that puts out from the main range in a northerly direction. It seems to have been a rounded, broad-backed ridge which has been sculptured into its present irregular form by short residual glaciers, some of which, a mile or two long, are still at work.

As I lingered, gazing on the vast show, luminous shadowy clouds seemed to increase in glory of colour and motion, now fondling the highest peaks with infinite tenderness of touch, now hovering above them like eagles over their nests.

When night was drawing near, I ran down the flowery slopes exhilarated, thanking God for the gift of this great day. The setting sun fired the clouds. All the world seemed new-born. Every thing, even the commonest, was seen in new light and was looked at with new interest as if never seen before. The plant people seemed glad, as if rejoicing with me, the little ones as well as the trees, while every feature of the peak and its travelled boulders seemed to know what I had been about and the depth of my joy, as if they could read faces.

CHAPTER EIGHT

Exploration of the Stickeen Glaciers

NEXT DAY I planned an excursion to the so-called Dirt Glacier, the most interesting to Indians and steamer men of all the Stickeen glaciers from its mysterious floods. I left the steamer Gertrude for the glacier delta an hour or two before sunset. The captain kindly loaned me his canoe and two of his Indian deck hands, who seemed much puzzled to know what the rare service required of them might mean, and on leaving bade a merry adieu to their companions. We camped on the west side of the river opposite the front of the glacier, in a spacious valley surrounded by snowy mountains. Thirteen small glaciers were in sight and four waterfalls. It was a fine, serene evening, and the highest peaks were wearing turbans of flossy, gossamer cloud-stuff. I had my supper before leaving the steamer, so I had only to make a camp-fire, spread my blanket, and lie down. The Indians had their own bedding and lay beside their own fire.

The Dirt Glacier is noted among the river men as being subject to violent flood outbursts once or twice a year, usually in the late summer. The delta of this glacier stream is three or four miles wide where it fronts the river, and the many rough channels with which it is guttered and the uprooted trees and huge boulders that roughen its surface manifest the power of the floods that swept them to their places; but under ordinary conditions the glacier discharges its drainage water into the river through only four or five of the delta-channels.

Our camp was made on the south or lower side of the delta, below all the draining streams, so that I would not have to ford any of them on my way to the glacier. The Indians chose a sand-pit to sleep in; I chose a level spot back of a drift log. I had but little to say to my companions as they could speak no English, nor I much Thlinkit or Chinook. In a few minutes after landing they retired to their pit and were soon asleep and asnore. I lingered by the fire until after ten o'clock, for the night sky was clear, and the great white mountains in the starlight seemed nearer than by day and to be looking down like guardians of the valley, while the waterfalls, and the torrents escaping from beneath the big glacier, roared in a broad, low monotone, sounding as if close at hand, though, as it proved next day, the nearest was three miles away. After wrapping myself in my blankets, I still gazed into the marvellous sky and made out to sleep only about two hours. Then, without waking the noisy sleepers, I arose, ate a piece of bread, and set out in my shirt-sleeves, determined to make the most of the time at my disposal. The captain was to pick us up about noon at a woodpile about a mile from here; but if in the mean time the steamer should run aground and he should need his canoe, a three-whistle signal would be given.

Following a dry channel for about a mile, I came suddenly upon the main outlet of the glacier, which in the imperfect light seemed as large as the river, about one hundred and fifty feet wide, and perhaps three or four feet deep. A little farther up it was only about fifty feet wide and rushing on with impetuous roaring force in its rocky channel, sweeping forward sand, gravel, cobblestones and boulders, the bump and rumble sounds of the largest of these rolling stones being readily heard in the midst of the roaring. It was too swift and rough to ford, and no bridge tree could be found, for the great floods had cleared everything out of their way. I was therefore compelled to keep on up the right bank, however difficult the way. Where a strip of bare boulders lined the margin, the walking was easy, but where the current swept close along the ragged edge of the forest, progress was difficult and slow on account of snow-crinkled and interlaced thickets of alder and willow, reinforced with fallen trees and thorny devil's-club (*Echinopanax horridum*), making a jungle all but impenetrable. The mile of this extravagantly difficult growth through which I struggled, inch by inch, will not soon be forgotten. At length arriving within a few hundred yards of the glacier, full of panax barbs, I found that both the glacier and its unfordable stream were pressing hard against a shelving cliff, dangerously steep, leaving no margin, and compelling me to scramble along its face before I could get on to the glacier. But by sunrise all these cliff, jungle and torrent troubles were overcome and I gladly found myself free on the magnificent ice-river.

The curving, out-bulging front of the glacier is about two miles wide, two hundred feet high, and its surface for a mile or so above the front is strewn with moraine detritus, giving it a strangely dirty, dusky look, hence its name, the 'Dirt Glacier', this detritus-laden portion being all that is seen in passing up the river. A mile or two beyond the moraine-covered part I was surprised to find alpine plants growing on the ice, fresh and green, some of them in full flower. These curious glacier gardens, the first I had seen, were evidently planted by snow avalanches from the high walls. They were well watered, of course, by the melting surface of the ice and fairly well nourished by humus still attached to the roots, and in some places formed beds of considerable thickness. Seedling trees and bushes also were growing among the flowers. Admiring these novel floating gardens, I struck out for the middle of the pure white glacier, where the ice seemed smoother, and then held straight on for about eight miles, where I reluctantly turned back to meet the steamer, greatly regretting that I had not brought a week's supply of hardtack to allow me to explore the glacier to its head, and then trust to some passing canoe to take me down to Buck Station, from which I could explore the Big Stickeen Glacier.

Altogether, I saw about fifteen or sixteen miles of the main trunk. The grade is almost regular, and the walls on either hand are about from two to three thousand feet high, sculptured like those of Yosemite Valley. I found no difficulty of an extraordinary kind. Many a crevasse had to be crossed, but most of them were narrow and easily jumped, while the few wide ones that lay in my way were crossed on sliver bridges or avoided by passing around them. The structure of the glacier was strikingly revealed on its melting surface. It is made up of thin vertical or inclined sheets or slabs set on edge and welded together. They represent, I think, the successive snowfalls from heavy storms on the tributaries. One of the tributaries on the right side, about three miles above the front, has been entirely melted off from the trunk and has receded two or three miles, forming an independent glacier. Across the mouth of this abandoned part of its channel the main glacier flows, forming a dam which gives rise to a lake. On the head of the detached tributary there are some five or six small residual glaciers, the drainage of which, with that of the snowy mountain slopes above them, discharges into the lake, whose outlet is through a channel or channels beneath the damming glacier. Now these sub-channels are occasionally blocked and the water rises until it flows alongside of the glacier, but as the dam is a moving one, a grand outburst is sometimes made, which, draining the large lake, produces a flood of amazing power, sweeping down immense quantities of moraine material and raising the river all the way down to its mouth, so that several trips may occasionally be made by the steamers after the season of low water has laid them up for the year. The occurrence of these floods are, of course, well known to the Indians and steamboat men, though they know nothing of their cause. They simply remark, 'The Dirt Glacier has broken out again'.

I greatly enjoyed my walk up this majestic ice-river, charmed by the pale-blue, ineffably fine light in the crevasses, moulins, and wells, and the innumerable azure pools in basins of azure ice, and the network of surface streams, large and small, gliding, swirling with wonderful grace of motion in their frictionless channels, calling forth devout admiration at almost every step and filling the mind with a sense of Nature's endless beauty and power. Looking ahead from the middle of the glacier, you see the broad white flood, though apparently rigid as iron, sweeping in graceful curves between its high mountain-like walls, small glaciers hanging in the hollows on either side, and snow in every form above them, and the great down-plunging granite buttresses and headlands of the walls marvellous in bold massive sculpture; forests in side canyons to within fifty feet of the glacier; avalanche pathways overgrown with alder and willow; innumerable cascades keeping up a solemn harmony of water sounds blending with those of the glacier moulins and rills; and as far as the eye can reach, tributary glaciers at short intervals silently descending from their high, white fountains to swell the grand central ice-river.

In the angle formed by the main glacier and the lake that gives rise to the river floods, there is a massive granite dome sparsely feathered with trees, and just beyond this yosemitic rock is a mountain, perhaps ten thousand feet high, laden with ice and snow which seemed pure pearly white in the morning light. Last evening as seen from camp it was adorned with a cloud streamer, and both the streamer and the peak were flushed in the alpenglow. A mile or two above this mountain, on the opposite side of the glacier, there is a rock like the Yosemite Sentinel; and in general all the wall rocks as far as I saw them are more or less yosemitic in form and colour and streaked with cascades.

But wonderful as this noble ice-river is in size and depth and in power displayed, far more wonderful was the vastly greater glacier three or four thousand feet, or perhaps a mile, in depth, whose size and general history is inscribed on the sides of the walls and over the tops of the rocks in characters which have not yet been greatly dimmed by the weather. Comparing its present size with that when it was in its prime, is like comparing a small rivulet to the same stream when it is a roaring torrent.

The return trip to the camp past the shelving cliff and through the weary devil's-club jungle was made in a few hours. The Indians had gone off picking berries, but were on the watch for me and hailed me as I approached. The captain had called for me, and, after waiting three hours, departed for Wrangell without leaving any food, to make sure, I suppose, of a quick return of his Indians and canoe. This was no serious matter, however, for the swift current swept us down to Buck Station, some thirty-five miles distant, by eight o'clock. Here I remained to study the 'Big Stickeen Glacier', but the Indians set out for Wrangell soon after supper, though I invited them to stay till morning.

The weather that morning, 27 August, was dark and rainy, and I tried to persuade myself that I ought to rest a day before setting out on new ice work. But just across the river the 'Big Glacier' was staring me in the face, pouring its majestic flood through a broad mountain gateway and expanding in the spacious river valley to a width of four or five miles, while dim in the grey distance loomed its high mountain fountains. So grand an invitation displayed in characters so telling was of course irresistible, and body-care and weather-care vanished.

Mr Choquette, the keeper of the station, ferried me across the river, and I spent the day in getting general views and planning the work that had been long in mind. I first traced the broad, complicated terminal moraine to its southern extremity, climbed up the west side along the lateral moraine three or four miles, making my way now on the glacier, now on the moraine-covered bank, and now compelled to climb up through the timber and brush in order to pass some rocky headland, until I reached a point commanding a good general view of the lower end of the glacier. Heavy, blotting rain then began to fall, and I retraced my steps, oftentimes stopping to admire the blue ice-caves into which glad, rejoicing streams from the mountain-side were hurrying as if going home, while the glacier seemed to open wide its crystal gateways to welcome them.

The following morning blotting rain was still falling, but time and work was too precious to mind it. Kind Mr Choquette put me across the river in a canoe, with a lot of biscuits his Indian wife had baked for me and some dried salmon, a little sugar and tea, a blanket, and a piece of light sheeting for shelter from rain during the night, all rolled into one bundle.

'When shall I expect you back?' inquired Choquette, when I bade him good-bye.

'Oh, any time,' I replied. 'I shall see as much as possible of the glacier, and I know not how long it will hold me.'

'Well, but when will I come to look for you, if anything happens? Where are you going to try to go? Years ago Russian officers from Sitka went up the glacier from here and none ever returned. It's a mighty dangerous glacier, all full of damn deep holes and cracks. You've no idea what ticklish deceiving traps are scattered over it.'

'Yes, I have,' I said. 'I have seen glaciers before, though none so big as this one. Do not look for me until I make my appearance on the river-bank. Never mind me. I am used to caring for myself.' And so, shouldering my bundle, I trudged off through the moraine boulders and thickets.

My general plan was to trace the terminal moraine to its extreme north end, pitch my little tent, leave the blanket and most of the hardtack, and from this main camp go and come as hunger required or allowed.

After examining a cross-section of the broad moraine, roughened by concentric masses, marking interruptions in the recession of the glacier of perhaps several centuries, in which the successive moraines were formed and shoved together in closer or wider order, I traced the moraine to its northeastern extremity and ascended the glacier for several miles along the left margin, then crossed it at the grand cataract and down the right side to the river, and along the moraine to the point of beginning.

On the older portions of this moraine I discovered several kettles in process of formation and was pleased to find that they conformed in the most striking way with the theory I had already been led to make from observations on the old kettles which form so curious a feature of the drift covering Wisconsin and Minnesota and some of the larger moraines of the residual glaciers in the California Sierra. I found a pit eight or ten feet deep with raw shifting sides countersunk abruptly in the rough moraine material, and at the bottom, on sliding down by the aid of a lithe spruce tree that was being undermined, I discovered, after digging down a foot or two, that the bottom was resting on a block of solid blue ice which had been buried in the moraine perhaps a century or more, judging by the age of the tree that had grown above it. Probably more than another century will be required to complete the formation of this kettle by the slow melting of the buried ice-block. The moraine material of course was falling in as the ice melted, and the sides maintained an angle as steep as the material would lie. All sorts of theories have been advanced for the formation of these kettles, so abundant in the drift over a great part of the United States, and I was glad to be able to set the question at rest, at least as far as I was concerned.

The glacier and the mountains about it are on so grand a scale and so generally inaccessible in the ordinary sense, it seemed to matter but little what course I pursued. Everything was full of interest, even the weather, though about as unfavourable as possible for wide views, and scrambling through the moraine jungle brush kept one as wet as if all the way was beneath a cascade.

I pushed on, with many a rest and halt to admire the bold and marvellously sculptured ice-front, looking all the grander and more striking in the grey mist with all the rest of the glacier shut out, until I came to a lake about two hundred yards wide and two miles long with scores of small bergs floating in it, some aground, close inshore against the moraine, the light playing on their angles and shimmering in their blue caves in ravishing tones. This proved to be the largest of the series of narrow lakelets that lie in shallow troughs between the moraine and the glacier, a miniature Arctic Ocean, its ice-cliffs played upon by whispering, rippling wavelets and its small berg floes drifting in its currents or with the wind, or stranded here and there along its rocky moraine shore.

Hundreds of small rills and good-sized streams were falling into the lake from the glacier, singing in low tones, some of them pouring in sheer falls over blue cliffs from narrow ice-valleys, some spouting from pipelike channels in the solid front of the glacier, others gurgling out of arched openings at the base. All these water-streams were riding on the parent ice-stream, their voices joined in one grand anthem telling the wonders of their near and far-off mountains. The lake itself is resting in a basin of ice, and the forested moraine, though seemingly cut off from the glacier and probably more than a century old, is in great part resting on buried ice left behind as the glacier receded, and melting slowly on account of the protection afforded by the moraine detritus, which keeps shifting and falling on the inner face long after it is overgrown with lichens, mosses, grasses, bushes, and even good-sized trees; these changes going on with marvellous deliberation until in fullness of time the whole moraine settles down upon its bed-rock foundation.

The outlet of the lake is a large stream, almost a river in size, one of the main draining streams of the glacier. I attempted to ford it where it begins to break in rapids in passing over the moraine, but found it too deep and rough on the bottom. I then tried to ford at its head, where it is wider and glides smoothly out of the lake, bracing myself against the current with a pole, but found it too deep, and when the icy water reached my shoulders I cautiously struggled back to the moraine. I next followed down through the rocky jungle to a place where in breaking across the moraine dam it was only about thirty-five feet wide. Here I found a spruce tree, which I felled for a bridge; it reached across, about ten feet of the top holding in the bank brush. But the force of the torrent, acting on the submerged branches and the slender end of the trunk, bent it like a bow and made it very unsteady, and after testing it by going out about a third of the way over, it seemed likely to be carried away when bent deeper into the current by my weight. Fortunately, I discovered another larger tree well situated a little farther down, which I felled, and though a few feet in the middle was submerged, it seemed perfectly safe.

As it was now getting late, I started back to the lakeside where I had left my bundle, and in trying to hold a direct course found the interlaced jungle still more difficult than it was along the bank of the torrent. For over an hour I had to creep and struggle close to the rocky ground like a fly in a spider-web without being able to obtain a single glimpse of any guiding feature of the landscape. Finding a little willow taller than the surrounding alders, I climbed it, caught sight of the glacier-front, took a compass bearing, and sunk again into the dripping, blinding maze of brush, and at length emerged on the lake-shore seven hours after leaving it, all this time as wet as though I had been swimming, thus completing a trying day's work. But everything was deliciously fresh, and I found new and old plant friends, and lessons on Nature's Alaska moraine landscape-gardening that made everything bright and light.

It was now near dark, and I made haste to make up my flimsy little tent. The ground was desperately rocky. I made out, however, to level down a strip large enough to lie on, and by means of slim alder stems bent over it and tied together soon had a home. While thus busily engaged I was startled by a thundering roar across the lake. Running to the top of the moraine, I discovered that the tremendous noise was only the outcry of a newborn berg about fifty or sixty feet in diameter, rocking and wallowing in the waves it had raised as if enjoying its freedom after its long grinding work as a part of the glacier. After this fine last lesson I managed to make a small fire out of wet twigs, got a cup of tea, stripped off my dripping clothing, wrapped myself in a blanket and lay brooding on the gains of the day and plans for the morrow, glad, rich, and almost comfortable.

It was raining hard when I awoke, but I made up my mind to disregard the weather, put on my dripping clothing, glad to know it was fresh and clean; ate biscuits and a piece of dried salmon without attempting to make a tea fire; filled a bag with hardtack, slung it over my shoulder, and with my indispensable ice-axe plunged once more into the dripping jungle. I found my bridge holding bravely in place against the swollen torrent, crossed it and beat my way around pools and logs and through two hours of tangle back to the moraine on the north side of the outlet – a wet weary battle but not without enjoyment. The smell of the washed ground and vegetation made every breath a pleasure, and I found *Calypso borealis*, the first I had seen on this side of the continent, one of my darlings, worth any amount of hardship; and I saw one of my Douglas squirrels on the margin of a grassy pool. The drip of the rain on the various leaves was pleasant to hear. More especially marked were the flat low-toned bumps and splashes of large drops from the trees on the broad horizontal leaves of *Echinopanax horridum*, like the drumming of thunder-shower drops on veratrum and palm leaves, while the mosses were indescribably beautiful, so fresh, so bright, so cheerily green, and all so low and calm and silent, however heavy and wild the wind and the rain blowing and pouring above them. Surely never a particle of dust has touched leaf or crown of all these blessed mosses; and how bright were the red rims of the cladonia cups beside them, and the fruit of the dwarf cornel! And the wet berries, Nature's precious jewellry, how beautiful they were! – huckleberries with pale bloom and a crystal drop on each; red and yellow salmon-berries, with clusters of smaller drops; and the glittering, berry-like raindrops, adorning the interlacing arches of bent grasses and sedges around the edges of the pools, every drop a mirror with all the landscape in it. A' that and a' that and twice as muckle's a' that in this glorious Alaska day, recalling, however different, George Herbert's 'Sweet day, so cool, so calm, so bright'.

In the gardens and forests of this wonderful moraine one might spend a whole joyful life.

When I at last reached the end of the great moraine and the front of the mountain that forms the north side of the glacier basin, I tried to make my way along its side, but, finding the climbing tedious and difficult, took to the glacier and fared well, though a good deal of step-cutting was required on its ragged, crevassed margin. When night was drawing nigh, I scanned the steep mountainside in search of an accessible bench, however narrow, where a bed and a fire might be gathered for a camp. About dark great was my delight to find a shelf with a few small mountain hemlocks growing in cleavage joints. Projecting knobs below it enabled me to build a platform for a fireplace and a bed and by industrious creeping from one fissure to another, cutting bushes and small trees and sliding them down to within reach of my rock-shelf, I made out to collect wood enough to last through the night. In an hour or two I had a cheery fire, and spent the night in turning from side to side, steaming and drying after being wet two days and a night. Fortunately this night it did not rain, but it was very cold.

Pushing on next day, I climbed to the top of the glacier by ice-steps and along its side to the grand cataract two miles wide where the whole majestic flood of the glacier pours like a mighty surging river down a steep declivity in its channel. After gazing a long time on the glorious show, I discovered a place beneath the edge of the cataract where it flows over a hard, resisting granite rib, into which I crawled and enjoyed the novel and instructive view of a glacier pouring over my head, showing not only its grinding, polishing action, but how it breaks off large angular boulder-masses – a most telling lesson in earth sculpture, confirming many I had already learned in the glacier basins of the High Sierra of California. I then crossed to the south side, noting the forms of the huge blocks into which the glacier was broken in passing over the brow of the cataract, and how they were welded.

The weather was now clear, opening views according to my own heart far into the high snowy fountains. I saw what seemed the farthest mountains, perhaps thirty miles from the front, everywhere winter-bound, but thick forested, however steep, for a distance of at least fifteen miles from the front, the trees, hemlock and spruce, clinging to the rock by root-holds among cleavage joints. The greatest discovery was in methods of denudation displayed beneath the glacier.

After a few more days of exhilarating study I returned to the river-bank opposite Choquette's landing. Promptly at sight of the signal I made, the kind Frenchman came across for me in his canoe. At his house I enjoyed a rest while writing out notes; then examined the smaller glacier fronting the one I had been exploring, until a passing canoe bound for Fort Wrangell took me aboard.

CHAPTER NINE

A Canoe Voyage to Northward

I ARRIVED at Wrangell in a canoe with a party of Cassiar miners in October while the icy regions to the northward still burned in my mind. I had met several prospectors who had been as far as Chilcat at the head of Lynn Canal, who told wonderful stories about the great glaciers they had seen there. All the high mountains up there, they said, seemed to be made of ice, and if glaciers 'are what you are after, that's the place for you,' and to get there 'all you have to do is to hire a good canoe and Indians who know the way'.

But it now seemed too late to set out on so long a voyage. The days were growing short and winter was drawing nigh when all the land would be buried in snow. On the other hand, though this wilderness was new to me, I was familiar with storms and enjoyed them. The main channels extending along the coast remain open all winter, and, their shores being well forested, I knew that it would be easy to keep warm in camp, while abundance of food could be carried. I determined, therefore, to go ahead as far north as possible, to see and learn what I could, especially with reference to future work. When I made known my plans to Mr Young, he offered to go with me, and, being acquainted with the Indians, procured a good canoe and crew, and with a large stock of provisions and blankets, we left Wrangell 14 October, eager to welcome weather of every sort, as long as food lasted.

I was anxious to make an early start, but it was half-past two in the afternoon before I could get my Indians together – Toyatte, a grand old Stickeen nobleman, who was made captain, not only because he owned the canoe, but for his skill in woodcraft and seamanship; Kadachan, the son of a Chilcat chief; John, a Stickeen, who acted as interpreter; and Sitka Charley. Mr Young, my companion, was an adventurous evangelist, and it was the opportunities the trip might afford to meet the Indians of the different tribes on our route with reference to future missionary work, that induced him to join us.

When at last all were aboard and we were about to cast loose from the wharf, Kadachan's mother, a woman of great natural dignity and force of character, came down the steps alongside the canoe oppressed with anxious fears for the safety of her son. Standing silent for a few moments, she held the missionary with her dark, bodeful eyes, and with great solemnity of speech and gesture accused him of using undue influence in gaining her son's consent to go on a dangerous voyage among unfriendly tribes; and like an ancient sibyl foretold a long train of bad luck from storms and enemies, and finished by saying, 'If my son comes not back, on you will be his blood, and you shall pay. I say it.'

Mr Young tried in vain to calm her fears, promising Heaven's care as well as his own for her precious son, assuring her that he would faithfully share every danger that he encountered, and if need be die in his defence.

'We shall see whether or not you die', she said, and turned away.

Toyatte also encountered domestic difficulties. When he stepped into the canoe I noticed a cloud of anxiety on his grand old face, as if his doom now drawing near was already beginning to overshadow him. When he took leave of his wife, she refused to shake hands with him, wept bitterly, and said that his enemies, the Chilcat chiefs, would be sure to kill him in case he reached their village. But it was not on this trip that the old hero was to meet his fate, and when we were fairly free in the wilderness and a gentle breeze pressed us joyfully over the shining waters these gloomy forebodings vanished.

We first pursued a westerly course, through Sumner Strait, between Kupreanof and Prince of Wales Islands, then, turning northward, sailed up the Kiku Strait through the midst of innumerable picturesque islets, across Prince Frederick's Sound, up Chatham Strait, thence northwestward through Icy Strait and around the then uncharted Glacier Bay. Thence returning through Icy Strait, we sailed up the beautiful Lynn Canal to the Davidson Glacier and the lower village of the Chilcat tribe and returned to Wrangell along the coast of the mainland, visiting the icy Sum Dum Bay and the Wrangell Glacier on our route. Thus we made a journey more than eight hundred miles long, and though hardships and perhaps dangers were encountered, the great wonderland made compensation beyond our most extravagant hopes. Neither rain nor snow stopped us, but when the wind was too wild, Kadachan and the old captain stayed on guard in the camp and John and Charley went into the woods deer-hunting, while I examined the adjacent rocks and woods. Most of our camp-grounds were in sheltered nooks where good firewood was abundant, and where the precious canoe could be safely drawn up beyond reach of the waves. After supper we sat long around the fire, listening to the Indian's stories about the wild animals, their hunting-adventures, wars, traditions, religion, and customs. Every Indian party we met we interviewed, and visited every village we came to.

Our first camp was made at a place called the Island of the Standing Stone, on the shore of a shallow bay. The weather was fine. The mountains of the mainland were unclouded, excepting one, which had a horizontal ruff of dull slate colour, but its icy summit covered with fresh snow towered above the cloud, flushed like its neighbours in the alpenglow. All the large islands in sight were densely forested, while many small rock islets in front of our camp were treeless or nearly so. Some of them were distinctly glaciated even below the tide-line, the effects of wave washing and general weathering being scarce appreciable as yet. Some of the larger islets had a few trees, others only grass. One looked in the distance like a two-masted ship flying before the wind under press of sail.

Next morning the mountains were arrayed in fresh snow that had fallen during the night down to within a hundred feet of the sea-level. We made a grand fire, and after an early breakfast pushed merrily on all day along beautiful forested shores embroidered with autumn-coloured bushes. I noticed some pitchy trees that had been deeply hacked for kindling-wood and torches, precious conveniences to belated voyagers on stormy nights. Before sundown we camped in a beautiful nook of Deer Bay, shut in from every wind by grey-bearded trees and fringed with rose bushes, rubus, potentilla, asters, etc. Some of the lichen tresses depending from the branches were six feet in length.

A dozen rods or so from our camp we discovered a family of Kake Indians snugly sheltered in a portable bark hut, a stout middle-aged man with his wife, son, and daughter, and his son's wife. After our tent was set and fire made, the head of the family paid us a visit and presented us with a fine salmon, a pair of mallard ducks, and a mess of potatoes. We paid a return visit with gifts of rice and tobacco, etc. Mr Young spoke briefly on mission affairs and inquired whether their tribe would be likely to welcome a teacher or missionary. But they seemed unwilling to offer an opinion on so important a subject. The following words from the head of the family was the only reply:

'We have not much to say to you fellows. We always do to Boston men as we have done to you, give a little of whatever we have, treat everybody well and never quarrel. This is all we have to say.'

Our Kake neighbours set out for Fort Wrangell next morning, and we pushed gladly on toward Chilcat. We passed an island that had lost all its trees in a storm, but a hopeful crop of young ones was springing up to take their places. I found no trace of fire in these woods. The ground was covered with leaves, branches, and fallen trunks perhaps a dozen generations deep, slowly decaying, forming a grand mossy mass of ruins, kept fresh and beautiful. All that is repulsive about death was here hidden beneath abounding life. Some rocks along the shore were completely covered with crimson-leafed huckleberry bushes; one species still in fruit might well be called the winter huckleberry. In a short walk I found vetches eight feet high leaning on raspberry bushes, and tall ferns and *Smilacina unifolia* with leaves six inches wide growing on yellow-green moss, producing a beautiful effect.

Our Indians seemed to be enjoying a quick and merry reaction from the doleful domestic dumps in which the voyage was begun. Old and young behaved this afternoon like a lot of truant boys on a lark. When we came to a pond fenced off from the main channel by a moraine dam, John went ashore to seek a shot at ducks. Creeping up behind the dam, he killed a mallard fifty or sixty feet from the shore and attempted to wave it within reach by throwing stones back of it. Charley and Kadachan went to his help, enjoying the sport, especially enjoying their own blunders in throwing in front of it and thus driving the duck farther out. To expedite the business John then tried to throw a rope across it, but failed after repeated trials, and so did each in turn, all laughing merrily at their awkward bungling. Next they tied a stone to the end of the rope to carry it further and with better aim, but the result was no better. Then majestic old Toyatte tried his hand at the game. He tied the rope to one of the canoe-poles, and taking aim threw it, harpoon fashion, beyond the duck, and the general merriment was redoubled when the pole got loose and floated out to the middle of the pond. At length John stripped, swam to the duck, threw it ashore, and brought in the pole in his teeth, his companions meanwhile making merry at his expense by splashing the water in front of him and making the dead duck go through the motions of fighting and biting him in the face as he landed.

The morning after this delightful day was dark and threatening. A high wind was rushing down the strait dead against us, and just as we were about ready to start, determined to fight our way by creeping close inshore, pelting rain began to fly. We concluded therefore to wait for better weather. The hunters went out for deer and I to see the forests. The rain brought out the fragrance of the drenched trees, and the wind made wild melody in their tops, while every brown bole was embroidered by a network of rain rills. Perhaps the most delightful part of my ramble was along a stream that flowed through a leafy arch beneath overleaning trees which met at the top. The water was almost black in the deep pools and fine clear amber in the shallows. It was the pure, rich wine of the woods with a pleasant taste, bringing spicy spruce groves and widespread bog and beaver meadows to mind. On this amber stream I discovered an interesting fall. It is only a few feet high, but remarkably fine in the curve of its brow and blending shades of colour, while the mossy, bushy pool into which it plunges is inky black, but wonderfully brightened by foam bells larger than common that drift in clusters on the smooth water around the rim, each of them carrying a picture of the overlooking trees leaning together at the tips like the teeth of moss capsules before they rise.

I found most of the trees here fairly loaded with mosses. Some broadly palmated branches had beds of yellow moss so wide and deep that when wet they must weigh a hundred pounds or even more. Upon these moss-beds ferns and grasses and even good-sized seedling trees grow, making beautiful hanging gardens in which the curious spectacle is presented of old trees holding hundreds of their own children in their arms, nourishing by rain and dew and the decaying leaves showered down to them by their parents. The branches upon which these beds of mossy soil rest become flat and irregular like weathered roots or the antlers of deer, and at length die; and when the whole tree has thus been killed it seems to be standing on its head with roots in the air. A striking example of this sort stood near the camp and I called the missionary's attention to it.

'Come, Mr Young,' I shouted. 'Here's something wonderful, the most wonderful tree you ever saw; it is standing on its head.'

'How in the world', said he in astonishment, 'could that tree have been plucked up by the roots, carried high in the air, and dropped down head foremost into the ground. It must have been the work of a tornado.'

Toward evening the hunters brought in a deer. They had seen four others, and at the camp-fire talk said that deer abounded on all the islands of considerable size and along the shores of the mainland. But few were to be found in the interior on account of wolves that ran them down where they could not readily take refuge in the water. The Indians, they said, hunted them on the islands with trained dogs which went into the woods and drove them out, while the hunters lay in wait in canoes at the points where they were likely to take to the water. Beaver and black bear also abounded on this large island. I saw but few birds there, only ravens, jays, and wrens. Ducks, gulls, bald eagles, and jays are the commonest birds hereabouts. A flock of swans flew past, sounding their startling human-like cry which seemed yet more striking in this lonely wilderness. The Indians said that geese, swans, cranes, etc., making their long journeys in regular order thus called aloud to encourage each other and enable them to keep stroke and time like men in rowing or marching (a sort of 'Row, brothers, row', or 'Hip, hip' of marching soldiers).

18 October was about half sunshine, half rain and wet snow, but we paddled on through the midst of the innumerable islands in more than half comfort, enjoying the changing effects of the weather on the dripping wilderness. Strolling a little way back into the woods when we went ashore for luncheon, I found fine specimens of cedar, and here and there a birch, and small thickets of wild apple. A hemlock, felled by Indians for bread-bark, was only twenty inches thick at the butt, a hundred and twenty feet long, and about five hundred and forty years old at the time it was felled. The first hundred of its rings measured only four inches, showing that for a century it had grown in the shade of taller trees and at the age of one hundred years was yet only a sapling in size. On the mossy trunk of an old prostrate spruce about a hundred feet in length thousands of seedlings were growing. I counted seven hundred on a length of eight feet, so favourable is this climate for the development of tree seeds and so fully do these trees obey the command to multiply and replenish the earth. No wonder these islands are densely clothed with trees. They grow on solid rocks and logs as well as on fertile soil. The surface is first covered with a plush of mosses in which the seeds germinate; then the interlacing roots form a sod, fallen leaves soon cover their feet, and the young trees, closely crowded together, support each other, and the soil becomes deeper and richer from year to year.

I greatly enjoyed the Indian's camp-fire talk this evening on their ancient customs, how they were taught by their parents ere the whites came among them, their religion, ideas connected with the next world, the stars, plants, the behaviour and language of animals under different circumstances, manner of getting a living, etc. When our talk was interrupted by the howling of a wolf on the opposite side of the strait, Kadachan puzzled the minister with the question, 'Have wolves souls?' The Indians believe that they have, giving as foundation for their belief that they are wise creatures who know how to catch seals and salmon by swimming slyly upon them with their heads hidden in a mouthful of grass, hunt deer in company, and always bring forth their young at the same and most favourable time of the year. I inquired how it was that with enemies so wise and powerful the deer were not all killed. Kadachan replied that wolves knew better than to kill them all and thus cut off their most important food-supply. He said they were numerous on all the large islands, more so than on the mainland, that Indian hunters were afraid of them and never ventured far into the woods alone, for these large grey and black wolves attacked man whether they were hungry or not. When attacked, the Indian hunter, he said, climbed a tree or stood with his back against a tree or rock as a wolf never attacks face to face. Wolves, and not bears, Indians regard as masters of the woods, for they sometimes attack and kill bears, but the wolverine they never attack, 'for', said John, 'wolves and wolverines are companions in sin and equally wicked and cunning'.

On one of the small islands we found a stockade, sixty by thirty-five feet, built, our Indians said, by the Kake tribe during one of their many warlike quarrels. Toyatte and Kadachan said these forts were common throughout the canoe waters, showing that in this foodful, kindly wilderness, as in all the world beside, man may be man's worst enemy.

We discovered small bits of cultivation here and there, patches of potatoes and turnips, planted mostly on the cleared sites of deserted villages. In spring the most industrious families sailed to their little farms of perhaps a quarter of an acre or less, and ten or fifteen miles from their villages. After preparing the ground, and planting it, they visited it again in summer to pull the weeds and speculate on the size of the crop they were likely to have to eat with their fat salmon. The Kakes were then busy digging their potatoes, which they complained were this year injured by early frosts.

We arrived at Klugh-Quan, one of the Kupreanof Kake villages, just as a funeral party was breaking up. The body had been burned and gifts were being distributed – bits of calico, handkerchiefs, blankets, etc., according to the rank and wealth of the deceased. The death ceremonies of chiefs and head men, Mr Young told me, are very weird and imposing, with wild feasting, dancing and singing. At this little place there are some eight totem poles of bold and intricate design, well executed, but smaller than those of Stickeens. As elsewhere throughout the archipelago, the bear, raven, eagle, salmon, and porpoise are the chief figures. Some of the poles have square cavities, mortised into the back, which are said to contain the ashes of members of the family. These recesses are closed by a plug. I noticed one that was caulked with a rag where the joint was imperfect.

Strolling about the village, looking at the tangled vegetation, sketching the totems, etc., I found a lot of human bones scattered on the surface of the ground or partly covered. In answer to my inquiries, one of our crew said they probably belonged to Sitka Indians slain in war. These Kakes are shrewd, industrious, and rather good-looking people. It was at their largest village that an American schooner was seized and all the crew except one man murdered. A gunboat sent to punish them burned the village. I saw the anchor of the ill-fated vessel lying near the shore.

Though all the Thlinkit tribes believe in witch-craft, they are less superstitious in some respects than many of the lower classes of whites. Chief Yana Taowk seemed to take pleasure in kicking the Sitka bones that lay in his way, and neither old nor young showed the slightest trace of superstitious fear of the dead at any time.

It was at the northmost of the Kupreanof Kake villages that Mr Young held his first missionary meeting, singing hymns, praying, and preaching, and trying to learn the number of the inhabitants and their readiness to receive instruction. Neither here nor in any of the other villages of the different tribes that we visited was there anything like a distinct refusal to receive school-teachers or ministers. On the contrary, with but one or two exceptions, all with apparent good faith declared their willingness to receive them, and many seemed heartily delighted at the prospect of gaining light on subjects so important and so dark to them. All had heard ere this of the wonderful work of the Reverend Mr Duncan at Metlakatla, and even those chiefs who were not at all inclined to anything like piety were yet anxious to procure schools and churches that their people should not miss the temporal advantages of knowledge, which with their natural shrewdness they were not slow to recognize. 'We are all children', they said, 'groping in the dark. Give us this light and we will do as you bid us.'

The chief of the first Kupreanof Kake village we came to was a venerable-looking man, perhaps seventy years old, with massive head and strongly marked features, a bold Roman nose, deep, tranquil eyes, shaggy eyebrows, a strong face set in a halo of long grey hair. He seemed delighted at the prospect of receiving a teacher for his people. 'This is just what I want', he said. 'I am ready to bid him welcome'.

'This', said Yana Taowk, chief of the larger north village, 'is a good work you bring us. We will be glad to come out of our darkness into your light. You Boston men must be favourites of the Great Father. You know all about God, and ships and guns and the growing of things to eat. We will sit quiet and listen to the words of any teacher you send us.'

While Mr Young was preaching, some of the congregation smoked, talked to each other, and answered the shouts of their companions outside, greatly to the disgust of Toyatte and Kadachan, who regarded the Kakes as manner-less barbarians. A little girl, frightened at the strange exercises, began to cry and was turned out of doors. She cried in a strange, low, wild tone, quite unlike the screech crying of the children of civilization.

The following morning we crossed Prince Frederick Sound to the west coast of Admiralty Island. Our frail shell of a canoe was tossed like a bubble on the swells coming in from the ocean. Still, I suppose, the danger was not so great as it seemed. In a good canoe, skilfully handled, you may safely sail from Victoria to Chilcat, a thousand-mile voyage frequently made by Indians in their trading operations before the coming of the whites. Our Indians, however, dreaded this crossing so late in the season. They spoke of it repeatedly before we reached it as the one great danger of our voyage.

John said to me just as we left the shore, 'You and Mr Young will be scared to death on this broad water'.

'Never mind us, John', we merrily replied, 'perhaps some of you brave Indian sailors may be the first to show fear'.

Toyatte said he had not slept well a single night thinking of it, and after we rounded Cape Gardner and entered the comparatively smooth Chatham Strait, they all rejoiced, laughing and chatting like frolicsome children.

We arrived at the first of the Hootsenoo villages on Admiralty Island shortly after noon and were welcomed by everybody. Men, women, and children made haste to the beach to meet us, the children staring as if they had never before seen a Boston man. The chief, a remarkably good-looking and intelligent fellow, stepped forward, shook hands with us Boston fashion, and invited us to his house. Some of the curious children crowded in after us and stood around the fire staring like half-frightened wild animals. Two old women drove them out of the house, making hideous gestures, but taking good care not to hurt them. The merry throng poured through the round door, laughing and enjoying the harsh gestures and threats of the women as all a joke, indicating mild parental government in general. Indeed, in all my travels I never saw a child, old or young, receive a blow or even a harsh word. When our cook began to prepare luncheon our host said through his interpreter that he was sorry we could not eat Indian food, as he was anxious to entertain us. We thanked him, of course, and expressed our sense of his kindness. His brother, in the mean time, brought a dozen turnips, which he peeled and sliced and served in a clean dish. These we ate raw as dessert, reminding me of turnip-field feasts when I was a boy in Scotland. Then a box was brought from some corner and opened. It seemed to be full of tallow or butter. A sharp stick was thrust into it, and a lump of something five or six inches long, three or four wide, and an inch thick was dug up, which proved to be a section of the back fat of a deer, preserved in fish oil and seasoned with boiled spruce and other spicy roots. After stripping off the lard-like oil, it was cut into small pieces and passed round. It seemed white and wholesome, but I was unable to taste it even for manner's sake. This disgust, however, was not noticed, as the rest of the company did full justice to the precious tallow and smacked their lips over it as a great delicacy. A lot of potatoes about the size of walnuts, boiled and peeled and added to a potful of salmon, made a savoury stew that all seemed to relish. An old, cross-looking, wrinkled crone presided at the steaming chowder-pot, and as she peeled the potatoes with her fingers she, at short intervals, quickly thrust one of the best into the mouth of a little wild-eyed girl that crouched beside her, a spark of natural love which charmed her withered face and made all the big gloomy house shine. In honour of our visit, our host put on a genuine white shirt. His wife also dressed in her best and put a pair of dainty trousers on her two-year-old boy, who seemed to be the pet and favourite of the large family and indeed of the whole village. Toward evening messengers were sent through the village to call everybody to a meeting. Mr Young delivered the usual missionary sermon and I also was called on to say something. Then the chief arose and made an eloquent reply, thanking us for our good words and for the hopes we had inspired of obtaining a teacher for their children. In particular, he said, he wanted to hear all we could tell him about God.

This village was an offshoot of a larger one, ten miles to the north, called Killisnoo. Under the prevailing patriarchal form of government each tribe is divided into comparatively few families; and because of quarrels, the chief of this branch moved his people to this little bay, where the beach offered a good landing for canoes. A stream which enters it yields abundance of salmon, while in the adjacent woods and mountains berries, deer, and wild goats abound.

'Here', he said, 'we enjoy peace and plenty; all we lack is a church and a school, particularly a school for the children'. His dwelling so much with benevolent aspect on the children of the tribe showed, I think, that he truly loved them and had a right intelligent insight concerning their welfare. We spent the night under his roof, the first we had ever spent with Indians, and I never felt more at home. The loving kindness bestowed on the little ones made the house glow.

Next morning, with the hearty good wishes of our Hootsenoo friends, and encouraged by the gentle weather, we sailed gladly up the coast, hoping soon to see the Chilcat glaciers in their glory. The rock hereabouts is mostly a beautiful blue marble, waveworn into a multitude of small coves and ledges. Fine sections were thus revealed along the shore, which with their colours, brightened with showers and late-blooming leaves and flowers, beguiled the weariness of the way. The shingle in front of these marble cliffs is also mostly marble, well polished and rounded and mixed with a small percentage of glacier-borne slate and granite erratics.

We arrived at the upper village about half-past one o'clock. Here we saw Hootsenoo Indians in a very different light from that which illumined the lower village. While we were yet half a mile or more away, we heard sounds I had never before heard – a storm of strange howls, yells, and screams rising from a base of gasping, bellowing grunts and groans. Had I been alone, I should have fled as from a pack of fiends, but our Indians quietly recognized this awful sound, if such stuff could be called sound, simply as the 'whiskey howl' and pushed quietly on. As we approached the landing, the demoniac howling so greatly increased I tried to dissuade Mr Young from attempting to say a single word in the village, and as for preaching one might as well try to preach in Tophet. The whole village was afire with bad whiskey. This was the first time in my life that I learned the meaning of the phrase 'a howling drunk'. Even our Indians hesitated to venture ashore, notwithstanding whiskey storms were far from novel to them. Mr Young, however, hoped that in this Indian Sodom at least one man might be found so righteous as to be in his right mind and able to give trustworthy information. Therefore I was at length prevailed on to yield consent to land. Our canoe was drawn up on the beach and one of the crew left to guard it. Cautiously we strolled up the hill to the main row of houses, now a chain of alcoholic volcanoes. The largest house, just opposite the landing, was about forty feet square, built of immense planks, each hewn from a whole log, and, as usual, the only opening was a mere hole about two and a half feet in diameter, closed by a massive hinged plug like the breach of a cannon. At the dark door-hole a few black faces appeared and were suddenly withdrawn. Not a single person was to be seen on the street. At length a couple of old, crouching men, hideously blackened, ventured out and stared at us, then, calling to their companions, other black and burning heads appeared, and we began to fear that like the Alloway Kirk witches the whole legion was about to sally forth. But, instead, those outside suddenly crawled and tumbled in again. We were thus allowed to take a general view of the place and return to our canoe unmolested. But ere we could get away, three old women came swaggering and grinning down to the beach, and Toyatte was discovered by a man with whom he had once had a business misunderstanding, who, burning for revenge, was now jumping and howling and threatening as only a drunken Indian may, while our heroic old captain, in severe icy majesty, stood erect and motionless, uttering never a word. Kadachan, on the contrary, was well nigh smothered with the drunken caresses of one of his father's *tillicums* (friends), who insisted on his going back with him into the house. But reversing the words of St Paul in his account of his shipwreck, it came to pass that we at length got safe to sea and by hard rowing managed to reach a fine harbour before dark, fifteen sweet, serene miles from the howlers.

Our camp this evening was made at the head of a narrow bay bordered by spruce and hemlock woods. We made our beds beneath a grand old Sitka spruce five feet in diameter, whose broad, winglike branches were outspread immediately above our heads. The night picture as I stood back to see it in the firelight was this one great tree, relieved against the gloom of the woods back of it, the light on the low branches revealing the shining needles, the brown, sturdy trunk grasping an outswelling mossy bank, and a fringe of illuminated bushes within a few feet of the tree with the firelight on the tips of the sprays.

Next morning, soon after we left our harbour, we were caught in a violent gust of wind and dragged over the seething water in a passionate hurry, though our sail was close-reefed, flying past the grey headlands in most exhilarating style, until fear of being capsized made us drop our sail and run into the first little nook we came to for shelter. Captain Toyatte remarked that in this kind of wind no Indian would dream of travelling, but since Mr Young and I were with him he was willing to go on, because he was sure that the Lord loved us and would not allow us to perish.

We were now within a day or two of Chilcat. We had only to hold a direct course up the beautiful Lynn Canal to reach the large Davidson and other glaciers at its head in the canyons of the Chilcat and Chilcoot Rivers. But rumours of trouble among the Indians there now reached us. We found a party taking shelter from the stormy wind in a little cove, who confirmed the bad news that the Chilcats were drinking and fighting, that Kadachan's father had been shot, and that it would be far from safe to venture among them until blood-money had been paid and the quarrels settled. I decided, therefore, in the mean time to turn westward and go in search of the wonderful 'ice-mountains' that Sitka Charley had been telling us about. Charley, the youngest of my crew, noticing my interest in glaciers, said that when he was a boy he had gone with his father to hunt seals in a large bay full of ice, and that though it was long since he had been there, he thought he could find his way to it. Accordingly, we pushed eagerly on across Chatham Strait to the north end of Icy Strait, toward the new and promising ice-field.

On the south side of Icy Strait we ran into a picturesque bay to visit the main village of the Hoona tribe. Rounding a point on the north shore of the bay, the charmingly located village came in sight, with a group of the inhabitants gazing at us as we approached. They evidently recognized us as strangers or visitors from the shape and style of our canoe, and perhaps even determining that white men were aboard, for these Indians have wonderful eyes. While we were yet half a mile off, we saw a flag unfurled on a tall mast in front of the chief's house. Toyatte hoisted his United States flag in reply, and thus arrayed we made for the landing. Here we were met and received by the chief, Kashoto, who stood close to the water's edge, barefooted and bareheaded, but wearing so fine a robe and standing so grave, erect, and serene, his dignity was complete. No white man could have maintained sound dignity under circumstances so disadvantageous. After the usual formal salutations, the chief, still standing as erect and motionless as a tree, said that he was not much acquainted with our people and feared that his house was too mean for visitors so distinguished as we were. We hastened of course to assure him that we were not proud of heart, and would be glad to have the honour of his hospitality and friendship. With a smile of relief he then led us into his large fort house to the seat of honour prepared for us. After we had been allowed to rest unnoticed and unquestioned for fifteen minutes or so, in accordance with good Indian manners in case we should be weary or embarrassed, our cook began to prepare luncheon; and the chief expressed great concern at his not being able to entertain us in Boston fashion.

Luncheon over, Mr Young as usual requested him to call his people to a meeting. Most of them were away at outlying camps gathering winter stores. Some ten or twelve men, however, about the same number of women, and a crowd of wondering boys and girls were gathered in, to whom Mr Young preached the usual gospel sermon. Toyatte prayed in Thlinkit, and the other members of the crew joined in the hymn-singing. At the close of the mission exercises the chief arose and said that he would now like to hear what the other white chief had to say. I directed John to reply that I was not a missionary, that I came only to pay a friendly visit and see the forests and mountains of their beautiful country. To this he replied, as others had done in the same circumstances, that he would like to hear me on the subject of their country and themselves; so I had to get on my feet and make some sort of a speech, dwelling principally on the brotherhood of all races of people, assuring them that God loved them and that some of their white brethren were beginning to know them and become interested in their welfare; that I seemed this evening to be among old friends with whom I had long been acquainted, though I had never been here before; that I would always remember them and the kind reception they had given us; advised them to heed the instructions of sincere self-denying mission men who wished only to do them good and desired nothing but their friendship and welfare in return. I told them that in some far-off countries, instead of receiving the missionaries with glad and thankful hearts, the Indians killed and ate them; but I hoped, and indeed felt sure, that his people would find a better use for missionaries than putting them, like salmon, in pots for food. They seemed greatly interested, looking into each other's faces with emphatic nods and a-ahs and smiles.

The chief then slowly arose and, after standing silent a minute or two, told us how glad he was to see us; that he felt as if his heart had enjoyed a good meal; that we were the first to come humbly to his little out-of-the-way village to tell his people about God; that they were all like children groping in darkness, but eager for light; that they would gladly welcome a missionary and teacher and use them well; that he could easily believe that whites and Indians were the children of one Father just as I had told them in my speech; that they differed little and resembled each other a great deal, calling attention to the similarity of hands, eyes, legs, etc., making telling gestures in the most natural style of eloquence and dignified composure. 'Oftentimes', he said, 'when I was on the high mountains in the fall, hunting wild sheep for meat, and for wool to make blankets, I have been caught in snowstorms and held in camp until there was nothing to eat, but when I reached my home and got warm, and had a good meal, then my body felt good. For a long time my heart has been hungry and cold, but to-night your words have warmed my heart, and given it a good meal, and now my heart feels good.'

The most striking characteristic of these people is their serene dignity in circumstances that to us would be novel and embarrassing. Even the little children behave with natural dignity, come to the white men when called, and restrain their wonder at the strange prayers, hymn-singing, etc. This evening an old woman fell asleep in the meeting and began to snore; and though both old and young were shaken with suppressed mirth, they evidently took great pains to conceal it. It seems wonderful to me that these so-called savages can make one feel at home in their families. In good breeding, intelligence, and skill in accomplishing whatever they try to do with tools they seem to me to rank above most of our uneducated white labourers. I have never yet seen a child ill-used, even to the extent of an angry word. Scolding, so common a curse in civilization, is not known here at all. On the contrary the young are fondly indulged without being spoiled. Crying is very rarely heard.

In the house of this Hoona chief a pet marmot (Parry's) was a great favourite with old and young. It was therefore delightfully confiding and playful and human. Cats were petted, and the confidence with which these cautious, thoughtful animals met strangers showed that they were kindly treated.

There were some ten or a dozen houses, all told, in the village. The count made by the chief for Mr Young showed some seven hundred and twenty-five persons in the tribe.

CHAPTER TEN

The Discovery of Glacier Bay

FROM HERE, on 24 October, we set sail for Guide Charley's ice-mountains. The handle of our heaviest axe was cracked, and as Charley declared that there was no firewood to be had in the big ice-mountain bay, we would have to load the canoe with a store for cooking at an island out in the Strait a few miles from the village. We were therefore anxious to buy or trade for a good sound axe in exchange for our broken one. Good axes are rare in rocky Alaska. Soon or late an unlucky stroke on a stone concealed in moss spoils the edge. Finally one in almost perfect condition was offered by a young Hoona for our broken-handled one and a half-dollar to boot; but when the broken axe and money were given he promptly demanded an additional twenty-five cents' worth of tobacco. The tobacco was given him, then he required a half-dollar's worth more of tobacco, which was also given; but when he still demanded something more, Charley's patience gave way and we sailed in the same condition as to axes as when we arrived. This was the only contemptible commercial affair we encountered among these Alaskan Indians.

We reached the wooded island about one o'clock, made coffee, took on a store of wood, and set sail direct for the icy country, finding it very hard indeed to believe the woodless part of Charley's description of the Icy Bay, so heavily and uniformly are all the shores forested wherever we had been. In this view we were joined by John, Kadachan and Toyatte, none of them on all their lifelong canoe travels having ever seen a woodless country.

We held a northwesterly course until long after dark, when we reached a small inlet that sets in near the mouth of Glacier Bay, on the west side. Here we made a cold camp on a desolate snow-covered beach in stormy sleet and darkness. At daybreak I looked eagerly in every direction to learn what kind of place we were in; but gloomy rain-clouds covered the mountains, and I could see nothing that would give me a clue, while Vancouver's chart, hitherto a faithful guide, here failed us altogether. Nevertheless, we made haste to be off; and fortunately, for just as we were leaving the shore, a faint smoke was seen across the inlet, toward which Charley, who now seemed lost, gladly steered. Our sudden appearance so early that grey morning had evidently alarmed our neighbours, for as soon as we were within hailing distance an Indian with his face blackened fired a shot over our heads, and in a blunt, bellowing voice roared, 'Who are you?'

Our interpreter shouted, 'Friends and the Fort Wrangell missionary'.

Then men, women, and children swarmed out of the hut, and awaited our approach on the beach. One of the hunters having brought his gun with him, Kadachan sternly rebuked him, asking with superb indignation whether he was not ashamed to meet a missionary with a gun in his hands. Friendly relations, however, were speedily established, and as a cold rain was falling, they invited us to enter their hut. It seemed very small and was jammed full of oily boxes and bundles; nevertheless, twenty-one persons managed to find shelter in it about a smoky fire. Our hosts proved to be Hoona seal-hunters laying in their winter stores of meat and skins. The packed hut was passably well ventilated, but its heavy, meaty smells were not the same to our noses as those we were accustomed to in the sprucy nooks of the evergreen woods. The circle of black eyes peering at us through a fog of reek and smoke made a novel picture. We were glad, however, to get within reach of information, and of course asked many questions concerning the ice-mountains and the strange bay, to most of which our inquisitive Hoona friends replied with counter-questions as to our object in coming to such a place, especially so late in the year. They had heard of Mr Young and his work at Fort Wrangell, but could not understand what a missionary could be doing in such a place as this. Was he going to preach to the seals and gulls, they asked, or to the ice-mountains? And could they take his word? Then John explained that only the friend of the missionary was seeking ice-mountains, that Mr Young had already preached many good words in the villages we had visited, their own among the others, that our hearts were good and every Indian was our friend. Then we gave them a little rice, sugar, tea, and tobacco, after which they began to gain confidence and to speak freely. They told us that the big bay was called by them Sit-a-da-kay, or Ice Bay; that there were many large ice-mountains in it, but no gold-mines; and that the ice-mountain they knew best was at the head of the bay, where most of the seals were found.

Notwithstanding the rain, I was anxious to push on and grope our way beneath the clouds as best we could, in case worse weather should come; but Charley was ill at ease, and wanted one of the seal-hunters to go with us, for the place was much changed. I promised to pay well for a guide, and in order to lighten the canoe proposed to leave most of our heavy stores in the hut until our return. After a long consultation one of them consented to go. His wife got ready his blanket and a piece of cedar matting for his bed, and some provisions – mostly dried salmon, and seal sausage made of strips of lean meat plaited around a core of fat. She followed us to the beach, and just as we were pushing off said with a pretty smile, 'It is my husband that you are taking away. See that you bring him back.'

We got under way about 10 am. The wind was in our favour, but a cold rain pelted us, and we could see but little of the dreary, treeless wilderness which we had now fairly entered. The bitter blast, however, gave us good speed; our bedraggled canoe rose and fell on the waves as solemnly as a big ship. Our course was northwestward, up the southwest side of the bay, near the shore of what seemed to be the mainland, smooth marble islands being on our right. About noon we discovered the first of the great glaciers, the one I afterward named for James Geikie, the noted Scotch geologist. Its lofty blue cliffs, looming through the draggled skirts of the clouds, gave a tremendous impression of savage power, while the roar of the new-born icebergs thickened and emphasized the general roar of the storm. An hour and a half beyond the

Geikie Glacier we ran into a slight harbour where the shore is low, dragged the canoe beyond the reach of drifting icebergs, and, much against my desire to push ahead, encamped, the guide insisting that the big ice-mountain at the head of the bay could not be reached before dark, that the landing there was dangerous even in daylight, and that this was the only safe harbour on the way to it. While camp was being made, I strolled along the shore to examine the rocks and the fossil timber that abounds here. All the rocks are freshly glaciated, even below the sea-level, nor have the waves as yet worn off the surface polish, much less the heavy scratches and grooves and lines of glacial contour.

The next day being Sunday, the minister wished to stay in camp; and so, on account of the weather, did the Indians. I therefore set out on an excursion, and spent the day alone on the mountain-slopes above the camp, and northward, to see what I might learn. Pushing on through rain and mud and sludgy snow, crossing many brown, boulder-choked torrents, wading, jumping, and wallowing in snow up to my shoulders was mountaineering of the most trying kind. After crouching cramped and benumbed in the canoe, poulticed in wet or damp clothing night and day, my limbs had been asleep. This day they were awakened and in the hour of trial proved that they had not lost the cunning learned on many a mountain peak of the High Sierra. I reached a height of fifteen hundred feet, on the ridge that bounds the second of the great glaciers. All the landscape was smothered in clouds and I began to fear that as far as wide views were concerned I had climbed in vain. But at length the clouds lifted a little, and beneath their grey fringes I saw the berg-filled expanse of the bay, and the feet of the mountains that stand about it, and the imposing fronts of five huge glaciers, the nearest being immediately beneath me. This was my first general view of Glacier Bay, a solitude of ice and snow and newborn rocks, dim, dreary, mysterious. I held the ground I had so dearly won for an hour or two, sheltering myself from the blast as best I could, while with benumbed fingers I sketched what I could see of the landscape, and wrote a few lines in my notebook. Then, breasting the snow again, crossing the shifting avalanche slopes and torrents, I reached camp about dark, wet and weary and glad.

While I was getting some coffee and hardtack, Mr Young told me that the Indians were discouraged, and had been talking about turning back, fearing that I would be lost, the canoe broken, or in some other mysterious way the expedition would come to grief if I persisted in going farther. They had been asking him what possible motive I could have in climbing mountains when storms were blowing; and when he replied that I was only seeking knowledge, Toyatte said, 'Muir must be a witch to seek knowledge in such a place as this and in such miserable weather'.

After supper, crouching about a dull fire of fossil wood, they became still more doleful, and talked in tones that accorded well with the wind and waters and growling torrents about us, telling sad old stories of crushed canoes, drowned Indians, and hunters frozen in snowstorms. Even brave old Toyatte, dreading the treeless, forlorn appearance of the region, said that his heart was not strong, and that he feared his canoe, on the safety of which our lives depended, might be entering a skookum-house (jail) of ice, from which there might be no escape; while the Hoona guide said bluntly that if I was so fond of danger, and meant to go close up to the noses of the ice-mountains, he would not consent to go any farther; for we should all be lost, as many of his tribe had been, by the sudden rising of bergs from the bottom. They seemed to be losing heart with every howl of the wind, and fearing that they might fail me now that I was in the midst of so grand a congregation of glaciers, I made haste to reassure them, telling them that for ten years I had wandered alone among mountains and storms, and good luck always followed me; that with me, therefore, they need fear nothing. The storm would soon cease and the sun would shine to show us the way we should go, for God cares for us and guides us as long as we are trustful and brave, therefore all childish fear must be put away. This little speech did good. Kadachan, with some show of enthusiasm, said he liked to travel with good-luck people; and dignified old Toyatte declared that now his heart was strong again, and he would venture on with me as far as I liked for my 'wawa' was 'delait' (my talk was very good). The old warrior even became a little sentimental, and said that even if the canoe was broken he would not greatly care, because on the way to the other world he would have good companions.

Next morning it was still raining and snowing, but the south wind swept us bravely forward and swept the bergs from our course. In about an hour we reached the second of the big glaciers, which I afterwards named for Hugh Miller. We rowed up its fiord and landed to make a slight examination of its grand frontal wall. The berg-producing portion we found to be about a mile and a half wide, and broken into an imposing array of jagged spires and pyramids, and flat-topped towers and battlements, of many shades of blue, from pale, shimmering, limpid tones in the crevasses and hollows, to the most startling, chilling, almost shrieking vitriol blue on the plain mural spaces from which bergs had just been discharged. Back from the front for a few miles the glacier rises in a series of wide steps, as if this portion of the glacier had sunk in successive sections as it reached deep water, and the sea had found its way beneath it. Beyond this it extends indefinitely in a gently rising prairie-like expanse, and branches along the slopes and canyons of the Fairweather Range.

From here a run of two hours brought us to the head of the bay, and to the mouth of the northwest fiord, at the head of which lie the Hoona sealing-grounds, and the great glacier now called the Pacific, and another called the Hoona. The fiord is about five miles long, and two miles wide at the mouth. Here our Hoona guide had a store of dry wood, which we took aboard. Then, setting sail, we were driven wildly up the fiord, as if the storm-wind were saying, 'Go, then, if you will, into my icy chamber; but you shall stay in until I am ready to let you out.' All this time sleety rain was falling on the bay, and snow on the mountains; but soon after we landed the sky began to open. The camp was made on a rocky bench near the front of the Pacific Glacier, and the canoe was carried beyond the reach of the bergs and berg-waves. The bergs were now crowded in a dense pack against the discharging front, as if the storm-wind had determined to make the glacier take back her crystal off-spring and keep them at home.

While camp affairs were being attended to, I set out to climb a mountain for comprehensive views; and before I had reached a height of a thousand feet the rain ceased, and the clouds began to rise from the lower altitudes, slowly lifting their white skirts, and lingering in majestic, wing-shaped masses about the mountains that rise out of the broad, icy sea, the highest of all the white mountains, and the greatest of all the glaciers I had yet seen. Climbing higher for a still broader outlook, I made notes and sketched, improving the precious time while sunshine streamed through the luminous fringes of the clouds and fell on the green waters of the fiord, the glittering bergs, the crystal bluffs of the vast glacier, the intensely white, far-spreading fields of ice, and the ineffably chaste and spiritual heights of the Fairweather Range, which were now hidden, now partly revealed, the whole making a picture of icy wildness unspeakably pure and sublime.

Looking southward, a broad ice-sheet was seen extending in a gently undulating plain from the Pacific Fiord in the foreground to the horizon, dotted and ridged here and there with mountains which were as white as the snow-covered ice in which they were half, or more than half, submerged. Several of the great glaciers of the bay flow from this one grand fountain. It is an instructive example of a general glacier covering the hills and dales of a country that is not yet ready to be brought to the light of day – not only covering but creating a landscape with the features it is destined to have when, in the fullness of time, the fashioning ice-sheet shall be lifted by the sun, and the land become warm and fruitful. The view to the westward is bounded and almost filled by the glorious Fairweather Mountains, the highest among them springing aloft in sublime beauty to a height of nearly sixteen thousand feet, while from base to summit every peak and spire and dividing ridge of all the mighty host was spotless white, as if painted. It would seem that snow could never be made to lie on the steepest slopes and precipices unless plastered on when wet, and then frozen. But this snow could not have been wet. It must have been fixed by being driven and set in small particles like the storm-dust of drifts, which, when in this condition, is fixed not only on sheer cliffs, but in massive, overcurling cornices. Along the base of this majestic range sweeps the Pacific Glacier, fed by innumerable cascading tributaries, and discharging into the head of its fiord by two mouths only partly separated by the brow of an island rock about one thousand feet high, each nearly a mile wide.

Dancing down the mountain to camp, my mind glowing like the sunbeaten glaciers, I found the Indians seated around a good fire, entirely happy now that the farthest point of the journey was safely reached and the long, dark storm was cleared away. How hopefully, peacefully bright that night were the stars in the frosty sky, and how impressive was the thunder of the icebergs, rolling, swelling, reverberating through the solemn stillness! I was too happy to sleep.

About daylight next morning we crossed the fiord and landed on the south side of the rock that divides the wall of the great glacier. The whiskered faces of seals dotted the open spaces between the bergs, and I could not prevent John and Charley and Kadachan from shooting at them. Fortunately, few, if any, were hurt. Leaving the Indians in charge of the canoe, I managed to climb to the top of the wall by a good deal of step-cutting between the ice and dividing rock, and gained a good general view of the glacier. At one favourable place I descended about fifty feet below the side of the glacier, where its denuding, fashioning action was clearly shown. Pushing back from here, I found the surface crevassed and sunken in steps, like the Hugh Miller Glacier, as if it were being undermined by the action of tide waters. For a distance of fifteen or twenty miles the river-like ice-flood is nearly level, and when it recedes, the ocean water will follow it, and thus form a long extension of the fiord, with features essentially the same as those now extending into the continent farther south, where many great glaciers once poured into the sea, though scarce a vestige of them now exists. Thus the domain of the sea has been, and is being, extended in these ice-sculptured lands, and the scenery of their shores enriched. The brow of the dividing rock is about a thousand feet high, and is hard beset by the glacier. A short time ago it was at least two thousand feet below the surface of the over-sweeping ice; and under present climatic conditions it will soon take its place as a glacier-polished island in the middle of the fiord, like a thousand others in the magnificent archipelago. Emerging from its icy sepulchre, it gives a most telling illustration of the birth of a marked feature of a landscape. In this instance it is not the mountain, but the glacier, that is in labour, and the mountain itself is being brought forth.

The Hoona Glacier enters the fiord on the south side, a short distance below the Pacific, displaying a broad and far-reaching expanse, over which many lofty peaks are seen; but the front wall, thrust into the fiord, is not nearly so interesting as that of the Pacific, and I did not observe any bergs discharged from it.

In the evening, after witnessing the unveiling of the majestic peaks and glaciers and their baptism in the down-pouring sunbeams, it seemed inconceivable that nature could have anything finer to show us. Nevertheless, compared with what was to come the next morning, all that was as nothing. The calm dawn gave no promise of anything uncommon. Its most impressive features were the frosty clearness of the sky and a deep, brooding stillness made all the more striking by the thunder of the newborn bergs. The sunrise we did not see at all, for we were beneath the shadows of the fiord cliffs; but in the midst of our studies, while the Indians were getting ready to sail, we were startled by the sudden appearance of a red light burning with a strange unearthly splendour on the topmost peak of the Fairweather Mountains. Instead of vanishing as suddenly as it had appeared, it spread and spread until the whole range down to the level of the glaciers was filled with the celestial fire. In colour it was at first a vivid crimson, with a thick, furred appearance, as fine as the alpenglow, yet indescribably rich and deep – not in the least like a garment or mere external flush or bloom through which one might expect to see the rocks or snow, but every mountain apparently was glowing from the heart like molten metal fresh from a furnace. Beneath the frosty shadows of the fiord we stood hushed and awe-stricken, gazing at the holy vision; and had we seen the heavens opened and God made manifest, our attention could not have been more tremendously strained. When the highest peak began to burn, it did not seem to be steeped in sunshine, however glorious, but rather as if it had been thrust into the body of the sun itself. Then the supernal fire slowly descended, with a sharp line of demarcation separating it from the cold, shaded region beneath; peak after peak, with their spires and ridges and cascading glaciers, caught the heavenly glow, until all the mighty host stood transfigured, hushed, and thoughtful, as if awaiting the coming of the Lord. The white, rayless light of morning, seen when I was alone amid the peaks of the California Sierra, had always seemed to me the most telling of all the terrestrial manifestations of God. But here the mountains themselves were made divine, and declared His glory in terms still more impressive. How long we gazed I never knew. The glorious vision passed away in a gradual, fading change through a thousand tones of colour to pale yellow and white, and then the work of the ice-world went on again in everyday beauty. The green waters of the fiord were filled with sun-spangles; the fleet of icebergs set forth on their voyages with the upspringing breeze; and on the innumerable mirrors and prisms of these bergs, and on those of the shattered crystal walls of the glaciers, common white light and rainbow light began to burn, while the mountains shone in their frosty jewellry, and loomed again in the thin azure in serene terrestrial majesty. We turned and sailed away, joining the outgoing bergs, while 'Gloria in excelsis' still seemed to be sounding over all the white landscape, and our burning hearts were ready for any fate, feeling that, whatever the future might have in store, the treasures we had gained this glorious morning would enrich our lives forever.

When we arrived at the mouth of the fiord, and rounded the massive granite headland that stands guard at the entrance on the north side, another large glacier, now named the Reid, was discovered at the head of one of the northern branches of the bay. Pushing ahead into this new fiord, we found that it was not only packed with bergs, but that the spaces between the bergs were crusted with new ice, compelling us to turn back while we were yet several miles from the discharging frontal wall. But though we were not then allowed to set foot on this magnificent glacier, we obtained a fine view of it, and I made the Indians cease rowing while I sketched its principal features. Thence, after steering northeastward a few miles, we discovered still another large glacier, now named the Carroll. But the fiord into which this glacier flows was, like the last, utterly inaccessible on account of ice, and we had to be content with a general view and sketch of it, gained as we rowed slowly past at a distance of three or four miles. The mountains back of it and on each side of its inlet are sculptured in a singularly rich and striking style of architecture, in which subordinate peaks and gables appear in wonderful profusion, and an imposing conical mountain with a wide, smooth base stands out in the main current of the glacier, a mile or two back from the discharging ice-wall.

We now turned southward down the eastern shore of the bay, and in an hour or two discovered a glacier of the second class, at the head of a comparatively short fiord that winter had not yet closed. Here we landed, and climbed across a mile or so of rough boulder-beds, and back upon the wildly broken, receding front of the glacier, which, though it descends to the level of the sea, no longer sends off bergs. Many large masses, detached from the wasting front by irregular melting, were partly buried beneath mud, sand, gravel, and boulders of the terminal moraine. Thus protected, these fossil icebergs remain unmelted for many years, some of them for a century or more, as shown by the age of trees growing above them, though there are no trees here as yet. At length melting, a pit with sloping sides is formed by the falling in of the overlying moraine material into the space at first occupied by the buried ice. In this way are formed the curious depressions in drift-covered regions called kettles or sinks. On these decaying glaciers we may also find many interesting lessons on the formation of boulders and boulder-beds, which in all glaciated countries exert a marked influence on scenery, health and fruitfulness.

Three or four miles farther down the bay, we came to another fiord, up which we sailed in quest of more glaciers, discovering one in each of the two branches into which the fiord divides. Neither of these glaciers quite reaches tide-water. Notwithstanding the apparent fruitfulness of their fountains, they are in the first stage of decadence, the waste from melting and evaporation being greater now than the supply of new ice from their snowy fountains. We reached the one in the north branch, climbed over its wrinkled brow, and gained a good view of the trunk and some of the tributaries, and also of the sublime grey cliffs of its channel.

Then we sailed up the south branch of the inlet, but failed to reach the glacier there, on account of a thin sheet of new ice. With the tent-poles we broke a lane for the canoe for a little distance; but it was slow work, and we soon saw that we could not reach the glacier before dark. Nevertheless, we gained a fair view of it as it came sweeping down through its gigantic gateway of massive Yosemite rocks three or four thousand feet high. Here we lingered until sundown, gazing and sketching; then turned back, and encamped on a bed of cobblestones between the forks of the fiord.

We gathered a lot of fossil wood and after supper made a big fire, and as we sat around it the brightness of the sky brought on a long talk with the Indians about the stars; and their eager, childlike attention was refreshing to see as compared with the deathlike apathy of weary town-dwellers, in whom natural curiosity has been quenched in toil and care and poor shallow comfort.

After sleeping a few hours, I stole quietly out of the camp, and climbed the mountain that stands between the two glaciers. The ground was frozen, making the climbing difficult in the steepest places; but the views over the icy bay, sparkling beneath the stars, were enchanting. It seemed then a sad thing that any part of so precious a night had been lost in sleep. The starlight was so full that I distinctly saw not only the berg-filled bay, but most of the lower portions of the glaciers, lying pale and spirit-like amid the mountains. The nearest glacier in particular was so distinct that it seemed to be glowing with light that came from within itself. Not even in dark nights have I ever found any difficulty in seeing large glaciers; but on this mountain-top, amid so much ice, in the heart of so clear and frosty a night, everything was more or less luminous, and I seemed to be poised in a vast hollow between two skies of almost equal brightness. This exhilarating scramble made me glad and strong and I rejoiced that my studies called me before the glorious night succeeding so glorious a morning had been spent!

I got back to camp in time for an early breakfast, and by daylight we had everything packed and were again under way. The fiord was frozen nearly to its mouth, and though the ice was so thin it gave us but little trouble in breaking a way for the canoe, yet it showed us that the season for exploration in these waters was well-nigh over. We were in danger of being imprisoned in a jam of icebergs, for the water-spaces between them freeze rapidly, binding the floes into one mass. Across such floes it would be almost impossible to drag a canoe, however industriously we might ply the axe, as our Hoona guide took great pains to warn us. I would have kept straight down the bay from here, but the guide had to be taken home, and the provisions we left at the bark hut had to be got on board. We therefore crossed over to our Sunday storm-camp, cautiously boring a way through the bergs. We found the shore lavishly adorned with a fresh arrival of assorted bergs that had been left stranded at high tide. They were arranged in a curving row, looking intensely clear and pure on the grey sand, and, with the sunbeams pouring through them, suggested the jewel-paved streets of the New Jerusalem.

On our way down the coast, after examining the front of the beautiful Geikie Glacier, we obtained our first broad view of the great glacier afterwards named the Muir, the last of all the grand company to be seen, the stormy weather having hidden it when we first entered the bay. It was now perfectly clear, and the spacious prairie-like glacier, with its many tributaries extending far back into the snowy recesses of its fountains, made a magnificent display of its wealth, and I was strongly tempted to go and explore it at all hazards. But winter had come, and the freezing of its fiords was an insurmountable obstacle. I had, therefore, to be content for the present with sketching and studying its main features at a distance.

When we arrived at the Hoona hunting-camp, men, women, and children came swarming out to welcome us. In the neighbourhood of this camp I carefully noted the lines of demarcation between the forested and deforested regions. Several mountains here are only in part deforested, and the lines separating the bare and the forested portions are well defined. The soil, as well as the trees, had slid off the steep slopes, leaving the edge of the woods raw-looking and rugged.

At the mouth of the bay a series of moraine islands show that the trunk glacier that occupied the bay halted here for some time and deposited this island material as a terminal moraine; that more of the bay was not filled in shows that, after lingering here, it receded comparatively fast. All the level portions of trunks of glaciers occupying ocean fiords, instead of melting back gradually in times of general shrinking and recession, as inland glaciers with sloping channels do, melt almost uniformly over all the surface until they become thin enough to float. Then, of course, with each rise and fall of the tide, the sea water, with a temperature usually considerably above the freezing-point, rushes in and out beneath them, causing rapid waste of the nether surface, while the upper is being wasted by the weather, until at length the fiord portions of these great glaciers become comparatively thin and weak and are broken up and vanish almost simultaneously.

Glacier Bay is undoubtedly young as yet. Vancouver's chart, made only a century ago, shows no trace of it, though found admirably faithful in general. It seems probable, therefore, that even then the entire bay was occupied by a glacier of which all those described above, great though they are, were only tributaries. Nearly as great a change has taken place in Sum Dum Bay since Vancouver's visit, the main trunk glacier there having receded from eighteen to twenty-five miles from the line marked on his chart. Charley, who was here when a boy, said that the place had so changed that he hardly recognized it, so many new islands had been born in the meantime and so much ice had vanished. As we have seen, this Icy Bay is being still farther extended by the recession of the glaciers. That this whole system of fiords and channels was added to the domain of the sea by glacial action is to my mind certain.

We reached the island from which we had obtained our store of fuel about half-past six and camped here for the night, having spent only five days in Sitadaka, sailing round it, visiting and sketching all the six glaciers excepting the largest, though I landed only on three of them, – the Geikie, Hugh Miller, and Grand Pacific – the freezing of the fiords in front of the others rendering them inaccessible at this late season.

CHAPTER ELEVEN

The Country of the Chilcats

ON 30 OCTOBER we visited a camp of Hoonas at the mouth of a salmon-chuck. We had seen some of them before, and they received us kindly. Here we learned that peace reigned in Chilcat. The reports that we had previously heard were, as usual in such cases, wildly exaggerated. The little camp hut of these Indians was crowded with the food-supplies they had gathered – chiefly salmon, dried and tied in bunches of convenient size for handling and transporting to their villages, bags of salmon-roe, boxes of fish-oil, a lot of mountain-goat mutton, and a few porcupines. They presented us with some dried salmon and potatoes, for which we gave them tobacco and rice. About 3 pm we reached their village, and in the best house, that of a chief, we found the family making whiskey. The still and mash were speedily removed and hidden away with apparent shame as soon as we came in sight. When we entered and passed the regular greetings, the usual apologies as to being unable to furnish Boston food for us and inquiries whether we could eat Indian food were gravely made. Toward six or seven o'clock Mr Young explained the object of his visit and held a short service. The chief replied with grave deliberation, saying that he would be heartily glad to have a teacher sent to his poor ignorant people, upon whom he now hoped the light

of a better day was beginning to break. Hereafter he would gladly do whatever the white teachers told him to do and would have no will of his own. This
under the whiskey circumstances seemed too good to be true. He thanked us
over and over again for coming so far to see him, and complained that Port
Simpson Indians, sent out on a missionary tour by Mr Crosby, after making a
good-luck board for him and nailing it over his door, now wanted to take it
away. Mr Young promised to make him a new one, should this threat be
executed, and remarked that since he had offered to do his bidding he hoped
he would make no more whiskey. To this the chief replied with fresh complaints concerning the threatened loss of his precious board, saying that he
thought the Port Simpson Indians were very mean in seeking to take it away,
but that now he would tell them to take it as soon as they liked for he was
going to get a better one at Wrangell. But no effort of the missionary could
bring him to notice or discuss the whiskey business. The luck board nailed
over the door was about two feet long and had the following inscription: 'The
Lord will bless those who do his will. When you rise in the morning, and when
you retire at night give him thanks. Heccla Hockla Popla.'

This chief promised to pray like a white man every morning, and to bury
the dead as the whites do. 'I often wondered', he said, 'where the dead went
to. Now I am glad to know'; and at last acknowledged the whiskey, saying he
was sorry to have been caught making the bad stuff. The behaviour of all,
even the little ones circled around the fire, was very good. There was no
laughter when the strange singing commenced. They only gazed like curious,
intelligent animals. A little daughter of the chief with the glow of the firelight
on her eyes made an interesting picture, head held aslant. Another in the
group, with upturned eyes, seeming to half understand the strange words
about God, might have passed for one of Raphael's angels.

The chief's house was about forty feet square, of the ordinary fort kind, but
better built and cleaner than usual. The side-room doors were neatly panel-
led, though all the lumber had been nibbled into shape with a small narrow
Indian adze. We had our tent pitched on a grassy spot near the beach, being
afraid of wee beasties; which greatly offended Kadachan and old Toyatte,
who said, 'If this is the way you are to do up at Chilcat, we will be ashamed of
you.' We promised them to eat Indian food and in every way behave like
good Chilcats.

We set out direct for Chilcat in the morning against a brisk head wind. By
keeping close inshore and working hard, we made about ten miles by two or
three o'clock, when, the tide having turned against us, we could make scarce
any headway, and therefore landed in a sheltered cove a few miles up the west
side of Lynn Canal. Here I discovered a fine growth of yellow cedar, but none
of the trees were very large, the tallest only seventy-five to one hundred feet
high. The flat, drooping, plume-like branchlets hang edgewise, giving the
trees a thin, open, airy look. Nearly every tree that I saw in a long walk was
more or less marked by the knives and axes of the Indians, who use the bark
for matting, for covering house-roofs, and making temporary portable huts.
For this last purpose sections five or six feet long and two or three wide are
pressed flat and secured from warping or splitting by binding them with thin

strips of wood at the end. These they carry about with them in their canoes, and in a few minutes they can be put together against slim poles and made into a rainproof hut. Every paddle that I have seen along the coast is made of the light, tough, handsome yellow wood of this tree. It is a tree of moderately rapid growth and usually chooses ground that is rather boggy and mossy. Whether its network of roots makes the bog or not, I am unable as yet to say.

Three glaciers on the opposite side of the canal were in sight, descending nearly to sea-level, and many smaller ones that melt a little below timber-line. While I was sketching these, a canoe hove in sight, coming on at a flying rate of speed before the wind. The owners, eager for news, paid us a visit. They proved to be Hoonas, a man, his wife, and four children, on their way home from Chilcat. The man was sitting in the stern steering and holding a sleeping child in his arms. Another lay asleep at his feet. He told us that Sitka Jack had gone up to the main Chilcat village the day before he left, intending to hold a grand feast and potlatch, and that whiskey up there was flowing like water. The news was rather depressing to Mr Young and myself, for we feared the effect of the poison on Toyatte's old enemies. At 8.30 pm we set out again on the turn of the tide, though the crew did not relish this night work. Naturally enough, they liked to stay in camp when wind and tide were against us, but didn't care to make up lost time after dark however wooingly wind and tide might flow and blow. Kadachan, John and Charley rowed, and Toyatte steered and paddled, assisted now and then by me. The wind moderated and almost died away, so that we made about fifteen miles in six hours, when the tide turned and snow began to fall. We ran into a bay nearly opposite Berner's Bay, where three or four families of Chilcats were camped, who shouted when they heard us landing and demanded our names. Our men ran to the huts for news before making camp. The Indians proved to be hunters, who said there were plenty of wild sheep on the mountains back a few miles from the head of the bay. This interview was held at three o'clock in the morning, a rather early hour. But Indians never resent any such disturbance provided there is anything worthwhile to be said or done. By four o'clock we had our tents set, a fire made and some coffee, while the snow was falling fast. Toyatte was out of humour with this night business. He wanted to land an hour or two before we did, and then, when the snow began to fall and we all wanted to find a camping-ground as soon as possible, he steered out into the middle of the canal, saying grimly that the tide was good. He turned, however, at our orders, but read us a lecture at the first opportunity, telling us to start early if we were in a hurry, but not to travel in the night like thieves.

After a few hours' sleep, we set off again, with the wind still against us and the sea rough. We were all tired after making only about twelve miles, and camped in a rocky nook where we found a family of Hoonas in their bark hut beside their canoe. They presented us with potatoes and salmon and a big bucketful of berries, salmon-roe, and grease of some sort, probably fish-oil, which the crew consumed with wonderful relish.

A fine breeze was blowing next morning from the south, which would take us to Chilcat in a few hours, but unluckily the day was Sunday and the good wind was refused. Sunday, it seemed to me, could be kept as well by sitting in the canoe and letting the Lord's wind waft us quietly on our way. The day was rainy and the clouds hung low. The trees here are remarkably well developed, tall and straight. I observed three or four hemlocks which had been struck by lightning – the first I noticed in Alaska. Some of the species on windy outjutting rocks become very picturesque, almost as much so as old oaks, the foliage becoming dense and the branchlets tufted in heavy plume-shaped horizontal masses.

Monday was a fine clear day, but the wind was dead ahead, making hard, dull work with paddles and oars. We passed a long stretch of beautiful marble cliffs enlivened with small merry waterfalls, and toward noon came in sight of the front of the famous Chilcat or Davidson Glacier, a broad white flood reaching out two or three miles into the canal with wonderful effect. I wanted to camp beside it but the head wind tired us out before we got within six or eight miles of it. We camped on the west side of a small rocky island in a narrow cove. When I was looking among the rocks and bushes for a smooth spot for a bed, I found a human skeleton. My Indians seemed not in the least shocked or surprised, explaining that it was only the remains of a Chilcat slave. Indians never bury or burn the bodies of slaves, but just cast them away anywhere. Kind Nature was covering the poor bones with moss and leaves, and I helped in the pitiful work.

The wind was fair and joyful in the morning, and away we glided to the famous glacier. In an hour or so we were directly in front of it and beheld it in all its crystal glory descending from its white mountain fountains and spreading out in an immense fan three or four miles wide against its tree-fringed terminal moraine. But, large as it is, it long ago ceased to discharge bergs.

The Chilcats are the most influential of all the Thlinkit tribes. Whenever on our journey I spoke of the interesting characteristics of other tribes we had visited, my crew would invariably say, 'Oh, yes, these are pretty good Indians, but wait till you have seen the Chilcats'. We were now only five or six miles distant from their lower village, and my crew requested time to prepare themselves to meet their great rivals. Going ashore on the moraine with their boxes that had not been opened since we left Fort Wrangell, they sat on boulders and cut each other's hair, carefully washed and perfumed themselves and made a complete change in their clothing, even to white shirts, new boots, new hats, and bright neckties. Meanwhile, I scrambled across the broad, brushy, forested moraine, and on my return scarcely recognized my crew in their dress suits. Mr Young also made some changes in his clothing, while I, having nothing dressy in my bag, adorned my cap with an eagle's feather I found on the moraine, and thus arrayed we set forth to meet the noble Thlinkits.

We were discovered while we were several miles from the village, and as we entered the mouth of the river we were hailed by a messenger from the chief, sent to find out who we were and the objects of our extraordinary visit.

'Who are you?' he shouted in a heavy, far-reaching voice. 'What are your names? What do you want? What have you come for?'

On receiving replies, he shouted the information to another messenger, who was posted on the river-bank at a distance of a quarter of a mile or so, and he to another and another in succession, and by this living telephone the news was delivered to the chief as he sat by his fireside. A salute was then fired to welcome us, and a swarm of musket-bullets, flying scarce high enough for comfort, pinged over our heads. As soon as we reached the landing at the village, a dignified young man stepped forward and thus addressed us:

'My chief sent me to meet you, and to ask if you would do him the honour to lodge in his house during your stay in our village?'

We replied, of course, that we would consider it a great honour to be entertained by so distinguished a chief.

The messenger then ordered a number of slaves, who stood behind him, to draw our canoe out of the water, carry our provisions and bedding into the chief's house, and then carry the canoe back from the river where it would be beyond the reach of floating ice. While we waited, a lot of boys and girls were playing on a meadow near the landing – running races, shooting arrows, and wading in the icy river without showing any knowledge of our presence beyond quick stolen glances. After all was made secure, he conducted us to the house, where we found seats of honour prepared for us.

The old chief sat barefooted by the fireside, clad in a calico shirt and blanket, looking down, and though we shook hands as we passed him he did not look up. After we were seated, he still gazed into the fire without taking the slightest notice of us for about ten or fifteen minutes. The various members of the chief's family, also – men, women, and children – went about their usual employment and play as if entirely unconscious that strangers were in the house, it being considered impolite to look at visitors or speak to them before time had been allowed them to collect their thoughts and prepare any message they might have to deliver.

At length, after the politeness period had passed, the chief slowly raised his head and glanced at his visitors, looked down again, and at last said, through our interpreter:

'I am troubled. It is customary when strangers visit us to offer them food in case they might be hungry, and I was about to do so, when I remembered that the food of you honourable white chiefs is so much better than mine that I am ashamed to offer it.'

We, of course, replied that we would consider it a great honour to enjoy the hospitality of so distinguished a chief as he was.

Hearing this, he looked up, saying, 'I feel relieved'; or, in John the interpreter's words, 'He feels good now, he says he feels good'.

He then ordered one of his family to see that the visitors were fed. The young man who was to act as steward took up his position in a corner of the house commanding a view of all that was going on, and ordered the slaves to make haste to prepare a good meal; one to bring a lot of the best potatoes from the cellar and wash them well; another to go out and pick a basketful of fresh berries; another to broil a salmon; while others made a suitable fire, pouring oil on the wet wood to make it blaze. Speedily the feast was prepared and passed around. The first course was potatoes, the second fish-oil and salmon, next berries and rose-hips; then the steward shouted the important news, in a loud voice like a herald addressing an army, 'That's all!' and left his post.

Then followed all sorts of questions from the old chief. He wanted to know what Professor Davidson had been trying to do a year or two ago on a mountain-top back of the village, with many strange things looking at the sun when it grew dark in the daytime; and we had to try to explain eclipses. He asked us if we could tell him what made the water rise and fall twice a day, and we tried to explain that the sun and moon attracted the sea by showing how a magnet attracted iron.

Mr Young, as usual, explained the object of his visit and requested that the people might be called together in the evening to hear his message. Accordingly all were told to wash, put on their best clothing, and come at a certain hour. There was an audience of about two hundred and fifty, to whom Mr Young preached. Toyatte led in prayer, while Kadachan and John joined in the singing of several hymns. At the conclusion of the religious exercises the chief made a short address of thanks, and finished with a request for the message of the other chief. I again tried in vain to avoid a speech by telling the interpreter to explain that I was only travelling to see the country, the glaciers, and mountains and forests, etc., but these subjects, strange to say, seemed to be about as interesting as the gospel, and I had to deliver a sort of lecture on the fine foodful country God had given them and the brotherhood of man, along the same general lines I had followed at other villages. Some five similar meetings were held here, two of them in the daytime, and we began to feel quite at home in the big block-house with our hospitable and warlike friends.

At the last meeting an old white-haired shaman of grave and venerable aspect, with a high wrinkled forehead, big, strong Roman nose and light-coloured skin, slowly and with great dignity arose and spoke for the first time.

'I am an old man', he said, 'but I am glad to listen to those strange things you tell, and they may well be true, for what is more wonderful than the flight of birds in the air? I remember the first white man I ever saw. Since that long, long-ago time I have seen many, but never until now have I ever truly known and felt a white man's heart. All the white men I have heretofore met wanted to get something from us. They wanted furs and they wished to pay for them as small a price as possible. They all seemed to be seeking their own good – not our good. I might say that through all my long life I have never until now heard a white man speak. It has always seemed to me while trying to speak to traders and those seeking gold-mines that it was like speaking to a person across a broad stream that was running fast over stones and making so loud a noise that scarce a single word could be heard. But now, for the first time, the Indian and the white man are on the same side of the river, eye to eye, heart to heart. I have always loved my people. I have taught them and ministered to them as well as I could. Hereafter, I will keep silent and listen to the good words of the missionaries, who know God and the places we go to when we die so much better than I do.'

At the close of the exercises, after the last sermon had been preached and the last speech of the Indian chief and headsmen had been made, a number of the sub-chiefs were talking informally together. Mr Young, anxious to know what impression he had made on the tribe with reference to mission work, requested John to listen and tell him what was being said.

'They are talking about Mr Muir's speech', he reported. 'They say he knows how to talk and beats the preacher far.' Toyatte also, with a teasing smile, said: 'Mr Young, mika tillicum hi yu tola wawa' (Your friend leads you far in speaking).

Later, when the sending of a missionary and teacher was being considered, the chief said they wanted me, and, as an inducement, promised that if I would come to them they would always do as I directed, follow my councils, give me as many wives as I liked, build a church and school, and pick all the stones out of the paths and make them smooth for my feet.

They were about to set out on an expedition to the Hootsenoos to collect blankets as indemnity or blood-money for the death of a Chilcat woman from drinking whiskey furnished by one of the Hootsenoo tribe. In case of their refusal to pay, there would be fighting, and one of the chiefs begged that we would pray them good luck, so that no one would be killed. This he asked as a favour, after begging that we would grant permission to go on this expedition, promising that they would avoid bloodshed if possible. He spoke in a very natural and easy tone and manner, always serene and so much of a polished diplomat that all polish was hidden. The younger chief stood while speaking, the elder sat on the floor. None of the congregation had a word to say, though they gave approving nods and shrugs.

The house was packed at every meeting, two a day. Some climbed on the roof to listen around the smoke opening. I tried in vain to avoid speech-making, but, as usual, I had to say something at every meeting. I made five speeches here, all of which seemed to be gladly heard, particularly what I said on the different kinds of white men and their motives, and their own kindness and good manners in making strangers feel at home in their houses.

The chief had a slave, a young and good-looking girl, who waited on him, cooked his food, lighted his pipe for him, etc. Her servitude seemed by no means galling. In the morning, just before we left on the return trip, interpreter John overhead him telling her that after the teacher came from Wrangell, he was going to dress her well and send her to school and use her in every way as if she were his own daughter. Slaves are still owned by the richest of the Thlinkits. Formerly, many of them were sacrificed on great occasions, such as the opening of a new house or the erection of a totem pole. Kadachan ordered John to take a pair of white blankets out of his trunk and wrap them about the chief's shoulders, as he sat by the fire. This gift was presented without ceremony or saying a single word. The chief scarcely noticed the blankets, only taking a corner in his hand, as if testing the quality of the wool. Toyatte had been an inveterate enemy and fighter of the Chilcats, but now, having joined the church, he wished to forget the past and bury all the hard feuds and be universally friendly and peaceful. It was evident, however, that he mistrusted the proud and warlike Chilcats and doubted the acceptance of his friendly advances, and as we approached their village became more and more thoughtful.

'My wife said that my old enemies would be sure to kill me. Well, never mind. I am an old man and may as well die as not.' He was troubled with palpitations, and oftentimes, while he suffered, he put his hand over his heart and said, 'I hope the Chilcats will shoot me here'.

Before venturing up the river to the principal village, located some ten miles up the river, we sent Sitka Charley and one of the young Chilcats as messengers to announce our arrival and inquire whether we would be welcome to visit them, informing the chief that both Kadachan and Toyatte were Mr Young's friends and mine, that we were 'all one meat' and any harm done them would also be done to us.

While our messengers were away, I climbed a pure-white, dome-crowned mountain about fifty-five hundred feet high and gained noble telling views to the northward of the main Chilcat glaciers and the multitude of mighty peaks from which they draw their sources. At a height of three thousand feet I found a mountain hemlock, considerably dwarfed, in company with Sitka spruce and the common hemlock, the tallest about twenty feet high, sixteen inches in diameter. A few stragglers grew considerably higher, say at about four thousand feet. Birch and two-leaf pine were common.

The messengers returned next day, bringing back word that we would all be heartily welcomed excepting Toyatte; that the guns were loaded and ready to be fired to welcome us, but that Toyatte, having insulted a Chilcat chief not long ago in Wrangell, must not come. They also informed us in their message that they were very busy merrymaking with other visitors, Sitka Jack and his friends, but that if we could get up to the village through the running ice on the river, they would all be glad to see us; they had been drinking and Kadachan's father, one of the principal chiefs, said plainly that he had just waked up out of a ten days' sleep. We were anxious to make this visit, but, taking the difficulties and untoward circumstances into account, the danger of being frozen in at so late a time, while Kadachan would not be able to walk back on account of a shot in his foot, the danger also from whiskey, the awakening of old feuds on account of Toyatte's presence, etc., we reluctantly concluded to start back on the home journey at once. This was on Friday and a fair wind was blowing, but our crew, who loved dearly to rest and eat in these big hospitable houses, all said that Monday would be *hyas klosh* for the starting-day. I insisted, however, on starting Saturday morning, and succeeded in getting away from our friends at ten o'clock. Just as we were leaving, the chief who had entertained us so handsomely requested a written document to show that he had not killed us, so in case we were lost on the way home he could not be held accountable in any way for our death.

CHAPTER TWELVE

The Return to Fort Wrangell

THE DAY of our start for Wrangell was bright and the Hoon, the north wind strong. We passed around the east side of the larger island which lies near the south extremity of the point of land between the Chilcat and the Chilcoot channels and thence held a direct course down the east shore of the canal. At sunset we encamped in a small bay at the head of a beautiful harbour three or four miles south of Berner's Bay, and the next day, being Sunday, we remained in camp as usual, though the wind was fair and it is not a sin to go home. The Indians spent most of the day in washing, mending, eating, and singing hymns with Mr Young, who also gave them a Bible lesson, while I wrote notes and sketched. Charley made a sweathouse and all the crew got good baths. This is one of the most delightful little bays we have thus far enjoyed, girdled with tall trees whose branches almost meet, and with views of pure-white mountains across the broad, river-like canal.

Seeing smoke back in the dense woods, we went ashore to seek it and discovered a Hootsenoo whiskey-factory in full blast. The Indians said that an old man, a friend of theirs, was about to die and they were making whiskey for his funeral.

Our Indians were already out of oily flesh, which they regard as a necessity and consume in enormous quantities. The bacon was nearly gone and they eagerly inquired for flesh at every camp we passed. Here we found skinned carcasses of porcupines and a heap of wild mutton lying on the confused hut floor. Our cook boiled the porcupines in a big pot with a lot of potatoes we obtained at the same hut, and although the potatoes were protected by their skins, the awfully wild penetrating porcupine flavour found a way through the skins and flavoured them to the very heart. Bread and beans and dried fruit we had in abundance, and none of these rank aboriginal dainties ever came nigh any meal of mine. The Indians eat the hips of wild roses entire like berries, and I was laughed at for eating only the outside of this fruit and rejecting the seeds.

When we were approaching the village of the Auk tribe, venerable Toyatte seemed to be unusually pensive, as if weighed down by some melancholy thought. This was so unusual that I waited attentively to find out the cause of his trouble.

When at last he broke silence it was to say, 'Mr Young, Mr Young' – he usually repeated the name – 'I hope you will not stop at the Auk village'.

'Why, Toyatte?' asked Mr Young.

'Because they are a bad lot, and preaching to them can do no good.'

'Toyatte', said Mr Young, 'have you forgotten what Christ said to his disciples when he charged them to go forth and preach the gospel to everybody; and that we should love our enemies and do good to those who use us badly?'

'Well', replied Toyatte, 'if you preach to them, you must not call on me to pray, because I cannot pray for Auks.'

'But the Bible says we should pray for all men, however bad they may be.'

'Oh, yes, I know that, Mr Young; I know it very well. But Auks are not men, good or bad – they are dogs.'

It was now nearly dark and quite so ere we found a harbour, not far from the fine Auk Glacier which descends into the narrow channel that separates Douglas Island from the mainland. Two of the Auks followed us to our camp after eight o'clock and inquired into our object in visiting them, that they might carry the news to their chief. One of the chief's houses is opposite our camp a mile or two distant, and we concluded to call on him next morning.

I wanted to examine the Auk Glacier in the morning, but tried to be satisfied with a general view and sketch as we sailed around its wide fan-shaped front. It is one of the most beautiful of all the coast glaciers that are in the first stage of decadence. We called on the Auk chief at daylight, when he was yet in bed, but he arose goodnaturedly, put on a calico shirt, drew a blanket around his legs, and comfortably seated himself beside a small fire that gave light enough to show his features and those of his children and the three women that one by one came out of the shadows. All listened attentively to Mr Young's message of goodwill. The chief was a serious, sharp-featured, dark-complexioned man, sensible-looking and with good manners. He was very sorry, he said, that his people had been drinking in his absence and had used us so ill; he would like to hear us talk and would call his people together if we would return to the village. This offer we had to decline. We gave him good words and tobacco and bade him good-bye.

The scenery all through the channel is magnificent, something like Yosemite Valley in its lofty avalanche-swept wall cliffs, especially on the mainland side, which are so steep few trees can find footing. The lower island side walls are mostly forested. The trees are heavily draped with lichens, giving the woods a remarkably grey, ancient look. I noticed a good many two-leafed pines in boggy spots. The water was smooth, and the reflections of the lofty walls striped with cascades were charmingly distinct.

It was not easy to keep my crew full of wild flesh. We called at an Indian summer camp on the mainland about noon, where there were three very squalid huts crowded and jammed full of flesh of many colours and smells, among which we discovered a lot of bright fresh trout, lovely creatures about fifteen inches long, their sides adorned with vivid red spots. We purchased five of them and a couple of salmon for a box of gun-caps and a little tobacco. About the middle of the afternoon we passed through a fleet of icebergs, their number increasing as we neared the mouth of the Taku Fiord, where we camped, hoping to explore the fiord and see the glaciers where the bergs, the first we had seen since leaving Icy Bay, are derived.

We left camp at six o'clock, nearly an hour before daybreak. My Indians were glad to find the fiord barred by a violent wind, against which we failed to make any headway; and as it was too late in the season to wait for better weather, I reluctantly gave up this promising work for another year, and directed the crew to go straight ahead down the coast. We sailed across the mouth of the happy inlet at fine speed, keeping a man at the bow to look out for the smallest of the bergs, not easily seen in the dim light, and another bailing the canoe as the tops of some of the white caps broke over us. About two o'clock we passed a large bay or fiord, out of which a violent wind was blowing, though the main Stephens Passage was calm. About dusk, when we were all tired and anxious to get into camp, we reached the mouth of Sum Dum Bay, but nothing like a safe landing could we find. Our experienced captain was indignant, as well he might be, because we did not see fit to stop early in the afternoon at a good camp-ground he had chosen. He seemed determined to give us enough of night sailing as a punishment to last us for the rest of the voyage. Accordingly, though the night was dark and rainy and the bay full of icebergs, he pushed grimly on, saying that we must try to reach an Indian village on the other side of the bay or an old Indian fort on an island in the middle of it. We made slow, weary, anxious progress while Toyatte, who was well acquainted with every feature of this part of the coast and could find his way in the dark, only laughed at our misery. After a mile or two of this dismal night work we struck across toward the island, now invisible, and came near being wrecked on a rock which showed a smooth round back over which the waves were breaking. In the hurried Indian shouts that followed and while we were close against the rock, Mr Young shouted, as he leaned over against me, 'It's a whale, a whale!' evidently fearing its tail, several specimens of these animals, which were probably still on his mind, having been seen in the forenoon. While we were passing along the east shore of the island we saw a light on the opposite shore, a joyful sight, which Toyatte took for a fire in the Indian village, and steered for it. John stood in the bow, as guide through the bergs. Suddenly, we ran aground on a sand bar. Clearing this, and running back half a mile or so, we again stood for the light, which now shone brightly. I thought it strange that Indians should have so large a fire. A broad white mass dimly visible back of the fire Mr Young took for the glow of the fire on the clouds. This proved to be the front of a glacier. After we had effected a landing and stumbled up toward the fire over a ledge of slippery, algæ-covered rocks, and through the ordinary tangle of shore grass, we were astonished to find white men instead of Indians, the first we had seen for a month. They proved to be a party of seven gold-seekers from Fort Wrangell. It was now about eight o'clock and they were in bed, but a jolly Irishman got up to make coffee for us and find out who we were, where we had come from, where going, and the objects of our travels. We unrolled our chart and asked for information as to the extent and features of the bay. But our benevolent friend took great pains to pull wool over our eyes, and made haste to say that if 'ice and sceneries' were what we were looking for, this was a very poor, dull place. There were 'big rocks, gulches and sceneries' of a far better quality down the coast on the way to Wrangell. He and his party were prospecting, he said, but thus far they had found only a few colours and they proposed going over to Admiralty Island in the morning to try their luck.

In the morning, however, when the prospectors were to have gone over to the island, we noticed a smoke half a mile back on a large stream, the outlet of the glacier we had seen the night before, and an Indian told us that the white men were building a big log house up there. It appeared that they had found a promising placer mine in the moraine and feared we might find it and spread the news. Daylight revealed a magnificent fiord that brought Glacier Bay to mind. Miles of bergs lay stranded on the shores, and the waters of the branch fiords, not on Vancouver's chart, were crowded with them as far as the eye could reach. After breakfast we set out to explore an arm of the bay that trends southeastward, and managed to force a way through the bergs about ten miles. Farther we could not go. The pack was so close no open water was in sight, and, convinced at last that this part of my work would have to be left for another year, we struggled across to the west side of the fiord and camped.

I climbed a mountain next morning, hoping to gain a view of the great fruitful glaciers at the head of the fiord or, at least, of their snowy fountains. But in this also I failed; for at a distance of about sixteen miles from the mouth of the fiord a change to the northward in its general trend cut off all its upper course from sight.

Returning to camp baffled and weary, I ordered all hands to pack up and get out of the ice as soon as possible. And how gladly was that order obeyed! Toyatte's grand countenance glowed like a sun-filled glacier, as he joyfully and teasingly remarked that 'the big Sum Dum ice-mountain had hidden his face from me and refused to let me pay him a visit'. All the crew worked hard boring a way down the west side of the fiord, and early in the afternoon we reached comparatively open water near the mouth of the bay. Resting a few minutes among the drifting bergs, taking last lingering looks at the wonderful place I might never see again, and feeling sad over my weary failure to explore it, I was cheered by a friend I little expected to meet here. Suddenly, I heard the familiar whirr of an ouzel's wings, and, looking up, saw my little comforter coming straight from the shore. In a second or two he was with me, and flew three times around my head with a happy salute, as if saying, 'Cheer up, old friend, you see I am here and all's well'. He then flew back to the shore, alighted on the topmost jag of a stranded iceberg, and began to nod and bow as though he were on one of his favourite rocks in the middle of a sunny California mountain cataract.

Mr Young regretted not meeting the Indians here, but mission work also had to be left until next season. Our happy crew hoisted sail to a fair wind, shouted 'Good-bye, Sum Dum!' and soon after dark reached a harbour a few miles north of Hobart Point.

We made an early start the next day, a fine, calm morning, glided smoothly down the coast, admiring the magnificent mountains arrayed in their winter robes, and early in the afternoon reached a lovely harbour on an island five or six miles north of Cape Fanshawe. Toyatte predicted a heavy winter storm, though only a mild rain was falling as yet. Everybody was tired and hungry, and as the voyage was nearing the end, I consented to stop here. While the shelter tents were being set up and our blankets stowed under cover, John went out to hunt and killed a deer within two hundred yards of the camp.

When we were at the camp-fire in Sum Dum Bay, one of the prospectors, replying to Mr Young's complaint that they were oftentimes out of meat, asked Toyatte why he and his men did not shoot plenty of ducks for the minister. 'Because the duck's friend would not let us', said Toyatte; 'when we want to shoot, Mr Muir always shakes the canoe'.

Just as we were passing the south headland of Port Houghton Bay, we heard a shout, and a few minutes later saw four Indians in a canoe paddling rapidly after us. In about an hour they overtook us. They were an Indian, his son, and two women with a load of fish-oil and dried salmon to sell and trade at Fort Wrangell. They camped within a dozen yards of us; with their sheets of cedar bark and poles they speedily made a hut, spread spruce boughs in it for a carpet, unloaded the canoe, and stored their goods under cover. Toward evening the old man came smiling with a gift for Toyatte – a large fresh salmon, which was promptly boiled and eaten by our captain and crew as if it were only a light refreshment like a biscuit between meals. A few minutes after the big salmon had vanished, our generous neighbour came to Toyatte with a second gift of dried salmon, which after being toasted a few minutes tranquilly followed the fresh one as though it were a mere mouthful. Then, from the same generous hands, came a third gift – a large milk-panful of huckleberries and grease boiled together – and, strange to say, this wonderful mess went smoothly down to rest on the broad and deep salmon foundation. Thus refreshed, and appetite sharpened, my sturdy crew made haste to begin on the buck, beans, bread, etc., and boiling and roasting, managed to get comfortably full on but little more than half of it by sundown, making a good deal of sport of my pity for the deer and refusing to eat any of it and nicknaming me the ice *ancou* and the deer and duck's *tillicum*.

Sunday was a wild, driving, windy day with but little rain but big promise of more. I took a walk back in the woods. The timber here is very fine, about as large as any I have seen in Alaska, much better than farther north. The Sitka spruce and the common hemlock, one hundred and fifty and two hundred feet high, are slender and handsome. The Sitka spruce makes good firewood even when green, the hemlock very poor. Back a little way from the sea, there was a good deal of yellow cedar, the best I had yet seen. The largest specimen that I saw and measured on the trip was five feet three inches in diameter and about one hundred and forty feet high. In the evening Mr Young gave the Indians a lesson, calling in our Indian neighbours. He told them the story of Christ coming to save the world. The Indians wanted to know why the Jews had killed him. The lesson was listened to with very marked attention. Toyatte's generous friend caught a devil-fish about three feet in diameter to add to his stores of food. It would be very good, he said, when boiled in berry and colicon-oil soup. Each arm of this savage animal with its double row of button-like suction discs closed upon any object brought within reach with a grip nothing could escape. The Indians tell me that devil-fish live mostly on crabs, mussels and clams, the shells of which they easily crunch with their strong, parrot-like beaks. That was a wild, stormy, rainy night. How the rain soaked us in our tents!

'Just feel that', said the minister in the night, as he took my hand and plunged it into a pool about three inches deep in which he was lying.

'Never mind', I said, 'it is only water. Everything is wet now. It will soon be morning and we will dry at the fire.'

Our Indian neighbours were, if possible, still wetter. Their hut had been blown down several times during the night. Our tent leaked badly, and we were lying in a mossy bog, but around the big camp-fire we were soon warm and half dry. We had expected to reach Wrangell by this time. Toyatte said the storm might last several days longer. We were out of tea and coffee, much to Mr Young's distress. On my return from a walk I brought in a good big bunch of glandular ledum and boiled it in the teapot. The result of this experiment was a bright, clear amber-coloured, rank-smelling liquor which I did not taste, but my suffering companion drank the whole potful and praised it. The rain was so heavy we decided not to attempt to leave camp until the storm somewhat abated, as we were assured by Toyatte that we would not be able to round Cape Fanshawe, a sheer, outjutting headland, the nose as he called it, past which the wind sweeps with great violence in these southeastern storms. With what grateful enthusiasm the trees welcomed the life-giving rain! Strong, towering spruces, hemlocks, and cedars tossed their arms, bowing, waving, in every leap, quivering and rejoicing together in the grey, roaring storm. John and Charley put on their gun-coats and went hunting for another deer, but returned later in the afternoon with clean hands, having fortunately failed to shed any more blood. The wind still held in the south, and Toyatte, grimly trying to comfort us, told us that we might be held here a week or more, which we should not have minded much, for we had abundance of provisions. Mr Young and I shifted our tent and tried to dry blankets. The wind moderated considerably, and at 7 am we started but met a rough sea and so stiff a wind we barely succeeded in rounding the cape by all hands pulling their best. Thence we struggled down the coast, creeping close to the shore and taking advantage of the shelter of protecting rocks, making slow, hard-won progress until about the middle of the afternoon, when the sky opened and the blessed sun shone out over the beautiful waters and forests with rich amber light; and the high, glacier-laden mountains, adorned with fresh snow, slowly came to view in all their grandeur, the bluish-grey clouds crawling and lingering and dissolving until every vestige of them vanished. The sunlight made the upper snow-fields pale creamy yellow, like that seen on the Chilcat mountains the first day of our return trip. Shortly after the sky cleared, the wind abated and changed around to the north, so that we ventured to hoist our sail, and then the weary Indians had rest. It was interesting to note how speedily the heavy swell that had been rolling for the last two or three days was subdued by the comparatively light breeze from the opposite direction. In a few minutes the sound was smooth and no trace of the storm was left, save the fresh snow and the discoloration of the water. All the water of the sound as far as I noticed was pale coffee-colour like that of the streams in boggy woods. How much of this colour was due to the inflow of the flooded streams many times increased in size and number by the rain, and how much to the beating of the waves along the shore stirring up vegetable matter in shallow bays, I cannot determine. The effect, however, was very marked.

About four o'clock we saw smoke on the shore and ran in for news. We found a company of Taku Indians, who were on their way to Fort Wrangell, some six men and about the same number of women. The men were sitting in a bark hut, handsomely reinforced and embowered with fresh spruce boughs. The women were out at the side of a stream, washing their many bits of calico. A little girl, six or seven years old, was sitting on the gravelly beach, building a playhouse of white quartz pebbles, scarcely caring to stop her work to gaze at us. Toyatte found a friend among the men, and wished to encamp beside them for the night, assuring us that this was the only safe harbour to be found within a good many miles. But we resolved to push on a little farther and make use of the smooth weather after being stormbound so long, much to Toyatte and his companion's disgust. We rowed about a couple of miles and ran into a cozy cove where wood and water were close at hand. How beautiful and homelike it was! plushy moss for mattresses decked with red cornel berries, noble spruce standing guard about us and spreading kindly protecting arms. A few ferns, aspidiums, polypodiums, with dewberry vines, coptis, pyrola, leafless huckleberry bushes, and ledum grow beneath the trees. We retired at eight o'clock, and just then Toyatte, who had been attentively studying the sky, presaged rain and another southeaster for the morrow.

The sky was a little cloudy next morning, but the air was still and the water smooth. We all hoped that Toyatte, the old weather prophet, had misread the sky signs. But before reaching Point Vanderpeut the rain began to fall and the dreaded southeast wind to blow, which soon increased to a stiff breeze, next thing to a gale, that lashed the sound into ragged white caps. Cape Vanderpeut is part of the terminal of an ancient glacier that once extended six or eight miles out from the base of the mountains. Three large glaciers that once were tributaries still descend nearly to the sea-level, though their fronts are back in narrow fiords, eight or ten miles from the sound. A similar point juts out into the sound five or six miles to the south, while the missing portion is submerged and forms a shoal.

All the cape is forested save a narrow strip about a mile long, composed of large boulders against which the waves beat with loud roaring. A bar of foam a mile or so farther out showed where the waves were breaking on a submerged part of the moraine, and I supposed that we would be compelled to pass around it in deep water, but Toyatte, usually so cautious, determined to cross it, and after giving particular directions, with an encouraging shout every oar and paddle was strained to shoot through a narrow gap. Just at the most critical point a big wave heaved us aloft and dropped us between two huge rounded boulders, where, had the canoe been a foot or two closer to either of them, it must have been smashed. Though I had offered no objection to our experienced pilot's plan, it looked dangerous, and I took the precaution to untie my shoes so they could be quickly shaken off for swimming. But after crossing the bar we were not yet out of danger, for we had to struggle hard to keep from being driven ashore while the waves were beating us broadside on. At length we discovered a little inlet, into which we gladly escaped. A pure-white iceberg, weathered to the form of a cross, stood amid drifts of kelp and the black rocks of the wave-beaten shore in sign of safety and welcome. A good fire soon warmed and dried us into common comfort.

Our narrow escape was the burden of conversation as we sat around the fire. Captain Toyatte told us of two similar adventures while he was a strong young man. In both of them his canoe was smashed and he swam ashore out of the surge with a gun in his teeth. He says that if we had struck the rocks he and Mr Young would have been drowned, all the rest of us probably would have been saved. Then, turning to me, he asked me if I could have made a fire in such a case without matches, and found a way to Wrangell without canoe or food.

We started about daybreak from our blessed white cross harbour, and, after rounding a bluff cape opposite the mouth of Wrangell Narrows, a fleet of icebergs came in sight, and of course I was eager to trace them to their source. Toyatte naturally enough was greatly excited about the safety of his canoe and begged that we should not venture to force a way through the bergs, risking the loss of the canoe and our lives now that we were so near the end of our long voyage.

'Oh, never fear, Toyatte', I replied. 'You know we are always lucky – the weather is good. I only want to see the Thunder Glacier for a few minutes, and should the bergs be packed dangerously close, I promise to turn back and wait until next summer.'

Thus assured, he pushed rapidly on until we entered the fiord, where we had to go cautiously slow. The bergs were close packed almost throughout the whole extent of the fiord, but we managed to reach a point about two miles from the head – commanding a good view of the down-plunging lower end of the glacier and blue, jagged ice-wall. This was one of the most imposing of the first-class glaciers I had as yet seen, and with its magnificent fiord formed a fine triumphant close for our season's ice work. I made a few notes and sketches and turned back in time to escape from the thickest packs of bergs before dark. Then Kadachan was stationed in the bow to guide through the open portion of the mouth of the fiord and across Soutchoi Strait. It was not until several hours after dark that we were finally free from ice. We occasionally encountered stranded packs on the delta, which in the starlight seemed to extend indefinitely in every direction. Our danger lay in breaking the canoe on small bergs hard to see and in getting too near the larger ones that might split or roll over.

'Oh, when will we escape from this ice?' moaned much-enduring old Toyatte.

We ran aground in several places in crossing the Stickeen delta, but finally succeeded in groping our way over muddy shallows before the tide fell, and encamped on the boggy shore of a small island, where we discovered a spot dry enough to sleep on, after tumbling about in a tangle of bushes and mossy logs.

We left our last camp 21 November at daybreak. The weather was calm and bright. Wrangell Island came into view beneath a lovely rosy sky, all the forest down to the water's edge silvery grey with a dusting of snow. John and Charley seemed to be seriously distressed to find themselves at the end of their journey while a portion of the stock of provisions remained uneaten. 'What is to be done about it?' they asked, more than half in earnest. The fine,

strong, and specious deliberation of Indians was well illustrated on this
eventful trip. It was fresh every morning. They all behaved well, however,
exerted themselves under tedious hardships without flinching for days or
weeks at a time; never seemed in the least nonplussed; were prompt to act in
every exigency; good as servants, fellow travellers, and even friends.

We landed on an island in sight of Wrangell and built a big smoky signal fire
for friends in town, then set sail, unfurled our flag, and about noon completed
our long journey of seven or eight hundred miles. As we approached the
town, a large canoeful of friendly Indians came flying out to meet us, cheering
and handshaking in lusty Boston fashion. The friends of Mr Young had
intended to come out in a body to welcome him back, but had not had time to
complete their arrangements before we landed. Mr Young was eager for
news. I told him there could be no news of importance about a town. We only
had real news, drawn from the wilderness. The mail steamer had left Wrangell
eight days before, and Mr Vanderbilt and family had sailed on her to Portland.
I had to wait a month for the next steamer, and though I would have liked to
go again to Nature, the mountains were locked for the winter and canoe
excursions no longer safe.

So I shut myself up in a good garret alone to wait and work. I was invited to
live with Mr Young but concluded to prepare my own food and enjoy quiet
work. How grandly long the nights were and short the days! At noon the sun
seemed to be about an hour high, the clouds coloured like sunset. The
weather was rather stormy. North winds prevailed for a week at a time,
sending down the temperature to near zero and chilling the vapour of the bay
into white reek, presenting a curious appearance as it streamed forward on
the wind, like combed wool. At Sitka the minimum was eight degrees plus; at
Wrangell, near the storm-throat of the Stickeen, zero. This is said to be the
coldest weather ever experienced in southeastern Alaska.

CHAPTER THIRTEEN

Alaska Indians

LOOKING BACK on my Alaska travels, I have always been glad that good luck
gave me Mr Young as a companion, for he brought me into confiding contact
with the Thlinkit tribes, so that I learned their customs, what manner of men
they were, how they lived and loved, fought and played, their morals, religion,
hopes and fears, and superstitions, how they resembled and differed in their
characteristics from our own and other races. It was easy to see that they
differed greatly from the typical American Indian of the interior of this
continent. They were doubtless derived from the Mongol stock. Their down-
slanting oval eyes, wide cheek-bones, and rather thick, outstanding upper lips
at once suggest their connection with the Chinese or Japanese. I have not

seen a single specimen that looks in the least like the best of the Sioux, or indeed of any of the tribes to the east of the Rocky Mountains. They also differ from other North American Indians in being willing to work, when free from contamination of bad whites. They manage to feed themselves well, build good substantial houses, bravely fight their enemies, love their wives and children and friends, and cherish a quick sense of honour. The best of them prefer death to dishonour, and sympathize with their neighbours in their misfortunes and sorrows. Thus when a family loses a child by death, neighbours visit them to cheer and console. They gather around the fire and smoke, talk kindly and naturally, telling the sorrowing parents not to grieve too much, reminding them of the better lot of their child in another world and of the troubles and trials the little ones escape by dying young, all this in a perfectly natural, straightforward way, wholly unlike the vacant, silent, hesitating behaviour of most civilized friends, who oftentimes in such cases seem nonplussed, awkward, and afraid to speak, however sympathetic.

The Thlinkits are fond and indulgent parents. In all my travels I never heard a cross, fault-finding word, or anything like scolding inflicted on an Indian child, or ever witnessed a single case of spanking, so common in civilized communities. They consider the want of a son to bear their name and keep it alive the saddest and most deplorable ill-fortune imaginable.

The Thlinkit tribes give a hearty welcome to Christian missionaries. In particular they are quick to accept the doctrine of the atonement, because they themselves practice it, although to many of the civilized whites it is a stumbling-block and rock of offence. As an example of their own doctrine of atonement they told Mr Young and me one evening that twenty or thirty years ago there was a bitter war between their own and the Sitka tribe, great fighters, and pretty evenly matched. After fighting all summer in a desultory, squabbling way, fighting now under cover, now in the open, watching for every chance for a shot, none of the women dared venture to the salmon-streams or berry-fields to procure their winter stock of food. At this crisis one of the Stickeen chiefs came out of his block-house fort into an open space midway between their fortified camps, and shouted that he wished to speak to the leader of the Sitkas.

When the Sitka chief appeared he said:

'My people are hungry. They dare not go to the salmon-streams or berry-fields for winter supplies, and if this war goes on much longer most of my people will die of hunger. We have fought long enough; let us make peace. You brave Sitka warriors go home, and we will go home, and we will all set out to dry salmon and berries before it is too late.'

The Sitka chief replied:

'You may well say let us stop fighting, when you have had the best of it. You have killed ten more of my tribe than we have killed of yours. Give us ten Stickeen men to balance our blood-account; then, and not till then, will we make peace and go home.'

'Very well', replied the Stickeen chief, 'you know my rank. You know that I am worth ten common men and more. Take me and make peace.'

This noble offer was promptly accepted; the Stickeen chief stepped forward and was shot down in sight of the fighting bands. Peace was thus established, and all made haste to their homes and ordinary work. That chief literally gave himself a sacrifice for his people. He died that they might live. Therefore, when missionaries preached the doctrine of atonement, explaining that when all mankind had gone astray, had broken God's laws and deserved to die, God's son came forward, and, like the Stickeen chief, offered himself as a sacrifice to heal the cause of God's wrath and set all the people of the world free, the doctrine was readily accepted.

'Yes, your words are good', they said. 'The Son of God, the Chief of chiefs, the Maker of all the world, must be worth more than all mankind put together; therefore, when His blood was shed, the salvation of the world was made sure.'

A telling illustration of the ready acceptance of this doctrine was displayed by Shakes, head chief of the Stickeens at Fort Wrangell. A few years before my first visit to the Territory, when the first missionary arrived, he requested Shakes to call his people together to hear the good word he had brought them. Shakes accordingly sent out messengers throughout the village, telling his people to wash their faces, put on their best clothing, and come to the block-house to hear what their visitor had to say. When all were assembled, the missionary preached a Christian sermon on the fall of man and the atonement whereby Christ, the Son of God, the Chief of chiefs, had rede-eemed all mankind, provided that this redemption was voluntarily accepted with repentance of their sins and the keeping of his commandments.

When the misionary had finished his sermon, Chief Shakes slowly arose, and, after thanking the missionary for coming so far to bring them good tidings and taking so much unselfish interest in the welfare of his tribe, he advised his people to accept the new religion, for he felt satisfied that because the white man knew so much more than the Indian, the white man's religion was likely to be better than theirs.

'The white man', said he, 'makes great ships. We, like children, can only make canoes. He makes his big ships go with the wind, and he also makes them go with fire. We chop down trees with stone axes; the Boston man with iron axes, which are far better. In everything the ways of the white man seem to be better than ours. Compared with the white man we are only blind children, knowing not how best to live either here or in the country we go to after we die. So I wish you to learn this new religion and teach it to your children, that you may all go when you die into that good heaven country of the white man and be happy. But I am too old to learn a new religion, and besides, many of my people who have died were bad and foolish people, and if this word the missionary has brought us is true, and I think it is, many of my people must be in that bad country the missionary calls 'Hell', and I must go there also, for a Stickeen chief never deserts his people in time of trouble. To that bad country, therefore, I will go, and try to cheer my people and help them as best I can to endure their misery.'

Toyatte was a famous orator. I was present at the meeting at Fort Wrangell at which he was examined and admitted as a member of the Presbyterian Church. When called upon to answer the questions as to his ideas of God, and the principal doctrines of Christianity, he slowly arose in the crowded audience, while the missionary said, 'Toyatte, you do not need to rise. You can answer the questions seated.'

To this he paid no attention, but stood several minutes without speaking a word, never for a moment thinking of sitting down like a tired woman while making the most important of all the speeches of his life. He then explained in detail what his mother had taught him as to the character of God, the great Maker of the world; also what the shamans had taught him; the thoughts that often came to his mind when he was alone on hunting expeditions, and what he first thought of the religion which the missionaries had brought them. In all his gestures, and in the language in which he expressed himself, there was a noble simplicity and earnestness and majestic bearing which made the sermons and behaviour of the three distinguished divinity doctors present seem commonplace in comparison.

Soon after our return to Fort Wrangell this grand old man was killed in a quarrel in which he had taken no other part than that of peacemaker. A number of the Taku tribe came to Fort Wrangell, camped near the Stickeen village, and made merry, manufacturing and drinking *hootchenoo*, a vile liquor distilled from a mash made of flour, dried apples, sugar and molasses and drunk hot from the still. The manufacture of *hootchenoo* being illegal, and several of Toyatte's tribe having been appointed deputy constables to prevent it, they went to the Taku camp and destroyed as much of the liquor as they could find. The Takus resisted, and during the quarrel one of the Stickeens struck a Taku in the face – an unpardonable offence. The next day messengers from the Taku camp gave notice to the Stickeens that they must make atonement for that blow, or fight with guns. Mr Young, of course, was eager to stop the quarrel and so was Toyatte. They advised the Stickeen who had struck the Taku to return to their camp and submit to an equal blow in the face from the Taku. He did so; went to the camp, said he was ready to make atonement, and invited the person whom he had struck to strike him. This the Taku did with so much force that the balance of justice was again disturbed. The attention of the Takus was called to the fact that this atoning blow was far harder than the one to be atoned for, and immediately a sort of general free fist-fight began, and the quarrel was thus increased in bitterness rather than diminished.

Next day the Takus sent word to the Stickeens to get their guns ready, for tomorrow they would come up and fight them, thus boldy declaring war. The Stickeens in great excitement assembled and loaded their guns for the coming strife. Mr Young ran hither and thither amongst the men of his congregation, forbidding them to fight, reminding them that Christ told them when they were struck to offer the other cheek instead of giving a blow in return, doing everything in his power to still the storm, but all in vain. Toyatte stood outside one of the big block-houses with his men about him, awaiting the onset of the Takus. Mr Young tried hard to get him away to a place of safety, reminding him that he belonged to his church and no longer had any right to fight. Toyatte calmly replied:

'Mr Young, Mr Young, I am not going to fight. You see I have no gun in my hand; but I cannot go inside of the fort to a place of safety like women and children while my young men are exposed to the bullets of their enemies. I must stay with them and share their dangers, but I will not fight. But you, Mr Young, *you* must go away; you are a minister and you are an important man. It would not do for you to be exposed to bullets. Go to your home in the fort; pretty soon "hi yu poogh"' (much shooting).

At the first fire Toyatte fell, shot through the breast. Thus died for his people the noblest old Roman of them all.

On this first Alaska excursion I saw Toyatte under all circumstances – in rain and snow, landing at night in dark storms, making fires, building shelters, exposed to all kinds of discomfort, but never under any cicumstances did I ever see him do anything, or make a single gesture, that was not dignified, or hear him say a word that might not be uttered anywhere. He often deplored the fact that he had no son to take his name at his death, and expressed himself as very grateful when I told him that his name would not be forgotten – that I had named one of the Stickeen glaciers for him.

Part 2

The Trip of 1880

CHAPTER FOURTEEN

Sum Dum Bay

I ARRIVED early on the morning of the eighth of August on the steamer California to continue my explorations of the fiords to the northward which were closed by winter the previous November. The noise of our cannon and whistle was barely sufficient to awaken the sleepy town. The morning shout of one good rooster was the only evidence of life and health in all the place. Everything seemed kindly and familiar – the glassy water; evergreen islands; the Indians with their canoes and baskets and blankets and berries; the jet ravens, prying and flying about the streets and spruce trees; and the bland, hushed atmosphere brooding tenderly over all.

How delightful it is, and how it makes one's pulses bound to get back into this reviving northland wilderness! How truly wild it is, and how joyously one's heart responds to the welcome it gives, its waters and mountains shining and glowing like enthusiastic human faces! Gliding along the shores of its network of channels, we may travel thousands of miles without seeing any mark of man, save at long intervals some little Indian village or the faint smoke of a camp-fire. Even these are confined to the shore. Back a few yards from the beach the forests are as trackless as the sky, while the mountains, wrapped in their snow and ice and clouds, seem never before to have been looked at.

For those who really care to get into hearty contact with the coast region, travel by canoe is by far the better way. The larger canoes carry from one to three tons, rise lightly over any waves likely to be met on the inland channels, go well under sail, and are easily paddled alongshore in calm weather or against moderate winds, while snug harbours where they may ride at anchor or be pulled up on a smooth beach are to be found almost everywhere. With plenty of provisions packed in boxes, and blankets and warm clothing in

rubber or canvas bags, you may be truly independent, and enter into partner-
ship with Nature; to be carried with the winds and currents, accept the noble
invitations offered all along your way to enter the mountain fiords, the homes
of the waterfalls and glaciers, and encamp almost every night beneath
hospitable trees.

I left Fort Wrangell the 16th of August, accompanied by Mr Young, in a
canoe about twenty-five feet long and five wide, carrying two small square
sails and manned by two Stickeen Indians – Captain Tyeen and Hunter Joe –
and a half-breed named Smart Billy. The day was calm, and bright, fleecy,
clouds hung about the lowest of the mountain-brows, while far above the
clouds the peaks were seen stretching grandly away to the northward with
their ice and snow shining in as calm a light as that which was falling on the
glassy waters. Our Indians welcomed the work that lay before them, dipping
their oars in exact time with hearty good will as we glided past island after
island across the delta of the Stickeen into Soutchoi Channel.

By noon we came in sight of a fleet of icebergs from Hutli Bay. The Indian
name of this icy fiord is Hutli, or Thunder Bay, from the sound made by the
bergs in falling and rising from the front of the inflowing glacier.

As we floated happily on over the shining waters, the beautiful islands, in
ever-changing pictures, were an unfailing source of enjoyment; but chiefly
our attention was turned upon the mountains. Bold granite headlands with
their feet in the channel, or some broad-shouldered peak of surpassing grandeur, would fix the eye, or some one of the larger glaciers, with far-reaching
tributaries clasping entire groups of peaks and its great crystal river pouring
down through the forest between grey ridges and domes. In these grand
picture lessons the day was spent, and we spread our blankets beneath a
Menzies spruce on moss two feet deep.

Next morning we sailed around an outcurving bank of boulders and sand
ten miles long, the terminal moraine of a grand old glacier on which last
November we met a perilous adventure. It is located just opposite three large
converging glaciers which formerly united to form the vanished trunk of the
glacier to which the submerged moraine belonged. A few centuries ago it
must have been the grandest feature of this part of the coast, and, so well
preserved are the monuments of its greatness, the noble old ice-river may be
seen again in imagination about as vividly as if present in the flesh, with snow-
clouds crawling about its fountains, sunshine sparkling on its broad flood, and
its ten-mile ice-wall planted in the deep waters of the channel and sending off
its bergs with loud resounding thunder.

About noon we rounded Cape Fanshawe, scudding swiftly before a fine
breeze, to the delight of our Indians, who had now only to steer and chat.
Here we overtook two Hoona Indians and their families on their way home
from Fort Wrangell. They had exchanged five sea-otter furs, worth about a
hundred dollars apiece, and a considerable number of fur-seal, land-otter,
marten, beaver and other furs and skins, some $800 worth, for a new canoe
valued at eighty dollars, some flour, tobacco, blankets and a few barrels of
molasses for the manufacture of whiskey. The blankets were not to wear, but
to keep as money, for the almighty dollar of these tribes is a Hudson's Bay
blanket. The wind died away soon after we met, and as the two canoes glided

slowly side by side, the Hoonas made minute inquiries as to who we were and what we were doing so far north. Mr Young's object in meeting the Indians as a missionary they could in part understand, but mine in searching for rocks and glaciers seemed past comprehension, and they asked our Indians whether gold-mines might not be the main object. They remembered, however, that I had visited their Glacier Bay ice-mountains a year ago, and seemed to think there might be, after all, some mysterious interest about them of which they were ignorant. Toward the middle of the afternoon they engaged our crew in a race. We pushed a little way ahead for a time, but, though possessing a considerable advantage, as it would seem, in our long oars, they at length overtook us and kept up until after dark, when we camped together in the rain on the bank of a salmon-stream among dripping grass and bushes some twenty-five miles beyond Cape Fanshawe.

These cold northern waters are at times about as brilliantly phosphorescent as those of the warm South, and so they were this evening in the rain and darkness, with the temperature of the water at forty-nine degrees, the air fifty-one. Every stroke of the oar made a vivid surge of white light, and the canoes left shining tracks.

As we neared the mouth of the well-known salmon-stream where we intended making our camp, we noticed jets and flashes of silvery light caused by the startled movement of the salmon that were on their way to the spawning-grounds. These became more and more numerous and exciting, and our Indians shouted joyfully, 'Hi yu salmon! Hi yu muck-a-muck!' while the water about the canoe and beneath the canoe was churned by thousands of fins in silver fire. After landing two of our men to commence camp-work, Mr Young and I went up the stream with Tyeen to the foot of a rapid, to see him catch a few salmon for supper. The stream was so filled with them there seemed to be more fish than water in it, and we appeared to be sailing in boiling, seething silver light marvellously relieved in the jet darkness. In the midst of the general auroral glow and the specially vivid flashes made by the frightened fish darting ahead and to right and left of the canoe, our attention was suddenly fixed by a long, steady, comet-like blaze that seemed to be made by some frightful monster that was pursuing us. But when the portentous object reached the canoe, it proved to be only our little dog, Stickeen.

After getting the canoe into a side eddy at the foot of the rapids, Tyeen caught half a dozen salmon in a few minutes by means of a large hook fastened to the end of a pole. They were so abundant that he simply groped for them in a random way, or aimed at them by the light they themselves furnished. That food to last a month or two may thus be procured in less than an hour is a striking illustration of the fruitfulness of these Alaskan waters.

Our Hoona neighbours were asleep in the morning at sunrise, lying in a row, wet and limp like dead salmon. A little boy about six years old, with no other covering than a remnant of a shirt, was lying peacefully on his back like Tam o'Shanter, despising wind and rain and fire. He is up now, looking happy and fresh, with no clothes to dry and no need of washing while this weather lasts. The two babies are firmly strapped on boards, leaving only their heads and hands free. Their mothers are nursing them, holding the boards on end, while they sit on the ground with their breasts level with the little prisoners' mouths.

This morning we found out how beautiful a nook we had got into. Besides the charming picturesqueness of its lines, the colours about it, brightened by the rain, made a fine study. Viewed from the shore, there was first a margin of dark-brown algæ, then a bar of yellowish-brown, next a dark bar on the rugged rocks marking the highest tides, then a bar of granite boulders with grasses in the seams, and above this a thick, bossy, overleaning fringe of bushes coloured red and yellow and green. A wall of spruces and hemlocks draped and tufted with grey and yellow lichens and mosses embowered the camp-ground and overarched the little river, while the camp-fire smoke, like a stranded cloud, lay motionless in their branches. Down on the beach ducks and sandpipers in flocks of hundreds were getting their breakfasts, bald eagles were seen perched on dead spars along the edge of the woods, heavy-looking and overfed, gazing stupidly like gorged vultures, and porpoises were blowing and lunging outside.

As for the salmon, as seen this morning urging their way up the swift current – tens of thousands of them, side by side, with their backs out of the water in shallow places now that the tide was low – nothing that I could write might possibly give anything like a fair conception of the extravagance of their numbers. There was more salmon apparently, bulk for bulk, than water in the stream. The struggling multitudes, crowding one against another, could not get out of our way when we waded into the midst of them. One of our men amused himself by seizing them above the tail and swinging them over his head. Thousands could thus be taken by hand at low tide, while they were making their way over the shallows among the stones.

Whatever may be said of other resources of the Territory, it is hardly possible to exaggerate the importance of the fisheries. Not to mention cod, herring, halibut, etc., there are probably not less than a thousand salmon-streams in southeastern Alaska as large or larger than this one (about forty feet wide) crowded with salmon several times a year. The first run commenced that year in July, while the king salmon, one of the five species recognized by the Indians, was in the Chilcat River about the middle of the November before.

From this wonderful salmon-camp we sailed joyfully up the coast to explore icy Sum Dum Bay, beginning my studies where I left off the previous November. We started about six o'clock, and pulled merrily on through fog and rain, the beautiful wooded shore on our right, passing bergs here and there, the largest of which, though not over two hundred feet long, seemed many times larger as they loomed grey and indistinct through the fog. For the first five hours the sailing was open and easy, nor was there anything very exciting to be seen or heard, save now and then the thunder of a falling berg rolling and echoing from cliff to cliff, and the sustained roar of cataracts.

About eleven o'clock we reached a point where the fiord was packed with ice all the way across, and we ran ashore to fit a block of wood on the cutwater of our canoe to prevent its being battered or broken. While Captain Tyeen, who had had considerable experience among berg ice, was at work on the canoe, Hunter Joe and Smart Billy prepared a warm lunch.

The sheltered hollow where we landed seems to be a favourite camping-ground for the Sum Dum seal-hunters. The pole-frames of tents, tied with cedar bark, stood on level spots strewn with seal bones, bits of salmon, and spruce bark.

We found the work of pushing through the ice rather tiresome. An opening of twenty or thirty yards would be found here and there, then a close pack that had to be opened by pushing the smaller bergs aside with poles. I enjoyed the labour, however, for the fine lessons I got, and in an hour or two we found zigzag lancs of water, through which we paddled with but little interruption, and had leisure to study the wonderful variety of forms the bergs presented as we glided past them. The largest we saw did not greatly exceed two hundred feet in length, or twenty-five or thirty-feet in height above the water. Such bergs would draw from one hundred and fifty to two hundred feet of water. All those that have floated long undisturbed have a projecting base at the water-line, caused by the more rapid melting of the immersed portion. When a portion of the berg breaks off, another base line is formed, and the old one, sharply cut, may be seen rising at all angles, giving it a marked character. Many of the oldest bergs are beautifully ridged by the melting out of narrow furrows strictly parallel throughout the mass, revealing the bedded structure of the ice, acquired perhaps centuries ago, on the mountain snow fountains. A berg suddenly going to pieces is a grand sight, especially when the water is calm and no motion is visible save perchance the slow drift of the tide-current. The prolonged roar of its fall comes with startling effect, and heavy swells are raised that haste away in every direction to tell what has taken place, and tens of thousands of its neighbours rock and swash in sympathy, repeating the news over and over again. We were too near several larger ones that fell apart as we passed them, and our canoe had narrow escapes. The seal-hunters, Tyeen says, are frequently lost in these sudden berg accidents.

In the afternoon, while we were admiring the scenery, which, as we ap-proached the head of the fiord, became more and more sublime, one of our Indians callcd attention to a flock of wild goats on a mountain overhead, and soon afterwards we saw two other flocks, at a height of about fifteen hundred feet, relieved against the mountains as white spots. They are abundant here and throughout the Alaskan Alps in general, feeding on the grassy slopes above the timber-line. Their long, yellowish hair is shed at this time of year and they were snowy white. None of nature's cattle are better fed or better protected from the cold. Tyeen told us that before the introduction of guns they used to hunt them with spears, chasing them with their wolf-dogs, and thus bringing thcm to bay among the rocks, where they were easily approached and killed.

The upper half of the fiord is about from a mile to a mile and a half wide, and shut in by sublime Yosemite cliffs, nobly sculptured, and adorned with waterfalls and fringes of trees, bushes, and patches of flowers; but amid so crowded a display of novel beauty it was not easy to concentrate the attention long enough on any portion of it without giving more days and years than our lives could afford. I was determined to see at least the grand fountain of all this ice. As we passed headland after headland, hoping as each was rounded we should obtain a view of it, it still remained hidden.

'Ice-mountain hi yu kumtux hide' – glaciers know how to hide extremely well – said Tyeen, as he rested for a moment after rounding a huge granite shoulder of the wall whence we expected to gain a view of the extreme head of the fiord. The bergs, however, were less closely packed and we made good progress, and at half-past eight o'clock, fourteen and a half hours after setting out, the great glacier came in sight at the head of a branch of the fiord that comes in from the northeast.

The discharging front of this fertile, fast-flowing glacier is about three quarters of a mile wide, and probably eight or nine hundred feet deep, about one hundred and fifty feet of its depth rising above the water as a grand blue barrier wall. It is much wider a few miles farther back, the front being jammed between sheer granite walls from thirty-five hundred to four thousand feet high. It shows grandly from where it broke on our sight, sweeping boldly forward and downward in its majestic channel, swaying from side to side in graceful fluent lines around stern unflinching rocks. While I stood in the canoe making a sketch of it, several bergs came off with tremendous dashing and thunder, raising a cloud of ice-dust and spray to a height of a hundred feet or more.

'The ice-mountain is well disposed toward you', said Tyeen. 'He is firing his big guns to welcome you'.

After completing my sketch and entering a few notes, I directed the crew to pull around a lofty burnished rock on the west side of the channel, where, as I knew from the trend of the canyon, a large glacier once came in; and what was my delight to discover that the glacier was still there and still pouring its ice into a branch of the fiord. Even the Indians shared my joy and shouted with me. I expected only one first-class glacier here, and found two. They are only about two miles apart. How glorious a mansion that precious pair dwell in! After sunset we made haste to seek a camp-ground. I would fain have shared these upper chambers with the two glaciers, but there was no landing-place in sight, and we had to make our way back a few miles in the twilight to the mouth of the side canyon where we had seen timber on the way up. There seemed to be a good landing as we approached the shore, but, coming nearer, we found that the granite fell directly into deep water without leading any level margin, though the slope a short distance back was not very steep.

After narrowly scanning the various seams and steps that roughened the granite, we concluded to attempt a landing rather than grope our way further down the fiord through the ice. And what a time we had climbing on hands and knees up the slippery glacier-polished rocks to a shelf some two hundred feet above the water and dragging provisions and blankets after us! But it proved to be a glorious place, the very best camp-ground of all the trip – a perfect garden, ripe berries nodding from a fringe of bushes around its edges charmingly displayed in the light of our big fire. Close alongside there was a lofty mountain capped with ice, and from the blue edge of the ice-cap there were sixteen silvery cascades in a row, falling about four thousand feet, each one of the sixteen large enough to be heard at least two miles.

How beautiful was the firelight on the nearest larkspurs and geraniums and daisies of our garden! How hearty the wave greeting on the rocks below brought to us from the two glaciers! And how glorious a song the sixteen cascades sang!

The cascade songs made us sleep all the sounder, and we were so happy as to find in the morning that the berg waves had spared our canoe. We set off in high spirits down the fiord and across to the right side to explore a remarkably deep and narrow branch of the main fiord that I had noted on the way up, and that, from the magnitude of the glacial characters on the two colossal rocks that guard the entrance, promised a rich reward for our pains.

After we had sailed about three miles up this side fiord, we came to what seemed to be its head, for trees and rocks swept in a curve around from one side to the other without showing any opening, although the walls of the canyon were seen extending back indefinitely, one majestic brow beyond the other.

When we were tracing this curve, however, in a leisurely way, in search of a good landing, we were startled by Captain Tyeen shouting, 'Skookum chuck! Skookum chuck!' (strong water, strong water), and found our canoe was being swept sideways by a powerful current, the roar of which we had mistaken for a waterfall. We barely escaped being carried over a rocky bar on the boiling flood, which, as we afterwards learned, would have been only a happy shove on our way. After we had made a landing a little distance back from the brow of the bar, we climbed the highest rock near the shore to seek a view of the channel beyond the inflowing tide rapids, to find out whether or no we could safely venture in. Up over rolling, mossy, bushy burnished rock waves we scrambled for an hour or two, which resulted in a fair view of the deep-blue waters of the fiord stretching on and on along the feet of the most majestic Yosemite rocks we had yet seen. This determined our plan of shooting the rapids and exploring it to its furthest recesses. This novel interruption of the channel is a bar of exceedingly hard resisting granite, over which the great glacier that once occupied it swept, without degrading it to the general level, and over which tide-waters now rush in and out with the violence of a mountain torrent.

Returning to the canoe, we pushed off, and in a few moments were racing over the bar with lightning speed through hurrahing waves and eddies and sheets of foam, our little shell of a boat tossing lightly as a bubble. Then, rowing across a belt of back-flowing water, we found ourselves on a smooth mirror reach between granite walls of the very wildest and most exciting description, surpassing in some ways those of the far-famed Yosemite Valley.

As we drifted silent and awe-stricken beneath the shadows of the mighty cliffs, which, in their tremendous height and abruptness, seemed to overhang at the top, the Indians gazing intently, as if they, too, were impressed with the strange, awe-inspiring grandeur that shut them in, one of them at length broke the silence by saying. 'This must be a good place for woodchucks; I hear them calling'.

When I asked them, further on, how they thought this gorge was made, they gave up the question, but offered an opinion as to the formation of rain and soil. The rain, they said, was produced by the rapid whirling of the earth by a stout mythical being called Yek. The water of the ocean was thus thrown up, to descend again in showers, just as it is thrown off a wet grindstone. They did not, however, understand why the ocean water should be salt, while the rain from it is fresh. The soil, they said, for the plants to grow on is formed by the washing of the rain on the rocks and gradually accumulating. The grinding action of ice in this connection they had not recognized.

Gliding on and on, the scenery seemed at every turn to become more lavishly fruitful in forms as well as more sublime in dimensions – snowy falls booming in splendid dress; colossal domes and battlements and sculptured arches of a fine neutral-grey tint, their bases laved by the blue fiord water; green ferny dells; bits of flower-bloom on ledges; fringes of willow and birch; and glaciers above all. But when we approached the base of a majestic rock like the Yosemite Half Dome at the head of the fiord, where two short branches put out, and came in sight of another glacier of the first order sending off bergs, our joy was complete. I had a most glorious view of it, sweeping in grand majesty from high mountain fountains, swaying around one mighty bastion after another, until it fell into the fiord in shattered overleaning fragments. When we had feasted awhile on this unhoped-for treasure, I directed the Indians to pull to the head of the left fork of the fiord, where we found a large cascade with a volume of water great enough to be called a river, doubtless the outlet of a receding glacier not in sight from the fiord.

This is in form and origin a typical Yosemite valley, though as yet its floor is covered with ice and water – ice above and beneath, a noble mansion in which to spend a winter and a summer! It is about ten miles long, and from three quarters of a mile to a mile wide. It contains ten large falls and cascades, the finest one on the left side near the head. After coming in an admirable rush over a granite brow where it is first seen at a height of nine hundred or a thousand feet, it leaps a sheer precipice of about two hundred and fifty feet, then divides and reaches the tide-water in broken rapids over boulders. Another about a thousand feet high drops at once on to the margin of the glacier two miles back from the front. Several of the others are upwards of three thousand feet high, descending through narrow gorges as richly feathered with ferns as any channel that water ever flowed in, though tremendously abrupt and deep. A grander array of rocks and waterfalls I have never yet beheld in Alaska.

The amount of timber on the walls is about the same as that on the Yosemite walls, but owing to greater moisture, there is more small vegetation – bushes, ferns, mosses, grasses, etc.; though by far the greater portion of the area of the wall-surface is bare and shining with the polish it received when occupied by the glacier that formed the fiord. The deep-green patches seen on the mountains back of the walls at the limits of vegetation are grass, where the wild goats, or chamois rather, roam and feed. The still greener and more luxuriant patches farther down in gullies and on slopes where the declivity is not excessive, are made up mostly of willows, birch, and huckleberry bushes, with a varying amount of prickly ribes and rubus and echinopanax. This growth, when approached, especially on the lower slopes near the level of the sea at the jaws of the great side canyons, is found to be the most impenetrable and tedious and toilsome combination of fighting bushes that the weary explorer ever fell into, incomparably more punishing than the buckthorn and manzanita tangles of the Sierra.

The cliff gardens of this hidden Yosemite are exceedingly rich in colour. On almost every rift and bench, however small, as well as on the wider table-rocks where a little soil has lodged, we found gay multitudes of flowers, far more brilliantly coloured than would be looked for in so cool and beclouded a region – larkspurs, geraniums, painted-cups, blue-bells, gentians, saxifrages, epilobiums, violets, parnassia, veratrum, spiranthes and other orchids, fritillaria, smilax, asters, daisies, bryanthus, cassiope, linnæa, and a great variety of flowering ribes and rubus and heathworts. Many of the above, though with soft stems and leaves, are yet as brightly painted as those of the warm sunlands of the south. The heathworts in particular are very abundant and beautiful, both in flower and fruit, making delicate green carpets for the rocks, flushed with pink bells, or dotted with red and blue berries. The tallest of the grasses have ribbon leaves well tempered and arched, and with no lack of bristly spikes and nodding purple panicles. The alpine grasses of the Sierra, making close carpets on the glacier meadows, I have not yet seen in Alaska.

The ferns are less numerous in species than in California, but about equal in the number of fronds. I have seen three aspidiums, two woodsias, a lomaria, polypodium, cheilanthes and several species of pteris.

In this eastern arm of Sum Dum Bay and its Yosemite branch, I counted from my canoe, on my way up and down, thirty small glaciers back of the walls, and we saw three of the first order; also thirty-seven cascades and falls, counting only those large enough to make themselves heard several miles. The whole bay, with its rocks and woods and ice, reverberates with their roar. How many glaciers may be disclosed in the other great arm that I have not seen as yet, I cannot say, but, judging from the bergs it sends down, I guess not less than a hundred pour their turbid streams into the fiord, making about as many joyful, bouncing cataracts.

About noon we began to retrace our way back into the main fiord, and arrived at the gold-mine camp after dark, rich and weary.

On the morning of 21 August I set out with my three Indians to explore the right arm of this noble bay, Mr Young having decided, on account of mission work, to remain at the gold-mine. So here is another fine lot of Sum Dum ice – thirty-five or forty square miles of bergs, one great glacier of the first class descending into the fiord at the head, the fountain whence all these bergs were derived, and thirty-one smaller glaciers that do not reach tide-water; also nine cascades and falls, large size, and two rows of Yosemite rocks from three to four thousand feet high, each row about eighteen or twenty miles long, burnished and sculptured in the most telling glacier style, and well trimmed with spruce groves and flower gardens; a' that and more of a kind that cannot here be catalogued.

For the first five or six miles there is nothing excepting the icebergs that is very striking in the scenery as compared with that of the smooth unencumbered outside channels, where all is so evenly beautiful. The mountain-wall on the right as you go up is more precipitous than usual, and a series of small glaciers is seen along the top of it, extending their blue-crevassed fronts over the rims of pure-white snow fountains, and from the end of each front a hearty stream coming in a succession of falls and rapids over the terminal moraines, through patches of dwarf willows, and then through the spruce woods into the bay, singing and dancing all the way down. On the opposite side of the bay from here there is a small side bay about three miles deep, with a showy group of glacier-bearing mountains back of it. Everywhere else the view is bounded by comparatively low mountains densely forested to the very top.

After sailing about six miles from the mine, the experienced mountaineer could see some evidence of an opening from this wide lower portion, and on reaching it, it proved to be the continuation of the main west arm, contracted between stupendous walls of grey granite, and crowded with bergs from shore to shore, which seem to bar the way against everything but wings. Headland after headland, in most imposing array, was seen plunging sheer and bare from dizzy heights, and planting its feet in the ice-encumbered water without leaving a spot on which one could land from a boat, while no part of the great glacier that pours all these miles of ice into the fiord was visible. Pushing our way slowly through the packed bergs, and passing headland after headland, looking eagerly forward, the glacier and its fountain mountains were still beyond sight, cut off by other projecting headland capes, toward which I urged my way, enjoying the extraordinary grandeur of the wild unfinished Yosemite. Domes swell against the sky in fine lines as lofty and perfect in form as those of the California valley, and rock-fronts stand forward, as sheer and nobly sculptured. No ice-work that I have ever seen surpasses this, either in the magnitude of the features or effectiveness of composition.

On some of the narrow benches and tables of the walls rows of spruce trees and two-leaved pines were growing, and patches of considerable size were found on the spreading bases of those mountains that stand back inside the canyons, where the continuity of the walls is broken. Some of these side canyons are cut down to the level of the water and reach far back, opening views into groups of glacier fountains that give rise to many a noble stream; while all along the tops of the walls on both sides small glaciers are seen, still busily engaged in the work of completing their sculpture. I counted twenty-five from the canoe. Probably the drainage of fifty or more pours into this fiord. The average elevation at which they melt is about eighteen hundred feet above sea-level, and all of them are residual branches of the grand trunk that filled the fiord and overflowed its walls when there was only one Sum Dum glacier.

The afternoon was wearing away as we pushed on and on through the drifting bergs without our having obtained a single glimpse of the great glacier. A Sum Dum seal-hunter, whom we met groping his way deftly through the ice in a very small, unsplitable cottonwood canoe, told us that the ice-mountain was yet fifteen miles away. This was toward the middle of the afternoon, and I gave up sketching and making notes and worked hard with the Indians to reach it before dark. About seven o'clock we approached what seemed to be the extreme head of the fiord, and still no great glacier in sight – only a small one, three or four miles long, melting a thousand feet above the sea. Presently, a narrow side opening appeared between tremendous cliffs sheer to a height of four thousand feet or more, trending nearly at right angles to the general trend of the fiord, and apparently terminated by a cliff, scarcely less abrupt or high, at a distance of a mile or two. Up this bend we toiled against wind and tide, creeping closely along the wall on the right side, which, as we looked upward, seemed to be leaning over, while the waves beating against the bergs and rocks made a discouraging kind of music. At length, toward nine o'clock, just before the grey darkness of evening fell, a long, triumphant shout told that the glacier, so deeply and desperately hidden, was at last hunted back to its benmost bore. A short distance around a second bend in the canyon, I reached a point where I obtained a good view of it as it pours its deep, broad flood into the fiord in a majestic course from between the noble mountains, its tributaries, each of which would be regarded else-where as a grand glacier, converging from right and left from a fountain set far in the silent fastnesses of the mountains.

'There is your lost friend', said the Indians laughing; 'he says, "Sagh-a-ya'"' (how do you do)? And while berg after berg was being born with thundering uproar, Tyeen said, 'Your friend has klosh tumtum (good heart). Hear! Like the other big-hearted one he is firing his guns in your honour.'

I stayed only long enough to make an outline sketch, and then urged the Indians to hasten back some six miles to the mouth of a side canyon I had noted on the way up as a place where we might camp in case we should not find a better. After dark we had to move with great caution through the ice. One of the Indians was stationed in the bow with a pole to push aside the smaller fragments and look out for the most promising openings, through which he guided us, shouting, 'Friday! Tucktay!' (shoreward, seaward) about ten times a minute. We reached this landing-place after ten o'clock, guided in the darkness by the roar of a glacier torrent. The ground was all boulders and it was hard to find a place among them, however small, to lie on. The Indians anchored the canoe well out from the shore and passed the night in it to guard against berg-waves and drifting waves, after assisting me to set my tent in some sort of way among the stones well back beyond the reach of the tide. I asked them as they were returning to the canoe if they were not going to eat something. They answered promptly:

'We will sleep now, if your ice friend will let us. We will eat to-morrow, but we can find some bread for you if you want it.'

'No', I said, 'go to rest. I, too, will sleep now and eat tomorrow.' Nothing was attempted in the way of light or fire. Camping that night was simply lying down. The boulders seemed to make a fair bed after finding the best place to take their pressure.

During the night I was awakened by the beating of the spent ends of berg-waves against the side of my tent, though I had fancied myself well beyond their reach. These special waves are not raised by wind or tide, but by the fall of large bergs from the snout of the glacier, or sometimes by the overturning or breaking of large bergs that may have long floated in perfect poise. The highest berg-waves oftentimes travel half a dozen miles or farther before they are much spent, producing a singularly impressive uproar in the far recesses of the mountains on calm dark nights when all beside is still. Far and near they tell the news that a berg is born, repeating their story again and again, compelling attention and reminding us of earthquake-waves that roll on for thousands of miles, taking their story from continent to continent.

When the Indians came ashore in the morning and saw the condition of my tent they laughed heartily and said, 'Your friend [meaning the big glacier] sent you a good word last night, and his servant knocked at your tent and said, "Sagh-a-ya, are you sleeping well?"'

I had fasted too long to be in very good order for hard work, but while the Indians were cooking, I made out to push my way up the canyon before break-fast to seek the glacier that once came into this fiord, knowing from the size and muddiness of the stream that drains it that it must be quite large and not far off. I came in sight of it after a hard scramble of two hours through thorny chaparral and across steep avalanche taluses of rocks and snow. The front reaches across the canyon from wall to wall, covered with rocky detritus, and looked dark and forbidding in the shadow cast by the cliffs, while from a low, cavelike hollow its draining stream breaks forth, a river in size, with a reverberating roar that stirs all the canyon. Beyond, in a cloudless blaze of sunshine, I saw many tributaries, pure and white as new-fallen snow, drawing their sources from clusters of peaks and sweeping down waving slopes to unite their crystal currents with the trunk glacier in the central canyon. This fine glacier reaches to within two hundred and fifty feet of the level of the sea, and would even yet reach the fiord and send off bergs but for the waste it suffers in flowing slowly through the trunk canyon, the declivity of which is very slight.

Returning, I reached camp and breakfast at ten o'clock; then had everything packed into the canoe, and set off leisurely across the fiord to the mouth of another wide and low canyon, whose lofty outer cliffs, facing the fiord, are telling glacial advertisements. Gladly I should have explored it all, traced its streams of water and streams of ice, and entered its highest chambers, the homes and fountains of the snow. But I had to wait. I only stopped an hour or two, and climbed on to the top of a rock through the common underbrush whence I had a good general view. The front of the main glacier is not far distant from the fiord, and sends off small bergs into a lake. The walls of its tributary canyons are remarkably jagged and high, cut in red variegated rock, probably slate. On the way back to the canoe I gathered ripe salmon-berries an inch and a half in diameter, ripe huckleberries, too, in great abundance, and several interesting plants I had not before met in the territory.

About noon, when the tide was in our favour, we set out on the return trip to the gold-mine camp. The sun shone free and warm. No wind stirred. The water spaces between the bergs were smooth as glass, reflecting the unclouded sky, and doubling the ravishing beauty of the bergs as the sunlight streamed through their innumerable angles in rainbow colours.

Soon a light breeze sprang up, and dancing lily spangles on the water mingled their glory of light with that burning on the angles of the ice.

On days like this, true sun-days, some of the bergs show a purplish tinge, though most are white from the disintegrating of their weathered surfaces. Now and then a new-born one is met that is pure blue crystal throughout, freshly broken from the fountain or recently exposed to the air by turning over. But in all of them, old and new, there are azure caves and rifts of ineffable beauty, in which the purest tones of light pulse and shimmer, lovely and untainted as anything on earth or in the sky.

As we were passing the Indian village I presented a little tobacco to the headmen as an expression of regard, while they gave us a few smoked salmon, after putting many questions concerning my exploration of their bay and bluntly declaring their disbelief in the ice business.

About nine o'clock we arrived at the gold camp, where we found Mr Young ready to go on with us the next morning, and thus ended two of the brightest and best of all my Alaska days.

CHAPTER FIFTEEN

From Taku River to Taylor Bay

I NEVER saw Alaska looking better than it did when we bade farewell to Sum Dum on 22 August and pushed on northward up the coast toward Taku. The morning was clear, calm, bright – not a cloud in all the purple sky, nor wind, however gentle, to shake the slender spires of the spruces or dew-laden grass around the shores. Over the mountains and over the broad white bosoms of the glaciers the sunbeams poured, and rosy as ever, fell on fields of ripening wheat, drenching the forests and kindling the glassy waters and icebergs into a perfect blaze of coloured light. Every living thing seemed joyful, and nature's work was going on in glowing enthusiasm, not less appreciable in the deep repose that brooded over every feature of the landscape, suggesting the coming fruitfulness of the icy land and showing the advance that has already been made from glacial winter to summer. The care-laden commercial lives we lead close our eyes to the operations of God as a workman, though openly carried on that all who will look may see. The scarred rocks here and the moraines make a vivid showing of the old winter-time of the glacial period, and mark the bounds of the *mer-de-glace* that once filled the bay and covered the surrounding mountains. Already that sea of ice is replaced by water, in which multitudes of fishes are fed, while the hundred glaciers lingering about the bay and the streams that pour from them are busy night and day bringing in sand and mud and stones, at the rate of tons every minute, to fill it up. Then, as the seasons grow warmer, there will be fields here for the plough.

Our Indians, exhilarated by the sunshine, were garrulous as the gulls and plovers, and pulled heartily at the oars, evidently glad to get out of the ice with a whole boat.

'Now for Taku', they said, as we glided over the shining water. 'Good-bye, Ice-Mountains; good-bye, Sum Dum.' Soon a light breeze came, and they unfurled the sail and laid away their oars and began, as usual in such free times, to put their goods in order, unpacking and sunning provisions, guns, ropes, clothing, etc. Joe has an old flintlock musket suggestive of Hudson's Bay times, which he wished to discharge and reload. So, stepping in front of the sail, he fired at a gull that was flying past before I could prevent him, and it fell slowly with outspread wings alongside the canoe, with blood dripping from its bill. I asked him why he had killed the bird, and followed the question by a severe reprimand for his stupid cruelty, to which he could offer no other excuse than that he had learned from the whites to be careless about taking life. Captain Tyeen denounced the deed as likely to bring bad luck.

Before the whites came most of the Thlinkits held with Agassiz, that animals have souls, and that it was wrong and unlucky to even speak disrespectfully of the fishes or any of the animals that supplied them with food. A case illustrating their superstitious beliefs in this connection occurred at Fort Wrangell while I was there the year before. One of the sub-chiefs of the Stickeens had a little son five or six years old, to whom he was very much attached, always taking him with him in his short canoe-trips, and leading him by the hand while going about town. Last summer the boy was taken sick, and gradually grew weak and thin, whereupon his father became alarmed, and feared, as is usual in such obscure cases, that the boy had been bewitched. He first applied in his trouble to Dr Carliss, one of the missionaries, who gave medicine, without effecting the immediate cure that the fond father demanded. He was, to some extent, a believer in the powers of missionaries, both as to material and spiritual affairs, but in so serious an exigency it was natural that he should go back to the faith of his fathers. Accordingly, he sent for one of the shamans, or medicine-men, of his tribe, and submitted the case to him, who, after going through the customary incantations, declared that he had discovered the cause of the difficulty.

'Your boy', he said, 'has lost his soul, and this is the way it happened. He was playing among the stones down on the beach when he saw a crawfish in the water, and made fun of it, pointing his finger at it and saying, "Oh, you crooked legs! Oh, you crooked legs! You can't walk straight; you go sidewise", which made the crab so angry that he reached out his long nippers, seized the lad's soul, pulled it out of him and made off with it into deep water. And', continued the medicine-man, 'unless his stolen soul is restored to him and put back in its place he will die. Your boy is really dead already; it is only his lonely empty body that is living now, and though it may continue to live in this way for a year or two, the boy will never be of any account, not strong, nor wise, nor brave.'

The father then inquired whether anything could be done about it; was the soul still in possession of the crab, and if so, could it be recovered and re-installed in his forlorn son? Yes, the doctor rather thought it might be charmed back and re-united, but the job would be a difficult one, and would probably cost about fifteen blankets.

After we were fairly out of the bay into Stephens Passage, the wind died away, and the Indians had to take to their oars again, which ended our talk. On we sped over the silvery level, close alongshore. The dark forests extending far and near, planted like a field of wheat, might seem monotonous in general views, but the appreciative observer, looking closely, will find no lack of interesting variety, however far he may go. The steep slopes on which they grow allow almost evf ·y individual tree, with its peculiarities of form and colour, to be seen like an audience on seats rising above one another – the blue-green, sharply-tapering spires of the Menzies spruce, the warm yellow-green Mertens spruce with their finger-like tops all pointing in the same direction, or drooping gracefully like leaves of grass, and the airy, feathery, brownish-green Alaska cedar. The outer fringe of bushes along the shore and hanging over the brows of the cliffs, the white mountains above, the shining water beneath, the changing sky over all, form pictures of divine beauty in which no healthy eye may ever grow weary.

Toward evening at the head of a picturesque bay we came to a village belonging to the Taku tribe. We found it silent and deserted. Not a single shaman or policeman had been left to keep it. These people are so happily rich as to have but little of a perishable kind to keep, nothing worth fretting about. They were away catching salmon, our Indians said. All the Indian villages hereabouts are thus abandoned at regular periods every year, just as a tent is left for a day, while they repair to fishing, berrying and hunting stations, occupying each in succession for a week or two at a time, coming and going from the main, substantially built villages. Then, after their summer's work is done, the winter supply of salmon dried and packed, fish-oil and seal-oil stored in boxes, berries and spruce bark pressed into cakes, their trading-trips completed, and the year's stock of quarrels with the neighbouring tribe patched up in some way, they devote themselves to feasting, dancing and hootchenoo drinking. The Takus, once a powerful and warlike tribe, were at this time, like most of the neighbouring tribes, whiskied nearly out of existence. They had a larger village on the Taku River, but, according to the census taken that year by the missionaries, they numbered only 269 in all – 109 men, 79 women, and 81 children, figures that show the vanishing condition of the tribe at a glance.

Our Indians wanted to camp for the night in one of the deserted houses, but I urged them on into the clean wilderness until dark, when we landed on a rocky beach fringed with devil's-clubs, greatly to the disgust of our crew. We had to make the best of it, however, as it was too dark to seek farther. After supper was accomplished among the boulders, they retired to the canoe, which they anchored a little way out, beyond low tide, while Mr Young and I at the expense of a good deal of scrambling and panax stinging, discovered a spot on which we managed to sleep.

The next morning, about two hours after leaving our thorny camp, we rounded a great mountain rock nearly a mile in height and entered the Taku fiord. It is about eighteen miles long and from three to five miles wide, and extends directly back into the heart of the mountains, draining hundreds of glaciers and streams. The ancient glacier that formed it was far too deep and broad and too little concentrated to erode one of those narrow canyons, usually so impressive in sculpture and architecture, but it is all the more interesting on this account when the grandeur of the ice work accomplished is recognized. This fiord, more than any other I have examined, explains the formation of the wonderful system of channels extending along the coast from Puget Sound to about latitude 59 degrees, for it is a marked portion of the system – a branch of Stephens Passage. Its trends and general sculpture are as distinctly glacial as those of the narrowest fiord, while the largest tributaries of the great glacier that occupied it are still in existence. I counted some forty-five altogether, big and little, in sight from the canoe in sailing up the middle of the fiord. Three of them, drawing their sources from magnificent groups of snowy mountains, came down to the level of the sea and formed a glorious spectacle. The middle one of the three belongs to the first class, pouring its majestic flood, shattered and crevassed, directly into the fiord, and crowding about twenty-five square miles of it with bergs. The next below it also sends off bergs occasionally, though a narrow strip of glacial detritus separates it from the tide-water. That forenoon a large mass fell from it, damming its draining stream, which at length broke the dam, and the resulting flood swept forward thousands of small bergs across the mud-flat into the fiord. In a short time all was quiet again; the flood-waters receded, leaving only a large blue scar on the front of the glacier and stranded bergs on the moraine flat to tell the tale.

These two glaciers are about equal in size – two miles wide – and their fronts are only about a mile and a half apart. While I sat sketching them from a point among the drifting icebergs where I could see far back into the heart of their distant fountains, two Taku seal-hunters, father and son, came gliding toward us in an extremely small canoe. Coming alongside with a goodnatured 'Sagh-a-ya', they inquired who we were, our objects, etc., and gave us information about the river, their village, and two other large glaciers that descend nearly to the sea-level a few miles up the river canyon. Crouching in their little shell of a boat among the great bergs, with paddle and barbed spear, they formed a picture as arctic and remote from anything to be found in civilization as ever was sketched for us by the explorers of the Far North.

Making our way through the crowded bergs to the extreme head of the fiord, we entered the mouth of the river, but were soon compelled to turn back on account of the strength of the current. The Taku River is a large stream, nearly a mile wide at the mouth, and, like the Stickeen, Chilcat and Chilcoot, draws its sources from far inland, crossing the mountain-chain from the interior through a majestic canyon, and draining a multitude of glaciers on its way.

The Taku Indians, like the Chilcats, with a keen appreciation of the advantages of their position for trade, hold possession of the river and compel the Indians of the interior to accept their services as middle-men, instead of allowing them to trade directly with the whites.

When we were baffled in our attempt to ascend the river, the day was nearly done, and we began to seek a camp-ground. After sailing two or three miles along the left side of the fiord, we were so fortunate as to find a small nook described by the two Indians, where firewood was abundant, and where we could drag our canoe up the bank beyond reach of the berg-waves. Here we were safe, with a fine outlook across the fiord to the great glaciers and near enough to see the birth of the icebergs and the wonderful commotion they make, and hear their wild, roaring rejoicing. The sunset sky seemed to have been painted for this one mountain mansion, fitting it like a ceiling. After the fiord was in shadow the level sunbeams continued to pour through the miles of bergs with ravishing beauty, reflecting and refracting the purple light like cut crystal. Then all save the tips of the highest became dead white. These, too, were speedily quenched, the glowing points vanishing like stars sinking beneath the horizon. And after the shadows had crept higher, submerging the glaciers and the ridges between them, the divine alpenglow still lingered on their highest fountain peaks as they stood transfigured in glorious array. Now the last of the twilight purple has vanished, the stars begin to shine, and all trace of the day is gone. Looking across the fiord the water seems perfectly black, and the two great glaciers are seen stretching dim and ghostly into the shadowy mountains now darkly massed against the starry sky.

Next morning it was raining hard, everything looked dismal, and on the way down the fiord a growling head wind battered the rain in our faces, but we held doggedly on and by 10 am got out of the fiord into Stephens Passage. A breeze sprung up in our favour that swept us bravely on across the passage and around the end of Admiralty Island by dark. We camped in a boggy hollow on a bluff among scraggy, usnea-bearded spruces. The rain, bitterly cold and driven by a stormy wind, thrashed us well while we floundered in the stumpy bog trying to make a fire and supper.

When daylight came we found our camp-ground a very savage place. How we reached it and established ourselves in the thick darkness it would be difficult to tell. We crept along the shore a few miles against strong head winds, then hoisted sail and steered straight across Lynn Canal to the mainland, which we followed without great difficulty, the wind having moderated toward evening. Near the entrance to Icy Strait we met a Hoona who had seen us last year and who seemed glad to see us. He gave us two salmon, and we made him happy with tobacco and then pushed on and camped near Sitka Jack's deserted village.

Though the wind was still ahead next morning, we made about twenty miles before sundown and camped on the west end of Farewell Island. We bumped against a hidden rock and sprung a small leak that was easily stopped with resin. The salmon-berries were ripe. While climbing a bluff for a view of our course, I discovered moneses, one of my favourites and saw many well-travelled deer-trails, though the island is cut off from the mainland and other islands by at least five or six miles of icy, berg-encumbered water.

We got under way early next day – a grey, cloudy morning with rain and wind. Fair and head winds were about evenly balanced throughout the day. Tides run fast here, like great rivers. We rowed and paddled around Point Wimbledon against both wind and tide, creeping close to the feet of the huge, bold rocks of the north wall of Cross Sound, which here were very steep and awe-inspiring as the heavy swells from the open sea coming in past Cape Spencer dashed white against them, tossing our frail canoe up and down lightly as a feather. The point reached by vegetation shows that the surf dashes up to a height of about seventy-five or a hundred feet. We were awestricken and began to fear that we might be upset should the ocean waves rise still higher. But little Stickeen seemed to enjoy the storm, and gazed at the foam-wreathed cliffs like a dreamy, comfortable tourist admiring the sunset. We reached the mouth of Taylor Bay about two or three o'clock in the afternoon, when we had a view of the open ocean before we entered the bay. Many large bergs from Glacier Bay were seen drifting out to sea past Cape Spencer. We reached the head of the fiord now called Taylor Bay at five o'clock and camped near an immense glacier with a front about three miles wide stretching across from wall to wall. No icebergs are discharged from it, as it is separated from the water of the fiord at high tide by a low, smooth mass of outspread, overswept moraine material, netted with torrents and small shallow rills from the glacier-front, with here and there a lakelet, and patches of yellow mosses and garden spots bright with epilobium, saxifrage, grass-tufts, sedges and creeping willows on the higher ground. But only the mosses were sufficiently abundant to make conspicuous masses of colour to relieve the dull slaty grey of the glacial mud and gravel. The front of the glacier, like all those which do not discharge icebergs, is rounded like a brow, smooth-looking in general views, but cleft and furrowed, nevertheless, with chasms and grooves in which the light glows and shimmers in glorious beauty.

The granite walls of the fiord, though very high, are not deeply sculptured. Only a few deep side canyons with trees, bushes, grassy and flowery spots interrupt their massive simplicity, leaving but few of the cliffs absolutely sheer and bare like those of Yosemite, Sum Dum or Taku. One of the side canyons is on the left side of the fiord, the other on the right, the tributaries of the former leading over by a narrow tide-channel to the bay next to the eastward, and by a short portage over into a lake into which pours a branch glacier from the great glacier. Still another branch from the main glacier turns to the right. Counting all three of these separate fronts, the width of this great Taylor Bay Glacier must be about seven or eight miles.

While camp was being made, Hunter Joe climbed the eastern wall in search of wild mutton, but found none. He fell in with a brown bear, however, and got a shot at it, but nothing more. Mr Young and I crossed the moraine slope, splashing through pools and streams up to the ice-wall, and made the interesting discovery that the glacier had been advancing of late years, ploughing up and shoving forward moraine soil that had been deposited long ago, and overwhelming and grinding and carrying away the forests on the sides and front of the glacier. Though not now sending off icebergs, the front is probably far below sea-level at the bottom, thrust forward beneath its wave-washed moraine.

Along the base of the mountain-wall we found abundance of salmonberries, the largest measuring an inch and a half in diameter. Strawberries, too, are found hereabouts. Some which visiting Indians brought us were as fine in size and colour and flavour as any I ever saw anywhere. After wandering and wondering an hour or two, admiring the magnificent rock and crystal scenery about us, we returned to camp at sundown, planning a grand excursion for the morrow.

I set off early in the morning of 30 August before anyone else in camp had stirred, not waiting for breakfast, but only eating a piece of bread. I had intended getting a cup of coffee, but a wild storm was blowing and calling, and I could not wait. Running out against the rain-laden gale and turning to catch my breath I saw that the minister's little dog had left his bed in the tent and was coming boring through the storm, evidently determined to follow me. I told him to go back, that such a day as this had nothing for him.

'Go back', I shouted, 'and get your breakfast'. But he simply stood with his head down, and when I began to urge my way again, looking around, I saw he was still following me. So I at last told him to come on if he must and gave him a piece of the bread I had in my pocket.

Instead of falling, the rain, mixed with misty shreds of clouds, was flying in level sheets, and the wind was roaring as I had never heard wind roar before. Over the icy levels and over the woods, on the mountains, over the jagged rocks and spires and chasms of the glacier it boomed and moaned and roared, filling the fiord in even, grey, structureless gloom, inspiring and awful. I first struggled up in the face of the blast to the east end of the ice-wall, where a patch of forest had been carried away by the glacier when it was advancing. I noticed a few stumps well out on the moraine flat, showing that its present bare, raw condition was not the condition of fifty or a hundred years ago. In front of this part of the glacier there is a small moraine lake about half a mile in length, around the margin of which are a considerable number of trees standing knee-deep, and of course dead. This also is a result of the recent advance of the ice.

Pushing up through the ragged edge of the woods on the left margin of the glacier, the storm seemed to increase in violence, so that it was difficult to draw breath in facing it; therefore I took shelter back of a tree to enjoy it and wait, hoping that it would at last somewhat abate. Here the glacier, descending over an abrupt rock, falls forward in grand cascades, while a stream swollen by the rain was now a torrent – wind, rain, ice-torrent and water-torrent in one grand symphony.

At length the storm seemed to abate somewhat, and I took off my heavy rubber boots, with which I had waded the glacial streams on the flat, and laid them with my overcoat on a log, where I might find them on my way back, knowing I would be drenched anyhow, and firmly tied my mountain shoes, tightened my belt, shouldered my ice-axe, and, thus free and ready for rough work, pushed on, regardless as possible of mere rain. Making my way up a steep granite slope, its projecting polished bosses encumbered here and there by boulders and the ground and bruised ruins of the ragged edge of the forest that had been uprooted by the glacier during its recent advance, I traced the side of the glacier for two or three miles, finding everywhere evidence of its having encroached on the woods, which here run back along its edge for fifteen or twenty miles. Under the projecting edge of this vast ice-river I could see down beneath it to a depth of fifty feet or so in some places, where logs and branches were being crushed to pulp, some of it almost fine enough for paper, though most of it stringy and coarse.

After thus tracing the margin of the glacier for three or four miles, I chopped steps and climbed to the top, and as far as the eye could reach, the nearly level glacier stretched indefinitely away in the grey cloudy sky, a prairie of ice. The wind was now almost moderate, though rain continued to fall, which I did not mind, but a tendency to mist in the drooping draggled clouds made me hesitate about attempting to cross to the opposite shore. Although the distance was only six or seven miles, no traces at this time could be seen of the mountains on the other side, and in case the sky should grow darker, as it seemed inclined to do, I feared that when I got out of sight of land and perhaps into a maze of crevasses I might find difficulty in winning a way back.

Lingering awhile and sauntering about in sight of the shore, I found this eastern side of the glacier remarkably free from large crevasses. Nearly all I met were so narrow I could step across them almost anywhere, while the few wide ones were easily avoided by going up or down along their sides to where they narrowed. The dismal cloud ceiling showed rifts here and there, and, thus encouraged, I struck out for the west shore, aiming to strike it five or six miles above the front wall, cautiously taking compass bearings at short intervals to enable me to find my way back should the weather darken again with mist or rain or snow. The structure lines of the glacier itself were, however, my main guide. All went well. I came to a deeply furrowed section about two miles in width where I had to zigzag in long, tedious tacks and make narrow doublings, tracing the edges of wide longitudinal furrows and chasms until I could find a bridge connecting their sides, oftentimes making the direct distance ten times over. The walking was good of its kind, however, and by dint of patient doubling and axe-work on dangerous places, I gained the opposite shore in about three hours, the width of the glacier at this point being about seven miles. Occasionally, while making my way, the clouds lifted a little, revealing a few bald, rough mountains sunk to the throat in the broad, icy sea which encompassed them on all sides, sweeping on forever and forever as we count them, wearing them away, giving them the shape they are destined to take when in the fullness of time they shall be parts of new landscapes.

Ere I lost sight of the east-side mountains, those on the west came in sight, so that holding my course was easy, and, though making haste, I halted for a moment to gaze down into the beautiful pure blue crevasses and to drink at the lovely blue wells, the most beautiful of all Nature's water-basins, or at the rills and streams outspread over the ice-land prairie, never ceasing to admire their lovely colour and music as they glided and swirled in their blue crystal channels and potholes, and the rumbling of the moulins, or mills, where streams poured into blue-walled pits of unknown depth, some of them as regularly circular as if bored with augers. Interesting, too, were the cascades over blue cliffs, where streams fell into crevasses or slid almost noiselessly down slopes so smooth and frictionless their motion was concealed. The round or oval wells, however, from one to ten feet wide, and from one to twenty or thirty feet deep, were perhaps the most beautiful of all, the water so pure as to be almost invisible. My widest view did not probably exceed fifteen miles, the rain and mist making distances seem greater.

On reaching the farther shore and tracing it a few miles to northward, I found a large portion of the glacier-current sweeping out westward in a bold and beautiful curve around the shoulder of a mountain as if going direct to the open sea. Leaving the main trunk, it breaks into a magnificent uproar of pinnacles and spires and up-heaving, splashing wave-shaped masses, a crystal cataract incomparably greater and wilder than a score of Niagaras.

Tracing its channel three or four miles, I found that it fell into a lake, which it fills with bergs. The front of this branch of the glacier is about three miles wide. I first took the lake to be the head of an arm of the sea, but, going down to its shore and tasting it, I found it fresh, and by my aneroid perhaps less than a hundred feet above sea-level. It is probably separated from the sea only by a moraine dam. I had not time to go around its shores, as it was now near five o'clock and I was about fifteen miles from camp, and I had to make haste to recross the glacier before dark, which would come on about eight o'clock. I therefore made haste up to the main glacier, and, shaping my course by compass and the structure lines of the ice, set off from the land out on to the grand crystal prairie again. All was so silent and so concentrated, owing to the low dragging mist, the beauty close about me was all the more keenly felt, though tinged with a dim sense of danger, as if coming events were casting shadows. I was soon out of sight of land, and the evening dusk that on cloudy days precedes the real night gloom came stealing on and only ice was in sight, and the only sounds, save the low rumbling of the mills and the rattle of falling stones at long intervals, were the low, terribly earnest moanings of the wind or distant waterfalls coming through the thickening gloom. After two hours of hard work I came to a maze of crevasses of appalling depth and width which could not be passed apparently either up or down. I traced them with firm nerve developed by the danger, making wide jumps, poising cautiously on dizzy edges after cutting footholds, taking wide crevasses at a grand leap at once frightful and inspiring. Many a mile was thus travelled, mostly up and down the glacier, making but little real headway, running much of the time as the danger of having to pass the night on the ice became more and more imminent. This I could do, though with the weather and my rain-soaked condition it would be trying at best. In treading the mazes of this crevassed section I had frequently to cross bridges that were only knife-edges for twenty or thirty feet, cutting off the sharp tops and leaving them flat so that little Stickeen could follow me. These I had to straddle, cutting off the top as I progressed and hitching gradually ahead like a boy riding a rail fence. All this time the little dog followed me bravely, never hesitating on the brink of any crevasse that I had jumped, but now that it was becoming dark and the crevasses became more troublesome, he followed close at my heels instead of scampering far and wide, where the ice was at all smooth, as he had in the forenoon. No land was now in sight. The mist fell lower and darker and snow began to fly. I could not see far enough up and down the glacier to judge how best to work out of the bewildering labyrinth, and how hard I tried while there was yet hope of reaching camp that night! A hope which was fast growing dim like the sky. After dark, on such ground, to keep from freezing, I could only jump up and down until morning on a piece of flat ice between the crevasses, dance to the boding music of the winds and waters, and as I was already tired and hungry I would be in bad condition for such ice work. Many times I was put to my mettle, but with a firm-braced nerve, all the more unflinching as the dangers thickened, I worked out of that terrible ice-web, and with blood fairly up Stickeen and I ran over common danger without fatigue. Our very hardest trial was in getting across the very last of the sliver bridges. After examining the first of the two widest crevasses, I followed its edge half a mile or so up and down and discovered that its narrowest spot was about eight feet wide, which was the limit of what I was able to jump. Moreover, the side I was on – that is, the west side – was about a foot higher than the other, and I feared that in case I should be stopped by a still wider impassable crevasse ahead that I would hardly be able to take back that jump from its lower side. The ice beyond, however, as far as I could see it, looked temptingly smooth. Therefore, after carefully making a socket for my foot on the rounded brink, I jumped, but found that I had nothing to spare and more than ever dreaded having to retrace my way. Little Stickeen jumped this, however, without apparently taking a second look at it, and we ran ahead joyfully over smooth, level ice, hoping we were now leaving all danger behind us. But hardly had we gone a hundred or two yards when to our dismay we found ourselves on the very widest of all the longitudinal crevasses we had yet encountered. It was about forty feet wide. I ran anxiously up the side of it to northward eagerly hoping that I could get around its head, but my worst fears were realized when at a distance of about a mile or less it ran into the crevasse that I had just jumped. I then ran down the edge for a mile or more below the point where I had first met it, and found that its lower end also united with the crevasse I had jumped, showing dismally that we were on an island two or three hundred yards wide and about two miles long and the only way of escape from this island was by turning back and jumping again that crevasse which I dreaded, or venturing ahead across the giant crevasse by the very worst of the sliver bridges I had ever seen. It was so badly weathered and melted down that it formed a knife-edge, and extended across from side to side in a low, drooping curve like that made by a loose rope attached at each end at the same height. But the worst difficulty was that the ends of the down-curving sliver were attached to the sides at a depth of about eight or ten feet below the surface of the glacier. Getting down to the end of the bridge, and then after crossing it getting up the other side, seemed hardly possible. However, I decided to dare the dangers of the fearful sliver rather than to attempt to retrace my steps. Accordingly I dug a low groove in the rounded edge for my knees to rest in and, leaning over, began to cut a narrow foothold on the steep, smooth side. When I was doing this, Stickeen came up behind me, pushed his head over my shoulder, looked into the crevasses and along the narrow knife-edge, then turned and looked in my face, muttering and whining as if trying to say, 'Surely you are not going down there'. I said, 'Yes, Stickeen, this is the only way'. He then began to cry and ran wildly along the rim of the crevasse, searching for a better way, then, returning baffled, of course, he came behind me and lay down and cried louder and louder.

After getting down one step I cautiously stooped and cut another and another in succession until I reached the point where the sliver was attached to the wall. There, cautiously balancing, I chipped down the upcurved end of the bridge until I had formed a small level platform about a foot wide, then, bending forward, got astride of the end of the sliver, steadied myself with my knees, then cut off the top of the sliver, hitching myself forward an inch or two at a time, leaving it about four inches wide for Stickeen. Arrived at the farther end of the sliver, which was about seventy-five feet long, I chipped another little platform on its upcurved end, cautiously rose to my feet, and with infinite pains cut narrow notch steps and finger-holds in the wall and finally got safely across. All this dreadful time poor little Stickeen was crying as if his heart was broken, and when I called to him in as reassuring a voice as I could muster, he only cried the louder, as if trying to say that he never, never could get down there – the only time that the brave little fellow appeared to know what danger was. After going away as if I was leaving him, he still howled and cried without venturing to try to follow me. Returning to the edge of the crevasse, I told him that I must go, that he could come if he only tried, and finally in despair he hushed his cries, slid his little feet slowly down into my footsteps out on the big sliver, walked slowly and cautiously along the sliver as if holding his breath, while the snow was falling and the wind was moaning and threatening to blow him off. When he arrived at the foot of the slope below me, I was kneeling on the brink ready to assist him in case he should be unable to reach the top. He looked up along the row of notched steps I had made, as if fixing them in his mind, then with a nervous spring he whizzed up and passed me out on to the level ice, and ran and cried and barked and rolled about fairly hysterical in the sudden revulsion from the depth of despair to triumphant joy. I tried to catch him and pet him and tell him how good and brave he was, but he would not be caught. He ran round and round, swirling like autumn leaves in an eddy, lay down and rolled head over heels. I told him we still had far to go and that we must now stop all nonsense and get off the ice before dark. I knew by the ice-lines that every step was now taking me nearer the shore and soon it came in sight. The headland four or five miles back from the front, covered with spruce trees, loomed faintly but surely through the mist and light fall of snow not more than two miles away. The ice now proved good all the way across, and we reached the lateral moraine just at dusk, then with trembling limbs, now that the danger was over, we staggered and tumbled down the bouldery edge of the glacier and got over the dangerous rocks by the cascades while yet a faint light lingered. We were safe, and then, too, came limp weariness such as no ordinary work ever produces, however hard it may be. Wearily we stumbled down through the woods, over logs and and brush and roots, devil's-clubs pricking us at every faint blundering tumble. At last we got out on the smooth mud slope with only a mile of slow but sure dragging of weary limbs to camp. The Indians had been firing guns to guide me and had a fine supper and fire ready, though fearing they would be compelled to seek us in the morning, a care not often applied to me. Stickeen and I were too tired to eat much, and, strange to say, too tired to sleep. Both of us, springing up in the night again and again, fancied we were still on that dreadful ice bridge in the shadow of death.

Nevertheless, we arose next morning in newness of life. Never before had rocks and ice and trees seemed so beautiful and wonderful, even the cold, biting rain-storm that was blowing seemed full of loving kindness, wonderful compensation for all that we had endured, and we sailed down the bay through the grey, driving rain rejoicing.

CHAPTER SIXTEEN

Glacier Bay

WHILE STICKEEN and I were away, a Hoona, one of the head men of the tribe, paid Mr Young a visit, and presented him with porpoise meat and berries and much interesting information. He naturally expected a return visit, and when we called at his house, a mile or two down the fiord, he said his wives were out in the rain gathering fresh berries to complete a feast prepared for us. We remained, however, only a few minutes, for I was not aware of this arrangement or of Mr Young's promise until after leaving the house. Anxiety to get around Cape Wimbeldon was the cause of my haste, fearing the storm might increase. On account of this ignorance, no apologies were offered him, and the upshot was that the good Hoona became very angry. We succeeded, however, in the evening of the same day, in explaining our haste, and by sincere apologies and presents made peace.

After a hard struggle we got around stormy Wimbeldon and into the next fiord to the northward (Klunastucksana – Dundas Bay). A cold, drenching rain was falling, darkening but not altogether hiding its extraordinary beauty, made up of lovely reaches and side fiords, feathery headlands and islands, beautiful every one and charmingly collocated. But how it rained, and how cold it was, and how weary we were pulling most of the time against the wind! The branches of this bay are so deep and so numerous that, with the rain and low clouds concealing the mountain landmarks, we could hardly make out the main trends. While groping and gazing among the islands through the misty rain and clouds, we discovered wisps of smoke at the foot of a sheltering rock in front of a mountain, where a choir of cascades were chanting their rain songs. Gladly we made for this camp, which proved to belong to a rare old Hoona sub-chief, so tall and wide and dignified in demeanour he looked grand even in the sloppy weather, and every inch a chief in spite of his bare legs and the old shirt and draggled, ragged blanket in which he was dressed. He was given to much handshaking, gripping hard, holding on and looking you gravely in the face while most emphatically speaking in Thlinkit, not a word of which we understood until interpreter John came to our help. He turned from one to the other of us, declaring, as John interpreted, that our presence did him good like food and fire, that he would welcome white men, especially teachers, and that he and all his people compared to ourselves were only children. When Mr Young informed him that a missionary was about to be sent to his people, he said he would call them all together four times and explain that a teacher and preacher were coming and that they therefore must put away all foolishness and prepare their hearts to receive them and their words. He then introduced his three children, one a naked lad five or six years old who, as he fondly assured us, would soon be a chief, and later to his wife, an intelligent-looking woman of whom he seemed proud. When we arrived she was out at the foot of the cascade mountain gathering salmon-berries. She came in dripping and loaded. A few of the fine berries saved for the children she presented, proudly and fondly beginning with the youngest, whose only clothing was a nose-ring and a string of beads. She was lightly apparelled in a cotton gown and bit of blanket, thoroughly bedraggled, but after unloading her berries she retired with a dry calico gown around the corner of a rock and soon returned fresh as a daisy and with becoming dignity took her place by the fireside. Soon two other berry-laden women came in, seemingly enjoying the rain like the bushes and trees. They put on little clothing so that they may be the more easily dried, and as for the children, a thin shirt of sheeting is the most they encumber themselves with, and get wet and half dry without seeming to notice it while we shiver with two or three dry coats. They seem to prefer being naked. The men also wear but little in wet weather. When they go out for all day they put on a single blanket, but in choring around camp, getting firewood, cooking, or looking after their precious canvas, they seldom wear anything, braving wind and rain in utter nakedness to avoid the bother of drying clothes. It is a rare sight to see the children bringing in big chunks of firewood on their shoulders, balancing in crossing boulders with firmly set bow-legs and bulging back muscles.

We gave Ka-hood-oo-shough, the old chief, some tobacco and rice and coffee, and pitched our tent near his hut among tall grass. Soon after our arrival the Taylor Bay sub-chief came in from the opposite direction from ours, telling us that he came through a cut-off passage not on our chart. As stated above, we took pains to conciliate him and soothe his hurt feelings. Our words and gifts, he said, had warmed his sore heart and made him glad and comfortable.

The view down the bay among the islands was, I thought, the finest of this kind of scenery that I had yet observed.

The weather continued cold and rainy. Nevertheless Mr Young and I and our crew, together with one of the Hoonas, an old man who-acted as guide, left camp to explore one of the upper arms of the bay, where we were told there was a large glacier. We managed to push the canoe several miles up the stream that drains the glacier to a point where the swift current was divided among rocks and the banks were overhung with alders and willows. I left the canoe and pushed up the right bank past a magnificent waterfall some twelve hundred feet high, and over the shoulder of a mountain, until I secured a good view of the lower part of the glacier. It is probably a lobe of the Taylor Bay or Brady Glacier.

On our return to camp, thoroughly drenched and cold, the old chief came to visit us, apparently as wet and cold as ourselves.

'I have been thinking of you all day', he said, 'and pitying you, knowing how miserable you were, and as soon as I saw your canoe coming back I was ashamed to think that I had been sitting warm and dry at my fire while you were out in the storm; therefore I made haste to strip off my dry clothing and put on these wet rags to share your misery and show how much I love you.'

I had another long talk with Ka-hood-oo-shough the next day.

'I am not able', he said, 'to tell you how much good your words have done me. Your words are good, and they are strong words. Some of my people are foolish, and when they make their salmon-traps they do not take care to tie the poles firmly together, and when the big rain-floods come the traps break and are washed away because the people who made them are foolish people. But your words are strong words and when storms come to try them they will stand the storms.'

There was much hand shaking as we took our leave and assurances of eternal friendship. The grand old man stood on the shore watching us and waving farewell until we were out of sight.

We now steered for the Muir Glacier and arrived at the front on the east side the evening of the third, and camped on the end of the moraine, where there was a small stream. Captain Tyeen was inclined to keep at a safe distance from the tremendous threatening cliffs of the disharging wall. After a good deal of urging he ventured within half a mile of them, on the east side of the fiord, where with Mr Young I went ashore to seek a camp-ground on the moraine, leaving the Indians in the canoe. In a few minutes after we landed a huge berg sprung aloft with awful commotion, and the frightened Indians incontinently fled down the fiord, plying their paddles with admirable energy in the tossing waves until a safe harbour was reached around the south end of the moraine. I found a good place for a camp in a slight hollow where a few spruce stumps afforded firewood. But all efforts to get Tyeen out of his harbour failed. 'Nobody knew', he said, 'how far the angry ice mountain could throw waves to break his canoe'. Therefore I had my bedding and some provisions carried to my stump camp, where I could watch the bergs as they were discharged and get night views of the brow of the glacier and its sheer jagged face all the way across from side to side of the channel. One night the water was luminous and the surge from discharging icebergs churned the water into silver fire, a glorious sight in the darkness. I also went back up the east side of the glacier five or six miles and ascended a mountain between its first two eastern tributaries, which, though covered with grass near the top, was exceedingly steep and difficult. A bulging ridge near the top I discovered was formed of ice, a remnant of the glacier when it stood at this elevation which had been preserved by moraine material and later by a thatch of dwarf bushes and grass.

Next morning at daybreak I pushed eagerly back over the comparatively smooth eastern margin of the glacier to see as much as possible of the upper fountain region. About five miles back from the front I climbed a mountain twenty-five hundred feet high, from the flowery summit of which, the day being clear, the vast glacier and its principal branches were displayed in one magnificent view. Instead of a stream of ice winding down a mountain-walled valley like the largest of the Swiss glaciers, the Muir looks like a broad undulating prairie streaked with medial moraines and gashed with crevasses, surrounded by numberless mountains from which flow its many tributary glaciers. There are seven main tributaries from ten to twenty miles long and from two to six miles wide where they enter the trunk, each of them fed by many secondary tributaries; so that the whole number of branches, great and small, pouring from the mountain fountains perhaps number upward of two hundred, not counting the smallest. The area drained by this one grand glacier can hardly be less than seven or eight hundred miles, and probably contains as much ice as all the eleven hundred Swiss glaciers combined. Its length from the frontal wall back to the head of its farthest fountain seemed to be about forty or fifty miles, and the width just below the confluence of the main tributaries about twenty-five miles. Though apparently motionless as the mountains, it flows on forever, the speed varying in every part with the seasons, but mostly with the depth of the current, and the declivity, smoothness and directness of the different portions of the basin. The flow of the central cascading portion near the front, as determined by Professor Reid, is at the rate of from two and a half to five inches an hour, or from five to ten feet a day. A strip of the main trunk about a mile in width, extending along the eastern margin about fourteen miles to a lake filled with bergs, has so little motion and is so little interrupted by crevasses, a hundred horsemen might ride abreast over it without encountering very much difficulty.

But far the greater portion of the vast expanse looking smooth in the distance is torn and crumpled into a bewildering network of hummocky ridges and blades, separated by yawning gulfs and crevasses, so that the explorer, crossing it from shore to shore, must always have a hard time. In hollow spots here and there in the heart of the icy wilderness are small lakelets fed by swift-glancing streams that flow without friction in blue shining channels, making delightful melody, singing and ringing in silvery tones of peculiar sweetness, radiant crystals like flowers ineffably fine growing in dazzling beauty along their banks. Few, however, will be likely to enjoy them. Fortunately to most travellers the thundering ice-wall, while comfortably accessible, is also the most strikingly interesting portion of the glacier.

The mountains about the great glacier were also seen from this standpoint in exceedingly grand and telling views, ranged and grouped in glorious array. Along the valleys of the main tributarie to the north-westward I saw far into their shadowy depths, one noble peak in its snowy robes appearing beyond another in fine perspective. One of the most remarkable of them, fashioned like a superb crown with delicately fluted sides, stands in the middle of the second main tributary, counting from left to right. To the westward the magnificent Fairweather Range is displayed in all its glory, lifting its peaks and glaciers into the blue sky. Mount Fairweather, though not the highest, is the noblest and most majestic in port and architecture of all the sky-dwelling company. La Perouse, at the south end of the range, is also a magnificent mountain, symmetrically peaked and sculptured, and wears its robes of snow and glaciers in noble style. Lituya, as seen from here, is an immense tower, severely plain and massive. It makes a fine and terrible and lonely impression. Crillon, though the loftiest of all (being nearly sixteen thousand feet high), presents no well-marked features. Its ponderous glaciers have ground it away into long, curling ridges until, from this point of view, it resembles a huge twisted shell. The lower summits about the Muir Glacier, like this one, the first that I climbed, are richly adorned and enlivened with flowers, though they make but a faint show in general views. Lines and dashes of bright green appear on the lower slopes as one approaches them from the glacier, and a fainter green tinge may be noticed on the subordinate summits at a height of two thousand or three thousand feet. The lower are mostly alder bushes and the topmost a lavish profusion of flowering plants, chiefly cassiope, vaccinium, pyrola, erigeron, gentiana, campanula, anemone, larkspur and columbine, with a few grasses and ferns. Of these cassiope is at once the commonest and the most beautiful and influential. In some places its delicate stems make mattresses more than a foot thick over several acres, while the bloom is so abundant that a single handful plucked at random contains hundreds of its pale pink bells. The very thought of this Alaska garden is a joyful exhilaration. Though the storm-beaten ground it is growing on is nearly half a mile high, the glacier centuries ago flowed over it as a river flows over a boulder; but out of all the cold darkness and glacial crushing and grinding comes this warm, abounding beauty and life to teach us that what we in our faithless ignorance and fear call destruction is creation finer and finer.

When night was approaching I scrambled down out of my blessed garden to the glacier, and returned to my lonely camp, and, getting some coffee and bread, again went up the moraine to the east end of the great ice-wall. It is about three miles long, but the length of the jagged, berg-producing portion that stretches across the fiord from side to side like a huge green-and-blue barrier is only about two miles and rises above the water to a height of from two hundred and fifty to three hundred feet. Soundings made by Captain Carroll show that seven hundred and twenty feet of the wall is below the surface, and a third unmeasured portion is buried beneath the moraine detritus deposited at the foot of it. Therefore, were the water and rocky detritus cleared away, a sheer precipice of ice would be presented nearly two miles long and more than a thousand feet high. Seen from a distance, as you come up the fiord, it seems comparatively regular in form, but it is far otherwise; bold, jagged capes jut forward into the fiord, alternating with deep re-entering angles and craggy hollows with plain bastions, while the top is roughened with innumerable spires and pyramids and sharp hacked blades leaning and toppling or cutting straight into the sky.

The number of bergs given off varies somewhat with the weather and the tides, the average being about one every five or six minutes, counting only those that roar loud enough to make themselves heard at a distance of two or three miles. The very largest, however, may under favourable conditions be heard ten miles or even farther. When a large mass sinks from the upper fissured portion of the wall, there is first a keen, prolonged, thundering roar, which slowly subsides into a low muttering growl, followed by numerous smaller grating clashing sounds from the agitated bergs that dance in the waves about the newcomer as if in welcome; and these again are followed by the swash and roar of the waves that are raised and hurled up the beach against the moraines. But the largest and most beautiful of the bergs, instead of thus falling from the upper weathered portion of the wall, rise from the submerged portion with a still grander commotion, springing with tremendous voice and gestures nearly to the top of the wall, tons of water streaming like hair down their sides, plunging and rising again and again before they finally settle in perfect poise, free at last, after having formed part of the slow-crawling glacier for centuries. And as we contemplate their history, as they sail calmly away down the fiord to the sea, how wonderful it seems that ice formed from pressed snow on the far-off mountains two or three hundred years ago should still be pure and lovely in colour after all its travel and toil in the rough mountain quarries, grinding and fashioning the features of predestined landscapes.

When sunshine is sifting through the midst of the multitude of icebergs that fill the fiord and through the jets of radiant spray ever rising from the tremendous dashing and splashing of the falling and upspringing bergs, the effect is indescribably glorious. Glorious, too, are the shows they make in the night when the moon and stars are shining. The berg-thunder seems far louder than by day, and the projecting buttresses seem higher as they stand forward in the pale light, relieved by gloomy hollows, while the new-born bergs are dimly seen, crowned with faint lunar rainbows in the up-dashing spray. But it is in the darkest nights when storms are blowing and the waves are phosphorescent that the most impressive displays are made. Then the long range of ice-bluffs is plainly seen stretching through the gloom in wierd, unearthly splendour, luminous wave foam dashing against every bluff and drifting berg; and ever and anon amid all this wild auroral splendour some huge new-born berg dashes the living water into yet brighter foam, and the streaming torrents pouring from its sides are worn as robes of light, while they roar in awful accord with the winds and waves, deep calling unto deep, glacier to glacier, from fiord to fiord over all the wonderful bay.

After spending a few days here, we struck across to the main Hoona village on the south side of Icy Strait, thence by a long cut-off with one short portage to Chatham Strait, and thence down through Peril Strait, sailing all night, hoping to catch the mail steamer at Sitka. We arrived at the head of the strait about daybreak. The tide was falling, and rushing down with the swift current as if descending a majestic cataract was a memorable experience. We reached Sitka the same night, and there I paid and discharged my crew, making allowance for a couple of days or so for the journey back home to Fort Wrangell, while I boarded the steamer for Portland and thus ended my exploration for this season.

Part 3

The Trip of 1890

CHAPTER SEVENTEEN

In Camp at Glacier Bay

I LEFT San Francisco for Glacier Bay on the steamer City of Pueblo, 14 June 1890, at 10 am, this being my third trip to southeastern Alaska and fourth to Alaska, including northern and western Alaska as far as Unalaska and Pt Barrow and the northeastern coast of Siberia. The bar at the Golden Gate was smooth, the weather cool and pleasant. The redwoods in sheltered coves approach the shore closely, their dwarfed and shorn tops appearing here and there in ravines along the coast up to Oregon. The wind-swept hills, beaten with scud, are of course bare of trees. Along the Oregon and Washington coast the trees get nearer the sea, for spruce and contorted pine endure the briny winds better than the redwoods. We took the inside passage between the shore and Race Rocks, a long range of islets on which many a good ship has been wrecked. The breakers from the deep Pacific, driven by the gale, made a glorious display of foam on the bald islet rocks, sending spray over the tops of some of them a hundred feet high or more in sublime, curving jagged-edged and flame-shaped sheets. The gestures of these upspringing, purple-tinged waves as they dashed and broke were sublime and serene, combining displays of graceful beauty of motion and form with tremendous power – a truly glorious show. I noticed several small villages on the green slopes between the timbered mountains and the shore. Long Branch made quite a display of new houses along the beach, north of the mouth of the Columbia.

I had pleasant company on the Pueblo and sat at the chief engineer's table, who was a good and merry talker. An old San Francisco lawyer, rather stiff and dignified, knew my father-in-law, Dr Strentzel. Three ladies, opposed to the pitching of the ship, were absent from table the greater part of the way. My best talker was an old Scandinavian sea-captain, who was having a new bark built at Port Blakely – an interesting old salt, every sentence of his conversation flavoured with sea-brine, bluff and hearty as a sea-wave, keen-eyed, courageous, self-reliant, and so stubbornly sceptical he refused to believe even in glaciers.

'After you see your bark', I said, 'and find everything being done to your mind, you had better go on to Alaska and see the glaciers'.

'Oh, I haf seen many glaciers already'.

'But are you sure that you know what a glacier is?' I asked.

'Vell, a glacier is a big mountain all covered up with ice'.

'Then a river', said I, 'must be a big mountain all covered with water'.

I explained what a glacier was and succeeded in exciting his interest. I told him he must reform, for a man who neither believed in God nor glaciers must be very bad, indeed the worst of all unbelievers.

At Port Townsend I met Mr Loomis, who had agreed to go with me as far as the Muir Glacier. We sailed from here on the steamer Queen. We touched again at Victoria, and I took a short walk into the adjacent woods and gardens and found the flowery vegetation in its glory, especially the large wild rose for which the region is famous, and the spiræa and English honeysuckle of the gardens.

18 June. We sailed from Victoria on the Queen at 10.30 am. The weather all the way to Fort Wrangell was cloudy and rainy, but the scenery is delight-ful even in the dullest weather. The marvellous wealth of forests, islands, and waterfalls, the cloud-wreathed heights, the many avalanche slopes and slips, the pearl-grey tones of the sky, the browns of the woods, their purple flower edges and mist fringes, the endless combinations of water and land and ever-shifting clouds – none of these greatly interest the tourists. I noticed one of the small whales that frequent these channels and mentioned the fact, then called attention to a charming group of islands, but they turned their eyes from the islands, saying 'Yes, yes, they are very fine, but where did you see the whale?'

The timber is larger and apparently better every way as you go north from Victoria, that is on the islands, perhaps on account of fires from less rain to the southward. All the islands have been overswept by the ice-sheet and are but little changed as yet, save a few of the highest summits which have been sculptured by local residual glaciers. All have approximately the form of greatest strength with reference to the overflow of an ice-sheet, excepting those mentioned above, which have been more or less eroded by local residual glaciers. Every channel also has the form of greatest strength with reference to ice-action. Islands, as we have seen, are still being born in Glacier Bay and elsewhere to the northward.

I found many pleasant people aboard, but strangely ignorant on the subject of earth-sculpture and landscape-making. Professor Niles, of the Boston Institute of Technology, is aboard; also Mr Russell and Mr Kerr of the Geological Survey, who are now on their way to Mount St Elias, hoping to reach the summit; and a granddaughter of Peter Burnett, the first governor of California.

We arrived at Wrangell in the rain at 10.30 pm. There was a grand rush on shore to buy curiosities and see totem poles. The shops were jammed and mobbed, high prices paid for shabby stuff manufactured expressly for tourist trade. Silver bracelets hammered out of dollars and half dollars by Indian smiths are the most popular articles, then baskets, yellow cedar toy canoes, paddles, etc. Most people who travel look only at what they are directed to look at. Great is the power of the guidebook-maker, however ignorant. I inquired for my old friends Tyeen and Shakes, who were both absent.

20 June. We left Wrangell early this morning and passed through the Wrangell Narrows at high tide. I noticed a few bergs near Cape Fanshawe from Wrangell Glacier. The water ten miles from Wrangell is coloured with particles derived mostly from the Stickeen River glaciers and Le Conte Glacier. All the waters of the channels north of Wrangell are green or yellowish from glacier erosion. We had a good view of the glaciers all the way to Juneau, but not of their high, cloud-veiled fountains. The stranded bergs on the moraine bar at the mouth of Sum Dum Bay looked just as they did when I first saw them ten years ago.

Before reaching Juneau, the Queen proceeded up the Taku Inlet that the passengers might see the fine glacier at its head, and ventured to within half a mile of the berg-discharging front, which is about three quarters of a mile wide. Bergs fell but seldom, perhaps one in half an hour. The glacier makes a rapid descent near the front. The inlet, therefore, will not be much extended beyond its present limit by the recession of the glacier. The grand rocks on either side of its channel show ice-action in telling style. The Norris Glacier, about two miles below the Taku, is a good example of a glacier in the first stage of decadence. The Taku River enters the head of the inlet a little to the east of the glaciers, coming from beyond the main coast range. All the tourists are delighted at seeing a grand glacier in the flesh. The scenery is very fine here and in the channel at Juneau. On Douglas Island there is a large mill of 240 stamps, all run by one small water-wheel, which, however, is acted on by water at enormous pressure. The forests around the mill are being rapidly nibbled away. Wind is here said to be very violent at times, blowing away people and houses and sweeping scud far up the mountain-side. Winter snow is seldom more than a foot or two deep.

21 June. We arived at Douglas Island at five in the afternoon and went sight-seeing through the mill. Six hundred tons of low-grade quartz are crushed per day. Juneau, on the mainland opposite the Douglas Island mills, is quite a village, well supplied with stores, churches, etc. A dance-house in which Indians are supposed to show native dances of all sorts is perhaps the best-patronized of all the places of amusement. A Mr Brooks, who prints a paper here, gave us some information on Mount St Elias, Mount Wrangell and the Cook Inlet and Prince William Sound region. He told Russell that he would never reach the summit of St Elias, that it was inaccessible. He saw no glaciers that discharged bergs into the sea at Cook Inlet, but many in Prince William Sound.

22 June. Leaving Juneau at noon, we had a good view of the Auk Glacier at the mouth of the channel between Douglas Island and the mainland, and of

Eagle Glacier a few miles north of the Auk on the east side of Lynn Canal. Then the Davidson Glacier came in sight, finely curved, striped with medial moraines, and girdled in front by its magnificent tree-fringed terminal moraine; and besides these many others of every size and pattern on the mountains bounding Lynn Canal, most of them comparatively small, completing their sculpture. The mountains on either hand and at the head of the canal are strikingly beautiful at any time of the year. The sky today is mostly clear, with just clouds enough hovering about the mountains to show them to best advantage as they stretch onward in sustained grandeur like two separate and distinct ranges, each mountain with its glaciers and clouds and fine sculpture glowing bright in smooth, graded light. Only a few of them exceed five thousand feet in height; but as one naturally associates great height with ice-and-snow-laden mountains and with glacial sculpture so pronounced, they seem much higher. There are now two canneries at the head of Lynn Canal. The Indians furnish some of the salmon at ten cents each. Everybody sits up to see the midnight sky. At this time of the year there is no night here, though the sun drops a degree or two below the horizon. One may read at twelve o'clock San Francisco time.

23 June. Early this morning we arrived in Glacier Bay. We passed through crowds of bergs at the mouth of the bay, though, owing to wind and tide, there were but few at the front of Muir Glacier. A fine, bright day, the last of a group of a week or two, as shown by the dryness of the sand along the shore and on the moraine – rare weather hereabouts. Most of the passengers went ashore and climbed the moraine on the east side to get a view of the glacier from a point a little higher than the top of the front wall. A few ventured on a mile or two farther. The day was delightful, and our one hundred and eighty passengers were happy, gazing at the beautiful blue of the bergs and the shattered pinnacled crystal wall, awed by the thunder and commotion of the falling and rising icebergs, which ever and anon sent spray flying several hundred feet into the air and raised swells that set all the fleet of bergs in motion and roared up the beach, telling the story of the birth of every iceberg far and near. The number discharged varies much, influenced in part no doubt by the tides and weather and seasons, sometimes one every five minutes for half a day at a time on the average, though intervals of twenty or thirty minutes may occur without any considerable fall, then three or four immense discharges will take place in as many minutes. The sound they make is like heavy thunder, with a prolonged roar after deep thudding sounds – a perpetual thunderstorm easily heard three or four miles away. The roar in our tent and the shaking of the ground one or two miles distant from points of discharge seems startlingly near.

I had to look after camp-supplies and left the ship late this morning, going with a crowd to the glacier; then, taking advantage of the fine weather, I pushed off alone into the silent icy prairie to the east, to Nunatak Island, about five hundred feet above the ice. I discovered a small lake on the larger of the two islands, and many battered and ground fragments of fossil wood, large and small. They seem to have come from trees that grew on the island perhaps centuries ago. I mean to use this island as a station in setting out stakes to measure the glacial flow. The top of Mount Fairweather is in sight at a distance of perhaps thirty miles, the ice all smooth on the eastern border, wildly broken in the central portion. I reached the ship at 2.30 pm. I had intended getting back at noon and sending letters and bidding friends good-bye, but could not resist this glacier saunter. The ship moved off as soon as I was seen on the moraine bluff, and Loomis and I waved our hats in farewell to the many wavings of handkerchiefs of acquaintances we had made on the trip.

Our goods – blankets, provisions, tent, etc. – lay in a rocky moraine hollow within a mile of the great terminal wall of the glacier, and the discharge of the rising and falling icebergs kept up an almost continuous thundering and echoing, while a few gulls flew about on easy wing or stood like specks of foam on the shore. These were our neighbours.

After my twelve-mile walk, I ate a cracker and planned the camp. I found that one of my boxes had been left on the steamer, but still we have more than enough of everything. We obtained two cords of dry wood at Juneau which Captain Carroll kindly had his men carry up the moraine to our camp-ground. We piled the wood as a wind-break, then laid a floor of lumber brought from Seattle for a square tent, nine feet by nine. We set the tent, stored our provisions in it, and made our beds. This work was done by 11.30 pm, good daylight lasting to this time. We slept well in our roomy cotton house, dreaming of California home nests in the wilderness of ice.

25 June. A rainy day. For a few hours I kept count of the number of bergs discharged, then sauntered along the beach to the end of the crystal wall. A portion of the way is dangerous, the moraine bluff being capped by an overlying lobe of the glacier, which as it melts sends down boulders and fragments of ice, while the strip of sandy shore at high tide is only a few rods wide, leaving but little room to escape from the falling moraine material and the berg-waves. The view of the ice-cliffs, pinnacles, spires and ridges was very telling, a magnificent picture of nature's power and industry and love of beauty. About a hundred or a hundred and fifty feet from the shore a large stream issues from an arched, tunnel-like channel in the wall of the glacier, the blue of the ice hall being of an exquisite tone, contrasting with the strange, sooty, smoky, brown-coloured stream. The front wall of the Muir Glacier is about two and a half or three miles wide. Only the central portion about two miles wide discharges icebergs. The two wings advanced over the washed and stratified moraine deposits have little or no motion melting and receding as fast, or perhaps faster, than it advances. They have been advanced at least a mile over the old re-formed moraines, as is shown by the overlying, angular, recent moraine deposits, now being laid down, which are continuous with the medial moraines of the glacier.

In the old stratified moraine banks, trunks and branches of trees showing but little sign of decay occur at a height of about a hundred feet above tide-water. I have not yet compared this fossil wood with that of the opposite shore deposits. That the glacier was once withdrawn considerably back of its present limit seems plain. Immense torrents of water had filled in the inlet with stratified moraine-material, and for centuries favourable climatic conditions allowed forests to grow upon it. At length the glacier advanced, probably three or four miles, uprooting and burying the trees which had grown undisturbed for centuries. Then came a great thaw, which produced the flood that deposited the uprooted trees. Also the trees which grew around the shores above reach of floods were shed off, perhaps by the thawing of the soil that was resting on the buried margin of the glacier, left on its retreat and protected by a covering of moraine-material from melting as fast as the exposed surface of the glacier. What appear to be remnants of the margin of the glacier when it stood at a much higher level still exist on the left side and probably all along its banks on both sides just below its present terminus.

26 June. We fixed a mark on the left wing to measure the motion if any. It rained all day, but I had a grand tramp over mud, ice and rock to the east wall of the inlet. Brown metamorphic slate, close-grained in places, dips away from the inlet, presenting edges to ice-action, which has given rise to a singularly beautiful and striking surface, polished and grooved and fluted.

All the next day it rained. The mountains were smothered in dull-coloured mist and fog, the great glacier looming through the gloomy grey fog fringes with wonderful effect. The thunder of bergs booms and rumbles through the foggy atmosphere. It is bad weather for exploring but delightful nevertheless, making all the strange, mysterious region yet stranger and more mysterious.

28 June. A light rain. We were visited by two parties of Indians. A man from each canoe came ashore, leaving the women in the canoe to guard against the berg-waves. I tried my Chinook and made out to say that I wanted to hire two of them in a few days to go a little way back on the glacier and round the bay. They are seal-hunters and promised to come again with 'Charley', who 'hi yu kumtux wawa Boston' – knew well how to speak English.

I saw three huge bergs born. Spray rose about two hundred feet. Lovely reflections showed of the pale-blue tones of the ice-wall and mountains in the calm water. Mirages are common, making the stranded bergs along the shore look like the sheer frontal wall of the glacier from which they were discharged.

I am watching the ice-wall, berg life and behaviour, etc. Yesterday and to-day a solitary small flycatcher was feeding about camp. A sandpiper on the shore, loons, ducks, gulls and crows, a few of each and a bald eagle are all the birds I have noticed thus far. The glacier is thundering gloriously.

30 June. Clearing clouds and sunshine. In less than a minute I saw three large bergs born. First there is usually a preliminary thundering of com-paratively small masses as the large mass begins to fall, then the grand crash and boom and reverberating roaring. Oftentimes three of four heavy main throbbing thuds and booming explosions are heard as the main mass falls in several pieces, and also secondary thuds and thunderings as the mass or masses plunge and rise again and again ere they come to rest. Seldom, if ever, do the towers, battlements and pinnacles into which the front of the glacier is broken fall forward headlong from their bases like falling trees at the water-level or above or below it. They mostly sink vertically or nearly so, as if undermined by the melting action of the water of the inlet, occasionally maintaining their upright position after sinking far below the level of the water and rising again a hundred feet or more into the air with water stream-ing like hair down their sides from their crowns, then launch forward and fall flat with yet another thundering report, raising spray in magnificent, flame-like, radiating jets and sheets, occasionally to the very top of the front wall. Illumined by the sun, the spray and angular crystal masses are indescribably beautiful. Some of the discharges pour in fragments from clefts in the wall like waterfalls, white and mealy-looking, even dusty with minute swirling ice-particles, followed by a rushing succession of thunder-tones combining into a huge, blunt, solemn roar. Most of these crumbling discharges are from the excessively shattered central part of the ice-wall; the solid deep-blue masses from the ends of the wall forming the large bergs rise from the bottom of the glacier.

Many lesser reports are heard at a distance of a mile or more from the fall of pinnacles into crevasses or from the opening of new crevasses. The berg discharges are very irregular, from three to twenty-two an hour. On one rising tide, six hours, there were sixty bergs discharged, large enough to thunder and be heard at distances of from three quarters to one and a half miles; and on one succeeding falling tide, six hours, sixty-nine were discharged.

1 July. We were awakened at four o'clock this morning by the whistle of the steamer George W. Elder. I went out on the moraine and waved my hand in salute and was answered by a toot from the whistle. Soon a party came ashore and asked if I was Professor Muir. The leader, Professor Harry Fielding Reid of Cleveland, Ohio, introduced himself and his companion, Mr Cushing, also of Cleveland and six or eight young students who had come well provided with instruments to study the glacier. They landed seven or eight tons of freight and pitched camp beside ours. I am delighted to have companions so congenial – we have now a village.

As I set out to climb the second mountain, three thousand feet high, on the east side of the glacier, I met many tourists returning from a walk on the smooth east margin of the glacier, and had to answer many questions. I had a hard climb, but wonderful views were developed and I sketched the glacier from this high point and most of its upper fountains.

Many fine alpine plants grew here, an anemone on the summit, two species of cassiope in shaggy mats, three or four dwarf willows, large blue hairy lupines eighteen inches high, parnassia, phlox, solidago, dandelion, white-flowered bryanthus, daisy, pedicularis, epilobium, etc., with grasses, sedges, mosses and lichens, forming a delightful deep spongy sod. Woodchucks stood erect and piped dolefully for an hour 'Chee-chee!' with jaws absurdly stretched to emit so thin a note – rusty-looking, seedy fellows, also a smaller striped species which stood erect and cheeped and whistled like a Douglas squirrel. I saw three or four species of birds. A finch flew from her nest at my feet; and I almost stepped on a family of young ptarmigan ere they scattered, little bunches of downy brown silk, small but able to run well. They scattered along a snow-bank, over boulders, through willows, grass and flowers, while the mother, very lame, tumbled and sprawled at my feet. I stood still until the little ones began to peep; the mother answered 'Too-too-too' and showed admirable judgment and devotion. She was in brown plumage with white on the wing primaries. She had fine grounds on which to lead and feed her young.

Not a cloud in the sky today; a faint film to the north vanished by noon, leaving all the sky full of soft, hazy light. The magnificent mountains around the widespread tributaries of the glacier; the great, gently undulating, prairie-like expanse of the main trunk, bluish on the east, pure white on the west and north; its trains of moraines in magnificent curving lines and many colours – black, grey, red and brown; the stormy, cataract-like, crevassed sections; the hundred fountains; the lofty, pure white Fairweather Range; the thunder of the plunging bergs; the fleet of bergs sailing tranquilly in the inlet – formed a glowing picture of nature's beauty and power.

2 July. I crossed the inlet with Mr Reid and Mr Adams today. The stratified drift on the west side all the way from top to base contains fossil wood. On the east side, as far as I have seen it, the wood occurs only in one stratum at a height of about a hundred and twenty feet in sand and clay. Some in a bank of the west side are rooted in clay soil. I noticed a large grove of stumps in a washed-out channel near the glacier-front but had no time to examine closely. Evidently a flood carrying great quantities of sand and gravel had overwhelmed and broken off these trees, leaving high stumps. The deposit, about a hundred feet or more above them, had been recently washed out by one of the draining streams of the glacier, exposing a part of the old forest floor certainly two or three centuries old.

I climbed along the right bank of the lowest of the tributaries and set a signal flag on a ridge fourteen hundred feet high. This tributary is about one and a fourth or one and a half miles wide and has four secondary tributaries. It reaches tide-water but gives off no bergs. Later I climbed the large Nunatak Island, seven thousand feet high, near the west margin of the glacier. It is composed of crumbling granite draggled with washed boulders, but has some enduring bosses which on sides and top are polished and scored rigidly, showing that it had been heavily overswept by the glacier when it was thousands of feet deeper than now, like a submerged boulder in a river-channel. This island is very irregular in form, owing to the variations in the structure joints of the granite. It has several small lakelets and has been loaded with glacial drift, but by the melting of the ice about its flanks is shedding it off, together with some of its own crumbling surface. I descended a deep rock gully on the north side, the rawest, dirtiest, dustiest, most dangerous that I have seen hereabouts. There is also a large quantity of fossil wood scattered on this island, especially on the north side, that on the south side having been cleared off and carried away by the first tributary glacier, which, being lower and melting earlier, has allowed the soil of the moraine material to fall, together with its forest and be carried off. That on the north side is now being carried off or buried. The last of the main ice foundation is melting and the moraine material re-formed over and over again, and the fallen tree-trunks, decayed or half decayed or in a fair state of preservation, are also unburied and buried again or carried off to the terminal or lateral moraine.

I found three small seedling Sitka spruces, feeble beginnings of a new forest. The circumference of the island is about seven miles. I arrived at camp about midnight, tired and cold. Sailing across the inlet in a cranky rotten boat through the midst of icebergs was dangerous, and I was glad to get ashore.

4 July. I climbed the east wall to the summit, about thirty-one hundred feet or so, by the northern-most ravine next to the yellow ridge, finding about a mile of snow in the upper portion of the ravine and patches on the summit. A few of the patches probably lie all the year, the ground beneath them is so plantless. On the edge of some of the snow-banks I noticed cassiope. The thin, green, mosslike patches seen from camp are composed of a rich, shaggy growth of cassiope, white-flowered bryanthus, dwarf vaccinium with bright pink flowers, saxifrages, anemones, blue-bells, gentians, small erigeron, pedicularis, dwarf willow and a few species of grasses. Of these, *Cassiope tetragona* is far the most influential and beautiful. Here it forms mats a foot thick and an acre or more in area, the sections being measured by the size and drainage of the soil-patches. I saw a few plants anchored in the less crumbling parts of the steep-faced bosses and steps – parnassia, potentilla, hedysarum, lutkea, etc. The lower, rough-looking patches half-way up the mountain are mostly alder bushes ten or fifteen feet high. I had a fine view of the top of the mountain-mass which forms the boundary wall of the upper portion of the inlet on the west side, and of several glaciers, tributary to the first of the eastern tributaries of the main Muir Glacier. Five or six of these tributaries were seen, most of them now melted off from the trunk and independent. The highest peak to the eastward has an elevation of about five thousand feet or a little less. I also had glorious views of the Fairweather Range, La Pérouse, Crillon, Lituya, and Fairweather. Mount Fairweather is the most beautiful of all the giants that stand guard about Glacier Bay. When the sun is shining on it from the east or south its magnificent glaciers and colours are brought out in most telling display. In the late afternoon its features become less distinct. The atmosphere seems pale and hazy, though around to the north and northeastward of Fairweather innumerable white peaks are displayed, the highest fountain-heads of the Muir Glacier crowded together in bewildering array, most exciting and inviting to the mountaineer. Altogether I have had a delightful day, a truly glorious celebration of the fourth.

6 July. I sailed three or four miles down the east coast of the inlet with the Reid party's cook, who is supposed to be an experienced camper and prospector, and landed at a stratified moraine-bank. It was here that I camped in 1880, a point at that time less than half a mile from the front of the glacier, now one and a half miles. I found my Indian's old camp made just ten years ago and Professor Wright's of five years ago. Their alder-bough beds and fireplace were still marked and but little decayed. I found thirty-three species of plants in flower, not counting willows – a showy garden on the shore only a few feet above high tide, watered by a fine stream. Lutkea, hedysarum, parnassia, epilobium, bluebell, solidago, habenaria, strawberry with fruit half grown, arctostaphylos, mertensia, erigeron, willows, tall grasses and alder are the principal species. There are many butterflies in this garden. Gulls are breeding near here. I saw young in the water today.

On my way back to camp I discovered a group of monumental stumps in a washed-out valley of the moraine and went ashore to observe them. They are in the dry course of a flood-channel about eighty feet above mean tide and four or five hundred yards back from the shore, where they have been pounded and battered by boulders rolling against them and over them, making them look like gigantic shaving-brushes. The largest is about three feet in diameter and probably three hundred years old. I mean to return and examine them at leisure. A smaller stump, still firmly rooted, is standing astride of an old crumbling trunk, showing that at least two generations of trees flourished here undisturbed by the advance or retreat of the glacier or by its draining stream-floods. They are Sitka spruces and the wood is mostly in a good state of preservation. How these trees were broken off without being uprooted is dark to me at present. Perhaps most of their companions were uprooted and carried away.

7 July. Another fine day; scarce a cloud in the sky. The icebergs in the bay are miraged in the distance to look like the frontal wall of a great glacier. I am writing letters in anticipation of the next steamer, the Queen.

She arrived about 2.30 pm with two hundred and thirty tourists. What a show they made with their ribbons and kodaks! All seemed happy and enthusiastic, though it was curious to see how promptly all of them ceased gazing when the dinner-bell rang, and how many turned from the great thundering crystal world of ice to look curiously at the Indians that came alongside to sell trinkets, and how our little camp and kitchen arrangements excited so many to loiter and waste their precious time prying into our poor hut.

8 July. A fine clear day. I went up the glacier to observe stakes and found that a marked point near the middle of the current had flowed about a hundred feet in eight days. On the medial moraine one mile from the front there was no measureable displacement. I found a raven devouring a tom-cod that was alive on a shallow at the mouth of the creek. It had probably been wounded by a seal or eagle.

10 July. I have been getting acquainted with the main features of the glacier and its fountain mountains with reference to an exploration of its main tributaries and the upper part of its prairie-like trunk, a trip I have long had in mind. I have been building a sled and must now get fully ready to start without reference to the weather. Yesterday evening I saw a large blue berg just as it was detached sliding down from the front. Two of Professor Reid's party rowed out to it as it sailed past the camp, estimating it to be two hundred and forty feet in length and one hundred feet high.

CHAPTER EIGHTEEN

My Sled-trip on the Muir Glacier

I STARTED off the morning of 11 July on my memorable sled-trip to obtain general views of the main upper part of the Muir Glacier and its seven principal tributaries, feeling sure that I would learn something and at the same time get rid of a severe bronchial cough that followed an attack of the grippe and had troubled me for three months. I intended to camp on the glacier every night, and did so, and my throat grew better every day until it was well, for no lowland microbe could stand such a trip. My sled was about three feet long and made as light as possible. A sack of hardtack, a little tea and sugar and a sleeping-bag were firmly lashed on it so that nothing could drop off however much it might be jarred and dangled in crossing crevasses.

Two Indians carried the baggage over the rocky moraine to the clear glacier at the side of one of the eastern Nunatak Islands. Mr Loomis accompanied me to this first camp and assisted in dragging the empty sled over the moraine. We arrived at the middle Nunatak Island about nine o'clock. Here I sent back my Indian carriers, and Mr Loomis assisted me the first day in hauling the loaded sled to my second camp at the foot of Hemlock Mountain, returning the next morning.

13 July. I skirted the mountain to eastward a few miles and was delighted to discover a group of trees high up on its ragged rocky side, the first trees I had seen on the shores of Glacier Bay or on those of any of its glaciers. I left my sled on the ice and climbed the mountain to see what I might learn. I found that all the trees were mountain hemlock (*Tsuga mertensiana*), and were evidently the remnant of an old well-established forest, standing on the only ground that was stable, all the rest of the forest below it having been sloughed off with the soil from the disintegrating slate bed rock. The lowest of the trees stood at an elevation of about two thousand feet above the sea, the highest at about three thousand feet or a little higher. Nothing could be more striking than the contrast between the raw, crumbling, deforested portions of the mountain, looking like a quarry that was being worked, and the forested part with its rich, shaggy beds of cassiope and bryanthus in full bloom and its sumptuous cushions of flower-enamelled mosses. These garden-patches are full of gay colours of gentian, erigeron, anemone, larkspur and columbine and are enlivened with happy birds and bees and marmots. Climbing to an elevation of twenty-five hundred feet, which is about fifteen hundred feet above the level of the glacier at this point, I saw and heard a few marmots and three ptarmigans that were as tame as barnyard fowls. The sod is sloughing off on the edges, keeping it ragged. The trees are storm-bent from the southeast. A few are standing at an elevation of nearly three thousand feet; at twenty-five hundred feet, pyrola, veratrum, vaccinium, fine grasses, sedges, willows, mountain-ash, buttercups and acres of the most luxuriant cassiope are in bloom.

A lake encumbered with icebergs lies at the end of Divide Glacier. A spacious, level-floored valley beyond it, eight or ten miles long, with forested mountains on its west side, perhaps discharges to the southeastward into Lynn Canal. The divide of the glacier is about opposite the third of the eastern tributaries. Another berg-dotted lake into which the drainage of the Braided Glacier flows, lies a few miles to the westward and is one and a half miles long. Berg Lake is next the remarkable Girdled Glacier to the southeastward.

When the ice-period was in its prime, much of the Muir Glacier that now flows northward into Howling Valley flowed southward into Glacier Bay as a tributary of the Muir. All the rock contours show this, and so do the medial moraines. Berg Lake is crowded with bergs because they have no outlet and melt slowly. I heard none discharged. I had a hard time crossing the Divide Glacier, on which I camped. Half a mile back from the lake I gleaned a little fossil wood and made a fire on moraine boulders for tea. I slept fairly well on the sled. I heard the roar of four cascades on a shaggy green mountain on the west side of Howling Valley and saw three wild goats fifteen hundred feet up in the steep grassy pastures.

14 July. I rose at four o'clock this cloudy and dismal morning and looked for my goats, but saw only one. I thought there must be wolves where there were goats, and in a few minutes heard their low, dismal, far-reaching howling. One of them sounded very near and came nearer until it seemed to be less than a quarter of a mile away on the edge of the glacier. They had evidently seen me, but I was unable to catch sight of any of them. About half an hour later, while I was eating breakfast, they began howling again, so near I began to fear they had a mind to attack me, and I made haste to the shelter of a big square boulder, where, though I had no gun, I might be able to defend myself from a front attack with my alpenstock. After waiting half an hour or so to see what these wild dogs meant to do, I ventured to proceed on my journey to the foot of Snow Dome, where I camped for the night.

There are six tributaries on the northwest side of Divide arm, counting to the Grey Glacier, next after Granite Canyon Glacier going northwest. Next is Dirt Glacier, which is dead. I saw bergs on the edge of the main glacier a mile back from here which seem to have been left by the draining of a pool in a sunken hollow. A circling rim of driftwood, back twenty rods on the glacier, marks the edge of the lakelet shore where the bergs lie scattered and stranded. It is now half past ten o'clock and getting dusk as I sit by my little fossil-wood fire writing these notes. A strange bird is calling and complaining. A stream is rushing into a glacier well on the edge of which I am camped, back a few yards from the base of the mountain for fear of falling stones. A few small ones are rattling down the steep slope. I must go to bed.

15 July. I climbed the dome to plan a way, scan the glacier, and take bearings, etc., in case of storms. The main divide is about fifteen hundred feet; the second divide, about fifteen hundred also, is about one and one half miles southeastward. The flow of water on the glacier noticeably diminished last night though there was no frost. It is now already increasing. Stones begin to roll into the crevasses and into new positions, sliding against each other, half turning over or falling on moraine ridges. Mud pellets with small pebbles slip and roll slowly from ice-hummocks again and again. How often and by how many ways are boulders finished and finally brought to anything like permanent form and place in beds for farms and fields, forests and gardens. Into crevasses and out again, into moraines, shifted and reinforced and reformed by avalanches, melting from pedestals, etc. Rain, frost and dew help in the work; they are swept in rills, caught and ground in pot-hole mills. Moraines of washed pebbles, like those on glacier margins, are formed by snow avalanches deposited in crevasses, then weathered out and projected on the ice as shallow raised moraines. There is one such at this camp.

A ptarmigan is on a rock twenty yards distant, as if on show. It has red over the eye, a white line, not conspicuous, over the red, belly white, white markings over the upper parts on ground of brown and black wings, mostly white as seen when flying, but the coverts the same as the rest of the body. Only about three inches of the folded primaries show white. The breast seems to have golden iridescent colours, white under the wings. It allowed me to approach within twenty feet. It walked down a sixty degree slope of the rock, took flight with a few whirring wingbeats, then sailed with wings perfectly motionless four hundred yards down a gentle grade and vanished over the brow of a cliff. Ten days ago Loomis told me that he found a nest with nine eggs. On the way down to my sled I saw four more ptarmigans. They utter harsh notes when alarmed. 'Crack, chuck, crack', with the *r* rolled and prolonged. I also saw fresh and old goat-tracks and some bones that suggest wolves.

There is a pass through the mountains at the head of the third glacier. Fine mountains stand at the head on each side. The one on the northeast side is the higher and finer every way. It has three glaciers, tributary to the third. The third glacier has altogether ten tributaries, five on each side. The mountain on the left side of White Glacier is about six thousand feet high. The moraines of Girdled Glacier seem scarce to run anywhere. Only a little material is carried to Berg Lake. Most of it seems to be at rest as a terminal on the main glacier-field, which here has little motion. The curves of these last as seen from this mountain-top are very beautiful.

It has been a glorious day, all pure sunshine. An hour or more before sunset the distant mountains, a vast host, seemed more softly ethereal than ever, pale blue, ineffably fine, all angles and harshness melted off in the soft evening light. Even the snow and the grinding, cascading glaciers became divinely tender and fine in this celestial amethystine light. I got back to camp at 7.15, not tired. After my hardtack supper I could have climbed the mountain again and got back before sunrise, but dragging the sled tires me. I have been out on the glacier examining a moraine-like mass about a third of a mile from camp. It is perhaps a mile long, a hundred yards wide, and is thickly strewn with wood. I think that it has been brought down the mountain by a heavy snow avalanche, loaded on the ice, then carried away from the shore in the direction of the flow of the glacier. This explains detached moraine-masses. This one seems to have been derived from a big roomy cirque or amphitheatre on the northwest side of this Snow Dome Mountain.

To shorten the return journey I was tempted to glissade down what appeared to be a snow-filled ravine, which was very steep. All went well until I reached a bluish spot which proved to be ice, on which I lost control of myself and rolled into a gravel talus at the foot without a scratch. Just as I got up and was getting myself orientated, I heard a loud fierce scream, uttered in an exulting, diabolical tone of voice which startled me, as if an enemy, having seen me fall, was glorying in my death. Then suddenly two ravens came swooping from the sky and alighted on the jag of rock within a few feet of me, evidently hoping that I had been maimed and that they were going to have a feast. But as they stared at me, studying my condition, impatiently waiting for bone-picking time, I saw what they were up to and shouted, 'Not yet, not yet!'

16 July. At 7 am I left camp to cross the main glacier. Six ravens came to the camp as soon as I left. What wonderful eyes they must have! Nothing that moves in all this icy wilderness escapes the eyes of these brave birds. This is one of the loveliest mornings I ever saw in Alaska; not a cloud or faintest hint of one in all the wide sky. There is a yellowish haze in the east, white in the west, mild and mellow as a Wisconsin Indian Summer, but finer, more ethereal, God's holy light making all divine.

In an hour or so I came to the confluence of the first of the seven grand tributaries of the main Muir Glacier and had a glorious view of it as it comes sweeping down in wild cascades from its magnificent, pure white, mountain-girt basin to join the main crystal sea, its many fountain peaks, clustered and crowded, all pouring forth their tribute to swell its grand current. I crossed its front a little below its confluence, where its shattered current, about two or three miles wide, is reunited, and many rills and good-sized brooks glide gurgling and ringing in pure blue channels, giving delightful animation to the icy solitude.

Most of the ice-surface crossed today has been very uneven, and hauling the sled and finding a way over hummocks has been fatiguing. At times I had to lift the sled bodily and to cross many narrow, nerve-trying, ice-sliver bridges, balancing astride of them and cautiously shoving the sled ahead of me with tremendous chasms on either side. I had made perhaps not more than six or eight miles in a straight line by six o'clock this evening when I reached ice so hummocky and tedious I concluded to camp and not try to take the sled any farther. I intend to leave it here in the middle of the basin and carry my sleeping-bag and provisions the rest of the way across to the west side. I am cozy and comfortable here resting in the midst of glorious icy scenery, though very tired. I made out to get a cup of tea by means of a few shavings and splinters whittled from the bottom board of my sled, and made a fire in a little can, a small campfire, the smallest I ever made or saw, yet it answered well enough as far as tea was concerned. I crept into my sack before eight o'clock as the wind was cold and my feet wet. One of my shoes is about worn out. I may have to put on a wooden sole. This day has been cloudless throughout, with lovely sunshine, a purple evening and morning. The circumference of mountains beheld from the midst of this world of ice is marvellous, the vast plain reposing in such soft tender light, the fountain mountains so clearly cut, holding themselves aloft with their loads of ice in supreme strength and beauty of architecture. I found a skull and most of the other bones of a goat on the glacier about two miles from the nearest land. It had probably been chased out of its mountain home by wolves and devoured here. I carried its horns with me. I saw many considerable depressions in the glacial surface, also a pitlike hole, irregular, not like the ordinary wells along the slope of the many small dirt-clad hillocks, faced to the south. Now the sun is down and the sky is saffron yellow, blending and fading into purple around to the south and north. It is a curious experience to be lying in bed writing these notes, hummock waves rising in every direction, their edges marking a multitude of crevasses and pits, while all around the horizon rise peaks innumerable of most intricate style of architecture. Solemnly growling and grinding moulins contrast with the sweet low-voiced whispering and warbling of a network of rills, singing like water-ouzels, glinting, gliding with indescribable softness and sweetness of voice. They are all around, one within a few feet of my hard sled bed.

17 July. Another glorious cloudless day is dawning in yellow and purple and soon the sun over the eastern peak will blot out the blue peak shadows and make all the vast white ice prairie sparkle. I slept well last night in the middle of the icy sea. The wind was cold but my sleeping-bag enabled me to lie neither warm nor intolerably cold. My three-months cough is gone. Strange that with such work and exposure one should know nothing of sore throats and of what are called colds. My heavy, thick-soled shoes, resoled just before starting on the trip six days ago, are about worn out and my feet have been wet every night. But no harm comes of it, nothing but good. I succeeded in getting a warm breakfast in bed. I reached over the edge of my sled, got hold of a small cedar stick that I had been carrying, whittled a lot of thin shavings from it, stored them on my breast, then set fire to a piece of paper in a shallow tin can, added a pinch of shavings, held the cup of water that always stood at my bedside over the tiny blaze with one hand, and fed the fire by adding little pinches of shavings until the water boiled, then pulling my bread sack within reach, made a good warm breakfast, cooked and eaten in bed. Thus refreshed, I surveyed the wilderness of crevassed, hummocky ice and concluded to try to drag my little sled a mile or two farther, then, finding encouragement, persevered, getting it across innumerable crevasses and streams and around several lakes and over and through the midst of hummocks, and at length reached the western shore between five and six o'clock this evening, extremely fatigued. This I consider a hard job well done, crossing so wildly broken a glacier, fifteen miles of it from Snow Dome Mountain, in two days with a sled weighing altogether not less than a hundred pounds. I found innumerable crevasses, some of them brimful of water. I crossed in most places just where the ice was close pressed and welded after descending cascades and was being shoved over an upward slope, thus closing the crevasses at the bottom, leaving only the upper sun-melted bevelled portion open for water to collect in.

Vast must be the drainage from this great basin. The waste in sunshine must be enormous, while in dark weather rains and winds also melt the ice and add to the volume produced by the rain itself. The winds also, though in temperature they may be only a degree or two above freezing-point, dissolve the ice as fast, or perhaps faster, than clear sunshine. Much of the water caught in tight crevasses doubtless freezes during the winter and gives rise to many of the irregular veins seen in the structure of the glacier. Saturated snow also freezes at times and is incorporated with the ice, as only from the lower part of the glacier is the snow melted during the summer. I have noticed many traces of this action. One of the most beautiful things to be seen on the glacier is the myriads of minute and intensely brilliant radiant lights burning in rows on the banks of streams and pools and lakelets from the tips of crystals melting in the sun, making them look as if bordered with diamonds. These gems are rayed like stars and twinkle; no diamond radiates keener or more brilliant light. It was perfectly glorious to think of this divine light burning over all this vast crystal sea in such ineffably fine effulgence, and over how many other of icy Alaska's glaciers where nobody sees it. To produce these effects I fancy the ice must be melting rapidly, as it was being melted today. The ice in these pools does not melt with anything like an even surface, but in long branches and leaves, making fairy forests of points, while minute bubbles of air are constantly being set free. I am camped tonight on what I call Quarry Mountain from its raw, loose, plantless condition, seven or eight miles above the front of the glacier. I found enough fossil wood for tea. Glorious is the view to the eastward from this camp. The sun has set, a few clouds appear, and a torrent rushing down a gully and under the edge of the glacier is making a solemn roaring. No tinkling, whistling rills this night. Ever and anon I hear a falling boulder. I have had a glorious and instructive day, but am excessively weary and to bed I go.

18 July. I felt tired this morning and meant to rest today. But after breakfast at 8 am I felt I must be up and doing, climbing, sketching new views up the great tributaries from the top of Quarry Mountain. Weariness vanished and I could have climbed, I think, five thousand feet. Anything seems easy after sled-dragging over hummocks and crevasses, and the constant nerve-strain in jumping crevasses so as not to slip in making the spring. Quarry Mountain is the barest I have ever seen, a raw quarry with infinite abundance of loose decaying granite all on the go. Its slopes are excessively steep. A few patches of epilobium make gay purple spots of colour. Its seeds fly everywhere seeking homes. Quarry Mountain is cut across into a series of parallel ridges by oversweeping ice. It is still overswept in three places by glacial flows a half to three quarters of a mile wide, finely arched at the top of the divides. I have been sketching, though my eyes are much inflamed and I can scarce see. All the lines I make appear double. I fear I shall not be able to make the few more sketches I want tomorrow, but must try. The day has been gloriously sunful, the glacier pale yellow toward five o'clock. The hazy air, white with a yellow tinge, gives an Indian-summerish effect. Now the blue evening shadows are creeping out over the icy plain, some ten miles long, with sunny yellow belts between them. Boulders fall now and again with dull, blunt booming, and the gravel pebbles rattle.

19 July. Nearly blind. The light is intolerable and I fear I may be long unfitted for work. I have been lying on my back all day with a snow poultice bound over my eyes. Every object I try to look at seems double; even the distant mountain-ranges are doubled, the upper an exact copy of the lower, though somewhat faint. This is the first time in Alaska that I have had too much sunshine. About four o'clock this afternoon, when I was waiting for the evening shadows to enable me to get nearer the main camp, where I could be more easily found in case my eyes should become still more inflamed and I should be unable to travel, thin clouds cast a grateful shade over all the glowing landscape. I gladly took advantage of these kindly clouds to make an effort to cross the few miles of the glacier that lay between me and the shore of the inlet. I made a pair of goggles but am afraid to wear them. Fortunately the ice here is but little broken, therefore I pulled my cap well down and set off about five o'clock. I got on pretty well and camped on the glacier in sight of the main camp, which from here in a straight line is only five or six miles away. I went ashore on Granite Island and gleaned a little fossil wood with which I made tea on the ice.

20 July. I kept wet bandages on my eyes last night as long as I could, and feel better this morning, but all the mountains still seem to have double summits, giving a curiously unreal aspect to the landscape. I packed everything on the sled and moved three miles farther down the glacier, where I want to make measurements. Twice today I was visited on the ice by a hummingbird, attracted by the red lining of the bear-skin sleeping-bag.

I have gained some light on the formation of gravel-beds along the inlet. The material is mostly sifted and sorted by successive rollings and washings along the margins of the glacier-tributaries, where the supply is abundant beyond anything I ever saw elsewhere. The lowering of the surface of a glacier when its walls are not too steep leaves a part of the margin buried and protected from the wasting sunshine beneath the lateral moraines. Thus a marginal valley is formed, clear ice on one side, or nearly so, buried ice on the other. As melting goes on, the marginal trough, or valley, grows deeper and wider, since both sides are being melted, the land side slower. The dead, protected ice in melting first sheds off the large boulders, as they are not able to lie on slopes where smaller ones can. Then the next larger ones are rolled off and pebbles and sand in succession. Meanwhile this material is subjected to torrent-action, as if it were cast into a trough. When floods come it is carried forward and stratified, according to the force of the current, sand, mud, or larger material. This exposes fresh surfaces of ice and melting goes on again, until enough material has been undermined to form a veil in front; then follows another washing and carrying-away and depositing where the current is allowed to spread. In melting, protected margin terraces are oftentimes formed. Perhaps these terraces mark successive heights of the glacial surface. From terrace to terrace the grist of stone is rolled and sifted. Some, meeting only feeble streams, have only the fine particles carried away and deposited in smooth beds; others, coarser, from swifter streams, overspread the fine beds, while many of the large boulders no doubt roll back upon the glacier to go on their travels again.

It has been cloudy mostly today, though sunny in the afternoon, and my eyes are getting better. The steamer Queen is expected in a day or two, so I must try to get down to the inlet tomorrow and make signal to have some of the Reid party ferry me over. I must hear from home, write letters, get rest and more to eat.

Near the front of the glacier the ice was perfectly free, apparently, of anything like a crevasse, and in walking almost carelessly down it I stopped opposite the large granite Nunatak Island, thinking that I would there be partly sheltered from the wind. I had not gone a dozen steps toward the island when I suddenly dropped into a concealed water-filled crevasse, which on the surface showed not the slightest sign of its existence. This crevasse like many others was being used as the channel of a stream, and at some narrow point the small cubical masses of ice into which the glacier surface disintegrates were jammed and extended back farther and farther till they completely covered and concealed the water. Into this I suddenly plunged, after crossing thousands of really dangerous crevasses, but never before had I encountered a danger so completely concealed. Down I plunged over head and ears, but of course bobbed up again, and after a hard struggle succeeded in dragging myself out over the farther side. Then I pulled my sled over close to Nunatak cliff, made haste to strip off my clothing, threw it in a sloppy heap and crept into my sleeping-bag to shiver away the night as best I could.

21 July. Dressing this rainy morning was a miserable job, but might have been worse. After wringing my sloppy underclothing, getting it on was far from pleasant. My eyes are better and I feel no bad effect from my icy bath. The last trace of my three months' cough is gone. No lowland grippe microbe could survive such experiences.

I have had a fine telling day examining the ruins of the old forest of Sitka spruce that no great time ago grew in a shallow mud-filled basin near the southwest corner of the glacier. The trees were protected by a spur of the mountain that puts out here, and when the glacier advanced they were simply flooded with fine sand and overborne. Stumps by the hundred, three to fifteen feet high, rooted in a stream of fine blue mud on cobbles, still have their bark on. A stratum of decomposed bark, leaves, cones and old trunks is still in place. Some of the stumps are on rocky ridges of gravelly soil about one hundred and twenty-five feet above sea. The valley has been washed out by the stream now occupying it, one of the glacier's draining streams a mile long or more and an eighth of a mile wide.

I got supper early and was just going to bed, when I was startled by seeing a man coming across the moraine, Professor Reid, who had seen me from the main camp and who came with Mr Loomis and the cook in their boat to ferry me over. I had not intended making signals for them until tomorrow but was glad to go. I had been seen also by Mr Case and one of his companions, who were on the western mountain-side above the fossil forest, shooting ptarmigans. I had a good rest and sleep and leisure to find out how rich I was in new facts and pictures and how tired and hungry I was.

CHAPTER NINETEEN

Auroras

A FEW days later I set out with Professor Reid's party to visit some of the other large glaciers that flow into the bay, to observe what changes have taken place in them since October, 1879, when I first visited and sketched them. We found the upper half of the bay closely choked with bergs, through which it was exceedingly difficult to force a way. After slowly struggling a few miles up the east side, we dragged the whale-boat and canoe over rough rocks into a fine garden and comfortably camped for the night.

The next day was spent in cautiously picking a way across to the west side of the bay; and as the strangely scanty stock of provisions was already about done, and the ice-jam to the northward seemed impenetrable, the party decided to return to the main camp by a comparatively open, roundabout way to the southward, while with the canoe and a handful of food-scraps I pushed on northward. After a hard, anxious struggle, I reached the mouth of the Hugh Miller fiord about sundown, and tried to find a camp-spot on its steep, boulder-bound shore. But no landing-place where it seemed possible to drag the canoe above high-tide mark was discovered after examining a mile or more of this dreary forbidding barrier, and as night was closing down, I decided to try to grope my way across the mouth of the fiord in the starlight to an open sandy spot on which I had camped in October, 1879, a distance of about three or four miles.

With the utmost caution I picked my way through the sparkling bergs, and after an hour or two of this nerve-trying work, when I was perhaps less than half-way across and dreading the loss of the frail canoe which would include the loss of myself, I came to a pack of very large bergs which loomed threateningly, offering no visible thoroughfare. Paddling and pushing to right and left, I at last discovered a sheer-walled opening about four feet wide and perhaps two hundred feet long, formed apparently by the splitting of a huge iceberg. I hesitated to enter this passage, fearing that the slightest change in the tide-current might close it, but ventured nevertheless, judging that the dangers ahead might not be greater than those I had already passed. When I had got about a third of the way in, I suddenly discovered that the smooth-walled ice-lane was growing narrower, and with desperate haste backed out. Just as the bow of the canoe cleared the sheer walls they came together with a growling crunch. Terror-stricken, I turned back, and in an anxious hour or two gladly reached the rock-bound shore that had at first repelled me, determined to stay on guard all night in the canoe or find some place where with the strength that comes in a fight for life I could drag it up the boulder wall beyond ice danger. This at last was happily done about midnight, and with no thought of sleep I went to bed rejoicing.

My bed was two boulders, and as I lay wedged and bent on their up-bulging sides, beguiling the hard, cold time in gazing into the starry sky and across the sparkling bay, magnificent upright bars of light in bright prismatic colours suddenly appeared, marching swiftly in close succession along the northern horizon from west to east as if in diligent haste, an auroral display very different from any I had ever before beheld. Once long ago in Wisconsin I saw the heavens draped in rich purple auroral clouds fringed and folded in most magnificent forms; but in this glory of light, so pure, so bright, so enthusiastic in motion, there was nothing in the least cloud-like. The short colour-bars, apparently about two degrees in height, though blending, seemed to be as well defined as those of the solar spectrum.

How long these glad, eager soldiers of light held on their way I cannot tell; for sense of time was charmed out of mind and the blessed night circled away in measureless rejoicing enthusiasm.

In the early morning after so inspiring a night I launched my canoe feeling able for anything, crossed the mouth of the Hugh Miller fiord, and forced a way three or four miles along the shore of the bay, hoping to reach the Grand Pacific Glacier in front of Mount Fairweather. But the farther I went, the ice-pack, instead of showing inviting little open streaks here and there, became so much harder jammed that on some parts of the shore the bergs, drifting south with the tide, were shoving one another out of the water beyond high-tide line. Farther progress to northward was thus rigidly stopped, and now I had to fight for a way back to my cabin, hoping that by good tide luck I might reach it before dark. But at sundown I was less than half-way home, and though very hungry was glad to land on a little rock island with a smooth beach for the canoe and a thicket of alder bushes for fire and bed and a little sleep. But shortly after sundown, while these arrangements were being made, lo and behold another aurora enriching the heavens! and though it proved to be one of the ordinary almost colourless kind, thrusting long, quivering lances toward the zenith from a dark cloudlike base, after last night's wonderful display one's expectations might well be extravagant and I lay wide awake watching.

On the third night I reached my cabin and food. Professor Reid and his party came in to talk over the results of our excursions, and just as the last one of the visitors opened the door after bidding good-night, he shouted, 'Muir, come look here. Here's something fine.'

I ran out in auroral excitement, and sure enough here was another aurora, as novel and wonderful as the marching rainbow-coloured columns – a glowing silver bow spanning the Muir Inlet in a magnificent arch right under the zenith, or a little to the south of it, the ends resting on the top of the mountain-walls. And though colourless and steadfast, its intense, solid, white splendour, noble proportions and fineness of finish excited boundless admiration. In form and proportion it was like a rainbow, a bridge of one span five miles wide; and so brilliant, so fine and solid and homogeneous in every part, I fancy that if all the stars were raked together into one windrow, fused and welded and run through some celestial rolling-mill, all would be required to make this one glowing white colossal bridge.

After my last visitor went to bed, I lay down on the moraine in front of the cabin and gazed and watched. Hour after hour the wonderful arch stood perfectly motionless, sharply defined and substantial-looking as if it were a permanent addition to the furniture of the sky. At length while it yet spanned the inlet in serene unchanging splendour, a band of fluffy, pale grey, quivering ringlets came suddenly all in a row over the eastern mountain-top, glided in nervous haste up and down the under side of the bow and over the western mountain-wall. They were about one and a half times the apparent diameter of the bow in length, maintained a vertical posture all the way across, and slipped swiftly along as if they were suspended like a curtain on rings. Had these lively auroral fairies marched across the fiord on the top of the bow instead of shuffling along the under side of it, one might have fancied they were a happy band of spirit people on a journey making use of the splendid bow for a bridge. There must have been hundreds of miles of them; for the time required for each to cross from one end of the bridge to the other seemed only a minute or less, while nearly an hour elapsed from their first appearance until the last of the rushing throng vanished behind the western mountain, leaving the bridge as bright and solid and steadfast as before they arrived. But later, half an hour or so, it began to fade. Fissures or cracks crossed it diagonally through which a few stars were seen, and gradually it became thin and nebulous until it looked like the Milky Way, and at last vanished, leaving no visible monument of any sort to mark its place.

I now returned to my cabin, replenished the fire, warmed myself, and prepared to go to bed, though too aurorally rich and happy to go to sleep. But just as I was about to retire, I thought I had better take another look at the sky, to make sure that the glorious show was over; and, contrary to all reasonable expectations, I found that the pale foundation for another bow was being laid right overhead like the first. Then losing all thought of sleep, I ran back to my cabin, carried out blankets and lay down on the moraine to keep watch until daybreak, that none of the sky wonders of the glorious night within reach of my eyes might be lost.

I had seen the first bow when it stood complete in full splendour, and its gradual fading decay. Now I was to see the building of a new one from the beginning. Perhaps in less than half an hour the silvery material was gathered, condensed, and welded into a glowing, evenly proportioned arc like the first and in the same part of the sky. Then in due time over the eastern mountain-wall came another throng of restless electric auroral fairies, the infinitely fine pale-grey garments of each lightly touching those of their neighbours as they swept swiftly along the under side of the bridge and down over the western mountain like the merry band that had gone the same way before them, all keeping quivery step and time to music too fine for mortal ears.

While the gay throng was gliding swiftly along, I watched the bridge for any change they might make upon it, but not the slightest could I detect. They left no visible track, and after all had passed the glowing arc stood firm and apparently immutable, but at last faded slowly away like its glorious predecessor.

Excepting only the vast purple aurora mentioned above, said to have been visible over nearly all the continent, these two silver bows in supreme, serene, supernal beauty surpassed everything auroral I ever beheld.

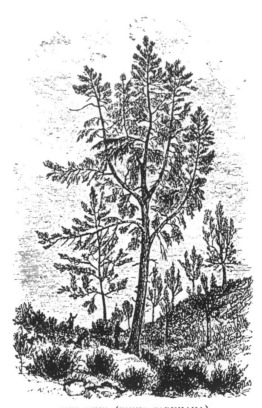

NUT PINE (PINUS SABINIANA).

STEEP TRAILS

Steep Trails

First published by Houghton Mifflin Co., Boston, 1918

EDGE OF THE TIMBER LINE ON MOUNT SHASTA.

Contents

FOREST OF SEQUOIA, SUGAR PINE, AND DOUGLAS SPRUCE.

CHAPTER ONE

Wild Wool

MORAL IMPROVERS have calls to preach. I have a friend who has a call to plough, and woe to the daisy sod or azalea thicket that falls under the savage redemption of his keen steel shares. Not content with the so-called subjugation of every terrestrial bog, rock and moorland, he would fain discover some method of reclamation applicable to the ocean and the sky, that in due calendar time they might be brought to bud and blossom as the rose. Our efforts are of no avail when we seek to turn his attention to wild roses, or to the fact that both ocean and sky are already about as rosy as possible – the one with stars, the other with dulse and foam, and wild light. The practical developments of his culture are orchards and clover-fields wearing a smiling, benevolent aspect, truly excellent in their way, though a near view discloses something barbarous in them all. Wildness charms not my friend, charm it never so wisely: and whatsoever may be the character of his heaven, his earth seems only a chaos of agricultural possibilities calling for grubbing-hoes and manures.

Sometimes I venture to approach him with a plea for wildness, when he good-naturedly shakes a big mellow apple in my face, reiterating his favourite aphorism, 'Culture is an orchard apple; Nature is a crab'. Not all culture, however, is equally destructive and inappreciative. Azure skies and crystal waters find loving recognition, and few there be who would welcome the axe among mountain pines, or would care to apply any correction to the tones and costumes of mountain waterfalls. Nevertheless, the barbarous notion is almost universally entertained by civilized man, that there is in all the manufactures of Nature something essentially coarse which can and must be eradicated by human culture. I was, therefore, delighted in finding that the wild wool growing upon mountain sheep in the neighbourhood of Mount Shasta was much finer than the average grades of cultivated wool. This *fine* discovery was made some three months ago,[1] while hunting among the Shasta sheep between Shasta and Lower Klamath Lake. Three fleeces were obtained – one that belonged to a large ram about four years old, another to a ewe about the same age, and another to a yearling lamb. After parting their beautiful wool on the side and many places along the back, shoulders and hips, and examining it closely with my lens, I shouted: 'Well done for wildness! Wild wool is finer than tame!'

My companions stooped down and examined the fleeces for themselves, pulling out tufts and ringlets, spinning them between their fingers, and

---

[1] This essay was written early in 1875. [Editor.]

measuring the length of the staple, each in turn paying tribute to wildness. It *was* finer, and no mistake; finer than Spanish Merino. Wild wool *is* finer than tame.

'Here', said I, 'is an argument for fine wildness that needs no explanation. Not that such arguments are by any means rare, for all wildness is finer than tameness, but because fine wool is appreciable by everybody alike – from the most speculative president of national wool-growers' associations all the way down to the gude-wife spinning by her ingle-side'.

Nature is a good mother, and sees well to the clothing of her many bairns – birds with smoothly imbricated feathers, beetles with shining jackets and bears with shaggy furs. In the tropical south, where the sun warms like a fire, they are allowed to go thinly clad; but in the snowy northland she takes care to clothe warmly. The squirrel has socks and mittens and a tail broad enough for a blanket; the grouse is densely feathered down to the ends of his toes; and the wild sheep, besides his undergarment of fine wool, has a thick overcoat of hair that sheds off both the snow and the rain. Other provisions and adaptations in the dresses of animals, relating less to climate than to the more mechanical circumstances of life, are made with the same consummate skill that characterizes all the love-work of Nature. Land, water and air, jagged rocks, muddy ground, sand-beds, forests, underbrush, grassy plains, etc., are considered in all their possible combinations while the clothing of her beautiful wildlings is preparing. No matter what the circumstances of their lives may be, she never allows them to go dirty or ragged. The mole, living always in the dark and in the dirt, is yet as clean as the otter or the wave-washed seal; and our wild sheep, wading in snow, roaming through bushes, and leaping among jagged storm-beaten cliffs, wears a dress so exquisitely adapted to its mountain life that it is always found as unruffled and stainless as a bird.

On leaving the Shasta hunting-grounds I selected a few specimen tufts, and brought them away with a view to making more leisurely examinations; but, owing to the imperfectness of the instruments at my command, the results thus far obtained must be regarded only as rough approximations.

As already stated, the clothing of our wild sheep is composed of fine wool and coarse hair. The hairs are from about two to four inches long, mostly of a dull bluish-grey colour, though varying somewhat with the seasons. In general characteristics they are closely related to the hairs of the deer and antelope, being light, spongy and elastic, with a highly polished surface, and though somewhat ridged and spiraled, like wool, they do not manifest the slightest tendency to felt or become taggy. A hair two and a half inches long, which is perhaps near the average length, will stretch about one fourth of an inch before breaking. The diameter decreases rapidly both at the top and bottom, but is maintained throughout the greater portion of the length with a fair degree of regularity. The slender tapering point in which the hairs terminate is nearly black: but, owing to its fineness as compared with the main trunk, the quantity of blackness is not sufficient to affect greatly the general colour. The number of hairs growing upon a square inch is about ten thousand; the number of wool fibres is about twenty-five thousand, or two and a half times that of the hairs. The wool fibres are white and glossy, and beautifully spired into ringlets. The average length of the staple is about an inch and a half. A fibre of this length, when growing undisturbed down among the hairs, measures about an inch; hence the degree of curliness may easily be inferred. I regret exceedingly that my instruments do not enable me to measure the diameter of the fibres, in order that their degrees of fineness might be definitely compared with each other and with the finest of the domestic breeds; but that the three wild fleeces under consideration are considerably finer than the average grades of Merino shipped from San Francisco is, I think, unquestionable.

When the fleece is parted and looked into with a good lens, the skin appears of a beautiful pale-yellow colour, and the delicate wool fibres are seen growing up among the strong hairs, like grass among stalks of corn, every individual fibre being protected about as specially and effectively as if enclosed in a separate husk. Wild wool is too fine to stand by itself, the fibres being about as frail and invisible as the floating threads of spiders, while the hairs against which they lean stand erect like hazel wands; but, notwithstanding their great dissimilarity in size and appearance, the wool and hair are forms of the same thing, modified in just that way and to just that degree that renders them most perfectly subservient to the well-being of the sheep. Furthermore, it will be observed that these wild modifications are entirely distinct from those which are brought chancingly into existence through the accidents and caprices of culture; the former being inventions of God for the attainment of definite ends. Like the modifications of limbs – the fin for swimming, the wing for flying, the foot for walking – so the fine wool for warmth, the hair for additional warmth and to protect the wool, and both together for a fabric to wear well in mountain roughness and wash well in mountain storms.

The effects of human culture upon wild wool are analogous to those produced upon wild roses. In the one case there is an abnormal development of petals at the expense of the stamens, in the other an abnormal development of wool at the expense of the hair. Garden roses frequently exhibit stamens in which the transmutation to petals may be observed in various stages of accomplishment, and analogously the fleeces of tame sheep occasionally contain a few wild hairs that are undergoing transmutation to wool. Even wild wool presents here and there a fibre that appears to be in a state of change. In the course of my examinations of the wild fleeces mentioned above, three fibres were found that were wool at one end and hair at the other. This, however, does not necessarily imply imperfection, or any process of change similar to that caused by human culture. Water-lilies contain parts variously developed into stamens at one end, petals at the other, as the constant and normal condition. These half wool, half hair fibres may therefore subserve some fixed requirement essential to the perfection of the whole, or they may simply be the fine boundary-lines where an exact balance between the wool and the hair is attained.

I have been offering samples of mountain wool to my friends, demanding in return that the fineness of wildness be fairly recognized and confessed, but the returns are deplorably tame. The first question asked is, 'Now truly, wild sheep, wild sheep, have you any wool?' while they peer curiously down among the hairs through lenses and spectacles. 'Yes, wild sheep, you *have* wool; but Mary's lamb had more. In the name of use, how many wild sheep, think you, would be required to furnish wool sufficient for a pair of socks?' I endeavour to point out the irrelevancy of the latter question, arguing that wild wool was not made for man but for sheep, and that, however deficient as clothing for other animals, it is just the thing for the brave mountain-dweller that wears it. Plain, however, as all this appears, the quantity question rises again and again in all its commonplace tameness. For in my experience it seems well-nigh impossible to obtain a hearing on behalf of Nature from any other standpoint than that of human use. Domestic flocks yield more flannel per sheep than the wild, therefore it is claimed that culture has improved upon wildness; and so it has as far as flannel is concerned, but all to the contrary as far as a sheep's dress is concerned. If every wild sheep inhabiting the Sierra were to put on tame wool, probably only a few would survive the dangers of a single season. With their fine limbs muffled and buried beneath a tangle of hairless wool, they would become short-winded, and fall an easy prey to the strong mountain wolves. In descending precipices they would be thrown out of balance and killed, by their taggy wool catching upon sharp points of rocks. Disease would also be brought on by the dirt which always finds a lodgment in tame wool, and by the draggled and water-soaked condition into which it falls during stormy weather.

No dogma taught by the present civilization seems to form so insuperable an obstacle in the way of a right understanding of the relations which culture sustains to wildness as that which regards the world as made especially for the uses of man. Every animal, plant and crystal controverts it in the plainest terms. Yet it is taught from century to century as something ever new and precious, and in the resulting darkness the enormous conceit is allowed to go unchallenged.

I have never yet happened upon a trace of evidence that seemed to show that any one animal was ever made for another as much as it was made for itself. Not that Nature manifests any such thing as selfish isolation. In the making of every animal the presence of every other animal has been recognized. Indeed, every atom in creation may be said to be acquainted with and married to every other, but with universal union there is a division sufficient in degree for the purposes of the most intense individuality; no matter, therefore, what may be the note which any creature forms in the song of existence, it is made first for itself, then more and more remotely for all the world and worlds.

Were it not for the exercise of individualizing cares on the part of Nature, the universe would be felted together like a fleece of tame wool. But we are governed more than we know, and most when we are wildest. Plants, animals and stars are all kept in place, bridled along appointed ways, *with* one another, and *through the midst* of one another – killing and being killed, eating and being eaten, in harmonious proportions and quantities. And it is right that we should thus reciprocally make use of one another, rob, cook and consume, to the utmost of our healthy abilities and desires. Stars attract one another as they are able, and harmony results. Wild lambs eat as many wild flowers as they can find or desire, and men and wolves eat the lambs to just the same extent.

This consumption of one another in its various modifications is a kind of culture varying with the degree of directness with which it is carried out, but we should be careful not to ascribe to such culture any improving qualities upon those on whom it is brought to bear. The water-ouzel plucks moss from the river-bank to build its nest, but it does not improve the moss by plucking it. We pluck feathers from birds, and less directly wool from wild sheep, for the manufacture of clothing and cradle-nests, without improving the wool for the sheep, or the feathers for the bird that wore them. When a hawk pounces upon a linnet and proceeds to pull out its feathers, preparatory to making a meal, the hawk may be said to be cultivating the linnet, and he certainly does effect an improvement as far as hawk-food is concerned; but what of the songster? He ceases to be a linnet as soon as he is snatched from the woodland choir; and when, hawklike, we snatch the wild sheep from its native rock, and, instead of eating and wearing it at once, carry it home, and breed the hair out of its wool and the bones out of its body, it ceases to be a sheep.

These breeding and plucking processes are similarly improving as regards the secondary uses aimed at; and, although the one requires but a few minutes for its accomplishment, the other many years or centuries, they are essentially alike. We eat wild oysters alive with great directness, waiting for no cultivation, and leaving scarce a second of distance between the shell and the lip; but we take wild sheep home and subject them to the many extended processes of husbandry, and finish by boiling them in a pot – a process which completes all sheep improvements as far as man is concerned. It will be seen, therefore, that wild wool and tame wool – wild sheep and tame sheep – arc terms not properly comparable, nor are they in any correct sense to be considered as bearing any antagonism toward each other; they are different things, planned and accomplished for wholly different purposes.

Illustrative examples bearing upon this interesting subject may be multiplied indefinitely, for they abound everywhere in the plant and animal kingdoms wherever culture has reached. Recurring for a moment to apples. The beauty and completeness of a wild apple tree living its own life in the woods is heartily acknowledged by all those who have been so happy as to form its acquaintance. The fine wild piquancy of its fruit is unrivalled, but in the great question of quantity as human food wild apples are found wanting. Man, therefore, takes the tree from the woods, manures and prunes and grafts, plans and guesses, adds a little of this and that, selects and rejects, until apples of every conceivable size and softness are produced, like nut-galls in response to the irritating punctures of insects. Orchard apples are to me the most eloquent words that culture has ever spoken, but they reflect no imperfection upon Nature's spicy crab. Every cultivated apple is a crab, not improved, *but cooked*, variously softened and swelled out in the process, mellowed, sweetened, spiced and rendered pulpy and foodful, but as utterly unfit for the uses of nature as a meadowlark killed and plucked and roasted. Give to Nature every cultured apple – codling, pippin, russet – and every sheep so laboriously compounded – muffled Southdowns, hairy Cotswolds, wrinkled Merinos – and she would throw the one to her caterpillars, the other to her wolves.

It is now some thirty-six hundred years since Jacob kissed his mother and set out across the plains of Padan-aram to begin his experiments upon the flocks of his uncle, Laban; and, notwithstanding the high degree of excellence he attained as a wool-grower, and the innumerable painstaking efforts subsequently made by individuals and associations in all kinds of pastures and climates, we still seem to be as far from definite and satisfactory results as we ever were. In one breed the wool is apt to wither and crinkle like hay on a sunbeaten hillside. In another, it is lodged and matted together like the lush tangled grass of a manured meadow. In one the staple is deficient in length, in another in fineness; while in all there is a constant tendency toward disease, rendering various washings and dippings indispensable to prevent its falling out. The problem of the quality and quantity of the carcass seems to be as doubtful and as far removed from a satisfactory solution as that of the wool. Desirable breeds blundered upon by long series of groping experiments are often found to be unstable and subject to disease – bots, foot-rot, blind-staggers, etc. – causing infinite trouble, both among breeders and manufacturers. Would it not be well, therefore, for someone to go back as far as possible and take a fresh start?

The source or sources whence the various breeds were derived is not positively known, but there can be hardly any doubt of their being descendants of the four or five wild species so generally distributed throughout the mountainous portions of the globe, the marked differences between the wild and domestic species being readily accounted for by the known variability of the animal, and by the long series of painstaking selection to which all its characteristics have been subjected. No other animal seems to yield so submissively to the manipulations of culture. Jacob controlled the colour of his flocks merely by causing them to stare at objects of the desired hue; and possibly Merinos may have caught their wrinkles from the perplexed brows of their breeders. The California species (*Ovis montana*)[1] is a noble animal, weighing when full-grown some three hundred and fifty pounds, and is well worthy the attention of wool-growers as a point from which to make a new departure, for pure wildness is the one great want, both of men and of sheep.

[1] The wild sheep of California are now classified as *Ovis nelsoni*. Whether those of the Shasta region belonged to the latter species, or to the bighorn species of Oregon, Idaho and Washington, is still an unsettled question. [Editor.]

CHAPTER TWO

A Geologist's Winter Walk[1]

AFTER REACHING Turlock, I sped afoot over the stubble fields and through miles of brown hemizonia and purple erigeron, to Hopeton, conscious of little more than that the town was behind and beneath me, and the mountains above and before me; on through the oaks and chaparral of the foothills to Coulterville; and then ascended the first great mountain step upon which grows the sugar pine. Here I slackened pace, for I drank the spicy, resiny wind, and beneath the arms of this noble tree I felt that I was safely home. Never did pine trees seem so dear. How sweet was their breath and their song and how grandly they winnowed the sky! I tingled my fingers among their tassels, and rustled my feet among their brown needles and burrs, and was exhilarated and joyful beyond all I can write.

When I reached Yosemite, all the rocks seemed talkative, and more telling and lovable than ever. They are dear friends, and seemed to have warm blood gushing through their granite flesh; and I love them with a love intensified by long and close companionship. After I had bathed in the bright river, sauntered over the meadows, conversed with the domes, and played with the pines, I still felt blurred and weary, as if tainted in some way with the sky of your streets. I determined, therefore, to run out for a while to say my prayers in the higher mountain temples. 'The days are sunful', I said, 'and, though now winter, no great danger need be encountered, and no sudden storm will block my return, if I am watchful'.

The morning after this decision, I started up the canyon of Tenaya, caring little about the quantity of bread I carried; for, I thought, a fast and a storm and a difficult canyon were just the medicine I needed. When I passed Mirror Lake, I scarcely noticed it, for I was absorbed in the great Tissiack – her crown a mile away in the hushed azure; her purple granite drapery flowing in soft and graceful folds down to my feet, embroidered gloriously around with deep, shadowy forest. I have gazed on Tissiack a thousand times – in days of solemn storms, and when her form shone divine with the jewellery of winter, or was veiled in living clouds; and I have heard her voice of winds, and snowy, tuneful waters when floods were falling; yet never did her soul reveal itself more impressively than now. I hung about her skirts, lingering timidly, until the higher mountains and glaciers compelled me to push up the canyon.

This canyon is accessible only to mountaineers, and I was anxious to carry my barometer and clinometer through it, to obtain sections and altitudes, so I chose it as the most attractive highway. After I had passed the tall groves that

[1] An excerpt from a letter to a friend, written in 1872. [Editor.]

stretch a mile above Mirror Lake, and scrambled around the Tenaya Fall, which is just at the head of the lake groves, I crept through the dense and spiny chaparral that plushes the roots of the mountains here for miles in warm green, and was ascending a precipitous rock-front, smoothed by glacial action, when I suddenly fell – for the first time since I touched foot to Sierra rocks. After several somersaults, I became insensible from the shock, and when consciousness returned I found myself wedged among short, stiff bushes, trembling as if cold, not injured in the slightest.

Judging by the sun, I could not have been insensible very long; probably not a minute, possibly an hour; and I could not remember what made me fall, or where I had fallen from; but I saw that if I had rolled a little farther, my mountain-climbing would have been finished, for just beyond the bushes the canyon wall steepened and I might have fallen to the bottom. 'There', said I, addressing my feet, to whose separate skill I had learned to trust night and day on any mountain, 'that is what you get by intercourse with stupid town stairs, and dead pavements'. I felt degraded and worthless. I had not yet reached the most difficult portion of the canyon, but I determined to guide my humbled body over the most nerve-trying places I could find; for I was now awake, and felt confident that the last of the town fog had been shaken from both head and feet.

I camped at the mouth of a narrow gorge which is cut into the bottom of the main canyon, determined to take earnest exercise next day. No plushy boughs did my ill-behaved bones enjoy that night, nor did my bumped head get a spicy cedar plume pillow mixed with flowers. I slept on a naked boulder, and when I awoke all my nervous trembling was gone.

The gorged portion of the canyon, in which I spent all the next day, is about a mile and a half in length; and I passed the time in tracing the action of the forces that determined this peculiar bottom gorge, which is an abrupt, ragged-walled, narrow-throated canyon, formed in the bottom of the wide-mouthed, smooth and bevelled main canyon. I will not stop now to tell you more; some day you may see it, like a shadowy line, from Clouds' Rest. In high water, the stream occupies all the bottom of the gorge, surging and chafing in glorious power from wall to wall. But the sound of the grinding was low as I entered the gorge, scarcely hoping to be able to pass through its entire length. By cool efforts, along glassy, ice-worn slopes, I reached the upper end in a little over a day, but was compelled to pass the second night in the gorge, and in the moonlight I wrote you this short pencil-letter in my notebook:

The moon is looking down into the canyon, and how marvellously the great rocks kindle to her light! Every dome, and brow, and swelling boss touched by her white rays, glows as if lighted with snow. I am now only a mile from last night's camp; and have been climbing and sketching all day in this difficult but instructive gorge. It is formed in the bottom of the main canyon, among the roots of Clouds' Rest. It begins at the filled-up lake-basin where I camped last night, and ends a few hundred yards above, in another basin of the same kind. The walls everywhere are craggy and vertical, and in some places they overlean. It is only from twenty to sixty feet wide, and not, though black and broken enough, the thin, crooked mouth of some mysterious abyss; but it was eroded, for in many places I saw its solid, seamless floor.

I am sitting on a big stone, against which the stream divides, and goes brawling by its rapids on both sides; half of my rock is white in the light, half in shadow. As I look from the opening jaws of this shadowy gorge, South Dome is immediately in front – high in the stars, her face turned from the moon, with the rest of her body gloriously muffled in waved folds of granite. On the left, sculptured from the main Cloud's Rest ridge, are three magnificent rocks, sisters of the great South Dome. On the right is the massive, moonlit front of Mount Watkins, and between, low down on the farthest distance, is Sentinel Dome, girdled and darkened with forest. In the near foreground Tenaya Creek is singing against boulders that are white with snow and moonbeams. Now look back twenty yards, and you will see a waterfall fair as a spirit; the moonlight just touches it, bringing it into relief against a dark background of shadow. A little to the left, and a dozen steps this side of the fall, a flickering light marks my camp – and a precious camp it is. A huge, glacier-polished slab, falling from the smooth, glossy flank of Cloud's Rest, happened to settle on edge against the wall of the gorge. I did not know that this slab was glacier-polished until I lighted my fire. Judge of my delight. I think it was sent here by an earthquake. It is about twelve feet square. I wish I could take it home[1] for a hearthstone. Beneath this slab is the only place in this torrent-swept gorge where I could find sand sufficient for a bed.

I expected to sleep on the boulders, for I spent most of the afternoon on the slippery wall of the canyon, endeavouring to get around this difficult part of the gorge, and was compelled to hasten down here for water before dark. I shall sleep soundly on this sand; half of it is mica. Here, wonderful to behold, are a few green stems of prickly rubus, and a tiny grass. They are here to meet us. Ay, even here in this darksome gorge, 'frightened and tormented' with raging torrents and choking avalanches of snow. Can it be? As if rubus and the grass leaf were not enough of God's tender prattle words of love, which we so much need in these mighty temples of power, yonder in the 'benmost bore' are two blessed adiantums. Listen to them! How wholly infused with God is this one big word of love that we call the world! Good-night. Do you see the fire-glow on my ice-smoothed slab, and on my two ferns and the rubus and grass panicles? And do you hear how sweet a sleep-song the fall and cascades are singing?

The water-ground chips and knots that I found fastened between the rocks kept my fire alive all through the night. Next morning I rose nerved and ready for another day of sketching and noting, and any form of climbing. I escaped from the gorge about noon, after accomplishing some of the most delicate feats of mountaineering I ever attempted; and here the canyon is all broadly open again – the floor luxuriantly forested with pine, and spruce, and silver fir, and brown-trunked librocedrus. The walls rise in Yosemite forms, and Tenaya Creek comes down seven hundred feet in a white brush of foam. This is a little Yosemite valley. It is about two thousand feet above the level of the main Yosemite, and about twenty-four hundred below Lake Tenaya.

I found the lake frozen, and the ice was so clear and unruffled that the surrounding mountains and the groves that look down upon it were reflected almost as perfectly as I ever beheld them in the calm evening mirrors of summer. At a little distance, it was difficult to believe the lake frozen at all; and when I walked out on it, cautiously stamping at short intervals to test the strength of the ice, I seemed to walk mysteriously, without adequate faith, on the surface of the water. The ice was so transparent that I could see through it

---

[1] Muir at this time was making Yosemite Valley his home. [Editor.]

the beautifully wave-rippled, sandy bottom, and the scales of mica glinting back the down-pouring light. When I knelt down with my face close to the ice, through which the sunbeams were pouring, I was delighted to discover myriads of Tyndall's six-rayed water flowers, magnificently coloured.

A grand old mountain mansion is this Tenaya region! In the glacier period it was a *mer de glace*, far grander than the *mer de glace* of Switzerland, which is only about half a mile broad. The Tenaya *mer de glace* was not less than two miles broad, late in the glacier epoch, when all the principal dividing crests were bare; and its depth was not less than fifteen hundred feet. Ice-streams from Mounts Lyell and Dana, and all the mountains between, and from the nearer Cathedral Peak, flowed hither, welded into one, and worked together. After eroding this Tenaya Lake basin, and all the splendidly sculptured rocks and mountains that surround and adorn it, and the great Tenaya Canyon, with its wealth of all that makes mountains sublime, they were welded with the vast South, Lyell and Illilouette glaciers on one side, and with those of Hoffman on the other – thus forming a portion of a yet grander *mer de glace* in Yosemite Valley.

I reached the Tenaya Canyon, on my way home, by coming in from the northeast, rambling down over the shoulders of Mount Watkins, touching bottom a mile above Mirror Lake. From thence home was but a saunter in the moonlight.

After resting one day, and the weather continuing calm, I ran up over the left shoulder of South Dome and down in front of its grand split face to make some measurements, completed my work, climbed to the right shoulder, struck off along the ridge for Cloud's Rest, and reached the topmost heave of her sunny wave in ample time to see the sunset.

Cloud's Rest is a thousand feet higher than Tissiack. It is a wavelike crest upon a ridge, which begins at Yosemite with Tissiack, and runs continuously eastward to the thicket of peaks and crests around Lake Tenaya. This lofty granite wall is bent this way and that by the restless and weariless action of glaciers just as if it had been made of dough. But the grand circumference of mountains and forests are coming from far and near, densing into one close assemblage; for the sun, their god and father, with love ineffable, is glowing a sunset farewell. Not one of all the assembled rocks or trees seemed remote. How impressively their faces shone with responsive love!

I ran home in the moonlight with firm strides; for the sun-love made me strong. Down through the junipers; down through the firs; now in jet shadows, now in white light; over sandy moraines and bare, clanking rocks; past the huge ghost of South Dome rising weird through the firs; past the glorious fall of Nevada, the groves of Illilouette; through the pines of the valley; beneath the bright crystal sky blazing with stars. All of this mountain wealth in one day! – one of the rich ripe days that enlarge one's life; so much of the sun upon one side of it, so much of the moon and stars on the other.

CHAPTER THREE

Summer Days at Mount Shasta

MOUNT SHASTA rises in solitary grandeur from the edge of a comparatively
low and lightly sculptured lava plain near the northern extremity of the
Sierra, and maintains a far more impressive and commanding individuality
than any other mountain within the limits of California. Go where you may,
within a radius of from fifty to a hundred miles or more, there stands before
you the colossal cone of Shasta, clad in ice and snow, the one grand, unmistakable landmark – the pole-star of the landscape. Far to the southward
Mount Whitney lifts its granite summit four or five hundred feet higher than
Shasta, but it is nearly snowless during the late summer, and is so feebly
individualized that the traveller may search for it in vain among the many
rival peaks crowded along the axis of the range to north and south of it, which
all alike are crumbling residual masses brought into relief in the degradation
of the general mass of the range. The highest point on Mount Shasta, as
determined by the State Geological Survey, is 14,440ft. above mean tide.
That of Whitney, computed from fewer observations, is about 14,900ft. But
inasmuch as the average elevation of the plain out of which Shasta rises is only
about four thousand feet above the sea, while the actual base of the peak of
Mount Whitney lies at an elevation of eleven thousand feet, the individual
height of the former is about two and a half times as great as that of the latter.

Approaching Shasta from the south, one obtains glimpses of its snowy cone
here and there through the trees from the tops of hills and ridges; but it is not
until Strawberry Valley is reached, where there is a grand out-opening of the
forests, that Shasta is seen in all its glory, from base to crown clearly revealed
with its wealth of woods and waters and fountain snow, rejoicing in the bright
mountain sky, and radiating beauty on all the subject landscape like a sun.
Standing in a fringing thicket of purple spiraea in the immediate foreground is
a smooth expanse of green meadow with its meandering stream, one of the
smaller affluents of the Sacramento; then a zone of dark, close forest, its
countless spires of pine and fir rising above one another on the swelling base
of the mountain in glorious array; and, over all, the great white cone sweeping far into the thin, keen sky – meadow, forest and grand icy summit
harmoniously blending and making one sublime picture evenly balanced.

The main lines of the landscape are immensely bold and simple, and so
regular that it needs all its shaggy wealth of woods and chaparral and its finely
tinted ice and snow and brown jutting crags to keep it from looking
conventional. In general views of the mountain three distinct zones may be
readily defined. The first, which may be called the Chaparral Zone, extends
around the base in a magnificent sweep nearly a hundred miles in length on its

lower edge, and with a breadth of about seven miles. It is a dense growth of chaparral from three to six or eight feet high, composed chiefly of manzanita, cherry, chincapin and several species of ceanothus, called deerbrush by the hunters, forming, when in full bloom, one of the most glorious flower-beds conceivable. The continuity of this flowery zone is interrupted here and there, especially on the south side of the mountain, by wide swaths of coniferous trees, chiefly the sugar and yellow pines, Douglas spruce, silver fir and incense cedar, many specimens of which are two hundred feet high and five to seven feet in diameter. Goldenrods, asters, gilias, lilies and lupines, with many other less conspicuous plants, occur in warm sheltered openings in these lower woods, making charming gardens of wildness where bees and butterflies are at home and many a shy bird and squirrel.

The next higher is the Fir Zone, made up almost exclusively of two species of silver fir. It is from two to three miles wide, has an average elevation above the sea of some six thousand feet on its lower edge and eight thousand on its upper, and is the most regular and best defined of the three.

The Alpine Zone has a rugged, straggling growth of storm-beaten dwarf pines (*Pinus albicaulis*), which forms the upper edge of the timber-line. This species reaches an elevation of about nine thousand feet, but at this height the tops of the trees rise only a few feet into the thin frosty air, and are closely pressed and shorn by wind and snow; yet they hold on bravely and put forth an abundance of beautiful purple flowers and produce cones and seeds. Down towards the edge of the fir belt they stand erect, forming small, well-formed trunks, and are associated with the taller two-leafed and mountain pines and the beautiful Williamson spruce. Bryanthus, a beautiful flowering heathwort, flourishes a few hundred feet above the timber-line, accompanied with kalmia and spiræa. Lichens enliven the faces of the clifs with their bright colours, and in some of the warmer nooks of the rocks, up to a height of eleven thousand feet, there are a few tufts of dwarf daisies, wall-flowers and penstemons; but, notwithstanding these bloom freely, they make no appreciable show at a distance, and the stretches of rough brown lava beyond the storm-beaten trees seem as bare of vegetation as the great snow-fields and glaciers of the summit.

Shasta is a fire-mountain, an old volcano gradually accumulated and built up into the blue deep of the sky by successive eruptions of ashes and molten lava which, shot high in the air and falling in darkening showers, and flowing from chasms and craters, grew outward and upward like the trunk of a knotty, bulging tree. Not in one grand convulsion was Shasta given birth, nor in any one special period of volcanic storm and stress, though mountains more than a thousand feet in height have been cast up like mole-hills in a night – quick contributions to the wealth of the landscapes, and most emphatic statements, on the part of Nature, of the gigantic character of the power that dwells beneath the dull, dead-looking surface of the earth. But sections cut by the glaciers, displaying some of the internal framework of Shasta, show that comparatively long periods of quiescence intervened between many distinct eruptions, during which the cooling lavas ceased to flow, and took their places as permanent additions to the bulk of the growing mountain. Thus with alternate haste and deliberation eruption succeeded eruption, until Mount Shasta surpassed even its present sublime height.

Then followed a strange contrast. The glacial winter came on. The sky that so often had been darkened with storms of cinders and ashes and lighted by the glare of volcanic fires was filled with crystal snow-flowers, which, loading the cooling mountain, gave birth to glaciers that, uniting edge to edge, at length formed one grand conical glacier – a down-crawling mantle of ice upon a fountain of smouldering fire, crushing and grinding its brown, flinty lavas, and thus degrading and remodelling the entire mountain from summit to base. How much denudation and degradation has been effected we have no means of determining, the porous, crumbling rocks being ill adapted for the reception and preservation of glacial inscriptions.

The summit is now a mass of ruins, and all the finer striations have been effaced from the flanks by post-glacial weathering, while the irregularity of its lavas as regards susceptibility to erosion, and the disturbance caused by inter- and post-glacial eruptions, have obscured or obliterated those heavier characters of the glacial record found so clearly inscribed upon the granite pages of the High Sierra between latitude 36°30' and 39°. This much, however, is plain: that the summit of the mountain was considerably lowered, and the sides were deeply grooved and fluted while it was a centre of dispersal for the glaciers of the circumjacent region. And when at length the glacial period began to draw near its close, the ice mantle was gradually melted off around the base of the mountain, and in receding and breaking up into its present fragmentary condition the irregular heaps and rings of moraine matter were stored upon its flanks on which the forests are growing. The glacial erosion of most of the Shasta lavas gives rise to detritus composed of rough subangular boulders of moderate size and porous gravel and sand, which yields freely to the transporting power of running water. Several centuries ago immense quantities of this lighter material were washed down from the higher slopes by a flood of extraordinary magnitude, caused probably by the sudden melting of the ice and snow during an eruption, giving rise to the deposition of conspicuous delta-like beds around the base. And it is upon these flood-beds of moraine soil, thus suddenly and simultaneously laid down and joined edge to edge, that the flowery chaparral is growing.

Thus, by forces seemingly antagonistic and destructive, Nature accomplishes her beneficent designs – now a flood of fire, now a flood of ice, now a flood of water; and again in the fullness of time an outburst of organic life – forest and garden, with all their wealth of fruit and flowers, the air stirred into one universal hum with rejoicing insects, a milky way of wings and petals, girdling the new-born mountain like a cloud, as if the vivifying sunbeams beating against its sides had broken into a foam of plant-bloom and bees.

But with such grand displays as Nature is making here, how grand are her reservations, bestowed only upon those who devotedly seek them! Beneath the smooth and snowy surface the fountain fires are still aglow, to blaze forth afresh at their appointed times. The glaciers, looking so still and small at a distance, represented by the artist with a patch of white paint laid on by a single stroke of his brush, are still flowing onward, unhalting, with deep crystal currents, sculpturing the mountain with stern, resistless energy. How many caves and fountains that no eye has yet seen lie with all their fine furniture deep down in the darkness, and how many shy wild creatures are at home beneath the grateful lights and shadows of the woods, rejoicing in their fullness of perfect life!

Standing on the edge of the Strawberry Meadows in the sun-days of summer, not a foot or feather or leaf seems to stir; and the grand, towering mountain with all its inhabitants appears in rest, calm as a star. Yet how profound is the energy ever in action, and how great is the multitude of claws and teeth, wings and eyes, wide-awake and at work and shining! Going into the blessed wilderness, the blood of the plants throbbing beneath the life-giving sunshine seems to be heard and felt; plant-growth goes on before our eyes, and every tree and bush and flower is seen as a hive of restless industry. The deeps of the sky are mottled with singing wings of every colour and tone – clouds of brilliant chrysididæ dancing and swirling in joyous rhythm, golden-barred vespidæ, butterflies, grating cicadas and jolly rattling grasshoppers – fairly enamelling the light, and shaking all the air into music. Happy fellows they are, every one of them, blowing tiny pipe and trumpet, plodding and prancing, at work or at play.

Though winter holds the summit, Shasta in summer is mostly a massy, bossy mound of flowers coloured like the alpenglow that flushes the snow. There are miles of wild roses, pink bells of huckleberry and sweet manzanita, every bell a honey-cup, plants that tell of the north and of the south; tall nodding lilies, the crimson sarcodes, rhododendron, cassiope and blessed linnæa; phlox, calycanthus, plum, cherry, cratægus, spiræa, mints and clovers in endless variety; ivesia, larkspur and columbine; golden aplopappus, linosyris,[1] bahia, wyethia, arnica, brodiæa, etc. – making sheets and beds of light edgings of bloom in lavish abundance for the myriads of the air dependent on their bounty.

The common honey-bees, gone wild in this sweet wilderness, gather tons of honey into the hollows of the trees and rocks, clambering eagerly through bramble and hucklebloom, shaking the clustered bells of the generous manzanita, now humming aloft among polleny willows and firs, now down on the ashy ground among small gilias and buttercups, and anon plunging into banks of snowy cherry and buckthorn. They consider the lilies and roll into them, pushing their blunt polleny faces against them like babies on their mother's bosom; and fondly, too, with eternal love does Mother Nature clasp her small bee-babies and suckle them, multitudes at once, on her warm Shasta breast. Besides the common honey-bee there are many others here, fine burly, mossy fellows, such as were nourished on the mountains many a flowery century before the advent of the domestic species – bumble-bees, mason-bees, carpenter-bees and leaf-cutters. Butterflies, too, and moths of every size and pattern; some wide-winged like bats, flapping slowly and sailing in easy curves; others like small flying violets shaking about loosely in short zigzag flights close to the flowers, feasting in plenty night and day.

---

[1] An obsolete genus of plants now replaced in the main by *Chrysothamnus* and *Ericameria*. [Editor.]

Deer in great abundance come to Shasta from the warmer foothills every spring to feed in the rich, cool pastures, and bring forth their young in the ceanothus tangles of the chaparral zone, retiring again before the snowstorms of winter, mostly to the southward and westward of the mountain. In like manner the wild sheep of the adjacent region seek the lofty inaccessible crags of the summit as the snow melts, and are driven down to the lower spurs and ridges where there is but little snow, to the north and east of Shasta.

Bears, too, roam this foodful wilderness, feeding on grass, clover, berries, nuts, ant-eggs, fish, flesh or fowl, – whatever comes in their way – with but little troublesome discrimination. Sugar and honey they seem to like best of all, and they seek far to find the sweets; but when hard pushed by hunger they make out to gnaw a living from the bark of trees and rotten logs, and might almost live on clean lava alone.

Notwithstanding the California bears have had as yet but little experience with honey-bees, they sometimes succeed in reaching the bountiful stores of these industrious gatherers and enjoy the feast with majestic relish. But most honey-bees in search of a home are wise enough to make choice of a hollow in a living tree far from the ground, whenever such can be found. There they are pretty secure, for though the smaller brown and black bears climb well, they are unable to gnaw their way into strong hives, while compelled to exert themselves to keep from falling and at the same time endure the stings of the bees about the nose and eyes, without having their paws free to brush them off. But woe to the unfortunates who dwell in some prostrate trunk, and to the black bumble-bees discovered in their mossy, mouselike nests in the ground. With powerful teeth and claws these are speedily laid bare, and almost before time is given for a general buzz the bees, old and young, larvæ, honey, stings, nest and all, are devoured in one ravishing revel.

The antelope may still be found in considerable numbers to the northeastward of Shasta, but the elk, once abundant, have almost entirely gone from the region. The smaller animals, such as the wolf, the various foxes, wildcats, coon, squirrels and the curious wood rat that builds large brush huts, abound in all the wilder places; and the beaver, otter, mink, etc., may still be found along the sources of the rivers. The blue grouse and mountain quail are plentiful in the woods and the sage-hen on the plains about the northern base of the mountain, while innumerable smaller birds enliven and sweeten every thicket and grove.

There are at least five classes of human inhabitants about the Shasta region: the Indians, now scattered, few in numbers and miserably demoralized, though still offering some rare specimens of savage manhood; miners and prospectors, found mostly to the north and west of the mountain, since the region about its base is overflowed with lava; cattle-raisers, mostly on the open plains to the northeastward and around the Klamath Lakes; hunters and trappers, where the woods and waters are wildest; and farmers, in Shasta Valley on the north side of the mountain, wheat, apples, melons, berries, all the best production of farm and garden growing and ripening there at the foot of the great white cone, which seems at times during changing storms ready to fall upon them – the most sublime farm scenery imaginable.

The Indians of the McCloud River that have come under my observation differ considerably in habits and features from the Diggers and other tribes of the foothills and plains, and also from the Pah Utes and Modocs. They live chiefly on salmon. They seem to be closely related to the Tlingits of Alaska, Washington and Oregon, and may readily have found their way here by passing from stream to stream in which salmon abound. They have much better features than the Indians of the plains, and are rather wide awake, speculative and ambitious in their way, and garrulous, like the natives of the northern coast.

Before the Modoc War they lived in dread of the Modocs, a tribe living about the Klamath Lake and the Lava Beds, who were in the habit of crossing the low Sierra divide past the base of Shasta on freebooting excursions, stealing wives, fish and weapons from the Pitts and McClouds. Mothers would hush their children by telling them that the Modocs would catch them.

During my stay at the Government fish-hatching station on the McCloud I was accompanied in my walks along the river-bank by a McCloud boy about ten years of age, a bright, inquisitive fellow, who gave me the Indian names of the birds and plants that we met. The water-ouzel he knew well and he seemed to like the sweet singer, which he called 'Sussinny'. He showed me how strips of the stems of the beautiful maidenhair fern were used to adorn baskets with handsome brown bands, and pointed out several plants good to eat, particularly the large saxifrage growing abundantly along the river-margin. Once I rushed suddenly upon him to see if he would be frightened; but he unflinchingly held his ground, struck a grand heroic attitude, and shouted, 'Me no 'fraid; me Modoc!'

Mount Shasta, so far as I have seen, has never been the home of Indians, not even their hunting-ground to any great extent, above the lower slopes of the base. They are said to be afraid of fire-mountains and geyser-basins as being the dwelling-places of dangerously powerful and unmanageable gods. However, it is food and their relations to other tribes that mainly control the movements of Indians; and here their food was mostly on the lower slopes, with nothing except the wild sheep to tempt them higher. Even these were brought within reach without excessive climbing during the storms of winter.

On the north side of Shasta, near Sheep Rock, there is a long cavern, sloping to the northward, nearly a mile in length, thirty or forty feet wide, and fifty feet or more in height, regular in form and direction like a railroad tunnel, and probably formed by the flowing away of a current of lava after the hardening of the surface. At the mouth of this cave, where the light and shelter is good, I found many of the heads and horns of the wild sheep, and the remains of campfires, no doubt those of Indian hunters who in stormy weather had camped there and feasted after the fatigues of the chase. A wild picture that must have formed on a dark night – the glow of the fire, the circle of crouching savages around it seen through the smoke, the dead game, and the weird darkness and half-darkness of the walls of the cavern, a picture of cave-dwellers at home in the stone age!

Interest in hunting is almost universal, so deeply is it rooted as an inherited instinct ever ready to rise and make itself known. Fine scenery may not stir a fibre of mind or body, but how quick and how true is the excitement of the pursuit of game! Then up flames the slumbering volcano of ancient wildness, all that has been done by church and school through centuries of cultivation is for the moment destroyed, and the decent gentleman or devout saint becomes a howling, bloodthirsty, demented savage. It is not long since we all were cave-men and followed game for food as truly as wildcat or wolf, and the long repression of civilization seems to make the rebound to savage love of blood all the more violent. This frenzy, fortunately, does not last long in its most exaggerated form, and after a season of wildness refined gentlemen from cities are not more cruel than hunters and trappers who kill for a living.

Dwelling apart in the depths of the woods are the various kinds of mountaineers – hunters, prospectors and the like – rare men, 'queer characters', and well worth knowing, Their cabins are located with reference to game and the ledges to be examined, and are constructed almost as simply as those of the wood rats made of sticks laid across each other without compass or square. But they afford good shelter from storms, and so are 'square' with the need of their builders. These men as a class are singularly fine in manners, though their faces may be scarred and rough like the bark of trees. On entering their cabins you will promptly be placed on your good behaviour, and, your wants being perceived with quick insight, complete hospitality will be offered for body and mind to the extent of the larder.

These men know the mountains far and near, and their thousand voices, like the leaves of a book. They can tell where the deer may be found at any time of year or day, and what they are doing; and so of all the other furred and feathered people they meet in their walks; and they can send a thought to its mark as well as a bullet. The aims of such people are not always the highest, yet how brave and manly and clean are their lives compared with too many in crowded towns mildewed and dwarfed in disease and crime! How fine a chance is here to begin life anew in the free fountains and sky-lands of Shasta, where it is so easy to live and to die! The future of the hunter is likely to be a good one; no abrupt change about it, only a passing from wilderness to wilderness, from one high place to another.

Now that the railroad has been built up the Sacramento, everybody with money may go to Mount Shasta, the weak as well as the strong, fine-grained, succulent people, whose legs have never ripened, as well as sinewy mountaineers seasoned long in the weather. This, surely, is not the best way of going to the mountains, yet it is better than staying below. Many still small voices will not be heard in the noisy rush and din, suggestive of going to the sky in a chariot of fire or a whirlwind, as one is shot to the Shasta mark in a booming palace-car cartridge; up the rocky canyon, skimming the foaming river, above the level reaches, above the dashing spray – fine exhilarating translation, yet a pity to go so fast in a blur, where so much might be seen and enjoyed.

The mountains are fountains, not only of rivers and fertile soil, but of men. Therefore we are all, in some sense, mountaineers, and going to the mountains is going home. Yet how many are doomed to toil in town shadows while the white mountains beckon all along the horizon! Up the canyon to Shasta would be a cure for all care. But many on arrival seem at a loss to know what to do with themselves, and seek shelter in the hotel, as if that were the Shasta they had come for. Others never leave the rail, content with the window views, and cling to the comforts of the sleeping-car like blind mice to their mothers. Many are sick and have been dragged to the healing wilderness unwillingly for body-good alone. Were the parts of the human machine detachable like Yankee inventions, how strange would be the gatherings on the mountains of pieces of people out of repair!

How sadly unlike the whole-hearted ongoing of the seeker after gold is this partial, compulsory mountaineering! – as if the mountain treasuries contained nothing better than gold! Up the mountains they go, high-heeled and high-hatted, laden like Christian with mortifications and mortgages of divers sorts and degrees, some suffering from the sting of bad bargains, others exulting in good ones; hunters and fishermen with gun and rod and leggins; blythe and jolly troubadours to whom all Shasta is romance; poets singing their prayers; the weak and the strong, unable or unwilling to bear mental taxation. But, whatever the motive, all will be in some measure benefited. None may wholly escape the good of Nature, however imperfectly exposed to her blessings. The minister will not preach a perfectly flat and sedimentary sermon after climbing a snowy peak; and the fair play and tremendous impartiality of Nature, so tellingly displayed, will surely affect the after pleadings of the lawyer. Fresh air at least will get into everybody, and the cares of mere business will be quenched like the fires of a sinking ship.

Possibly a branch railroad may some time be built to the summit of Mount Shasta like the road on Mount Washington. In the mean time tourists are dropped at Sisson's, about twelve miles from the summit, whence as headquarters they radiate in every direction to the so-called 'points of interest'; sauntering about the flowery fringes of the Strawberry Meadows, bathing in the balm of the woods, scrambling, fishing, hunting; riding about Castle Lake, the McCloud River, Soda Springs, Big Spring, deer pastures and elsewhere. Some demand bears, and make excited inquiries concerning their haunts, how many there might be altogether on the mountain, and whether they are grizzly, brown or black. Others shout, 'Excelsior', and make off at once for the upper snow-fields. Most, however, are content with comparatively level ground and moderate distances, gathering at the hotel every evening laden with trophies – great sheaves of flowers, cones of various trees, cedar and fir branches covered with yellow lichens, and possibly a fish or two, or quail, or grouse.

But the heads of deer, antelope, wild sheep and bears are conspicuously rare or altogether wanting in tourist collections in the 'paradise of hunters'. There is a grand comparing of notes and adventures. Most are exhilarated and happy, though complaints may occasionally be heard – 'The mountain does not look so very high after all, nor so very white; the snow is in patches like rags spread out to dry,' reminding one of Sydney Smith's joke against Jeffrey, 'D——n the Solar System; bad light, planets too indistinct'. But far the greater number are in good spirits, showing the influence of holiday enjoyment and mountain air. Fresh roses come to cheeks that long have been pale, and sentiment often begins to blossom under the new inspiration.

The Shasta region may be reserved as a national park, with special reference to the preservation of its fine forests and game. This should by all means be done; but, as far as game is concerned, it is in little danger from tourists, notwithstanding many of them carry guns, and are in some sense hunters. Going in noisy groups, and with guns so shining, they are oftentimes confronted by inquisitive Douglas squirrels, and are thus given opportunities for shooting; but the larger animals retire at their approach and seldom are seen. Other gun people, too wise or too lifeless to make much noise, move slowly along the trails and about the open spots of the woods, like benumbed beetles in a snowdrift. Such hunters are themselves hunted by the animals, which in perfect safety follow them out of curiosity.

During the bright days of midsummer the ascent of Shasta is only a long, safe saunter, without fright or nerve-strain, or even serious fatigue, to those in sound health. Setting out from Sisson's on horseback, accompanied by a guide leading a pack-animal with provisions, blankets and other necessaries, you follow a trail that leads up to the edge of the timberline, where you camp for the night, eight or ten miles from the hotel, at an elevation of about ten thousand feet. The next day, rising early, you may push on to the summit and return to Sisson's. But it is better to spend more time in the enjoyment of the grand scenery on the summit and about the head of the Whitney Glacier, pass the second night in camp, and return to Sisson's on the third day. Passing around the margin of the meadows and on through the zones of the forest, you will have good opportunities to get ever-changing views of the mountain and its wealth of creatures that bloom and breathe.

The woods differ but little from those that clothe the mountains to the southward, the trees being slightly closer together and generally not quite so large, marking the incipient change from the open sunny forests of the Sierra to the dense damp forests of the northern coast, where a squirrel may travel in the branches of the thick-set trees hundreds of miles without touching the ground. Around the upper belt of the forest you may see gaps where the ground has been cleared by avalanches of snow, thousands of tons in weight, which, descending with grand rush and roar, brush the trees from their paths like so many fragile shrubs or grasses.

At first the ascent is very gradual. The mountain begins to leave the plain in slopes scarcely perceptible, measuring from two to three degrees. These are continued by easy gradations mile after mile all the way to the truncated, crumbling summit, where they attain a steepness of twenty to twenty-five degrees. The grand simplicity of these lines is partially interrupted on the north subordinate cone that rises from the side of the main cone about three thousand feet from the summit. This side cone, past which your way to the summit lies, was active after the breaking-up of the main ice-cap of the glacial period, as shown by the comparatively unwasted crater in which it terminates and by streams of fresh-looking, unglaciated lava that radiate from it as a centre.

The main summit is about a mile and a half in diameter from southwest to northeast, and is nearly covered with snow and *névé*, bounded by crumbling peaks and ridges, among which we look in vain for any sure plan of an ancient crater. The extreme summit is situated on the southern end of a narrow ridge that bounds the general summit on the east. Viewed from the north, it appears as an irregular blunt point about ten feet high, and is fast disappearing before the stormy atmospheric action to which it is subjected.

At the base of the eastern ridge, just below the extreme summit, hot sulphurous gases and vapour escape with a hissing, bubbling noise from a fissure in the lava. Some of the many small vents cast up a spray of clear hot water, which falls back repeatedly until wasted in vapour. The steam and spray seem to be produced simply by melting snow coming in the way of the escaping gases, while the gases are evidently derived from the heated interior of the mountain, and may be regarded as the last feeble expression of the mighty power that lifted the entire mass of the mountain from the volcanic depths far below the surface of the plain.

The view from the summit in clear weather extends to an immense distance in every direction. Southeastward, the low volcanic portion of the Sierra is seen like a map, both flanks as well as the crater-dotted axis, as far as Lassen's[1] Butte, a prominent landmark and an old volcano like Shasta, between ten and eleven thousand feet high, and distant about sixty miles. Some of the higher summit peaks near Independence Lake, one hundred and eighty miles away, are at times distinctly visible. Far to the north, in Oregon, the snowy volcanic cones of Mounts Pitt, Jefferson and the Three Sisters rise in clear relief, like majestic monuments, above the dim dark sea of the northern woods. To the northeast lie the Rhett and Klamath Lakes, the Lava Beds and a grand display of hill and mountain and grey rocky plains. The Scott, Siskiyou and Trinity Mountains rise in long, compact waves to the west and southwest, and the valley of the Sacramento and the coast mountains, with their marvellous wealth of woods and waters, are seen; while close around the base of the mountain lie the beautiful Shasta Valley, Strawberry Valley, Huckleberry Valley and many others, with the headwaters of the Shasta, Sacramento and McCloud Rivers. Some observers claim to have seen the ocean from the summit of Shasta, but I have not yet been so fortunate.

The Cinder Cone near Lassen's Butte is remarkable as being the scene of the most recent volcanic eruption in the range. It is a symmetrical truncated cone covered with grey cinders and ashes, with a regular crater in which a few pines an inch or two in diameter are growing. It stands between two small lakes which previous to the last eruption, when the cone was built, formed one lake. From near the base of the cone a flood of extremely rough black vesicular lava extends across what was once a portion of the bottom of the lake into the forest of yellow pine.

This lava-flow seems to have been poured out during the same eruption that gave birth to the cone, cutting the lake in two, flowing a little way into the

---

[1] An early local name for what is now known as Lassen Peak, or Mount Lassen. In 1914 its volcanic activity was resumed with spectacular eruptions of ashes, steam and gas. [Editor.]

woods and overwhelming the trees in its way, the ends of some of the charred trunks still being visible, projecting from beneath the advanced snout of the flow where it came to rest; while the floor of the forest for miles around is so thickly strewn with loose cinders that walking is very fatiguing. The Pitt River Indians tell of a fearful time of darkness, probably due to this eruption, when the sky was filled with falling cinders which, as they thought, threatened every living creature with destruction, and say that when at length the sun appeared through the gloom it was red like blood.

Less recent craters in great numbers dot the adjacent region, some with lakes in their throats, some overgrown with trees, others nearly bare – telling monuments of Nature's mountain fires so often lighted throughout the northern Sierra. And, standing on the top of icy Shasta, the mightiest fire-monument of them all, we can hardly fail to look forward to the blare and glare of its next eruption and wonder whether it is nigh. Elsewhere men have planted gardens and vineyards in the craters of volcanoes quiescent for ages, and almost without warning have been hurled into the sky. More than a thousand years of profound calm have been known to intervene between two violent eruptions. Seventeen centuries intervened between two consecutive eruptions on the island of Ischia. Few volcanoes continue permanently in eruption. Like gigantic geysers, spouting hot stone instead of hot water, they work and sleep, and we have no sure means of knowing whether they are only sleeping or dead.

CHAPTER FOUR

A Perilous Night on Shasta's Summit

TOWARD THE end of summer, after a light, open winter, one may reach the summit of Mount Shasta without passing over much snow, by keeping on the crest of a long narrow ridge, mostly bare, that extends from near the campground at the timber-line. But on my first excursion to the summit the whole mountain, down to its low swelling base, was smoothly laden with loose fresh snow, presenting a most glorious mass of winter mountain scenery, in the midst of which I scrambled and revelled or lay snugly snowbound, enjoying the fertile clouds and the snow-bloom in all their growing, drifting grandeur.

I had walked from Redding, sauntering leisurely from station to station along the old Oregon stage-road, the better to see the rocks and plants, birds and people, by the way, tracing the rushing Sacramento to its fountains around icy Shasta. The first rains had fallen on the lowlands, and the first snows on the mountains, and everything was fresh and bracing, while an abundance of balmy sunshine filled all the noonday hours. It was the calm afterglow that usually succeeds the first storm of the winter. I met many of the birds that had reared their young and spent their summer in the Shasta woods and chaparral. They were then on their way south to their winter homes, leading their young full-fledged and about as large and strong as the parents. Squirrels, dry and elastic after the storms, were busy about their stores of pine nuts, and the latest goldenrods were still in bloom, though it was now past the middle of October. The grand colour glow – the autumnal jubilee of ripe leaves – was past prime, but, freshened by the rain, was still making a fine show along the banks of the river and in the ravines and the dells of the smaller streams.

At the salmon-hatching establishment on the McCloud River I halted a week to examine the limestone belt, grandly developed there, to learn what I could of the inhabitants of the river and its banks, and to give time for the fresh snow that I knew had fallen on the mountain to settle somewhat, with a view to making the ascent. A pedestrian on these mountain roads, especially so late in the year, is sure to excite curiosity, and many were the interrogations concerning my ramble. When I said that I was simply taking a walk, and that icy Shasta was my mark. I was invariably admonished that I had come on a dangerous quest. The time was far too late, the snow was too loose and deep to climb, and I should be lost in drifts and slides. When I hinted that new snow was beautiful and storms not so bad as they were called, my advisers shook their heads in token of superior knowledge and declared the ascent of 'Shasta Butte' through loose snow impossible. Nevertheless, before noon of the second of November I was in the frosty azure of the utmost summit.

When I arrived at Sisson's everything was quiet. The last of the summer visitors had flitted long before, and the deer and bears also were beginning to seek their winter homes. My barometer and the sighing winds and filmy, half-transparent clouds that dimmed the sunshine gave notice of the approach of another storm, and I was in haste to be off and get myself established somewhere in the midst of it, whether the summit was to be attained or not. Sisson, who is a mountaineer, speedily fitted me out for storm or calm as only a mountaineer could, with warm blankets and a week's provisions so generous in quantity and kind that they easily might have been made to last a month in case of my being closely snow-bound. Well I knew the weariness of snow-climbing, and the frosts, and the dangers of mountaineering so late in the year; therefore I could not ask a guide to go with me, even had one been willing. All I wanted was to have blankets and provisions deposited as far up in the timber as the snow would permit a pack-animal to go. There I could build a storm nest and lie warm, and make raids up and around the mountain in accordance with the weather.

Setting out on the afternoon of November first, with Jerome Fay, mountaineer and guide, in charge of the animals, I was soon plodding wearily upward through the muffled winter woods, the snow of course growing steadily deeper and looser, so that we had to break a trail. The animals began to get discouraged, and after night and darkness came on they became entangled in a bed of rough lava, where, breaking through four or five feet of mealy snow, their feet were caught between angular boulders. Here they were in danger of being lost, but after we had removed packs and saddles and assisted their efforts with ropes, they all escaped to the side of a ridge about a thousand feet below the timber-line.

To go farther was out of the question, so we were compelled to camp as best we could. A pitch-pine fire speedily changed the temperature and shed a blaze of light on the wild lava-slope and the straggling storm-bent pines around us. Melted snow answered for coffee, and we had plenty of venison to roast. Toward midnight I rolled myself in my blankets, slept an hour and a half, arose and ate more venison, tied two days' provisions to my belt, and set out for the summit, hoping to reach it ere the coming storm should fall. Jerome accompanied me a little distance above camp and indicated the way as well as he could in the darkness. He seemed loath to leave me, but, being reassured that I was at home and required no care, he bade me good-bye and returned to camp, ready to lead his animals down the mountain at daybreak.

After I was above the dwarf pines, it was fine practice pushing up the broad unbroken slopes of snow, alone in the solemn silence of the night. Half the sky was clouded; in the other half the stars sparkled icily in the keen, frosty air; while everywhere the glorious wealth of snow fell away from the summit of the cone in flowing folds, more extensive and continuous than any I had ever seen before. When day dawned the clouds were crawling slowly and becoming more massive, but gave no intimation of immediate danger, and I pushed on faithfully, though holding myself well in hand, ready to return to the timber; for it was easy to see that the storm was not far off. The mountain rises ten thousand feet above the general level of the country, in blank exposure to the deep upper currents of the sky, and no labyrinth of peaks and canyons I had ever been in seemed to me so dangerous as these immense slopes, bare against the sky.

The frost was intense, and drifting snow-dust made breathing at times rather difficult. The snow was as dry as meal, and the finer particles drifted freely, rising high in the air, while the larger portions of the crystals rolled like sand. I frequently sank to my armpits between buried blocks of loose lava, but generally only to my knees. When tired with walking I still wallowed slowly upward on all fours. The steepness of the slope – thirty-five degrees in some places – made any kind of progress fatiguing, while small avalanches were being constantly set in motion in the steepest places. But the bracing air and the sublime beauty of the snowy expanse thrilled every nerve and made absolute exhaustion impossible. I seemed to be walking and wallowing in a cloud; but, holding steadily onward, by half-past ten o'clock I had gained the highest summit.

I held my commanding foothold in the sky for two hours, gazing on the glorious landscapes spread maplike around the immense horizon, and tracing the outlines of the ancient lava-streams extending far into the surrounding plains, and the pathways of vanished glaciers of which Shasta had been the centre. But, as I had left my coat in camp for the sake of having my limbs free in climbing, I soon was cold. The wind increased in violence, raising the snow in magnificent drifts that were drawn out in the form of wavering banners glowing in the sun. Toward the end of my stay a succession of small clouds struck against the summit rocks like drifting icebergs, darkening the air as they passed, and producing a chill as definite and sudden as if ice-water had been dashed in my face. This is the kind of cloud in which snow-flowers grow, and I turned and fled.

Finding that I was not closely pursued, I ventured to take time on the way down for a visit to the head of the Whitney Glacier and the 'Crater Butte'. After I reached the end of the main summit ridge the descent was but little more than one continuous soft, mealy, muffled slide, most luxurious and rapid, though the hissing, swishing speed attained was obscured in great part by flying snow-dust – a marked contrast to the boring seal-wallowing upward struggle. I reached camp about an hour before dusk, hollowed a strip of loose ground in the lee of a large block of red lava, where firewood was abundant, rolled myself in my blankets and went to sleep.

Next morning, having slept little the night before the ascent and being weary with climbing after the excitement was over, I slept late. Then, awaking suddenly, my eyes opened on one of the most beautiful and sublime scenes I ever enjoyed. A boundless wilderness of storm-clouds of different degrees of ripeness were congregated over all the lower landscape for thousands of square miles, coloured grey, and purple, and pearl, and deep-glowing white, amid which I seemed to be floating; while the great white cone of the mountain above was all aglow in the free, blazing sunshine. It seemed not so much an ocean as a *land* of clouds – undulating hill and dale, smooth purple plains, and silvery mountains of cumuli, range over range, diversified with peak and dome and hollow fully brought out in light and shade.

I gazed enchanted, but cold grey masses, drifting like dust on a wind-swept plain, began to shut out the light, forerunners of the coming storm I had been so anxiously watching. I made haste to gather as much wood as possible, snugging it as a shelter around my bed. The storm side of my blankets was fastened down with stakes to reduce as much as possible the sifting-in of drift and the danger of being blown away. The precious bread-sack was placed safely as a pillow, and when at length the first flakes fell I was exultingly ready to welcome them. Most of my firewood was more than half rosin and would blaze in the face of the fiercest drifting; the winds could not demolish my bed, and my bread could be made to last indefinitely; while in case of need I had the means of making snowshoes and could retreat or hold my ground as I pleased.

Presently the storm broke forth into full snowy bloom, and the thronging crystals darkened the air. The wind swept past in hissing floods, grinding the snow into meal and sweeping down into the hollows in enormous drifts all the heavier particles, while the finer dust was sifted through the sky, increasing the icy gloom. But my fire glowed bravely as if in glad defiance of the drift to quench it, and, notwithstanding but little trace of my nest could be seen after the snow had levelled and buried it, I was snug and warm, and the passionate uproar produced a glad excitement.

Day after day the storm continued, piling snow on snow in weariless abundance. There were short periods of quiet, when the sun would seem to look eagerly down through rents in the clouds, as if to know how the work was advancing. During these calm intervals I replenished my fire – sometimes without leaving the nest, for fire and woodpile were so near this could easily be done – or busied myself with my notebook, watching the gestures of the trees in taking the snow, examining separate crystals under a lens, and learning the methods of their deposition as an enduring fountain for the streams. Several times, when the storm ceased for a few minutes, a Douglas squirrel came frisking from the foot of a clump of dwarf pines, moving in sudden interrupted spurts over the bossy snow; then, without any apparent guidance, he would dig rapidly into the drift where were buried some grains of barley that the horses had left. The Douglas squirrel does not strictly belong to these upper woods, and I was surprised to see him out in such weather. The mountain sheep also, quite a large flock of them, came to my camp and took shelter beside a clump of matted dwarf pines a little above my nest.

The storm lasted about a week, but before it was ended Sisson became alarmed and sent up the guide with animals to see what had become of me and recover the camp outfit. The news spread that 'there was a man on the mountain', and he must surely have perished, and Sisson was blamed for allowing any one to attempt climbing in such weather; while I was as safe as anybody in the lowlands, lying like a squirrel in a warm, fluffy nest, busied about my own affairs and wishing only to be let alone. Later, however, a trail could not have been broken for a horse, and some of the camp furniture would have had to be abandoned. On the fifth day I returned to Sisson's, and from that comfortable base made excursions, as the weather permitted, to the Black Butte, to the foot of the Whitney Glacier, around the base of the mountain, to Rhett and Klamath Lakes, to the Modoc region and elsewhere, developing many interesting scenes and experiences.

But the next spring, on the other side of this eventful winter, I saw and felt still more of the Shasta snow. For then it was my fortune to get into the very heart of a storm, and to be held in it for a long time.

On the 28 April [1875] I led a party up the mountain for the purpose of making a survey of the summit with reference to the location of the Geodetic monument. On the 30th, accompanied by Jerome Fay, I made another ascent to make some barometrical observations, the day intervening between the two ascents being devoted to establishing a camp on the extreme edge of the timber-line. Here, on our red trachyte bed, we obtained two hours of shallow sleep broken for occasional glimpses of the keen, starry night. At two o'clock we rose, breakfasted on a warmed tin-cupful of coffee and a piece of frozen venison broiled on the coals, and started for the summit. Up to this time there was nothing in sight that betokened the approach of a storm; but on gaining the summit, we saw toward Lassen's Butte hundreds of square miles of white cumuli boiling dreamily in the sunshine far beneath us, and causing no alarm.

The slight weariness of the ascent was soon rested away, and our glorious morning in the sky promised nothing but enjoyment. At 9 am the dry thermometer stood at 34° in the shade and rose steadily until at 1 pm it stood at 50°, probably influenced somewhat by radiation from the sun-warmed cliffs. A common bumble-bee, not at all benumbed, zigzagged vigorously about our heads for a few moments, as if unconscious of the fact that the nearest honey flower was a mile beneath him.

In the mean time clouds were growing down in Shasta Valley – massive swelling cumuli, displaying delicious tones of purple and grey in the hollows of their sun-beaten bosses. Extending gradually southward around on both sides of Shasta, these at length united with the older field towards Lassen's Butte, thus encircling Mount Shasta in one continuous cloud-zone. Rhett and Klamath Lakes were eclipsed beneath clouds scarcely less brilliant than their own silvery disks. The Modoc Lava Beds, many a snow-laden peak far north in Oregon, the Scott and Trinity and Siskiyou Mountains, the peaks of the Sierra, the blue Coast Range, Shasta Valley, the dark forests filling the valley of the Sacramento, all in turn were obscured or buried, leaving the lofty cone on which we stood solitary in the sunshine between two skies – a sky of spotless blue above, a sky of glittering cloud beneath. The creative sun shone glorious on the vast expanse of cloudland; hill and dale, mountain and valley springing into existence responsive to his rays and steadily developing in beauty and individuality. One huge mountain-cone of cloud, corresponding to Mount Shasta in these newborn cloud-ranges, rose close alongside with a visible motion, its firm, polished bosses seeming so near and substantial that we almost fancied we might leap down upon them from where we stood and make our way to the lowlands. No hint was given, by anything in their appearance, of the fleeting character of these most sublime and beautiful cloud mountains. On the contrary they impressed one as being lasting additions to the landscape.

The weather of the springtime and summer, throughout the Sierra in general, is usually varied by slight local rains and dustings of snow, most of which are obviously far too joyous and life-giving to be regarded as storms – single clouds growing in the sunny sky, ripening in an hour, showering the heated landscape, and passing away like a thought, leaving no visible bodily remains to stain the sky. Snow-storms of the same gentle kind abound among the high peaks, but in spring they not unfrequently attain larger proportions, assuming a violence and energy of expression scarcely surpassed by those bred in the depths of winter. Such was the storm now gathering about us.

It began to declare itself shortly after noon, suggesting to us the idea of at once seeking our safe camp in the timber and abandoning the purpose of making an observation of the barometer at 3 pm – two having already been made, at 9 am, and 12 noon, while simultaneous observations were made at Strawberry Valley. Jerome peered at short intervals over the ridge, contemplating the rising clouds with anxious gestures in the rough wind, and at length declared that if we did not make a speedy escape we should be compelled to pass the rest of the day and night on the summit. But anxiety to complete my observations stifled my own instinctive promptings to retreat, and held me to my work. No inexperienced person was depending on me, and I told Jerome that we two mountaineers should be able to make our way down through any storm likely to fall.

Presently thin, fibrous films of cloud began to blow directly over the summit from north to south, drawn out in long fairy webs like carded wool, forming and dissolving as if by magic. The wind twisted them into ringlets and whirled them in a succession of graceful convolutions like the outside sprays of Yosemite Falls in flood-time; then, sailing out into the thin azure over the precipitous brink of the ridge they were drifted together like wreaths of foam on a river. These higher and finer cloud fabrics were evidently produced by the chilling of the air from its own expansion caused by the upward deflection of the wind against the slopes of the mountain. They steadily increased on the north rim of the cone, forming at length a thick, opaque, ill-defined embankment from the icy meshes of which snow-flowers began to fall, alternating with hail. The sky speedily darkened, and just as I had completed my last observation and boxed my instruments ready for the descent, the storm began in serious earnest. At first the cliffs were beaten with hail, every stone of which, as far as I could see, was regular in form, six-sided pyramids with rounded base, rich and sumptuous-looking, and fashioned with loving care, yet seemingly thrown away on those desolate crags down which they went rolling, falling, sliding in a network of curious streams.

After we had forced our way down the ridge and past the group of hissing fumaroles, the storm became inconceivably violent. The thermometer fell 22° in a few minutes, and soon dropped below zero. The hail gave place to snow, and darkness came on like night. The wind, rising to the highest pitch of violence, boomed and surged amid the desolate crags; lightning-flashes in quick succession cut the gloomy darkness; and the thunders, the most tremendously loud and appalling I ever heard, made an almost continuous roar, stroke following stroke in quick, passionate succession, as though the mountain were being rent to its foundations and the fires of the old volcano were breaking forth again.

Could we at once have begun to descend the snow-slopes leading to the timber, we might have made good our escape, however dark and wild the storm. As it was, we had first to make our way along a dangerous ridge nearly a mile and a half long, flanked in many places by steep ice-slopes at the head of the Whitney Glacier on one side and by shattered precipices on the other. Apprehensive of this coming darkness, I had taken the precaution, when the storm began, to make the most dangerous points clear to my mind, and to mark their relations with reference to the direction of the wind. When, therefore, the darkness came on, and the bewildering drift, I felt confident that we could force our way through it with no other guidance. After passing the 'Hot Springs' I halted in the lee of a lava-block to let Jerome, who had fallen a little behind, come up. Here he opened a council in which, under circumstances sufficiently exciting but without evincing any bewilderment, he maintained, in opposition to my views, that it was impossible to proceed. He firmly refused to make the venture to find the camp, while I, aware of the dangers that would necessarily attend our efforts, and conscious of being the cause of his present peril, decided not to leave him.

Our discussions ended, Jerome made a dash from the shelter of the lava-block and began forcing his way back against the wind to the 'Hot Springs', wavering and struggling to resist being carried away, as if he were fording a rapid stream. After waiting and watching in vain for some flaw in the storm that might be urged as a new argument in favour of attempting the descent, I was compelled to follow. 'Here', said Jerome, as we shivered in the midst of the hissing, sputtering fumaroles, 'we shall be safe from frost'. 'Yes', said I, 'we can lie in this mud and steam and sludge, warm at least on one side; but how can we protect our lungs from the acid gases, and how, after our clothing is saturated, shall we be able to reach camp without freezing, even after the storm is over? We shall have to wait for sunshine, and when will it come?'

The tempered area to which we had committed ourselves extended over about one fourth of an acre, but it was only about an eighth of an inch in thickness, for the scalding gas-jets were shorn off close to the ground by the oversweeping flood of frosty wind. And how lavishly the snow fell only mountaineers may know. The crisp crystal flowers seemed to touch one another and fairly to thicken the tremendous blast that carried them. This was the bloom-time, the summer of the cloud, and never before have I seen even a mountain cloud flowering so profusely.

When the bloom of the Shasta chaparral is falling, the ground is sometimes covered for hundreds of square miles to a depth of half an inch. But the bloom of this fertile snow-cloud grew and matured and fell to a depth of two feet in a few hours. Some crystals landed with their rays almost perfect, but most of them were worn and broken by striking against one another, or by rolling on the ground. The touch of these snow-flowers in calm weather is infinitely gentle – glinting, swaying, settling silently in the dry mountain air, or massed in flakes soft and downy. To lie out alone in the mountains of a still night and be touched by the first of these small silent messengers from the sky is a memorable experience, and the fineness of that touch none will forget. But the storm-blast laden with crisp, sharp snow seems to crush and bruise and stupefy with its multitude of stings, and compels the bravest to turn and flee.

The snow fell without abatement until an hour or two after what seemed to be the natural darkness of the night. Up to the time the storm first broke on the summit its development was remarkably gentle. There was a deliberate growth of clouds, a weaving of translucent tissue above, then the roar of the wind and the thunder, and the darkening flight of snow. Its subsidence was not less sudden. The clouds broke and vanished, not a crystal was left in the sky, and the stars shone out with pure and tranquil radiance.

During the storm we lay on our backs so as to present as little surface as possible to the wind, and to let the drift pass over us. The mealy snow sifted into the folds of our clothing and in many places reached the skin. We were glad at first to see the snow packing about us, hoping it would deaden the force of the wind; but it soon froze into a stiff, crusty heap as the temperature fell, rather augmenting our novel misery.

When the heat became unendurable, on some spot where steam was escaping through the sludge, we tried to stop it with snow and mud, or shifted a little at a time by shoving with our heels; for to stand in blank exposure to the fearful wind in our frozen-and-broiled condition seemed certain death. The acrid incrustations sublimed from the escaping gases frequently gave way, opening new vents to scald us; and, fearing that if at any time the wind should fall, carbonic acid, which often formed a considerable portion of the gaseous exhalations of volcanoes, might collect in sufficient quantities to cause sleep and death. I warned Jerome against forgetting himself for a single moment, even should his sufferings admit of such a thing.

Accordingly, when during the long, dreary watches of the night we roused from a state of half-consciousness, we called each other by name in a frightened, startled way, each fearing the other might be benumbed or dead. The ordinary sensations of cold give but a faint conception of that which comes on after hard climbing with want of food and sleep in such exposure as this. Life is then seen to be a fire, that now smoulders, now brightens, and may be easily quenched. The weary hours wore away like dim half-forgotten years, so long and eventful they seemed, though we did nothing but suffer. Still the pain was not always of that bitter, intense kind that precludes thought and takes away all capacity for enjoyment. A sort of dreamy stupor came on at times in which we fancied we saw dry, resinous logs suitable for campfires, just as after going days without food men fancy they see bread.

Frozen, blistered, famished, benumbed, our bodies seemed lost to us at times – all dead but the eyes. For the duller and fainter we became the clearer was our vision, though only in momentary glimpses. Then, after the sky cleared, we gazed at the stars, blessed immortals of light, shining with marvellous brightness with long lance rays, near-looking and new-looking, as if never seen before. Again they would look familiar and remind us of star-gazing at home. Oftentimes imagination coming into play would present charming pictures of the warm zone below, mingled with others near and far. Then the bitter wind and the drift would break the blissful vision and dreary pains cover us like clouds. 'Are you suffering much?' Jerome would inquire with pitiful faintness. 'Yes', I would say, striving to keep my voice brave, 'frozen and burned; but never mind, Jermone, the night will wear away at last, and tomorrow we go a-Maying, and what campfires we will make, and what sun-baths we will take!'

The frost grew more and more intense, and we became icy and covered over with a crust of frozen snow, as if we had lain cast away in the drift all winter. In about thirteen hours – every hour like a year – day began to dawn, but it was long ere the summit's rocks were touched by the sun. No clouds were visible from where we lay, yet the morning was dull and blue, and bitterly frosty; and hour after hour passed by while we eagerly watched the pale light stealing down the ridge to the hollow where we lay. But there was not a trace of that warm, flushing sunrise splendour we so long had hoped for.

As the time drew near to make an effort to reach camp, we became concerned to know what strength was left us, and whether or no we could walk; for we had lain flat all this time without once rising to our feet. Mountaineers, however, always find in themselves a reserve of power after great exhaustion. It is a kind of second life, available only in emergencies like this; and, having proved its existence, I had no great fear that either of us would fail, though one of my arms was already benumbed and hung powerless.

At length, after the temperature was somewhat mitigated on this memorable first of May, we arose and began to struggle homeward. Our frozen trousers could scarcely be made to bend at the knee, and we waded the snow with difficulty. The summit ridge was fortunately wind-swept and nearly bare, so we were not compelled to lift our feet high, and on reaching the long home slopes laden with loose snow we made rapid progress, sliding and shuffling and pitching headlong, our feebleness accelerating rather than diminishing our speed. When we had descended some three thousand feet the sunshine warmed our backs and we began to revive. At 10 am we reached the timber and were safe.

Half an hour later we heard Sisson shouting down among the firs, coming with horses to take us to the hotel. After breaking a trail through the snow as far as possible he had tied his animals and walked up. We had been so long without food that we cared but little about eating, but we eagerly drank the coffee he prepared for us. Our feet were frozen, and thawing them was painful, and had to be done very slowly by keeping them buried in soft snow for several hours, which avoided permanent damage. Five thousand feet below the summit we found only three inches of new snow, and at the base of the mountain only a slight shower of rain had fallen, showing how local our storm had been, notwithstanding its terrific fury. Our feet were wrapped in sacking, and we were soon mounted and on our way down into the thick sunshine – 'God's Country', as Sisson calls the Chaparral Zone. In two hours' ride the last snow-bank was left behind. Violets appeared along the edges of the trail, and the chaparral was coming into bloom, with young lilies and larkspurs about the open places in rich profusion. How beautiful, seemed the golden sunbeams streaming through the woods between the warm brown boles of the cedars and pines! All my friends among the birds and plants seemed like *old* friends, and we felt like speaking to every one of them as we passed, as if we had been a long time away in some far, strange country.

In the afternoon we reached Strawberry Valley and fell asleep. Next morning we seemed to have risen from the dead. My bedroom was flooded with sunshine, and from the window I saw the great white Shasta cone clad in forests and clouds and bearing them loftily in the sky. Everything seemed full and radiant with the freshness and beauty and enthusiasm of youth. Sisson's children came in with flowers and covered my bed, and the storm on the mountain-top vanished like a dream.

CHAPTER FIVE

Shasta Rambles and Modoc Memories

ARCTIC BEAUTY and desolation, with their blessings and dangers, all may be found here, to test the endurance and skill of adventurous climbers; but far better than climbing the mountain is going around its warm, fertile base, enjoying its bounties like a bee circling around a bank of flowers. The distance is about a hundred miles, and will take some of the time we hear so much about – a week or two – but the benefits will compensate for any number of weeks. Perhaps the profession of doing good may be full, but everybody should be kind at least to himself. Take a course of good water and air, and in the eternal youth of Nature you may renew your own. Go quietly, alone; no harm will befall you. Some have strange, morbid fears as soon as they find themselves with Nature, even in the kindest and wildest of her solitudes, like very sick children afraid of their mother – as if God were dead and the devil were king.

One may make the trip on horseback, or in a carriage, even; for a good level road may be found all the way round, by Shasta Valley, Sheep Rock, Elk Flat, Huckleberry Valley, Squaw Valley, following for a considerable portion of the way the old Emigrant Road, which lies along the east disk of the mountain, and is deeply worn by the wagons of the early gold-seekers, many of whom chose this northern route as perhaps being safer and easier, the pass here being only about six thousand feet above sea-level. But it is far better to go afoot. Then you are free to make wide waverings and zigzags away from the roads to visit the great fountain streams of the rivers, the glaciers also, and the wildest retreats in the primeval forests, where the best plants and animals dwell, and where many a flower-bell will ring against your knees, and friendly trees will reach out their fronded branches and touch you as you pass. One blanket will be enough to carry, or you may forego the pleasure and burden altogether, as wood for fires is everywhere abundant. Only a little food will be required. Berries and plums abound in season, and quail and grouse and deer – the magnificent shaggy mule deer as well as the common species.

As you sweep around so grand a centre, the mountain itself seems to turn, displaying its riches like the revolving pyramids in jewellers' windows. One glacier after another comes into view, and the outlines of the mountain are ever changing, though all the way around, from whatever point of view, the form is maintained of a grand, simple cone with a gently sloping base and rugged, crumbling ridges separating the glaciers and the snow-fields more or less completely. The play of colours, from the first touches of the morning sun on the summit, down the snow-fields and the ice and lava until the forests are aglow, is a never-ending delight, the rosy lava and the fine flushings of the snow being ineffably lovely. Thus one saunters on and on in the glorious radiance in utter peace and forgetfulness of time.

Yet, strange to say, there are days even here somewhat dull-looking, when the mountain seems uncommunicative, sending out no appreciable invitation, as if not at home. At such times its height seems much less, as if, crouching and weary, it were taking rest. But Shasta is always at home to those who love her, and is ever in a thrill of enthusiastic activity – burning fires within, grinding glaciers without, and fountains ever flowing. Every crystal dances responsive to the touches of the sun, and currents of sap in the growing cells of all the vegetation are ever in a vital whirl and rush, and though many feet and wings are folded, how many are astir! And the wandering winds, how busy they are, and what a breadth of sound and motion they make, glinting and bubbling about the crags of the summit, sifting through the woods, feeling their way from grove to grove, ruffling the loose hair on the shoulders of the bears, fanning and rocking young birds in their cradles, making a trumpet of every corolla, and carrying their fragrance around the world.

In unsettled weather, when storms are growing, the mountain looms immensely higher, and its miles of height become apparent to all, especially in the gloom of the gathering clouds, or when the storm is done and they are rolling away, torn on the edges and melting while in the sunshine. Slight rain-storms are likely to be encountered in a trip round the mountain, but one may easily find shelter beneath well-thatched trees that shed the rain like a roof. Then the shining of the wet leaves is delightful, and the steamy fragrance, and the burst of bird-song from a multitude of thrushes and finches and warblers that have nests in the chaparral.

The nights, too, are delightful, watching with Shasta beneath the great starry dome. A thousand thousand voices are heard, but so finely blended they seem a part of the night itself, and make a deeper silence. And how grandly do the great logs and branches of your campfire give forth the heat and light that during their long century-lives they have so slowly gathered from the sun, storing it away in beautiful dotted cells and beads of amber gum! The neighbouring trees look into the charmed circle as if the noon of another day had come, familiar flowers and grasses that chance to be near seem far more beautiful and impressive than by day, and as the dead trees give forth their light all the other riches of their lives seem to be set free and with the rejoicing flames rise again to the sky. In setting out from Strawberry Valley, by bearing off to the northwestward a few miles you may see

> '. . . beneath dim aisles, in odorous beds,
> The slight Linnæa hang its twin-born heads,
> And [bless] the monument of the man of flowers,
> Which breathes his sweet fame through the
>   northern bowers.'

This is one of the few places in California where the charming linnæa is found, though it is common to the northward through Oregon and Washington. Here, too, you may find the curious but unlovable darlingtonia, a carnivorous plant that devours bumble-bees, grasshoppers, ants, moths and other insects, with insatiable appetite. In approaching it, its suspicious-looking yellow-spotted hood and watchful attitude will be likely to make you go cautiously through the bog where it stands, as if you were approaching a dangerous snake. It also occurs in a bog near Sothern's Station on the stage-road, where I first saw it, and in other similar bogs throughout the mountains hereabouts.

The 'Big Spring' of the Sacramento is about a mile and a half above Sisson's, issuing from the base of a drift-covered hill. It is lined with emerald algæ and mosses, and shaded with alder, willow and thorn bushes, which give it a fine setting. Its waters, apparently unaffected by flood or drought, heat or cold, fall at once into white rapids with a rush and dash, as if glad to escape from the darkness to begin their wild course down the canyon to the plain.

Muir's Peak, a few miles to the north of the spring, rises about three thousand feet above the plain on which it stands, and is easily climbed. The view is very fine and well repays the slight walk to its summit, from which much of your way about the mountain may be studied and chosen. The view obtained of the Whitney Glacier should tempt you to visit it, since it is the largest of the Shasta glaciers and its lower portion abounds in beautiful and interesting cascades and crevasses. It is three or four miles long and terminates at an elevation of about nine thousand five hundred feet above sea-level, in moraine-sprinkled ice-cliffs sixty feet high. The long grey slopes leading up to the glacier seem remarkably smooth and unbroken. They are much interrupted, nevertheless, with abrupt, jagged precipitous gorges, which, though offering instructive sections of the lavas for examination, would better be shunned by most people. This may be done by keeping well down on the base until fronting the glacier before beginning the ascent.

The gorge through which the glacier is drained is raw-looking, deep and narrow, and indescribably jagged. The walls in many places overhang; in others they are bevelled, loose and shifting where the channel has been eroded by cinders, ashes, strata of firm lavas and glacial drift, telling of many a change from frost to fire and their attendant floods of mud and water. Most of the drainage of the glacier vanishes at once in the porous rocks to reappear in springs in the distant valley, and it is only in time of flood that the channel carries much water; then there are several fine falls in the gorge, six hundred feet or more in height. Snow lies in it the year round at an elevation of eight thousand five hundred feet, and in sheltered spots a thousand feet lower. Tracing this wild changing channel-gorge, gully, or canyon, the sections will show Mount Shasta as a huge palimpsest, containing the records, layer upon layer, of strangely contrasted events in its fiery-icy history. But look well to your footing, for the way will test the skill of the most cautious mountaineers.

Regaining the low ground at the base of the mountain and holding on in your grand orbit, you pass through a belt of juniper woods, called 'The Cedars', to Sheep Rock at the foot of the Shasta Pass. Here you strike the old emigrant road, which leads over the low divide to the eastern slopes of the mountain. In a north-northwesterly direction from the foot of the pass you may chance to find Pluto's Cave, already mentioned; but it is not easily found, since its several mouths are on a level with the general surface of the ground, and have been made simply by the falling-in of portions of the roof. Far the most beautiful and richly furnished of the mountain caves of California occur in a thick belt of metamorphic limestone that is pretty generally developed along the western flank of the Sierra from the McCloud River to the Kaweah, a distance of nearly four hundred miles. These volcanic caves are not wanting in interest, and it is well to light a pitch-pine torch and take a walk in these dark ways of the underworld whenever opportunity offers, if for no other reason to see with new appreciation on returning to the sunshine the beauties that lie so thick about us.

Sheep Rock is about twenty miles from Sisson's, and is one of the principal winter pasture-grounds of the wild sheep, from which it takes its name. It is a mass of lava presenting to the grey sage plain of Shasta Valley a bold craggy front two thousand feet high. Its summit lies at an elevation of five thousand five hundred feet above the sea, and has several square miles of comparatively level surface, where bunch-grass grows and the snow does not lie deep, thus allowing the hardy sheep to pick up a living through the winter months when deep snows have driven them down from the lofty ridges of Shasta.

From here it might be well to leave the immediate base of the mountain for a few days and visit the Lava Beds made famous by the Modoc War. They lie about forty miles to the northeastward, on the south shore of Rhett or Tule[1] Lake, at an elevation above sea-level of about forty-five hundred feet. They are a portion of a flow of dense black vesicular lava, dipping northeastward at a low angle, but little changed as yet by the weather, and about as destitute of soil as a glacial pavement. The surface, though smooth in a general way as seen from a distance, is dotted with hillocks and rough crater-like pits, and traversed by a network of yawning fissures, forming a combination of topographical conditions of very striking character. The way lies by Mount Bremer, over stretches of grey sage plains, interrupted by rough lava-slopes timbered with juniper and yellow pine, and with here and there a green meadow and a stream.

This is a famous game region, and you will be likely to meet small bands of antelope, mule deer and wild sheep. Mount Bremer is the most noted stronghold of the sheep in the whole Shasta region. Large flocks dwell here from year to year, winter and summer, descending occasionally into the adjacent sage plains and lava-beds to feed, but ever ready to take refuge in the jagged crags of their mountain at every alarm. While travelling with a company of hunters I saw about fifty in one flock.

The Van Bremer brothers, after whom the mountain is named, told me that they once climbed the mountain with their rifles and hounds on a grand hunt; but, after keeping up the pursuit for a week, their boots and clothing gave way, and the hounds were lamed and worn out without having run down a single sheep, notwithstanding they ran night and day. On smooth spots, level or ascending, the hounds gained on the sheep, but on descending ground, and over rough masses of angular rocks they fell hopelessly behind. Only half a dozen sheep were shot as they passed the hunters stationed near their paths circling round the rugged summit. The full-grown bucks weigh nearly three hundred and fifty pounds.

The mule deer are nearly as heavy. Their long, massive ears give them a very striking appearance. One large buck that I measured stood three feet and seven inches high at the shoulders, and when the ears were extended horizontally the distance across from tip to tip was two feet and one inch.

From the Van Bremer ranch the way to the Lava Beds leads down the Bremer Meadows past many a smooth grassy knoll and jutting cliff, along the shore of Lower Klamath Lake, and thence across a few miles of sage plain to the brow of the wall-like bluff of lava four hundred and fifty feet above Tule Lake. Here you are looking southeastward, and the Modoc landscape, which at once takes possession of you, lies revealed in front. It is composed of three principal parts; on your left lies the bright expanse of Tule Lake, on your right an evergreen forest, and between the two are the black Lava Beds.

When I first stood there, one bright day before sundown, the lake was fairly blooming in purple light, and was so responsive to the sky in both calmness and colour it seemed itself a sky. No mountain shore hides its loveliness. It

---

[1] Pronounced Too'-lay.

lies wide open for many a mile, veiled in no mystery but the mystery of light. The forest also was flooded with sun-purple, not a spire moving, and Mount Shasta was seen towering above it rejoicing in the ineffable beauty of the alpenglow. But neither the glorified woods on the one hand, nor the lake on the other, could at first hold the eye. That dark mysterious lava plain between them compelled attention. Here you trace yawning fissures, there clusters of sombre pits; now you mark where the lava is bent and corrugated in swelling ridges and domes, again where it breaks into a rough mass of loose blocks. Tufts of grass grow far apart here and there and small bushes of hardy sage, but they have a singed appearance and can do little to hide the blackness. Deserts are charming to those who know how to see them – all kinds of bogs, barrens and heathy moors; but the Modoc Lava Beds have for me an uncanny look. As I gazed the purple deepened over all the landscape. Then fell the gloaming, making everything still more forbidding and mysterious. Then, darkness like death.

Next morning the crisp, sunshiny air made even the Modoc landscape less hopeless, and we ventured down the bluff to the edge of the Lava Beds. Just at the foot of the bluff we came to a square enclosed by a stone wall. This is a graveyard where lie buried thirty soldiers, most of whom met their fate out in the Lava Beds, as we learn by the boards marking the graves – a gloomy place to die in, and deadly-looking even without Modocs. The poor fellows that lie here deserve far more pity than they have ever received. Picking our way over the strange ridges and hollows of the beds, we soon came to a circular flat about twenty yards in diameter, on the shore of the lake, where the comparative smoothness of the lava and a few handfuls of soil have caused the grass tufts to grow taller. This is where General Canby was slain while seeking to make peace with the treacherous Modocs.

Two or three miles farther on is the main stronghold of the Modocs, held by them so long and defiantly against all the soldiers that could be brought to the attack. Indians usually choose to hide in tall grass and bush and behind trees, where they can crouch and glide like panthers, without casting up defences that would betray their positions; but the Modoc castle is in the rock. When the Yosemite Indians made raids on the settlers of the lower Merced, they withdrew with their spoils into Yosemite Valley; and the Modocs boasted that in case of war they had a stone house into which no white man could come as long as they cared to defend it. Yosemite was not held for a single day against the pursuing troops; but the Modocs held their fort for months, until, weary of being hemmed in, they chose to withdraw.

It consists of numerous redoubts formed by the unequal subsidence of portions of the lava-flow, and a complicated network of redans abundantly supplied with salient and re-entering angles, being united each to the other and to the redoubts by a labyrinth of open and covered corridors, some of which expand at intervals into spacious caverns, forming as a whole the most complete natural Gibraltar I ever saw. Other castles scarcely less strong are connected with this by subterranean passages known only to the Indians, while the unnatural blackness of the rock out of which Nature has constructed these defences, and the weird, inhuman physiognomy of the whole region are well calculated to inspire terror.

Deadly was the task of storming such a place. The breech-loading rifles of the Indians thrust through chinks between the rocks were ready to pick off every soldier who showed himself for a moment, while the Indians lay utterly invisible. They were familiar with byways both over and under ground, and could at any time sink suddenly out of sight like squirrels among the loose boulders. Our bewildered soldiers heard them shooting, now before, now behind them, as they glided from place to place through fissures and subterranean passes, all the while as invisible as Gyges wearing his magic ring. To judge from the few I have seen, Modocs are not very amiable-looking people at best. When, therefore, they were crawling stealthily in the gloomy caverns, unkempt and begrimed and with the glare of war in their eyes, they must have seemed very demons of the volcanic pit.

Captain Jack's cave is one of the many sombre cells of the castle. It measures twenty-five or thirty feet in diameter at the entrance, and extends but a short distance in a horizontal direction. The floor is littered with the bones of the animals slaughtered for food during the war. Some eager archæologist may hereafter discover this cabin and startle his world by announcing another of the Stone Age caves. The sun shines freely into its mouth, and graceful bunches of grass and eriogonums and sage grow about it, doing what they can toward its redemption from degrading associations and making it beautiful.

Where the lava meets the lake there are some fine curving bays, beautifully embroidered with rushes and polygonums, a favourite resort of waterfowl. On our return, keeping close along shore, we caused a noisy plashing and beating of wings among cranes and geese. The ducks, less wary, kept their places, merely swimming in and out through openings in the rushes, rippling the glassy water, and raising spangles in their wake. The countenance of the lava-beds became less and less forbidding. Tufts of pale grasses, relieved on the jet rocks, looked like ornaments on a mantel, thick-furred mats of emerald mosses appeared in damp spots next the shore, and I noticed one tuft of small ferns. From year to year in the kindly weather the beds are thus gathering beauty – beauty for ashes.

Returning to Sheep Rock and following the old emigrant road, one is soon back again beneath the snows and shadows of Shasta, and the Ash Creek and McCloud Glaciers come into view on the east side of the mountain. They are broad, rugged, crevassed cloudlike masses of down-grinding ice, pouring forth streams of muddy water as measures of the work they are doing in sculpturing the rocks beneath them; very unlike the long, majestic glaciers of Alaska that riverlike go winding down the valleys through the forests to the sea. These, with a few others as yet nameless, are lingering remnants of once great glaciers that occupied the canyons now taken by the rivers, and in a few centuries will, under present conditions, vanish altogether.

The rivers of the granite south half of the Sierra are outspread on the peaks in a shining network of small branches, that divide again and again into small dribbling, purling, oozing threads drawing their sources from the snow and ice of the surface. They seldom sink out of sight, save here and there in moraines or glaciers, or, early in the season, beneath banks and bridges of snow, soon to issue again. But in the north half, laden with rent and porous lava, small tributary streams are rare, and the rivers, flowing for a time beneath the sky of rock, at length burst forth into the light in generous volume from seams and caverns, filtered, cool and sparkling, as if their bondage in darkness, safe from the vicissitudes of the weather in their youth, were only a blessing.

Only a very small portion of the water derived from the melting ice and snow of Shasta flows down its flanks on the surface. Probably ninety-nine per cent of it is at once absorbed and drained away beneath the porous lava-folds of the mountain to gush forth, filtered and pure, in the form of immense springs, so large, some of them, that they give birth to rivers that start on their journey beneath the sun, full-grown and perfect without any childhood. Thus the Shasta River issues from a large lakelike spring in Shasta Valley, and about two thirds of the volume of the McCloud gushes forth in a grand spring on the east side of the mountain, a few miles back from its immediate base.

To find the big spring of the McCloud, or 'Mud Glacier,' which you will know by its size (it being the largest on the east side), you make your way through sunny, parklike woods of yellow pine, and a shaggy growth of chaparral, and come in a few hours to the river flowing in a gorge of moderate depth, cut abruptly down into the lava plain. Should the volume of the stream where you strike it seem small, then you will know that you are above the spring; if large, nearly equal to its volume at its confluence with the Pitt River, then you are below it; and in either case have only to follow the river up or down until you come to it.

Under certain conditions you may hear the roar of the water rushing from the rock at a distance of half a mile, or even more; or you may not hear it until within a few rods. It comes in a grand, eager gush from a horizontal seam in the face of the wall of the river-gorge in the form of a partially interrupted sheet nearly seventy-five yards in width, and at a height above the river-bed of about forty feet, as nearly as I could make out without the means of exact measurement. For about fifty yards this flat current is in one unbroken sheet, and flows in a lacework of plashing, unleaping spray over boulders that are clad in green silky algæ and water-mosses to meet the smaller part of the river, which takes its rise farther up. Joining the river at right angles to its course, it at once swells its volume to three times its size above the spring.

The vivid green of the boulders beneath the water is very striking, and colours the entire stream with the exception of the portions broken into foam. The colour is chiefly due to a species of algæ which seems common in springs of this sort. That any kind of plant can hold on and grow beneath the wear of so boisterous a current seems truly wonderful, even after taking into consideration the freedom of the water from cutting drift, and the constancy of its volume and temperature throughout the year. The temperature is about 45°, and the height of the river above the sea is here about three thousand feet. Asplenium, epilobium, heuchera, hazel, dogwood and alder make a luxurious fringe and setting; and the forests of Douglas spruce along the banks are the finest I have ever seen in the Sierra.

From the spring you may go with the river – a fine travelling companion –

down to the sportsman's fishing station, where, if you are getting hungry, you may replenish your stores; or, bearing off around the mountain by Huckleberry Valley, complete your circuit without interruption, emerging at length from beneath the outspread arms of the sugar pine at Strawberry Valley, with all the new wealth and health gathered in your walk; not tired in the least, and only eager to repeat the round.

Tracing rivers to their fountains makes the most charming of travels. As the life-blood of the landscapes, the best of the wilderness comes to their banks, and not one dull passage is found in all their eventful histories. Tracing the McCloud to its highest springs, and over the divide to the fountains of Fall River, near Fort Crook, thence down that river to its confluence with the Pitt, on from there to the volcanic region about Lassen's Butte, through the Big Meadows among the sources of the Feather River, and down through forests of sugar pine to the fertile plains of Chico – this is a glorious saunter and imposes no hardship. Food may be had at moderate intervals, and the whole circuit forms one ever-deepening, broadening stream of enjoyment.

Fall River is a very remarkable stream. It is only about ten miles long, and is composed of springs, rapids, and falls – springs beautifully shaded at one end of it, a showy fall one hundred and eighty feet high at the other, and a rush of crystal rapids between. The banks are fringed with rubus, rose, plum, cherry, spiræa, azalea, honeysuckle, hawthorn, ash, alder, elder, aster, goldenrod, beautiful grasses, sedges, rushes, mosses and ferns with fronds as large as the leaves of palms – all in the midst of a richly forested landscape. Nowhere within the limits of California are the forests of yellow pine so extensive and exclusive as on the headwaters of the Pitt. They cover the mountains and all the lower slopes that border the wide, open valleys which abound there, pressing forward in imposing ranks, seemingly the hardiest and most firmly established of all the northern coniferæ.

The volcanic region about Lassen's Butte I have already in part described. Miles of its flanks are dotted with hot springs, many of them so sulphurous and boisterous and noisy in their boiling that they seem inclined to become geysers like those of the Yellowstone.

The ascent of Lassen's Butte is an easy walk, and the views from the summit are extremely telling. Innumerable lakes and craters surround the base; forests of the charming Williamson spruce fringe lake and crater alike; the sunbeaten plains to east and west make a striking show, and the wilderness of peaks and ridges stretch indefinitely away on either hand. The lofty, icy Shasta, towering high above all, seems but an hour's walk from you, though the distance in an air-line is about sixty miles.

The 'Big Meadows' lie near the foot of Lassen's Butte, a beautiful spacious basin set in the heart of the richly forested mountains, scarcely surpassed in the grandeur of its surroundings by Tahoe. During the Glacial Period it was a *mer de glace*, then a lake and now a level meadow shining with bountiful springs and streams. In the number and size of its big spring fountains it excels even Shasta. One of the largest that I measured forms a lakelet nearly a hundred yards in diameter, and, in the generous flood it sends forth offers one of the most telling symbols of Nature's affluence to be found in the mountains.

The great wilds of our country, once held to be boundless and inexhaustible, are being rapidly invaded and overrun in every direction, and everything destructible in them is being destroyed. How far destruction may go it is not easy to guess. Every landscape, low and high, seems doomed to be trampled and harried. Even the sky is not safe from scath – blurred and blackened whole summers together with the smoke of fires that devour the woods.

The Shasta region is still a fresh unspoiled wilderness, accessible and available for travellers of every kind and degree. Would it not then be a fine thing to set it apart like the Yellowstone and Yosemite as a National Park for the welfare and benefit of all mankind, preserving its fountains and forests and all its glad life in primeval beauty? Very little of the region can ever be more valuable for any other use – certainly not for gold nor for grain. No private right or interest need suffer, and thousands yet unborn would come from far and near and bless the country for its wise and benevolent forethought.

CHAPTER SIX

The City of the Saints[1]

THE MOUNTAINS rise grandly round about this curious city, the Zion of the new Saints, so grandly that the city itself is hardly visible. The Wahsatch Range, snow-laden and adorned with glacier-sculptured peaks, stretches continuously along the eastern horizon, forming the boundary of the Great Salt Lake Basin; while across the valley of the Jordan southwestward from here, you behold the Oquirrh Range, about as snowy and lofty as the Wahsatch. To the northwest your eye skims the blue levels of the great lake, out of the midst of which rise island mountains and beyond, at a distance of fifty miles, is seen the picturesque wall of the lakeside mountains blending with the lake and the sky.

The glacial developments of these superb ranges are sharply sculptured peaks and crests, with ample wombs between them where the ancient snows of the glacial period were collected and transformed into ice, and ranks of profound shadowy canyons, while moraines commensurate with the lofty fountains extend into the valleys, forming far the grandest series of glacial monuments I have yet seen this side of the Sierra.

In beginning this letter I meant to describe the city, but in the company of these noble old mountains, it is not easy to bend one's attention upon anything else. Salt Lake cannot be called a very beautiful town, neither is there anything ugly or repulsive about it. From the slopes of the Wahsatch foothills, or old lake benches, toward Fort Douglas it is seen to occupy the sloping gravelly delta of City Creek, a fine, hearty stream that comes pouring

[1] Letter dated 'Salt Lake City, Utah, May 15, 1877.' [Editor.]

from the snows of the mountains through a majestic glacial canyon; and it is just where this stream comes forth into the light on the edge of the valley of the Jordan that the Mormons have built their new Jerusalem.

At first sight there is nothing very marked in the external appearance of the town excepting its leafiness. Most of the houses are veiled with trees, as if set down in the midst of one grand orchard; and seen at a little distance they appear like a field of glacier boulders overgrown with aspens, such as one often meets in the upper valleys of the California Sierra, for only the angular roofs are clearly visible.

Perhaps nineteen twentieths of the houses are built of bluish-grey adobe bricks, and are only one or two stories high, forming fine cottage homes which promise simple comfort within. They are set well back from the street, leaving room for a flower garden, while almost every one has a thrifty orchard at the sides and around the back. The gardens are laid out with great simplicity, indicating love for flowers by people comparatively poor, rather than deliberate efforts of the rich for showy artistic effects. They are like the pet gardens of children, about as artless and humble, and harmonize with the low dwellings to which they belong. In almost every one you find daisies, and mint, and lilac bushes, and rows of plain English tulips. Lilacs and tulips are the most characteristic flowers, and nowhere have I seen them in greater perfection. As Oakland is pre-eminently a city of roses, so is this Mormon Saints' Rest a city of lilacs and tulips. The flowers, at least, are saintly, and they are surely loved. Scarce a home, however obscure, is without them, and the simple, unostentatious manner in which they are planted and gathered in pots and boxes about the windows shows how truly they are prized.

The surounding commons, the marshy levels of the Jordan, and dry, gravelly lake benches on the slopes of the Wahsatch foothills are now gay with wild flowers, chief among which are a species of phlox, with an abundance of rich pink corollas, growing among sagebrush in showy tufts, and a beautiful papilionaceous plant, with silky leaves and large clusters of purple flowers, banner, wings and keel exquisitely shaded, a mertensia, hydrophyllum, white boragewort, orthocarpus, several species of violets and a tall scarlet gilia. It is delightful to see how eagerly all these are sought after by the children, both boys and girls. Every day that I have gone botanizing I have met groups of little Latter-Days with their precious bouquets, and at such times it was hard to believe the dark, bloody passages of Mormon history.

But to return to the city. As soon as City Creek approaches its upper limit its waters are drawn off right and left, and distributed in brisk rills, one on each side of every street, the regular slopes of the delta upon which the city is built being admirably adapted to this system of street irrigation. These streams are all pure and sparkling in the upper streets, but, as they are used to some extent as sewers, they soon manifest the consequence of contact with civilization, though the speed of their flow prevents their becoming offensive, and little Saints not over particular may be seen drinking from them everywhere.

The streets are remarkably wide and the buildings low, making them appear yet wider than they really are. Trees are planted along the sidewalks – elms, poplars, maples and a few catalpas and hawthorns; yet they are mostly small and irregular, and nowhere form avenues half so leafy and imposing as one would be led to expect. Even in the business streets there is but little regularity in the buildings – now a row of plain adobe structures, half store, half dwelling, then a high mercantile block of red brick or sandstone, and again a row of adobe cottages nestled back among apple trees. There is one immense store with its sign upon the roof, in letters big enough to be read miles away, 'Z.C.M.I.' (Zion's Co-operative Mercantile Institution), while many a small, codfishy corner grocery bears the legend 'Holiness to the Lord, Z.C.M.I.' But little evidence will you find in this Zion, with its fifteen thousand souls, of great wealth, though many a Saint is seeking it as keenly as any Yankee Gentile. But on the other hand, searching throughout all the city, you will not find any trace of squalor or extreme poverty.

Most of the women I have chanced to meet, especially those from the country, have a weary, repressed look, as if for the sake of their religion they were patiently carrying burdens heavier than they were well able to bear. But, strange as it must seem to Gentiles, the many wives of one man, instead of being repelled from one another by jealousy, appear to be drawn all the closer together, as if the real marriage existed between the wives only. Groups of half a dozen or so may frequently be seen on the streets in close conversation, looking as innocent and unspeculative as a lot of heifers, while the masculine Saints pass them by as if they belonged to a distinct species. In the Tabernacle last Sunday, one of the elders of the church, in discoursing upon the good things of life, the possessions of Latter-Day Saints, enumerated fruitful fields, horses, cows, wives and implements, the wives being placed as above, between the cows and implements, without receiving any superior emphasis.

Polygamy, as far as I have observed, exerts a more degrading influence upon husbands than upon wives. The love of the latter finds expression in flowers and children, while the former seem to be rendered incapable of pure love of anything. The spirit of Mormonism is intensely exclusive and un-American. A more withdrawn, compact, sealed-up body of people could hardly be found on the face of the earth than is gathered here, notwithstanding railroads, telegraphs and the penetrating lights that go sifting through society everywhere in this revolutionary, question-asking century. Most of the Mormons I have met seem to be in a state of perpetual apology, which can hardly be fully accounted for by Gentile attacks. At any rate it is unspeakably offensive to any free man.

'We Saints,' they are continually saying, 'are not as bad as we are called. We don't murder those who differ with us, but rather treat them with all charity. You may go through our town night or day and no harm shall befall you. Go into our houses and you will be well used. We are as glad as you are that Lee was punished,' etc. While taking a saunter the other evening we were overtaken by a characteristic Mormon, 'an 'umble man,' who made us a very deferential salute and then walked on with us about half a mile. We discussed whatsoever of Mormon doctrines came to mind with American freedom, which he defended as best he could, speaking in an excited but deprecating tone. When hard pressed he would say: 'I don't understand these deep things,

but the elders do. I'm only an 'umble tradesman.' In taking leave he thanked
us for the pleasure of our querulous conversation, removed his hat and bowed
lowly in a sort of Uriah Heep manner, and then went to his humble home.
How many humble wives it contained, we did not learn.

Fine specimens of manhood are by no means wanting, but the number of
people one meets here who have some physical defect or who attract one's
attention by some mental peculiarity that manifests itself through the eyes, is
astonishingly great in so small a city. It would evidently be unfair to attribute
these defects to Mormonism, though Mormonism has undoubtedly been the
magnet that elected and drew these strange people together from all parts of
the world.

But however 'the peculiar doctrines' and 'peculiar practices' of Mormonism
have affected the bodies and the minds of the old Saints, the little Latter-Day
boys and girls are as happy and natural as possible, running wild, with plenty
of good hearty parental indulgence, playing, fighting, gathering flowers in
delightful innocence; and when we consider that most of the parents have
been drawn from the thickly settled portion of the Old World, where they
have long suffered the repression of hunger and hard toil, these Mormon
children, 'Utah's best crop,' seem remarkably bright and promising.

From children one passes naturally into the blooming wilderness, to the
pure religion of sunshine and snow, where all the good and the evil of this
strange people lifts and vanishes from the mind like mist from the mountains.

CHAPTER SEVEN

A Great Storm in Utah[1]

UTAH HAS just been blessed with one of the grandest storms I have ever
beheld this side of the Sierra. The mountains are laden with fresh snow; wild
streams are swelling and booming adown the canyons, and out in the valley of
the Jordan a thousand rain-pools are gleaming in the sun.

With reference to the development of fertile storms bearing snow and rain,
the greater portion of the calendar springtime of Utah has been winter. In all
the upper canyons of the mountains the snow is now from five to ten feet deep
or more, and most of it has fallen since March. Almost every other day during
the last three weeks small local storms have been falling on the Wahsatch and
Oquirrh Mountains, while the Jordan Valley remained dry and sun-filled. But
on the afternoon of Thursday, the 17th ultimo, wind, rain and snow filled the
whole basin, driving wildly over valley and plain from range to range, bestowing
their benefactions in most cordial and harmonious storm-measures. The oldest
Saints say they have never witnessed a more violent storm of this kind since

---

[1] Letter dated 'Salt Lake City, Utah, May 19, 1877.' [Editor.]

the first settlement of Zion, and while the gale from the northwest, with which the storm began, was rocking their adobe walls, uprooting trees and darkening the streets with billows of dust and sand, some of them seemed inclined to guess that the terrible phenomenon was one of the signs of the times of which their preachers are so constantly reminding them, the beginning of the out-pouring of the treasured wrath of the Lord upon the Gentiles for the killing of Joseph Smith. To me it seemed a cordial outpouring of Nature's love; but it is easy to differ with Salt Latter-Days in everything – storms, wives, politics and religion.

About an hour before the storm reached the city I was so fortunate as to be out with a friend on the banks of the Jordan enjoying the scenery. Clouds, with peculiarly restless and self-conscious gestures, were marshalling them-selves along the mountain-tops, and sending out long, overlapping wings across the valley; and even where no cloud was visible, an obscuring film absorbed the sunlight, giving rise to a cold, bluish darkness. Nevertheless, distant objects along the boundaries of the landscape were revealed with wonderful distinctness in this weird, subdued, cloud-sifted light. The moun-tains, in particular, with the forests on their flanks, their mazy lacelike canyons, the wombs of the ancient glaciers, and their marvellous profusion of ornate sculpture, were most impressively manifest. One would fancy that a man might be clearly seen walking on the snow at a distance of twenty or thirty miles.

While we were revelling in this rare, ungarish grandeur, turning from range to range, studying the darkening sky and listening to the still small voices of the flowers at our feet, some of the denser clouds came down, crowning and wreathing the highest peaks and dropping long grey fringes whose smooth linear structure showed that snow was beginning to fall. Of these partial storms there were soon ten or twelve, arranged in two rows, while the main Jordan Valley between them lay as yet in profound calm. At 4.30 pm a dark brownish cloud appeared close down on the plain towards the lake, extending from the northern extremity of the Oquirrh Range in a northeasterly direction as far as the eye could reach. Its peculiar colour and structure excited our attention without enabling us to decide certainly as to its character, but we were not left long in doubt, for in a few minutes it came sweeping over the valley in wild uproar, a torrent of wind thick with sand and dust, advancing with a most majestic front, rolling and overcombing like a gigantic sea-wave. Scarcely was it in plain sight ere it was upon us, racing across the Jordan, over the city and up the slopes of the Wahsatch, eclipsing all the landscapes in its course – the bending trees, the dust streamers and the wild onrush of every-thing movable giving it an appreciable visibility that rendered it grand and inspiring.

This gale portion of the storm lasted over an hour, then down came the blessed rain and the snow all through the night and the next day, the snow and rain alternating and blending in the valley. It is long since I have seen snow coming into a city. The crystal flakes falling in the foul streets was a pitiful sight.

Notwithstanding the vaunted refining influences of towns, purity of all kinds – pure hearts, pure streams, pure snow – must here be exposed to terrible trials. City Creek, coming from its high glacial fountains, enters the streets of this Mormon Zion pure as an angel, but how does it leave it? Even roses and lilies in gardens most loved are tainted with a thousand impurities as soon as they unfold. I heard Brigham Young in the Tabernacle the other day warning his people that if they did not mend their manners angels would not come into their houses, though perchance they might be sauntering by with little else to do than chat with them. Possibly there may be Salt Lake families sufficiently pure for angel society, but I was not pleased with the reception they gave the small snow angels that God sent among them the other night. Only the children hailed them with delight. The old Latter-Days seemed to shun them. I should like to see how Mr Young, the Lake Prophet, would meet such messengers.

But to return to the storm. Toward the evening of the 18th it began to wither. The snowy skirts of the Wahsatch Mountains appeared beneath the lifting fringes of the clouds, and the sun shone out through coloured windows, producing one of the most glorious after-storm effects I ever witnessed. Looking across the Jordan, the grey sagey slopes from the base of the Oquirrh Mountains were covered with a thick, plushy cloth of gold, soft and ethereal as a cloud, not merely tinted and gilded like a rock with autumn sunshine, but deeply muffled beyond recognition. Surely nothing in heaven, nor any mansion of the Lord in all his worlds, could be more gloriously carpeted. Other portions of the plain were flushed with red and purple, and all the mountains and the clouds above them were painted in corresponding loveliness. Earth and sky, round and round the entire landscape, was one ravishing revelation of colour, infinitely varied and inter-blended.

I have seen many a glorious sunset beneath lifting storm-clouds on the mountains, but nothing comparable with this. I felt as if new-arrived in some other far-off world. The mountains, the plains, the sky, all seemed new. Other experiences seemed but to have prepared me for this, as souls are prepared for heaven. To describe the colours on a single mountain would, if it were possible at all, require many a volume – purples, and yellows and delicious pearly greys divinely toned and inter-blended, and so richly put on one seemed to be looking down through the ground as through a sky. The disbanding clouds lingered lovingly about the mountains, filling the canyons like tinted wool, rising and drooping around the topmost peaks, fondling their rugged bases, or, sailing alongside, trailed their lustrous fringes through the pines as if taking a last view of their accomplished work. Then came darkness, and the glorious day was done.

This afternoon the Utah mountains, and valleys seem to belong to our own very world again. They are covered with common sunshine. Down here on the banks of the Jordan, larks and redwings are swinging on the rushes; the balmy air is instinct with immortal life; the wild flowers, the grass and the farmers' grain are fresh as if, like the snow, they had come out of heaven, and the last of the angel clouds are fleeing from the mountains.

CHAPTER EIGHT

Bathing in Salt Lake[1]

WHEN THE north wind blows, bathing in Salt Lake is a glorious baptism, for then it is all wildly awake with waves, blooming like a prairie in snowy crystal foam. Plunging confidently into the midst of the grand uproar you are hugged and welcomed, and swim without effort, rocking and heaving up and down, in delightful rhythm, while the winds sing in chorus and the cool, fragrant brine searches every fibre of your body; and at length you are tossed ashore with a glad Godspeed, braced and salted and clean as a saint.

The nearest point on the shore-line is distant about ten miles from Salt Lake City, and is almost inaccessible on account of the boggy character of the ground, but, by taking the Western Utah Railroad, at a distance of twenty miles you reach what is called Lake Point, where the shore is gravelly and wholesome and abounds in fine retreating bays that seem to have been made on purpose for bathing. Here the northern peaks of the Oquirrh Range plant their feet in the clear blue brine, with fine curving insteps, leaving no space for muddy levels. The crystal brightness of the water, the wild flowers and the lovely mountain scenery make this a favourite summer resort for pleasure and health seekers. Numerous excursion trains are run from the city, and parties, some of them numbering upwards of a thousand, come to bathe, and dance, and roam the flowery hillsides together.

But at the time of my first visit in May, I fortunately found myself alone. The hotel and bathhouse, which form the chief improvements of the place, were sleeping in winter silence, notwithstanding the year was in full bloom. It was one of those genial sun-days when flowers and flies come thronging to the light, and birds sing their best. The mountain-ranges, stretching majestically north and south, were piled with pearly cumuli, the sky overhead was pure azure, and the wind-swept lake was all aroll and aroar with whitecaps.

I sauntered along the shore until I came to a sequestered cove, where buttercups and wild peas were blooming close down to the limit reached by the waves. Here, I thought, is just the place for a bath; but the breakers seemed terribly boisterous and forbidding as they came rolling up the beach, or dashed white against the rocks that bounded the cove on the east. The outer ranks, ever broken, ever builded, formed a magnificent rampart, sculptured and corniced like the hanging wall of a bergschrund, and appeared hopelessly insurmountable, however easily one might ride the swelling waves beyond. I feasted awhile on their beauty, watching their coming in from afar like faithful messengers, to tell their stories one by one; then I turned

[1] Letter dated 'Lake Point, Utah, May 20, 1877.' [Editor.]

915

reluctantly away, to botanize and wait a calm. But the calm did not come that day, nor did I wait long. In an hour or two I was back again to the same little cove. The waves still sang the old storm song, and rose in high crystal walls, seemingly hard enough to be cut in sections, like ice.

Without any definite determination I found myself undressed, as if some one else had taken me in hand; and while one of the largest waves was ringing out its message and spending itself on the beach, I ran out with open arms to the next, ducked beneath its breaking top, and got myself into right lusty relationship with the brave old lake. Away I sped in free, glad motion, as if, like a fish I had been afloat all my life, now low out of sight in the smooth, glassy valleys, now bounding aloft on firm combing crests, while the crystal foam beat against my breast with keen, crisp clashing, as if composed of pure salt. I bowed to every wave, and each lifted me right royally to its shoulders, almost setting me erect on my feet, while they all went speeding by like living creatures, blooming and rejoicing in the brightness of the day, and chanting the history of their grand mountain home.

A good deal of nonsense has been written concerning the difficulty of swimming in this heavy water. 'One's head would go down, and heels come up, and the acrid brine would burn like fire.' I was conscious only of a joyous exhilaration, my limbs seemingly heeding their own business, without any discomfort or confusion; so much so, that without previous knowledge my experience on this occasion would not have led me to detect anything peculiar. In calm weather, however, the sustaining power of the water might probably be more marked. This was by far the most exciting and effective wave excursion I ever made this side of the Rocky Mountains; and when at its close I was heaved ashore among the sunny grasses and flowers, I found myself a new creature indeed, and went bounding along the beach with blood all aglow, reinforced by the best salts of the mountains, and ready for any race.

Since the completion of the transcontinental and Utah railways, this magnificent lake in the heart of the continent has become as accessible as any watering-place on either coast; and I am sure that thousands of travellers, sick and well, would throng its shores every summer were its merits but half known. Lake Point is only an hour or two from the city, and has hotel accommodations and a steamboat for excursions; and then, besides the bracing waters, the climate is delightful. The mountains rise into the cool sky furrowed with canyons almost yosemitic in grandeur, and filled with a glorious profusion of flowers and trees. Lovers of science, lovers of wildness, lovers of pure rest will find here more than they may hope for.

As for the Mormons one meets, however their doctrines be regarded, they will be found as rich in human kindness as any people in all our broad land, while the dark memories that cloud their earlier history will vanish from the mind as completely as when we bathe in the fountain azure of the Sierra.

CHAPTER NINE

Mormon Lilies[1]

LILIES ARE rare in Utah; so also are their companions the ferns and orchids, chiefly on account of the fiery saltness of the soil and climate. You may walk the deserts of the Great Basin in the bloom time of the year, all the way across from the snowy Sierra to the snowy Wahsatch, and your eyes will be filled with many a gay malva, and poppy, and abronia, and cactus, but you may not see a single true lily, and only a very few liliaceous plants of any kind. Not even in the cool, fresh glens of the mountains will you find these favourite flowers, though some of these desert ranges almost rival the Sierra in height. Nevertheless, in the building and planting of this grand Territory the lilies were not forgotten. Far back in the dim geologic ages, when the sediments of the old seas were being gathered and outspread in smooth sheets like leaves of a book, and when these sediments became dry land, and were baked and crumbled into the sky as mountain-ranges; when the lava-floods of the Fire Period were being lavishly poured forth from innumerable rifts and craters; when the ice of the Glacial Period was laid like a mantle over every mountain and valley – throughout all these immensely protracted periods, in the throng of these majestic operations, Nature kept her flower children in mind. She considered the lilies, and, while planting the plains with sage and the hills with cedar, she has covered at least one mountain with golden erythroniums and fritillarias as its crowning glory, as if willing to show what she could do in the lily line even here.

Looking southward from the south end of Salt Lake, the two northmost peaks of the Oquirrh Range are seen swelling calmly into the cool sky without any marked character, excepting only their snow crowns, and a few small weedy-looking patches of spruce and fir, the simplicity of their slopes preventing their real loftiness from being appreciated. Grey, sagey plains circle around their bases, and up to a height of a thousand feet or more their sides are tinged with purple, which I afterwards found is produced by a close growth of dwarf oak just coming into leaf. Higher you may detect faint tintings of green on a grey ground, from young grasses and sedges; then come the dark pine woods filling glacial hollows, and over all the smooth crown of snow.

While standing at their feet, the other day, shortly after my memorable excursion among the salt waves of the lake, I said: 'Now I shall have another baptism. I will bathe in the high sky, among cool wind-waves from the snow.' From the more southerly of the two peaks a long ridge comes down, bent like

[1] Letter dated 'Salt Lake, July, 1877.' [Editor.]

a bow, one end in the hot plains, the other in the snow of the summit. After carefully scanning the jagged towers and battlements with which it is roughened, I determined to make it my way, though it presented but a feeble advertisement of its floral wealth. This apparent barrenness, however, made no great objection just then, for I was scarce hoping for flowers, old or new, or even for fine scenery. I wanted in particular to learn what the Oquirrh rocks were made of, what trees composed the curious patches of forest; and, perhaps more than all, I was animated by a mountaineer's eagerness to get my feet into the snow once more, and my head into the clear sky, after lying dormant all winter at the level of the sea.

But in every walk with Nature one receives far more than he seeks. I had not gone more than a mile from Lake Point ere I found the way profusely decked with flowers, mostly compositæ and purple leguminosæ, a hundred corollas or more to the square yard, with a corresponding abundance of winged blossoms above them, moths and butterflies, the leguminosæ of the insect kingdom. This floweriness is maintained with delightful variety all the way up through rocks and bushes to the snow – violets, lilies, gilias, œnotheras, wallflowers, ivesias, saxifrages, smilax and miles of blooming bushes, chiefly azalea, honeysuckle, brier rose, buckthorn and eriogonum, all meeting and blending in divine accord.

Two liliaceous plants in particular, *Erythronium grandiflorum* and *Vritillaria pudica*, are marvellously beautiful and abundant. Never before, in all my walks, have I met so glorious a throng of these fine showy liliaceous plants. The whole mountain-side was aglow with them, from a height of fifty-five hundred feet to the very edge of the snow. Although remarkably fragile, both in form and in substance, they are endowed with plenty of deep-seated vitality, enabling them to grow in all kinds of places – down in leafy glens, in the lee of wind-beaten ledges and beneath the brushy tangles of azalea, and oak and prickly roses – everywhere forming the crowning glory of the flowers. If the neighbouring mountains are as rich in lilies, then this may well be called the Lily Range.

After climbing about a thousand feet above the plain I came to a picturesque mass of rock, cropping up through the underbrush on one of the steepest slopes of the mountain. After examining some tufts of grass and saxifrage that were growing in its fissured surface, I was going to pass it by on the upper side, where the bushes were more open, but a company composed of the two lilies I have mentioned were blooming on the lower side, and though they were as yet out of sight, I suddenly changed my mind and went down to meet them, as if attracted by the ringing of their bells. They were growing in a small, nestlike opening between the rock and the bushes, and both the erythronium and the fritillaria were in full flower. These were the first of the species I had seen, and I need not try to tell the joy they made. They are both lowly plants – lowly as violets – the tallest seldom exceeding six inches in height, so that the most searching winds that sweep the mountains scarce reach low enough to shake their bells.

The fritillaria has five or six linear, obtuse leaves, put on irregularly near the bottom of the stem, which is usually terminated by one large bell-shaped flower; but its more beautiful companion, the erythronium, has two radical leaves only, which are large and oval, and shine like glass. They extend horizontally in opposite directions, and form a beautiful glossy ground, over which the one large down-looking flower is swung from a simple stem, the petals being strongly recurved, like those of *Lilium superbum*. Occasionally a specimen is met which has from two to five flowers hung in a loose panicle. People oftentimes travel far to see curious plants like the carnivorous darlingtonia, the fly-catcher, the walking fern, etc. I hardly know how the little bells I have been describing would be regarded by seekers of this class, but every true flower-lover who comes to consider these Utah lilies will surely be well rewarded, however long the way.

Pushing on up the rugged slopes, I found many delightful seclusions – moist nooks at the foot of cliffs, and lilies in every one of them, not growing close together like daisies, but well apart, with plenty of room for their bells to swing free and ring. I found hundreds of them in full bloom within two feet of the snow. In winter only the bulbs are alive, sleeping deep beneath the ground, like field mice in their nests; then the snow-flowers fall above them, lilies over lilies, until the spring winds blow, and these winter lilies wither in turn; then the hiding erythroniums and fritillarias rise again, responsive to the first touches of the sun.

I noticed the tracks of deer in many places among the lily gardens, and at the height of about seven thousand feet I came upon the fresh trail of a flock of wild sheep, showing that these fine mountaineers still flourish here above the range of Mormon rifles. In the planting of her wild gardens, Nature takes the feet and teeth of her flocks into account, and makes use of them to trim and cultivate, and keep them in order, as the bark and buds of the tree are tended by woodpeckers and linnets.

The evergreen woods consist, as far as I observed, of two species, a spruce and a fir, standing close together, erect and arrowy in a thrifty, compact growth; but they are quite small, say from six to twelve or fourteen inches in diameter, and about forty feet in height. Among their giant relatives of the Sierra the very largest would seem mere saplings. A considerable portion of the south side of the mountain is planted with a species of aspen, called 'quaking asp' by the wood-choppers. It seems to be quite abundant on many of the eastern mountains of the basin, and forms a marked feature of their upper forests.

Wading up the curves of the summit was rather toilsome, for the snow, which was softened by the blazing sun, was from ten to twenty feet deep, but the view was one of the most impressively sublime I ever beheld. Snowy, ice-sculptured ranges bounded the horizon all around, while the great lake, eighty miles long and fifty miles wide, lay fully revealed beneath a lily sky. The shore-lines, marked by a ribbon of white sand, were seen sweeping around many a bay and promontory in elegant curves, and picturesque islands rising to mountain heights, and some of them capped with pearly cumuli. And the wide prairie of water glowing in the gold and purple of evening presented all the colours that tint the lips of shells and the petals of lilies – the most beautiful lake this side of the Rocky Mountains. Utah Lake, lying thirty-five miles to the south, was in full sight also, and the river Jordan, which links the two together, may be traced in silvery gleams throughout its whole course.

Descending the mountain, I followed the windings of the main central glen on the north, gathering specimens of the cones and sprays of the evergreens, and most of the other new plants I had met; but the lilies formed the crowning glory of my bouquet – the grandest I had carried in many a day. I reached the hotel on the lake about dusk with all my fresh riches, and my first mountain ramble in Utah was accomplished. On my way back to the city, the next day, I met a grave old Mormon with whom I had previously held some Latter-Day discussions. I shook my big handful of lilies in his face and shouted, 'Here are the true saints, ancient and Latter-Day, enduring forever!' After he had recovered from his astonishment he said, 'They are nice'.

The other liliaceous plants I have met in Utah are two species of zigadenas, *Fritillaria atropurpurea*, *Calochortus Nuttallii*, and three or four handsome alliums. One of these lilies, the calochortus, several species of which are well known in California as the 'Mariposa tulips', has received great consideration at the hands of the Mormons, for to it hundreds of them owe their lives. During the famine years between 1853 and 1858, great destitution prevailed, especially in the southern settlements, on account of drought and grasshoppers, and throughout one hungry winter in particular, thousands of the people subsisted chiefly on the bulbs of these tulips, called 'sego' by the Indians, who taught them its use.

Liliaceous women and girls are rare among the Mormons. They have seen too much hard, repressive toil to admit of the development of lily beauty either in form or colour. In general they are thickset, with large feet and hands, and with sun-browned faces, often curiously freckled like the petals of *Fritillaria atropurpurea*. They are fruit rather than flower – good brown bread. But down in the San Pitch Valley at Gunnison, I discovered a genuine lily, happily named Lily Young. She is a granddaughter of Brigham Young, slender and graceful, with lily-white cheeks tinted with clear rose. She was brought up in the old Salt Lake Zion House, but by some strange chance has been transplanted to this wilderness, where she blooms alone, the 'Lily of San Pitch'. Pitch is an old Indian, who, I suppose, pitched into the settlers and thus acquired fame enough to give name to the valley. Here I feel uneasy about the name of this lily, for the compositors have a perverse trick of making me say all kinds of absurd things wholly unwarranted by plain copy, and I fear that the 'Lily of San Pitch' will appear in print as the widow of Sam Patch. But, however this may be, among my memories of this strange land, that Oquirrh mountain, with its golden lilies, will ever rise in clear relief, and associated with them will always be the Mormon lily of San Pitch.

CHAPTER TEN

The San Gabriel Valley[1]

THE SUN valley of San Gabriel is one of the brightest spots to be found in all our bright land, and most of its brightness is wildness – wild south sunshine in a basin rimmed about with mountains and hills. Cultivation is not wholly wanting, for here are the choicest of all the Los Angeles orange groves, but its glorious abundance of ripe sun and soil is only beginning to be coined into fruit. The drowsy bits of cultivation accomplished by the old missionaries and the more recent efforts of restless Americans are scarce as yet visible and when comprehended in general views form nothing more than mere freckles on the smooth brown bosom of the Valley.

I entered the sunny south half a month ago, coming down along the cool sea, and landing at Santa Monica. An hour's ride over stretches of bare, brown plain, and through cornfields and orange groves, brought me to the handsome, conceited little town of Los Angeles, where one finds Spanish adobes and Yankee shingles meeting and overlapping in very curious antagonism. I believe there are some fifteen thousand people here, and some of their buildings are rather fine, but the gardens and the sky interested me more. A palm is seen here and there poising its royal crown in the rich light, and the banana, with its magnificent ribbon leaves, producing a marked tropical effect – not semi-tropical, as they are so fond of saying here, while speaking of their fruits. Nothing I have noticed strikes me as semi, save the brusque little bits of civilization with which the wilderness is chequered. These are semi-barbarous or less; everything else in the region has a most exuberant pronounced wholeness. The city held me but a short time, for the San Gabriel Mountains were in sight, advertising themselves grandly along the northern sky, and I was eager to make my way into their midst.

At Pasadena I had the rare good fortune to meet my old friend Doctor Congar, with whom I had studied chemistry and mathematics fifteen years ago. He exalted San Gabriel above all other inhabitable valleys, old and new, on the face of the globe. 'I have rambled', said he, 'ever since we left college, tasting innumerable climates, and trying the advantages offered by nearly every new State and Territory. Here I have made my home, and here I shall stay while I live. The geographical position is exactly right, soil and climate perfect, and everything that heart can wish comes to our efforts – flowers, fruits, milk and honey and plenty of money. And there', he continued, pointing just beyond his own precious possessions, 'is a block of land that is for sale; buy it and be my neighbour; plant five acres with orange trees, and

[1] Letter dated 'September 1, 1877'. [Editor.]

by the time your last mountain is climbed their fruit will be your fortune'. He then led me down the valley, through the few famous old groves in full bearing, and on the estate of Mr Wilson showed me a ten-acre grove eighteen years old, the last year's crop from which was sold for twenty thousand dollars. 'There', said he, with triumphant enthusiasm, 'what do you think of that? Two thousand dollars per acre per annum for land worth only one hundred dollars'.

The number of orange trees planted to the acre is usually from forty-nine to sixty-nine; they then stand from twenty-five to thirty feet apart each way, and, thus planted, thrive and continue fruitful to a comparatively great age. J. DeBarth Shorb, an enthusiastic believer in Los Angeles and oranges, says, 'We have trees on our property fully forty years old, and eighteen inches in diameter, that are still vigorous and yielding immense crops of fruit, although they are only twenty feet apart'. Seedlings are said to begin to bear remunerative crops in their tenth year, but by superior cultivation this long unproductive period may be somewhat lessened, while trees from three to five years old may be purchased from the nurserymen, so that the newcomer who sets out an orchard may begin to gather fruit by the fifth or sixth year. When first set out, and for some years afterward, the trees are irrigated by making rings of earth around them, which are connected with small ditches, through which the water is distributed to each tree. Or, where the ground is nearly level, the whole surface is flooded from time to time as required. From 309 trees, twelve years old from the seed, DeBarth Shorb says that in the season of 1874 he obtained an average of $20.50 per tree, or $1435 per acre, over and above cost of transportation to San Francisco, commission on sales, etc. He considers $1000 per acre a fair average at present prices, after the trees have reached the age of twelve years. The average price throughout the county for the last five years has been about $20 or $25 per thousand; and, inasmuch as the area adapted to orange culture is limited, it is hoped that this price may not greatly fall for many years.

The lemon and lime are also cultivated here to some extent, and considerable attention is now being given to the Florida banana, and the olive, almond and English walnut. But the orange interest heavily overshadows every other, while vines have of late years been so unremunerative they are seldom mentioned.

This is pre-eminently a fruit land, but the fame of its productions has in some way far outrun the results that have as yet been attained. Experiments have been tried, and good beginnings made, but the number of really valuable, well-established groves is scarce as one to fifty, compared with the newly planted. Many causes, however, have combined of late to give the business a wonderful impetus, and new orchards are being made every day, while the few old groves, aglow with golden fruit, are the burning and shining lights that direct and energize the sanguine newcomers.

After witnessing the bad effect of homelessness, developed to so destructive an extent in California, it would reassure every lover of his race to see the hearty home-building going on here and the blessed contentment that naturally follows it. Travel-worn pioneers, who have been tossed about like boulders in flood-time, are thronging hither as to a kind of terrestrial heaven, resolved to rest. They build, and plant, and settle, and so come under natural influences. When a man plants a tree he plants himself. Every root is an anchor, over which he rests with grateful interest, and becomes sufficiently calm to feel the joy of living. He necessarily makes the acquaintance of the sun and the sky. Favourite trees fill his mind, and, while tending them like children, and accepting the benefits they bring, he becomes himself a benefactor. He sees down through the brown common ground teeming with coloured fruits, as if it were transparent, and learns to bring them to the surface. What he wills he can raise by true enchantment. With slips and rootlets, his magic wands, they appear at his bidding. These, and the seeds he plants, are his prayers, and, by them brought into right relations with God, he works grander miracles every day than ever were written.

The Pasadena Colony, located on the southwest corner of the well-known San Pasqual Rancho, is scarce three years old, but it is growing rapidly, like a pet tree, and already forms one of the best contributions to culture yet accomplished in the county. It now numbers about sixty families, mostly drawn from the better class of vagabond pioneers, who, during their rolling-stone days have managed to gather sufficient gold moss to purchase from ten to forty acres of land. They are perfectly hilarious in their newly found life, work like ants in a sunny noonday, and, looking far into the future, hopefully count their orange chicks ten years or more before they are hatched; supporting themselves in the meantime on the produce of a few acres of alfalfa, together with garden vegetables and the quick-growing fruits, such as figs, grapes, apples, etc., the whole reinforced by the remaining dollars of their land purchase money. There is nothing more remarkable in the character of the colony than the literary and scientific taste displayed. The conversation of most I have met here is seasoned with a smack of mental ozone, Attic salt, which struck me as being rare among the tillers of California soil. People of taste and money in search of a home would do well to prospect the resources of this aristocratic little colony.

If we look now at these southern valleys in general, it will appear at once that with all their advantages they lie beyond the reach of poor settlers, not only on account of the high price of irrigable land – one hundred dollars per acre and upwards – but because of the scarcity of labour. A settler with three or four thousand dollars would be penniless after paying for twenty acres of orange land and building ever so plain a house, while many years would go by ere his trees yielded an income adequate to the maintenance of his family.

Nor is there anything sufficiently reviving in the fine climate to form a reliable inducement for very sick people. Most of this class, from all I can learn, come here only to die, and surely it is better to die comfortably at home, avoiding the thousand discomforts of travel, at a time when they are so hard to bear. It is indeed pitiful to see so many invalids, already on the verge of the grave, making a painful way to quack climates, hoping to change age to youth, and the darkening twilight of their day to morning. No such health-fountain has been found, and this climate, fine as it is, seems, like most others, to be adapted for well people only. From all I could find out regarding its influence upon patients suffering from pulmonary difficulties, it is seldom beneficial to any great extent in advanced cases. The cold sea-winds are less fatal to this class of sufferers than the corresponding winds further north, but, notwithstanding they are tempered on their passage inland over warm, dry ground, they are still more or less injurious.

The summer climate of the fir and pine woods of the Sierra Nevada would, I think, be found infinitely more reviving; but because these woods have not been advertised like patent medicines, few seem to think of the spicy, vivifying influences that pervade their fountain freshness and beauty.

CHAPTER ELEVEN

The San Gabriel Mountains[1]

AFTER SAYING so much for human culture in my last, perhaps I may now be allowed a word for wildness – the wildness of this southland, pure and untamable as the sea.

In the mountains of San Gabriel, overlooking the lowland vines and fruit groves, Mother Nature is most ruggedly, thornily savage. Not even in the Sierra have I ever made the acquaintance of mountains more rigidly inaccessible. The slopes are exceptionally steep and insecure to the foot of the explorer, however great his strength or skill may be, but thorny chaparral constitutes their chief defence. With the exception of little park and garden spots not visible in comprehensive views, the entire surface is covered with it, from the highest peaks to the plain. It swoops into every hollow and swells over every ridge, gracefully complying with the varied topography, in shaggy, ungovernable exuberance, fairly dwarfing the utmost efforts of human culture out of sight and mind.

But in the very heart of this thorny wilderness, down in the dells, you may find gardens filled with the fairest flowers, that any child would love, and unapproachable linns lined with lilies and ferns, where the ouzel builds its mossy hut and sings in chorus with the white falling water. Bears, also, and panthers, wolves, wildcats, wood rats, squirrels, foxes, snakes and innumerable birds, all find grateful homes here, adding wildness to wildness in glorious profusion and variety.

Where the coast ranges and the Sierra Nevada come together we find a very complicated system of short ranges, the geology and topography of which is yet hidden, and many years of laborious study must be given for anything like a complete interpretation of them. The San Gabriel is one or more of these ranges, forty or fifty miles long, and half as broad, extending from the Cajon Pass on the east, to the Santa Monica and Santa Susanna ranges on the west.

---

[1] Letter written during the first week of September, 1877. [Editor.]

San Antonio, the dominating peak, rises towards the eastern extremity of the range to a height of about six thousand feet, forming a sure landmark throughout the valley and all the way down to the coast, without, however, possessing much striking individuality. The whole range, seen from the plain, with the hot sun beating upon its southern slopes, wears a terribly forbidding aspect. There is nothing of the grandeur of snow, or glaciers, or deep forests, to excite curiosity or adventure; no trace of gardens or waterfalls. From base to summit all seems grey, barren, silent – dead, bleached bones of mountains, overgrown with scrubby bushes, like grey moss. But all mountains are full of hidden beauty, and the next day after my arrival at Pasadena I supplied myself with bread and eagerly set out to give myself to their keeping.

On the first day of my excursion I went only as far as the mouth of Eaton Canyon, because the heat was oppressive, and a pair of new shoes were chafing my feet to such an extent that walking began to be painful. While looking for a camping-ground among the boulder beds of the canyon, I came upon a strange, dark man of doubtful parentage. He kindly invited me to camp with him, and led me to his litle hut. All my conjectures as to his nationality failed, and no wonder, since his father was Irish and mother Spanish, a mixture not often met even in California. He happened to be out of candles, so we sat in the dark while he gave me a sketch of his life, which was exceedingly picturesque. Then he showed me his plans for the future. He was going to settle among these canyon boulders, and make money, and marry a Spanish woman. People mine for irrigating water along the foothills as for gold. He is now driving a prospecting tunnel into a spur of the mountains back of his cabin. 'My prospect is good', he said, 'and if I strike a strong flow, I shall soon be worth five or ten thousand dollars. That flat out there', he continued, referring to a small, irregular patch of gravelly detritus that had been sorted out and deposited by Eaton Creek during some flood season, 'is large enough for a nice orange grove, and, after watering my own trees, I can sell water down the valley; and then the hillside back of the cabin will do for vines, and I can keep bees, for the white sage and black sage up the mountains is full of honey. You see, I've got a good thing'. All this prospective affluence in the sunken, boulder-choked flood-bed of Eaton Creek! Most home-seekers would as soon think of settling on the summit of San Antonio.

Half an hour's easy rambling up the canyon brought me to the foot of 'The Fall', famous throughout the valley settlements as the finest yet discovered in the range. It is a charming little thing, with a voice sweet as a songbird's, leaping some thirty-five or forty feet into a round, mirror pool. The cliff back of it and on both sides is completely covered with thick, furry mosses, and the white fall shines against the green like a silver instrument in a velvet case. Here come the Gabriel lads and lassies from the commonplace orange groves, to make love and gather ferns and dabble away their hot holidays in the cool pool. They are fortunate in finding so fresh a retreat so near their homes. It is the Yosemite of San Gabriel. The walls, though not of the true Yosemite type either in form or sculpture, rise to a height of nearly two thousand feet. Ferns are abundant on all the rocks within reach of the spray, and picturesque maples and sycamores spread a grateful shade over a rich profusion of wild flowers that grow among the boulders from the edge of the pool a mile or more down the dell-like bottom of the valley, the whole forming a charming little poem of wildness – the vestibule of these shaggy mountain temples.

The foot of the fall is about a thousand feet above the level of the sea, and here climbing begins. I made my way out of the valley on the west side, followed the ridge that forms the western rim of the Eaton Basin to the summit of one of the principal peaks, thence crossed the middle of the basin, forcing a way over its many subordinate ridges, and out over the eastern rim, and from first to last during three days spent in this excursion, I had to contend with the richest, most self-possessed and uncompromising chaparral I have ever enjoyed since first my mountaineering began.

For a hundred feet or so the ascent was practicable only by means of bosses of the club moss that clings to the rock. Above this the ridge is weathered away to a slender knife-edge for a distance of two or three hundred yards, and thence to the summit it is a bristly mane of chaparral. Here and there small openings occur, commanding grand views of the valley and beyond to the ocean. These are favourite outlooks and resting-places for the wild animals, in particular for bears, wolves and wild-cats. In the densest places I came upon wood-rat villages whose huts were from four to eight feet high, built in the same style of architecture as those of the muskrats.

The day was nearly done. I reached the summit and I had time to make only a hasty survey of the topography of the wild basin now outspread maplike beneath, and to drink in the rare loveliness of the sunlight before hastening down in search of water. Pushing through another mile of chaparral, I emerged into one of the most beautiful parklike groves of live oak I ever saw. The ground beneath was planted only with aspidiums and brier roses. At the foot of the grove I came to the dry channel of one of the tributary streams, but, following it down a short distance, I descried a few specimens of the scarlet mimulus; and I was assured that water was near. I found about a bucketful in a granite bowl, but it was full of leaves and beetles, making a sort of brown coffee that could be rendered available only by filtering it through sand and charcoal. This I resolved to do in case the night came on before I found better. Following the channel a mile farther down to its confluence with another, larger tributary, I found a lot of boulder pools, clear as crystal, and brimming full, linked together by little glistening currents just strong enough to sing. Flowers in full bloom adorned the banks, lilies ten feet high, and luxuriant ferns arching over one another in lavish abundance, while a noble old live oak spread its rugged boughs over all, forming one of the most perfect and most secluded of Nature's gardens. Here I camped, making my bed on smooth cobblestones.

Next morning, pushing up the channel of a tributary that takes its rise on Mount San Antonio, I passed many lovely gardens watered by oozing currentlets, every one of which had lilies in them in the full pomp of bloom, and a rich growth of ferns, chiefly woodwardias and aspidiums and maidenhairs; but toward the base of the mountain the channel was dry, and the chaparral closed over from bank to bank, so that I was compelled to creep more than a mile on hands and knees.

In one spot I found an opening in the thorny sky where I could stand erect, and on the further side of the opening discovered a small pool. 'Now, *here*', I said, 'I must be careful in creeping, for the birds of the neighbourhood come here to drink, and the rattlesnakes come here to catch them'. I then began to cast my eye along the channel, perhaps instinctively feeling a snaky atmosphere, and finally discovered one rattler between my feet. But there was a bashful look in his eye, and a withdrawing, deprecating kink in his neck that showed plainly as words could tell that he would not strike, and only wished to be let alone. I therefore passed on, lifting my foot a little higher than usual, and left him to enjoy his life in this his own home.

My next camp was near the heart of the basin, at the head of a grand system of cascades from ten to two hundred feet high, one following the other in close succession and making a total descent of nearly seventeen hundred feet. The rocks above me leaned over in a threatening way and were full of seams, making the camp a very unsafe one during an earthquake.

Next day the chaparral, in ascending the eastern rim of the basin, was, if possible, denser and more stubbornly bayoneted than ever. I followed bear trails, where in some places I found tufts of their hair that had been pulled out in squeezing a way through; but there was much of a very interesting character that far overpaid all my pains. Most of the plants are identical with those of the Sierra, but there are quite a number of Mexican species. One coniferous tree was all I found. This is a spruce of a species new to me, *Douglasii macrocarpa*.[1]

My last camp was down at the narrow, notched bottom of a dry channel, the only open way for the life in the neighbourhood. I therefore lay between two fires, built to fence out snakes and wolves.

From the summit of the eastern rim I had a glorious view of the valley out to the ocean, which would require a whole book for its description. My bread gave out a day before reaching the settlements, but I felt all the fresher and clearer for the fast.

CHAPTER TWELVE

Nevada Farms[2]

To the farmer who comes to this thirsty land from beneath rainy skies, Nevada seems one vast desert, all sage and sand, hopelessly irredeemable now and forever. And this, under present conditions, is severely true. For notwithstanding it has gardens, grainfields and hayfields generously productive, these compared with the arid stretches of valley and plain, as beheld in

[1] [The spruce, or hemlock, then known as *Abies Douglasii* var. *macrocarpa* is now called *Pseudotsuga macrocarpa*.]
[2] Written at Ward, Nevada, in September, 1878. [Editor.]

general views from the mountain-tops, are mere specks lying inconspicuously here and there, in out-of-the-way places, often thirty or forty miles apart.

In leafy regions, blessed with copious rains, we learn to measure the productive capacity of the soil by its natural vegetation. But this rule is almost wholly inapplicable here, for, notwithstanding its savage nakedness, scarce at all veiled by a sparse growth of sage and linosyris,[1] the desert soil of the Great Basin is as rich in the elements that in rainy regions rise and ripen into food as that of any other State in the Union. The rocks of its numerous mountain-ranges have been thoroughly crushed and ground by glaciers, thrashed and vitalized by the sun, and sifted and outspread in lake-basins by powerful torrents that attended the breaking-up of the glacial period, as if in every way Nature had been making haste to prepare the land for the husbandman. Soil, climate, topographical conditions, all that the most exacting could demand, are present, but one thing, water, is wanting. The present rainfall would be wholly inadequate for agriculture, even if it were advantageously distributed over the lowlands, while in fact the greater portion is poured out on the heights in sudden and violent thunder-showers called 'cloud-bursts'; the waters of which are fruitlessly swallowed up in sandy gulches and deltas a few minutes after their first boisterous appearance. The principal mountain-chains, trending nearly north and south, parallel with the Sierra and the Wahsatch, receive a good deal of snow during winter, but no great masses are stored up as fountains for large perennial streams capable of irrigating considerable areas. Most of it is melted before the end of May and absorbed by moraines and gravelly taluses, which send forth small rills that slip quietly down the upper canyons through narrow strips of flowery verdure, most of them sinking and vanishing before they reach the base of their fountain ranges. Perhaps not one in ten of the whole number flow out into the open plains, not a single drop reaches the sea, and only a few are large enough to irrigate more than one farm of moderate size.

It is upon these small outflowing rills that most of the Nevada ranches are located, lying countersunk beneath the general level, just where the mountains meet the plains, at an average elevation of five thousand feet above sea-level. All the cereals and garden vegetables thrive here, and yield bountiful crops. Fruit, however, has been, as yet, grown successfully in only a few specially favoured spots.

Another distinct class of ranches are found sparsely distributed along the lowest portions of the plains, where the ground is kept moist by springs, or by narrow threads of moving water called rivers, fed by some one or more of the most vigorous of the mountain rills that have succeeded in making their escape from the mountains. These are mostly devoted to the growth of wild hay, though in some the natural meadow grasses and sedges have been supplemented by timothy and alfalfa; and where the soil is not too strongly impregnated with salts, some grain is raised. Reese River Valley, Big Smoky Valley, and White River Valley offer fair illustrations of this class. As compared with the foothill ranches, they are larger and less inconspicuous, as they

---

[1] See footnote on p. 884.

lie in the wide, unshadowed levels of the plains – wavy-edged flecks of green in a wilderness of grey.

Still another class equally well defined, both as to distribution and as to products, is restricted to that portion of western Nevada and the eastern border of California which lies within the redeeming influences of California waters. Three of the Sierra rivers descend from their icy fountains into the desert like angels of mercy to bless Nevada. These are the Walker, Carson and Truckee; and in the valleys through which they flow are found by far the most extensive hay and grain fields within the bounds of the State. Irrigating streams are led off right and left through innumerable channels, and the sleeping ground, starting at once into action, pours forth its wealth without stint.

But notwithstanding the many porous fields thus fertilized, considerable portions of the waters of all these rivers continue to reach their old deathbeds in the desert, indicating that in these salt valleys there still is room for coming farmers. In middle and eastern Nevada, however, every rill that I have seen in a ride of three thousand miles, at all available for irrigation, has been claimed and put to use.

It appears, therefore, that under present conditions the limit of agricultural development in the dry basin between the Sierra and the Wahsatch has been already approached, a result caused not alone by natural restrictions as to the area capable of development, but by the extraordinary stimulus furnished by the mines to agricultural effort. The gathering of gold and silver, hay and barley, have gone on together. Most of the mid-valley bogs and meadows, and foothill rills capable of irrigating from ten to fifty acres, were claimed more than twenty years ago.

A majority of these pioneer settlers are plodding Dutchmen, living content in the back lanes and valleys of Nature; but the high price of all kinds of farm products tempted many of even the keen Yankee prospectors, made wise in California, to bind themselves down to this sure kind of mining. The wildest of wild hay, made chiefly of carices and rushes, was sold at from two to three hundred dollars per ton on ranches. The same kind of hay is still worth from fifteen to forty dollars per ton, according to the distance from mines and comparative security from competition. Barley and oats are from forty to one hundred dollars a ton, while all sorts of garden products find ready sale at high prices.

With rich mine markets and salubrious climate, the Nevada farmer can make more money by loose, ragged methods than the same class of farmers in any other State I have yet seen, while the almost savage isolation in which they live seems grateful to them. Even in those cases where the advent of neighbours brings no disputes concerning water-rights and ranges, they seem to prefer solitude, most of them having been elected from adventurers from California – the pioneers of pioneers. The passing stranger, however, is always welcomed and supplied with the best the home affords, and around the fireside, while he smokes his pipe, very little encouragement is required to bring forth the story of the farmer's life – hunting, mining, fighting, in the early Indian times, etc. Only the few who are married hope to return to

California to educate their children, and the ease with which money is made renders the fulfillment of these hopes comparatively sure.

After dwelling thus long on the farms of this dry wonderland, my readers may be led to fancy them of more importance as compared with the unbroken fields of Nature than they really are. Making your way along any of the wide grey valleys that stretch from north to south, seldom will your eye be interrupted by a single mark of cultivation. The smooth lake-like ground sweeps on indefinitely, growing more and more dim in the glowing sunshine, while a mountain-range from eight to ten thousand feet high bounds the view on either hand. No singing water, no green sod, no moist nook to rest in – mountain and valley alike naked and shadowless in the sun-glare; and though, perhaps, travelling a well-worn road to a gold or silver mine, and supplied with repeated instructions, you can scarce hope to find any human habitation from day to day, so vast and impressive is the hot, dusty, alkaline wildness.

But after riding some thirty or forty miles, and while the sun may be sinking behind the mountains, you come suddenly upon signs of cultivation. Clumps of willows indicate water, and water indicates a farm. Approaching more nearly, you discover what may be a patch of barley spread out unevenly along the bottom of a flood-bed, broken perhaps, and rendered less distinct by boulder-piles and the fringing willows of a stream. Speedily you can confidently say that the grain-patch is surely such; its ragged bounds become clear; a sand-roofed cabin comes to view littered with sun-cracked implements and with an outer girdle of potato, cabbage and alfalfa patches.

The immense expanse of mountain-girt valleys, on the edges of which these hidden ranches lie, make even the largest fields seem comic in size. The smallest, however, are by no means insignificant in a pecuniary view. On the east side of the Toyabe Range I discovered a jolly Irishman who informed me that his income from fifty acres, reinforced by a sheep-range on the adjacent hills, was from seven to nine thousand dollars per annum. His irrigating brook is about four feet wide and eight inches deep, flowing about two miles per hour.

On Duckwater Creek, Nye County, Mr Irwin has reclaimed a Tule swamp several hundred acres in extent, which is now chiefly devoted to alfalfa. On twenty-five acres he claims to have raised this year thirty-seven tons of barley. Indeed, I have not yet noticed a meagre crop of any kind in the State. Fruit alone is conspicuously absent.

On the California side of the Sierra grain will not ripen at a much greater elevation than four thousand feet above sea-level. The valleys of Nevada lie at a height of from four to six thousand feet, and both wheat and barley ripen, wherever water may be had, up to seven thousand feet. The harvest, of course, is later as the elevation increases. In the valleys of the Carson and Walker Rivers, four thousand feet above the sea, the grain harvest is about a month later than in California. In Reese River Valley, six thousand feet, it begins near the end of August. Winter grain ripens somewhat earlier, while occasionally one meets a patch of barley in some cool, high-lying canyon that will not mature before the middle of September.

Unlike California, Nevada will probably be always richer in gold and silver than in grain. Utah farmers hope to change the climate of the east side of the basin by prayer, and point to the recent rise in the waters of the Great Salt Lake as a beginning of moister times. But Nevada's only hope, in the way of any considerable increase in agriculture, is from artesian wells. The cleft and porous character of the mountain rocks, tilted at every angle, and the presence of springs bursting forth in the valleys far from the mountain sources, indicate accumulations of water from the melting snows that have escaped evaporation, which, no doubt, may in many places now barren be brought to the surface in flowing wells. The experiment has been tried on a small scale with encouraging success. But what is now wanted seems to be the boring of a few specimen wells of a large size out in the main valleys. The encouragement that successful experiments of this kind would give to emigration seeking farms forms an object well worthy the attention of the Government. But all that California farmers in the grand central valley require is the preservation of the forests and the wise distribution of the glorious abundance of water from the snow stored on the west flank of the Sierra.

Whether any considerable area of these sage plains will ever thus be made to blossom in grass and wheat, experience will show. But in the mean time Nevada is beautiful in her wildness, and if tillers of the soil can thus be brought to see that possibly Nature may have other uses even for *rich* soil besides the feeding of human beings, then will these foodless 'deserts' have taught a fine lesson.

CHAPTER THIRTEEN

Nevada Forests[1]

WHEN THE traveller from California has crossed the Sierra and gone a little way down the eastern flank, the woods come to an end about as suddenly and completely as if, going westward, he had reached the ocean. From the very noblest forests in the world he emerges into free sunshine and dead alkaline lake-levels. Mountains are seen beyond, rising in bewildering abundance, range beyond range. But however closely we have been accustomed to associate forests and mountains, these always present a singularly barren aspect, appearing grey and forbidding and shadeless, like heaps of ashes dumped from the blazing sky.

But wheresoever we may venture to go in all this good world, nature is ever found richer and more beautiful than she seems, and nowhere may you meet with more varied and delightful surprises than in the byways and recesses of this sublime wilderness – lovely asters and abronias on the dusty plains, rose-gardens around the mountain wells, and resiny woods, where all seemed so

[1] Written at Eureka, Nevada, in October, 1878. [Editor.]

desolate, adorning the hot foothills as well as the cool summits, fed by cordial and benevolent storms of rain and hail and snow; all of these scant and rare as compared with the immeasurable exuberance of California, but still amply sufficient throughout the barest deserts for a clear manifestation of God's love.

Though Nevada is situated in what is called the 'Great Basin', no less than sixty-five groups and chains of mountains rise within the bounds of the State to a height of about from eight thousand to thirteen thousand feet above the level of the sea, and as far as I have observed, every one of these is planted, to some extent, with coniferous trees, though it is only upon the highest that we find anything that may fairly be called a forest. The lower ranges and the foothills and slopes of the higher are roughened with small scrubby junipers and nut pines, while the dominating peaks, together with the ridges that swing in grand curves between them, are covered with a closer and more erect growth of pine, spruce and fir, resembling the forests of the Eastern States both as to size and general botanical characteristics. Here is found what is called the heavy timber, but the tallest and most fully developed sections of the forests, growing down in sheltered hollows on moist moraines, would be regarded in California only as groves of saplings, and so, relatively, they are, for by careful calculation we find that more than a thousand of these trees would be required to furnish as much timber as may be obtained from a single specimen of our Sierra giants.

The height of the timber-line in eastern Nevada, near the middle of the Great Basin, is about eleven thousand feet above sea-level; consequently the forests, in a dwarfed, storm-beaten condition, pass over the summits of nearly every range in the State, broken here and there only by mechanical conditions of the surface rocks. Only three mountains in the State have as yet come under my observation whose summits rise distinctly above the tree-line. These are Wheeler's Peak, twelve thousand three hundred feet high, Mount Moriah, about twelve thousand feet, and Granite Mountain, about the same height, all of which are situated near the boundary-line between Nevada and Utah Territory.

In a rambling mountaineering journey of eighteen hundred miles across the state, I have met nine species of coniferous trees – four pines, two spruces, two junipers and one fir – about one third the number found in California. By far the most abundant and interesting of these is the *Pinus Fremontiana*,[1] or nut pine. In the number of individual trees and extent of range this curious little conifer surpasses all the others combined. Nearly every mountain in the State is planted with it from near the base to a height of from eight thousand to nine thousand feet above the sea. Some are covered from base to summit by this one species, with only a sparse growth of juniper on the lower slopes to break the continuity of these curious woods, which, though dark-looking at a little distance, are yet almost shadeless, and without any hint of the dark glens and hollows so characteristic of other pine woods. Tens of thousands of acres occur in one continuous belt. Indeed, viewed comprehensively, the entire

[1] Now called *Pinus monophylla*, or one-leaf pinyon. [Editor.]

State seems to be pretty evenly divided into mountain-ranges covered with
nut pines and plains covered with sage -- now a swath of pines stretching from
north to south, now a swath of sage; the one black, the other grey; one
severely level, the other sweeping on complacently over ridge and valley and
lofty crowning dome.

The real character of a forest of this sort would never be guessed by the
inexperienced observer. Travelling across the sage levels in the dazzling
sunlight, you gaze with shaded eyes at the mountains rising along their edges,
perhaps twenty miles away, but no invitation that is at all likely to be
understood is discernible. Every mountain, however high it swells into the
sky, seems utterly barren. Approaching nearer, a low brushy growth is seen,
strangely black in aspect, as though it had been burned. This is a nut pine
forest, the bountiful orchard of the red man. When you ascend into its midst
you find the ground beneath the trees, and in the openings also, nearly naked,
and mostly rough on the surface -- a succession of crumbling ledges of lava,
limestones, slate and quartzite, coarsely strewn with soil weathered from
them. Here and there occurs a bunch of sage or linosyris, or a purple aster, or
a tuft of dry bunch-grass.

The harshest mountain-sides, hot and waterless, seem best adapted to the
nut pine's development. No slope is too steep, none too dry; every situation
seems to be gratefully chosen, if only it be sufficiently rocky and firm to afford
secure anchorage for the tough, grasping roots. It is a sturdy, thickset little
tree, usually about fifteen feet high when full grown, and about as broad as
high, holding its knotty branches well out in every direction in stiff zigzags,
but turning them gracefully upward at the ends in rounded bosses. Though
making so dark a mass in the distance, the foliage is a pale greyish green, in
stiff, awl-shaped fascicles. When examined closely these round needles seem
inclined to be two-leaved, but they are mostly held firmly together, as if to
guard against evaporation. The bark on the older sections is nearly black, so
that the boles and branches are clearly traced against the prevailing grey of
the mountains on which they delight to dwell.

The value of this species to Nevada is not easily overestimated. It furnishes
fuel, charcoal and timber for the mines, and, together with the enduring
juniper, so generally associated with it, supplies the ranches with abundance
of firewood and rough fencing. Many a square mile has already been denuded
in supplying these demands, but, so great is the area covered by it, no
appreciable loss has as yet been sustained. It is pretty generally known that
this tree yields edible nuts, but their importance and excellence as human
food is infinitely greater than is supposed. In fruitful seasons like this one, the
pine-nut crop of Nevada is, perhaps, greater than the entire wheat crop of
California, concerning which so much is said and felt throughout the food-
markets of the world.

The Indians alone appreciate this portion of Nature's bounty and celebrate
the harvest home with dancing and feasting. The cones, which are a bright
grass-green in colour and about two inches long by one and a half in diameter,
are beaten off with poles just before the scales open, gathered in heaps of
several bushels, and lightly scorched by burning a thin covering of brushwood

over them. The resin, with which the cones are bedraggled, is thus burned off, the nuts slightly roasted, and the scales made to open. Then they are allowed to dry in the sun, after which the nuts are easily thrashed out and are ready to be stored away. They are about half an inch long by a quarter of an inch in diameter, pointed at the upper end, rounded at the base, light-brown in general colour, and handsomely dotted with purple, like birds' eggs. The shells are thin, and may be crushed between the thumb and finger. The kernels are white and waxy-looking, becoming brown by roasting, sweet and delicious to every palate, and are eaten by birds, squirrels, dogs, horses and man. When the crop is abundant the Indians bring in large quantities for sale; they are eaten around every fireside in the State, and oftentimes fed to horses instead of barley.

Looking over the whole continent, none of Nature's bounties seems to me so great as this in the way of food, none so little appreciated. Fortunately for the Indians and wild animals that gather around Nature's board, this crop is not easily harvested in a monopolizing way. If it could be gathered like wheat the whole would be carried away and dissipated in towns, leaving the brave inhabitants of these wilds to starve.

Long before the harvest-time, which is in September and October, the Indians examine the trees with keen discernment, and inasmuch as the cones require two years to mature from the first appearance of the little red rosettes of the fertile flowers, the scarcity or abundance of the crop may be predicted more than a year in advance. Squirrels, and worms and Clarke crows, make haste to begin the harvest. When the crop is ripe the Indians make ready their long beating-poles; baskets, bags, rags, mats, are gotten together. The squaws out among the settlers at service, washing and drudging, assemble at the family huts; the men leave their ranch work; all, old and young, are mounted on ponies, and set off in great glee to the nut lands, forming cavalcades curiously picturesque. Flaming scarfs and calico skirts stream loosely over the knotty ponies, usually two squaws astride of each, with the small baby midgets bandaged in baskets slung on their backs, or balanced upon the saddle-bow, while the nut-baskets and water-jars project from either side, and the long beating-poles, like old-fashioned lances, angle out in every direction.

Arrived at some central point already fixed upon, where water and grass is found, the squaws with baskets, the men with poles, ascend the ridges to the laden trees, followed by the children; beating begins with loud noise and chatter; the burs fly right and left, lodging against stones and sagebrush; the squaws and children gather them with fine natural gladness; smoke-columns speedily mark the joyful scene of their labours as the roasting-fires are kindled; and, at night, assembled in circles, garrulous as jays, the first grand nut feast begins. Sufficient quantities are thus obtained in a few weeks to last all winter.

The Indians also gather several species of berries and dry them to vary their stores, and a few deer and grouse are killed on the mountains, besides immense numbers of rabbits and hares; but the pine-nuts are their main dependence – their staff of life, their bread.

Insects also, scarce noticed by man, come in for their share of this fine bounty. Eggs are deposited, and the baby grubs, happy fellows, find themselves in a sweet world of plenty, feeding their way through the heart of the cone from one nut-chamber to another, secure from rain and wind and heat, until their wings are grown and they are ready to launch out into the free ocean of air and light.

CHAPTER FOURTEEN

Nevada's Timber Belt[1]

THE PINE woods on the tops of the Nevada mountains are already shining and blooming in winter snow, making a most blessedly refreshing appearance to the weary traveller down on the grey plains. During the fiery days of summer the whole of this vast region seems so perfectly possessed by the sun that the very memories of pine trees and snow are in danger of being burned away, leaving one but little more than dust and metal. But since these first winter blessings have come, the wealth and beauty of the landscapes have come fairly into view, and one is rendered capable of looking and seeing.

The grand nut-harvest is over, as far as the Indians are concerned, though perhaps less than one bushel in a thousand of the whole crop has been gathered. But the squirrels and birds are still busily engaged, and by the time that Nature's ends are accomplished, every nut will doubtless have been put to use.

All of the nine Nevada conifers mentioned in my last letter are also found in California, excepting only the Rocky Mountain spruce, which I have not observed westward of the Snake Range. So greatly, however, have they been made to vary by differences of soil and climate, that most of them appear as distinct species. Without seeming in any way dwarfed or repressed in habit, they nowhere develop to anything like California dimensions. A height of fifty feet and diameter of twelve or fourteen inches would probably be found to be above the average size of those cut for lumber. On the margin of the Carson and Humboldt Sink the larger sage bushes are called 'heavy timber'; and to the settlers here any tree seems large enough for saw-logs.

Mills have been built in the most accessible canyons of the higher ranges, and sufficient lumber of an inferior kind is made to supply most of the local demand. The principal lumber trees of Nevada are the white pine (*Pinus flexilis*), foxtail pine, and Douglas spruce, or 'red pine', as it is called here. Of these the first named is most generally distributed, being found on all the higher ranges throughout the State. In botanical characters it is nearly allied to the Weymouth, or white, pine of the Eastern States, and to the sugar and

[1] Written at Pioche, Nevada, in October, 1878. [Editor.]

mountain pines of the Sierra. In open situations it branches near the ground
and tosses out long down-curving limbs all around, often gaining in this way a
very strikingly picturesque habit. It is seldom found lower than nine thousand
feet above the level of the sea, but from this height it pushes upward over the
roughest ledges to the extreme limit of tree growth – about eleven thousand
feet.

On the Hot Creek, White Pine and Golden Gate ranges we find a still
hardier and more picturesque species, called the foxtail pine, from its long
dense leaf-tassels. About a foot or eighteen inches of the ends of the branches
are densely packed with stiff outstanding needles, which radiate all around
like an electric fox- or squirrel-tail. The needles are about an inch and a half
long, slightly curved, elastic and glossily polished; so that the sunshine sifting
through them makes them burn with a fine silvery lustre, while their number
and elastic temper tell delightfully in the singing winds.

This tree is pre-eminently picturesque, far surpassing not only its companion species of the mountains in this respect, but also the most noted of the
lowland oaks and elms. Some stand firmly erect, feathered with radiant tail
tassels down to the ground, forming slender, tapering towers of shining
verdure; others with two or three specialized branches pushed out at right
angles to the trunk and densely clad with the tasselled sprays, take the form of
beautiful ornamental crosses. Again, in the same woods you find trees that
are made up of several boles united near the ground, and spreading in easy
curves at the sides in a plane parallel to the axis of the mountain, with the
elegant tassels hung in charming order between them, the whole making a
perfect harp, ranged across the main wind-lines just where they may be most
effective in the grand storm harmonies. And then there is an infinite variety of
arching forms, standing free or in groups, leaning away from or toward each
other in curious architectural structures – innumerable tassels drooping under
the arches and radiating above them, the outside glowing in the light, masses
of deep shade beneath, giving rise to effects marvellously beautiful – while on
the roughest ledges of crumbling limestone are lowly old giants, five or six
feet in diameter, that have braved the storms of more than a thousand years.
But, whether old or young, sheltered or exposed to the wildest gales, this tree
is ever found to be irrepressibly and extravagantly picturesque, offering a
richer and more varied series of forms to the artist than any other species I
have yet seen.

One of the most interesting mountain excursions I have made in the State
was up through a thick spicy forest of these trees to the top of the highest
summit of the Troy Range, about ninety miles to the south of Hamilton. The
day was full of perfect Indian-summer sunshine, calm and bracing. Jays and
Clarke crows made a pleasant stir in the foothill pines and junipers; grasshoppers danced in the hazy light, and rattled on the wing in pure glee, reviving
suddenly from the torpor of a frosty October night to exuberant summer joy.
The squirrels were working industriously among the falling nuts; ripe willows
and aspens made gorgeous masses of colour on the russet hillsides and along
the edges of the small streams that threaded the higher ravines; and on the
smooth sloping uplands, beneath the foxtail pines and firs, the ground was

covered with brown grasses, enriched with sunflowers, columbines and lark-spurs and patches of linosyris, mostly frost-nipped and gone to seed, yet making fine bits of yellow and purple in the general brown.

At a height of about ninety-five hundred feet we passed through a mag-nificent grove of aspens, about a hundred acres in extent, through which the mellow sunshine sifted in ravishing splendour, showing every leaf to be as beautiful in colour as the wing of a butterfly, and making them tell gloriously against the evergreens. These extensive groves of aspen are a marked feature of the Nevada woods. Some of the lower mountains are covered with them, giving rise to remarkably beautiful effects in general views – waving, trembl-ing masses of pale, translucent green in spring and summer, yellow and orange in autumn, while in winter, after every leaf has fallen, the white bark of the boles and branches seen in mass seems like a cloud of mist that has settled close down on the mountain, conforming to all its hollows and ridges like a mantle, yet roughened on the surface with innumerable ascending spires.

Just above the aspens we entered a fine, close growth of foxtail pine, the tallest and most evenly planted I had yet seen. It extended along a waving ridge tending north and south and down both sides with but little interruption for a distance of about five miles. The trees were mostly straight in the bole, and their shade covered the ground in the densest places, leaving only small openings to the sun. A few of the tallest specimens measured over eighty feet, with a diameter of eighteen inches; but many of the younger trees, growing in tufts, were nearly fifty feet high, with a diameter of only five or six inches, while their slender shafts were hidden from top to bottom by a close, fringy growth of tasselled branchlets. A few white pines and balsam firs occur here and there, mostly around the edges of sunny openings, where they enrich the air with their rosiny fragrance, and bring out the peculiar beauties of the predominating foxtails by contrast.

Birds find grateful homes here – grouse, chickadees and linnets, of which we saw large flocks that had a delightfully enlivening effect. But the wood-peckers are remarkably rare. Thus far I have noticed only one species, the golden-winged; and but few of the streams are large enough or long enough to attract the blessed ouzel, so common in the Sierra.

On Wheeler's Peak, the dominating summit of the Snake Mountains, I found all the conifers I had seen on the other ranges of the State, excepting the foxtail pine, which I have not observed further east than the White Pine range, but in its stead the beautiful Rocky Mountain spruce. First, as in the other ranges, we find the juniper and nut pine; then, higher, the white pine and balsam fir; then the Douglas spruce and this new Rocky Mountain spruce, which is common eastward from here, though this range is, as far as I have observed, its western limit. It is one of the largest and most important of Nevada conifers, attaining a height of from sixty to eighty feet and a diameter of nearly two feet, while now and then an exceptional specimen may be found in shady dells a hundred feet high or more.

The foliage is bright yellowish and bluish green, according to exposure and age, growing all around the branchlets, though inclined to turn upward from the under sides, like that of the plushy firs of California, making remarkably handsome fernlike plumes. While yet only mere saplings five or six inches thick at the ground, they measure fifty or sixty feet in height and are beautifully clothed with broad, level, fronded plumes down to the base, preserving a strict arrowy outline, though a few of the larger branches shoot out in free exuberance, relieving the spire from any unpicturesque stiffness of aspect, while the conical summit is crowded with thousands of rich brown cones to complete its beauty.

We made the ascent of the peak just after the first storm had whitened its summit and brightened the atmosphere. The foot-slopes are like those of the Troy range, only more evenly clad with grasses. After tracing a long, rugged ridge of exceedingly hard quartzite, said to be veined here and there with gold, we came to the North Dome, a noble summit rising about a thousand feet above the timber-line, its slopes heavily tree-clad all around but most perfectly on the north. Here the Rocky Mountain spruce forms the bulk of the forest. The cones were ripe; most of them had shed their winged seeds, and the shell-like scales were conspicuously spread, making rich masses of brown from the tops of the fertile trees down half-way to the ground, cone touching cone in lavish clusters. A single branch that might be carried in the hand would be found to bear a hundred or more.

Some portions of the wood were almost impenetrable, but in general we found no difficulty in mazing comfortably on over fallen logs and under the spreading boughs, while here and there we came to an opening sufficiently spacious for standpoints, where the trees around their margins might be seen from top to bottom. The winter sunshine streamed through the clustered spires, glinting and breaking into a fine dust of spangles on the spiky leaves and beads of amber gum, and bringing out the reds and greys and yellows of the lichened boles which had been freshened by the late storm; while the tip of every spire looking up through the shadows was dipped in deepest blue.

The ground was strewn with burs and needles and fallen trees; and, down in the dells, on the north side of the dome, where strips of aspen are imbedded in the spruces, every breeze sent the ripe leaves flying, some lodging in the spruce boughs, making them bloom again, while the fresh snow beneath looked like a fine painting.

Around the dome and well up toward the summit of the main peak, the snow-shed was well marked with tracks of the mule deer and the pretty stitching and embroidery of field mice, squirrels and grouse; and on the way back to camp I came across a strange track, somewhat like that of a small bear, but more spreading at the toes. It proved to be that of a wolverine. In my conversations with hunters, both Indians and white men assure me that there are no bears in Nevada, notwithstanding the abundance of pine-nuts, of which they are so fond, and the accessibility of these basin ranges from their favourite haunts in the Sierra Nevada and Wahsatch Mountains. The mule deer, antelope, wild sheep, wolverine and two species of wolves are all of the larger animals that I have seen or heard of in the State.

CHAPTER FIFTEEN

Glacial Phenomena in Nevada[1]

THE MONUMENTS of the Ice Age in the Great Basin have been greatly obscured and broken, many of the more ancient of them having perished altogether, leaving scarce a mark, however faint, of their existence – a condition of things due not alone to the long-continued action of post-glacial agents, but also in great part to the perishable character of the rocks of which they were made. The bottoms of the main valleys, once grooved and planished like the glacier pavements of the Sierra, lie buried beneath sediments and detritus derived from the adjacent mountains, and now form the arid sage plains; characteristic U-shaped canyons have become V-shaped by the deepening of their bottoms and straightening of their sides, and decaying glacier headlands have been undermined and thrown down in loose taluses, while most of the moraines and striæ and scratches have been blurred or weathered away. Nevertheless, enough remains of the more recent and the more enduring phenomena to cast a good light well back upon the conditions of the ancient ice-sheet that covered this interesting region, and upon the system of distinct glaciers that loaded the tops of the mountains and filled the canyons long after the ice-sheet had been broken up.

The first glacial traces that I noticed in the basin are on the Wassuck, Augusta and Toyabe ranges, consisting of ridges and canyons, whose trends, contours and general sculpture are in great part specifically glacial, though deeply blurred by subsequent denudation. These discoveries were made during the summer of 1876–77. And again, on the 17th of last August, while making the ascent of Mount Jefferson, the dominating mountain of the Toquima range, I discovered an exceedingly interesting group of moraines, canyons with V-shaped cross sections, wide *névé* amphitheatres, moutonnéed rocks, glacier meadows and one glacier lake, all as fresh and telling as if the glaciers to which they belonged had scarcely vanished.

The best preserved and most regular of the moraines are two laterals about two hundred feet in height and two miles long, extending from the foot of a magnificent canyon valley on the north side of the mountain and trending first in a northerly direction, then curving around to the west, while a well-characterized terminal moraine, formed by the glacier towards the close of its existence, unites them near their lower extremities at a height of eighty-five hundred feet. Another pair of older lateral moraines, belonging to a glacier of which the one just mentioned was a tributary, extend in a general

[1] Written at Eureka, Nevada, in November, 1878. [Editor.]

north-westerly direction nearly to the level of Big Smoky Valley, about fifty-five hundred feet above sea-level.

Four other canyons, extending down the eastern slopes of this grand old mountain into Monito Valley, are hardly less rich in glacial records, while the effects of the mountain-shadows in controlling and directing the movements of the residual glaciers to which all these phenomena belonged are everywhere delightfully apparent in the trends of the canyons and ridges, and in the massive sculpture of the *névě*-wombs at their heads. This is a very marked and imposing mountain, attracting the eye from a great distance. It presents a smooth and gently curved outline against the sky, as observed from the plains, and is whitened with patches of enduring snow. The summit is made up of irregular volcanic tables, the most extensive of which is about two and a half miles long, and like the smaller ones is broken abruptly down on the edges by the action of the ice. Its height is approximately eleven thousand three hundred feet above the sea.

A few days after making these interesting discoveries, I found other well-preserved glacial traces on Arc Dome, the culminating summit of the Toyabe Range. On its northeastern slopes there are two small glacier lakes, and the basins of two others which have recently been filled with down-washed detritus. One small residual glacier lingered until quite recently beneath the coolest shadows of the dome, the moraines and *névé*-fountains of which are still as fresh and unwasted as many of those lying at the same elevation on the Sierra – ten thousand feet – while older and more wasted specimens may be traced on all the adjacent mountains. The sculpture, too, of all the ridges and summits of this section of the range is recognized at once as glacial, some of the larger characters being still easily readable from the plains at a distance of fifteen or twenty miles.

The Hot Creek Mountains, lying to the east of the Toquima and Monito ranges, reach the culminating point on a deeply serrate ridge at a height of ten thousand feet above the sea. This ridge is found to be made up of a series of imposing towers and pinnacles which have been eroded from the solid mass of the mountain by a group of small residual glaciers that lingered in their shadows long after the larger ice rivers had vanished. On its western declivities are found a group of well-characterized moraines, canyons and *roches moutonnées*, all of which are unmistakably fresh and telling. The moraines in particular could hardly fail to attract the eye of any observer. Some of the short laterals of the glaciers that drew their fountain snows from the jagged recesses of the summit are from one to two hundred feet in height, and scarce at all wasted as yet, notwithstanding the countless storms that have fallen upon them, while cool rills flow between them, watering charming gardens of arctic plants – saxifrages, larkspurs, dwarf birch, ribes and parnassia, etc. – beautiful memories of the Ice Age, representing a once greatly extended flora.

In the course of explorations made to the eastward of here, between the 38th and 40th parallels, I observed glacial phenomena equally fresh and demonstrative on all the higher mountains of the White Pine, Golden Gate and Snake Ranges, varying from those already described only as determined by differences of elevation, relations to the snow-bearing winds, and the physical characteristics of the rock-formations.

On the Jeff Davis group of the Snake Range, the dominating summit of which is nearly thirteen thousand feet in elevation, and the highest ground in the basin, every marked feature is a glacier monument – peaks, valleys, ridges, meadows and lakes. And because here the snow-fountains lay at a greater height, while the rock, an exceedingly hard quartzite, offered superior resistance to post-glacial agents, the ice-characters are on a larger scale, and are more sharply defined than any we have noticed elsewhere, and it is probably here that the last lingering glacier of the basin was located. The summits and connecting ridges are mere blades and points, ground sharp by the glaciers that descended on both sides to the main valleys. From one standpoint I counted nine of these glacial channels with their moraines sweeping grandly out to the plains to deep sheer-walled névé-fountains at their heads, making a most vivid picture of the last days of the Ice Period.

I have thus far directed attention only to the most recent and appreciable of the phenomena; but it must be borne in mind that less recent and less obvious traces of glacial action abound on *all* the ranges throughout the entire basin, where the fine striæ and grooves have been obliterated, and most of the moraines have been washed away, or so modified as to be no longer recognizable, and even the lakes and meadows, so characteristic of glacial regions, have almost entirely vanished. For there are other monuments, far more enduring than these, remaining tens of thousands of years after the more perishable records are lost. Such are the canyons, ridges and peaks themselves, the glacial peculiarities of whose trends and contours cannot be hid from the eye of the skilled observer until changes have been wrought upon them far more destructive than those to which these basin ranges have yet been subjected.

It appears, therefore, that the last of the basin glaciers have but recently vanished, and that the almost innumerable ranges trending north and south between the Sierra and the Wahsatch Mountains were loaded with glaciers that descended to the adjacent valleys during the last glacial period, and that it is to this mighty host of ice-streams that all the more characteristic of the present features of these mountain-ranges are due.

But grand as is this vision delineated in these old records, this is not all; for there is not wanting evidence of a still grander glaciation extending over all the valleys now forming the sage plains as well as the mountains. The basins of the main valleys alternating with the mountain-ranges, and which contained lakes during at least the closing portion of the Ice Period, were eroded wholly, or in part, from a general elevated tableland, by immense glaciers that flowed north and south to the ocean. The mountains as well as the valleys present abundant evidence of this grand origin.

The flanks of all the interior ranges are seen to have been heavily abraded and ground away by the ice acting in a direction parallel with their axes. This action is most strikingly shown upon projecting portions where the pressure has been greatest. These are shorn off in smooth planes and bossy outswelling curves, like the outstanding portions of canyon-walls. Moreover, the extremities of the ranges taper out like those of dividing ridges which have been ground away by dividing and confluent glaciers. Furthermore, the horizontal sections of separate mountains, standing isolated in the great valleys, are lens-shaped like those of mere rocks that rise in the channels of ordinary canyon glaciers, and which have been overflowed or past-flowed, while in many of the smaller valleys *roches moutonnées* occur in great abundance.

Again, the mineralogical and physical characters of the two ranges bounding the sides of many of the valleys indicate that the valleys were formed simply by the removal of the material between the ranges. And again, the rim of the general basin, where it is elevated, as for example on the southwestern portion, instead of being a ridge sculptured on the sides like a mountain-range, is found to be composed of many short ranges, parallel to one another, and to the interior ranges, and so modelled as to resemble a row of convex lenses set on edge and half buried beneath a general surface, without manifesting any dependence upon synclinal or anticlinal axes – a series of forms and relations that could have resulted only from the outflow of vast basin glaciers on their courses to the ocean.

I cannot, however, present all the evidence here bearing upon these interesting questions, much less discuss it in all its relations. I will, therefore, close this letter with a few of the more important generalizations that have grown up out of the facts that I have observed. First, at the beginning of the glacial period the region now known as the Great Basin was an elevated tableland, not furrowed as at present with mountains and valleys, but comparatively bald and featureless.

Second, this tableland, bounded on the east and west by lofty mountain-ranges, but comparatively open on the north and south, was loaded with ice, which was discharged to the ocean northward and southward, and in its flow brought most, if not all, the present interior ranges and valleys into relief by erosion.

Third, as the glacial winter drew near its close the ice vanished from the lower portions of the basin, which then became lakes, into which separate glaciers descended from the mountains. Then these mountain glaciers vanished in turn, after sculpturing the ranges into their present condition.

Fourth, the few immense lakes extending over the lowlands, in the midst of which many of the interior ranges stood as islands, became shallow as the ice vanished from the mountains, and separated into many distinct lakes, whose waters no longer reached the ocean. Most of these have disappeared by the filling of their basins with detritus from the mountains, and now form sage plains and 'alkali flats'.

The transition from one to the other of these various conditions was gradual and orderly: first, a nearly simple tableland; then a grand *mer de glace* shedding its crawling silver currents to the sea, and becoming gradually more wrinkled as unequal erosion roughened its bed, and brought the highest peaks and ridges above the surface; then a land of lakes, an almost continuous sheet of water stretching from the Sierra to the Wahsatch, adorned with innumerable island mountains; then a slow desiccation and decay to present conditions of sage and sand.

CHAPTER SIXTEEN

Nevada's Dead Towns[1]

NEVADA IS one of the very youngest and wildest of the States; nevertheless it is already strewn with ruins that seem as grey and silent and time-worn as if the civilization to which they belonged had perished centuries ago. Yet, strange to say, all these ruins are results of mining efforts made within the last few years. Wander where you may throughout the length and breadth of this mountain-barred wilderness, you everywhere come upon these dead mining towns, with their tall chimney-stacks, standing forlorn amid broken walls and furnaces, and machinery half buried in sand, the very names of many of them already forgotten amid the excitements of later discoveries, and now known only through tradition – tradition ten years old.

While exploring the mountain-ranges of the State during a considerable portion of three summers, I think that I have seen at least five of these deserted towns and villages for every one in ordinary life. Some of them were probably only camps built by bands of prospectors, and inhabited for a few months or years, while some specially interesting canyon was being explored, and then carelessly abandoned for more promising fields. But many were real towns, regularly laid out and incorporated, containing well-built hotels, churches, school-houses, post-offices and jails, as well as the mills on which they all depended; and whose well-graded streets were filled with lawyers, doctors, brokers, hangmen, real-estate agents, etc., the whole population numbering several thousand.

A few years ago the population of Hamilton is said to have been nearly eight thousand; that of Treasure Hill, six thousand; of Shermantown, seven thousand; of Swansea, three thousand. All of these were incorporated towns with mayors, councils, fire departments and daily newspapers. Hamilton has now about one hundred inhabitants, most of whom are merely waiting in dreary inaction for something to turn up. Treasure Hill has about half as many, Shermantown one family and Swansea none, while on the other hand the graveyards are far too full.

In one canyon of the Toyabe range, near Austin, I found no less than five dead towns without a single inhabitant. The streets and blocks of 'real estate' graded on the hillsides are rapidly falling back into the wilderness. Sage-brushes are growing up around the forges of the blacksmith shops, and lizards bask on the crumbling walls.

While travelling southward from Austin down Big Smoky Valley, I noticed a remarkably tall and imposing column, rising like a lone pine out of the

[1] Date and place of writing not given. Published in the *San Francisco Evening Bulletin*, 15 January 1879. [Editor.]

sage-brush on the edge of a dry gulch. This proved to be a smokestack of solid masonry. It seemed strangely out of place in the desert, as if it had been transported entire from the heart of some noisy manufacturing town and left here by mistake. I learned afterwards that it belonged to a set of furnaces that were built by a New York company to smelt ore that never was found. The tools of the workmen are still lying in place beside the furnaces, as if dropped in some sudden Indian or earthquake panic and never afterwards handled. These imposing ruins, together with the desolate town, lying a quarter of a mile to the northward, present a most vivid picture of wasted effort. Coyotes now wander unmolested through the brushy streets, and of all the busy throng that so lavishly spent their time and money here only one man remains – a lone bachelor with one suspender.

Mining discoveries and progress, retrogression and decay, seem to have been crowded more closely against each other here than on any other portion of the globe. Some one of the band of adventurous prospectors who came from the exhausted placers of California would discover some rich ore – how much or little mattered not at first. These specimens fell among excited seekers after wealth like sparks in gunpowder, and in a few days the wilderness was disturbed with the noisy clang of miners and builders. A little town would then spring up, and before anything like a careful survey of any particular lode would be made, a company would be formed, and expensive mills built. Then, after all the machinery was ready for the ore, perhaps little, or none at all, was to be found. Meanwhile another discovery was reported, and the young town was abandoned as completely as a camp made for a single night; and so on, until some really valuable lode was found, such as those of Eureka, Austin, Virginia, etc., which formed the substantial groundwork for a thousand other excitements.

Passing through the dead town of Schellbourne last month, I asked one of the few lingering inhabitants why the town was built. 'For the mines', he replied. 'And where are the mines?' 'On the mountains back here.' 'And why were they abandoned?' I asked. 'Are they exhausted?' 'Oh, no', he replied, 'they are not exhausted; on the contrary, they have never been worked at all, for unfortunately, just as we were about ready to open them, the Cherry Creek mines were discovered across the valley in the Egan range, and everybody rushed off there, taking what they could with them – houses, machinery and all. But we are hoping that somebody with money and speculation will come and revive us yet'.

The dead mining excitements of Nevada were far more intense and destructive in their action than those of California, because the prizes at stake were greater, while more skill was required to gain them. The long trains of gold-seekers making their way to California had ample time and means to recover from their first attacks of mining fever while crawling laboriously across the plains, and on their arrival on any portion of the Sierra gold belt, they at once began to make money. No matter in what gulch or canyon they worked, some measure of success was sure, however unskilful they might be. And though while making ten dollars a day they might be agitated by hopes of making twenty, or of striking their picks against hundred- or thousand-dollar nuggets, men of ordinary nerve could still work on with comparative steadiness, and remain rational.

But in the case of the Nevada miner, he too often spent himself in years of weary search without gaining a dollar, travelling hundreds of miles from mountain to mountain, burdened with wasting hopes of discovering some hidden vein worth millions, enduring hardships of the most destructive kind, driving innumerable tunnels into the hillsides, while his assayed specimens again and again proved worthless. Perhaps one in a hundred of these brave prospectors would 'strike it rich', while ninety-nine died alone in the mountains or sank out of sight in the corners of saloons, in a haze of whiskey and tobacco smoke.

The healthful ministry of wealth is blessed; and surely it is a fine thing that so many are eager to find the gold and silver that lie hid in the veins of the mountains. But in the search the seekers too often become insane, and strike about blindly in the dark like raving madmen. Seven hundred and fifty tons of ore from the original Eberhardt mine on Treasure Hill yielded a million and a half dollars, the whole of this immense sum having been obtained within two hundred and fifty feet of the surface, the greater portion within one hundred and forty feet. Other ore-masses were scarcely less marvellously rich, giving rise to one of the most violent excitements that ever occurred in the history of mining. All kinds of people – shoemakers, tailors, farmers, etc., as well as miners – left their own right work and fell in a perfect storm of energy upon the White Pine Hills, covering the ground like grasshoppers, and seeming determined by the very violence of their efforts to turn every stone to silver. But with few exceptions, these mining storms pass away about as suddenly as they rise, leaving only ruins to tell of the tremendous energy expended, as heaps of giant boulders in the valley tell of the spent power of the mountain floods.

In marked contrast with this destructive unrest is the orderly deliberation into which miners settle in developing a truly valuable mine. At Eureka we were kindly led through the treasure chambers of the Richmond and Eureka Consolidated, our guides leisurely leading the way from level to level, calling attention to the precious ore-masses which the workmen were slowly breaking to pieces with their picks, like navvies wearing away the day in a railroad cutting; while down at the smelting works the bars of bullion were handled with less eager haste than the farmer shows in gathering his sheaves.

The wealth Nevada has already given to the world is indeed wonderful, but the only grand marvel is the energy expended in its development. The amount of prospecting done in the face of so many dangers and sacrifices, the innumerable tunnels and shafts bored into the mountains, the mills that have been built – these would seem to require a race of giants. But, in full view of the substantial results achieved, the pure waste manifest in the ruins one meets never fails to produce a saddening effect.

The dim old ruins of Europe, so eagerly sought after by travellers, have something pleasing about them, whatever their historical associations; for they at least lend some beauty to the landscape. Their picturesque towers and arches seem to be kindly adopted by nature, and planted with wild flowers and wreathed with ivy; while their rugged angles are soothed and freshened and embossed with green mosses, fresh life and decay mingling in pleasing measures, and the whole vanishing softly like a ripe, tranquil day fading into night. So, also, among the older ruins of the East there is a fitness felt. They have served their time, and like the weather-beaten mountains are wasting harmoniously. The same is in some degree true of the dead mining towns of California.

But those lying to the eastward of the Sierra throughout the ranges of the Great Basin waste in the dry wilderness like the bones of cattle that have died of thirst. Many of them do not represent any good accomplishment, and have no right to be. They are monuments of fraud and ignorance – sins against science. The drifts and tunnels in the rocks may perhaps be regarded as the prayers of the prospector, offered for the wealth he so earnestly craves; but, like prayers of any kind not in harmony with nature, they are unanswered. But, after all, effort however misapplied, is better than stagnation. Better toil blindly, beating every stone in turn for grains of gold, whether they contain any or not, than lie down in apathetic decay.

The fever period is fortunately passing away. The prospector is no longer the raving, wandering ghoul of ten years ago, rushing in random lawlessness among the hills, hungry and footsore; but cool and skilful, well supplied with every necessary, and clad in his right mind. Capitalists, too, and the public in general, have become wiser, and do not take fire so readily from mining sparks; while at the same time a vast amount of real work is being done, and the ratio between growth and decay is constantly becoming better.

CHAPTER SEVENTEEN

Puget Sound

WASHINGTON TERRITORY, recently admitted[1] into the Union as a State, lies between latitude 46° and 49° and longitude 117° and 125°, forming the northwest shoulder of the United States. The majestic range of the Cascade Mountains naturally divides the State into two distinct parts, called Eastern and Western Washington, differing greatly from each other in almost every way, the western section being less than half as large as the eastern, and, with its copious rains and deep fertile soil, being clothed with forests of evergreens, while the eastern section is dry and mostly treeless, though fertile in many parts, and producing immense quantities of wheat and hay. Few States are more fertile and productive in one way or another than Washington, or more strikingly varied in natural features or resources.

[1] 11 November 1889; Muir's description probably was written toward the end of the same year. [Editor.]

Within her borders every kind of soil and climate may be found – the densest woods and dryest plains, the smoothest levels and roughest mountains. She is rich in square miles (some seventy thousand of them), in coal, timber and iron, and in sheltered inland waters that render these resources advantageously accessible. She also is already rich in busy workers, who work hard, though not always wisely, hacking, burning, blasting their way deeper into the wilderness, beneath the sky, and beneath the ground. The wedges of development are being driven hard, and none of the obstacles or defences of nature can long withstand the onset of this immeasurable industry.

Puget Sound, so justly famous the world over for the surpassing size and excellence and abundance of its timber, is a long, many-fingered arm of the sea reaching southward from the head of the Strait of Juan de Fuca into the heart of the grand forests of the western portion of Washington, between the Cascade Range and the mountains of the coast. It is less than a hundred miles in length, but so numerous are the branches into which it divides, and so many its bays, harbours and islands, that its entire shore-line is said to measure more than eighteen hundred miles. Throughout its whole vast extent ships move in safety, and find shelter from every wind that blows, the entire mountain-girt sea forming one grand unrivalled harbour and centre for commerce.

The forest trees press forward to the water around all the windings of the shores in most imposing array, as if they were courting their fate, coming down from the mountains far and near to offer themselves to the axe, thus making the place a perfect paradise for the lumberman. To the lover of nature the scene is enchanting. Water and sky, mountain and forest, clad in sunshine and clouds, are composed in landscapes sublime in magnitude, yet exquisitely fine and fresh, and full of glad, rejoicing life. The shining waters stretch away into the leafy wilderness, now like the reaches of some majestic river and again expanding into broad roomy spaces like mountain lakes, their farther edges fading gradually and blending with the pale blue of the sky. The wooded shores with an outer fringe of flowering bushes sweep onward in beautiful curves around bays, and capes, and jutting promontories innumerable; while the islands, with soft, waving outlines, lavishly adorned with spruces and cedars, thicken and enrich the beauty of the waters; and the white spirit mountains looking down from the sky keep watch and ward over all, faithful and changeless as the stars.

All the way from the Strait of Juan de Fuca up to Olympia, a hopeful town situated at the head of one of the farthest-reaching of the fingers of the Sound, we are so completely inland and surrounded by mountains that it is hard to realize that we are sailing on a branch of the salt sea. We are constantly reminded of Lake Tahoe. There is the same clearness of the water in calm weather without any trace of the ocean swell, the same picturesque winding and sculpture of the shore-line and flowery, leafy luxuriance; only here the trees are taller and stand much closer together, and the backgrounds are higher and far more extensive. Here, too, we find greater variety amid the marvellous wealth of islands and inlets, and also in the changing views dependent on the weather. As we double cape after cape and round the uncounted islands, new combinations come to view in endless variety, sufficient to fill and satisfy the lover of wild beauty through a whole life.

Oftentimes in the stillest weather, when all the winds sleep and no sign of storms is felt or seen, silky clouds form and settle over all the land, leaving in sight only a circle of water with indefinite bounds like views in mid-ocean; then, the clouds lifting, some islet will be presented standing alone, with the tops of its trees dipping out of sight in pearly grey fringes; or, lifting higher, and perhaps letting in a ray of sunshine through some rift overhead, the whole island will be set free and brought forward in vivid relief amid the gloom, a girdle of silver light of dazzling brightness on the water about its shores, then darkening again and vanishing back into the general gloom. Thus island after island may be seen, singly or in groups, coming and going from darkness to light like a scene of enchantment, until at length the entire cloud ceiling is rolled away, and the colossal cone of Mount Rainier is seen in spotless white looking down over the forests from a distance of sixty miles, but so lofty and so massive and clearly outlined as to impress itself upon us as being just back of a strip of woods only a mile or two in breadth.

For the tourist sailing to Puget Sound from San Francisco there is but little that is at all striking in the scenery within reach by the way until the mouth of the Strait of Juan de Fuca is reached. The voyage is about four days in length and the steamers keep within sight of the coast, but the hills fronting the sea up to Oregon are mostly bare and uninviting, the magnificent redwood forests stretching along this portion of the California coast seeming to keep well back, away from the heavy winds, so that very little is seen of them; while there are no deep inlets or lofty mountains visible to break the regular monotony. Along the coast of Oregon the woods of spruce and fir come down to the shore, kept fresh and vigorous by copious rains, and become denser and taller to the northward until, rounding Cape Flattery, we enter the Strait of Fuca, where, sheltered from the ocean gales, the forests begin to hint the grandeur they attain in Puget Sound. Here the scenery in general becomes exceedingly interesting; for now we have arrived at the grand mountain-walled channel that forms the entrance to that marvellous network of inland waters that extends along the margin of the continent to the northward for a thousand miles.

This magnificent inlet was named for Juan de Fuca, who discovered it in 1592 while seeking a mythical strait, supposed to exist somewhere in the north, connecting the Atlantic and Pacific. It is about seventy miles long, ten or twelve miles wide, and extends to the eastward in a nearly straight line between the south end of Vancouver Island and the Olympic Range of mountains on the mainland.

Cape Flattery, the western termination of the Olympic Range, is terribly rugged and jagged, and in stormy weather is utterly inaccessible from the sea. Then the ponderous rollers of the deep Pacific thunder amid its caverns and cliffs with the foam and uproar of a thousand Yosemite waterfalls. The bones of many a noble ship lie there, and many a sailor. It would seem unlikely that any living thing should seek rest in such a place, or find it. Nevertheless, frail and delicate flowers bloom there, flowers of both the land and the sea; heavy, ungainly seals disport in the swelling waves, and find grateful retreats back in the inmost bores of its storm-lashed caverns; while in many a chink and hollow of the highest crags, not visible from beneath, a great variety of water-fowl make homes and rear their young.

But not always are the inhabitants safe, even in such wave-defended castles as these, for the Indians of the neighbouring shores venture forth in the calmest summer weather in their frail canoes to spear the seals in the narrow gorges amid the grinding, gurgling din of the restless waters. At such times also the hunters make out to scale many of the apparently inaccessible cliffs for the eggs and young of the gulls and other water-birds, occasionally losing their lives in these perilous adventures, which give rise to many an exciting story told around the camp-fires at night when the storms roar loudest.

Passing through the strait, we have the Olympic Mountains close at hand on the right, Vancouver Island on the left, and the snowy peak of Mount Baker straight ahead in the distance. During calm weather, or when the clouds are lifting and rolling off the mountains after a storm, all these views are truly magnificent. Mount Baker is one of that wonderful series of old volcanoes that once flamed along the summits of the Sierras and Cascades from Lassen to Mount St Elias. Its fires are sleeping now, and it is loaded with glaciers, streams of ice having taken the place of streams of glowing lava. Vancouver Island presents a charming variety of hill and dale, open sunny spaces and sweeps of dark forest rising in swell beyond swell to the high land in the distance.

But the Olympic Mountains most of all command attention, seen tellingly near and clear in all their glory, rising from the water's edge into the sky to a height of six or eight thousand feet. They bound the strait on the south side throughout its whole extent, forming a massive sustained wall, flowery and bushy at the base, zigzag of snowy peaks along the top, which have ragged-edged fields of ice and snow beneath them, enclosed in wide amphitheatres opening to the waters of the strait through spacious forest-filled valleys enlivened with fine, dashing streams. These valleys mark the courses of the Olympic glaciers at the period of their greatest extension, when they poured their tribute into that portion of the great northern ice-sheet that over-swept the south end of Vancouver Island and filled the strait with flowing ice as it is now filled with ocean water.

The steamers of the Sound usually stop at Esquimalt on their way up, thus affording tourists an opportunity to visit the interesting town of Victoria, the capital of British Columbia. The Victoria harbour is too narrow and difficult of access for the larger class of ships; therefore a landing has to be made at Esquimalt. The distance, however, is only about three miles, and the way is delightful, winding on through a charming forest of Douglas spruce, with here and there groves of oak and madrone, and a rich undergrowth of hazel, dogwood, willow, alder, spiræa, rubus, huckleberry and wild rose. Pretty cottages occur at intervals along the road, covered with honeysuckle, and many an upswelling rock, freshly glaciated and furred with yellow mosses and lichen, telling interesting stories of the icy past.

Victoria is a quiet, handsome, breezy town, beautifully located on finely modulated ground at the mouth of the Canal de Haro, with charming views in front, of islands and mountains and far-reaching waters, ever changing in the shifting lights and shades of the clouds and sunshine. In the background there are a mile or two of field and forest and sunny oak openings; then comes the forest primeval, dense and shaggy and well-nigh impenetrable.

Notwithstanding the importance claimed for Victoria as a commercial centre and the capital of British Columbia, it has a rather young, loose-jointed appearance. The government buildings and some of the business blocks on the main streets are well built and imposing in bulk and architecture. These are far less interesting and characteristic, however, than the mansions set in the midst of spacious pleasure-grounds and the lovely home cottages embowered in honeysuckle and climbing roses. One soon discovers that this is no Yankee town. The English faces and the way that English is spoken alone would tell that; while in business quarters there is a staid dignity and moderation that is very noticeable, and a want of American push and hurrah. Love of land and of privacy in homes is made manifest in the residences, many of which are built in the middle of fields and orchards or large city blocks, and in the loving care with which these home-grounds are planted. They are very beautiful. The fineness of the climate, with its copious measure of warm moisture distilling in dew and fog, and gentle, bathing, laving rain, give them a freshness and floweriness that is worth going far to see.

Victoria is noted for its fine drives, and every one who can should either walk or drive around the outskirts of the town, not only for the fine views out over the water but to see the cascades of bloom pouring over the gables of the cottages, and the fresh wild woods with their flowery, fragrant underbrush. Wild roses abound almost everywhere. One species, blooming freely along the woodland paths, is from two or three inches in diameter, and more fragrant than any other wild rose I ever saw excepting the sweetbriar. This rose and three species of spiræa fairly fill the air with fragrance after a shower. And how brightly then do the red berries of the dogwood shine out from the warm yellow-green of leaves and mosses!

But still more interesting and significant are the glacial phenomena displayed hereabouts. All this exuberant tree, bush and herbaceous vegetation, cultivated or wild, is growing upon moraine beds outspread by waters that issued from the ancient glaciers at the time of their recession, and scarcely at all moved or in any way modified by post-glacial agencies. The town streets and the roads are graded in moraine material, among scratched and grooved rock-bosses that are as unweathered and telling as any to be found in the glacier-channels of Alaska. The harbour also is clearly of glacial origin. The rock islets that rise here and there, forming so marked a feature of the harbour, are unchanged *roches moutonnées*, and the shores are grooved, scratched and rounded, and in every way as glacial in all their characteristics as those of a newborn glacial lake.

Most visitors to Victoria go to the stores of the Hudson's Bay Company, presumably on account of the romantic associations, or to purchase a bit of fur or some other wild-Indianish trinket as a memento. At certain seasons of the year, when the hairy harvests are gathered in, immense bales of skins may be seen in these unsavoury warehouses, the spoils of many thousand hunts over mountain and plain, by lonely river and shore. The skins of bears, wolves, beavers, otters, fishers, martens, lynxes, panthers, wolverine, reindeer, moose, elk, wild goats, sheep, foxes, squirrels and many others of our 'poor earth-born companions and fellow-mortals' may here be found.

Vancouver is the southmost and the largest of the countless islands forming the greater archipelago that stretches a thousand miles to the northward. Its shores have been known a long time, but little is known of its lofty mountainous interior on account of the difficulties in the way of explorations – lake, bogs and shaggy tangled forests. It is mostly a pure, savage wilderness, without roads or clearings, and silent so far as man is concerned. Even the Indians keep close to the shore, getting a living by fishing, dwelling together in villages, and travelling almost wholly by canoes. White settlements are few and far between. Good agricultural lands occur here and there on the edge of the wilderness, but they are hard to clear, and have received but little attention thus far. Gold, the grand attraction that lights the way into all kinds of wildernesses and makes rough places smooth, has been found, but only in small quantities, too small to make much motion. Almost all the industry of the island is employed upon lumber and coal, in which, so far as is known, its chief wealth lies.

Leaving Victoria for Port Townsend, after we are fairly out on the free open water, Mount Baker is seen rising solitary over a dark breadth of forest, making a glorious show in its pure white raiment. It is said to be about eleven thousand feet high, is loaded with glaciers, some of which come well down into the woods, and never, so far as I have heard, has been climbed, though in all probability it is not inaccessible. The task of reaching its base through the dense woods will be likely to prove of greater difficulty than the climb to the summit.

In a direction a little to the left of Mount Baker and much nearer, may be seen the island of San Juan, famous in the young history of the country for the quarrels concerning its rightful ownership between the Hudson's Bay Company and Washington Territory, quarrels which nearly brought on war with Great Britain. Neither party showed any lack of either pluck or gunpowder. General Scott was sent out by President Buchanan to negotiate, which resulted in a joint occupancy of the island. Small quarrels, however, continued to arise until the year 1874, when the peppery question was submitted to the Emperor of Germany for arbitration. Then the whole island was given to the United States.

San Juan is one of a thickset cluster of islands that fills the waters between Vancouver and the mainland, a little to the north of Victoria. In some of the intricate channels between these islands the tides run at times like impetuous rushing rivers, rendering navigation rather uncertain and dangerous for the small sailing-vessels that ply between Victoria and the settlements on the coast of British Columbia and the larger islands. The water is generally deep enough everywhere, too deep in most places for anchorage, and, the winds shifting hither and thither or dying away altogether, the ships, getting no direction from their helms, are carried back and forth or are caught in some eddy where two currents meet and whirled round and round to the dismay of the sailors, like a chip in a river whirlpool.

All the way over to Port Townsend the Olympic Mountains well maintain their massive, imposing grandeur, and present their elaborately carved summits in clear relief, many of which are out of sight in coming up the strait on account of our being too near the base of the range. Turn to them as often as we may, our admiration only grows the warmer the longer we dwell upon them. The highest peaks are Mount Constance and Mount Olympus, said to be about eight thousand feet high.

In two or three hours after leaving Victoria, we arrive at the handsome little town of Port Townsend, situated at the mouth of Puget Sound, on the west side. The residential portion of the town is set on the level top of the bluff that bounds Port Townsend Bay, while another nearly level space of moderate extent, reaching from the base of the bluff to the shore-line, is occupied by the business portion, thus making a town of two separate and distinct stories, which are connected by long, ladder-like flights of stairs. In the streets of the lower storey, while there is no lack of animation, there is but little business noise as compared with the amount of business transacted. This in great part is due to the scarcity of horses and wagons. Farms and roads back in the woods are few and far between. Nearly all the tributary settlements are on the coast, and communication is almost wholly by boats, canoes and schooners. Hence country stages and farmers' wagons and buggies, with the whirr and din that belong to them, are wanting.

This being the port of entry, all vessels have to stop here, and they make a lively show about the wharves and in the bay. The winds stir the flags of every civilized nation, while the Indians in their long-beaked canoes glide about from ship to ship, satisfying their curiosity or trading with the crews. Keen traders these Indians are, and few indeed of the sailors or merchants from any country ever get the better of them in bargains. Curious groups of people may often be seen in the streets and stores, made up of English, French, Spanish, Portuguese, Scandinavians, Germans, Greeks, Moors, Japanese and Chinese, of every rank and station and style of dress and behaviour; settlers from many a nook and bay and island up and down the coast; hunters from the wilderness; tourists on their way home by the Sound and the Columbia River or to Alaska or California.

The upper storey of Port Townsend is charmingly located, wide bright waters on one side, flowing evergreen woods on the other. The streets are well laid out and well tended, and the houses, with their luxuriant gardens about them, have an air of taste and refinement seldom found in towns set on the edge of a wild forest. The people seem to have come here to make true homes, attracted by the beauty and fresh breezy healthfulness of the place as well as by business advantages, trusting to natural growth and advancement instead of restless 'booming' methods. They perhaps have caught some of the spirit of calm moderation and enjoyment from their English neighbours across the water. Of late, however, this sober tranquillity has begun to give way, some whiffs from the whirlwind of real-estate speculation up the Sound having at length touched the town and ruffled the surface of its calmness.

A few miles up the bay is Fort Townsend, which makes a pretty picture with the green woods rising back of it and the calm water in front. Across the mouth of the Sound lies the long, narrow Whidbey Island, named by Vancouver for one of his lieutenants. It is about thirty miles in length, and is remarkable in this region of crowded forests and mountains as being comparatively open and low. The soil is good and easily worked, and a considerable portion of the island has been under cultivation for many years. Fertile fields, open, parklike groves of oak, and thick masses of evergreens succeed one another in charming combinations to make this 'the garden spot of the Territory.'

Leaving Port Townsend for Seattle and Tacoma, we enter the Sound and sail down into the heart of the green, aspiring forests, and find, look where we may, beauty ever changing, in lavish profusion. Puget Sound, 'the Mediterranean of America' as it is sometimes called, is in many respects one of the most remarkable bodies of water in the world. Vancouver, who came here nearly a hundred years ago and made a careful survey of it, named the larger northern portion of it 'Admiralty Inlet' and one of the long, narrow branches 'Hood's Canal,' applying the name 'Puget Sound' only to the comparatively small southern portion. The latter name, however, is now applied generally to the entire inlet, and is commonly shortened by the people hereabouts to 'The Sound'. The natural wealth and commercial advantages of the Sound region were quickly recognized, and the cause of the activity prevailing here is not far to seek. Vancouver, long before civilization touched these shores, spoke of it in terms of unstinted praise. He was sent out by the British government with the principal object in view of 'acquiring accurate knowledge as to the nature and extent of any water communication which may tend in any considerable degree to facilitate an intercourse for the purposes of commerce between the northwest coast and the country on the opposite side of the continent,' vague traditions having long been current concerning a strait supposed to unite the two oceans. Vancouver reported that he found the coast from San Francisco to Oregon and beyond to present a nearly straight solid barrier to the sea, without openings, and we may well guess the joy of the old navigator on the discovery of these waters after so long and barren a search to the southward.

His descriptions of the scenery – Mounts Baker, Rainier, St Helen's, etc. – were as enthusiastic as those of the most eager landscape-lover of the present day, when scenery is in fashion. He says in one place: 'To describe the beauties of this region will, on some future occasion, be a very grateful task for the pen of a skilful panegyrist. The serenity of the climate, the immeasurable pleasing landscapes, and the abundant fertility that unassisted nature puts forth, require only to be enriched by the industry of man with villages, mansions, cottages and other buildings, to render it the most lovely country that can be imagined. The labour of the inhabitants would be amply rewarded in the bounties which nature seems ready to bestow on cultivation.' 'A picture so pleasing could not fail to call to our remembrance certain delightful and beloved situations in old England.' So warm, indeed, were the praises he sung that his statements were received in England with a good deal of hesitation. But they were amply corroborated by Wilkes and others who followed many years later. 'Nothing,' says Wilkes, 'can exceed the beauty of these waters and their safety. Not a shoal exists in the Straits of Juan de Fuca, Admiralty Inlet, Puget Sound or Hood's Canal, that can in any way interrupt their navigation by a 74-gun ship. I venture nothing in saying there is no country in the world that possesses waters like these.' And again, quoting from the United States Coast Survey, 'For depth of water, boldness of approaches, freedom from hidden dangers, and the immeasurable sea of gigantic timber coming down to the very shores, these waters are unsurpassed, unapproachable.'

The Sound region has a fine, fresh, clean climate, well washed both winter and summer with copious rains and swept with winds and clouds that come from the mountains and the sea. Every hidden nook in the depths of the woods is searched and refreshed, leaving no stagnant air; beaver meadows and lake-basins and low and willowy bogs, all are kept wholesome and sweet the year round. Cloud and sunshine alternate in bracing, cheering succession, and health and abundance follow the storms. The outer sea-margin is sublimely dashed and drenched with ocean brine, the spicy scud sweeping at times far inland over the bending woods, the giant trees waving and chanting in hearty accord as if surely enjoying it all.

Heavy, long-continued rains occur in the winter months. Then every leaf, bathed and brightened, rejoices. Filtering drops and currents through all the shaggy undergrowth of the woods go with tribute to the small streams, and these again to the larger. The rivers swell, but there are no devastating floods; for the thick felt of roots and mosses holds the abounding waters in check, stored in a thousand thousand fountains. Neither are there any violent hurricanes here. At least, I never have heard of any, nor have I come upon their tracks. Most of the streams are clear and cool always, for their waters are filtered through deep beds of mosses, and flow beneath shadows all the way to the sea. Only the streams from the glaciers are turbid and muddy. On the slopes of the mountains where they rush from their crystal caves, they carry not only small particles of rock-mud, worn off the sides and bottoms of the channels of the glaciers, but grains of sand and pebbles and large boulders tons in weight, rolling them forward on their way rumbling and bumping to their appointed places at the foot of steep slopes, to be built into rough bars and beds, while the smaller material is carried farther and outspread in flats, perhaps for coming wheat-fields and gardens, the finest of it going out to sea, floating on the tides for weeks and months ere it finds rest on the bottom.

Snow seldom falls to any great depth on the lowlands, though it comes in glorious abundance on the mountains. And only on the mountains does the temperature fall much below the freezing-point. In the warmest summer weather a temperature of eighty-five degrees or even more occasionally is reached, but not for long at a time, as such heat is speedily followed by a breeze from the sea. The most charming days here are days of perfect calm, when all the winds are holding their breath and not a leaf stirs. Then the surface of the Sound shines like a silver mirror over all its vast extent, reflecting its lovely islands and shores; and long sheets of spangles flash and dance in the wake of every swimming seabird and boat. The sun, looking down on the tranquil landscape, seems conscious of the presence of every living thing on which he is pouring his blessings, while they in turn, with perhaps the exception of man, seem conscious of the presence of the sun as a benevolent father and stand hushed and waiting.

CHAPTER EIGHTEEN

The Forests of Washington

WHEN WE force our way into the depths of the forests, following any of the rivers back to their fountains, we find that the bulk of the woods is made up of the Douglas spruce (*Pseudotsuga Douglasii*), named in honour of David Douglas, an enthusiastic botanical explorer of early Hudson's Bay times. It is not only a very large tree but a very beautiful one, with lively bright-green drooping foliage, handsome pendent cones, and a shaft exquisitely straight and regular. For so large a tree it is astonishing how many find nourishment and space to grow on any given area. The magnificent shafts push their spires into the sky close together with as regular a growth as that of a well-tilled field of grain. And no ground has been better tilled for the growth of trees than that on which these forests are growing. For it has been thoroughly ploughed and rolled by the mighty glaciers from the mountains, and sifted and mellowed and outspread in beds hundreds of feet in depth by the broad streams that issued from their fronts at the time of their recession, after they had long covered all the land.

The largest tree of this species that I have myself measured was nearly twelve feet in diameter at a height of five feet from the ground, and, as near as I could make out under the circumstances, about three hundred feet in length. It stood near the head of the Sound not far from Olympia. I have seen a few others, both near the coast and thirty or forty miles back in the interior, that were from eight to ten feet in diameter, measured above their bulging insteps; and many from six to seven feet. I have heard of some that were said to be three hundred and twenty-five feet in height and fifteen feet in diameter, but none that I measured were so large, though it is not at all unlikely that such colossal giants do exist where conditions of soil and exposure are surpassingly favourable. The average size of all the trees of this species found up to an elevation on the mountain-slopes of, say, two thousand feet above sea-level, taking into account only what may be called mature trees two hundred and fifty to five hundred years of age, is perhaps, at a vague guess, not more than a height of one hundred and seventy-five or two hundred feet and a diameter of three feet; though, of course, throughout the richest sections the size is much greater.

In proportion to its weight when dry, the timber from this tree is perhaps stronger than that of any other conifer in the country. It is tough and durable and admirably adapted in every way for shipbuilding, piles and heavy timbers in general. But its hardness and liability to warp render it much inferior to white or sugar pine for fine work. In the lumber-markets of California it is known as 'Oregon pine' and is used almost exclusively for spars, bridge-timbers, heavy planking and the framework of houses.

The same species extends northward in abundance through British Columbia and southward through the coast and middle regions of Oregon and California. It is also a common tree in the canyons and hollows of the Wahsatch Mountains in Utah, where it is called 'red pine' and on portions of the Rocky Mountains and some of the short ranges of the Great Basin. Along the coast of California it keeps company with the redwood wherever it can find a favourable opening. On the western slope of the Sierra, with the yellow pine and incense cedar, it forms a pretty well-defined belt at a height of from three thousand to six thousand feet above the sea, and extends into the San Gabriel and San Bernardino Mountains in southern California. But, though widely distributed, it is only in these cool, moist northlands that it reaches its finest development, tall, straight, elastic and free from limbs to an immense height, growing down to tide-water, where ships of the largest size may lie close alongside and load at the least possible cost.

Growing with the Douglas we find the white spruce, or 'Sitka pine,' as it is sometimes called. This also is a very beautiful and majestic tree, frequently attaining a height of two hundred feet or more and a diameter of five or six feet. It is very abundant in southeastern Alaska, forming the greater part of the best forests there. Here it is found mostly around the sides of beaver-dam and other meadows and on the borders of the streams, especially where the ground is low. One tree that I saw felled at the head of the Hop-Ranch meadows on the upper Snoqualmie River, though far from being the largest I have seen, measured a hundred and eighty feet in length and four and a half in diameter, and was two hundred and fifty-seven years of age.

In habit and general appearance it resembles the Douglas spruce, but it is somewhat less slender and the needles grow close together all around the branchlets and are so stiff and sharp-pointed on the younger branches that they cannot well be handled without gloves. The timber is tough, close-grained, white and looks more like pine than any other of the spruces. It splits freely, makes excellent shingles and in general use in house-building takes the place of pine. I have seen logs of this species a hundred feet long and two feet in diameter at the upper end. It was named in honour of the old Scotch botanist Archibald Menzies, who came to this coast with Vancouver in 1792.[1]

The beautiful hemlock spruce with its warm yellow-green foliage is also common in some portions of these woods. It is tall and slender and exceedingly graceful in habit before old age comes on, but the timber is inferior and is seldom used for any other than the roughest work, such as wharf-building.

[1] [This tree, now known to botanists as *Picea sitchensis*, was named *Abies Menziessi* by Lindley in 1833.]

The Western arbor-vitae[1] (*Thuja gigantea*) grows to a size truly gigantic on low rich ground. Specimens ten feet in diameter and a hundred and forty feet high are not at all rare. Some that I have heard of are said to be fifteen and even eighteen feet thick. Clad in rich, glossy plumes, with grey lichens covering their smooth, tapering boles, perfect trees of this species are truly noble objects and well worthy the place they hold in these glorious forests. It is of this tree that the Indians make their fine canoes.

Of the other conifers that are so happy as to have place here, there are three firs, three or four pines, two cypresses, a yew and another spruce, the *Abies Pattoniana*.[2] This last is perhaps the most beautiful of all the spruces, but, being comparatively small and growing only far back on the mountains, it receives but little attention from most people. Nor is there room in a work like this for anything like a complete description of it, or of the others I have just mentioned. Of the three firs, one (*Picea grandis*),[3] grows near the coast and is one of the largest trees in the forest, sometimes attaining a height of two hundred and fifty feet. The timber, however, is inferior in quality and not much sought after while so much that is better is within reach. One of the others (*P. amabilis*, var. *nobilis*) forms magnificent forests by itself at a height of about three thousand to four thousand feet above the sea. The rich plushy, plumelike branches grow in regular whorls around the trunk, and on the topmost whorls, standing erect, are the large, beautiful cones. This is far the most beautiful of all the firs. In the Sierra Nevada it forms a considerable portion of the main forest belt on the western slope, and it is there that it reaches its greatest size and greatest beauty. The third species (*P. subalpina*) forms, together with *Abies Pattoniana*, the upper edge of the timber-line on the portion of the Cascades opposite the Sound. A thousand feet below the extreme limit of tree-growth it occurs in beautiful groups amid parklike openings where flowers grow in extravagant profusion.

The pines are nowhere abundant in the State. The largest, the yellow pine (*Pinus ponderosa*), occurs here and there on margins of dry gravelly prairies, and only in such situations have I yet seen it in this State. The others (*P. monticola* and *P. contorta*) are mostly restricted to the upper slopes of the mountains, and though the former of these two attains a good size and makes excellent lumber, it is mostly beyond reach at present and is not abundant. One of the cypresses (*Cupressus Lawsoniana*)[4] grows near the coast and is a fine large tree, clothed like the arbor-vitæ in a glorious wealth of flat, feathery branches. The other is found here and there well up toward the edge of the timber-line. This is the fine Alaska cedar (*C. Nootkatensis*), the lumber from which is noted for its durability, fineness of grain and beautiful yellow colour, and for its fragrance, which resembles that of sandal-wood. The Alaska Indians make their canoe-paddles of it and weave matting and coarse cloth from the fibrous brown bark.

---

[1] Also known as 'canoe cedar,' and described in Jepson's *Silva of California* under the more recent specific name *Thuja plicata*. [Editor.]
[2] Now classified as *Tsuga mestensiana* Sarg. [Editor.]
[3] Now *Abies grandis* Lindley. [Editor.]
[4] *Chemæcyparis lawsoniana* Parl. (Port Orford cedar) in Jepson's *Silva*. [Editor.]

Among the different kinds of hardwood trees are the oak, maple, madrofia, birch, alder and wild apple, while large cottonwoods are common along the rivers and shores of the numerous lakes.

The most striking of these to the traveller is the Menzies arbutus, or madrofia, as it is popularly called in California. Its curious red and yellow bark, large thick glossy leaves and panicles of waxy-looking greenish-white urn-shaped flowers render it very conspicuous. On the boles of the younger trees and on all the branches, the bark is so smooth and seamless that it does not appear as bark at all, but rather the naked wood. The whole tree, with the exception of the larger part of the trunk, looks as though it had been thoroughly peeled. It is found sparsely scattered along the shores of the Sound and back in the forests also on open margins, where the soil is not too wet, and extends up the coast on Vancouver Island beyond Nanaimo. But in no part of the State does it reach anything like the size and beauty of proportions that it attains in California, few trees here being more than ten or twelve inches in diameter and thirty feet high. It is, however, a very remarkable-looking object, standing there like some lost or runaway native of the tropics, naked and painted, beside that dark mossy ocean of northland conifers. Not even a palm tree would seem more out of place here.

The oaks, so far as my observation has reached, seem to be most abundant and to grow largest on the islands of the San Juan and Whidbey Archipelago. One of the three species of maples that I have seen is only a bush that makes tangles on the banks of the rivers. Of the other two one is a small tree, crooked and moss-grown, holding out its leaves to catch the light that filters down through the close-set spires of the great spruces. It grows almost everywhere throughout the entire extent of the forest until the higher slopes of the mountains are reached, and produces a very picturesque and delightful effect; relieving the bareness of the great shafts of the evergreens, without being close enough in its growth to hide them wholly, or to cover the bright mossy carpet that is spread beneath all the dense parts of the woods.

The other species is also very picturesque and at the same time very large, the largest tree of its kind that I have ever seen anywhere. Not even in the great maple woods of Canada have I seen trees either as large or with so much striking, picturesque character. It is widely distributed throughout western Washington, but is never found scattered among the conifers in the dense woods. It keeps together mostly in magnificent groves by itself on the damp levels along the banks of streams or lakes where the ground is subject to overflow. In such situations it attains a height of seventy-five to a hundred feet and a diameter of four to eight feet. The trunk sends out large limbs toward its neighbours, laden with long drooping mosses beneath and rows of ferns on their upper surfaces, thus making a grand series of richly ornamented interlacing arches, with the leaves laid thick overhead, rendering the underwood spaces delightfully cool and open. Never have I seen a finer forest ceiling or a more picturesque one, while the floor, covered with tall ferns and rubus and thrown into hillocks by the bulging roots, matches it well. The largest of these maple groves that I have yet found is on the right bank of the Snoqualmie River, about a mile above the falls. The whole country hereabouts is picturesque, and interesting in many ways, and well worthy a visit by tourists passing through the Sound region, since it is now accessible by rail from Seattle.

Looking now at the forests in a comprehensive way, we find in passing through them again and again from the shores of the Sound to their upper limits, that some portions are much older than others, the trees much larger, and the ground beneath them strewn with immense trunks in every stage of decay, representing several generations of growth, everything about them giving the impression that these are indeed the 'forests primeval', while in the younger portions, where the elevation of the ground is the same as to the sea-level and the species of trees are the same as well as the quality of the soil, apart from the moisture which it holds, the trees seem to be and are mostly of the same age, perhaps from one hundred to two or three hundred years, with no grey-bearded, venerable patriarchs – forming tall, majestic woods without any grandfathers.

When we examine the ground we find that it is as free from those mounds of brown crumbling wood and mossy ancient fragments as are the growing trees from very old ones. Then, perchance, we come upon a section farther up the slopes towards the mountains that has no trees more than fifty years old, or even fifteen or twenty years old. These last show plainly enough that they have been devastated by fire, as the black, melancholy monuments rising here and there above the young growth bear witness. Then, with this fiery, suggestive testimony, on examining those sections whose trees are a hundred years old or two hundred, we find the same fire-records, though heavily veiled with mosses and lichens, showing that a century or two ago the forests that stood there had been swept away in some tremendous fire at a time when rare conditions of drought made their burning possible. Then, the bare ground sprinkled with the winged seeds from the edges of the burned district, a new forest sprang up, nearly every tree starting at the same time or within a few years, thus producing the uniformity of size we find in such places; while, on the other hand, in those sections of ancient aspect containing very old trees both standing and fallen, we find no traces of fire, nor from the extreme dampness of the ground can we see any possibility of fire ever running there.

Fire, then, is the great governing agent in forest-distribution and to a great extent also in the conditions of forest-growth. Where fertile lands are very wet one half the year and very dry the other, there can be no forests at all. Where the ground is damp, with drought occurring only at intervals of centuries, fine forests may be found, other conditions being favourable. But it is only where fires never run that truly ancient forests of pitchy coniferous trees may exist. When the Washington forests are seen from the deck of a ship out in the middle of the Sound, or even from the top of some high, commanding mountain, the woods seem everywhere perfectly solid. And so in fact they are in general found to be. The largest openings are those of the lakes and prairies, the smaller of beaver-meadows, bogs and the rivers; none of them large enough to make a distinct mark in comprehensive views.

Of the lakes there are said to be some thirty in King's County alone; the largest, Lake Washington, being twenty-six miles long and four miles wide.

Another, which enjoys the duckish name of Lake Squak, is about ten miles long. Both are pure and beautiful, lying imbedded in the green wilderness. The rivers are numerous and are but little affected by the weather, flowing with deep, steady currents the year round. They are short, however, none of them drawing their sources from beyond the Cascade Range. Some are navigable for small steamers on their lower courses, but the openings they make in the woods are very narrow, the tall trees on their banks leaning over in some places, making fine shady tunnels.

The largest of the prairies that I have seen was south of Tacoma on the line of the Portland and Tacoma Railroad. The ground is dry and gravelly, a deposit of water-washed cobbles and pebbles derived from moraines – conditions which readily explain the absence of trees here and on other prairies adjacent to Yelm. Berries grow in lavish abundance, enough for man and beast with thousands of tons to spare. The woods are full of them, especially about the borders of the waters and meadows where the sunshine may enter. Nowhere in the north does Nature set a more bountiful table. There are huckleberries of many species, red, blue and black, some of them growing close to the ground, others on bushes eight to ten feet high; also salal berries, growing on a low, weak-stemmed bush, a species of gaultheria, seldom more than a foot or two high. This has pale pea-green glossy leaves two or three inches long and half an inch wide and beautiful pink flowers, urn-shaped, that make a fine, rich show. The berries are black when ripe, are extremely abundant, and, with the huckleberries, form an important part of the food of the Indians, who beat them into paste, dry them, and store them away for winter use, to be eaten with their oily fish. The salmon-berry also is very plentiful, growing in dense prickly tangles. The flowers are as large as wild roses and of the same colour, and the berries measure nearly an inch in diameter. Besides these there are gooseberries, currants, raspberries, blackberries, and, in some favoured spots, strawberries. The mass of the underbrush of the woods is made up in great part of these berry-bearing bushes, together with white-flowered spiræa twenty feet high, hazel, dogwood, wild rose, honeysuckle, symphoricarpus, etc. But in the depths of the woods, where little sunshine can reach the ground, there is but little underbrush of any kind, only a very light growth of huckleberry and rubus and young maples in most places. The difficulties encountered by the explorer in penetrating the wilderness are presented mostly by the streams and bogs, with their tangled margins, and the fallen timber and thick carpet of moss covering all the ground.

Notwithstanding the tremendous energy displayed in lumbering and the grand scale on which it is being carried on, and the number of settlers pushing into every opening in search of farmlands, the woods of Washington are still almost entirely virgin and wild, without trace of human touch, savage or civilized. Indians, no doubt, have ascended most of the rivers on their way to the mountains to hunt the wild sheep and goat to obtain wool for their clothing, but with food in abundance on the coast they had little to tempt them into the wilderness, and the monuments they have left in it are scarcely more conspicuous than those of squirrels and bears; far less so than those of the beavers, which in damming the streams have made clearings and meadows which will continue to mark the landscape for centuries. Nor is there much in these woods to tempt the farmer or cattle-raiser. A few settlers established homes on the prairies or open borders of the woods and in the valleys of the Chehalis and Cowlitz before the gold days of California. Most of the early immigrants from the Eastern States, however, settled in the fertile and open Willamette Valley of Oregon. Even now, when the search for land is so keen, with the exception of the bottom lands around the Sound and on the lower reaches of the rivers, there are comparatively few spots of cultivation in western Washington. On every meadow or opening of any kind someone will be found keeping cattle, planting hop-vines, or raising hay, vegetables and patches of grain. All the large spaces available, even back near the summits of the Cascade Mountains, were occupied long ago. The new-comers, building their cabins where the beavers once built theirs, keep a few cows and industriously seek to enlarge their small meadow patches by chopping, girdling and burning the edge of the encircling forest, gnawing like beavers, and scratching for a living among the blackened stumps and logs, regarding the trees as their greatest enemies – a sort of larger pernicious weed immensely difficult to get rid of.

But all these are as yet mere spots, making no visible scar in the distance and leaving the grand stretches of the forest as wild as they were before the discovery of the continent. For many years the axe has been busy around the shores of the Sound and chips have been falling in perpetual storm like flakes of snow. The best of the timber has been cut for a distance of eight or ten miles from the water and to a much greater distance along the streams deep enough to float the logs. Railroads too, have been built to fetch in the logs from the best bodies of timber otherwise inaccessible except at great cost. None of the ground, however, has been completely denuded. Most of the young trees have been left, together with the hemlocks and other trees undesirable in kind or in some way defective, so that the neighbouring trees appear to have closed over the gaps made by the removal of the larger and better ones, maintaining the general continuity of the forest and leaving no sign on the sylvan sea, at least as seen from a distance.

In felling the trees they cut them off usually at a height of six to twelve feet above the ground, so as to avoid cutting through the swollen base, where the diameter is so much greater. In order to reach this height the chopper cuts a notch about two inches wide and three or four deep and drives a board into it, on which he stands while at work. In case the first notch, cut as high as he can reach, is not high enough, he stands on the board that has been driven into the first notch and cuts another. Thus the axeman may often be seen at work standing eight or ten feet above the ground. If the tree is so large that with his long-handled axe the chopper is unable to reach to the farther side of it, then a second chopper is set to work, each cutting halfway across. And when the tree is about to fall, warned by the faint crackling of the strained fibres, they jump to the ground, and stand back out of danger from flying limbs, while the noble giant that had stood erect in glorious strength and beauty century after century, bows low at last and with gasp and groan and booming throb falls to earth.

Then with long saws the trees are cut into logs of the required length, peeled, loaded upon wagons capable of carrying a weight of eight or ten tons, hauled by a long string of oxen to the nearest available stream or railroad, and floated or carried to the Sound. There the logs are gathered into booms and towed by steamers to the mills, where workmen with steel spikes in their boots leap lightly with easy poise from one to another and by means of long pike-poles push them apart and, selecting such as are at the time required, push them to the foot of the chute and drive dogs into the ends, when they are speedily hauled in by the mill machinery alongside the saw-carriage and placed and fixed in position. Then with sounds of greedy hissing and growling they are rushed back and forth like enormous shuttles, and in an incredibly short time they are lumber and are aboard the ships lying at the mill wharves.

Many of the long, slender boles so abundant in these woods are saved for spars, and so excellent is their quality that they are in demand in almost every shipyard of the world. Thus these trees, felled and stripped of their leaves and branches, are raised again, transplanted and set firmly erect, given roots of iron and a new foliage of flapping canvas, and sent to sea. On they speed in glad, free motion, cheerily waving over the blue, heaving water, responsive to the same winds that rocked them when they stood at home in the woods. After standing in one place all their lives they now, like sight-seeing tourists, go round the world, meeting many a relative from the old home forest, some like themselves, wandering free, clad in broad canvas foliage, others planted head downward in mud, holding wharf platforms aloft to receive the wares of all nations.

The mills of Puget Sound and those of the redwood region of California are said to be the largest and most effective lumber-makers in the world. Tacoma alone claims to have eleven sawmills, and Seattle about as many; while at many other points on the Sound, where the conditions are particularly favourable, there are immense lumbering establishments, as at Ports Blakely, Madison, Discovery, Gamble, Ludlow, etc., with a capacity all together of over three million feet a day. Nevertheless, the observer coming up the Sound sees not nor hears anything of this fierce storm of steel that is devouring the forests, save perhaps the shriek of some whistle or the columns of smoke that mark the position of the mills. All else seems as serene and unscathed as the silent watching mountains.

CHAPTER NINETEEN

People and Towns of Puget Sound

AS ONE strolls in the woods about the logging-camps, most of the lumbermen are found to be interesting people to meet, kind and obliging and sincere, full of knowledge concerning the bark and sapwood and heartwood of the trees they cut, and how to fell them without unnecessary breakage, on ground where they may be most advantageously sawed into logs and loaded for removal. The work is hard, and all of the older men have a tired, somewhat haggard appearance. Their faces are doubtful in colour, neither sickly nor quite healthy-looking, and seamed with deep wrinkles like the bark of the spruces, but with no trace of anxiety. Their clothing is full of rosin and never wears out. A little of everything in the woods is stuck fast to these loggers, and their trousers grow constantly thicker with age. In all their movements and gestures they are heavy and deliberate like the trees above them, and they walk with a swaying, rocking gait altogether free from quick, jerky fussiness, for chopping and log-rolling have quenched all that. They are also slow of speech, as if partly out of breath, and when one tries to draw them out on some subject away from logs, all the fresh, leafy, outreaching branches of the mind seem to have been withered and killed with fatigue, leaving their lives little more than dry lumber. Many a tree have these old axe-men felled, but, round-shouldered and stooping, they too are beginning to lean over. Many of their companions are already beneath the moss, and among those that we see at work some are now dead at the top (bald), leafless, so to speak, and tottering to their fall.

A very different man, seen now and then at long intervals but usually invisible, is the free roamer of the wilderness – hunter, prospector, explorer, seeking he knows not what. Lithe and sinewy, he walks erect, making his way with the skill of wild animals, all his senses in action, watchful and alert, looking keenly at everything in sight, his imagination well nourished in the wealth of the wilderness, coming into contact with free nature in a thousand forms, drinking at the fountains of things, responsive to wild influences, as trees to the winds. Well he knows the wild animals his neighbours, what fishes are in the streams, what birds in the forests, and where food may be found. Hungry at times and weary, he has corresponding enjoyment in eating and resting, and all the wilderness is home. Some of these rare, happy rovers die alone among the leaves. Others half settle down and change in part into farmers; each, making choice of some fertile spot where the landscape attracts him, builds a small cabin, where, with few wants to supply from garden or field, he hunts and farms in turn, going perhaps once a year to the settlements, until night begins to draw near, and, like forest shadows, thickens into darkness and his day is done. In these Washington wilds, living alone, all sorts of men may perchance be found – poets, philosophers and even full-blown transcendentalists, though you may go far to find them.

Indians are seldom to be met with away from the Sound, excepting about the few out-lying hop-ranches, to which they resort in great numbers during the picking-season. Nor in your walks in the woods will you be likely to see many of the wild animals, however far you may go, with the exception of the Douglas squirrel and the mountain goat. The squirrel is everywhere, and the goat you can hardly fail to find if you climb any of the high mountains. The deer, once very abundant, may still be found on the islands and along the shores of the Sound, but the large grey wolves render their existence next to impossible at any considerable distance back in the woods of the mainland, as they can easily run them down unless they are near enough to the coast to make their escape by plunging into the water and swimming to the islands off shore. The elk and perhaps also the moose still exist in the most remote and inaccessible solitudes of the forest, but their numbers have been greatly reduced of late, and even the most experienced hunters have difficulty in finding them. Of bears there are two species, the black and the large brown, the former by far the more common of the two. On the shaggy bottom-lands where berries are plentiful, and along the rivers while salmon are going up to spawn, the black bear may be found, fat and at home. Many are killed every year, both for their flesh and skins. The large brown species like higher and opener ground. He is a dangerous animal, a near relative of the famous grizzly, and wise hunters are very fond of letting him alone.

The towns of Puget Sound are of a very lively, progressive and aspiring kind, fortunately with abundance of substance about them to warrant their ambition and make them grow. Like young sapling sequoias, they are sending out their roots far and near for nourishment, counting confidently on longevity and grandeur of stature. Seattle and Tacoma are at present far in the lead of all others in the race for supremacy, and these two are keen, active rivals, to all appearances well matched. Tacoma occupies near the head of the Sound a site of great natural beauty. It is the terminus of the Northern Pacific Railroad, and calls itself the 'City of Destiny'. Seattle is also charmingly located about twenty miles down the Sound from Tacoma, on Elliott Bay. It is the terminus of the Seattle, Lake-Shore and Eastern Railroad, now in process of construction, and calls itself the 'Queen City of the Sound' and the 'Metropolis of Washington'. What the populations of these towns number I am not able to say with anything like exactness. They are probably about the same size and they each claim to have about twenty thousand people; but their figures are so rapidly changing, and so often mixed up with counts that refer to the future that exact measurements of either of these places are about as hard to obtain as measurements of the clouds of a growing storm. Their edges run back for miles into the woods among the trees and stumps and brush which hide a good many of the houses and the stakes which mark the lots; so that, without being as yet very large towns, they seem to fade away into the distance.

But, though young and loose-jointed, they are fast taking on the forms and manners of old cities, putting on airs, as some would say, like boys in haste to be men. They are already towns 'with all modern improvements, first-class in every particular', as is said of hotels. They have electric motors and lights, paved broadways and boulevards, substantial business blocks, schools, churches, factories and foundries. The lusty, titanic clang of boiler-making may be heard there, and plenty of the languid music of pianos mingling with the babel noises of commerce carried on in a hundred tongues. The main streets are crowded with bright, wide-awake lawyers, ministers, merchants, agents for everything under the sun; ox-drivers and loggers in stiff, gummy overalls; back-slanting dudes, well-tailored and shiny; and fashions and bonnets of every feather and colour bloom gayly in the noisy throng and advertize London and Paris. Vigorous life and strife are to be seen everywhere. The spirit of progress is in the air. Still it is hard to realize how much good work is being done here of a kind that makes for civilization – the enthusiastic, exulting energy displayed in the building of new towns, railroads and mills, in the opening of mines of coal and iron and the development of natural resources in general. To many, especially in the Atlantic States, Washington is hardly known at all. It is regarded as being yet a far wild west – a dim, nebulous expanse of woods – by those who do not know that railroads and steamers have brought the country out of the wilderness and abolished the old distances. It is now near to all the world and is in possession of a share of the best of all that civilization has to offer, while on some of the lines of advancement it is at the front.

Notwithstanding the sharp rivalry between different sections and towns, the leading men mostly pull together for the general good and glory– building, buying, borrowing, to push the country to its place; keeping arithmetic busy in counting population present and to come, ships, towns, factories, tons of coal and iron, feet of lumber, miles of railroad– Americans, Scandinavians, Irish, Scotch and Germans being joined together in the white heat of work like religious crowds in time of revival who have forgotten sectarianism. It is a fine thing to see people in hot earnest about anything; therefore, however extravagant and high the brag ascending from Puget Sound, in most cases it is likely to appear pardonable and more.

Seattle was named after an old Indian chief who lived in this part of the Sound. He was very proud of the honour and lived long enough to lead his grandchildren about the streets. The greater part of the lower business portion of the town, including a long stretch of wharves and warehouses built on piles, was destroyed by fire a few months ago,[1] with immense loss. The people, however, are in no wise discouraged, and ere long the loss will be gain, inasmuch as a better class of buildings, chiefly of brick, are being erected in place of the inflammable wooden ones, which, with comparatively few exceptions, were built of pitchy spruce.

With their own scenery so glorious ever on show, one would at first thought suppose that these happy Puget Sound people would never go sightseeing from home like less favoured mortals. But they do all the same. Some go boating on the Sound or on the lakes and rivers, or with their families make excursions at small cost on the steamers. Others will take the train to the Franklin and Newcastle or Carbon River coal-mines for the sake of the thirty- or forty-mile rides through the woods, and a look into the black depths of the underworld. Others again take the steamers for Victoria, Fraser River, or Vancouver, the new ambitious town at the terminus of the Canadian Railroad, thus getting views of the outer world in a near foreign country. One of the regular summer resorts of this region where people go for fishing, hunting and the healing of diseases, is the Green River Hot Springs, in the Cascade Mountains, sixty-one miles east of Tacoma, on the line of the Northern Pacific Railroad. Green River is a small rocky stream with picturesque banks, and derives its name from the beautiful pale-green hue of its waters.

[1] 1889.

Among the most interesting of all the summer rest and pleasure places is the famous 'Hop Ranch' on the upper Snoqualmie River, thirty or forty miles eastward from Seattle. Here the dense forest opens, allowing fine free views of the adjacent mountains from a long stretch of ground which is half meadow, half prairie, level and fertile, and beautifully diversified with outstanding groves of spruces and alders and rich flowery fringes of spiræa and wild roses, the river meandering deep and tranquil through the midst of it. On the portions most easily cleared some three hundred acres of hop-vines have been planted and are now in full bearing, yielding, it is said, at the rate of about a ton of hops to the acre. They are a beautiful crop, these vines of the north, pillars of verdure in regular rows, seven feet apart and eight or ten feet in height; the long, vigorous shoots sweeping round in fine, wild freedom, and the light, leafy cones hanging in loose, handsome clusters.

Perhaps enough of hope might be raised in Washington for the wants of all the world, but it would be impossible to find pickers to handle the crop. Most of the picking is done by Indians, and to this fine, clean, profitable work they come in great numbers in their canoes, old and young, of many different tribes, bringing wives and children and household goods, in some cases from a distance of five or six hundred miles, even from far Alaska. Then they too grow rich and spend their money on red cloth and trinkets. About a thousand Indians are required as pickers at the Snoqualmie ranch alone, and a lively and merry picture they make in the field, arrayed in bright, showy calicoes, lowering the rustling vine-pillars with incessant song-singing and fun. Still more striking are their queer camps on the edges of the fields or over on the riverbank, with the firelight shining on their wild, jolly faces. But woe to the ranch should fire-water get there!

But the chief attractions here are not found in the hops, but in trout-fishing and bear-hunting, and in the two fine falls on the river. Formerly the trip from Seattle was a hard one, over corduroy roads; now it is reached in a few hours by rail along the shores of Lake Washington and Lake Squak, through a fine sample section of the forest and past the brow of the main Snoqualmie Fall. From the hotel at the ranch village the road to the fall leads down the right bank of the river through the magnificent maple woods I have mentioned elsewhere, and fine views of the fall may be had on that side, both from above and below. It is situated on the main river, where it plunges over a sheer precipice, about two hundred and forty feet high, in leaving the level meadows of the ancient lake-basin. In a general way it resembles the well-known Nevada Fall in Yosemite, having the same twisted appearance at the top and the free plunge in numberless comet-shaped masses into a deep pool seventy-five or eighty yards in diameter. The pool is of considerable depth, as is shown by the radiating well-beaten foam and mist, which is of a beautiful rose colour at times, of exquisite fineness of tone, and by the heavy waves that lash the rocks in front of it.

Though to a Californian the height of this fall would not seem great, the volume of water is heavy, and all the surroundings are delightful. The maple forest, of itself worth a long journey, the beauty of the river-reaches above and below, and the views down the valley afar over the mighty forests, with all its lovely trimmings of ferns and flowers, make this one of the most interesting falls I have ever seen. The upper fall is about seventy-five feet high, with bouncing rapids at head and foot, set in a romantic dell thatched with dripping mosses and ferns and embowered in dense evergreens and blooming bushes, the distance to it from the upper end of the meadows being about eight miles. The road leads through majestic woods with ferns ten feet high beneath some of the thickets, and across a gravelly plain deforested by fire many years ago. Orange lilies are plentiful, and handsome shining mats of the kinnikinic, sprinkled with bright scarlet berries.

From a place called 'Hunt's,' at the end of the wagon-road, a trail leads through lush, dripping woods (never dry) to Thuja and Mertens, Menzies and Douglas spruces. The ground is covered with the best moss-work of the moist lands of the north, made up mostly of the various species of hypnum, with some liverworts, marchantia, jungermannia, etc., in broad sheets and bosses, where never a dust-particle floated, and where all the flowers, fresh with mist and spray, are wetter than water-lilies. The pool at the foot of the fall is a place surpassingly lovely to look at, with the enthusiastic rush and song of the falls, the majestic trees overhead leaning over the brink like listeners eager to catch every word of the white refreshing waters, the delicate maiden-hairs and aspleniums with fronds outspread gathering the rainbow sprays, and the myriads of hooded mosses, every cup fresh and shining.

CHAPTER TWENTY

An Ascent of Mount Rainier

AMBITIOUS CLIMBERS, seeking adventures and opportunities to test their strength and skill, occasionally attempt to penetrate the wilderness on the west side of the Sound, and push on to the summit of Mount Olympus. But the grandest excursion of all to be made hereabouts is to Mount Rainier, to climb to the top of its icy crown. The mountain is very high,[1] fourteen thousand four hundred feet, and laden with glaciers that are terribly roughened and interrupted by crevasses and ice-cliffs. Only good climbers should attempt to gain the summit, led by a guide of proved nerve and endurance. A good trail has been cut through the woods to the base of the mountain on the north; but the summit of the mountain never has been reached from this side, though many brave attempts have been made upon it.

Last summer I gained the summit from the south side, in a day and a half from the timber-line, without encountering any desperate obstacles that could not in some way be passed in good weather. I was accompanied by Keith, the

---

[1] A careful re-determination of the height of Rainier, made by Professor A. G. McAdie in 1905, gave an altitude of 14,394 feet. The Standard Dictionary wrongly describes it as 'the highest peak (14,363 feet) within the United States.' The United States Baedeker and railroad literature overstate its altitude by more than a hundred feet. [Editor.]

artist, Professor Ingraham, and five ambitious young climbers from Seattle. We were led by the veteran mountaineer and guide Van Trump, of Yelm, who many years before guided General Stevens in his memorable ascent, and later Mr Bailey, of Oakland. With a cumbersome abundance of campstools and blankets we set out from Seattle, travelling by rail as far as Yelm Prairie, on the Tacoma and Oregon road. Here we made our first camp and arranged with Mr Longmire, a farmer in the neighbourhood, for pack and saddle animals. The noble King Mountain was in full view from here, glorifying the bright, sunny day with his presence, rising in godlike majesty over the woods, with the magnificent prairie as a foreground. The distance to the mountain from Yelm in a straight line is perhaps fifty miles; but by the mule and yellow-jacket trail we had to follow it is a hundred miles. For, notwithstanding a portion of this trail runs in the air, where the wasps work hardest, it is far from being an air-line as commonly understood.

By night of the third day we reached the Soda Springs on the right bank of the Nisqually, which goes roaring by, grey with mud, gravel and boulders from the caves of the glaciers of Rainier, now close at hand. The distance from the Soda Springs to the Camp of the Clouds is about ten miles. The first part of the way lies up the Nisqually Canyon, the bottom of which is flat in some places and the walls very high and precipitous, like those of the Yosemite Valley. The upper part of the Canyon is still occupied by one of the Nisqually glaciers, from which this branch of the river draws its source, issuing from a cave in the grey, rock-strewn snout. About a mile below the glacier we had to ford the river, which caused some anxiety, for the current is very rapid and carried forward large boulders as well as lighter material, while its savage roar is bewildering.

At this point we left the canyon, climbing out of it by a steep zigzag up the old lateral moraine of the glacier, which was deposited when the present glacier flowed past at this height, and is about eight hundred feet high. It is now covered with a superb growth of *Picea amabilis;*[1] so also is the corresponding portion of the right lateral. From the top of the moraine, still ascending, we passed for a mile or two through a forest of mixed growth, mainly silver fir, Patton spruce, and mountain pine, and then came to the charming park region, at an elevation of about five thousand feet above sea-level. Here the vast continuous woods at length begin to give way under the dominion of climate, though still at this height retaining their beauty and giving no sign of stress of storm, sweeping upward in belts of varying width, composed mainly of one species of fir, sharp and spiry in form, leaving smooth, spacious parks, with here and there separate groups of trees standing out in the midst of the openings like islands in a lake. Every one of these parks, great and small, is a garden filled knee-deep with fresh, lovely flowers of every hue, the most luxuriant and the most extravagantly beautiful of all the alpine gardens I ever beheld in all my mountain-top wanderings.

We arrived at the Cloud Camp at noon, but no clouds were in sight, save a few gauzy ornamental wreaths adrift in the sunshine. Out of the forest at last

---

[1] Doubtless the red silver fir, now classified as *Abies amabilis*. [Editor.]

there stood the mountain, wholly unveiled, awful in bulk and majesty, filling all the view like a separate, new-born world, yet withal so fine and so beautiful it might well fire the dullest observer to desperate enthusiasm. Long we gazed in silent admiration, buried in tall daisies and anemones by the side of a snowbank. Higher we could not go with the animals and find food for them and wood for our own camp-fires, for just beyond this lies the region of ice, with only here and there an open spot on the ridges in the midst of the ice, with dwarf alpine plants, such as saxifrages and drabas, which reach far up between the glaciers, and low mats of the beautiful bryanthus, while back of us were the gardens and abundance of everything that heart could wish. Here we lay all the afternoon, considering the lilies and the lines of the mountains with reference to a way to the summit.

At noon next day we left camp and began our long climb. We were in light marching order, save one who pluckily determined to carry his camera to the summit. At night, after a long easy climb over wide and smooth fields of ice, we reached a narrow ridge, at an elevation of about ten thousand feet above the sea, on the divide between the glaciers of the Nisqually and the Cowlitz. Here we lay as best we could, waiting for another day, without fire of course, as we were now many miles beyond the timber-line and without much to cover us. After eating a little hardtack, each of us levelled a spot to lie on among lava-blocks and cinders. The night was cold, and the wind coming down upon us in stormy surges drove gritty ashes and fragments of pumice about our ears while chilling to the bone. Very short and shallow was our sleep that night; but day dawned at last, early rising was easy, and there was nothing about breakfast to cause any delay. About four o'clock we were off, and climbing began in earnest. We followed up the ridge on which we had spent the night, now along its crest, now on either side, or on the ice leaning against it, until we came to where it becomes massive and precipitous. Then we were compelled to crawl along a seam or narrow shelf, on its face, which we traced to its termination in the base of the great ice-cap. From this point all the climbing was over ice, which was here desperately steep but fortunately was at the same time carved into innumerable spikes and pillars which afforded good footholds, and we crawled cautiously on, warm with ambition and exercise.

At length, after gaining the upper extreme of our guiding ridge, we found a good place to rest and prepare ourselves to scale the dangerous upper curves of the dome. The surface almost everywhere was bare, hard, snowless ice, extremely slippery; and, though smooth in general, it was interrupted by a network of yawning crevasses, outspread like lines of defence against any attempt to win the summit. Here every one of the party took off his shoes and drove stout steel caulks about half an inch long into them, having brought tools along for the purpose, and not having made use of them until now so that the points might not get dulled on the rocks ere the smooth dangerous ice was reached. Besides being well shod each carried an alpenstock, and for special difficulties we had a hundred feet of rope and an axe.

Thus prepared, we stepped forth afresh, slowly groping our way through tangled lines of crevasses, crossing on snow bridges here and there after cautiously testing them, jumping at narrow places, or crawling around the ends of the largest, bracing well at every point with our alpenstocks and setting our spiked shoes squarely down on the dangerous slopes. It was nerve-trying work, most of it, but we made good speed nevertheless, and by noon all stood together on the utmost summit, save one who, his strength failing for a time, came up later.

We remained on the summit nearly two hours, looking about us at the vast maplike views, comprehending hundreds of miles of the Cascade Range, with their black interminable forests and white volcanic cones in glorious array reaching far into Oregon; the Sound region also, and the great plains of eastern Washington, hazy and vague in the distance. Clouds began to gather. Soon of all the land only the summits of the mountains, St Helen's, Adams and Hood, were left in sight, forming islands in the sky. We found two well-formed and well-preserved craters on the summit, lying close together like two plates on a table with their rims touching. The highest point of the mountain is located between the craters, where their edges come in contact. Sulphurous fumes and steam issue from several vents, giving out a sickening smell that can be detected at a considerable distance. The unwasted condition of these craters, and, indeed, to a great extent, of the entire mountain, would tend to show that Rainier is still a comparatively young mountain. With the exception of the projecting lips of the craters and the top of a subordinate summit a short distance to the northward, the mountain is solidly capped with ice all around; and it is this ice-cap which forms the grand central fountain whence all the twenty glaciers of Rainier flow, radiating in every direction.

The descent was accomplished without disaster, though several of the party had narrow escapes. One slipped and fell, and as he shot past me seemed to be going to certain death. So steep was the ice-slope no one could move to help him, for fortunately, keeping his presence of mind, he threw himself on his face and digging his alpenstock into the ice, gradually retarded his motion until he came to rest. Another broke through a slim bridge over a crevasse, but his momentum at the time carried him against the lower edge and only his alpenstock was lost in the abyss. Thus crippled by the loss of his staff, we had to lower him the rest of the way down the dome by means of the rope we carried. Falling rocks from the upper precipitous part of the ridge were also a source of danger, as they came whizzing past in successive volleys; but none told on us, and when we at length gained the gentle slopes of the lower ice-fields, we ran and slid at our ease, making fast, glad time, all care and danger past, and arrived at our beloved Cloud Camp before sundown.

We were rather weak from want of nourishment, and some suffered from sunburn, notwithstanding the partial protection of glasses and veils; other-wise, all were unscathed and well. The view we enjoyed from the summit could hardly be surpassed in sublimity and grandeur; but one feels far from home so high in the sky, so much so that one is inclined to guess that, apart from the acquisition of knowledge and the exhilaration of climbing, more pleasure is to be found at the foot of mountains than on their frozen tops. Doubly happy, however, is the man to whom lofty mountain-tops are within reach, for the lights that shine there illumine all that lies below.

CHAPTER TWENTY ONE

The Physical and Climatic Characteristics of Oregon

OREGON IS a large, rich, compact section of the west side of the continent, containing nearly a hundred thousand square miles of deep, wet evergreen woods, fertile valleys, icy mountains and high, rolling, wind-swept plains, watered by the majestic Columbia River and its countless branches. It is bounded on the north by Washington, on the east by Idaho, on the south by California and Nevada, and on the west by the Pacific Ocean. It is a grand, hearty, wholesome, foodful wilderness and, like Washington, once a part of the Oregon Territory, abounds in bold, far-reaching contrasts as to scenery, climate, soil and productions. Side by side there is drought on a grand scale and overflowing moisture; flinty, sharply cut lava-beds, gloomy and forbidding, and smooth, flowery lawns; cool bogs, exquisitely plushy and soft, overshadowed by jagged crags barren as icebergs; forests seemingly boundless and plains with no tree in sight; presenting a wide range of conditions, but as a whole favourable to industry. Natural wealth of an available kind abounds nearly everywhere, inviting the farmer, the stock-raiser, the lumberman, the fisherman, the manufacturer and the miner, as well as the free walker in search of knowledge and wildness. The scenery is mostly of a comfortable, assuring kind, grand and inspiring without too much of that dreadful overpowering sublimity and exuberance which tend to discourage effort and cast people into inaction and superstition.

Ever since Oregon was first heard of in the romantic, adventurous, hunting, trapping Wild West days, it seems to have been regarded as the most attractive and promising of all the Pacific countries for farmers. While yet the whole region as well as the way to it was wild, ere a single road or bridge was built, undaunted by the trackless thousand-mile distances and scalping, cattle-stealing Indians, long trains of covered wagons began to crawl wearily westward, crossing how many plains, rivers, ridges and mountains, fighting the painted savages and weariness and famine. Setting out from the frontier of the old West in the spring as soon as the grass would support their cattle, they pushed on up the Platte, making haste slowly, however, that they might not be caught in the storms of winter ere they reached the promised land. They crossed the Rocky Mountains to Fort Hall; thence followed down the Snake River for three or four hundred miles, their cattle limping and failing on the rough lava plains; swimming the streams too deep to be forded, making boats out of wagon-boxes for the women and children and goods, or where trees could be had, lashing together logs for rafts. Thence, crossing the Blue Mountains and the plains of the Columbia, they followed the river to the Dalles. Here winter would be upon them, and before a wagon-road was built across the Cascade Mountains the toil-worn emigrants would be compelled to leave their cattle and wagons until the following summer, and, in the mean time, with the assistance of the Hudson's Bay Company, make their way to the Willamette Valley on the river with rafts and boats.

How strange and remote these trying times have already become! They are now dim as if a thousand years had passed over them. Steamships and locomotives with magical influence have well-nigh abolished the old distances and dangers, and brought forward the New West into near and familiar companionship with the rest of the world.

Purely wild for unnumbered centuries, a paradise of oily, salmon-fed Indians, Oregon is now roughly settled in part and surveyed, its rivers and mountain-ranges, lakes, valleys and plains have been traced and mapped in a general way, civilization is beginning to take root, towns are springing up and flourishing vigorously like a crop adapted to the soil, and the whole kindly wilderness lies invitingly near with all its wealth open and ripe for use.

In sailing along the Oregon coast one sees but few more signs of human occupation than did Juan de Fuca three centuries ago. The shore bluffs rise abruptly from the waves, forming a wall apparently unbroken, though many short rivers from the coast range of mountains and two from the interior have made narrow openings on their way to the sea. At the mouths of these rivers good harbours have been discovered for coasting vessels, which are of great importance to the lumbermen, dairymen and farmers of the coast region. But little or nothing of these appear in general views, only a simple grey wall nearly straight, green along the top, and the forest stretching back into the mountains as far as the eye can reach.

Going ashore, we find few long reaches of sand where one may saunter, or meadows, save the brown and purple meadows of the sea, overgrown with slippery kelp, swashed and swirled in the restless breakers. The abruptness of the shore allows the massive waves that have come from far over the broad Pacific to get close to the bluffs ere they break, and the thundering shock shakes the rocks to their foundations. No calm comes to these shores. Even in the finest weather when the ships off shore are becalmed and their sails hang loose against the mast, there is always a wreath of foam at the base of these bluffs. The breakers are ever in bloom and crystal brine is ever in the air.

A scramble along the Oregon sea-bluffs proves as richly exciting to lovers of wild beauty as heart could wish. Here are three hundred miles of pictures of rock and water in black and white, or grey and white, with more or less of green and yellow, purple and blue. The rocks, glistening in sunshine and foam, are never wholly dry – many of them marvels of wave-sculpture and most imposing in bulk and bearing, standing boldly forward, monuments of a thousand storms, types of permanence, holding the homes and places of refuge of multitudes of seafaring animals in their keeping, yet ever wasting away. How grand the songs of the waves about them, every wave a fine hearty storm in itself, taking its rise on the breezy plains of the sea, perhaps thousands of miles away, travelling with majestic, slow-heaving deliberation, reaching the end of its journey, striking its blow, bursting into a mass of white and pink bloom, then falling spent and withered to give place to the next in the endless procession, thus keeping up the glorious show and glorious song through all times and seasons forever!

Terribly impressive as is this cliff and wave scenery when the skies are bright and kindly sunshine makes rainbows in the spray, it is doubly so in dark, stormy nights, when, crouching in some hollow on the top of some jutting headland, we may gaze and listen undisturbed in the heart of it. Perhaps now and then we may dimly see the tops of the highest breakers, looking ghostly in the gloom; but when the water happens to be phosphorescent, as it oftentimes is, then both the sea and the rocks are visible, and the wild, exulting, up-dashing spray burns every particle of it, and is combined into one glowing mass of white fire; while back in the woods and along the bluffs and crags of the shore the storm-wind roars, and the rain-floods, gathering strength and coming from far and near, rush wildly down every gulch to the sea, as if eager to join the waves in their grand, savage harmony; deep calling unto deep in the heart of the great, dark night, making a sight and a song unspeakably sublime and glorious.

In the pleasant weather of summer, after the rainy season is past and only occasional refreshing showers fall, washing the sky and bringing out the fragrance of the flowers and the evergreens, then one may enjoy a fine, free walk all the way across the State from the sea to the eastern boundary on the Snake River. Many a beautiful stream we should cross in such a walk, singing through forest and meadow and deep rocky gorge, and many a broad prairie and plain, mountain and valley, wild garden and desert, presenting landscape beauty on a grand scale and in a thousand forms, and new lessons without number, delightful to learn. Oregon has three mountain-ranges which run nearly parallel with the coast, the most influential of which, in every way, is the Cascade Range. It is about six thousand to seven thousand feet in average height, and divides the State into two main sections called Eastern and Western Oregon, corresponding with the main divisions of Washington; while these are again divided, but less perfectly, by the Blue Mountains and the Coast Range. The eastern section is about two hundred and thirty miles wide, and is made up in great part of the treeless plains of the Columbia, which are green and flowery in spring, but grey, dusty, hot and forbidding in summer. Considerable areas, however, on these plains, as well as some of the valleys countersunk below the general surface along the banks of the streams, have proved fertile and produce large crops of wheat, barley, hay and other products.

In general views the western section seems to be covered with one vast, evenly planted forest, with the exception of the few snow-clad peaks of the Cascade Range, these peaks being the only points in the landscape that rise above the timber-line. Nevertheless, embosomed in this forest and lying in the great trough between the Cascades and coast mountains, there are some of the best bread-bearing valleys to be found in the world. The largest of these are the Willamette, Umpqua and Rogue River Valleys. Inasmuch as a considerable portion of these main valleys was treeless, or nearly so, as well as surpassingly fertile, they were the first to attract settlers; and the Willamette, being at once the largest and nearest to tide water, was settled first of all, and now contains the greater portion of the population and wealth of the state.

The climate of this section, like the corresponding portion of Washington, is rather damp and sloppy throughout the winter months, but the summers are bright, ripening the wheat and allowing it to be garnered in good condition. Taken as a whole, the weather is bland and kindly, and like the forest trees the crops and cattle grow plump and sound in it. So also do the people; children ripen well and grow up with limbs of good size and fibre and, unless overworked in the woods, live to a good old age, hale and hearty.

But, like every other happy valley in the world, the sunshine of this one is not without its shadows. Malarial fevers are not unknown in some places, and untimely frosts and rains may at long intervals in some measure disappoint the hopes of the husbandman. Many a tale, good-natured or otherwise, is told concerning the overflowing abundance of the Oregon rains. Once an English traveller, as the story goes, went to a store to make some purchases and on leaving found that rain was falling; therefore, not liking to get wet, he stepped back to wait till the shower was over. Seeing no signs of clearing, he soon became impatient and inquired of the storekeeper how long he thought the shower would be likely to last. Going to the door and looking wisely into the grey sky and noting the direction of the wind, the latter replied that he thought the shower would probably last about six months, an opinion that of course disgusted the fault-finding Briton with the 'blawsted country,' though in fact it is but little if at all wetter or cloudier than his own.

No climate seems the best for everybody. Many there be who waste their lives in a vain search for weather with which no fault may be found, keeping themselves and their families in constant motion, like floating seaweeds that never strike root, yielding compliance to every current of news concerning countries yet untried, believing that everywhere, anywhere, the sky is fairer and the grass grows greener than where they happen to be. Before the Oregon and California railroad was built, the overland journey between these States across the Siskiyou Mountains in the old-fashioned emigrant wagon was a long and tedious one. Nevertheless, every season dissatisfied climate-seekers, too wet and too dry, might be seen plodding along through the dust in the old ''49 style,' making their way one half of them from California to Oregon, the other half from Oregon to California. The beautiful Sisson meadows at the base of Mount Shasta were a favourite halfway resting-place, where the weary cattle were turned out for a few days to gather strength for better climates, and it was curious to hear those perpetual pioneers comparing notes and seeking information around the camp-fires.

'Where are you from?' some Oregonian would ask.

'The Joaquin.'

'It's dry there, ain't it?'

'Well, I should say so. No rain at all in summer and none to speak of in winter, and I'm dried out. I just told my wife I was on the move again, and I'm going to keep moving till I come to a country where it rains once in a while, like it does in every reg'lar white man's country; and that, I guess, will be Oregon, if the news be true.'

'Yes, neighbour, you's heading in the right direction for rain,' the Oregonian would say. 'Keep right on to Yamhill and you'll soon be damp enough. It rains there more than twelve months in the year; at least, no saying but it wifl. I've just come from there, plumb drowned out, and I told my wife to jump into the wagon and we would start out and see if we couldn't find a dry day somewhere. Last fall the hay was out and the wood was out, and the cabin leaked, and I made up my mind to try California the first chance.'

'Well, if you be a horned toad or coyote,' the seeker of moisture would reply, 'then maybe you can stand it. Just keep right on by the Alabama Settlement to Tulare and you can have my place on Big Dry Creek and welcome. You'll be drowned there mighty seldom. The wagon spokes and tyres will rattle and tell you when you come to it.'

'All right, partner, we'll swap square, you can have mine in Yamhill and the rain thrown in. Last August a painter sharp came along one day wanting to know the way to Willamette Falls, and I told him: "Young man, just wait a little and you'll find falls enough without going to Oregon City after them. The whole dog-gone Noah's flood of a country will be a fall and melt and float away some day."' And more to the same effect.

But no one need leave Oregon in search of fair weather. The wheat and cattle region of eastern Oregon and Washington on the upper Columbia plains is dry enough and dusty enough more than half the year. The truth is, most of these wanderers enjoy the freedom of gypsy life and seek not homes but camps. Having crossed the plains and reached the ocean, they can find no farther west within reach of wagons, and are therefore compelled now to go north and south between Mexico and Alaska, always glad to find an excuse for moving, stopping a few months or weeks here and there, the time being measured by the size of the camp-meadow, conditions of the grass, game and other indications. Even their so-called settlements of a year or two, when they take up land and build cabins, are only another kind of camp, in no common sense homes. Never a tree is planted, nor do they plant themselves, but like good soldiers in time of war are ever ready to march. Their journey of life is indeed a journey with very matter-of-fact thorns in the way, though not wholly wanting in compensation.

One of the most influential of the motives that brought the early settlers to these shores, apart from that natural instinct to scatter and multiply which urges even sober salmon to climb the Rocky Mountains, was their desire to find a country at once fertile and winterless, where their flocks and herds could find pasture all the year, thus doing away with the long and tiresome period of haying and feeding necessary in the eastern and old western States and Territories. Cheap land and good land there was in abundance in Kansas, Nebraska, Minnesota and Iowa; but there the labour of providing for animals of the farm was very great, and much of that labour was crowded together into a few summer months, while to keep cool in summers and warm in the icy winters was well-nigh impossible to poor farmers.

Along the coast and throughout the greater part of western Oregon in general, snow seldom falls on the lowlands to a greater depth than a few inches, and never lies long. Grass is green all winter. The average temperature for the year in the Willamette Valley is about 52°, the highest and lowest being about 100° and 20°, though occasionally a much lower temperature is reached.

The average rainfall is about fifty or fifty-five inches in the Willamette Valley, and along the coast seventy-five inches, or even more at some points – figures that bring many a dreary night and day to mind, however fine the effect on the great evergreen woods and the fields of the farmers. The rainy season begins in September or October and lasts until April or May. Then the whole country is solemnly soaked and poulticed with the grey, streaming clouds and fogs, night and day, with marvellous constancy. Towards the beginning and end of the season a good many bright days occur to break the pouring gloom, but whole months of rain, continuous, or nearly so, are not at all rare. Astronomers beneath these Oregon skies would have a dull time of it. Of all the year only about one fourth of the days are clear, while three fourths have more or less of fogs, clouds, or rain.

The fogs occur mostly in the fall and spring. They are grand, far-reaching affairs of two kinds, the black and the white, some of the latter being very beautiful, and the infinite delicacy and tenderness of their touch as they linger to caress the tall evergreens is most exquisite. On farms and highways and in streets of towns, where work has to be done, there is nothing picturesque or attractive in any obvious way about the grey, serious-faced rain-storms. Mud abounds. The rain seems dismal and heedless and gets in everybody's way. Every face is turned from it, and it has but few friends who recognize its boundless beneficence. But back in the untrodden woods where no axe has been lifted, where a deep, rich carpet of brown and golden mosses covers all the ground like a garment, pressing warmly about the feet of the trees and rising in thick folds softly and kindly over every fallen trunk, leaving no spot naked or uncared-for, there the rain is welcomed, and every drop that falls finds a place and use as sweet and pure as itself. An excursion into the woods when the rain harvest is at its height is a noble pleasure, and may be safely enjoyed at small expense, though very few care to seek it. Shelter is easily found beneath the great trees in some hollow out of the wind, and one need carry but little provision, none at all of a kind that a wetting would spoil. The colours of the woods are then at their best, and the mighty hosts of the forest, every needle tingling in the blast, wave and sing in glorious harmony.

'' 'T were worth ten years of peaceful life, one glance at this array.'

The snow that falls in the lowland woods is usually soft, and makes a fine show coming through the trees in large, feathery tufts, loading the branches of the firs and spruces and cedars and weighing them down against the trunks until they look slender and sharp as arrows, while a strange, muffled silence prevails, giving a peculiar solemnity to everything. But these lowland snow-storms and their effects quickly vanish; every crystal melts in a day or two, the bent branches rise again, and the rain resumes its sway.

While these gracious rains are searching the roots of the lowlands, cor-responding snows are busy along the heights of the Cascade Mountains. Month after month, day and night the heavens shed their icy bloom in stormy, measureless abundance, filling the grand upper fountains of the rivers to last through the summer. Awful then is the silence that presses down over the mountain forests. All the smaller streams vanish from sight, hushed and obliterated. Young groves of spruce and pine are bowed down as by a gentle hand and put to rest, not again to see the light or move leaf or limb until the grand awakening of the springtime, while the larger animals and most of the birds seek food and shelter in the foothills on the borders of the valleys and plains.

The lofty volcanic peaks are yet more heavily snow-laden. To their upper zones no summer comes. They are white always. From the steep slopes of the summit the new-fallen snow, while yet dry and loose, descends in magnificent avalanches to feed the glaciers, making meanwhile the most glorious manifestations of power. Happy is the man who may get near them to see and hear. In some sheltered camp nest on the edge of the timberline one may lie snug and warm, but after the long shuffle on snowshoes we may have to wait more than a month ere the heavens open and the grand show is unveiled. In the mean time, bread may be scarce, unless with careful forecast a sufficient supply has been provided and securely placed during the summer. Nevertheless, to be thus deeply snowbound high in the sky is not without generous compensation for all the cost. And when we at length go down the long white slopes to the levels of civilization, the pains vanish like snow in sunshine, while the noble and exalting pleasures we have gained remain with us to enrich our lives forever.

The fate of the high-flying mountain snowflowers is a fascinating study, though little may we see of their works and ways while their storms go on. The glinting, swirling swarms fairly thicken the blast, and all the air, as well as the rocks and trees, is as one smothering mass of bloom, through the midst of which at close intervals come the low, intense thunder-tones of the avalanches as they speed on their way to fill the vast fountain hollows. Here they seem at last to have found rest. But this rest is only apparent. Gradually the loose crystals by the pressure of their own weight are welded together into clear ice, and, as glaciers, march steadily, silently on, with invisible motion, in broad, deep currents, grinding their way with irresistible energy to the warmer lowlands, where they vanish in glad, rejoicing streams.

In the sober weather of Oregon lightning makes but little show. Those magnificent thunder-storms that so frequently adorn and glorify the sky of the Mississippi Valley are wanting here. Dull thunder and lightning may occasionally be seen and heard, but the imposing grandeur of great storms marching over the landscape with streaming banners and a network of fire is almost wholly unknown.

Crossing the Cascade Range, we pass from a green to a grey country, from a wilderness of trees to a wilderness of open plains, level or rolling or rising here and there into hills and short mountain spurs. Though well supplied with rivers in most of its main sections, it is generally dry. The annual rainfall is only from about five to fifteen inches, and the thin winter garment of snow seldom lasts more than a month or two, though the temperature in many places falls from five to twenty-five degrees below zero for a short time. That the snow is light over eastern Oregon, and the average temperature not intolerably severe, is shown by the fact that large droves of sheep, cattle and horses live there through the winter without other food or shelter than they find for themselves on the open plains or down in the sunken valleys and gorges along the streams.

When we read of the mountain-ranges of Oregon and Washington with detailed descriptions of their old volcanoes towering snow-laden and glacier-laden above the clouds, one may be led to imagine that the country is far icier and whiter and more mountainous than it is. Only in winter are the Coast and Cascade Mountains covered with snow. Then as seen from the main interior valleys they appear as comparatively low, bossy walls stretching along the horizon and making a magnificent display of their white wealth. The Coast Range in Oregon does not perhaps average more than three thousand feet in height. Its snow does not last long, most of its soil is fertile all the way to the summits, and the greater part of the range may at some time be brought under cultivation. The immense deposits on the great central uplift of the Cascade Range are mostly melted off before the middle of summer by the comparatively warm winds and rains from the coast, leaving only a few white spots on the highest ridges, where the depth from drifting has been greatest, or where the rate of waste has been diminished by specially favourable conditions as to exposure. Only the great volcanic cones are truly snow-clad all the year, and these are not numerous and make but a small portion of the general landscape.

As we approach Oregon from the coast in summer, no hint of snowy mountains can be seen, and it is only after we have sailed into the country by the Columbia, or climbed some one of the commanding summits, that the great white peaks send us greeting and make telling advertisements of themselves and of the country over which they rule. So, also, in coming to Oregon from the east the country by no means impresses one as being surpassingly mountainous, the abode of peaks and glaciers. Descending the spurs of the Rocky Mountains into the basin of the Columbia, we see hot, hundred-mile plains, roughened here and there by hills and ridges that look hazy and blue in the distance, until we have pushed well to the westward. Then one white point after another comes into sight to refresh the eye and the imagination; but they are yet a long way off, and have much to say only to those who know them or others of their kind. How grand they are, though insignificant-looking on the edge of the vast landscape! What noble woods they nourish, and emerald meadows and gardens! What springs and streams and waterfalls sing about them, and to what a multitude of happy creatures they give homes and food!

The principal mountains of the range are Mounts Pitt, Scott and Thielson, Diamond Peak, the Three Sisters, Mounts Jefferson, Hood, St Helens, Adams, Rainier, Aix and Baker. Of these the seven first named belong to Oregon, the others to Washington. They rise singly at irregular distances from one another along the main axis of the range or near it, with an elevation of from about eight thousand to fourteen thousand four hundred feet above the level of the sea. From few points in the valleys may more than three or four of them be seen, and of the more distant ones of these only the tops appear. Therefore, speaking generally, each of the lowland landscapes of the State contains only one grand snowy mountain.

The heights back of Portland command one of the best general views of the forests and also of the most famous of the great mountains both of Oregon and Washington. Mount Hood is in full view, with the summits of Mounts Jefferson, St Helens, Adams and Rainier in the distance. The city of Portland is at our feet, covering a large area along both banks of the Willamette, and, with its fine streets, schools, churches, mills, shipping, parks and gardens, makes a telling picture of busy, aspiring civilization in the midst of the green wilderness in which it is planted. The river is displayed to fine advantage in the foreground of our main view, sweeping in beautiful curves around rich, leafy islands, its banks fringed with willows.

A few miles beyond the Willamette flows the renowned Columbia, and the confluence of these two great rivers is at a point only about ten miles below the city. Beyond the Columbia extends the immense breadth of the forest, one dim, black, monotonous field, with only the sky, which one is glad to see is not forested, and the tops of the majestic old volcanoes to give diversity to the view. That sharp, white, broad-based pyramid on the south side of the Columbia, a few degrees to the south of east from where you stand, is the famous Mount Hood. The distance to it in a straight line is about fifty miles. Its upper slopes form the only bare ground, bare as to forests, in the landscape in that direction. It is the pride of Oregonians, and when it is visible is always pointed out to strangers as the glory of the country, the mountain of mountains. It is one of the grand series of extinct volcanoes extending from Lassen's Butte[1] to Mount Baker, a distance of about six hundred miles, which once flamed like gigantic watch-fires along the coast. Some of them have been active in recent times, but no considerable addition to the bulk of Mount Hood has been made for several centuries, as is shown by the amount of glacial denudation it has suffered. Its summit has been ground to a point, which gives it a rather thin, pinched appearance. It has a wide-flowing base, however, and is fairly well proportioned. Though it is eleven thousand feet high, it is too far off to make much show under ordinary conditions in so extensive a landscape. Through a great part of the summer it is invisible on account of smoke poured into the sky from burning woods, logging-camps, mills, etc., and in winter for weeks at a time, or even months, it is in the clouds. Only in spring and early summer and in what there may chance to be of bright weather in winter is it or any of its companions at all clear or telling. From the Cascades on the Columbia it may be seen at a distance of twenty miles or thereabouts, or from other points up and down the river, and with the magnificent foreground it is very impressive. It gives the supreme touch of grandeur to all the main Columbia views, rising at every turn, solitary, majestic, awe-inspiring, the ruling spirit of the landscape. But, like mountains everywhere, it varies greatly in impressiveness and apparent height at different times and seasons, not alone from differences as to the dimness or

---

[1] Lassen Peak on recent maps. [Editor.]

transparency of the air. Clear, or arrayed in clouds, it changes both in size and general expression. Now it looms up to an immense height and seems to draw near in tremendous grandeur and beauty, holding the eyes of every beholder in devout and awful interest. Next year or next day, or even in the same day, you return to the same point of view, perhaps to find that the glory has departed, as if the mountain had died and the poor dull, shrunken mass of rocks and ice had lost all power to charm.

Never shall I forget my first glorious view of Mount Hood one calm evening in July, though I had seen it many times before this. I was then sauntering with a friend across the new Willamette bridge between Portland and East Portland for the sake of the river views, which are here very fine in the tranquil summer weather. The scene on the water was a lively one. Boats of every description were gliding, glinting, drifting about at work or play, and we leaned over the rail from time to time, contemplating the gay throng. Several lines of ferry-boats were making regular trips at intervals of a few minutes, and river steamers were coming and going from the wharves, laden with all sorts of merchandise, raising long diverging swells that made all the light pleasure-craft bow and nod in hearty salutation as they passed. The crowd was being constantly increased by new arrivals from both shores, sailboats, rowboats, racing-shells, rafts, were loaded with gayly dressed people, and here and there some adventurous man or boy might be seen as a merry sailor on a single plank or spar, apparently as deep in enjoyment as were any on the water. It seemed as if all the town were coming to the river, renouncing the cares and toils of the day, determined to take the evening breeze into their pulses, and be cool and tranquil ere going to bed.

Absorbed in the happy scene, given up to dreamy, random observation of what lay immediately before me, I was not conscious of anything occurring on the outer rim of the landscape. Forest, mountain and sky were forgotten, when my companion suddenly directed my attention to the eastward, shouting, 'Oh, look! look!' in so loud and excited a tone of voice that passers-by, saunterers like ourselves, were startled and looked over the bridge as if expecting to see some boat upset. Looking across the forest, over which the mellow light of the sunset was streaming, I soon discovered the source of my friend's excitement. There stood Mount Hood in all the glory of the alpenglow, looming immensely high, beaming with intelligence, and so impressive that one was overawed as if suddenly brought before some superior being newly arrived from the sky.

The atmosphere was somewhat hazy, but the mountain seemed neither near nor far. Its glaciers flashed in the divine light. The rugged, storm-worn ridges between them and the snowfields of the summit, these perhaps might have been traced as far as they were in sight, and the blending zones of colour about the base. But so profound was the general impression, partial analysis did not come into play. The whole mountain appeared as one glorious manifestation of divine power, enthusiastic and benevolent, glowing like a countenance with ineffable repose and beauty, before which we could only gaze in devout and lowly admiration.

The far-famed Oregon forests cover all the western section of the State, the mountains as well as the lowlands, with the exception of a few gravelly spots and open spaces in the central portions of the great cultivated valleys. Beginning on the coast, where their outer ranks are drenched and buffeted by wind-driven scud from the sea, they press on in close, majestic ranks over the coast mountains, across the broad central valleys, and over the Cascade Range, broken and halted only by the few great peaks that rise like islands above the sea of evergreens.

In descending the eastern slopes of the Cascades the rich, abounding, triumphant exuberance of the trees is quickly subdued; they become smaller, grow wide apart, leaving dry spaces without moss covering or underbrush, and before the foot of the range is reached, fail altogether, stayed by the drought of the interior almost as suddenly as on the western margin they are stayed by the sea. Here and there at wide intervals on the eastern plains patches of a small pine (*Pinus contorta*) are found, and a scattering growth of juniper, used by the settlers mostly for fence-posts and firewood. Along the stream-bottoms there is usually more or less of cottonwood and willow, which, though yielding inferior timber, is yet highly prized in this bare region. On the Blue Mountains there is pine, spruce, fir and larch in abundance for every use, but beyond this range there is nothing that may be called a forest in the Columbia River basin, until we reach the spurs of the Rocky Mountains; and these Rocky Mountain forests are made up of trees which, compared with the giants of the Pacific Slope, are mere saplings.

CHAPTER TWENTY TWO

The Forests of Oregon and Their Inhabitants

LIKE THE forests of Washington, already described, those of Oregon are in great part made up of the Douglas spruce,[1] or Oregon pine (*Abies Douglasii*). A large number of mills are at work upon this species, especially along the Columbia, but these as yet have made but little impression upon its dense masses, the mills here being small as compared with those of the Puget Sound region. The white cedar, or Port Orford cedar (*Cupressus Lawsoniana*, or *Chamæcyparis Lawsoniana*), is one of the most beautiful of the evergreens, and produces excellent lumber, considerable quantities of which are shipped to the San Francisco market. It is found mostly about Coos Bay, along the Coquille River, and on the northern slopes of the Siskiyou Mountains, and extends down the coast into California. The silver firs, the spruces and the colossal arbor-vitæ, or white cedar[2] (*Thuja gigantea*), described in the chapter on Washington, are also found here in great beauty and perfection, the

---

[1] *Pseudoisuga taxifolia.* Brit. [Editor.]
[2] *Thuja plicata* Don. [Editor.]

largest of these (*Picea grandis*, Loud.; *Abies grandis*, Lindl.) being confined mostly to the coast region, where it attains a height of three hundred feet, and a diameter of ten or twelve feet. Five or six species of pines are found in the State, the most important of which, both as to lumber and as to the part they play in the general wealth and beauty of the forests, are the yellow and sugar pines (*Pinus ponderosa* and *P. Lambertiana*). The yellow pine is most abundant on the eastern slopes of the Cascades, forming there the main bulk of the forest in many places. It is also common along the borders of the open spaces in Willamette Valley. In the southern portion of the State the sugar pine, which is the king of all the pines and the glory of the Sierra forests, occurs in considerable abundance in the basins of the Umpqua and Rogue Rivers, and it was in the Umpqua Hills that this noble tree was first discovered by the enthusiastic botanical explorer David Douglas, in the year 1826.

This is the Douglas for whom the noble Douglas spruce is named, and many a fair blooming plant also, which will serve to keep his memory fresh and sweet as long as beautiful trees and flowers are loved. The Indians of the lower Columbia River watched him with lively curiosity as he wandered about in the woods day after day, gazing intently on the ground or at the great trees, collecting specimens of everything he saw, but, unlike all the eager fur-gathering strangers they had hitherto seen, caring nothing about trade. And when at length they came to know him better, and saw that from year to year the growing things of the woods and prairies, meadows and plains were his only object of pursuit, they called him the 'Man of Grass,' a title of which he was proud.

He was a Scotchman and first came to this coast in the spring of 1825 under the auspices of the London Horticultural Society, landing at the mouth of the Columbia after a long, dismal voyage of eight months and fourteen days. During this first season he chose Fort Vancouver, belonging to the Hudson's Bay Company, as his headquarters, and from there made excursions into the glorious wilderness in every direction, discovering many new species among the trees as well as among the rich underbrush and smaller herbaceous vegetation. It was while making a trip to Mount Hood this year that he discovered the two largest and most beautiful firs in the world (*Picea amabilis* and *P. nobilis* – now called *Abies*), and from the seeds which he then collected and sent home tall trees are now growing in Scotland.

In one of his trips that summer, in the lower Willamette Valley, he saw in an Indian's tobacco-pouch some of the seeds and scales of a new species of pine, which he learned were gathered from a large tree that grew far to the southward. Most of the following season was spent on the upper waters of the Columbia, and it was not until September that he returned to Fort Vancouver, about the time of the setting-in of the winter rains. Nevertheless, bearing in mind the great pine he had heard of, and the seeds of which he had seen, he made haste to set out on an excursion to the headwaters of the Willamette in search of it; and how he fared on this excursion and what dangers and hardships he endured is best told in his own journal, part of which I quote as follows:

October 26th, 1826. Weather dull. Cold and cloudy. When my friends in England are made acquainted with my travels I fear they will think that I have told them nothing but my miseries. ... I quitted my camp early in the morning to survey the neighbouring country, leaving my guide to take charge of the horses until my return in the evening. About an hour's walk from the camp I met an Indian, who on perceiving me instantly strung his bow, placed on his left arm a sleeve of raccoon skin and stood on the defensive. Being quite sure that conduct was prompted by fear and not by hostile intentions, the poor fellow having probably never seen such a being as myself before, I laid my gun at my feet on the ground and waved my hand for him to come to me, which he did slowly and with great caution. I then made him place his bow and quiver of arrows beside my gun, and striking a light gave him a smoke out of my own pipe and a present of a few beads. With my pencil I made a rough sketch of the cone and pine tree which I wanted to obtain and drew his attention to it, when he instantly pointed with his hand to the hills fifteen or twenty miles distant towards the south; and when I expressed my intention of going thither, cheerfully set about accompanying me. At midday I reached my long-wished-for pines and lost no time in examining them and endeavouring to collect specimens and seeds. New and strange things seldom fail to make strong impressions and are therefore frequently overrated; so that, lest I should never see my friends in England to inform them verbally of this most beautiful and immensely grand tree, I shall here state the dimensions of the largest I could find among several that had been blown down by the wind. At three feet from the ground its circumference is fifty-seven feet, nine inches; at one hundred and thirty-four feet, seventeen feet five inches; the extreme length two hundred and forty-five feet. ... As it was impossible either to climb the tree or hew it down, I endeavoured to knock off the cones by firing at them with ball, when the report of my gun brought eight Indians, all of them painted with red earth, armed with bows, arrows, bone-tipped spears, and flint knives. They appeared anything but friendly. I explained to them what I wanted and they seemed satisfied and sat down to smoke; but presently I saw one of them string his bow and another sharpen his flint knife with a pair of wooden pincers and suspend it on the wrist of his right hand. Further testimony of their intentions was unnecessary. To save myself by flight was impossible, so without hesitation I stepped back about five paces, cocked my gun, drew one of the pistols out of my belt, and holding it in my left hand, the gun in my right, showed myself determined to fight for my life. As much as possible I endeavoured to preserve my coolness, and thus we stood looking at one another without making any movement or uttering a word for perhaps ten minutes, when one at last, who seemed to be the leader, gave a sign that they wished for some tobacco; this I signified they should have if they fetched a quantity of cones. They sent off immediately in search of them, and no sooner were they all out of sight than I picked up my three cones and some twigs of the trees and made the quickest possible retreat, hurrying back to my camp, which I reached before dusk. The Indian who last undertook to be my guide to the trees I sent off before gaining my encampment, lest he should betray me. How irksome is the darkness of night to one under such circumstances. I cannot speak a word to my guide, nor have I a book to divert my thoughts, which are continually occupied with the dread lest the hostile Indians should trace me hither and make an attack. I now write lying on the grass with my gun cocked beside me, and penning these lines by the light of my *Columbian candle*, namely, an ignited piece of rosin-wood.

Douglas named this magnificent species *Pinus Lambertiana*, in honour of his friend Dr Lambert, of London. This is the noblest pine thus far discovered in the forests of the world, surpassing all others not only in size but in beauty and majesty. Oregon may well be proud that its discovery was made within her borders, and that, though it is far more abundant in California, she has the largest known specimens. In the Sierra the finest sugar pine forests lie at an elevation of about five thousand feet. In Oregon they occupy much lower ground, some of the trees being found but little above tide-water.

No lover of trees will ever forget his first meeting with the sugar pine. In most coniferous trees there is a sameness of form and expression which at length becomes wearisome to most people who travel far in the woods. But the sugar pines are as free from conventional forms as any of the oaks. No two are so much alike as to hide their individuality from any observer. Every tree is appreciated as a study in itself and proclaims in no uncertain terms the surpassing grandeur of the species. The branches, mostly near the summit, are sometimes nearly forty feet long, feathered richly all around with short, leafy branchlets, and tasselled with cones a foot and a half long. And when these superb arms are outspread, radiating in every direction, an immense crownlike mass is formed which, poised on the noble shaft and filled with sunshine, is one of the grandest forest objects conceivable. But though so wild and unconventional when full-grown, the sugar pine is a remarkably regular tree in youth, a strict follower of coniferous fashions, slim, erect, tapering, symmetrical, every branch in place. At the age of fifty or sixty years this shy, fashionable form begins to give way. Special branches are thrust out away from the general outlines of the trees and bent down with cones. Henceforth it becomes more and more original and independent in style, pushes boldly aloft into the winds and sunshine, growing ever more stately and beautiful, a joy and inspiration to every beholder.

Unfortunately, the sugar pine makes excellent lumber. It is too good to live, and is already passing rapidly away before the woodman's axe. Surely out of all of the abounding forest wealth of Oregon a few specimens might be spared to the world, not as dead lumber, but as living trees. A park of moderate extent might be set apart and protected for public use forever, containing at least a few hundreds of each of these noble pines, spruces and firs. Happy will be the men who, having the power and the love and benevolent forecast to do this, will do it. They will not be forgotten. The trees and their lovers will sing their praises, and generations yet unborn will rise up and call them blessed.

Dotting the prairies and fringing the edges of the great evergreen forests we find a considerable number of hardwood trees, such as the oak, maple, ash, alder, laurel, madrone, flowering dogwood, wild cherry and wild apple. The white oak (*Quercus Garryana*) is the most important of the Oregon oaks as a timber tree, but not nearly so beautiful as Kellogg's oak (*Q. Kelloggii*). The former is found mostly along the Columbia River, particularly about the Dalles, and a considerable quantity of useful lumber is made from it and sold, sometimes for eastern white oak, to wagon-makers. Kellogg's oak is a magnificent tree and does much for the picturesque beauty of the Umpqua and Rogue River Valleys where it abounds. It is also found in all the Yosemite valleys of the Sierra, and its acorns form an important part of the food of the Digger Indians. In the Siskiyou Mountains there is a live oak (*Q. chrysolepis*), wide-spreading and very picturesque in form, but not very common. It extends southward along the western flank of the Sierra and is there more abundant and much larger than in Oregon, oftentimes five to eight feet in diameter.

The maples are the same as those in Washington, already described, but I have not seen any maple groves here equal in extent or in the size of the trees to those on the Snoqualmie River.

The Oregon ash is now rare along the stream-banks of western Oregon, and it grows to a good size and furnishes lumber that is for some purposes equal to the white ash of the Western States.

Nuttall's flowering dogwood makes a brave display with its wealth of showy involucres in the spring along cool streams. Specimens of the flowers may be found measuring eight inches in diameter.

The wild cherry (*Prunus emarginata*, var. *mollis*) is a small, handsome tree seldom more than a foot in diameter at the base. It makes valuable lumber and its black, astringent fruit furnishes a rich resource as food for the birds. A smaller form is common in the Sierra, the fruit of which is eagerly eaten by the Indians and hunters in time of need.

The wild apple (*Pyrus rivularis*) is a fine, hearty, handsome little tree that grows well in rich, cool soil along streams and on the edges of beaver-meadows from California through Oregon and Washington to southeastern Alaska. In Oregon it forms dense, tangled thickets, some of them almost impenetrable. The largest trunks are nearly a foot in diameter. When in bloom it makes a fine show with its abundant clusters of flowers, which are white and fragrant. The fruit is very small and savagely acid. It is wholesome, however, and is eaten by birds, bears, Indians and many other adventurers, great and small.

Passing from beneath the shadows of the woods where the trees grow close and high, we step into charming wild gardens full of lilies, orchids, heathworts, roses, etc., with colours so gay and forming such sumptuous masses of bloom, they make the gardens of civilization, however lovingly cared for, seem pathetic and silly. Around the great fire-mountains, above the forests and beneath the snow, there is a flowery zone of marvellous beauty planted with anemones, erythroniums, daisies, bryanthus, kalmia, vaccinium, cassiope, saxifrages, etc., forming one continuous garden fifty or sixty miles in circumference, and so deep and luxuriant and closely woven it seems as if Nature, glad to find an opening, were economizing space and trying to see how many of her bright-eyed darlings she can get together in one mountain wreath.

Along the slopes of the Cascades, where the woods are less dense, especially about the headwaters of the Willamette, there are miles of rhododendron, making glorious outbursts of purple bloom, and down on the prairies in rich, damp hollows the blue-flowered camassia grows in such profusion that at a little distance its dense masses appear as beautiful blue lakes imbedded in the green, flowery plains; while all about the streams and the lakes and the beaver-meadows and the margins of the deep woods there is a magnificent tangle of gaultheria and huckleberry bushes with their myriads of pink bells, reinforced with hazel, cornel, rubus of many species, wild plum, cherry and crab apple; besides thousands of charming bloomers to be found in all sorts of places throughout the wilderness whose mere names are refreshing, such as linnæa, menziesia, pyrola, chimaphila, brodiæa, smilacina, fritillaria, calochortus, trillium, clintonia, veratrum, cypripedium, goodyera, spiranthes, habenaria and the rare and lovely 'Hider of the North,' *Calypso borealis*, to find which is alone a sufficient object for a journey into the wilderness. And besides these there is a charming underworld of ferns and mosses flourishing gloriously beneath all the woods.

Everybody loves wild woods and flowers more or less. Seeds of all these Oregon evergreens and of many of the flowering shrubs and plants have been sent to almost every country under the gun, and they are now growing in carefully tended parks and gardens. And now that the ways of approach are open one would expect to find these woods and gardens full of admiring visitors revelling in their beauty like bees in a clover-field. Yet few care to visit them. A portion of the bark of one of the California trees, the mere dead skin, excited the wondering attention of thousands when it was set up in the Crystal Palace in London, as did also a few peeled spars, the shafts of mere saplings from Oregon or Washington. Could one of these great silver firs or sugar pines three hundred feet high have been transplanted entire to that exhibition, how enthusiastic would have been the praises accorded to it!

Nevertheless, the countless hosts waving at home beneath their own sky, beside their own noble rivers and mountains, and standing on a flower-enamelled carpet of mosses thousands of square miles in extent, attract but little attention. Most travellers content themselves with what they may chance to see from car windows, hotel verandas, or the deck of a steamer on the lower Columbia – clinging to the battered highways like drowning sailors to a life-raft. When an excursion into the woods is proposed, all sorts of exaggerated or imaginary dangers are conjured up, filling the kindly, soothing wilderness with colds, fevers, Indians, bears, snakes, bugs, impassable rivers and jungles of brush, to which is always added quick and sure starvation.

As to starvation, the woods are full of food, and a supply of bread may easily be carried for habit's sake, and replenished now and then at outlying farms and camps. The Indians are seldom found in the woods, being confined mainly to the banks of the rivers, where the greater part of their food is obtained. Moreover, the most of them have been either buried since the settlement of the country or civilized into comparative innocence, industry, or harmless laziness. There are bears in the woods, but not in such numbers nor of such unspeakable ferocity as town-dwellers imagine, nor do bears spend their lives in going about the country like the devil, seeking whom they may devour. Oregon bears, like most others, have no liking for man either as meat or as society; and while some may be curious at times to see what manner of creature he is, most of them have learned to shun people as deadly enemies. They have been poisoned, trapped, and shot at until they have become shy, and it is no longer easy to make their acquaintance. Indeed, since the settlement of the country, notwithstanding far the greater portion is yet wild, it is difficult to find any of the larger animals that once were numerous and comparatively familiar, such as the bear, wolf, panther, lynx, deer, elk and antelope.

As early as 1843, while the settlers numbered only a few thousands, and before any sort of government had been organized, they came together and held what they called 'a wolf meeting,' at which a committee was appointed to devise means for the destruction of wild animals destructive to tame ones, which committee in due time begged to report as follows:

It being admitted by all that bears, wolves, panthers, etc., are destructive to the useful animals owned by the settlers of this colony, your committee would submit the following resolutions as the sense of this meeting, by which the community may be governed in carrying on a defensive and destructive war on all such animals:

Resolved, 1st. – That we deem it expedient for the community to take immediate measures for the destruction of all wolves, panthers and bears, and such other animals as are known to be destructive to cattle, horses, sheep and hogs.

2d. – That a bounty of fifty cents be paid for the destruction of a small wolf, $3.00 for a large wolf, $1.50 for a lynx, $2.00 for a bear and $5.00 for a panther.

This centre of destruction was in the Willamette Valley. But for many years prior to the beginning of the operations of the 'Wolf Organization' the Hudson's Bay Company had established forts and trading-stations over all the country, wherever fur-gathering Indians could be found, and vast numbers of these animals were killed. Their destruction has since gone on at an accelerated rate from year to year as the settlements have been extended, so that in some cases it is difficult to obtain specimens enough for the use of naturalists. But even before any of these settlements were made, and before the coming of the Hudson's Bay Company, there was very little danger to be met in passing through this wilderness as far as animals were concerned, and but little of any kind as compared with the dangers encountered in crowded houses and streets.

When Lewis and Clark made their famous trip across the continent in 1804–05, when all the Rocky Mountain region was wild, as well as the Pacific Slope, they did not lose a single man by wild animals, nor, though frequently attacked, especially by the grizzlies of the Rocky Mountains, were any of them wounded seriously. Captain Clark was bitten on the hand by a wolf as he lay asleep; that was one bite among more than a hundred men while travelling through eight to nine thousand miles of savage wilderness. They could hardly have been so fortunate had they stayed at home. They wintered on the edge of the Clatsop plains, on the south side of the Columbia River near its mouth. In the woods on that side they found game abundant, especially elk, and with the aid of the friendly Indians who furnished salmon and 'wapatoo' (the tubers of *Sagittaria variabilis*), they were in no danger of starving.

But on the return trip in the spring they reached the base of the Rocky Mountains when the range was yet too heavily snow-laden to be crossed with horses. Therefore they had to wait some weeks. This was at the head of one of the northern branches of Snake River, and, their scanty stock of provisions being nearly exhausted, the whole party was compelled to live mostly on bears and dogs; deer, antelope and elk, usually abundant, were now scarce because the region had been closely hunted over by the Indians before their arrival.

Lewis and Clark had killed a number of bears and saved the skins of the more interesting specimens, and the variations they found in size, colour of the hair, etc., made great difficulty in classification. Wishing to get the opinion of the Chopumish Indians, near one of whose villages they were encamped, concerning the various species, the explorers unpacked their bundles and spread out for examination all the skins they had taken. The Indian hunters immediately classed the white, the deep and the pale grizzly red, the grizzly dark-brown – in short, all those with the extremities of the hair of a white or frosty colour without regard to the colour of the ground or foil – under the name of *hoh-host*. The Indians assured them that these were all of the same species as the white bear, that they associated together, had longer nails than the others, and never climbed trees. On the other hand, the black skins, those that were black with white hairs intermixed or with a white breast, the uniform bay, the brown, and the light reddish-brown, were classed under the name *yack-ah*, and were said to resemble each other in being smaller and having shorter nails, in climbing trees, and being so little vicious that they could be pursued with safety.

Lewis and Clark came to the conclusion that all those with white-tipped hair found by them in the basin of the Columbia belonged to the same species as the grizzlies of the upper Missouri; and that the black and reddish-brown, etc., of the Rocky Mountains belong to a second species equally distinct from the grizzly and the black bear of the Pacific Coast and the East, which never vary in colour.

As much as possible should be made by the ordinary traveller of these descriptions, for he will be likely to see very little of any species for himself; not that bears no longer exist here, but because, being shy, they keep out of the way. In order to see them and learn their habits one must go softly and alone, lingering long in the fringing woods on the banks of the salmon streams, and in the small openings in the midst of thickets where berries are most abundant.

As for rattlesnakes, the other grand dread of town-dwellers when they leave beaten roads, there are two, or perhaps three, species of them in Oregon. But they are nowhere to be found in great numbers. In western Oregon they are hardly known at all. In all my walks in the Oregon forest I have never met a single specimen, though a few have been seen at long intervals.

When the country was first settled by the whites, fifty years ago, the elk roamed through the woods and over the plains to the east of the Cascades in immense numbers; now they are rarely seen except by experienced hunters who know their haunts in the deepest and most inaccessible solitudes to which they have been driven. So majestic an animal forms a tempting mark for the sportsman's rifle. Countless thousands have been killed for mere amusement and they already seem to be nearing extinction as rapidly as the buffalo. The antelope also is vanishing from the Columbia plains before the farmers and cattle-men. Whether the moose still lingers in Oregon or Washington I am unable to say.

On the highest mountains of the Cascade Range the wild goat roams in comparative security, few of his enemies caring to go so far in pursuit and to hunt on ground so high and so dangerous. He is a brave, sturdy, shaggy mountaineer of an animal, enjoying the freedom and security of crumbling ridges and overhanging cliffs above the glaciers, oftentimes beyond the reach of the most daring hunter. They seem to be as much at home on the ice and snow-fields as on the crags, making their way in flocks from ridge to ridge on the great volcanic mountains by crossing the glaciers that lie between them, travelling in single file guided by an old experienced leader, like a party of climbers on the Alps. On these ice-journeys they pick their way through networks of crevasses and over bridges of snow with admirable skill, and the mountaineer may seldom do better in such places than to follow their trail, if he can. In the rich alpine gardens and meadows they find abundance of food, venturing sometimes well down in the prairie openings on the edge of the timber-line, but holding themselves ever alert and watchful, ready to flee to their highland castles at the faintest alarm. When their summer pastures are buried beneath the winter snows, they make haste to the lower ridges, seeking the wind-beaten crags and slopes where the snow cannot lie at any great depth, feeding at times on the leaves and twigs of bushes when grass is beyond reach.

The wild sheep is another admirable alpine rover, but comparatively rare in the Oregon mountains, choosing rather the drier ridges to the southward on the Cascades and to the eastward among the spurs of the Rocky Mountain chain.

Deer give beautiful animation to the forests, harmonizing finely in their colour and movements with the grey and brown shafts of the trees and the swaying of the branches as they stand in groups at rest, or move gracefully and noiselessly over the mossy ground about the edges of beaver-meadows and flowery glades, daintily culling the leaves and tips of the mints and aromatic bushes on which they feed. There are three species, the black-tailed, white-tailed, and mule deer; the last being restricted in its range to the open woods and plains to the eastward of the Cascades. They are nowhere very numerous now, killing for food, for hides, or for mere wanton sport, having well-nigh exterminated them in the more accessible regions, while elsewhere they are too often at the mercy of the wolves.

Gliding about in their shady forest homes, keeping well out of sight, there is a multitude of sleek fur-clad animals living and enjoying their clean, beautiful lives. How beautiful and interesting they are is about as difficult for busy mortals to find out as if their homes were beyond sight in the sky. Hence the stories of every wild hunter and trapper are eagerly listened to as being possibly true, or partly so, however thickly clothed in successive folds of exaggeration and fancy. Unsatisfying as these accounts must be, a tourist's frightened rush and scramble through the woods yields far less than the hunter's wildest stories, while in writing we can do but little more than to give a few names, as they come to mind, — beaver, squirrel, coon, fox, marten, fisher, otter, ermine, wildcat – only this instead of full descriptions of the bright-eyed furry throng, their snug home nests, their fears and fights and loves, how they get their food, rear their young, escape their enemies, and keep themselves warm and well and exquisitely clean through all the pitiless weather.

For many years before the settlement of the country the fur of the beaver brought a high price, and therefore it was pursued with weariless ardour. Not even in the quest for gold has a more ruthless, desperate energy been developed. It was in those early beaver-days that the striking class of adventurers called 'free trappers' made their appearance. Bold, enterprising men, eager to make money, and inclined at the same time to relish the license of a savage life, would set forth with a few traps and a gun and a hunting-knife, content at first to venture only a short distance up the beaver-streams nearest to the settlements, and where the Indians were not likely to molest them. There they would set their traps, while the buffalo, antelope, deer, etc., furnished a royal supply of food. In a few months their pack-animals would be laden with thousands of dollars' worth of fur.

Next season they would venture farther, and again farther, meanwhile growing rapidly wilder, getting acquainted with the Indian tribes, and usually marrying among them. Thenceforward no danger could stay them in their exciting pursuit. Wherever there were beaver they would go, however far or wild – the wilder the better, provided their scalps could be saved. Oftentimes they were compelled to set their traps and visit them by night and lie hid during the day, when operating in the neighbourhood of hostile Indians. Not then venturing to make a fire or shoot game, they lived on the raw flesh of the beaver, perhaps seasoned with wild cresses or berries. Then, returning to the trading-stations, they would spend their hard earnings in a few weeks of dissipation and 'good time,' and go again to the bears and beavers, until at length a bullet or arrow would end all. One after another would be missed by some friend or trader at the autumn rendezvous, reported killed by the Indians, and – forgotten. Some men of this class have, from superior skill or fortune, escaped every danger, lived to a good old age, and earned fame, and, by their knowledge of the topography of the vast West then unexplored, have been able to render important service to the country; but most of them laid their bones in the wilderness after a few short, keen seasons. So great were the perils that beset them, the average length of the life of a 'free trapper' has been estimated at less than five years. From the Columbia waters beaver and beaver men have almost wholly passed away, and the men once so striking a part of the view have left scarcely the faintest sign of their existence. On the other hand, a thousand meadows on the mountains tell the story of the beavers, to remain fresh and green for many a century, monuments of their happy, industrious lives.

But there is a little airy, elfin animal in these woods, and in all the evergreen woods of the Pacific Coast, that is more influential and interesting than even the beaver. This is the Douglas squirrel (*Sciurus Douglasi*). Go where you will throughout all these noble forests, you everywhere find this little squirrel the master-existence. Though only a few inches long, so intense is his fiery vigour and restlessness, he stirs every grove with wild life, and makes himself more important than the great bears that shuffle through the berry tangles beneath him. Every tree feels the sting of his sharp feet.

Nature has made him master-forester, and committed the greater part of the coniferous crops to his management. Probably over half of all the ripe cones of the spruces, firs and pines are cut off and handled by this busy harvester. Most of them are stored away for food through the winter and spring, but a part are pushed into shallow pits and covered loosely, where some of the seeds are no doubt left to germinate and grow up. All the tree squirrels are more or less birdlike in voice and movements, but the Douglas is pre-eminently so, possessing every squirrelish attribute, fully developed and concentrated. He is the squirrel of squirrels, flashing from branch to branch of his favourite evergreens, crisp and glossy and sound as a sunbeam. He stirs the leaves like a rustling breeze, darting across openings in arrowy lines, launching in curves, glinting deftly from side to side in sudden zigzags, and swirling in giddy loops and spirals around the trunks, now on his haunches, now on his head, yet ever graceful and performing all his feats of strength and skill without apparent effort. One never tires of this bright spark of life, the brave little voice crying in the wilderness. His varied, piney gossip is as savoury to the air as balsam to the palate. Some of his notes are almost flutelike in softness, while others prick and tingle like thistles. He is the mockingbird of squirrels, barking like a dog, screaming like a hawk, whistling like a blackbird or linnet, while in bluff, audacious noisiness he is a jay. A small thing, but filling and animating all the woods.

Nor is there any lack of wings, notwithstanding few are to be seen on short, noisy rambles. The ouzel sweetens the shady glens and canyons where waterfalls abound, and every grove or forest, however silent it may seem when we chance to pay it a hasty visit, has its singers – thrushes, linnets, warblers – while hummingbirds glint and hover about the fringing masses of bloom around stream and meadow openings. But few of these will show themselves or sing their songs to those who are ever in haste and getting lost, going in gangs formidable in colour and accoutrements, laughing, hallooing, breaking limbs off the trees as they pass, awkwardly struggling through briery thickets, entangled like bluebottles in spider-webs, and stopping from time to time to fire off their guns and pistols for the sake of the echoes, thus frightening all the life about them for miles. It is this class of hunters and travellers who report that there are 'no birds in the woods or game animals of any kind larger than mosquitoes'.

Besides the singing-birds mentioned above, the handsome Oregon grouse may be found in the thick woods, also the dusky grouse and Franklin's grouse, and in some places the beautiful mountain partridge, or quail. The white-tailed ptarmigan lives on the lofty snow peaks above the timber, and the prairie-chicken and sage-cock on the broad Columbia plains from the Cascade Range back to the foothills of the Rocky Mountains. The bald eagle is very common along the Columbia River, or wherever fish, especially salmon, are plentiful, while swans, herons, cranes, pelicans, geese, ducks of many species and water-birds in general abound in the lake region, on the main streams, and along the coast, stirring the waters and sky into fine, lively pictures, greatly to the delight of wandering lovers of wildness.

CHAPTER TWENTY THREE

The Rivers of Oregon

TURNING FROM the woods and their inhabitants to the rivers, we find that while the former are rarely seen by travellers beyond the immediate borders of the settlements, the great river of Oregon draws crowds of visitors, and is never without enthusiastic admirers to sound its praises. Every summer since the completion of the first overland railroad, tourists have been coming to it in ever increasing numbers, showing that in general estimation the Columbia is one of the chief attractions of the Pacific Coast. And well it deserves the admiration so heartily bestowed upon it. The beauty and majesty of its waters, and the variety and grandeur of the scenery through which it flows, lead many to regard it as the most interesting of all the great rivers of the continent, notwithstanding the claims of the other members of the family to which it belongs and which nobody can measure – the Fraser, McKenzie, Saskatchewan, the Missouri, Yellowstone, Platte and the Colorado, with their glacier and geyser fountains, their famous canyons, lakes, forests and vast flowery prairies and plains. These great rivers and the Columbia are intimately related. All draw their upper waters from the same high fountains on the broad, rugged uplift of the Rocky Mountains, their branches interlacing like the branches of trees. They sing their first songs together on the heights; then, collecting their tributaries, they set out on their grand journey to the Atlantic, Pacific, or Arctic Ocean.

The Columbia, viewed as one from the sea to the mountains, is like a rugged, broad-topped, picturesque old oak about six hundred miles long and nearly a thousand miles wide measured across the spread of its upper branches, the main limbs gnarled and swollen with lakes and lakelike expansions, while innumerable smaller lakes shine like fruit among the smaller branches. The main trunk extends back through the Coast and Cascade Mountains in a general easterly direction for three hundred miles, when it divides abruptly into two grand branches which bend off to the northeastward and southeastward.

The south branch, the longer of the two, called the Snake, or Lewis, River, extends into the Rocky Mountains as far as the Yellowstone National Park, where its head tributaries interlace with those of the Colorado, Missouri and Yellowstone. The north branch, still called the Columbia, extends through Washington far into British territory, its highest tributaries reaching back through long parallel spurs of the Rockies between and beyond the headwaters of the Fraser, Athabasca and Saskatchewan. Each of these main branches, dividing again and again, spreads a network of channels over the vast complicated mass of the great range throughout a section nearly a thousand miles in length, searching every fountain, however small or great, and gathering a glorious harvest of crystal water to be rolled through forest and plain in one majestic flood to the sea, reinforced on the way by tributaries that drain the Blue Mountains and more than two hundred miles of the Cascade and Coast Ranges. Though less than half as long as the Mississippi, it is said to carry as much water. The amount of its discharge at different seasons, however, has never been exactly measured, but in time of flood its current is sufficiently massive and powerful to penetrate the sea to a distance of fifty or sixty miles from shore, its waters being easily recognized by the difference in colour and by the drift of leaves, berries, pine cones, branches and trunks of trees that they carry.

That so large a river as the Columbia, making a telling current so far from shore, should remain undiscovered while one exploring expedition after another sailed past seems remarkable, even after due allowance is made for the cloudy weather that prevails hereabouts and the broad fence of breakers drawn across the bar. During the last few centuries, when the maps of the world were in great part blank, the search for new worlds was a fashionable business, and when such large game was no longer to be found, islands lying unclaimed in the great oceans, inhabited by useful and profitable people to be converted or enslaved, became attractive objects; also new ways to India, seas, straits, El Dorados, fountains of youth and rivers that flowed over golden sands.

Those early explorers and adventurers were mostly brave, enterprising, and, after their fashion, pious men. In their clumsy sailing-vessels they dared to go where no chart or lighthouse showed the way, where the set of the currents, the location of sunken outlying rocks and shoals, were all unknown, facing fate and weather, undaunted however dark the signs, heaving the lead and thrashing the men to their duty and trusting to Providence. When a new shore was found on which they could land, they said their prayers with superb audacity, fought the natives if they cared to fight, erected crosses and took possession in the names of their sovereigns, establishing claims, such as they were, to everything in sight and beyond, to be quarrelled for and battled for, and passed from hand to hand in treaties and settlements made during the intermissions of war.

The branch of the river that bears the name of Columbia all the way to its head takes its rise in two lakes about ten miles in length that lie between the Selkirk and main ranges of the Rocky Mountains in British Columbia, about eighty miles beyond the boundary-line. They are called the Upper and Lower Columbia Lakes. Issuing from these, the young river holds a nearly straight course for a hundred and seventy miles in a northwesterly direction to a plain called 'Boat Encampment', receiving many beautiful affluents by the way from the Selkirk and main ranges, among which are the Beaver-Foot, Blackberry, Spill-e-Mee-Chene and Gold Rivers. At Boat Encampment it receives two large tributaries, the Canoe River from the northwest, a stream about a hundred and twenty miles long; and the Whirlpool River from the north, about a hundred and forty miles in length.

The Whirlpool River takes its rise near the summit of the main axis of the range on the fifty-fourth parallel, and is the northmost of all the Columbia waters. About thirty miles above its confluence with the Columbia it flows through a lake called the Punch-Bowl, and thence it passes between Mounts Hooker and Brown, said to be fifteen thousand and sixteen thousand feet high, making magnificent scenery; though the height of the mountains thereabouts has been considerably over-estimated. From Boat Encampment the river, now a large, clear stream, said to be nearly a third of a mile in width, doubles back on its original course and flows southward as far as its confluence with the Spokane in Washington, a distance of nearly three hundred miles in a direct line, most of the way through a wild, rocky, picturesque mass of mountains, charmingly forested with pine and spruce – though the trees seem strangely small, like second growth saplings, to one familiar with the western forests of Washington, Oregon and California.

About forty-five miles below Boat Encampment are the Upper Dalles, or Dalles de Mort, and thirty miles farther the Lower Dalles, where the river makes a magnificent uproar and interrupts navigation. About thirty miles below the Lower Dalles the river expands into Upper Arrow Lake, a beautiful sheet of water forty miles long and five miles wide, straight as an arrow and with the beautiful forests of the Selkirk range rising from its east shore, and those of the Gold range from the west. At the foot of the lake are the Narrows, a few miles in length, and after these rapids are passed, the river enters Lower Arrow Lake, which is like the Upper Arrow, but is even longer and not so straight.

A short distance below the Lower Arrow the Columbia receives the Kootenay River, the largest affluent thus far on its course and said to be navigable for small steamers for a hundred and fifty miles. It is an exceedingly crooked stream, heading beyond the upper Columbia lakes, and, in its mazy course, flowing to all points of the compass, it seems lost and baffled in the tangle of mountain spurs and ridges it drains. Measured around its loops and bends, it is probably more than five hundred miles in length. It is also rich in lakes, the largest, Kootenay Lake, being upwards of seventy miles in length with an average width of five miles. A short distance below the confluence of the Kootenay, near the boundary-line between Washington and British Columbia, another large stream comes in from the east, Clarke's Fork, or the Flathead River. Its upper sources are near those of the Missouri and South Saskatchewan, and in its course it flows through two large and beautiful lakes, the Flathead and the Pend d'Oreille. All the lakes we have noticed thus far would make charming places of summer resort; but Pend d'Oreille, besides being surpassingly beautiful, has the advantage of being easily accessible, since it is on the main line of the Northern Pacific Railroad in the Territory of Idaho. In the purity of its waters it reminds one of Tahoe, while its many picturesque islands crowned with evergreens, and its winding shores forming an endless variety of bays and promontories lavishly crowded with spirey spruce and cedar, recall some of the best of the island scenery of Alaska.

About thirty-five miles below the mouth of Clarke's Fork the Columbia is joined by the Ne-whoi-al-pit-ku River from the northwest. Here too are the great Chaudière, or Kettle Falls on the main river, with a total descent of about fifty feet. Fifty miles farther down, the Spokane River, a clear, dashing stream, comes in from the east. It is about one hundred and twenty miles long, and takes its rise in the beautiful Lake Cœur d'Alène, in Idaho, which receives the drainage of nearly a hundred miles of the western slopes of the Bitter Root Mountains, through the St Joseph and Cœur d'Alène Rivers. The lake is about twenty miles long, set in the midst of charming scenery, and, like Pend d'Oreille, is easy of access and is already attracting attention as a summer place for enjoyment, rest and health.

The famous Spokane Falls are in Washington, about thirty miles below the lake, where the river is outspread and divided and makes a grand descent from a level basaltic plateau, giving rise to one of the most beautiful as well as one of the greatest and most available of water-powers in the State. The city of the same name is built on the plateau along both sides of the series of cascades and falls, which, rushing and sounding through the midst, give singular beauty and animation. The young city is also rushing and booming. It is founded on a rock, levelled and prepared for it, and its streets require no grading or paving. As a power to whirl the machinery of a great city and at the same time to train the people to a love of the sublime and beautiful as displayed in living water, the Spokane Falls are unrivalled, at least as far as my observation has reached. Nowhere else have I seen such lessons given by a river in the streets of a city, such a glad, exulting, abounding outgush, crisp and clear from the mountains, dividing, falling, displaying its wealth, calling aloud in the midst of the busy throng, and making glorious offerings for every use of utility or adornment.

From the mouth of the Spokane the Columbia, now out of the woods, flows to the westward with a broad, stately current for a hundred and twenty miles to receive the Okinagan, a large, generous tributary a hundred and sixty miles long, coming from the north and drawing some of its waters from the Cascade Range. More than half its course is through a chain of lakes, the largest of which at the head of the river is over sixty miles in length. From its confluence with the Okinagan the river pursues a southerly course for a hundred and fifty miles, most of the way through a dreary, treeless, parched plain to meet the great south fork. The Lewis, or Snake River is nearly a thousand miles long and drains nearly the whole of Idaho, a territory rich in scenery, gold mines, flowery, grassy valleys and deserts, while some of the highest tributaries reach into Wyoming, Utah and Nevada. Throughout a great part of its course it is countersunk in a black lava plain and shut in by mural precipices a thousand feet high, gloomy, forbidding and unapproachable, although the gloominess of its canyon is relieved in some manner by its many falls and springs, some of the springs being large enough to appear as the outlets of subterranean rivers. They gush out from the faces of the sheer black walls and descend foaming with brave roar and beauty to swell the flood below.

From where the river skirts the base of the Blue Mountains its surroundings are less forbidding. Much of the country is fertile, but its canyon is everywhere deep and almost inaccessible. Steamers make their way up as far as Lewiston, a hundred and fifty miles, and receive cargoes of wheat at different points through chutes that extend down from the tops of the bluffs. But though the Hudson's Bay Company navigated the north fork to its courses, they depended altogether on pack-animals for the transportation of supplies and furs between the Columbia and Fort Hall on the head of the south fork, which shows how desperately unmanageable a river it must be.

A few miles above the mouth of the Snake the Yakima, which drains a considerable portion of the Cascade Range, enters from the northwest. It is about a hundred and fifty miles long, but carries comparatively little water, a great part of what it sets out with from the base of the mountains being consumed in irrigated fields and meadows in passing through the settlements along its course, and by evaporation on the parched desert plains. The grand flood of the Columbia, now from half a mile to a mile wide, sweeps on to the westward, holding a nearly direct course until it reaches the mouth of the Willamette, where it turns to the northward and flows fifty miles along the main valley between the Coast and Cascade Ranges ere it again resumes its westward course to the sea. In all its course from the mouth of the Yakima to the sea, a distance of three hundred miles, the only considerable affluent from the northward is the Cowlitz, which heads in the glaciers of Mount Rainier.

From the south and east it receives the Walla-Walla and Umatilla, rather short and dreary-looking streams, though the plains they pass through have proved fertile, and their upper tributaries in the Blue Mountains, shaded with tall pines, firs, spruces and the beautiful Oregon larch (*Larix brevifolia*), lead into a delightful region. The John Day River also heads in the Blue Mountains, and flows into the Columbia sixty miles below the mouth of the Umatilla. Its valley is in great part fertile, and is noted for the interesting fossils discovered in it by Professor Condon in sections cut by the river through the overlying lava-beds.

The Deschutes River comes in from the south about twenty miles below the John Day. It is a large, boisterous stream, draining the eastern slope of the Cascade Range for nearly two hundred miles, and from the great number of falls on the main trunk, as well as on its many mountain tributaries, well deserves its name. It enters the Columbia with a grand roar of falls and rapids, and at times seems almost to rival the main stream in the volume of water it carries. Near the mouth of the Deschutes are the Falls of the Columbia, where the river passes a rough bar of lava. The descent is not great, but the immense volume of water makes a grand display. During the flood-season the falls are obliterated and skilful boatmen pass over them in safety; while the Dalles, some six or eight miles below, may be passed during low water but are utterly impassable in flood-time. At the Dalles the vast river is jammed together into a long, narrow slot of unknown depth cut sheer down in the basalt.

This slot, or trough, is about a mile and a half long and about sixty yards wide at the narrowest place. At ordinary times the river seems to be set on edge and runs swiftly but without much noisy surging with a descent of about twenty feet to the mile. But when the snow is melting on the mountains the river rises here sixty feet, or even more during extraordinary freshets, and spreads out over a great breadth of massive rocks through which have been cut several other gorges running parallel with the one usually occupied.

All these inferior gorges now come into use, and the huge, roaring torrent, still rising and spreading, at length overwhelms the high jagged rock walls between them, making a tremendous display of chafing, surging, shattered currents, counter-currents and hollow whirls that no words can be made to describe. A few miles below the Dalles the storm-tossed river gets itself together again, looks like water, becomes silent, and with stately, tranquil deliberation goes on its way, out of the grey region of sage and sand into the Oregon woods. Thirty-five or forty miles below the Dalles are the Cascades of the Columbia, where the river in passing through the mountains makes another magnificent display of foaming, surging rapids, which form the first obstruction to navigation from the ocean, a hundred and twenty miles distant. This obstruction is to be overcome by locks, which are now being made.

Between the Dalles and the Cascades the river is like a lake a mile or two wide, lying in a valley, or canyon, about three thousand feet deep. The walls of the canyon lean well back in most places, and leave here and there small strips, or bays of level ground along the water's edge. But towards the Cascades, and for some distance below them, the immediate banks are guarded by walls of columnar basalt, which are worn in many places into a great variety of bold and picturesque forms, such as the Cashe Rock, the Rooster Rock, the Pillars of Hercules, Cape Horn, etc., while back of these rise the sublime mountain-walls, forest-crowned and fringed more or less from top to base with pine, spruce and shaggy underbrush, especially in the narrow gorges and ravines, where innumerable small streams come dancing and drifting down, misty and white, to join the mighty river. Many of these falls on both sides of the canyon of the Columbia are far larger and more interesting in every way than would be guessed from the slight glimpses one gets of them while sailing past on the river or from the car windows. The Multnoman Falls are particularly interesting, and occupy fern-lined gorges of marvellous beauty in the basalt. They are said to be about eight hundred feet in height and, at times of high water when the mountain snows are melting, are well worthy of a place beside the famous falls of the Yosemite Valley.

According to an Indian tradition, the river of the Cascades once flowed through the basalt beneath a natural bridge that was broken down during a mountain war, when the old volcanoes, Hood and St Helen's, on opposite sides of the river, hurled rocks at each other, thus forming a dam. That the river has been dammed here to some extent, and within a comparatively short period, seems probable to say the least, since great numbers of submerged trees standing erect may be found along both shores, while, as we have seen, the whole river for thirty miles above the Cascades looks like a lake or mill-pond. On the other hand, it is held by some that the submerged groves were carried into their places by immense landslides.

Much of interest in this connection must necessarily be omitted for want of space. About forty miles below the Cascades the river receives the Willamette, the last of its great tributaries. It is navigable for ocean vessels as far as Portland, ten miles above its mouth, and for river steamers a hundred miles farther. The Falls of the Willamette are fifteen miles above Portland, where the river, coming out of dense woods, breaks its way across a bar of black basalt and falls forty feet in a passion of snowy foam, showing to fine advantage against its background of evergreens.

Of the fertility and beauty of the Willamette all the world has heard. It lies between the Cascade and Coast Ranges, and is bounded on the south by the Calapooya Mountains, a cross-spur that separates it from the valley of the Umpqua.

It was here the first settlements for agriculture were made and a provisional government organized, while the settlers, isolated in the far wilderness, numbered only a few thousand and were labouring under the opposition of the British Government and the Hudson's Bay Company. Eager desire in the acquisition of territory on the part of these pioneer state-builders was more truly boundless than the wilderness they were in, and their unconscionable patriotism was equalled only by their belligerence. For here, while negotiations were pending for the location of the northern boundary, originated the celebrated 'Fifty-four forty or fight', about as reasonable a war-cry as the 'North Pole or fight'. Yet sad was the day that brought the news of the signing of the treaty fixing their boundary along the forty-ninth parallel, thus leaving the little land-hungry settlement only a mere quarter-million of miles!

As the Willamette is one of the most foodful of valleys, so is the Columbia one of the most foodful of rivers. During the fisher's harvest-time salmon from the sea come in countless millions, urging their way against falls, rapids and shallows, up into the very heart of the Rocky Mountains, supplying everybody by the way with most bountiful masses of delicious food, weighing from twenty to eighty pounds each, plump and smooth like loaves of bread ready for the oven. The supply seemed inexhaustible, as well it might. Large quantities were used by the Indians as fuel, and by the Hudson's Bay people as manure for their gardens at the forts. Used, wasted, canned and sent in shiploads to all the world, a grand harvest was reaped every year while nobody sowed. Of late, however, the salmon crop has begun to fail, and millions of young fry are now sown like wheat in the river every year, from hatching-establishments belonging to the Government.

All of the Oregon waters that win their way to the sea are tributary to the Columbia, save the short streams of the immediate coast, and the Umpqua and Rogue Rivers in southern Oregon. These both head in the Cascade Mountains and find their way to the sea through gaps in the Coast Range, and both drain large and fertile and beautiful valleys. Rogue River Valley is peculiarly attractive. With a fine climate, and kindly, productive soil, the scenery is delightful. About the main, central open portion of the basin, dotted with picturesque groves of oak, there are many smaller valleys charmingly environed, the whole surrounded in the distance by the Siskiyou, Coast, Umpqua and Cascade Mountains. Besides the cereals nearly every sort of fruit flourishes here, and large areas are being devoted to peach, apricot, nectarine and vine culture. To me it seems above all others the garden valley of Oregon and the most delightful place for a home. On the eastern rim of the valley, in the Cascade Mountains, about sixty miles from Medford in a direct line, is the remarkable Crater Lake, usually regarded as the one grand wonder of the region. It lies in a deep, sheer-walled basin about seven thousand feet above the level of the sea, supposed to be the crater of an extinct volcano.

Oregon as it is today is a very young country, though most of it seems old. Contemplating the Columbia sweeping from forest to forest, across plain and desert, one is led to say of it, as did Byron of the ocean –

'Such as Creation's dawn beheld, thou rollest now.'

How ancient appear the crumbling basaltic monuments along its banks, and the grey plains to the east of the Cascades! Nevertheless, the river as well as its basin in anything like their present condition are comparatively but of yesterday. Looming no further back in the geological records than the Tertiary Period, the Oregon of that time looks altogether strange in the few suggestive glimpses we may get of it – forests in which palm trees wave their royal crowns, and strange animals roaming beneath them or about the reedy margins of lakes, the oreodon, the lophiodon and several extinct species of the horse, the camel and other animals.

Then came the fire period with its darkening showers of ashes and cinders and its vast floods of molten lava, making quite another Oregon from the fair and fertile land of the preceding era. And again, while yet the volcanic fires show signs of action in the smoke and flame of the higher mountains, the whole region passes under the dominion of ice, and from the frost and darkness and death of the Glacial Period, Oregon has but recently emerged to the kindly warmth and life of today.

CHAPTER TWENTY FOUR

The Grand Canyon of the Colorado

HAPPY NOWADAYS is the tourist with earth's wonders, new and old, spread invitingly open before him, and a host of able workers as his slaves making everything easy, padding plush about him, grading roads for him, boring tunnels, moving hills out of his way, eager, like the Devil, to show him all the kingdoms of the world and their glory and foolishness, spiritualizing travel for him with lightning and steam, abolishing space and time and almost everything else. Little children and tender, pulpy people, as well as storm-seasoned explorers, may now go almost everywhere in smooth comfort, cross oceans and deserts scarce accessible to fishes and birds, and, dragged by steel horses, go up high mountains, riding gloriously beneath starry showers of sparks, ascending like Elijah in a whirlwind and chariot of fire.

First of the wonders of the great West to be brought within reach of the tourist were the Yosemite and the Big Trees, on the completion of the first transcontinental railway; next came the Yellowstone and icy Alaska, by the northern roads; and last the Grand Canyon of the Colorado, which, naturally the hardest to reach, has now become, by a branch of the Santa Fé, the most accessible of all.

Of course, with this wonderful extension of steel ways through our wildness there is loss as well as gain. Nearly all railroads are bordered by belts of desolation. The finest wilderness perishes as if stricken with pestilence. Bird and beast people, if not the dryads, are frightened from the groves. Too often the groves also vanish, leaving nothing but ashes. Fortunately, nature has a few big places beyond man's power to spoil – the ocean, the two icy ends of the globe, and the Grand Canyon.

When I first heard of the Santa Fé trains running to the edge of the Grand Canyon of Arizona, I was troubled with thoughts of the disenchantment likely to follow. But last winter, when I saw those trains crawling along through the pines of the Coconino Forest and close up to the brink of the chasm at Bright Angel, I was glad to discover that in the presence of such stupendous scenery they are nothing. The locomotives and trains are mere beetles and caterpillars, and the noise they make is as little disturbing as the hooting of an owl in the lonely woods.

In a dry, hot, monotonous forested plateau, seemingly boundless, you come suddenly and without warning upon the abrupt edge of a gigantic sunken landscape of the wildest, most multitudinous features, and those features, sharp and angular, are made out of flat beds of limestone and sandstone forming a spiry, jagged, gloriously coloured mountain-range countersunk in a level grey plain. It is a hard job to sketch it even in scrawniest outline; and, try as I may, not in the least sparing myself, I cannot tell the hundredth part of the wonders of its features – the side-canyons, gorges, alcoves, cloisters and amphitheatres of vast sweep and depth, carved in its magnificent walls; the throng of great architectural rocks it contains resembling castles, cathedrals, temples and palaces, towered and spired and painted, some of them nearly a mile high, yet beneath one's feet. All this, however, is less difficult than to give any idea of the impression of wild, primeval beauty and power one receives in merely gazing from its brink. The view down the gulf of colour and over the rim of its wonderful wall, more than any other view I know, leads us to think of our earth as a star with stars swimming in light, every radiant spire pointing the way to the heavens.

But it is impossible to conceive what the canyon is, or what impression it makes, from descriptions or pictures, however good. Naturally it is untellable even to those who have seen something perhaps a little like it on a small scale in this same plateau region. One's most extravagant expectations are indefinitely surpassed, though one expects much from what is said of it as 'the biggest chasm on earth' – 'so big is it that all other big things – Yosemite, the Yellowstone, the Pyramids, Chicago – all would be lost if tumbled into it.' Naturally enough, illustrations as to size are sought for among other canyons like or unlike it, with the common result of worse confounding confusion. The prudent keep silence. It was once said that the 'Grand Canyon could put a dozen Yosemites in its vest pocket'.

The justly famous Grand Canyon of the Yellowstone is, like the Colorado, gorgeously coloured and abruptly countersunk in a plateau, and both are mainly the work of water. But the Colorado's canyon is more than a thousand times larger, and as a score or two of new buildings of ordinary size would not appreciably change the general view of a great city, so hundreds of Yellowstones might be eroded in the sides of the Colorado Canyon without noticeably augmenting its size or the richness of its sculpture.

But it is not true that the great Yosemite rocks would be thus lost or hidden. Nothing of their kind in the world, so far as I know, rivals El Capitan and Tissiack, much less dwarfs or in any way belittles them. None of the sandstone or limestone precipices of the canyon that I have seen or heard of approaches in smooth, flawless strength and grandeur the granite face of El Capitan or the Tenaya side of Cloud's Rest. These colossal cliffs, types of permanence, are about three thousand and six thousand feet high; those of the canyon that are sheer are about half as high, and are types of fleeting change; while glorious-domed Tissiack, noblest of mountain buildings, far from being over-shadowed or lost in this rosy, spiry canyon company, would draw every eye, and, in serene majesty, 'aboon them a'' she would take her place – castle, temple, palace, or tower. Nevertheless a noted writer, comparing the Grand Canyon in a general way with the glacial Yosemite, says: 'And the Yosemite – ah, the lovely Yosemite! Dumped down into the wilderness of gorges and mountains, it would take a guide who knew of its existence a long time to find it.' This is striking, and shows up well above the levels of commonplace description; but it is confusing, and has the fatal fault of not being true. As well try to describe an eagle by putting a lark in it. 'And, the lark – ah, the lovely lark! Dumped down the red, royal gorge of the eagle, it would be hard to find.' Each in its own place is better, singing at heaven's gate, and sailing the sky with the clouds.

Every feature of Nature's big face is beautiful – height and hollow, wrinkle, furrow, and line – and this is the main master-furrow of its kind on our continent, incomparably greater and more impressive than any other yet discovered, or likely to be discovered, now that all the great rivers have been traced to their heads.

The Colorado River rises in the heart of the continent on the dividing ranges and ridges between the two oceans, drains thousands of snowy mountains through narrow or spacious valleys, and thence through canyons of every colour, sheer-walled and deep, all of which seem to be represented in this one grand canyon of canyons.

It is very hard to give anything like an adequate conception of its size; much more of its colour, its vast wall-sculpture, the wealth of ornate architectural buildings that fill it, or, most of all, the tremendous impression it makes. According to Major Powell, it is about two hundred and seventeen miles long, from five to fifteen miles wide from rim to rim, and from about five thousand to six thousand feet deep. So tremendous a chasm would be one of the world's greatest wonders even if, like ordinary canyons cut in sedimentary rocks, it were empty and its walls were simple. But instead of being plain, the walls are so deeply and elaborately carved into all sorts of recesses – alcoves, cirques, amphitheatres and side-canyons – that, were you to trace the rim closely around on both sides, your journey would be nearly a thousand miles long. Into all these recesses the level, continuous beds of rock in ledges and benches, with their various colours, run like broad ribbons, marvellously beautiful and effective even at a distance of ten or twelve miles. And the vast space these glorious walls enclose, instead of being empty, is crowded with gigantic architectural rock-forms gorgeously coloured and adorned with towers and spires like works of art.

Looking down from this level plateau, we are more impressed with a feeling of being on the top of everything than when looking from the summit of a mountain. From side to side of the vast gulf, temples, palaces, towers and spires come soaring up in thick array half a mile or nearly a mile above their sunken, hidden bases, some to a level with our standpoint, but none higher. And in the inspiring morning light all are so fresh and rosy-looking that they seem new-born; as if, like the quick-growing crimson snow-plants of the California woods, they had just sprung up, hatched by the warm, brooding, motherly weather.

In trying to describe the great pines and sequoias of the Sierra, I have often thought that if one of these trees could be set by itself in some city park, its grandeur might there be impressively realized; while in its home forests, where all magnitudes are great, the weary, satiated traveller sees none of them truly. It is so with these majestic rock structures.

Though mere residual masses of the plateau, they are dowered with the grandeur and repose of mountains, together with the finely chiselled carving and modelling of man's temples and palaces, and often, to a considerable extent, with their symmetry. Some, closely observed, look like ruins; but even these stand plumb and true, and show architectural forms loaded with lines strictly regular and decorative, and all are arrayed in colours that storms and time seem only to brighten. They are not placed in regular rows in line with the river, but 'a' through ither', as the Scotch say, in lavish, exuberant crowds, as if nature in wildest extravagance held her bravest structures as common as gravel-piles. Yonder stands a spiry cathedral nearly five thousand feet in height, nobly symmetrical, with sheer buttressed walls and arched doors and windows, as richly finished and decorated with sculptures as the great rock temples of India or Egypt. Beside it rises a huge castle with arched gateway, turrets, watch-towers, ramparts, etc., and to right and left palaces, obelisks and pyramids fairly fill the gulf, all colossal and all lavishly painted and carved. Here and there a flat-topped structure may be seen, or one imperfectly domed; but the prevailing style is ornate Gothic, with many hints of Egyptian and Indian.

Throughout this vast extent of wild architecture – nature's own capital city – there seem to be no ordinary dwellings. All look like grand and important public structures, except perhaps some of the lower pyramids, broad-based and sharp-pointed, covered with down-flowing talus like loosely set tents with hollow, sagging sides. The roofs often have disintegrated rocks heaped and draggled over them, but in the main the masonry is firm and laid in regular courses, as if done by square and rule.

Nevertheless they are ever changing: their tops are now a dome, now a flat table or a spire, as harder or softer strata are reached in their slow degradation, while the sides, with all their fine mouldings, are being steadily undermined and eaten away. But no essential change in style or colour is thus effected. From century to century they stand the same. What seems confusion among the rough earthquake-shaken crags nearest one comes to order as soon as the main plan of the various structures appears. Every building, however complicated and laden with ornamental lines, is at one with itself and every one of its neighbours, for the same characteristic controlling belts of colour and solid strata extend with wonderful constancy for very great distances, and pass through and give style to thousands of separate structures, however their smaller characters may vary.

Of all the various kinds of ornamental work displayed – carving, tracery on cliff-faces, mouldings, arches, pinnacles – none is more admirably effective or charms more than the webs of rain-channelled taluses. Marvellously extensive, without the slightest appearance of waste or excess, they cover roofs and dome-tops and the base of every cliff, belt each spire and pyramid and massy, towering temple, and in beautiful continuous lines go sweeping along the great walls in and out around all the intricate system of side-canyons, amphitheatres, cirques and scallops into which they are sculptured. From one point hundreds of miles of this fairy embroidery may be traced. It is all so fine and orderly that it would seem that not only had the clouds and streams been kept harmoniously busy in the making of it, but that every raindrop sent like a bullet to a mark had been the subject of a separate thought, so sure is the outcome of beauty through the stormy centuries. Surely nowhere else are there illustrations so striking of the natural beauty of desolation and death, so many of nature's own mountain buildings wasting in glory of high desert air – going to dust. See how steadfast in beauty they all are in their going. Look again and again how the rough, dusty boulders and sand of disintegration from the upper ledges wreathe in beauty the next and next below with these wonderful taluses, and how the colours are finer and faster the waste. We oftentimes see Nature giving beauty for ashes – as in the flowers of a prairie after fire – but here the very dust and ashes are beautiful.

Gazing across the mighty chasm, we at last discover that it is not its great depth nor length, nor yet these wonderful buildings, that most impresses us. It is its immense width, sharply defined by precipitous walls plunging suddenly down from a flat plain, declaring in terms instantly apprehended that the vast gulf is a gash in the once unbroken plateau, made by slow, orderly erosion and removal of huge beds of rocks. Other valleys of erosion are as great – in all their dimensions some are greater – but none of these produces an effect on the imagination at once so quick and profound, coming without study, given at a glance. Therefore by far the greatest and most influential feature of this view from Bright Angel or any other of the canyon views is the opposite wall. Of the one beneath our feet we see only fragmentary sections in cirques and amphitheatres and on the sides of the out-jutting promontories between them, while the other, though far distant, is beheld in all its glory of colour and noble proportions – the one supreme beauty and wonder to which the eye is ever turning. For while charming with its beauty it tells the story of the stupendous erosion of the canyon – the foundation of the unspeakable impression made on everybody. It seems a gigantic statement for even nature to make, all in one mighty stone word, apprehended at once like a burst of light, celestial colour its natural vesture, coming in glory to mind and heart as to a home prepared for it from the very beginning. Wildness so godful, cosmic, primeval, bestows a new sense of earth's beauty and size. Not even from high mountains does the world seem so wide, so like a star in glory of light on its way through the heavens.

I have observed scenery-hunters of all sorts getting first views of yosemites, glaciers, White Mountain ranges, etc. Mixed with the enthusiasm which such scenery naturally excites, there is often weak gushing, and many splutter aloud like little waterfalls. Here, for a few moments at least, there is silence, and all are in dead earnest, as if awed and hushed by an earthquake – perhaps until the cook cries 'Breakfast!' or the stable-boy 'Horses are ready!' Then the poor unfortunates, slaves of regular habits, turn quickly away, gasping and muttering as if wondering where they had been and what had enchanted them.

Roads have been made from Bright Angel Hotel through the Coconino Forest to the ends of outstanding promontories, commanding extensive views up and down the canyon. The nearest of them, three or four miles east and west, are O'Neill's Point and Rowe's Point; the latter, besides commanding the eternally interesting canyon, gives wide-sweeping views southeast and west over the dark forest roof to the San Francisco and Mount Trumbull volcanoes – the bluest of mountains over the blackest of level woods.

Instead of thus riding in dust with the crowd, more will be gained by going quietly afoot along the rim at different times of day and night, free to observe the vegetation, the fossils in the rocks, the seams beneath overhanging ledges once inhabited by Indians, and to watch the stupendous scenery in the changing lights and shadows, clouds, showers and storms. One need not go hunting the so-called 'points of interest'. The verge anywhere, everywhere, is a point of interest beyond one's wildest dreams.

As yet, few of the promontories or throng of mountain buildings in the canyon are named. Nor among such exuberance of forms are names thought of by the bewildered, hurried tourist. He would be as likely to think of names for waves in a storm. The Eastern and Western Cloisters, Hindu Amphitheatre, Cape Royal, Powell's Plateau, Grand View Point, Point Sublime, Bissell and Moran Points, the Temple of Set, Vishnu's Temple, Shiva's Temple, Twin Temples, Tower of Babel, Hance's Column – these fairly good names given by Dutton, Holmes, Moran and others are scattered over a large stretch of the canyon wilderness.

All the canyon rock-beds are lavishly painted, except a few neutral bars and the granite notch at the bottom occupied by the river, which makes but little sign. It is a vast wilderness of rocks in a sea of light, coloured and glowing like oak and maple woods in autumn, when the sun-gold is richest. I have just said that it is impossible to learn what the canyon is like from descriptions and pictures. Powell's and Dutton's descriptions present magnificent views not only of the canyon but of all the grand region round about it; and Holmes's drawings, accompanying Dutton's report, are wonderfully good.

Surely faithful and loving skill can go no farther in putting the multitudinous decorated forms on paper. But the *colours*, the living, rejoicing *colours*, chanting morning and evening in chorus to heaven! Whose brush or pencil, however lovingly inspired, can give us these? And if paint is of no effect, what hope lies in pen-work? Only this: some may be incited by it to go and see for themselves.

No other range of mountainous rock-work of anything like the same extent have I seen that is so strangely, boldly, lavishly coloured. The famous Yellowstone Canyon below the falls comes to mind; but, wonderful as it is, and well deserved as is its fame, compared with this it is only a bright rainbow ribbon at the roots of the pines. Each of the series of level, continuous beds of carboniferous rocks of the canyon has, as we have seen, its own characteristic colour. The summit limestone-beds are pale yellow; next below these are the beautiful rose-coloured cross-bedded sandstones; next there are a thousand feet of brilliant red sandstones; and below these the red wall limestones, over two thousand feet thick, rich massy red, the greatest and most influential of the series, and forming the main colour-fountain. Between these are many neutral-tinted beds. The prevailing colours are wonderfully deep and clear, changing and blending with varying intensity from hour to hour, day to day, season to season; throbbing, wavering, glowing, responding to every passing cloud or storm, a world of colour in itself, now burning in separate rainbow bars streaked and blotched with shade, now glowing in one smooth, all-pervading ethereal radiance like the alpenglow, uniting the rocky world with the heavens.

The dawn, as in all the pure, dry desert country is ineffably beautiful; and when the first level sunbeams string the domes and spires, with what a burst of power the big, wild days begin! The dead and the living, rocks and hearts alike, awake and sing the new-old song of creation. All the massy headlands and salient angles of the walls, and the multitudinous temples and palaces, seem to catch the light at once, and cast thick black shadows athwart hollow and gorge, bringing out details as well as the main massive features of the architecture; while all the rocks, as if wild with life, throb and quiver and glow in the glorious sunburst, rejoicing. Every rock temple then becomes a temple of music; every spire and pinnacle an angel of light and song, shouting colour hallelujahs.

As the day draws to a close, shadows, wondrous, black and thick, like those of the morning, fill up the wall hollows, while the glowing rocks, their rough angles burned off seem soft and hot to the heart as they stand submerged in purple haze, which now fills the canyon like a sea. Still deeper, richer, more divine grow the great walls and temples, until in the supreme flaming glory of sunset the whole canyon is transfigured, as if all the life and light of centuries of sunshine stored up and condensed in the rocks was now being poured forth as from one glorious fountain, flooding both earth and sky.

Strange to say, in the full white effulgence of the midday hours the bright colours grow dim and terrestrial in common grey haze; and the rocks, after the manner of mountains, seem to crouch and drowse and shrink to less than half their real stature, and have nothing to say to one, as if not at home. But it is fine to see how quickly they come to life and grow radiant and communicative as soon as a band of white clouds come floating by. As if shouting for joy, they seem to spring up to meet them in hearty salutation, eager to touch them and beg their blessings. It is just in the midst of these dull midday hours that the canyon clouds are born.

A good storm-cloud full of lightning and rain on its way to its work on a sunny desert day is a glorious object. Across the canyon, opposite the hotel, is a little tributary of the Colorado called Bright Angel Creek. A fountain-cloud still better deserves the name 'Angel of the Desert Wells' – clad in bright plumage, carrying cool shade and living water to countless animals and plants ready to perish, noble in form and gesture, seeming able for anything, pouring life-giving, wonder-working floods from its alabaster fountains, as if some sky-lake had broken. To every gulch and gorge on its favourite ground is given a passionate torrent, roaring, replying to the rejoicing lightning – stones, tons in weight, hurrying away as if frightened, showing something of the way Grand Canyon work is done. Most of the fertile summer clouds of the canyon are of this sort, massive, swelling cumuli, growing rapidly, displaying delicious tones of purple and grey in the hollows of their sun-beaten houses, showering favoured areas of the heated landscape, and vanishing in an hour or two. Some, busy and thoughtful-looking, glide with beautiful motion along the middle of the canyon in flocks, turning aside here and there, lingering as if studying the needs of particular spots, exploring side-canyons, peering into hollows like birds seeking nest-places, or hovering aloft on outspread wings. They scan all the red wilderness, dispensing their blessings of cool shadows and rain where the need is the greatest, refreshing the rocks, their offspring as well as the vegetation, continuing their sculpture, deepening gorges and sharpening peaks. Sometimes, blending all together, they weave a ceiling from rim to rim, perhaps opening a window here and there for sunshine to stream through, suddenly lighting some palace or temple and making it flare in the rain as if on fire.

Sometimes, as one sits gazing from a high, jutting promontory, the sky all clear, showing not the slightest wisp or pencilling, a bright band of cumuli will appear suddenly, coming up the canyon in single file, as if tracing a well-known trail, passing in review, each in turn darting its lances and dropping its shower, making a row of little vertical rivers in the air above the big brown one. Others seem to grow from mere points, and fly high above the canyon, yet following its course for a long time, noiseless, as if hunting, then suddenly darting lightning at unseen marks, and hurrying on. Or they loiter here and there as if idle, like labourers out of work, waiting to be hired.

Half a dozen or more showers may oftentimes be seen falling at once, while far the greater part of the sky is in sunshine, and not a raindrop comes nigh one. These thunder-showers from as many separate clouds, looking like wisps of long hair, may vary greatly in effects. The pale, faint streaks are showers that fail to reach the ground, being evaporated on the way down through the dry, thirsty air, like streams in deserts. Many, on the other hand, which in the distance seem insignificant, are really heavy rain, however local; these are the grey wisps well zigzagged with lightning. The darker ones are torrent rain, which on broad, steep slopes of favourable conformation give rise to so-called 'cloud-bursts'; and wonderful is the commotion they cause. The gorges and gulches below them, usually dry, break out in loud uproar, with a sudden downrush of muddy, boulder-laden floods. Down they all go in one simultaneous gush, roaring like lions rudely awakened, each of the tawny brood actually kicking up a dust at the first onset.

During the winter months snow falls over all the high plateau, usually to a considerable depth, whitening the rim and the roofs of the canyon buildings. But last winter, when I arrived at Bright Angel in the middle of January, there was no snow in sight, and the ground was dry, greatly to my disappointment, for I had made the trip mainly to see the canyon in its winter garb. Soothingly I was informed that this was an exceptional season, and that the good snow might arrive at any time. After waiting a few days, I gladly hailed a broad-browed cloud coming grandly on from the west in big promising blackness, very unlike the white sailors of the summer skies. Under the lee of a rim-ledge, with another snow-lover, I watched its movements as it took possession of the canyon and all the adjacent region in sight. Trailing its grey fringes over the spiry tops of the great temples and towers, it gradually settled lower, embracing them all with ineffable kindness and gentleness of touch, and fondled the little cedars and pines as they quivered eagerly in the wind like young birds begging their mothers to feed them. The first flakes and crystals began to fly about noon, sweeping straight up the middle of the canyon, and swirling in magnificent eddies along the sides. Gradually the hearty swarms closed their ranks, and all the canyon was lost in grey gloom except a short section of the wall and a few trees beside us, which looked glad with snow in their needles and about their feet as they leaned out over the gulf. Suddenly the storm opened with magical effect to the north over the canyon of Bright Angel Creek, inclosing a sunlit mass of the canyon architecture, spanned by great white concentric arches of cloud like the bows of a silvery aurora. Above these and a little back of them was a series of upboiling purple clouds, and high above all, in the background, a range of noble cumuli towered aloft like snow-laden mountains, their pure pearl bosses flooded with sunshine. The whole noble picture, calmly glowing, was framed in thick grey gloom, which soon closed over it; and the storm went on, opening and closing until night covered all.

Two days later, when we were on a jutting point about eighteen miles east of Bright Angel and one thousand feet higher, we enjoyed another storm of equal glory as to cloud effects, though only a few inches of snow fell. Before the storm began we had a magnificent view of this grander upper part of the canyon and also of the Coconino Forest and the Painted Desert. The march of the clouds with their storm banners flying over this sublime landscape was unspeakably glorious, and so also was the breaking up of the storm next morning – the mingling of silver-capped rock, sunshine and cloud.

Most tourists make out to be in a hurry even here; therefore their days or hours would be best spent on the promontories nearest the hotel. Yet a surprising number go down the Bright Angel Trail to the brink of the inner gloomy granite gorge overlooking the river. Deep canyons attract like high mountains; the deeper they are, the more surely are we drawn into them. On foot, of course, there is no danger whatever, and, with ordinary precautions, but little on animals. In comfortable tourist faith, unthinking, unfearing, down go men, women and children on whatever is offered, horse, mule, or burro, as if saying with Jean Paul, 'fear nothing but fear' – not without reason, for these canyon trails down the stairways of the gods are less dangerous than they seem, less dangerous than home stairs. The guides are cautious, and so are the experienced, much-enduring beasts. The scrawniest Rosinantes and wizened-rat mules cling hard to the rocks endwise or sidewise, like lizards or ants. From terrace to terrace, climate to climate, down one creeps in sun and shade, through gorge and gully and grassy ravine, and, after a long scramble on foot, at last beneath the mighty cliffs one comes to the grand, roaring river.

To the mountaineer the depth of the canyon, from five thousand to six thousand feet, will not seem so very wonderful, for he has often explored others that are about as deep. But the most experienced will be awestruck by the vast extent of strange, countersunk scenery, the multitude of huge rock monuments of painted masonry built up in regular courses towering above, beneath and round about him. By the Bright Angel Trail the last fifteen hundred feet of the descent to the river has to be made afoot down the gorge of Indian Garden Creek. Most of the visitors do not like this part, and are content to stop at the end of the horse-trail and look down on the dull-brown flood from the edge of the Indian Garden Plateau. By the new Hance Trail, excepting a few daringly steep spots, you can ride all the way to the river, where there is a good spacious camp-ground in a mesquite grove. This trail, built by brave Hance, begins on the highest part of the rim, eight thousand feet above the sea, a thousand feet higher than the head of Bright Angel Trail, and the descent is a little over six thousand feet, through a wonderful variety of climate and life. Often late in the fall, when frosty winds are blowing and snow is flying at one end of the trail, tender plants are blooming in balmy summer weather at the other. The trip down and up can be made afoot easily in a day. In this way one is free to observe the scenery and vegetation, instead of merely clinging to his animal and watching its steps. But all who have time should go prepared to camp awhile on the river-bank, to rest and learn something about the plants and animals and the mighty flood roaring past. In cool, shady amphitheatres at the head of the trail there are groves of white silver fir and Douglas spruce, with ferns and saxifrages that recall snowy mountains; below these, yellow pine, nut pine, juniper, hop-hornbeam, ash, maple, holly-leaved berberis, cowania, spiræa, dwarf oak and other small shrubs and trees. In dry gulches and on taluses and sun-beaten crags are sparsely scattered yuccas, cactuses, agave, etc. Where springs gush from the rocks there are willow thickets, grassy flats and bright, flowery gardens, and in the hottest recesses the delicate abronia, mesquite, woody compositæ and arborescent cactuses.

The most striking and characteristic part of this widely varied vegetation are the cactaceæ – strange, leafless, old-fashioned plants with beautiful flowers and fruit, in every way able and admirable. While grimly defending themselves with innumerable barbed spears, they offer both food and drink to man and beast. Their juicy globes and disks and fluted cylindrical columns are almost the only desert wells that never go dry, and they always seem to rejoice the more and grow plumper and juicier the hotter the sunshine and sand. Some are spherical, like rolled-up porcupines, crouching in rock-hollows beneath a mist of grey lances, unmoved by the wildest winds. Others, standing as erect as bushes and trees or tall branchless pillars crowned with magnificent flowers, their prickly armour sparkling, look boldly abroad over the glaring desert, making the strangest forests ever seen or dreamed of. *Cereus giganteus*, the grim chief of the desert tribe, is often thirty or forty feet high in southern Arizona. Several species of tree yuccas in the same deserts, laden in early spring with superb white lilies, form forests hardly less wonderful, though here they grow singly or in small lonely groves. The low, almost stemless *Yucca baccata*, with beautiful lily flowers and sweet banana-like fruit, prized by the Indians, is common along the canyon-rim, growing on lean, rocky soil beneath mountain-mahogany, nut pines and junipers, beside dense flowery mats of *Spiræa cæspitosa* and the beautiful pinnate-leaved *Spiræa millefolia*. The nut pine (*Pinus edulis*) scattered long the upper slopes and roofs of the canyon buildings, is the principal tree of the strange dwarf Coconino Forest. It is a picturesque stub of a pine about twenty-five feet high, usually with dead, lichened limbs thrust through its rounded head, and grows on crags and fissured rock tables, braving heat and frost, snow and drought, and continuing patiently, faithfully fruitful for centuries. Indians and insects and almost every desert bird and beast come to it to be fed.

To civilized people from corn and cattle and wheat-field countries the canyon at first sight seems as uninhabitable as a glacier crevasse, utterly silent and barren. Nevertheless it is the home of a multitude of our fellow-mortals, men as well as animals and plants. Centuries ago it was inhabited by tribes of Indians, who, long before Columbus saw America, built thousands of stone houses in its crags, and large ones, some of them several stories high, with hundreds of rooms on the mesas of the adjacent regions. Their cliff-dwellings, almost numberless, are still to be seen in the canyon, scattered along both sides from top to bottom and throughout its entire length, built of stone and mortar in seams and fissures like swallows' nests, or on isolated ridges and peaks. The ruins of larger buildings are found on open spots by the river, but most of them aloft on the brink of the wildest, giddiest precipices, sites evidently chosen for safety from enemies, and seemingly accessible only to the birds of the air. Many caves were also used as dwelling-places, as were mere seams on cliff-fronts formed by unequal weathering and with or without outer or side walls; and some of them were covered with coloured pictures of animals. The most interesting of these cliff-dwellings had pathetic little ribbon-like strips of garden on narrow terraces, where irrigating-water could be carried to them – most romantic of sky-gardens, but eloquent of hard times.

In recesses along the river and on the first plateau flats above its gorge were fields and gardens of considerable size, where irrigating-ditches may still be traced. Some of these ancient gardens are still cultivated by Indians, descendants of cliff-dwellers, who raise corn, squashes, melons, potatoes, etc., to reinforce the produce of the many wild food-furnishing plants – nuts, beans, berries, yucca and cactus fruits, grass and sunflower seeds, etc. – and the flesh of animals – deer, rabbits, lizards, etc. The canyon Indians I have met here seem to be living much as did their ancestors, though not now driven into rock-dens. They are able, erect men, with commanding eyes, which nothing that they wish to see can escape. They are never in a hurry, have a strikingly measured, deliberate, bearish manner of moving the limbs and turning the head, are capable of enduring weather, thirst, hunger and over-abundance, and are blessed with stomachs which triumph over everything the wilderness may offer. Evidently their lives are not bitter.

The largest of the canyon animals one is likely to see is the wild sheep, or Rocky Mountain bighorn, a most admirable beast, with limbs that never fail, at home on the most nerve-trying precipices, acquainted with all the springs and passes and broken-down jumpable places in the sheer ribbon cliffs, bounding from crag to crag in easy grace and confidence of strength, his great horns held high above his shoulders, wild red blood beating and hissing through every fibre of him like the wind through a quivering mountain pine.

Deer also are occasionally met in the canyon, making their way to the river when the wells of the plateau are dry. Along the short spring streams beavers are still busy, as is shown by the cottonwood and willow timber they have cut and peeled, found in all the river drift-heaps. In the most barren cliffs and gulches there dwell a multitude of lesser animals, well-dressed, clear-eyed, happy little beasts – wood rats, kangaroo rats, gophers, wood mice, skunks, rabbits, bob-cats and many others, gathering food, or dozing in their sun-warmed dens. Lizards, too, of every kind and colour are here enjoying life on the hot cliffs, and making the brightest of them brighter.

Nor is there any lack of feathered people. The golden eagle may be seen, and the osprey, hawks, jays, hummingbirds, the mourning dove and cheery familiar singers – the black-headed grosbeak, robin, bluebird, Townsend's thrush and many warblers, sailing the sky and enlivening the rocks and bushes through all the canyon wilderness.

Here at Hance's river-camp or a few miles above it brave Powell and his brave men passed their first night in the canyon on their adventurous voyage of discovery thirty-three[1] years ago. They faced a thousand dangers, open or hidden, now in their boats gladly sliding down swift, smooth reaches, now rolled over and over in back-combing surges of rough, roaring cataracts, sucked under in eddies, swimming like beavers, tossed and beaten like cast-away drift – stout-hearted, undaunted, doing their work through it all. After a month of this they floated smoothly out of the dark, gloomy, roaring abyss into light and safety two hundred miles below. As the flood rushes past us, heavy-laden with desert mud, we naturally think of its sources, its countless silvery branches outspread on thousands of snowy mountains along the crest of the continent, and the life of them, the beauty of them, their history and romance. Its topmost springs are far north and east in Wyoming and

---

[1] Muir wrote this description in 1902; Major J. W. Powell made his descent through the canyon, with small boats, in 1869. [Editor.]

Colorado, on the snowy Wind River, Front, Park and Sawatch Ranges, dividing the two ocean waters, and the Elk, Wahsatch, Uinta and innumerable spurs streaked with streams, made famous by early explorers and hunters. It is a river of rivers – the Du Chesne, San Rafael, Yampa, Dolores, Gunnison, Cochetepa, Uncompahgre, Eagle and Roaring Rivers, the Green and the Grand, and scores of others with branches innumerable, as mad and glad a band as ever sang on mountains, descending in glory of foam and spray from snow-banks and glaciers through their rocky moraine-dammed, beaver-dammed channels. Then, all emerging from dark balsam and pine woods and coming together, they meander through wide, sunny park valleys, and at length enter the great plateau and flow in deep canyons, the beginning of the system culminating in this grand canyon of canyons.

Our warm canyon camp is also a good place to give a thought to the glaciers which still exist at the heads of the highest tributaries. Some of them are of considerable size, especially those on the Wind River and Sawatch Ranges in Wyoming and Colorado. They are remnants of a vast system of glaciers which recently covered the upper part of the Colorado basin, sculptured its peaks, ridges and valleys to their present forms, and extended far out over the plateau region – how far I cannot now say. It appears, therefore, that, however old the main trunk of the Colorado may be, all its widespread upper branches and the landscapes they flow through are new-born, scarce at all changed as yet in any important feature since they first came to light at the close of the Glacial Period.

The so-called Grand Colorado Plateau, of which the Grand Canyon is only one of the well-proportioned features, extends with a breadth of hundreds of miles from the flanks of the Wahsatch and Park Mountains to the south of the San Francisco Peaks. Immediately to the north of the deepest part of the canyon it rises in a series of subordinate plateaus, diversified with green meadows, marshes, bogs, ponds, forests and grovy park valleys, a favourite Indian hunting-ground, inhabited by elk, deer, beaver, etc. But far the greater part of the plateau is good sound desert, rocky, sandy, or fluffy with loose ashes and dust, dissected in some places into a labyrinth of stream-channel chasms like cracks in a dry clay-bed, or the narrow slit crevasses of glaciers – blackened with lava-flows, dotted with volcanoes and beautiful buttes, and lined with long continuous escarpments – a vast bed of sediments of an ancient sea-bottom, still nearly as level as when first laid down after being heaved into the sky a mile or two high.

Walking quietly about in the alleys and byways of the Grand Canyon city, we learn something of the way it was made; and all must admire effects so great from means apparently so simple; rain striking light hammer-blows or heavier in streams, with many rest Sun-days; soft air and light, gentle sappers and miners, toiling forever; the big river sawing the plateau asunder, carrying away the eroded and ground waste, and exposing the edges of the strata to the weather; rain torrents sawing cross-streets and alleys, exposing the strata in the same way in hundreds of sections, the softer, less resisting beds weathering and receding faster, thus undermining the harder beds, which fall, not only in small weathered particles, but in heavy sheer-cleaving masses, assisted down from time to time by kindly earthquakes, rain torrents rushing the fallen material to the river, keeping the wall rocks constantly exposed. Thus the canyon grows wider and deeper. So also do the side-canyons and amphitheatres, while secondary gorges and cirques gradually isolate masses of the promontories, forming new buildings, all of which are being weathered and pulled and shaken down while being built, showing destruction and creation as one. We see the proudest temples and palaces in stateliest attitudes, wearing their sheets of detritus as royal robes, shedding off showers of red and yellow stones like trees in autum shedding their leaves, going to dust like beautiful days to night, proclaiming as with the tongues of angels the natural beauty of death.

Every building is seen to be a remnant of once continuous beds of sediments – sand and slime on the floor of an ancient sea, and filled with the remains of animals – and every particle of the sandstones and limestones of these wonderful structures to be derived from other landscapes, weathered and rolled and ground in the storms and streams of other ages. And when we examine the escarpments, hills, buttes and other monumental masses of the plateau on either side of the canyon, we discover that an amount of material has been carried off in the general denudation of the region compared with which even that carried away in the making of the Grand Canyon is as nothing. Thus each wonder in sight becomes a window through which other wonders come to view. In no other part of this continent are the wonders of geology, the records of the world's auld lang syne, more widely opened, or displayed in higher piles. The whole canyon is a mine of fossils, in which five thousand feet of horizontal strata are exposed in regular succession over more than a thousand square miles of wall-space, and on the adjacent plateau region there is another series of beds twice as thick, forming a grand geological library – a collection of stone books covering thousands of miles of shelving, tier on tier, conveniently arranged for the student. And with what wonderful scriptures are their pages filled – myriad forms of successive floras and faunas, lavishly illustrated with coloured drawings, carrying us back into the midst of the life of a past infinitely remote. And as we go on and on, studying this old, old life in the light of the life beating warmly about us, we enrich and lengthen our own.

APPENDICES

APPENDIX I

Zanita – Tale of the Yo-semite

by Thérèse Yelverton

A remarkable fictional portrait of John Muir as 'Kenmuir' was produced in the first two chapters of a novel published in 1872. It was written as a result of a visit to Yosemite during Muir's first full year in residence there in 1870. Thérèse Yelverton was sent to meet Muir by his Oakland friend and correspondent, Jeanne Carr. The novelist stayed throughout the summer into the late autumn, using Muir as a guide to locations for her novel, but also making notes on his conversations and his journals.

The male biographers of Muir regard Mrs Yelverton as a classic temptress who threatens Muir's sexual innocence. James Mitchell Clarke refers to her as 'a more dubious emissary from the world of culture'. Frederick Turner describes her as 'vivacious, attractive, romantic, and she became so enamoured of the blue-eyed miller/guide that she made him a character in a novel she was then writing. Her idealized portrait of Muir in Zanita strongly suggests she had developed more than a literary interest in him.' The evidence for her threat to Muir's emotional life seems to carry over from her toughness in fighting a bigamist in a much publicised case.

At the end of the Crimean War, Maria Theresa Longworth had married a Captain Yelverton, who, a few months later had left her to marry a wealthier woman. For nine years Mrs Yelverton fought the now Count of Avonmore through the courts to first win her case as the real Countess, and then lose on his appeal to the House of Lords. Having used up all her inherited money she took on a career as a travel writer and novelist. It may well be, as David Robertson asserts in *West of Eden*, that she became 'infatuated' with Muir, but his published letters do not show him finding excuses to run away from her as Clarke suggests. The editor of *The Life and Letters of John Muir*, Badè, suggests that the novel not only gives an accurate portrait of Muir in 1870, but that it indicates in chapter four 'that Muir knew at least as early as 1870 that ice had overridden Glacier Point, a fact of some historical interest since the origin of the name is not certainly known.'

Muir's comment on 'some of the manuscript' which he had seen was characteristically perceptive and self-deprecating:

> As for Kenmuir, I don't think she knew enough of wild nature to pen him well, but I have often worn shirts, soiled, ragged and buttonless, but with a spray ... stuck somewhere, or a carex, or chance flower. It is about all the vanity I persistently indulge in, at least in bodily adornments.

Perhaps the romanticism of Thérèse Yelverton's writing only echoes that of John Muir for the Yosemite.

CHAPTER ONE

Kenmuir

SOME OF THE most potential episodes of our lives are ushered in by apparently trivial circumstances. A fancy, a whim, a caprice, even a movement without any separate act of volition, an accidental glance across the street, a false step over the stones, are often the foundations upon which some vitally important bridge of our lives has to be constructed.

Trifling incidents not infrequently give birth to the most stupendous events.

Thus the life-drama which I am about to narrate fell out in consequence of the gratification of what might have appeared at the time a very innocent whim.

Caprice had been attributed to me all my life through: as a school-girl, by my companions, and as a woman, by my husband; until I had come to believe it formed a part of my character.

Yet any individual exercise of the propensity never warmed me at the time, and it was not until my husband classified my action as a piece of caprice, that I came to regard it in that light.

The very beginning and root of my story grew out of one of these trifling fancies. My husband was a Professor of Geology in a College of California, and much of the pleasantest part of my life was spent in bearing him company in his geological excursions.

We usually spent the vacations in delightful rambles, occasionally accompanied by a few of the more studious and inquiring of his pupils, sometimes by a fellow Professor, and sometimes alone.

I used to long for Commencement Day quite as eagerly as any overworked student. The city, and everything connected with the city, had by that time become abhorrent to me. I hated the noise, the dirt, the talk, the dress, my household cares, and the dry parched look of everything, and longed for the fresh green sward, the music of streams, the song of birds, the sunset rambles and the still hush of moonlight nights; in fine for all the delights of the country.

For, although a most practical body in the matter of shirt buttons, darning, and improvised dishes of unctuous flavour, yet there was a latent stratum of romance in my composition which, *de temps en temps*, would bubble up amid my daily cares and wrestle for a recognition, and enfranchisement of its own.

What then was my disappointment when the Professor announced that he would be detained by business for a week or ten days after the term had closed.

'This is a terrible disappointment to you I know, my dear,' said my husband, who never thwarted me in anything. 'But do you not think you could make a start on your own account, and stop at some pretty place for a few days, when I could join you?'

Of the two evils this seemed to be the least objectionable. And so it was settled that I should start for Mariposa alone, where I duly arrived, and was enjoying myself with my usual zest for the country, when the idea, or caprice, seized upon me that it would be a very pleasant thing to go on a little exploring expedition on my own behalf, and prospect for the Professor ere he arrived. I thought if I could secure a horse and guide, I would wander forth in search of that marvellous Valley of Yo-semite, so recently discovered by white men, and already exciting so much interest in the world at large, as well as in scientific circles.

I knew my husband had some intention of measuring the colossal trees, reported to be three or four hundred feet in height, and the granite giant, showing a vertical front of four thousand. I thought it would be pleasant to forestall him. Acting upon this freak of fancy, I set out with my guide, Horse-shoe Bill, who, as he informed me, derived his title, like many of the nobility, from having located in, and possessed himself of, a certain Horseshoe Bay.

We rode from early morn until eve through the most glorious country it had ever been my fate to traverse. Mountain rose above mountain, and tower above tower of rocky peaks; and, away up, mingling with the snowy clouds, peered the no less snowy caps of the distant Sierra Nevadas. Here and there we could see green valleys nestling in among the mountains, and deep canyons filled with dark pines.

'O, them's nowhar to the Valley whar I'm agoin' to take you; and we can most see some of it now. Them three peaks as you see a topplin' over one another, a sort of playin' leap-frog, the Indians call Pom-pom-pas-us.'

Looking in the direction to which he pointed, I beheld a chaos of mountain tops and deep chasms, all seemingly thrown inextricably together, and apparently inaccessible. My heart began to fail me as to my further progress, when a peculiar looking object foreign to the scenery caught my eye.

'What on earth is that?' I exclaimed, reining up my not unwilling mustang, and pointing to the singular creature extending itself as though about to take wing from the very verge of a pinnacle overhanging a terrific precipice. 'Is it a man, or a tree, or a bird?'

'It's a man, you bet,' replied my guide, chuckling. 'No tree or shrub as big as my fist ever found footing there. It's than darned idiot Kenmuir, and the sooner he dashes out that rum mixture of his he calls brains the sooner his troubles'll be over, that's my idea.'

'Its not mine though,' I said decisively, 'for if he is really crazy we are the more bound to take care of him. Suppose you give a shrill whistle to attract his attention.'

'He'll not bother for that, he'll know it's me; but if you ride around this here point he'll see you belike; that'll be a novel sight for him,' said the guide, who was by no means an ill-natured man: only thoroughly imbued with a recklessness of human life, which years spent in the wild wood seems to engender in the most humane.

Adopting his suggestion, we quickly rounded the point, when the singular figure was soon swaying to and fro with extended arms as if moved by the wind, the head thrown back as in swimming, and the long brown hair falling wildly about his face and neck.

The point on which he stood was a smooth jutting rock only a few inches in width, and a stone thrown over it would fall vertically into the valley five thousand feet below. My heart beat fast with horrible dread as my guide coolly explained this fact to me. I hardly dared to fix my eyes upon the figure lest I should see it disappear, or remove them, lest it should be gone when I looked again. In my desperation, I exerted that power of will which is said to convey itself through space without material aid. I strove to communicate with him by intangible force. The charm seemed to work well. He turned quickly towards me, and, with a spring like an antelope, was presently on *terra firma* and approaching us.

'There, you'll have plenty on him now,' said Horseshoe Bill. 'He loafs about this here valley gatherin' stocks and stones, as I may say, to be Scriptural, and praisin' the Lord for makin' of him such a born fool. Well some folks is easy satisfied!'

As the little figure approached, skipping over the rough boulders, poising with the balance of an athlete, or skirting a shelf of rock with the cautious activity of a goat, never losing for a moment the rhythmic motion of his flexile form, I began to think that his attitude on the overhanging rock might not, after all, have been so chimerical; and my resolves, as to how I should treat this phase of insanity, began to waver very sensibly, and I fell back on that mental rear-guard,—good intensions; but when he stood before me with a pleasant 'Good day, madam,' my perplexity increased ten-fold, for his bright intelligent face revealed no trace of insanity, and his open blue eyes of honest questioning, and glorious auburn hair might have stood as a portrait of the angel Raphael. His figure was about five feet nine, well knit, and bespoke that active grace which only trained muscles can assume.

The guide increased my confusion by exclaiming, 'Hallo, Kenmuir! the lady wants to speak to you.'

I wished the guide at Jericho for giving me such false notions. Why had he induced me to believe this man a raving maniac, only to compel me, like old Dogberry, to write myself down an ass. I could have as soon reproached one of the clouds gyrating round the crest of the mountain with running into danger.

'Can I do anything for you?' asked Kenmuir gently.

'She wants to know what you were doing out on that bloody knob over-hanging eternity?'

'Praising God,' solemnly replied Kenmuir.

'Thought that would start him,' interrupted the guide.

'Praising God, madam, for his mighty works, his glorious earth, and the sublimity of these fleecy clouds, the majesty of that great roaring torrent,' pointing to the Nevada, 'that leaps from rock to rock in exultant joy, and laves them, and kisses them with caresses of downiest foam. O, no mother ever pressed her child in tenderer embrace, or sung to it in more harmonious melody; and my soul joins in with all this shout of triumphant gladness, this burst of glorious life; this eternity of truth and beauty and joy; rejoices in the gorgeous canopy above us, in the exquisite carpet with which the valley is spread of living, palpitating, breathing splendor. Hearken to the hymn of praise which resounds upwards from every tiny sedge, every petal and calyx of myriads and myriads of flowers, all perfect, all replete with the divine impress of Omnipotent power. Shall man alone be silent and callous? Come, madam, let me lead you to Pal-li-li-ma, the point I have just left, where you can have a more complete view of this miracle of nature, for I am sure you also can worship in this temple of our Lord.'

Here was a pretty fix for a Professor's wife, and a sensible woman! I was about to put myself in the identical situation which but a few moments before had induced me to consider the man who occupied it a lunatic.

Horseshoe Bill remarked my puzzled expression, and laughed, 'Ho, he'll guide you right enough; he knows every inch of the road as well as I do. You needn't be afeard; he'll take you to the shanty I told you of, where you can locate for the night, and I'll make tracks back again, if so be you don't want me.'

One thought of the maniac shot through my mind, not as a fear, but a souvenir. I looked on the face of Kenmuir, shining with a pure and holy enthusiasm, and it reminded me of the face of a Christ I had seen years ago in some little old Italian village; not a picture of any note, but possessing such a tender, loving, benignant expression, that I had never forgotten it; and had then thought that the artist must have intended it for the Salvator Mundi before he became the Man of Sorrows.

With this picture brought forcibly to my mind, I resigned myself cheerfully, and followed his lead to the great projecting rock called the Glacier Point, or Pal-li-li-ma, where I had first seen him, and where there are still traces of ancient glaciers, which he said 'are no doubt the instruments the Almighty used in the formation of this valley.'

As we proceeded slowly and carefully, my thoughts dwelt with deep interest on the individual in advance of me. Truly his garments had the tatterdemalion style of a Mad Tom. The waist of his trousers was eked out with a grass band; a long flowing sedge rush stuck in the solitary button-hole of his shirt, the sleeves of which were ragged and forlorn, and his shoes appeared to have known hard and troublous times. What if he had been, at some previous period, insane, and still retained the curious mania of believing that human beings might through righteousness float in ambient air? What if he should insist on our making the experiment this evening together? What would my husband say if he knew all, and saw me here committed to the sole care of this man with the beautiful countenance, and with no other guarantee, in a wilderness of mighty rocks, gigantic trees, and awful precipices, a hundred miles from anywhere! This was a very awkward thought to deal with, and there was no justification I could think of. What inconvenient but useful creatures husbands are sometimes! If we should go over the rocks together, of course there would be an 'end of everything,' as Sir Peter Teazle says; but in case I should survive, and recount the whole matter to him, as I could not help doing, then he would upbraid me with riding off at the risk of my neck, on my favourite hobby-horse, Physiognomy.

But, in the course of conversation with my *cicerone*, I soon divined that his refinement was innate, his education collegiate, not only from his scientific treatment of his subject, but his correct English. Kenmuir, I decided in my mind, was a gentleman; and behind this bold rampart I resolved to intrench myself against the sarcastic tiltings of the Professor.

As we approached the point, Kenmuir said, with a gleeful laugh, 'I do not intend to take you out on the overhanging rock, where I was standing, but to a very nice little corner, where you can sit your horse comfortably, unless you really want to dismount.'

I thanked him, and, smiling at the arch allusion, said I would remain seated. The scene from Pal-li-li-ma was a marvel of grandeur and sublimity, and fully warranted the lavish enthusiasm of my new friend. Around us vast mountains of granite arose one above another in stupendous proportions, and over them leaped the mighty cataracts with majestic sweep.

'These are the Lord's fountains,' said Kenmuir, clasping his hands in the intensity of his delight, 'and away up above, elevated amid clouds, are the crests of the God-like peaks covered with eternal snows. These are the reservoirs whence He pours his floods to cheer the earth, to refresh man and beast, to have every sedge and tiny moss; from those exalted pinnacles flow the source of life, and joy, and supreme bliss to millions of breathing things below; to the dreamy-eyed cattle that you see four thousand feet in the valley beneath us, standing knee-deep in the limpid pool; to the tiny insects that are skimming in ecstatic merriment around every glistening ribbon of water as it falls. Look! and see these silvery threads of water all hurrying down so swiftly, yet so gracefully, to bathe the upturned face of nature, and varnish with new brilliancy her enamelled breast. Beyond is the Lord's workshop. With these resistless glaciers he formed a royal road — from the heights of the topmost Sierras which you now see covered with snow, roseate from the sun's last beams — into the valley at our feet. Yet all is lovely in form, and harmonious in colour. Look at that ledge of rock — the hardest of granite — how exquisitely it is tapestried with helianthemum. Would you like a bunch?'

And before I could reply, the rash man had leapt down, and alighted like a bird on a perch, and grasped a bunch of ferns, which he stroked affectionately, and carefully stowed away in the grass cincture, whilst there was but a half foot of rock between him and 'etarnity,' as the guide expressed it.

CHAPTER TWO

A Strange Guide

'Now,' said Kenmuir, 'lest you should think I have brought you to this wilderness to make you be food for ghouls and water kelpies, I will point out the spot where you are to spend the night, and as many more as you wish.'

I looked round in dismay. 'We seem a million miles from anywhere.'

' Upwards, yes,' he replied — 'but look down, and will see a yellow spot, surrounded by what appears a few willow sticks, but which are in reality tall pines, with the river winding round like a golden cord —that is the homestead. We will go down by the trail, which is almost level.'

By which I found he meant a pathway, next thing to stairs, down which my horse clambered very adroitly.

And thus through forests of gigantic pines, which Kenmuir would climb like a cat to reach some particular cone, and point out its wonderful structure; through groves of azaleas, making the air heavy with odorous sweetness, where Kenmuir would disappear altogether, returning with some previous specimen, all which he carried to me like a faithful dog, going twice the actual distance in his erratic gyrations. Then we came across a patch of great tigerlilies which we were both anxious to cull; and at last we entered on a green sward smooth as any lawn, set round (as in a garden) by Mariposa lilies, so called from their resemblance to a butterfly.

The piece of level ground was in front of a massive rock resembling an old country house, with gables and quaint chimneys overgrown with honeysuckle, which completed the delusion. Kenmuir threw up his arms in ecstasy, and declared it was a facsimile of his father's manse in the braw old country of Perthshire.

'Then you are a Scotchman?' I exclaimed.

'Yes; did you not know that by my name?'

'Names," I said, "are not so indicative in this country as in yours. There you may almost tell if a man comes of a good stock, by his name. Whereas, here the greatest aristocrat might rejoice in the name of *Squaddles* with impunity. The old country is more fastidious about emphonious sounds, and I think they are right; for I cannot help attaching a peculiar quality to peculiar sounds.'

'What would you judge your host of this way to be — his name is Oswald Naunton?'

'That is a name which requires a great deal of consideration. It is original. I never heard it before, and I am sure he will not be a common-place man. Then there is poetic rhythm, which would suggest something harmonious and symmetrical in the character. Both smartness and pride combined; a man from whom you might safely ask a favour, but from whom you could extort nothing.'

' Ha! ha!' laughed Kenmuir, 'you're a fine guesser.'

'I am not guessing in the least. You give me a real name and I will give you the rhythmical interpretation.'

'Then you don't believe a rose would smell as sweet if it were called a tulip?'

'I will not discuss botany with you; but I say the rose by another name would not have played the same role in the world, would not have had the same poetical *entourage*. Lovers would not have offered it to their belles as emblems of their passion had it been called catnip!'

The twilight now had deepened to moonlight. For although we could not see any moon, she had risen, and was taking a ramble behind the cliffs. Yet her light swam over the whole scenery in magic waves, transforming it to the most unearthly vision of weird enchantment. Every notch and projection caught the soft loving light which fell in perfect streams over the mighty Tutock-ah-nu-lah, which seemed to have pierced the pale clear blue of the heavens and let out floods of its glistening moonlight.

'Do you not perceive the balmy odours of the pines? They also mark the height and distance of these stupendous adamantine bulwarks. What are the towers of Notre Dame, which they so singularly resemble, compared to these cathedral spires rising in proud majesty three thousand feet with the flying buttresses and ancient caryatides supporting the projecting arches!'

'Yes,' I put in. 'I believe I see a procession of monks ascending to the great entrance of the church.'

'Those are pine-trees two hundred feet high, growing up the ravine. Look at the rich carving and fretwork on the walls, and the tall minarets dazzling in the moon's rays.'

'And I hear the *muezzin* calling to prayer.'

'That is an owl,' answered Kenmuir; 'and he says, 'Do! do! oh, do do!' *Do* what, I wonder?'

'Go on,' I suggested, 'for we have stopped here a full quarter of an hour, and our host will have retired for the night.'

'We will wake him up,' said Kenmuir, 'but he will not be asleep such a night as this, he has too much soul.'

'Still we had better move on,' I said, recollecting what my former guide had turned back to say in a stage whisper — 'Don't let him stop, or he'll talk till judgment day; and don't let him stoop to pick up any new specimen, or you'll never be through with him for a month.'

So we moved on softly, listening to the crackle of the pine straw which covered the earth through the park-like forest.

Kenmuir had got one more temptation—the moon-flower.

'Did you ever see them open to the moon? They gradually untwist the outer leaves, then suddenly burst right open like a flash of light. I have watched them many an hour; they belong to the family œnothera.'

'Stay! I'll hold your horse,' he said, as I made a quiet attempt to keep jogging on.

'Now, my dear sir,' I exclaimed, 'how long do you think it will take the flower to open? or do you think you can inspire it with the amiable idea to do so within sixty seconds, because longer than that I cannot wait, and I'm all on the *qui vive* to see if my *nomenclatology*, that is what I call my new science, for it has a right to an 'ology, is correct as regards Mr. Naunton.'

The flower did not open, and we sped on again, our shadows clearly defined on the grassy meadows which were studded with flowers, whose broad discs were like stars of the first magnitude.

'Do you see that light? That proves they are not gone to bed, and your fears may rest.'

Through the trees a bright light was glimmering; not unwelcome it appeared, for beside the excitement which so much novelty and magnificence are sure to arouse in certain temperaments, the bodily fatigue of so many hours of up-hill and down-hill climbing on horseback, made the prospect of rest very thoroughly congenial.

What romantic temperament has not fed the soul with the marvellous and supernatural on such a night as this; when arriving either late at night or by moonlight in some unknown part of the country, he has pictured himself benighted and lost in the forest or the fog; the night owl, or the will-o'-the-wisp, has been his only guide, and when a light has at length startled his aching sight, has imagined it the gleam of the lantern of some midnight assassins burying their dead; or fancied it proceeding from some monastery, where silence was the discipline, and where the brown cowled monk, who attended upon us dumbly, pointed to the pallet in a bare cell as the resting-place for the night.

Who has not frightened himself with a vague superstition, like children with a made-up bogle, the more to enjoy the pleasures of security.

But this evening there was no need to conjure up any phantom of the brain; no occasion to counterfeit any romance; the reality was too importunately present.

Here was I, a lone woman having transgressed her husband's directions to await him in a civilized place, alone in the wildest part of the wild world, with a stranger—the like of whom I had never met in all my travels—wandering on an untrodden path to a habitation of which I knew next to nothing. It was certainly as extraordinary and romantic a situation as any lover of fiction could have framed. But my ruminations were cut short by our actual arrival, and a wild hallo from Kenmuir to arouse the inmates.

APPENDIX II

The Making of the Eight Wilderness-Discovery Books

THE STORY OF MY BOYHOOD AND YOUTH (1913)

In 1902 Muir had published two books and, was making a list of others he planned. Sixth and last came 'possibly my autobiography which for ten years or more all sorts of people have been begging me to write. My life, however, has been so smooth and regular and reasonable, so free from blundering exciting adventures, the story hardly seems worth while in the midst of so much that is infinitely more important.' In fact this first volume shocked many readers by its details of the cruel regime of school and home. The book might never have been written at all had Muir not been bullied into it by E. H. Harriman, the railway tycoon with whom he had visited Alaska, while staying at the Harriman Lodge on Klamath Lake, Oregon in 1908. Harriman instructed his secretary to follow Muir on all his walks, taking dictated notes which Muir later reworked for the 1912 serial publication of this book.

A THOUSAND MILE WALK TO THE GULF (1916)

After Muir's death in 1914 his literary executor, William Frederick Badè, wanted to fill in the autobiographical gap Muir had left between *The Story of my Boyhood and Youth* and *My First Summer in the Sierra*, so he published the contents of the small brown leather-bound journal that Muir had carried in his pocket on the journey which took him to California. To make the final link with the Sierra, Badè included as a last chapter an article, "Twenty Hill Hollow", which had been published in the *Overland Monthly* of July 1872. This journal represents the earliest extended writing by Muir that we have. The freshness of its vivid details and the forcefulness of its reflections on the rights of nature are remarkable not only in coming from a young man, but in being written on the move.

MY FIRST SUMMER IN THE SIERRA (1911)

In June 1910 Muir wrote to the editor of *The Dial*, 'I have been hidden down here in Los Angeles for a month or two and have managed to get off a little book to Houghton Mifflin.' This was a reworking of the battered blue notebooks from a summer forty years earlier that Turner refers to as a 'conversion experience'. He believes that Muir 'made few substantive changes'. But Michael Cohen argues that, whilst '*First Summer* is an honest and truthful book, it is also narrated with all the skill a novelist might muster.' He believes that 'the old Muir was not only selecting and editing the journals but also deciding on their sequence . . . Sometimes he even put words into the young man's mouth which were obviously those of a more mature man.' Whatever the process, this remains for many readers Muir's best book.

THE MOUNTAINS OF CALIFORNIA (1894)

This is Muir's first book and, as he wrote to a friend, 'you will say that I should have written it long ago; but I begrudged the time of my young mountain-climbing days.' To his editor he wrote in April 1894: 'The book, begotten heaven knows when, is finished and out of me, therefore hurrah, etc., and thanks to you, very friend, for benevolent prodding. Six of the sixteen chapters are new, and the others are nearly so, for I have worked hard on every one of them, leaning them against each other, adding lots of new stuff, and killing adjectives and adverbs of redundant growth – the *verys*, *intenses*, *gloriouses*, *ands*, and *buts*, by the score. I feel sure the little alpine thing will not disappoint you. Anyhow I've done the best I could. Read the opening chapter when you have time. In it I have ventured to drop into the poetry that I like, but have taken good care to place it between bluffs and buttresses of bald, glacial, geological facts.'

The great success of this book encouraged Muir to launch into another: 'I am trying to write another book, but it is harder than mountaineering.'

OUR NATIONAL PARKS (1901)

This second book of Muir's is made up of ten articles originally published in the *Atlantic Monthly* between August 1897 and September 1901. They constitute a campaign that in the year prior to publication resulted in Congress approving a bill establishing the National Park system and in the year following publication lead to the foundation of the Sierra Club. 'I've been writing about the forests, mostly, doing what little I can to save them . . . But I make slow, hard work of it – slow and hard as glaciers'.

Muir's editor later wrote to him, 'I thank God that you do not write in glib, acrobatic fashion: anybody can do that. Half the people in the world are doing it all the time, to my infinite regret and confusion. . . . The two books on the Parks and on Alaska will not need any special season's sales, nor other accidental circumstances: they'll be Literature!'

The chronological order of original publication dates of the articles was as follows: Chapter X – August 1897; Chapter I – January 1898; Chapter II – April 1898; Chapter VI – November 1898; Chapter VII – December 1898; Chapter III – August 1899; Chapter IV – April 1900; Chapter V – August 1900; Chapter VIII – April 1901; Chapter IX – September 1901.

THE YOSEMITE (1912)

'Next month I mean to bring together a lot of Yosemite material into a handbook for travellers, which ought to have been written long ago. But the reason why it is needed now was that public opinion, based upon visits to Yosemite Valley, should raise its voice against the desecration of "other Yosemites".' This book takes the reader through Yosemite Valley to the threatened Hetch Hetchy. As usual, the writing process itself was thought of in terms of the real thing: 'As for myself, I've been reading old musty dusty Yosemite notes until I'm tired and blinky blind, trying to arrange them in lateral, medial, and terminal moraines on my den floor. I never imagined I had accumulated so vast a number. The long trains and embankments and heaped up piles are truly appalling. I thought that in a quiet day or two I might select all that would be required for a guidebook; but the stuff seems enough for a score of big jungle books, and it's very hard, I find, to steer through it on anything like a steady course in reasonable time.'

Under pressure to complete 'before leaving for the Amazon' Muir was still writing the book in Garrison, New York: 'I am now shut up in a magnificent room pegging away at that book, and working as hard as I ever did in my life. I do not know what has got into me, making so many books all at once. It is not natural . . .'

TRAVELS IN ALASKA (1915)

In the dark January days of 1895 (not 1896 as Turner says) Muir began work on his Alaska adventures. His journal entry for 19 January reads: 'Rain, wind, black weather with tedious monotony, but it matters not as far as my fields are concerned. In writing scenery I am in Alaska and the mind goes there with marvellous vividness. I see the mountains and the glaciers flowing down their gorges and broad shell-shaped hollows.' On 6 February he noted: 'This day I finished "The Discovery of Glacier Bay". Will mail it tomorrow to *The Century*. It seems strange that a paper that reads smoothly and may be finished in ten minutes should require months to write.' This chapter was published in *The Century* in June 1895, as was another in September 1897. But by that year the urgent demand for the articles that became *Our National Parks* resulted in Muir only returning to his Alaska book in the stormy and foggy winter of his last year.

Despite being ill and tired Muir often worked from seven in the morning until ten at night, aided now by a secretary who stored each finished chapter in an orange crate. When he died on Christmas Eve 1914 the almost completed manuscript was beside his bed. It was Marion Randall Parsons, his secretary, who brought the book to publication the following year.

STEEP TRAILS (1918)

Muir's literary executor, William Frederick Badè, compiled this important collection of essays after Muir's death. Part of his Editor's Note gives the following information:

The papers brought together in this volume have, in a general way, been arranged in chronological sequence. They span a period of twenty-nine years of Muir's life, during which they appeared as letters and articles, for the most part in publications of limited and local circulation. The Utah and Nevada sketches, and the two San Gabriel papers, were contributed, in the form of letters to the *San Francisco Evening Bulletin* toward the end of the seventies. Written in the field, they preserve the freshness of the author's first impression of those regions. Much of the material in the chapters on Mount Shasta first took similar shape in 1874. Subsequently it was rewritten and much expanded for inclusion in *Picturesque California, and the Region West of the Rocky Mountains*, which Muir began to edit in 1888. In the same work appeared the description of Washington and Oregon. The charming little essay "Wild Wool" was written for the *Overland Monthly* in 1875. "A Geologist's Winter Walk" is an extract from a letter to a friend, who, appreciating its fine literary quality, took the responsibility of sending it to the *Overland Monthly* without the author's knowledge The concluding chapter on "The Grand Canyon of the Colorado". was published in the *Century Magazine* in 1902, and exhibits Muir's powers of description at their maturity.

Some of these papers were revised by the author during the later years of his life, and these revisions are a part of the form in which they now appear. The chapters on Mount Shasta, Oregon, and Washington will be found to contain occasional sentences and a few paragraphs that were included, more or less verbatim, in *The Mountains of California* and *Our National Parks*.

APPENDIX III

Selected Bibliography

The Eight Wilderness-Discovery Books in order of publication

The Mountains of California (Century, New York 1894)
Our National Parks (Houghton Mifflin, Boston 1901)
My First Summer in the Sierra (Houghton Mifflin, Boston 1911)
The Yosemite (Century, New York 1912)
The Story of My Boyhood and Youth (Houghton Mifflin, Boston 1913)
Travels in Alaska (Houghton Mifflin, Boston 1915)
A Thousand Mile Walk to the Gulf (Houghton Mifflin, Boston 1916)
Steep Trails (Houghton Mifflin, Boston 1918)

Other Books by John Muir

Stickeen (1909; Houghton Mifflin, Boston, 1923)
Edward Henry Harriman (Doubleday, Page & Co., New York, 1911)
A memorial pamphlet about the organiser of the 1899 Alaskan Expedition which Muir joined.
The Cruise of the Corwin (Houghton Mifflin, Boston, 1917)
Newspaper articles and journals material from the Alaska trip of 1881.

Letters and Journals

Letters to a Friend: Written to Mrs Ezra S Carr, 1866–1879 edited by W. F. Badè (1915)

The Life and Letters of John Muir edited by W. F. Badè, 2 Vols. (1924)

John of the Mountains: The Unpublished Journals of John Muir edited by Linnie Marsh Wolfe, (1938: University of Wisconsin Press, 1979)

John Muir, To Yosemite and Beyond: Writings from the Years 1863–1875 edited by R. Engberg and D. Weslin, (University of Wisconsin Press, 1980)

Books about Muir

Rediscovering America: John Muir in his Time and Ours by Frederick Turner (Sierra Club Books, San Francisco 1985)

The Pathless Way: John Muir and American Wilderness by Michael P. Cohen (University of Wisconsin Press, 1984) A rigorous discussion of the complete range of Muir's ideas in the context of modern thinking and current dilemmas.

The American Conservation Movement: John Muir and his Legacy by Stephen Fox (University of Wisconsin Press, 1981)

Wilderness and the American Mind by Roderick Nash (Yale University Press, 1967) A seminal book on the history of the American notion of wilderness.

John Muir in Yosemite by Shirley Sargent (Flying Spur, Yosemite, 1971)

The Rights of Nature: A History of Environmental Ethics by Roderick Nash (University of Wisconsin Press, 1989) A brief, but important discussion of Muir as a political activist with radical environmental ethics.

The Idea of Wilderness: From Prehistory to the Age of Ecology by Max Oelschlaeger (Yale University Press, 1991)

JOHN MUIR
His Life and Letters and Other Writings
Edited by Terry Gifford. Contents include:
The Life and Letters of John Muir by William Frederick Badè
Studies in the Sierra, Six Letters from Scotland, Picturesque California (essays),
The Proposed Yosemite National Park, The Cruise of the Corwin, Stickeen,
Alaska Days with John Muir by Samuel Hall Young, *Edward Henry Harriman,*
Muir as Others Saw Him (assessments of Muir's writings and work).

The companion omnibus to this collection, containing virtually all the remaining Muir writings. Of particular interest is *Studies in the Sierra* – dealing with how Yosemite Valley and its surrounds were formed and shaped. In this rare piece Muir confidently questions existing orthodoxies providing one of the most entertaining geographical commentaries ever written.

Badè's biography is valuable for its plethora of letter exchanges which, with *Studies in the Sierra*, give us a large body of Muir's early writings when he was in the full flush of enthusiasm for his new found world of Sierra splendour.   *912 pp, 36 b/w & colour photos*

Bâton Wicks ISBN 1-898575-07-7 £20   **The Mountaineers** ISBN 0-89886-463-1 $38

Chronology

1838   John Muir born 126/128 High Street, Dunbar, East Lothian, Scotland.

1849   John Muir's parents and family move to Fountain Lake, Wisconsin, USA.

1855   The Muirs move to new farm at Hickory Hill, Wisconsin.

1860   John Muir leaves home for University of Wisconsin.

1861   American Civil War begins.

1862   John Muir teaches during part of his second year at University. Thoreau dies.

1865   Assassination of Abraham Lincoln.

1866   End of the American Civil War. John Muir returns to Indianapolis from his Canadian exile during the Civil War.

1867   Muir damages an eye in an industrial accident. Walks from Louisville to Florida.

1868   First visit to Yosemite.

1871   Muir publishes *Yosemite Glaciers*. Emerson visits Yosemite.

1872   First articles for *Overland Monthly*; meets William Keith. Yellowstone Park established.

1876   Muir lives in San Francisco with Swetts, *God's First Temples* signals his involvement in the conservation debates. Custer defeated at Little Bighorn.

1879   Muir becomes engaged to Louie Strentzel. First Alaskan expedition.

1880   Muir marries Louie Wanda Strentzel.

1881   Muir's daughter, Annie Wanda, is born; Muir travels to Alaska on the Corwin.

1882   Emerson dies.

1885   Daniel Muir dies.

1886   Muir's second daughter, Helen, is born.

1888   Louie urges Muir to return to his literary and conservation projects.

1890   Return to public debate begins with two articles for *Century Magazine*. Death of Dr John Strentzel. Sioux defeated at Wounded Knee. Disappearance of American frontier noted in Official Census.

1890   U.S. Congress approves a Bill setting up the National Park system. Sequoia National Park established.

1892   The Sierra Club founded. Yosemite National Park established. Forest reserves created in three states.

1893   Muir revisits Dunbar.

1894   *Mountains of California* published.

1896   Honorary degree from Harvard. Muir joins Forestry Commission. Annie G. Muir dies.

1897   Honorary degree from the University of Wisconsin.

1901   Theodore Roosevelt becomes President after McKinley's assassination. Muir writes to him regarding American natural resources. *Our National Parks* published.

1903   Roosevelt camps in Yosemite with Muir. First federal wildlife reserve established.

1905   Louie Muir dies. California recedes Yosemite to U.S.

1906   Sierra Valley National Park and Petrified Forest National Monument (Arizona) established. San Francisco earthquake.

1908   Muir Woods National Monument

1911   John Muir leaves on South American expedition. *My First Summer in the Sierra* published. Death of William Keith.

1912   *The Yosemite* published.

1913   Hetch Hetchy finally granted to San Francisco ending a lengthy dispute. *The Story of My Boyhood and Youth* published. Death of John Swetts.